Primer on the Metabolic Bone Diseases and Disorders of Mineral Metabolism

Sixth Edition

An Official Publication of the American Society for Bone and Mineral Research

Primer on the Metabolic Bone Diseases and Disorders of Mineral Metabolism

Sixth Edition

FOUNDING EDITOR

Murray J. Favus, M.D.
Pritzker School of Medicine
The University of Chicago
Chicago, Illinois

ASSOCIATE EDITORS

Daniel D. Bikle, M.D., Ph.D.
VA Medical Center
University of California
San Francisco, California

Sylvia Christakos, Ph.D.
University of Medicine and Dentistry of New Jersey
New Jersey Medical School
Newark, New Jersey

Steven R. Goldring, M.D.
Harvard Medical School
Boston, Massachusetts

Theresa A. Guise, M.D.
University of Virginia
Charlottesville, Virginia

Michael F. Holick, Ph.D., M.D.
Boston University School of Medicine
Boston, Massachusetts

Suzanne M. Jan de Beur, M.D.
John Hopkins University
Baltimore, Maryland

Frederick S. Kaplan, M.D.
University of Pennsylvania Hospital
Philadelphia, Pennsylvania

Michael Kleerekoper, M.D., F.A.C.E.
Wayne State University
Detroit, Michigan

Nancy Lane, M.D.
University of California
San Francisco, California

Craig B. Langman, M.D.
Northwestern University Medical School
Children's Memorial Hospital
Chicago, Illinois

Jane B. Lian, Ph.D.
University of Massachusetts
Medical School
Worcester, Massachusetts

Pamela Gehron Robey, Ph.D.
National Institute of Dental and Craniofacial Research
National Institutes of Health
Bethesda, Maryland

Elizabeth Shane, M.D.
Columbia University
College of Physicians and Surgeons
New York, New York

Andrew F. Stewart, M.D.
University of Pittsburgh School of Medicine
Pittsburgh, Pennsylvania

Michael P. Whyte, M.D.
Shriners Hospital for Children
Washington University School of Medicine
St. Louis, Missouri

Published by the American Society for Bone and Mineral Research
Washington, D.C.

Cover Designer: David Spratte, Third Eye Studio
Printer: Cadmus Professional Communications

©2006 by American Society for Bone and Mineral Research. Published by:

American Society for Bone and Mineral Research
2025 M Street, NW, Suite 800
Washington, DC 20036-3309
www.asbmr.org

Printed in the USA

Library of Congress Cataloging-in-Publication Data

Primer on the metabolic bone diseases and disorders of mineral metabolism / [founding editor, Murray J. Favus ; associate editors, Daniel D. Bikle . . . et al.]. — 6th ed.
　　p. ; cm.
　Includes bibliographical references and index.
　ISBN-13: 978-0-9778882-0-7 (pbk. : alk. paper)
　ISBN-10: 0-9778882-0-7 (pbk. : alk. paper)
　1. Bones—Metabolism—Disorders. 2. Mineral metabolism—Disorders. 3. Bones—Diseases. I. Favus, Murray J. II. American Society for Bone and Mineral Research.
　[DNLM: 1. Bone Diseases, Metabolic. 2. Bone and Bones—metabolism.
3. Minerals—metabolism. WE 250 P953 2006]

RC931.M45P75 2006
616.7'16—dc22

2006016950
CIP

Contents

Section V. Disorders of Serum Minerals
(Section Editors: Elizabeth Shane and Andrew F. Stewart)

Section VI. Osteoporosis
(Section Editors: Michael Kleerekoper and Nancy Lane)

Section VII. Metabolic Bone Diseases
(Section Editors: Craig B. Langman and Michael P. Whyte)

Section VIII. Cancer and Bone
(Section Editors: Andrew F. Stewart and Theresa Guise)

Section IX. Genetic, Developmental, and Dysplastic Skeletal Disorders
(Section Editor: Michael P. Whyte)

Contributing Authors

John S. Adams, M.D.
Sundaye O. Akintoye, D.D.S.
Ziyad Al-Aly, M.D.
Uri S. Alon, M.D.
Andrew Arnold, M.D.
Jane E. Aubin, Ph.D.
M. Janet Barger-Lux, M.S.
Paolo Bianco, M.D.
John P. Bilezikian, M.D.
Nick Bishop, MRCP, M.D.
Dennis Black, Ph.D.
Jean-Jacques Body, M.D., Ph.D.
Adele L. Boskey, Ph.D.
Alan Boyde, Ph.D.
Arthur E. Broadus, M.D., Ph.D.
Edward M. Brown, M.D.
Susan V. Bukata, M.D.
David A. Bushinsky, M.D.
Pauline Camacho, M.D.
Thomas O. Carpenter, M.D.
Charles H. Chesnut III, M.D.
Gregory A. Clines, M.D., Ph.D.
Adi Cohen, M.D., M.H.S.
David E. C. Cole, M.D., Ph.D.
Michael T. Collins, M.D.
Cyrus Cooper, M.A., D.M., F.R.C.P.
Felicia Cosman, M.D.
Gilbert J. Cote, Ph.D.
Bess Dawson-Hughes, M.D.
Leonard J. Deftos, M.D., J.D.
Marie B. Demay, M.D.
Linda L. Demer, M.D., Ph.D.
David W. Dempster, Ph.D.
Robert W. Downs, Jr., M.D.
Susannah Earl, B.M., S.H.O.
Richard Eastell, M.D., F.R.C.P.
Peter Ebeling, M.D., F.R.A.C.P.
Thomas A. Einhorn, M.D.
John A. Eisman, B.B.S., Ph.D.
Kristine E. Ensrud, M.D., M.P.H.
Murray J. Favus, M.D.
Robert F. Gagel, M.D.
Michele Garabedian, M.D., Ph.D.
Louis C. Gerstenfeld, Ph.D.
Vicente Gilsanz, M.D.
David L. Glaser, M.D.
David Goltzman, M.D.
Esther A. Gonzalez, M.D.
Susan L. Greenspan, M.D.
Theresa A. Guise, M.D.
Nicholas Harvey, M.A., M.B., M.R.C.P.
Robert P. Heaney, M.D., F.A.C.P., F.A.I.N.
Martin Hewison, Ph.D.
Angela Hirbe, B.A.
Michael F. Holick, M.D., Ph.D.

Mara J. Horwitz, M.D.
Keith A. Hruska, M.D.
Dinaz Irani, M.D.
Suzanne M. Jan de Beur, M.D.
Marjorie K. Jeffcoat, D.M.D.
Sheila J. Jones, Ph.D.
Harald Jüppner, M.D.
Frederick S. Kaplan, M.D.
Douglas P. Kiel, M.D., M.P.H.
Samuel C. Kim, M.D.
Michael Kleerekoper, M.D., F.A.C.E.
John Klingensmith, Ph.D.
Christopher S. Kovacs, M.D., F.R.C.P.C.
Paul H. Krebsbach, D.D.S., Ph.D.
Henry M. Kronenberg, M.D.
Rajiv Kumar, M.D.
Ramsay L. Kuo, M.D.
Craig B. Langman, M.D.
Jacob Lemann Jr., M.D.
Mary B. Leonard, M.D.
Michael A. Levine, M.D.
Jane B. Lian, Ph.D.
Robert Lindsay, M.B.Ch.B., Ph.D., F.R.C.P.
James E. Lingeman, M.D.
Marjorie M. Luckey, M.D.
Joan C. Marini, M.D., Ph.D.
Kevin J. Martin, M.B.B.Ch.
Stephen J. Marx, M.D.
Brian R. Matlaga, M.D., M.P.H.
Nicole L. Miller, M.D.
Paul D. Miller, M.D., F.A.C.P.
David G. Monroe, Ph.D.
Elizabeth Morgan, B.A.
Dorothy A. Nelson, Ph.D.
Robert A. Nissenson, Ph.D.
Shane A. Norris, Ph.D.
Regis J. O'Keefe, M.D.
Bjorn R. Olsen, M.D., Ph.D.
Eric S. Orwoll, M.D.
John M. Pettifor, M.B.B.Ch., Ph.D.
Richard L. Prince, M.D.
Frank Rauch, M.D.
Andrew Ravanelli, B.S.
Robert R. Recker, M.D., F.A.C.P., F.A.C.E.
Kurt Redlich, M.D.
Ian R. Reid, M.D., F.R.A.C.P.
Pamela Gehron Robey, Ph.D.
G. David Roodman, M.D., Ph.D.
Clifford J. Rosen, M.D.
F. Patrick Ross, Ph.D.
Clinton Rubin, Ph.D.
Janet Rubin, M.D.
Robert K. Rude, M.D.
Philip N. Sambrook, M.D.
Georg Schett, M.D.

John T. Schousboe, M.D., M.S.
Frank J. Secreto, Ph.D.
Elizabeth Shane, M.D.
Eileen M. Shore, M.D.
Shonni J. Silverberg, M.D.
Stuart L. Silverman, M.D.
James P. Simmer, D.D.S., Ph.D.
Ethel S. Siris, M.D.
Josef Smolen, M.D.
Thomas C. Spelsberg, Ph.D.
Stuart Sprague, D.O.
Gary S. Stein, Ph.D.

Andrew F. Stewart, M.D.
Brent C. Taylor, Ph.D., M.P.H.
Peter J. Tebben, M.D.
Rajesh V. Thakker, M.D., F.R.C.P.
Leslie F. Thomas, M.D.
Dwight A. Towler, M.D., Ph.D.
Özge Uluçkan, B.S.
Tamara J. Vokes, M.D.
Jean Wactawski-Wende, Ph.D.
Katherine Weilbaecher, M.D.
Michael P. Whyte, M.D.
John J. Wysolmerski, M.D.

Preface to the Sixth Edition

The mission of the ASBMR *Primer on the Metabolic Bone Diseases and Disorders of Mineral Metabolism* is to present core knowledge in this field in a comprehensive yet concise fashion. In the 3 years since publication of the fifth edition, substantial new information has advanced our understanding of bone biology, mineral homeostasis, hormonal regulation, and the associated disease states.

The sixth edition reflects these rapid and exciting advances in the basic sciences and translational research. For instance, under the guidance of Theresa Guise, we added a new section on Bone Cancer Biology. While we addressed malignancy and bone in earlier editions, the significance of recent advances in this field mandated creation of a new section of the *Primer*. In addition, Bob Gagel spearheaded the expansion of our analysis of bone genetics, with a new chapter and more detailed Appendix, providing readers with information we couldn't even envision when we assembled the first *Primer* in the late 1980s. Some chapters have been consolidated and others have been expanded to continue the role of the *Primer* as an essential resource.

Since its first printing in 1990, the *Primer* has proven useful to medical students, graduate students, residents and fellows in training, and clinical and basic investigators. We believe this edition will prove even more valuable for the many scientists, trainees, and physician practitioners who are intrigued and challenged by the complexities of the bone, its regulatory hormones, and the related diseases.

Our understanding of bone and mineral metabolism reaches across diverse areas of study: molecular biology, physiology, genetics, nutrition, structural biology, hormonal regulation, and cell signaling in many organs and tissues including bone, cartilage, parathyroid, kidney, intestine, marrow, skin, muscle, and the immune system. The changes and updates incorporated into the sixth edition have improved the *Primer* as a source of information for those in many disciplines (internal medicine, pediatrics, orthopedics, primary care, obstetrics and gynecology, endocrinology, rheumatology, and nephrology) who develop and implement advances in research and treatment of bone and mineral disorders.

With the sixth edition now published, I end my work with the *Primer*. Serving the Society as Editor of the first six editions of the *Primer* has been an honor and a most stimulating experience that I reflect on with much satisfaction. As I turn the editorship over to Cliff Rosen, I know that the *Primer* will continue to be the most complete and up-to-date source of information in the field. The *Primer* has evolved with each edition, and I am confident that Cliff will continue to improve the *Primer* as it serves to educate a new generation of bone and mineral investigators and physicians. All the best Cliff.

Murray J. Favus
University of Chicago

Acknowledgement

A remarkable feature of the sixth edition's editorial board is that Sylvia Christakos, Michael Kleerekoper, Craig Langman, Elizabeth Shane, Andrew Stewart, and Michael Whyte have worked on the *Primer* since its inception. Since publication of the first edition in 1990, each has contributed in many ways to the growth of the bone and mineral field. Yet, when called on, they have dedicated valuable time and effort to bring out the next editions. Their experience and judgment have allowed for the successful evolution of the *Primer* as the field continues to change. Also, I want to express my sincere appreciation to the other editors who have served on one or more editorial boards with dedication, including (editions in parentheses): Daniel Bikle (5, 6), Robert Gagel (1, 2), Steven Goldring (3, 4, 5, 6), Theresa Guise (6), Geoffrey Hendy (3), Michael Holick (3, 4, 5, 6), Suzanne Jan de Beur (6), Frederick Kaplan (3, 4, 5, 6), Sundeep Khosla (3, 4), Nancy Lane (5, 6), Jane Lian (3, 4, 5, 6), Pamela Robey (5, 6), and Dolores Shoback (3, 4, 5). I am indebted to all the editors for lending their expertise, knowledge, tenacity, and timely good humor in getting us through the publication process.

Of course, it is the contributing authors who have made the *Primer* a valuable source of information in the bone field. The editorial board is deeply indebted to the many authors who over the years have articulated in print the state of their areas of expertise. This impressive group has successfully taken on the challenge of organizing the ever-expanding scientific information into a coherent presentation.

The sixth edition of the *Primer* is the product of a tripartite collaboration involving an experienced editorial board, skilled authors, and an enthusiastic and supportive ASBMR editorial staff. The ASBMR staff, seasoned by the initial experience of self-publication with the fifth edition, has improved the publication process in many ways that benefited the authors and editors. The ASBMR staff, under the effective leadership of Adrienne Lea, must also be credited with expanding the distribution of the *Primer* and so delivering it into the hands of so many more students, trainees, scientists, and physician practitioners than we ever envisioned. I must also mention the significant work of Matt Kilby, who served as the point person for the staff and did a superb job in every way. I will miss working with the many talented and creative people that have served the Society as editors, authors, and publishing staff. On completion of the publication process, I can only hope that each will take a moment to thumb through the new *Primer* and reflect on the time and effort that was required to bring it to publication. I hope that you too will experience the good feelings of satisfaction and accomplishment.

Murray J. Favus
University of Chicago

The American Society for Bone and Mineral Research

The American Society for Bone and Mineral Research is delighted to publish the sixth edition of the *Primer on the Metabolic Bone Disease and Disorders of Mineral Metabolism*. This book is one of the signatures of our society, one of which we should be justly proud. We owe its success to the foresight and dedication of Dr. Murray Favus, who has been the editor since the inception of the *Primer*, to the dedicated group of editors, and to all those society members who have contributed chapters over the years.

The first edition of the *Primer* was published in 1990, the vision of Murray and the members of the ASBMR Education Committee. As a member of the Education Committee during that period and one of the original members of the *Primer* Editorial Board, I can personally attest to Murray's dedication to this project. He convinced the Council that such a book would greatly advance the educational mission of the ASBMR and increase the visibility of our society among practicing physicians, clinical investigators, and basic scientists. He raised the funds necessary to produce the *Primer*. He personally read every contribution, and I also recall that, with virtually no assistance, Murray compiled the entire index to the first edition.

We also owe Murray a debt of gratitude for overseeing the next five editions of the *Primer*. Each brought with it a specific set of challenges to be overcome, and Murray overcame each and every one. His efforts have turned the *Primer* into one of the most widely used sources of information on metabolic bone diseases. This is the last edition for Murray and his editorial team. ASBMR Past-President Clifford J. Rosen will take over the reins for the seventh edition. We thank Murray, the Associate Editors, and all of the contributors to the past and current editions. We are grateful for their dedication and commitment of time, energy, and knowledge to this important educational resource.

Elizabeth Shane

Elizabeth Shane
President
American Society for Bone and Mineral Research

Morphogenesis, Structure, and Cell Biology of Bone
(Section Editors: Jane B. Lian and Steven R. Goldring)

Chapter 1.   Bone Embryology

Bjorn R. Olsen

Department of Cell Biology, Harvard Medical School, Department of Developmental Biology, Harvard School of Dental Medicine, Boston, Massachusetts

INTRODUCTION

The cells that make up the vertebrate skeleton are derived from three lineages. Neural crest cells give rise to the branchial arch derivatives of the craniofacial skeleton, paraxial mesoderm contributes to the craniofacial skeleton and forms most of the axial skeleton (through the sclerotome division of the somites), and cells in the lateral plate mesoderm contribute to the skeleton of the limbs. In areas where bones are formed, mesenchymal cells from these sources condense and form regions of high cell density that represent outlines of future skeletal elements. During this condensation process, important changes take place in the extracellular matrix between the cells allowing cells to establish contact with each other and activate signaling pathways that regulate cell differentiation. Classical experiments have shown that, by the time mesenchymal condensations appear, the cells within them have already acquired properties that give them positional identity. Mechanisms that ensure the development of a complex skeleton with elements of unique size, shape, and anatomical identity can therefore be traced back to molecular and cellular events in precondensed mesenchyme.

MEMBRANOUS AND ENDOCHONDRAL BONE FORMATION

As mesenchymal cells within condensations differentiate, they can follow one of two paths. They can either differentiate into bone-forming cells, osteoblasts, or they can differentiate into chondrocytes and secrete the characteristic extracellular matrix of hyaline cartilage. Differentiation into osteoblasts occurs in areas of membranous ossification, such as in the calvaria of the skull, the maxilla, and the mandible, and in the subperiosteal bone-forming layer of long bones. Differentiation into chondrocytes occurs in the remaining skeleton where cartilage models of the future bones are formed. These models, frequently described by their German term anlagen, are subsequently replaced by bone in a process called endochondral ossification.

The choice of mesenchymal cells to differentiate into osteoblasts or chondrocytes is regulated by what is known as canonical Wnt signaling. In this case, binding of members of the large family of extracellular Wnt cytokines to Frizzled receptors and Lrp 5/6 co-receptors on cells stimulates intracellular events that prevent proteolytic degradation of β-catenin in the cytoplasm. This stable β-catenin can enter the cell nucleus and control (by a process mediated by specific transcription factors) transcription of downstream target genes. In areas of membranous ossification, Wnt signaling (induced in part by signaling through another important cytokine, sonic hedgehog) results in high levels of β-catenin in mesenchymal cells.[1] This induces the expression of genes that are required for osteoblastic cell differentiation and inhibits transcription of genes needed for chondrocytic differentiation. One of the induced transcription factors, CBFA1/RUNX2,[2-4] in turn induces the expression of another transcription factor called osterix (OSX),[5] and these two factors are critical for the differentiation of mesenchymal cells to osteoblasts. The importance of β-catenin for membranous bone formation is dramatically shown by experiments in which the gene for β-catenin has been genetically inactivated in limb and head mesenchymal cells during early embryonic development.[6,7] In the absence of β-catenin, the mesenchymal cells differentiate into chondrocytes instead of osteoblasts!

The formation of membranous bones occurs within mesenchymal condensations that are rich in blood vessels. As the bones grow by appositional growth, sprouting of capillaries (angiogenesis) is an essential part of the process. Angiogenesis is controlled by both pro-angiogenic and anti-angiogenic factors. An important pro-angiogenic factor, vascular endothelial growth factor (VEGF-A), is expressed by vascular endothelial cells and osteoblasts, and its binding to receptors on both cell types results in a stimulation of angiogenesis that is coupled to stimulation of bone formation.[8]

The differentiation of chondrocytes and formation of cartilage anlagen occur in mesenchymal condensations with low levels of β-catenin (Fig. 1). This results in upregulated expression of the transcription factor SOX9 and other members of the SOX family.[9] As a consequence of the activities of these transcription factors, cells become large and round in the center of the mesenchymal condensations. They develop organelles for high level synthesis and secretion of proteins (endoplasmic reticulum and Golgi complex) and switch from production of an extracellular matrix containing collagens I and III to a matrix containing the cartilage-specific collagens II, IX, and XI. The cartilage anlagen grow by interstitial and appositional growth so that they over time come to resemble the future bones in shape and size. While they normally are replaced by bone through endochondral ossification, they can grow into shapes that resemble the final bones even in the absence of bone formation. This is dramatically seen in mice that carry two inactivated alleles of the gene for CBFA1/RUNX2.[3,4] As mentioned above, this factor is critical for osteoblastic differentiation,[2] and in mice without functional CBFA1/RUNX2, no osteoblasts are formed. In these mice, the cartilaginous anlagen are not ossified, yet they form a nearly complete "skeleton" of the correctly shaped elements, consisting entirely of cartilage. The patterning of the endochondral skeleton therefore depends on processes that regulate the spatial differentiation and growth of cartilage. In humans, heterozygosity for loss-of-function mutations in *CBFA1/RUNX2* is associated with cleidocranial dysplasia.[10] Affected individuals exhibit short stature, hypoplasia/aplasia of the clavicle, hypoplasia of the pelvis, delayed ossification and closure of cranial sutures, and defects in tooth eruption and tooth number (supernumerary teeth in the permanent dentition).

In contrast to membranous bones that form within vascularized regions of mesenchyme, cartilage anlagen of endochondral bones form within mesenchymal condensations from which blood vessels are excluded (Fig. 1). Experiments with forced overexpression of a pro-angiogenic factor such as VEGF-A within the avascular mesenchymal condensations of endochondral limb bones show that angiogenesis within these regions inhibits chondrocyte differentiation.[11] Cartilage anlagen are therefore avascular from the start and they continue to grow in the absence of blood vessels within the cartilage. Curiously, the chondrocytes in the anlagen express VEGF-A at a low level.[12,13] This level of expression is insufficient for stimulating ingrowth of capillaries from the tissue (perichon-

---

The author has no conflicts of interest.

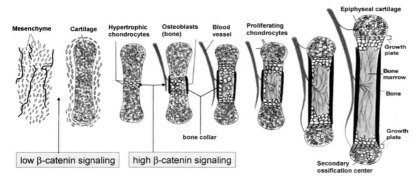

Mesenchyme Cartilage Hypertrophic chondrocytes Osteoblasts (bone) Blood vessel Proliferating chondrocytes Epiphyseal cartilage Growth plate Bone marrow Bone Growth plate Secondary ossification center

low β-catenin signaling   high β-catenin signaling

bone collar

FIG. 1. Diagram showing the steps of endochondral ossification, from vascularized mesenchyme (left) to an endochondral bone with a primary ossification center (right). Cartilage models form within avascular regions of mesenchyme where β-catenin levels are low, and the cartilages become invaded by blood vessels only after hypertrophy of chondrocytes. VEGF-A, expressed at a high level by hypertrophic chondrocytes, plays an essential role in this invasion and the establishment of the primary ossification center. Chondrocyte hypertrophy and the formation of a perichondrial bone collar require high levels of β-catenin. A low-level expression of VEGF-A in the epiphyseal chondrocytes is required for their survival. Based on Horton WA 1990 The biology of bone growth. Growth Genet Horm **6:**1–3 with permission.[57]

drium) around the cartilage. However, it is essential for survival of the proliferating chondrocytes in the end regions (epiphyses) of the developing endochondral bones, and inactivation of VEGF-A expression in chondrocytes at an early developmental stage results in massive chondrocytic cell death in these epiphyseal regions.[13]

As development of endochondral bones proceeds, chondrocytes at the center of the avascular anlagen cease to proliferate and differentiate (in a process requiring Wnt signaling and upregulated levels of β-catenin in the cells) to hypertrophy. At the same time, mesenchymal progenitor cells in the perichondrium differentiate into osteoblasts and form a bone collar around the hypertrophic portion (diaphysis) of the cartilage anlage. The hypertrophic chondrocytes express high levels of the transcription factor CBFA1/RUNX2, and this results in upregulated expression of several genes that are not expressed by the smaller, proliferating chondrocytes in the epiphyseal regions. Among these genes is VEGF-A, which is expressed at high levels in hypertrophic chondrocytes, and connective tissue growth factor (Ctgf).[14,15] The two factors are important for invasion of blood vessels, osteoblastic progenitor cells, and cartilage/bone-resorbing cells from the perichondrium into the hypertrophic cartilage. This invasion results in formation of a primary ossification center, characterized by erosion of the hypertrophic cartilage and its replacement with bone marrow and trabecular bone. The primary ossification center does not form when VEGF-A expression is inactivated, indicating that VEGF-A is crucial for this critical step in endochondral ossification.[13]

REGULATION OF MESENCHYMAL CONDENSATION AND CHONDROCYTE DIFFERENTIATION IN THE AXIAL SKELETON

During the fourth week of human development, cells of the paraxial mesoderm condense to the segmented structures called somites on either side of the neural tube and the notochord (Fig. 2). Within the somites, cells undergo transition from a mesenchymal to an epithelial phenotype, and this is followed by transition back to mesenchyme and migration of cells in the most ventral region of the somites into an area surrounding the notochord (Fig. 2). These cells form the sclerotomes.

Sclerotome cells differentiate into chondrocytes that form the anlagen of vertebral bodies. The notochord subsequently disappears within the vertebral bodies, but remains as the nucleus pulposus within intervertebral discs. The neural arches of the vertebrae are formed by sclerotome cells that migrate dorsally around the neural tube, whereas sclerotome cells that migrate laterally form the rib anlagen in the thoracic region. In the anterior body wall, mesenchymal cell condensations on each side of the midline form the sternal anlagen. Cells within

these condensations form two cartilaginous bars that later fuse into the sternum. Condensations above the sternum give rise to the manubrium and pairs of lateral condensations form the anterior cartilaginous portions of the ribs that are connected with the sternum.

The condensation, segmentation, and mesenchymal–epithelial transformation of paraxial mesoderm cells to somites is controlled in part by signaling between neighboring cells involving the cell surface receptor Notch1 and ligands that bind to it.[16,17] Notch1 is a large transmembrane protein with several repeated amino acid sequence domains. The ligands that bind to Notch1 and activate signaling pathways that are downstream of Notch1 are themselves transmembrane molecules with signaling potential.[18] The interactions between Notch1 and its ligands therefore require cell–cell contact. In mice carrying inactivated alleles for a mouse homolog of the *Drosophila* Notch ligand Delta[19] and in mice with inactivated *Notch1* genes,[5] early defects in the condensation and patterning of somites lead to defects in the vertebral column. Also, genes that control the expression of Notch1 or are controlled by Notch1 have been shown to be important for early stages of vertebral column development.[20,21] In humans, loss-of-function mutations in the Notch ligand δ-like 3 (DLL3) cause the recessive form of spondylocostal dysostosis, characterized by short stature, vertebral abnormalities in the form of semivertebrae, and deletions and fusions of ribs.[22] Mutations resulting in haplo-insufficiency of the Notch ligand Jagged 1 (JAG1) are associated with Alagille syndrome.[23,24] Affected individuals have abnormally shaped vertebral bodies (butterfly vertebrae) and abnormalities of the liver, heart, eye, and facial structures.

Differentiation of cells within sclerotomes to cartilage-producing chondrocytes is also under complex regulation. A master regulator of sclerotome cell differentiation and therefore of vertebral column formation is the secreted cytokine sonic hedgehog.[25] Sonic hedgehog is produced by the notochord as a protein that undergoes proteolytic self-cleavage and gets a cholesterol residue attached before it becomes an active cytokine.[26,27] That its signaling activity is absolutely required for sclerotome differentiation is evident from the phenotype of mice that carry inactivated sonic hedgehog alleles.[28] Such mice develop without a vertebral column and the posterior portions of the ribs. However, they do form a sternum and the anterior portions of ribs, the shoulder, and pelvic girdles, showing that the anlagen for those portions of the skeleton are not controlled by sonic hedgehog. Another important regulator is the transcription factor PAX1, which is, at least in part, induced by sonic hedgehog. A mutation in *PAX1* in humans causes a neural tube defect,[29] and mutations in mice lead to defective sclerotome differentiation and abnormalities in the vertebral column.[30]

A

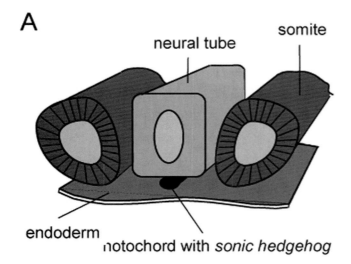

neural tube

somite

endoderm

notochord with *sonic hedgehog*

Early stage

B

dermatome

neural tube

migrating sclerotome cells myotome

Late stage

FIG. 2. Diagrams showing differentiation of somites in the trunk region of the embryo. (A) The ectoderm has been removed to reveal the somites adjacent to the neural tube. At this stage, the cells of the somites have an epithelial organization. (B) Later, cells from the medial region of the somites migrate toward the notochord and form the sclerotomes. The remainder differentiate into dermatome (skin) and myotome (striated muscle). Modified from Hogan B, Beddington R, Costantini F, Lacy E 1994 Manipulating the Mouse Embryo—A Laboratory Manual, 2nd ed. Cold Spring Harbor Laboratory Press, p.77 with permission.

SKELETAL MORPHOGENESIS IN THE LIMB

Skeletal development in the limb starts with formation of limb buds, outgrowths of the lateral body wall, appearing early in the second month of human development as a result of proliferation of mesenchymal cells from the lateral plate mesoderm. A group of tall, specialized epithelial cells, called the apical ectodermal ridge (AER), caps the limb bud. As the limb bud grows and cartilage anlagen of future bones develop within it, the developing limb is patterned along three axes: a proximal to distal axis, a dorsal to ventral axis, and a posterior to anterior axis.

Patterning along the proximal to distal axis is largely controlled by factors produced by the AER.[31] These include fibroblast growth factors that are important for stimulating proliferation and patterning of the underlying mesenchyme.[32,33] They are therefore essential for normal limb outgrowth. As the limb grows out, mesenchymal cells condense in the center to form the cartilage anlagen of the limb bones. The anlagen develop in a proximal to distal direction, and their development can be described as a series of bifurcations and segmentations that follow an axis along the humerus, through the ulna and the distal carpal (or tarsal in the foot) anlagen (Fig. 3).[34]

In the lower arm (leg) and hands (feet), the patterning of the anlagen from one side to the other is regulated by a cascade of signaling molecules and transcription factors. The most important of these include sonic hedgehog, secreted by a small group of cells (called the zone of polarizing activity) located at the posterior (ulnar) aspect of the developing limb bud, homeobox transcription factors, and members of the TGF-β superfamily of signaling molecules.[35] How all these and many other molecules are working together as an orchestrated system to generate the normal limb skeletal pattern is not known in detail, but recent studies are rapidly filling in the missing pieces.

Mutations in many of these genes result in striking abnormalities in the limb skeleton. For example, mutations involving expansions of a polyalanine stretch in the transcription factor *HOXD13* cause polysyndactyly (extra fingers) in humans[36]; other polysyndactyly syndromes have been shown to be caused by mutations in an intracellular, downstream target of sonic hedgehog signaling, a transcription factor called *GLI3*.[37,38] Mutations in a TGF-β homolog (GDF5/CDMP1) cause abnormal shortening of distal limb bones, perhaps as a result of a defect in formation of joints between bones.[39] Mutations in *Noggin*, an extracellular molecule that binds and inactivates GDF5/CDMP1 and other members of the TGF-β superfamily of molecules, are associated with proximal symphalangism, characterized by fusion of proximal joints between digits and early onset conductive deafness, and multiple dysostoses syndrome, including fusion of multiple joints in hands and feet, elbows, and hips and of intervertebral joints.[40]

Several studies also provide insights into mechanisms that ensure patterning along the dorsal–ventral axis. As a consequence of such studies, the basis for the Nail-patella syndrome in humans, characterized by dysplasia of nails and absent or hypoplastic patellae, has been found to be mutations in a transcription factor called *LMX1B*.[41]

Molecules and signaling pathways controlling the formation of digits in hands and feet are rapidly being identified from studies of human brachydactylies, a group of disorders characterized by shortening of fingers and toes. Several different clinical subtypes of brachydactyly are recognized; heterozygous mutations in the cytokine Indian hedgehog, receptor tyrosine kinase ROR2, and GDF5/CDMP1 have been described in subtypes A1, B, and C, respectively.[39,42,43]

CHONDROCYTE PROLIFERATION AND DIFFERENTIATION IN GROWTH PLATES

During endochondral ossification, cartilage anlagen are replaced by bone marrow and bone. In this process, epiphyseal growth plates are formed. A sequence of chondrocyte proliferation, differentiation to hypertrophy, and cell death (apoptosis) within the growth plate results in longitudinal bone growth and thus the final steps in bone morphogenesis. Proliferation and differentiation of growth plate chondrocytes are controlled in several ways. An important brake on chondrocyte proliferation is local signaling through fibroblast growth factor (FGF) (most likely

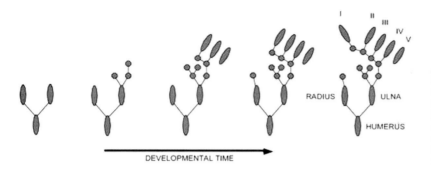

FIG. 3. Diagram showing branching and segmentation of mesenchymal condensations during limb development. As the limb bud grows (indicated by the horizontal arrow from left to right), the condensations develop in a distinct sequence to form the cartilage anlagen of the future bones (humerus, radius, ulna, carpal bones, and metacarpal bones for the five fingers [I–V]). Based on Shubin and Alberch 1986.[34]

Fgf18[44]) interaction with the cell surface tyrosine kinase receptor FGFR3. Activating mutations in *FGFR3* cause decreased bone growth in achondroplasia and hypochondroplasia in humans.[45,46] The cytokine PTH-related peptide (PTHrP) has an inhibitory effect on chondrocyte differentiation to hypertrophy,[47] and both activating and loss-of-function mutations in the PTHrP receptor (a cell surface G-protein–coupled receptor) cause decreased bone growth and distinct forms of dwarfism because of either inhibition of chondrocyte hypertrophy (Jansen's metaphyseal chondrodysplasia) or accelerated chondrocyte hypertrophy (Blomstrand's chondrodysplasia) in growth plates.[48,49] Signaling from the PTHrP receptor involves an inhibitory effect on the expression of a secreted signaling molecule called Indian hedgehog.[47] Indian hedgehog is homologous to sonic hedgehog and acts on cells through the same type of receptor as sonic hedgehog. Indian hedgehog induces expression of PTHrP so the two molecules seem to be involved in a self-regulating feedback loop within growth plates.[47] In addition, Indian hedgehog is a positive regulator of chondrocyte proliferation and induces (directly or indirectly) osteoblastic differentiation in the perichondrium (the bone collar) during endochondral ossification.[50]

As discussed above, chondrocyte hypertrophy leads to the synthesis of an extracellular matrix that is significantly different from that of the rest of growth plate cartilage. This hypertrophic matrix is readily degraded, and the high level expression of VEGF-A by the hypertrophic chondrocytes stimulates continued ingrowth of blood vessels, osteoclasts, and osteoblasts from the underlying bone marrow.[8,14,51] A member of a distinct subfamily of collagenous molecules, collagen X, is expressed at high levels by hypertrophic chondrocytes.[52] Because this collagen is not expressed by any other cell type, it is routinely used as a specific marker for hypertrophic chondrocytes. Genetic analyses of collagen X in mice show that this extracellular matrix component is required for normal growth plate function and longitudinal bone growth.[53,54] It may also be important for normal differentiation of hematopoietic progenitor cells in the adjacent bone marrow.[55] Mutations in collagen X in humans cause a distinct form of dwarfism, Schmid type metaphyseal chondrodysplasia.[56]

ACKNOWLEDGMENTS

The studies of skeletal and vascular development in the author's own laboratory were supported by National Institutes of Health Grants AR 36819 and AR 36820.

REFERENCES

1. Hu H, Hilton MJ, Tu X, Yu K, Ornitz DM, Long F 2005 Sequential roles of Hedgehog and Wnt signaling in osteoblast development. Development **132:**49–60.

2. Ducy P, Zhang R, Geoffroy V, Ridall AL, Karsenty G 1997 Osf2/Cbfa1: A transcriptional activator of osteoblast differentiation. Cell **89:**747–754.

3. Otto F, Thornell AP, Crompton T, Denzel A, Gilmour KC, Rosewell IR, Stamp GW, Beddington RS, Mundlos S, Olsen BR, Selby PB, Owen MJ 1997 Cbfa1, a candidate gene for cleidocranial dysplasia syndrome, is essential for osteoblast differentiation and bone development. Cell **89:**765–771.

4. Komori T, Yagi H, Nomura S, Yamaguchi A, Sasaki K, Deguchi K, Shimizu Y, Bronson RT, Gao YH, Inada M, Sato M, Okamoto R, Kitamura Y, Yoshiki S, Kishimoto T 1997 Targeted disruption of Cbfa1 results in a complete lack of bone formation owing to maturational arrest of osteoblasts. Cell **89:**755–764.

5. Nakashima K, Zhou X, Kunkel G, Zhang Z, Deng JM, Behringer RR, de Crombrugghe B 2002 The novel zinc finger-containing transcription factor osterix is required for osteoblast differentiation and bone formation. Cell **108:**17–29.

6. Day TF, Guo X, Garrett-Beal L, Yang Y 2005 Wnt/beta catenin signaling in mesenchymal progenitors controls osteoblast and chondrocyte differentiation during vertebrate skeletogenesis. Dev Cell **8:**739–750.

7. Hill TP, Spater D, Taketo MM, Birchmeier W, Hartmann C 2005 Canonical Wnt/beta-catenin signaling prevents osteoblasts from differentiating into chondrocytes. Dev Cell **8:**727–738.

8. Zelzer E, Olsen BR 2005 Multiple roles of vascular endothelial growth factor (VEGF) in skeletal development, growth, and repair. Curr Topics Dev Biol **65:**169–187.

9. Akiyama H, Chaboissier MC, Martin JF, Schedl A, de Crombrugghe B 2002 The transcription factor Sox9 has essential roles in successive steps of the chondrocyte differentiation pathway and is required for expression of Sox5 and Sox6. Genes Dev **16:**2813–2828.

10. Mundlos S, Otto F, Mundlos C, Mulliken JB, Aylsworth AS, Albright S, Lindhout D, Cole WG, Henn W, Knoll JHM, Owen MJ, Zabel BU, Mertelsmann R, Olsen BR 1997 Mutations involving the transcription factor CBFA1 cause cleidocranial dysplasia. Cell **89:**773–779.

11. Yin M, Pacifici M 2001 Vascular regression is required for mesenchymal condensation and chondrogenesis in the developing limb. Dev Dyn **222:**522–533.

12. Schipani E, Ryan HE, Didrickson S, Kobayashi T, Knight M, Johnson RS 2001 Hypoxia in cartilage: HIF-1alpha is essential for chondrocyte growth arrest and survival. Genes Dev **15:**2865–2876.

13. Zelzer E, Mamluk R, Ferrara N, Johnson RS, Schipani E, Olsen BR 2004 VEGFA is necessary for chondrocyte survival during bone development. Development **131:**2161–2171.

14. Zelzer E, Glotzer DJ, Hartmann C, Thomas D, Fukai N, Shay S, Olsen BR 2001 Tissue specific regulation of VEGF expression by Cbfa1/Runx2 during bone development. Mech Dev **106:**97–106.

15. Ivkovic S, Yoon BS, Popoff SN, Safadi FF, Libuda DE, Stephenson RC, Daluiski A, Lyons KM 2003 Connective tissue growth factor coordinates chondrogenesis and angiogenesis during skeletal development. Development **130:**2779–2791.

16. Gossler A, Hrabe de Angelis M 1998 Somitogenesis. Curr Top Dev Biol **38:**225–287.

17. Conlon RA, Reaume AG, Rossant J 1995 Notch1 is required for the coordinate segmentation of somites. Development **121:**1533–1545.

18. Lendahl U 1998 A growing family of Notch ligands. Bioessays **20:**103–107.

19. Kusumi K, Sun ES, Kerrebrock AW, Bronson RT, Chi DC, Bulotsky MS, Spencer JB, Birren BW, Frankel WN, Lander ES 1998 The mouse pudgy mutation disrupts Delta homologue Dll3 and initiation of early somite boundaries. Nat Genet **19:**274–278.

20. Wong PC, Zheng H, Chen H, Becher MW, Sirinathsinghji DJ, Trumbauer ME, Chen HY, Price DL, Van der Ploeg LH, Sisodia SS 1997 Presenilin

1 is required for Notch1 and DII1 expression in the paraxial mesoderm. Nature **387**:288–292.

21. Saga Y, Hata N, Koseki H, Taketo MM 1997 Mesp2: A novel mouse gene expressed in the presegmented mesoderm and essential for segmentation initiation. Genes Dev **11**:1827–1839.

22. Bulman MP, Kusumi K, Frayling TM, McKeown C, Garrett C, Lander ES, Krumlauf R, Hattersley AT, Ellard S, Turnpenny PD 2000 Mutations in the human Delta homologue, DLL3, cause axial skeletal defects in spondylocostal dysostosis. Nat Genet **24**:438–441.

23. Oda T, Elkahloun AG, Pike BL, Okajima K, Krantz ID, Genin A, Piccoli DA, Meltzer PS, Spinner NB, Collins FS, Chandrasekharappa SC 1997 Mutations in the human Jagged1 gene are responsible for Alagille syndrome. Nat Genet **16**:235–242.

24. Li L, Krantz ID, Deng Y, Genin A, Banta AB, Collins CC, Qi M, Trask BJ, Kuo WL, Cochran J, Costa T, Pierpont ME, Rand EB, Piccoli DA, Hood L, Spinner NB 1997 Alagille syndrome is caused by mutations in human Jagged1, which encodes a ligand for Notch1. Nat Genet **16**:243–251.

25. Johnson RL, Laufer E, Riddle RD, Tabin C 1994 Ectopic expression of Sonic hedgehog alters dorsal-ventral patterning of somites. Cell **79**:1165–1173.

26. Porter JA, von Kessler DP, Ekker SC, Young KE, Lee JJ, Moses K, Beachy PA 1995 The product of hedgehog autoproteolytic cleavage active in local and long-range signalling. Nature **374**:363–366.

27. Porter JA, Young KE, Beachy PA 1996 Cholesterol modification of hedgehog signaling proteins in animal development. Science **274**:255–259.

28. Chiang C, Litingtung Y, Lee E, Young KE, Corden JL, Westphal H, Beachy PA 1996 Cyclopia and defective axial patterning in mice lacking Sonic hedgehog gene function. Nature **383**:407–413.

29. Hol FA, Geurds MP, Chatkupt S, Shugart YY, Balling R, Schrander-Stumpel CT, Johnson WG, Hamel BC, Mariman EC 1996 PAX genes and human neural tube defects: An amino acid substitution in PAX1 in a patient with spina bifida. J Med Genet **33**:655–660.

30. Wilm B, Dahl E, Peters H, Balling R, Imai K 1998 Targeted disruption of Pax1 defines its null phenotype and proves haploinsufficiency. Proc Natl Acad Sci USA **95**:8692–8697.

31. Robertson KE, Tickle C 1997 Recent molecular advances in understanding vertebrate limb development. Br J Plast Surg **50**:109–115.

32. Niswander L, Jeffrey S, Martin GR, Tickle C 1994 A positive feedback loop coordinates growth and patterning in the vertebrate limb. Nature **317**:609–612.

33. Crossley PH, Minowada G, MacArthur CA, Martin GR 1996 Roles for FGF8 in the induction, initiation, and maintenance of chick limb development. Cell **84**:127–136.

34. Shubin NH, Alberch P 1986 A morphogenetic approach to the origin and basic organization of the tetrapod limb. Evol Biol **20**:319–387.

35. Johnson RL, Tabin CJ 1997 Molecular models for vertebrate limb development. Cell **90**:979–990.

36. Muragaki Y, Mundlos S, Upton J, Olsen BR 1996 Altered growth and branching patterns in synpolydactyly caused by mutations in HOXD13. Science **272**:548–551.

37. Wild A, Kalff-Suske M, Vortkamp A, Bornholdt D, Konig R, Grzeschik KH 1997 Point mutations in human GLI3 cause Greig syndrome. Hum Mol Genet **6**:1979–1984.

38. Kang S, Graham JM, Jr., Olney AH, Biesecker LG 1997 GLI3 frameshift mutations cause autosomal dominant Pallister-Hall syndrome. Nat Genet **15**:266–268.

39. Polinkovsky A, Robin NH, Thomas JT, Irons M, Lynn A, Goodman FR, Reardon W, Kant SG, Brunner HG, van der Burgt I, Chitayat D, McGaughran J, Donnai D, Luyten FP, Warman ML 1997 Mutations in CDMP1 cause autosomal dominant brachydactyly type C. Nat Genet **17**:18–19.

40. Gong Y, Krakow D, Marcelino J, Wilkin D, Chitayat D, Babul-Hirji R, Hudgins L, Cremers CW, Cremers FP, Brunner HG, Reinker K, Rimoin DL, Cohn DH, Goodman FR, Reardon W, Patton M, Francomano CA, Warman ML 1999 Heterozygous mutations in the gene encoding noggin affect human joint morphogenesis. Nat Genet **21**:302–304.

41. Dreyer SD, Zhou G, Baldini A, Winterpacht A, Zabel B, Cole W, Johnson RL, Lee B 1998 Mutations in LMX1B cause abnormal skeletal patterning and renal dysplasia in nail patella syndrome. Nat Genet **19**:47–50.

42. McCready ME, Sweeney E, Fryer AE, Donnai D, Baig A, Racacho L, Warman ML, Hunter AG, Bulman DE 2002 A novel mutation in the IHH gene causes brachydactyly type A1: A 95- year-old mystery resolved. Hum Genet **111**:368–375.

43. Oldridge M, Fortuna AM, Maringa M, Propping P, Mansour S, Pollitt C, DeChiara TM, Kimble RB, Valenzuela DM, Yancopoulos GD, Wilkie AO 2000 Dominant mutations in ROR2, encoding an orphan receptor tyrosine kinase, cause brachydactyly type B. Nat Genet **24**:275–278.

44. Ohbayashi N, Shibayama M, Kurotaki Y, Imanishi M, Fujimori T, Itoh N, Takada S 2002 FGF18 is required for normal cell proliferation and differentiation during osteogenesis and chondrogenesis. Genes Dev **16**:870–879.

45. Shiang R, Thompson LM, Zhu YZ, Church DM, Fielder TJ, Bocian M, Winokur ST, Wasmuth JJ 1994 Mutations in the transmembrane domain of FGFR3 cause the most common genetic form of dwarfism, achondroplasia. Cell **78**:335–342.

46. Bellus GA, McIntosh I, Smith EA, Aylsworth AS, Kaitila I, Horton WA, Greenhaw GA, Hecht JT, Francomano CA 1995 A recurrent mutation in the tyrosine kinase domain of fibroblast growth factor receptor 3 causes hypochondroplasia. Nat Genet **10**:357–359.

47. Vortkamp A, Lee K, Lanske B, Segre GV, Kronenberg HM, Tabin CJ 1996 Regulation of rate of cartilage differentiation by Indian hedgehog and PTH-related protein. Science **273**:613–622.

48. Schipani E, Langman CB, Parfitt AM, Jensen GS, Kikuchi S, Kooh SW, Cole WG, Juppner H 1996 Constitutively activated receptors for parathyroid hormone and parathyroid hormone-related peptide in Jansen's metaphyseal chondrodysplasia. N Engl J Med **335**:708–714.

49. Jobert AS, Zhang P, Couvineau A, Bonaventure J, Roume J, Le Merrer M, Silve C 1998 Absence of functional receptors for parathyroid hormone and parathyroid hormone-related peptide in Blomstrand chondrodysplasia. J Clin Invest **102**:34–40.

50. Long F, Zhang XM, Karp S, Yang Y, McMahon AP 2001 Genetic manipulation of hedgehog signaling in the endochondral skeleton reveals a direct role in the regulation of chondrocyte proliferation. Development **128**:5099–5108.

51. Gerber HP, Vu TH, Ryan AM, Kowalski J, Werb Z, Ferrara N 1999 VEGF couples hypertrophic cartilage remodeling, ossification and angiogenesis during endochondral bone formation. Nat Med **5**:623–628.

52. Linsenmayer TF, Eavey RD, Schmid TM 1988 Type X collagen: A hypertrophic cartilage-specific molecule. Pathol Immunopathol Res **7**:14–19.

53. Jacenko O, LuValle P, Olsen BR 1993 Spondylometaphyseal dysplasia in mice carrying a dominant negative mutation in a matrix protein specific for cartilage-to-bone transition. Nature **365**:56–61.

54. Kwan KM, Pang MK, Zhou S, Cowan SK, Kong RY, Pfordte T, Olsen BR, Sillence DO, Tam PP, Cheah KS 1997 Abnormal compartmentalization of cartilage matrix components in mice lacking collagen X: Implications for function. J Cell Biol **136**:459–471.

55. Gress CJ, Jacenko O 2000 Growth plate compressions and altered hematopoiesis in collagen X null mice. J Cell Biol **149**:983–993.

56. Warman ML, Abbott MH, Apte SS, Hefferon T, McIntosh I, Cohn DH, Hecht JT, Olsen BR, Francomano CA 1993 A type X collagen mutation causes Schmid metaphyseal chondrodysplasia. Nat Genet **5**:79–82.

57. Horton WA 1990 The biology of bone growth. Growth Genet Horm **6**:1–3.

Chapter 2. Anatomy and Functions of the Adult Skeleton

David W. Dempster

Regional Bone Center, Helen Hayes Hospital, West Haverstraw, New York

INTRODUCTION

The adult human skeleton is comprised of 213 bones, each of which is sculpted by a process called modeling, and each is constantly renewed by a process termed remodeling. Depending on its location, each bone supports one or more specific functions, including structural support and movement, protection of vital organs, and maintenance of mineral homeostasis. Remodeling plays a key role in the latter and also provides a mechanism for preservation of bone strength by replacing old fatigued bone by new mechanically sound bone. Remodeling is achieved by the sequential action of osteoclasts and osteoblasts and the process is regulated by osteocytes. The rate of remodeling and balance between resorption and formation in each remodeling unit differs depending on anatomical location and also as a function of age and in disease states. Knowledge of the fundamental principles of remodeling provides an excellent framework for understanding age-related changes in bone structure and geometry, as well as the pathogenesis of metabolic bone diseases and the effects of drugs used to treat them.

MACROSCOPIC ANATOMY

Anatomists distinguish between two main types of bones: flat bones, such as the skull, mandible, and scapula, and long bones such as the femur, tibia, and radius. A process called membranous bone formation forms flat bones and long bones develop by a combination of a process called endochondral bone formation and membranous bone formation. These two modes of bone development are described elsewhere. Long bones consist of a hollow tube (shaft or diaphysis), which flairs at the ends to form the cone-shaped metaphyses, the regions below the growth plate, and the epiphyses, the regions above the growth plate (Fig. 1). The shaft is comprised primarily of cortical bone, whereas the metaphysis and epiphysis contain cancellous bone that is surrounded by a shell of cortical bone. Approximately 80% of the adult skeleton is composed of cortical bone and 20% is cancellous, but the relative proportions of the two types of bone vary considerably among different skeletal sites. For example the ratio of cancellous:cortical bone is estimated to be 75:25 in human vertebrae, 50:50 in the femoral head, and 95:5 in the diaphysis of the radius (Fig. 2).

Bones have an outer fibrous sheath called the periosteum, and the inner surface, which is in direct contact with the marrow, is referred to as the endosteum. The periosteum is an envelope of fibrous connective tissue that covers all bone surfaces except at the joints where the bone is lined by articular cartilage. The periosteum contains the blood vessels that nourish the bone, as well as nerve endings and osteoblasts and osteoclasts. The periosteum is anchored to the bone by strong, collagenous fibers called Sharpeys' fibers that penetrate into the bone tissue. The endosteum is a membranous sheath that also contains blood vessels, osteoblasts and osteoclasts. In addition to lining the marrow cavity, the endosteum also envelopes the surface of cancellous bone and lines the blood vessel canals (Volkman's canals) that run through the bone.

CORTICAL AND TRABECULAR BONE STRUCTURE AND FUNCTIONS

At a macroscopic level, cortical bone appears dense and solid, whereas cancellous bone is a honeycomb-like network of interconnected trabecular plates and bars surrounding bone marrow (Fig. 1). At the microscopic level, both cortical and cancellous are composed of basic structural units or osteons (Fig. 3). In cortical bone, the osteons are commonly referred to as Haversian systems after Clopton Havers, the 17th century English anatomist who first observed the canals in the center of the structures. Haversian systems are cylindrical in shape and form an anatomizing network like the branches of a tree.[1] Their walls are formed by concentric sheaths or lamellae, reminiscent of a tree trunk in cross-section. Trabecular osteons, also referred to as packets, are saucer-shaped, ~35 mm in thickness, and are also composed of stacks of lamellae.

When it comes to function, the skeleton can be considered as a prototype for multitasking. The long bones serve as levers for the muscles, supporting locomotion and all other forms of motion. The flat bones, such as the ribs and those of the skull, serve as armor for the vital organs that they surround. It is common knowledge that the skeleton serves as the body's main repository for calcium and plays a key role in homeostatic regulation of serum calcium concentration. It is less well known that the skeleton plays a similar role with regard to acid–base balance.[2] Bone also serves as a rich source of growth factors and cytokines, a prime example of which is the finding that osteoblasts produce a number of factors that are important for the differentiation and survival of hematopoietic stem cells.[3]

From a functional standpoint, cancellous bone is generally considered to be more metabolically active than is cortical bone, which is viewed largely in its mechanical role. However, this is probably a misconception and may also be species-, and situation-dependent. For example, medullary bone in birds, which is cancellous in structure, serves as a labile source of calcium that is mobilized during eggshell calcification.[4] On the other hand, during antler formation in deer, it is the cortical bone that supplies the necessary extra calcium.[5] Increased demands for calcium during pregnancy and lactation in humans are met primarily from non–weight-bearing bone,[6] whereas bone is preferentially lost from cortical sites in primary hyperparathyroidism.[7]

MODELING

The term bone modeling describes the process whereby bones are shaped or reshaped by independent action of osteoblasts and osteoclasts. This occurs, for example, during growth or in the adult to change the shape of the bone in response to mechanical loads (mechanical adaptation). The radius in the playing arm of competitive, young tennis players has a thicker cortex and greater diameter than the contralateral radius as a result of modeling.[8] Bone modeling is distinguished from remodeling by the fact that bone formation is not tightly coupled to prior bone resorption. In adult humans, bone modeling occurs less frequently than bone remodeling, particularly in cancellous bone, but it does take place in normal subjects[9] and may be increased in hypoparathyroidism and renal bone disease.[10,11] Anabolic agents for the treatment of osteoporosis,

---

The author has reported no conflicts of interest.

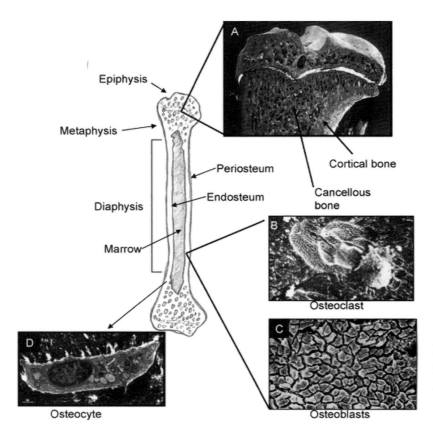

FIG. 1. (A) Scanning electron micrograph of a rat tibial growth plate. (B) Scanning electron micrograph of a human osteoclast cultured for 24 h on a bone slice (reproduced with permission from *J Bone Miner Res* 1989;**4**:259–268. (C) Scanning electron micrograph of osteoblasts on the endosteal surface of a rat long bone. (D) Transmission electron micrograph of a rat osteocyte.

such as PTH(1-34), are also capable of stimulating modeling.[12]

REMODELING

Half a century ago, Dr. A. M. Cooke wrote eloquently that "The skeleton, out of site and often out of mind, is a formidable mass of tissue occupying about 9% of the body by bulk and no less than 17% by weight. The stability and immutability of dry bones and their persistence for centuries, and even millions of years after the soft tissues have turned to dust, give us a false impression of bone during life. Its fixity after death is in sharp contrast to its ceaseless activity during life."[13] In the adult skeleton, the "ceaseless activity" largely refers to the process of bone remodeling. One of the more remarkable features of mammalian bone is its ability to constantly rejuvenate itself through the process of remodeling, which begins in utero and continues until death. Remodeling is accomplished by the collaborative and sequential efforts of a group of cells that are collectively termed the bone remodeling unit (BRU).[14–18] There are four distinct phases in the remodeling cycle: activa-

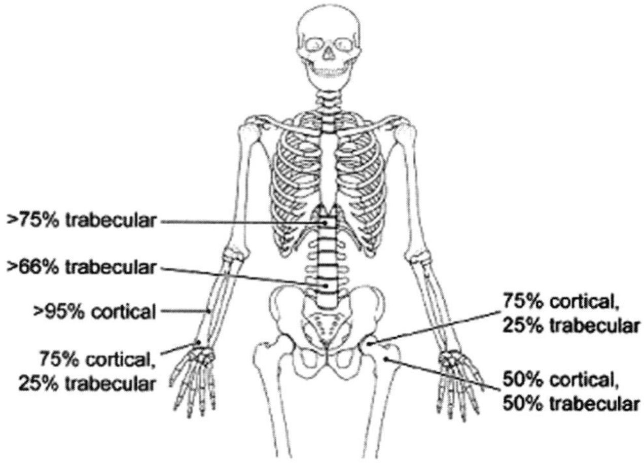

FIG. 2. Proportion of cancellous and cortical bone at different skeletal sites. Reproduced with permission from ASBMR Primer, 5th ed.

>75% trabecular

>66% trabecular

>95% cortical

75% cortical, 25% trabecular

75% cortical, 25% trabecular

50% cortical, 50% trabecular

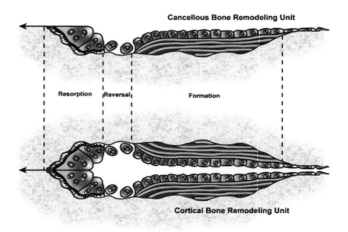

Dempster DW.

FIG. 3. Cross-sectional diagrams of BRUs in cancellous bone (top) and cortical bone (bottom). The arrow indicates the direction of movement through space. Note that the cancellous BRU is essentially one half of the cortical BRU.

tion, resorption, reversal, and formation (Fig. 3). Activation describes the initiating event that transforms a previously quiescent bone surface into a remodeling one. Activation involves recruitment of mononucleated osteoclast precursors from cells in the monocyte–macrophage lineage in the circulation,[19] infiltration of the bone lining cell layer, and fusion of the mononuclear cells to form multinucleated preosteoclasts. The degree to which remodeling activation at a particular site on the bone surface is preselected and the extent to which it is random is unclear. There is some evidence that a proportion of the remodeling is targeted toward specific sites that need to be repaired (see below), but most remodeling is likely to be random.[20,21] The pre-osteoclasts affix themselves to the bone matrix through avid binding between integrin receptors in their membranes and RGD-containing peptides in the organic matrix, creating an annular sealing zone. In forming the seal, the osteoclast creates the bone-resorbing compartment, a unique microenvironment, between itself and the bone matrix. Osteoclast formation, activation, and activity of osteoclasts are all regulated by local cytokines such as RANKL, interleukins -1 and-6 (IL-1 and IL-6), and colony-stimulating factors (CSFs), and systemic hormones such as PTH, 1,25-dihydroxyvitamin D_3, and calcitonin.[19,22–25] During the resorption phase of the cycle, specific types of proton pumps in the osteoclast membrane transfer protons to the resorbing compartment lowering its pH considerably. pH values as low as 4.0 have been detected in this compartment.[26] Acidification of the resorbing compartment is accompanied by secretion of a number of lysosomal enzymes, such as TRACP and cathepsin K, as well as matrix metalloproteases including MMP-9 (collagenase) and gelatinase.[27] The acidic solution, containing enzymes that are most active at low pH, effectively dissolves and digests the mineral and organic phases of the matrix, creating saucer-shaped resorption cavities called Howship's lacunae on the surface of the cancellous bone and cylindrical tunnels within the cortex (Fig. 3). Initially, the resorption is accomplished by multinucleated osteoclasts, but there is both in vivo and in vitro evidence to suggest that excavation of the resorption cavity is completed by mononucleated cells.[28,29] The resorption phase ends with osteoclast apoptosis[30] and is followed by reversal. During reversal, the resorption lacuna is populated by mononuclear cells, including monocytes, osteocytes that have been liberated from the bone by osteoclasts, and pre-osteoblasts that are being recruited to begin the formation phase of the cycle.[31] It is during the reversal phase that all-important coupling signals are sent out to summon osteoblasts into the resorption cavities to replace the bone that has been removed. Without an efficient coupling mechanism, each remodeling transaction would result in net loss of bone. The exact nature of the coupling signal(s) is currently undefined, but there are a number of hypotheses. One attractive theory is that osteoclasts release growth factors from the bone matrix during the resorption phase and that these factors act as chemo-attractants for osteoblast precursors and stimulate osteoblast proliferation and differentiation. This hypothesis explains the correct spatial localization of the osteoblasts and recruitment of the requisite number of osteoblasts to replace the volume of bone that has been removed, which, in turn, will determine the amount of growth factor released. Bone matrix–derived growth factors, such as TGF-β, IGF-I and II, bone morphogenetic proteins (BMPs), platelet-derived growth factors (PDGF), and fibroblast growth factor (FGF) are all likely candidates for coupling factors.[32–36] TGF-β prolongs osteoblast life span in vitro by inhibiting apoptosis, and evidence that TGF-β plays an important role in bone remodeling comes from the demonstration that the concentration of TGF-β human bone is positively correlated with histomorphometric indices of bone resorption and bone formation and with serum

levels of osteocalcin and bone-specific alkaline phosphatase.[37] In addition to stimulating formation during the reversal phase, it is likely that TGF-β released from bone also plays a role in shutting down resorption by inhibiting RANKL production by osteoblasts.[38] Another plausible mechanism for coupling of formation to resorption is that it is a strain-regulated phenomenon.[39] In this theory, it is suggested that, as bone remodeling units traverse through cortical bone, strain levels are reduced ahead of the osteoclasts and are increased behind them. Similarly, strain is thought to be higher at the base of Howship's lacunae in cancellous bone and reduced in the surrounding bone. It is theorized that this gradient of strain leads to sequential activation of osteoclasts and osteoblasts, with osteoclasts being activated in response to reduced strain and osteoblasts in response to increased strain. This hypothesis also has the potential to account for alignment of osteons to the dominant load direction.[40] Another recently proposed idea is that the osteoclast itself plays a role in coupling.[41,42]

Formation is a two-step process in which the osteoblasts initially synthesize the organic matrix and then regulate its mineralization. Once the collagenous organic matrix is secreted, the osteoblasts trigger mineralization by releasing small, membrane-bound vesicles, called matrix vesicles, that establish suitable conditions for initial mineral deposition by concentrating calcium and phosphate ions and enzymatically degrading inhibitors of mineralization, such as pyrophosphate and proteoglycans that are present in the extracellular matrix.[43] As bone formation continues, osteoblasts become entombed in the matrix as osteocytes. Although buried in the matrix, the osteocytes maintain intimate contact with one another, as well as with the cells on the bone surface, by means of gap junctions between the cytoplasmic processes that extend through small tubes in the matrix called canaliculae. Each osteocyte becomes part of a large, 3D, functional syncitium, which can "sense" a change in the mechanical properties of the surrounding bone and transmit this information to the cells on the surface to initiate or regulate bone remodeling when necessary.[44,45] It has therefore been suggested that, from this perspective, bone cells behave like a neuronal network.[46]

When the osteoblasts have completed their matrix-forming function, they endure a number of fates. Approximately 50–70% die by apoptosis, and the remainder are either incorporated into the matrix as osteocytes or remain on the surface as bone-lining cells. The bone-lining cells were once thought to serve primarily to regulate the flow of ions into and out of the bone extracellular fluid and, in so doing, constitute the anatomical basis of the blood–bone barrier. However, it has recently been shown that under certain circumstances, for example, stimulation by PTH or mechanical force, bone-lining cells can revert back to osteoblasts.[47,48] Another potentially important function of the lining cells is to create specialized compartments on the surface of trabecular bone in which bone remodeling occurs.[49]

The net result of each remodeling cycle is the production of a new osteon (Fig. 4). Note that the process of bone remodeling is essentially identical in cancellous and cortical bone. The BRUs in cancellous bone are equivalent to cortical BRUs split in half longitudinally[50] (Fig. 3). The difference between the volume of bone removed by the osteoclasts and that replaced by the osteoblasts is referred to as the "bone balance." BRUs on the periosteal surface of cortical bone produce a slightly positive bone balance so that, with aging, the periosteal circumference increases as the effect of the small positive balance in each BRU accumulates. Remodeling units on the endosteal surface of cortical bone are in negative balance so that the marrow cavity enlarges with age. Furthermore, the balance is more negative on the endosteal surface than it is on the peri-

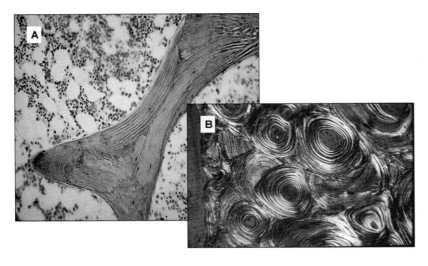

FIG. 4. Basic structural units in (A) cancellous bone and (B) cortical bone. Reproduced with permission from Dempster DW, Lindsay R 1993 Pathogenesis of osteoporosis. Lancet **341**:797–801 with permission from Elsevier.

osteal surface and, as a result, cortical thickness decreases with age. The bone balance on cancellous surfaces is also negative, resulting in a gradual thinning of the trabecular plates with the passage of time.[14]

FUNCTIONS OF BONE REMODELING

Two principal functions of bone remodeling are known, although it has been suggested that there must be other, as yet unknown functions or reasons why the human skeleton undergoes such extensive remodeling.[51] The primary functions of bone remodeling are presumed to be the preventive maintenance of mechanical strength by continuously replacing fatigued bone by new, mechanically sound bone, and, second, an important role in mineral homeostasis by providing access to the skeletal stores of calcium and phosphorus, as described above. While the turnover rate of 2–3% per year in cortical bone is consistent with maintenance of mechanical properties, the turnover rate in cancellous bone is much higher than would be required for this purpose, suggesting that this is driven more by its role in mineral metabolism.[18] In situations where calcium demand is high, activation of new remodeling units may be required, but it has been suggested that short-term mineral homeostasis may only require the presence of a minimum number of osteoclasts whose activity can be regulated. Continual remodeling activity therefore ensures the presence of this contingent of osteoclasts. Remodeling also ensures a constant continuous supply of new bone of low mineral density, which is needed for ionic exchange at quiescent surfaces.[18] The best evidence to date for a role of bone remodeling in the maintenance of the mechanical integrity of the skeleton has come from studies in dogs.[52,53] Long bones were loaded to induce fatigue damage and then studied histologically. A statistically significant association between microcracks and resorption spaces was observed, with up to six times as many cracks associated with resorption spaces as predicted by chance alone.[54] This could be explained by a propensity of microcracks to form close to resorption spaces. However, further experiments showed that the activation of remodeling was in response to the appearance of microcracks.[53] This was shown by loading the left forelimbs of dogs 8 days before death and loading the right forelimbs immediately before death. If cracks simply localize at sites of resorption, the number of cracks associated with resorption spaces would be expected to be identical in each limb. The results showed the same number of microcracks in each limb, but that the limb that was loaded a week before displayed more resorption spaces and a greater

association between microcracks and resorption than the limb that was loaded immediately before death. The reasonable conclusion is that microcracks initiate resorption. One possible mechanism for this targeted remodeling is that microcracks cause debonding of cortical osteons.[55] As a result, there is a decrease in stress and strain in that region of the osteon, which is detected by the osteocytes and communicated to the surface lining cells. The lining cells trigger activation of a bone remodeling unit from the Haversian canal and this moves toward, and ultimately replaces the damaged area with a new osteon. Fatigue damage may also promote osteocyte apoptosis and it has been suggested that this is the initial trigger for targeted remodeling.[56–59]

REFERENCES

1. Stout SD, Brunsden BS, Hildebolt CF, Commean PK, Smith KE, Tappen NC 1999 Computer-assisted 3D reconstruction of serial sections of cortical bone to determine the 3D structure of osteons. Calcif Tissue Int **65**:280–284.
2. Arnett T 2003 Regulation of bone cell function by acid-base balance. Proc Nutr Soc **62**:511–520.
3. Taichman RS 2005 Blood and bone: Two tissues whose fates are intertwined to create the hematopoietic stem-cell niche. Blood **105**:2631–2639.
4. Whitehead CC 2004 Overview of bone biology in the egg-laying hen. Poult Sci **83**:193–199.
5. Banks WJ Jr, Epling GP, Kainer RA, Davis RW 1968 Antler growth and osteoporosis. I. Morphological and morphometric changes in the costal compacta during the antler growth cycle. Anat Rec **162**:387–398.
6. Bowman BM, Miller SC 2001 Skeletal adaptations during mammalian reproduction. J Musculoskelet Neuronal Interact **1**:347–355.
7. Bilezikian JP, Brandi ML, Rubin M, Silverberg SJ 2005 Primary hyperparathyroidism: New concepts in clinical, densitometric and biochemical features. J Intern Med **257**:6–8.
8. Haapasalo H, Kontulainen S, Sievanen H, Kannus P, Jarvinen M, Vuori I 2000 Exercise-induced bone gain is due to enlargement in bone size without a change in volumetric bone density: A peripheral quantitative computed tomography study of the upper arms of male tennis players. Bone **27**:351–357.
9. Kobayashi S, Takahashi HE, Ito A, Saito N, Nawata M, Horiuchi H, Ohta H, Ito A, Iorio R, Yamamoto N, Takaoka K 2003 Trabecular minimodeling in human iliac bone. Bone **32**:163–169.
10. Ubara Y, Tagami T, Nakanishi S, Sawa N, Hoshino J, Suwabe T, Katori H, Takemoto F, Hara S, Takaichi K 2005 Significance of minimodeling in dialysis patients with adynamic bone disease. Kidney Int **68**:833–839.
11. Ubara Y, Fushimi T, Tagami T, Sawa N, Hoshino J, Yokota M, Katori H, Takemoto F, Hara S 2003 Histomorphometric features of bone in patients with primary and secondary hypoparathyroidism. Kidney Int **63**:1809–1816
12. Lindsay R, Cosman F, Zhou H, Bostrom M, Shen V, Cruz J, Nieves JW, Dempster DW 2006 A novel tetracycline labeling schedule for longitudi-

nal evaluation of the short-term effects of anabolic therapy with a single iliac crest bone biopsy: Early actions of teriparatide. J Bone Miner Res **21:**366–373.

13. Cooke AM 1955 Osteoporosis. Lancet **1:**878–882.

14. Frost HM 1986 Intermediary Organization of the Skeleton. CRC Press, Boca Raton, FL, USA.

15. Parfitt AM 2002 Physiologic and pathogenetic significance of bone histomorphometric data. In: Coe FL, Favus MJ (eds.) Disorders of Bone Miner Metabolism, 2nd ed. Lippincott Williams and Wilkins, Baltimore, MD, USA, pp. 469–485.

16. Dempster DW 2002 Bone remodeling. In: Coe FL, Favus MJ (eds.) Disorders of Bone Miner Metabolism, 2nd ed. Lippincott Williams and Wilkins, Baltimore, MD, USA, pp. 315–343.

17. Dempster DW 1995 Bone remodeling. In: Riggs BL, Melton LJ III (eds.) Osteoporosis: Etiology, Diagnosis, and Management, 2nd ed. Raven Press, New York, NY, USA, pp. 67–91.

18. Parfitt AM 1995 Problems in the application of in vitro systems to the study of human bone remodeling. Calcif Tissue Int **56**(Suppl 1):S5–S7.

19. Roodman, GD 1999 Cell biology of the osteoclast. Exp Hematol **27:** 1229–1241.

20. Burr, DB 2002 Targeted and nontargeted remodeling. Bone **30:**2–4.

21. Parfitt, AM 2002 Targeted and nontargeted bone remodeling: Relationship to basic multicellular unit origination and progression. Bone **30:**5–7.

22. Roodman, GD 2004 Mechanisms of bone metastasis. N Engl J Med **350:**1655–1664.

23. Simonet WS, Lacey DL 2003 Osteoclast differentiation and activation. Nature **423:**337–342.

24. Troen BR 2003 Molecular mechanisms underlying osteoclast formation and activation. Exp Gerontol **38:**605–614.

25. Blair, HC, Athanasou, NA 2004 Recent advances in osteoclast biology and pathological bone resorption. Histol Histopathol **19:**189–199.

26. Silver IA, Murrills RJ, Etherington DJ 1988 Microelectrode studies on the acid microenvironment beneath adherent macrophages and osteoclasts. Exp Cell Res **175:**266–276.

27. Delaisse JM, Andersen TL, Engsig MT, Henriksen K, Troen T, Blavier L 2003 Matrix metalloproteinases (MMP) and cathepsin K contribute differently to osteoclastic activities. Microsc Res Tech **61:**504–513.

28. Eriksen EF 1986 Normal and pathological remodeling of human trabecular bone: Three-dimensional reconstruction of the remodeling sequence in normals and in metabolic bone disease. Endocrine Rev **7:**379–408.

29. Dempster DW, Hughes-Begos C, Plavetic-Chee K, Brandao-Burch A, Cosman F, Nieves J, Neubort S, Lu S, Iida-Klein A, Arnett T, Lindsay R 2005 Normal human osteoclasts formed from peripheral blood monocytes express PTH type 1 receptors and are stimulated by PTH in the absence of osteoblasts. J Cell Biochem **95:**139–148.

30. Reddy SV 2004 Regulatory mechanisms operative in osteoclasts. Crit Rev Eukaryot Gene Expr **14:**255–270.

31. Baron R, Vignery A, Tran Van P 1980 The significance of lacunar erosion without osteoclasts: Studies on the reversal phase of the remodeling sequence. Metab Bone Dis Rel Res **2S:**35–40.

32. Bonewald LF, Mundy GR 1990 Role of transforming growth factor beta in bone remodeling. Clin Orthop Rel Res **250:**261–276.

33. Mohan S, Baylink DJ 1996 Insulin-like growth factor system components and the coupling of bone formation to resorption. Horm Res **45**(Suppl 1):59–62.

33. Hock, JM, Centrella, M, Canalis, E 1998 Insulin-like growth factor I (IGF-I) has independent effects on bone matrix formation and cell replication. Endocrinology **122:**254–260.

34. Fiedler, J, Roderer, G, Gunther, KP, Brenner, RE 2002 BMP-2, BMP-4, and PDGF-bb stimulate chemotactic migration of primary human mesenchymal progenitor cells. J Cell Biochem **87:**306–312.

35. Tanaka, H, Wakisaka, A, Ogasa, H, Kawai, S, Liang, CT 2003 Effects of basic fibroblast growth factor on osteoblast-related gene expression in the process of medullary bone formation induced in rat femur. J Bone Miner Metab **21:**74–79.

36. Locklin, RM, Oreffo, RO, Triffitt, JT 1999 Effects of TGFbeta and bFGF on the differentiation of human bone marrow stromal fibroblasts. Cell Biol Int **23:**185–194.

37. Pfeilschifter J, Diel I, Scheppach B, Bretz A, Krempien R, Erdmann J, Schmidd G, Reske N, Bismar H, Seck T, Krempien B, Ziegler R 1998 Concentration of transforming growth factor beta in human bone tissue: Relationship to age, menopause, bone turnover, and bone volume. J Bone Miner Res **13:**716–730.

38. Fox SW, Lovibond AC 2005 Current insights into the role of transforming growth factor-beta in bone resorption. Mol Cell Endocrinol **243:**19–26.

39. Smit TH, Burger EH 2000 Is BMU-coupling a strain-regulated phenomenon? A finite element analysis. J Bone Miner Res **15:**301–307.

40. Smit TH, Burger EH, Huyghe JM 2002 A case for strain-induced fluid flow as a regulator of BMU-coupling and osteonal alignment. J Bone Miner Res **17:**2021–2029.

41. Martin TJ, Sims NA 2005 Osteoclast-derived activity in the coupling of bone formation to resorption. Trends Mol Med **11:**76–81.

42. Karsdal MA, Henriksen K, Sorensen MG, Gram J, Schaller S, Dziegiel MH, Christophersen P, Martin TJ, Christiansen C, Bollerslev J 2005 Acidification of the osteoclastic resorption compartment provides insight into the coupling of bone formation to bone resorption. Am J Pathol **166:**467–476.

43. Anderson HC 2003 Matrix vesicles and calcification. Curr Rheumatol Rep **5:**222–226.

44. Huiskes, R, Ruimerman, R, van Lenthe, GH, Janssen, JD 2000 Effects of mechanical forces on maintenance and adaptation of form in trabecular bone. Nature **405:**704–706.

45. Burger, EH, Klein-Nulend J, Smit TH 2003 Strain-derived canalicular fluid flow regulates osteoclast activity in a remodeling osteon—a proposal. J Biomech **36:**1452–1459.

46. Turner CH, Robling AG, Duncan RL, Burr DB 2002 Do bone cells behave like a neuronal network? Calcif Tissue Int **70:**435–442.

47. Dobnig H, Turner RT 1995 Evidence that intermittent treatment with parathyroid hormone increases bone formation in adult rats by activation of bone lining cells. Endocrinology **136:**3632–3638.

48. Chow JW, Wilson AJ, Chambers TJ, Fox SW 1998 Mechanical loading stimulates bone formation by reactivation of bone lining cells in 13-week-old rats. J Bone Miner Res **13:**1760–1767.

49. Hauge EM, Qvesel D, Eriksen EF, Mosekilde L, Melsen F 2001 Cancellous bone remodeling occurs in specialized compartments lined by cells expressing osteoblastic markers. J Bone Miner Res **16:**1575–1582.

50. Parfitt AM 1994 Osteonal and hemiosteonal remodeling: The spatial and temporal framework for signal traffic in adult bone. J Cell Biochem **55:**273–276.

51. Currey JD 2002 Bones: Structure and Mechanics. Princeton University Press, Princeton, NJ, USA.

52. Burr DB, Martin RB, Schaffler MB, Radin EL 1985 Bone remodeling in response to in vivo fatigue microdamage. J Biomech **18:**189–200.

53. Mori S, Burr DB 1993 Increased intracortical remodeling following fatigue damage. Bone **14:**103–109.

54. Burr DB, Forwood MR, Fyhrie DP, Martin RB, Schaffler MB, Turner CH 1997 Perspective: Bone microdamage and skeletal fragility in osteoporotic and stress fractures. J Bone Miner Res **12:**6–15.

55. Martin RB, Burr DB 1989 Structure, Function, and Adaptation of Compact Bone. Raven Press, New York, NY, USA.

56. Noble BS, Peet N, Stevens HY, Brabbs A, Mosley JR, Reilly GC, Reeve J, Skerry TM, Lanyon LE 2003 Mechanical loading: Biphasic osteocyte survival and targeting of osteoclasts for bone destruction in rat cortical bone. Am J Physiol Cell Physiol **284:**C934–C943.

57. Verborgt O, Tatton NA, Majeska RJ, Schaffler MB 2002 Spatial distribution of Bax and Bcl-2 in osteocytes after bone fatigue: Complementary roles in bone remodeling regulation? J Bone Miner Res **17:**907–914.

58. Verborgt O, Gibson GJ, Schaffler MB 2000 Loss of osteocyte integrity in associated with microdamage and bone remodeling after fatigue in vivo. J Bone Miner Res **15:**60–67.

59. Noble BS, Stevens H, Loveridge N, Reeve J 1997 Identification of apoptotic changes in osteocytes in normal and pathological bone. Bone **20:**273–282.

Chapter 3. Extracellular Matrix and Biomineralization of Bone

Pamela Gehron Robey[1] and Adele L. Boskey[2]

[1]Craniofacial and Skeletal Diseases Branch, National Institute of Dental and Craniofacial Research, National Institutes of Health, and Department of Health and Human Services, Bethesda, Maryland; and [2]Musculoskeletal Integrity Program, Hospital for Special Surgery, and Department of Biochemistry and Program in Physiology, Biophysics and Systems Biology, Weill Medical College and Graduate School of Cornell University, New York, New York

INTRODUCTION

Bone composes the largest proportion of the body's connective tissue mass. Unlike most other connective tissue matrices, bone matrix is physiologically mineralized and is unique in that it is constantly regenerated throughout life as a consequence of bone turnover. Information on the gene and protein structure and potential function of bone extracellular matrix constituents has exploded during the last few decades. This information has been described in great detail elsewhere,[1,2] to which the reader is referred for specific references, which are too numerous to be listed adequately here. This chapter summarizes salient features of the classes of bone matrix proteins, and the tables list specific details for the individual components.

COLLAGEN

The basic building block of the bone matrix fiber network is type I collagen, which is a triple-helical molecule containing two identical α1(I) chains and a structurally similar, but genetically different, α2(I) chain[3] (Table 1). Collagen α chains are characterized by a Gly-X-Y repeating triplet (where X is usually proline, and Y is often hydroxyproline), and by several post-translational modifications including (1) hydroxylation of certain lysyl residues (2) glycosylation of lysyl or hydroxylysyl residues with glucose or galactose residues or both, and (3) formation of intra- and intermolecular covalent cross-links that differ from those found in soft connective tissues. Measurement of these bone-derived collagen cross-links in urine have proved to be good measures of bone resorption.[4] Bone matrix proper consists predominantly of type I collagen; however, trace amounts of type III, V, and FACIT collagens may be present during certain stages of bone formation and may contribute to the regulation of collagen fibril diameter (Table 1).

NONCOLLAGENOUS PROTEINS

Noncollagenous proteins (NCPs) compose 10–15% of the total bone protein content. Approximately one fourth of the total NCP content is exogenously derived. This fraction is largely composed of serum-derived proteins, such as albumin and α_2-HS-glycoprotein (Table 2), which are acidic in character and bind to bone matrix because of their affinity to hydroxyapatite. Although these proteins are not endogenously synthesized, they may exert effects on matrix mineralization, and α_2-HS-glycoprotein, which is the human analoga of fetuin, also may regulate bone cell proliferation. The remainder of this exogenous fraction is composed of growth factors and a large variety of other molecules present in trace amounts, which also may influence local bone cell activity.[2]

Bone-forming cells synthesize and secrete as many molecules of NCP as of collagen, on a mole-to-mole basis. These molecules can be broken down into four general (and sometimes overlapping) groups: (1) proteoglycans, (2) glycosylated proteins, (3) glycosylated proteins with potential cell-attachment activities, and (4) γ-carboxylated (gla) proteins. The physiological roles for individual bone protein constituents are not well defined; however, many seem to be multifunctional, participating not only in regulating the deposition and turnover of mineral, but also in the control of osteoblastic and osteoclastic metabolism.

PROTEOGLYCANS, LEUCINE-RICH REPEAT PROTEINS, AND HYALURONAN

Proteoglycans are macromolecules that contain acidic polysaccharide side chains (glycosaminoglycans) attached to a central core protein, and bone matrix contains several members of this family.[5] During initial stages of bone formation, the large chondroitin sulfate proteoglycan, versican, and the glycosaminoglycan, hyaluronan (which is not attached to a protein core), are produced and may delineate areas that will become bone (Table 3) With continued osteogenesis, versican is replaced by two small chondroitin sulfate proteoglycans, decorin and biglycan, composed of tandem repeats of a leucine-rich repeat sequence. These two proteoglycans belong to a family of small proteoglycans, known as SLRPs (small leucine-rich proteoglycans). Decorin has been implicated in the regulation of collagen fibrillogenesis and is distributed predominantly in the ECM space of connective tissues and in bone, whereas biglycan tends to be found in pericellular locales. Although their exact physiological functions are not known, they are assumed to be important for the integrity of most connective tissue matrices. Deletion of the biglycan gene in transgenic animals leads to a significant decrease in the development of trabecular bone, indicating that it is a positive regulator of bone formation.[6] One function might rise from the ability of decorin and biglycan to bind and modulate the activity of the TGF-β family in the extracellular space, thereby influencing cell proliferation and differentiation. Other SLRPs (which may or may not bear glycosaminoglycans), such as fibromodulin, osteoglycin, osteoadherin, lumican, and asporin are found in bone matrix but at lower levels than decorin and biglycan and may function in other aspects of bone metabolism[7] (Table 3).

GLYCOPROTEINS

One of the hallmarks of bone formation is the synthesis of high levels of alkaline phosphatase (Table 4). This enzyme, primarily bound to the cell surface through a phosphoinositol linkage, can be cleaved from the cell surface and may be found within mineralized matrix. The function of alkaline phosphatase in bone cell biology has been the matter of much speculation and remains undefined.[8] However deletion of the tissue nonspecific form of alkaline phosphatase results in an abnormal pattern of calcification, confirming the significance of this enzyme in the mineralization process.[9]

The most abundant NCP produced by bone cells is osteonectin, a phosphorylated glycoprotein accounting for ~2% of the total protein of developing bone in most animal species. Os-

The authors have reported no conflicts of interest.

TABLE 1. CHARACTERISTICS OF COLLAGEN-RELATED GENES AND PROTEINS FOUND IN BONE MATRIX

Protein/gene	Function	Disease/animal model
Type I—17q21.23, 7q22.1 [α1(I)₂α2(I)] [α1(I)₃]	Most abundant protein in bone matrix (90% of organic matrix), serves as scaffolding, binds and orients other proteins that nucleate hydroxyapatite deposition	Osteogenesis imperfecta; oim mouse; mov 14 mouse; brtl knock-in mouse; bones mechanically weak; mineral crystals small; some mineral outside collagen
Type X—6q21 [α1(X)₃]	Present in hypertrophic cartilage but does not seem to regulate matrix mineralization	Human mutations—Schmid metaphyseal chondrodysplasia knockout mouse—no apparent skeletal phenotype
Type III—2q31 [α1(III)]₃ Type V—9q34.2-34.3; 2q24.3-31, 19q13.2 [α1(V)₂α2(V)] [α1(V) α2(V) α3(V)]	Present in bone in trace amounts, may regulate collagen fibril diameter, their paucity in bone may explain the large diameter size of bone collagen fibrils	Human mutations—different forms of Ehlers-Danlos syndrome

teonectin is transiently produced in nonbone tissues that are rapidly proliferating, remodeling, or undergoing profound changes in tissue architecture and is found constitutively in certain types of epithelial cells, cells associated with the skeleton, and in platelets. Its function(s) in bone may be multiple, with potential association with osteoblast growth, proliferation, or both, as well as with matrix mineralization.[2,10] A transgenic mouse deficient in osteonectin exhibits a defect in bone formation.[11] Tetranectin deletion results in no abnormalities in bone formation, but by 6 months, mice lacking tetranectin develop a curvature of the spine that is not associated with muscle abnormalities, implying some role of this protein in stabilizing the vertebral bodies,[12] but its precise function is unknown. Bone cells produce another set of glycoproteins, tenascin-C and -W, which seem to regulate both the organization of the matrix and the activity of cells, although tenascin-C–deficient mice do not have a skeletal phenotype, perhaps because of compensation by tenascin-W.[13]

SMALL INTEGRIN-BINDING LIGAND, N-GLYCOSLATED PROTEIN AND OTHER GLYCOPROTEINS WITH CELL ATTACHMENT ACTIVITY

All connective tissue cells interact with their extracellular environment in response to stimuli that direct and/or coordinate specific cell functions, such as migration, proliferation, and differentiation. These particular interactions involve cell attachment through transient or stable focal adhesions to extracellular macromolecules, which are mediated by cell surface receptors (primarily integrins) that subsequently transduce intracellular signals. Bone cells synthesize at least nine proteins

that may mediate cell attachment: members of the small integrin-binding ligand, N-glycoslated protein (SIBLING) family (osteopontin, bone sialoprotein, dentin matrix protein-1, MEPE; Table 5), type I collagen, fibronectin, thrombospondin(s) (predominantly TSP-2 with lower levels of TSP1,3,4 and COMP), vitronectin, fibrillin, BAG-75 (Table 6), and osteoadherin (which is also a proteoglycan).[1,2,5,14] Many of these proteins are phosphorylated and/or sulfated, and all contain RGD (Arg-Gly-Asn), the cell attachment consensus sequence that binds to the integrin class of cell surface molecules. However, in some cases, cell attachment seems to be independent of RGD, indicating the presence of other sequences or mechanisms of cell attachment. Both osteopontin and bone sialoprotein are known to anchor osteoclasts to bone, and in addition to supporting cell attachment, bind Ca^{2+} with extremely high affinity through polyacidic amino acid sequences. It is not immediately clear why there are such a plethora of RGD-containing proteins in bone; however, the pattern of expression varies from one RGD protein to another, as does the pattern of the different integrins that bind to these proteins. This variability indicates that cell–matrix interactions change as a function of maturational stage, suggesting that they also may play a role in osteoblastic maturation.[2,15]

γ-CARBOXYLIC ACID–CONTAINING PROTEINS

Three bone-matrix NCPs, matrix γ-carboxylic acid (gla) protein (MGP), osteocalcin (bone gla protein [BGP]), both of which are made endogenously, and protein S (made primarily in the liver but also made by osteogenic cells), are post-translationally modified by the action of vitamin K–dependent γ-carboxylases[2] (Table 7). The production of di-carboxylic

TABLE 2. GENE AND PROTEIN CHARACTERISTICS OF SERUM PROTEINS FOUND IN BONE MATRIX

Protein/gene	Function	Disease/animal model
Albumin—4q11-q13 69 kDa, non-glycosylated, one sulfhydryl, 17 disulfide bonds, high affinity hydrophobic binding pocket	Inhibits hydroxyapatite crystal growth	
α2-HS glycoprotein—3q27 Precursor protein of cleaved to form A and B chains that are disulfide linked, ala-ala and pro-pro repeat sequences, N-linked oligosaccharides, cystatin-like domains	Promotes endocytosis, has opsonic properties, chemoattractant for monocytic cells, bovine analog (fetuin) is a growth factor	Knockout mouse—adult ectopic calcification

Table 3. Gene and Protein Characteristics of Glycosaminoglycan-Containing Molecules, Leucine Rich Repeat Proteins (LRRs), and Hyaluronan

Protein/gene	Function	Disease/animal model
Aggrecan—15q26.1 ~2.5 × 10⁶-kDa intact protein, ~180–370,000 kDa core, ~100 CS chains of 25 kDa, and some KS chains of similar size, G1, G2 and G3 globular domains with hyaluronan binding sites, EGF and CRP-like sequences	Matrix organization, retention of water and ions, resilience to mechanical forces	Brachymorphic mouse (mutation), accelerated growth plate calcification, nanomelic chick (mutation)—abnormal bone shape,
Versican (PG-100)—5q14.3 ~1 × 10⁶-kDa intact protein, ~360-kDa core, ~12 CS chains of 45 kDa, G1 and G3 globular domains with hyaluronan binding sites, EGF and CRP-like sequences	May "capture" space that is destined to become bone	Heart defect mouse (insertion leading to null), homozygous embryonic lethal, appears to regulation pre-chondrogenic condensation
Decorin (class 1 SLRP)—12q21.3 ~130-kDa intact protein, ~38–45-kDa core with 10 leucine rich repeat sequences, 1 CS chain of 40 kDa	Binds to collagen and regulates fibril diameter, binds to TGF-β and may modulate activity, inhibits cell attachment to fibronectin	Knockout—no apparent skeletal phenotype, DCN/BGN double knockout—progeroid form of Ehler's-Danlos syndrome
Biglycan (class 1 SLRP)—Xq28 ~270-kDa intact protein, ~38–45-kDa core protein with 12 leucine rich repeat sequences, 2 CS chains of 40 kDa	Binds to collagen, may bind to TGF-β, pericellular environment, may be a genetic determinant of peak bone mass	Knockout mouse, Turners syndrome—osteopenia; thin bones, decreased mineral content, increased crystal size; short stature, thin bones; Kleinfelder's syndrome—excessive height
Asporin (class 1 SLRP)—9q22 67 kDa, most likely no GAG chains		
Fibromodulin (class 2 SLRP)—1q32 59-kDa intact protein, 42-kDa core protein, one N-linked KS chain	Binds to collagen, regulates fibril formation, binds to TGF-β	Fibromodulin/biglycan double knockout—joint laxity and formation of supernumery sesmoid bones
Osteoadherin/osteomodulin (class 2 SLRP)—9q22.3 85-kDa intact protein, 47-kDa core protein, RGD sequence	May mediate cell attachment	
Lumican (class 2 SLRP)—12q21.3-q22 70- to 80-kDa intact protein, 37-kDa core protein	Binds to collagen, may regulate fibril formation	Lumican/fibromodulin double knockout mouse—ectopic calcification
Osteoglycin/mimecan (class 3 SLRP)—9q22 299 aa precursor, 105 aa mature protein, no GAG in bone, keratan sulfate in other tissues	Binds to TGF-β	Knockout mouse—no apparent skeletal defect
Hyaluronan—multigene complex Glycosaminoglycan without a core protein, assembled by multiple proteins associated outside of the cell	May work with versican molecule to capture space destined to become bone	

glutamyl (gla) residues enhances calcium binding. MGP is found in many connective tissues, whereas osteocalcin is bone and dentin specifically. MGP-deficient mice develop calcification in extraskeletal sites such as in the aorta[16] and excessive calcification in skeletal sites. Osteocalcin-deficient mice have increased BMD compared with normal mice.[17] In human bone, osteocalcin is concentrated in osteocytes, and its release may be a signal in the bone turnover cascade. Osteocalcin measurements in serum have proved valuable as a marker of bone turnover in metabolic disease states.[4]

BONE MINERALIZATION

The composition of bone enables it to perform its unique mechanical, protective, and homeostatic functions. While this composition varies with age, anatomic location, diet, and health status, in general, mineral accounts for 50–70% of adult mammalian bone, the organic matrix for 20–40%, water for 5–10%, and lipids for <3%. The mineral, a calcium- and hydroxide-deficient analog of the geologic mineral, hydroxyapatite [Ca₁₀(PO₄)₆(OH)₂], provides mechanical rigidity and load bearing strength to the bone composite. In contrast to large geologic hydroxyapatite crystals, bone mineral crystals are extremely small (~200 Å in their largest dimension). Bone mineral contains numerous impurities (carbonate, magnesium, acid phosphate) and vacancies (missing OH⁻), and is usually referred to as a poorly crystalline, carbonate-substituted apatite.[18] These small imperfect crystals are more soluble than geologic apatite enabling bone to act as a reservoir for calcium, phosphate, and magnesium ions.

The organic matrix, predominantly type I collagen, provides elasticity and flexibility to bone and also determines its structural organization. Both the collagen and the non-collagenous proteins associated with the collagen influence the way bone mineralization occurs and the way bone remodels. The cells that are responsible for bone formation, repair, and remodeling respond to hormonal, mechanical, and other extrinsic signals. Lipids, found in the membranes of these cells control the flux of ions and also are directly involved mineralization. Water, found within the cells and in the extracellular matrix, is important for maintenance of tissue properties and nutrition.

Bone mineral is initially deposited at discrete sites in the

Table 4. Gene and Protein Characteristics of Glycoproteins in Bone Matrix

Protein/gene	Function	Disease/animal models
Alkaline Phosphatase (bone-liver-kidney isozyme)—1p36.1-p34 Two identical subunits of ~80 kDa, disulfide bonded, tissue specific post translational modifications	Potential Ca^{++} carrier, hydrolyzes inhibitors of mineral deposition such as pyrophosphates	Hypophosphatasia (decreased activity), TNAP knockout mouse—growth impaired; decreased mineralization
Osteonectin/SPARC—5q31.3-q32 ~35–45 kDa, intramolecular disulfide bonds, α helical amino terminus with multiple low affinity Ca^{++} binding sites, two EF hand high affinity Ca^{++} sites, ovomucoid homology, glycosylated, phosphorylated, tissue specific modifications	Regulates collagen fibrillogenesis, binds to growth factors, may influence cell cycle, positive regulator of bone formation	Knockout mouse—altered collagen cross-linking; decreased trabecular connectivity; decreased mineral content; increased crystal size
Tetranectin—3p22-p21.3 21-kDa protein composed of four identical subunits of 5.8 kDa, sequence homologies with asialoprotein receptor and G3 domain of aggrecan	Binds to plasminogen, may regulate matrix mineralization	Knockout mouse—no long bone phenotype, spinal deformity, increased mineralization in implant model
Tenascin-C—9q33 Hexameric structure, six identical chains of 320 kDa, cys rich, EGF-like repeats, FN type III repeats	Interferes with cell-FN interactions	Knockout mouse—no apparent skeletal phenotype
Tenascin-W Hexameric structure like tenascin C with 9 FN type III repeats	Expressed in same tissues as Tenascin C during bone development; may be involved in regulating osteogenesis	

collagenous matrix.[18] As bone matures, the mineral crystals become larger and more perfect (containing fewer impurities). The increase in crystal dimension is caused both by the actual addition of ions to the crystals (crystal growth) and by aggregation of the crystals.[19,20] The initial sites of mineralization are the "hole" zones between the collagen fibrils.[18] There is still debate as to whether bone mineral forms concurrently in the protected environment of membrane bound bodies known as extracellular matrix vesicles, as it does in calcifying cartilage and mineralizing turkey tendons.[2,21] Because the body fluids are undersaturated with respect to apatite (i.e., apatite will not precipitate spontaneously), the bone matrix must contain one or more components, which facilitate apatite deposition.

Table 5. Gene and Protein Characteristics of SIBLINGs in Bone

Protein/gene	Function	Disease/animal models
Osteopontin—4q21 ~44–75 kDa, polyaspartyl stretches, no disulfide bonds, glycosylated, phosphorylated, RGD located 2/3 from the N-terminal	Binds to cells, inhibits mineralization in bone and soft tissues; inhibits remodeling; involved in tumorogenesis; inhibits nitric oxide synthase, may regulate resistance to viral infection	Knockout mouse—decreased crystal size; increased mineral content; not subject to osteoclast remodeling
Bone sialoprotein—4q21 ~46–75 kDa, polyglutamyl stretches, no disulfide bonds, 50% carbohydrate, tyrosine-sulfated, RGD near the C terminus	Binds to cells, initiates mineralization in vitro	Knockout mouse—no published data on phenotype.
DMP-1—4q21 513 amino acids predicted; acidic, RGD 2/3 from N-terminus	In vitro regulator of mineralization	Knockout mouse—craniofacial and growth plate abnormalities; decreased mineral content, increased crystal size
MEPE—4q21.1 525 amino acids predicted, ~48–57 kDa, acidic proteolysis resistant domain (ASARM)	Possible regulator of phosphate metabolism	Knockout mouse—increased bone formation, decrease in age-related trabecular bone loss, possible involvement in renal phosphate wasting diseases in humans
DSPP—4q21.3 Codes for both phosphophoryn (DPP) and dentin sialoprotein (DSP), DPP—85% acidic, phosphoserine-rich, DPP similar to BSP and OPN		Knockout mouse—dentin and enamel abnormalities—no obvious bone phenotype

TABLE 6. GENE AND PROTEIN CHARACTERISTICS OF OTHER RGD-CONTAINING GLYCOPROTEINS

Protein/gene	Function	Disease/animal models
Thrombospondins (1-4, COMP)—15q15, 6q27, 1q21, 5q13, 19p13.1 ~450-kDa molecule, three identical disulfide linked subunits of ~150–180 kDa, homologies to fibrinogen, properdin, EGF, collagen, von Willebrand, P. falciparum and calmodulin, RGD at the C terminal globular domain	Cell attachment (but usually not spreading), binds to heparin, platelets, types I and V collagens, thrombin, fibrinogen, laminin, plasminogen and plasminogen activator inhibitor, histidine rich glycoprotein	TSP-2 knockout mouse—large collagen fibrils, thickened bones; spinal deformities
Fibronectin—2q34 ~400 kDa with two nonidentical subunits of ~200 kDa, composed of type I, II, and III repeats, RGD in the 11th type III repeat 2/3 from N terminus	Binds to cells, fibrin heparin, gelatin collagen	Knockout mouse—lethal before skeletal development
Vitronectin—17q11 ~70 kDa, RGD close to N terminus, homology to somatomedin B, rich in cysteines, sulfated, phosphorylated	Cell attachment protein, binds to collagen, plasminogen and plasminogen activator inhibitor, and to heparin	
Fibrillin 1 and 2-15q21.1, 5q23-q31 350 kDa, EGF-like domains, RGD, cysteine motifs	Regulates elastic fiber formation	Fibrillin 1 mutations—Marfan's syndrome, Fibrillin 2 mutations—congenital contractural arachnodactyly

INITIAL MINERAL DEPOSITION

The membrane bound extracellular bodies released from chondrocytes (and osteoblasts) known as "extracellular matrix vesicles" can facilitate initial mineral deposition by accumulating calcium and phosphate ions in a protected environment. Additionally, they provide enzymes that can degrade inhibitors of mineralization (e.g., ATP, pyrophosphate, proteoglycans), which are found in the surrounding matrix. They also contain a "nucleational core," consisting of proteins and a complex of acidic phospholipids, calcium, and inorganic phosphate, which can induce apatite formation.[2,21] Because these matrix vesicles are not directly associated with the collagen fibrils, the question of how mineral crystals form at discrete sites on the collagen fibrils remains. It is thought that there may be some association of vesicle mineral with the mineral in the collagen matrix, or that the matrix vesicle mineral may serve as a source of calcium and phosphate ions to support initial collagen based mineralization.

In general, crystals form when the component ions of the crystal lattice, or clusters of those ions, come together with the proper orientation and with sufficient energy to generate the first stable crystal (critical nucleus). The formation of this miniature crystal, perhaps only one or two unit cells in size,[20] is the most energy-demanding step of crystallization. Nucleation is followed by the addition of ions and ion clusters to the critical nucleus as the crystal grows. Growth may occur in one or more dimensions, or additional crystals may start to form at "kink" sites on the crystal, in a fashion analogous to glycogen branching. This so-called "secondary nucleation" allows for exponential proliferation of crystals.

There is some debate as to whether noncrystalline calcium phosphate clusters (amorphous calcium phosphate) deposits before hydroxyapatite crystals, analogous to the way in which calcium carbonate in shells forms initially as an amorphous phase and is converted to crystalline forms.[22] However, to date, amorphous calcium phosphate has not been identified in embryonic bone or bone formed in cell culture, and it is currently believed that, because of the actions of anionic proteins, apatite crystals may form directly.

Macromolecules may facilitate the direct formation of the critical nucleus, sequester ions increasing the local concentrations, or bind one or more ions creating a structure on which "heterogenous nucleation" occurs. As crystals proliferate, the macromolecules may bind to crystal surfaces, blocking growth in one or more directions, thereby regulating the size, shape, or (if secondary nucleation is blocked) the number of crystals.

Several possible promoters (nucleators) of bone mineral formation have been identified based on solution studies and studies of animals in which the proteins have been ablated (knockouts), overexpressed (knock-ins), or mutated (transgenics) (see Tables 1–7 for specific proteins). Originally, collagen was thought to be the bone mineral nucleator, but later studies

TABLE 7. GENE AND PROTEIN CHARACTERISTICS OF GAMMA-CARBOXY GLUTAMIC ACID-CONTAINING PROTEINS IN BONE MATRIX

Protein/gene	Function	Disease/animal model
Matrix Gla Protein—12p13.1-p12.3 ~15 kDa, five gla residues, one disulfide bridge, phosphoserine residues	A negative regulator of mineralization	Knockout mouse—excessive cartilage calcification, osteochondral lesions
Osteocalcin—1q25-q31 ~5 kDa, one disulfide bridge, gla residues located in α helical region	Regulates activity of osteoclasts and their precursors, may mark the turning point between bone formation and resorption	Knockout mouse, osteopetrotic mouse (mutation)—thickened bones, decreased crystal size, increased mineral content
Protein S—3p11.2 ~72 kDa	Primarily a liver product, but may be made by osteogenic cells	Deficiency in human—osteopenia

TABLE 8. TECHNIQUES FOR DETERMINING BONE MINERAL AND MATRIX PROPERTIES

Technique	Information derived	Tissue type needed	Comments
X-ray diffraction	Average mineral crystal size	Homogenized tissue	No information on matrix
Transmission electron microscopy	Crystal orientation Size of individual crystals	Small tissue segments	With immuno-gold labeling can localize matrix proteins
Backscatter electron imaging	High resolution distribution of mineral density	Thick tissue segments	No information on nature of crystals or matrix
Small angle scattering	Crystal size, morphology, and orientation; fibrous protein size	Thick tissue segments	No information on nature of crystals
Atomic force microscopy	Size of individual crystals Organization of matrix	Small tissue segments	With nano-indentation can measure elastic modulus
Mechanical testing	Ability of tissue to withstand torsion or compressive loads	Machined tissue segments or whole bones	
Dual photon absorptiometry	Two-dimensional tissue density	In situ measurements	DXA–BMD measurement
μCT	Three-dimensional density, tissue connectivity, bone architecture	Small tissue segments or small bones	Can be done with live small animals
Histomorphometry	Cellular activity	Stained tissue sections	Destructive technique
Infrared microscopy and imaging	Mineral composition, mineral and matrix properties (7-μm spatial resolution)	Embedded tissue sections	Nondestructive; can get information on cell activity, lipids, and sugars from same spectrum
Raman microscopy and imaging	Mineral composition, mineral and matrix properties (0.5-μm spatial resolution)	Wet, nonembedded tissue samples	Techniques being developed to allow penetration through skin (same as above)
Nuclear MRI	Composition of bone, mineral orientation	In situ measurements	P-imaging needed for crystal analysis; noninvasive

showed that removal of noncollagenous proteins from bone collagen matrices prevented these matrices from causing apatite formation.[23] Removal of protein phosphate from demineralized bones reduced their nucleational ability in a concentration-dependent fashion, implying that one of the bone mineral nucleators was a phosphoprotein.

As discussed above, the phosphoproteins of bone include collagen itself, the SIBLINGs (osteopontin, bone sialoprotein [BSP], matrix extracellular phosphoglycoprotein [MEPE], dentin matrix protein-1 [DMP-1]), osteonectin, and bone acidic glycoprotein-75 (BAG-75).[2] Of these, to date, only BSP and DMP1 have been shown to act as apatite nucleators.[1] Both DMP1 and BSP can also inhibit apatite proliferation and growth in solution. Table 8 lists the bone matrix proteins that have been shown to affect apatite formation and growth in cell-free solution or in cell cultures. As can be seen from Table 8, most of these macromolecules are anionic, and thus can bind Ca^{+2} in solution or on the apatite crystal surface.

Several enzymes that regulate phosphoprotein phosphorylation and dephosphorylation have also been associated with the mineralization process.[2] Of these, the phosphoprotein kinases, which regulate phosphoprotein phosphorylation, and alkaline phosphatase and other phosphoprotein phosphatases seem to be most important. Alkaline phosphatase hydrolyzes phosphate esters, increasing the local phosphate concentration, enhancing the rate and extent of mineralization. Blocking phosphoprotein phosphorylation in culture decreases rates of mineralization, and cells that lack alkaline phosphatase do not mineralize in certain culture systems unless transfected with that enzyme. Patients with hypophosphatasia, a deficiency of alkaline phos-

phatase, also show abnormal bone mineralization. Whether the function of alkaline phosphatase is simply to increase local phosphate concentrations; to remove phosphate containing inhibitors of apatite growth (such as ATP); or to modify phosphoproteins, thereby controlling their ability to act as nucleators, is still undetermined.

GROWTH, PROLIFERATION, AND MATURATION OF MINERAL CRYSTALS

The growth of bone mineral crystals is governed in part by the constraints of the collagen matrix on which the mineral is deposited. Non-collagenous proteins that bind to the mineral crystals can also regulate their sizes and shapes. These proteins are also important in recruiting bone resorbing cells (osteoclasts) to the apatite crystal surface.[2] As bone apatite crystals grow and mature, substances in addition to proteins and lipids can affect their fates. They may be introduced through the diet, given therapeutically, or may accumulate from dialysis fluids. For example, of the dietary cations, both Mg^{+2} and Sr^{+2} can be incorporated directly into the bone mineral substituting for Ca^{+2} in the crystal lattice, yielding mineral crystals that are smaller and less perfect than those formed in their absence. Cadmium (Cd^{2+}) a toxic pollutant, when ingested, has a similar effect on bone mineral. Carbonate ($CO_3^=$), part of the body fluids, is a common constituent impurity of bone mineral, substituting for both OH^- and PO_4^{-3}, as well as adsorbing on to the crystal surface. Citrate is another impurity that adsorbs onto the surface of bone mineral. With age the total amount of

TABLE 9. EFFECT OF BONE MATRIX PROTEINS ON MINERALIZATION IN VITRO

Promote or support apatite formation	Inhibits mineralization	Dual function (nucleate and inhibit)	No known effect on mineralization
Type I collagen	Aggrecan	Biglycan	Decorin
Proteolipid (matrix vesicle nucleational core)	α2-HS glycoprotein	Osteonectin	BAG-75
57K DMP1	Matrix gla protein (MGP)	Fibronectin	Lumican
	Osteopontin	Bone sialoprotein	Tetranectin
	Osteocalcin	α2-HS glycoprotein	Osteoadherin
		DMP1	Thrombospondin
			Intact DMP1

carbonate increases, but the surface (labile) carbonate decreases with maturation of the mineral.[24]

While each of these impurities tend to make the crystals smaller, more imperfect, and more soluble, fluoride incorporation increases the size and therefore decreases the solubility of the apatite crystals. This in part was the basis for fluoride supplementation in osteoporosis therapy, because larger crystals are more resistant to osteoclastic turnover. Another type of antiresorptive agent used in osteoporosis, the bisphosphonates, can bind to the surface of apatite crystals, and thereby block dissolution, as well as altering the activity of bone resorbing cells. Thus, bisphosphonate-treated crystals are stabilized and not apparently altered in size.[25,26] Tetracycline and other fluorescent compounds used to measure bone formation rates are Ca-chelators, which bind with high affinity to the surface of the most recently formed mineral. Because the newest formed crystals are small, their surface to volume ratios are very high, and the amount of label bound is similarly high.

EFFECTS OF MINERAL ALTERATION ON BONE PROPERTIES

While the inclusion of "foreign" ions into the bone apatite lattice can influence the properties of bone, cellular activities can also influence mineral properties. For example, where mineral deposition is retarded (e.g., hypophosphatemic rickets), crystals tend to be larger than normal.[27] Crystals are smaller in osteopetrotic bone[28] where remodeling is impaired and the small crystals persist rather than being resorbed. In osteoporosis, where bone formation may be impaired and resorption accelerated, the larger crystals persist.[29] In skeletal fluorosis, and, in general, as bone fluoride content increases, mineral content is increased, and crystals are increased in length and decreased in width.[25]

The size and distribution of mineral crystals in the bone matrix influences bone mechanical properties.[26,30] Bone strength is dependent on bone architecture, as well as numerous other factors. The mechanical strength of bone is correlated with BMD,[31] a measurement that describes the amount of bone in a given area without providing information on architecture, mineral content, or crystal properties. However, there is not a 100% correlation between BMD and mechanical strength, and it is suggested that material properties (crystal size and composition, collagen maturity, etc.) may be important determinants.[26] It should be clear from the diseases mentioned above that if there are too few crystals or crystals are too small, the mechanical strength will be compromised. Similarly, if there are too many crystals or crystals are excessively large, as in the case of skeletal fluorosis, bones many become brittle (unable to bear load). Thus, there is an optimal crystal size distribution, as well as an optimal amount of mineral. There are multiple methods for characterizing the composition of bone mineral and matrix and these are listed in Table 8.

MINERAL FORMATION IN CELL CULTURE

Osteoblasts in vitro synthesize an extracellular matrix that mineralizes in the presence of an exogenous phosphate source. Cell culture studies for the most part have focused on the factors controlling osteoblast differentiation and proliferation and microarray analyses of expression of matrix proteins.[32,33] Only a few of these studies,[34–37] however, have shown that the mineral formed was bonelike apatite. Numerous methods can be used to prove that bonelike apatite is present. The least rigorous are the histochemical stains (von Kossa for phosphate or alizarin red for calcium). The von Kossa silver stain gives positive reactions with anions that complex silver and all phosphate-containing materials. The alizarin red stain, specific for calcium, similarly cannot distinguish calcium complexed to the organic matrix from calcium bound to phosphate. Even when these two stains are co-localized, this does not prove that apatite is present.[35] Similarly more sophisticated electron microscopic methods such as microprobe analyses, or chemical analyses of Ca and PO$_4$ contents, cannot conclusively establish the presence of apatite. Electron micrographs showing the presence of thin plates or needles associated with collagen fibrils provide more convincing evidence of the presence of apatite, but morphology can be confusing, and calcium phosphates can take on other shapes (apatite in Greek means "deceiving"). Thus, the electron micrographs must be accompanied by electron diffraction analyses that provide definite structure verification, or by other diffraction methods (X-ray, synchrotron, or neutron), which provide unambiguous proof that the mineral phase examined is apatite.[34–39] NMR and spectroscopic methods can also provide unambiguous identification of apatite. Infrared and Raman spectra also reveal the relative proportions and properties of the organic matrix, data not obtainable from diffraction methods.

Table 9 includes those bone matrix proteins that have been shown to affect mineral deposition in culture, as well as in solution, and Tables 1–7 list animal models and human diseases in which the absence, modification, or overexpression of these proteins affects bone mineral properties. It thus should be apparent that the bone cells, the bone matrix, and the extracellular environment can influence mineralization, and in turn, because the mineral properties affect mechanical strength, the properties of bone.

ACKNOWLEDGMENTS

Dr. Boskey's work described in this report was supported by National Institutes of Health Grants DE 04141, AR 037661, and AR 041325.

REFERENCES

1. Qin C, Baba O, Butler WT 2004 Post-translational modifications of sibling proteins and their roles in osteogenesis and dentinogenesis. Crit Rev Oral Biol Med **15:**126–136.
2. Gokhale JA, Robey PG, Boskey AL 2001 The biochemistry of bone. In: Marcus R, Feldman D, Kelsey J (eds.) Osteoporosis, vol. 1. Academic Press, San Diego, CA, USA, pp. 107–188.
3. Brodsky B, Persikov AV 2005 Molecular structure of the collagen triple helix. Adv Protein Chem **70:**301–339.
4. Seibel MJ 2003 Biochemical markers of bone remodeling. Endocrinol Metab Clin North Am **32:**83–113.
5. Robey PG 2002 Bone proteoglycans and glycoproteins. In: Bilezikian JP, Raisz LA, Rodan GA (eds.) Principles of Bone Biology. Academic Press, San Diego, CA, USA, pp. 225–238.
6. Xu T, Bianco P, Fisher LW, Longenecker G, Smith E, Goldstein S, Bonadio J, Boskey A, Heegaard AM, Sommer B, Satomura K, Dominguez P, Zhao C, Kulkarni AB, Robey PG, Young MF 1998 Targeted disruption of the biglycan gene leads to an osteoporosis-like phenotype in mice. Nat Genet **20:**78–82.
7. Hocking AM, Shinomura T, McQuillan DJ 1998 Leucine-rich repeat glycoproteins of the extracellular matrix. Matrix Biol **17:**1–19.
8. Henthorn PS 1996 Alkaline phosphatase. In: Bilezikian JP, Raisz LA, Rodan GA (eds.) Principles of bone biology. Academic Press, San Diego, CA, USA, pp. 197–216.
9. Anderson HC, Sipe JB, Hessle L, Dhanyamraju R, Atti E, Camacho NP, Millan JL 2004 Impaired calcification around matrix vesicles of growth plate and bone in alkaline phosphatase-deficient mice. Am J Pathol **164:** 841–847.
10. Brekken RA, Sage EH 2001 SPARC, a matricellular protein: At the crossroads of cell-matrix communication. Matrix Biol **19:**816–827.
11. Delany AM, Amling M, Priemel M, Howe C, Baron R, Canalis E 2000 Osteopenia and decreased bone formation in osteonectin-deficient mice. J Clin Invest **105:**915–923.
12. Iba K, Durkin ME, Johnsen L, Hunziker E, Damgaard-Pedersen K, Zhang H, Engvall E, Albrechtsen R, Wewer UM 2001 Mice with a targeted deletion of the tetranectin gene exhibit a spinal deformity. Mol Cell Biol **21:**7817–7825.
13. Chiquet-Ehrismann R, Tucker RP 2004 Connective tissues: Signalling by tenascins. Int J Biochem Cell Biol **36:**1085–1089.
14. Fisher LW, Fedarko NS 2003 Six genes expressed in bones and teeth encode the current members of the SIBLING family of proteins. Connect Tissue Res **44**(Suppl 1)**:**33–40.
15. Robey PG, Bianco P 2002 The cell and molecular biology of bone formation. In: Coe FL, Favus MJ (eds.) Disorders of Mineral Metabolism. Williams & Wilkin, Philadelphia, PA, USA, pp. 199–226.
16. Luo G, Ducy P, McKee MD, Pinero GJ, Loyer E, Behringer RR, Karsenty G 1997 Spontaneous calcification of arteries and cartilage in mice lacking matrix GLA protein. Nature **386:**78–81.
17. Boskey AL, Gadaleta S, Gundberg C, Doty SB, Ducy P, Karsenty G 1998 Fourier transform infrared microspectroscopic analysis of bones of osteocalcin-deficient mice provides insight into the function of osteocalcin. Bone **23:**187–196.
18. Glimcher MJ 1998 The nature of the mineral phase in bone: Biological and clinical implications. In: Avioli LV, Krane SM (eds.) Metabolic Bone Disease and Clinically Related Disorders, 3rd ed. Academic Press, San Diego, CA, USA, pp. 23–51.
19. Landis WJ 1995 The strength of a calcified tissue depends in part on the molecular structure and organization of its constituent mineral crystals in their organic matrix. Bone **16:**533–544.
20. Eppell SJ, Tong W, Katz JL, Kuhn L, Glimcher MJ 2001 Shape and size of isolated bone mineralites measured using atomic force microscopy. J Orthop Res **19:**1027–1034.
21. Anderson HC 2003 Matrix vesicles and calcification. Curr Rheumatol Rep **5:**222–226.
22. Weiner S, Sagi I, Addadi L 2005 Structural biology. Choosing the crystallization path less traveled. Science **309:**1027–1028.
23. Termine JD, Belcourt AB, Conn KM, Kleinman HK 1981 Mineral and collagen-binding proteins of fetal calf bone. J Biol Chem **256:**10403–10408.
24. Rey C, Shimizu M, Collins B, Glimcher MJ 1991 Resolution-enhanced Fourier transform infrared spectroscopy study of the environment of phosphate ion in the early deposits of a solid phase of calcium phosphate in bone and enamel and their evolution with age: 2. Investigations in the nu3PO4 domain. Calcif Tissue Int **49:**383–388.
25. Fratzl P, Schreiber S, Roschger P, Lafage MH, Rodan G, Klaushofer K 1996 Effects of sodium fluoride and alendronate on the bone mineral in minipigs: A small-angle X-ray scattering and backscattered electron imaging study. J Bone Miner Res **11:**248–253.
26. Boskey AL 2003 Bone mineral crystal size. Osteoporos Int **14**(Suppl 5)**:**16–21.
27. Boskey AL, Gilder H, Neufeld E, Ecarot B, Glorieux FH 1991 Phospholipid changes in the bones of the hypophosphatemic mouse. Bone **12:**345–351.
28. Boskey AL, Marks SC Jr 1985 Mineral and matrix alterations in the bones of incisors-absent (*ia/ia*) osteopetrotic rats. Calcif Tissue Int **37:**287–292.
29. Paschalis EP, Betts F, DiCarlo E, Mendelsohn R, Boskey AL 1997 FTIR microspectroscopic analysis of human iliac crest biopsies from untreated osteoporotic bone. Calcif Tissue Int **61:**487–492.
30. Martin RB 1993 Aging and strength of bone as a structural material. Calcif Tissue Int **53:**34–40.
31. Currey JD, Brear K, Zioupos P 1996 The effects of ageing and changes in mineral content in degrading the toughness of human femora. J Biomech **29:**257–260.
32. Siggelkow H, Rebenstorff K, Kurre W, Niedhart C, Engel I, Schulz H, Atkinson MJ, Hufner M 1999 Development of the osteoblast phenotype in primary human osteoblasts in culture: Comparison with rat calvarial cells in osteoblast differentiation. J Cell Biochem **75:**22–35.
33. Raouf A, Ganss B, McMahon C, Vary C, Roughley PJ, Seth A 2002 Lumican is a major proteoglycan component of the bone matrix. Matrix Biol **21:**361–367.
34. Ecarot-Charrier B, Glorieux FH, van der Rest M, Pereira G 1983 Osteoblasts isolated from mouse calvaria initiate matrix mineralization in culture. J Cell Biol **96:**639–643.
35. Bonewald LF, Harris SE, Rosser J, Dallas MR, Dallas SL, Camacho NP, Boyan B, Boskey A 2003 von Kossa staining alone is not sufficient to confirm that mineralization in vitro represents bone formation. Calcif Tissue Int **72:**537–547.
36. Gerstenfeld LC, Chipman SD, Kelly CM, Hodgens KJ, Lee DD, Landis WJ 1988 Collagen expression, ultrastructural assembly, and mineralization in cultures of chicken embryo osteoblasts. J Cell Biol **106:**979–989.
37. Rey C, Kim HM, Gerstenfeld L, Glimcher MJ 1996 Characterization of the apatite crystals of bone and their maturation in osteoblast cell culture: Comparison with native bone crystals. Connect Tissue Res **35:**343–349.
38. Kato Y, Boskey A, Spevak L, Dallas M, Hori M, Bonewald LF 2001 Establishment of an osteoid preosteocyte-like cell MLO-A5 that spontaneously mineralizes in culture. J Bone Miner Res **16:**1622–1633.
39. Chaudhary LR, Hofmeister AM, Hruska KA 2004 Differential growth factor control of bone formation through osteoprogenitor differentiation. Bone **34:**402–411.

Chapter 4. Bone Formation: Maturation and Functional Activities of Osteoblast Lineage Cells

Jane E. Aubin,[1] Jane B. Lian,[2] and Gary S. Stein[2]

[1]Department of Molecular and Medical Genetics, University of Toronto, Toronto, Ontario, Canada; and [2]Department of Cell Biology and Cancer Center, University of Massachusetts Medical School, Worcester, Massachusetts

INTRODUCTION

Bone is a dynamic connective tissue, comprising an exquisite assembly of functionally distinct cell populations that are required to support the structural, biochemical, and mechanical integrity of bone and its central role in mineral homeostasis. The responsiveness of bone to mechanical forces and metabolic regulatory signals that accommodate requirements for maintaining the organ and connective tissue functions of bone are operative throughout life. As such, bone tissue undergoes remodeling, a continual process of resorption and renewal. The principal cells that mediate the bone forming processes of the mammalian skeleton are: osteoprogenitor cells that contribute to maintaining the osteoblast population and bone mass; osteoblasts that synthesize the bone matrix on bone forming surfaces; osteocytes, organized throughout the mineralized bone matrix that support bone structure; and the protective bone surface lining cells (Fig. 1). The fidelity of bone tissue structure and metabolic functions necessitates exchange of regulatory signals among these cell populations.

It should be emphasized that within the osteoblast lineage, subpopulations of cells can respond selectively to physiologic signals. Studies show that osteoblasts from axial and appendicular bone exhibit different responses to hormonal, mechanical, and developmental cues. The extent to which this reflects the local, cellular and tissue environment or inherent properties of the cells selected at an early stage during osteoblast differentiation remains to be determined. Subtle yet important differences may reflect selective responses of osteoblasts that relate to either homeostatic functions or the establishment and maintenance of bone structure.

Bone formation involves osteoblast maturation that requires a spectrum of signaling proteins including morphogens, hormones, growth factors, cytokines, matrix proteins, transcription factors, and their co-regulatory proteins. They act coordinately to support the temporal expression (i.e., sequential activation, suppression, and modulation) of other genes that represent the phenotypic, structural, and functional properties of osteoblasts during the differentiation process. Several approaches are being used to identify and functionally characterize factors that play key roles in the growth, commitment, and differentiation of mesenchymal stem cells to the osteochondrogenic lineage and osteoblasts. These include expression studies in bone tissue by in situ analyses for mRNA and protein, characterization of gene abnormalities in human skeletal disorders, and functional studies with mice lacking the gene or transgenic mouse models expressing wildtype or mutant proteins to reveal skeletal defects. Lineage allocation and tracing strategies in mice and cell culture models augment these approaches. Examples of regulatory proteins characterized in vivo and in vitro for their effects on stem cells, committed progenitors, and differentiating osteoblasts are listed in Table 1. This chapter will present the basic concepts and requirements for osteoblast determination and differentiation from progenitor cells, the functional activities of bone-forming cells, and how these cells are regulated for the control of bone formation. Through an understanding of the molecular and cellular mechanisms supporting progression of osteoblast differentiation and functional activities of distinct cell populations, a basis can be provided for improved diagnosis of skeletal disease and treatment that is targeted to specific cells in bone tissue.

OSTEOGENIC CELL POPULATIONS

Osteoprogenitor Cells: Origin and Regulation

By definition, stem cells are pluripotent and have self-renewal capacity, repopulating multiple cell lineages in a tissue environment. Osteoprogenitor cells will arise under the appropriate stimulus from stem cells present in many tissues in the adult organism. The bone marrow stroma contains cells with robust proliferative potential that will form single colonies (CFU-Fs) with the capacity to form bone, cartilage, adipocytes, and fibrous tissue when transplanted in vivo in diffusion chambers.[1–3] These CFU-Fs are now most commonly referred to as mesenchymal stem cells (MSCs) and are distinguished from the hematopoietic stem cell (HSC) lineage. It is estimated that only a low percentage (15%) of all CFU-F have stem cell-like properties or are bone colony–forming cells.[4,5] These data are consistent with the view that CFU-F belong to a lineage hierarchy in which only some of the cells are multipotential stem or primitive progenitors while others have more limited differentiation capacity (Fig. 2). Cells with features similar to adult bone marrow MSCs have also been isolated from adult peripheral blood,[6] fetal cord blood,[7] fetal liver, blood, and bone marrow,[8] and tooth pulp.[9] Muscle satellite cells have also recently been found to be multipotential, undergoing myogenic, osteogenic, and adipogenic differentiation in vitro.[10]

The potential for use of MSCs to treat genetic disorders and for tissue engineering for reconstruction of bone tissue has fueled attempts to identify markers for isolation and purification of the MSC populations, but this has been challenging. Immunoselection and flow cytometry procedures have been applied for enrichment of osteoprogenitor cells from whole marrow. Historically, the STRO-1 antibody was used to isolate CFU populations in human bone marrow.[11] Figure 1 lists other now frequently used antibodies, and the current view is that combinations of multiple positive markers and absence of HSC markers achieve better enrichment of MSCs than single antibody strategies. To date, no single specific marker has been identified for selecting all osteoprogenitor cells or for characterizing maintenance of their progenitor phenotype. A competent signature of markers may be maximally effective. However, primordial stem cells can be reliably identified by individual cell surface proteins. For MSC-based therapeutic applications, maintaining the undifferentiated stem cell like properties may be an important consideration for long-term engraftment expansion and repopulation of a tissue by these cells in vivo, as well as for maintained expression of transgenes.

Factors maintaining the undifferentiated state are beginning to be characterized and allow for approaches to expand a potential mesenchymal stem cell and osteoprogenitor population in vitro and in vivo (Table 1). Among these factors are those that promote the self-renewal or proliferation of MSCs (e.g., Sca-1,[12] IL-18[13]) and generally this continual cell cycling is inhibitory to terminal differentiation. Other factors such as osteoblast stimulat-

Dr. Aubin is on the Scientific Advisory Board for Enobia. All other authors have reported no conflicts of interest.

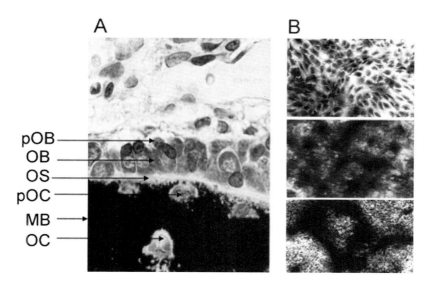

FIG. 1. Osteoblast differentiation (A) in vivo and (B) in vitro. (A) Cellular organization of bone formation. OP, osteoprogenitors; OB, osteoblasts; OS, osteoid; pre-OC, pre-osteocytes; MB, mineralized bone matrix; OC, osteocyte. (B) Recapitulation of osteoblast differentiation in cultured cells isolated from fetal rat calvarial bone. Proliferating osteoprogenitors (top), post-proliferative osteoblasts in nodules expressing alkaline phosphatase activity (middle); mineral deposition (von Kossa stain) of the ECM (bottom).

ing factor-1/pleiotrophin[14] are chemotactic for osteoprogenitors, stimulate colony formation, and increase the percent of alkaline phosphatase positive cells. IL-11, whose overexpression in mice causes thicker cortical bones, higher BMD, and greater bone mechanical strength, also increases the number of alkaline phosphatase–positive cells and colonies.[15] Some growth factors (e.g., IGF and connective tissue growth factor) and peptide hormones (e.g., PTH, growth hormone) display more widespread effects, stimulating proliferation of MSCs and osteoprogenitors but also promoting differentiation of osteoblasts. Growth factors, cytokines, and peptide hormones transduce their signals through nonreceptor kinases or membrane receptors that lead to phosphorylation of intracellular proteins through kinases. The contributions of specific kinases to cell responses are being dissected by in vitro studies with pathway inhibitors.

It should be noted that committed phenotypes from MSCs may dedifferentiate during proliferation and postmitotically assume a different phenotype dependent on the local cellular environment.[16] In this manner, pericytes can also be induced into the osteogenic lineage.[17] Mechanisms that directly inhibit the commitment of pluripotent MSCs to the osteoblast lineage also appear to be operative. This was observed on inactivation of Menin-1, the product of the *multiple endocrine neoplasia type-I* genes.[18] Such observations and the identification of the molecular pathways described above for proliferation and commitment have led to the concept of "plasticity" and transdifferentiation of stromal and other adult stem and precursor cell types.

Mechanisms Regulating Commitment to the Osteoblast Lineage

Commitment of MSCs to tissue-specific cell types is orchestrated by morphogens, developmental signaling pathways, and transcriptional regulators that serve as "master switches" (Table 1; Figs. 1 and 2). The canonical Wnt/β-catenin pathway provides early developmental cues that indirectly mediate the initial cascade of gene expression for skeletal development, bone formation, and osteoblast differentiation.[19,20] Specific Wnt pathway components with key roles in osteoblasts have recently been identified. Identification of the human mutation activating LRP5, a Wnt co-receptor protein, as a high bone mass trait gene has intensified research in this area.[21,22] Multiple skeletal defects are also manifested in mice with mutations in Wnts, the co-receptor LRP5, or the downstream transcriptional regulator β-catenin.[23–26] The data indicate that

Wnts play a widespread role in skeletogenesis from embryonic skeletal patterning, through fetal skeletal development, and adult skeletal remodeling. In vitro experiments also implicate Wnt signaling in chondrogenesis and osteogenesis; however, there remain conflicting data on whether Wnts are uniformly stimulatory or inhibitory for osteoblast differentiation.[27] It seems most likely that this reflects diverse functions of Wnts at different stages of skeletogenesis, but at least part of their role may be to serve as a molecular switch between maintaining the self-renewal and stemness of MSCs and differentiation, as they do in the hematopoietic lineage.[28,29] There is also recent data to support a role for Wnt10b as a regulator of fate choice, i.e., a stimulator of osteoblastogenesis and inhibitor of adipogenesis from bipotential mesenchymal precursors in vitro and in mice.[30] Wnt10b shifts cell fate toward the osteoblast lineage by suppression of the adipogenic transcription factors C/EBPα and PPARγ and induction of the osteogenic transcription factors Runx2, Dlx5, Osterix, and Runx2.[31]

Bone morphogenetic proteins (members of the TGF-β family), BMP-2, BMP-4, and BMP-7 (also called OP-1) are potent inducers of osteogenesis in vivo and in vitro that function through a specific receptor complex BMPRIA/BMPRIB and intracellular receptor Smads (R-Smads) that heterodimerize with a DNA-binding Smad4 and/or other transcription factors to regulate gene expression.[32] BMP activity is regulated by inhibitory Smads and several antagonists including noggin and chordin that affect skeletal development.[33] Because of the early embryonic lethality of BMP null mutants, elucidation of their precise functions in osteoblastogenesis and bone formation is being approached through analysis of deficiencies and mutations of the receptors and intracellular SMAD signaling components.[34,35] Multiple BMP target genes, induced within a few hours of treatment include transcription factors essential for osteogenesis [e.g., runt homology domain (Runx) factors, homeodomain proteins (Msx2, Dlx3, Dlx2, Dlx5), and Osterix] that all promote commitment to the osteogenic lineage.[36,37] BMPs are currently being used clinically to augment fracture repair.[38]

In summary, the bone microenvironment supports a continual supply of osteoprogenitor cells by extracellular matrix accumulation of circulating and osteoblast synthesized cytokines, growth factors, non-collagenous proteins and other molecules that cooperatively function to recruit progenitor cells. The commitment and differentiation of these cells is induced by morphogenic/developmental proteins that signal to tran-

Table 1. Regulation of Osteoblastogenesis and Bone Formation

Osteoprogenitor cell commitment and expansion (signaling proteins, growth factors)

BMP 2/4/7	Chondro-osteoprogenitor cell specification
Indian hedgehog (Ihh)	Promotes osteogenic cell phenotype for bone collar formation
β catenin	Levels control canonical Wnt signaling for commitment to Chondrocytes (low β catenin) or osteoblasts (high β catenin)
IL-18	Stromal cell cytokine; interferon γ inducing factor that is mitogenic for chondrocytes and osteoblasts
Pleiotrophin	Osteoblast stimulating factor 1. Transgenic mice have increased bone formation
Biglycan and decorin	Modulates proliferation and survival of stromal cells
Menin	A Smad3 and Runx2 interacting protein required for commitment
Twist and dermo	HLH transcription factors support osteoprogenitor phenotype
Stromal-derived factor-1 (CXCL 12)	Promotes growth and survival of marrow stromal stem cells

Transcriptional regulators

Homeodomain proteins

Msx1/2	Control many aspects of craniofacial development and negative regulator of genes expressed in mature osteoblasts
Dlx3/5/6	Roles in limb development and positive regulator of osteoblast differentiation

SP factors

Osterix	Essential for late stage of bone formation in vivo
SP-3	Contributes to ossification in vivo

Activating transcription factors

ATF 2	Role in endochondral ossification
ATF 4	Maintains bone mass through regulation of osteoblast genes
Activating Protein1 (AP-1)	AP-1 factors respond to growth and mechanical stimuli
Cfos, Fra1, ΔFosB Jun B, Jun D	Interact as fos/jun heterodimers or jun homodimers at AP-1 sites in most osteoblast genes
Runt homology domain TFs	Essential for cell differentiation and organogenesis
Runx1 (Cbfa2/AML1)	Required for hematopoiesis; expressed in chondrocytes and osteoprogenitors
Runx2(Cbfa1/AML3)	Required for bone formation
Runx3(Cbfa3/AML2)	Required for gut and neural development; expressed in hypertrophic chondrocytes
NF-κB	Role in apoptosis of osteoblasts; negative regulator of osteoblast differentiation
LEF/TCF	Transduces the Wnt/B-catenin signal to target genes in the nucleus

Growth factors

IGF-1/IGF-2	Anabolic regulators; IGF-1 required for anabolic effects of PTH
PDGF	Stimulates migration and proliferation; inhibits differentiation
EGF	Stimulates MSCs to differentiate
Endothelin	Peptide produced by endothelial cells; increases bone nodules in vitro

Hormones

PTH	Numerous anabolic effects via regulation of many types of osteoblast genes
1,25(OH)2D3	Upregulates many osteoblast genes that are components of the ECM
Glucocorticoid	Promotes osteoprogenitor cell differentiation, but increases apoptosis of mature osteoblasts;
Sex Steroids	General anabolic effects on bone
Progesterone	Stimulates proliferation and formation of bone colonies in vitro
Estrogen	Increases IGF-1; stimulates osteoprogenitor proliferation and collagen synthesis
Androgen	Increases differentiation of post-proliferative osteoblasts and mineralization
Growth hormone	Stimulates proliferation and differentiation
Thyroid stimulating hormone	Decreases Wnt/Lrp5 signaling, and inhibits osteoblast differentiation and collagen synthesis

Signaling molecules

Prostaglandin E2	Rapidly secreted in response to mechanical stimuli via EP4 receptor to increase BMP2 expression
Oncostatin M	Increases IGF-1 and alkaline phosphatase, promoting osteoprogenitor differentiation
Sclerostin	A BMP antagonist secreted by osteocytes to inhibit osteoblast differentiation and activity, but suppressed by intermittent PTH
Leptin	Dual activities: as a hypothalamic factor it is antiosteogenic in vivo, but with exogenous treatment of leptin deficient mice, chondrocytes and osteoblasts, anabolic effects are exhibited.
Adrenomedullin	A member of the calcitonin peptide family has mitogenic effects on osteoblasts
Pregnancy-associated plasma protein A	An IGFBP-4 protease and therefore regulates IGF-1 release as IGFBP4 is highly expressed in osteoblasts

scription factors for activation of osteogenic genes for synthesis of a bone matrix that provides additional extracellular matrix-mediated cues for osteoblast maturation.

Osteoblasts: Synthesize the Bone Matrix

Committed pre-osteoblasts are recognizable near the bone surface by their proximity to surface osteoblasts and by histochemical detection of alkaline phosphatase enzyme activity, one of the earliest markers of the osteoblast phenotype. The active mature osteoblast on the bone surface is distinguished by its morphological and ultrastructural properties, which are typical of a cell engaged in secretion of a connective tissue matrix, having a large nucleus, enlarged Golgi, and extensive endoplasmic reticulum. The osteoblast is highly enriched in alkaline phosphatase and vectorially secretes type I collagen and specialized bone matrix proteins as unmineralized osteoid toward the bone forming front. On quiescent bone surfaces, single layers of flattened osteoblasts or bone lining cells are observed. These inactive lining cells form either the endosteum separating bone from the marrow or they underlie the periosteum directly on the mineralized surfaces.

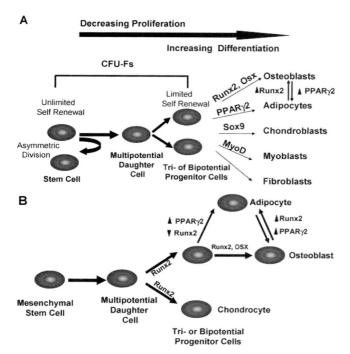

FIG. 2. Stem cell commitment to mesenchymal phenotypes. A schematic of stem cell commitment through either (A) a single-step process or (B) a multistep hierarchical process with increasing lineage restriction to various end-stage mesenchymal cell types. Stem cells have unlimited self-renewal through asymmetric divisions with daughter cells assuming properties of a pluripotent progenitor cell (CFU-Fs). Some of the known transcription factors playing key regulatory roles in the mesenchymal lineages are indicated. Also depicted is apparent plasticity between osteoblasts and adipocytes.

The osteoblasts and lining cells are in close contact with each other, joined by adherens junctions. Cadherins are calcium-dependent transmembrane proteins that are an integral part of the adherens junctions and, together with tight junctions and desmosomes, join cells by anchorage through their cytoskeleton. The changes in relative abundance of the different cadherins in mesenchymal cells seem to define their differentiation pathway.[39] Major cadherins expressed in osteoblasts include N-cadherin and cadherin-11, which are critical for embryonic limb development (Table 1). N-cadherin is important for cell–cell adhesion mediated by BMP2, and such cell–cell interactions promote differentiation of the early osteoprogenitor and osteoblast survival.[40]

Bone matrix synthesis by the osteoblast supports both cell–cell and cell–matrix interactions that are mediated by transmembrane proteins (e.g., Notch-1) and several classes of adhesion proteins. Integrins, which couple the extracellular matrix to the structural proteins of the cytoskeleton, mediate signals to modulate cell differentiation, cytoskeletal organization, cell adhesion, cell shape change, and cell spreading. The $\beta1$ integrins play key roles in early bone development and during osteoblast differentiation by binding various collagens and inducing signals that lead to expression of osteoblast phenotypic genes. Recently, it was found that osteoblast differentiation is accelerated by interaction of the type I collagen matrix with $\alpha1\beta1$ or $\alpha2\beta1$ integrins, which activate the mitogen-activated protein kinase (MAPK) signaling pathway. This intracellular pathway is emerging as a key regulator of osteoblast differentiation.

The temporal expression of proteins involved in extracellular matrix biosynthesis and matrix mineralization provides a panel of osteoblast phenotypic markers that reflect stages of osteoblast differentiation (Fig. 3). Based on bone nodule formation in vitro, the process has been subdivided into three stages: (1) proliferation, (2) extracellular matrix development and maturation, and (3) mineralization, with characteristic changes in gene expression at each stage; some apoptosis can also be seen in mature nodules. While Fig. 3 presents only three major stages of maturation, additional stages of maturation are becoming apparent with newer methodologies.[41] In many studies, genes associated with cell growth and exit from the cell cycle [e.g., histones, cell cycle regulators (cyclins, cdk, and cdi), proto-oncogenes such as c-*fos* and c-*myc*] characterize the proliferative stage. Cell cycle inhibitors, such as p27 and p21, promote osteochondroprogenitor cell differentiation. Expression of the most frequently assayed osteoblast-associated genes type I collagen, alkaline phosphatase, osteopontin, osteocalcin, bone sialoprotein, and PTH/PTH-related protein (PTHrP) receptor (PTH1R) is asynchronously upregulated and/or downregulated as the progenitor cells differentiate and matrix matures and mineralizes. In general, alkaline phosphatase and PTH1R are early markers of osteoprogenitors that increase as osteoblasts mature and deposit matrix but decline again as osteoblasts transition to osteocytes, whereas osteocalcin is a late marker that is upregulated only in post-proliferative mature osteoblasts associated with mineralizing osteoid (Fig. 3).

When the pre-osteoblast ceases to proliferate, a key signaling event occurs for development of the large cuboidal differentiated osteoblast on the bone surface from the spindle shaped osteoprogenitor. The osteoblast is responsible for synthesis of the extracellular matrix (ECM) leading to a "matrix maturation" stage when induced expression of alkaline phosphatase and specialized bone proteins render the ECM competent for mineral deposition. The composition and organization of the bone ECM is critical for structural and functional fidelity of bone tissue for constituents of the ECM. Mineralization results in upregulated expression of several non-collagenous enriched proteins, thereby providing markers of the mature osteoblast (e.g., osteocalcin, osteopontin, bone sialoprotein). These calcium and phosphate binding proteins may function in regulating the ordered deposition of mineral, amount of the hydroxyapatite crystals, or crystal size. High-throughput screening analyses and microarray gene profiling approaches are identifying an increasing number of regulatory factors and signature genes for specific stages of osteoblast maturation.

The developmental sequence of gene expression in osteoblasts can be visualized at the single cell level in developing osteoblasts in vitro and in bone tissue by in situ methods.[41] It has been evident for some time that not all osteoblasts associated with bone nodules in vitro or in bone tissue are identical. Extensive diversity in expressed gene repertoires is not a consequence or an artifact of the in vitro environment as confirmed by analysis of osteoblastic cells in vivo where individual osteoblasts differentially express various osteoblast-associated molecules at both mRNA and protein levels. The observed differences in mRNA and protein expression repertoires in different osteoblasts may contribute to the heterogeneity in trabecular microarchitecture seen at different skeletal sites, to anatomic site-specific differences in disease manifestation such as seen in osteoporosis, and to regional variations in the ability of osteoblasts to respond to therapeutic agents.

Osteocytes: Mechanotransduction Properties Support Bone Structure and Function

The osteocyte is the terminal differentiation stage of the osteoblast and supports bone structure and metabolic functions. A distinguishing morphological feature of osteocytes is the location of each osteocyte in lacunae and the numerous cellular extensions of filapodia processes that lie in canaliculi. The canaliculi and

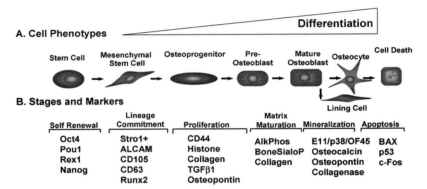

FIG. 3. Growth and differentiation of osteoblasts. Schematic illustration of (A) osteoblast lineage cells and (B) frequently used markers of the stages of maturation. Selected examples are shown.

cytoplasmic connections with adjacent cells help to ensure osteocyte viability as the mineralizing osteoid renders the ECM impermeable. Osteocytes isolated directly from bone tissue retain the filapodial processes in vitro.[42,43] In bone, osteocytes seem negative for alkaline phosphatase, but produce large amounts of osteocalcin, galectin-3, and CD44, a cell adhesion receptor for hyaluronate, and several bone matrix proteins that may be involved in cellular extensions.[43,44] Osteocytes have the capacity to synthesize certain matrix molecules to support cellular adhesive properties and regulate the deposition of mineral to maintain the necessary surrounding barrier of bone fluid in their lacunae and canalicular network for diffusion of physiological elements. They also function in osteolysis and contain lysosomal vacuoles and other features of phagocytic cells.

Osteocytes within the mineralized matrix are in direct communication with each other and surface osteoblasts through their cellular processes. They form a continuum by connection at the tip of their cell processes through gap junctions. Connexins are the integral membrane proteins that form the gap junctions between cells to allow direct communications through intercellular channels. Osteocytes are metabolically and electrically coupled through gap junction protein complexes principally comprised of Connexin 43. Gap junction formation is essential for osteocyte maturation, activity, and survival.[45–47] The primary function of the osteoblast (or lining cell)–osteocyte continuum is considered to be mechanosensory [i.e., to transduce stress signals (stretching, bending) to biological activity]. The flow of extracellular fluid in response to mechanical forces throughout the canaliculi induces a spectrum of cellular responses in osteocytes.[42] Rapid fluxes of bone calcium across these junctions are thought to facilitate transmission of information between osteoblasts on the bone surface and osteocytes within the structure of bone itself.[48,49] Signaling pathways mediating the mechanotransducing properties of osteocytes from the extracellular matrix through the cytoskeleton and finally to the nucleus to modulate gene transcription are beginning to be characterized. They involve prostaglandin E$_2$ and cyclooxygenase 2, kinases, Runx2, and NO-mediated responsiveness of the bone to systemic factors and mechanical forces.

Osteocytes can reside for long periods, even decades in humans, in healthy bone that is not turned over. In aging bone, empty lacunae are observed suggesting osteocytes may undergo apoptosis.[50] Disruption of intercellular communication systems, as gap junctions or cell–matrix interactions, will lead to apoptosis and nonviable bone that will be resorbed. Apoptosis or programmed cell death is important for skeletal development, as well as the growth and maintenance of bone tissue.[51] The timely apoptosis of mesenchymal cells is required for digit formation, and apoptosis of hypertrophic chondrocytes is necessary for endochondral bone formation, whereas osteoclast apoptosis is one control mechanism for the regulation of bone resorption. However, osteocyte apoptosis

may be deleterious to bone structure. In vivo quantitation of apoptotic cells in the mouse and mouse models of accelerated aging and osteopenic bone induced by ovariectomy or glucocorticoid treatment confirm that programmed cell death contributes to active bone loss. Notably, bisphosphonates and estrogens, which inhibit bone resorption and are used to treat osteoporosis, have been found to inhibit osteoblast and osteocyte apoptosis.[50,52] Importantly mechanical loading of bone in a physiologic range in the rat reduces osteocyte apoptosis.[53] In summary, the organization of osteocytes in direct contact with osteoblasts or surface lining cells is consistent with the concept that bone cells support bone structure and responses to physiological signals and can communicate their responses for bone formation and resorption.

REGULATION OF OSTEOBLAST DIFFERENTIATION AND FUNCTIONAL ACTIVITIES

Transcriptional Mechanisms Control Osteoblastogenesis

Many classes of DNA binding proteins have been shown to regulate the transcription and required expression levels of bone phenotypic genes during the development of bone tissue. For example, steroid receptors, the homeodomain proteins, and other classes of transcription factors shown in Table 1 are among the early regulators of transcription in osteoprogenitors. Transcription factors further interact with co-regulatory proteins that can provide the necessary control for either activating or repressing gene expression dependent on the maturation stage of the osteoblasts or their physiologic responsive at a particular bone site.[54] Knowledge of these regulatory factors provides a basis for understanding bone related disorders. Examples include cleidocranial dysplasia resulting from mutations in Runx2,[55] Coffin-Lowry Syndrome related to ATF4 inactivation,[56,57] and the osteopenia associated with diabetes that results from inadequate expression of bone-related transcriptional regulators.[58] Transcription factors mediate physiologic control of gene expression by serving as scaffolds through protein–protein interactions for organization and assembly of regulatory complexes at strategic sites on target gene promoters. Specificity is determined by promoter context of the DNA sequence, structure of the gene, and temporal–spatial organization of the regulatory machinery within the nucleus.

The developmental expression patterns of transcription factors during osteoblast maturation reflect their roles as key determinants of osteoblast differentiation. The helix-loop-helix (HLH) proteins (Id, Twist, Dermo) are expressed at peak levels in proliferating progenitor cells and have been proposed to play a role in maintaining the osteoprogenitor population.[59,60] Because HLH proteins function as repressors of genes representing the mature osteoblast phenotype and are in effect negative regulators of osteoblast differentiation, they must be downregulated for osteoblast differentiation to proceed. Members of the family of activating proteins (APs) dimerize to form complexes at AP-1 recognition sites that occur in most genes. AP-1 factors are expressed primarily during growth (e.g., c-fos, c-jun), but also at later stages of osteoblast differentiation (e.g., junD, fra-2). The complexes either activate or repress gene transcription, thereby contributing to temporal expression of osteogenic genes. Homeodomain proteins are critical determinants of pattern formation and craniofacial and limb development.[27] These transcription factors become re-expressed during osteoblast differentiation (Table 1). Msx2 is expressed maximally in the mesenchymal/osteoprogenitor population and subsequently downregulated in the mature bone forming cells, whereas Dlx3 and Dlx5 expression are sustained in the post-proliferative osteoblast and increased during the mineralization stage.[61] Relatively few of the homeodomain proteins that have revealed phenotypes at the early stage of skeletal formation in null or transgenic mice[62] have been studied directly in osteoblasts.

Requirements for the runt homology domain factor Runx2 (Cbfa1/AML3/PEBPα1)[63] and the zinc finger protein Osterix (Table 1) in bone formation and osteoblast differentiation have been established by genetic studies.[37,64–68] Null mutations of either factor results in absence of a mineralized skeleton and perinatal lethality. Because Runx2 expression occurs earlier than Osterix (i.e., it is unaltered in Osterix$^{-/-}$ mice), these two factors may represent a temporal sequence of regulation essential for the early and final stages of osteoblast differentiation. Runx2 is a key regulator of cell growth[69,70] and commitment to the osteoblast lineage,[65,67,71] for maturation of chondrocytes to the hypertrophic stage, and mineralization of the cartilage,[72,73] endothelial cell migration,[74] and vascular invasion by directly upregulating vascular endothelial growth factor.[75] Runx2 target genes include those contributing not only to bone formation (osteocalcin, osteopontin, bone sialoprotein, galectin, TGFβ receptor I, and dentin sialophosphoprotein-1),[65,67,76–80] but also to bone turnover (collagenase 3, osteoprotegerin, and RANKL).[81–83] The two other Runx factors are expressed in the skeleton. Runx1 (AML1/Cbfa2), which is essential for hematopoiesis, is present in periosteum and perichondrium and seems to promote chondrogenesis.[84,85] Runx3 (AML2/Cbfa3) supports chondrocyte maturation.[73,86]

Studies on Runx2 have established new paradigms for understanding properties of a master gene regulatory switch for lineage determination[87] (Fig. 2). Runx2 remains associated with chromosomes during mitosis contributing to bone phenotype stability.[88] Runx2 binds to specific DNA sequence with a partner protein, CBFβ1, which is also required for normal bone formation.[89] Runx2 interacts with numerous co-regulatory proteins in subnuclear domains for gene activation and repression including factors that remodel chromatin [e.g., p300 and other factors with histone acetyl transferase activity (HAT) to activate gene transcription or attenuate levels of expression by recruiting histone deacetylase enzymes HDAC; see Table 1 for their effects on osteoblast differentiation]. Other co-regulatory proteins include the Wnt pathway regulator LEF-1,[90] AP-1 factors,[91,92] C/EBP,[93,94] the vitamin D receptor,[95] TGFβ/BMP-responsive SMAD proteins,[96,97] and the WW domain proteins.[98,99] Thus, Runx factors also integrate key signaling pathways for osteogenesis. A key property of Runx factors is its DNA binding domain and specific nuclear matrix signal that targets Runx2 to subnuclear domains, facilitating the formation of multimeric complexes with Runx2 partner proteins. Mutations in these functional domains and consequential loss of co-regulatory protein interactions result in absence of a mineralized skeleton in the mouse[68] and accounts for several of the cleidocranial dysplasia disorders (CCD) variants.[55,100]

The potency of transcription factors in lineage determination and differentiation is reflected by their ability to cause trans-differentiation of cells to other phenotypes when they are overexpressed or suppressed. For example, forced overexpression of peroxisome proliferation-activated receptor γ2 (PPARγ2) in osteoblasts will change their phenotype to adipocytes, whereas forced expression of Runx2 in adipocytes or other nonosseous cells results in acquisition of a differentiated osteoblast phenotype[101–103] (Fig. 2). It has been suggested that the inverse relationship sometimes seen between expression of the osteoblast and adipocytic phenotypes in marrow stroma (e.g., in osteoporosis) may reflect the ability of single or combinations of agents to alter the commitment or at least the differentiation pathway that multi or bipotential cells will transit. At some point in the future, transcription factors may be used to promote osteogenesis from stem cell populations.

Regulation of Osteoblast Maturation, Activity and Apoptosis

As already raised, steroid and polypeptide hormones, growth factors, and cytokines regulate not only the growth of osteoprogenitors and/or their progression to mature osteoblasts, but also regulate osteoblast activity and apoptosis. This regulation is often not at a single differentiation stage but occurs at multiple points in the maturational sequence and often with biphasic or opposite activities at different times or on different bone compartments. Thus, a single factor may increase osteoprogenitor proliferation but also stimulate or inhibit later differentiation stages sometimes in an anatomic site-specific manner. For example, PTH stimulates growth of osteoprogenitor populations, while also inhibiting osteoblast and osteocyte apoptosis.[50] However, in a study with overexpression of a constitutively active PTH1R, opposite effects were observed in trabecular and endosteal osteoblast populations (increased osteoblast activity) versus periosteal osteoblast populations (decreased activity),[104] reminiscent of the differential effects of PTH in trabecular versus cortical bone in primary hyperparathyroidism.[105] Many of these regulatory factors also act as local autocrine and paracrine regulators. Thus, PTHrP functions as a local cytokine-regulating cell growth for differentiation during development.[106] Numerous mouse genetic models have defined the role of this pathway, integrated with other developmental regulators, such as Indian hedgehog (Ihh), in the control of chondrocyte proliferation and maturation for endochondral bone formation and osteoblast differentiation.

Glucocorticoids promote the differentiation of human and rat marrow mesenchymal cells to osteoblasts in vitro as established by many studies. Recently, the enzyme 11β-hydroxysteroid dehydrogenase type 1 (11β-HSD1) regulating conversion of cortisone into active cortisol is controlled by osteoblast differentiation[107] and transgenic mice overexpressing 11β-HSD1 type 2 in osteoblasts has revealed an anabolic role for endogenous glucocorticoids in bone.[108] However, when used therapeutically, glucocorticoids can have negative effects on bone formation and can contribute to osteoporosis at least in part by inducing osteoblast and osteocyte apoptosis.[50,109] Vitamin D [1,25(OH)$_2$D$_3$] is a potent regulator of gene transcription, increasing or decreasing expression of numerous osteoblast phenotypic genes that are consistent with more differentiated osteoblasts, (e.g., enhanced osteocalcin synthesis).[110] The sex steroids have anabolic effects on bone and osteoblasts. Retinoic acid has a well-established role in skeletal development of the embryo; recently an orphan receptor for retinoic acid (ROR) has been recognized for contributing to bone formation in the postnatal mouse (Table 1).[111,112] Adrenomedullin increases cellular proliferation in cultured calvaria, suggesting stimulated osteoblast growth.[113] Leptin acts as a systemic factor that contributes to decreased bone mass in a null mouse model acting through the hypothalamus.[114] Leptin is secreted largely by adipose tissue, but also by human osteoblasts at the mineralization stage[115] and has been reported to have anabolic effects on osteoblasts and stromal cells promoting their differentiation in vitro,[115,116] but also inducing apoptosis of stromal cells.[117] Nonetheless, leptin reduced bone loss in ovariectomized rats,[118] and positive correlations between circulating leptin levels and BMD in postmenopausal and nonobese women have been reported.[119] It is thus apparent that leptin is an important regulator of bone cell function, but seems to control bone growth and osteoblast activities through several distinct mechanisms.

Cytokines of the LIF/IL-6 family, which signal through gp130, play a role not only in osteoclastogenesis, but also in bone formation. Lack of gp130 signaling alters osteoblast phenotype and activity,[120] and loss of SHP2/ras/MAPK activation by gp130 induces high bone turnover with increased formation and resorption.[121] Transgenic mice overexpressing the IL-11 cytokine exhibit higher BMD and greater bone mechanical strength, apparently as a result of the ability of IL-11 to act locally to stimulate the number of osteoprogenitors and bone formation by regulating transcription of BMP-2 target genes (e.g., smad6).[15] Overexpression of oncostatin M (OSM) in mouse knees induces, in addition to synovial inflammation, increased periosteal bone apposition,[122] which may be the in vivo correlate of the stimulatory effect of OSM seen on osteoprogenitors in rat calvarial-derived populations.[123] However, the signaling pathways induced and cellular mechanisms invoked to achieve these bone effects are complex. Overall, the data suggest that IL-11, OSM, LIF, and other family members, act differently not only at different differentiation stages but also differently on the periosteum/suture and bone tissue–derived cell populations compared with stromal/endosteal cells.[123]

The conflicting data on whether Wnt proteins are stimulatory or inhibitory for osteoblast differentiation is likely to reflect diverse functions of Wnts at different stages of skeletogenesis, and more data in different models will be required to expand our understanding of their complex role in osteogenesis. While canonical signaling promotes early stage osteogenesis (commitment to osteoblasts), recent data suggest that Lef1, a transcriptional regulator of the Wnt/β-catenin signaling cascade, promotes osteoprogenitor differentiation,[31] but delays osteoblast maturation and mineralization.[124] There is also accumulating evidence that Wnts regulate apoptosis of osteogenic cells. For example, Wnts prevent apoptosis of both uncommitted osteoprogenitors and differentiated osteoblasts by β-catenin–dependent as well as –independent signaling cascades involving Src/ERK and PI3K/Akt.[125] Thus, regulation of Wnt activity during osteoblast maturation is important. Secreted frizzled-related protein (sFRP)-1, an antagonist of canonical Wnt signaling, is a negative regulator of human osteoblast and osteocyte survival.[126]

A large number of in vitro and mouse experiments have shown a broad role of TGF-β1 throughout osteoblast differentiation and bone formation. Despite conflicting data and evidence for biphasic/concentration-dependent effects, it is generally accepted that TGF-β1 increases bone formation in vitro mainly by recruiting osteoprogenitors both by inducing chemotaxis and stimulating their proliferation, thus expanding the pool of committed osteoblasts. It also promotes the early stages of differentiation, while blocking later phases of differentiation, mineralization and osteoblast apoptosis.[127]

Among important concepts in regulation of osteoblast differentiation and activity is the idea that local or endogenous production of particular growth factors and cytokines undergoes changes required for osteoprogenitor differentiation to proceed and osteoblasts to modify their activity. For example,

IGF-I expression is markedly increased during early osteoblast recruitment, but declines quite markedly as these cells undergo differentiation. Data from both IGF-I– or IGF-I receptor–deficient mice and mice with targeted overexpression of IGF-I in osteoblasts show that IGF-I is involved not only in embryonic bone development but also postnatal bone formation and remodeling.[128,129] Much remains to be clarified about the effects of IGF-I and IGF-II on osteoblast precursor proliferation and/or osteoblast activity, but it does seem that targeted overexpression of IGF-I in osteoblasts results in increased trabecular bone volume, increased osteoblast function with accelerated formation, and decreased mineralization lag time, but no change in the number of osteoblast precursors.[128] When overexpression is targeted to both pre-osteoblasts and osteoblasts, osteoblast number increased, cortical bone thickness increased, but trabecular bone volume decreased, possibly because of increased turnover. IGF-I also acts as a potent antiapoptotic factor particularly for differentiated osteoblasts and osteocytes. Targeted deletion of the type I IgfR gene in mature osteoblasts results in a mineralization defect associated with lower BMD, but an increase in osteoblast precursor cells.[129]

Other Functional Activities of Osteoblast Lineage Cells

The functional properties and regulated activity of bone cells evolve during progression of osteoblast differentiation. As described above, they form the structural components of bone, producing a mineralized matrix and a cellular syncytium to respond to physiologic and mechanical demands on the skeleton. An equally important function of osteoblasts, as well as the pre-osteoblasts, which lie in close proximity, and osteocytes is their responsiveness to endocrine factors and the production of paracrine and autocrine factors for the recruitment of osteoprogenitors, the growth of pre-osteoblasts, and the regulation of osteoclastic resorption of the mineralized bone matrix.

The bone microenvironment seems to be essential for two components of osteoclastogenesis: (1) maturation and fusion of the mononuclear precursor to the multinucleated osteoclast and (2) activation and regulation of the activity of the functional osteoclast. The requirement for stromal osteoprogenitors or osteoblasts in mediating osteoclast differentiation is linked to the role of osteotrophic hormones and cytokines in regulating development of pre-osteoclasts and the multinucleated phenotype. Osteoblast lineage cells secrete osteoprotegerin, a soluble inhibitor of osteoclastogenesis and have receptors for RANKL, PTH, and 1,25(OH)$_2$D$_3$, which will promote osteoclast activity and bone turnover. Osteoblasts are the major source of the colony-stimulating factor 1 (CSF1) and also secrete some cytokines, which participate in osteoclastogenesis. Prostaglandins produced by bone cells, a potent stimulator of bone formation, as well as resorption, exemplifies the complexity of cellular responses in bone. The regulation of bone resorption and coupling of osteoblast and osteoclast activities is detailed elsewhere.

The role of osteoblastic cells as supporting cells for the bone marrow and hematopoietic stem cells (HSCs) has also begun to receive new attention because of two recent papers in which novel transgenic mouse models, one using the conditional deletion of the BMPR1A gene[130] and the other using overexpression of an active PTH/PTHrP receptor (PPR) mutant within osteoblasts.[131] The studies show parallel, concordant increases in the generation of trabecular osteoblasts and the number of HSCs in vivo and in vitro with a physical proximity of HSCs to endosteal osteoblasts and interaction between them. These data support the notion that osteoblasts are a major, defining component of the HSC niche within the bone marrow.[130,131]

REFERENCES

1. Friedenstein AJ 1990 Osteogenic stem cells in the bone marrow. In: Heersche JNM, Kanis JA (eds.) Bone Miner Research. Elsevier Science Publishers, Amsterdam, The Netherlands, pp. 243–270.
2. Pittenger MF, Mackay AM, Beck SC, Jaiswal RK, Douglas R, Mosca JD, Moorman MA, Simonetti DW, Craig S, Marshak DR 1999 Multilineage potential of adult human mesenchymal stem cells. Science **284:**143–147.
3. Jiang Y, Jahagirdar BN, Reinhardt RL, Schwartz RE, Keene CD, Ortiz-Gonzalez XR, Reyes M, Lenvik T, Lund T, Blackstad M, Du J, Aldrich S, Lisberg A, Low WC, Largaespada DA, Verfaillie CM 2002 Pluripotency of mesenchymal stem cells derived from adult marrow. Nature **418:**41–49.
4. Aubin JE 1999 Osteoprogenitor cell frequency in rat bone marrow stromal populations: Role for heterotypic cell-cell interactions in osteoblast differentiation. J Cell Biochem **72:**396–410.
5. Wu X, Peters JM, Gonzalez FJ, Prasad HS, Rohrer MD, Gimble JM 2000 Frequency of stromal lineage colony forming units in bone marrow of peroxisome proliferator-activated receptor-alpha-null mice. Bone **26:**21–26.
6. Huss R, Lange C, Weissinger EM, Kolb HJ, Thalmeier K 2000 Evidence of peripheral blood-derived, plastic-adherent CD34(-/low) hematopoietic stem cell clones with mesenchymal stem cell characteristics. Stem Cells **18:**252–260.
7. Erices A, Conget P, Minguell JJ 2000 Mesenchymal progenitor cells in human umbilical cord blood. Br J Haematol **109:**235–242.
8. Campagnoli C, Roberts IA, Kumar S, Bennett PR, Bellantuono I, Fisk NM 2001 Identification of mesenchymal stem/progenitor cells in human first-trimester fetal blood, liver, and bone marrow. Blood **98:**2396–2402.
9. Miura M, Gronthos S, Zhao M, Lu B, Fisher LW, Robey PG, Shi S 2003 SHED: Stem cells from human exfoliated deciduous teeth. Proc Natl Acad Sci USA **100:**5807–5812.
10. Asakura A, Komaki M, Rudnicki M 2001 Muscle satellite cells are multipotential stem cells that exhibit myogenic, osteogenic, and adipogenic differentiation. Differentiation **68:**245–253.
11. Gronthos S, Graves SE, Ohta S, Simmons PJ 1994 The STRO-1+ fraction of adult human bone marrow contains the osteogenic precursors. Blood **84:**4164–4173.
12. Bonyadi M, Waldman SD, Liu D, Aubin JE, Grynpas MD, Stanford WL 2003 Mesenchymal progenitor self-renewal deficiency leads to age-dependent osteoporosis in Sca-1/Ly-6A null mice. Proc Natl Acad Sci USA **100:**5840–5845.
13. Cornish J, Gillespie MT, Callon KE, Horwood NJ, Moseley JM, Reid IR 2003 Interleukin-18 is a novel mitogen of osteogenic and chondrogenic cells. Endocrinology **144:**1194–1201.
14. Yang X, Tare RS, Partridge KA, Roach HI, Clarke NM, Howdle SM, Shakesheff KM, Oreffo RO 2003 Induction of human osteoprogenitor chemotaxis, proliferation, differentiation, and bone formation by osteoblast stimulating factor-1/pleiotrophin: Osteoconductive biomimetic scaffolds for tissue engineering. J Bone Miner Res **18:**47–57.
15. Takeuchi Y, Watanabe S, Ishii G, Takeda S, Nakayama K, Fukumoto S, Kaneta Y, Inoue D, Matsumoto T, Harigaya K, Fujita T 2002 Interleukin-11 as a stimulatory factor for bone formation prevents bone loss with advancing age in mice. J Biol Chem **277:**49011–49018.
16. Park SR, Oreffo RO, Triffitt JT 1999 Interconversion potential of cloned human marrow adipocytes in vitro. Bone **24:**549–554.
17. Doherty MJ, Ashton BA, Walsh S, Beresford JN, Grant ME, Canfield AE 1998 Vascular pericytes express osteogenic potential in vitro and in vivo. J Bone Miner Res **13:**828–838.
18. Sowa H, Kaji H, Canaff L, Hendy GN, Tsukamoto T, Yamaguchi T, Miyazono K, Sugimoto T, Chihara K 2003 Inactivation of menin, the product of the multiple endocrine neoplasia type 1 gene, inhibits the commitment of multipotential mesenchymal stem cells into the osteoblast lineage. J Biol Chem **278:**21058–21069.
19. Logan CY, Nusse R 2004 The Wnt signaling pathway in development and disease. Annu Rev Cell Dev Biol **20:**781–810.
20. Church VL, Francis-West P 2002 Wnt signalling during limb development. Int J Dev Biol **46:**927–936.
21. Boyden LM, Mao J, Belsky J, Mitzner L, Farhi A, Mitnick MA, Wu D, Insogna K, Lifton RP 2002 High bone density due to a mutation in LDL-receptor-related protein 5. N Engl J Med **346:**1513–1521.
22. Little RD, Recker RR, Johnson ML 2002 High bone density due to a mutation in LDL-receptor-related protein 5. N Engl J Med **347:**943–944.
23. Kato M, Patel MS, Levasseur R, Lobov I, Chang BH, Glass DA, Hartmann C, Li L, Hwang TH, Brayton CF, Lang RA, Karsenty G, Chan L 2002 Cbfa1-independent decrease in osteoblast proliferation, osteopenia, and persistent embryonic eye vascularization in mice deficient in Lrp5, a Wnt coreceptor. J Cell Biol **157:**303–314.
24. Holmen SL, Zylstra CR, Mukherjee A, Sigler RE, Faugere MC, Bouxsein ML, Deng L, Clemens TL, Williams BO 2005 Essential role of beta-catenin in post natal bone acquisition. J Biol Chem **280:**21162–21168.
25. Day TF, Guo X, Garrett-Beal L, Yang Y 2005 Wnt/beta-Catenin Signaling in Mesenchymal Progenitors Controls Osteoblast and Chondrocyte Differentiation during Vertebrate Skeletogenesis. Dev Cell **8:**739–750.
26. Hill TP, Spater D, Taketo MM, Birchmeier W, Hartmann C 2005 Canonical Wnt/beta-catenin signaling prevents osteoblasts from differentiating into chondrocytes. Dev Cell **8:**727–738.
27. de la Fuente, Helms JA 2005 Head, shoulders, knees, and toes. Dev Biol **282:**294–306.
28. Reya T, Duncan AW, Ailles L, Domen J, Scherer DC, Willert K, Hintz L, Nusse R, Weissman IL 2003 A role for Wnt signalling in self-renewal of haematopoietic stem cells. Nature **423:**409–414.
29. Willert K, Brown JD, Danenberg E, Duncan AW, Weissman IL, Reya T, Yates JR, III, Nusse R 2003 Wnt proteins are lipid-modified and can act as stem cell growth factors. Nature **423:**448–452.
30. Bennett CN, Longo KA, Wright WS, Suva LJ, Lane TF, Hankenson KD, MacDougald OA 2005 Regulation of osteoblastogenesis and bone mass by Wnt10b. Proc Natl Acad Sci USA **102:**3324–3329.
31. Gaur T, Lengner CJ, Hovhannisyan H, Bhat RA, Bodine PVN, Komm BS, Javed A, van Wijnen AJ, Stein JL, Stein GS, Lian JB 2005 Canonical WNT signaling promotes osteogenesis by directly stimulating RUNX2 gene expression. J Biol Chem **280:**33132–33140.
32. ten Dijke P, Fu J, Schaap P, Roelen BA 2003 Signal transduction of bone morphogenetic proteins in osteoblast differentiation. J Bone Joint Surg Am **85**(Suppl 3):34–38.
33. Canalis E, Economides AN, Gazzerro E 2003 Bone morphogenetic proteins, their antagonists, and the skeleton. Endocr Rev **24:**218–235.
34. Yi SE, Daluiski A, Pederson R, Rosen V, Lyons KM 2000 The type I BMP receptor BMPRIB is required for chondrogenesis in the mouse limb. Development **127:**621–630.
35. Settle SH, Jr., Rountree RB, Sinha A, Thacker A, Higgins K, Kingsley DM 2003 Multiple joint and skeletal patterning defects caused by single and double mutations in the mouse Gdf6 and Gdf5 genes. Dev Biol **254:**116–130.
36. Balint E, Lapointe D, Drissi H, van der Meijden C, Young DW, van Wijnen AJ, Stein JL, Stein GS, Lian JB 2003 Phenotype discovery by gene expression profiling: Mapping of biological processes linked to BMP-2-mediated osteoblast differentiation. J Cell Biochem **89:**401–426.
37. Nakashima K, Zhou X, Kunkel G, Zhang Z, Deng JM, Behringer RR, de Crombrugghe B 2002 The novel zinc finger-containing transcription factor osterix is required for osteoblast differentiation and bone formation. Cell **108:**17–29.
38. Seeherman H, Wozney JM 2005 Delivery of bone morphogenetic proteins for orthopedic tissue regeneration. Cytokine Growth Factor Rev **16:**329–345.
39. Shin CS, Lecanda F, Sheikh S, Weitzmann L, Cheng SL, Civitelli R 2000 Relative abundance of different cadherins defines differentiation of mesenchymal precursors into osteogenic, myogenic, or adipogenic pathways. J Cell Biochem **78:**566–577.
40. Stains JP, Civitelli R 2005 Cell-cell interactions in regulating osteogenesis and osteoblast function. Birth Defects Res C Embryo Today **75:**72–80.
41. Liu F, Malaval L, Aubin JE 2003 Global amplification polymerase chain reaction reveals novel transitional stages during osteoprogenitor differentiation. J Cell Sci **116:**1787–1796.
42. Nijweide PJ, Burger EH, Klein-Nulend J 2002 The osteocyte. In: Bilezikian JP, Raisz LG, Rodan GA (eds.) Principles of Bone Biology, 2nd ed. Academic Press, San Diego, CA, USA, pp. 93–107.
43. Bonewald LF 1999 Establishment and characterization of an osteocyte-like cell line, MLO-Y4. J Bone Miner Metab **17:**61–65.
44. Jamal HH, Aubin JE 1996 CD44 expression in fetal rat bone: in vivo and in vitro analysis. Exp Cell Res **223:**467–477.
45. Schiller PC, D'Ippolito G, Brambilla R, Roos BA, Howard GA 2001 Inhibition of gap-junctional communication induces the trans-differentiation of osteoblasts to an adipocytic phenotype in vitro. J Biol Chem **276:**14133–14138.
46. Furlan F, Lecanda F, Screen J, Civitelli R 2001 Proliferation, differentiation and apoptosis in connexin43-null osteoblasts. Cell Commun Adhes **8:**367–371.
47. Plotkin LI, Manolagas SC, Bellido T 2002 Transduction of cell survival signals by connexin-43 hemichannels. J Biol Chem **277:**8648–8657.
48. Rubin CT, Lanyon LE 1987 Osteoregulatory nature of mechanical stimuli: Function as a determinant for adaptive bone remodeling. J Orthop Res **5:**300–310.
49. Jorgensen NR, Teilmann SC, Henriksen Z, Civitelli R, Sorensen OH, Steinberg TH 2003 Activation of L-type calcium channels is required for gap junction-mediated intercellular calcium signaling in osteoblastic cells. J Biol Chem **278:**4082–4086.
50. Boyce BF, Xing L, Jilka RJ, Bellido T, Weinstein RS, Parfitt AM, Mano-

lagas SC 2002 Apoptosis in bone cells. In: Bilezikian JP, Raisz LG, Rodan GA (eds.) Principles of Bone Biology, 2nd ed. Academic Press, San Diego, CA, USA, pp. 151–168.

51. Xing L, Boyce BF 2005 Regulation of apoptosis in osteoclasts and osteoblastic cells. Biochem Biophys Res Commun 328:709–720.

52. Plotkin LI, Aguirre JI, Kousteni S, Manolagas SC, Bellido T 2005 Bisphosphonates and estrogens inhibit osteocyte apoptosis via distinct molecular mechanisms downstream of extracellular signal-regulated kinase activation. J Biol Chem 280:7317–7325.

53. Noble BS, Peet N, Stevens HY, Brabbs A, Mosley JR, Reilly GC, Reeve J, Skerry TM, Lanyon LE 2003 Mechanical loading: Biphasic osteocyte survival and targeting of osteoclasts for bone destruction in rat cortical bone. Am J Physiol Cell Physiol 284:C934–C943.

54. Lian JB, Javed A, Zaidi SK, Lengner C, Montecino M, van Wijnen AJ, Stein JL, Stein GS 2004 Regulatory controls for osteoblast growth and differentiation: Role of Runx/Cbfa/AML factors. Crit Rev Eukaryot Gene Expr 14:1–41.

55. Otto F, Kanegane H, Mundlos S 2002 Mutations in the RUNX2 gene in patients with cleidocranial dysplasia. Hum Mutat 19:209–216.

56. Yang X, Matsuda K, Bialek P, Jacquot S, Masuoka HC, Schinke T, Li L, Brancorsini S, Sassone-Corsi P, Townes TM, Hanauer A, Karsenty G 2004 ATF4 is a substrate of RSK2 and an essential regulator of osteoblast biology; implication for Coffin-Lowry Syndrome. Cell 117:387–398.

57. Yu VW, Ambartsoumian G, Verlinden L, Moir JM, Prud'homme J, Gauthier C, Roughley PJ, St-Arnaud R 2005 FIAT represses ATF4-mediated transcription to regulate bone mass in transgenic mice. J Cell Biol 169:591–601.

58. Lu H, Kraut D, Gerstenfeld LC, Graves DT 2003 Diabetes interferes with the bone formation by affecting the expression of transcription factors that regulate osteoblast differentiation. Endocrinology 144:346–352.

59. Lee MS, Lowe GN, Strong DD, Wergedal JE, Glackin CA 1999 TWIST, a basic helix-loop-helix transcription factor, can regulate the human osteogenic lineage. J Cell Biochem 75:566–577.

60. Bialek P, Kern B, Yang X, Schrock M, Sosic D, Hong N, Wu H, Yu K, Ornitz DM, Olson EN, Justice MJ, Karsenty G 2004 A twist code determines the onset of osteoblast differentiation. Dev Cell 6:423–435.

61. Hassan MQ, Javed A, Morasso MI, Karlin J, Montecino M, van Wijnen AJ, Stein GS, Stein JL, Lian JB 2004 Dlx3 transcriptional regulation of osteoblast differentiation: Temporal recruitment of Msx2, Dlx3, and Dlx5 homeodomain proteins to chromatin of the osteocalcin gene. Mol Cell Biol 24:9248–9261.

62. Bendall AJ, Abate-Shen C 2000 Roles for Msx and Dlx homeoproteins in vertebrate development. Gene 247:17–31.

63. van Wijnen AJ, Stein GS, Gergen JP, Groner Y, Hiebert SW, Ito Y, Liu P, Neil JC, Ohki M, Speck N 2004 Nomenclature for Runt-related (RUNX) proteins. Oncogene 23:4209–4210.

64. Komori T, Yagi H, Nomura S, Yamaguchi A, Sasaki K, Deguchi K, Shimizu Y, Bronson RT, Gao Y-H, Inada M, Sato M, Okamoto R, Kitamura Y, Yoshiki S, Kishimoto T 1997 Targeted disruption of Cbfa1 results in a complete lack of bone formation owing to maturational arrest of osteoblasts. Cell 89:755–764.

65. Ducy P, Zhang R, Geoffroy V, Ridall AL, Karsenty G 1997 Osf2/Cbfa1: A transcriptional activator of osteoblast differentiation. Cell 89:747–754.

66. Otto F, Thornell AP, Crompton T, Denzel A, Gilmour KC, Rosewell IR, Stamp GWH, Beddington RSP, Mundlos S, Olsen BR, Selby PB, Owen MJ 1997 Cbfa1, a candidate gene for cleidocranial dysplasia syndrome, is essential for osteoblast differentiation and bone development. Cell 89:765–771.

67. Banerjee C, McCabe LR, Choi J-Y, Hiebert SW, Stein JL, Stein GS, Lian JB 1997 Runt homology domain proteins in osteoblast differentiation: AML-3/CBFA1 is a major component of a bone specific complex. J Cell Biochem 66:1–8.

68. Choi J-Y, Pratap J, Javed A, Zaidi SK, van Wijnen AJ, Lian JB, Stein JL, Jones SN, Stein GS 2000 In vivo replacement of the Runx2/Cbfa1 gene with a mutant gene lacking a subnuclear targeting signal and transcriptional regulatory functions results in severe skeletal abnormalities. J Bone Miner Res 15:S157.

69. Rossi F, MacLean HE, Yuan W, Francis RO, Semenova E, Lin CS, Kronenberg HM, Cobrinik D 2002 p107 and p130 coordinately regulate proliferation, Cbfa1 expression, and hypertrophic differentiation during endochondral bone development. Dev Biol 247:271–285.

70. Galindo M, Pratap J, Young DW, Hovhannisyan H, Im HJ, Choi JY, Lian JB, Stein JL, Stein GS, van Wijnen AJ 2005 The bone-specific expression of RUNX2 oscillates during the cell cycle to support a G1 related antiproliferative function in osteoblasts. J Biol Chem 280:20274–20285.

71. Zaidi SK, Young DW, Pockwinse SH, Javed A, Lian JB, Stein JL, van Wijnen AJ, Stein GS 2003 Mitotic partitioning and selective reorganization of tissue specific transcription factors in progeny cells. Proc Natl Acad Sci USA 100:14852–14857.

72. Enomoto H, Enomoto-Iwamoto M, Iwamoto M, Nomura S, Himeno M, Kitamura Y, Kishimoto T, Komori T 2000 Cbfa1 is a positive regulatory factor in chondrocyte maturation. J Biol Chem 275:8695–8702.

73. Stricker S, Fundele R, Vortkamp A, Mundlos S 2002 Role of runx genes in chondrocyte differentiation. Dev Biol 245:95–108.

74. Sun L, Vitolo M, Passaniti A 2001 Runt-related gene 2 in endothelial cells: Inducible expression and specific regulation of cell migration and invasion. Cancer Res 61:4994–5001.

75. Zelzer E, Glotzer DJ, Hartmann C, Thomas D, Fukai N, Soker S, Olsen BR 2001 Tissue specific regulation of VEGF expression during bone development requires Cbfa1/Runx2. Mech Dev 106:97–106.

76. Stock M, Schafer H, Stricker S, Gross G, Mundlos S, Otto F 2003 Expression of galectin-3 in skeletal tissues is controlled by Runx2. J Biol Chem 278:17360–17367.

77. Ji C, Casinghino S, Chang DJ, Chen Y, Javed A, Ito Y, Hiebert SW, Lian JB, Stein GS, McCarthy TL, Centrella M 1998 CBFa(AML/PEBP2)-related elements in the TGF-beta type I receptor promoter and expression with osteoblast differentiation. J Cell Biochem 69:353–363.

78. Javed A, Barnes GL, Jassanya BO, Stein JL, Gerstenfeld L, Lian JB, Stein GS 2001 Runt homology domain transcription factors (Runx, Cbfa, and AML) mediate repression of the bone sialoprotein promoter: Evidence for promoter context-dependent activity of Cbfa proteins. Mol Cell Biol 21:2891–2905.

79. Sato M, Morii E, Komori T, Kawahata H, Sugimoto M, Terai K, Shimizu H, Yasui T, Ogihara H, Yasui N, Ochi T, Kitamura Y, Ito Y, Nomura S 1998 Transcriptional regulation of osteopontin gene in vivo by PEBP2alphaA/CBFA1 and ETS1 in the skeletal tissues. Oncogene 17:1517–1525.

80. Chen S, Gu TT, Sreenath T, Kulkarni AB, Karsenty G, MacDougall M 2002 Spatial expression of Cbfa1/Runx2 isoforms in teeth and characterization of binding sites in the DSPP gene. Connect Tissue Res 43:338–344.

81. Thirunavukkarasu K, Halladay DL, Miles RR, Yang X, Galvin RJ, Chandrasekhar S, Martin TJ, Onyia JE 2000 The osteoblast-specific transcription factor Cbfa1 contributes to the expression of osteoprotegerin, a potent inhibitor of osteoclast differentiation and function. J Biol Chem 275:25163–25172.

82. Geoffroy V, Kneissel M, Fournier B, Boyde A, Matthias P 2002 High bone resorption in adult aging transgenic mice overexpressing cbfa1/runx2 in cells of the osteoblastic lineage. Mol Cell Biol 22:6222–6233.

83. Jimenez MJ, Balbin M, Lopez JM, Alvarez J, Komori T, Lopez-Otin C 1999 Collagenase 3 is a target of Cbfa1, a transcription factor of the runt gene family involved in bone formation. Mol Cell Biol 19:4431–4442.

84. Wang Y, Belflower RM, Dong YF, Schwarz EM, O'Keefe RJ, Drissi H 2005 Runx1/AML1/Cbfa2 mediates onset of mesenchymal cell differentiation toward chondrogenesis. J Bone Miner Res 20:1624–1636.

85. Lian JB, Balint E, Javed A, Drissi H, Vitti R, Quinlan EJ, Zhang L, van Wijnen AJ, Stein JL, Speck N, Stein GS 2003 Runx1/AML1 hematopoietic transcription factor contributes to skeletal development in vivo. J Cell Physiol 196:301–311.

86. Yoshida CA, Yamamoto H, Fujita T, Furuichi T, Ito K, Inoue K, Yamana K, Zanma A, Takada K, Ito Y, Komori T 2004 Runx2 and Runx3 are essential for chondrocyte maturation, and Runx2 regulates limb growth through induction of Indian hedgehog. Genes Dev 18:952–963.

87. Gori F, Thomas T, Hicok KC, Spelsberg TC, Riggs BL 1999 Differentiation of human marrow stromal precursor cells: Bone morphogenetic protein-2 increases OSF2/CBFA1, enhances osteoblast commitment, and inhibits late adipocyte maturation. J Bone Miner Res 14:1522–1535.

88. Zaidi SK, Young DW, Choi JY, Pratap J, Javed A, Montecino M, Stein JL, van Wijnen AJ, Lian JB, Stein GS 2005 The dynamic organization of gene-regulatory machinery in nuclear microenvironments. EMBO Rep 6:128–133.

89. Miller J, Horner A, Stacy T, Lowrey C, Lian JB, Stein G, Nuckolls GH, Speck NA 2002 The core-binding factor beta subunit is required for bone formation and hematopoietic maturation. Nat Genet 32:645–649.

90. Kahler RA, Westendorf JJ 2003 Lymphoid enhancer factor-1 and beta-catenin inhibit Runx2-dependent transcriptional activation of the osteocalcin promoter. J Biol Chem 278:11937–11944.

91. D'Alonzo RC, Selvamurugan N, Karsenty G, Partridge NC 2002 Physical Interaction of the Activator Protein-1 Factors c-Fos and c-Jun with Cbfa1 for Collagenase-3 Promoter Activation. J Biol Chem 277:816–822.

92. Hess J, Porte D, Munz C, Angel P 2001 AP-1 and Cbfa/Runt physically interact and regulate PTH-dependent MMP13 expression in osteoblasts through a new OSE2/AP-1 composite element. J Biol Chem 276:20029–20038.

93. Ji C, Chen Y, Centrella M, McCarthy TL 1999 Activation of the insulin-like growth factor-binding protein-5 promoter in osteoblasts by cooperative E box, CCAAT enhancer-binding protein, and nuclear factor-1 deoxyribonucleic acid-binding sequences. Endocrinology 140:4564–4572.

94. Gutierrez S, Javed A, Tennant D, van Rees M, Montecino M, Stein GS, Stein JL, Lian JB 2002 CCAAT/enhancer-binding proteins (C/EBP) β and δ Activate osteocalcin gene transcription and synergize with Runx2 at the C/EBP element to regulate bone-specific expression. J Biol Chem 277:1316–1323.

95. Sierra J, Villagra A, Paredes R, Cruzat F, Gutierrez S, Javed A, Arriagada G, Olate J, Imschenetzky M, van Wijnen AJ, Lian JB, Stein GS, Stein JL 2003 Regulation of the bone-specific osteocalcin gene by p300 requires Runx2/Cbfa1 and the vitamin D3 receptor but not p300 intrinsic histone acetyltransferase activity. Mol Cell Biol 23:3339–3351.

96. Zaidi SK, Sullivan AJ, van Wijnen AJ, Stein JL, Stein GS, Lian JB 2002 Integration of Runx and Smad regulatory signals at transcriptionally active subnuclear sites. Proc Natl Acad Sci USA 99:8048–8053.

97. Zhang YW, Yasui N, Ito K, Huang G, Fujii M, Hanai J, Nogami H, Ochi T, Miyazono K, Ito Y 2000 A RUNX2/PEBP2αA/CBFA1 mutation displaying impaired transactivation and Smad interaction in cleidocranial dysplasia. Proc Natl Acad Sci USA 97:10549–10554.

98. Zaidi SK, Sullivan AJ, Medina R, Ito Y, van Wijnen AJ, Stein JL, Lian JB, Stein GS 2004 Tyrosine phosphorylation controls Runx2-mediated subnuclear targeting of YAP to repress transcription. EMBO J 23:790–799.

99. Cui CB, Cooper LF, Yang X, Karsenty G, Aukhil I 2003 Transcriptional coactivation of bone-specific transcription factor Cbfa1 by TAZ. Mol Cell Biol 23:1004–1013.

100. Zhang YW, Bae SC, Takahashi E, Ito Y 1997 The cDNA cloning of the transcripts of human PEBP2alphaA/CBFA1 mapped to 6p12.3-p21.1, the locus for cleidocranial dysplasia. Oncogene 15:367–371.

101. Lecka-Czernik B, Gubrij I, Moerman EJ, Kajkenova O, Lipschitz DA, Manolagas SC, Jilka RL 1999 Inhibition of Osf2/Cbfa1 expression and terminal osteoblast differentiation by PPARgamma2. J Cell Biochem 74:357–371.

102. Jeon MJ, Kim JA, Kwon SH, Kim SW, Park KS, Park SW, Kim SY, Shin CS 2003 Activation of peroxisome proliferator-activated receptor-gamma inhibits the Runx2-mediated transcription of osteocalcin in osteoblasts. J Biol Chem 278:23270–23277.

103. Nuttall ME, Patton AJ, Olivera DL, Nadeau DP, Gowen M 1998 Human trabecular bone cells are able to express both osteoblastic and adipocytic phenotype: Implications for osteopenic disorders. J Bone Miner Res 13:371–382.

104. Calvi LM, Sims NA, Hunzelman JL, Knight MC, Giovannetti A, Saxton JM, Kronenberg HM, Baron R, Schipani E 2001 Activated parathyroid hormone/parathyroid hormone-related protein receptor in osteoblastic cells differentially affects cortical and trabecular bone. J Clin Invest 107:277–286.

105. Parisien M, Silverberg SJ, Shane E, de la CL, Lindsay R, Bilezikian JP, Dempster DW 1990 The histomorphometry of bone in primary hyperparathyroidism: Preservation of cancellous bone structure. J Clin Endocrinol Metab 70:930–938.

106. Karaplis AC, Goltzman D 2000 PTH and PTHrP effects on the skeleton. Rev Endocr Metab Disord 1:331–341.

107. Eijken M, Hewison M, Cooper MS, de Jong FH, Chiba H, Stewart PM, Uitterlinden AG, Pols HA, Van Leeuwen JP 2005 11beta-Hydroxysteroid dehydrogenase expression and glucocorticoid synthesis are directed by a molecular switch during osteoblast differentiation. Mol Endocrinol 19:621–631.

108. Sher LB, Woitge HW, Adams DJ, Gronowicz GA, Krozowski Z, Harrison JR, Kream BE 2004 Transgenic expression of 11beta-hydroxysteroid dehydrogenase type 2 in osteoblasts reveals an anabolic role for endogenous glucocorticoids in bone. Endocrinology 145:922–929.

109. Kream BE, Lukert BP 2002 Clinical and basic aspects of glucocorticoid action in bone. In: Bilezikian JP, Raisz LG, Rodan GA (eds.) Principles of Bone Biology, 2nd ed. Academic Press, San Diego, CA, USA, pp. 723–740.

110. Van Leeuwen JP, van Driel M, van den Bemd GJ, Pols HA 2001 Vitamin D control of osteoblast function and bone extracellular matrix mineralization. Crit Rev Eukaryot Gene Expr 11:199–226.

111. Meyer T, Kneissel M, Mariani J, Fournier B 2000 In vitro and in vivo evidence for orphan nuclear receptor RORalpha function in bone metabolism. Proc Natl Acad Sci USA 97:9197–9202.

112. Jarvis CI, Staels B, Brugg B, Lemaigre-Dubreuil Y, Tedgui A, Mariani J 2002 Age-related phenotypes in the staggerer mouse expand the RORalpha nuclear receptor's role beyond the cerebellum. Mol Cell Endocrinol 186:1–5.

113. Cornish J, Callon KE, Coy DH, Jiang NY, Xiao L, Cooper GJ, Reid IR 1997 Adrenomedullin is a potent stimulator of osteoblastic activity in vitro and in vivo. Am J Physiol 273:E1113–E1120.

114. Elefteriou F, Takeda S, Ebihara K, Magre J, Patano N, Kim CA, Ogawa Y, Liu X, Ware SM, Craigen WJ, Robert JJ, Vinson C, Nakao K, Capeau J, Karsenty G 2004 Serum leptin level is a regulator of bone mass. Proc Natl Acad Sci USA 101:3258–3263.

115. Gordelaze JO, Drevon CA, Syversen U, Reseland JE 2002 Leptin stimulates human osteoblastic cell proliferation, de novo collagen synthesis, and mineralization: Impact on differentiation markers, apoptosis, and osteoclastic signaling. J Cell Biochem 85:825–836.

116. Thomas T, Gori F, Khosla S, Jensen MD, Burguera B, Riggs BL 1999 Leptin acts on human marrow stromal cells to enhance differentiation to osteoblasts and to inhibit differentiation to adipocytes. Endocrinology 140:1630–1638.

117. Kim GS, Hong JS, Kim SW, Koh JM, An CS, Choi JY, Cheng SL 2003 Leptin induces apoptosis via ERK/cPLA2/cytochrome c pathway in human bone marrow stromal cells. J Biol Chem 278:21920–21929.

118. Burguera B, Hofbauer LC, Thomas T, Gori F, Evans GL, Khosla S, Riggs BL, Turner RT 2001 Leptin reduces ovariectomy-induced bone loss in rats. Endocrinology 142:3546–3553.

119. Pasco JA, Henry MJ, Kotowicz MA, Collier GR, Ball MJ, Ugoni AM, Nicholson GC 2001 Serum leptin levels are associated with bone mass in nonobese women. J Clin Endocrinol Metab 86:1884–1887.

120. Shin HI, Divieti P, Sims NA, Kobayashi T, Miao D, Karaplis AC, Baron R, Bringhurst R, Kronenberg HM 2004 Gp130-mediated signaling is necessary for normal osteoblastic function in vivo and in vitro. Endocrinology 145:1376–1385.

121. Sims NA, Jenkins BJ, Quinn JM, Nakamura A, Glatt M, Gillespie MT, Ernst M, Martin TJ 2004 Glycoprotein 130 regulates bone turnover and bone size by distinct downstream signaling pathways. J Clin Invest 113:379–389.

122. de Hooge AS, van de Loo FA, Bennink MB, de Jong DS, Arntz OJ, Lubberts E, Richards CD, vandDen Berg WB 2002 Adenoviral transfer of murine oncostatin M elicits periosteal bone apposition in knee joints of mice, despite synovial inflammation and up-regulated expression of interleukin-6 and receptor activator of nuclear factor-kappa B ligand. Am J Pathol 160:1733–1743.

123. Malaval L, Liu F, Vernallis AB, Aubin JE 2005 GP130/OSMR is the only LIF/IL-6 family receptor complex to promote osteoblast differentiation of calvaria progenitors. J Cell Physiol 204:585–593.

124. Kahler RA, Galindo M, Lian J, Stein GS, van Wijnen AJ, Westendorf JJ 2005 Lymphocyte enhancer-binding factor 1 (Lef1) inhibits terminal differentiation of osteoblasts. J Cell Biochem [Epub ahead of print].

125. Almeida M, Han L, Bellido T, Manolagas SC, Kousteni S 2005 Wnt proteins prevent apoptosis of both uncommitted osteoblast progenitors and differentiated osteoblasts by beta-catenin-dependent and -independent signaling cascades involving Src/ERK and phosphatidylinositol 3-kinase/Akt. J Biol Chem 280:41342–41351.

126. Bodine PV, Billiard J, Moran RA, Ponce-de-Leon H, McLarney S, Mangine A, Scrimo MJ, Bhat RA, Stauffer B, Green J, Stein GS, Lian JB, Komm BS 2005 The Wnt antagonist secreted frizzled-related protein-1 controls osteoblast and osteocyte apoptosis. J Cell Biochem 96:1212–1230.

127. Janssens K, ten DP, Janssens S, Van HW 2005 Transforming growth factor-beta1 to the bone. Endocr Rev 26:743–774.

128. Zhao G, Monier-Faugere MC, Langub MC, Geng Z, Nakayama T, Pike JW, Chernausek SD, Rosen CJ, Donahue LR, Malluche HH, Fagin JA, Clemens TL 2000 Targeted overexpression of insulin-like growth factor I to osteoblasts of transgenic mice: Increased trabecular bone volume without increased osteoblast proliferation. Endocrinology 141:2674–2682.

129. Zhang M, Xuan S, Bouxsein ML, von Stechow D, Akeno N, Faugere MC, Malluche H, Zhao G, Rosen CJ, Efstratiadis A, Clemens TL 2002 Osteoblast-specific knockout of the insulin-like growth factor (IGF) receptor gene reveals an essential role of IGF signaling in bone matrix mineralization. J Biol Chem 277:44005–44012.

130. Zhang J, Niu C, Ye L, Huang H, He X, Tong WG, Ross J, Haug J, Johnson T, Feng JQ, Harris S, Wiedemann LM, Mishina Y, Li L 2003 Identification of the haematopoietic stem cell niche and control of the niche size. Nature 425:836–841.

131. Calvi LM, Adams GB, Weibrecht KW, Weber JM, Olson DP, Knight MC, Martin RP, Schipani E, Divieti P, Bringhurst FR, Milner LA, Kronenberg HM, Scadden DT 2003 Osteoblastic cells regulate the haematopoietic stem cell niche. Nature 425:841–846.

Chapter 5. Osteoclast Biology and Bone Resorption

F. Patrick Ross

Washington University School of Medicine, Department of Pathology and Immunology, St. Louis, Missouri

CELL BIOLOGY OF THE OSTEOCLAST

Pathological bone loss, regardless of etiology, invariably represents an increase in the rate at which the skeleton is degraded by osteoclasts relative to its formation by osteoblasts. Thus, prevention of conditions such as osteoporosis requires an understanding of the molecular mechanisms of bone resorption.

The osteoclast, the exclusive bone resorptive cell (Fig. 1), is a member of the monocyte/macrophage family and a polykaryon that can be generated in vitro from mononuclear phagocyte precursors resident in a number of tissues.[1] There is, however, general agreement that the principal physiological osteoclast precursor is the bone marrow macrophage. Two cytokines are essential and sufficient for basal osteoclastogenesis, the first being RANKL[1,2] and the second being macrophage colony-stimulating factor (M-CSF), also designated CSF-1.[3] These two proteins, which exist as both membrane-bound and soluble forms, are produced by marrow stromal cells and their derivative osteoblasts, and thus physiological recruitment of osteoclasts from their mononuclear precursors requires the presence of these non-hematopoietic, bone-residing cells.[1] RANKL, a member of the TNF superfamily, is the key osteoclastogenic cytokine, because osteoclast formation requires its presence or its priming of precursor cells. M-CSF contributes to the proliferation, survival, and differentiation of osteoclast precursors, as well as the survival and cytoskeletal rearrangement required for efficient bone resorption (Fig. 2). The discovery of RANKL was preceded by identification of its physiological inhibitor osteoprotegerin (OPG), to which it binds with high affinity.[4] In contrast, M-CSF is a moiety long known to regulate the broader biology of myeloid cells, including osteoclasts[3] (see Fig. 2).

Our understanding of how osteoclasts resorb bone derives from two major sources: biochemical and genetic.[2] The unique osteoclastogenic properties of RANKL permit generation of pure populations of osteoclasts in culture and hence the performance of meaningful biochemical and molecular experiments that provide insights into the molecular mechanisms by which osteoclasts resorb bone. Further evidence has come from our capacity to generate mice lacking specific genes, plus the positional cloning of genetic abnormalities in people with abnormal osteoclast function. Key to the resorptive event is the capacity of the osteoclast to form a microenvironment between itself and the underlying bone matrix (Fig. 3A). This compartment, which is isolated from the general extracellular space, is acidified by an electrogenic proton pump (H^+-ATPase) and a Cl^- channel to a pH of ~4.5.[5] The acidified milieu mobilizes the mineralized component of bone, exposing its organic matrix, consisting largely of type 1 collagen that is subsequently degraded by the lysosomal enzyme, cathepsin K. The critical role that the proton pump, Cl^- channel, and cathepsin K play in osteoclast function is underscored by the fact that dysfunction of each results in human diseases of excess bone mass, namely osteopetrosis or pyknodysostosis.[2,5]

The above model of bone degradation clearly depends on physical intimacy between the osteoclast and bone matrix, a role provided by integrins. Integrins are $\alpha\beta$ heterodimers with long extracellular and single transmembrane domains.[6] In most instances, the integrin cytoplasmic region is relatively short, consisting of 40–70 amino acids. Integrins are the principal cell/matrix attachment molecules and they mediate osteoclast/bone recognition. Members of the $\beta1$ family of integrins, which recognize collagen, fibronectin, and laminin are present on osteoclasts, but $\alpha v\beta3$ is the principal integrin mediating bone resorption.[7] This heterodimer, like all members of the αv integrin family, recognizes the amino acid motif Arg-Gly-Asp (RGD), which is present in a variety of bone residing proteins such as osteopontin and bone sialoprotein. Thus, osteoclasts attach to and spread on these substrates in an RGD-dependent manner and, most importantly, competitive ligands arrest bone resorption in vivo. Definitive proof of the pivotal role that $\alpha v\beta3$ in the resorptive process came with the generation of $\beta3$ integrin knockout mouse, which develops a progressive increase in bone mass because of osteoclast dysfunction.[7] Based on a combination of these in vitro and in vivo observations, small molecule inhibitors of osteoclast function that target $\alpha v\beta3$ have been developed.[8]

Bone resorption also requires a polarization event in which the osteoclast delivers effector molecules like HCl and cathepsin K into the resorptive microenvironment. Osteoclasts are characterized by a unique cytoskeleton, which mediates the resorptive process. Specifically, when the cell contacts bone, it generates two polarized structures, which enable it to degrade skeletal tissue. In the first instance, a subset of acidified vesicles containing specific cargo, including cathepsin K and other matrix metallo-proteases, are transported, probably through microtubules, to the bone-apposed plasma membrane,[9] to which they fuse in a manner not currently understood. Insertion of these vesicles into the plasmalemma results in formation of a villous structure, unique to the osteoclast, the ruffled membrane. This resorptive organelle contains the abundant H^+ transporting machinery to create the acidified microenvironment, while the accompanying exocytosis serves as the means by which cathepsin K is secreted (Fig. 3B).

In addition to inducing ruffled membrane formation, contact with bone also prompts the osteoclast to polarize its fibrillar actin into a circular structure known as the "actin ring." A separate "sealing zone" surrounds and isolates the acidified resorptive microenvironment in the active cell, but its composition is almost completely unknown. The actin ring, like the ruffled membrane, is a hallmark of the degradative capacity of the osteoclast, because structural abnormalities of either occur in conditions of arrested resorption.[10] In most cells, such as fibroblasts, matrix attachment prompts formation of stable structures known as focal adhesions that contain both integrins and a host of signaling and cytoskeletal molecules, which mediate contact and formation of actin stress fibers. In keeping with the substitution of the actin ring for stress fibers in osteoclasts, these cells form podosomes instead of focal adhesions. Podosomes, which in resorbing osteoclasts are present in the actin ring, consist of an actin core surrounded by $\alpha v\beta3$ and associated cytoskeletal proteins.

The integrin $\beta3$ subunit knockout mouse serves as an important tool for determining the role of $\alpha v\beta3$ in the capacity of the osteoclast to resorb bone. Failure to express $\alpha v\beta3$ results in a dramatic osteoclast phenotype, particularly regarding the actin cytoskeleton. The $\beta3^{-/-}$ osteoclast forms abnormal ruffled membranes in vivo and, whether generated in vitro or directly isolated from bone, the mutant cells fail to spread when plated on immobilized RGD ligand or mineralized matrix in

The author has reported no conflicts of interest.

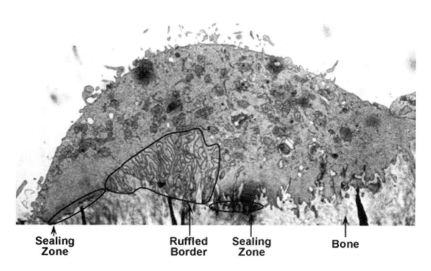

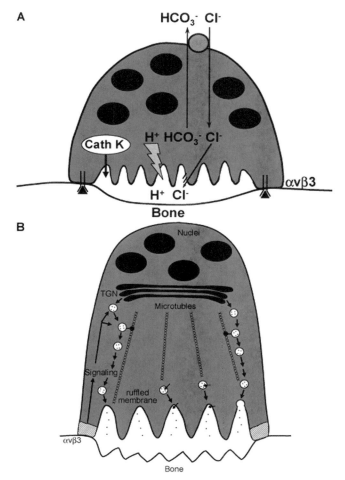

FIG. 1. The osteoclast as a resorptive cell. Transmission electron microscopy of a multinucleated primary rat osteoclast on bone. Note the extensive ruffled border, close apposition of the cell to bone, and the partially degraded matrix between the sealing zones. Courtesy of H. Zhao.

physiological amounts of RANKL and M-CSF. Confirming their attenuated resorptive activity, $\beta3^{-/-}$ osteoclasts generate fewer and shallower resorptive lacunae on dentin slices than do their wildtype counterparts. In keeping with attenuated bone resorption, in vivo, $\beta3^{-/-}$ mice are substantially hypocalcemic.[5]

Integrin Signaling

While integrins were viewed initially as merely cell attachment molecules, it is now apparent that their capacity to transmit signals to and from the cell interior is equally important, an event that requires that the integrin convert from a default low affinity state to one in which its capacity to bind matrix is significantly enhanced. The process, termed activation, arises

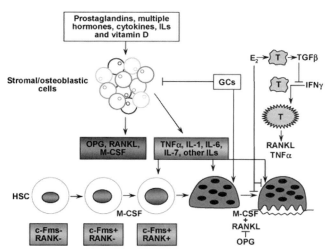

FIG. 2. Role of cytokines, hormones, steroids, and prostaglandins in osteoclast formation. Under the influence of other cytokines (data not shown), hematopoietic stem cell (HSCs) commit to the myeloid lineage, express c-Fms and RANK, the receptors for M-CSF and RANKL, respectively, and differentiate into osteoclasts. Mesenchymal cells in the marrow respond to a range of stimuli, secreting a mixture of pro- and anti-osteoclastogenic proteins, the latter primarily OPG. Glucocorticoids suppress bone resorption indirectly but possibly also target osteoclasts and/or their precursors. Estrogen, by a complex mechanism, inhibits activation of T cells, decreasing their secretion of RANKL and TNF-α; the sex steroid also inhibits osteoblast and osteoclast differentiation and lifespan. A key factor regulating bone resorption is the RANKL/OPG ratio.

FIG. 3. Mechanism of osteoclastic bone resorption. (A) The osteoclast adheres to bone through the integrin $\alpha v\beta3$, creating a sealing zone, into which is secreted hydrochloric acid and acidic proteases such as cathepsin K, MMP9, and MMP13. The acid is generated by the combined actions of a vacuolar H^+ ATPase, its coupled chloride channel and a basolateral chloride-bicarbonate exchanger. Carbonic anhydrase converts CO_2 into H^+ and HCO_3^- (data not shown). (B) Integrin engagement results in signals that target acidifying vesicles ($\blacklozenge$ = proton pump complex) containing specific cargo (black dots) to the bone-apposed face of the cell. Fusion of these vesicles with the plasma membrane generates a polarized cell capable of secreting the acid and proteases required for bone resorption.

from either integrin ligation of their multivalent ligands or indirectly by growth factor signaling.[11]

$\alpha v \beta 3$ is absent from osteoclast precursors, but their differentiation under the action of RANKL results in marked up-regulation of this heterodimer. The capacity of integrins to transmit intracellular signals to the cytoskeleton heightened interest in the cytoplasmic molecules mediating these events in osteoclasts and $\alpha v \beta 3$ signaling in this context is reasonably well understood. The initial signaling event involves the proto-oncogene c-src which, acting as a kinase and an adaptor protein, regulates formation of lamellipodia and disassembly of podosomes, indicating that c-src controls formation of resorptive organelles of the cell, such as the ruffled membrane, and also arrests migration on the bone surface. There is continuing debate surrounding the molecules which link c-src to the cytoskeleton, one proposal being that the focal adhesion kinase family member Pyk2, acting in concert with c-Cbl, a proto-oncogene and ubiquitin ligase.[12] A strong alternative candidate is Syk, a nonreceptor tyrosine kinase that is recruited to the active conformation of $\alpha v \beta 3$ in osteoclasts in a c-src–dependent manner, where it targets Vav3,[7] a member of the large family of guanine nucleotide exchange factors (GEFs) that convert Rho GTPases from their inactive GDP to their active GTP conformation.

Small GTPases

The Rho family of GTPases is central to remodeling of the actin cytoskeleton in many cell types,[13] and as such plays a central role in osteoclastic bone resorption. On attachment to bone, Rho and Rac bind GTP and translocate to the cytoskeleton. While both small GTPases impact the actin cytoskeleton, Rac and Rho exert distinctive effects. Rho signaling mediates formation of the actin ring and a constitutively active form of the GTPase stimulates podosome formation, osteoclast motility, and bone resorption, whereas dominant negative Rho arrests these events.[14] Rac stimulation in osteoclast precursors prompts appearance of lamellipodia, thus forming the migratory front of the cell to which $\alpha v \beta 3$ moves when activated.[15] In sum, it is likely that Rho's effect is principally on cell adhesion, whereas Rac mediates the cytoskeleton's migratory machinery. Importantly, absence of Vav3 blunts Rac but not Rho activity in the osteoclast.[16]

FACTORS REGULATING OSTEOCLAST FORMATION AND/OR FUNCTION

Proteins

In addition to the two key osteoclastogenic cytokines M-CSF and RANKL, a number of other proteins play important roles in osteoclast biology, either in physiological and/or pathophysiological circumstances.

As discussed earlier, osteoprotogerin, a high affinity ligand for RANKL that acts as a soluble inhibitor of RANKL, is secreted by cells of mesenchymal origin, both basally and in response to other regulatory signals, including cytokines and bone-targeting steroids.[4] Pro-inflammatory cytokines suppress OPG expression while simultaneously enhancing that of RANKL, with the net effect being a marked increase in osteoclast formation and function. Genetic deletion of OPG in both mouse and humans leads to profound osteopetrosis, whereas overexpression of the molecule under the control of a hepatic promoter results in severe osteoporosis. Together, these observation indicate that circulating OPG modulates the bone resorptive activity of RANKL and help to explain the increased bone loss in clinical situations accompanied by increased levels of TNF-α, interleukin (IL)-1, PTH, or PTH-related protein

(PTHrP). Serum PTH levels are increased in hyperparathyroidism of whatever etiology, whereas PTHrP is secreted by bone-targeting lung and breast carcinoma.[17,18] TNF antibodies or a soluble TNF receptor-IgG fusion protein potently suppress the bone loss in disorders of inflammatory osteolysis such as rheumatoid arthritis.[19] The molecular basis of this observation seems to be that the inflammatory cytokine synergizes with RANKL in a unique manner, most likely because RANKL and TNF each activate a number of key downstream effector pathways, leading to nuclear localization of a range of osteoclastogenic transcription factors (see Fig. 6). Recent evidence suggests a new paradigm linking TNF, IL-1, and the natural secreted inhibitor for the latter cytokine, IL-1 receptor antagonist, which blocks IL-1 function. Specifically, it seems that, at least in murine osteoclasts and their precursors, many of the effects of TNF are mediated through its stimulation of IL-1, which in turn increases expression and secretion of IL-1ra, a set of events that represent a complex control pathway. The significance of IL receptor antagonist is shown by the fact an IgG fusion protein containing the active component of this molecule has been developed and enhances the ability of anti-TNF-α antibodies to decrease bone loss in rheumatoid arthritis.[20]

Elegant studies suggest that interferon gamma (IFN-γ) is an important suppressor of osteoclast formation and function.[21] Nevertheless, these findings seem to be in conflict with other in vivo observations, including the report that IFNγ treatment of children with osteopetrosis ameliorates the disease[22] and the fact that a number of in vivo studies indicate that IFN-γ stimulates bone resorption.[23] This conundrum highlights the importance of discriminating between in vitro culture experiments using single cytokines and results in vivo. Many additional studies have implicated a range of other cytokines in the regulation of the osteoclast. These include a range of interleukins, granulocyte macrophage-colony stimulating factor (GM-CSF), IFN-β, stromal-derived growth factor 1 (SDF-1), macrophage inflammatory protein 1α (MIPα), and monocyte chemotactic protein 1 (MCP-1)[24–27] but at this time the results are either contradictory, as for GM-CSF in the murine versus human systems, or lack direct proof in humans. Future studies are likely to clarify the currently confusing data set. Finally, interactions between immune receptors such as DAP12 and FcγR and their ligands on cells of the stromal and myeloid/lymphoid lineages are important for transmission of RANK-derived signals.[21]

Small Molecules

1,25-dihydroxyvitamin D has all the characteristics of a steroid hormone, including a high affinity nuclear receptor that binds as a heterodimer with the retinoid X receptor to regulate transcription of a set of specific target genes. The active form of vitamin D, generated by successive hydroxylation in the liver and kidney, is a well-established stimulator of bone resorption when present at supraphysiological levels. Studies over many years indicate that this steroid hormone increases mesenchymal cell transcription of the *RANKL* gene while diminishing that of OPG.[4] Separately, 1,25-dihydroxyvitamin D suppresses synthesis of the pro-osteoclastogenic hormone PTH[28] and enhances calcium uptake. Taken together, two latter effects would seem to be antiresorptive, but many studies in humans indicate the net osteolytic action resulting from high levels of the steroid hormone, suggesting that its ability to stimulate osteoclast function overrides any bone anabolic actions.

Loss of estrogen (E2), most often seen in the context of menopause, is a major reason for the development of significant bone loss in aging. Interestingly, it is now clear that estrogen is the main sex steroid regulating bone mass in both men and women.[29] The mechanisms by which estrogen mediates its osteolytic effects are still incompletely understood, but significant advances have been made over the last decade. The original hypothesis, now considered to only part of the explanation, is that decreased serum E2 led to increased production, by circulating macrophages, of osteoclastogenic cytokines such as IL-6, TNF, and IL-1. These molecules then act on stromal cells and osteoclast precursors to enhance bone resorption by regulating expression of pro-(RANKL, M-CSF) and anti-(OPG) osteoclastogenic cytokines (in the case of mesenchymal cells) and by synergizing with RANKL itself (in the case of myeloid osteoclast precursors; see Fig. 2). However, the realization that lymphocytes play a key role in mediating several aspects of bone biology has led to a growing realization that the cellular and molecular targets for E2 are more widespread than previously believed. A recent compelling model proposes that E2 impacts the resorptive component of bone turnover (the steroid has separate effects on osteoblasts), at least in part by modulating production by T cells of RANKL and TNF.[23] This effect is itself indirect, with E2 suppressing antigen presentation by dendritic cells and macrophages by enhancing expression by the same cells of TGF-β. Antigen presentation activates T cells, thereby enhancing their production of RANKL and TNF. As discussed previously, the first molecule is the key osteoclastogenic cytokine, whereas the second potentiates RANKL action. This newly discovered interface between T cells and bone resorption also clarifies aspects of inflammatory osteolysis. Finally, some studies indicate that E2 modulates signaling in pre-OCs, and that acting through reactive oxygen species, it increases the lifespan and/or function of mature osteoclasts.[30]

Both endogenous glucocortocoids and their synthetic analogs, which have been and continue to be a major mainstay of immunosuppressive therapy, are members of a third steroid hormone family having a major impact on bone biology.[31] One consequence of their chronic mode of administration is severe osteoporosis arising from decreased bone formation and resorption with the latter still (low turnover osteoporosis). The majority of the evidence focuses on the osteoblast as the prime target with the steroid increasing apoptosis of these bone-forming cells. However, numerous human studies document a rapid initial decrease in bone resorption, suggesting that the osteoclast and/or its precursors may also be targets. The molecular basis for this latter finding is unclear. However, because osteoblasts are a requisite part of the resorptive cycle, one consequence of their long-term diminution could be decreased osteoclast formation and/or function secondary to lower levels of RANKL and/or M-CSF production. Alternatively, glucocorticoids have been shown to decrease osteoclast apoptosis.[32]

A wide range of clinical information shows that excess prostaglandins stimulate bone loss, but once again, the cellular basis has not been established conclusively. Prostaglandins target stromal and osteoblastic cells, stimulating expression of RANKL and suppressing that of OPG.[33] This increase in the RANKL/OPG ratio, seen in a variety of human studies, is sufficient of itself to explain the clinical findings of increased osteoclastic activity. However, highlighting again the dilemma of interpreting in vitro studies, there have been a number of studies in which prostaglandins regulate osteoclastogenesis per se in murine cell culture.

Phosphoinositides play distinct and important roles in organization of the osteoclast cytoskeleton.[34] Binding of M-CSF or RANKL to their cognate receptors, c-Fms and RANK, or activation of αvβ3, recruits phosphoinositol-3-kinase (PI3-K) to the plasma membrane, where it converts membrane-bound

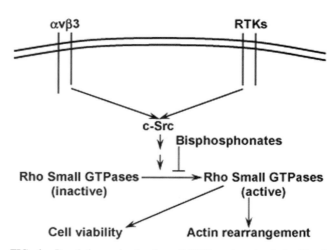

FIG. 4. Regulation and role of small GTPases in osteoclasts. Signals from αvβ3 and/or receptor tyrosine kinases (RTKs) activate small GTPases of the Rho family in a c-src–dependent manner. Bisphosphonates, the potent antiresorptive drugs, block addition of hydrophobic moieties onto the GTPases, preventing their membrane targeting and activation. The active GTPases also regulate cell viability and thus bisphosphonates induce osteoclast death.[46]

phosphatidylinositol-4,5-bisphosphate into phosphatidylinositol-3,4,5-trisphosphate (Fig. 4). The latter compound is recognized by specific motifs in a wide range of cytoskeletally active proteins,[35] and thus PI3-K plays a central role in organizing the cytoskeleton of the osteoclast, including its ruffled membrane. Akt is a downstream target of PI3-K and plays an important role in osteoclast function, particularly by mediating RANKL and/or M-CSF stimulated proliferation and/or survival.[34]

Cell–Cell Interactions in Bone Marrow

Recent evidence indicates that a number of additional cell types are important for osteoclast biology in a range of situations (Fig. 5). First, as discussed previously, T cells play a key role in estrogen loss, but also are important in a range of inflammatory diseases, most notably rheumatoid arthritis[36] and periodontal disease.[37] Given the fact that both osteoclast precursors and the various lymphocyte subsets, such as T, B, and NK cells, arise from the same stem cell, it is not surprising that some of the same receptors and ligands that mediate the immune process also govern the maturation of osteoclast precursors and the capacity of the mature cell to degrade bone. This interface has given rise to the new discipline of osteoimmunology, which promises to provide important and exciting findings in the future.

Second, while it is well-established that mesenchymal cells are major mediators of cytokine and prostaglandin action on osteoclasts, it has become clear recently that cells of the same lineage, residing on cortical and trabecular bone, are the site of a hematopoietic stem cell (HSC) niche.[38] Specifically, HSCs reside close to osteoblasts as a result of multiple interactions involving receptors and ligands on both cells types.[26] Furthermore, the mesenchymally derived cells secrete both membrane-bound and soluble factors that contribute to survival and proliferation of multipotent osteoclast precursors, as well as molecules that influence osteoclast formation and function. Both committed osteoblasts and the numerous stromal cells in bone marrow produce a range of proteins both basally and in response to hormones and growth factors, resulting in modulation of the capacity of HSCs to become functional osteoclasts.

Third, cancer cells facilitate their infiltration into the marrow cavity by stimulating osteoclast formation and function. An initial stimulus is PTHrP generation by lung and breast cancer cells,[17,18,39] thus enhancing mesenchymal production of RANKL and M-CSF, while decreasing that of OPG. The resulting increase in matrix dissolution releases bone-residing cytokines and growth factors, which, feeding back on the cancer cells, increase their growth and/or survival. This loop has been termed "the vicious cycle."[18] Multiple myeloma seems to use a different but related strategy, namely secretion of MIPα and MCP-1, both of which are chemotactic and proliferative for osteoclast precursors.[40,41] The latter compound has been reported to be secreted by osteoclasts in response to RANKL and enhances osteoclast formation.[27] It seems likely further future studies experiments will uncover additional molecules mediating bone loss in metastatic disease.

Intracellular Signaling Pathways

The discussions above have not described in detail the intracellular signals by which osteoclasts are formed or those by which they degrade bone. The final major section of this review lays out the important pathways involved. Briefly, three major protein classes are involved: adaptors, kinases, and transcription factors (Fig. 6), with one significant exception, RANKL-induced release of Ca^{2+}, a pathway that activates the calmodulin-dependent phosphatase calcineurin. NFAT1c is a major substrate for this enzyme, resulting in its nuclear translocation and subsequent activation of osteoclast-specific genes. Importantly, the potent immunosuppressive drugs FK506 and cyclosporine inhibit calcineurin activity and therefore may target the osteoclast.[42]

The multiplicity of adaptors that link the various receptors to downstream signals precludes providing a meaningful summary, and so in Fig. 6 we summarize only the modulatory effects of kinases and transcription factors, which together regulate receptor-driven proliferation and/or survival of precursors. Proliferation is mediated by the surface receptors αvβ3

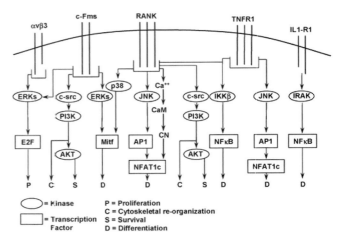

FIG. 6. Osteoclast signaling pathways. Summary of the major receptors, downstream kinases, and effector transcription factors that regulate osteoclast formation and function. Proliferation (P) of precursors is driven chiefly through ERKs and their downstream cyclin targets and E2F; maximal activation of this pathway requires combined signals from c-Fms and the integrin αvβ3. As expected, given its rapid nature, regulation of the cytoskeleton (C) is independent of nuclear control but depends on a series of kinases and their cytoskeletal-regulating targets, whereas differentiation (D) is regulated largely by controlling gene expression. The calcium/calmodulin (CaM)/calcineurin (CN) axis enhances nuclear translocation of NFAT1c the most distal transcription factor characterized to date. For further details consult the text or Refs. 2, 3, 7, 21, 34, 44, and 48–50.

and c-Fms,[7,43] re-organization of the cytoskeleton by αvβ3, c-Fms, and RANK,[2,7] differentiation of mature osteoclasts from myeloid progenitors by c-Fms, RANK, TNFR1, and IL-1R1,[2,43,44] and their function by RANK, TNFR1, and IL-1R1.[44,45] Figure 6 and its legend provide details of the intracellular pathways involved. Not shown is the fact that multiple other cytokines and growth factors, targeting the same or other less prominent pathways or acting indirectly, probably contribute to overall control of bone resorption.[24]

Human Genetics

The text above might suggest that numerous mutations linked to the osteoclast are likely to have been discovered. In fact, few such genetic changes have been defined, with >50% of those reported being in the chloride channel that modulates acid secretion (Fig. 3). Sporadic reports relating to RANK are also known, while total loss of OPG in humans leads to devastating osteoporosis. For further details, see the Appendix titled "Summary of Gene Disorders of Serum Mineral Metabolism or Skeleton Formation."

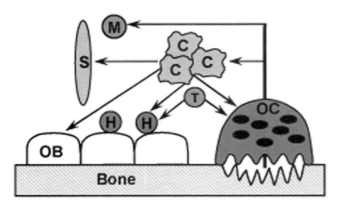

FIG. 5. Cell–cell interactions in bone marrow. Hematopoietic stem cells (H), the precursors of both T cells (T) and osteoclasts (OC), reside in a stem cell niche provided by osteoblasts (OB), which, together with stromal cells (S), derive from mesenchymal stem cells (M). Bone degradation results in release of matrix-associated growth factors (thick vertical line), which stimulate mesenchymal cells and thus bone formation. This "coupling" is an essential consequence of osteoclast activity.[47] After activation, T cells secrete molecules that stimulate osteoclastogenesis and function. Cancer cells (C) release cytokines that activate bone resorption; in turn, matrix-derived factors stimulate cancer cell proliferation, the so-called "vicious cycle."

REFERENCES

1. Suda T, Takahashi N, Udagawa N, Jimi E, Gillespie MT, Martin TJ 1999 Modulation of osteoclast differentiation and function by the new members of the tumor necrosis factor receptor and ligand families. Endocr Rev **20:**345–357.
2. Boyle WJ, Simonet WS, Lacey DL 2003 Osteoclast differentiation and activation. Nature **423:**337–342.
3. Pixley FJ, Stanley ER 2004 CSF-1 regulation of the wandering macrophage: Complexity in action. Trends Cell Biol **14:**628–638.
4. Kostenuik PJ, Shalhoub V 2001 Osteoprotegerin: A physiological and pharmacological inhibitor of bone resorption. Curr Pharm Des **7:**613–635.
5. Teitelbaum SL, Ross FP 2003 Genetic regulation of osteoclast development and function. Nat Rev Genet **4:**638–649.

6. Hynes RO 2002 Integrins: Bidirectional, allosteric signaling machines. Cell **110:**673–687.
7. Ross FP, Teitelbaum SL 2005 αvβ3 and macrophage colony-stimulating factor: Partners in osteoclast biology. Immunol Rev **208:**88–105.
8. Teitelbaum SL 2005 Osteoporosis and integrins. J Clin Endocrinol Metab **90:**2466–2468.
9. Teitelbaum SL, Abu-Amer Y, Ross FP 1995 Molecular mechanisms of bone resorption. J Cell Biochem **59:**1–10.
10. Vaananen HK, Zhao H, Mulari M, Halleen JM 2000 The cell biology of osteoclast function. J Cell Sci **113:**377–381.
11. Schwartz MA, Ginsberg MH 2002 Networks and crosstalk: Integrin signalling spreads. Nat Cell Biol **4:**E65–E68.
12. Horne WC, Sanjay A, Bruzzaniti A, Baron R 2005 The role(s) of Src kinase and Cbl proteins in the regulation of osteoclast differentiation and function. Immunol Rev **208:**106–125.
13. Jaffe AB, Hall A 2005 Rho GTPases: Biochemistry and biology. Annu Rev Cell Dev Biol **21:**247–269.
14. Chellaiah MA 2005 Regulation of actin ring formation by rho GTPases in osteoclasts. J Biol Chem **280:**32930–32943.
15. Fukuda A, Hikita A, Wakeyama H, Akiyama T, Oda H, Nakamura K, Tanaka S 2005 Regulation of osteoclast apoptosis and motility by small GTPase binding protein Rac1. J Bone Miner Res **20:**2245–2253.
16. Faccio R, Teitelbaum SL, Fujikawa K, Chappel JC, Zallone A, Tybulewicz VL, Ross FP, Swat W 2005 Vav3 regulates osteoclast function and bone mass. Nat Med **11:**284–290.
17. Martin TJ 2002 Manipulating the environment of cancer cells in bone: A novel therapeutic approach. J Clin Invest **110:**1399–1401.
18. Clines GA, Guise TA 2005 Hypercalcaemia of malignancy and basic research on mechanisms responsible for osteolytic and osteoblastic metastasis to bone. Endocr Relat Cancer **12:**549–583.
19. Zwerina J, Redlich K, Schett G, Smolen JS 2005 Pathogenesis of rheumatoid arthritis: Targeting cytokines. Ann NY Acad Sci **1051:**716–729.
20. Zwerina J, Hayer S, Tohidast-Akrad M, Bergmeister H, Redlich K, Feige U, Dunstan C, Kollias G, Steiner G, Smolen J, Schett G 2004 Single and combined inhibition of tumor necrosis factor, interleukin-1, and RANKL pathways in tumor necrosis factor-induced arthritis: Effects on synovial inflammation, bone erosion, and cartilage destruction. Arthritis Rheum **50:**277–290.
21. Takayanagi H 2005 Mechanistic insight into osteoclast differentiation in osteoimmunology. J Mol Med **83:**170–179.
22. Key LL, Rodriguiz RM, Willi SM, Wright NM, Hatcher HC, Eyre DR, Cure JK, Griffin PP, Ries WL 1995 Long-term treatment of osteopetrosis with recombinant human interferon gamma. N Engl J Med **332:**1594–1599.
23. Cenci S, Toraldo G, Weitzmann MN, Roggia C, Gao Y, Qian WP, Sierra O, Pacifici R 2003 Estrogen deficiency induces bone loss by increasing T cell proliferation and lifespan through IFN-γ-induced class II transactivator. Proc Natl Acad Sci USA **100:**10405–10410.
24. Udagawa N 2003 The mechanism of osteoclast differentiation from macrophages: Possible roles of T lymphocytes in osteoclastogenesis. J Bone Miner Metab **21:**337–343.
25. Boyce BF, Yamashita T, Yao Z, Zhang Q, Li F, Xing L 2005 Roles for NF-kappaB and c-Fos in osteoclasts. J Bone Miner Metab **23**(Suppl):11–15.
26. Taichman RS 2005 Blood and bone: Two tissues whose fates are intertwined to create the hematopoietic stem-cell niche. Blood **105:**2631–2639.
27. Kim MS, Day CJ, Selinger CI, Magno CL, Stephens SRJ, Morrison NA 2006 MCP-1-induced human osteoclast-like cells are tartrate-resistant acid phosphatase, NFATc1, and calcitonin receptor-positive but require receptor activator of NFκB ligand for bone resorption. J Biol Chem **281:**1274–1285.
28. Goltzman D, Miao D, Panda DK, Hendy GN 2004 Effects of calcium and of the vitamin D system on skeletal and calcium homeostasis: Lessons from genetic models. J Steroid Biochem Mol Biol **89–90:**485–489.
29. Syed F, Khosla S 2005 Mechanisms of sex steroid effects on bone. Biochem Biophys Res Commun **328:**688–696.
30. Eastell R 2005 Role of oestrogen in the regulation of bone turnover at the menarche. J Endocrinol **185:**223–234.
31. Canalis E, Bilezikian JP, Angeli A, Giustina A 2004 Perspectives on glucocorticoid-induced osteoporosis. Bone **34:**593–598.
32. Weinstein RS, Chen J-R, Powers CC, Stewart SA, Landes RD, Bellido T, Jilka RL, Parfitt AM, Manolagas SC 2002 Promotion of osteoclast survival and antagonism of bisphosphonate-induced osteoclast apoptosis by glucocorticoids. J Clin Invest **109:**1041–1048.
33. Kobayashi T, Narumiya S 2002 Function of prostanoid receptors: Studies on knockout mice. Prostaglandins Other Lipid Mediat **68–69:**557–573.
34. Golden LH, Insogna KL 2004 The expanding role of PI3-kinase in bone. Bone **34:**3–12.
35. DiNitto JP, Cronin TC, Lambright DG 2003 Membrane recognition and targeting by lipid-binding domains. Sci STKE **2003:**re16.
36. Nakashima T, Wada T, Penninger JM 2003 RANKL and RANK as novel therapeutic targets for arthritis. Curr Opin Rheumatol **15:**280–287.
37. Taubman MA, Valverde P, Han X, Kawai T 2005 Immune response: The key to bone resorption in periodontal disease. J Periodontol **76:**2033–2041.
38. Suda T, Arai F, Hirao A 2005 Hematopoietic stem cells and their niche. Trends Immunol **26:**426–433.
39. Bendre M, Gaddy D, Nicholas RW, Suva LJ 2003 Breast cancer metastasis to bone: It is not all about PTHrP. Clin Orthop Relat Res **415:**S39–S45.
40. Hata H 2005 Bone lesions and macrophage inflammatory protein-1 alpha (MIP-1a) in human multiple myeloma. Leuk Lymphoma **46:**967–972.
41. Kim MS, Day CJ, Morrison NA 2005 MCP-1 is induced by receptor activator of nuclear factorκB ligand, promotes human osteoclast fusion, and rescues granulocyte macrophage colony-stimulating factor suppression of osteoclast formation. J Biol Chem **280:**16163–16169.
42. Seales EC, Micoli KJ, McDonald JM 2006 Calmodulin is a critical regulator of osteoclastic differentiation, function, and survival. J Cell Biochem **97:**45–55.
43. Ross FP 2006 M-CSF, c-Fms and signaling in osteoclasts and their precursors. Ann NY Acad Sci (in press).
44. Feng X 2005 Regulatory roles and molecular signaling of TNF family members in osteoclasts. Gene **350:**1–13.
45. Blair HC, Robinson LJ, Zaidi M 2005 Osteoclast signalling pathways. Biochem Biophys Res Commun **328:**728–738.
46. Rogers MJ 2004 From molds and macrophages to mevalonate: A decade of progress in understanding the molecular mode of action of bisphosphonates. Calcif Tissue Int **75:**451–461.
47. Martin TJ, Sims NA 2005 Osteoclast-derived activity in the coupling of bone formation to resorption. Trends Mol Med **11:**76–81.
48. Wagner EF, Eferl R 2005 Fos/AP-1 proteins in bone and the immune system. Immunol Rev **208:**126–140.
49. Lee ZH, Kim H-H 2003 Signal transduction by receptor activator of nuclear factor kappa B in osteoclasts. Biochem Biophys Res Commun **305:**211–214.
50. Hershey CL, Fisher DE 2004 Mitf and Tfe3: Members of a b-HLH-ZIP transcription factor family essential for osteoclast development and function. Bone **34:**689–696.

Chapter 6. Biomechanics and Mechanobiology of Bone

Clinton Rubin[1] and Janet Rubin[2]

[1]Department of Biomedical Engineering, State University of New York, Stony Brook, New York; and [2]Department of Medicine,
University of North Carolina-Chapel Hill, Chapel Hill, North Carolina

INTRODUCTION

The primary responsibility of the skeleton is to provide structural support for the body. In this role, the skeleton is the basis of posture, opposes muscular contraction conveying locomotion, withstands the daily challenges of load bearing, and protects internal organs. The structural success of the skeleton, achieved through the interdependent contributions of the skeleton's morphology and mechanical properties, is determined both by genetic determinants of bone architecture and the tissue's sensitivity to mechanical signals; bone structure is enhanced by exercise or compromised by disuse. The quality of the tissue is as important to bone structure as quantity[1]; connectivity and orientation of trabeculae, as well as cortical bone's resistance to microdamage, helps define a bone's resistance to failure independent of a need to increase bone mass.

The success of the skeleton as a structure is jeopardized by genetic disorders such as osteogenesis imperfecta, metabolic diseases such as Paget's, or osteoporosis, the bone loss that parallels aging or menopause. Importantly, any decrease in the structural quality of the skeleton is accompanied by a proportional increase in skeletal fragility, whereas even subtle improvements in bone quality can result in significant reductions in fracture occurrence. Whereas the great majority of therapies for bone disease work through modulation (inhibition or promotion) of a specific bone cell function, the success of any particular intervention is evaluated as a biomechanical outcome—the ability to reduce the incidence of fractures. In summary, to appreciate the structural consequences of bone and mineral disorders and to understand how new interventions may ameliorate the impact of bone loss or reduced bone quality, it is essential to understand how the mechanical parameters responsible for the skeleton's structural success, how metabolic conditions and/or aging compromise these features, and how mechanical signals influence those cells responsible for achieving and maintaining the mechanical integrity of bone tissue. To appreciate the structural risks that accompany metabolic bone diseases and the manner in which the skeleton can adapt to alterations in its mechanical loading environment, it is important to review the biomechanics of bone, such as the principles of strain, stress, load, and failure and to consider the bone cell population that regulates and responds to mechanical challenges by modeling and remodeling a successful structure.

BIOMECHANICAL PRINCIPLES OF BONE

Strain

When a force is applied to any material, such as bone, it deforms. The amount of deformation in the material relative to its original length is the strain in the material. Strain is a dimensionless unit formally defined as the change in length divided by its original length ($\epsilon = \Delta L/L$). When a material is pulled, it gets longer (tensile strain), and when pushed together, the material shortens (compressive strain). Shear strain is the angle, measured in radians, through which a material has been deformed by forces acting parallel, rather than opposed, to the material. Shear strain arises when layers of a material slide

against another, as might occur with torsion or bending. Peak compressive strains in bone during vigorous activity can reach as high as 3500 microstrain ($\mu\epsilon$) in compression (0.35% strain), 1000 $\mu\epsilon$ in tension, and 1500 $\mu\epsilon$ in shear (Fig. 1). Despite a wide range of activities, peak strains reached in the diaphyseal shafts of long bones are very similar across a spectrum of vertebrates.[2] In contrast, tensile strain in tendon might reach 25% during vigorous activity, while strain in ligaments approaches 5%.

Stress

To determine the material properties of bone (how stiff or strong it is), a machined sample is subjected to a known tensile or compressive force. Such controlled loading conditions aids in the direct comparison of the properties of one material (e.g., cortical bone from the femur of an 80-year-old woman) to another (e.g., cortical bone from a 20-year-old woman), or to facilitate comparisons between laboratories, and such tests indicate the magnitude of the force applied to a material of a defined cross-sectional area. The force per unit area is the stress ($\sigma = $ Force/Area) and is reported in pascals, which are newtons per square meter (Nm^{-2}; where 1 N is the unit of force required to accelerate a mass of 1 kg 1 m/s/s). The compressive stress caused in the third metacarpal of a thoroughbred racehorse during a gallop[3] is on the order of 63,000,000 Pa, or 63 MPa, indicating that a force of 63,000,000N are effectively acting on 1 m^2 of bone.

Modulus

The degree to which a material deforms depends not only on the magnitude of the force and moments (turning, twisting, or rotational effect of a force is a moment, where the magnitude is the product of force times distance; M = Nm) applied to the structure, but also on the stiffness of the constituent materials. In the case of bone, stiffness is determined by the relative proportions of the hydroxyapatite crystals and the collagen fibers in the composite, as well as their organization and maturity. During the initial stages of a load:displacement test to define a bone's material properties, there is a linear increase in strain as the stress increases (Fig. 2), known as the elastic region. Should the load be removed during this phase of the test, the specimen will return to its original size and shape almost immediately, without incurring permanent damage. The linear relation between strain and stress is called Hooke's Law, which can be paraphrased as *ut tensio, sic vis*, which means, literally, *as the extension, so the force*.

The slope of the elastic region of the stress–strain curve reflects the stiffness of the material, otherwise known as the material's elastic modulus ($E = \sigma/\epsilon$). The stiffer the material, the steeper the slope of the line describing its stress–strain curve. A force of 100N pulling on a tendon will result in far greater strain (the tendon will be stretched more) than the same force pulling on a sample of bone of the same dimensions. While the stress (force per unit area) is identical, the modulus of bone is much higher than tendon (the slope of the stress–strain curve is much steeper), resulting in much less deformation in the bone tissue from the load.

A material like rubber, which has identical mechanical property values in all directions, is isotropic. A material like bone,

Dr. C. Rubin is a consultant for, owns stock in, and has received funding from Juvent, Inc. Dr. J. Rubin has reported no conflicts of interest.

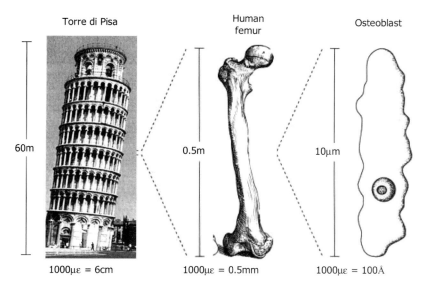

Torre di Pisa   Human femur   Osteoblast

60m   0.5m   10µm

1000µε = 6cm   1000µε = 0.5mm   1000µε = 100Å

FIG. 1. Strain is defined as a (load-induced) change in length relative to the structure's original length; 1000 $\mu\epsilon$, or 0.1% strain, reflects the amount of strain experienced by bone tissue during an activity such as walking. For a structure such as the 60-m Leaning Tower of Pisa, 1000 $\mu\epsilon$ would represent a 6-cm change in length over the unloaded length of the entire structure. In a human femur, 1000 $\mu\epsilon$ would reflect a 0.5-mm change in the bone's original 500 mm length. At the level of a 10-mm bone-lining cell resting on the periosteum of that femur, the 1000 $\mu\epsilon$ induced by walking would relate to a 100-Å change in the cell's original length. The mechanisms responsible for perceiving and responding to such small biomechanical signals, whatever they may be, must be extremely sensitive.

which has distinct mechanical properties in different directions, is anisotropic. The modulus of mature cortical bone is on the order of 18 GPa in the longitudinal direction, 12 GPa in the transverse direction, and 3.3 GPa in shear, meaning it is stiffest in the longitudinal direction and relatively compliant in shear.[4] The material properties of cancellous bone are even more complex, because trabecular orientation, connectivity, and density greatly influence the stiffness, and depending on location can range from 0.1 to 3.5 GPa.[5] Reductions in the degree of mineralization (e.g., immature or woven bone), increases in porosity (e.g., osteoporosis), or damage (accumulation of microdamage) will greatly compromise the stiffness of the bone and thereby lower the elastic modulus. Under such

conditions, a given load (walking up the stairs), inconsequential to the healthy skeleton, can be catastrophic to one of compromised structural quality.

Yield Failure

When the increase in strain is no longer linearly related to the applied stress, the elastic properties of the material have been superseded, and the material is unable to resume its original shape (Fig. 2). This indicates that the specimen has moved into the plastic region and that permanent damage has begun to accrue within the material. In terms of bone, yield failure first arises through ultrastructural microcracks within the hydroxyapatite and the disruption of the collagen fibrils. The yield strain of cortical bone in compression is on the order of 6800 $\mu\epsilon$, suggesting that a safety factor of 2 exists between peak strains caused by normal functional activity and the point where damage begins to accumulate.[6] The yield stress for cortical bone is ~130 MPa, which is where substantial cracking of the tissue would occur. The failure properties of bone experiencing tensile strain, defined predominantly by the collagen component of the material, is far lower than failure properties for compressive strain, where the mineral portion helps to support the load.

Ultimate Failure

As loading continues in the plastic region, the material will eventually experience ultimate failure, where the specimen fails catastrophically. The point at which the bone breaks can either be viewed as exceeding the ultimate strain (~15,000 $\mu\epsilon$ for cortical bone) or the ultimate stress (140 MPa in tension, 200 MPa in compression, and 65 MPa in shear). Because of this disparity, the nature of the failure test is very important to control, and factors that might contribute to fracture in humans are very important to consider (i.e., the contribution of bending and torsional moments during the impact of a fall). In considering a load test of bone, once in the plastic region of the material, the stress exceeds the ability of the bone to support it, and frank fracture occurs, reducing the load to zero.

Ductility

The ability of a material to withstand plastic deformation without rupture is a measure of the material's ductility, reflect-

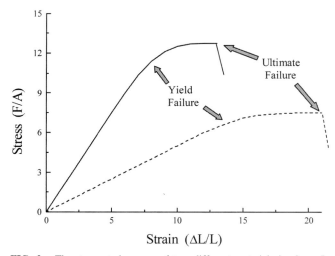

FIG. 2. The stress-strain curve of two different materials is given. In material A (solid line), the material is more stiff, as depicted by the steeper slope of the line ($E = \sigma/\epsilon$). Thus, for a given stress, there is less strain. However, the yield strain of material A is lower than that of material B (dashed line), as depicted by the point where the relationship between stress and strain is no longer linear (yield failure). As well, the ultimate strain of material A is lower than that of material B, as depicted by the point where there is catastrophic failure of the material, i.e., there is no longer any stress necessary to cause strain (ultimate failure). Material A is more brittle than material B. The area beneath the curves reflects the toughness of the materials.

ing its ability to resist the propagation of cracks. A ductile material is one that can change form without breaking; a tendon is more ductile than bone because it can readily change shape and still retain its structure. A material that manages little postyield behavior before ultimate failure is considered brittle, such as would occur with glass or ceramic. While osteoporosis is often referred to as the brittle bone disease, in reality there is little experimental evidence that supports an actual reduction in the ductility of bone material examined from patients with this disease[7]; there is just less bone to resist a given force per unit area (stress during functional activity is just that much closer to yield stress). Perhaps a better example of brittle bone is provided by osteogenesis imperfecta, where a qualitative and/or quantitative deficiency in type I collagen in the material reduces its ductility,[8] condemning it to ultimate failure soon after the material has begun to yield.

Toughness

The toughness of a material is, in essence, its resistance to fracture when suddenly stressed: the ability of a femur to avoid fracture at impact, although some damage has been incurred. As revealed by the stress–strain curve (how a material of a given area deforms for a given load), the area under the curve reflects the amount of work, or energy per unit volume, possessed by the material at any given point on the curve, and a tough material can absorb a great deal of load before cracking (or failing). At ultimate failure, the area under the curve defines the energy required to break the object, or toughness. A major contributor to the toughness of cortical bone is its composite nature of haversian, circumferential, and interstitial lamellae. The analogy of a bundle of straws versus a plastic stick illustrates how the architecture of a composite anisotropic structure outperforms a single uniform isotropic material in resisting loads and avoiding yield and ultimate strain. The plastic stick breaks with relatively little bending because high strains are generated within the periphery of the material. A bundle of straws comprised of the same mass and subjected to the same bending conditions will continue to strain rather than break, as each independent element slips relative to adjacent bundles.

Bone, as an organ, has a requirement to be both stiff and tough. There is, however, an inevitable trade-off between these two attributes, because they must be attained through a balance between the resistance to crack propagation provided by collagen, cement lines, and lacunae, and the resistance to deformation provided by the mineral. Comparatively small changes in the mineral content of bone tissue can have significant effects on its properties as a material, as shown by Curry[9] in his determination of the mechanical properties of bones' with diverse functional responsibilities. By comparing the bovine femur, the deer antler, and the whale tympanic bulla, he showed that the mineral content changed to accommodate a specific functional responsibility. In the extreme, the mineral content ranged from 86% in the bulla, which requires high acoustic impedance, to 59% in the antler, which must resist high impact loads. The consequence of this high mineral content is revealed by comparing the relative toughness of these bones; the bulla is only 3% as tough as the antler.

Bone as a Composite Material

Bone's composite structure allows it to withstand compressive and tensile loads, as well as bending and torsional moments to such a degree that its overall strength approaches that of cast iron while remaining, essentially, as light as wood.[10] The inorganic phase of bone, with hydroxyapatite crystals arrayed in a protein matrix, provides the ability to resist compression. Individual calcium phosphate crystals of multiple sizes are imbedded in and around the fibrils of the collagen type I lattice.[11] Hydroxyapatite crystals, while effectively resisting compressive loads, have a poor ability to withstand tensile loads. As in concrete, a material that excels at resisting compression but is poor in resisting tension, tensile elements (e.g., steel reinforcing rods) are added to create a composite material that can cope with complex loading environments. In the case of bone, this tensile strength arises from collagen fibrils organized into lamellae.

The collagen orientation between adjacent lamellae can rotate by as much as 90°, permitting the tissue to resist forces and moments acting from several different directions, much like the added strength in plywood realized by the distinct orientation of the fibers in each specific ply.[12] While the ultrastructural organization of the skeleton is, to a certain extent, defined by the genome, the functional environment also contributes to the organization and distribution of lamellae as well the osteons that house them.[13] This directed deposition of collagen adds to the anisotropy of the bone. Given that >80% of functional strains are caused by bending (and thus a high percentage of strain is tensile), the structural quality of the bone may ultimately be determined by the quality of the collagen and the organization of the microarchitecture. Thus, the age-related deterioration of collagen would directly contribute to the declining material properties of the skeleton, just as a compromised inorganic phase of bone, which might occur under conditions such as rickets, may compromise the structural strength of bone.

Alterations in either the organic (e.g., collagen) or inorganic (e.g., hydroxyapatite) matrix components can bring about changes in bone strength. Mutations in the collagen gene give rise to several genetic skeletal problems, some of which increase fracture risk. In some forms of osteogenesis imperfecta, mutations in the primary structure of type I procollagen lead to brittle bone.[14] Another disorder of collagen resulting in excessively fragile bone is fibrogenesis imperfecta ossium[15]; a rare disease where remodeling results in a disorganized, collagen-deficient tissue. While the number of hydroxyapatite crystals contributes to the ability to resist compression, density is not everything. Fluoroapatite, which incorporates into the mineral phase of bone during fluoride poisoning, is denser than hydroxyapatite, but is brittle and shatters easily under load.[16]

Areal Properties

Areal properties, which define the overall mass and morphology of the structure, are as important in determining the ultimate success of the skeleton as the material properties. Size, density, girth, and architecture effectively describe areal properties at the gross level, such as can be seen in the 35% increase in cross-sectional area of the serving arm of the professional tennis player compared with the arm that simply throws the ball into the air.[17] Other more subtle properties are also key contributors to the structural efficacy of bone, including the long bone curvature, the geometry of the cross-sectional area, and the trabecular organization (e.g., connectivity and orientation).

Compressive loading of bone purely in the axial (longitudinal) direction results in very little strain for a given load; consider how strong a pencil is when you press straight down on the long axis of the shaft. At the same time, it is important to consider how easily the pencil is snapped when it is subject to bending. Consider now the neck of the femur while climbing a flight of stairs—the functional demands of the skeleton are very complex, and subject not only to axial conditions, but to bending and torsional moments. Recognizing the complex nature of the functional environment, it is clear that a strategy of minimal mass will not serve as a successful structure. Instead, the morphology of the bone must be designed to resist a wide assortment of loading conditions, perhaps to control and regulate the manner in which a bone is loaded, rather than necessarily to minimize the strain.[18]

Even the simplest of loading operations creates a complex strain and stress environment in any material, made even more complicated in isotropic materials such as bone. Axial loads applied to a slightly curved beam will cause tensile strain on the convex side and compressive strain on the concave side. The strains are greatest at these extremes, and decrease to zero in the middle of the beam. This area is called the neutral axis, where strain is essentially zero. The flexural rigidity of the material, EI, represents the amount of force per unit cross-sectional area required to deform the material a given amount, where E is elastic modulus (see above) and I is the second moment of area. The second moment, or moment of inertia, reflects the contribution of each bit of material to the stiffness, in each position in the cross-section of the beam ($I = \Sigma y^2 dA$, where y is the distance of each element of area A from the neutral axis). Therefore, the further the material is relative to the neutral axis, the better placed it will be to resist bending. This areal property is a powerful means of rapidly increasing flexural rigidity for a small investment of material. For example, in the elderly, it has been shown that very small increases in periosteal expansion that parallel aging will cause an increase in the second moment of inertia, making it more resistive to bending loads and may—to a certain degree—compensate for the inevitable loss of bone loss and thinning of the cortex.[19]

This brief overview of the mechanical principles of bone structure is intended to help define the architectural elements of a structure that determine the skeleton's ability to withstand loading. As important to the study of a bone quantity and quality, however, is to address the biological aspects of the bone tissue that allow it to perceive and respond to mechanical signals, permitting local adaptation to the functional loading environment to achieve an idealized structure for the demands placed on it. The next phase of this review will consider the bone cell population that coordinates a modeling/remodeling response to changes in its functional demands and the specific mechanical factors that are important in regulating this response.

MECHANOBIOLOGY OF BONE

Mechanically Responsive Bone Cells

The ability of bone cells to respond to mechanical signals, including stromal cells, osteoblasts, and osteocytes, have all been documented. However, even given the importance of bone cell sensitivity to mechanical signals, it is often difficult to isolate the critical cell responsible for orchestrating the response: for example, exposure to microgravity results in a decreased number of osteoblasts—but what cell senses and responds to the loss of gravity—the stromal cell, the differentiated osteoblast, or the interconnected osteocyte? Li et al.[20] found that marrow stromal cells change their proliferation rate and gene expression patterns in response to mechanical stimulation. With respect to osteoclast number: stromal cell expression of the osteoclastogenic factor, RANKL, is sensitive to mechanical force,[21] suggesting that the number of osteoclasts present is controlled through mechanical regulation sensed by stromal cells. As well, the osteoclast itself has been shown to respond to mechanical signals, adding another layer of control by which mechanical force may limit bone resorption.[22] Other cells present in bone, such as endothelial and smooth muscle

cells in the penetrating vasculature, might also contribute to the skeleton's adaptive response to loading. After all, endothelial cells respond to shear stress and tensile strain generated by increased heart rate during exercise, by producing NO,[23] which has been shown to have pleomorphic effects on the skeleton.

Appreciation of the fact that >95% of the bone cells in the adult skeleton are osteocytes has stimulated consideration of their role in defining the mechanosensitivity of the skeleton.[24] The sequestered osteocyte, although losing size and organelles in differentiation from the osteoblast, adopts a new phenotype that allows connection to a dense network of other osteocytes and bone lining cells through cytoplasmic extensions that radiate outward from the central vascular canal. These interconnecting canaliculi may be pathways for chemical, electrical, and stress-generated fluid communication through the dense bone matrix. The antenna-like three-dimensional morphology of this osteocyte syncytium is—theoretically—ideally configured to perceive and perhaps even amplify biophysical stimuli.[25]

The volume of bone occupied by this syncytium is ~5% by the canaliculi network and 2% for the lacunae spaces. However, the connectivity of this network deteriorates markedly with age and may well contribute to the progressive loss of sensitivity of bone tissue to chemical and physical signals.[26] The surface area of the canalicular and system has been estimated to be at least 250 m^2/liter of calcified bone matrix and communicates with a submicroscopic, interfibrillar space representing 35,000 mm^2/mm^3. Thus, exchange of mineral, nutrients, and chemical and physical stimuli through this enormous network is both rapid and substantial and certainly essential to the homeostatic control of the tissue.

Mechanical Factors That Regulate the Bone Cell Response

Some component of the complex loading environment must be recognized by bone cell populations and transduced into cellular signals that regulate bone formation and resorption relative to the "form follows function" goals of the skeleton. However, which specific factors regulate the response? The loads that arise from functional activity generate strain in the bone tissue, pressure in the intramedullary cavity and within the cortices, transient pressure waves and shear forces through canaliculi, and even dynamic electric fields as interstitial fluid flows past charged bone crystals. What has been shown is that bone remodeling is sensitive to changes in strain magnitude,[27] the number of loading cycles,[28] the distribution of the loading,[29] and the rate of strain.[30] Importantly, the signal must be dynamic (time-varying) to influence the bone cell response; static loads are ignored by the skeleton, and the anabolic potential of a load regime increases when rest periods are inserted between mechanical events.[31] Even extremely low levels of bone strain, if induced at relatively high frequencies such as might arise through the spectral content of muscle contractibility,[32] have been shown to be anabolic to bone tissue,[33] enhancing not only the quantity of bone (bone mass) but quality of bone (bone strength; Fig. 3).

Whatever the mechanical factor, at the level of small volumes of tissue, all loads and bending moments resolve into strain and must be at least indirectly to deformation of the material. However, the strain levels that are actually "experienced" by bone cells in vivo is unclear and has even been proposed to be 10× that experienced by the matrix.[34] Furthermore, as bone cells are subject to flow of interstitial fluid through a pressure differential of the circulatory system as well as through applied mechanical loading,[35] they are subject to

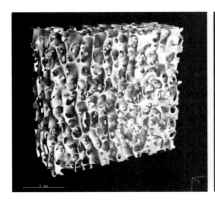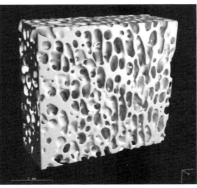

FIG. 3. μCT of the distal femur of adult (8 years old) sheep, comparing a control animal (left) to an animal subject to 20 minutes/day of 30 Hz (cycles per second) of a low-level (0.3g) mechanical vibration for 1 year.[39] The large increase in trabecular BMD results in enhanced bone strength, achieved with tissue strains three orders of magnitude below those that cause damage to the tissue. These data suggest that specific mechanical parameters may represent a non-pharmacologic basis for the treatment of osteoporosis.[40]

shear stresses and dynamic changes in pressure. In summary, the complex loading environment of the skeleton generates a diverse range of mechanical forces that are ultimately inseparable.

Using cultured osteocytes, Burger et al.[36] have shown osteocytes to be preferentially sensitive to shear strain, as opposed to hydrostatic pressure, suggesting that the osteocyte can differentiate between specific components of the mechanical milieu. Recent experiments even indicate that physiologic levels of strain actually reduce the rate of osteocyte apoptosis, suggesting matrix deformation is critical even to the survival of these cells.[37] However, it is also clear that too much strain will induce microdamage in the matrix and exacerbate the death of cells adjacent to the damaged matrix.[38] This "too much of a good thing" indicates a specific "window" where the strain signals would be beneficial to the viability of the cell population. Considering that factors other than matrix strain, per se, may be driving the adaptive response, recent work has shown that extremely low-level loading, generating strains less than 10 $\mu\epsilon$, can be anabolic to bone tissue if induced at a sufficiently high frequency.[39] Exploiting bone's sensitivity to physical signals, much in the same way as exercise can help modulate bone mass, these extremely low-level mechanical signals may provide a unique, non-pharmacologic means of preventing osteoporosis.[40] Thus, rather than deformation per se, these data support the notion that byproducts of the strain signal, such as shear stress arising from fluid flow or strain-generated potentials, may play an important role in regulating the biology of the adaptive response. However, how do the cells sense these mechanical signals?

Mechanoreceptors

Peak strains of 3000 $\mu\epsilon$ achieved during functional activity, once resolved to the level of the cell, imply deformations on the order of Angstroms ($Å = 10^{-10}$ m, or one one-hundred millionth of a centimeter); certainly, whatever cellular system perceives these physical (e.g., mechanical, electrical) signals must be exquisitely sensitive. The ability of cells to interpret their physical environment requires that their mechanoreceptors must either be in contact with the outside, through the cell membrane and its attachment to substrate, or that the mechanoreceptor be able to sense changes in a loading-induced physical intermediary such as fluid shear on the apical membrane. While there are examples of channels that are regulated by movement of mechanosensory bristles or by tension waves,[41] a unified model of the most proximal events that lead to intracellular signal transduction in nonsensory tissues does not yet exist. Multiple candidates for various sensing paradigms have been suggested.

Alterations in ion channel activity in osteoblasts have been associated with bone cell activation, whether through alteration in conductance stimulated by PTH,[42] or by stretch/strain of the membrane or distortion of the cell.[43] Patch-clamp techniques have been used to show at least three classes of mechanosensitive ion channels in human osteoblasts.[44] Mechanically activated channels have been studied in limb bone cultures: gadolinium chloride, which blocks some stretch/shear-sensitive cation channels, was able to block load-related increases in prostacyclin (PGI)2 and NO.[45]

Membrane deformation and shear across the membrane, as well as pressure transients, are transmitted to the cytoskeleton and ultimately to the cell–matrix adhesion proteins that anchor the cell in place.[46] Integrins are membrane spanning proteins that couple the cell to its extracellular environment. A large number of additional adhesion-associated linker proteins with both structural and biochemical roles are potential molecular mechanotransducers. The architecture of the cytoskeleton itself, and its network of microfilaments and microtubules that link adhesion receptors to the cell nucleus, is such that it may also play a role in perceiving small deformations of the cell and directly informing the nucleus of mechanical challenges.[47] Rearrangement in proteins of the cell cytoskeleton can lead to adaptive responses.

Connexins are membrane-spanning proteins that form regulated channels that allow the direct exchange of small molecules with adjacent cells resulting in intercellular communication; an ideal feature considering that the loading of bone tissue may need to be spatially integrated across cell populations. Intercellular communication through gap junctions has been suggested to be the central feature of the osteocyte syncytium and critical to the transmission of information about the mechanical challenges at a given anatomic location and permit a sensing cell to control an effector at some distance removed from the mechanosensing event.[48]

Cells possess a complex organizational structure that supports compartmentalization of signals within an equally complex plasma membrane. While aspects of the plasma membrane can still be represented by the Singer-Nicholson fluid mosaic concept of a neutral lipid bilayer, this sandwich has been found to contain several phases of lipid including gel, liquid-ordered, and liquid-disordered states. The organized structure of so-called lipid rafts creates a complex association between the inner and outer membrane leaflets where transmembrane proteins are found. The organized membrane may have greater significance for mechanical response than for parsing signals arising from liganded receptors. In the vascular endothelium, for instance, increased flow causes the translocation of signaling molecules to special forms of lipid rafts, the caveolae; if caveolae are disassembled, both proximal and downstream

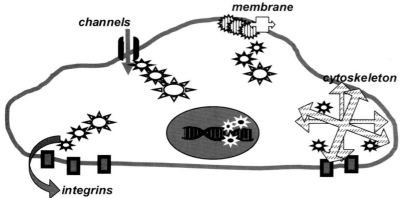

FIG. 4. Skeletal loading generates deformation of the hard tissue with strain across the cell's substrate, pressure in the intramedullary cavity and within the cortices with transient pressure waves, shear forces through canaliculi which cause drag over cells, and dynamic electric fields as interstitial fluid flows past charged bone crystals. Some composite of these physical signals interacts with the morphology of the cell through interactions such as potentiated by the membrane–matrix or membrane–nucleus structures or distortion of the membrane itself to regulate transcriptional activity of the cell.

signaling events, including activation of the mitogen-activated protein kinase (MAPK) pathway, are abrogated.[49]

With the multiplicity of mechanical signals presented to the cell, it is likely that no one mechanosensor or receptor mechanism is responsible for all of the integrated cell responses to the mechanical environment (Fig. 4). At the very least, these sensors are likely to interact with each other in integrating information that the cell receives through chemical and the mechanical signals.

Mechanical Signaling Networks

Because the distal responses to mechanical factors are similar to those elicited by ligand-receptor pairing, and result in changes in gene expression, mechanotransduction must eventually end up using similar intracellular signaling cascades. Mechanical forces have been shown to activate every type of signal transduction cascade, from increases in intracellular cAMP inositol 1,4,5 triphosphate (IP3), intracellular calcium, guanine regulatory proteins, and MAPK, detailed in a recent review.[50]

SUMMARY

An appreciation of both the biomechanical and mechanobiology of bone is critical to an improved understanding of the pathogenesis of metabolic bone disease, the potential to reduce risk factors for fracture through pharmacologic intervention, and the emerging possibility of controlling bone mass and morphology through mechanical signals. Indeed, not only does bone geometry and material properties between individuals, as defined by the genome, play a role in defining resistance to loading failures, there may be genome-specific sensitivities to mechanical loading, and thus predispose some individuals to high risk.[51] As important as inherent mechanical properties may be, it is also essential to appreciate that bone is extremely sensitive to its mechanical environment, and to a large extent, it is this functional milieu that defines skeletal morphology and ultrastructural organization postpartum. This "form follows function" aspect of skeletal tissue helps us to understand how mechanically based prophylaxes such as exercise serves as an anabolic agent to bone, and how disuse, cast immobilization, bed rest, and microgravity place the skeleton at severe risk of fracture.[52]

Clinicians, musculoskeletal scientists, and bioengineers must appreciate that the most devastating complication of bone disease is the structural collapse of the skeleton. There is every reason to believe that not only can an understanding of biomechanics help determine the pathogenesis of skeletal failure and mechanisms of treatment, but that biomechanical strategies can retard, prevent, or even reverse the structural demise of the skeleton. As importantly, scientists beginning to generate bone with molecular triggers will need to assure that the new bone is mechanically adequate to the functional demands placed on it. Skeletal science must strive to incorporate and integrate a multidisciplinary understanding of the biomechanical functions of the skeleton and consider them not only in terms of the engineering basis of the bone material, but the biological response of the bone tissue to the potent mechanical stimuli that arise from function.

REFERENCES

1. Bouxsein ML 2003 Bone quality: Where do we go from here? Osteoporos Int **14**(Suppl 5):118–127.
2. Rubin CT, Lanyon LE 1984 Dynamic strain similarity in vertebrates; an alternative to allometric limb bone scaling. J Theor Biol **107**:321–327.
3. Gross TS, McLeod KJ, Rubin CT 1992 Characterizing bone strain distributions in vivo using three triple rosette strain gages. J Biomech **25**:1081–1087.
4. Reilly DT, Burstein AH 1975 The elastic and ultimate properties of compact bone tissue. J Biomech **8**:393–405.
5. Goldstein SA, Goulet R, McCubbrey D 1993 Measurement and significance of three-dimensional architecture to the mechanical integrity of trabecular bone. Calcif Tissue Int **53**(Suppl 1):S127–S132.
6. Carter DR, Caler WE 1983 Cycle-dependent and time-dependent bone fracture with repeated loading. J Biomech Eng **105**:166–170.
7. Turner CH, Burr DB 1993 Basic biomechanical measurements of bone: A tutorial. Bone **14**:595–608.
8. Prockop DJ, Baldwin CT, Constantinou CD 1990 Mutations in type I procollagen genes that cause osteogenesis imperfecta. Adv Hum Genet **19**:105–132.
9. Currey JD 1979 Mechanical properties of bone tissues with greatly differing functions. J Biomech **12**:313–319.
10. Vincent JF 1982 Structural biomaterials. MacMillan Press, London, UK.
11. Weiner S, Traub W 1992 Bone structure: From angstroms to microns. FASEB J **6**:879–885.
12. Weiner S, Arad T, Sabanay I, Traub W 1997 Rotated plywood structure of primary lamellar bone in the rat: Orientations of the collagen fibril arrays. Bone **20**:509–514.
13. Skedros JG, Mason MW, Nelson MC, Bloebaum RD 1996 Evidence of structural and material adaptation to specific strain features in cortical bone. Anat Rec **246**:47–63.
14. Misof K, Landis WJ, Klaushofer K, Fratzl P 1997 Collagen from the

osteogenesis imperfecta mouse model (oim) shows reduced resistance against tensile stress. J Clin Invest **100:**40–45.

15. Carr AJ, Smith R, Athanasou N, Woods CG 1995 Fibrogenesis imperfecta ossium. J Bone Joint Surg Br **77:**820–829.

16. Turner CH, Owan I, Brizendine EJ, Zhang W, Wilson ME, Dunipace AJ 1996 High fluoride intakes cause osteomalacia and diminished bone strength in rats with renal deficiency. Bone **19:**595–601.

17. Jones HH, Priest JD, Hayes WC, Tichenor CC, Nagel DA 1977 Humeral hypertrophy in response to exercise. J Bone Joint Surg Am **59:**204–208.

18. Fritton S, Rubin C 2001 In vivo measurement of bone deformation using strain gages. In: Cowen S (ed.) Bone Mechanics. CRC Press, Boca Raton, FL, USA, pp. 1–41.

19. Ruff CB, Hayes WC 1982 Subperiosteal expansion and cortical remodeling of the human femur and tibia with aging. Science **217:**945–948.

20. Li YJ, Batra NN, You L, Meier SC, Coe IA, Yellowley CE, Jacobs CR 2004 Oscillatory fluid flow affects human marrow stromal cell proliferation and differentiation. J Orthop Res **22:**1283–1289.

21. Rubin J, Fan X, Biskobing DM, Taylor WR, Rubin CT 1999 Osteoclastogenesis is repressed by mechanical strain in an in vitro model. J Orthop Res **17:**639–645.

22. Wiltink A, Nijweide PJ, Scheenen WJ, Ypey DL, Van Duijn B 1995 Cell membrane stretch in osteoclasts triggers a self-reinforcing Ca2+ entry pathway. Pflugers Arch **429:**663–671.

23. Davis ME, Cai H, Drummond GR, Harrison DG 2001 Shear stress regulates endothelial nitric oxide synthase expression through c-Src by divergent signaling pathways. Circ Res **89:**1073–1080.

24. Cowin SC, Weinbaum S 1998 Strain amplification in the bone mechanosensory system. Am J Med Sci **316:**184–188.

25. Han Y, Cowin SC, Schaffler MB, Weinbaum S 2004 Mechanotransduction and strain amplification in osteocyte cell processes. Proc Natl Acad Sci USA **101:**16689–16694.

26. Rubin CT, Bain SD, McLeod KJ 1992 Suppression of the osteogenic response in the aging skeleton. Calcif Tissue Int **50:**306–313.

27. Rubin CT, Lanyon LE 1985 Regulation of bone mass by mechanical strain magnitude. Calcif Tissue Int **37:**411–417.

28. Rubin CT, Lanyon LE 1984 Regulation of bone formation by applied dynamic loads. J Bone Joint Surg Am **66:**397–402.

29. Lanyon LE, Goodship AE, Pye CJ, MacFie JH 1982 Mechanically adaptive bone remodelling. J Biomech **15:**141–154.

30. O'Connor JA, Lanyon LE, MacFie H 1982 The influence of strain rate on adaptive bone remodeling. J Biomech **15:**767–781.

31. Srinivasan S, Weimer DA, Agans SC, Bain SD, Gross TS 2002 Low-magnitude mechanical loading becomes osteogenic when rest is inserted between each load cycle. J Bone Miner Res **17:**1613–1620.

32. Huang RP, Rubin CT, McLeod KJ 1999 Changes in postural muscle dynamics as a function of age. J Gerontol A Biol Sci Med Sci **54:**B352–B357.

33. Rubin C, Turner AS, Bain S, Mallinckrodt C, McLeod K 2001 Anabolism: Low mechanical signals strengthen long bones. Nature **412:**603–604.

34. Nicolella DP, Moravits DE, Gale AM, Bonewald LF, Lankford J 2005 Osteocyte lacunae tissue strain in cortical bone. J Biomech (in press).

35. Piekarski K, Munro M 1977 Transport mechanism operating between blood supply and osteocytes in long bones. Nature **269:**80–82.

36. Burger EH, Klein-Nulend J, Veldhuijzen JP 1991 Modulation of osteogenesis in fetal bone rudiments by mechanical stress in vitro. J Biomech **24**(Suppl 1):101–109.

37. Gross TS, Akeno N, Clemens TL, Komarova S, Srinivasan S, Weimer DA, Mayorov S 2001 Selected contribution: Osteocytes upregulate HIF-1alpha in response to acute disuse and oxygen deprivation. J Appl Physiol **90:**2514–2519.

38. Verborgt O, Gibson GJ, Schaffler MB 2000 Loss of osteocyte integrity in association with microdamage and bone remodeling after fatigue in vivo. J Bone Miner Res **15:**60–67.

39. Rubin C, Turner AS, Muller R, Mittra E, McLeod K, Lin W, Qin YX 2002 Quantity and quality of trabecular bone in the femur are enhanced by a strongly anabolic, noninvasive mechanical intervention. J Bone Miner Res **17:**349–357.

40. Ward K, Alsop C, Caulton J, Rubin C, Adams J, Mughal Z 2004 Low magnitude mechanical loading is osteogenic in children with disabling conditions. J Bone Miner Res **19:**360–369.

41. Morris CE 1990 Mechanosensitive ion channels. J Membr Biol **113:**93–107.

42. Ferrier J, Ward A, Kanehisa J, Heersche JN 1986 Electrophysiological responses of osteoclasts to hormones. J Cell Physiol **128:**23–26.

43. Duncan RL, Hruska KA, Misler S 1992 Parathyroid hormone activation of stretch-activated cation channels in osteosarcoma cells (UMR-106.01). FEBS Lett **307:**219–223.

44. Davidson RM, Tatakis DW, Auerbach AL 1990 Multiple forms of mechanosensitive ion channels in osteoblast-like cells. Pflugers Arch **416:**646–651.

45. Rawlinson SC, Pitsillides AA, Lanyon LE 1996 Involvement of different ion channels in osteoblasts' and osteocytes' early responses to mechanical strain. Bone **19:**609–614.

46. Katsumi A, Orr AW, Tzima E, Schwartz MA 2004 Integrins in mechanotransduction. J Biol Chem **279:**12001–12004.

47. Ingber DE 2005 Mechanical control of tissue growth: Function follows form. Proc Natl Acad Sci USA **102:**11571–11572.

48. Yellowley CE, Li Z, Zhou Z, Jacobs CR, Donahue HJ 2000 Functional gap junctions between osteocytic and osteoblastic cells. J Bone Miner Res **15:**209–217.

49. Rizzo V, Sung A, Oh P, Schnitzer JE 1998 Rapid mechanotransduction in situ at the luminal cell surface of vascular endothelium and its caveolae. J Biol Chem **273:**26323–26329.

50. Rubin J, Rubin C, Jacobs CR 2006 Mechanical signaling in bone (in press).

51. Judex S, Donahue LR, Rubin CT 2002 Genetic predisposition to osteoporosis is paralleled by an enhanced sensitivity to signals anabolic to the skeleton. FASEB J **16:**1280–1282.

52. Lang T, LeBlanc A, Evans H, Lu Y, Genant H, Yu A 2004 Cortical and trabecular bone mineral loss from the spine and hip in long-duration spaceflight. J Bone Miner Res **19:**1006–1012.

Chapter 7.   Fracture Healing: The Biology of Bone Repair and Regeneration

Louis C. Gerstenfeld and Thomas A. Einhorn

Department of Orthopaedic Surgery, Orthopaedic Research Laboratory, Boston University Medical Center, Boston, Massachusetts

CELL BIOLOGY OF FRACTURE HEALING

Bone healing is unique in that, once a fracture is sustained, either by trauma or surgical osteotomy, the injured bone regenerates its original structural geometry and biomechanical integrity. The process of fracture healing is comprised of four phases: (1) inflammatory response; (2) mesenchymal stem cell recruitment and skeletal cell differentiation, leading to formation of cartilage and bone; (3) cartilage resorption and primary bone formation; and (4) secondary bone formation and remodeling in which the newly formed callus is shaped to restore the anatomical structure and support mechanical loads. It is generally accepted that the molecular mechanism(s) that control the processes of bone healing largely recapitulates those that

Dr. Einhorn is on the Osteoporosis Advisory Board at Eli Lilly. Dr. Gerstenfeld has stock in Amgen.

Origin of Cells & Signals

Stages of Fracture Healing
Biological Processes

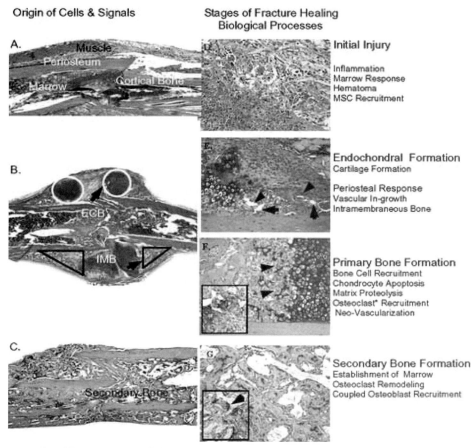

Initial Injury
Inflammation
Marrow Response
Hematoma
MSC Recruitment

Endochondral Formation
Cartilage Formation

Periosteal Response
Vascular In-growth
Intramembraneous Bone

Primary Bone Formation
Bone Cell Recruitment
Chondrocyte Apoptosis
Matrix Proteolysis
Osteoclast* Recruitment
Neo-Vascularization

Secondary Bone Formation
Establishment of Marrow
Osteoclast Remodeling
Coupled Osteoblast Recruitment

FIG. 1. Anatomic characterization of fracture repair. (A–C) Overview of the morphogenetic fields of tissue development and the proximate tissue interactions. (A) Histological section of the fracture site immediately after fracture. Potential tissue origins of mesenchymal stem cells and morphogenetic signals are denoted by the arrows and are denoted in the figure. (B) Histological section of the fracture site at 7 days after fracture. The two types of bone formation processes are denoted as endochondral bone formation (ECB) and intramembraneous bone formation (IMB). The two processes in a symmetrical manner around the fracture site. (C) Histological section of the fracture site at 28 days after fracture. Late stage of bone repair predominated by secondary bone formation and coupled remodeling. (D–G) Summary of the multiple stages of fracture healing. Histological sections are presented for each stage and a summary of the various processes that are associated with each stage. All histological specimens are from sagittal sections of mouse tibia transverse fractures and were stained with safranin O and fast green. Micrographic images are at ×200 magnification. (D) Section for the initial injury was taken from the fracture site 24 h after injury. (E) Section depicting the initial periosteal response and endochondral formation is from 7 days after injury. Arrows denote vascular in growth from the peripheral areas of the periosteum. (F) Section depicting the period of primary bone formation is from 14 days after injury. Arrows denote neovascular growth areas of the underlying new bone. Inset depicts ×400 images of an osteoclast (*chondroclast) resorbing an area of calcified cartilage. (G) Sections depicting the period of secondary bone formation are from 21 days after injury. Callus sites. Inset depicts ×400 images of an osteoclast resorbing an area of primary bone.

were operative during the embryological development of the skeleton[1] as described in earlier chapters.

Postnatal bone regeneration has unique attributes that distinguish it from prenatal skeletal development. First, inflammation and immune function play a substantial role in initiating bone healing. Second, because fracture involves disruption of a pre-existing skeletal unit, there is a structural context in which the morphogenetic factors function as defined by the pre-existing anatomy of the bone. Thus, the bone regenerates with the exact or near-exact geometric and structural attributes of the uninjured bone. Finally, the postnatal biomechanical environment is one of the most important epigenetic modifiers of tissue morphogenesis, and the rate of skeletal healing is greatly affected by the mechanical strain environment to which it is exposed. The primary factors affecting the rate of fracture repair are the underlying physiological and biomechanical conditions that either promote or retard the transition of the cells through each of the phases of healing. Therefore, a failure to transition through an individual phase of the healing process will lead to either delayed healing or nonunion.

The cell types and the structural arrangements of tissues that establish the morphogenetic fields during healing are summarized in Fig. 1. The fracture site sets up the overall spatial relationships of the morphogenetic fields during tissue regeneration. This is shown by the endochondral bone formation response involving two discrete circular-shaped centers of cartilage that form on both sides of the fracture and which taper proximally and distally along the cortices of the bone (best seen in the top middle microphotograph in A and B). Concurrently, a crescent-shaped region of intramembranous bone formation is initiated in the periosteal tissues at the proximal and distal ends of the area that taper inward toward the fracture, deep to the ring of cartilage tissue. Thus, two distinct types of bone formation processes contribute to bone healing: one around the central region of the fracture (endochondral) and one more peripheral and adja-

MOLECULAR REGULATION OF FRACTURE REPAIR

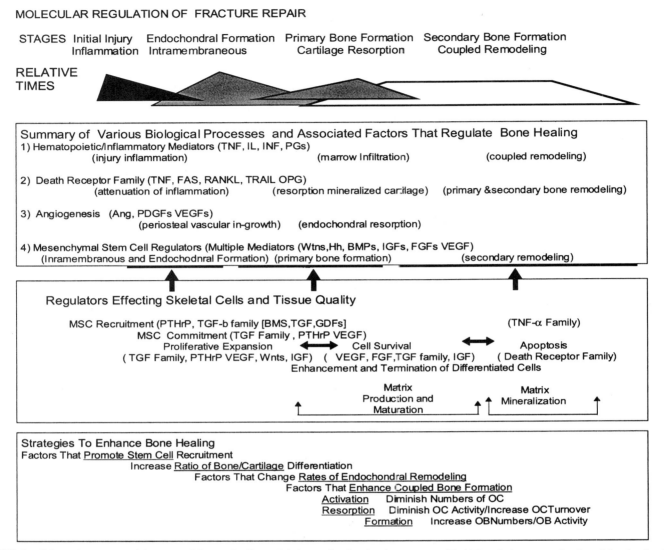

FIG. 2. Schematic summary of the stages of fracture healing and their associated molecular processes. (Top) The relative temporal and spatial scale of each of the stages of the fracture healing process are denoted by basic geometric shapes that connote both the relative intensity and time in which key stages of the healing of the molecular processes that define each of the stages. Time frames in each of the panels are matched for cross reference. (Middle) Biological processes and factors associated with each stage of bone healing. This panel denotes the basic biological processes that are occurring across the time-course and the types of individual molecular factors that regulate these processes are indicated. (Bottom) Major regulatory factors that affect skeletal cell formation and bone tissue quality. Three waves of MSC recruitment and differentiation are denoted by the corresponding lines and arrows. Each round of anabolic activity would be potentially regulated by similar temporal series of events, but the individual regulatory factors would be unique to that stage of bone healing.

cent to the cortices of bone (intramembranous). The instructive interactions initiated between cells during bone repair must occur among the external soft tissues adjacent to the fracture, the underlying cortical bone and marrow, and the developing endochondral and intramembranous tissues comprising the callus (Fig. 1A).

REGULATORY MECHANISMS OF BONE HEALING

A further understanding of the molecular mechanisms that regulate bone healing and regeneration are of immense clinical importance. The increasing interest in the use of pharmacologic modifiers of the healing processes makes elucidation of these mechanisms essential to establishing the safety of specific drugs in the context of clinical care. A schematic summary of the biological responses that contribute to bone healing, the types of factors that are involved, and the biological strategies that might be used to enhance bone healing are shown in Fig. 2. While these biological processes are presented to provide a logical framework within which to temporally and spatially relate the activities of the various factors, many of these processes overlap and are interrelated.

Hematopoietic/Inflammatory Mediators and the Role of Death Receptors During Bone Healing

Unlike the processes associated with embryologic development and postnatal growth that are regulated by ontogenetic, endocrinological, or neurological mechanisms, fracture healing after traumatic or surgical injury is initiated locally in response to regulatory mechanisms associated with inflammation and the innate immune response.[2] The hematopoietic/inflammatory and death receptor mediators are considered together because their activities are coordinated during repair. The collaboration of these factors' activities is also representative of three successive waves of tissue resorption/remodeling that occur during the time-course of bone healing.

Immediately after injury, there is a massive influx of macrophages and other cells associated with an innate immune response. During this period, the hematoma and necrotic tissues associated with bleeding and soft tissue injury begin to clear.[3] Descriptive studies examining the expression of various inflammatory factors have shown that prostaglandins (PGs), interleukin (IL-1), IL-6, IL-11, TNF-α, TNF-β, lymphotoxin-β (LT-β), macrophage-colony stimulating factor (M-CSF), RANKL, osteoprotegerin (OPG), and IFN-γ are all induced within the first 3 days after fracture.[2,4,5] While the importance of cytokines and small molecule mediators such as PGs are well known as they relate to immune cell function, they also play key roles in the initiation of the repair process.

One of the best studied examples showing the crucial role these factors play during bone repair concerns the role of cyclooxygenase-2 (COX-2). These studies are also illustrative of the intimate relationship between the hematopoietic elements and factors that regulate the cells responsible for skeletal tissue formation. In studies in rats comparing both a nonselective nonsteroidal anti-inflammatory drug (NSAID) and a COX-2 selective drug, impaired fracture healing was observed with a greater effect seen for the COX-2 selective drug.[6] Moreover, in studies of mice homozygous for a null mutation in the COX-2 gene, induced prostaglandin production was shown to be essential for the optimal mesenchymal cell differentiation during skeletal repair.[6,7] The histology of the fractures in the COX-2-null mice showed a persistence of undifferentiated mesenchyme and a marked reduction in osteoblastogenesis resulting in a high rate of nonunion. In a number of retrospective human studies examining the effects of NSAIDs in various clinical situations of bone healing, some negative effects were observed. Finally, it is interesting to note that recent studies have focused on the selective use of PG receptor agonists that have been used to specifically promote bone healing.[8]

At later stages of fracture healing, the major functions of the hematopoietic/inflammatory and death receptor mediators are associated with two periods of tissue remodeling. The first occurs at the end of the endochondral phase at which time mineralized cartilage is removed and primary bone formation takes place. The second occurs after woven bone has been laid down and remodeling is required to restore the injured bone to its original shape and structure. The role of TNF-α and its receptors has been the focus of a number of studies because this cytokine is both a major inflammatory mediator and has been implicated in bone remodeling. While it is acutely expressed at very high levels immediately after injury, its expression is largely absent during the initial periods of endochondral differentiation. However, when chondrocyte hypertrophy and mineralized cartilage resorption begins, its expression re-emerges.[4] During this same period, the key regulators of osteoclastogenesis, RANKL, OPG, and M-CSI, increase in expression. Two of these, RANKL and OPG, are also members of the TNF-α superfamily. RANKL, OPG, and M-CSF become elevated.[4,5] Once mineralized cartilage resorption is completed and woven bone formation has occurred, a subsequent phase of bone resorption takes place in which IL-1 and IL-6 increase in their expression but OPG, M-CSF, and RANKL levels decline. Indeed the role of interactions of hematopoietic/lymphopoietic and osteogenic microenvironments in regulating the homeostatic balance of bone remodeling is emerging as a major area of research interest and changes in cytokines that alter lymphopoiesis have been shown to affect bone homeostasis as well as immune function.[9]

The death receptors (TNF superfamily of cytokines) are the central arbitrators of a tissue's microenvironment by promoting the survival of one population of cells, yet destining another to undergo apoptosis. After tissue injury, this family of cytokines plays many crucial roles in all aspects of bone healing. During the initial immune response induced by tissue injury, TNFR1 and Fas mediate activation-induced cell death of macrophages, T cells, and B cells and thereby regulate the timing of the innate and acquired immune responses.[10] The pathological manifestations of inappropriate control of the apoptotic processes and a failure to initiate programmed cell death in one or another population of immune cells may trigger autoimmune disease.[11]

The death receptor family has been shown to play a pivotal role in the regulation of many different types of developmental processes. During postnatal tissue repair, these cytokines may also replace the function of other morphogenetic factors that act during embryogenesis.[12] Alternatively, these factors may act to initiate postnatal repair or regenerative processes that are not operative during embryological development. It is also now well established that chondrocytes undergo apoptosis during normal endochondral development and during arthritic disease.[13] Currently three members of the TNF family of cytokines have been implicated, including Fas ligand, TNF-α and TRAIL.[14,15] Treatment of human articular chondrocytes with Fas ligand in vitro causes apoptosis and the Fas system has been shown to be present in both growth plate chondrocytes and during endochondral development during fracture healing.[14,16] In previous studies, chondrocytes in fracture callus[16] have been shown to express Fas, and articular chondrocytes in joints have been shown to undergo programmed cell death in response to TNF-α.[5,14] The relationship between the apoptotic process and the normal progression of endochondral development is observable in data that have now been gathered from many naturally or genetically engineered defects that affect growth cartilage development. The hallmark of almost all of these defects is either a foreshortening or expansion of the growth plates. One such example is the expansion of the growth plate in genetically engineered mice deficient in matrix metalloproteinase (MMP)-9.[17] It is interesting to note that such basic defects in mineralized cartilage removal as in seen in the absence of MMP-9 are also seen in during fracture healing. This show how processes that are operative during development do indeed recapitulate themselves during postnatal skeletal repair.[18]

Processes of Angiogenesis in Bone Repair

Vascularization of the growth plate is one of the underlying mechanisms that couples chondrogenesis and osteogenesis. As discussed above, essential components of the terminal stages of chondrogenesis are chondrocyte hypertrophy, apoptosis, and the recruitment and activation of chondroclasts that resorb the mineralized cartilage matrix allowing for the formation of primary bone by osteoblasts. Morphological evidence suggests that chondrocyte apoptosis occurs readily after the invasion of endothelial cells[13,19] and that chondrocyte death is induced by diffusible factors arising either from the vasculature or hematopoietic elements brought in during angiogenesis.[20]

The intimate relationship between the in growth of vascular tissues and the differentiation and development of skeletal tissues has made the role of angiogenic mediators a central focus of many studies of bone healing. Fracture healing, as well as any tissue repair process, results in increased blood flow to the surrounding tissues. Thus, it may be speculated that the initial interactions of the vascular elements and the initiation and propagation of the periosteal response are the primary driving mechanisms that facilitate intramembranous bone formation. It has also been suggested that periovascular mesenchymal cells that exist in blood vessel walls may contribute to this process.[21] Functional demonstration of the importance of vascularization during fracture repair has been shown in several recent studies suggesting that treatment with broad spectrum angiogenic inhibitors completely prevents fracture healing and the formation of callus and periosteal woven bone.[22] In contrast, treatment of fractures with vascular endothelial growth factor (VEGF) improves bone healing, leading to a more rapid regain of mechanical strength and increased mineralization of the callus.[22]

While a large focus has been placed on the role of VEGF, angiogenesis seems to also be regulated by angiopoietin-dependent signaling. Interestingly, both Ang 1 and Ang 2 have been localized to bone cells during development,[23] distraction osteogenesis, and fracture healing.[24,25] In studies of murine fracture repair or distraction osteogenesis, Ang 1 and Ang 2, as well as their Tie receptors, were shown to be expressed throughout the healing time-course concurrent with both VEGF-A and VEGF-C. These regulators of angiogenesis showed expression throughout the chondrogenic phase of healing and reached maximal levels of expression during the late phases of endochondral remodeling and bone formation. Unlike the VEGF family that promotes new vessel formation through the stimulation of endothelial cell division, Ang 2 promotes blood vessel destabilization and regression in the absence of VEGF-A or basic fibroblast growth factor (FGF).[26] Because recent findings have suggested that Ang 2 in the presence of VEGF will promote new vessel formation both by inducing remodeling of capillary basal lamina and stimulating endothelial cell sprouting and migration,[26] the predominant expression of Ang2 during bone repair suggests a similar role in this process.

It is interesting to note that the angiogenic, hematopoietic, and death receptor mediators show collaborative interactions. Studies of fracture repair in mice deficient in TNF-α receptor–dependent signaling show greatly diminished vascular endothelial growth inhibitor (VEGI) expression. VEGI, in fact, is a death receptor ligand that interacts with death receptor 4 and is the primary regulator of the progression of vascularization. It plays a dual role in the maintenance of growth arrest of endothelial cells in G0/G1 interfaces while inducing apoptosis in any cells that enter the S phase.[27,28] Taken together, these results suggest that after injury, existent vessels are first dissociated into a pool of nondividing endothelial cells through the actions of Ang 2 and VEGI. At the time endochondral remodeling is initiated, VEGF levels rise and VEGI levels fall, stimulating cell division and allowing endothelial cells to contribute to neoangiogenic processes.

Regulators of Cell Physiology and Bone Quality

While the roles of these regulatory factors may influence several essential tissue repair processes, there is a group of factors that are specific in their actions to enhance cellular recruitment, proliferation, and differentiation (Fig. 2, middle). Indeed, they may be the most important anabolic factors in bone development because they ultimately determine the spatial organization of the skeleton and thereby control tissue structure and material properties.

The TGF-β superfamily of proteins, which includes TGF-β (1, 2, and 3), the bone morphogenetic family of factors (BMPS), and the growth and development factors (GDFs), seems to be involved in the overall recruitment and differentiation of mesenchymal stem cells. The PTH/PTH-related protein (PTHrP) and Hedgehog (Hh) families of factors primarily regulate committed chondrocyte differentiation and the progression of endochondral bone formation, although PTH, when administered intermittently, also seems to have an anabolic effect through its actions on coupled remodeling. The Wnt, FGF, and IGF families, each by different mechanisms, all primarily control the proliferative expansion of the different mesenchymal stem cell populations.

The BMP family is perhaps one of the most extensively studied groups of morphogenetic factors involved in bone healing. After Urist's landmark demonstration that the implantation of demineralized bone at extraskeletal sites induces de novo formation of cartilage and bone,[29] investigators have sought to understand the osteoinductive activity of demineralized bone matrix (DBM), and this culminated in the cloning and sequencing of individual BMPs.[30] The subsequent expression of BMPs in recombinant systems permitted their use in a variety of animal models and led to the demonstration of their abilities to enhance fracture healing and the repair of skeletal defects repair.[30–32] At this time, both rhBMP-7 (OP-1) and rhBMP-2 have been approved for use in patients to enhance bone repair in specific clinical settings.

Despite numerous studies showing that exogenous BMP may enhance fracture healing, our understanding of their role in the normal physiology of skeletal repair and regeneration remains incomplete. Several studies have attempted to define the role of endogenous BMPs in normal fracture healing. Using RT-PCR amplification, Nakase et al.[33] were the first to show the temporal and spatial distribution of BMP-4 during bone repair. Recently, Cho et al.[34] has shown that specific members of the TGF-β super family, including the BMPs, may act in combination to promote the various stages of intramembranous and endochondral bone formation observed during fracture healing. Taken together, these studies suggest that the coordinated expression of multiple BMPs and their receptors during fracture healing is important in both skeletal development and repair. Further study is needed to determine the critical roles of the individual BMPs within this coordinated network of fracture healing.

The roles of PTH and PTHrP as autocrine/parcrine regulators of endochondral bone formation during axial skeletal development may be of particular importance in bone healing.[35] Studies examining PTHrP during long bone growth and in various human pathologies have shown that the PTH/PTHrP receptor mediates the effects of Indian hedgehog and controls the progression of terminal hypertrophic chondrocyte differentiation.[36] These studies suggest that PTH signaling plays an essential role in a variety of mechanisms of bone formation including endochondral ossification.

Although the effects of PTH are usually associated with bone resorption, the response of osteoclasts to PTH are most likely mediated through osteoblastic activity, and the receptors for PTH are found in the cell membranes of osteoblasts.[37] Indeed, while continuous exposure to PTH leads to an increase in osteoclast number and activity, low intermittent doses stimulate osteoblasts and result in increased bone formation in humans.[38] Thus, the characteristic effects of this hormone on the skeleton, which are produced primarily by its amino terminal portion (1-34), are anabolic with respect to bone. These finding led to clinical trials showing that intermittent PTH treatment increases BMD and reduces the risk of vertebral and nonvertebral fractures in postmenopausal women.[39,40]

The approval of PTH(1-34) as an anabolic treatment for osteoporosis provided the major impetus to examine PTH in various models of bone healing. Several recent reports have examined effects on fracture healing with doses ranging from 10 to 200 μg/kg in rat models, and all showed significant increases in both mechanical and histological properties of the calluses.[41–43] In other studies, using models of impaired bone metabolism, PTH analogs were shown to reverse the inhibition of bone healing observed in ovariectomized rats[44] and rabbits treated with corticosteroids.[45] Finally, one report showed that PTH(1-34) increased bone in growth and pull-out strength in porous metallic implants.[46] The one drawback of most of these studies was that doses of this hormone were much higher than those which would be tolerated in humans. In one of the earliest studies using low intermittent daily subcutaneous injections of 10 μg/kg of recombinant human PTH(1-34) [rhPTH(1-34)] administered over a 28-day period of fracture healing, a larger cartilaginous callus was observed but no delay in chondrocyte differentiation was seen during fracture healing.[43] Such findings clearly suggested that these low doses could have a positive effect on fracture healing. Subsequently, studies using the recombinant human PTH [sqb]PTH(1-34); teriparatide; Forteo] at doses that were pharmakinetically comparable with those used in patients were carried out.[47] In this study, multiple time-points starting after a 21-day course of PTH treatment were assessed. Significantly improved healing as assessed by biomechanical testing and μCT was seen at the end of the endochondral period of repair. By later time-points, even the lowest dose treatment groups showed significant increases in BMC, BMD, and total osseous tissue volume. While dosing was discontinued on day 21, these data show that daily systemic administration of low-dose PTH(1-34) enhanced fracture healing by increasing BMD and BMC and produced a sustained anabolic effect throughout the remodeling phase of repair.

EFFECT OF TISSUE STRUCTURE AND FRACTURE SITE STABILITY

As noted above, one of the most unique features of bone healing is that is that it is a regenerative process such that the original geometry and internal architecture of the tissue is restored. It follows that there must be some underlying relationship among the gradients of morphogenesis that promote the developmental processes, the original anatomy of the tissue, and the biomechanical demands imposed on the injury repair mechanisms. One of the most obvious characteristics of the repair phenomenon is the resultant symmetry of bone reparative tissue around the fracture site. It may be speculated that the signals responsible arise either from the marrow or are released from the injured bone matrix. Indeed, how the injury itself influences these responses in the tissues may be of considerable relevance because the field of inflammatory signals is propagated from the point of origin of the injury.[4]

The role of the biomechanical environment in guiding the bone repair processes has received attention. Studies in which bending and shear loading were introduced at an osteotomy site were shown to selectively drive chondrogenesis versus osteogenesis.[48] Other studies have similarly shown that mechanical instability leads to persistence of cartilage tissue at the fracture site by upregulating molecular signals such as Indian hedgehog that control chondrogenesis.[49] It has also been shown that the time-course of healing and whether the injured bone goes on to union are also greatly affected by initial shear motion at the fracture site and the stability of fixation.[50] Finally, there are considerable data suggesting that some aspects of mechanical stimulation promote healing.[51]

The structural geometry of callus development might also be dependent on the muscular anatomy and vascularity of the tissues. The question of how the morphogenetic fields are established and how biomechanical factors drive both tissue differentiation and the geometry of the callus are of considerable importance in identifying the molecular signals induced by the fracture and relating them to the origins of skeletal stem cells that conduct the repair. The answers to these questions may help to determine how present and future therapeutic compounds can be introduced at the correct time and for the appropriate duration.

FUTURE PERSPECTIVES

It is now well established that multiple morphogenetic factors regulate skeletal development and the technological advances that have made these factors available for the treatment of fractures have already had important clinical impact. However, the use of some of these factors has had mixed success, and none have been shown to uniformly promote healing. Indeed, the major objective in the enhancement of fracture healing is a regain in biomechanical competency of the bone. This involves much more than simply promoting stem cell recruitment, proliferation, and differentiation. It also requires restoration of the appropriate skeletal geometry and tissue material properties. Hence, future directions involve identifying novel factors to promote repair and the appropriate times and durations in which to introduce them. Finally, while there has been considerable focus on the factors themselves, it is now clear that their activation and association with receptors and signal transduction pathways is key aspect to their success. Understanding and correcting the challenges of human host responsiveness to growth-promoting factor is perhaps the most important future direction of fracture healing research.

REFERENCES

1. Ferguson C, Alpern E, Miclau T, Helms JA 1999 Does adult fracture repair recapitulate embryonic skeletal formation?. Mech Dev **87:**57–66.
2. Barnes GL, Kostenuik PJ, Gerstenfeld LC, Einhorn TA 1999 Growth factor regulation of fracture repair. J Bone Miner Res **14:**1805–1815.
3. Bolander ME 1992 Regulation of fracture repair by growth factors. Proc Soc Exp Biol Med **200:**165–170.
4. Kon T, Cho TJ, Aizawa T, Yamazaki M, Nooh N, Graves D, Gerstenfeld LC, Einhorn TA 2001 Expression of osteoprotegerin, receptor activator of NF-kappaB ligand (osteoprotegerin ligand) and related proinflammatory cytokines during fracture healing. J Bone Miner Res **16:**1004–1014.
5. Gerstenfeld LC, Cho TJ, Kon T, Aizawa T, Tsay A, Fitch J, Barnes GL, Graves DT, Einhorn TA 2003 Impaired fracture healing in the absence of TNF-alpha signaling: The role of TNF-alpha in endochondral cartilage resorption. J Bone Miner Res **18:**1584–1592.
6. Simon AM, Manigrasso MB, O'Connor JP 2002 Cyclo-oxygenase-2 function is essential for bone fracture healing. J Bone Miner Res **17:**963–976.
7. Zhang X, Schwarz EM, Young DA, Puzas JE, Rosier RN, O'Keefe RJ 2002 Cycloxygenase-2 regulates mesenchymal cell differentiation into the osteoblast lineage and is critically involved in bone repair. J Clin Invest **109:**1405–1415.
8. Paralkar VM, Borovecki F, Ke HZ, Cameron KO, Lefker B, Grasser WA, Owen TA, Li M, DaSilva-Jardine P, Zhou M, Dunn RL, Dumont F, Korsmeyer R, Krasney P, Brown TA, Plowchalk D, Vukicevic S, Thompson DD 2003 An EP2 receptor-selective prostaglandin E2 agonist induces bone healing. Proc Natl Acad Sci USA **100:**6736–6740.
9. Calvi LM, Adams GB, Weibrecht KW, Weber JM, Olson DP, Knight MC, Martin RP, Schipani E, Divieti P, Bringhurst FR, Milner LA, Kronenberg HM, Scadden DT 2003 Osteoblastic cells regulate the hematopoietic stem cell niche. Nature **425:**841–846.
10. Schultz DR, Harrington WJ Jr 2003 Apoptosis: Programmed cell death at a molecular level. Semin Arthritis Rheum **32:**345–369.
11. Vaux DL, Flavell RA 2000 Apoptosis genes and autoimmunity. Curr Opin Immunol **12:**719–724.
12. Danial NN, Korsmeyer SJ 2004 Cell death: Critical control points. Cell **116:**205–219.
13. Farnum CE, Willsman NJ 1989 Cellular turnover at the chondro-osseous junction of growth plate cartilage: Analysis by serial sections at the light microscopical level. J Orthop Res **7:**654–666.
14. Cho TJ, Lehmann W, Edgar C, Sadeghi C, Hou A, Einhorn TA, Gerstenfeld LC 2003 Tumor necrosis factor alpha activation of the apoptotic cascade in murine articular chondrocytes is associated with the induction of metalloproteinases and specific pro-resorptive factors. Arthritis Rheum **48:**2845–2854.
15. Lee SW, Lee HJ, Chung WT, Choi SM, Rhyu SH, Kim DK, Kim KT, Kim JY, Kim JM, Yoo YH 2004 TRAIL induces apoptosis of chondrocytes and influences the pathogenesis of experimentally induced rat osteoarthritis. Arthritis Rheum **50:**534–542.

16. Lee FY, Choi YW, Behrens FF, DeFouw DO, Einhorn TA 1998 Programmed removal of chondrocytes during endochondral fracture healing. J Orthopedic Res **6:**144–150.

17. Vu TH, Shipley JM, Bergers G, Berger JE, Helms JA, Hanahan D, Shapiro SD, Senior RM, Werb Z 1998 MMP-9/gelatinase B is a key regulator of growth plate angiogenesis and apoptosis of hypertrophic chondrocytes. Cell **93:**411–422.

18. Colnot C, Thompson Z, Miclau T, Werb Z, Helms JA 2003 Altered fracture repair in the absence of MMP9. Development **130:**4123–4133.

19. Hunziker EB, Schenk RK, Cruz-Orive LM 1987 Quantitation of chondrocyte performance in growth-plate cartilage during longitudinal bone growth. J Bone Joint Surg Am **69:**162–173.

20. Gerstenfeld LC, Shapiro FD 1996 Expression of bone-specific genes by hypertrophic chondrocytes: Implication of the complex functions of the hypertrophic chondrocyte during endochondral bone development. J Cell Biochem **62:**1–9.

21. Bouletreau PJ, Warren SM, Spector JA, Peled ZM, Gerrets RP, Greenwald JA, Longaker MT 2002 Hypoxia and VEGF up-regulate BMP-2 mRNA and protein expression in microvascular endothelial cells: Implications for fracture healing. Plast Reconstr Surg **109:**2384–2397.

22. Street J, Bao M, deGuzman L, Bunting S, Peale FV Jr., Ferrara N, Steinmetz H, Hoeffel J, Cleland JL, Daugherty A, van Bruggen N, Redmond HP, Carano RA, Filvaroff EH 2002 Vascular endothelial growth factor stimulates bone repair by promoting angiogenesis and bone turnover. Proc Natl Acad Sci USA **99:**9656–9661.

23. Horner A, Bord S, Kelsall AW, Coleman N, Compston JE 2001 Tie2 ligands angiopoietin-1 and angiopoietin-2 are coexpressed with vascular endothelial cell growth factor in growing human bone. Bone **28:**65–71.

24. Carvalho RS, Einhorn TA, Lehmann W, Edgar C, Al-Yamani A, Apazidis A, Pacicca D, Clemens TL, Gerstenfeld LC 2004 The role of angiogenesis in a murine tibial model of distraction osteogenesis. Bone **34:**849–861.

25. Lehmann W, Edgar CM, Wang K, Cho TJ, Barnes GL, Kakar S, Graves DT, Rueger JM, Gerstenfeld LC, Einhorn TA 2005 Tumor necrosis factor alpha (TNF-alpha) coordinately regulates the expression of specific matrix metalloproteinases (MMPS) and angiogenic factors during fracture healing. Bone **36:**300–310.

26. Maisonpierre PC, Suri C, Jones PF, Bartunkova S, Wiegand SJ, Radziejewski C, Compton D, McClain J, Aldrich TH, Papadopoulos N, Daly TJ, Davis S, Sato TN, Yancopoulos GD 1997 Angiopoietin-2, a natural antagonist for Tie 2 that disrupts in vivo angiogenesis. Science **277:**55.

27. Yu J, Tian S, Metheny-Barlow L, Chew LJ, Hayes AJ, Pan H, Yu GL, Li LY 2001 Modulation of endothelial cell growth arrest and apoptosis by vascular endothelial growth inhibitor. Circ Res **89:**1161–1167.

28. Haridas V, Shrivastava A, Su J, Yu GL, Ni J, Liu D, Chen SF, Ni Y, Ruben SM, Gentz R, Aggarwal BB 1999 VEGI, a new member of the TNF family activates nuclear factor-kappa B and c-Jun N-terminal kinase and modulates cell growth. Oncogene **18:**6496–6504.

29. Urist MR 1965 Bone: Formation by autoinduction. Science **150:**893–899.

30. Wozney JM 1989 Bone morphogenetic proteins. Prog Growth Factor Res **1:**267–280.

31. Yasko AW, Lane JM, Fellinger EJ, Rosen V, Wozney JM, Wang EA 1992 The healing of segmental bone defects, induced by recombinant human bone morphogenetic protein (rhBMP-2). J Bone Joint Surg Am **74:**659–671.

32. Einhorn TA, Majeska RJ, Mohaideen A, Kagel EM, Bouxsein ML, Turek TJ, Wozney JM 2003 A single percutaneous injection of recombinant human bone morphogenetic protein-2 accelerates fracture repair. J Bone Joint Surg Am **85:**1425–1435.

33. Nakase T, Nomura S, Yoshikawa H, Hashimoto J, Hirota S, Kitamura Y, Oikawa S, Ono K, Takaoka K 1994 Transient and localized expression of bone morphogenetic protein 4 messenger RNA during fracture healing. J Bone Miner Res **9:**651–659.

34. Cho T-J, Gerstenfeld LC, Einhorn TA 2002 Differential temporal expression of members of the transforming growth factor beta superfamily during murine fracture healing. J Bone Miner Res **17:**513–520.

35. Lanske B, Karaplis AC, Lee K, Luz A, Vortkamp A, Pirro A, Karperien M, Defize LH, Ho C, Mulligan RC, Abou-Samra AB, Juppner H, Segre GV, Kronenberg HM 1996 PTH/PTHrP receptor in early development and Indian hedgehog-regulated bone growth. Science **273:**663–666.

36. Vortkamp A, Lee K, Lanske B, Segre GV, Kronenberg HM, Tabin CJ 1996 Regulation of rate of cartilage differentiation by Indian hedgehog and PTH-related protein. Science **273:**613–622.

37. Rubin MR, Bilezikian JP 2003 The anabolic effects of parathyroid hormone therapy. Clin Geriatr Med **19:**415–432.

38. Dempster DW, Cosman F, Kurland ES, Zhou H, Nieves J, Woelfert L, Shane E, Plavetic K, Muller R, Bilezikian J, Lindsay R 2001 Effects of daily treatment with parathyroid hormone on bone microarchitecture and turnover in patients with osteoporosis: A paired biopsy study. J Bone Miner Res **16:**1846–1853.

39. Neer RM, Arnaud CD, Zanchetta JR, Prince R, Gaich GA, Reginster JY, Hodsman AB, Eriksen EF, Ish-Shalom S, Genant HK, Wang O, Mitlak BH 2001 Effect of parathyroid hormone (1–34) on fractures and bone mineral density in postmenopausal women with osteoporosis. N Engl J Med **344:**1434–1441.

40. Black DM, Greenspan SL, Ensrud KE, Palermo L, McGowan JA, Lang TF, Garnero P, Bouxsein ML, Bilezikian JP, Rosen CJ, PaTH Study Investigators 2003 The effects of parathyroid hormone and alendronate alone or in combination in postmenopausal osteoporosis. N Engl J Med **349:**1207–1215.

41. Andreassen TT, Ejersted C, Oxlund H 1999 Intermittent parathyroid hormone (1–34) treatment increases callus formation and mechanical strength of healing rat fractures. J Bone Miner Res **14:**960–968.

42. Holzer G, Majeska RJ, Lundy MW, Hartke JR, Einhorn TA 1999 Parathyroid hormone enhances fracture healing. Clin Orthop **366:**258–263.

43. Nakajima A, Shimoji N, Shiomi K, Shimizu S, Moriya H, Einhorn TA, Yamazaki M 2002 Mechanisms for the enhancement of fracture healing in rats treated with intermittent low-dose human parathyroid hormone (1–34). J Bone Miner Res **17:**2038–2047.

44. Kim HW, Jahng JS 1999 Effect of intermittent administration of parathyroid hormone on fracture healing in ovariectomized rats. Iowa Orthop J **19:**71–77.

45. Bostrom MP, Gamradt SC, Asnis P, Vickery BH, Hill E, Avnur Z, Waters RV 2000 Parathyroid hormone-related protein protein analog RS-66271 is an effective therapy for impaired bone healing in rabbits on corticosteroid therapy. Bone **2:**437–442.

46. Skripitz R, Andreassen TT, Aspenberg P 2000 Parathyroid hormone (1–34) increases the density of rat cancellous bone in a bone chamber. A dose-response study. J Bone Joint Surg Br **82:**138–141.

47. Alkhiary YM, Gerstenfeld LC, Krall E, Westmore M, Sato M, Mitlak BH, Einhorn TA 2005 Enhancement of experimental fracture healing by systemic administration of recombinant human parathyroid hormone (PTH 1–34). J Bone Joint Surg Am **87:**731–741.

48. Cullinane DM, Fredrick A, Eisenberg SR, Pacicca D, Elman MV, Lee C, Salisbury K, Gerstenfeld LC, Einhorn TA 2002 Induction of a neoarthrosis by precisely controlled motion in an experimental mid-femoral defect. J Orthop Res **20:**579–586.

49. Le AX, Miclau T, Hu D, Helms JA 2001 Molecular aspects of healing in stabilized and non-stabilized fractures. J Orthop Res **19:**78–84.

50. Schell H, Epari DR, Kassi JP, Bragulla H, Bail HJ, Duda GN 2005 The course of bone healing is influenced by the initial shear fixation stability. J Orthop Res **23:**1022–1028.

51. Mark H, Nilsson A, Nannmark U, Rydevik B 2004 Effects of fracture fixation stability on ossification in healing fractures. Clin Orthop Relat Res **419:**245–250.

Skeletal Physiology
(Section Editors: Elizabeth Shane and Michael Kleerekoper)

Chapter 8.   Skeletal Physiology: Fetus and Neonate

Christopher S. Kovacs

Faculty of Medicine-Endocrinology, Health Sciences Centre, Memorial University of Newfoundland, St. John's, Newfoundland, Canada

INTRODUCTION

Because of obvious limitations in studying human fetuses and (to a lesser degree) neonates, human regulation of fetal and neonatal mineral homeostasis must be largely inferred from studies in animals. Some observations in animals may not apply to humans. This chapter briefly reviews existing human and animal data, including older studies of surgically manipulated animals and recent studies of mice engineered to lack calciotropic hormones or receptors. Detailed references are available in two comprehensive reviews.[1,2]

FETUS

Much of normal mineral and bone homeostasis in the adult can be explained by the interactions of PTH, 1,25-dihydroxyvitamin D or calcitriol (1,25-D), calcitonin, and the sex steroids. In contrast to the adult, comparatively little has been known about how mineral and bone homeostasis is regulated in the fetus. Fetal mineral metabolism has been uniquely adapted to meet the specific needs of this developmental period, including the requirement to maintain an extracellular level of calcium (and other minerals) that is physiologically appropriate for fetal tissues and to provide sufficient calcium (and other minerals) to fully mineralize the skeleton before birth. Mineralization occurs rapidly in late gestation, such that a human accretes 80% of the required 30 g of calcium in the third trimester, whereas a rat accretes 95% of the required 12.5 mg of calcium in the last 5 days of its 3-week gestation.

Minerals Ions and Calciotropic Hormones

A consistent finding among human and other mammalian fetuses is a total and ionized calcium concentration that is significantly higher than the maternal level during late gestation. Similarly, serum phosphate is significantly elevated, and serum magnesium is minimally elevated above the maternal concentration. The physiological importance of these elevated levels is not known. A calcium level equal to the maternal calcium concentration (and not above it) seems to be sufficient to ensure adequate mineralization of the fetal skeleton, and fetal survival to term is unaffected by extremes of hypocalcemia in several animal models. The increased calcium level is robustly maintained despite chronic, severe maternal hypocalcemia of a variety of causes. For example, adult humans and mice with nonfunctional vitamin D receptors have severe hypocalcemia, but murine fetuses with the same abnormality have normal serum calcium concentrations.[3]

Calciotropic hormone levels are also maintained at levels that differ from the adult. These differences seem to reflect the relatively different roles that these hormones play in the fetus and are not an artifact of altered metabolism or clearance of these hormones. Intact PTH levels are much lower than maternal PTH levels near the end of gestation, but it is unknown whether fetal PTH levels are low throughout gestation after the formation of the parathyroids or only in late gestation. The low level of PTH is critically important, because fetal mice lacking parathyroids and PTH have marked hypocalcemia and undermineralized skeletons.[4] Circulating 1,25-D levels are also lower than the maternal level in late gestation and seem to be

largely if not completely derived from fetal sources. The low circulating levels of 1,25-D in the fetus may be a response to high serum phosphate and suppressed PTH levels in late gestation. With respect to 1,25-D, the low levels of this hormone may reflect its relative unimportance for fetal mineral homeostasis, because both vitamin D deficiency and absence of vitamin D receptors do not impair serum mineral concentrations or the mineralization of the fetal skeleton.[3] Fetal calcitonin levels are higher than maternal levels and are thought to reflect increased synthesis of the hormone. Apart from responding appropriately to changes in the serum calcium concentration, there is little evidence of an essential role for calcitonin in fetal mineral homeostasis.[5]

PTH-related protein (PTHrP) is normally not present in the human adult circulation (outside of pregnancy and lactation), but in cord blood, PTHrP levels are up to 15-fold higher than that of PTH. PTHrP is produced in many tissues and plays multiple roles during embryonic and fetal development. The absence of PTHrP (in the *Pthrp*-null fetal mouse) leads to abnormalities of chondrocyte differentiation and skeletal development,[6] modest hypocalcemia,[7] and reduced placental calcium transfer. Such *Pthrp*-null fetuses have increased PTH levels[8] but still remain modestly hypocalcemic, indicating that PTH does not make up for lack of PTHrP in maintaining a normal calcium concentration in the fetal circulation.

The role (if any) of the sex steroids in fetal skeletal development and mineral accretion is unknown, largely because the relevant analyses have not been performed in the relevant mouse models, and corresponding human data are absent. Estrogen receptor α and β knockout mice have been shown to have altered skeletal metabolism that develops postnatally, but the fetal skeleton has not been examined in detail. Similarly, postnatal skeletal roles of RANK, RANKL, and osteoprotegerin have been shown in relevant knockout mice, but the role that this system plays in fetal mineral metabolism is not yet known.

Fetal Parathyroids

Intact parathyroid glands are required for maintenance of normal fetal calcium, magnesium, and phosphate levels; lack of parathyroids and PTH causes a greater fall in the fetal blood calcium than lack of PTHrP. Fetal parathyroids are also required for normal accretion of mineral by the skeleton and may be required for regulation of placental mineral transfer. Studies in fetal lambs have indicated that the fetal parathyroids may contribute to mineral homeostasis by producing both PTH and PTHrP, whereas a detailed study of rats indicates that the fetal parathyroids produce only PTH. Whether human fetal parathyroids produce PTH alone or PTH and PTHrP together is unclear.

Calcium Sensing Receptor

The calcium sensing receptor (CaSR) sets the serum calcium level in adults by regulating PTH, but it does not seem to set the serum calcium level in fetuses. Instead, the fetal serum calcium is driven above the maternal level by the action of PTHrP, while in turn, the CaSR appropriately suppresses PTH in response to this elevated calcium level (Fig. 1A). In the absence of PTHrP (*Pthrp*-null mice), the fetal serum calcium falls to the normal adult level, and the serum PTH is increased,

---

The author has reported no conflicts of interest.

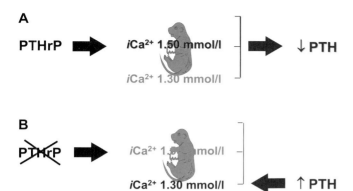

FIG. 1. Fetal blood calcium regulation. (A) Normal high fetal calcium level, which is dependent on PTHrP, activates the parathyroid CaSR, and PTH is suppressed. (B) In the absence of PTHrP, the fetal calcium level falls to a level that is now set by the parathyroid CaSR; PTH is stimulated to maintain the ionized calcium at the normal adult level (maternal). (Reprinted from Pediatric Bone, Glorieux FH, Pettifor JM, Jüppner H, Fetal mineral homeostasis, pp. 271–302, 2003, with permission from Elsevier.)

consistent with the normal function of the CaSR to maintain the calcium concentration at the adult level (Fig. 1B). Inactivating mutations of the CaSR (*Casr*-null fetuses) lead to increases in serum calcium, PTH, 1,25-D, and bone turnover of fetuses, resulting in a lower skeletal calcium content by term. The CaSR is also expressed within placenta as shown in humans and mice, and this may indicate that the CaSR participates in the regulation of placental mineral transfer. *Casr*-null fetuses have a reduced rate of placental calcium transfer, but whether this is a direct consequence of the loss of placental CaSR is not known.[9]

Fetal Kidneys and Amniotic Fluid

Fetal kidneys partly regulate calcium homeostasis by adjusting the relative reabsorption and excretion of calcium, magnesium, and phosphate in response to the filtered load and other factors, such as PTHrP and PTH. The fetal kidneys also synthesize 1,25-D, but because absence of vitamin D receptors in fetal mice does not impair fetal calcium homeostasis or placental calcium transfer, it seems likely that renal production of 1,25-D is relatively unimportant.

Renal calcium handling in fetal life may be less important compared with the adult for the regulation of calcium homeostasis because calcium excreted by the kidneys is not permanently lost. Fetal urine is the major source of fluid and solute in the amniotic fluid, and fetal swallowing of amniotic fluid is a pathway by which excreted calcium can be made available again to the fetus.

Placental Mineral Ion Transport

As noted above, the bulk of placental calcium and other mineral transfer occurs late in gestation at a rapid rate. Active transport of calcium, magnesium, and phosphate across the placenta is necessary for the fetal requirement to be met; only placental calcium transfer has been studied in detail. Analogous to calcium transfer across the intestinal mucosa, it has been theorized that calcium diffuses into calcium-transporting cells through maternal-facing basement membranes, is carried across these cells by calcium-binding proteins, and is actively extruded at the fetal-facing basement membranes by Ca^{2+}-ATPase.

Data from animal models indicates that a normal rate of

maternal-to-fetal calcium transfer can usually be maintained despite the presence of maternal hypocalcemia or maternal hormone deficiencies such as aparathyroidism, vitamin D deficiency, and absence of the vitamin D receptor. Whether the same is true for human pregnancies is less certain. A "normal" rate of maternal–fetal calcium transfer does not necessarily imply that the fetus is unaffected by maternal hypocalcemia. Instead, it is an indication of the resilience of the fetal–placental unit to be able to extract the required amount of calcium from a maternal circulation that has a severely lower calcium concentration than normal.

Fetal regulation of placental calcium transfer has been studied in a number of different animal models. Thyroparathyroidectomy in fetal lambs results in a reduced rate of placental calcium transfer, suggesting that the parathyroids are required for this process.[10] In contrast, mice lacking parathyroids as a consequence of ablation of the *Hoxa3* gene have a normal rate of placental calcium transfer.[4] The discrepancy between these findings in lambs and mice may be caused by whether or not the parathyroids are an important source of PTHrP in the circulation. Studies in fetal lambs and in *Pthrp*-null fetal mice are in agreement that PTHrP, and in particular mid-molecular forms of PTHrP, stimulate placental calcium transfer.[7,11,12] PTH does not seem to be involved in this process, and there is little evidence that calcitonin or 1,25-D are required either.[3,5]

Fetal Skeleton

A complete cartilaginous skeleton with digits and intact joints is present by the eighth week of gestation in humans. Primary ossification centers form in the vertebrae and long bones between the 8th and 12th weeks, but it is not until the third trimester that the bulk of mineralization occurs. At the 34th week of gestation, secondary ossification centers form in the femurs, but otherwise most epiphyses are cartilaginous at birth, with secondary ossification centers appearing in other bones in the neonate and child.[13]

The skeleton must undergo substantial growth and be sufficiently mineralized by the end of gestation to support the organism, but as in the adult, the fetal skeleton participates in the regulation of mineral homeostasis. Calcium accreted by the fetal skeleton can be subsequently resorbed to help maintain the concentration of calcium in the blood. Functioning fetal parathyroid glands are needed for normal skeletal mineral accretion, and both hypoparathyroidism (thyroparathyroidectomized fetal lambs and aparathyroid fetal mice) and hyperparathyroidism (including *Casr*-null fetal mice) reduce the net amount of skeletal mineral accreted by term.

Further comparative study of fetal mice lacking parathyroids or PTHrP has clarified the relative and interlocking roles of PTH and PTHrP in the regulation of the development and mineralization of the fetal skeleton. PTHrP produced locally in the growth plate directs the development of the cartilaginous scaffold that is later broken down and transformed into endochondral bone,[14] whereas PTH controls the mineralization of bone through its contribution to maintaining the fetal blood calcium and magnesium.[8] In the absence of PTHrP, a severe chondrodysplasia results,[6] but the fetal skeleton is fully mineralized.[8] In the absence of parathyroids and PTH, endochondral bone forms normally but is significantly undermineralized.[8] The blood calcium and magnesium were also significantly reduced in aparathyroid fetuses, and this may explain why lack of PTH impaired skeletal mineralization. That is, by reducing the amount of mineral presented to the skeletal surface and to osteoblasts, lack of PTH thereby impaired mineral accretion by the skeleton. When both parathyroids and PTHrP are deleted, the typical *Pthrp*-null chondrodysplasia results, but the skeleton is smaller and contains less mineral.[8] Therefore, normal mineralization of the fetal skeleton requires intact fetal parathyroid glands and adequate delivery of minerals to the fetal circulation. While both PTH and PTHrP are involved, PTH plays the more critical role in ensuring full mineralization of the skeleton before term.

Fetal Response to Maternal Hyperparathyroidism

In humans, maternal primary hyperparathyroidism has been associated with adverse fetal outcomes, including spontaneous abortion and stillbirth, which are thought to result from suppression of the fetal parathyroid glands. Because PTH cannot cross the placenta, fetal parathyroid suppression may result from increased calcium flux across the placenta to the fetus, facilitated by maternal hypercalcemia. Similar suppression of fetal parathyroids occurs when the mother has hypercalcemia because of familial hypocalciuric hypercalcemia. Chronic elevation of the maternal serum calcium in mice results in suppression of the fetal PTH level,[9] but fetal outcome is not notably affected by this.

Fetal Response to Maternal Hypoparathyroidism

Maternal hypoparathyroidism during human pregnancy can cause fetal hyperparathyroidism. This is characterized by fetal parathyroid gland hyperplasia, generalized skeletal demineralization, subperiosteal bone resorption, bowing of the long bones, osteitis fibrosa cystica, rib and limb fractures, low birth weight, spontaneous abortion, stillbirth, and neonatal death. Similar skeletal findings have been reported in the fetuses and neonates of women with pseudohypoparathyroidism, renal tubular acidosis, and chronic renal failure. These changes in human skeletons differ from what has been found in animal models of maternal hypocalcemia, in which the fetal skeleton and the blood calcium is generally normal.

Integrated Fetal Calcium Homeostasis

The evidence discussed in the preceding sections suggests the following summary models.

Calcium Source. The main flux of calcium and other minerals is across the placenta and into fetal bone, but calcium is also made available to the fetal circulation through several routes (Fig. 2). The kidneys reabsorb calcium; calcium excreted by the kidneys into the urine and amniotic fluid may be swallowed and reabsorbed; calcium is also resorbed from the developing skeleton. Some calcium returns to the maternal circulation (backflux). The maternal skeleton is a potential source of mineral, and it may be compromised in mineral deficiency states to provide to the fetus.

Blood Calcium Regulation. The fetal blood calcium is set at a level higher than the maternal level through the actions of PTHrP and PTH acting in concert (among other potential factors; Fig. 3). The CaSR suppresses PTH in response to the high calcium level, but the low level of PTH is critically required for maintaining the blood calcium and facilitating mineral accretion by the skeleton. 1,25-D synthesis and secretion are, in turn, suppressed by low PTH and high blood calcium and phosphate. The parathyroids may play a central role by producing PTH and PTHrP or may produce PTH alone while PTHrP is produced by the placenta and other fetal tissues.

PTH and PTHrP, both present in the fetal circulation, independently and additively regulate the fetal blood calcium, with PTH having the greater effect. Neither hormone can make up

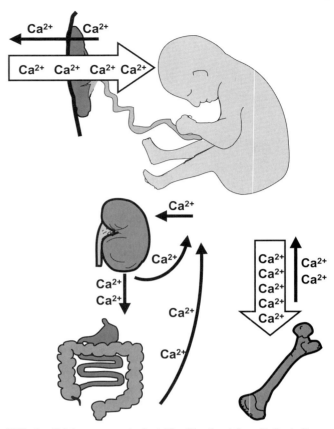

FIG. 2. Calcium sources in fetal life. (Reprinted from Pediatric Bone, Glorieux FH, Pettifor JM, Jüppner H, Fetal mineral homeostasis, pp. 271–302, 2003, with permission from Elsevier.)

for absence of the other: if one is missing the blood calcium is reduced, and if both are missing, the blood calcium is reduced even further. PTH may contribute to the blood calcium through actions on the PTH/PTHrP (PTH1) receptor in classic target tissues (kidney, bone), whereas PTHrP may contribute through placental calcium transfer and actions on the PTH1 receptor and other receptors.

The normal elevation of the fetal blood calcium above the maternal calcium concentration was historically taken as proof that placental calcium transfer is an active process. However, the fetal blood calcium level is not simply determined by the rate of placental calcium transfer because placental calcium transfer is normal in aparathyroid mice and increased in mice lacking the PTH1 receptor, but both phenotypes have significantly reduced blood calcium levels.[4,7] Also, *Casr*-null fetuses have reduced placental calcium transfer but markedly increased blood calcium levels.[9]

Placental Calcium Transfer. Placental calcium transfer is regulated by PTHrP but not by PTH (Fig. 4), and the placenta (and possibly the parathyroids) is likely an important source of PTHrP.

Skeletal Mineralization. PTH and PTHrP have separate roles with respect to skeletal development and mineralization (Fig. 5). PTH normally acts systemically to direct the mineralization of the bone matrix by maintaining the blood calcium at the adult level and possibly by direct actions on osteoblasts within the bone matrix. In contrast, PTHrP acts both locally within the growth plate to direct endochondral bone development and

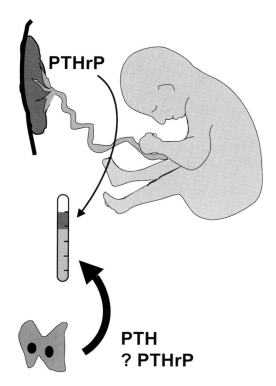

FIG. 3. Fetal blood calcium regulation. PTH has a more dominant effect on fetal blood calcium regulation than PTHrP, with blood calcium represented schematically as a thermometer (light gray, contribution of PTH; dark gray, contribution of PTHrP). In the absence of PTHrP, the blood calcium falls to the maternal level. In the absence of PTH (*Hoxa3*-null that has absent PTH but normal circulating PTHrP levels), the blood calcium falls well below the maternal calcium concentration. In the absence of both PTHrP and PTH (*Hoxa3/Pthrp* double mutant) the blood calcium falls even further than in the absence of PTH alone. (Reprinted from Pediatric Bone, Glorieux FH, Pettifor JM, Jüppner H, Fetal mineral homeostasis, pp. 271–302, 2003, with permission from Elsevier.)

outside of bone to affect skeletal development and mineralization by contributing to the regulation of the blood calcium and placental calcium transfer. PTH has the more critical role in maintaining skeletal mineral accretion.

The rate of placental calcium transfer has been historically considered to be the rate-limiting step for skeletal mineral accretion. However, this is not correct because accretion of mineral was reduced in the presence of both normal and increased placental calcium transfer.[1] The rate-limiting step seems to be the blood calcium level, which in turn is largely determined by PTH. The level of blood calcium achieved in the *Pthrp*-null—that is, the normal adult level—is sufficient to allow normal accretion of mineral, whereas lower levels of blood calcium impair it.

NEONATE

On cutting the umbilical cord and abruptly losing the placental calcium infusion (and placental sources of PTHrP), a rapid adjustment in the regulation of mineral homeostasis occurs over hours to days. The neonate becomes dependent on intestinal calcium intake, skeletal calcium stores, and renal calcium reabsorption to maintain a normal blood calcium at a time of continued skeletal growth. PTH and 1,25-D become

more important, whereas PTHrP becomes less involved in neonatal calcium homeostasis.

Mineral Ions and Calciotropic Hormones

Birth marks the onset of a fall in the total and ionized calcium concentration, likely provoked by loss of the placental calcium pump and placental-derived PTHrP and a rise in pH induced by the onset of breathing. Studies in rodents indicate a fall in total and ionized calcium levels to 60% of the fetal value by 6–12 h after birth and a subsequent rise to the normal adult value over the succeeding week. Although data are less complete in humans, the progression in ionized and total calcium values seems to be similar. The ionized calcium in normal neonates falls from the umbilical cord level of 1.45 mM to a mean of 1.20 mM by 24 h after birth.[15] Babies delivered by elective cesarian-section were found to have lower blood calcium and higher PTH levels at birth compared with babies delivered by spontaneous vaginal delivery,[16] indicating that the mode of delivery can affect early neonatal mineral homeostasis.

Phosphate initially rises over the first 24 h of postnatal life in humans and then gradually declines. The intact PTH level has been found to rise briskly to within or near the normal adult range by 24–48 h after birth.[2] The increase in PTH follows the early postnatal drop in the serum ionized calcium and precedes the subsequent rise in ionized calcium and 1,25-D and the fall in phosphate. During the first 48 h, the parathyroid glands have been found to respond sluggishly to more severe falls in the ionized calcium, such as that caused by exchange transfusion with citrated blood. The degree of responsiveness to acute hypocalcemia seems to increase with postnatal age.

In humans, 1,25-D rises to adult levels over the first 48 h of postnatal life, likely in response to the rise in PTH. Serum

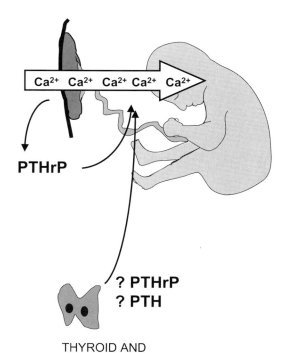

FIG. 4. Placental calcium transfer is regulated by PTHrP but not by PTH; whether the parathyroids produce PTHrP or not is uncertain. (Reprinted from Pediatric Bone, Glorieux FH, Pettifor JM, Jüppner H, Fetal mineral homeostasis, pp. 271–302, 2003, with permission from Elsevier.)

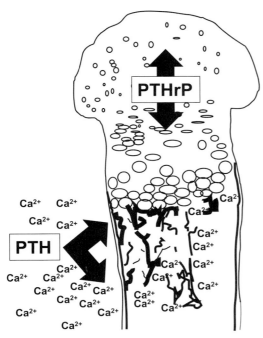

FIG. 5. Schematic model of the relative contribution of PTH and PTHrP to endochondral bone formation and skeletal mineralization. PTHrP is produced within the cartilaginous growth plate and directs the development of this scaffold that will later be broken down and replaced by bone. PTH reaches the skeleton systemically from the parathyroids and directs the accretion of mineral by the developing bone matrix. (Reprinted from Pediatric Bone, Glorieux FH, Pettifor JM, Jüppner H, Fetal mineral homeostasis, pp. 271–302, 2003, with permission from Elsevier.)

calcitonin rises 2- to 10-fold over cord blood levels over the same time interval and then gradually declines. Infants that are premature, asphyxiated, or hypocalcemic have the highest postnatal calcitonin levels; consequently, hypercalcitoninemia has been suggested to cause neonatal hypocalcemia. However, other studies indicate that the postnatal rise in calcitonin levels does not correlate to the fall in serum calcium.

PTHrP secretion from placenta, amnion, and umbilical cord is lost at birth; secretion from the parathyroid glands (if ever present) is also apparently lost sometime after birth, because PTHrP circulates at low to undetectable levels during normal adult life in humans and animals. Animal studies suggest that PTHrP may persist in the neonatal circulation for some time, whether secreted by the parathyroids or caused by absorption of PTHrP from milk (milk contains PTHrP at concentrations 10,000-fold higher than the level in the fetal circulation). Whether PTHrP present in milk contributes to the regulation of neonatal mineral homeostasis is unknown.

Intestinal Absorption of Calcium

In newborns, intestinal calcium absorption is a passive, nonsaturable process that is not dependent on vitamin D and 1,25-D. The high lactose content of milk has been shown to specifically increase the efficiency of intestinal calcium absorption and net bioavailability of dietary calcium through effects on paracellular diffusion in the distal small bowel. With increasing postnatal age, the vitamin D receptor begins to appear in intestinal cells, and mucosal levels of the calcium-binding protein calbindin$_{9K}$-D increase sharply. Around the same time, vitamin D–dependent active transport of calcium becomes noticeable, whereas passive transfer of calcium declines. By the time of weaning in rodents, the intestine is less permeable

to passive absorption of calcium, and active transport has become the dominant means by which calcium is transferred into the intestinal mucosa. Data from newborn humans are less complete, but the onset of 1,25-D–dependent active transport of calcium follows a similar postnatal course. The normal postnatal maturation of the neonatal intestine may limit the ability of preterm humans to accrete sufficient calcium for skeletal mineralization and to regulate the blood calcium.

Renal Handling of Calcium

Although data are limited, urinary calcium excretion rises in humans over the first 2 weeks, consistent with a concurrent 2-fold rise in glomerular filtration rate. The neonatal kidney show a response to exogenously administered PTH that increases with postnatal age.

Skeletal Calcium Metabolism

In humans, the neonatal skeleton continues to accrete calcium at a rate of about 150 mg/kg/day, similar to the rate of the late-term fetus. Vitamin D deficiency or loss of the vitamin D receptor (which has no or minimal effect on mineral homeostasis of the fetus) becomes obvious during the neonatal period because of the onset of dependence on intestinal calcium transport for supply of calcium. In human vitamin D deficiency, hypocalcemia appears late in the first or second week, and rickets develops after 2–3 months.

Although parathyroidectomy and vitamin D deficiency in rats and loss of vitamin D receptors in mice will eventually result in hypocalcemia and hyperphosphatemia, by the time of weaning, neonatal rats and mice still have normal serum mineral concentrations and skeletal mineral content. These findings suggest that factors other than PTH and vitamin D (such as lactose and, perhaps, PTHrP in milk) may be required for normal accretion of calcium in the first several weeks when the pup is suckling and intestinal calcium absorption is not yet fully dependent on 1,25-D.

Premature infants are prone to develop metabolic bone disease of prematurity, a form of rickets precipitated by loss of the placental calcium pump at a time when the skeleton is accreting calcium at a peak rate. It is not caused by vitamin D deficiency, but seems to be the consequence of inadequate calcium and phosphate intake to meet the demands of the mineralizing neonatal skeleton. Special oral or parenteral formulas that are high in calcium and phosphorus content will correct the demineralization process and allow normal skeletal accretion of these minerals.

Neonatal Response to Maternal Hyper- or Hypoparathyroidism

Maternal hyperparathyroidism results in suppression of the neonatal parathyroid glands for some time after birth (the suppression can be permanent), and hypocalcemia, tetany, and even death may occur. The mechanism of the prolonged suppression is not known, but may be caused by chronic exposure to increased flux of calcium across the placenta during fetal development. Suppression has been observed in infants of women with familial hypocalciuric hypercalcemia.

Maternal hypoparathyroidism in humans has resulted in neonatal parathyroid gland hyperplasia, as noted above in the fetal section. The serum calcium level of the neonate has usually been reported to be normal while the PTH level (older assays) has been found to be elevated. The skeletal findings generally resolve over the first several months after birth, but acute interventions may be required to raise or lower the blood calcium in the neonate. In addition, subtotal parathyroidectomy may be required to control more severe, autonomous disease.

Maternal hypocalcemia of any cause may result in parathyroid gland hyperplasia and hyperparathyroidism in the fetus and neonate. In women with pseudohypoparathyroidism, children that do not inherit the genetic disorder are usually normal at birth, although transient neonatal hyperparathyroidism has been reported in some cases. Furthermore, children that did inherit the condition may also be normal at birth and gradually develop the full biochemical features of pseudohypoparathyroidism over the first several years of life.

Neonatal Hypocalcemia

Neonatal hypocalcemia typically presents as seizures that onset between 4 and 28 days of age. The preterm infant is particularly prone to hypocalcemia, having lost the placental calcium infusion at a time when the skeleton is rapidly accreting calcium, and the intestinal calcium absorption is relatively inefficient. In addition to prematurity, other causes of neonatal hypocalcemia include congenital hypoparathyroidism, magnesium deficiency, maternal diabetes, vitamin D deficiency or resistance, and hyperphosphatemia.

Neonatal hypocalcemia can occur as a complication of maternal diabetes in pregnancy in up to 50% of cases, although tight control of the maternal glucose during pregnancy reduces the incidence. The cause of hypocalcemia is likely to be multifactorial but may include neonatal hypomagnesemia as a consequence of maternal glucosuria during pregnancy. Studies in rats have also suggested that maternal diabetes reduces placental mineral transport and skeletal mineral accretion, which in turn predisposes the neonate to develop hypocalcemia and hypomagnesemia.

REFERENCES

1. Kovacs CS 2003 Fetal mineral homeostasis. In: Glorieux FH, Pettifor JM, Jüppner H (eds.) Pediatric Bone: Biology and Diseases. Academic Press, San Diego, CA, USA, pp. 271–302.
2. Kovacs CS, Kronenberg HM 1997 Maternal-fetal calcium and bone metabolism during pregnancy, puerperium and lactation. Endocr.Rev **18**: 832–872.
3. Kovacs CS, Woodland ML, Fudge NJ, Friel JK 2005 The vitamin D receptor is not required for fetal mineral homeostasis or for the regulation of placental calcium transfer. Am J Physiol Endocrinol Metab **289**:E133–E144.
4. Kovacs CS, Manley NR, Moseley JM, Martin TJ, Kronenberg HM 2001 Fetal parathyroids are not required to maintain placental calcium transport. J Clin Invest **107**:1007–1015.
5. McDonald KR, Fudge NJ, Woodrow JP, Friel JK, Hoff AO, Gagel RF, Kovacs CS 2004 Ablation of calcitonin/calcitonin gene related peptide-α impairs fetal magnesium but not calcium homeostasis. Am J Physiol Endocrinol Metab **287**:E218–E226.
6. Karaplis AC, Luz A, Glowacki J, Bronson RT, Tybulewicz VL, Kronenberg HM, Mulligan RC 1994 Lethal skeletal dysplasia from targeted disruption of the parathyroid hormone-related peptide gene. Genes Dev **8**:277–289.
7. Kovacs CS, Lanske B, Hunzelman JL, Guo J, Karaplis AC, Kronenberg HM 1996 Parathyroid hormone-related peptide (PTHrP) regulates fetal-placental calcium transport through a receptor distinct from the PTH/PTHrP receptor. Proc Natl Acad Sci USA **93**:15233–15238.
8. Kovacs CS, Chafe LL, Fudge NJ, Friel JK, Manley NR 2001 PTH regulates fetal blood calcium and skeletal mineralization independently of PTHrP. Endocrinology **142**:4983–4993.
9. Kovacs CS, Ho-Pao CL, Hunzelman JL, Lanske B, Fox J, Seidman JG, Seidman CE, Kronenberg HM 1998 Regulation of murine fetal-placental calcium metabolism by the calcium-sensing receptor. J Clin Invest **101**:2812–2820.
10. Care AD, Caple IW, Abbas SK, Pickard DW 1986 The effect of fetal thyroparathyroidectomy on the transport of calcium across the ovine placenta to the fetus. Placenta **7**:417–424.
11. Care AD, Abbas SK, Pickard DW, Barri M, Drinkhill M, Findlay JB, White IR, Caple IW 1990 Stimulation of ovine placental transport of calcium and magnesium by mid-molecule fragments of human parathyroid hormone-related protein. Exp Physiol **75**:605–608.
12. Rodda CP, Kubota M, Heath JA, Ebeling PR, Moseley JM, Care AD, Caple IW, Martin TJ 1988 Evidence for a novel parathyroid hormone-related protein in fetal lamb parathyroid glands and sheep placenta: Comparisons with a similar protein implicated in humoral hypercalcaemia of malignancy. J Endocrinol **117**:261–271.
13. Moore KL, Persaud TVN 1998 The Developing Human, 6th ed. Saunders, Philadelphia, PA, USA.
14. Karsenty G 2001 Chondrogenesis just ain't what it used to be. J Clin Invest **107**:405–407.
15. Loughead JL, Mimouni F, Tsang RC 1988 Serum ionized calcium concentrations in normal neonates. Am J Dis Child **142**:516–518.
16. Bagnoli F, Bruchi S, Garosi G, Pecciarini L, Bracci R 1990 Relationship between mode of delivery and neonatal calcium homeostasis. Eur J Pediatr **149**:800–803.

Chapter 9.   Childhood and Adolescence

Dorothy A. Nelson,[1] Shane A. Norris,[2] and Vicente Gilsanz[3]

[1]Internal Medicine, Wayne State University, Detroit, Michigan; [2]MRC Mineral Metabolism Research Unit, University of the Witwatersrand, Johannesburg, South Africa; and [3]Radiology, Children's Hospital of Los Angeles, Los Angeles, California

INTRODUCTION

Childhood and adolescence are characterized by longitudinal growth as well as by changes in skeletal size and shape. Bone mass increases dramatically during growth, and it is becoming increasingly clear that the amount of bone accrued during these life periods may be an important determinant of future resistance to fractures. Thus, considerable interest is placed on defining the determinants that account for the physiological variations in skeletal growth, because they will provide the best means for identification of individuals and populations that are at greatest risk of osteoporosis and other disorders of bone and mineral metabolism.

The development of precise noninvasive methods for measuring BMC and BMD has significantly improved our ability to study the influence of genetic and environmental factors on the attainment of bone mass. Pediatric applications of the most commonly used methods, DXA and QCT will be discussed below. Inherent differences in these measurement methods have sometimes led investigators to different conclusions about the timing and characteristics of bone growth and accumulation of bone mass. Nevertheless, bone densitometry can be an

Dr. Nelson receives research funding from Pfizer and Aventis/Procter & Gamble. All other authors have reported no conflicts of interest.

effective tool in children both within the clinical and research setting provided that the results are presented in a clinically useful format or the results are interpreted independent of body size and growth.

ACCUMULATION OF BONE MASS AND PEAK BONE MASS

Skeletal mass increases from ~70–95 g at birth to 2400–3300 g in young women and men, respectively.[1] These gains are achieved through longitudinal growth, which results from a combination of bone modeling and remodeling. These processes occur at different rates and at different times at primary and secondary sites of bone formation.

Longitudinal studies of total body BMC measurements show that gains in bone mass are very rapid during adolescence and that up to 25% of peak bone mass (PBM) is acquired during the 2-year period across peak height velocity.[2] At peak height velocity, boys and girls have reached 90% of their adult stature but only 57% of their adult BMC. At least 90% of PBM is acquired by age 18.[2]

The human skeleton contains ~85% cortical bone and 15% cancellous bone, and studies have shown that the patterns of gain during growth (like those of the rate of bone loss with aging) differ considerably between these two skeletal compartments.[3,4] The density of cancellous bone is strongly influenced by hormonal and/or metabolic factors associated with sexual development during late adolescence.[5] On average, cancellous BMD in the spine increases by 13% during puberty in white boys and girls. After controlling for puberty, vertebral BMD fails to correlate significantly with age, sex, weight, height, surface area, or body mass index (BMI).[5] The increase in the density of cancellous bone during the later stages of puberty is likely a reflection of a greater thickness of the trabeculae.

The factors that account for the increase in cancellous vertebral BMD during late puberty remain to be determined. It is reasonable to suspect that many of the physical changes undergone, such as the accelerated growth spurt and the increases in body and bone mass, are, at least in part, mediated by the actions of sex steroids.[6] Some of these effects may be caused by changes in protein and calcium metabolism induced by sex steroids, or, alternatively, they may be secondary to the cascade of events triggered by the increase in growth hormone (GH) and insulin growth factor I (IGF-I) production observed after sex steroid exposure.

The exact age at which values for bone mass reach their peak at various skeletal sites has not yet been determined with certainty. It is likely that the timing of peak values differs between the axial and appendicular skeletons and between men and women. Moreover, differences among studies are, in part, a reflection of the different modalities used for measuring bone mass.

In the axial skeleton, PBM may be achieved by the end of the second decade of life. Studies in women using CT have shown that the density and the size of vertebral bone reach their peak soon after the time of sexual and skeletal maturity,[5,7] which corroborates anatomical data that indicate trabecular bone loss as early as the third decade of life, and no change in the cross-sectional area of the vertebral body from 15 to 90 years of age.[8,9] The data regarding whether vertebral cross-sectional area in men continues to grow after cessation of longitudinal growth are controversial; while some authors find no change in the cross-sectional dimensions after skeletal maturity, others have suggested that vertebral size increases with age throughout adulthood.[9]

In the appendicular skeleton, the range of ages published in cross-sectional studies for the timing of PBM has varied significantly from 17–18 years of age to as late as 35 years of age.[10–13] Longitudinal DXA studies indicate that the rate of increase in skeletal mass slows markedly in late adolescence and that peak values in the femoral neck, such as those in the spine, are achieved near the end of puberty in normal females.[7,14]

According to the "mechanostat" theory, bone mass accrual is tightly controlled by mechanical loads on bone generated from muscle forces.[15,16] Growing muscle and body weight in children exert a load on the skeleton that causes strain (change in dimensions and/or shape of the bone in response to the force load) on bone. Furthermore, strain seems to be an important signaling mechanism in bone to help control bone's structural adaptations to the mechanical use.[15] Microstrains (μE) between 800 and 1600 preserve bone, whereas loads on bone that regularly exceeds 1600 μE result in bone becoming stronger. Absorptiometric data from a study in Argentina showed that, in children, both bone and muscle mass increase linearly until puberty, but in girls at 12 years of age, DXA-derived bone mass begins increasing faster than muscle mass. It is hypothesized that an estrogen response may result in the storing of more bone than needed for strictly mechanical reasons in adolescent girls, possibly to provide calcium stores for later use during pregnancy and lactation.[17–19]

GENETIC INFLUENCE ON BONE ACCUMULATION DURING GROWTH

Heredity factors are important determinants of bone mass. Convergent data from mother-daughter pairs, sib pairs, and twin studies have estimated the heritability of bone mass to account for 60–80% of its variance.[20–22] The magnitude of the genetic effect varies with age and between skeletal sites; it is higher in the young than in the elderly and in the spine than in the extremities.[23] Further support for this genetic influence comes from studies showing reduced bone mass in daughters of osteoporotic women compared with controls,[22] in men and women with first-degree relatives who have osteoporosis,[24] and, more recently, in studies reporting a link between several "candidate" genes and bone mass.

In a study of a large group of female subjects, polymorphisms of the *vitamin D receptor* (*VDR*) gene at a *Bsm*I restriction site were associated with BMD in prepubertal and adolescent girls.[25] Girls with the BB genotype had significantly lower spinal BMD SD scores than girls with the Bb and bb genotypes.[25] In contrast, polymorphisms at the start codon site of the *VDR* gene, detected with the *Fok*I restriction enzyme, were not associated with BMD at any skeletal site in prepubertal girls.[26] An association between femoral and spinal BMD and the VDR genotype at the *Apa*I and *Bsm*I restriction sites has been shown using CT in prepubertal American girls of Hispanic descent.[27] In this study, girls with aa and bb genotypes showed significantly higher volumetric BMD values than girls with the other genotypes, both at the spine and the femur. A polymorphism in the Sp1-binding site of the gene encoding for collagen type Ia1 was also found to explain some of the variability in vertebral BMD in this cohort of prepubertal girls.[28] In contrast, no relationship between the VDR genotype at the *Bsm*I site and forearm BMD or rates of gain of BMD was found in Norwegian boys and girls.[29] It would seem that *VDR* polymorphisms are weak determinants of bone mass. This is not surprising because VDR is likely to be confounded by the effect of numerous other genes that influence bone homeostasis and skeletal development in a growing individual. However, the recent emergence of candidate genes (*calcium-sensing re-*

ceptor gene, *α2HS-glycoprotein* gene, *estrogen receptor α* gene, *calcitonin* gene, *PTH* gene, *collagen Iα1* gene, *TGFβ* genes, and others) has opened new concepts in the understanding of the pathophysiology of bone development and loss, but much research is still needed for us to detangle the complexity of gene–gene and gene–environment interactions on bone mass.[30]

Effect of Sex

Observations using CT indicate that, throughout life, females have smaller vertebral cross-sectional area compared with males, even after accounting for differences in body size. On average, the cross-sectional area of the vertebral bodies is 11% smaller in prepubertal girls than in prepubertal boys matched for age, height, and weight.[31] This disparity increases with growth and is greatest at skeletal maturity, when the cross-sectional dimensions of the vertebrae are ~25% smaller in women than in men, even after taking into consideration differences in body size.[32] Thus, the phenotypic basis for the 4- to 8-fold higher incidence of vertebral fractures in women compared with that in men may lie in the smaller size of the female vertebra.

In contrast, the cross-sectional dimensions of the femur do not differ between males and females matched for age, height, and weight.[33] The cross-sectional and cortical bone areas at the midshaft of the femur are primarily related to body weight, regardless of sex, a notion consistent with analytical models proposing that long bone cross-sectional growth is strongly driven by mechanical loads.[33,34]

Recent evidence also indicates that BMD is similar in boys and girls before puberty. Data obtained with DXA in two large samples of healthy subjects clearly indicated that there were no sex differences in BMC and BMD during the prepubertal period.[35,36] In the study by Nguyen et al.,[35] BMD values during puberty in girls were higher in the pelvis and spine, whereas measures in postpubertal boys were higher in the whole skeleton. Peak BMC and BMD was achieved between the ages of 20 and 25 years and occurred much earlier in girls than in boys.

Effect of Ethnicity

Most reports of ethnic differences in bone mass during childhood, based on absorptiometric methods, have indicated a higher bone mass among blacks compared with whites.[36–39] This has led to the generalization that black population groups have greater bone mass and strength compared with white population groups as an attempt to explain the lower fracture rates observed in black population groups. However, not all U.S. studies have observed ethnic differences in BMC and BMD in children.[40,41] Furthermore, black Gambian children have a smaller bone mass than British children,[42] and black children in South Africa have a similar appendicular bone mass to white children.[43] Prepubertal black children in South Africa have greater BMC at the femoral neck than their white peers and similar BMC at the lumbar spine and whole body and lower BMC at the midradius than their white peers. Thus, it is important to recognize that bone mass varies within and among ethnic groups depending on a variety of genetic and environmental factors.

Pediatric studies using CT indicate that, regardless of sex, ethnicity has significant and differential effects on the density and the size of the bones in the axial and appendicular skeletons.[44] In the axial skeleton, the density of cancellous bone in the vertebral bodies is greater in black than in U.S. white adolescents. This difference first becomes apparent during late stages of puberty and persists throughout life.[45] Based on CT data, cancellous BMD is similar in black and white children before puberty, but during puberty it increases in all adolescents. The magnitude of the increase from prepubertal to postpubertal values is, however, substantially greater in black than in white subjects (34% versus 11%, respectively).[44] The cross-sectional areas of the vertebral bodies, however, do not differ between black and white children.[44] Thus, theoretically, the structural basis for the lower vertebral bone strength and the greater incidence of fractures in the axial skeleton of white subjects resides in their lower cancellous BMD. In contrast, in the appendicular skeleton, ethnicity influences the cross-sectional areas of the femora but not the cortical bone area or the material density of cortical bone.[44] Although values for femoral cross-sectional area increase with height, weight, and other anthropometric parameters in all children, this measurement is substantially greater in black children.[44] Because the same amount of cortical bone placed further from the center of the bone results in greater bone strength, the skeletal advantage for blacks in the appendicular skeleton is likely the consequence of the greater cross-sectional size of the bones.[34]

Limited data from Asian and Hispanic youth suggest that their bone mass is similar to that of whites but much lower than that of black children.[41] Differences in bone and body size account for much of the apparent observed ethnic differences in BMD among non-Hispanic, Hispanic, and Asian children.[41]

TRACKING OF BONE MASS

The lack of a meaningful clinical pediatric outcome measure related to BMD examinations is currently a major limitation for their value in children. Unfortunately, studies assessing the relationship of childhood fractures to bone measures have been inconclusive. While several studies have suggested that children with fractures have a deficiency in bone acquisition compared with those who do not fracture, other factors, such as level of activity and the risk associated with youthful behavior, limit the predictive value of bone measures. However, establishing the degree that these determinations can be tracked throughout growth will help us to define the constancy of a child's expected measurements relative to population percentiles. The amount of bone that is gained during adolescence is the main contributor to PBM, which, in turn, is believed to be a major determinant of osteoporosis and fracture risk in the elderly. Available data indicate that the morphological traits that contribute to the strength of the bone track throughout life, from childhood to adulthood.[35,46,47] Longitudinal CT measurements of the cross-sectional areas of the vertebrae and femora and of cancellous BMD in healthy children indicated that measures at early puberty predicted values at sexual maturity.[47] When baseline values were divided into quartiles, a linear relation across pubertal stages was observed for each quartile (Fig. 1). The regression lines differed among quartiles, paralleled each other, and did not overlap. Therefore, individual volumetric BMD and bone size tracked through growth, maintaining the same position in the normal distribution at the end of puberty as was present in the prepubertal period. Establishing whether DXA values also maintain their rank order across time will aid in the identification of those children who are prone to develop low values for PBM and who may be at greater risk for osteoporosis later in life. Available data support the notion of significant tracking for pediatric DXA measures. Indeed, strong correlations between baseline and follow-up DXA values 2 years later have been observed in prepubertal girls.

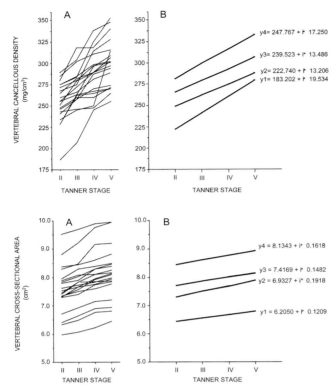

FIG. 1. Longitudinal measurements of vertebral cancellous BMD (top) and vertebral cross-sectional area (bottom) in 20 girls from Tanner stages 2–5 of sexual development. Values are shown (A) for each girl and (B) for each quartile.

PEDIATRIC BONE MASS MEASUREMENT

DXA

The most commonly used quantitative radiologic method to assess bone mass in children, as in adults, is DXA. The standard software from most DXA manufacturers, however, was designed with adult patients in mind, so special software for pediatrics has been developed by some manufacturers. The software may require longer scanning time, which can make cooperation from children difficult, resulting in motion artifacts and other inaccuracies.[48]

The preferred anatomic sites for DXA measurements in adults (lumbar spine, proximal femur, and forearm) are problematic when measured in the growing skeleton where size and shape change with age. There is also tremendous variability in growth and body size at any given chronologic age. Because of these factors that affect regional BMD in children, whole body BMC has been recommended for pediatric studies.[49]

Normative data for DXA values in pediatrics are available in the literature and are included in some DXA software packages. It should, however, be noted that different DXA manufacturers display substantial variation in BMD values of the same bone. Therefore, caution is advised before using published normative data for clinical use, and institutional and device-specific norms are preferable to published references.

Bone mass determinations in children with DXA have been done at all ages, including newborns[50] and infants.[51,52] In general, values measured at different skeletal sites increase from infancy to adulthood (Fig. 2).[14,40,53,54] The relationship between age and BMC in the lumbar spine seems to be represented by a segmented polynomial curve; a rapid increase during childhood is followed by an even greater increase during puberty that ends in the third decade of life.[7,14,55,56] Similar relationships may be seen in the femoral neck[14,53,55] and the entire skeleton.[53,55] However, radial DXA values in children have not been found to be influenced by puberty.[55]

Radiation exposure involved in DXA examinations is extremely low. The subject effective dose has been estimated to be ~0.4 μSv for lumbar spine measurements and ~5.4 μSv for whole skeleton scans.[57] In children, the precision of DXA measurements ranges from 0.8% to 2.5% in most studies.[50,51]

Several limitations of DXA must be stressed with reference to bone measurements during childhood, when major changes in body composition, body size, and skeletal mass occur. DXA is a projectional technique, and its measurements are based on the 2D projection of a 3D structure. Thus, DXA values are a function of three skeletal parameters: the size of the bone being examined, the volume of the bone, and its mineral density.[58] These values are frequently expressed as measurements of the bone content per surface area (g/cm^2), as determined by scan radiographs. However, scan radiographs only provide an approximation of the size of the bone, and any correction based on these radiographs is only a very rough estimate of the "density." Consequently, the interpretation of DXA-derived areal BMD poses major challenges in children because of

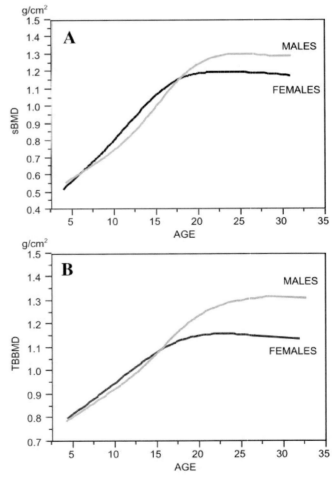

FIG. 2. Changes in BMD values of (A) the lumbar spine and (B) whole body with chronological age. The acceleration during adolescence is followed by a plateau phase in early adulthood. DXA measurements performed in 319 healthy subjects (156 female, 163 male) from 4 to 32 years of age are shown (courtesy of Stefano Mora, MD, Milan, Italy).

changes in bone and body size related to age and pubertal development. A number of approaches have been suggested to overcome this disadvantage with the use of correction factors. A simple correction involves adjusting BMD for the height of the subject. Another method is the determination of bone mineral apparent density (BMAD), which can be calculated in a variety of ways: by dividing BMC by the 3D bone volume calculated from the 2D DXA-derived bone area, assuming the cross-sectional area of the vertebrae is a cube[56,58,59]; or by assuming that the shape approximates a cylinder with a circular base,[54,60] or a cylinder with an elliptic base area.[61] Other size adjustments for BMC include use of lean tissue mass, etc. However, all of these methods are subject to error because there is no closed formula that defines the shape of the vertebrae. Similarly, although correction formulas have been proposed for the femur and the midradius,[54,62] they are also prone to error, because they cannot account for the marked changes in the size and shape of the bone during growth.

Inaccuracies in DXA values can also result from the unknown composition of the soft tissues adjacent to the bone being analyzed. Because corrections for soft tissues are based on a homogenous distribution of fat around the bone, changes in DXA measurements are observed if fat is distributed inhomogeneously around the bone measured. It has been calculated that inhomogeneous fat distribution in soft tissues, resulting in a difference of a 2-cm fat layer between soft tissue area and bone area, will influence DXA measurements by 10%.[63] While this is not of concern when studying subjects whose weight and body size remain constant, longitudinal DXA values in children are subject to considerable error, and measurements may reflect the changes in body size and composition that occur with growth more than true changes in BMD. This disadvantage especially limits the use of DXA in studies of children with eating disorders, such as obesity or anorexia nervosa.

QCT

QCT bone measurements can be obtained at any skeletal site with a standard clinical CT scanner using an external bone mineral reference phantom for calibration and specially developed software. The ability of QCT to assess both the volume and the density of bone in the axial and appendicular skeletons, without influence from body or skeletal size, is the major advantage of this modality when used in children. Unfortunately, CT scanners are expensive, large, nonportable machines that require costly maintenance and considerable technological expertise for proper function. Moreover, this equipment is usually located in the radiology department and is under constant clinical demand, creating a lack of accessibility. These disadvantages have partially been overcome by the recent development of smaller, mobile, less expensive peripheral QCT (pQCT) scanners designed exclusively for bone measurements. These smaller scanners, however, can only assess the bones of the appendicular skeleton; reference data of the distal radius are available for children.[64]

The radiation exposure from QCT measurements is related to the technique used and can be as low as 150 mrem (1.5 mSv) localized to the region of interest in the appendicular or axial skeleton. The total body equivalent dose of radiation is ~4–9 mrems (40–90 μSv), and this figure includes the radiation associated with screening digital radiographs used to localize the site of measurement.[57] This amount of radiation is far lower than that associated with other CT imaging procedures, accounting for the wide range of published figures for the radiation dose associated with CT measurements. It is also less than many other commonly used radiographic diagnostic tests.

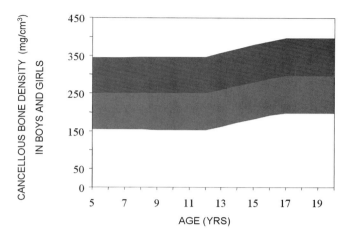

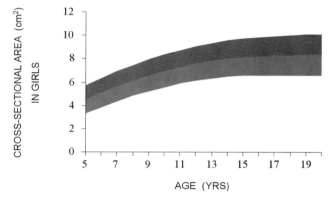

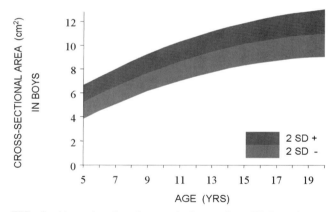

FIG. 3. Normative data for vertebral cancellous BMD and cross-sectional area in children and adolescents. Values for BMD are similar for boys and girls, whereas those for cross-sectional area differ.

In the axial skeleton, QCT has principally been used to determine cancellous bone density (mg/cm³) in the vertebral bodies, and less frequently, the dimensions of the vertebrae (Fig. 3). It should be noted that because the vertebrae of children contain proportionally more bone and less fat than that of elderly subjects, both the precision and accuracy of QCT cancellous BMD determinations in children are far better than those reported for adults. CVs for determinations of cancellous BMD, vertebral body height, and vertebral cross-sectional area have been calculated as 1.5%, 1.3%, and 0.8%, respectively.[31] Unfortunately, the cortical bone in the vertebral body is not thick enough to avoid inaccuracies associated with bone averaging errors.

In the appendicular skeleton, three bone parameters can be measured by QCT: the cross-sectional area (cm^2) of the bone, the cortical bone area (cm^2), and the cortical bone density.[65,66] To this effect, the outer and inner boundaries of the cortex are identified by specially developed software at the place of the maximum slope of the profile through the bone. The area within the outer cortical shell represents the cross-sectional area, whereas the area between the outer and inner shells represents the cortical bone area. The mean CT numbers of the pixels within the inner and outer cortical shells provide the average density of the bone. The CVs for repeated QCT measurements of cortical BMD, cortical bone area, and cross-sectional area of the femur range between 0.6% and 1.5%.[33,65,66] Unfortunately, the reproducibility of measurements of cancellous BMD is poor because of the large anatomical variability of the metaphysis of the long bone.

ENVIRONMENTAL AND HORMONAL INFLUENCE ON BONE ACCUMULATION DURING GROWTH

Physical Activity

The beneficial effects of exercise on bone mass are well documented through multiple observational and retrospective studies indicating that weight-bearing activities increase bone mass. Studies of prepubertal female gymnasts showed a larger cross-sectional area of the forearm, despite a shorter stature,[67] and that areal BMD values expressed as SD scores were significantly greater than zero (the predicted mean of the controls) in the arms, legs, and spine, all weight-bearing sites.[67] In other studies, children and adolescents who were physically active accrued more bone mineral than their sedentary peers,[2,68] and a more recent study showed that physical activity levels measured by accelerometry and parental report were positively associated with total body BMC and BMD measurements in preschool children.[69]

Studies comparing the effects of different physical exercises on bone indicated that high impact exercises resulted in the greatest increases in bone mass in adolescents.[70] Similarly, gymnasts had higher spine and femur BMD than swimmers or sedentary girls.[71] Amateur athletes involved in weight-bearing sports (rugby, soccer, endurance running, fighting sports, bodybuilding) had higher values for total body and legs BMD than amateur sportsmen involved in active loading activities (swimming, rowing).[72]

Several randomized trials involving weight-bearing activity interventions for bone mass gains have been conducted in children and adolescents.[73–77] Exercise session attendance ranged from 50% to 97%; exercise adherence is therefore a potentially serious threat to the internal validity of the results. However, the most recent studies showed very high rates of adherence. With one exception at 36+ months,[73] the duration of the interventions was 6–12 months. All studies reported significant changes in femoral BMD, and four studies indicated increases in lumbar spine BMD and BMC in the intervention groups.

Whether the beneficial effect of physical activity on the growing skeleton is maintained in adulthood is unknown, because no prospective study has been designed to address this question. However, the results of most, but not all, retrospective analyses indicate that, indeed, the enhancement of bone acquisition during growth because of exercise interventions may be long lasting. Lifetime tennis players, playing at a lower level of intensity then during youth, have remarkably higher forearm BMC than control subjects.[78] Retired soccer players have high BMD during the first 10–20 years after cessation of sport, but their BMD is lower compared with active players.[79]

Other studies suggest that BMD values are maintained at ~0.5–1.0 SD above the age-predicted mean in athletes who have been retired for 10–20 years.[67,80,81] Peri- and postmenopausal women who participated in sport activities during adolescence showed BMD measurements at the lumbar spine and femur that were remarkably higher than those of women who did not participate in physical activities during youth.[82] In a recent follow-up study of 27 years, lifetime physical activity was related to adult BMD, indicating the importance of continuing exercise after growth.[83] In contrast, a decrease in spinal BMD has been reported in runners who ceased exercising.[84] Similarly, cessation of exercise led to the return of BMD values to pretraining levels in 12 women who performed unilateral leg press for a year.[85]

Calcium Intake

The earliest data suggesting an influence of dietary calcium on PBM came from a study of two Croatian populations with substantially different calcium intakes.[86] The differences seen in bone mass were present at 30 years of age, suggesting that the effects of dietary calcium probably occurred during growth rather than in adulthood. Moreover, some epidemiological studies have shown an increased prevalence of osteoporosis in regions where dietary calcium intake is extremely low.[87]

The most convincing evidence that calcium consumption influences rates of bone mineral accrual rates comes from controlled supplementation trials in young healthy subjects. These studies showed that subjects given additional calcium for 1–3 years had greater gains than did controls.[88–93] Although bone size increased as a result of added dietary calcium in two studies,[83,92] the response to calcium varied with skeletal site, pretreatment calcium consumption, and pubertal stage. Greater bone mineral gains have been generally reported at cortical skeletal sites in prepubertal subjects and in girls whose habitual dietary intake was <850 mg/day.[92]

Whether short-term increases in bone mineral observed in these trials will translate into a clinically relevant reduction in osteoporosis risk is yet unknown. The magnitude of gains in BMC or BMD in most studies was modest (<5%). Moreover, the beneficial effect of calcium supplementation does not seem to last, and most studies reported that the benefits of intervention disappeared once the treatment was stopped. However, in other studies, the benefits persisted 12 months after discontinuation of supplement.[92]

Hormonal Status

The presence of low bone mass in patients with abnormal pubertal development shows the critical role that pubertal hormone changes have on mineral acquisition. Adult patients with hypogonadotropic hypogonadism commonly have low BMD values, resulting from inadequate bone mineral accrual during puberty.[94] Androgen receptors mediate the effects of testosterone in bone but their function is generally exerted after conversion to estrogen by a specific aromatase present in osteoblastic cells.[95] Thus, the more important sex steroid involved in skeletal maturation is estrogen.[96] Amenorrheic teens have lower lumbar BMD than girls with normal menses.[97] In addition, male patients with aromatase deficiency, or estrogen receptor defects resulting in complete resistance, have a phenotype that includes tall stature, normal secondary sexual characteristics, severe osteoporosis, and skeletal immaturity (delayed physeal closure), despite normal serum levels of testosterone.[98] Idiopathic delayed puberty has also been implicated as a cause of reduced peak bone mass.[99]

The effect that pregnancy and lactation have on bone acquisition in teenagers is yet to be fully defined. Normal pregnancy places a demand on calcium homeostasis, because the fetus and the placenta draw calcium from the maternal circulation to mineralize the fetal skeleton, and low BMD has been reported during pregnancy. Whether pregnancy during adolescence negatively influences BMD and PBM is the subject of great importance and is yet to be elucidated.

Reduced BMD is commonly seen in GH–deficient children who fail to acquire bone mineral at the expected rate.[100] Part of the bone mass deficit in these patients is caused by reduced bone size. Much of the GH action on bone is mediated through IGF-I, which functions as a bone trophic hormone that positively affects osteoblasts and stimulates collagen synthesis. In humans, IGF-I serum levels have been found to be positively correlated to bone size measured at the midshaft of the femur.[101]

CONCLUSION

Skeletal mass is accrued throughout childhood and adolescence and is largely determined by genetic and/or familial factors. A child's sex affects bone mass after puberty, while many ethnic differences seem to be present throughout growth. The influence of gonadal steroids is of major importance during puberty, while many factors such as other hormonal influences, physical activity type and intensity, and dietary calcium intake affect bone acquisition throughout growth. Bone mass measurements such as DXA and CT, while limited in some respects for pediatric applications, can be very important in assessing a child's skeletal status and growth.

REFERENCES

1. Trotter M, Hixon BB 1974 Sequential changes in weight, density, and percentage ash weight of human skeletons from an early fetal period through old age. Anat Rec **179:**1–18.
2. Bailey DA, McKay HA, Mirwald RL, Crocker PR, Faulkner RA 1999 A six-year longitudinal study of the relationship of physical activity to bone mineral accrual in growing children: The University of Saskatchewan bone mineral accrual study. J Bone Miner Res **14:**1672–1679.
3. Riggs BL, Wahner HW, Dunn WL, Mazess RB, Offord KP, Mellon LJ 1981 Differential changes in bone mineral density of the appendicular skeleton with aging. J Clin Invest **67:**328–335.
4. Mora S, Goodman WG, Loro ML, Roe TF, Sayre J, Gilsanz V 1994 Age-related changes in cortical and cancellous vertebral bone density in girls: Assessment with quantitative CT. AJR Am J Roentgenol **162:**405–409.
5. Gilsanz V, Gibbens DT, Carlson M, Boechat MI, Cann CE, Schulz EE 1988 Peak trabecular vertebral density: A comparison of adolescent and adult females. Calcif Tissue Int **43:**260–262.
6. Mauras N, Haymond MW, Darmaun D, Vieira NE, Abrams SA, Yergey A 1994 Calcium and protein kinetics in prepubertal boys—positive effects of testosterone. J Clin Invest **93:**1014–1019.
7. Theintz G, Buchs B, Rizzoli R, Slosman D, Clavien H, Sizonenko PC, Bonjour JP 1992 Longitudinal monitoring of bone mass accumulation in healthy adolescents: Evidence for a marked reduction after 16 years of age at the levels of lumbar spine and femoral neck in female subjects. J Clin Endocrinol Metab **75:**1060–1065.
8. Marcus R, Kosen J, Pfefferbaum A, Horning A 1983 Age-related loss of trabecular bone in premenopausal women: A biopsy study. Calcif Tiss Int **35:**406–409.
9. Mosekilde L 1989 Sex differences in age-related loss of vertebral trabecular bone mass and structure—biomechanical consequences. Bone **10:**425–432.
10. Halioua L, Anderson JJB 1990 Age and anthropometric determinants of radial bone mass in premenopausal Caucasian women: A cross-sectional study. Osteoporos Int **1:**50–55.
11. Gordon CL, Halton JM, Atkinson S, Webber CE 1991 The contributions of growth and puberty to peak bone mass. Growth Dev Aging **55:**257–262.
12. Recker RR, Davies KM, Hinders SM, Heaney RP, Stegman MR, Kimmel DB 1992 Bone gain in young adult women. J Am Med Assoc **268:**2403–2408.
13. Matkovic V, Jelic T, Wardlaw GM, Ilich JZ, Goel PK, Wright JK, Andon MB, Smith KT, Heaney RP 1994 Timing of peak bone mass in Caucasian females and its implication for the prevention of osteoporosis. J Clin Invest **93:**799–808.
14. Bonjour JP, Theintz G, Buchs B, Slosman B, Rizzoli R 1991 Critical years and stages of puberty for spinal and femoral bone mass accumulation during adolescence. J Clin Endocrinol Metab **73:**555–563.
15. Frost HM 1996 Bone development during childhood: Insights from a new paradigm. In: Schonau E (ed.) New Developments in Diagnostics and Therapy. Elsevier Science, Amsterdam, The Netherlands, pp. 3–39.
16. Frost HM 1997 Perspectives: Why do long distance runners not have more bone? A vital biomechanical explanation and an estrogen effect. J Bone Miner Metab **15:**9–16.
17. Zanchetta JR, Plotkin H, Alvarez-Figueira ML 1995 ztiBone mass in children: Normative values for the 2–20 year-old population. Bone **16**(Suppl):393–399.
18. Neu CM, Manz F, Rauch F, Merkel A, Schoenau E 2001 Bone densities and bone size at the distal radius in healthy children and adolescents: A study using peripheral quantitative computed tomography. Bone **28:**227–232.
19. Schoenau E, Neu MC, Manz F 2004 Muscle mass during childhood—relationship to skeletal development. J Musculoskelet Neuron Interact **4:**105–108.
20. Christian JC, Yu PL, Slemenda CW, Johnston CC 1989 Heritability of bone mass: A longitudinal study in ageing male twins. Am J Hum Genet **44:**429–433.
21. Pocock NA, Eisman JA, Hopper JL, Yeates MG, Sambrook PN, Ebert S 1991 Genetic determinants of bone mass in adults: A twin study. J Clin Invest **80:**706–710.
22. Seeman E, Hopper JL, Bach LA, Cooper ME, Parkinson E, McKay J, Jerums G 1989 Reduced bone mass in daughters of women with osteoporosis. N Engl J Med **320:**554–558.
23. Slemenda CW, Christian JC, Williams CJ, Norton JA, Johnston CC Jr 1991 Genetic determinants of bone mass in adult women: A reevaluation of the twin model and the potential importance of gene interaction on heritability estimates. J Bone Miner Res **6:**561–567.
24. Evans RA, Marel GH, Lancaster EK, Kos S, Evans M, Wong YP 1988 Bone mass is low in relatives of osteoporotic patients. Ann Intern Med **109:**870–873.
25. Ferrari SL, Rizzoli R, Slosman DO, Bonjour JP 1998 Do dietary calcium and age explain the controversy surrounding the relationship between bone mineral density and vitamin D receptor gene polymorphism? J Bone Miner Res **13:**363–370.
26. Ferrari SL, Rizzoli R, Manen D, Slosman DA, Bonjour JP 1998 Vitamin D receptor gene start codon polymorphisms (*Fok*I) and bone mineral density: Interaction with age, dietary calcium, and 3′-end region polymorphisms. J Bone Miner Res **13:**925–930.
27. Sainz J, Van Tornout JM, Loro ML, Sayre J, Roe TF, Gilsanz V 1997 Vitamin D receptor gene polymorphisms and bone density in prepubertal girls. N Engl J Med **337:**77–82.
28. Sainz J, Van Tornout JM, Sayre J, Kaufman F, Gilsanz V 1999 Association of collagen type 1 a1 gene polymorphism with bone density in early childhood. J Clin Endocrinol Metab **84:**853–855.
29. Gunnes M, Berg JP, Hasle J, Lehmann EH 1997 Lack of relationship between vitamin D receptor genotype and forearm bone gain in healthy children, adolescents, and young adults. J Clin Endocrinol Metab **82:**851–855.
30. Rizzoli R, Bonjour J-P, Ferrari SL 2001 Osteoporosis, genetics and hormones. J Molecul Endocrinol **26:**79–94.
31. Gilsanz V, Boechat MI, Roe TF, Loro ML, Sayre JW, Goodman WG 1994 Gender differences in vertebral body sizes in children and adolescents. Radiology **190:**673–677.
32. Gilsanz V, Boechat MI, Gilsanz R, Loro ML, Roe TF, Goodman WG 1994 Gender differences in vertebral sizes in adults: Biomechanical implications. Radiology **190:**678–682.
33. Gilsanz V, Kovanlikaya A, Costin G, Roe TF, Sayre J, Kaufman F 1997 Differential effect of gender on the size of the bones in the axial and appendicular skeletons. J Clin Endocrinol Metab **82:**1603–1607.
34. Van der Meulen MCH, Beaupre GS, Carter DR 1993 Mechanobiologic influences in long bone cross-sectional growth. Bone **14:**635–642.
35. Nguyen TV, Maynard LM, Towne B, Roche AF, Wisemandle W, Li J, Guo SS, Chumlea WC, Siervogel RM 2001 Sex differences in bone mass acquisition during growth. J Clin Densitom **4:**147–157.
36. Nelson DA, Simpson PM, Johnson CC, Barondness DA, Kleerekoper M 1997 The accumulation of whole body skeletal mass in third- and fourth-grade children: Effects of age, gender, ethnicity and body composition. Bone Miner **20:**73–78.
37. Bell NH, Shary J, Stevens J, Garza M, Gordon L, Edwards J 1991

Demonstration that bone mass is greater in black than in white children. J Bone Miner Res **6:**719–723.

38. Li JY, Specker BL, Ho ML, Tsang RC 1989 Bone mineral content in black and white children 1 to 6 years of age. Early appearance of race and sex differences. Am J Dis Child **143:**1346–1349.

39. Thomas KA, Cook SD, Bennett JT, Whitecloud TSHI, Rice JC 1991 Femoral neck and lumbar spine mineral densities in a normal population 3–20 years of age. J Pediatric Orthopad **11:**48–58.

40. Southard RN, Morris JD, Mahan JD, Hayes JR, Torch MA, Sommer A, Zipf WB 1991 Bone mass in healthy children: Measurements with quantitative DXA. Radiology **179:**735–738.

41. Bachrach LK, Hastie T, Wang MC, Balasubramanian N, Marcus R 1999 Bone mineral acquisition in healthy asian, hispanic, black, and caucasian youth: A longitudinal study. J Clin Endocrinol Metab **84:**4702–4712.

42. Prentice A, Laskey MA, Shaw J, Cole TJ, Fraser DR 1990 Bone mineral content of Gambian and British children aged 0–36 months. Bone Miner **10:**211–224.

43. Patel DN, Pettifor JM, Becker PJ, Grieve C, Leschner K 1992 The effect of ethnic group on appendicular bone mass in children. J Bone Miner Res **7:**263–272.

44. Gilsanz V, Skaggs DL, Kovanlikaya A, Sayre J, Loro ML, Kaufman F, Korenman SG 1998 Differential effect of race on the axial and appendicular skeletons of children. J Clin Endocrinol Metab **83:**1420–1427.

45. Kleerekoper M, Nelson DA, Flynn MJ, Pawluszka AS, Jacobsen G, Peterson EL 1994 Comparison of radiographic absorptiometry with dual energy x-ray absorptiometry and quantitative computed tomography in normal older white and black children. J Bone Miner Res **9:**1745–1750.

46. Ferrari S, Rizzoli R, Slosman D, Bonjour JP 1998 Familial resemblance for bone mineral mass is expressed before puberty. J Clin Endocrinol Metab **83:**358–361.

47. Loro ML, Sayre J, Roe TF, Goran MI, Kaufman FR, Gilsanz V 2000 Early identification of children predisposed to low peak bone mass and osteoporosis later in life. J Clin Endocrinol Metab **85:**3908–3918.

48. Koo WWK, Massom LR, Walters J 1995 Validation of accuracy and precision of dual energy x-ray absorptiometry for infants. J Bone Miner Res **10:**1111–1115.

49. Nelson DA, Koo WK 1995 Interpretation of bone mass measurements in the growing skeleton. Calcif Tissue Int **65:**1–3.

50. Braillon PM, Salle BL, Brunet J, Glorieux FH, Delmas PD, Meunier PJ 1992 Dual energy x-ray absorptiometry measurement of bone mineral content in newborns: Validation of the technique. Pediatr Res **32:**77–80.

51. Koo WW, Walters J, Bush AJ 1995 Technical considerations of dual-energy x-ray absorptiometry-based bone mineral measurements for pediatric subjects. J Bone Miner Res **10:**1998–2004.

52. Rupich RC, Specker BL, Lieuw-A-Fa M, Ho M 1996 Gender and race differences in bone mass during infancy. Calcif Tissue Int **58:**395–397.

53. Faulkner RA, Bailey DA, Drinkwater DT, McKay HA, Arnold C, Wilkinson AA 1996 Bone densitometry in canadian children. Calcif Tissue Int **59:**344–351.

54. Kröger H, Kotaniemi A, Vainio P, Alhava E 1992 Bone densitometry of the spine and femur in children by dual-energy x-ray absorptiometry. Bone Miner **17:**75–85.

55. Zanchetta JR, Plotkin H, Alvarez-Filgueira ML 1995 Bone mass in children: Normative values for the 2–20-year-old population. Bone **14:**3S–399S.

56. Katzman DK, Bachrach LK, Carter DR, Marcus R 1991 Clinical and anthropometric correlates of bone mineral acquisition in healthy adolescent girls. J Clin Endocrinol Metab **73:**1332–1339.

57. Kalender WA 1992 Effective dose values in bone mineral measurements by photon absorptiometry and computed tomography. Osteoporos Int **2:**82–87.

58. Carter DR, Bouxsein ML, Marcus R 1992 New approaches for interpreting projected bone densitometry data. J Bone Miner Res **7:**137–145.

59. Jergas M, Breitenseher M, Gluer CC, Genant HK 1995 Estimates of volumetric bone density from projectional measurements improve the discriminatory capability of dual x-ray absorptiometry. J Bone Miner Res **10:**1101–1110.

60. Salle BL, Braillon P, Glorieux FG, Brunet J, Cavero E, Meunier PJ 1992 Lumbar bone mineral content measured by dual energy X-ray absorptiometry in newborns and infants. Acta Paediatr **81:**953–958.

61. Peel NFA, Eastell R 1994 Diagnostic value of estimated volumetric bone mineral density of the lummbar spine in osteoporosis. J Bone Miner Res **9:**317–320.

62. Lu PW, Cowell CT, Lloyd-Jones SA, Briody JN, Howman-Giles R 1996 Volumetric bone mineral density in normal subjects, aged 5–27 years. J Clin Endocrinol Metab **81:**1586–1590.

63. Hangartner TN 1990 Influence of fat on bone measurements with dual-energy absorptiometry. Bone Miner **9:**71–78.

64. Rauch F, Schoenau E 2005 Peripheral quantitative computed tomography of the distal radius in young subjects—new reference data and interpretation of results. J Musculoskelet Neuronal Interact **5:**119–126.

65. Hangartner TN, Gilsanz V 1996 Evaluation of cortical bone by computed tomography. J Bone Miner Res **11:**1518–1525.

66. Kovanlikaya A, Loro ML, Hangartner TN, Reynolds RA, Roe TF, Gilsanz V 1996 Osteopenia in children: CT assessment. Radiology **198:**781–784.

67. Bass S, Pearce G, Bradney M, Hendrich E, Delmas PD, Harding A, Seeman E 1998 Exercise before puberty may confer residual benefits in bone density in adulthood: Studies in active prepubertal and retired female gymnasts. J Bone Miner Res **13:**500–507.

68. Cooper C, Cawley M, Bhalla A, Egger P, Ring F, Morton L, Barker D 1995 Childhood growth, physical activity, and peak bone mass in women. J Bone Miner Res **10:**940–947.

69. Janz KF, Burns TL, Torner JC, Levy SM, Paulos R, Willing MC, Warren JJ 2001 Physical activity and bone measures in young children: The Iowa bone development study. Pediatrics **107:**1387–1393.

70. Lima F, DeFalco V, Baima J, Carazzato JG, Pereira RM 2001 Effect of impact load and active load on bone metabolism and body composition of adolescent athletes. Med Sci Sports Exerc **33:**1318–1323.

71. Courteix D, Lespessailles E, Peres SL, Obert P, Germain P, Benhamou CL 1998 Effect of physical training on bone mineral density in prepubertal girls: A comparative study between impact-loading and non-impact-loading sports. Osteoporos Int **8:**152–158.

72. Morel J, Combe B, Francisco J, Bernard J 2001 Bone mineral density of 704 amateur sportsmen involved in different physical activities. Osteoporos Int **12:**152–157.

73. Sundberg M, Gardsell P, Johnell O, Karlsson MK, Ornstein E, Sandstedt B, Sernbo I 2001 Peripubertal moderate exercise increases bone mass in boys but not in girls: A population-based intervention study. Osteoporos Int **12:**230–238.

74. Petit MA, McKay HA, MacKelvie KJ, Heinonen A, Khan KM, Beck TJ 2002 A randomized school-based jumping intervention confers site and maturity specific benefits on bone structural properties in girls: A hip structural analysis study. J Bone Miner Res **17:**363–372.

75. Fuchs RK, Buauer JJ, Snow CM 2001 Jumping improves hip and lumbar spine bone mass in prepubescent children: A randomized controlled trial. J Bone Miner Res **16:**148–156.

76. Bradney M, Pearce G, Naughton G, Sullivan C, Bass S, Beck T, Carlson J, Seeman E 1998 Moderate exercise during growth in prepubertal boys: Changes in bone mass, size, volumetric density, and bone strength: A controlled prospective study. J Bone Miner Res **13:**1814–1821.

77. Binkley T, Specker B 2004 Increased periosteal circumference remains present 12 months after as exercise intervention in preschool children. Bone **35:**1383–1388.

78. Huddleston AL, Rockwell D, Kulund DN, Harrison RB 1980 Bone mass in lifetime tennis athletes. JAMA **244:**1107–1109.

79. Karlsson MK, Linden C, Karlsson C, Johnell O, Obrant K, Seeman E 2000 Exercise during growth and bone mineral density and fractures in old age. Lancet **355:**469–470.

80. Khan KM, Grren RM, Saul A, Bennell KL, Crichton KJ, Hopper JL 1996 Retired elite female ballet dancers and nonathletic controls have similar bone mineral density at weight bearing sites. J Bon Miner Res **11:**1566–1574.

81. Etherington J, Harris PA, Nandra D, Hart DJ, Wolman RL, Doyle DV, Spector TD 1996 The effect of weight-bearing exercise on bone mineral density: A study of female ex-elite athletes and the general population. J Bone Miner Res **11:**1333–1338.

82. Puntila E, Kroger H, Lakke T, Honkanen R, Tupperainen M 1997 1997 Physical activity in adolescence and bone density in peri- and postmenopausal women: A population based study. Bone **21:**363–367.

83. Delvaux K, Lefevre J, Philippaerts R, Dequeker J, Thomis M, Vanreusel B, Claessens A, Eynde BV, Beunen G, Lysens R 2001 Bone mass and lifetime physical activity in Flemish males: A 27 year follow-up study. Med Sci Sports Exerc **33:**1868–1875.

84. Michel BA, Lane NE, Bjorkengren A, Bloch DA, Fries JF 1992 Impact of running on lumbar bone density: A 5-year longitudinal study. J Rheumatol **19:**1759–1763.

85. Vuori I, Heinonen A, Sievanan H, Kannus P, Pasanen M, Oja P 1994 Effect of unilateral strength training and detraining on bone mineral density and content in young women: A study of mechanical loading and deloading on human bones. Calcif Tissue Int **55:**59–67.

86. Matkovic V, Kostial K, Simonovic I, Buzinz R, Brodarec A, Nordin BE 1979 Bone status and fracture rates in two regions of Yugoslavia. Am J Clin Nutr **32:**540–549.

87. Heaney RP 1992 Calcium in the prevention and treatment of osteoporosis. J Intern Med **231:**169–180.

88. Lee WTK, Leung SSF, Leung DM, Cheng JC 1996 A follow-up study on the effects of calcium-supplement withdrawal and puberty on bone acquisition in children. Am J Clin Nutr **64:**71–77.
89. Lloyd T, Andon MB, Rollings N, Martel JK, Landis JR, Demers LM, Eggli DF, Kieselhorst K, Kulin HE 1993 Calcium supplementation and bone mineral density in adolescent girls. JAMA **270:**841–844.
90. Johnston CC Jr, Miller JZ, Slemenda CW, Reister TK, Hui S, Christian JC, Peacock M 1992 Calcium supplementation and increases in bone mineral density in children. N Engl J Med **327:**82–87.
91. Chan GM, Hoffman K, McMurry M 1995 Effects of dairy products on bone and body composition in pubertal girls. J Pediatr **126:**551–556.
92. Bonjour JP, Carrie AL, Ferrari S, Clavien H, Slosman D, Theintz G, Rizzoli 1997 Calcium-enriched foods and bone mass growth in prepubertal girls: A randomized double blind, placebo-controlled trial. J Clin Invest **99:**1287–1294.
93. Nowson CA, Green RM, Hopper JL, Sherwin AJ, Young D, Kaymakci B, Guest CS, Smid M, Larkins RG, Wark J 1997 A co-twin study of the effect of calcium supplementation on bone density during adolescence. Osetoporos Int **7:**219–225.
94. Finkelstein JS, Klibanski A, Neer RM, Greenspan SL, Rosenthal DI, Crowley WF Jr 1987 Osteoporosis in men with idiopathic hypogonadotropic hypogonadism. Ann Intern Med **106:**354–361.
95. Abu EO, Horner A, Kusec V, Triffitt JT, Compston JE 1997 The localization of androgen receptors in human bone. J Clin Endocrinol Metab **82:**3493–3497.
96. Frank GR 1995 The role of estrogen in pubertal skeletal physiology: Epiphyseal maturation and mineralization of the skeleton. Acta Paediatr **84:**627–630.
97. Hergenroeder AC 1995 Bone mineralization, hypothalamic amenorrhea, and sex steroid therapy in female adolescents and young adults. J Pediatr **126:**683–689.
98. Carani C, Qin K, Simoni M, Faustini-Fustini M, Serpente S, Boyd J, Korach KS, Simpson ER 1997 Effect of testosterone and estradiol in a man with aromatase deficiency. N Engl J Med **337:**91–95.
99. Finkelstein JS, Klibanski A, Neer RM 1996 A longitudinal evaluation of bone mineral density in adult men with histories of delayed puberty. J Clin Endocrinol Metab **81:**1152–1155.
100. Baroncelli GI, Bertelloni S, Ceccarelli C, Saggese G 1998 Measurement of volumetric bone mineral density accurately determines degree of lumbar undermineralization in children with growth hormone deficiency. J Clin Endocrinol Metab **83:**3150–3154.
101. Mora S, Pitukcheewanont P, Nelson JC, Gilsanz V 1999 Serum levels of insulin-like growth factor-I and the density, volume and cross-sectional area of bone in children. J Clin Endocrinol Metab **84:**2780–2783.

Chapter 10. Skeletal Physiology: Pregnancy and Lactation

Christopher S. Kovacs[1] and Henry M. Kronenberg[2]

[1]Faculty of Medicine-Endocrinology, Health Sciences Centre, Memorial University of Newfoundland, St. John's, Newfoundland, Canada; and [2]Endocrine Unit, Massachusetts General Hospital and Harvard Medical School, Boston, Massachusetts

INTRODUCTION

Normal pregnancy places a demand on the calcium homeostatic mechanisms of the human female, because the fetus and placenta draw calcium from the maternal circulation to mineralize the fetal skeleton. Similar demands are placed on the lactating woman, to supply sufficient calcium to the breast milk and enable continued skeletal growth in a nursing infant. Despite a similar magnitude of calcium demand presented to pregnant and lactating women, the adjustments made in each of these reproductive periods differ significantly (Fig. 1). These hormone-mediated adjustments normally satisfy the daily calcium needs of the fetus and infant without long-term consequences to the maternal skeleton. Detailed references on this subject are available in two comprehensive reviews.[1,2]

PREGNANCY

In total, the developing fetal skeleton gains up to 33 g of calcium, and ~80% of the accretion occurs during the third trimester when the fetal skeleton is rapidly mineralizing. This calcium demand seems to be largely met by a doubling of maternal intestinal calcium absorption, mediated by 1,25-dihydroxyvitamin D and other factors.

Mineral Ions and Calciotropic Hormones

Normal pregnancy results in altered levels of calcium and the calciotropic hormones as schematically depicted in Fig. 2.[1] The total serum calcium falls early in pregnancy because of a fall in the serum albumin. This decrease should not be mistaken for true hypocalcemia, because the ionized calcium (the physiologically important fraction) remains constant. Serum phosphate levels are also normal during pregnancy.

The serum PTH level, when measured with a two-site immunoradiometric assay, falls to the low-normal range (i.e., 10–30% of the mean nonpregnant value) during the first trimester, but increases steadily to the midnormal range by term. Total 1,25-dihydroxyvitamin D levels double early in pregnancy and maintain this increase until term; free 1,25-dihydroxyvitamin D levels are increased from the third trimester and possibly earlier. The rise in 1,25-dihydroxyvitamin D may be largely independent of changes in PTH, because PTH levels are typically decreasing at the time of the increase in 1,25-dihydroxyvitamin D. The maternal kidneys likely account for most, if not all, of the rise in 1,25-dihydroxyvitamin D during pregnancy, although the decidua, placenta, and fetal kidneys may contribute a small amount. The relative contribution of the maternal kidneys is based on several lines of evidence,[1] including the report of an anephric woman on hemodialysis who had low 1,25-dihydroxyvitamin D levels before and during a pregnancy. The renal 1α-hydroxylase is upregulated in response to factors such as PTH-related protein (PTHrP), estradiol, prolactin, and placental lactogen. Serum calcitonin levels are also increased during pregnancy.

PTHrP levels are increased during pregnancy, as determined by assays that detect PTHrP fragments encompassing amino acids 1–86. Because PTHrP is produced by many tissues in the fetus and mother (including the placenta, amnion, decidua, umbilical cord, fetal parathyroids, and breast), it is not clear which source(s) contribute to the rise detected in the maternal circulation. PTHrP may contribute to the elevations in 1,25-dihydroxyvitamin D and suppression of PTH that are noted during pregnancy. PTHrP may have other roles during pregnancy, such as regulating placental calcium transport in the fetus.[1,3] Also, PTHrP may have a role in protecting the maternal skeleton during pregnancy, because the carboxy-terminal

The authors have reported no conflicts of interest.

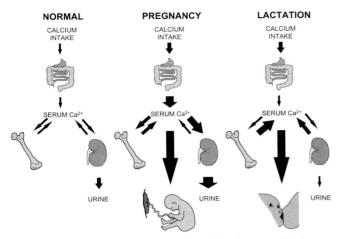

FIG. 1. Schematic illustration contrasting calcium homeostasis in human pregnancy and lactation compared with normal. The thickness of arrows indicates a relative increase or decrease with respect to the normal and nonpregnant state. (Modified with permission of The Endocrine Society from Kovacs CS, Kronenberg HM 1997 Maternal-fetal calcium and bone metabolism during pregnancy, puerperium and lactation. Endocr Rev **18:** 832–872. Copyright 1997, The Endocrine Society.)

portion of PTHrP (osteostatin) has been shown to inhibit osteoclastic bone resorption.[4]

Pregnancy induces significant changes in the levels of other hormones, including the sex steroids, prolactin, placental lactogen, and IGF-1. Each of these may have direct or indirect effects on calcium and bone metabolism during pregnancy, but these issues have been largely unexplored.

Intestinal Absorption of Calcium

Intestinal absorption of calcium is doubled during pregnancy from as early as 12 weeks of gestation (the earliest time-point studied); this seems to be a major maternal adaptation to meet the fetal need for calcium. This increase may be largely the result of a 1,25-dihydroxyvitamin D–mediated increase in intestinal calbindin$_{9K}$-D and other proteins; prolactin and placental lactogen (and possibly other factors) may also mediate part of the increase in intestinal calcium absorption. The increased absorption of calcium early in pregnancy may allow the maternal skeleton to store calcium in advance of the peak fetal demands that occur later in pregnancy.

Renal Handling of Calcium

The 24-h urine calcium excretion is increased as early as the 12th week of gestation (the earliest time-point studied), and the amounted excreted may exceed the normal range. The elevated calcitonin levels of pregnancy might also promote renal calcium excretion. Because fasting urine calcium values are normal or low, the increase in 24-h urine calcium likely reflects the increased intestinal absorption of calcium (absorptive hypercalciuria).

Skeletal Calcium Metabolism

Animal models indicate that histomorphometric parameters of bone turnover are increased during pregnancy and that BMC may increase; however, comparable histomorphometric data are not available for human pregnancy. In one study,[5] 15 women who electively terminated a pregnancy in the first trimester (8–10 weeks) had bone biopsy evidence of increased bone resorption, including increased resorption surface and increased numbers of resorption cavities. These findings were

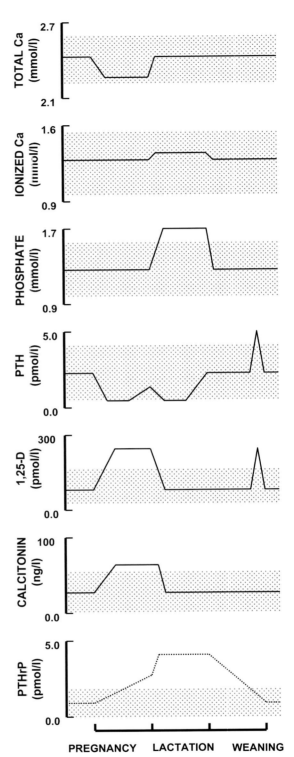

FIG. 2. Schematic illustration of the longitudinal changes in calcium, phosphate, and calciotropic hormone levels that occur during pregnancy and lactation. Normal adult ranges are indicated by the shaded areas. The progression in PTHrP levels has been depicted by a dashed line to reflect that the data are less complete; the implied comparison of PTHrP levels in late pregnancy and lactation are uncertain extrapolations because no reports followed patients serially. In both situations, PTHrP levels are elevated. (Adapted with permission of The Endocrine Society from Kovacs CS, Kronenberg HM 1997 Maternal-fetal calcium and bone metabolism during pregnancy, puerperium, and lactation. Endocr Rev **18:**832–872. Copyright 1997, The Endocrine Society.)

not present in biopsy specimens obtained from nonpregnant controls or in biopsy specimens obtained at term from 13 women who had elective cesarian-sections.

Most human studies of skeletal calcium metabolism in pregnancy have examined changes in serum markers of bone formation and urine markers of bone resorption. These studies are fraught with a number of confounding variables, including lack of prepregnancy baseline values; effects of hemodilution in pregnancy on serum markers; increased glomular filtration rate (GFR); altered creatinine excretion; placental, uterine, and fetal contribution to the levels of markers in blood; degradation and clearance by the placenta; and lack of diurnally timed or fasted specimens. Given these limitations, many studies have reported that urinary markers of bone resorption (24-h collection) are increased from early to mid-pregnancy (including deoxypyridinoline, pyridinoline, and hydroxyproline). Conversely, serum markers of bone formation (generally not corrected for hemodilution or increased GFR) are often decreased from prepregnancy or nonpregnant values in early or mid-pregnancy, rising to normal or above before term (including osteocalcin, procollagen I carboxypeptides, and bone-specific alkaline phosphatase). It is conceivable that the bone formation markers are artifactually lowered by normal hemodilution and increased renal clearance of pregnancy, obscuring any real increase in the level of the markers. Total alkaline phosphatase rises early in pregnancy due largely to contributions from the placental fraction; it is not a useful marker of bone formation in pregnancy.

Based on the scant bone biopsy data and the measurements of bone markers (with aforementioned confounding factors), one may cautiously conclude that bone resorption is increased in pregnancy from as early as the 10th week of gestation. There is comparatively little maternal–fetal calcium transfer occurring at this stage of pregnancy compared with the peak rate of calcium transfer in the third trimester. One might have anticipated that markers of bone resorption would increase particularly in the third trimester, but in fact, no marked increase is seen at that time.

Changes in skeletal calcium content have been assessed through the use of sequential BMD studies during pregnancy. Because of concerns about fetal radiation exposure, few such studies have been done. Such studies are confounded by the changes in body composition and weight during normal pregnancy that can lead to artifactual changes in the BMD reading obtained. Using single and/or dual-photon absorptiometry (SPA/DPA), several prospective studies did not find a significant change in cortical or trabecular BMD during pregnancy.[1] Several recent studies have used DXA before conception (range, 1–8 months prior, but not always stated) and after delivery (range, 1–6 weeks postpartum).[2] Most studies involved 16 or fewer subjects. One study found no change in lumbar spine BMD measurements obtained preconception and within 1–2 weeks after delivery, whereas the other studies reported decreases of 4–5% in lumbar spine BMD, with the postpartum measurement taken between 1 and 6 weeks after delivery. Because the puerperium is associated with BMD losses of 1–3% per month, it is possible that obtaining the second measurement 2–6 weeks after delivery contributed to the bone loss documented in many of the studies. Other longitudinal studies have found a progressive decrease during pregnancy in indices thought to correlate with BMD, as determined by ultrasonographic measurements at another peripheral site, the os calcis. None of all the aforementioned studies can address the question as to whether skeletal calcium content is increased early in pregnancy in advance of the third trimester. Further studies, with larger numbers of patients, will be needed to clarify the extent of bone loss during pregnancy.

It seems certain that any acute changes in bone metabolism during pregnancy do not cause long-term changes in skeletal calcium content or strength. Numerous studies of osteoporotic or osteopenic women have failed to find a significant association of parity with BMD or fracture risk.[1,6] Although many of these studies could not separate out the effects of parity from those of lactation, it may be reasonable to conclude that if parity has any effect on BMD or fracture risk later in life, it must be only a very modest effect.

Osteoporosis in Pregnancy

Occasionally, a woman may present with fragility fractures and low BMD during or shortly after pregnancy; the possibility that the woman had low BMD before pregnancy cannot be excluded. Some women may experience excessive resorption of calcium from the skeleton because of changes in mineral metabolism induced by pregnancy and other factors such as low dietary calcium intake and vitamin D insufficiency. The apparently increased rate of bone resorption in pregnancy may contribute to fracture risk, because a high rate of bone turnover is an independent risk factor for fragility fractures outside of pregnancy. Therefore, fragility fractures in pregnancy or the puerperium may be a consequence of preexisting low BMD and increased bone resorption, among other possible factors. During lactation, additional changes in mineral metabolism occur that may further increase fracture risk in some women.

Focal, transient osteoporosis of the hip is a rare, self-limited form of pregnancy-associated osteoporosis. It is probably not a manifestation of altered calciotropic hormone levels or mineral balance during pregnancy, but rather might be a consequence of local factors. The theories proposed to explain the condition include femoral venous stasis caused by the gravid uterus, reflex sympathetic dystrophy, ischemia, trauma, viral infections, marrow hypertrophy, immobilization, and fetal pressure on the obturator nerve. These patients present with unilateral or bilateral hip pain, limp, and/or hip fracture in the third trimester. There is objective evidence of reduced BMD of the symptomatic femoral head and neck, which has been shown by MRI to be the consequence of increased water content of the femoral head and the marrow cavity; a joint effusion may also be present. The symptoms and the radiological appearance usually resolve within 2–6 months postpartum.

Primary Hyperparathyroidism

Although probably a rare condition (there are no data available on its prevalence), primary hyperparathyroidism in pregnancy has been associated in the literature with an alarming rate of adverse outcomes in the fetus and neonate, including a 30% rate of spontaneous abortion or stillbirth. The adverse postnatal outcomes are thought to result from suppression of the fetal and neonatal parathyroid glands; this suppression may occasionally be prolonged after birth for months. To prevent these adverse outcomes, surgical correction of primary hyperparathyroidism during the second trimester has been almost universally recommended. Several case series have found elective surgery to be well tolerated and to dramatically reduce the rate of adverse events compared with the earlier cases reported in the literature. Many of the women in those early cases had a relatively severe form of primary hyperparathyroidism that is not often seen today (symptomatic with nephrocalcinosis and renal insufficiency). While mild, asymptomatic primary hyperparathyroidism during pregnancy has been followed conservatively with successful outcomes, complications continue to occur; therefore, in the absence of definitive data, surgery during the second trimester remains the most common recommendation.[7]

Familial Hypocalciuric Hypercalcemia

Although familial hypocalciuric hypercalcemia (FHH) has not been reported to adversely affect the mother during pregnancy, maternal hypercalcemia can cause fetal and neonatal parathyroid suppression with subsequent tetany.

Hypoparathyroidism and Pseudohypoparathyroidism

Early in pregnancy, hypoparathyroid women may have fewer hypocalcemic symptoms and require less supplemental calcium. This is consistent with a limited role for PTH in the pregnant woman and suggests that an increase in 1,25-dihydroxyvitamin D and/or increased intestinal calcium absorption will occur in the absence of PTH. However, it is clear from other case reports that some pregnant hypoparathyroid women may require increased calcitriol replacement to avoid worsening hypocalcemia. It is important to maintain a normal ionized calcium level in pregnant women because maternal hypocalcemia has been associated with the development of intrauterine fetal hyperparathyroidism and fetal death. Levels of ionized calcium rather than that of total calcium should be followed, because of the fall of serum albumin during pregnancy. Late in pregnancy, hypercalcemia may occur in hypoparathyroid women unless the calcitriol dosage is substantially reduced or discontinued. This effect may be mediated by the increasing levels of PTHrP in the maternal circulation in late pregnancy.

In limited case reports of pseudohypoparathyroidism, pregnancy has been noted to normalize the serum calcium level, reduce the PTH level by one-half, and increase the 1,25-dihydroxyvitamin D level 2- to 3-fold.[8] The mechanism by which these changes occur despite pseudohypoparathyroidism remains unclear.

LACTATION

The typical daily loss of calcium in breast milk has been estimated to range from 280 to 400 mg, although daily losses as great as 1000 mg calcium have been reported. A temporary demineralization of the skeleton seems to be the main mechanism by which lactating humans meet these calcium requirements. This demineralization does not seem to be mediated by PTH or 1,25-dihydroxyvitamin D, but may be mediated by PTHrP in the setting of a fall in estrogen levels.

Mineral Ions and Calciotropic Hormones

The normal lactational changes in maternal calcium, phosphate, and calciotropic hormone levels are schematically depicted in Fig. 2.[1] The mean ionized calcium level of exclusively lactating women is increased, although it remains within the normal range. Serum phosphate levels are also higher during lactation, and the level may exceed the normal range. Because reabsorption of phosphate by the kidneys seems to be increased, the increased serum phosphate levels may, therefore, reflect the combined effects of increased flux of phosphate into the blood from diet and from skeletal resorption in the setting of decreased renal phosphate excretion.

Intact PTH, as determined by a two-site immunoradiometric assay (IRMA) assay, has been found to be reduced 50% or more during the first several months of lactation. It rises to normal at weaning, but may rise above normal after weaning. In contrast to the high 1,25-dihydroxyvitamin D levels of pregnancy, maternal free and bound 1,25-dihydroxyvitamin D levels fall to normal within days of parturition and remain there throughout lactation. Calcitonin levels fall to normal after the first 6 weeks postpartum. Mice lacking the calcitonin gene lose twice the normal amount of BMC during lactation, which indicates that physiological levels of calcitonin may protect the maternal skeleton from excessive resorption during this time

period.[9,10] Whether calcitonin plays a similar role in human physiology is unknown.

PTHrP levels, as measured by two-site IRMA assays, are significantly higher in lactating women than in nonpregnant controls. The source of PTHrP may be the breast, because PTHrP has been detected in breast milk at concentrations exceeding 10,000 times the level found in the blood of patients with hypercalcemia of malignancy or normal human controls. Furthermore, lactating mice with the *PTHrP* gene ablated only from mammary tissue have lower blood levels of PTHrP than control lactating mice.[11] Studies in animals suggest that PTHrP may regulate mammary development and blood flow and the calcium content of milk. In addition, PTHrP reaching the maternal circulation from the lactating breast may cause resorption of calcium from the maternal skeleton, renal tubular reabsorption of calcium, and (indirectly) suppression of PTH. In support of this hypothesis, deletion of the *PTHrP* gene from mammary tissue at the onset of lactation resulted in more modest losses of BMC during lactation in mice.[11] In humans, PTHrP levels correlate with the amount of BMD lost, negatively with PTH levels, and positively with the ionized calcium levels of lactating women.[12–14] Furthermore, observations in aparathyroid women provide evidence of the impact of PTHrP in calcium homeostasis during lactation (see below).

Intestinal Absorption of Calcium

Intestinal calcium absorption decreases to the nonpregnant rate from the increased rate of pregnancy. This corresponds to the fall in 1,25-dihydroxyvitamin D levels to normal.

Renal Handling of Calcium

In humans, the glomerular filtration rate falls during lactation, and the renal excretion of calcium is typically reduced to levels as low as 50 mg/24 h. This suggests that the tubular reabsorption of calcium must be increased to account for reduced calcium excretion in the setting of increased serum calcium.

Skeletal Calcium Metabolism

Histomorphometric data from animals consistently show increased bone turnover during lactation, and losses of 35% or more of bone mineral are achieved during 2–3 weeks of normal lactation in the rat.[1] Comparative histomorphometric data are lacking for humans, and in place of that, serum markers of bone formation and urinary markers of bone resorption have been assessed in numerous cross-sectional and prospective studies of lactation. Some of the confounding factors discussed with respect to pregnancy apply to the use of these markers in lactating women. In this instance, the GFR is reduced, and the intravascular volume is contracted. Urinary markers of bone resorption (24-h collection) have been reported to be elevated 2- to 3-fold during lactation and are higher than the levels attained in the third trimester. Serum markers of bone formation (not adjusted for hemoconcentration or reduced GFR) are generally high during lactation and increased over the levels attained during the third trimester. Total alkaline phosphatase falls immediately postpartum because of loss of the placental fraction, but may still remain above normal because of the elevation in the bone-specific fraction. Despite the confounding variables, these findings suggest that bone turnover is significantly increased during lactation.

Serial measurements of BMD during lactation (by SPA, DPA, or DXA) have shown a fall of 3–10.0% in BMC after 2–6 months of lactation at trabecular sites (lumbar spine, hip, femur, and distal radius), with smaller losses at cortical sites.[1,6] The loss occurs at a peak rate of 1–3% per month, far

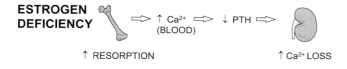

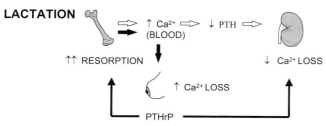

FIG. 3. Acute estrogen deficiency (e.g., GnRH analog therapy) increases skeletal resorption and raises the blood calcium; in turn, PTH is suppressed and renal calcium losses are increased. During lactation, the combined effects of PTHrP (secreted by the breast) and estrogen deficiency increase skeletal resorption, reduce renal calcium losses, and raise the blood calcium, but calcium is directed into breast milk. (Reprinted with permission of The Endocrine Society from Kovacs CS, Kronenberg HM 1997 Maternal-fetal calcium and bone metabolism during pregnancy, puerperium and lactation. Endocr Rev **18:**832–872. Copyright 1997, The Endocrine Society.)

exceeding the rate of 1–3% per year that can occur in women with postmenopausal osteoporosis who are considered to be losing bone rapidly. Loss of bone mineral from the maternal skeleton seems to be a normal consequence of lactation and may not be preventable by raising the calcium intake above the recommended dietary allowance. Several studies have shown that calcium supplementation does not significantly reduce the amount of bone lost during lactation.[15–18] Not surprisingly, the lactational decrease in BMD correlates with the amount of calcium lost in the breast milk.[19]

The mechanisms controlling the rapid loss of skeletal calcium content are not well understood. The reduced estrogen levels of lactation are clearly important but are unlikely to be the sole explanation. To estimate the effects of estrogen deficiency during lactation, it is worth noting the alterations in calcium and bone metabolism that occur in reproductive age women who have estrogen deficiency induced by gonadotropin-releasing hormone (GnRH) agonist therapy for endometriosis and other conditions. Six months of acute estrogen deficiency induced by GnRH agonist therapy leads to 1–4% losses in trabecular (but not cortical) BMD, increased urinary calcium excretion, and suppression of 1,25-dihydroxyvitamin D and PTH levels.[1] In lactation, women are not as estrogen deficient but lose more BMD (at both trabecular and cortical sites), have normal (as opposed to low) 1,25-dihydroxyvitamin D levels, and have reduced (as opposed to increased) urinary calcium excretion. The difference between isolated estrogen deficiency and lactation may be caused by the effects of other factors (such as PTHrP) that add to the effects of estrogen withdrawal in lactation (Fig. 3).

The BMD losses of lactation seem to be substantially reversed during weaning.[1,6,16] This corresponds to a gain in BMD of 0.5–2% per month in the woman who has weaned her infant. The mechanism for this restoration of BMD is uncertain and largely unexplored. In the long term, the consequences of lactation-induced depletion of bone mineral seem clinically unimportant. The vast majority of epidemiologic studies of pre- and postmenopausal women have found no adverse effect of a history of lactation on peak bone mass, BMD, or hip fracture risk.

Osteoporosis of Lactation

Rarely, a woman will suffer a fragility fracture during lactation, and osteoporotic readings will be confirmed by DXA. Like osteoporosis in pregnancy, this may represent a coincidental, unrelated disease; the woman may have had low BMD before conception. Alternatively, some cases might represent an exacerbation of the normal degree of skeletal demineralization that occurs during lactation and a continuum from changes in BMD and bone turnover that may have occurred during pregnancy. For example, excessive PTHrP release from the lactating breast into the maternal circulation could cause excessive bone resorption, osteoporosis, and fractures in some of these cases. PTHrP levels were high in one case of lactational osteoporosis and were found to remain elevated for months after weaning.[20]

Hypoparathyroidism and Pseudohypoparathyroidism

Levels of calcitriol/calcium supplementation required for treatment of hypoparathyroid women fall early in the postpartum period, especially if the woman breastfeeds, and hypercalcemia may occur if the calcitriol dosage is not substantially reduced.[21] As observed in one recent case, this is consistent with PTHrP reaching the maternal circulation in amounts sufficient to allow stimulation of 1,25-dihydroxyvitamin D synthesis and maintenance of normal (or slightly increased) maternal serum calcium.[22]

The management of pseudohypoparathyroidism has been less well documented. Because these patients are likely resistant to the renal actions of PTHrP and the placental sources of 1,25-dihydroxyvitamin D are lost at parturition, the calcitriol requirements might well increase and may require further adjustments during lactation.

IMPLICATIONS

In both pregnancy and lactation, novel regulatory systems specific to these settings complement the usual regulators of calcium homeostasis. The studies of pregnant women suggest that the fetal calcium demand is met in large part by intestinal calcium absorption, which more than doubles from early in pregnancy, correlating with the increase in 1,25-dihydroxyvitamin D. The studies of biochemical markers of bone turnover, DXA, and ultrasound are not conclusive, but are compatible with the possibility that the maternal skeleton does contribute calcium to the developing fetus. In comparison, the studies in lactating women suggest that skeletal calcium resorption is a dominant mechanism by which calcium is supplied to the breast milk, whereas renal calcium conservation is also apparent. These changes seem to be driven by PTHrP in association with estrogen deficiency. These observations indicate that the maternal adaptations to pregnancy and lactation have evolved differently over time, such that dietary calcium absorption dominates in pregnancy, whereas the temporary borrowing of calcium from the skeleton seems to dominate during lactation. Lactation seems to program an obligatory skeletal calcium loss irrespective of maternal calcium intake, but the calcium is completely restored to the skeleton after weaning. The rapidity of calcium loss and regain by the skeleton of the lactating woman are through mechanisms that are, at best, only partly understood. A full elucidation of the mechanisms of bone loss and restoration in the lactating woman might lead to the development of novel approaches to the treatment of osteoporosis and other metabolic bone diseases. Finally, while it is apparent that some women will experience fragility fractures as a consequence of pregnancy or lactation, the vast majority of women can be assured that the changes in calcium and bone metabolism during pregnancy and lactation are normal, healthy, and without adverse consequences in the long term.

REFERENCES

1. Kovacs CS, Kronenberg HM 1997 Maternal-fetal calcium and bone metabolism during pregnancy, puerperium and lactation. Endocr Rev 18:832–872.
2. Kovacs CS, El-Hajj Fuleihan G 2005 Calcium and bone disorders during pregnancy and lactation. Endocrinol Metab Clin North Am 35:21–51.
3. Kovacs CS, Lanske B, Hunzelman JL, Guo J, Karaplis AC, Kronenberg HM 1996 Parathyroid hormone-related peptide (PTHrP) regulates fetal-placental calcium transport through a receptor distinct from the PTH/PTHrP receptor. Proc Natl Acad Sci USA 93:15233–15238.
4. Cornish J, Callon KE, Nicholson GC, Reid IR 1997 Parathyroid hormone-related protein-(107–139) inhibits bone resorption in vivo. Endocrinology 138:1299–1304.
5. Purdie DW, Aaron JE, Selby PL 1988 Bone histology and mineral homeostasis in human pregnancy. Br J Obstet Gynaecol 95:849–854.
6. Sowers M 1996 Pregnancy and lactation as risk factors for subsequent bone loss and osteoporosis. J Bone Miner Res 11:1052–1060.
7. Schnatz PF, Curry SL 2002 Primary hyperparathyroidism in pregnancy: Evidence-based management. Obstet Gynecol Surv 57:365–76.
8. Breslau NA, Zerwekh JE 1986 Relationship of estrogen and pregnancy to calcium homeostasis in pseudohypoparathyroidism. J Clin Endocrinol Metab 62:45–51.
9. Woodrow JP, Noseworthy CS, Fudge NJ, Hoff AO, Gagel RF, Kovacs CS 2003 Calcitonin/calcitonin gene-related peptide protect the maternal skeleton from excessive resorption during lactation. J Bone Miner Res 18:S2; S37.
10. Woodrow JP, Hoff AO, Gagel RF, Kovacs CS 2004 Calcitonin treatment rescues calcitonin-null mice from excessive bone resorption during lactation. J Bone Miner Res 19:S1;SA518.
11. VanHouten JN, Dann P, Stewart AF, Watson CJ, Pollak M, Karaplis AC, Wysolmerski JJ 2003 Mammary-specific deletion of parathyroid hormone-related protein preserves bone mass during lactation. J Clin Invest 112:1429–1436.
12. Kovacs CS, Chik CL 1995 Hyperprolactinemia caused by lactation and

13. Dobnig H, Kainer F, Stepan V, Winter R, Lipp R, Schaffer M, Kahr A, Nocnik S, Patterer G, Leb G 1995 Elevated parathyroid hormone-related peptide levels after human gestation: Relationship to changes in bone and mineral metabolism. J Clin Endocrinol Metab 80:3699–3707.
14. Sowers MF, Hollis BW, Shapiro B, Randolph J, Janney CA, Zhang D, Schork A, Crutchfield M, Stanczyk F, Russell-Aulet M 1996 Elevated parathyroid hormone-related peptide associated with lactation and bone density loss. J Am Med Assoc 276:549–554.
15. Kolthoff N, Eiken P, Kristensen B, Nielsen SP 1998 Bone mineral changes during pregnancy and lactation: A longitudinal cohort study. Clin Sci (Colch) 94:405–412.
16. Polatti F, Capuzzo E, Viazzo F, Colleoni R, Klersy C 1999 Bone mineral changes during and after lactation. Obstet Gynecol 94:52–56.
17. Kalkwarf HJ, Specker BL, Bianchi DC, Ranz J, Ho M 1997 The effect of calcium supplementation on bone density during lactation and after weaning. N Engl J Med 337:523–528.
18. Cross NA, Hillman LS, Allen SH, Krause GF 1995 Changes in bone mineral density and markers of bone remodeling during lactation and postweaning in women consuming high amounts of calcium. J Bone Miner Res 10:1312–1320.
19. Laskey MA, Prentice A, Hanratty LA, Jarjou LM, Dibba B, Beavan SR, Cole TJ 1998 Bone changes after 3 mo of lactation: Influence of calcium intake, breast-milk output, and vitamin D-receptor genotype. Am J Clin Nutr 67:685–692.
20. Reid IR, Wattie DJ, Evans MC, Budayr AA 1992 Post-pregnancy osteoporosis associated with hypercalcaemia. Clin Endocrinol (Oxf) 37:298–303.
21. Caplan RH, Beguin EA 1990 Hypercalcemia in a calcitriol-treated hypoparathyroid woman during lactation. Obstet Gynecol 76:485–489.
22. Mather KJ, Chik CL, Corenblum B 1999 Maintenance of serum calcium by parathyroid hormone-related peptide during lactation in a hypoparathyroid patient. J Clin Endocrinol Metab 84:424–427.

pituitary adenomas is associated with altered serum calcium, phosphate, parathyroid hormone (PTH), and PTH-related peptide levels. J Clin Endocrinol Metab 80:3036–3042.

Chapter 11. Menopause

Ian R. Reid

Department of Medicine, University of Auckland, Auckland, New Zealand

INTRODUCTION

Menopause refers to the cessation of menstruation, which occurs at ~48–50 years of age in healthy women. The decline in ovarian hormone production is gradual and starts several years before the last period. Changes in bone mass and calcium metabolism are evident during this perimenopausal transition. Estrogen is the ovarian product that has the greatest impact on mineral metabolism, although both progesterone and ovarian androgens may have some influence. Menopause ushers in a period of bone loss that extends until the end of life and that is the central contributor to the development of osteoporotic fractures in older women.

EFFECTS ON BONE

Before menopause, there is virtually no bone loss in most regions of the skeleton, and fracture rates are stable. The most obvious effect of menopause on bone is an increase in the incidence of fractures; in the forearms and vertebrae, this is clearly apparent within the first postmenopausal decade. It is attributable to the rapid decline in bone mass that occurs in the perimenopausal years. Bone loss is more marked in trabecular than in cortical bone because the former has a far greater surface area over which bone resorption can take place. Thus, the fractures that occur early in menopause are in trabecular-rich regions of the skeleton such as the distal forearm and vertebrae. The loss of bone and increase in fracture rates are preventable with estrogen replacement.

The perimenopausal increase in bone loss is driven by increased bone resorption.[1] Bone biopsy specimens in normal postmenopausal women show an increase in the proportion of bone surfaces at which resorption is taking place and an increase in the depth of resorption pits. These changes follow from an increase in the activation frequency of remodeling units and a prolongation of their resorptive phase. Indices of bone resorption are twice the levels found in premenopausal women, whereas markers of bone formation are only ~50% above premenopausal levels,[2] leading to negative bone balance. The resulting loss of bone leads to the perforation and loss of trabeculae and increased porosity in cortical bone. The changes in histomorphometric indices and biochemical markers can be returned to premenopausal levels with estrogen replacement therapy.

The changes in bone turnover that accompany menopause are in part accounted for by the direct actions of estrogen on bone cells. Estrogen receptors are present in both osteoblasts and osteoclasts. Estrogen promotes the development of osteoblasts in preference to adipocytes from their common precursor cell,[3] increases osteoblast proliferation,[4] and increases pro-

The author has reported no conflicts of interest.

duction of a number of osteoblast proteins (e.g., IGF-1, type I procollagen, TGF-β, and BMP-6). Thus, estrogen tends to have an anabolic effect on the isolated osteoblast, which is complemented by its inhibition of apoptosis in osteocytes[5] and osteoblasts.[6] In vivo, however, the initiation of estrogen replacement therapy is usually associated with a reduction in osteoblast numbers and activity.[7] This is accounted for by the tight coupling of osteoblast activity to that of osteoclasts and the overriding effect of estrogen to reduce osteoclastic bone resorption. However, there is now evidence that high concentrations of estrogen increase some histomorphometric indices of osteoblast activity (e.g., mean wall thickness) in humans, possibly by increasing osteoblast synthesis of growth factors.[8]

Estrogen's suppression of osteoclast activity is contributed to by increased osteoclast apoptosis,[9] by reduced osteoblast/stromal cell production of RANKL, and by increased production of osteoprotegerin.[10] These direct effects are buttressed by estrogen action on bone marrow stromal and mononuclear cells and on T cells. The former produce cytokines, such as IL-1, IL-6, and TNF-α, which are potent stimulators of osteoclast recruitment and/or activity.[11] Estrogen decreases production of each of these cytokines[12] and modulates levels of IL-1 receptors.[13] Bone loss after ovariectomy is reduced by blockers of these cytokines. IL-1 and TNF-α may act in part by regulating stromal cell production of IL-6 and macrophage colony-stimulating factor.[14] Estrogen's reduction in bone resorption is also contributed to by its increasing levels of NO and TGF-β, both of which are potent inhibitors of osteoclast differentiation and bone resorption.[15] TGF-β acts through regulation of T-cell production of TNF-α,[16] and estrogen also influences T-cell proliferation through interferon-γ.[17] These effects on osteoclasts and bone marrow cytokines are supported by estrogen's regulation of the release of systemic factors, such as growth hormone.[18]

EFFECTS ON CALCIUM METABOLISM

The bone loss that follows menopause is accompanied by negative changes in external calcium balance, which are approximately equally contributed to by decreases in intestinal calcium absorption and by increases in urinary calcium loss.[19] Menopause is associated with reduced circulating concentrations of total, but not free, 1,25-dihydroxyvitamin D [1,25(OH)$_2$D], implying that its main effect is on vitamin D binding protein. However, intestinal mucosal cells contain estrogen receptors and respond directly to 17β-estradiol with enhanced calcium transport,[20] probably through regulation of the epithelial calcium channel CaT1,[21] suggesting estrogen's effects are independent of vitamin D.

In the kidney, it is clear that tubular reabsorption of calcium is higher in the presence of estrogen[22,23]. One study[23] found higher PTH concentrations in the presence of estrogen and inferred that this was the mechanism of the renal calcium conservation. However, higher PTH levels have not been the finding in a number of other studies. Thus, it is likely that estrogen directly modulates renal tubular calcium absorption through its own receptor in the kidney, as suggested by in vitro studies of renal tubule cells that show a stimulatory effect of 17β-estradiol on calcium membrane transport.[24]

The changes in the handling of calcium by the gut and kidney could each be a cause of postmenopausal bone loss or they could represent homeostatic responses to it. If the former was the case, PTH concentrations would be elevated in postmenopausal women to maintain plasma calcium concentrations in the face of intestinal and renal losses. This, in turn, would cause bone loss. If, on the other hand, bone loss were the primary event, suppression of PTH would be expected, leading

to secondary declines in intestinal and renal calcium absorption. The effect of menopause on PTH concentrations has been addressed many times without any consistent pattern emerging. This suggests that estrogen has direct effects on bone, kidney and gut, and the opposing effects of these actions on PTH secretion leads to inconsistent changes in PTH concentrations. Furthermore, estrogen may directly modulate PTH secretion.[25,26]

There are small but consistently demonstrable effects of menopause on circulating concentrations of calcium. Total calcium is 0.05 mM higher after menopause.[22,27] This is partly attributable to a contraction of the plasma volume and resulting increase in albumin concentrations that occurs in the absence of estrogen,[28,29] and partly to an increase in plasma bicarbonate that leads to an increase in the complexed fraction of plasma calcium. The higher bicarbonate levels of postmenopausal women are attributable to a respiratory acidosis that results from the loss of the respiratory stimulatory effects of progesterone on the central nervous system, an action that is potentiated by estrogen.[30,31] Despite changes in protein-bound and complexed calcium fractions, ionized calcium concentrations are usually found to be the same in pre- and postmenopausal women.

SUMMARY

The effects of menopause on skeletal physiology are summarized in Fig. 1. The major effect is an increase in bone turnover, which is dominantly an increase in bone resorption. This results in bone loss that may be contributed to by reductions in both intestinal and renal tubular absorption of calcium. Bone loss persists throughout the entire postmenopausal period and results in a high risk of fractures in those women whose peak bone mass was in the lower part of the normal range.

REFERENCES

1. Heaney RP, Recker RR, Saville PD 1978 Menopausal changes in bone remodeling. J Lab Clin Med **92:**964–970.
2. Garnero P, Sornayrendu E, Chapuy MC, Delmas PD 1996 Increased bone turnover in late postmenopausal women is a major determinant of osteoporosis. J Bone Miner Res **11:**337–349.
3. Okazaki R, Inoue D, Shibata M, Saika M, Kido S, Ooka H, Tomiyama H, Sakamoto Y, Matsumoto T 2002 Estrogen promotes early osteoblast differentiation and inhibits adipocyte differentiation in mouse bone marrow stromal cell lines that express estrogen receptor (ER) alpha or beta. Endocrinology **143:**2349–2356.
4. Fujita M, Urano T, Horie K, Ikeda K, Tsukui T, Fukuoka H, Tsutsumi O, Ouchi Y, Inoue S 2002 Estrogen activates cyclin-dependent kinases 4 and 6 through induction of cyclin D in rat primary osteoblasts. Biochem Biophys Res Commun **299:**222–228.
5. Tomkinson A, Reeve J, Shaw RW, Noble BS 1997 The death of osteocytes via apoptosis accompanies estrogen withdrawal in human bone. J Clin Endocrinol Metab **82:**3128–3135.
6. Gohel A, McCarthy MB, Gronowicz G 1999 Estrogen prevents glucocorticoid-induced apoptosis in osteoblasts in vivo and in vitro. Endocrinology **140:**5339–5347.
7. Vedi S, Compston JE 1996 The effects of long-term hormone replacement therapy on bone remodeling in postmenopausal women. Bone **19:**535–539.
8. Bord S, Beavan S, Ireland D, Horner A, Compston JE 2001 Mechanisms by which high-dose estrogen therapy produces anabolic skeletal effects in postmenopausal women: Role of locally produced growth factors. Bone **29:**216–222.
9. Kameda T, Mano H, Yuasa T, Mori Y, Miyazawa K, Shiokawa M, Nakamaru Y, Hiroi E, Hiura K, Kameda A, Yang NN, Hakeda Y, Kumegawa M 1997 Estrogen inhibits bone resorption by directly inducing apoptosis of the bone-resorbing osteoclasts. J Exp Med **186:**489–495.
10. Syed F, Khosla S 2005 Mechanisms of sex steroid effects on bone. Biochem Biophys Res Comm **328:**688–696.
11. Manolagas SC, Jilka RL 1995 Mechanisms of disease: Bone marrow,

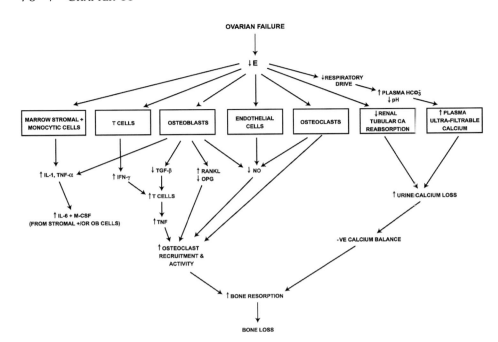

FIG. 1. The potential pathways by which menopause leads to bone loss. For simplicity, a contribution from loss of any anabolic effect of estrogen on the osteoblast is not shown. The fall in ovarian production of androgens and progesterone also contributes to some of these changes.

cytokines, and bone remodeling—emerging insights into the pathophysiology of osteoporosis. N Engl J Med **332**:305–311.

12. Rogers A, Eastell R 1998 Effects of estrogen therapy of postmenopausal women on cytokines measured in peripheral blood. J Bone Miner Res **13**:1577–1586.

13. Sunyer T, Lewis J, Collin-Osdoby P, Osdoby P 1999 Estrogen's bone-protective effects may involve differential IL-1 receptor regulation in human osteoclast-like cells. J Clin Invest **103**:1409–1418.

14. Kimble RB, Srivastava S, Ross FP, Matayoshi A, Pacifici R 1996 Estrogen deficiency increases the ability of stromal cells to support murine osteoclastogenesis via an interleukin-1-and tumor necrosis factor-mediated stimulation of macrophage colony-stimulating factor production. J Biol Chem **271**:28890–28897.

15. Ralston SH 1997 The Michael-Mason-Prize essay 1997—nitric oxide and bone—what a gas. Br J Rheumatol **36**:831–838.

16. Gao YH, Qian WP, Dark K, Toraldo G, Lin ASP, Guldberg RE, Flavell RA, Weitzmann MN, Pacifici R 2004 Estrogen prevents bone loss through transforming growth factor beta signaling in T cells. Proc Natl Acad Sci USA **101**:16618–16623.

17. Cenci S, Toraldo G, Weitzmann MN, Roggia C, Gao YH, Qian WP, Sierra O, Pacifici R 2003 Estrogen deficiency induces bone loss by increasing T cell proliferation and lifespan through IFN-gamma-induced class II transactivator. Proc Natl Acad Sci USA **100**:10405–10410.

18. Friend KE, Hartman ML, Pezzoli SS, Clasey JL, Thorner MO 1996 Both oral and transdermal estrogen increase growth hormone release in post-menopausal women: A clinical research center study. J Clin Endocrinol Metab **81**:2250–2256.

19. Heaney RP, Recker RR, Saville PD 1978 Menopausal changes in calcium balance performance. J Lab Clin Med **92**:953–963.

20. Arjandi BH, Salih MA, Herbert DC, Sims SH, Kalu DN 1993 Evidence for estrogen receptor-linked calcium transport in the intestine. Bone Miner **21**:63–74.

21. Van Cromphaut SJ, Rummens K, Stockmans I, Van Herck E, Dijcks FA, Ederveen A, Carmeliet P, Verhaeghe J, Bouillon R, Carmeliet G 2003 Intestinal calcium transporter genes are upregulated by estrogens and the reproductive cycle through vitamin D receptor-independent mechanisms. J Bone Miner Res **18**:1725–1736.

22. Nordin BEC, Wlshart JM, Clifton PM, McArthur R, Scopacasa F, Need AG, Morris HA, O'Loughlin PD, Horowitz M 2004 A longitudinal study of bone-related biochemical changes at the menopause. Clin Endocrinol (Oxf) **61**:123–130.

23. McKane WR, Khosla S, Burritt MF, Kao PC, Wilson DM, Ory SJ, Riggs BL 1995 Mechanism of renal calcium conservation with estrogen replacement therapy in women in early postmenopause: A clinical research center study. J Clin Endocrinol Metab **80**:3458–3464.

24. Dick IM, Liu J, Glendenning P, Prince RL 2003 Estrogen and androgen regulation of plasma membrane calcium pump activity in immortalized distal tubule kidney cells. Molec Cell Endocrinol **212**:11–18.

25. Duarte B, Hargis GK, Kukreja SC 1988 Effects of estradiol and progesterone on parathyroid hormone secretion from human parathyroid tissue. J Clin Endocrinol Metab **66**:584–587.

26. Greenberg C, Kukreja SC, Bowser EN, Hargis GK, Henderson WJ, Williams GA 1987 Parathyroid hormone secretion: Effect of estradiol and progesterone. Metabolism **36**:151–154.

27. Sokoll LJ, Dawson-Hughes B 1989 Effect of menopause and aging on serum total and ionized calcium and protein concentrations. Calcif Tissue Int **44**:181–185.

28. Aitken JM, Lindsay R, Hart DM 1974 The redistribution of body sodium in women on long-term estrogen therapy. Clin Sci Mol Med **47**:179–187.

29. Minkoff JR, Young G, Grant B, Marcus R 1986 Interactions of medroxy-progesterone acetate with estrogen on the calcium-parathyroid axis in post-menopausal women. Maturitas **8**:35–45.

30. Bayliss DA, Millhorn DE 1992 Central neural mechanisms of progesterone action: Application to the respiratory system. J Appl Physiol **73**:393–404

31. Orr-Walker BJ, Horne AM, Evans MC, Grey AB, Murray MAF, McNeil AR, Reid IR 1999 Hormone replacement therapy causes a respiratory alkalosis in normal postmenopausal women. J Clin Endocrinol Metab **84**:1997–2001.

Chapter 12.   Age-Related Osteoporosis

Clifford J. Rosen[1] and Douglas P. Kiel[2]

[1]St. Joseph Hospital, Bangor, Maine; and [2]Institute for Aging Research, Hebrew SeniorLife, Boston, Massachusetts

INTRODUCTION

Age-related fractures are the most common manifestation of osteoporosis and are responsible for the greatest proportion of the morbidity and mortality from this disease. Over the next quarter century, as the population ages, fracture prevalence will also rise. Biochemical, biomechanical, and nonskeletal factors contribute to fragility fractures in the elderly. In this overview, we will focus on the quantitative and qualitative changes in the skeleton as well as the nonskeletal pathways that contribute to osteoporotic fractures in older individuals.

AGE-RELATED CHANGES IN BONE QUALITY AND QUANTITY THAT CONTRIBUTE TO FRACTURE RISK

Numerous studies have documented a progressive reduction in BMD at nearly every skeletal site with aging[1]; however, fracture risk also climbs with age, independent of BMD.[2] Therefore, other skeletal and nonskeletal factors must contribute to overall fracture risk. Recent advances in imaging technology and the availability of more longitudinal studies reveal significant changes in trabecular architecture and connectivity that can be linked to bone strength and ultimately fracture risk in the elderly.[3] Other qualitative factors that are influenced by age include the degree of mineralization, microcrack number and frequency, anisotropy, skeletal geometry, and the periosteal response to trabecular bone loss. The latter is particularly intriguing because the loss of trabecular elements may result in a compensatory increase in the cortical shell diameter.[4] This characteristic is more pronounced in the aging male rather than female and probably serves to protect the skeleton during active bone loss. Finally, recent attention has focused on the role of marrow fat in the bone marrow compartment because adipogenesis at this site increases with aging.[5] . These age-related changes can be visualized by MRI and could have structural consequences, although neither the function nor the fate of marrow adipocytes is known.[6]

Currently. it is difficult, if not impossible, to clinically measure qualitative characteristics of bone; however, risk factors such as age and previous fracture capture some of these qualitative determinants of fracture risk. In contrast to the limited ability to measure qualitative changes in bone, quantifying BMD and loss of BMD can be easily assessed by DXA measurements. BMD changes with aging contribute to the risk of future fracture. For example, over a lifespan, women lose ~42% of their spinal and 58% of their femoral bone mass.[1] Surprisingly, rates of bone loss in the eighth and ninth decades of life may be comparable with or even exceed those found in the immediate peri- and postmenopausal period of some women.[7,8] This is caused by uncoupling in the bone remodeling cycle of older individuals, resulting in a marked increase in bone resorption but no change or a decrease in bone formation.[7,9] The latter scenario is particularly intriguing because aging is associated with a significant increase in stromal cell differentiation into the fat lineage and greater marrow adiposity, which may be associated with fewer stromal cells committed to the osteoblast lineage. Alterations in bone turnover can be detected by biochemical markers of bone remodeling that include bone resorption indices (e.g., urinary and serum breakdown products of type I collagen) and bone formation markers (e.g., osteocalcin, procollagen peptide, bone specific alkaline phosphatase). In general, bone turnover markers are significantly higher in older rather than younger postmenopausal women, and these indices are inversely related to BMD.[10] For example, in the EPIDOS trial of elderly European females, the highest levels of osteocalcin, N-telopeptide, C-telopeptide, and bone-specific alkaline phosphatase were noted for those in the lowest tertile of femoral BMD.[11] Also, increased bone resorption indices were associated with a greater fracture risk independent of BMD.[11] For those women in EPIDOS with low BMD and a high bone resorption rate, there was a nearly 5-fold greater risk of a hip fracture. Similar findings have been noted in other cohorts composed of elderly individuals.[12]

In contrast to consistently high bone resorption indices, bone formation markers in the elderly are more variable. Serum osteocalcin levels are high in elderly individuals, but this may be indicative of an increase in bone turnover rather than reflecting a true rise in bone formation.[11] On the other hand, bone-specific alkaline phosphatase and procollagen peptide levels have been reported to be high, normal or low in elderly men and women.[13] Bone histomorphometric indices in the elderly are also quite variable. Morphologically, the age-associated increase in marrow fat may or may not contribute to the heterogeneity in formation markers. Thus, although there is strong evidence for an age-associated rise in bone resorption, changes in bone formation are inconsistent. Notwithstanding the limitations of biochemical markers, it is generally assumed there is uncoupling of the remodeling unit that leads to bone loss, altered skeletal architecture, and an increased propensity to fractures.

FACTORS THAT CONTRIBUTE TO AGE-RELATED BONE LOSS

Nutritional

Increased bone resorption in older individuals can be attributed to a number of factors including calcium and/or vitamin D deficiency. Both are very common in the elderly and are caused by a number of conditions, including abrupt dietary changes, lack of sunlight exposure, malabsorption, use of certain drugs, cachexia, and anorexia. The result of low calcium intake is persistent secondary hyperparathyroidism, which in turn leads to increased bone resorption, often accentuated by occult vitamin D deficiency, especially in women living in northern latitudes.[14] It is estimated that upward of 80% of elderly postmenopausal women may have vitamin D deficiency as defined by a 25-hydroxyvitamin D of <20 ng/ml (50 nM).[15,16] Low vitamin D levels could result not only in reduced bone mass but also altered muscle function.

In a meta-analysis of clinical trials of calcium supplementation for postmenopausal women, lumbar BMD was shown to be slightly increased in women who were supplemented.[17] Calcium treatment alone, however, does not reduce vertebral or nonvertebral fractures and debate continues about whether vitamin D alone, in doses of ≥800 IU/day, can prevent fractures.[18–20] Certainly there is some evidence to suggest that vitamin D supplementation can improve muscle function, thereby indirectly reducing fracture risk.[20] The National

Dr. Rosen has received grant funding from Procter & Gamble, Merck, Aventis, Lilly, NPS, Allelix, GlaxoSmithKline, Novartis, and Wyeth. Dr. Kiel has been a consultant for Eli Lilly, Novartis, GlaxoSmithKline Beecham, Merck, and Procter & Gamble.

Academy of Science recommends a minimal daily requirement for calcium intake in people >65 years of age to be 1500 mg/day and for vitamin D to be 600 IU/day.[21] It is likely that this 600 IU/day recommendation for vitamin D will be increased to 800 IU/day in the coming years.

A balanced diet that includes micro- and macronutrients is essential for the overall health of the older individual. Besides calcium and vitamin D, other nutritional factors may play a role in age-related osteoporosis. Although total protein intake seems to be beneficial to the skeleton, there is still a debate as to whether high animal protein intake creates an acidic environment in bone, leading to loss of calcium from the skeleton.[22–24] Protein/calorie malnutrition stimulates bone resorption and impairs bone formation both directly and through other mechanisms such as reduced serum IGF-I.[25] Vitamin K deficiency may contribute to an increased risk of osteoporotic fractures, possibly through effects on the carboxylation of bone proteins such as osteocalcin.[26] Other micronutrients such as the B vitamins and vitamin C have been linked to osteoporotic risk in some but not all studies. At least one observational study suggested that increased vitamin A intake might be associated with low BMD.[18,27] A case control study showed a significant relationship between excessive intake of vitamin A and age-related fractures.[28]

Hormonal

Estrogen deficiency has long been recognized as a major cause of bone loss in the first decade after menopause. More recently, investigators have identified a strong relationship between endogenous estrogen and bone mass in elderly men and women. In one prospective study, Slemenda et al.[29] noted that both estrogens and androgens were independent predictors of bone loss in older postmenopausal women. In both the Rancho Bernardo cohort and the Framingham Cohort, estradiol levels were strongly related to BMD at the spine, hip, and forearm.[30,31]

Males also suffer from age-related bone loss, and evidence suggests that absolute estrogen levels, rather than testosterone concentrations, are essential for maintenance of BMD. In the Rancho Bernardo cohort, serum estradiol levels in elderly men correlated closely with bone mass at several sites,[30] and low estradiol levels in men were associated with increased risk of hip fracture. Recently, Falahati et al.[32,33] showed that small amounts of estradiol were essential for preventing bone resorption in men, in part by upregulating osteoprotegerin (OPG). Endogenous testosterone also plays a role in regulating bone turnover, possibly more on the formation side than in respect to resorption. Serum testosterone levels decline with age at a rate of ~1.2%/year, whereas sex hormone binding globulin (SHBG) levels rise. Males treated with androgen antagonists or gonadotropin agonists for prostate cancer metastases rapidly lose bone mass and may be at high risk for subsequent osteoporotic fractures.[34] Overall, it seems likely that both androgens and estrogens are important in the elderly male. Whether changes in male hormone levels are causally related to age-related bone loss in men will have to await large scale prospective studies.

Changes in other circulating factors may be related to bone loss in the elderly. For example, growth hormone (GH) secretion declines 14% per decade and is the principle cause for low serum IGF-I concentrations in both elderly men and women.[35] Serum IGF-I concentrations in some studies but not others are directly related to BMD, and in one study, low IGF-I was an independent predictor of hip fracture.[36] Similarly, the adrenal androgens, dehydroepiandrosterone (DHEA) and DHEA-S, also decline precipitously with age and are 10–20% of young adult serum levels.[37] OPG levels are also lower in the elderly than in younger postmenopausal woman, but whether this can lead to increased bone loss has yet to be shown.[2] Aging is also

associated with a generalized cytokinemia, including greater serum levels of interleukin-6 (IL-6) and TNF, as well as C-reactive protein (CRP). Whether these changes are a function of other disease processes and therefore may contribute to bone loss in the elderly have not been established.

Heritable and Environmental Factors

Age-related bone loss can be dramatic in some individuals, and this decline cannot be attributed solely to hormonal or nutritional factors. Several investigators have hypothesized that there is genetic programming, which when triggered by environmental factors, may lead to bone loss, especially in the elderly. Some animal models, but not others, have shown a heritable component to age-related bone loss.[38] Recently, Bouxsein et al.[39] showed that, after ovariectomy, inbred strains of mice lost bone at very different rates. This would suggest that genetic programming may be operative in determining the rate of bone loss with estrogen deprivation. In humans, the multiplicity of environmental factors makes the determination of fracture heritability complicated, although recent publications also suggest a genetic component.[40,41] On the other hand, environmental factors, including inactivity and loss of muscle mass, smoking, alcohol, and medications such as glucocorticoids and anticonvulsants, may contribute to an excessive rate of bone loss in some elderly.

FRACTURES AND FALLS IN THE ELDERLY

In elderly individuals, decreased bone strength, as reflected by BMD, is only one of many important contributors to overall hip fracture risk. Other factors include propensity to fall, inability to correct a postural imbalance, characteristics of the faller such as height and muscle activity, the orientation of the fall, adequacy of local tissue shock absorbers, and characteristics of the impact surface. The resistance of a skeletal structure to failure (i.e., fracture) depends on the geometry of the bone, the material properties of the calcified tissue, and the location and direction of the loads to which the bone is subjected (i.e., during a fall or other activities). Estimations of the forces generated within the bone in response to a given load can be estimated using basic engineering principles. Those forces can be compared with the strengths of the tissue. The ratio of the impact force expected during a fall to the force required to cause the bone to fail incorporates the two major determinants of fracture risk. When this ratio is close to or more than 1, the structure is at great risk of failure.

In the elderly, this ratio is 0.3 at the femoral neck for simple stance and normal ambulation. For stair climbing, it is about 0.6. In falls, the ratio ranges from 1 to >70.[42] These calculations are complicated by considerable uncertainty about the loads to which hips are actually subjected during falls. For example, skeletal structures at high risk for age-related fracture, such as the hip, change their geometry with aging and bone remodeling, making it difficult to ascertain the true force of failure in vivo. Most of the energy from a fall dissipates before actual injury, and yet the residual force at impact remains two orders of magnitude greater than the energy required to fracture elderly femurs. This would suggest that a simple fall is easily capable of fracturing the proximal femur.

Falls in older people are rarely due to a single cause. Falls usually occur when a threat to the normal homeostatic mechanisms that maintain postural stability is superimposed on underlying age-related declines in balance, ambulation, and cardiovascular function. In some cases, this may involve an acute illness such as a fever or infection or an environmental stress such as a newly initiated drug or an unsafe walking surface. Regardless of the nature of the stress, an elderly person may not be able to compensate because of either age-related declines in function or severe chronic disease. It is unlikely for an extrinsic stress to completely explain the circumstances of a fall. Older persons, by virtue of their age alone, experience declines in physiologic function, have greater numbers of chronic diseases, acute illnesses, and hospitalizations, and use multiple medications. Superimposed on these age-related characteristics, challenges to postural control may have a greater impact in aged persons according to their risk-taking behavior and opportunity to fall. Thus, those individuals who are completely immobile may not be at risk of falling despite multiple predisposing factors. On the other hand, persons who are either vigorous or only slightly frail may be at higher risk compared with individuals in between those extremes, due in part to more risk taking and inability to compensate for postural changes. Despite the importance of falls, BMD still remains a major predictor of fracture risk[2] regardless of age.[43] Recent evidence also implicates low vitamin D as an important contributor to the risk of falls and fractures and to lower extremity function.[20,44,45] Moreover, vitamin D supplementation may reduce fracture risk by enhancing muscle strength, particularly in the lower extremity.

In one large study for hip fracture risk in elderly women, the subjects were grouped into three categories according to number of risk factors for fracture other than BMD. Across all three risk groups, BMD remained an important predictor for fracture.[2]

APPROACH TO FRACTURE PREVENTION IN THE ELDERLY PATIENT

Because older persons have lower BMD to start, are continuing to lose bone, and are in the age group most likely to fracture, interventions would be expected to be most cost-effective when initiated in these individuals. The interventions can be divided into two groups: (1) those that reduce the applied load to the skeleton (fall prevention, passive protective systems) and (2) those that preserve or increase BMD.

Interventions That Reduce the Applied Load

Interventions to prevent falls must be predicated on an assessment of fall risk. This should include a history of falls because a history of falls is the single most important risk factor for a subsequent fall. If that history is positive, additional information can be obtained surrounding the events of the fall, because this information may identify important factors for targeting risk factor modification strategies. The physical assessment of fall risk should include orthostatic vital sign measurement, a test of visual acuity, hearing, cardiac exam, extremity exam, and a test of the postural stability system as a whole using any of several recently developed assessment tools such as the "Get Up and Go" test[46,47] and the Short Portable Physical Performance Battery.[48] Because some of the unfavorable outcomes of major fractures such as hip fractures are highly dependent on the premorbid status of an older patient, fracture prevention efforts should include a thorough assessment of underlying disability and frailty of the older person, because these factors influence long-term outcomes.[49]

For fall prevention interventions, the pooled results from several studies suggest that an intervention in which older people are assessed by a health professional trained to identify intrinsic and environmental risk factors is likely to reduce the fall rate (OR = 0.79; 95% CI, 0.65–0.96).[50,51] Because falls to the side that impact on the hip are the primary determinant of hip fracture,[52] protective trochanteric padding devices have been developed. Over the past 5 years, randomized, controlled trials have largely confirmed that hip protectors can reduce hip fracture, but subject compliance has been low.[53]

Interventions That Preserve or Increase BMD

In addition to the attention to adequate basic nutritional factors, the use of therapeutic agents in the treatment of osteoporosis in the elderly person may be useful. Because older persons are at the greatest risk of fracture and because fracture reduction has been shown for the bisphosphonates,[54–56] estrogen therapy,[57,58] nasal calcitonin,[59] risedronate,[55] and PTH,[60] potentially fewer elderly persons would have to be treated for less duration to prevent fractures than a younger population at lower risk of fracture.[61–64]

REFERENCES

1. Riggs BL, Wahner HW, Seeman E, Offord KP, Dunn WL, Mazess RB, Johnson KA, Melton LJ III 1982 Changes in bone mineral density of the proximal femur and spine with aging. Differences between the postmenopausal and senile osteoporosis syndromes. J Clin Invest 70:716–723.
2. Cummings SR, Nevitt MC, Browner WS, Stone K, Fox KM, Ensrud KE, Cauley J, Black D, Vogt TM 1995 Risk factors for hip fracture in white women. Study of Osteoporotic Fractures Research Group. N Engl J Med 332:767–773.
3. Bouxsein ML 2003 Bone quality: Where do we go from here? Osteoporos Int 14(Suppl 5):118–127.
4. Ahlborg HG, Johnell O, Turner CH, Rannevik G, Karlsson MK 2003 Bone loss and bone size after menopause. N Engl J Med 349:327–334.
5. Justesen J, Stenderup K, Ebbesen EN, Mosekilde L, Steiniche T, Kassem M 2001 Adipocyte tissue volume in bone marrow is increased with aging and in patients with osteoporosis. Biogerontology 2:165–171.
6. Wehrli FW, Hopkins JA, Hwang SN, Song HK, Snyder PJ, Haddad JG 2000 Cross-sectional study of osteopenia with quantitative MR imaging and bone densitometry. Radiology 217:527–538.
7. Ensrud KE, Palermo L, Black DM, Cauley J, Jergas M, Orwoll ES, Nevitt MC, Fox KM, Cummings SR 1995 Hip and calcaneal bone loss increase with advancing age: Longitudinal results from the study of osteoporotic fractures. J Bone Miner Res 10:1778–1787.
8. Hannan MT, Felson DT, Dawson-Hughes B, Tucker KL, Cupples LA, Wilson PW, Kiel DP 2000 Risk factors for longitudinal bone loss in elderly men and women: The Framingham Osteoporosis Study. J Bone Miner Res 15(4):710–720.
9. Ross PD, Knowlton W 1998 Rapid bone loss is associated with increased levels of biochemical markers. J Bone Miner Res 13:297–302.
10. Dresner-Pollak R, Parker RA, Poku M, Thompson J, Seibel MJ, Greenspan SL 1996 Biochemical markers of bone turnover reflect femoral bone loss in elderly women. Calcif Tissue Int 59:328–333.
11. Garnero P, Hausherr E, Chapuy MC, Marcelli C, Grandjean H, Muller C, Cormier C, Breart G, Meunier PJ, Delmas PD 1996 Markers of bone resorption predict hip fracture in elderly women: The EPIDOS Prospective Study. J Bone Miner Res 11:1531–1538.
12. Garnero P, Sornay-Rendu E, Claustrat B, Delmas PD 2000 Biochemical markers of bone turnover, endogenous hormones and the risk of fractures in postmenopausal women: The OFELY study. J Bone Miner Res 15:1526–1536.
13. Bollen AM, Kiyak HA, Eyre DR 1997 Longitudinal evaluation of a bone resorption marker in elderly subjects. Osteoporos Int 7:544–549.
14. Chapuy MC, Schott AM, Garnero P, Hans D, Delmas PD, Meunier PJ 1996 Healthy elderly French women living at home have secondary hyperparathyroidism and high bone turnover in winter. EPIDOS Study Group. J Clin Endocrinol Metab 81:1129–1133.
15. Heaney RP 2000 Vitamin D: How much do we need, and how much is too much? Osteoporos Int 11:553–555.
16. Rosen CJ 2005 Clinical practice. Postmenopausal osteoporosis. N Engl J Med 353:595–603.
17. Cranney A, Wells G, Willan A, Griffith L, Zytaruk N, Robinson V, Black D, Adachi J, Shea B, Tugwell P, Guyatt G 2002 Meta-analyses of therapies for postmenopausal osteoporosis. II. Meta-analysis of alendronate for the treatment of postmenopausal women. Endocr Rev 23:508–516.
18. Dawson-Hughes B, Harris SS, Krall EA, Dallal GE 1997 Effect of calcium and vitamin D supplementation on bone density in men and women 65 years of age or older. N Engl J Med 337:670–676.
19. Recker RR, Hinders S, Davies KM, Heaney RP, Stegman MR, Lappe JM, Kimmel DB 1996 Correcting calcium nutritional deficiency prevents spine fractures in elderly women. J Bone Miner Res 11:1961–1966.
20. Bischoff-Ferrari HA, Dawson-Hughes B, Willett WC, Staehelin HB, Bazemore MG, Zee RY, Wong JB 2004 Effect of Vitamin D on falls: A meta-analysis. JAMA 291:1999–2006.
21. 2001 Osteoporosis prevention, diagnosis, and therapy. JAMA 285:785–795.

22. Dawson-Hughes B, Harris SS 2002 Calcium intake influences the association of protein intake with rates of bone loss in elderly men and women. Am J Clin Nutr **75:**773–779.

23. Hannan MT, Tucker KL, Dawson-Hughes B, Cupples LA, Felson DT, Kiel DP 2000 Effect of dietary protein on bone loss in elderly men and women: The Framingham Osteoporosis Study. J Bone Miner Res **15:**2504–2512.

24. Tucker KL, Chen H, Hannan MT, Cupples LA, Wilson PW, Felson D, Kiel DP 2002 Bone mineral density and dietary patterns in older adults: The Framingham Osteoporosis Study. Am J Clin Nutr **76:**245–252.

25. Schurch MA, Rizzoli R, Slosman D, Vadas L, Vergnaud P, Bonjour JP 1998 Protein supplements increase serum insulin-like growth factor-I levels and attenuate proximal femur bone loss in patients with recent hip fracture. A randomized, double-blind, placebo-controlled trial. Ann Intern Med **128:**801–809.

26. McKeown NM, Jacques PF, Gundberg CM, Peterson JW, Tucker KL, Kiel DP, Wilson PW, Booth SL 2002 Dietary and nondietary determinants of vitamin K biochemical measures in men and women. J Nutr **132:**1329–1334.

27. Promislow JH, Goodman-Gruen D, Slymen DJ, Barrett-Connor E 2002 Retinol intake and bone mineral density in the elderly: The Rancho Bernardo Study. J Bone Miner Res **17:**1349–1358.

28. Michaelsson K, Lithell H, Vessby B, Melhus H 2003 Serum retinol levels and the risk of fracture. N Engl J Med **348:**287–294.

29. Slemenda CW, Longcope C, Zhou L, Hui SL, Peacock M, Johnston CC 1997 Sex steroids and bone mass in older men. Positive associations with serum estrogens and negative associations with androgens. J Clin Invest **100:**1755–1759.

30. Greendale GA, Edelstein S, Barrett-Connor E 1997 Endogenous sex steroids and bone mineral density in older women and men: The Rancho Bernardo Study. J Bone Miner Res **12:**1833–1843.

31. Amin S, Zhang Y, Sawin CT, Evans SR, Hannan MT, Kiel DP, Wilson PW, Felson DT 2000 Association of hypogonadism and estradiol levels with bone mineral density in elderly men from the Framingham study. Ann Intern Med **133:**951–963.

32. Khosla S, Atkinson EJ, Dunstan CR, O'Fallon WM 2002 Effect of estrogen versus testosterone on circulating osteoprotegerin and other cytokine levels in normal elderly men. J Clin Endocrinol Metab **87:**1550–1554.

33. Falahati-Nini A, Riggs BL, Atkinson EJ, O'Fallon WM, Eastell R, Khosla S 2000 Relative contributions of testosterone and estrogen in regulating bone resorption and formation in normal elderly men. J Clin Invest **106:**1553–1560.

34. Smith MR, Finkelstein JS, McGovern FJ, Zietman AL, Fallon MA, Schoenfeld DA, Kantoff PW 2002 Changes in body composition during androgen deprivation therapy for prostate cancer. J Clin Endocrinol Metab **87:**599–603.

35. Rosen CJ, Donahue LR, Hunter SJ 1994 Insulin-like growth factors and bone: The osteoporosis connection. Proc Soc Exp Biol Med **206:**83–102.

36. Bauer DC, Rosen CJ, Cauley J, Cummings SR 1997 Low serum IGF-I but not IGFBP-3 predicts hip and spine fractures. Bone **21:**561.

37. Barrett-Connor E, Kritz-Silverstein D, Edelstein SL 1993 A prospective study of dehydroepiandrosterone sulfate (DHEAS) and bone mineral density in older men and women. Am J Epidemiol **137:**201–206.

38. Halloran BP, Ferguson VL, Simske SJ, Burghardt A, Venton LL, Majumdar S 2002 Changes in bone structure and mass with advancing age in the male C57BL/6J mouse. J Bone Miner Res **17:**1044–1050.

39. Bouxsein ML, Myers KS, Shultz KL, Donahue LR, Rosen CJ, Beamer WG 2005 Ovariectomy-induced bone loss varies among inbred strains of mice. J Bone Miner Res **20:**1085–1092.

40. Deng HW, Mahaney MC, Williams JT, Li J, Conway T, Davies KM, Li JL, Deng H, Recker RR 2002 Relevance of the genes for bone mass variation to susceptibility to osteoporotic fractures and its implications to gene search for complex human diseases. Genet Epidemiol **22:**12–25.

41. Karasik D, Myers RH, Cupples LA, Hannan MT, Gagnon DR, Herbert A, Kiel DP 2002 Genome screen for quantitative trait loci contributing to normal variation in bone mineral density: The Framingham Study. J Bone Miner Res **17:**1718–11727.

42. Hayes WC 1991 Implications for assessment of fracture risk. In: Mow VC, Hayes WC (eds.) Basic Orthopaedic Biomechanics. Raven Press, New York, NY, USA, pp. 93–142.

43. Nevitt MC, Johnell O, Black DM, Ensrud K, Genant HK, Cummings SR 1994 Bone mineral density predicts non-spine fractures in very elderly women. Study of Osteoporotic Fractures Research Group. Osteoporos Int **4:**325–331.

44. Bischoff-Ferrari HA, Dietrich T, Orav EJ, Hu FB, Zhang Y, Karlson EW, Dawson-Hughes B 2004 Higher 25-hydroxyvitamin D concentrations are associated with better lower-extremity function in both active and inactive persons aged > or =60 y. Am J Clin Nutr **80:**752–758.

45. Bischoff-Ferrari HA, Willett WC, Wong JB, Giovannucci E, Dietrich T, Dawson-Hughes B 2005 Fracture prevention with vitamin D supplementation: A meta-analysis of randomized controlled trials. JAMA **293:**2257–2264.

46. Mathias S, Nayak US, Isaacs B 1986 Balance in elderly patients: The "get-up and go" test. Arch Phys Med Rehabil **67:**387–389.

47. Tinetti ME 1986 Performance-oriented assessment of mobility problems in elderly patients. J Am Geriatr Soc **34:**119–126.

48. Guralnik JM, Ferrucci L, Pieper CF, Leveille SG, Markides KS, Ostir GV, Studenski S, Berkman LF, Wallace RB 2000 Lower extremity function and subsequent disability: Consistency across studies, predictive models, and value of gait speed alone compared with the short physical performance battery. J Gerontol A Biol Sci Med Sci **55:**M221–M231.

49. Leibson CL, Tosteson AN, Gabriel SE, Ransom JE, Melton LJ 2002 Mortality, disability, and nursing home use for persons with and without hip fracture: A population-based study. J Am Geriatr Soc **50:**1644–1650.

50. Gillespie L, Gillespie W, Robertson M, Lamb S, Cumming R, Rowe B 2001 Interventions for preventing falls in elderly people. Cochrane Database Syst Rev **3:**CD000340.

51. Gillespie LD, Gillespie WJ, Robertson MC, Lamb SE, Cumming RG, Rowe BH 2003 Interventions for preventing falls in elderly people. Cochrane Database Syst Rev **4:**CD000340.

52. Greenspan SL, Myers ER, Kiel DP, Parker RA, Hayes WC, Resnick NM 1998 Fall direction, bone mineral density, and function: Risk factors for hip fracture in frail nursing home elderly. Am J Med **104:**539–545.

53. Parker MJ, Gillespie LD, Gillespie WJ 2003 Hip protectors for preventing hip fractures in the elderly. Cochrane Database Syst Rev **3:**CD001255.

54. Black DM, Cummings SR, Karpf DB, Cauley JA, Thompson DE, Nevitt MC, Bauer DC, Genant HK, Haskell WL, Marcus R, Ott SM, Torner JC, Quandt SA, Reiss TF, Ensrud KE 1996 Randomised trial of effect of alendronate on risk of fracture in women with existing vertebral fractures. Lancet **348:**1535–1541.

55. McClung MR, Geusens P, Miller PD, Zippel H, Bensen WG, Roux C, Adami S, Fogelman I, Diamond T, Eastell R, Meunier PJ, Reginster JY 2001 Effect of risedronate on the risk of hip fracture in elderly women. Hip Intervention Program Study Group. N Engl J Med **344:**333–340.

56. Chesnut IC, Skag A, Christiansen C, Recker R, Stakkestad JA, Hoiseth A, Felsenberg D, Huss H, Gilbride J, Schimmer RC, Delmas PD 2004 Effects of oral ibandronate administered daily or intermittently on fracture risk in postmenopausal osteoporosis. J Bone Miner Res **19:**1241–1249.

57. Cauley JA, Robbins J, Chen Z, Cummings SR, Jackson RD, LaCroix AZ, LeBoff M, Lewis CE, McGowan J, Neuner J, Pettinger M, Stefanick ML, Wactawski-Wende J, Watts NB 2003 Effects of estrogen plus progestin on risk of fracture and bone mineral density: The Women's Health Initiative randomized trial. JAMA **290:**1729–1738.

58. Rossouw JE, Anderson GL, Prentice RL, LaCroix AZ, Kooperberg C, Stefanick ML, Jackson RD, Beresford SA, Howard BV, Johnson KC, Kotchen JM, Ockene J 2002 Risks and benefits of estrogen plus progestin in healthy postmenopausal women: Principal results From the Women's Health Initiative randomized controlled trial. JAMA **288:**321–333.

59. Chesnut CH III, Silverman S, Andriano K, Genant H, Gimona A, Harris S, Kiel D, LeBoff M, Maricic M, Miller P, Moniz C, Peacock M, Richardson P, Watts N, Baylink D 2000 A randomized trial of nasal spray salmon calcitonin in postmenopausal women with established osteoporosis: The prevent recurrence of osteoporotic fractures study. PROOF Study Group. Am J Med **109:**267–276.

60. Neer RM, Arnaud CD, Zanchetta JR, Prince R, Gaich GA, Reginster JY, Hodsman AB, Eriksen EF, Ish-Shalom S, Genant HK, Wang O, Mitlak BH 2001 Effect of parathyroid hormone (1–34) on fractures and bone mineral density in postmenopausal women with osteoporosis. N Engl J Med **344:**1434–1441.

61. Lufkin EG, Wahner HW, O'Fallon WM, Hodgson SF, Kotowicz MA, Lane AW, Judd HL, Caplan RH, Riggs BL 1992 Treatment of postmenopausal osteoporosis with transdermal estrogen. Ann Intern Med **117:**1–9.

62. Overgaard K, Hansen MA, Jensen SB, Christiansen C 1992 Effect of salcatonin given intranasally on bone mass and fracture rates in established osteoporosis: A dose-response study. BMJ **305:**556–561.

63. Black DM, Cummings SR, Karpf DB, Cauley JA, Thompson DE, Nevitt MC, Bauer DC, Genant HK, Haskell WL, Marcus R, Ott SM, Torner JC, Quandt SA, Reiss TF, Ensrud KE 1996 Randomised trial of effect of alendronate on risk of fracture in women with existing vertebral fractures. Fracture Intervention Trial Research Group. Lancet **348:**1535–1541.

64. Liberman UA, Weiss SR, Broll J, Minne HW, Quan H, Bell NH, Rodriguez-Portales J, Downs RW, Jr., Dequeker J, Favus M 1995 Effect of oral alendronate on bone mineral density and the incidence of fractures in postmenopausal osteoporosis. The Alendronate Phase III Osteoporosis Treatment Study Group. N Engl J Med **333:**1437–1443.

Mineral Homeostasis
(Section Editors: Sylvia Christakos and Michael F. Holick)

Chapter 13.   Regulation of Calcium, Magnesium, and Phosphate Metabolism

Murray J. Favus,[1] David A. Bushinsky,[2] and Jacob Lemann Jr.[3]

[1]Section of Endocrinology, University of Chicago, Chicago, Illinois; [2]Nephrology Unit, University of Rochester School of Medicine, Rochester, New York; and [3]Nephrology Section, Tulane University School of Medicine, New Orleans, Louisiana

INTRODUCTION

The mineral ion homeostatic system maintains Ca, Mg, and P (because P does not exist as free P in biological systems, it will be referred to as phosphate and abbreviated PO_4) distribution and levels in the extracellular fluid and intracellular compartments while simultaneously providing sufficient absorption and retention to meet skeletal mineral requirements. Homeostasis is achieved by the coordinated interaction of the intestine, the site of net absorption; the kidney, the site of net excretion; and the skeleton, the largest repository of these ions in the body. Mineral fluxes across intestine, bone, and kidney and in and out of blood are regulated by PTH and 1,25-dihydroxyvitamin D_3 [$1,25(OH)_2D_3$], the hormonal or active form of vitamin D (also called calcitriol). There is emerging evidence that fibroblast growth factor (FGF)-23 may also be an important physiologic regulator of PO_4 homeostasis. External balance may vary with the stages of the life cycle, skeletal mineral requirements, supply of the minerals in the diet, and by a variety of disorders. For example, balance is neutral in adult, nonpregnant humans who have no daily net gain or loss of body Ca, Mg, or PO_4. Mineral balance becomes positive (intake and retention exceed urinary and intestinal losses) during skeletal growth during childhood and adolescence and during pregnancy and lactation. Negative balance (gastrointestinal and/or urinary losses exceed intake and retention) may occur during high rates of bone remodeling during estrogen deficiency, with aging, and with diseases such as hyperthyroidism and primary hyperparathyroidism. The adjustment or adaptation of the homeostatic system to maintain balance is mediated by PTH and $1,25(OH)_2D_3$ through changes in intestinal and renal tubule mineral transport. In the following sections, the distributions and fluxes of Ca, Mg, and PO_4 and hormonal regulations of mineral ion transport and balance are discussed.

CALCIUM

Total Body Distribution

Total body Ca content in adults (Fig. 1) is about 1000 g, of which 99% exists as the hydroxyapatite [$Ca_{10}(PO4)_6(OH)_2$] crystal in the mineral phase of bone. The crystal contributes to the mechanical weight-bearing properties of bone and also serves as a Ca and PO_4 reservoir that can be rapidly mobilized to support the numerous biological systems in which Ca or PO_4 are cofactors and regulators. The remaining 1% of total body Ca is in soft tissue and the extracellular fluid (ECF) space including blood. Serum total Ca concentration of 10^{-3} M exists in the ionized (50%) and protein-bound (40%) states and complexed mainly to citrate and PO_4 ions (10%). The biological actions of Ca are attributed to the ionized fraction, which is readily exchangeable with pools of Ca in bone, blood, and intracellular sites.

Cellular Distribution

Ionic cytosol Ca is maintained at about 10^{-6} M. Because blood and ECF Ca is 10^{-3} M, the 1000-fold chemical gradient favors Ca entry into the cell. The differential electrical charges across the cell plasma membrane of 50-mV gradient (cell interior negative) creates an electrical gradient that also favors Ca entry. Therefore, the major threat to cell viability is excessive Ca influx from the extracellular space along the electrochemical gradients. The defense against excess Ca influx into cells includes extrusion of Ca from the cell through energy-dependent Ca channels, Ca-dependent ATP-driven Ca pumps, and Na-Ca exchangers and active uptake into organelles including the endoplasmic reticulum and mitochondria. Ca-binding proteins and Ca transport proteins facilitate Ca transport into these cellular organelles. They also serve to buffer excess calcium preventing cell death. Ca-rich mitochondria and endoplasmic reticulum also serve as reservoirs to maintain cytosolic Ca when levels fall. Ca bound to the plasma membrane and the organelles may also be released in pulses in response to activation of receptors on the external surface of the plasma membrane.

Cell Ca homeostasis varies by cell function. For example, Ca facilitates the linking of excitation and contraction in skeletal and cardiac muscle through mobilization of the large Ca intracellular stores of the sarcoplasmic reticulum. In nonskeletal cells, Ca serves as a signal transducer, mediating signaling from activated plasma membrane receptors to carry out a variety of functions such as hormone secretion, neurotransmission, and kinase phosphorylation.

Homeostasis

Because diet Ca intake and skeletal Ca requirements vary widely from day to day and across the various stages of the life cycle, the homeostatic system is constantly adjusting to deliver sufficient Ca, Mg, and PO_4 from intestine and kidney into the ECF and blood and then to bone to meet changing skeletal growth requirements without disturbing the serum ionized Ca concentration [Ca^{2+}]. The serum Ca^{2+} fraction controls cellular biological functions, and therefore the homeostatic system maintains serum Ca^{2+} at the expense of BMC.

Serum Ca^{2+} may increase from Ca influx from intestinal absorption or bone resorption and decrease with Ca efflux into bone mineralization sites, secretion into the intestinal lumen, or filtration at the renal glomerulus and secretion along selected segments of the nephron. A decline in serum Ca^{2+} is potentially more likely and is therefore defended against by all of the actions of PTH. PTH secretion is regulated by the parathyroid cell plasma membrane Ca-sensing receptor (CaSR), which detects ambient serum Ca^{2+} and so regulates minute-to-minute PTH secretion. PTH increases Ca influx into the extracellular space through enhanced renal tubule reabsorption of filtered Ca that occurs within minutes; increased osteoclastic- and osteocytic-mediated bone resorption that appears within minutes to hours; and stimulation of intestinal Ca absorption indirectly through increased renal proximal tubule $1,25(OH)_2D_3$ synthesis that appears by 24 h after PTH secretion. Hypercalcemia suppresses CaSR signaling and thereby suppresses PTH secretion. Elevated serum Ca^{2+} stimulates distal nephron CaSR, which reduces net tubule Ca reabsorption, increases urine Ca excretion, and thus lowers serum Ca^{2+} to normal.

The authors have reported no conflicts of interest.

© 2006 American Society for Bone and Mineral Research

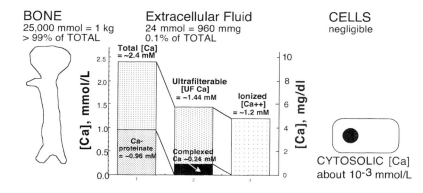

FIG. 1. Ca content and distribution in a 70-kg adult.

Intestinal Absorption

Ca intake is largely dependent on dairy product intake. Ca intake varies from a very low of 5.0 mmol (200 mg) per day to well above the recommended intake of 25 mmol (1000 mg) per day for adult males <65 years of age and premenopausal women. Net Ca absorption measured by the external balance technique shows the relationship between net absorption and dietary Ca intake (Fig. 2). Negative Ca balance appears when Ca net absorption falls below 5.0 mmol (200 mg) per day. Ca requirements increase with age, presumably to compensate for the decline in intestinal Ca absorption with age in both men and women. High rates of absorption occur in children, adolescents, young adults, and during pregnancy and lactation. When the diet is low in Ca, the efficiency of the absorptive process is enhanced to absorb the greatest portion of ingested Ca. Efficiency of absorption declines with age or when Ca intake is high. In humans, the efficiency of absorption can be measured as fractional Ca absorption using external 6-day balance studies, segmental perfusion after intubation with a multiple lumen tube, and single- and double-Ca stable- or radio- isotope kinetics. These studies reveal that only a fraction of dietary Ca is absorbed, ranging from 20% to 60% (Fig. 3). The range reflects age, Ca intake, skeletal requirements, vitamin D status, the state of the homeostatic system, and the bioavailability of Ca contained in foods. Despite the array of Ca absorption techniques used in clinical investigations, none are available for routine patient man-

agement. Fecal Ca losses estimated from balance studies are between 2.5 and 5.0 mmol (100 and 200 mg) per day (Fig. 3). The origins of fecal Ca include unabsorbed dietary Ca and secreted Ca contained in pancreatic and biliary juices and mucosal secretion. Fecal Ca is not regulated by hormones or serum Ca.

Sites, Mechanisms, and Regulation of Absorption

Transit time is rapid in the duodenum and jejunum; however, the large surface area in these regions are responsible for ~90% of Ca absorbed during adequate Ca intake. Increased Ca requirements stimulate Ca active transport primarily in duodenum and ileum and to a lesser extent in jejunum and all regions of colon to increase fractional Ca absorption from 25–45% to 55–70%.

The relationship between net intestinal Ca absorption (diet Ca intake − fecal Ca excretion) and diet Ca intake is derived from metabolic balance studies (Fig. 3). To maintain neutral or positive Ca balance, healthy adults require about 10 mmol (400 mg) Ca intake per day, because net Ca absorption is negative (fecal Ca exceeds diet Ca intake) or less than zero when diet Ca is less than 5.0 mmol (200 mg) per day (Fig. 2). As diet Ca intake increases from very low levels (<5.0 mmol or 200 mg/day), net Ca absorption increases and begins to plateau as Ca intake approaches 25 mmol (1000 mg) per day (will provide net absorption of about 7.5 mmol or 300 mg/day). The curvilinear relationship between net Ca absorption and Ca intake reflects the sum of two absorptive mechanisms: a cell-mediated, saturable active transport; and a passive, diffusional, paracellular absorption that is driven by trans-epithelial electrochemical gradients. The wide variation in net Ca absorption among healthy adults for any given level of Ca intake (Fig. 2), especially when Ca intake is above the 15–20 mmol (600–800 mg) per day range, is most likely caused by variation in the activity of the active transport component. Intestinal perfusion studies in humans show that net Ca absorption increases with luminal Ca concentration with a tendency to plateau at higher concentrations. Adults fed a low Ca diet for 1 month have greater net Ca absorption at the same level of luminal Ca concentration as those fed a diet adequate in Ca, which reflects stimulation of Ca active transport by $1,25(OH)_2D_3$. Very high Ca intakes increase primarily passive absorption, because serum $1,25(OH)_2D_3$ levels are low. Diffusional Ca flow along the paracellular pathway is in part dictated by the permeability of each intestinal segment, which is similar across duodenum, jejunum, and ileum, lowest in cecum, and intermediate across the colon. Major causes of increased and decreased Ca absorption are listed in Table 1.

At the cellular level, transcellular Ca transport (Fig. 4) is stimulated by $1,25(OH)_2D_3$ and upregulation of the intestinal epithelial vitamin D receptor (VDR). VDR-mediated increased expression of a number of vitamin D–dependent genes produce proteins that participate in the active transport process. Ca influx across the brush border membrane is facilitated by the

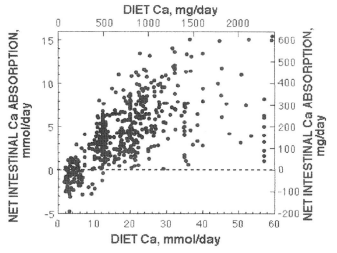

FIG. 2. Net intestinal Ca absorption in humans as measured by the external balance method in relation to dietary Ca intake. Adapted with permission from top right panel of Fig. 30.6. In: Coe FL, Favus MJ (eds.) Disorders of Bone and Mineral Metabolism, 2nd ed. Lippincott Williams & Wilkins, Philadelphia, PA, USA, 2002, pp.678.

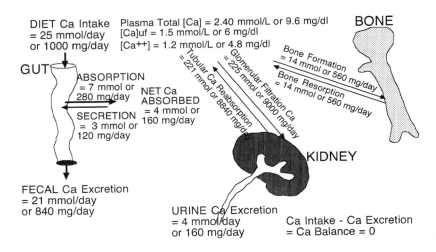

FIG. 3. Daily Ca turnover in a 70-kg adult.

channel created by the Ca transport protein 1 (TRPV6), which is induced by both $1,25(OH)_2D_3$ and estradiol independently through their cognate receptors. Within the cell (Fig. 4), Ca destined for transport is sequestered in vesicles containing the Ca binding protein calbindin 9 kDa. The vesicles then move to and fuse with the basolateral plasma membrane to begin the process of Ca extrusion out of the cell. Ca exit from the cell may involve both the low affinity, high capacity Na-Ca exchanger and an energy-dependent, high-affinity, limited capacity Ca, Mg-dependent ATPase (Fig. 4).

Renal Handling and Urinary Excretion

Filtration. Complexed and ionized Ca together are termed the ultrafilterable Ca and are freely filtered by the glomerulus with a Ca concentration of ~1.5 mM. The quantity of Ca filtered each day of over 270 mmol (10 g) is far greater than the Ca content of the entire ECF compartment and far more than net intestinal Ca absorption, which is ~4.0 mmol (160 mg) per day. To maintain neutral Ca balance, ~98% of the filtered Ca must be reabsorbed along the renal tubule. The substantial filtration followed by selective reabsorption allows precise control of excretion.

Reabsorption. Approximately 70% of filtered Ca is reabsorbed in the proximal tubule through predominately passive mechanisms. About 20% of filtered Ca is reabsorbed in the loop of Henle. Little Ca is reabsorbed in the thin descending and thin ascending limbs of the loop. However, the thick ascending limb of the loop of Henle (TALH) is the sight of paracellular Ca reabsorption driven by the Na-K-2 Cl transporter. Loop diuretics such as furosemide impair Ca reabsorption in this segment by decreasing lumen-positive voltage created by the transporter. The basolateral membrane of these cells contains the CaSR. An increase in peritubular Ca stimulates the CaSR, which reduces lumen positive voltage and thereby reduces Ca reabsorption. Also along this segment is the tight junction protein paracellin 1. Mutations of paracellin 1 result in a selective defect in paracellular Ca and Mg reabsorption. The distal convoluted tubule reabsorbs ~8% of filtered Ca and is the major site of physiologic regulation of urine Ca excretion. Active Ca reabsorption against electrochemical gradients involves entry across the apical membrane through the highly Ca-selective renal epithelial Ca channel 1 (TRPV5). The

TABLE 1. CAUSES OF INCREASED AND DECREASED INTESTINAL Ca ABSORPTION

Increased Ca absorption	Decreased Ca absorption
Increased renal $1,25(OH)_2D_3$ production	Decreased $1,25(OH)_2D_3$ production
Growth	Hypoparathyroidism
Pregnancy	Vitamin D deficiency
Lactation	Vitamin D–dependent rickets, type I
Primary hyperparathyroidism	Chronic renal insufficiency
Idiopathic hypercalciuria	Aging
Increased extrarenal $1,25(OH)_2D_3$	Normal $1,25(OH)_2D_3$ production
Sarcoidosis and other granulomatous disorders	Glucocorticoid excess
B-cell lymphoma	Thyroid hormone excess
	Intestinal malabsorption syndromes
With normal $1,25(OH)_2D_3$ production	Increased renal $1,25(OH)_2D_3$ production
Idiopathic hypercalciuria	Low dietary Ca intake

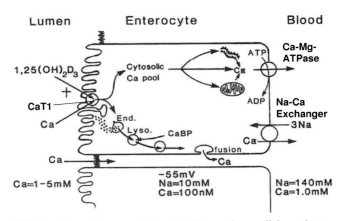

FIG. 4. Schematic representation of cellular and paracellular pathways for Ca transport across intestinal epithelium. Lumen-to-blood electrochemical gradients drive the paracellular pathway for Ca transport, and lumen-to-intracellular gradients are overcome by energy-dependent transcellular transport. The transcellular Ca sequestration model for intracellular Ca transport is shown. Molecules in bold are either ion channels, or transporters. CaBP is calbindin 9 kDa located within the Ca-transporting lysosomes. Reprinted with permission from Favus MJ 2002 Intestinal absorption of calcium, magnesium, and phosphorus. In: Coe FL, Favus MJ (eds.) Disorders of Bone and Mineral Metabolism, 2nd ed. Lippincott Williams Wilkins, Philadelphia, PA, USA, pp. 48–73.

channel is selectively more permeable to Ca than Na and is induced by $1,25(OH)_2D_3$, estradiol, and low Ca diet. Cytosolic Ca diffusion is facilitated by Ca binding to calbindin 28 kDa and calbindin 9 kDa, and active extrusion across the distal nephron plasma membrane is accomplished by the Na-Ca exchanger and a Ca-ATPase (PMCA1b). While Ca generally follows Na in this segment, reabsorption and excretion of Ca and Na can be dissociated. The collecting duct absorbs <5% of the filtered load. As a result of the reabsorption of Ca along the nephron, the final urine contains only ~2% of the filtered load.

Factors Affecting Reabsorption. Factors that may increase or decrease Ca excretion and their sites of action are listed in Table 2. Volume expansion increases and volume contraction decreases urine Ca and Na excretions through decreased and increased proximal tubule ion reabsorption, respectively. Increased dietary Ca increases urine Ca excretion with 6–8% of the increase in diet Ca appearing in the urine. Hypercalcemia increases ultrafilterable Ca but decreases glomerular filtration rate (GFR). In addition, hypercalcemia decreases proximal tubule, TALH, and distal convoluted tubule Ca reabsorption resulting in greater urinary excretion of Ca than Na. Ca activation of CaR in the TALH decreases Ca reabsorption, and Ca may also alter paracellin 1–regulated Ca and Mg permeability with decreased reabsorption of both ions. In the inner medulla collecting duct, the CaSR inhibits the water channel aquaphorin 2, which leads to polyuria, often observed in patients with hypercalcemia. PTH is the principle regulator of Ca reabsorption, with high PTH levels stimulating Ca reabsorption (Fig. 5). PTH reduces GFR and thus the filtered load of Ca, increases TALH active Ca transport, and opens the epithelial calcium channel (ECaC) in the distal convoluted tubule. Although PTH increases net Ca reabsorption, patients with primary hyperparathyroidism are often hypercalciuric, because increased tubule Ca reabsorption leads to hypercalcemia and an increased filtered load of Ca and resulting in hypercalciuria (Fig. 5). PTH-related peptide (PTHrP), which is secreted by a

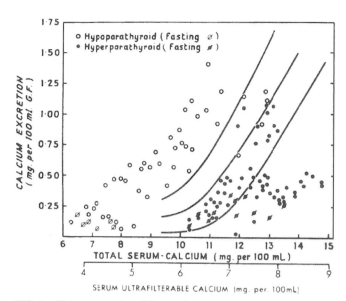

FIG. 5. Urinary excretion of Ca as a function of serum Ca concentration in normal subjects (solid line) and in patients with hypoparathyroidism (triangles) and hyperparathyroidism (circles). Dashed lines ± SD define normal range. Reprinted from Nordin BEC, Peacock M 1969 Role of kidney in regulation of plasma calcium. Lancet 2:1280–1283 with permission from Elsevier.

number of malignant cells, mimics the actions of PTH along the nephron. $1,25(OH)_2D_3$ actions on the kidney are complex and poorly understood. Vitamin D deficiency reduces Ca reabsorption independent of PTH levels. $1,25(OH)_2D_3$ increases CaSR expression, which decreases Ca reabsorption. Calbindin 28 kDa levels are increased and may increase Ca reabsorption. PO_4 administration reduces urine Ca excretion through increased distal Ca reabsorption and stimulation of PTH. Dietary PO_4 deprivation causes hypercalciuria in part by actions in the distal nephron. Acute and chronic metabolic acidosis increases urine Ca excretion, and alkalosis decreases urine Ca excretion. Endogenous acid production from the metabolism of sulfur-containing amino acids (methionine, cysteine) found in animal protein contributes to the postprandial increase in urine Ca.

Diuretics have variable effects on urine Ca excretion. Thiazide and related diuretics (hydrochlorothiazide, chlorthalidone), indapamide, and amiloride increase urine Na excretion and decrease urine Ca through an increase in renal tubule Ca reabsorption mainly in the distal convoluted tubule. These agents are useful in the treatment of Ca nephrolithiasis because they reduce hypercalciuria and urine Ca oxalate supersaturation. Loop diuretics (furosemide, torosemide, ethacrynic acid) increase urine Ca and Na excretion by inhibiting the Na-K-2 Cl transporter in the TALH. Hypercalciuria continues as long as urinary Na losses are replaced. These agents are useful in treatment of hypercalcemia.

Genetic disorders may increase or decrease renal Ca transport, including Bartter's syndrome associated with several mutations affecting TALH and hypocalciuria; Dent's disease caused by a defect in the proximal tubule affecting the chloride channel resulting in decreased tubule Ca reabsorption and hypercalciuria; inactivating mutations of the CaSR in familial hypocalciuric hypercalcemia (FHH) leading to increased renal tubule Ca reabsorption and hypocalciuria; activating mutations of the CaSR in autosomal dominant hypocalcemia associated with low PTH, decreased renal tubule Ca reabsorption, and hypercalciuria; and Gitelman's syndrome accompanied by hypocalciuria.

TABLE 2. FACTORS INFLUENCING RENAL Ca EXCRETION

Glomerular filtration
  Increased
    Hypercalcemia
  Decreased
    Hypocalcemia
    Renal insufficiency
Tubular reabsorption
  Increased
    ECF volume depletion
    Hypocalcemia
    Thiazide diuretics
    Phosphate administration
    Metabolic alkalosis
    Parathyroid hormone
    Parathyroid hormone related peptide
    Familial hypocalciuric hypercalcemia
  Decreased
    ECF volume expansion
    Hypercalcemia
    Dietary PO_4 deprivation
    Metabolic acidosis
    Loop diuretics
    Cyclosporin A
    Autosomal dominant hypocalcemia
    Dent's disease
    Bartter's syndrome

MAGNESIUM

Total Body Distribution

Adult tissues contain about 1.04 mol (25 g) of Mg, of which 66% is located within the skeleton, 33% is intracellular, and 1% is within the extracellular compartment. Although Mg is a major constituent of bone, it is not a consistent component of the hydroxyapatite crystal structure. Mg is primarily on the crystal surface, and a portion is in equilibrium with ECF Mg. Mg is the most abundant divalent cation in the intracellular compartment, where it serves as a co-factor in a number of biological systems that regulate enzymatic activities and neuromuscular functions. The concentration of cytosolic Mg of about 5×10^{-4} M is very close to the concentration in the extracellular fluid, and both pools are closely regulated by systems that have not been characterized. Serum Mg exists in the ionic state (55%), protein-bound (30%), and complexed (15%). Ionic Mg is the fraction that most closely correlates with Mg-dependent biological actions. Serum total or ionic Mg is not a good estimate of intracellular, soft tissue, or total body Mg content.

Cellular Distribution

Free, ionic cytosolic Mg represents 5–10% of total cellular Mg and is controlled through uptake of Mg by intracellular organelles. Sixty percent of cell Mg is located within the mitochondria where it functions as a cofactor in a number of enzyme systems involved in PO_4 transport, transcription, translation, and ATP use. The transporters and channels involved in maintaining the intracellular distribution of Mg are poorly understood.

Homeostasis

Mg blood levels are regulated largely by the quantitative influx and efflux of Mg across intestine, bone, and kidney rather than an elaborate hormonal system that has evolved for control of Ca. Blood ionic Mg is less potent than $[Ca^{2+}]$ in regulating PTH secretion. Serum Mg levels are regulated primarily in the kidney at the level of renal tubular Mg reabsorption.

Intestinal Absorption

Mg intake is generally adequate, because Mg is a constituent of foods of cellular origin and intake is proportional to total caloric intake. Net intestinal Mg absorption increases in direct proportion to dietary Mg intake. Above 2 mmol (28 mg) per day, Mg absorption exceeds Mg secretion, and Mg balance is positive. During usual Mg intake of 7–30 mmol (168–720 mg/day), fractional Mg absorption averages 35–40%. Net Mg absorption varies with dietary constituents such as P, which forms nonabsorbable complexes with Mg and thereby reduces Mg absorption. Unlike Ca absorption, Mg absorption is not stimulated by $1,25(OH)_2D_3$, and there is no correlation between serum $1,25(OH)_2D_3$ and net Mg absorption. Reduced Mg absorption occurs with diffuse intestinal disease or during chronic laxative abuse.

In both small intestine and colon, absorptive and secretory Mg fluxes have voltage-dependent and voltage-independent components, consistent with both cellular and paracellular pathways. Intestinal luminal Mg concentration drives passive diffusional absorption along the paracellular pathway. Saturable Mg absorption is small compared with the total Mg absorptive flux, indicating a modest cellular, regulated Mg flux.

Renal Handling and Urinary Excretion

Filtration. Ionized and complexed Mg are ~70% of total serum Mg and constitute the ultrafilterable Mg. Urine Mg averages about 24 mmol/day, indicating that ~95% of the GFR is reabsorbed before excretion.

TABLE 3. FACTORS INFLUENCING RENAL Mg REABSORPTION

Glomerular filtration
Increased
Hypermagnesemia
Decreased
Hypomagnesemia
Renal insufficiency
Tubular reabsorption
Increased
ECF volume depletion
Hypomagnesemia
Hypocalcemia
Metabolic alkalosis
Parathyroid hormone
Decreased
ECF volume expansion
Hypermagnesemia
Phosphate depletion
Hypercalcemia
Loop diuretics
Aminoglycoside antibiotics
Cisplantin
Cyclosporin A
Ethanol
Gitelman's syndrome

Reabsorption. In contrast to the 70% reabsorption of filtered Ca in the proximal tubule, this segment reabsorbs only ~15% of the Mg ultrafiltrate. About 70% of Mg is reabsorbed in the cortical TALH and no reabsorption in the medullary TALH. Mg may also stimulate CaR, resulting in decreased Mg reabsorption. Paracellin 1 in the tight junctions also regulates Mg reabsorption. The distal convoluted tubule reabsorbs ~10% of Mg through a transcellular transport process.

Factors Affecting Reabsorption. A number of factors may increase or decrease urine Mg reabsorption (Table 3). ECF volume expansion decreases Mg reabsorption and increases urine Mg because distal portions of the nephron are incapable of reabsorbing Mg. Hypermagnesemia increases urine Mg excretion in part through activation of CaSR. Hypomagnesemia increases TALH Mg reabsorption and decreases urine Mg. Hypercalcemia decreases Mg reabsorption in the proximal tubule and TALH. PTH increases Mg reabsorption, but in primary hyperparathyroidism, the hypercalcemia reduces Mg reabsorption. No other hormones are known to alter Mg reabsorption. Vitamin D and metabolites have no known action on Mg reabsorption. Thiazide diuretics have a minimal effect on Mg excretion. Loop diuretics markedly increase urine Mg excretion. Genetic disorders of renal Mg handling include: Gitelman's syndrome, which is associated with increased urinary Mg excretion because of a mutation of the chlorothiazide-sensitive NaCl co-transporter in the distal convoluted tubule; Bartter's syndrome, which is not associated with changes in serum Mg; and mutations of the CaR, which are associated with defective renal Mg transport.

PHOSPHORUS (PO_4)

Total Body Distribution

About 17,500 mmol (542 g) of PO_4 are found in adult humans (Fig. 6). Eighty-five percent of the total is contained in the hydroxyapatite crystals in bone and 15% is present in soft tissues, with only 0.1% in the extracellular fluids. In soft tissues, PO_4 is in the form of phosphate esters. Only modest

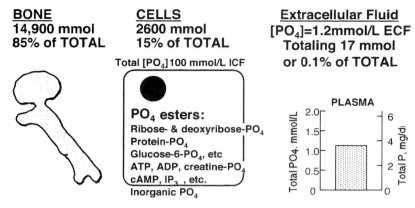

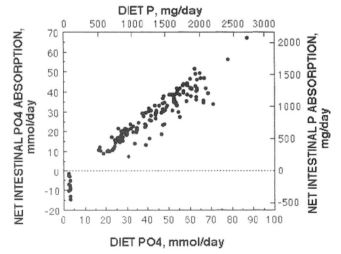

FIG. 6. Phosphate content and distribution in a 70-kg adult.

PO_4 gradients exist across the plasma membrane, with concentration in the extracellular fluids and cytosol of about 10^{-4} and 2×10^{-4} M, respectively. Unlike the tight control of serum Ca, serum PO_4 levels fluctuate widely depending on sex, age, dietary intake, rate of growth, and levels of several hormones. Serum PO_4 is largely determined by the efficiency of reabsorption of filtered PO_4. Serum PO_4 declines in the postprandial state and during intravenous glucose administration through insulin-mediated cellular PO_4 entry. P in serum is mainly in the inorganic form as PO_4 and exists in three fractions: ionic (55%), protein-bound (10%), and complexed to sodium, Ca, and Mg (35%). An adequate PO_4 concentration in serum is required to maintain the Ca × PO_4 ion product sufficient to support mineralization of bone. Low serum PO_4 levels may create a suboptimal Ca × PO_4 ion product and impair skeletal mineralization. A pathologically high Ca × PO_4 product in serum and extracellular fluids promotes ectopic or extraskeletal soft tissue calcification. A detailed discussion of the state of the three fractions of PO_4 in serum and the influence of protein binding and pH are found elsewhere in the primer.

Cellular Distribution

The majority of intracellular PO_4 ion is either bound or exists as inorganic phosphate esters, phospholipids in cell membranes, or phosphorylated intermediate molecules involved in a wide variety of biochemical processes including the generation, storage, and transfer of energy. Cytosolic free PO_4 ion concentration is quite low, whereas mitochondrial PO_4 represents a large proportion of total cellular PO_4, mainly in the form of Ca PO_4 salts.

Intestinal Absorption

PO_4 is found in most all food groups, and PO_4 absorption is directly related to dietary PO_4 intake (Fig. 7). Dietary PO_4 absorption is dependent on both passive transport driven by lumenal PO_4 concentration, which is maximal after a meal, and active, cell-mediated PO_4 transport stimulated by $1,25(OH)_2D_3$. Because PO_4 is a major component of all cells, dietary PO_4 intake is seldom <20 mmol (620 mg) per day. Using synthetic diets low in PO_4, metabolic balance studies show that net intestinal PO_4 secretion occurs when diet PO_4 is <10 mmol (310 mg) per day. However, when dietary PO_4 intake is within the usual range of 25–60 mmol (775–1860 mg) per day, 60–80% of dietary PO_4 is absorbed. Under conditions of normal dietary PO_4 intake, $1,25(OH)_2D_3$ does not stimulate jejunal PO_4 absorption. However, in patients with vitamin D deficiency or in chronic renal failure with low $1,25(OH)_2D_3$

production, the administration of $1,25(OH)_2D_3$ stimulates net PO_4 absorption. Even in patients with chronic renal failure who have low to undetectable serum $1,25(OH)_2D_3$ levels, there is significant net PO_4 absorption. In fact, the relationship between dietary PO_4 intake and net PO_4 absorption is the same in patients with chronic renal failure and in normal subjects. PO_4 absorption is reduced with diffuse small intestinal disease such as malabsorption syndromes.

Transepithelial PO_4 transport must overcome existing electrochemical gradients as the ion moves from intestinal lumen into the enterocyte. Entry across the brush border is driven either by an energy-dependent transport process or a secondary active transport process coupled to the flux of another ion such as Na. The linear increase in PO_4 uptake with luminal PO_4 and Na support the importance of Na-PO_4 co-transport across the intestinal brush border. $1,25(OH)_2D_3$ stimulates net intestinal PO_4 absorption through enhanced cellular brush border PO_4 uptake. The uptake process is saturable with an affinity coefficient of 1.0 mM. Thus, at luminal PO_4 concentrations >1.0 mM, diffusional PO_4 absorption predominates, but when lumen PO_4 concentration is low, as during low diet PO_4 intake, the transcellular mechanism is active. The saturable active trans-

FIG. 7. Net intestinal PO_4 absorption in relation to dietary P intake. Net intestinal P (mmol/day) = −5.4 + 0.77 × dietary P (mmol/day); r = 0.95. Adapted with permission from top panel of Fig. 42. In: Coe FL, Favus, MJ, Pak CYC, Parks JH, Preminger GM (eds.) Kidney Stones: Medical and Surgical Management, 1st ed. Lippincott-Raven, Philadelphia, PA, USA, 1996, p. 281.

port mechanism is present in proximal duodenum, jejunum, and to a lesser extent, in distal ileum. Net PO_4 absorption does not occur in colon.

Renal PO_4 Handling and Urinary Excretion

Filtration. Approximately 85% of serum PO_4 is ultrafilterable, and urine PO_4 excretion is ~25–33 mmol (750–1000 mg) per day. Thus, ~12.5% of glomerular filtrate is excreted in the urine.

Reabsorption. Eighty-five percent of PO_4 reabsorption occurs in the proximal tubule. The rate-limiting step in PO_4 reabsorption is located in the apical domain of the proximal tubule cells, which is also the site of active Na-PO_4 co-transport. The transporter moves PO_4 against trans-brush border electrochemical PO_4 gradients and follows a transcellular pathway that is dependent on low intracellular Na concentration. Three genes encode related Na gradient–dependent phosphate transporters (Npt1–Npt3), and the apical brush border membrane Npt2 accounts for ~85% of proximal tubule PO_4 reabsorption. Npt2 but not Npt1 is regulated, and a major regulator of Npt2 is FGF-23. Elevated levels of FGF-23 have been found in patients with disorders of hypophosphatemia and renal PO_4 wasting including X-linked hypophosphatemic rickets (XLH), tumor-induced osteomalacia, and autosomal dominant hypophosphatemic rickets. Other so-called phosphotonins have been identified that may also regulate Npt2. Beyond the proximal tubule, a small fraction of PO_4 reabsorption occurs in the distal convoluted tubule. Tubular maximum for the reabsorption of PO_4 is regulated and is approximately equal to the normal amount of PO_4 filtered by the glomerulus. Thus, any appreciable increase in filtered PO_4 increases urinary PO_4 excretion.

Factors Affecting Reabsorption. Dietary PO_4 intake, PTH, and FGF-23 are the major regulators of Na-dependent PO_4 reabsorption (Table 4) that determine the maximal capacity of the kidney to reabsorb filtered PO_4. Low PO_4 intake stimulates reabsorption, whereas high PO_4 intake inhibits reabsorption and increases urine PO_4. These alterations in proximal tubule PO_4 reabsorption over a range of PO_4 intakes are independent of changes in PTH, level of serum Ca, or ECF volume. Changes in PO_4 intake induce an inverse modulation in the maximal rate of the brush border Npt2 co-transporter within hours and thereby alter the level of PO_4 reabsorption. The effects of hypercalcemia and hypocalcemia are to decrease and increase renal PO_4 reabsorption, respectively. Part of the renal response to hypercalcemia is the associated decrease in GFR and therefore filtered PO_4. ECF volume expansion decreases proximal tubule Na and PO_4 reabsorption. PTH is a phosphaturic hormone and the principle regulator of renal PO_4 reabsorption and excretion. PTH decreases proximal tubule PO_4 reabsorption through suppression of the proximal tubule brush border Npt2 co-transporter. $1,25(OH)_2D_3$ increases intestinal PO_4 absorption and decreases renal PO_4 reabsorption. Insulin increases renal PO_4 reabsorption, and glucocorticoids and glucagon decrease renal PO_4 reabsorption. As discussed elsewhere, FGF-23 is a major circulating phosphaturic factor (phosphotonin) that is detectable in the circulation of normal subjects and in some hypophosphatemic disorders. Serum FGF-23 levels are positively correlated with serum PO_4 and suggest a role in normal physiologic control of renal PO_4 reabsorption.

TABLE 4. FACTORS INFLUENCING RENAL PO_4 REABSORPTION

Glomerular filtration
  Increased
    Hyperphosphatemia
    Mild hypercalcemia
  Decreased
    Hypophosphatemia
    Renal insufficiency
    Moderate hypercalcemia
Tubular reabsorption
  Increased
    Dietary PO_4 deprivation
    Hypercalcemia
    ECF volume depletion
    Chronic metabolic alkalosis
  Decreased
    PO_4 excess
    Hypocalcemia
    Acute metabolic alkalosis
    Chronic metabolic acidosis
    Parathyroid hormone
    Parathyroid hormone related protein
    FGF-23
    Calcitriol
    Thiazide diuretics
    X-linked hypophosphatemic rickets
    Autosomal dominant hypophosphatemic rickets
    Tumor-induced osteomalacia

MINERAL BALANCE AND ADAPTATION TO CHANGING REQUIREMENTS

Mineral balance refers to the state of retention or loss of Ca (Figs. 2 and 3), Mg, and PO_4 (Fig. 8) with respect to the external environment. Adaptation refers to adjustments in the mineral homeostatic system to meet mineral requirements and return the system to neutral balance. With respect to Ca, the homeostatic system is sufficiently flexible to maintain blood ionized Ca within the normal range during wide variations in dietary Ca intake and changing rates of bone mineralization. Thus, adaptations of the Ca homeostatic system occur while blood Ca remains stable. External mineral balance is determined by feeding subjects constant diets analyzed for Ca, Mg, and PO_4. Subjects are adapted to the diet for 7–10 days, especially if the quantity of the ions in the test diet differs significantly from a subject's usual intake. After a period of adaptation, a balance period of at least 6 days is conducted, during which time the diet is continued and all fecal and urine passed are analyzed for the ions. A nonabsorbable marker of fecal collection is administered with each meal to assess completeness of fecal collection. Dietary intake minus average daily fecal excretion during the balance period estimates net intestinal absorption of Ca, Mg, and PO_4 (Figs. 2, 3, and 8). Several examples of physiologic adaptation or pathological alteration in Ca, Mg, and PO_4 balances are presented below.

Neutral Balance

In neutral mineral balance, mineral ion absorptions match the sum of urinary and fecal mineral losses (Figs. 3 and 8). Neutral balance is found in adult men <65 years of age and in premenopausal, nonpregnant women after reaching peak bone mass.

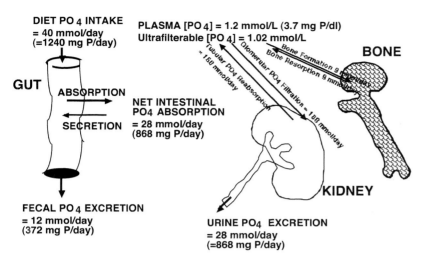

FIG. 8. Daily PO_4 turnover in a 70-kg adult

Positive Balance

In positive balance, mineral absorption and retention exceed fecal and urine mineral losses. Positive balance of Ca, Mg, and PO_4 occurs during skeletal growth during childhood and adolescence and during pregnancy and lactation. Adaptation such as during skeletal growth is characterized by increased efficiency of intestinal mineral absorption with greater influx of ions into the ECF space; reduction of urine mineral ion losses through increased renal tubule reabsorption to return mineral into the ECF space; and the resultant increased serum mineral ion levels that enhance delivery and deposition at skeletal mineralization sites. Increased mineral ion transport is stimulated indirectly by PTH and by direct actions of $1,25(OH)_2D_3$ through insertion of ion channels and transporters into epithelial membranes which enhance transepithelial fluxes.

Negative Balance

Negative mineral ion balance is defined by mineral loss (fecal plus urine) exceeding mineral retention and may be associated with clinically significant bone loss. Negative mineral ion balance with bone loss occurs in postmenopausal women and during estrogen deficiency at any age. Pregnancy is associated with negative mineral balance to the extent that minerals are transferred from the mother's skeleton across the placenta to the rapidly mineralizing fetal skeleton. However, balance studies performed on pregnant women reveal positive mineral balance because of the retention of mineral ions by the combined maternal-fetal unit. Bone loss and negative mineral ion balance occur during chronic glucocorticoid excess, hyperthyroidism, and vitamin D deficiency. In all three examples, intestinal mineral ion absorption is reduced, mineral fluxes into bone are exceeded by bone mineral ion efflux, and urinary ion excretion may be excessive (glucocorticoid excess and hyperthyroidism) or low (vitamin D deficiency).

SUGGESTED READING

1. Bringhurst FR 2001 Regulation of calcium and phosphate homeostasis. In: DeGroot LJ, Jameson JL (eds.) Endocrinology, 4th ed. Saunders, Philadelphia, PA, USA, pp. 1029–1052.
2. Nordin BEC, Peacock M 1969 Role of kidney in regulation of plasma calcium. Lancet 2:1280–1283.
3. Carafoli E 1987 Intracellular calcium homeostasis. Ann Rev Biochem 56:395–433.
4. Wasserman RH 2005 Vitamin D and the intestinal absorption of calcium: A view and overview. In: Feldman D, Pike JW, Glorieux FH (eds.)Vitamin D, 2nd ed. Elsevier, San Diego, CA, USA, pp. 441–428.
5. Favus MJ 2002 Intestinal absorption of calcium, magnesium, and phosphorus. In: Coe FL, Favus MJ (eds.) Disorders of Bone Mineral Metabolism, 2nd ed. Lippincott Williams Wilkins, Philadelphia, PA, USA, pp. 48–73.
6. Nordin BEC, Need AG, Morris HA, O'Loughlin PD, Horowitz M 2004 Effect of age on calcium absorption in postmenopausal women. Am J Clin Nutr 80:998–1002.
7. Ireland P, Fordtran JS 1973 Effect of dietary calcium and age on jejunal calcium absorption in human studied by intestinal perfusion. J Clin Invest 52:2672–2681.
8. Joost GJ, Muller D, Suzuki M, van Os CH, Bindels RJM 2000 Epithelial calcium channel: Gate-keeper of active calcium reabsorption. Curr Opin Nephrol Hypertens 9:335–340.
9. Favus MJ 1985 Factors that influence absorption and secretion of calcium in the small intestine and colon. Am J Physiol 248:G147–G157.
10. Bronner F, Pansu D, Stein WD 1986 An analysis of intestinal calcium transport across the rat intestine. Am J Physiol 250:G561–G569.
11. Birge J, Peck WA, Berman M, Whedon DG 1969 Study of calcium absorption in man: A kinetic analysis and physiologic model. J Clin Invest 48:1705–1713.
12. Christakos S, Prince R 2003 Estrogen, vitamin D, and calcium transport. J Bone Miner Res 18:1737–1739.
13. Sooy K, Kohut J, Christakos S 2000 The role of calbindin and 1,25-dihydroxyvitamin D_3 in the kidney. Curr Opin Nephrol Hypertens 9:341–347.
14. Hoenterop JG, Nilius B, Bindels RJ 2002 Molecular mechanism if active Ca^{2+} reabsorption in the distal nephron. Annu Rev Physiol 64:529–549.
15. Hebert SC, Brown EM, Harris HW 1997 Role of the Ca^{2+}-sensing receptor in divalent mineral ion homeostasis. J Exp Biol 200:295–302.
16. Yu ASL 2004 Renal transport of calcium, magnesium, and phosphate. In: Brenner BM (ed.) The Kidney, 7th ed. Saunders, Philadelphia, PA, USA, pp. 535–572.
17. Lee DBN, Walling MW, Corry DB, Coburn JW 1984 1,25-dihydroxyvitamin D_3 stimulates calcium and phosphate absorption by different mechanisms: Contrasting requirement for sodium. Adv Exp Med Biol 178:189–193.
18. Schmulen AC, Lerman M, Pak CY, Zerwekh J, Morawski S, Fordtran JS, Vergne-Marini P 1980 Effect of $1,25(OH)_2D_3$ on jejunal absorption of magnesium in patients with chronic renal disease. Am J Physiol 238:G349–G352.
19. Rude RK 1993 Magnesium metabolism and deficiency. Endocrinol Metab Clin North Am 22:377–390.
20. Tenenhouse HS, Portale AA 2005 Phosphate homeostasis. In: Feldman D, Pike JW, Glorieux FH (eds.)Vitamin D, 2nd ed. Elsevier, San Diego, CA, USA, pp. 453–476.
21. Shimada T, Kakitani M, Yamazaki Y, Hasegawa H, Takeuchi Y, Fujita T, Fukumoto S, Tomizuka K, Yamashita T 2004 Targeted ablation of Fgf23 demonstrates an essential physiological role of FGF23 in phosphate and vitamin D metabolism. J Clin Invest 113:561–568.
22. Beck L, Karaplis AC, Amizuka N, Hewson AS, Ozawa H, Tenenhouse HS 1998 Targeted inactivation of Npt2 in mice leads to severe renal phosphate wasting, hypercalciuria, and skeletal abnormalities. Proc Natl Acad Sci USA 95:5372–5377.

Chapter 14.   Gonadal Steroids and Receptors

Frank J. Secreto, David G. Monroe, and Thomas C. Spelsberg

Department of Biochemistry and Molecular Biology, Mayo Clinic College of Medicine, Rochester, Minnesota

INTRODUCTION

Since steroid hormones were discovered in the early 1900s, studies of their molecular actions have extended from the whole body, to the target tissues, to specific functions within those target tissues, to the specific cells, and finally to specific genes and their protein products. It is well accepted that sex steroids and other steroid family members play an important role in bone cell metabolism, including the regulation of osteoblast and osteoclast activities and reinforcing the coupling between these cells through paracrine factors. Gonadal steroids act on the skeleton to maintain proper bone homeostasis to prevent bone loss. The reduction of systemic estrogen secretion in postmenopausal women, for example, is primarily responsible for type I osteoporosis, a disease characterized by the rapid phase bone loss during the first 5–10 years after menopause. Estrogen replacement therapy reinstates the homeostasis between the osteoblasts and osteoclasts and prevents bone loss, thereby supporting the role of estrogen deficiency in osteoporosis. This chapter presents a brief overview of the structure and function of gonadal (sex) steroid hormones, their receptors, receptor co-regulators, and the mechanisms by which they regulate gene expression and cell function. Reviews, instead of original papers, are often used in this chapter to limit the numbers of references and to give further direction to the readers for each of the areas discussed in this chapter.

STEROID HORMONES

There are three categories of steroid hormones: glucocorticoids, mineralocorticoids, and the gonadal (sex) steroids (estrogens, androgens, and progesterone), each with different functions in the human body. Sex steroids are synthesized in response to signals from the brain. Certain signals from the central nervous system initiate a stimulus from the hypothalamus to the pituitary gland, which releases peptide hormones that target the reproductive organs. These peptide hormones, luteinizing hormone, and follicle-stimulating hormone, stimulate the synthesis of progesterone and estrogens in the female ovaries and testosterone in the male testes. Comprehensive reviews on these processes are available.[1–5] Traditionally, sex steroids were thought to only regulate activity in reproductive organs, but the discovery of steroid hormone receptors throughout the body has implicated varied patterns of functionality in many other tissues.

Biosynthesis of Steroid Hormones

The synthesis of steroid hormones from cholesterol involves pathways with 10 or more enzymes (Fig. 1A).[4,5] The level of steroid hormones in the bloodstream is primarily controlled by its rate of synthesis, because little of the steroid reserves are maintained. The increase of these hormones in the serum takes from hours to days, so cellular responses are delayed but last longer than the effects mediated by the peptide hormones. In ovulating women and during pregnancy, progesterone is secreted by the ovaries. Progesterone not only exhibits biological activity, but as shown in Fig. 1A, also serves as a precursor for all other steroid hormones. Estrone and estradiol are formed from androstenedione and testosterone, respectively (Fig. 1A).

This reaction is mediated by the enzyme aromatase, a cytochrome P-450 enzyme present in the ovary, as well as the testis, adipocytes, and osteoblast/osteocyte cells. Estradiol and estrone are in reversible equilibrium because of hepatic and intestinal 17β-hydroxysteroid dehydrogenases. The major circulating estrogen in postmenopausal women is estrone, which, in turn, follows two main pathways of metabolism, resulting in 16α-hydroxyestrone (active) and 2-hydroxyestrone (inactive/weak).[6] The balance in the ratio of these hydroxylated estrones along with the local production of estrogens by aromatase have been implicated as playing roles in several disease states, including breast cancer, osteoporosis, systemic lupus erythematosis, and liver cirrhosis.[7]

The steroidogenic pathway is essentially the same in the testes and in the ovaries, with the exception that testosterone is the major secretory product, although small amounts of estradiol are also secreted.[5] Testosterone is converted to more active metabolites in target tissues, such as gonads, brain, and bone. This modification is accomplished by two enzymes: 5α-reductase and aromatase.[5] As depicted in Fig. 1A, the 5α-reductase irreversibly converts testosterone to dihydroxytestosterone, which cannot be aromatized to estrogens. Conversely, aromatase irreversibly converts testosterone into estrogenic molecules.

Transport Through the Bloodstream

The major sex steroids in circulation are androgens and estrogens (estradiol and estrone). Because their chemical structure makes them fat soluble, most are bound to specific carrier proteins (e.g., serum [or sex hormone] binding globulins [SBGs]) for transportation through the bloodstream to hormone receptors that reside in target cells. Only 1–3% of the total circulating biologically active sex steroids are free in solution. Both the free steroid and the albumin-bound fraction (35–55%) can enter target tissues, thereby representing the "bioavailable" steroid pool. The remaining fraction, bound to the SBGs, is unable to enter the cells. The sex steroids enter all cells by simple diffusion through the cell membrane and subsequently bind to specific receptor molecules to regulate gene transcription.

Selective Estrogen Receptor Modulators

Steroid analogs, called selective receptor modulators (SRMs), have been developed to elicit tissue-specific rather than systemic effects, avoiding common side effects of steroid replacement therapy. Selective estrogen receptor (ER) modulators (SERMs) bind to estrogen receptors as a ligand, but act either as agonists or antagonists, depending on the cell/tissue-type (Fig. 1B). For example, the SERM, tamoxifen, is an antagonist in reproductive tissues with little effect on bone, and raloxifene is an agonist in bone with little effect in reproductive tissues. Other compounds (e.g., diethylstilbestrol) are not steroids but still bind with relative high affinity to the ER to mimic estrogen action in reproductive and bone tissues. The synthetic steroid, ICI 182,780, is a pure antiestrogen, binds to the ER and as a pure antagonist blocking all ER activity. Recent studies have shown that SERMs exert many of their actions by regulating a unique set of genes or differentially regulating the same genes as does estrogen.[8,9] The progesterone antagonist RU 486, along with the androgen receptor inhibitor, flutamide

---

The authors have reported no conflicts of interest.

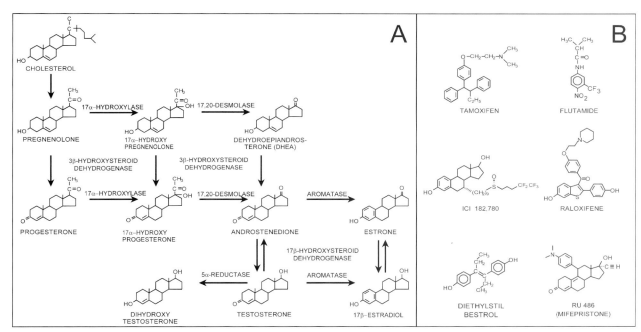

FIG. 1. (A) Pathways of steroid hormones biosynthesis from cholesterol. The initiation of steroid hormone synthesis involves the hydrolysis of cholesterol esters and the uptake of cholesterol into mitochondria of cells in the target organ. Dehydrogenation of pregnenolone produces progesterone, which serves as a precursor molecule for the generation of all other gonadal steroid hormones. (B) Chemical structures of common steroid analogs. [Adapted from Khosla et al. 1999 Dynamics of bone cartilage metabolism. In: Seibel M, Robins S, Bilezikian J (eds). Sex Steroid Effects on Bone Metabolism. pp. 233–245, with permission from Elsevier.[28]]

(aSARM), functions in a similar manner to SERMs. Further studies with SERM analogs, including their effects on steroid receptor structures and co-activator recruitment, are providing new alternatives to steroid replacement therapy.[3,10,11]

STEROID HORMONE RECEPTORS

Steroid hormones generate their intracellular signaling by binding to steroid-specific proteins called receptors. There are three steps in the general mechanism of action for steroid receptors: (1) binding of the steroid ligand to the receptor in the nucleus, (2) translocation of the steroid receptor complex to a specific site on the DNA, and (3) the regulation of gene transcription. Each type of steroid receptor is activated by a unique steroidal ligand. As shown in Fig. 2, steroid receptor proteins have multiple "domains," each of which has specific functions. All steroid receptor species share significant homology in terms of peptide sequence and functional domains. There are currently two sites, located in domains I and IV, identified as having transcriptional activation functions (TAFs). Additionally, a sequence of basic amino acids near the second zinc finger in domain III comprises a nuclear localization signal, allowing for the interaction of the receptor with nuclear transport proteins and subsequent entry into the nucleus. Other nuclear localization signals have been identified in the hormone-binding domain (IV) and are hormone-dependent.[12,13] As shown in Fig. 2B, the receptor domains have been further divided into six domains (A/B, C, D, E, and F) based on molecular structure and functions.

It should be mentioned that all species of sex steroid receptors, except for the androgen receptor, have two receptor isoforms (species) coded from the same or different genes (see Fig. 2B).[14] Furthermore, some isoforms have been shown to include several species or "variants" of each isoform.[15,16] Traditionally, it was thought that one isoform or splice variant

of a particular nuclear receptor acted as the primary mediator of gene expression, whereas the other variants antagonized the primary receptors effects. Recent data, however, suggest that ERα and ERβ regulate mainly distinct sets of genes and unique effects on cellular proliferation and other pathways.[8,9]

Heat Shock Proteins as Steroid Receptor Chaperones

In their inactive state, steroid receptors exist as part of a large complex in association with other non–steroid-binding proteins within cells not exposed to the steroid. Many of these proteins are members of the heat shock protein family that are classified by size (e.g., hsp90, hsp70, hsp60, hsp40, and hsp27) and act as molecular chaperones that bind to client proteins (e.g., receptors). Heat shock proteins assist in protein folding, intracellular transport, protein repair, and degradation of damaged proteins.[17,18] Overall, heat shock proteins are required for the activation and functionality of many proteins, including steroid receptors.

Receptor Activation

Each receptor reversibly binds its respective steroid with high affinity and specificity. However, few steroid receptors exhibit absolute ligand specificity (e.g., gonadal steroids can bind to more than one class of receptor) if the steroid ligands are at sufficiently high concentrations that encourages lower affinity interactions. This lack of steroid specificity among receptors is not unexpected in view of the significant homology among their ligand binding domains. The primary effect of ligand binding to domain IV is to "activate" the receptor molecule by inducing a conformational change in the whole protein, so that it can interact with DNA. This activation, as a result of ligand binding, involves the release of the chaperones (described above) and a conformational change in the receptor molecule, especially domain IV. This overall ligand-dependent

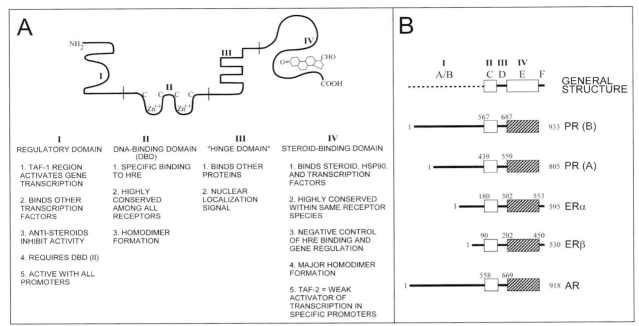

FIG. 2. (A) Structure and functional domains of steroid hormone receptors. Proceeding in the N-terminal to C-terminal direction, the receptors contain a variable domain (I or A/B), thought to be involved in cell type–specific regulation of gene transcription, a DNA binding domain (II or C) of 66–68 amino acids, which shows a high degree of homology among members of the steroid receptor family, a "hinge" domain (III or D), a steroid binding domain (IV or E), showing some homology, and variable regions (V or F) with little homology that somehow contribute to optimal function of the receptor. (B) Structural homology among sex steroid receptor family members. The sex steroid receptors range in size from 530 amino acids for the estrogen receptor to 933 amino acids for the progesterone receptor. Human progesterone receptors exist in two isoforms, A and B, generated by the same gene through differential promoters. The estrogen receptor also exists in two forms (ERα and ERβ); however, they arise from different genes, each with unique domains that allow for tissue- and ligand-specific functions. TAF, transcriptional activation function; DBD, DNA binding domain; HRE, hormone response element. [Adapted from Oursler et al. 1996 Osteoporosis. In: Marcus R, Feldman D, Kelsey J (eds.) Regulation of Bone Cell Function by Gonadal Steroids. pp. 237–260, with permission from Elsevier.[36]]

conformational change seems to be conserved across steroid family members.

CONTROL OF GENE EXPRESSION

The mechanism by which steroid hormone receptors exert their effects on target cells is 2-fold (Fig. 3). Initially, steroid hormones can act in a nongenomic manner through binding to steroid receptors associated with the plasma membrane. The resulting steroid receptor activation initiates a signal transduction cascade modulated by various kinase pathways that eventually alter the activities of select transcription factors. The second type of steroid action involves the better understood genomic pathway, by which steroid receptors in the cytoplasm and/or nucleus are activated after ligand binding and subsequently act as transcription factors to regulate gene expression. In the classical or canonical genomic pathway, ligand-bound steroid receptors bind to specific DNA sequences called hormone response elements (HREs), which are unique for each steroid receptor. In the non-canonical genomic pathway, activated receptors bind indirectly to the DNA through specific transcription factors (e.g., activating protein-1 [AP-1], signal protein-1 [SP-1]; see Fig. 3). Regulation of steroid receptor activity is further controlled by association with receptor co-regulator proteins (co-activators/co-repressors). Co-regulators bind to steroid receptors before and after receptor/DNA interactions and act with the general transcriptional machinery to either enhance or inhibit gene expression (Fig. 3).[14,19]

Genomic Pathway

Receptor Binding to DNA Element. The DNA binding domain of the receptor contains two "zinc fingers" (looped structures involving chelated metal ions) that are responsible for the binding to the HREs of target genes in what is termed the canonical pathway. A characteristic hexanucleotide inverted palindromic repeat allows the receptor to bind the DNA as a dimer. The orientation, sequence, and space between the hexanucleotide repeats are unique for each steroid hormone.[20] The receptors bound to the DNA through transcription factors (non-canonical pathway) also bind as dimers.

General Co-Regulator Function—Co-Activators and Co-Repressors. Steroid hormone receptor co-activators are involved in enhancing the transcriptional signal of the steroid hormone receptors after ligand binding.[11] Steroid receptor co-activator-1 (SRC1), the founding member of the SRC family (also called the p160 family), was originally identified as an interacting protein with the progesterone receptor (PR) ligand binding domain (LBD).[21] Further analysis showed that SRC1 exhibits transcriptional co-activation properties not only with the PR but also with nearly all type I nuclear hormone receptors. Two additional members of the p160 family of co-activators, SRC2 and SRC3, were also identified which interact with and co-activate numerous nuclear hormone receptors. The p160 family of proteins mediate the interactions with steroid hormone receptors through a centrally located receptor interaction domain (RID) of the p160 protein, which contains three α-helical LXXLL motifs necessary for interaction with steroid hormone receptors.[10,11,14] Binding of ligand to the receptor induces a conformational change that allows association of the RID domain with the LBD/AF-2 function of the steroid hormone receptor. Mutation or deletion of the SRC RID domains disrupts physical interaction with the steroid receptor LBD and

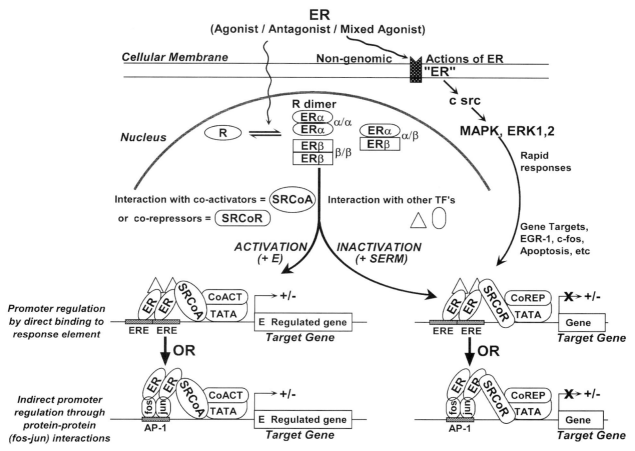

FIG. 3. Overall mechanism of action of steroid (estrogen) receptors. The inactive receptor is complexed to several heat-shock proteins (hsp). On binding of the steroid hormone, a conformational change in the receptor occurs causing the receptor to become "activated" and function as a transcriptional regulator in the genomic pathway. Alternatively, steroidal/nonsteroidal activation of a plasma membrane–associated receptor (steroid receptor or unknown membrane variant) can lead to rapid downstream cellular responses through nongenomic pathways. In the genomic pathway, the two isoforms of most sex steroid receptors (e.g., ERα or ERβ) form homo- or heterodimers and form large complexes with various co-regulators (co-activators or co-repressors), enabling the receptor to associate with targeted genes and regulate their expression. The binding of an agonist ligand to either receptor isoform causes a conformational change to occur in the ligand binding domain (LBD) of the steroid receptor followed by recruitment of primary co-activators (SRCoA), such as the SRC family of co-activators. This in turn, recruits other transcription factors (sometimes called "secondary" co-activators), such as p300/CBP, and histone acetylases to open the chromatin DNA, allowing for recruitment of the basal transcription complex and culminating in a productive transcriptional response. Some co-activators recruit HAT to destabilize histones and nucleosomes, whereas other co-activators contain this activity intrinsically. Binding of an antagonist ligand to the receptor, on the other hand, produces a conformational change in the LBD of the steroid receptor which recruits specific steroid receptor co-repressors (SRCoR) that cannot recruit the transcription co-activators necessary for a productive transcriptional response. These co-repressors recruit histone deacetylases (HDAC), which re-establishes the histone–DNA complexes and nucleosome structure and blocking DNA for transcription.

thus abolishes the transcriptional co-activation potential of the SRC molecule and the steroid receptor.[10,11,14] The p160 family of co-activators contains intrinsic transcriptional activation domains that contribute to the overall transcriptional activation elicited by the ligand-bound steroid hormone receptor. These domains function to recruit other molecules involved in activating transcription such as CBP/p300 (see Fig. 3). One interesting domain found in both SRC1 and SRC3 is the histone acetyltransferase (HAT) domain. This domain functions to modulate a condensed chromatin structure into a conformation permissive to transcriptional activation. HAT activity serves to transfer acetyl groups to specific lysines in histones and is thought to "loosen" the histone grip on DNA, facilitating the entry of other transcription factors (or the basal transcriptional machinery itself) to activate transcription. Thus, the various co-activators serve numerous functions in the processes of transcriptional activation.

Transcriptional repression by steroid hormone receptors is mediated by the recruitment of co-repressors that function by competing with co-activators for the ligand-bound LBD of steroid receptors. The co-repressor, REA (repressor of estrogen action), functions in this manner by directly competing with SRC1 in binding to the LBD.[22] Other transcriptional co-repressors bind the LBD either in the absence of ligand or in the presence of steroid receptor antagonists such as tamoxifen or ICI 182,780. The structure of co-repressors in many ways mirrors that of co-activators. Certain co-repressors contain histone deactylation interacting domains that seem to antagonize transcriptional activation by recruiting factors involved in histone deactylation, called HDACs (protein complexes that tightly pack DNA, rendering DNA elements inaccessible to transcription factors).[10,11,14] Thus, the activities of co-repressors and co-activators target similar processes in opposing manners (e.g., HAT activity versus HDAC activity). The regulation of co-activator and co-repressor function is a major component in determining the activation state of a gene. Figure 3 outlines the sequence of events that may occur when either a co-activator or a co-repressor is bound to the steroid receptor.

However, it must be noted that nuclear receptor activation is not a static process. Studies involving the promoter region of the E2-dependent gene pS2, showed that unliganded ER cycles on and off the promoter until bound by E2. Steroid binding results in a conformational change of the receptor, stabilizing the DNA/protein interaction, thus allowing for RNA polymerase and nuclear co-regulator association.[23] This process is highly transient and cyclic with receptors and co-regulators binding, dissociating, and rebinding with a 20-minute periodicity.[23]

Nongenomic Pathway. There is a growing body of evidence that steroids can alter cell metabolism by nongenomic effects (i.e., without direct interaction with DNA or transcription factor DNA complexes). More recent studies[24–26] have confirmed previous data showing that steroid hormones can act through nongenomic signaling pathways. These effects have been characterized by rapid responses ranging from seconds to minutes, involving steroid interaction with membrane receptors or steroid receptor activation in the absence of ligand. Nongenomic estrogen effects signal through the activation of cell surface receptors, leading to alterations in cAMP levels, calcium influx, and direct channel gating. Immediate early responses by estrogen can be mediated by ERα through the direct interaction with Src tyrosine kinase, leading to the activation of multiple signaling cascades, including mitogen-activated protein kinase (MAPK).[27] Mechanistically, covalent modifications of the steroid receptor, such as phosphorylation, are thought to be responsible for the activation of nuclear receptors by nonsteroid effectors.

PHYSIOLOGY OF STEROID EFFECTS ON BONE

The two major types of cells in bone that are responsible for the maintenance of normal bone density are osteoblasts (OBs) and osteoclasts (OCLs).[28–30] Normal bone remodeling processes involve bone resorption by OCLs and bone formation by OBs, which are tightly coupled to prevent a net loss of bone mass. Many factors that influence bone resorption can either act directly on the OCLs or indirectly through the OBs. Some of these factors are local regulators, including interleukins, TNF, prostaglandins, and TGF-β, or systemic factors, including PTH, vitamin D_3, calcitonin, glucocorticoids, and the sex steroid hormones.

Estrogens

Estrogen acts as a potent anabolic steroid regarding bone mass, reducing bone resorption indirectly by inhibiting osteoclastogenesis and directly by inhibiting OCL function. In postmenopausal women, there is an increase in bone remodeling activity in which resorption is no longer coupled with bone formation. After menopause, women lose bone mass at an average rate of 3% annually compared with 0.5–1.0% for similarly aged men.[31] Estrogen deficiency is recognized as the most important factor in the pathogenesis of postmenopausal bone loss, because estrogen replacement therapy has been shown to be effective in preventing and treating osteoporosis. The identification of estrogen receptors in human OBs and OCLs implicated estrogen as a direct effector on these bone cells, as opposed to previous theories that other calcitropic hormones were the primary mediators of the skeletal effects of estrogen deficiency.[28–30] Estrogens have recently been shown to play an important role in the selected physiology of men.[32] The strong influence of the local production of estrogens by the aromatase-cytochrome p450 enzyme in men and postmenopausal women are becoming more apparent.[7] Many of the late effects of steroid receptors are generated as secondary effects through the steroid regulated production of growth factors/cytokines, which in turn, can affect these target cells.

Progesterone

At menopause, there is a decrease in circulating levels of progesterone as well as estrogens,[6] which implicates progesterone in postmenopausal bone loss. However, in contrast to the abundance of work on the effects of estrogens on bone metabolism, there is little evidence of direct effects of progesterone on bone.[33] Clinical studies suggest that the effects of progesterone treatment on postmenopausal women are similar to those of estrogen, but combined estrogen and progesterone treatment has effects that differ from those of treatment with either steroid alone. Because of the adverse side effects of estrogen-alone therapy, alternative therapies, such as the combined estrogen and progesterone treatments, are being pursued. Although estrogen is usually required to induce their synthesis, progesterone receptors have been identified in human OB cells, so progesterone could exert direct effects on bone through its own receptor. Another possible mechanism for progesterone action is through interaction with glucocorticoid receptors. Progesterone can displace glucocorticoids from their receptors and vice versa.[34] Progesterone usually does not activate the glucocorticoid receptor and thus often blocks glucocorticoid responses.

Androgens

Like estrogens, androgens influence bone development and metabolism with dramatic clinical manifestations. Decreased androgen levels have been linked to lower bone density in men, and there is a strong correlation between hypogonadism in elderly men and hip fracture and spinal osteoporosis. Clinical studies also show that treatment of osteoporosis with androgens is effective in increasing bone density in both men and women. However, newer studies suggest that estrogens may play a greater (or equivalent) role than androgens in the male skeleton.[32] Human bone cells have androgen receptor concentrations similar to estrogen receptors and 5α-reductase and aromatase activity for the conversion of testosterone to dihydroxytestosterone and estrogen, respectively. Androgens decrease bone resorption by acting directly on human OCL cells. In addition, androgens also regulate the production of a number of bone-resorbing factors by mature OB or by marrow stromal cells, which contain OB progenitor cells. As with progesterone, further studies are needed to determine the complete role of androgens on bone metabolism.[35]

CONCLUSIONS

Steroid receptors act as cyto-nuclear transcription factors, whose structures are altered by ligand binding, such that the transcription activating domains of the receptor molecule are free to regulate gene expression. The binding of steroid analogs to these receptors can alter the receptor structure, thereby modulating which nuclear co-regulators are bound to the receptor and which TAF region is active. The particular type and relative amounts of steroid receptors in a cell determines the response as much as the circulating hormone levels (e.g., the ratio of ERα and ERβ in a given cell will significantly modulate the response to estrogen). The interaction of steroids with membrane receptors and the activation of steroid receptors in the absence of ligand through phosphorylation events can lead to alternative biological and physiological responses. Additionally, the ratio and presence or absence of specific nuclear co-regulators in a given cell or tissue type may alter steroid-dependent gene expression patterns. These molecular discoveries are aiding in the explanation of physiological actions of steroid hormones and their select steroid receptor modulators.

REFERENCES

1. Wilson JD, Foster DW, Kronenberg HM, Larsen PR 1998 Williams Textbook of Endocrinology, 9th ed. Saunders, Philadelphia, PA, USA.
2. Parl FF 2000 Estrogens, Estrogen Receptor, and Breast Cancer. IOS Press, Amsterdam, The Netherlands.
3. Lobo RA 1997 The postmenopausal state and estrogen deficiency. In: Lindsay R, Dempster DW, Jordan VC (eds.) Estrogens and Antiestrogens: Basic and Clinical Aspects. Lippincott-Raven, Philadelphia, PA, USA, pp. 63–74.
4. Ho CM, Strauss J III 2005 Ovarian hormone synthesis. In: De Groot L, Jameson JL (eds.) Endocrinology, vol. 3. Elsevier/Saunders, Philadelphia, PA, USA, pp. 2805–2903.
5. Handelsman DJ 2005 Androgen action and pharmacologic uses. In: De Groot L, Jameson JL (eds.) Endocrinology, vol. 3. Elsevier/Saunders, Philadelphia, PA, USA, pp. 3121–3139.
6. Schverberg A, Santoro N 2005 Mechanisms of menopause and menopausal transition. In: De Groot L, Jameson JL (eds.) Endocrinology, vol. 3. Elsevier/Saunders, Philadelphia, PA, USA, pp. 3021–3033.
7. Simpson ER, Misso M, Hewitt KN, Hill RA, Boon WC, Jones ME, Kovacic A, Zhou J, Clyne CD 2005 Estrogen—the good, the bad, and the unexpected. Endocr Rev 26:322–330.
8. Monroe DG, Secreto FJ, Subramaniam M, Getz BJ, Khosla S, Spelsberg TC 2005 Estrogen receptor alpha and beta heterodimers exert unique effects on estrogen- and tamoxifen-dependent gene expression in human U2OS osteosarcoma cells. Mol Endocrinol 19:1555–1568.
9. Monroe DG, Getz BJ, Johnsen SA, Riggs BL, Khosla S, Spelsberg TC 2003 Estrogen receptor isoform-specific regulation of endogenous gene expression in human osteoblastic cell lines expressing either ERalpha or ERbeta. J Cell Biochem 90:315–326.
10. Nettles KW, Greene GL 2004 Ligand control of coregulator recruitment to nuclear receptors. Annu Rev Physiol 67:309–333.
11. Smith CL, O'Malley BW 2004 Coregulator function: A key to understanding tissue specificity of selective receptor modulators. Endocr Rev 25:45–71.
12. Ing NH, O'Malley BW 1995 The steroid hormone receptor superfamily: Molecular mechanisms of action. In: Weintraub BD (ed.) Molecular Endocrinology: Basic Concepts and Clinical Correlations. Raven Press, New York, NY, USA, pp. 195–215.
13. Vegeto E, Wagner BL, Imhof MO, McDonnell DP 1996 The molecular pharmacology of ovarian steroid receptors. Vitam Horm 52:99–128.
14. McKenna NJ, Moore DD 2005 Nuclear receptors: Structure, function, and cofactors. In: De Groot L, Jameson JL (eds.) Endocrinology, vol. 1. Elsevier/Saunders, Philadelphia, PA, USA, pp. 277–287.
15. Denger S, Reid G, Kos M, Flouriot G, Parsch D, Brand H, Korach KS, Sonntag-Buck V, Gannon F 2001 ERalpha gene expression in human primary osteoblasts: Evidence for the expression of two receptor proteins. Mol Endocrinol 15:2064–2077.
16. Ogawa S, Inoue S, Watanabe T, Orimo A, Hosoi T, Ouchi Y, Muramatsu M 1998 Molecular cloning and characterization of human estrogen receptor betacx: A potential inhibitor ofestrogen action in human. Nucleic Acids Res 26:3505–3512.
17. Goetz MP, Toft DO, Ames MM, Erlichman C 2003 The Hsp90 chaperone complex as a novel target for cancer therapy. Ann Oncol 14:1169–1176.
18. Pratt WB, Toft DO 2003 Regulation of signaling protein function and trafficking by the hsp90/hsp70-based chaperone machinery. Exp Biol Med 228:111–133.
19. Wu RC, Smith CL, O'Malley BW 2005 Transcriptional regulation by steroid receptor co-activator phosphorylation. Endocr Rev 26:393–399.
20. O'Lone R, Frith MC, Karlsson EK, Hansen U 2004 Genomic targets of nuclear estrogen receptors. Mol Endocrinol 18:1859–1875.
21. Onate SA, Tsai SY, Tsai MJ, O'Malley BW 1995 Sequence and characterization of a co-activator for the steroid hormone receptor superfamily. Science 270:1354–1357.
22. Montano MM, Ekena K, Delage-Mourroux R, Chang W, Martini P, Katzenellenbogen BS 1999 An estrogen receptor-selective coregulator that potentiates the effectiveness of antiestrogens and represses the activity of estrogens. Proc Natl Acad Sci USA 96:6947–6952.
23. Metivier R, Penot G, Hubner MR, Reid G, Brand H, Kos M, Gannon F 2003 Estrogen receptor-alpha directs ordered, cyclical, and combinatorial recruitment of cofactors on a natural target promoter. Cell 115:751–763.
24. Lyttle CR, Komm BS, Cheskis BJ 2004 Estrogens: From classical endocrine action to tissue selective action. Ernst Schering Res Found Workshop 46:1–21.
25. Levin ER 2005 Integration of the extranuclear and nuclear actions of estrogen. Mol Endocrinol 19:1951–1959.
26. Bjornstrom L, Sjoberg M 2005 Mechanisms of estrogen receptor signaling: Convergence of genomic and nongenomic actions on target genes. Mol Endocrinol 19:833–842.
27. Song RX, Zhang Z, Santen RJ 2005 Estrogen rapid action via protein complex formation involving ERalpha and Src. Trends Endocrinol Metab 16:347–353.
28. Khosla S, Spelsberg TC, Riggs BL 1999 Sex steroid effects on bone metabolism. In: Seibel M, Robins S, Bilezikian J (eds.) Dynamics of Bone and Cartilage Metabolism. Academic Press, San Diego, CA, USA, pp. 233–245.
29. Rickard DJ, Harris SA, Turner RT, Khosla S, Spelsberg TC 2002 Estrogens and progestins. In: Bilezikian JP, Raisz LG, Rodan GA (eds.) Principles of Bone Biology, 2nd ed. Academic Press, San Diego, CA, USA, pp. 655–675.
30. Monroe DG, Secreto FJ, Khosla S, Spelsberg TC 2006 The classical estrogen receptor transcriptional pathway: Implications in human osteoblasts. In: Licata A (ed.) Clinical Reviews in Bone Miner Metabolism. Humana Press, Totowa, NJ, USA, 4:1–12.
31. Guthrie JR, Dennerstein L, Wark JD 2000 Risk factors for osteoporosis: A review. Medscape Womens Health 5:E1.
32. Khosla S, Melton LJ III, Riggs BL 2002 Clinical review 144: Estrogen and the male skeleton. J Clin Endocrinol Metab 87:1443–1450.
33. Prior J 1990 Progesterone as a bone-trophic hormone. Endocr Rev 11:386–398.
34. Leo JC, Guo C, Woon CT, Aw SE, Lin VC 2004 Glucocorticoid and mineralocorticoid cross-talk with progesterone receptor to induce focal adhesion and growth inhibition in breast cancer cells. Endocrinology 145:1314–1321.
35. Vanderschueren D, Bouillon R 1995 Androgens and bone. Calcif Tissue Int 56:341–346.
36. Oursler MJ, Kassem M, Turner RT, Riggs BL, Spelsberg TC 1996 Regulation of bone cell function by gonadal steroids. In: Marcus R, Feldman D, Kelsey J (eds.) Osteoporosis. Academic Press, San Diego, CA, USA, pp. 237–260.

Chapter 15. Parathyroid Hormone: Synthesis, Secretion, and Action

Edward M. Brown[1] and Harald Jüppner[2]

[1]Brigham and Women's Hospital, Harvard Medical School, Boston, Massachusetts; and [2]Endocrine Unit, Departments of Pediatrics and Medicine, Harvard Medical School, Massachusetts General Hospital, Boston, Massachusetts

INTRODUCTION

Parathyroid hormone (PTH), produced by the chief cells of the parathyroid gland, plays a central role in calcium homeostasis through its actions on bone, kidney, and, indirectly through stimulating the 1-hydroxylation of 25-hydroxyvitamin D_3, intestine. The three key physiological regulators of PTH secretion and synthesis and parathyroid cellular proliferation are extracellular calcium and phosphate ions and 1,25-dihydroxyvitamin D_3 [1,25$(OH)_2D_3$]. In response to decrements in extracellular calcium, increases in extracellular phosphate and/or reductions in 1,25$(OH)_2D_3$, the parathyroid chief cell secretes and synthesizes more PTH in the short term and undergoes cellular proliferation in the longer term. These three actions will increase blood calcium, reduce blood phosphate, and increase renal synthesis of 1,25$(OH)_2D_3$, thereby restoring these physiological perturbations to or toward normal. The effects of PTH are mediated by a G protein–coupled PTH/PTH-related protein (PTHrP) receptor. The actions of extracellular calcium on parathyroid function are also mediated by a G protein–coupled receptor, the extracellular calcium-sensing receptor (CaSR), that also modulates the actions of PTH on the kidney. 1,25$(OH)_2D_3$, in contrast, acts through a nuclear transcription factor, the vitamin D receptor (VDR), and the mechanism(s) underlying phosphate sensing are unknown. For the CaSR, PTH receptor, and VDR (discussed elsewhere), studies of naturally occurring mutations in humans as well as genetically modified mice have greatly clarified the functional roles of these receptors. In the case of the CaSR, drugs are now available that activate or inhibit the receptor and are already approved or in clinical trials for use in humans.

PTH and the active form of vitamin D, 1,25$(OH)_2D_3$, are the principal regulators of calcium homeostasis in humans and most likely all terrestrial vertebrates.[1,2] In bone, PTH stimulates the release of calcium and phosphate, and in the kidney, it promotes the reabsorption of calcium and inhibits that of phosphate. Furthermore, PTH increases the activity of the renal 1-α-hydroxylase, thereby enhancing the synthesis of 1,25$(OH)_2D_3$, which in turn increases the intestinal absorption of calcium and phosphate. As a result of these PTH-dependent actions, blood calcium concentration rises and blood phosphate concentration declines. The extracellular calcium concentration is the most important physiological regulator of the minute-to-minute secretion of PTH. A rise in blood calcium concentration decreases PTH secretion, whereas a reduction in blood calcium increases PTH release. 1,25$(OH)_2D_3$ and low phosphate, as well as an increase in calcium, all act to decrease the synthesis of PTH. The mutual regulatory interactions of PTH, calcium, 1,25$(OH)_2D_3$, and phosphate can thus maintain the blood calcium level constant, even in the presence of significant fluctuations in dietary calcium, bone metabolism, or renal function. In this chapter, we shall review the structure and biosynthesis of PTH, the regulation of its secretion, particularly by extracellular (Ca^{2+}_o) acting through the Ca^{2+}_o-sensing receptor (CaSR), the physiologic actions of PTH, and then examine the cellular and subcellular mechanisms responsible for those actions.

PTH

During evolution, the parathyroid glands first appeared as discrete organs in amphibians (i.e., with the migration of vertebrates from an aquatic to a terrestrial existence). In mammals, PTH is produced by the parathyroid glands, although its mRNA has also been detected in the rodent hypothalamus and thymus.[1] PTH is a single chain polypeptide that comprises 84 amino acids in all investigated mammalian species, whereas chicken PTH contains 88 residues. Although fish do not have parathyroid glands, two genes encoding distinct PTH molecules that are shorter than mammalian PTH species were recently identified in zebrafish and puffer fish.[3,4] Their mRNAs are expressed in lateral line cells, which are histologically related to the mammalian vestibular apparatus and the inner ear[3]; furthermore, amino-terminal fragments of both peptides activate mammalian and fish PTH/PTHrP receptors (Fig. 1). The amino-terminal region of PTH, which is associated with most of its known biological actions, shows high homology among the different vertebrate species. The middle and carboxy-terminal regions show greater sequence variation, and these portions of the PTH molecule seem to have distinct biological properties that are probably mediated through distinct receptors.[1] However, the physiological importance of these actions needs further clarification.

Within the first 34 residues, PTH shares significant amino acid sequence conservation with PTHrP, which was initially discovered as the cause of the syndrome of humoral hypercalcemia of malignancy.[1,5] Both peptides are derived from genes that presumably evolved through an ancient gene duplication event from a common precursor and thus share similarities in their intron-exon organization. PTH and PTHrP are furthermore distantly related to the tuberoinfundibular peptide of 39 residues (TIP39),[6] and the *TIP39* gene has an organization similar to those encoding PTH and PTHrP[7] (Fig. 2).

THE PARATHYROID CELL

Regulation of PTH Synthesis and Secretion and Parathyroid Cell Proliferation

Although a large number of factors modulate parathyroid function in vitro, only a few regulators are known to be of physiological relevance in vivo.[8] The extracellular concentration of calcium (Ca^{2+}_o) is the most important determinant of the minute-to-minute secretory rate of the parathyroid gland; low Ca^{2+}_o stimulates while high Ca^{2+}_o inhibits PTH secretion, PTH gene expression, and parathyroid cellular proliferation, actions mediated by the CaSR. 1,25$(OH)_2D_3$ inhibits expression of the PTH gene and may also directly reduce PTH secretion and parathyroid cellular proliferation. The molecular basis for vitamin D action, the VDR, a member of the superfamily of nuclear receptors, is discussed in subsequent chap-

---

The authors have reported no conflicts of interest.

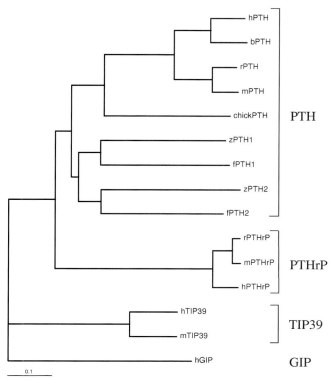

FIG. 1. Phylogenetic analysis of some precursors of PTH, PTHrP, and TIP39, and human GIP.[4]

ters. Phosphate, the most recently recognized direct modulator of parathyroid function, stimulates PTH gene expression, and, probably indirectly, PTH secretion, as well as parathyroid cellular proliferation[9] (Fig. 3). The mechanisms underlying phosphate-sensing by the parathyroid cell are not understood.

The parathyroid cell has a temporal hierarchy of responses to changes in Ca^{2+}_o, which can mount a progressively larger increase in PTH secretion in response to prolonged hypocalcemia.[8] To meet acute hypocalcemic challenges, PTH, stored in secretory vesicles, is rapidly secreted by exocytosis (e.g., over seconds to a few minutes). For the correction of prolonged hypocalcemia, parathyroid cells reduce the intracellular degra-

dation of PTH (over minutes to an hour or so), increase PTH gene expression (over several hours to a few days), and enhance the proliferative activity of parathyroid cells (over days to weeks or longer). Many, if not all, of these processes are controlled by the G protein–coupled, CaSR—described in more detail later—that recognizes extracellular calcium ions as its principal physiological ligand (Fig. 3). This CaSR is expressed on the surface of parathyroid cells and several other cell types that are involved in regulating mineral ion homeostasis.[10]

Physiological Regulation of PTH Secretion

There is a steep inverse sigmoidal relationship between PTH levels and Ca^{2+}_o in vivo and in vitro.[8] The steepness of this curve ensures large changes in PTH for small alterations in Ca^{2+}_o and contributes importantly to the near constancy with which Ca^{2+}_o is maintained in vivo. Parathyroid cells readily detect alterations in Ca^{2+}_o of only a few percent. The mid-point or set-point of this parathyroid function curve is a key determinant of the level at which Ca^{2+}_o is "set" in vivo. The parathyroid cell responds to changes in Ca^{2+}_o within a matter of seconds, and it has sufficient stored PTH to sustain a maximal secretory response for 60–90 minutes. $1,25(OH)_2D_3$ reduces PTH secretion in vitro,[11] whereas elevations in the extracellular phosphate concentration stimulate PTH secretion.[9] These changes in PTH secretion caused by $1,25(OH)_2D_3$ and phosphate are, however, not immediate and may reflect primary actions on PTH synthesis.

Regulation of Intracellular Degradation of PTH

The pool of stored, intracellular PTH in the parathyroid cell is finite, as just noted, lasting about 1 h. The cell must therefore have mechanisms to increase hormone synthesis and release in response to more sustained hypocalcemia. One such adaptive mechanism is to reduce the intracellular degradation of the hormone, thereby increasing the net amount of intact, biologically active PTH that is available for secretion. During hypocalcemia, the bulk of the hormone that is released from the parathyroid cell is intact PTH(1-84). As the level of Ca^{2+}_o increases, a greater fraction of intracellular PTH is degraded. With overt hypercalcemia, the majority of the secreted immunoreactive PTH consists of smaller carboxy-terminal fragments. However, at least two additional forms of PTH are also secreted, including a peptide that is truncated at the amino terminus and a modified, possibly phosphorylated form of

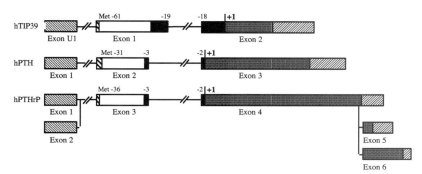

FIG. 2. Structures of the genes encoding human TIP39, human PTH, and human PTHrP. Boxed areas are exons and their names are shown underneath (because the start of exon U1 of the *TIP39* gene is unknown, the box is open on the left side), white boxes denote presequences, black boxes denote prosequences (for TIP39 presumed), gray stippled boxes denote the mature sequences; noncoding regions are shown as striped boxes. The small striped boxes preceding the white boxes denote untranslated exonic sequences (4 bp for TIP39; 5 bp for PTH; 22 bp for PTHrP). The positions of the initiator methionine based on the secreted peptide are noted above the graphs; the positions where pro-sequences are interrupted by an intron are noted above the graph. +1 denotes the relative position of the beginning of the secreted peptide.[7]

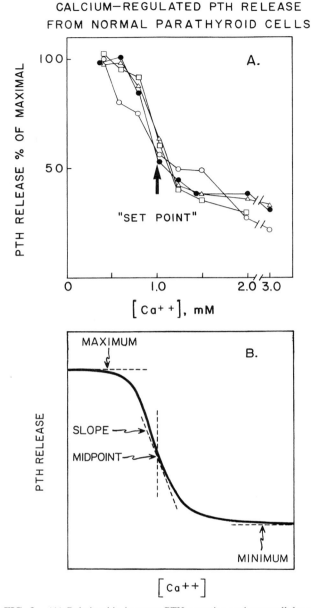

CALCIUM–REGULATED PTH RELEASE
FROM NORMAL PARATHYROID CELLS

FIG. 3. (A) Relationship between PTH secretion and extracellular calcium in normal human parathyroid cells. Dispersed parathyroid cells were incubated with the indicated levels of calcium and PTH was determined by radioimmunoassay. (Reproduced with permission from Brown EM 1980 Set-point for calcium: Its role in normal and abnormal parathyroid secretion. In: Cohn DV, Talmage RV, Matthews JL (eds.) Hormonal Control of Calcium Metabolism, Proceedings of the Seventh International Conference on Calcium Regulating Hormones, September 5–9, 1980, International Congress series No. 511, Excerpta Medica, Amsterdam, pp. 35–43. (B) The four parameters describing the inverse sigmoidal relationship between the extracellular calcium concentration and PTH release in vivo and in vitro: A, maximal secretory rate; B, slope of the curve at the midpoint; C, midpoint or set-point of the curve (the level of calcium producing one-half of the maximal decrease in secretory rate; D, minimal secretory rate.[61]

PTH(1-84).[12] The amino-terminally truncated form of PTH(1-84) seems to be identical to PTH(7-84),[12] which was previously shown to bind to a unique receptor, reduce in vitro the formation of osteoclast-like cells, and has hypocalcemic properties when tested in vivo.[13]

Physiological Control of PTH Gene Expression

The second adaptive mechanism of the parathyroid cell to sustained reductions in Ca^{2+}_o is to increase the cellular levels of PTH mRNA, which takes several hours. Reductions in Ca^{2+}_o increase, whereas elevations reduce, the cellular levels of PTH mRNA by affecting the transcription rate of the PTH gene as well as through additional, post-transcriptional mechanisms.[2] Available data suggest that phosphate ions also directly regulate PTH gene expression. Hypo- and hyperphosphatemia in the rat lower and raise, respectively, the levels of mRNA for PTH through a mechanism of action that is independent of changes in Ca^{2+}_o or $1,25(OH)_2D_3$.[2] This action of an elevated extracellular phosphate concentration could potentially contribute importantly to the secondary hyperparathyroidism frequently encountered in states with a chronically high serum phosphate, such as the secondary hyperparathyroidism in end-stage renal failure. It will be of interest to determine whether phosphate-sensing involves a receptor-mediated mechanism similar to that through which Ca^{2+}_o regulates parathyroid and kidney function.

Metabolites of vitamin D, principally $1,25(OH)_2D_3$, play an important role in the long-term regulation of parathyroid function and may act at several levels, including the control of PTH secretion,[11] as noted before, control of PTH, CaSR, and VDR expression,[8,14] as well as the regulation of parathyroid cellular proliferation.[2] By far the most important metabolite of vitamin D modulating parathyroid function is $1,25(OH)_2D_3$, which acts principally through an intracellular receptor that functions as a nuclear transcription factor, often in concert with other such transcription factors (i.e., those for retinoic acid or glucocorticoids). $1,25(OH)_2D_3$ reduces the levels of the mRNA encoding PTH through an action mediated by DNA sequences upstream from the PTH gene. $1,25(OH)_2D_3$-induced upregulation of the level of VDR expression in parathyroid could act as a feedforward mechanism to potentiate its own inhibitory action(s) on parathyroid function.[2] High Ca^{2+}_o and $1,25(OH)_2D_3$ coordinately increase the mRNA for the VDR.[8] Some of the "noncalcemic" analogs of $1,25(OH)_2D_3$ (e.g., 22-oxacalcitriol, calcipotriol, and 19-nor-1,25-dihydroxyvitamin D_2) inhibit PTH secretion while producing relatively little stimulation of intestinal calcium absorption and of bone resorption, the biological actions that underlie the hypercalcemic effects of $1,25(OH)_2D_3$.[15] Therefore, these synthetic vitamin D analogs may represent attractive candidates for treating the hyperparathyroidism of chronic renal insufficiency, because hypercalcemia resulting from the gastrointestinal and skeletal actions of $1,25(OH)_2D_3$ often becomes a factor limiting the treatment of such patients. In addition to the kidney, the parathyroid cell expresses the 25-hydroxyvitamin D_3 1-hydroxylase that forms $1,25(OH)_2D_3$ from 25-hydroxyvitamin D_3. Therefore, raising the level of 25-hydroxyvitamin D_3 (e.g., by administering vitamin D_3) may raise the level of $1,25(OH)_2D_3$ within the parathyroid cell in patients with end-stage renal failure and represent another means of lowering PTH levels in this setting.[16]

Physiological Regulation of Parathyroid Cellular Proliferation

The final adaptive mechanism contributing to changes in the overall level of parathyroid gland secretory activity is to adjust the rate of parathyroid cellular proliferation. Under normal conditions, there is little or no proliferative activity of parathyroid cells. The parathyroid glands, however, can enlarge greatly during states of chronic hypocalcemia, particularly in the setting of renal failure [probably because of a combination of hypocalcemia, hyperphosphatemia, and low levels of

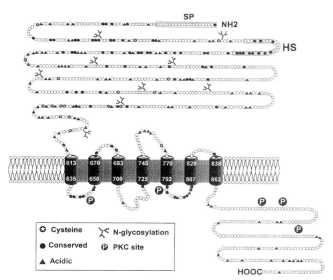

FIG. 4. Predicted structure of the human CaR. SP, signal peptide; HS, hydrophobic segment.[62]

1,25$(OH)_2D_3$ in the latter condition].[8] This enlargement cannot be accounted for solely by cellular hypertrophy, although the latter does contribute to the overall increase in glandular mass. The ability of calcium administration to prevent parathyroid hyperplasia in mice with deleted vitamin D receptors shows the importance of calcium in regulating parathyroid cell number.[17] Calcium acts to prevent hyperplasia through activation of the CaSR, because mutational inactivation of the CaSR in humans and mice leads to parathyroid hyperplasia at birth and because calcimimetic compounds that activate the CaSR can prevent parathyroid hyperplasia in experimental uremia.[18]

Molecular Basis for Ca^{2+}_o Sensing by the Parathyroid Cell

Recent studies have elucidated the mechanism by which Ca^{2+}_o regulates several of the aspects of parathyroid function described above. For many years, it was unclear how an ion could regulate cellular function, other than through actions on ion channels, membrane potential, and the like. The realization that the calcium ion could control the function of parathyroid and other cells through a G protein–coupled receptor (GPCR) contributed to the current awareness that a much wider range of agents affect cellular function through GPCRs than previously recognized (e.g., lipids, bile acids, citric acid cycle intermediates).

The CaSR is the molecular mechanism underlying the sensing of Ca^{2+}_o by the parathyroid chief cells as well as other cells involved in calcium homeostasis, particularly the kidney.[19] In effect, the CaSR acts as the body's thermostat for calcium or "calciostat." It is capable of detecting perturbations in the serum ionized calcium concentration of only a few percent and responding with the alterations in parathyroid function described above as well as changes in renal function that are designed to normalize Ca^{2+}_o. The CaSR has three structural domains: a large extracellular "sensing" domain (ECD), the seven membrane-spanning "serpentine" motif characteristic of the GPCRs, and a long intracellular, carboxyterminal (C)-tail (Fig. 4).[19] The ECD of the CaSR is heavily glycosylated, which is important for its efficient cell surface expression. The biologically active form of the receptor is a dimer, linked together by two disulfide bonds (at cys129 and cys131) between the ECDs of two monomers. The CaSR's ECD has important determinants for binding extracellular calcium ions, although the locations of these sites are currently unknown, and some binding of calcium to the transmembrane domains may occur as well. After the binding of calcium to the ECD, the initiation of CaSR signaling involves the binding of G proteins to the receptor's intracellular loops—especially the second and third loops—and the proximal portion of the C-tail.[20] In addition to activating phospholipases A_2, C, and D, the CaSR also activates various mitogen-activated protein kinases (MAPKs) and inhibits adenylate cyclase.[18]

While Ca^{2+}_o is undoubtedly the CaSR's principal physiological ligand in vivo, the receptor is activated by a number of other ligands, at least two of which—magnesium and certain amino acids[21]—are likely to be physiologically relevant. Although magnesium is ~2-fold less potent than calcium in its actions on the CaSR, and the level of Mg^{2+}_o is lower than that of Ca^{2+}_o, persons with inactivating or activating mutations of the receptor tend to have increases or decreases in their serum magnesium concentrations, respectively. These alterations in serum magnesium encompass changes within the normal range to frank hyper- or hypo-magnesemia. Thus, it is likely that the CaSR contributes to "setting" the normal level of extracellular magnesium.

More recent studies have shown that certain amino acids, especially aromatic amino acids, allosterically activate the CaSR,[21] effectively sensitizing the receptor to any given level of Ca^{2+}_o. It is possible, therefore, that the CaSR serves a more generalized role as a "nutrient" receptor, recognizing not only divalent cations but also amino acids. For instance, both calcium and aromatic amino acids increase gastrin release and acid production in the stomach—actions that are likely mediated by the CaSR.[19] There are additional circumstances in which calcium and protein metabolism seem to be linked in ways that could be mediated by the CaSR. A high protein intake promotes hypercalciuria, an action traditionally ascribed to the acid load generated by metabolism of the protein; however, stimulation of renal CaSRs by high circulating levels of amino acids could also contribute to the hypercalciuria. Furthermore, a low protein intake in normal subjects, as well as in patients with renal impairment, is associated with elevated levels of PTH.[22] This association could be mediated, in part, by the parathyroid glands sensing a reduction in "nutrient" availability (e.g., the sum of divalent cation and amino acids and responding with enhanced PTH secretion).

In addition to these endogenous ligands, allosteric activators of the CaSR, so-called "calcimimetics," have been developed, as have CaSR antagonists, termed "calcilytics."[23] Calcimimetics are currently in clinical trials for the treatment of primary hyperparathyroidism and have been approved for use in controlling secondary hyperparathyroidism in patients with chronic renal insufficiency undergoing dialysis treatment. They seem to provide an effective treatment in the latter setting and restore calcium to or toward normal in primary hyperparathyroidism. Calcilytics provide a means of stimulating endogenous PTH secretion by "tricking" the parathyroid glands into sensing hypocalcemia. They may provide an alternative to the injection of PTH and its analogs as an anabolic treatment of osteoporosis.[23]

Studies of mice homozygous for targeted disruption of the *CaSR* gene[24] and of patients with activating or inactivating mutations of the receptor[14] have firmly established the role of the CaSR in regulating several of the aspects of parathyroid function that were discussed above. With complete knockout of the CaSR, there is markedly abnormal Ca^{2+}_o-regulated PTH release, which is poorly, if at all, regulated by extracellular calcium. There is also marked parathyroid hyperplasia in this

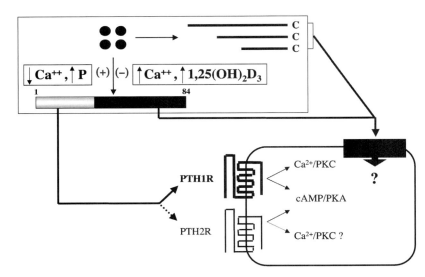

FIG. 5. PTH production and activation of different receptors. Intact PTH and different fragments are secreted from the parathyroid glands. Low ionized calcium and elevated phosphate increase PTH synthesis and secretion, whereas increased ionized calcium and 1,25(OH)$_2$D lead to a decrease; note that the regulatory actions of calcium are mediated through the calcium-sensing receptor. Different receptors interact with the amino- or carboxy-terminal portion of intact PTH. Through its amino-terminal portion, PTH activates the PTH/PTHrP receptor (PTH1R), a G protein–coupled receptor that mediates its actions through at least two different signaling pathways, cAMP/KPA and Ca^{2+}/PKC. The closely related PTH2 receptor (PTH2R) is most likely the primary receptor for the tuberoinfundibular peptide of 39 residues (TIP39); however, at least the human PTH2R is also activated by amino-terminal PTH. Another receptor, which has not yet been cloned, interacts only with the carboxy-terminal portion of PTH.

setting, establishing that the CaSR, directly or indirectly, regulates parathyroid cellular proliferation. Available data also suggest that the receptor mediates the inhibitory effect of high Ca$^{2+}{}_o$ on PTH gene expression. Additional studies will be needed to determine the receptor's role in the regulation of other aspects of parathyroid function by Ca$^{2+}{}_o$, such as intracellular degradation of PTH.

In addition to being expressed in the parathyroid chief cells, the CaSR is also expressed by the calcitonin-secreting C cells of the thyroid gland, where it mediates the stimulation of CT secretion by Ca$^{2+}{}_o$.[19] Calcitonin probably does not participate to a meaningful extent in maintaining calcium homeostasis in humans, but its hypocalcemic actions—exerted through inhibition of bone resorption and stimulation of renal calcium excretion—are robust in other species, particularly rodents. It serves, therefore, as part of a homeostatic loop in which hypercalcemia stimulates calcitonin secretion, whose hypocalcemic actions, when combined with the homeostatic action of lowering PTH levels, foster a return to normocalcemia.

Molecular Defects in the CaSR

Soon after the cloning of the CaSR, families with familial hypocalciuric hypercalcemia and neonatal severe hyperparathyroidism were found in most cases to harbor inactivating mutations in the *CaSR* gene. Subsequently, activating mutations in the receptor were identified as the cause of a form of hypoparathyroidism called autosomal dominant hypoparathyroidism (ADH or ADHP). In addition to providing the molecular basis for these inherited conditions of calcium metabolism, the clinical and biochemical features of these disorders has provided important insights into the CaSR's role in calcium and water metabolism as well as into the structure and function of the receptor.[14]

In familial hypocalciutic hypercalcemia (FHH), there is PTH-dependent hypercalcemia accompanied by PTH-independent hypocalciuria, firmly establishing the role of the CaSR in Ca$^{2+}{}_o$-regulated PTH release as well as in renal handling of calcium. Reduced CaSR activity, likely in the cortical thick ascending limb (CTAL), leads to constitutive reabsorption of calcium with a conspicuous lack of the usual calciuric action of hypercalcemia mediated by the receptor. These individuals also concentrate their urine more effectively than a patient with primary hyperparathyroidism and a comparable degree of hypercalcemia,[25] supporting the CaSR's role

in inhibiting the renal concentrating mechanism. Finally, the prominent lack of symptoms in FHH supports a role for the CaSR in mediating some of the symptomatology of hypercalcemia.

In contrast to FHH, neonatal severe hyperparathyroidism (NSHPT) is a severe disorder caused, in its worst cases, by the presence of homozygous or compound heterozygous mutations in the CaSR.[14] As in mice homozygous for knockout of the CaSR, there is marked, PTH-dependent hypercalcemia with hyperparathyroid bone disease. The disorder can be fatal without urgent parathyroidectomy. Thus, the total absence of normally functioning CaSRs can be incompatible with life. The clinical and biochemical manifestations of ADH are the converse of FHH, and the former might also be termed familial hypercalciuric hypocalcemia.[26] The presence of CaSRs with inappropriately high activity at any given level of Ca$^{2+}{}_o$ inhibits PTH secretion and promotes an excessive degree of urinary calcium excretion for a given level of Ca$^{2+}{}_o$. Of interest, as the level of serum calcium concentration is increased in these patients by treatment with 1,25(OH)D$_3$ and calcium supplementation, they can develop symptoms suggesting hypercalcemia, polydipsia, and polyuria, even while still hypocalcemic, again supporting the CaSR as a mediator of symptoms of hypercalcemia as well as the link between calcium and water metabolism noted above.

PTH ACTION

Receptors for PTH

PTH-dependent regulation of mineral ion homeostasis is largely mediated through the PTH/PTHrP receptor, which is coupled to adenylate cyclase through G$_s\alpha$ and to phospholipase C through the G$_q$ family of signaling proteins.[1,27] (see Fig. 5). While most PTH/PTHrP receptor–dependent actions involve activation of adenylyl cyclase, some actions seem to require phospholipase C–mediated events. These dual signaling properties are particularly relevant, because the PTH/PTHrP receptor was recently shown to interact in vitro, through a PDZ domain, with Na$^{(+)}$/H$^{(+)}$ exchange regulatory factors sodium-hydrogen exchanger regulatory factors (NHERF) 1 and NHERF2. In the presence of NHERF2 (but probably also NHERF1), the activated PTH/PTHrP receptor preferentially activated phospholipase C and inhibited adenylyl cyclase through stimulation of inhibitory G proteins (G$_{i/o}$ proteins).[28]

NHERF-dependent changes in PTH/PTHrP receptor signaling may thus account for some of different tissue- and cell-specific actions induced by PTH or PTHrP.

The PTH/PTHrP receptor belongs to a distinct family of G protein–coupled receptors and mediates with similar or indistinguishable efficacy biological actions of both PTH and PTHrP.[1,27] The PTH/PTHrP receptor is most abundantly expressed in the target tissues for PTH's actions (i.e., kidney and bone), but it is also found in a large variety of other fetal and adult tissues, and at particularly high concentrations in growth plate chondrocytes.[1,27] In tissues other than kidney and bone, the PTH/PTHrP receptor most likely mediates the para-/autocrine actions of PTHrP rather than the endocrine actions of PTH. Of considerable importance is the receptor's role in cartilage and bone development, because it mediates in this tissue the PTHrP-dependent regulation of chondrocyte proliferation and differentiation; thus, it has a major role in bone development and growth.[29]

The PTH/PTHrP receptor seems to be the most important receptor mediating the actions of PTH and PTHrP. There is considerable pharmacologic evidence, however, for the existence of other receptors that are activated by either PTH and/or PTHrP, including a receptor/binding protein that interacts with the carboxy-terminal portion of PTH and may be involved in mediating the hypocalcemic actions of this portion of the molecule.[13] However, most of these putative receptors have not yet been cloned and their biological functions, some of which may be unrelated to the control of calcium and phosphorus homeostasis, remain poorly characterized. Only cDNA encoding the PTH2 receptor has been isolated thus far.[1,27,30] Only the human PTH2 receptor, but not the homolog of this receptor from other species, is activated by PTH; PTHrP does not activate any of the different PTH2 receptor species unless residues 5 and 23 are replaced with the corresponding PTH-specific amino acids.[1,27] However, the natural ligand for the PTH2 receptor seems to be TIP39, a recently identified hypothalamic peptide.[6] Expression of the PTH2 receptor is restricted to relatively few tissues (i.e., placenta, pancreas, blood vessels, testis, and brain), and although most biological function(s) mediated through this receptor remain to be determined, it may have a role in the regulation of renal blood flow.[30,31]

Actions of PTH on Bone

PTH has complex and only partially understood actions on bone that require the presence of and often direct contact between several different specialized cell types, including osteoblasts, bone marrow stromal cells, hematopoietic precursors of osteoclasts, and mature osteoclasts.[32] Administration of PTH leads to the release of calcium from a rapidly turning-over pool of calcium near the surface of bone; after several hours, calcium is also released from an additional pool that turns over more slowly.[33] Chronic administration of PTH (or increased secretion of PTH associated with primary hyperparathyroidism) leads to an increase in osteoclast cell number and activity.[34] The release of calcium is accompanied by the release of phosphate and matrix components, such as degradation products of collagen. Paradoxically, particularly when given intermittently, PTH administration leads to the formation of increased amounts of trabecular bone[35,36]; these anabolic actions of PTH are currently being explored for the prevention and treatment of osteoporosis, either alone or in combination with a bisphosphonate.[37–39]

The osteoblast and its precursor, the marrow stromal cell, have central roles in directing both the catabolic (bone resorption) and anabolic (bone formation) actions of PTH (Fig. 6). Only a subset of stromal cells and osteoblasts synthesize

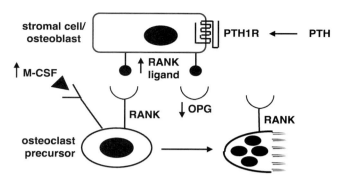

FIG. 6. PTH actions on bone. The PTH/PTHrP receptor (PTH1R) is expressed on stromal cells/osteoblasts. On receptor activation by PTH, expression of M-CSF and RANKL are increased, which enhances the formation of osteoclasts from precursors and the activity of already existing mature osteoclasts. In response to PTH, expression of OPG, a decoy receptor for RANKL, is decreased, thus reducing the activity of existing osteoclasts and the formation of mature osteoclasts from precursor cells.

mRNA encoding the PTH/PTHrP receptor.[1] Although cell lines capable of differentiating into osteoclasts have been shown to have PTH/PTHrP receptors, these receptors are not needed or sufficient for the stimulation of osteoclastic development by PTH. Elegant studies of co-cultures of osteoblasts/stromal cells and osteoclast precursors had shown that PTH affects osteoclast maturation and functions only indirectly through its actions on cells of the osteoblast lineage, which express abundant amounts of the PTH/PTHrP receptor.[32] A key osteoblastic protein that activates osteoclast development and activity of mature osteoclasts is RANKL (also termed osteoclast-differentiating factor [ODF], TRANCE, or osteoprotegerin ligand), a member of the TNF family of proteins, which is anchored by a single hydrophobic membrane-spanning domain to the cell surface of osteoblasts.[32] On interaction with RANK, a member of the TNF receptor family, expressed on pre-osteoclasts, these precursors differentiate into mature osteoclasts, if macrophage-colony stimulating factor (M-CSF) is also present.[32] RANKL also increases the bone-resorbing properties of mature osteoclasts. PTH stimulates the expression of RANKL on the cell surface of osteoblasts, and the same response is stimulated by other molecules [i.e., interleukin 11 (IL-11), prostaglandin E$_2$, and 1,25(OH)$_2$D] that were previously noted to stimulate the formation of osteoclasts. PTH also stimulates the synthesis of M-CSF.[32]

The interactions of osteoblastic RANKL and its osteoclastic receptor RANK are further controlled by a secreted protein, osteoprotegerin (OPG), a soluble "decoy" receptor with homology to RANK and other members of the TNF receptor family. The effects of overexpression of OPG in transgenic mice and the ablation of the *OPG* gene both suggest that this binding protein importantly modulates the communication between osteoblasts and osteoclasts.[32] PTH inhibits the expression of OPG in osteoblast cells. Thus, by increasing M-CSF and RANKL and inhibiting OPG expressed locally by cells of the osteoblast lineage, PTH stimulates osteoclastogenesis and the activity of mature osteoclasts.

The mechanisms whereby PTH increases bone formation are complicated and less well understood (see Fig. 4). PTH increases the number of osteoblasts by increasing the number of osteoprogenitors cells[40] as a result of a reduction in apoptosis of pre-osteoblasts and osteoblasts,[41] by increasing osteoblast proliferation, and perhaps by converting inactive bone-lining cells to active osteoblasts.[42] On the other hand, when added to cells in culture, PTH stops pre-osteoblastic cells from becoming mature osteoblasts. It also changes the activity of mature osteoblasts. In cell culture systems, PTH inhibits the production of collagen and other matrix proteins, perhaps partly by steering the key osteoblast transcription factor, RUNX2 (also called CBFA-1), to proteosome-mediated destruction.[42] The prominent action of PTH in vivo to increase bone formation may result from the production by osteoblasts of growth factors such as IGF-1 and fibroblast growth factor (FGF)-2, as well as from the release of growth factors from matrix after PTH-induced osteoclast action.[43]

With complicated actions both on bone formation and bone resorption, it is perhaps not surprising that the net effects of PTH on bone can be either anabolic (net increase in bone mass) or catabolic (net decrease in bone mass). Depending on the dose of PTH, the mode of administration (intermittent versus continuous), the animal species, and the specific site (trabecular bone versus cortical bone), PTH can be either anabolic or catabolic.

Actions of PTH in Kidney

In the kidney, PTH has three major biological functions that are essential for the regulation of mineral ion homeostasis: stimulating the reabsorption of calcium, inhibiting the reabsorption of phosphate, and enhancing the synthesis of $1,25(OH)_2D_3$. Each of these actions of PTH contributes to the maintenance of blood calcium, and to a lesser extent, phosphate concentrations within narrow limits.

Phosphate is normally reabsorbed from the glomerular filtrate both in the proximal and distal tubules, and reabsorption is inhibited by PTH at both these sites.[44] Best studied is its effect on proximal tubular cells where phosphate is transported into the cell against an electrochemical gradient. To accomplish this task, an ATP-dependent sodium pump, Na^+/K^+ ATPase, drives sodium from the cell. Because of the concentration gradient for sodium established by this pump and through the actions of two membrane-anchored co-transporters, NPT-2a and NPT-2c, sodium re-enters the cell along with phosphate.[44–46] PTH blocks this sodium-dependent phosphate co-transport by reducing the amount of the Npt2a and possibly Npt2c protein on the cell surface, primarily by increasing its internalization and subsequent lysosomal degradation, but also by decreasing its synthesis. PTH is only one of several determinants of Npt2a and Npt2c expression, as dietary phosphate restriction leads, independent of changes in blood concentrations of PTH, to a markedly enhanced renal phosphate reabsorption, and thus a virtual elimination of urinary phosphate losses.[44–46] Furthermore, FGF-23 is a recently identified, key regulator of phosphate homeostasis, which also has direct actions on Npt2a and Npt2c expression.[46,47] The complete lack of Npt2a expression through ablation of its gene leads to severe renal phosphate wasting and nephrocalcinosis.[47] Although these abnormalities are similar to those observed in hereditary hypophosphatemic rickets with hypercalciuria (HHRH), mutations in *Npt2a* were excluded in this disorder; instead homozygous or compound heterozygous mutations were identified in NPT2c.[49,50] Interestingly, heterozygous *NPT2a* mutations were recently identified in two patients with nephrolithiasis and osteoporosis associated with hypophosphatemia caused by impaired renal tubular reabsorption.[51] These seem to have a dominant negative effect, although the in vitro findings leading to this conclusion are controversial.[52]

In the distal tubule, PTH also inhibits phosphate reabsorption; the transporter(s) that are involved in this process have not yet been identified. Teleologically, the PTH-stimulated phosphaturia can be viewed as a way of handling the release of phosphate from bone that accompanies the PTH-stimulated release of calcium from bone. Furthermore, because of the quantitative dominance of the phosphaturia, blood phosphate falls in response to PTH. This hypophosphatemia reinforces the effect of PTH on bone, because low levels of blood phosphate stimulate bone resorption.

Most calcium reabsorption occurs in the proximal tubule, but only the calcium reabsorption in the distal nephron is PTH dependent.[44] In the CTAL, reabsorption of NaCl, Ca^{2+}, and Mg^{2+} takes place largely through a paracellular pathway and is driven by the lumen positive transepithelial potential in this nephron segment. PTH stimulates calcium reabsorption in the CTAL by increasing the value of this potential through a cAMP-dependent mechanism. PTH also is thought to enhance transcellular reabsorption of calcium in the CTAL.[44] In the distal convoluted tubule (DCT), reabsorption of calcium and magnesium take place through the transcellular route—a process that is augmented by PTH. Calcium initially enters the cells through a recently cloned, calcium-permeable channel in the luminal membrane called TRPV5[53] and exits the basolateral membrane through the Na^+/Ca^{2+} exchanger and/or Ca^{2+}-ATPase.

Although the kidneys reabsorb calcium more efficiently when stimulated by PTH, the absolute amount of calcium in the urine usually increases when the circulating concentrations of PTH are chronically elevated to levels sufficient to produce hypercalcemia, as in patients with primary hyperparathyroidism. However, this increase in urinary calcium excretion is caused by the substantial increase in the filtered load of calcium, which is caused by the hypercalcemia that results from increased bone resorption and increased intestinal absorption of calcium rather than by impaired renal tubular reabsorption of calcium.

PTH also activates the mitochondrial 25-hydroxyvitamin D_3-1-α-hydroxylase in proximal tubular cells; this leads to an elevation of the blood $1,25(OH)_2D_3$ concentration, which, in turn, is a potent inducer of intestinal calcium absorption (as well as of bone resorption).[44] This effect of PTH is not immediate, because the stimulation of $1,25(OH)_2D_3$ synthesis occurs over several hours and requires the synthesis of new mRNA and protein. Along with its action on the 1-α-hydroxylase, PTH decreases the activity of the renal 25-hydroxyvitamin D_3-24-hydroxylase, thus enhancing the effect on $1,25(OH)_2D_3$ synthesis. Other factors, particularly low blood phosphate concentration, also markedly increase the synthesis of this biologically active vitamin D metabolite, whereas hypercalcemia, as would be generated by sustained increases in PTH, directly suppresses, independent of blood levels of PTH or phosphate, the 1-α-hydroxylase activity, and thus limits in a homeostatic manner the production of $1,25(OH)_2D_3$.[44]

Because of its effectiveness in raising the blood calcium concentration, $1,25(OH)_2D_3$ is widely used, along with oral calcium supplementation, in the treatment of hypoparathyroidism and pseudohypoparathyroidism.[54,55] However, because $1,25(OH)_2D_3$ cannot mimic the renal, calcium-sparing effects of PTH, urinary calcium excretion can rise quickly as serum calcium approaches the normal range, particularly when the underlying hypoparathyroidism is caused by activating mutations in the calcium-sensing receptor, as in autosomal dominant hypocalcemia with hypercalciuria.[14] In both groups of patients, but particularly the latter, the blood calcium is best kept at or below the lower limit of the normal range, with periodic monitoring of 24-h urinary calcium excretion, to avoid the long-term consequences of hypercalciuria.

Direct, CaSR-Mediated Modulation of Renal Actions of PTH

In addition to being expressed by parathyroid chief cells and thyroidal C cells, the CaSR is also expressed in numerous nephron segments, where it modulates several of the renal actions of PTH. In this way, the receptors for PTH and extracellular calcium can exert mutually antagonistic actions on the kidney that enable integrated control of tubular function not only by PTH per se but also by a key regulator of PTH secretion (e.g., Ca^{2+}_o, acting through the CaSR). Thus, in addition to its long-recognized role in regulating PTH secretion, extracellular calcium also modulates PTH action. Calcium exerts numerous actions on the kidney, several of which are relevant to the physiology and pathophysiology of mineral ion metabolism.[14] For example, high Ca^{2+}_o inhibits the 1-hydroxylation of 25-hydroxyvitamin D_3, reduces renin secretion, promotes hypercalciuria, and reduces urinary concentrating ability. Recent data have implicated a mediatory role of the CaSR in several of these, as noted below.

Prominent sites of CaSR expression in the kidney are on the apical surface of the proximal tubular cells, the basolateral surface of the medullary (MTAL) and CTALs of Henle's loop as well as the macula densa.[56] It is present predominantly on the basolateral membrane of the DCT. In the most distal nephron, it resides on the apical surface of the inner medullary collecting duct (IMCD), where vasopressin increases renal tubular reabsorption of water during dehydration by promoting insertion of aquaporin-2–containing endosomes into the same apical membrane.

In the proximal tubule, available data indicate that the CaSR blunts the phosphaturic action of PTH, probably by inhibiting PTH-stimulated cAMP accumulation. It has not yet been determined whether the CaSR in the proximal tubule also mediates the inhibitory action of hypercalcemia on the 1-hydroxylation of 25-hydroxyvitamin D_3, which occurs not only indirectly through CaSR-induced reduction in PTH secretion, but also through a direct suppressive action of hypercalcemia on the proximal tubular cells.

In the MTAL, the CaSR inhibits NaCl reabsorption, thereby impairing generation of the hypertonic interstitium required for vasopressin to maximally stimulate water reabsorption in the IMCD. As will be discussed below, the CaSR also inhibits the action of vasopressin in the IMCD,[57] further limiting the capacity of the kidney to concentrate the urine. These two actions of the CaSR on the renal concentrating mechanism very likely account for the known inhibitory effect of hypercalcemia on urinary concentrating ability.[58]

The CaSR inhibits calcium reabsorption in both the CTAL and DCT, including that stimulated by PTH. Thus, in addition to decreasing renal calcium reabsorption by CaSR-mediated inhibition of PTH secretion, the CaSR also blocks the action of PTH on these nephron segments to further reduce renal calcium and magnesium reabsorption by a direct renal action of Ca^{2+}_o. In both nephron segments, the CaSR likely acts by reducing PTH-stimulated cAMP accumulation, but may also act through additional intracellular signaling pathways.

In the IMCD, available data strongly implicate the CaSR in modulating vasopressin-stimulated water reabsorption in a physiologically important manner.[57,58] Consistent with the CaSR's presence on the apical but not the basolateral surface of the IMCD, perfusion of the luminal (but not the basolateral side) of isolated IMCD segments with elevated levels of Ca^{2+}_o inhibits vasopressin-stimulated water flow by about 40%. Vasopressin stimulates water reabsorption in this nephron segment by promoting aquaporin-2–mediated reabsorption of water into the hypertonic medullary interstitium. Because vasopressin exerts its effect on aquaporin-2 trafficking by activating adenylate cyclase, the CaSR could inhibit this process, at least in part, by inhibiting vasopressin-stimulated cAMP accumulation, similar to its actions on PTH-stimulated cAMP accumulation noted above.[58] By inhibiting vasopressin-stimulated water flow, the CaSR would, in effect, set an upper limit to the level of Ca^{2+}_o that could be reached within the distal nephron, which could potentially reduce the risk of renal stone formation in hypercalciuric states, such as primary hyperparathyroidism.

Molecular Defects in the PTH/PTHrP Receptor

The endocrine actions of PTH, and the autocrine/paracrine actions of PTHrP, are mediated through the PTH/PTHrP receptor.[1] A single G protein–coupled receptor is thus essential for the biological roles of two distinct ligands, which are important for regulation of calcium homeostasis and for the regulation of chondrocyte proliferation and differentiation, respectively. As with the CaSR, genetic deletion of the PTH/PTH receptor gene in mice and the identification of naturally occurring mutations in this receptor in humans have shed considerable light on the receptor's physiological roles in vivo.

The ablation of one allele encoding the PTH/PTHrP receptor gene in mice revealed no discernible abnormality, whereas the ablation of both alleles resulted, depending on the mouse strain, in fetal death during mid- or late gestation and severe skeletal abnormalities.[29] Based on the functional properties of the PTH/PTHrP receptor and based on the findings in gene-ablated mice, it seemed likely that receptor mutations in humans would most likely affect mineral ion homeostasis and bone development.

Mutations in the PTH/PTHrP receptor were initially suspected as a cause of pseudohypoparathyroidism type Ib (PHP-Ib), in which patients exhibit PTH-resistant hypocalcemia and hyperphosphatemia.[54,55] However, these patients lack discernible growth plate abnormalities, indicating that the actions of PTHrP are appropriately mediated. It was therefore not surprising, at least in retrospect, that PTH/PTHrP receptor mutations could not be identified in PHP-Ib patients. The autosomal dominant form of PHP-Ib (AD-PHP-Ib) was subsequently mapped to the GNAS locus and was shown to be paternally imprinted.[54,55] Furthermore, patients affected by PHP-Ib revealed changes in the methylation pattern at one or several GNAS exons and their promoters.[59] Recently, several different deletions either up-stream of or within the GNAS locus were identified.[54,55] It remains uncertain, however, how these deletions affect methylation and lead to PTH resistance in the proximal renal tubules.

PTH/PTHrP receptor mutations have been identified in three rare genetic disorders: Jansen metaphyseal chondrodysplasia, Blomstrand lethal chondrodysplasia, and Eiken skeletal dysplasia. Activating mutations that lead to ligand-independent accumulation of cAMP were identified as the cause of the autosomal dominant Jansen disease, which is characterized by short-limbed dwarfism, severe hypercalcemia, and hypophosphatemia, despite normal or undetectable levels of PTH and PTHrP in the circulation. A milder form of this disease was found to be caused by a PTH/PTHrP receptor mutation that leads to less pronounced ligand-independent cAMP formation.[55] Inactivating PTH/PTHrP receptor mutations (homozygous or compound heterozygous) were identified in patients with Blomstrand disease, who are typically born prematurely and die at birth or shortly thereafter. These patients present with advanced bone maturation, accelerated chondrocyte differentiation, and, most likely, severe abnormalities in mineral ion homeostasis.[55] Homozygous PTH/PTHrP receptor mutations were furthermore identified in Eiken skeletal dysplasia, a nonlethal disorder affecting the skeleton.[60]

REFERENCES

1. Jüppner H, Gardella T, Brown E, Kronenberg H, Potts J Jr 2005 Parathyroid hormone and parathyroid hormone-related peptide in the regulation of calcium homeostasis and bone development. In: DeGroot L, Jameson J (eds.) Endocrinology. Saunders, Philadelphia, PA, USA, pp. 1377–1417.
2. Silver J, Naveh-Many T, Kronenberg HM 2002. Parathyroid hormone. In Bilezikian JP, Raisz LG, Rodan GA (eds.) Principles of Bone Biology. Academic Press, New York, NY, USA, pp. 407–422.
3. Hogan B, Danks J, Layton J, Hall N, Heath J, Lieschke G 2004 Duplicate zebrafish pth genes are expressed along the lateral line and in the central nervous system during embryogenesis. Endocrinology 146:547–551.
4. Gensure R, Ponugoti B, Gunes Y, Papasani M, Lanske B, Bastepe M, Rubin D, Jüppner H 2004 Isolation and characterization of two PTH-like molecules in zebrafish. Endocrinology 145:1634–1639.
5. Wysolmerski J, Stewart A 1998 The physiology of parathyroid hormone-related protein: An emerging role as a developmental factor. Annu Rev Physiol 60:431–460.
6. Usdin TB, Hoare SRJ, Wang T, Mezey E, Kowalak JA 1999 Tip39: A new neuropeptide and PTH2-receptor agonist from hypothalamus. Nat Neurosci 2:941–943.
7. John M, Arai M, Rubin D, Jonsson K, Jüppner H 2002 Identification and characterization of the murine and human gene encoding the tuberoinfundibular peptide of 39 residues (TIP39). Endocrinology 143:1047–1057.
8. Diaz R, El-Hajj GF, Brown E 1998. Regulation of Parathyroid Function. Oxford University Press, New York, NY, USA, pp. 607–662.
9. Slatopolsky E, Finch J, Denda M, Ritter C, Zhong M, Dusso A, MacDonald P, Brown A 1996 Phosphorus restriction prevents parathyroid gland growth. High phosphorus directly stimulates PTH secretion in vitro. J Clin Invest 97:2534–2540.
10. Brown EM, Gamba G, Riccardi D, Lombardi M, Butters R, Kifor O, Sun A, Hediger MA, Lytton J, Hebert SC 1993 Cloning and characterization of an extracellular Ca^{2+}-sensing receptor from bovine parathyroid. Nature 366:575–580.
11. Au W 1984 Inhibition by 1,25 dihydroxycholecalciferol of parathyroid gland in organ culture. Calcif Tiss Int 36:384–391.
12. D'Amour P, Brossard J, Rousseau L, Nguyen-Yamamoto L, Nassif E, Lazure C, Gauthier D, Lavigne J, Zahradnik R 2005 Structure of non-(1–84) PTH fragments secreted by parathyroid glands in primary and secondary hyperparathyroidism. Kidney Int 68:998–1007.
13. Murray TM, Rao LG, Divieti P, Bringhurst FR 2005 Parathyroid hormone secretion and action: Evidence for discrete receptors for the carboxyl-terminal region and related biological actions of carboxyl-terminal ligands. Endocr Rev 26:78–113.
14. Diaz R, Brown E 2005 Familial hypocalciuric hypercalcemia and other disorders due to calcium-sensing receptor mutations. In: DeGroot L, Jameson J (eds.) Endocrinology. Saunders, Philadelphia, PA, USA, pp. 1595–1609.
15. Slatopolsky E, Finch J, Ritter C, Denda M, Morrissey J, Brown A, DeLuca H 1995 A new analog of calcitrol, 19-nor-1,25-(OH)$_2$D$_2$, suppress parathyroid hormone secretion in uremic rats in the absence of hypercalcemia. Am J Kidney Dis 26:852–860.
16. Holick MF 2005 Vitamin D for health and in chronic kidney disease. Semin Dialysis 18:266–275.
17. Li YC, Amling M, Pirro AE, Priemel M, Meuse J, Baron R, Delling G, Demay MB 1998 Normalization of mineral ion homeostasis by dietary means prevents hyperparathyroidism, rickets, and osteomalacia, but not alopecia in vitamin D receptor-ablated mice. Endocrinology 139:4391–4396.
18. Wada M, Nagano N, Furuya Y, Chin J, Nemeth EF, Fox J 2000 Calcimimetic NPS R-568 prevents parathyroid hyperplasia in rats with severe secondary hyperparathyroidism. Kidney Int 57:50–58.
19. Brown EM, MacLeod RJ 2001 Extracellular calcium sensing and extracellular calcium signaling. Physiol Rev 81:239–297.
20. Chang W, Chen TH, Pratt S, Shoback D 2000 Amino acids in the second and third intracellular loops of the parathyroid Ca2+-sensing receptor mediate efficient coupling to phospholipase C. J Biol Chem 275:19955–19963.
21. Conigrave AD, Quinn SJ, Brown EM 2000 L-amino acid sensing by the extracellular Ca2+-sensing receptor. Proc Natl Acad Sci USA 97:4814–4819.
22. Kerstetter JE, Svastisalee CM, Caseria DM, Mitnick ME, Insogna KL 2000 A threshold for low-protein-diet-induced elevations in parathyroid hormone. Am J Clin Nutr 72:168–173.
23. Nemeth EF 2002 Pharmacological regulation of parathyroid hormone secretion. Curr Pharm Des 8:2077–2087.
24. Ho C, Conner DA, Pollak M, Ladd DJ, Kifor O, Warren H, Brown EM, Seidman CE, Seidman JG 1995 A mouse model for familial hypocalciuric hypercalcemia and neonatal severe hyperparathyroidism. Nature Genet 11:389–394.
25. Marx SJ, Attie MF, Stock JL, Spiegel AM, Levine MA 1981 Maximal urine-concentrating ability: Familial hypocalciuric hypercalcemia versus typical primary hyperparathyroidism. J Clin Endocrinol Metab 52:736–740.
26. Pearce SH, Williamson C, Kifor O, Bai M, Coulthard MG, Davies M, Lewis-Barned N, McCredie D, Powell H, Kendall-Taylor P 1996 A familial syndrome of hypocalcemia with hypercalciuria due to mutations in the calcium-sensing receptor. N Engl J Med 335:1115–1122.
27. Gardella TJ, Jüppner H, Bringhurst FR, Potts JT Jr 2002. Receptors for parathyroid hormone (PTH) and PTH-related peptide. In: Bilezikian J, Raisz L, Rodan G (eds.) Principles of Bone Biology. Academic Press, San Diego, CA, USA, pp. 389–405.
28. Mahon M, Donowitz M, Yun C, Segre G 2002 Na(+)/H(+) exchanger regulatory factor 2 directs parathyroid hormone 1 receptor signalling. Nature 417:858–861.
29. Kronenberg H 2003 Developmental regulation of the growth plate. Nature 423:332–336.
30. Usdin TB, Gruber C, Bonner TI 1995 Identification and functional expression of a receptor selectively recognizing parathyroid hormone, the PTH2 receptor. J Biol Chem 270:15455–15458.
31. Eichinger A, Fiaschi-Taesch N, Massfelder T, Fritsch S, Barthelmebs M, Helwig J 2002 Transcript expression of the tuberoinfundibular peptide (TIP)39/PTH2 receptor system and non-PTH1 receptor-mediated tonic effects of TIP39 and other PTH2 receptor ligands in renal vessels. Endocrinology 143:3036–3043.
32. Takahashi N, Udagawa N, Takami M, Suda T 2005 Cells of bone: Osteoclast generation. In: Bilezikian JP, Raisz LG, Rodan GA (eds.) Principles of Bone Biology. Academic Press, New York, NY, USA, pp. 109–126.
33. Talmage RV, Elliott JR 1958 Removal of calcium from bone as influenced by the parathyroids. Endocrinology 62:717–722.
34. Mundy GR, Roodman GD (eds.) 1987 Osteoclast Ontogeny and Function. Elsesvier, Amsterdam, The Netherlands.
35. Finkelstein JS 1996 Pharmacological mechanisms of therapeutics: Parathyroid hormone. In Bilezikian JP, Raisz LG, Rodan GA (eds.) Principles of Bone Biology. Academic Press, New York, NY, USA, pp. 993–1005.
36. Dempster DW, Cosman F, Parisien M, Shen V, Lindsay R 1993 Anabolic actions of parathyroid hormone on bone. Endocr Rev 14:690–709.
37. Neer R, Arnaud C, Zanchetta J, Prince R, Gaich G, Reginster J, Hodsman A, Eriksen E, Ish-Shalom S, Genant H 2001 Effect of parathyroid hormone (1–34) on fractures and bone mineral density in postmenopausal women with osteoporosis. N Engl J Med 344:1434–1441.
38. Black D, Greenspan S, Ensrud K, Palermo L, McGowan J, Lang T, Garnero P, Bouxsein M, Bilezikian J, Rosen C 2003 The effects of parathyroid hormone and alendronate alone or in combination in postmenopausal osteoporosis. N Engl J Med 349:1207–1215.
39. Finkelstein J, Hayes A, Hunzelman J, Wyland J, Lee H, Neer R 2003 The effects of parathyroid hormone, alendronate, or both in men with osteoporosis. N Engl J Med 349:1216–1226.
40. Aubin J, Triffitt J 2002 Mesenchymal stem cells and osteoblast differentiation. In: Bilezikian J, Raisz L, Rodan G (eds.) Principles of Bone Biology. Academic Press, San Diego, CA, USA, pp. 59–82.
41. Manolagas SC 2000 Birth and death of bone cells: Basic regulatory mechanisms and implications for the pathogenesis and treatment of osteoporosis. Endocr Rev 21:115–137.
42. Dobnig H, Turner RT 1995 Evidence that intermittent treatment with parathyroid hormone increases bone formation in adult rats by activation of bone lining cells. Endocrinology 136:3632–3638.
43. Canalis E, Centrella M, Burch W, McCarthy TL 1989 Insulin-like growth factor I mediates selective anabolic effects of parathyroid hormone in bone cultures. J Clin Invest 83:60–65.
44. Leder B, Bringhurst FR 2005 Regulation of calcium and phosphate homeostasis. In: DeGroot LJ, Jameson J (eds.) Endocrinology. Saunders, Philadelphia, PA, USA, pp. 1465–1498.
45. Murer H, Forster I, Biber J 2004 The sodium phosphate cotransporter family SLC34. Pflugers Arch 447:763–767.
46. Miyamoto K, Segawa H, Ito M, Kuwahata M 2004 Physiological regulation of renal sodium-dependent phosphate cotransporters. Jpn J Physiol 54:93–102.
47. Larsson T, Marsell R, Schipani E, Ohlsson C, Ljunggren Ö, Tenenhouse H, Jüppner H, Jonsson K 2004 Transgenic mice expressing fibroblast growth factor 23 under the control of the a1(I) collagen promoter exhibit

growth retardation, osteomalacia and disturbed phosphate homeostasis. Endocrinology 45:3077–3094.

48. Beck L, Karaplis AC, Amizuka N, Hewson AS, Ozawa H, Tenenhouse HS 1998 Targeted inactivation of Ntp2 in mice leads to severe renal phosphate wasting, hypercalciuria, and skeletal abnormalities. Proc Natl Acad Sci USA 95:5372–5377.

49. Bergwitz C, Roslin N, Tieder M, Loredo-Osti J, Bastepe M, Abu-Zahra H, Carpenter T, Anderson D, Garabédian M, Sermet I 2006 SLC34A3 mutations in patients with hereditary hypophosphatemic rickets with hypercalciuria (HHRH) predict a key role for the sodium-phosphate co-transporter NaPi-IIc in maintaining phosphate homeostasis and skeletal function. Am J Human Genet 78:179–192.

50. Lorenz-Depiereux B, Benet-Pages A, Eckstein G, Tenenbaum-Rakover Y, Wagenstaller J, Tiosano D, Gershoni-Baruch R, Albers N, Lichtner P, Schnabel D 2006 Hereditary hypophosphatemic rickets with hypercalciuria is caused by mutations in the sodium/phosphate cotransporter gene SLC34A3. Am J Human Genet 78:193–201.

51. Prié D, Huart V, Bakouh N, Planelles G, Dellis O, Gérard B, Hulin P, Benque-Blanchet F, Silve C, Grandchamp B 2002 Nephrolithiasis and osteoporosis associated with hypophosphatemia caused by mutations in the type 2a sodium-phosphate cotransporter. N Engl J Med 347:983–991.

52. Virkki L, Forster I, Hernando N, Biber J, Murer H 2003 Functional characterization of two naturally occurring mutations in the human sodium-phosphate cotransporter type IIa. J Bone Miner Res 18:2135–2141.

53. van Abel, M, Hoenderop JG, Bindels RJ 2005 The epithelial calcium channels TRPV5 and TRPV6: Regulation and implications for disease. Naunyn Schmiedebergs Arch Pharmacol 371:295–306.

54. Levine M 2005 Hypoparathyroidism and pseudohypoparathyroidism. In:

55. Thakker R, Jüppner H 2005 Genetics disorders of calcium homeostasis caused by abnormal regulation of parathyroid hormone secretion or responsiveness. In: DeGroot L, Jameson J (eds.) Endocrinology. Saunders, Philadelphia, PA, USA, pp. 1511–1532.

56. Riccardi D, Hall AE, Chattopadhyay N, Xu JZ, Brown EM, Hebert S 1998 Localization of the extracellular Ca2+/polyvalent cation-sensing protein in rat kidney. Am J Physiol 274:F611–F622.

57. Sands JM, Naruse M, Baum M, Jo I, Hebert SC, Brown EM, Harris HW 1997 Apical extracellular calcium/polyvalent cation-sensing receptor regulates vasopressin-elicited water permeability in rat kidney inner medullary collecting duct. J Clin Invest 99:1399–1405.

58. Hebert SC, Brown EM, Harris HW 1997 Role of the Ca(2+)-sensing receptor in divalent mineral ion homeostasis. J Exp Biol 200:295–302.

59. Bastepe M, Fröhlich L, Linglart A, Abu-Zahra H, Tojo K, Ward L, Jüppner H 2005 Deletion of the NESP55 differentially methylated region causes loss of maternal GNAS imprints and pseudohypoparathyroidism type Ib. Nat Genet 37:25–27.

60. Duchatelet S, Ostergaard E, Cortes D, Lemainque A, Julier C 2005 Recessive mutations in PTHR1 cause contrasting skeletal dysplasias in Eiken and Blomstrand syndromes. Hum Mol Genet 14:1–5.

61. Brown EM 1983 Four-parameter model of the sigmoidal relationship between the parathyroid hormone release and extracellular calcium concentration in normal and abnormal parathyroid tissue. J Clin Endocrinol Metab 56:572–581.

62. Brown E, Bai M, Pollak M 1997 Familial benign hypocalciuric hypercemia and other syndromes of altered responsiveness to extracellular calcium. In: Krane S, Avioli L (eds.) Metabolic Bone Diseases. Academic Press, San Diego, CA, USA, pp. 479–499.

DeGroot L, Jameson J (eds.) Endocrinology. Saunders, Philadelphia, PA, USA, pp. 1611–1636.

Chapter 16.   Parathyroid Hormone–Related Protein

Arthur E. Broadus[1] and Robert A. Nissenson[2]

[1]Departments of Medicine and Physiology, Yale University School of Medicine, New Haven, Connecticut; and [2]Departments of Medicine and Physiology, University of California and Veteran Affairs Medical Center, San Francisco, California

INTRODUCTION

In 1941, Fuller Albright proposed that tumors associated with hypercalcemia might produce a PTH-like factor. Forty years later, it was recognized that the factor in question interacts with the PTH receptor in the kidney, an observation that provided the strategy that was used to isolate and clone the PTH-related protein (PTHrP) in the mid-1980s.[1–3]

We now know that the PTH and PTHrP genes arose by duplication and are members of a small gene family.[1–5] What remains from this common heritage is a similar organization of the two genes and a stretch of homologous sequence at the N terminus of each mature peptide. Otherwise, the genes have evolved separately. The PTH gene has a simple structure, and its product is a classical systemic peptide hormone. The PTHrP gene has a complex structure, is widely expressed in normal tissues, and its product(s) seems to function principally in an autocrine or paracrine fashion.[4,5] A fundamental aspect of the divergence of these two genes has been the development of very different mechanisms of control. The key regulatory step in PTH physiology is calcium-gated PTHrP secretion. In contrast, PTHrP seems to be a constitutive secretory product, such that the key control point in PTHrP production/secretion is at the level of PTHrP mRNA expression, and this is very tightly regulated, as might well be expected for a predominantly constitutive product with powerful local regulatory effects.[4]

The PTHrP gene and its products also have several levels of structural complexity that do not apply to the PTH gene and its product. The human PTHrP gene encodes three alternatively spliced isoforms, of as yet unknown biological significance. In addition, the primary PTHrP translation product(s) is subject to cleavage and processing into N-terminal, mid-region, and C-terminal products. There is also a functional nuclear localization sequence (NLS) at approximately the junction of the proximal two thirds and distal one third of the molecule.[4–6] The N-terminal and mid-region products and the NLS-bearing products have clear functional correlates, as described below.

PTHrP FUNCTIONS

By the early 1990s, it had become evident that PTHrP must be a local regulatory molecule, and the widespread expression of the gene in fetal tissues led many to suppose that it might function in development. This supposition led several groups to turn to gene manipulation techniques in mice, and the results of these experiments provided convincing evidence that PTHrP functions as a developmental regulatory molecule. These functions include such diverse processes as control of the formation of endochondral bone, the development of the mammary epithelium, and the eruption of teeth.[7–10] In the adult, the best-studied PTHrP function is regulation of the tone of accommodative smooth muscle structures such as the uterus, bladder, and vasculature, in which the PTHrP gene is induced by mechanical stretch and serves to relax the smooth muscle structure in question.[11,12]

The authors have reported no conflicts of interest.

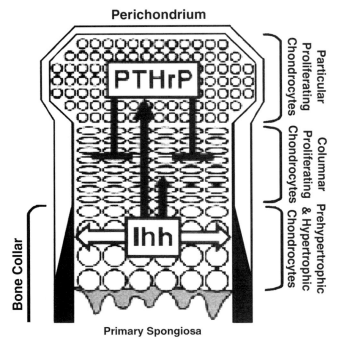

Perichondrium

PTHrP

Ihh

Bone Collar

Particular Proliferating Chondrocytes

Columnar Proliferating Chondrocytes

Prehypertrophic & Hypertrophic Chondrocytes

Primary Spongiosa

FIG. 1. PTHrP function in the cartilaginous growth plate. The chondrocyte differentiation program proceeds from undifferentiated chondrocytes above, through the proliferative chondrocytes in the columns, to the prehypertrophic and terminally differentiated hypertrophic chondrocytes below. PTHrP is expressed most abundantly in the proliferative chondrocytes at the junction of the periarticular and columnar populations and serves as a brake on the differentiation of the columnar chondrocytes to the hypertrophic stage. Indian hedgehog (Ihh) is produced by the chondrocytes as they hypertrophy and feeds back to increase PTHrP production, thereby slowing the rate at which the chondrocyte differentiation program proceeds. Absent PTHrP or PTH1R, the chondrocyte program proceeds too rapidly; the columns collapse, and premature mineralization and dwarfing take place. (Reproduced with permission from Chung U, Schipani E, McMahon AP, Kronenberg HM 2001 Indian hedgehog couples chondrogenesis to osteogenesis in endochondral bone development. J Clin Inv **107:**295–304.)

The Skeleton

Cartilage. At the time of its discovery, PTHrP represented a molecule in search of a function. The most powerful strategy for posing such a question is to knockout the gene in a mouse, and this experiment was reported in 1994.[7] The PTHrP-null mouse was something of a good news–bad news venture, the good news being that the mouse had a clear phenotype and the bad that this phenotype was a neonatal lethal.[7] Endochondral bone develops through a two-step process, the first step being the formation of a cartilaginous mold of the bone and the second a gradual replacement of the cartilage by bone; the most important biological consequence of this developmental strategy is the formation of the cartilaginous growth plate that provides the capacity for linear growth. The critical control point in this process is the chondrocyte differentiation program, a classical example of such a developmental program. In this program, chondrocytes progress through a series of stages to become terminally differentiated hypertrophic chondrocytes, which are mineralizing and apoptotic cells (Fig. 1). PTHrP normally regulates the rate at which this program proceeds, and its deletion results in a too rapid progression of the program that is associated with a classic chondrodysplasia (short-limbed dwarfism) that is lethal at birth.[7]

The details of PTHrP regulation and signaling in the growth plate are better understood than any other PTHrP regulatory function. PTHrP serves as the regulatory instrument of a higher-order developmental regulatory gene known as Indian hedgehog (Ihh), which is responsible for a number of different aspects of growth plate and bone cell development. This regulation functions as a classical negative feedback loop, with Ihh being produced by differentiating hypertrophic chondrocytes and feeding back through PTHrP to regulate the rate of chondrocyte differentiation through its differentiation program (Fig. 1). Thus, an increase in hypertrophic chondrocytes begats an increase in Ihh signaling and a PTHrP-mediated slowing of chondrocyte differentiation, and vice versa.[8]

PTHrP is also expressed in other cartilaginous sites. One is in the perichondrium that surrounds the costal cartilage,[13] which normally remains cartilaginous and enables expansion of the chest wall during breathing. It is presumably the loss of this PTHrP source that is responsible for the shield chest that causes the neonatal death of the PTHrP-null mouse.[13] Another site is the subarticular chondrocyte population just subjacent to the hyaline chondrocytes of the joint space.[13] PTHrP function here is unknown but might well be to prevent chondrocyte hypertrophy and mineralization of the joint space.

Bone. The abnormalities in the endochondral skeleton of the PTHrP-null mouse are seen as entirely a consequence of the absence of PTHrP regulation of chondrocyte development.[7,8] It was subsequently reported that heterozygous PTHrP-null mice are normal at birth but acquire trabecular osteopenia in their long bones at and beyond 3 months of age.[14] This observation has been recently confirmed in more detail as well as extended by the demonstration that conditional deletion of PTHrP in osteoblasts results in the same osteopenic phenotype.[15] In both models, bone formation and mineral apposition are reduced, as are the formation and survival of osteoblasts.[15] There is actually disagreement as to whether and/or in which osteoblast populations PTHrP is expressed, perhaps because of the use of different localization techniques or species/strains.[13–15] Nevertheless, the osteopenia in the two mouse models is intriguing and has led the authors to suggest that PTH and PTHrP may have quite distinct domains of influence regarding trabecular bone, PTHrP being a locally produced anabolic stimulus and PTH being a circulating resorptive agent charged with maintaining systemic mineral homeostasis.[15]

It turns out that PTHrP is also expressed in the periosteum and in the insertion sites of tendons and ligaments into cortical bone.[13] Periosteal bone formation is responsible for the accretion of bone at its periphery, a necessary consequence of bone growth as well as a compensatory mechanism to maintain skeletal strength when trabecular and/or endosteal bone is lost.[16] Tendon and ligament insertion sites are cemented in place by fibrous and/or fibrocartilaginous structures that are incorporated into mature cortical bone.[17] In certain of these sites, such as the tibial insertion of the medial collateral ligament, the insertion sites must migrate as the bone lengthens.[18] In all of these locations, PTHrP is not expressed in the underlying osteoblastic or bone cell populations but rather in the connective tissue cells in the outer layer of the periosteum or their equivalent at the myotendinous junction of the insertion sites. The function(s) of PTHrP in these locations is unknown, but the working hypotheses are that PTHrP may be induced in these sites by mechanical force[19] and serve to regulate localized bone formation and/or bone turnover.[13]

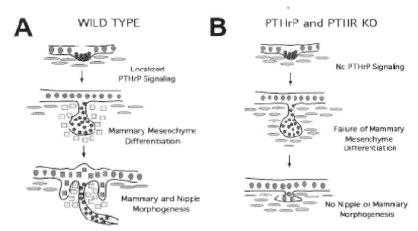

FIG. 2. PTHrP function in embryonic mammary epithelial development. (A) Normal mammary epithelial development, in which PTHrP (black dots) is expressed initially in an epidermal placode (top), subsequently in a bud (middle), and finally in branching epithelia that invade the mammary fat pad (bottom). PTHrP from the placode signals to the subjacent undifferentiated dermal mesenchymal cells (gray cigar-like cells) and drives their differentiation into specialized mammary mesenchymal cells (gray boxes). The mammary mesenchyme directs the formation of the nipple as well as the branching morphogenesis of the mammary bud. (B) Pattern in PTHrP-null (or PTH1R-null) mice. Here, the epithelial–mesenchymal signaling cascade is absent; the mammary mesenchyme fails to form, and the nascent mammary bud is resorbed. (Adapted with permission from Foley J, Dann P, Hong J, Cosgrove J, Dreyer BE, Rimm D, Dunbar ME, Philbrick WM, Wysolmerski JJ 2001 Parathyroid hormone-related protein maintains mammary epithelial fate and triggers nipple skin differentiation during embryonic breast development. Development **128:**513–525 and the Company of Biologists Ltd.)

Development of the Mammary Epithelium and Teeth and Reproductive Functions of PTHrP

By targeting an activated PTH/PTHrP receptor (PTH1R) or PTHrP itself to proliferative chondrocytes, it proved possible to "rescue" the PTHrP-knockout mouse from neonatal death.[9,10,20] In the PTHrP-targeted case, this generated a mouse that was PTHrP-sufficient in chondrocytes but PTHrP-null in all other sites.[9,10] These mice were small and fragile, but some survived and had a phenotype that in a human would be referred to as an ectodermal dysplasia. This phenotype included a failure of mammary epithelial development, a failure of tooth eruption, and abnormalities of a number of skin appendages such as the nails.[9,10,20–22] These structures share a common developmental history, each arising from a PTHrP-expressing epidermal placode/bud that signals the dermal mesenchyme to develop into a specialized connective tissue compartment that reciprocally drives the development of the epithelial structure in question. This kind of reciprocal paracrine signaling drives the formation of most epidermal appendages and is referred to as epithelial-mesenchymal morphogenesis. Many structures that form in this fashion continue their development postnatally, two cases in point being the mammary gland and the tooth.

Clearly, each of the abnormalities in the PTHrP-knockout and rescued PTHrP-knockout mice bespeaks a normal physiological function of PTHrP, and it would be presumed that a human syndrome that resulted from absent PTHrP signaling would be lethal and also would suffer from the combined abnormalities seen in these two mice. This proved to be the case in the form of Blomstrand chondrodysplasia, a rare and lethal syndrome that results from an inactivating mutation of the PTH1R and has a phenotype comprising the chondrodysplastic, mammary, and tooth impaction abnormalities seen in the mice.[23]

Mammary Gland. As just noted, mammary gland development begins early in embryonic life as a placode and then an inward bud of PTHrP-expressing epithelium that undergoes only limited development during fetal life. The adult mammary gland does not fully develop until adolescence, and it doesn't undergo full functional development until lactogenesis. It turns

out that PTHrP has a number of regulatory functions in the mammary gland at several distinct stages of its development and function.

During embryonic development, PTHrP derived from the mammary bud "instructs" the dermal mesenchymal cells to differentiate into a specialized subjacent mammary mesenchyme[9,22] (Fig. 2). The mammary mesenchyme supports the growth and branching of the bud into the mammary fat pad in which it forms the pre-adolescent mammary epithelial tree that is present at birth.[9,22] In the absence of PTHrP (or its receptor), the mammary mesenchyme does not differentiate; the mammary bud degenerates, and no mammary epithelial structures remain.

At adolescence, the immature mammary epithelia develops into the adult gland by a process of branching morphogenesis.[22] This process is driven by PTHrP-expressing cutting cones known as end buds that penetrate and branch through the PTH1R-expressing stroma until they reach the margins of the mammary fat pad, which defines the limits of the adult mammary gland. Excess PTHrP actually inhibits branching morphogenesis, and it is thought that PTHrP therefore may regulate the spacing of the branches, but the details of how PTHrP functions during adolescent mammary development are not fully understood.

Lactation places an enormous demand on maternal calcium homeostasis: in rodents, up to one third of maternal skeletal mineral is transferred to the offspring in a 3-week period.[22] It now seems that PTHrP derived from the mammary epithelium drives the mobilization of bone mineral that feeds this process. Furthermore, the mammary epithelium is capable of sensing the serum calcium concentration through the calcium receptor and secretes PTHrP accordingly, much as would a parathyroid chief cell.[24] This is proposed to function as a mammary bone feedback loop and may be the only circumstance in which PTHrP normally circulates. Examples of pregnancy/lactation-associated hypercalcemia caused by PTHrP have been described but are very rare.[5] PTHrP is found at very high concentrations in breast milk (20–50 nM, some three orders of magnitude higher than its circulating concentration in patients with humoral hypercalcemia of malignancy [HHM]), but its function in milk, if any, is unknown.[25]

Teeth. Teeth also develop from a PTHrP-expressing epithelial bud. By about embryonic day 14 in a mouse, the tooth has become encased in alveolar bone in what is aptly referred to as a dental crypt, from which it must escape. The process of tooth eruption is a remarkable example of uncoupled bone turnover in which osteoclasts form over the crown of the tooth and proceed to carve out the pathway through which the tooth will escape; bone formation at the base of the tooth subsequently propels it into the oral cavity.

It turns out that the teeth form quite normally in the rescued PTHrP-null mouse and that it is tooth eruption that fails.[10] The epithelial structure (known as the stellate reticulum) that surrounds the tooth in the crypt normally expresses abundant PTHrP just before eruption, which signals through connective tissue cells in the contiguous dental follicle to drive the formation of the crypt osteoclasts that sculpt the eruption pathway.[10,26] In the absence of PTHrP, the crypt osteoclasts do not form, and the tooth becomes progressively impacted in the crypt by encroaching alveolar bone.

The mammary epithelium and stellate reticulum are rapidly proliferating epithelial structures at the times when they deliver PTHrP into their developing microenvironments. Keratin-14 (K14) is a so-called proliferative keratin that also is expressed in proliferative epithelium. The K14 promoter was used to deliver PTHrP into the mammary epithelium and stellate reticulum in a second-generation crossing experiment that successfully rescued embryonic mammary epithelial development and also triggered tooth eruption.[9,10,22] This experiment reaffirmed the capacity of PTHrP from these epithelial structures to drive the developmental programs in question.

Skin. Human keratinocytes in primary culture were the first normal cells shown to express PTHrP, the lead here being the frequency of squamous cell carcinomas among patients with HHM.[27] While the functions of PTHrP in ectodermal derivatives such as the mammary gland and tooth are clear, there is disagreement as to what the function(s) of PTHrP might be in regulating the development/growth of hair and other epidermal appendages and, indeed, whether PTHrP is actually expressed in the interfollicular epidermis in vivo.[4,5,19,21,28]

Placental Calcium Transport. To subserve fetal mineral requirements, calcium is transported across the placenta through a pump that maintains a maternal–fetal gradient (i.e., the ambient calcium concentration is higher in the fetus). Regulation of placental calcium transport by PTHrP was initially suggested by the Melbourne group.[29] Physiological studies of this question have been carried out in sheep[29,30] and genetic studies in mice.[31,32] The gradient is lost in PTHrP-null mice and is restored by infusion of a mid-region fragment of PTHrP but not by an N-terminal fragment or PTH itself.[31] The same mid-region specificity has been shown in sheep.[30] There is general agreement that the placenta itself is a major source of the PTHrP[29–32] and that the calcium receptor is probably involved in gating placental PTHrP production.[22] A mid-region PTHrP receptor has yet to be identified.

PTHrP Expression and Function in Excitable Cells

In 1925, crude parathyroid extracts were infused into dogs and were found to decrease systemic blood pressure.[33] This triggered an interest in the putative regulation by PTH of smooth muscle, the heart, and neurons that persisted for ~60 years.[12] There was never a physiological rationale for such regulatory effects, in that PTH release from the parathyroid chief cell is gated by the ambient ionized calcium concentration in a classic negative feedback loop, and it circulates at some 1/1000th the concentration that these effects require. It now seems clear that PTHrP is the natural ligand that mediates such effects and that this regulation is local rather than systemic.

Smooth Muscle and the Cardiovascular System. PTHrP expression and regulation of smooth muscle cells can be summarized briefly as follows: (1) the PTHrP gene seems to be expressed by every smooth muscle cell/bed in the body; (2) in most if not all of these sites PTHrP is induced by mechanical stretch; (3) PTHrP effects are autocrine or paracrine and are mediated by the PTH1R; and (4) PTHrP functions to relax the smooth muscle cells or structure in question.[11,12] In the vasculature, PTHrP is also induced by vasoconstrictive agents such as angiotensin II and seems to have its principal effects on resistance vessels.[12] In general, PTHrP is seen as a local modulator of smooth muscle tone in specific vascular beds rather than as a systemic regulatory factor.[12,34] In accommodative smooth muscle structures such as the stomach, bladder, and uterus, stretch-induced PTHrP-driven smooth muscle relaxation allows the structure to accommodate gradual filling.[11,12] This can be shown in the uterus by simply inflating a balloon in one horn of the bicornuate rodent uterus. However, the major physiological peak in PTHrP expression in the uterus occurs at parturition,[11] and its exact role in the yin-yang control of smooth muscle function during this time is not understood.

PTHrP is also expressed in endothelial cells.[34–36] Several studies have shown that PTHrP can have potent antiangiogenic effects, which seem to be mediated by a combination of endothelial and smooth muscle actions.[35,36] Another recent series of experiments in rats revealed that PTHrP could be induced in the endothelium of cerebral microvessels by ischemia and that the vasodilatation induced by PTHrP downstream could limit the size of a cerebral infarct in a stroke model system.[37]

In isolated hearts, PTHrP has both positive ionotropic and chronotropic effects, but the ionotropy is thought to be secondary to a vasodilatation-induced increase in coronary flow.[12] PTHrP has been colocalized with atrial natriuretic peptide–containing granules in the rat atrium, but the functional implications of this finding are unknown.[12]

Central and Peripheral Nervous Systems. Both PTHrP and PTH1R are widely expressed in neurons of the cerebral cortex, hippocampus, and cerebellum.[38,39] Many of these PTHrP-expressing neuronal populations have in common abundant expression of excitatory amino acid (glutamate) receptors and L-type calcium channels and a known propensity to excitotoxicity, a form of neuronal damage that results from excessive excitation. In cerebellar granule cells, PTHrP expression is induced by depolarization-driven L channel calcium influx and seems to be capable of feeding back through the PTH1R to dampen L channel activity in an autocrine/paracrine fashion.[40] The net result is a neuroprotective feedback loop capable of combating excessive calcium-associated excitotoxicity.[40] The rescued PTHrP-null mouse displays an enhanced sensitivity to excitotoxic stimuli in vivo but is sufficiently fragile that it is not an ideal model system for such studies.[40]

PTHrP and the PTH1R are also expressed in neurons and glia of the peripheral nervous system (PNS). After peripheral nerve crush or sectioning, Schwann cells dedifferentiate, proliferate, and provide both a conduit and growth factors that enable axonal regeneration to occur.[41] PTHrP expression is dramatically increased in these dedifferentiated Schwann cells after injury and seems to retard the Schwann cell differentiation program much as it does the chondrocyte differentiation program, maintaining the immature Schwann cell population that is critical to PNS regeneration.

Pancreatic Islets. PTHrP is expressed in all four cell types of the pancreatic islet, most particularly the β cell.[22] β cells are classic neuroendocrine cells, in that they secrete insulin but are gated to do so electrophysiologically, the proximate secretory signal being L channel–mediated calcium influx. PTHrP is stored and cosecreted with insulin, but PTHrP does not seem to feed back on β-cell L channels as it does in some neurons (C. Macica, unpublished results, 2003). Overexpression of PTHrP in the β cells of transgenic mice is associated with an increased β-cell mass together with hyperinsulinemia and hypoglycemia,[42] but there is no obvious islet phenotype in the PTHrP-knockout or rescued PTHrP-knockout mouse.[22]

MECHANISM OF ACTION OF PTHrP

The discovery of PTHrP as the major mediator of HHM was based on its ability to replicate the actions of PTH on the PTH1R.[1,3,43] Indeed, most patients with HHM display elevated urinary excretion of nephrogenous cAMP,[44] reflecting the action of systemic PTHrP to stimulate renal adenylyl cyclase through the PTH1R. Purified PTHrP and synthetic amino-terminal fragments of PTHrP display an affinity for the PTH1R that is comparable with that of PTH.[45,46] In patients with HHM, the ability of tumor-derived PTHrP to mimic the skeletal and renal effects of excess PTH is attributable to PTHrP-induced activation of PTH1R signaling.

The physiological effects of PTHrP as a paracrine factor are also mediated, at least in part, by PTH1R signaling. Mice and humans with deletion of the PTH1R display chondrogenic defects that resemble those produced by PTHrP deletion in the mouse.[47] Null mutations in both genes produce neonatal death, but the chondrogenic defect in PTH1R-null mice is more severe than that seen in PTHrP-null mice. This suggests that a PTH1R ligand(s) other than PTHrP might contribute to the control of chondrocyte differentiation, at least in the absence of PTHrP. cAMP signaling seems to be critical for the actions of PTHrP to suppress chondrocyte maturation.[48] In support of this, deletion of the α-subunit of Gs (the G protein that couples the PTH1R to adenylyl cyclase) in chondrocytes was shown to phenocopy the effects of deletion of PTHrP.[49,50] This provides direct experimental evidence that cAMP signaling plays a central role in mediating the effects of PTHrP on cartilage development. cAMP signaling through the PTH1R is likely to be important for other physiological actions of PTHrP as well. For example, increased levels of cAMP reduce smooth muscle tone, and this mechanism almost certainly is essential for the actions of PTHrP as a paracrine smooth muscle relaxant.

Understanding PTHrP action is complicated by the fact that multiple forms of the peptide are synthesized by alternative splicing and that additional fragments arise from post-translational processing.[51,52] Three synthesized forms have been identified, and these consist of 139, 141, and 173 amino acids. These forms are identical through amino acid 139, and thus contain the same critical 1–34 sequence required for binding with high affinity to the PTH1R. Indeed, eight of the amino terminal residues of PTHrP are identical with the corresponding residues in PTH, and this underlies the ability of these two peptides to activate a common receptor (PTH1R). Different tissues and tumors display different patterns of expression of these secretory isoforms, but the biological significance of this remains obscure. The isoforms of PTHrP are cleaved by prohormone convertases, resulting in the production of multiple secreted peptides.[53–56] Cleavage products include an amino-terminal fragment that retains the ability to bind to and activate the PTH1R; a mid-region PTHrP fragment that may have biological actions that are distinct from those of intact or amino-terminal PTHrP (e.g., stimulation of placental calcium transport) and carboxy-terminal fragments that are detectable in the circulation. The functional importance of carboxy-terminal PTHrP peptides is not well defined. Such peptides are capable of producing calcium transients in hippocampal neurons,[57] and in some systems, produce inhibition of bone resorption.[58,59] These findings have led to the concept that PTHrP may be a polyhormone (i.e., the precursor of multiple biologically active peptides).[60]

In the arterial wall, PTHrP is expressed in proliferating vascular smooth muscle cells in culture and after balloon angioplasty in vivo.[61] The level of PTHrP is increased in atherosclerotic coronary arteries.[62] Exposure of rat vascular smooth muscle cells to PTHrP has an antimitotic effect, suggesting that locally released PTHrP would act to inhibit the response to a proliferative stimulus.[63] In contrast, when transfected into A10 rat vascular smooth muscle cells, PTHrP induces marked proliferation.[64] The proliferative response does not occur with transfection of mutant forms of PTHrP from which polybasic amino acid sequences between residues 88 and 106 had been deleted. These sequences have been shown to function as a nuclear localization sequence in other cells.[6] Wildtype PTHrP is targeted to the nucleus of A10 cells, but the deletion mutants fail to localize to the nucleus. Nuclear localization of PTHrP seems to require association of the peptide with importin-β.[65] Interestingly, a leucine-rich sequence in the C-terminal region of PTHrP seems to regulate nuclear export of the protein.[66] It has therefore been postulated that in addition to binding to cell surface receptors, PTHrP can have direct nuclear actions, termed intracrine actions. Because secreted fragments of PTHrP and its intracrine actions seem to have opposing effects on proliferation, PTHrP could interplay in a complex fashion with other proliferative factors in determining the response of the vascular wall to injury or atherosclerosis.

Potential intracrine actions of PTHrP have recently been shown to extend beyond vascular smooth muscle cells.[67,68] It is possible that this represents a major alternate signaling pathway for PTHrP in addition to G-protein signaling through the PTH1R, although this has yet to be definitively established. Intracrine signaling by PTHrP can occur through multiple mechanisms.[69] In some cases, secreted PTHrP may be taken up by cells through endocytosis, with subsequent trafficking of the protein to the nucleus.[70,71] It is not clear whether this endocytosis requires the binding of PTHrP to the PTH1R. A second possibility is that initiation of translation of PTHrP mRNA may occur through an alternative start site, resulting in the synthesis of a cytoplasmic form of the peptide capable of entering the nucleus.[72] Finally, PTHrP may be transported in retrograde fashion from the endoplasmic reticulum to the cytoplasm.[73] The nuclear localization of PTHrP seems to be regulated by phosphorylation of the protein, with PTHrP appearing either in the nuclear matrix or in the nucleolus, depending on the system.[70] In some cases, nuclear localization of PTHrP varies markedly as a function of the progression of cells through the cell cycle, suggesting a functional role of PTHrP in cell proliferation and/or survival.[74] Indeed, there is evidence that the intracrine actions of PTHrP can promote cell proliferation or survival, depending on the cell type.[6,75,76] Nuclear PTHrP may also function as a regulator of gene expression, as has recently been suggested in prostate cancer cells.[77] Additional studies are needed to determine how intracrine signaling cooperates with classical PTH1R signaling in mediating the pleiotropic biological effects of PTHrP.

CONCLUSIONS

PTHrP was isolated and cloned from human tumors associated with the syndrome of HHM in the late 1980s. PTHrP is not the first physiologically relevant peptide to have been found in such a bad neighborhood, a previous example being the isolation of growth hormone releasing hormone (GHRH) from a human pancreatic carcinoma by three independent groups in 1982.[78] The principal difference in the GHRH and the PTHrP stories was the outcome: GHRH already had a well-recognized job description before it was defined structurally in 1982, whereas PTHrP was identified in structural terms in 1987 well before any of its biological functions were recognized.

PTHrP is now known to have a variety of functions during both fetal and adult life. Among these one can begin to recognize several common themes: (1) virtually all such PTHrP effects involve paracrine pathways; (2) a number of these constitute classical epithelial–mesenchymal cascades; (3) in several sites, PTHrP seems to control the rate in which programs of differentiation proceed; (4) in several sites (e.g., the tooth and mammary bud), PTHrP serves to regulate the migration of an epithelial structure through a connective tissue/mesenchymal compartment; (5) in a number of systems (e.g., the growth plate, mammary epithelium and tooth), PTHrP regulates developmental events that occur and/or continue postnatally; (6) in several types (smooth muscle and some bone cells), PTHrP is mechanically induced; and (7) in a number of locations (e.g., placenta, the dental crypt, cartilage, and bone), PTHrP actions are calcium-related to one or another extent.

In the end, it is not so surprising that a constitutive secretory product that is widely expressed, particularly in proliferative epithelia, might turn out to be the mediator of a common "tumor-humor" syndrome.

REFERENCES

1. Suva LJ, Winslow GA, Wettenhall RE, Hammonds RG, Moseley JM, Diefenbach-Jagger H, Rodda CP, Kemp BE, Rodriguez H, Chen EY, Hudson PJ, Martin TJ, Wood WI 1987 A parathyroid hormone-related protein implicated in malignant hypercalcemia: Cloning and expression. Science 237:893–896.
2. Strewler GJ, Nissenson RA 1990 Hypercalcemia in malignancy. West J Med 153:635–640.
3. Broadus AE, Mangin M, Ikeda K, Insogna KL, Weir EC, Burtis WJ, Stewart AF 1988 Humoral hypercalcemia of cancer. Identification of a novel parathyroid hormone-like peptide. N Engl J Med 319:556–563.
4. Philbrick WM, Wysolmerski JJ, Galbraith S, Holt E, Orloff JJ, Yang KH, Vasavada RC, Weir EC, Broadus AE, Stewart AF 1996 Defining the roles of parathyroid hormone-related protein in normal physiology. Physiol Rev 76:127–173.
5. Strewler GJ 2000 The physiology of parathyroid hormone-related protein. N Engl J Med 342:177–185.
6. Henderson JE, Amizuka N, Warshawsky H, Biasotto D, Lanske BM, Goltzman D, Karaplis AC 1995 Nucleolar localization of parathyroid hormone-related peptide enhances survival of chondrocytes under conditions that promote apoptotic cell death. Mol Cell Biol 15:4064–4075.
7. Karaplis AC, Luz A, Glowacki J, Bronson RT, Tybulewicz VL, Kronenberg HM, Mulligan RC 1994 Lethal skeletal dysplasia from targeted disruption of the parathyroid hormone-related peptide gene. Genes Dev 8:277–289.
8. Kronenberg HM 2003 Developmental regulation of the growth plate. Nature 423:332–336.
9. Wysolmerski JJ, Philbrick WM, Dunbar ME, Lanske B, Kronenberg H, Broadus AE 1998 Rescue of the parathyroid hormone-related protein knockout mouse demonstrates that parathyroid hormone-related protein is essential for mammary gland development. Development 125:1285–1294.
10. Philbrick WM, Dreyer BE, Nakchbandi IA, Karaplis AC 1998 Parathyroid hormone-related protein is required for tooth eruption. Proc Natl Acad Sci USA 95:11846–11851.
11. Thiede MA, Daifotis AG, Weir EC, Brines ML, Burtis WJ, Ikeda K, Dreyer BE, Garfield RE, Broadus AE 1990 Intrauterine occupancy controls expression of the parathyroid hormone-related peptide gene in preterm rat myometrium. Proc Natl Acad Sci USA 87:6969–6973.
12. Clemens TL, Broadus AE 2002 Vascular, cardiovascular, and neurological actions of parathyroid hormone-related protein. In: Bilezikian JP, Raisz LG, Rodan GA (eds.) Principles of Bone Biology, 2nd ed. Academic Press, New York, NY, USA, pp. 261–274.
13. Chen X, Macica CM, Dreyer BE, Hammond VE, Hens JR, Philbrick WM, Broadus AE 2006 Initial characterization of PTH-related protein gene-driven lacZ expression in the mouse. J Bone Miner Res 21:113–123.
14. Amizuka N, Karaplis AC, Henderson JE, Warshawsky H, Lipman ML, Matsuki Y, Ejiri S, Tanaka M, Izumi N, Ozawa H, Goltzman D 1996 Haploinsufficiency of parathyroid hormone-related peptide (PTHrP) results in abnormal postnatal bone development. Dev Biol 175:166–176.
15. Miao D, He B, Jiang Y, Kobayashi T, Soroceanu MA, Zhao J, Su H, Tong X, Amizuka N, Gupta A, Genant HK, Kronenberg HM, Goltzman D, Karaplis AC 2005 Osteoblast-derived PTHrP is a potent endogenous bone anabolic agent that modifies the therapeutic efficacy of administered PTH 1–34. J Clin Invest 115:2402–2411.
16. Seeman E 2003 Periosteal bone formation—a neglected determinant of bone strength. N Engl J Med 349:320–323.
17. Benjamin M, Kumai T, Milz S, Boszczyk BM, Boszczyk AA, Ralphs JR 2002 The skeletal attachment of tendons—tendon "entheses". Comp Biochem Physiol A Mol Integr Physiol 133:931–945.
18. Wei X, Messner K 1996 The postnatal development of the insertions of the medial collateral ligament in the rat knee. Anat Embryol (Berl) 193:53–59.
19. Chen X, Macica CM, Ng KW, Broadus AE 2005 Stretch-induced PTH-related protein gene expression in osteoblasts. J Bone Miner Res 20:1454–1461.
20. Schipani E, Lanske B, Hunzelman J, Luz A, Kovacs CS, Lee K, Pirro A, Kronenberg HM, Juppner H 1997 Targeted expression of constitutively active receptors for parathyroid hormone and parathyroid hormone-related peptide delays endochondral bone formation and rescues mice that lack parathyroid hormone-related peptide. Proc Natl Acad Sci USA 94:13689–13694.
21. Foley J, Longely BJ, Wysolmerski JJ, Dreyer BE, Broadus AE, Philbrick WM 1998 PTHrP regulates epidermal differentiation in adult mice. J Invest Dermatol 111:1122–1128.
22. Wysolmerski JJ, Stewart AF, Martin TJ 2002 Physiological actions of parathyroid hormone (PTH) and PTH-related protein. In: Bilezikian JP, Raisz LG, Rodan GA (eds.) Principles of Bone Biology, 2nd ed. Academic Press, New York, NY, USA, pp. 515–530.
23. Wysolmerski JJ, Cormier S, Philbrick WM, Dann P, Zhang JP, Roume J, Delezoide AL, Silve C 2001 Absence of functional type 1 parathyroid hormone (PTH)/PTH-related protein receptors in humans is associated with abnormal breast development and tooth impaction. J Clin Endocrinol Metab 86:1788–1794.
24. VanHouten J, Dann P, McGeoch G, Brown EM, Krapcho K, Neville M, Wysolmerski JJ 2004 The calcium-sensing receptor regulates mammary gland parathyroid hormone-related protein production and calcium transport. J Clin Invest 113:598–608.
25. Budayr AA, Halloran BP, King JC, Diep D, Nissenson RA, Strewler GJ 1989 High levels of a parathyroid hormone-like protein in milk. Proc Natl Acad Sci USA 86:7183–7185.
26. Nakchbandi IA, Weir EE, Insogna KL, Philbrick WM, Broadus AE 2000 Parathyroid hormone-related protein induces spontaneous osteoclast formation via a paracrine cascade. Proc Natl Acad Sci USA 97:7296–7300.
27. Merendino JJ, Jr., Insogna KL, Milstone LM, Broadus AE, Stewart AF 1986 A parathyroid hormone-like protein from cultured human keratinocytes. Science 231:388–390.
28. Cho YM, Woodard GL, Dunbar M, Gocken T, Jimenez JA, Foley J 2003 Hair-cycle-dependent expression of parathyroid hormone-related protein and its type I receptor: Evidence for regulation at the anagen to catagen transition. J Invest Dermatol 120:715–727.
29. Abbas SK, Pickard DW, Rodda CP, Heath JA, Hammonds RG, Wood WI, Caple IW, Martin TJ, Care AD 1989 Stimulation of ovine placental calcium transport by purified natural and recombinant parathyroid hormone-related protein (PTHrP) preparations. Q J Exp Physiol 74:549–552.
30. Care AD, Abbas SK, Pickard DW, Barri M, Drinkhill M, Findley JB, White IR, Caple IW 1990 Stimulation of ovine placental transport of calcium and magnesium by mid-molecule fragments of human parathyroid hormone-related protein. Exp Physiol 75:605–608.

31. Kovacs CS, Lanske B, Hunzelman JL, Guo J, Karaplis AC, Kronenberg HM 1996 Parathyroid hormone-related peptide (PTHrP) regulates fetal-placental calcium transport through a receptor distinct from the PTH/PTHrP receptor. Proc Natl Acad Sci USA 93:15233–15238.

32. Kovacs CS, Manley NR, Moseley JM, Martin TJ, Kronenberg HM 2001 Fetal parathyroids are not required to maintain placental calcium transport. J Clin Invest 107:1007–1015.

33. Collip JB, Clark EP 1925 Further studies on the physiologic action of parathyroid hormone. J Biol Chem 64:485–507.

34. Massfelder T, Helwig JJ, Stewart AF 1996 Parathyroid hormone-related protein as a cardiovascular regulatory peptide. Endocrinology 137:3151–3153.

35. Bakre MM, Zhu Y, Yin H, Burton DW, Terkeltaub R, Deftos LJ, Varner JA 2002 Parathyroid hormone-related peptide is a naturally occurring, protein kinase A-dependent angiogenesis inhibitor. Nat Med 8:995–1003.

36. Fiaschi-Taesch N, Takane K, Masters SM, Stewart AF 2002 A virally delivered mutant of parathyroid hormone-related protein (PTHrP) completely prevents carotid restenosis. Circulation 106(Suppl 11):111–126.

37. Funk JL, Migliati E, Chen G, Wei H, Wilson J, Downey KJ, Mullarky PJ, Coull BM, McDonagh PF, Ritter LS 2003 Parathyroid hormone-related protein induction in focal stroke: A neuroprotective vascular peptide. Am J Physiol Regul Integr Comp Physiol 284:R1021–R1030.

38. Weir EC, Brines ML, Ikeda K, Burtis WJ, Broadus AE, Robbins RJ 1990 Parathyroid hormone-related peptide gene is expressed in the mammalian central nervous system. Proc Natl Acad Sci USA 87:108–112.

39. Weaver DR, Deeds JD, Lee K, Segre GV 1995 Localization of parathyroid hormone-related peptide (PTHrP) and PTH/PTHrP receptor mRNAs in rat brain. Brain Res Mol Brain Res 28:296–310.

40. Chatterjee O, Nakchbandi IA, Philbrick WM, Dreyer BE, Zhang JP, Kaczmarek LK, Brines ML, Broadus AE 2002 Endogenous parathyroid hormone-related protein functions as a neuroprotective agent. Brain Res 930:58–66.

41. Macica CM, Liang G, Lankford KL, Broadus AE 2006 Induction of parathyroid hormone-related peptide following peripheral nerve injury: Role as a modulator of Schwann cell phenotype. Glia 53:637–648.

42. Vasavada RC, Cavaliere C, D'Ercole AJ, Dann P, Burtis WJ, Madlener AL, Zawalich K, Zawalich W, Philbrick W, Stewart AF 1996 Overexpression of parathyroid hormone-related protein in the pancreatic islets of transgenic mice causes islet hyperplasia, hyperinsulinemia, and hypoglycemia. J Biol Chem 271:1200–1208.

43. Strewler GJ, Stern PH, Jacobs JW, Eveloff J, Klein RF, Leung SC, Rosenblatt M, Nissenson RA 1987 Parathyroid hormonelike protein from human renal carcinoma cells. Structural and functional homology with parathyroid hormone. J Clin Invest 80:1803–1807.

44. Stewart AF, Horst R, Deftos LJ, Cadman EC, Lang R, Broadus AE 1980 Biochemical evaluation of patients with cancer-associated hypercalcemia: Evidence for humoral and nonhumoral groups. N Engl J Med 303:1377–1383.

45. Nissenson RA, Diep D, Strewler GJ 1988 Synthetic peptides comprising the amino-terminal sequence of a parathyroid hormone-like protein from human malignancies. Binding to parathyroid hormone receptors and activation of adenylate cyclase in bone cells and kidney. J Biol Chem 263:12866–12871.

46. Orloff JJ, Wu TL, Stewart AF 1989 Parathyroid hormone-like proteins: Biochemical responses and receptor interactions. Endocr Rev 10:476–495.

47. Vortkamp A, Lee K, Lanske B, Segre GV, Kronenberg HM, Tabin CJ 1996 Regulation of rate of cartilage differentiation by Indian hedgehog and PTH-related protein. Science 273:613–622.

48. Ionescu AM, Schwarz EM, Vinson C, Puzas JE, Rosier R, Reynolds PR, O'Keefe RJ 2001 PTHrP modulates chondrocyte differentiation through AP-1 and CREB signaling. J Biol Chem 276:11639–11647.

49. Bastepe M, Weinstein LS, Ogata N, Kawaguchi H, Juppner H, Kronenberg HM, Chung UI 2004 Stimulatory G protein directly regulates hypertrophic differentiation of growth plate cartilage in vivo. Proc Natl Acad Sci USA 101:14794–14799.

50. Sakamoto A, Chen M, Kobayashi T, Kronenberg HM, Weinstein LS 2005 Chondrocyte-specific knockout of the G protein G(s)alpha leads to epiphyseal and growth plate abnormalities and ectopic chondrocyte formation. J Bone Miner Res 20:663–671.

51. Mangin M, Ikeda K, Dreyer BE, Broadus AE 1989 Isolation and characterization of the human parathyroid hormone-like peptide gene. Proc Natl Acad Sci USA 86:2408–2412.

52. Yasuda T, Banville D, Hendy GN, Goltzman D 1989 Characterization of the human parathyroid hormone-like peptide gene. Functional and evolutionary aspects. J Biol Chem 264:7720–7725.

53. Diefenbach-Jagger H, Brenner C, Kemp BE, Baron W, McLean J, Martin TJ, Moseley JM 1995 Arg21 is the preferred kexin cleavage site in parathyroid-hormone-related protein. Eur J Biochem 229:91–98.

54. Hook VY, Burton D, Yasothornsrikul S, Hastings RH, Deftos LJ 2001 Proteolysis of ProPTHrP(1–141) by "prohormone thiol protease" at multibasic residues generates PTHrP-related peptides: Implications for PTHrP peptide production in lung cancer cells. Biochem Biophys Res Commun 285:932–938.

55. Soifer NE, Dee KE, Insogna KL, Burtis WJ, Matovcik LM, Wu TL, Milstone LM, Broadus AE, Philbrick WM, Stewart AF 1992 Parathyroid hormone-related protein. Evidence for secretion of a novel mid-region fragment by three different cell types. J Biol Chem 267:18236–18243.

56. Orloff JJ, Reddy D, de Papp AE, Yang KH, Soifer NE, Stewart AF 1994 Parathyroid hormone-related protein as a prohormone: Posttranslational processing and receptor interactions. Endocr Rev 15:40–60.

57. Fukayama S, Tashjian AH Jr, Davis JN, Chisholm JC 1995 Signaling by N- and C-terminal sequences of parathyroid hormone-related protein in hippocampal neurons. Proc Natl Acad Sci USA 92:10182–10186.

58. Fenton AJ, Kemp BE, Kent GN, Moseley JM, Zheng MH, Rowe DJ, Britto JM, Martin TJ, Nicholson GC 1991 A carboxyl-terminal peptide from the parathyroid hormone-related protein inhibits bone resorption by osteoclasts. Endocrinology 129:1762–1768.

59. Cornish J, Callon KE, Nicholson GC, Reid IR 1997 Parathyroid hormone-related protein-(107–139) inhibits bone resorption in vivo. Endocrinology 138:1299–1304.

60. Mallette LE 1991 The parathyroid polyhormones: New concepts in the spectrum of peptide hormone action. Endocr Rev 12:110–117.

61. Ozeki S, Ohtsuru A, Seto S, Takeshita S, Yano H, Nakayama T, Ito M, Yokota T, Nobuyoshi M, Segre GV, Yamashita S, Yano K 1996 Evidence that implicates the parathyroid hormone-related peptide in vascular stenosis. Increased gene expression in the intima of injured carotid arteries and human restenotic coronary lesions. Arterioscler Thromb Vasc Biol 16:565–575.

62. Nakayama T, Ohtsuru A, Enomoto H, Namba H, Ozeki S, Shibata Y, Yokota T, Nobuyoshi M, Ito M, Sekine I, Yamashita S 1994 Coronary atherosclerotic smooth muscle cells overexpress human parathyroid hormone-related peptides. Biochem Biophys Res Commun 200:1028–1035.

63. Pirola CJ, Wang HM, Kamyar A, Wu S, Enomoto H, Sharifi B, Forrester JS, Clemens TL, Fagin JA 1993 Angiotensin II regulates parathyroid hormone-related protein expression in cultured rat aortic smooth muscle cells through transcriptional and post-transcriptional mechanisms. J Biol Chem 268:1987–1994.

64. Massfelder T, Dann P, Wu TL, Vasavada R, Helwig JJ, Stewart AF 1997 Opposing mitogenic and anti-mitogenic actions of parathyroid hormone-related protein in vascular smooth muscle cells: A critical role for nuclear targeting. Proc Natl Acad Sci USA 94:13630–13635.

65. Cingolani G, Bednenko J, Gillespie MT, Gerace L 2002 Molecular basis for the recognition of a nonclassical nuclear localization signal by importin beta. Mol Cell 10:1345–1353.

66. Pache JC, Burton DW, Deftos LJ, Hastings RH 2006 A carboxyl leucine-rich region of parathyroid hormone-related protein is critical for nuclear export. Endocrinology 147:990–998.

67. Amizuka N, Oda K, Shimomura J, Maeda T 2002 Biological action of parathyroid hormone (PTH)-related peptide (PTHrP) mediated either by the PTH/PTHrP receptor or the nucleolar translocation in chondrocytes. Anat Sci Int 77:225–236.

68. Shen X, Qian L, Falzon M 2004 PTH-related protein enhances MCF-7 breast cancer cell adhesion, migration, and invasion via an intracrine pathway. Exp Cell Res 294:420–433.

69. Fiaschi-Taesch NM, Stewart AF 2003 Minireview: Parathyroid hormone-related protein as an intracrine factor—trafficking mechanisms and functional consequences. Endocrinology 144:407–411.

70. Lam MH, House CM, Tiganis T, Mitchelhill KI, Sarcevic B, Cures A, Ramsay R, Kemp BE, Martin TJ, Gillespie MT 1999 Phosphorylation at the cyclin-dependent kinases site (Thr85) of parathyroid hormone-related protein negatively regulates its nuclear localization. J Biol Chem 274:18559–18566.

71. Aarts MM, Rix A, Guo J, Bringhurst R, Henderson JE 1999 The nucleolar targeting signal (NTS) of parathyroid hormone related protein mediates endocytosis and nucleolar translocation. J Bone Miner Res 14:1493–1503.

72. Nguyen M, He B, Karaplis A 2001 Nuclear forms of parathyroid hormone-related peptide are translated from non-AUG start sites downstream from the initiator methionine. Endocrinology 142:694–703.

73. Nguyen MT, Karaplis AC 1998 The nucleus: A target site for parathyroid hormone-related peptide (PTHrP) action. J Cell Biochem 70:193–199.

74. Lam MH, Olsen SL, Rankin WA, Ho PW, Martin TJ, Gillespie MT, Moseley JM 1997 PTHrP and cell division: Expression and localization of

PTHrP in a keratinocyte cell line (HaCaT) during the cell cycle. J Cell Physiol **173:**433–446.

75. de Miguel F, Fiaschi-Taesch N, Lopez-Talavera JC, Takane KK, Massfelder T, Helwig JJ, Stewart AF 2001 The C-terminal region of PTHrP, in addition to the nuclear localization signal, is essential for the intracrine stimulation of proliferation in vascular smooth muscle cells. Endocrinology **142:**4096–4105.

76. Falzon M, Du P 2000 Enhanced growth of MCF-7 breast cancer cells

overexpressing parathyroid hormone-related peptide. Endocrinology **141:**1882–1892.

77. Gujral A, Burton DW, Terkeltaub R, Deftos LJ 2001 Parathyroid hormone-related protein induces interleukin 8 production by prostate cancer cells via a novel intracrine mechanism not mediated by its classical nuclear localization sequence. Cancer Res **61:**2282–2288.

78. Frohman LA, Jansson JO 1986 Growth hormone-releasing hormone. Endocr Rev **7:**223–253.

Chapter 17. Vitamin D: Photobiology, Metabolism, Mechanism of Action, and Clinical Applications

Michael F. Holick[1] and Michele Garabedian[2]

[1]Section of Endocrinology, Diabetes and Metabolism, Department of Medicine, Boston University Medical Center, Boston, Massachusetts; and [2]Hospital St. Vincent de Paul, Paris, France

INTRODUCTION

Vitamin D is a secosteroid that is made in the skin by the action of sunlight.[1] Vitamin D (D represents either or both D_2 and D_3) is biologically inert and must undergo two successive hydroxylations in the liver and kidney to become the biologically active 1,25-dihydroxyvitamin D [1,25(OH)$_2$D].[1–4] 1,25(OH)$_2$D's main biological effect is to maintain the serum calcium within the normal range. It accomplishes this by increasing the efficiency of intestinal absorption of dietary calcium and by recruiting stem cells in the bone to become mature osteoclasts, which, in turn, mobilizes calcium stores from the bone into the circulation.[1–4] The renal production of 1,25(OH)$_2$D is tightly regulated by serum calcium levels and through the action of PTH and phosphorus (Fig. 1). There are a wide variety of inborn and acquired disorders in the metabolism of vitamin D that can lead to both hypo- and hypercalcemic conditions. 1,25(OH)$_2$D not only regulates calcium metabolism but also is capable of inhibiting the proliferation and inducing terminal differentiation of a variety of normal and cancer cells, modulating the immune system, enhancing insulin secretion, and downregulating the renin/angiotensin system.[1,2] Active vitamin D compounds are used for the treatment of osteoporosis, renal osteodystrophy, and psoriasis and are being developed to treat some cancers, hypertension, benign prostate hypertrophy, cardiovascular heart disease, and type I diabetes.[1–6]

PHOTOBIOLOGY OF VITAMIN D_3

During exposure to sunlight, cutaneous 7-dehydrocholesterol (7-DHC; provitamin D_3), the immediate precursor of cholesterol, absorbs solar radiation with energies between 290 and 315 nm (ultraviolet B [UVB]), transforming it into previtamin D_3 (Fig. 1).[1,2] Once formed, previtamin D_3 rapidly undergoes a membrane enhanced temperature dependent isomerization to vitamin D_3 (Fig. 1).[2] Vitamin D_3 is translocated from the skin into the circulation, where it is bound to the vitamin D–binding protein (DBP).[1,2]

There are no documented cases of vitamin intoxication caused by excessive exposure to sunlight, because once previtamin D_3 and vitamin D_3 are formed, they absorb solar UVB radiation and are transformed into several biologically inert photoproducts (Fig. 1).[1,2]

A variety of factors can alter the cutaneous production of vitamin D_3. Melanin, an excellent natural sunscreen, competes with 7-DHC for UVB photons, thereby reducing the production of vitamin D_3.[1,2] People of color require longer exposure (5- to 10-fold) to sunlight to make the same amount of vitamin D_3 as their white counterparts.[1,2] Aging diminishes the concentration of 7-DHC in the epidermis. Compared with a young adult, a person over the age of 70 years produced <30% of the amount of vitamin D_3 when exposed to the same amount of simulated sunlight.[1,2] Latitude, time of day, and season of the year dramatically affect the production of vitamin D_3 in the skin (Fig. 2). At latitudes of 42° N (Boston) and 48.5° N (Paris, France) or 52° N (Edmonton, Canada), sunlight is incapable of producing vitamin D_3 in the skin between the months of November through February and October through March,[1,2] respectively. Casual exposure to sunlight provides most (80–100%) of our vitamin D requirement. The inability of the sun to produce vitamin D_3 in the far northern and southern latitudes during the winter requires both children and adults to take a vitamin D supplement to prevent vitamin D deficiency. For children and young adults, the cutaneous production of vitamin D_3 during the spring, summer, and fall is often in excess and is stored in the fat so that it can be used during the winter months. However, both children and adults who always wear sun protection may not make enough vitamin D_3 and therefore do not have sufficient vitamin D stores for winter use and will become vitamin D deficient.[1] Exposure to sunlight at lower latitudes such as Los Angeles (24° N), Puerto Rico (18° N), and Buenos Aires (34° S) results in the cutaneous production of vitamin D_3 during the entire year (Fig. 2).[1,2] A sunscreen with a sun protection factor of 8 (SPF 8) reduced the cutaneous production of vitamin D_3 by 95%.[1,2] Chronic use of a sunscreen can result in vitamin D insufficiency.[1,2] Although sunscreen use is extremely valuable for the prevention of skin cancer and the damaging effects caused by excessive exposure to the sun, both children and adults who depend on sunlight for their vitamin D_3 should consider exposure of hands, face, and arms or arms and legs to suberythemal amounts of sunlight (25% of the amount that would cause a mild pinkness to the skin) two to three times a week before topically applying a sunscreen with an SPF of 15. Thus, they can take advantage of the beneficial

Dr. Holick is a consultant for the Nichols Institute. All other authors have reported no conflicts of interest.

effect of sunlight while preventing the damaging effects of chronic excessive exposure to sunlight.

FOOD SOURCES AND THE RECOMMENDED ADEQUATE INTAKE FOR VITAMIN D

Vitamin D is rare in foods. The major natural sources of vitamin D are oily fish such as salmon and mackerel (~400 IU/3.5 oz) as well as fish liver oils including cod liver oil.[1-3] Vitamin D can also be obtained from foods fortified with vitamin D including some cereals, bread products, yogurt, orange juice, and milk.[1,7] Other dairy products including ice cream and cheese are not fortified with vitamin D. In Europe, most countries except Sweden forbid vitamin D fortification of milk. However, margarine and some cereals are fortified with vitamin D in most European countries. Multivitamin and pharmaceutical preparations containing vitamin D are reliable sources of vitamin D. The new recommended adequate intake (AI) for vitamin D for infants, all children, and adults up to the age of 50 years is 200 IU (5 μg)/day. For adults 51–70 and 71+ years, the AIs are 400 and 600 IU/day, respectively.[7] There is mounting evidence that, in the absence of sunlight, the recommended AIs for vitamin D_3 for children and adults is inadequate without some sun exposure and they may need as much as 1000 IU of vitamin D_3 a day.[8-14]

METABOLISM OF VITAMIN D

Vitamin D_2, which comes from yeast and plants, and vitamin D_3, which is found in oily fish and cod liver oil and is made in the skin, are the major sources of vitamin D.[1,2,7] The differences between vitamin D_2 and vitamin D_3 are a double bond between C_{22} and C_{23}, and a methyl group on C_{24} for vitamin D_2. Vitamin D_2 is about 30% as effective as vitamin D_3 in maintaining vitamin D status.[13,14] Once vitamin D_2 or vitamin D_3 enters the circulation, it is bound to the vitamin D–binding protein and transported to the liver, where one or more cytochrome P_{450}-vitamin D-25-hydroxylase(s) (CYP27A1, CYP3A4, CYP2R1, CYP2J3) introduces a OH on carbon 25 to produce 25-hydroxyvitamin D [25(OH)D](Fig. 1).[1-3,10] 25(OH)D is the major circulating form of vitamin D. Because the hepatic vitamin D-25-hydroxylase is not tightly regulated, an increase in the cutaneous production of vitamin D_3 or ingestion of vitamin D will result in an increase in circulating levels of 25(OH)D.[1-3,7,10,14] Therefore, its measurement is used to determine whether a patient is vitamin D deficient, sufficient, or intoxicated.[1-3,7,10,14]

25(OH)D is biologically inert. It is transported to the kidney, where membrane-bound megalin transports the 25(OH)D-DBP complex into the renal tubule cell where the cytochrome P_{450}-mono-oxygenase, 25(OH)D-1α-hydroxylase (1-OHase; CYP27B1), metabolizes 25(OH)D to 1,25-dihydroxyvitamin D [1,25(OH)$_2$D] (Fig. 1).[1-4] Although the kidney is the major source of circulating 1,25(OH)$_2$D, there is strong evidence that a wide variety of tissues and cells including activated macrophages, osteoblasts, keratinocytes, prostate, colon, and breast express the 1-OHase and have the ability to produce 1,25(OH)$_2$D.[1-3,15] In addition, during pregnancy, the placenta produces 1,25(OH)$_2$D.[3] However, because anephric patients have very low or undetectable levels of 1,25(OH)$_2$D in their blood, the extrarenal sites of 1,25(OH)$_2$D production do not seem to play a role in calcium homeostasis. The exception is when macrophages make and excrete 1,25(OH)$_2$D into the circulation in patients with chronic granulomatous disorders such as sarcoidosis. This results in hypercalciuria and hypercalcemia.[3,15] The local production of 1,25(OH)$_2$D in tissues not associated with calcium homeostasis may be for the purpose of regulating a wide variety of biological functions including cell growth, apoptosis, angiogenesis, differentiation, and regulation of the immune system.[1-6,15]

When serum ionized calcium declines, there is an increase in the production and secretion of PTH. PTH has a variety of biological functions on calcium metabolism. It also regulates calcium homeostasis by enhancing the renal conversion of 25(OH)D to 1,25(OH)$_2$D (Fig. 1).[1-3] It does this by acting on the 1-OHase promoter and indirectly through its renal wasting of phosphorus resulting in decreased intracellular and blood levels of phosphorus.[1,3] Hypophosphatemia and hyperphosphatemia are associated with increased and decreased circulating concentrations of 1,25(OH)$_2$D, respectively.[16] Fibroblast growth factor (FGF)-23 is involved in phosphorus metabolism and markedly reduces the kidney's production of 1,25(OH)$_2$D.[17] Calcium deprivation will also enhance 1-OHase activity independent of the associated secondary hyperparathyroidism.[18] A variety of other hormones associated with growth and development of the skeleton or calcium regulation including growth hormone and prolactin indirectly increase the renal production of 1,25(OH)$_2$D. IGF-1 is a potent stimulator of 1,25(OH)$_2$D production and may explain the parallelism between serum 1,25(OH)$_2$D levels and growth velocity in children and adolescents.[19] Osteoporotic patients may lose their ability to upregulate the renal production of 1,25(OH)$_2$D by PTH.[20] This, along with a decrease in the amount of vitamin D receptor in elders' small intestine,[21] may help explain the age-related decrease in the efficiency of intestinal calcium absorption.

Both 25(OH)D and 1,25(OH)$_2$D undergo a 24-hydroxylation by the 25(OH)D-24-hydroxylase (CYP24) to form 24,25-dihydroxyvitamin D [24,25(OH)$_2$D] and 1,24,25-trihydroxyvitamin D, respectively.[1-4] 1,25(OH)$_2$D undergoes several hydroxylations in the side-chain by the 25(OH)D-24-hydroxylase causing the cleavage of the side-chain between carbons 23 and 24, resulting in the biologically inert water soluble acid, calcitroic acid (Fig. 1).[1-4] Although >50 different metabolites of vitamin D have been identified, only 1,25(OH)$_2$D is believed to be important for most if not all of the biological actions of vitamin D on calcium and bone metabolism.[1-4]

A wide variety of drugs including antiseizure medications, glucocorticoids, and rifampin enhance the catabolism of vitamin D. It is now recognized that when the pregnane-X-receptor (PXR) binds any one of these drugs and becomes activated, it can form a heterodimeric complex with retinoic acid X receptor (RXR). This complex binds to the VDR responsive element (VDRE) of the CYP24 and enhances the expression of the 24-OHase and the catabolism of 25(OH)D and 1,25(OH)$_2$D.[22] Thus, drugs and xenobiotics that activate PXR may also increase CYP24 activity, causing vitamin D deficiency and osteomalacia.

MOLECULAR BIOLOGY OF VITAMIN D

1,25(OH)$_2$D is a steroid hormone and acts similar to estrogen and other steroid hormones in inducing its biological responses.[1-4,23] 1,25(OH)$_2$D binds to the VDR in the cytoplasm causing conformational change to reorient the activation function 2 domain located in helix 12 of the receptor. This allows for it to interact with other cytoplasmic proteins and co-activators, which mediates its translocation along the microtubule with the hydrophilic nuclear localization sequence binding to importin α to enter the nucleus through the nuclear pore complex.[23,24] In the nucleus, the VDR–1,25(OH)$_2$D$_3$ complex binds with RXR (Fig. 3). This heterodimeric complex binds to the VDRE and initiates the binding of several initiation

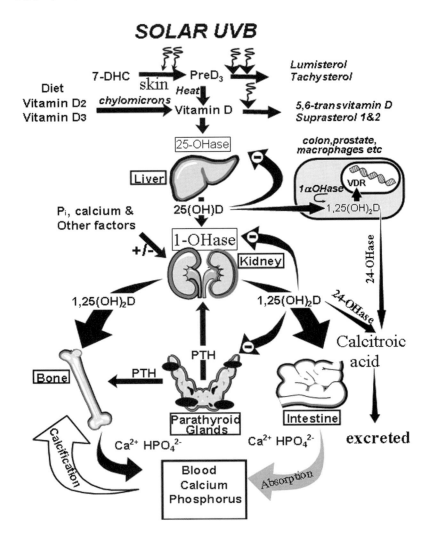

FIG. 1. The photochemical, thermal, and metabolic pathways for vitamin D. During exposure to sunlight, UVB 7-DHC is converted to previtamin D_3 (preD$_3$). PreD$_3$ undergoes thermal isomerization to vitamin D_3, and vitamin D from the diet, along with the skin's vitamin D, enters the circulation and is metabolized sequentially in the liver and kidney to 25(OH)D and 1,25(OH)$_2$D. Serum phosphorus (Pi) and PTH levels are major regulators of renal 1,25(OH)$_2$D production. The 24-OHase is responsible for the degradation of 1,25(OH)$_2$D to calciotropic acid. 25(OH)D can also enter other nonrenal tissues including macrophages, colon, prostate, and breast, where it undergoes transformation to 1,25(OH)$_2$D. It then interacts with its VDR to induce genes that regulate cell growth.

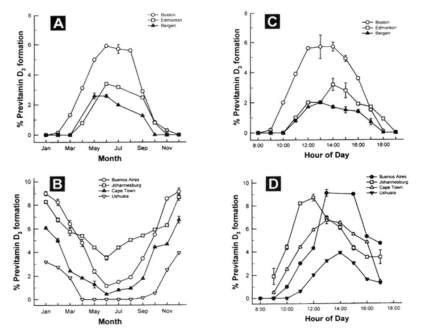

FIG. 2. Influence of season, time of day, and latitude on the synthesis of preD$_3$ in (A and C) the Northern and (B and D) Southern Hemispheres. The hour indicated in C and D is the end of the 1-h exposure time. Data for hour of the day were collected in July. Data represent means ± SE of duplicate determinations.

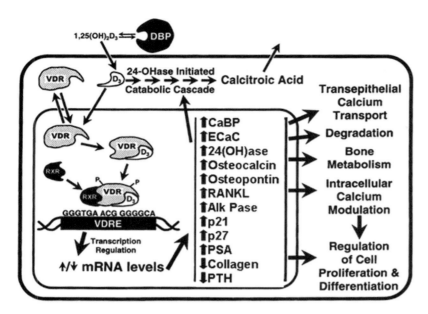

FIG. 3. A schematic representation of the mechanism of action of 1,25(OH)$_2$D in various target cells resulting in a variety of biological responses. The free form of 1,25(OH)$_2$D$_3$ enters the target cell and interacts with its nuclear VDR, which is phosphorylated (Pi). The 1,25(OH)$_2$D–VDR complex combines with the RXR to form a heterodimer, which in turn interacts with the VDRE, causing an enhancement or inhibition of transcription of vitamin D responsive genes including calcium-binding protein (CaBP), epithelial calcium channel (ECaC), 25(OH)D-24-hydroxylase (24-OHase), RANKL, alkaline phosphatase (alk PASE), prostate specific antogen (PSA), and PTH.

factors including the P160 co-activator proteins glucocorticoid receptor interacting protein 1 (GRIP-1), steroid receptor co-activator-1 (SRC-1), and vitamin D receptor interacting protein (DRIP)–thyroid receptor associated proteins (TRAP) complex along with a host of other coactivators that ultimately initiates transcription of the vitamin D responsive gene.[3,23]

The *VDR* gene has nine exons. The first exon includes several noncoding regions (Ia to If), whereas the eight following exons give rise to the classical VDR. Unlike other nuclear receptors of the same family, only a few isoforms of VDR have been identified, and their functional relevance remains unclear. Aside from the classical VDR, two N-terminal variances of the human VDR have been described. One is three amino acids shorter and is associated with the *Fok*I start codon polymorphism in the human VDR locus.[25] The other is 50 amino acids longer and results from the coding of the Id exon through alternative splicing.[26] Specific exon mutations and exon skipping have been identified, which caused resistance to 1,25(OH)$_2$D, causing vitamin D–resistant rickets (also known as vitamin D–dependent rickets type 2).[25]

Some VDR actions may not require its binding to 1,25(OH)$_2$D. When the ligand binding domain of the VDR was mutated so that it could no longer bind 1,25(OH)$_2$D$_3$, but was able to still interact with the RXR and the VDRE maintaining hair follicle homeostasis.[27] VDR can also bind non–vitamin D ligands including lithocholic acid, which is hepatotoxic and a potential carcinogenic bile acid and thus may mediate local cellular detoxification through induction of the CYP3A4 expression.[28] 1,25(OH)$_2$D may also be recognized by other receptors than VDR including MARRS, a multifunctional membrane associated protein isolated from chick intestine that stimulated phosphate uptake.[29] The functional importance of the interaction of these non–vitamin D ligands with VDR, however, is not well understood.[30]

There are also mutations in the exons and introns that can lead to polymorphisms of the *VDR* gene that do not cause any biologically significant alteration in the amino acid composition of the VDR.[31] These polymorphisms are thought to be important in the transcription of the *VDR* gene and/or stabilization of the resultant VDR mRNA. There is some evidence that these polymorphisms may lead to a differential responsiveness to 1,25(OH)$_2$D$_3$ in the intestine and bone, thereby playing a role in peak bone mass and the development and osteoporosis and other diseases.[32–34]

BIOLOGIC FUNCTIONS OF VITAMIN D IN THE INTESTINE AND BONE

The major physiologic function of vitamin D is to maintain serum calcium at a physiologically acceptable level to maximize a wide variety of metabolic functions, signal transduction, and neuromuscular activity.[1–3] It accomplishes this by interacting with its receptor in the small intestine. 1,25(OH)$_2$D enhances calcium entry by inducing the epithelial calcium channel (ECaC), a member of the vanillanoid receptor family (TRPV6).[3,35] 1,25(OH)$_2$D also induces several proteins in the small intestine, including calcium binding protein (calbindin D 9K), alkaline phosphatase, low affinity Ca ATPase, brush border actin, calmodulin, and several brush border proteins of 80–90 kDa.[3,35] These facilitate the movement of calcium through the cytoplasm and transfer the calcium across the basal lateral membrane into the circulation. 1,25(OH)$_2$D causes a biphasic response on intestinal calcium absorption in vitamin D–deficient animals. A rapid response occurs within 2 h and peaks by 6 h and another that begins after 12 h and peaks at 24 h, suggesting that there is a rapid action of 1,25(OH)$_2$D on intestinal calcium absorption and a more prolonged nuclear mediated response.[3,35] 1,25(OH)$_2$D also enhances the absorption of dietary phosphorus. Although calcium and phosphorus absorption occur along the entire length of the small intestine, most of the phosphorus transport occurs in the jejunum and ileum unlike calcium absorption, which principally occurs in the duodenum. The net result is that there is an increase in the efficiency of intestinal calcium and phosphorus absorption. In the vitamin D–deficient state, no more than 10–15% of dietary calcium and 60% of dietary phosphorus is absorbed the gastrointestinal tract. However, with adequate vitamin D, adults absorb 30–40% of dietary calcium and 70–80% of dietary phosphorus by the 1,25(OH)$_2$D-mediated processes. During pregnancy and lactation and during the growth spurt, circulating concentrations of 1,25(OH)$_2$D increase, thereby increasing the efficiency of intestinal calcium absorption by as much as 50–80%.[1–3,35]

When there is inadequate dietary calcium to satisfy the

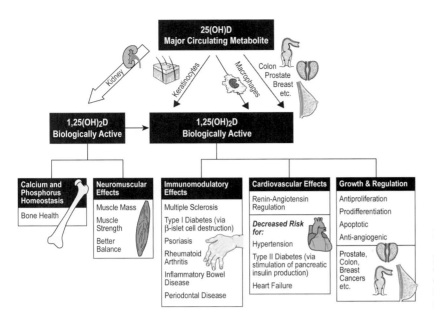

FIG. 4. Sources of vitamin D and its metabolism to 1,25(OH)₂D in the kidney and extrarenal tissues, including prostate gland, breast, colon, and immune cells. Once produced, 1,25(OH)₂D has a multitude of biological actions on calcium, muscle, and bone health, regulation of blood pressure and insulin production, regulation of immune function, and regulation of cell growth.

body's calcium requirement, 1,25(OH)$_2$D interacts with the VDR in osteoblasts resulting in signal transduction to induce RANKL expression. The pre-osteoclast has the receptor (RANK) for RANKL.[1–3,36,37] The direct contact of the pre-osteoclast's RANK with the osteoblast's RANKL results in signal transduction to induce pre-osteoclasts to become mature osteoclasts. The mature osteoclasts release hydrochloric acid and proteolytic enzymes to dissolve bone mineral and matrix releasing calcium into the extracellular space.

The major function of 1,25(OH)$_2$D for the bone mineralization process is to maintain a calcium-phosphorus product in the circulation that is in a supersaturated state, thereby resulting in the passive mineralization of the collagen matrix (osteoid) laid down by osteoblasts. 1,25(OH)$_2$D does not have a direct active role in the mineralization process; its responsibility is to maintain blood levels of calcium and phosphorus in the normal range for proper mineralization to occur.[1–3,37] 1,25(OH)$_2$D does have several additional direct effects on osteoblasts by increasing the expression of bone specific alkaline phosphatase, osteocalcin, osteonectin, osteoprotogerin, and a variety of cytokines.[3,36,37] In addition, 1,25(OH)$_2$D$_3$ alters the proliferation and apoptosis of skeletal cells including hypertrophic chondrocytes. These direct actions of 1,25(OH)$_2$D on bone cell homeostasis may explain the severity of rickets in patients with *VDR* mutations.[38] Vitamin D analogs have been developed that have a marked anabolic effect on bone and are being evaluated for the treatment of osteoporosis.[37]

NONCALCEMIC ACTIVITIES OF 1,25(OH)$_2$D$_3$

Most tissues and cells in the body have a VDR, including brain, prostate, breast, gonads, colon, pancreas, heart, monocytes, and activated T and B lymphocytes.[1–6,37] Although the exact physiologic function of 1,25(OH)$_2$D in these tissues is not fully understood, 1,25(OH)$_2$D has varied biological activities that have important physiologic implications and pharmacologic applications. 1,25(OH)$_2$D$_3$, and its analogs inhibit proliferation and induce terminal differentiation of normal cells, such as keratinocytes and cancer cells that express VDR including those of the prostate, colon, breast, lymphoproliferative system, and lung.[1–3,6,37] The antiproliferative and pro-

differentiating properties of 1,25(OH)$_2$D$_3$ and its analogs have been successfully developed to treat the hyperproliferative skin disorder psoriasis and are in development to treat prostate, breast, liver, and colon cancer.[5,39–41]

1,25(OH)$_2$D has been reported to downregulate renin production in the kidney, suggesting that 1,25(OH)$_2$D may influence blood pressure control.[42] β-islet cells have a VDR, and 1,25(OH)$_2$D$_3$ stimulates insulin production and secretion[1–3] either directly through its interaction with the β-islet cell's VDR or indirectly by raising the serum concentration of calcium.

Activated T and B lymphocytes, monocytes, and macrophages all respond to 1,25(OH)$_2$D, resulting in the modulation of their immune functions.[1–4,6,37] Thus, it has been suggested that vitamin D sufficiency may be important in decreasing risk of common autoimmune diseases such as multiple sclerosis, Crohn's disease, rheumatoid arthritis, and diabetes type 1[1–4,6,43–45] (Fig. 4).

NONRENAL SYNTHESIS OF 1,25(OH)$_2$D$_3$

The 1-OHase was cloned, and various point mutations have been identified for pseudovitamin D–deficient rickets (vitamin D–dependent rickets type 1).[3,46] In 1-OHase, knockout (KO) mice reproductive and immune dysfunction has been reported.[47] The cloning of the 1-OHase has provided the impetus to explore the expression of this mitochondrial enzyme in nonrenal tissues, including prostate, colon, skin, breast, lung, and osteoblasts.[1–3] Although the physiologic function of the extrarenal 1-OHase is not well understood, there is mounting evidence that the local cellular production of 1,25(OH)$_2$D may be important for regulation of cell growth, immune function, and other cellular activities (Fig. 4). It is believed that once 1,25(OH)$_2$D is made and carries out its physiologic function(s), it induces CYP24 and is rapidly catabolized to calcitroic acid and therefore does not enter into the circulation to increase circulating concentrations of 1,25(OH)$_2$D[1,2] (Fig. 1). Further studies are needed to help clarify the importance of the nonrenal 1-OHase in normal and cancer tissues.

REGULATION OF PTH SECRETION BY 1,25(OH)$_2$D

The parathyroid chief cell has a VDR and it responds to 1,25(OH)$_2$D$_3$ by decreasing the expression of the *PTH* gene and decreasing PTH synthesis and secretion. Patients with long-standing secondary and tertiary hyperparathyroidism can develop within the parathyroid glands, islands of PTH secreting cells that have little or no VDR. These cells are no longer responsive to the PTH-lowering effect of 1,25(OH)$_2$D.[48] Thus, the goal in patients with mild to moderate renal failure is to suppress secondary hyperparathyroidism. This can be accomplished by maintaining normal serum calcium concentrations first by controlling for hyperphosphatemia, which is one of the most potent downregulators of renal production of 1,25(OH)$_2$D$_3$. However, when the serum phosphorus levels are maintained in the normal range and there continues to be an increase in PTH levels in the circulation, the use of oral or intravenous 1,25(OH)$_2$D$_3$ and its less calcemic analogs 19-nor1,25-dihydroxyvitamin D$_2$, 1α-hydroxyvitamin D$_3$, 1α-hydroxyvitamin D$_2$, or 1,24-epi-dihydroxyvitamin D$_2$, to maintain serum calcium levels and directly suppress PTH expression is warranted.[49] One of the additional benefits of using an active vitamin D analog in chronic renal failure (CRF) patients is to decrease mortality presumably by decreasing cardiovascular events.[50] CRF patients who receive active vitamin D analog still need to be monitored for vitamin D deficiency.[51] It is known that parathyroid glands have 1-OHase activity, and thus increasing 25(OH)D may result in the local production of 1,25(OH)$_2$D in the parathyroid glands, which in turn, could downregulate PTH production.[52]

CLINICAL APPLICATIONS

Hypocalcemic Disorders

There are a variety of hypocalcemic disorders that are directly associated with acquired and inherited disorders in the acquisition of vitamin D, its metabolism to 1,25(OH)$_2$D, and the cellular recognition of 1,25(OH)$_2$D.[1–3,25,46,53] Vitamin D deficiency can be caused by a decreased synthesis of vitamin D$_3$ in the skin because of (1) excessive sunscreen use, (2) clothing of all sun-exposed areas, (3) aging, (4) changes in season of the year, and (5) increased latitude.[1–3,53] Intestinal malabsorption of vitamin D associated with fat malabsorption syndromes including Crohn's disease, sprue, Whipple's disease, and hepatic dysfunction are recognizable by low or undetectable circulating concentrations of 25(OH)D.[3,53] Increased vitamin D deposition in body fat is the cause of vitamin D deficiency in obesity.[1,2] Dilantin, phenobarbital, glucocorticoids, and a wide range of other drugs enhance the catabolism of 25(OH)D through the activation of PXR, requiring that these patients receive at least two to five times the AI for vitamin D to correct this abnormality.[22,53] Because the liver has such a large capacity to produce 25(OH)D, usually >90% of the liver has to be dysfunctional before it is incapable of making an adequate quantity of 25(OH)D. Often the fat malabsorption associated with the liver failure is the cause for vitamin D deficiency.[3,53] Patients with nephrotic syndrome excreting >4 g of protein/24 h can have lower 25(OH)D because of the co-excretion of the DBP with its 25(OH)D into the urine.[3,53]

Acquired disorders in the metabolism of 25(OH)D to 1,25(OH)$_2$D can cause hypocalcemia. Patients with chronic renal failure with a glomerular filtration rate (GFR) of <30% of normal have decreased reserved capacity to produce 1,25(OH)$_2$D.[1,3,49,53] Hyperphosphatemia and hypoparathyroidism will result in the decreased production of 1,25(OH)$_2$D.[3,16,53]

Conversely, hypophosphatemia may be associated with inappropriate low levels of 1,25(OH)$_2$D in the presence of excessive levels of FGF-23 that increases urinary phosphate excretion and inhibits the renal production of 1,25(OH)$_2$D.[3,17,54–56] This occurs in patients with abnormally high levels of FGF-23 because of the oncogenic production of the factor and in patients with hereditary activating mutations in the *FGF-23* gene (autosomal dominant hypophosphatemic rickets) and in patients with X-linked hypophosphatemic rickets caused by inactivation mutations in the *PHEX* gene.[53–56] The precise etiology for why 1,25(OH)$_2$D is low in these patients is not well understood.[56]

There are three rare inherited hypocalcemic disorders that are caused by a deficiency in the renal production of 1,25(OH)$_2$D: vitamin D–dependent rickets type I, a defect or deficiency in the VDR [1,25(OH)$_2$D-resistant syndrome], and elevated levels of a heterogenous nuclear ribonucleoprotein that specifically interacted with the VDRE, thus preventing the binding of the 1,25(OH)$_2$D-VDR-RXR to the VDRE, resulting in resistance to 1,25(OH)$_2$D$_3$ on calcium and bone metabolism.[3,25,46,53,57]

Hypercalcemic Disorders

Excessive ingestion of vitamin D (usually >10,000 IU/day) for many months can cause vitamin D intoxication that is recognized by markedly elevated levels of 25(OH)D (usually >150 ng/ml), and normal levels of 1,25(OH)$_2$D, hypercalcemia, and hyperphosphatemia.[3,53,58] Ingestion of excessive quantities of 25(OH)D$_3$, 1α-OH-D$_3$, 1,25(OH)$_2$D$_3$, dihydrotachysterol, and other active vitamin D analogs or exuberant use of topical 1,25(OH)$_2$D$_3$, calcipotriene (Dovonex; Leo Pharmaceutical Corp.), and other active vitamin D analogs for psoriasis can cause vitamin D intoxication.[5,53,58,72] Because activated macrophages convert 25(OH)D to 1,25(OH)$_2$D in an unregulated fashion, chronic granulomatous diseases such as sarcoidosis and tuberculosis are often associated with increased serum levels of 1,25(OH)$_2$D that results in hypercalciuria and hypercalcemia.[3,15,53] Rarely, lymphomas associated with hypercalcemia are caused by increased production of 1,25(OH)$_2$D by macrophages associated with the lymphoma. Primary hyperparathyroidism and hypophosphatemia are also associated with increase renal production of 1,25(OH)$_2$D.[3,16,49,53]

CONSEQUENCES AND TREATMENT OF VITAMIN D DEFICIENCY

Vitamin D plays a critical role in the mineralization of the skeleton at all ages. As the body depletes its stores of vitamin D because of lack of exposure to sunlight or a deficiency of vitamin D in the diet, the efficiency of intestinal calcium absorption decreases, causing a decrease in the serum ionized calcium concentrations, which signals the calcium sensor in the parathyroid glands to increase the synthesis and secretion of PTH.[1–3,49,53] PTH not only conserves calcium by increasing renal tubular reabsorption of calcium, but mobilizes stem cells to become active bone calcium resorbing osteoclasts. PTH also increases tubular excretion of phosphorus, causing hypophosphatemia. The net effect of vitamin D insufficiency and vitamin D deficiency is a normal serum calcium, elevated PTH and alkaline phosphatase, and low or low normal fasting serum phosphorus. The hallmark of vitamin D deficiency is a low level of 25(OH)D (<15 ng/ml) in the blood.[1–3,53,59] Most experts agree that to minimize PTH levels the 25(OH)D in adults should be >30 ng/ml.[1–3,59–62] The secondary hyperparathyroidism and low calcium-phosphorus product is thought to be responsible for the detective mineralization action of the osteoid, which is the hallmark of rickets/osteomalacia.[1,3,53,63] In addition, the secondary hyperparathyroidism causes increased osteoclastic activity, resulting in calcium wasting from the bone, which in turn can precipitate or exacerbate osteoporosis.

Vitamin D deficiency is a major cause of metabolic bone disease in older adults. Rickets is, once again, becoming a major health problem for infants of mothers of color who exclusively breast feed their children and do not supplement them with vitamin D.[1,53,63,64] Infants fed only nondairy milk substitutes that contain neither calcium nor vitamin D are also prone to developing rickets.[65] Vitamin D deficiency is underappreciated in both children and adults (1–3,12,66–69). The NHANES III survey revealed that 42% of black women 15–49 years of age were vitamin D deficient throughout the United States at the end of the winter.[67] Vitamin D deficiency is common in the elderly,[1,12,66] especially those who are infirm and in nursing homes.[1–3,12,53,66] Approximately 50% of free-living elders in Boston and Baltimore were found to be vitamin D deficient throughout the year.[1,53,66] Even healthy children and young adults are at risk. Forty-eight percent of preadolescent white girls (9–11 years of age)[66] and 52% of Hispanic and black adolescent boys and girls were reported to have a 25(OH)D of <20 ng/ml in New England.[69] In Europe where vitamin D fortification is scarce, 78% of Finnish girls (10–12 years of age) were vitamin D deficient.[70] In sunny climates where children and adults avoid sun exposure including Lebanon, Saudi Arabia, and India, a high incidence of rickets is reported.[66,71,72] A study in students and young medical doctors 18–29 years of age in Boston at the end of the winter revealed 32% were vitamin D deficient, and a significant number had secondary hyperparathyroidism.[66] Vitamin D deficiency not only robs the skeleton of precious calcium stores but causes osteomalacia. This disease, unlike osteoporosis, causes vague symptoms of bone pain, bone achiness, muscle aches and pains, and muscle weakness. These symptoms are often dismissed by physicians, and the patient is given the diagnosis of fibromyalgia, chronic fatigue syndrome, or simple depression.[66] Eighty-eight percent of Arab women with muscle pain, weakness, and bone pain[66] and 93% of children and adults 10–65 years of age with similar complaints were found to be vitamin D deficient.[73]

Casual exposure to sunlight is the best source of vitamin D. Because the skin has such a large capacity to produce vitamin D_3, children and adults of all ages can obtain their vitamin D requirement from exposure to sunlight. For young adults, a whole body exposure to one minimum erythemal dose (a slight pinkness to the skin) of simulated sunlight was found to be equivalent to taking a single oral dose of between 10,000 and 25,000 IU of vitamin D.[1,2] Therefore, children and adults only need minimum exposure of unprotected skin to sunlight followed by the application of a sunscreen or use of other sun protective measures, including clothing. In Boston, it is recommended that white men and women expose face and arms or arms and legs to sunlight three times a week for ~25% of time that it would cause a mild sunburn in the spring, summer, and fall.[1–3,66]

Patients with vitamin D deficiency require immediate attention with aggressive therapy. Trying to replete vitamin D deficiency with a multivitamin or with a few multivitamins containing 400 IU of vitamin D is not only not effective, but can be potentially dangerous because one multivitamin often contains the safe upper limit of vitamin A. The vitamin D tank is empty and requires rapid filling. This can be accomplished by giving pharmacologic doses of vitamin D orally; 50,000 IU of vitamin D_2 (equal to ~15,000 IU of vitamin D_3) once a week for 8 weeks will often correct vitamin D deficiency as

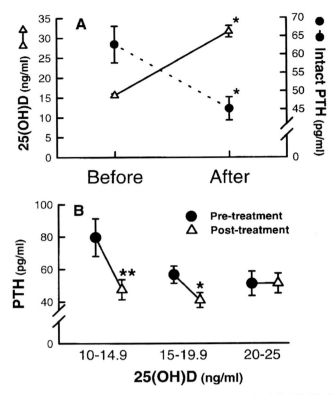

FIG. 5. (Top) Healthy adults 49–83 years of age received 50,000 IU of vitamin D_2 once a week for 8 weeks. Serum levels of 25(OH)D and intact PTH are shown before and after receiving vitamin D_2. (Bottom) These same patients with serum 25(OH)D >10 (considered to be the lowest limit of the normal range by many laboratories) and <25 ng/ml were stratified regarding their PTH levels before and immediately after therapy. The data clearly show significant declines in PTH when the initial serum 25(OH)D were between 11 and 19 ng/ml, suggesting that patients were deficient in vitamin D until the 25(OH)D was >20 ng/ml. Based on this and other data, the new recommendation is that patients should have a blood level of at least 20 ng/ml and preferably 30 ng/ml of 25(OH)D to maximize bone and cellular health.

measured by an increase in 25(OH)D >20 ng/ml[68] (Fig. 5). If this is not achieved, an additional 8-week course is reasonable. For patients who are chronically vitamin D deficient, they are often given 50,000 IU of vitamin D_2 once or twice a month after correction of their vitamin D deficiency. The fortification of some orange juices and other juice products with vitamin D[9] offers an additional source of vitamin D to those who do not drink milk. An effective alternative, especially for patients with malabsorption syndrome, is to be exposed to UVB radiation. In a nursing home setting, the installation of UVB-emitting lamps in an activity room was more effective then a multivitamin in maintaining 25(OH)D levels.[1,66] A patient with Crohn's disease, severe vitamin D deficiency osteomalacia, and attendant bone pain was effectively treated by being exposed to a sunbed three times a week.[1,66] The goal is to have blood levels of 25(OH)D of at least 30 ng/ml to achieve the maximum benefit for skeletal and cellular health.[1,10,11,61] For children with rickets, a single oral dose of 200,000 IU of vitamin D_3 is often effective in correcting the vitamin D deficiency.[63]

CONCLUSION

When evaluating patients for hypo- and hypercalcemic conditions, it is appropriate to consider the patient's vitamin D status as well as whether they suffer from either an acquired or inherited disorder in the acquisition and/or metabolism of vitamin D. Because the assay for vitamin D is not available to clinicians, the best assay to determine vitamin D status is 25(OH)D. The 1,25(OH)$_2$D assay is not only useless in determining vitamin D status, but it can also be misleading because 1,25(OH)$_2$D levels can be normal or elevated in a vitamin D–deficient patient. Only when there is a suspicion that there is an acquired or inherited disorder in the metabolism of 25(OH)D is it reasonable to measure circulating 1,25(OH)$_2$D concentrations. Although there are a variety of other metabolites of vitamin D in the circulation, the measurement of other vitamin D metabolites has not proved to be of any significant value. It has been suggested that there may be a correlation with the development of metabolic bone disease with the polymorphism for the *VDR* gene. Although these data are intriguing, the information is, at this time, of limited clinical value but may someday provide an insight as to a person's potential maximum BMD. The noncalcemic actions of 1,25(OH)$_2$D$_3$ have great promise for clinical applications in the future (Fig. 4). The activated vitamin D compounds 1,25(OH)$_2$D$_3$, 22-oxo-1,25(OH)$_2$D$_3$, 1,24(OH)$_2$D$_3$, and calcipotriene herald a new pharmacologic approach for treating psoriasis.[5] The recent report of a vitamin D analog that markedly increased BMD in rodents offers a novel approach of developing vitamin D analogs as anabolic drugs to treat osteoporosis.[37] High-dose vitamin D$_3$ therapy or combination therapy of 1,25(OH)$_2$D$_3$ and its analogs with other cancer drugs offers promise in treating many lethal cancers.[39,41,66] In addition, vitamin D analogs are being developed to treat or mitigate common autoimmune disorders including multiple sclerosis and diabetes type 1, as well as hypertension, cardiovascular heart disease, and prostatic hypertrophy. Clearly the vitamin D field of research remains robust.

ACKNOWLEDGMENTS

This work was supported in part by National Institutes of Health Grants AR 36963 and M01RR 00533 and the UV Foundation.

REFERENCES

1. Holick MF 2004 Vitamin D: Importance in the prevention of cancers, type 1 diabetes, heart disease, and osteoporosis. Am J Clin Nutr **79:**362–371.
2. Holick MF 2003 Calciotropic hormones and the skin: A millennium perspective. J Cell Biochem **88:**296–307.
3. Bouillon R 2001 Vitamin D: From photosynthesis, metabolism and action to clinical applications. In: Degroot LL, Jameson JL (eds.) Endocrinology, vol 2, 4th ed. Saunders, Philadelphia, PA, USA, pp. 1009–1028.
4. DeLuca HF, Cantorna MT 2001 Vitamin D: Its role and uses in immunology. FASEB **15:**2579–2585.
5. Holick MF 1998 Clinical efficacy of 1,25-dihydroxyvitamin D$_3$ and its analogues in the treatment of psoriasis. Retinoids **14:**12–17.
6. Mathieu C, Adorini L 2002 The coming of age of 1,25-dihydroxyvitamin D$_3$ analogs as immunomodulatory agents. Trends Molec Med **8:**174–179.
7. Standing Committee and the Scientific Evaluation of Dietary Reference Intakes, Food and Nutrition Board, Institute of Medicine 1999 Calcium and vitamin D. In: Dietary Reference Intakes for Calcium, Phosphorus, Magnesium, Vitamin D, and Fluoride. Institute of Medicine, National Academy Press, Washington, DC, USA, pp. 71–145.
8. Barger-Lux MJ, Heaney RP, Dowell S, Chen TC, Holick MF 1998 Vitamin D and its major metabolites: Serum levels after graded oral dosing in healthy men. Osteoporos Int **8:**222–230.
9. Tangpricha V, Koutkia P, Rieke SM, Chen TC, Perez A, Holick MF 2003 Fortification of orange juice with vitamin D: A novel approach to enhance vitamin D nutritional health. Am J Clin Nutr **77:**1478–1483.
10. Hollis BW 2005 Circulating 25-hydroxyvitamin D levels indicative of vitamin D sufficiency: Implications for establishing a new effective dietary intake recommendation for vitamin D. J Nutr **135:**317–322.
11. Bischoff-Ferrari HA, Willett WC, Wong JB, Giovannuci E, Dietrich T, Dawson-Hughes B 2005 Fracture prevention with vitamin D supplementation: A meta-analysis of randomized controlled trials. JAMA **293:**2257–2264.
12. Mosekilde L 2005 Vitamin D and the elderly. Clin Endocrinol (Oxf) **62:**265–281.
13. Vieth R 2004 Why the optimal requirement for vitamin D$_3$ is probably much higher than what is officially recommended for adults? J Steroid Biochem Mol Biol **88–89:**575–579.
14. Armas LAG, Hollis B, Heaney RP 2004 Vitamin D$_2$ is much less effective than vitamin D$_3$ in humans. J Clin Endocrinol Metab **89:**5387–5391.
15. Sharma OP 2000 Hypercalcemia in granulomatosis disorders: A clinical review. Curr Opin Pulmon Med **6:**442–447.
16. Portale AA, Halloran BP, Morris RC Jr 1989 Physiologic regulation of the serum concentration of 1,25-dihydroxyvitamin D by phosphorus in normal men. J Clin Invest **83:**1494–1499.
17. Shimada T, Hasegawa H, Yamazaki Y, Muto T, Hino R, Takeuchi Y 2004 FGF-23 is a potent regulator of vitamin D metabolism and phosphate homeostasis58. J Bone Miner Res **19:**429–435.
18. Mia D, He B, Lanske B, Bai XY, Tong XK, Hendy GN, Goltzman D, Karaplis AC 2004 Skeletal abnormalities in Pth-null mice are influenced by dietary calcium. Endocrinology **145:**2046–2053.
19. Menaa C, Vrtovsnik F, Friedlander G, Corvol M, Garabedian M 1995 Insulin-mike growth factor I, a unique calcium-dependent stimulator of 1,25-dihydroxyvitamin D$_3$ production. Studies in cultured mouse kidney cells. J Biol Chem **270:**25461–25467.
20. Halloran BP, Lonergan ET, Portale AA 1996 Aging and renal responsiveness to parathyroid hormone in healthy men. J Clin Endocrinol Metab **81:**2192–2197.
21. Ebeling PR, Sandgren ME, DiMagno EP, Lane AW, DeLuca HF, Riggs BL 1992 Evidence of an age-related decrease in intestinal responsiveness to vitamin D: Relationship between serum 1,25-dihydroxyvitamin D$_3$ and intestinal vitamin D receptor concentration in normal women. J Clin Endocrinol Metab **75:**176–182.
22. Pascussi JM, Robert A, Nguyen M, Walrant-Debray O, Garabedian M, Martin P, Pineau T, Saric J, Navarro F, Maurel P, Vilarem MJ 2005 Possible involvement of pregnane X receptor-enhanced CYP24 expression in drug-induced osteomacia. J Clin Invest **115:**177–186.
23. Haussler MR, Whitfield GK, Haussler CA, Hsieh JC, Thompson PD, Selznick SH, Dominguez CE, Jurutka PW, 1998 The nuclear vitamin D receptor: Biological and molecular regulatory properties revealed. J Bone Miner Res **13:**325–349.
24. Barsony J 2005 Vitamin D receptor and retinoid X receptor subcellular trafficking. In: Feldman D (ed.) Vitamin D, 2nd ed, vol. I. Academic Press, San Diego, CA, USA, pp. 363–379.
25. Malloy PJ, Feldman D 2003 Hereditary 1,25-dihydroxyvitamin D-resistant rickets. Endocr Dev **6:**175–199.
26. Sunn KL, Cock TA, Crofts LA, Eisman JM, Gardiner EM 2001 Novel N-terminal variant of human VDR. Mol Endocrinol **15:**1599–1609.
27. Skorija K, Cox M, Sisk JM, Dowd DR, Mac Donald PN, Thompson CC, Demay MB 2005 Ligand-independent actions of the vitamin D receptor maintain hair follicle homeostasis. Mol Endocrinol **19:**855–862.
28. Jurutka PW, Thompson PD, Whitfield GK, Eichhorst KR, Hall N, Dominguez CE, Hsieh JC, Haussler CA, Haussler MR 2005 Molecular and functional comparison of 1,25-dihydroxyvitamin D$_3$ and the novel vitamin D receptor ligand, lithocholic acid, in activating transcription of cytochrome P450 3A4. J Cell Biochem **94:**917–943.
29. Nemere I, Farch-Carson MC, Rohe B, Sterling TM, Norman AW, Boyan BD, Safford SE 2004 Ribozyme knockdown functionally links a 1,25(OH)$_2$D$_3$ membrane binding protein (1,25D3-MARRS) and phosphate uptake in intestinal cells. Proc Natl Acad Sci USA **101:**7392–7397.
30. Nagpal S, Na S, Rathnachalam R 2005 Non calcemic actions of vitamin D receptor ligands. Endocr Rev **26:**662–687.
31. Uitterlinden AG, Fang Y, Van Meurs JB, Pols HA, Van Leeuwen JP 2004 Genetics and biology of vitamin D receptor polymorphisms. Gene **338:**143–146.
32. d'Alesio A, Garabedian M, Sabatier JP, Guaydier-Souquieres G, Marcelli C, Lemaçon A, Walrant-Debray O, Jehan F 2005 Two single-nucleotide polymorphisms in the human vitamin D receptor promoter change protein-DNA complex formation and are associated with height and vitamin D status in adolescent girls. Hum Mol Genet **14:**3539–3548.
33. Cooper GS, Umbach DM 1996 Are vitamin D receptor polymorphisms associated with bone mineral density? A meta-analysis. J Bone Miner Res **11:**1841–1849.
34. Fang Y, Van Meurs JB, d'Alesio A, Jhamai M, Zhao H, Rivadeneira F, Hofman A, Van Leeuwen JP, Jehan F, Pols HA, Uitterlinden AG 2005

Promoter and 3′ UTR haplotypes in the vitamin D receptor (VDR) gene predispose to osteoporotic fractures: The Rotterdam Study. Am J Human Genet 77:807–823.

35. Christakos S, Dhawan P, Liu Y, Peng X, Porta A 2003 New Insights into the mechanisms of vitamin D action. J Cell Biochem 88:695–705.

36. Khosla S 2001 The OPG/RANKL/RANK system. Endocrinology 142:5050–5055.

37. DeLuca H 2004 Overview of general physiologic features and functions of vitamin D. Am J Clin Nutr 80:1689S–1696A.

38. Yagishita N, Yamamoto Y, Yoshizawa T, Sekine K, Uematsu Y, Murayama H, Nagai Y, Krezel W, Chambon P, Matsumoto T, Kato S 2001 Aberrant growth plate development in VDR/RXR gamma double mutant mice. Endocrinology 142:5332–5341.

39. Guyton KZ, Kensler TW, Posner GH 2001 Cancer chemoprevention using natural vitamin D and synthetic analogs. Annu Rev Pharmacol Toxicol 41:421–442.

40. Beer TM, Eilers KM, Garzotto M, Egorin MJ, Lowe BA, Henner WD 2003 Weekly high-dose calcitriol and docetaxel in metastatic androgen-independent prostate cancer. J Clin Oncol 21:123–128.

41. Dalhoff K, Dancey J, Astrup L, Skovsgaard T, Hamberg KJ, Lofts FJ, Rosmorduc O, Erlinger S, Bach Hansen J, Steward WP, Skov T, Burcharth F, Evans TR 2003 A phase II study of the vitamin D analogue Seocalcitol in patients with inoperable hepatocellular carcinoma. Br J Cancer 89:252–257.

42. Li Y, Kong J, Wei M, Chen ZF, Liu S, Cao LP 2002 1,25-dihydroxyvitamin D$_3$ is a negative endocrine regulator of the renin-angiotensin system. J Clin Invest 110:229–238.

43. Hypponen E, Laara E, Jarvelin M-R, Virtanen SM 2001 Intake of vitamin D and risk of type 1 diabetes: A birth-cohort study. Lancet 358:1500–1503.

44. Merlino LA, Curtis J, Mikuls TR, Cerhan JR, Criswell LA, Saag KG 2004 Vitamin D intake is inversely associated with rheumatoid arthritis. Athrit Rheum 50:72–77.

45. van der Mei I, Ponsonby A-L, Dwyer T, Blizzard L, Simmons R, Taylor BV 2003 Past exposure to sun, skim phenotype, and risk of multiple sclerosis: Case-control study. BMJ 327:316.

46. Kitanaka S, Takeyama KI, Murayama A, Sato T, Okumura K, Nogami M, Hasegawa Y, Nimi H, Yanagisawa J, Tanaka T, Kato S 1988 Inactivating mutations in the human 25-hydroxyvitamin D$_3$ 1α- hydroxylase gene in patients with pseudovitamin D-deficient rickets. N Engl J Med 338:653–661.

47. Sakai Y, kishimoto J, Demay MB 2001 Metabolic and cellular analysis of alopecia in vitamin D receptor knockout mice. J Clin Invest 107:961–966.

48. Fukuda N, Tanaka H, Tominaga R, Fukagawa M, Kurokawa K, Seino Y 1993 Decreased 1,25-dihydroxyvitamin D$_3$ receptor density is associated with a more severe form of parathyroid hyperplasia in chronic uremic patients. J Clin Invest 92:1436–1443.

49. Brown AJ, Coyne DW 2002 Vitamin D analogs: A new therapeutic agents for secondary hyperparathyroidism. Treat Endocrinol 1:313–327.

50. Teng M, Wolf M, Lowrie E, Ofsthun N, Lazarus JM, Thadhani R 2003 Survival of patients undergoing hemodialysis with paricalcitol or calcitriol therapy. N Engl J Med 349:446–456.

51. Holick MF 2005 Vitamin D for health and in chronic kidney disease. Semin Dialysis 18:266–275.

52. Segersten U, Corea P, Hewison M, Hellman P, Dralle H, Carling T, Akerstrom G, Westin G 2002 25-Hydroxyvitamin D$_3$-1α-hydroxylase expression in normal and pathological parathyroid glands. J Clin Endocrinol Metab 87:2967–2972.

53. Holick MF 2001 Evaluation and treatment of disorders in calcium, phosphorus, and magnesium metabolism. In: Noble J (ed.) Textbook of Primary Care Medicine, 3rd ed. Mosby, St. Louis, MO, USA, pp. 886–898.

54. Schiavi SC, Kumar R 2004 The phosphatonin pathway: New insights in phosphate homeostasis. Kidney Int 65:1–14.

55. Shimada T, Kakitani M, Yamazaki Y, Hasegawa H, Takeuchi Y, Fujita T, Fukumoto S, Tomizuka K, Yamashita T 2004 Targeted ablation of FGF23 demonstrates an essential physiological role of FGF23 in phosphate and vitamin D metabolism. J Clin Invest 113:561–568.

56. Rowe PS 2004 The wrickkened pathways of FGF23, MEPE and PHEX. Crit Rev Oral Biol Med 15:264–281.

57. Chen H, Hewison M, Hu B, Adams JS 2003 Heterogeneous nuclear ribonucleoprotein (hnRNP) binding to hormone response elements: A cause of vitamin D resistance. Proc Natl Acad Sci USA 100:6109–6114.

58. Vieth R 1999 The mechanisms of vitamin D toxicity. Bone Miner 11:267–272.

59. Dawson-Hughes B, Heaney RP, Holick MF, Lips P, Meunier PJ, Vieth R 2005 Estimates of optimal vitamin D status. Osteoporos Int 16:713–716.

60. Chapuy MC, Preziosi P, Maaner M, Arnaud S, Galan P, Hercberg S, Meunier PJ 1997 Prevalence of vitamin D insufficiency in an adult normal population. Osteoporos Int 7:439–443.

61. Heaney RPBA, Dowell MS, Hale CA 2003 Calcium absorption varies within the reference range for serum 25-hydroxyvitamin D. J Am Coll Nutr 2:142–146.

62. Holick MF, Siris ES, Binkley N, Beard MK, Khan A, Katzer JT, Petruschke RA, Chen E, de Papp AE 2005 Prevalence of vitamin D inadequacy among postmenopausal North American women receiving osteoporosis therapy. J Clin Endocrinol Metab 90:3215–3224.

63. Garabedian M, Bwn-Mekhbi H 1998 Rickets and vitamin D deficiency. In: Holick MF (ed.) Vitamin D: Physiology, Molecular Biology, and Clinical Applications. Humana Press, Totowa, NJ, USA, pp. 273–286.

64. Kreiter SR, Schwartz RP, Kirkman HN, Charlton PA, Calikoglu AS, Davenport M 2000 Nutritional rickets in African American breast-fed infants. J Pediatr 137:2–6.

65. Dagnelie PC, Vergote FJ, van Staveren WA, van den Berg H, Dingjan PG, Hautvast JG 1990 High prevalence of rickets in infants on macrobiotic diets. Am J Clin Nutr 51:202–208.

66. Holick MF 2006 High prevalence of vitamin D inadequacy and implications for health. Mayo Clin Rev 81:353–373.

67. Nesby-O'Dell S, Scanlon KS, Cogswell ME, Gillespie C, Hollis BW, Looker AC 2002 Hypovitaminosis D prevalence and determinants among African American and white women of reproductive age: Third national health and nutrition examination survey, 1988–1994. Am J Clin Nutr 76:187–192.

68. Malabanan A, Veronikis IE, Holick MF 1998 Redefining vitamin D insufficiency. Lancet 351:805–806.

69. Gordon CM, DePeter KC, Feldman HA, Estherann G., Emans SJ 2004 Prevalence of vitamin D deficiency among healthy adolescents. Arch Pediatr Adolesc Med 158:531–537.

70. Ala-Houhala M, Parvianen MT, Pyykko K, Visakorpi JK 1984 Serum 25-hydroxyvitamin D levels in Finnish children aged 2 to 17 years. Acta Paediatr Scand 73:232–236.

71. Taha SA, Dost SM, Sedrani SH 1984 25-Hydroxyvitamin D and total calcium: Extraordinarily low plasma concentrations in Saudi mothers and their neonates. Pediatr Res 18:739–741.

72. Marwaha RK, Tandon N, Reddy D, Aggarwal R, Singh R, Sawhney RC, Saluja B, Ganie MA, Singh S 2005 Vitamin D and bone mineral density status of healthy schoolchildren in northern India. Am J Clin Nutr 82:477–482.

73. Plotnikoff GA, Quigley JM 2003 Prevalence of severe hypovitaminosis D in patients with persistent, nonspecific musculoskeletal pain. Mayo Clin Proc 78:1463–1470.

Chapter 18. Calcitonin

Leonard J. Deftos

Department of Medicine, University of California at San Diego and San Diego Veterans Affairs Medical Center, San Diego, California

INTRODUCTION

Calcitonin (CT) is a 32 amino acid peptide secreted by thyroidal C cells and acting to inhibit osteoclasts in their resorptive function. This property has led to its use for disorders characterized by increased osteoclastic bone resorption, such as Paget's disease, osteoporosis, and the hypercalcemia of malignancy. The secretion of CT is regulated acutely by blood calcium and chronically by sex and perhaps age. Calcitonin is metabolized by the kidney and the liver. Calcitonin is also a tumor marker for medullary thyroid carcinoma, the signal tumor of multiple endocrine neoplasia (MEN) type II.[1-4]

BIOCHEMISTRY

Over a dozen species of CT, including human, have been sequenced. Common features include a 1–7 amino-terminal disulfide bridge, a glycine at residue 28, and a carboxy-terminal proline amide residue.[2-4] Five of the nine amino-terminal residues are identical in all CT species. The greatest divergence resides in the interior 27 amino acids. Basic amino acid substitutions enhance potency. Thus, the nonmammalian CTs have the most potency, even in mammalian systems. A biologically active fragment of CT has not been discovered.[5-7]

MOLECULAR BIOLOGY

The *CT* gene consists of six exons separated by introns.[2,4] Two distinct mature mRNAs are generated from differential splicing of the exon regions in the initial gene transcript. One translates as a 141-residue CT precursor and the other as a 128-residue precursor for calcitonin gene-related peptide (CGRP). CT is the major post-translationally processed peptide in C cells, whereas CGRP, a 37 amino acid peptide, is the major processed peptide in neurons. The main biological effect of CGRP is vasodilation, but it also functions as a neurotransmitter and does react with the CT receptor. The relevance of CGRP to skeletal metabolism is unknown, but it may be produced locally in skeletal tissue and exert a local regulatory effect. An alternative splicing pathway for the *CT* gene produces a carboxy-terminal C-pro CT with eight different terminal amino acids.[1-3]

BIOSYNTHESIS

Thyroidal C cells are the primary source of CT in mammals, and the ultimobranchial gland is the primary source in sub-mammals.[1,3] C cells are neural crest derivatives, and they also produce CGRP, the second *CT* gene product. Other tissue sources of CT have been described, notably the pituitary cells and widely distributed neuroendocrine cells.[2,4] Although CT may have paracrine effects at these sites, the nonthyroidal sources of CT are not likely to contribute to its peripheral concentration. However, malignant transformation can occur in both ectopic and eutopic cells that produce CT, and the peptide becomes a tumor marker.[1] The best example of the latter is medullary thyroid carcinoma, and of the former, small-cell lung cancer.[2,8]

BIOLOGIC EFFECTS

CT's main biological effect is to inhibit osteoclastic bone resorption.[1] Within minutes of its administration, CT causes the osteoclast to shrink in size and to decrease its bone-resorbing activity.[2] This dramatic and complex event is accompanied by the production of cAMP and by increased cytosolic calcium in the osteoclast.[2,3] In a situation where bone turnover is sufficiently high, CT will produce hypocalcemia and hypophosphatemia. Calcitonin has also been reported to inhibit osteocytes and stimulate osteoblasts, but these effects are controversial.[2,6] Analgesia is a commonly reported effect of CT treatment.[3,4] Calciuria, phosphaturia, and gastrointestinal effects on calcium flux have been reported for CT, but they occur at concentrations of the hormone that are supraphysiologic.[1-3] It should be noted, however, that the concentration of the peptide at its several sites of biosynthesis may be sufficiently high to explain some extraskeletal effects of CT by a paracrine mechanism.[1] Thus, CT may exert physiologic effects on the pituitary and CNS.[1,7] Furthermore, the demonstration of CT and CT receptors at intracranial sites may qualify CT as a neurotransmitter.[1,8] Other effects of CT have been reported. It has been observed to act as an anti-inflammatory agent, to promote fracture and wound healing, to be uricosuric, to be antihypertensive, and to impair glucose tolerance. The importance of these latter effects is yet to be determined.[1-4]

CALCITONIN AS A DRUG

CT's main biological action of inhibiting osteoclastic bone resorption has resulted in its successful use in disease states characterized by increased bone resorption and the consequent hypercalcemia.[2,3] Calcitonin is widely used in Paget's disease, in which osteoclastic bone resorption is dramatically increased; in osteoporosis, in which the increase of bone resorption may be more subtle; and in the treatment of hypercalcemia of malignancy.[2,5] Newer pharmacologic preparations of CT may have improved therapeutic effects.[2,4]

SECRETION AND METABOLISM

Ambient calcium concentration is the most important regulator of CT secretion.[1] When blood calcium rises acutely, there is a proportional increase in CT secretion, and an acute decrease in blood calcium produces a corresponding decrease in plasma CT.[1,2] The C cells seem to respond to sustained hypercalcemia by increasing CT secretion, but, if the hypercalcemia is severe and/or prolonged, the C cells probably exhaust their secretory reserve. Chronic hypocalcemia seems to decrease the secretory challenge to C cells and they increase their stores of CT; these stores can be released on appropriate stimulation.[2,4,9] The metabolism of CT is a complex process that involves many organ systems. Evidence has been reported for degradation of the hormone by kidney, liver, bone, and even the thyroid gland.[2-4] Like many other peptide hormones, CT disappears from plasma in a multiexponential manner that includes an early half-life measured in minutes. Inactivation of the hormone seems more important than renal excretion, because relatively little CT can be detected in urine. Metabolism of the peptide during inflammatory disease may result in the

---

The author has reported no conflicts of interest.

production of specific forms of CT that can be identified by selective immunoassays.[1]

GASTROINTESTINAL FACTORS

Gastrointestinal peptides, especially those of the gastrin-cholecystokinin family, are potent CT secretagogues when administered parenterally in supraphysiologic concentrations.[1,2,9] This observation has led to the postulate that there is an entero-C-cell regulatory pathway for CT secretion. However, only meals that contain sufficient calcium to raise the blood calcium have been shown to increase CT secretion in humans.[4] Nevertheless, pentagasrtin as well as glucagon can be used as stimulatory test for CT secretion.[2,9]

PROVOCATIVE TESTING FOR CT-PRODUCING TUMORS

The stimulatory effect of calcium and gastrointestinal (GI) peptides, especially pentagastrin, on CT secretion has led to their use as provocative tests for the secretion of CT in patients suspected of having medullary thyroid carcinoma (MTC), a neoplastic disorder of thyroidal C cells that can occur in a familial pattern as part of MEN type II.[1,9] Most tumors respond with increased CT secretion to the administration of either calcium or pentagastrin or their combination, but either agent can sometimes give misleading results. CT measurements can also be used to monitor the effectiveness of therapy, usually thyroidectomy, in patients with MTC.[1–3]

SEX AND AGE

Most investigators find that women have lower CT levels than men.[1,2,4] The effect of age on CT secretion is more controversial[1,2]: newborns seem to have a higher serum level of the hormone, and in adults, a progressive decline with age has been reported by several but not all laboratories.[1,4] The physiologic significance of the various circulating forms of CT measured by different assay procedures has not been defined.

MEDULLARY THYROID CARCINOMA

Medullary thyroid carcinoma is a tumor of the CT-producing C cells of the thyroid gland.[1,3,5] Although a rare tumor, it can occur in a familial pattern as part of MEN type II. Medullary thyroid carcinoma is generally regarded as intermediate between the aggressive behavior of anaplastic thyroid carcinoma and the more indolent behavior of papillary and follicular thyroid carcinoma. These tumors usually produce diagnostically elevated serum concentrations of CT. Therefore, immunoassay for CT in serum can be used to diagnose the presence of MTC with an exceptional degree of accuracy and specificity. To identify these patients with early disease, provocative tests for CT secretion have been developed.[2,9]

OTHER CT-PRODUCING NEOPLASMS

Neoplastic disorders of other neuroendocrine cells can also produce abnormally elevated amounts of CT. The best known example is small-cell lung cancer. However, other tumors, such as carcinoids and islet cell tumors of the pancreas, can also overexpress CT.[1,2,4]

RENAL DISEASE

There are increases in immunoassayable CT with both acute and chronic renal failure, but considerable disagreement exists regarding the mechanism and significance of these increases.[2,3] Because the secretion and/or metabolism of CT is ab-normal in renal disease, and because renal osteodystrophy is characterized by increased bone resorption, CT, which acts to inhibit bone resorption, has been implicated in the pathogenesis of uremic osteodystrophy.[1,2,4]

HYPERCALCIURIA

Elevated levels of CT have been shown in patients with hypercalciuria.[4,10] The physiologic significance of enhanced CT secretion is unknown, but it may represent a compensatory response to intestinal hyperabsorption of calcium.

BONE DISEASE

No skeletal disease has been conclusively attributed to CT abnormalities.[1,3,6] Although women have lower CT levels than men, there is conflicting evidence as to whether endogenous secretion of the hormone contributes to the pathogenesis of osteoporosis.[1] Nevertheless, CT has been of therapeutic benefit in osteoporosis.[3,4] Reduced CT reserve in women may contribute to the greater severity of osteitis fibrosa cystica in women with primary hyperparathyroidism.[1] Skeletal abnormalities have not been identified in patients after thyroidectomy.[1,2] However, the recent demonstration in pycnodysostosis of dysfunctional mutations of the gene for cathepsin K, responsible for collagen degradation by osteoclasts, and the high levels of serum calcitonin reported in this disease, suggest an intriguing link between skeletal dysplasia and calcitonin secretion.[1,4] For example, the increased calcitonin may be compensatory for the impaired osteoclastic resorption.

HYPERCALCEMIA AND HYPOCALCEMIA

Calcium challenge is a well-documented stimulus for CT secretion. Although increased CT secretion has only inconsistently been associated with chronic hypercalcemia, an exaggerated response of CT to secretagogues has been convincingly observed in several hypocalcemic states.[4,9]

CALCITONIN RECEPTOR

CT mediates its biological effects through the CT receptor (CRT).[4,8] CTRs are most robustly expressed in osteoclasts but also are expressed in several other sites, including the CNS. The mammalian CTRs share common structural and functional motifs, signal through several pathways, and can exist in several isoforms with insert sequences or deletions or both in their intracellular and extracellular domains. These isoforms arise from alternative splicing of receptor mRNA transcribed from a single gene. Some of the isoforms of the CTR seem to have differential ligand specificity, perhaps accounting for the pleiotropic effects of the hormone. Salmon calcitonin (SCT) apparently conforms best to the structural requirements for binding and signaling of mammalian CTRs, perhaps explaining its greater potency in humans and mammals and its sustained receptor binding and activation of cAMP.[1,2] An isoform of the CTR that is expressed in rat brain seems to preferentially recognize SCT, and binding sites for SCT are present at several sites in the CNS. It is thus speculated that an SCT-like ligand is produced by mammals. There is some evidence for this in both humans and murine. Finally, it is also notable that another nonmammalian CT, chicken CT (CCT), also seems more potent in humans than human CT and that a CCT-like ligand may be expressed in humans.[2,4]

LIGAND FAMILIES FOR CALCITONIN

Long known to be related to CGRP1 and 2, CT recently was recognized to be related in sequence to two other peptides, adrenomedullin and amylin.[1,8] Although all of these peptides share the feature of being neuromodulators, they also seem to have unique hormone actions. The effects of CT were described earlier. CGRP1 and CGRP2 are potent vasodilators an immunomodulators, with actions in the CNS and at many other targets. Adenomedullin also is a potent vasodilator with some CNS actions. The actions of amylin are related to carbohydrate metabolism, to gastric emptying, and to CNS function.[4,8]

RECEPTOR MODULATION

Despite their distinct bioactivities, the family of calcitonin-related ligands shows some cross-reactivity at each other's receptors, although they generally bear only partial homology.[2,4,8] The interaction of ligands among these receptors is influenced by newly discovered receptor-modulating proteins.[8] This modulation expands the repertoire of biological actions that can be mediated by receptors and their ligands. One modulator, termed CGRP-receptor component protein (CGRP-RCP), consists of a hydrophilic protein that is highly conserved across species and found in virtually all tissues. The second group of receptor modulators is a family of proteins termed receptor-activity-modifying proteins (RAMPs) and comprises three members, RAMPs1 to 3.[2,4,8] RAMPs interact with a distinct calcitonin receptor-like receptor (CRLR) and transports it to the cell-membrane surface.[4,8] RAMP1 transport of CRLR results in a terminally glycosylated receptor that recognizes CGRP, whereas RAMP2 and 3 expression produces a core glycosylated receptor that recognizes adrenomedullin. Receptor modulation is another molecular mechanism of genetic economy whereby specific ligands can acquire functions beyond those allowed by a simple lock-and-key model of receptor specificity.[8]

ROLE OF CALCITONIN IN MINERAL METABOLISM

The exact physiologic role of CT in calcium homeostasis and skeletal metabolism has not been established in humans, and many questions remain unanswered about the significance of this hormone in humans. Does CT secretion decline with age? Do gonadal steroids regulate the secretion of CT? Do the lower levels of serum CT in women contribute to the pathogenesis of age-related loss of bone mass and osteoporosis? Do extrathy-roidal sources of CT participate in the regulation of skeletal metabolism? Are there primary and secondary abnormalities of CT secretion in diseases of skeletal and calcium homeostasis? The conclusive answers to these questions await clinical studies with an assay procedure that directly measures the biological activity of CT in blood. Furthermore, accurate local measurements of CT and its effects may be necessary to elucidate the emerging role of CT as a paracrine and autocrine agent.

ACKNOWLEDGMENTS

This work was supported by the National Institutes of Health and the Department of Veterans Affairs.

REFERENCES

1. Deftos LJ, Gagel R 2000 Calcitonin and medullary thyroid carcinoma. In: Wyngarden JB, Bennett JC (eds.) Cecil Textbook of Medicine, 21st ed. WB Saunders, Philadelphia, PA, USA, pp. 1406–1409.
2. Deftos LJ 2002 Calcium and phosphate homeostasis, available at www.endotext.com. Accessed January 1, 2006.
3. Deftos LJ, Gagel R Calcitonin and medullary thyroid carcinoma. In: Goldman L, Ausiello D (eds.) Cecil Textbook of Medicine, 22nd ed. WB Saunders, Philadelphia, PA, USA (in press).
4. Deftos LJ 2003 Calcitonin In: Favus MJ (ed.) Primer on the Metabolic Bone Diseases and Disorders of Mineral Metabolism, 5th ed. Lippincott-Raven Press; New York, NY, USA, pp. 137–141
5. Deftos LJ, Sherman SI, Gagel RF 2001 Multiglandular endocrine disorders. In: Felig P, Frohman LA (eds.) Endocrinology and Metabolism, 4th ed. McGraw-Hill, New York, NY, USA, pp. 1703–1732.
6. Inzerillo AM, Zaidi M, Huang CL 2002 Calcitonin: The other thyroid hormone. Thyroid 12:791–798.
7. Zaidi M, Inzerillo AM, Moonga BS, Bevis JR, Huang CL-H 2002 Forty years of calcitonin—where are we now? A Tribute to the work of Iain Macintyre, FRS. Bone 30:655–663.
8. Hay, DB, Christopoulos G, Christopoulos, A, Poyner DR, Sexton PM 2005 Pharmacological discrimination of calcitonin receptor: Receptor activity modifying protein complexes. Molec Pharmacol 67:1655–1665.
9. Zwerman O, Piepkorn B, Engelbach M, Beyer J, Kann P 2002 Abnormal pentagastrin reponse in a patent with pseudohypoparathyroidism. Exp Clin Endocrinol Diabetes 111:49–50.
10. Bevilacqua, M, Dominguez LJ, Righini V, Toscano R, Sangaletti O, Vago T, Baldi G, Bianchi-Porro M 2005 Increased gastrin and calcitonin secretion after oral calcium or peptones administration in patients with hypercalciuria: A clue to an alteration in calcium-sensing receptor activity. J Clin Endocrinol Metab 90:1489–1494.

SECTION IV

Clinical Evaluation of Bone and Mineral Disorders
(Section Editors: Craig B. Langman and Suzanne M. Jan de Beur)

Chapter 19.   Bedside Evaluation of Bone and Mineral Disorders

Suzanne M. Jan de Beur[1] and Craig B. Langman[2]

[1]Department of Medicine, Johns Hopkins University School of Medicine, and Division of Endocrinology, Johns Hopkins Bayview Medical Center, Baltimore, Maryland; and [2]Department of Pediatrics, Feinberg School of Medicine, Northwestern University, and Kidney Diseases, Children's Memorial Hospital, Chicago, Illinois

INTRODUCTION

With the availability of treatments that can prevent, control, or cure most metabolic bone diseases, early recognition is essential. An experienced clinician can recognize and identify many bone disorders by history and physical examination alone. Unfortunately, because many of these diseases have a subtle and insidious onset and are not often recognized until they have reached a severe stage, the clinician's challenge is not only early diagnosis of existing disease, but also the identification of patients at risk. A careful history and thorough physical examination are the physician's most powerful tools in choosing whom to screen with diagnostic tests and deciding which patients will benefit most from preventive intervention or therapy.[1,2]

MEDICAL HISTORY

For the adult, an initial assessment should include the patient's age, sex, race, menopausal status, and a complete medical, pharmacologic, nutritional, and family history. For the child, a careful gestational history in the family with an emphasis on perinatal or neonatal mortality, current birth history, feeding history, and level of usual activity is warranted.

In some situations, the chief complaint leads directly to the search for a given diagnosis: for example, a hip fracture from osteoporosis, bowing deformity of the legs from rickets, numbness, and tingling around the mouth and in the tips of the fingers in a patient with hypocalcemia, or polyuria, lethargy, and hypertension with hypercalcemia. Other factors may provide strong evidence that an unspecified bone disease is present and prompt the physician to explore further. For example, severe back or bone pain, history of fracture with minimal trauma, prolonged immobilization, loss of height in elderly people, and sunlight deprivation all raise the index of suspicion for the presence of skeletal disease. In children, additional features of growth retardation or short stature, bone pain, muscle weakness, skeletal deformities, extraskeletal calcifications, and waddling gait are each suggestive of the presence of genetic or metabolic bone disease. The duration of symptoms is important: are they lifelong or of relatively recent onset? How severe are the symptoms? Are they static or progressive?

Information regarding dietary and lifestyle issues is important to elicit. Does the diet contain adequate calcium, phosphorus, and vitamin D? If the diet is insufficient, is there adequate sunlight exposure? Is there evidence of an eating disorder or unexplained weight loss or excessive and unplanned weight gain? Does the patient engage in regular weight-bearing exercise or engage in activities at play or work that involve a high risk of trauma? Was there a period of prolonged immobilization recently, or during childhood? Is there excessive alcohol consumption, because excessive alcohol intake is associated with hypomagnesemia, nutritional deficiencies of calcium, vitamin D, and protein, reduced sunlight exposure, and tendency to fall. Alcohol ingestion may directly impair osteoblast func-

tion as well. Does the patient have a history of tobacco use or currently smoke? How much caffeine is ingested daily, because high caffeine intake may increase the risk of osteoporotic hip fracture.

A medication history is of vital importance, because many medicines, including over-the-counter preparations, can adversely affect the skeleton. Glucocorticoids, (whether inhaled, taken orally, or administered systematically), thyroid hormone, anticonvulsants, and heparin may produce or worsen osteoporosis or other metabolic bone diseases. Current use of long-acting benzodiazepines may predispose to falls and increase fracture risk. Antacids containing aluminum may lead to aluminum-induced bone disease, typically in the setting of chronic kidney disease. Cancer chemotherapy, even years previously, may affect bone. Long-term lithium therapy is associated with hypercalcemia and PTH hypersecretion.[1] Prolonged use of sodium fluoride or the bisphosphonate etidronate can result in osteomalacia. Hypervitaminosis A is associated with excessive bone resorption and bone pain, and vitamin D excess can result in hypercalcemia. Gonadotropin-releasing hormone agonists induce an estrogen-deficient state when given in a continuous manner and may result in reduced bone mass. Diuretics can confound test interpretation by increasing or decreasing urine calcium or by increasing serum alkaline phosphatase activity.[2]

The patient should be asked about any history of endocrine, renal, or gastrointestinal disease. Hyper- and hypoparathyroidism, hyperthyroidism, Cushing's syndrome, and sex hormone deficiency all may affect bone remodeling. Gastrectomy, gastric stapling and bariatric surgery, intestinal malabsorption syndromes such as celiac disease, chronic obstructive biliary disease, and pancreatic insufficiency can result in bone loss. Chronic inflammatory conditions such as rheumatoid arthritis and inflammatory bowel disease are associated with reduced bone mass. Children with cystic fibrosis or chronic cholestatic liver disease are prone to fracturing bone disease, often with reduced BMD. Organ transplantation, whether solid or hematogenous (bone marrow, stem cell) predisposes to excessive fractures.

In women, a careful menstrual history is mandatory. She should be asked about periods of amenorrhea and the timing of onset of menses and menopause.

Data from the Study of Osteoporotic Fractures (SOF), a multicenter cohort of 9709 white women ≥65 years of age, identified historical factors that help to predict hip fracture in older women.[3] This study suggested that the risk of hip fracture is higher among women who have had previous fractures of any type after age 50 years, women who rate their own health as fair or poor, and women who spend ≤4 h a day on their feet. Among the SOF cohort, investigators found that, the more weight a woman had gained since age 25 years, the lower her risk of hip fracture. However, if a woman weighed less than she had at the age of 25 years, this doubled her risk of hip fractures. Women who were tall at the age of 25 years also had a greater risk.

In any patient under evaluation for reduced BMD a full risk factor assessment is critical. Briefly, this includes personal

---

The authors have reported no conflicts of interest.

TABLE 1. ASSOCIATIONS OF PHYSICAL FINDINGS AND METABOLIC OR GENETIC BONE DISEASES

Physical finding	Suggested diagnosis
Alopecia	Vitamin D–dependent rickets type II
Pallor	Marrow related disorders, malabsorption, nutritional disorders
Conjunctival pallor	Marrow related disorders, malabsorption, nutritional disorders
Proptosis	Hyperthyroidism
Enlarged skull	Paget disease, hypophosphatemic rickets
Dental defects	X-linked hypophosphatemic rickets, pseudohypoparathyroidism, hypophosphatasia
Round face	Cushing syndrome; Albright's hereditary osteodystrophy
Scleral icterus	Liver disease
Blue or gray sclerae	Osteogenesis imperfecta
Dorsocervial fat pad	Cushing syndrome
Goiter	Hyperthyroidism
Gynecomastia	Hyperprolactimenia, hypogonadism
Galactorrhea	Hyperprolactimenia
Spinal tenderness	Occult vertebral compression fracture
Violaceous stiae	Cushing syndrome
Centripetal obesity	Cushing syndrome
Abdominal scars	Gastrectomy, other gastrointestinal surgery that can lead to malabsorption
Proximal muscle wasting and weakness	Osteomalacia, Cushing syndrome, Muscular dystrophies
Small testes and/or soft testes	Hypogonadism
Bruises	Cushing syndrome, Ehlers-Danlos syndrome
Rash	Mastocytosis
Cafe au lait spots	McCune-Albright syndrome
Subcutaneous nodules	Hypoparathyroidism, pseudohypoparathyroidism, pseudopseudohypoparathyroidism
Brachydactyly	Pseudohypoparathyroidism
Arachnodactyly	Marfan syndrome
Anterior tibial tenderness	Osteomalacia
Deformed bones	Paget disease, rickets, X-linked hypophosphatemic rickets, fibrous dysplasia, renal osteodystrophy
Redness and warmth over a bone	Paget disease
Joint laxity	Marfan, Ehlers-Danlos syndrome
Arthritic changes in joints	Rheumatoid arthritis, inflammatory bowel disease
Vascular calcifications	Renal osteodystrophy

history of fractures, history of fracture in a first degree relative, adult height loss >1.5 in, adult body mass index (BMI) <21 kg/m^2, current cigarette smoking, or excessive alcohol consumption. When eliciting a fracture history, it is imperative to determine whether the fracture was associated with significant trauma or is a fragility fracture, that is, sustained during usual quotidian activities.

Because many of the metabolic bone disorders are heritable, a careful family history is important for purposes of screening and educating those at risk or for recommending genetic counseling. In the SOF cohort, women with a maternal history of hip fracture had a 2-fold increased risk of hip fracture, independent of bone mass, height, and weight.[3] In certain conditions, the diagnosis is firmly established when other family members are tested. Some genetic disorders associated with reduced bone mass, fractures, or osteomalacia include osteogenesis imperfecta, Ehlers-Danlos syndrome, Marfan syndrome, X-linked hypophosphatemic rickets, autosomal dominant hypophosphatemic rickets, and vitamin D–dependent rickets type II, among others.

PHYSICAL EXAMINATION

Height and weight should be measured in all patients, and, in children <3 years, head circumference. Children should have an evaluation of both statural growth and growth velocity by plotting on available charts for these purposes. A Tanner sexual maturity rating should be given to all children and adolescents. The clinician should look specifically for any bony deformities or masses, leg length inequality, vertebral tenderness, kyphosis, lordosis, or scoliosis, a surgical scar on the neck (suggesting previous thyroid or parathyroid surgery), and abnormal gait. Often a single physical finding leads to a specific diagnosis. Blue or gray sclerae in young infants suggest osteogenesis imperfecta. These patients also may have deafness, ligamentous laxity with joint hypermobility, diaphoresis, dental defects, and they may bruise easily. Café au lait spots are present in McCune-Albright syndrome, soft-tissue or mesenchymal tumors in tumor-induced osteomalacia, and premature loss of deciduous teeth in hypophosphatasia. Alopecia, ranging from sparse hair to total alopecia without eyelashes, occurs in two thirds of kindreds with vitamin D–dependent rickets type II. Round facies, centripetal obesity, easy bruising, dorsocervical fat pad, violaceous striae, and plethora point to the diagnosis of Cushing's syndrome. Proptotic eyes, goiter, and tremulousness suggests hyperthyroidism.

In rickets in children, a constellation of physical findings provides the diagnosis. The patient may have short stature, bony tenderness, softened skull (craniotabes), parietal flattening, and frontal bossing. There is often palpable enlargement of the costochondral junctions (the "rachitic rosary"), thickening of the wrists and ankles, flared wrists from metaphyseal widening, Harrison's groove (a horizontal depression along the lower border of the chest, corresponding to the costal insertions of the diaphragm), bowing deformity of the long bones from weight bearing, and waddling gait. The patient also may have reduced muscle strength and tone, lax ligaments, an indentation of the sternum in response to the force exerted by the diaphragm and intercostal muscles, delayed eruption of permanent teeth, and enamel defects. Rickets affect the most rapidly growing bone. Because the skull is growing rapidly at birth, craniotabes is found in congenital rickets. A rachitic rosary is prominent during the first year of life, when the rib cage grows rapidly. Late rickets, which occurs at the time of adolescent growth spurt, often results in a knock-knee deformity. In infants and young children, listlessness and irritability are common. In infants, floppiness and hypotonia are characteristic. Associated syndromic features in children should be evaluated as well during the examination, including ocular and otic abnormalities. In adults with osteomalacia, there are fewer physical findings but proximal weakness, waddling gait, and anterior tibial tenderness can be observed on examination.

Hypocalcemia is characterized by neuromuscular irritability. This may include varying degrees of tetany, which usually begins with numbness and tingling around the mouth and in the tips of the fingers, followed by muscle spasms in the extremities and face. There may be thumb adduction, metacarpophalangeal joint flexion, and interphalangeal joint extension. Latent tetany can be shown by eliciting Chvostek's sign or Trousseau's sign. Chvostek's sign is spasm of facial muscles elicited by tapping the facial nerve in the region of the parotid gland, just anterior to the ear lobe, below the zygomatic arch, or between the zygomatic arch and the corner of the mouth. The response ranges from a twitching of the lip at the corner of the mouth to a twitching of all the facial muscles on the stimulated side. Slightly positive reactions may occur in up to 10–15% of normal adults; it is commonly present in neonates without evidence of pathology. To elicit Trousseau's sign, a sphygmomanometer is inflated on the arm to 20 mm above the systolic blood pressure for 2–5 minutes. A positive response consists of carpal spasm with relaxation occurring 5–10 s after the cuff is deflated. Relaxation should not be immediate. Both Chvostek's and Trousseau's signs can be absent, however, even in severe hypocalcemia.

In patients with idiopathic hypoparathyroidism, the physician should look for signs of the polyglandular failure syndromes: chronic mucocutaneous candidiasis, adrenal insufficiency, alopecia, vitiligo, premature ovarian failure, diabetes mellitus, autoimmune thyroid disease, and pernicious anemia. Pseudohypoparathyroidism presents with a constellation of signs called Albright's hereditary osteodystrophy (AHO) as well as symptoms of long-standing hypocalcemia and hyperphosphatemia including carpopedal spasm, tetanic convulsions, paresthesias, and muscle cramps. Albright's hereditary osteodystrophy is manifest by round facies, short stature, obesity, shortening of the fourth and fifth digits (brachydactyly), subcutaneous ossification, dental hypoplasia, and mentally retardation. AHO can be seen with (pseudohypoparathyroidism) or without (pseudo-pseudohypoparathyroidism) the accompanying hypocalcemia and hyperphosphatemia.

Most patients with primary hyperparathyroidism usually have no abnormal physical findings. Enlarged parathyroid glands are usually palpable only when parathyroid carcinoma is present, and band keratopathy (calcium-phosphate deposition in the medial and lateral limbic margins of the cornea) is seen rarely and usually only by slit-lamp examination. Extreme elevations of serum calcium may produce an altered sensorium, hypertension, and nonspecific abdominal pain or renal colic from nephrolithiasis.

Patients with renal osteodystrophy often have characteristic physical findings. Spontaneous tendon rupture may occur in patients with advanced renal failure, almost always in association with marked secondary hyperparathyroidism. Bone deformities are common, especially in children, and in patients with severe aluminum toxicity. A funnel chest abnormality may be produced by rib deformities and kyphoscoliosis. Pseudoclubbing may result from enlargement of the distal tufts of the fingers as a result of osteitis fibrosa (severe secondary hyperparathyroidism). Bowing of long bones, genu valgum, and ulnar deviation of the wrist may be seen in children before epiphyseal closure has occurred, and slipped epiphyses may occur in the periadolescent period, especially in the femoral epiphysis.

Patients with Paget disease usually have no signs of the disease. Over many years, however, progressive cranial involvement can produce increased head size, whereas bowing and enlargement of the long bones may occur with disease of the femur and tibia. Slowly progressive hearing loss, vertigo, tinnitus, or a combination of these can occur in up to 25% of patients with skull involvement. Commonly, there is redness with increased skin temperature over an affected bone. Defects in Bruch's membrane of the retina, termed angioid streaks, may be observed in about 10% of patients. Deformity of the facial bones (leontiasis ossea) may be seen in Paget disease but is more common in fibrous dysplasia.

Patients with established osteoporosis often exhibit dorsal kyphosis or a gibbus (dowager's hump) and loss of height. They may have a protuberant abdomen (that the patient may confuse with obesity), ribs within the pelvic rim that may be bruised, paravertebral muscle spasm, and thin skin (McConkey's sign). The clinician should look for signs of secondary causes of osteoporosis (e.g., hypogonadism, Cushing's syndrome, and celiac disease, among others). In the SOF, four physical findings indicated an increased risk of hip fracture: the inability to rise from a chair without using one's arms, a resting pulse rate of >80 beats/minute, poor depth perception, and poorer low-frequency contrast sensitivity.[3] By combining these clinical findings with a careful history, assessment of risk factors, and bone density measurement, it may be possible to make a good assessment of hip fracture risk.

In men that are undergoing evaluation for osteoporosis, a testicular examination should be performed to alert the physician to hypogonadism that is acquired or congenital.

With the availability of sophisticated diagnostic techniques to assess BMD and remodeling, the clinician is faced with new and difficult decisions about test interpretation and resource allocation. A complete history and physical examination continue to be the clinician's most important guides, often providing crucial clues to the origin of skeletal disorders in children and adults.

REFERENCES

1. Bilezikian JP, Marcus R, Levine MA (eds.) 2001 The Parathyroids: Basic and Clinical Concepts. Academic Press, San Diego, CA, USA.
2. DeGroot LJ, Jameson JL (eds.) 2001 Endocrinology, 4th ed. WB Saunders, Philadelphia, PA, USA.
3. Cummings SR, Nevitt MC, Browner WS, Stone K, Fox KM, Ensrud KE, Cauley J, Black D, Vogt TM 1995 Risk factors for hip fracture in white women: Study of Osteoporotic Fractures Research Group. N Engl J Med **322:**767–773.

Chapter 20. Blood Calcium, Phosphate, and Magnesium

Tamara J. Vokes

Section of Endocrinology, Department of Medicine, University of Chicago, Chicago, Illinois

CALCIUM

Calcium in the blood is present in three forms (Fig. 1): bound to protein, complexed with inorganic acids, and free or ionized calcium.[1] Strictly speaking, ionized calcium is a misnomer because all serum/plasma calcium is ionized and associated with protein or anions by ionic binding. Thus, free calcium is a more accurate term. Only free calcium is physiologically active and is maintained in a narrow range by homeostatic mechanism. However, because the measurement of total calcium includes the large fraction that is bound to protein, alterations in protein concentrations or its affinity for calcium may result in abnormal calcium measurement in the absence of any abnormality in the calcium metabolism per se (Table 1). Calcium binds to anionic carboxylate groups on the albumin molecule with fewer than 20% of binding sites normally being occupied by calcium. Binding of calcium ions to protein is pH dependent. Thus, when pH increases, hydrogen ions dissociate from anionic sites on protein making them more available to calcium. The resulting increase in calcium binding to protein lowers free (ionized) calcium concentration. Conversely, in acidosis, increased binding of hydrogen ions to protein releases calcium from the protein binding sites resulting in increased free calcium. The approximate relationship between pH and free calcium is that an increase in pH of 0.1 lowers free calcium by 0.05 mM.

The concentration of calcium in the plasma (or serum) in the United States is usually expressed in milligrams per deciliters, and in other countries in millimols. Because the molecular weight of calcium is 40 and its valence is 2, the relationship between the units is given as:

$$mM = (mg/dl \times 10)/molecular\ weight$$

$$mEq/liter = mM \times valence$$

It follows that 1 mg/dl = 0.25 mM = 0.5 mEq/liter. The normal ranges for total and free calcium are dependent on the laboratory, specimen type, collection protocol, and method used for analysis. While in the past, 11 mg/dl was the accepted upper limit of normal, it is now appreciated that the upper limit is actually <10.5 mg/dl and most often 10.2 or 10.3 mg/dl. The usual normal range for total serum calcium is 8.8–10.3 mg/dl (2.2–2.6 mM and 4.4–5.2 mEq/liter) and for ionized calcium is 4.5–5.2 mg/dl (1.12–1.3 mM).

Calcium Measurement

In most clinical laboratories, total calcium is usually measured using automated spectrophotometric techniques that rely on formation of colored complexes between calcium and various metallochromic indicators or dyes.[1] Orthocresolphthalein complexone (CPC) and arsenazo III are the most widely used indicators. Atomic absorption spectrophotometry has higher precision and accuracy and is in most laboratories used as a reference method and for evaluating and trouble-shooting routine calcium measuring procedures. Serum is the preferred specimen, although heparinized plasma is also acceptable. Ci-

trate, oxalate, and EDTA should not be used as anticoagulants because they interfere by forming complexes with calcium. Calcium is stable in serum for days at 4°C and for months in the frozen state. In heparinized plasma, co-precipitation of calcium with fibrin or lipids can occur with storage or freezing. Hemolysis, icterus, lipemia, paraprotein, and magnesium interfere with photometric methods.[2] Hemolysis can cause a negative error because calcium concentration is lower in the red blood cells than in the serum. Usually, however, a more significant error is caused by spectral interference of hemoglobin, which may be positive or negative depending on the method. Because of this, measurement of calcium in hemolyzed specimens should be avoided, and if it has do be performed, blanking with EGTA is suggested. Lipemic specimens should be clarified by high-speed centrifugation.

While in the past, measurements of free (ionized) calcium were technically difficult, the newer calcium sensitive electrodes provide reliable, rapid, and precise automatic determinations.[3] However, proper handling of specimens is crucial and often a source of error.[4] Because of above-mentioned dependence of ionized calcium concentrations on pH, it is essential that the sample be collected anaerobically to prevent the loss of CO_2 and resulting increase in pH. If only aerobic specimens are available, the pH should be adjusted to patient's pH (or at least to pH 7.4) before analysis.[5] While adjusting pH to 7.4 may be appropriate for healthy subjects with normal acid–base balance, it may be misleading in patients with respiratory or metabolic acidosis or alkalosis.[6] For example, a patient with respiratory alkalosis and tetany may have normal free calcium adjusted to pH of 7.4 but low free calcium at a higher pH level.

The metabolic activity of the blood cells during storage also affects pH. Although hydrogen cation and lactate anion partly offset each other, the blood should be centrifuged within an hour to prevent the effect of acidosis on ionized calcium. The main advantage of using the anticoagulated blood is that it can be analyzed more rapidly. The values for free calcium in the whole blood tend to be slightly lower because of binding of calcium to heparin. To minimize this effect and prevent dilution of calcium by heparin, it is recommended to use calcium citrated heparin at a concentration of 50 IU/ml or lower or lithium heparin at 15 U/ml or lower. Dry heparin products virtually eliminate the interference by heparin. It is important that all syringes and tubes be completely filled to minimize

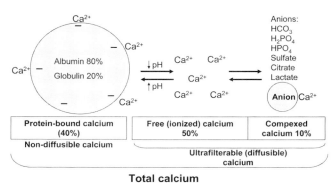

Total calcium

FIG. 1.   Approximate distribution of calcium in human plasma.

The author has reported no conflicts of interest.

TABLE 1. FACTORS OR ERRORS AFFECTING TOTAL AND/OR
FREE CALCIUM MEASUREMENTS

In vivo
    Tourniquet use and venous occlusion ($\uparrow$ total calcium)
    Changes in posture (recumbency– $\downarrow$ total calcium)
    Exercise ($\uparrow$ free calcium)
    Hyperventilation ($\downarrow$ free calcium)
    Fist clenching ($\uparrow$ free calcium)
    Effects of meals ($\uparrow$ calcium)
    Alterations in binding to protein
        Altered albumin concentration ($\uparrow$ total calcium with $\uparrow$ albumin)
        Abnormal protein (myeloma—rare) ($\uparrow$ total calcium)
        pH ($\uparrow$ pH causes $\downarrow$ free calcium)
        Heparin ($\downarrow$)
        Drugs (variable)
    Alterations in complex formation—citrate, bicarbonate, lactate,
        phosphate, pyruvate and β-hydroxybutirate, sulfate, and other
        anions that bind calcium ($\downarrow$ free calcium)
In vitro
    Inappropriate anticoagulants ($\downarrow$)
    Dilution or interference by heparin ($\downarrow$)
    Contamination with calcium (corks, glassware, etc.) ($\uparrow$)
    Specimen handling
        Changes in pH (specimen handling) ($\uparrow$ free calcium)
        Adsorption or precipitation of calcium ($\downarrow$)
    Spectrophotometric interference
        Hemolysis, icterus, lipemia (variable)

dilution and/or heparin effects.[7] Any specimen used for free calcium determination should be transported on ice or analyzed within minutes to prevent the effect of above-mentioned lactic acidosis on calcium binding to protein and acids.[4]

Factors That May Influence Calcium Measurement

A number of factors may influence calcium measurement, although they do not alter calcium metabolism (Table 1). Because a significant portion of total serum (plasma) calcium is bound to protein, changes in protein concentration will alter calcium level, although the concentration of free, physiologically important calcium is unchanged. Because 1 g/dl of protein binds ~0.8 mg/dl of calcium, a simple way for calculating "corrected serum calcium" is given by the formula:

$$\text{Corrected serum calcium (mg/dl)} = \text{Total calcium (mg/dl)} + 0.8\,(4 - \text{albumin in g/dl})$$

Low measured total serum calcium caused by a decrease in serum protein is most often seen in hypoalbuminemia because of hepatic or renal disease. On the other hand, dehydration increases serum albumin and total calcium measurement. Perhaps the most common cause of spurious hypercalcemia is a tight tourniquet that produces an elevation in serum albumin because of efflux of water from the vascular compartment during stasis.[8] The magnitude of this effect can be as much as 0.5–1 mg/dl. Therefore, if a tourniquet is required, it should only be used for a brief period of time. Fist clenching during blood draw should also be avoided because forearm exercise increases free calcium because of decreased pH associated with production of lactic acid by the exercising muscles.[8]

Erect posture has been reported to result in increase in total calcium of 0.2–0.8 mg/dl because of fluid shift.[9,10] In contrast, mild hypocalcemia is commonly observed in hospitalized patients because of hemodilution associated with

recumbency.[11] Prolonged bed rest, however, may be associated with true rather than spurious hypercalcemia caused by release of calcium from the bone caused by immobilization. Hyperventilation induces alkalosis, which may lower free calcium, whereas exercise may increases free calcium because of lowering of pH by lactic acid.[8,10]

While significant alterations in measured serum calcium are associated with changes in albumin, changes in serum globulins (which bind calcium only minimally) usually do not affect serum calcium measurements. An exception to this is a rare patient with multiple myeloma with a monoclonal paraprotein that binds calcium with high affinity, potentially leading to marked elevation in total but not free calcium concentrations.[12]

Physiologic variations in serum calcium level are related to circadian rhythm, alimentary status, and age. Total serum calcium is lower during the night, which is at least, in part, because of decrease in plasma protein caused by recumbency[13] (Fig. 2). However, even free calcium concentration fluctuates during the day,[14] which may be related to calcium intake (Fig. 3). The effect of food ingestion on calcium levels is a matter of debate, possibly because the magnitude of variability in serum calcium is greater if overall daily intake of calcium is lower.[14] It should be noted, however, that serum calcium is maintained in the normal range even at very low calcium intake. As a result, hypocalcemia is a relatively late manifestation of nutritional deficiency of cal-

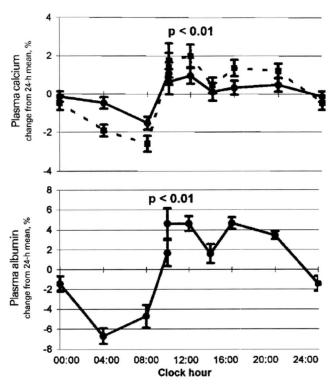

FIG. 2. Diurnal variation in plasma calcium (top panel: albumin adjusted, solid lines; unadjusted, broken lines) and protein (bottom panel). Means ± SE. (From Rejnmark L, Lauridsen AL, Vestergaard P, Heickendorff L, Andreasen F, Mosekilde L 2002 Diurnal rhythm of plasma 1,25-dihydroxyvitamin D and vitamin D-binding protein in postmenopausal women: relationship to plasma parathyroid hormone and calcium and phosphate metabolism. Eur J Endocrinol **146**:635–642.[24]) © Society of the European Journal of Endocrinology 2002. Reproduced with permission.

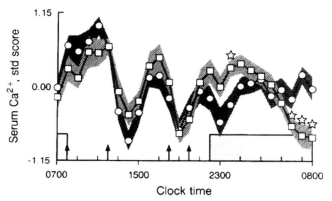

FIG. 3. Circadian variation in serum ionized calcium, expressed as standardized scores (standardized scores were obtained as follows: the mean and SD for the 26 time-points were determined for each subject and standardized scores were calculated for each time-point by subtracting the mean from each observation and dividing it by the SD; in the absence of true circadian rhythm, the mean standardized score would be zero). The group mean ± SE (shaded area) is shown for women (squares) and men (circles). Stars denote significant ($p < 0.04$) differences between men and women by two-sample t-test. Arrows indicate times of meals/snacks and the horizontal bar indicates the period of recumbency. (From Calvo MS, Eastell R, Offord KP, Bergstralh EJ, Burritt MF 1991 Circadian variation in ionized calcium and intact parathyroid hormone: evidence for sex differences in calcium homeostasis. J Clin Endocrinol Metab **72:**69–76.[25]) Copyright 1991, The Endocrine Society.

cium and vitamin D intake. Aging and menopausal status are not associated with clear alterations in calcium levels in well-nourished, vitamin D replete subjects.[14] In elderly men, there is a slight decrease in serum calcium, which is caused by a decrease in serum albumin.[15] In pregnancy, total serum calcium but not free calcium declines in parallel with serum albumin concentration.[16] Calcium levels are relatively higher in fetal blood (ionized calcium in the cord blood is 5.20–6.4 mg/dl), decline after birth, reaching a nadir at 24 h (4.40–5.44 mg/dl), and rise in the first few days of life to levels slightly above those seen in adults (4.80–5.52 mg/dl).[16–18]

Total or Free Calcium?

Free (ionized) calcium is easier to interpret and more likely to be useful for evaluation of calcium status.[19] However, it is more likely to be affected by improper specimen collection and handling described above. For relatively healthy outpatients, measuring total calcium and calculating "corrected" serum calcium may be adequate in many clinical situations. However, in sick and hospitalized patients, it is preferred to measure free calcium, which nowadays can be performed rapidly and accurately in most clinical laboratories.[3] Free calcium measurement is particularly useful in patients undergoing major surgery and/or receiving citrated blood products, heparin, bicarbonate, intravenous solutions, or calcium[3,19] (illustrative example of a patient undergoing liver transplantation is shown in Fig. 4). Similarly, free calcium is more useful in critically ill patients in intensive care units, who often have alterations in serum protein concentration, circulating factors that alter calcium binding to protein, and/or changes in acid/base status. Another clinical situation where free calcium measurements may be particularly useful is in patients with renal disease who have alterations in serum protein, pH, and calcium binding to

protein and organic and inorganic anions.[20] Finally, free calcium may also be preferred in neonates because it can be measured rapidly in small capillary specimens and because it is more reliable in the presence of hyperphosphatemia, alterations in pH, and persistence of α-fetoprotein after birth.[19,21]

PHOSPHORUS

Phosphorus in the blood is present in organic and inorganic forms.[1] Organic phosphorus is part of phospholipids and is not usually included in the measurement of phosphorus reported by the clinical laboratories. Inorganic phosphorus is in the form of phosphate that is routinely measured in the serum or plasma. Although only phosphate is measured, it's concentration in blood, urine, tissue, or food is expressed as amount of phosphorus contained in the specimen. A more precise terminology would be to report the value as phosphate expressed as milligrams per deciliter of phosphorus. Phosphate in the serum exists as both the monovalent and divalent phosphate anions $H_2PO_4^-$ and HPO_4^{2-}. The relative concentration of the two anions is dependent on the pH: the ratio of $H_2PO_4^-$ to HPO_4^{2-} is 1:1 in acidosis, 1:4 at pH of 7.4, and 1:9 in alkalosis. About 10–20% of plasma phosphate is protein bound. The remainder, which is filtered by the renal glomerulus, is either complexed with sodium, calcium, and magnesium (35%), or exists as free ions (55%). Because the atomic weight of phosphorus is 30.98, serum phosphorus concentration expressed in milligrams per deciliter can be converted to millimols by dividing by 3.1. Because the phosphate in the serum/plasma is a mixture of mono- and divalent ions, the composite valence is 1.8 at pH of 7.4, so that at this pH 1 mM of phosphorus is equal to 1.8 mEq. The normal value for phosphorus is laboratory specific, usually ~2.5–4.5 mg/dl (0.81–1.45 mM).

Phosphate Measurement

In most clinical laboratories, phosphate measurements are based on reaction of phosphate ions with molybdate. The colorless phosphomolybdate complexes can either be measured directly by UV absorption or reduced by various agents to produce molybdenum blue, which is measured using a photometric method. Serum is a preferred specimen, although phosphate can also be measured in heparinized

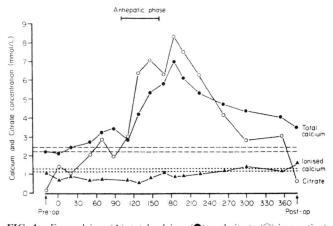

FIG. 4. Free calcium (▲), total calcium (●), and citrate (○) in a patient undergoing liver transplantation. The reference intervals are indicated by the upper (total calcium) and lower (free calcium) sets of dashed horizontal lines. The reference interval for citrate is 0.03–0.15 mM. (From Gray TA, Paterson CR 1988 The clinical value of ionized calcium assays. Ann Clin Biochem **25:**210–219 with permission.)

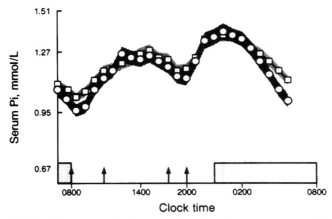

FIG. 5. Diurnal variation in serum phosphate. The group mean ± SE (shaded area) is shown for women (□) and men (○). Arrows indicate times of meals/snacks and the horizontal bar indicates the period of recumbency. (From Calvo MS, Eastell R, Offord KP, Bergstralh EJ, Burritt MF 1991 Circadian variation in ionized calcium and intact parathyroid hormone: Evidence for sex differences in calcium homeostasis. J Clin Endocrinol Metab 72:69–76.[25]) Copyright 1991, The Endocrine Society.

plasma where the levels are typically lower by ~0.2–0.3 mg/dl.[22] Other anticoagulants such as citrate, oxalate, and EDTA should not be used because they interfere with the formation of phosphomolybdate complexes. Serum or plasma should be separated promptly from the red blood cells to avoid spurious elevation in measured phosphate.[1] Because the intracellular concentration of phosphate is higher than that of plasma, prolonged storage of with cells or hemolysis increases phosphate concentration. Inorganic phosphate increases by 4–6 mg/dl per day in hemolyzed specimens stored at 4°C. Hydrolysis proceeds even faster at room temperature. Glucose phosphate, creatinine phosphate and other organic phosphates may also be hydrolyzed by assay conditions and result in overestimation of serum phosphate levels. Depending on the analytical method used for phosphate determination, positive or negative interference may occur in hemolyzed, icteric, and lipemic specimens.[2] Mannitol, fluoride, and monoclonal immunoglobulins have also been reported to interfere. If glassware is used in specimen processing or analysis, it should be thoroughly rinsed, because phosphate is a component of many detergents. In serum that has been separated from cells, phosphate is stable for days at 4°C and for months when frozen.

Factors That Influence Phosphate Measurement

Physiologic variations in serum phosphate levels are related to age, time of the day, and food intake. Serum phosphate levels are highest in infants in the first 3 months of life and gradually decrease to adult levels by late adolescence.[23] Serum phosphate levels are higher in childhood (4.0–7.0 mg/dl or 1.29–2.26 mM), lower (by about 0.7 mg/dl) in elderly men than in women,[24,25] and also lower in pregnancy.

In healthy subjects, there is a circadian rhythm to serum phosphate, with nadir achieved just before noon and higher levels in the afternoon and shortly after midnight[14,26] (Fig. 5). The amplitude of diurnal variability in phosphate level is ~1.2 mg/dl. Dietary intake of phosphate influences phosphate level measured during the day but not the fasting morning value, which is the optimal condition for phosphate measurement in most subjects. In contrast, the afternoon specimens are more likely to be affected by diet and may be more useful for

monitoring the efficacy of phosphate-binding agents given to patients with renal insufficiency.

Ingestion of a carbohydrate-rich meal or intravenous infusion of glucose and/or administration of insulin, lower serum phosphate because of movement into the cells.[27] This may be one of the reasons for the common finding of low serum phosphate in hospitalized patients who are often receiving glucose infusions. Alkalosis also decreases serum phosphate, with a reduction of as much as 2 mg/dl reported with acute respiratory alkalosis.[27] Infusion or endogenous release of epinephrine can acutely decrease the serum phosphorus concentration. Serum phosphate increases with exercise, acidosis, and intravenous calcium administration, the latter presumably because of efflux of phosphate from the red blood cells.

MAGNESIUM

Magnesium in the blood is distributed in a manner analogous to calcium: 30% is protein bound and not filtered by the glomerulus and the remainder is filtered and consists of free or ionized magnesium (55%) and complexed magnesium (15%). Similar to calcium, magnesium is bound principally to albumin with the affinity being influenced by pH. It is free (ionized) magnesium that is important for physiologic processes such as muscle contraction and cardiovascular function. The molecular weight of magnesium is 24 and its valence is 2. Thus, the concentration expressed in milligrams per deciliter can be converted to millimols by dividing by 2.4 and in milliequivalents per liter by dividing by 1.2. The normal range for total magnesium is 1.7–2.4 mg/dl (0.66–1.07 mM) and for free (ionized) magnesium is 0.44–0.59 mM.

Magnesium Measurement

In most clinical laboratories, total magnesium is measured using a spectrophotometric method that relies on metallochromic indicators or dyes that change color after selectively binding magnesium . Most commonly used indicators are calmagite (most common in automated analyzers), formazan dye, and methylthymol blue. Atomic absorption spectrometry provides greater accuracy and precision and is used in most laboratories as a reference method. Neutron activation with ^{27}Mg is the definitive method for magnesium analysis. Serum is the preferred specimen, but heparinized plasma can be used as well. However, lithium heparin, lithium zinc heparin, and newer heparins developed for determination of free calcium should be avoided because they significantly increase magnesium. Other anticoagulants such as citrate, oxalate, and EDTA should not be used because they form complexes with magnesium. Serum or plasma must be separated from cells as soon as possible because erythrocytes have about three times higher concentration of magnesium than plasma. Leakage of magnesium from the cells causes spurious elevation in serum levels. For the same reason, hemolyzed specimens are unacceptable. Interference by icterus and lipemia depends on the analytical method used. Lipemic specimens should be ultracentrifuged before analysis. Magnesium is stable in serum for days at 4°C and for months when frozen.

Ionized (free) magnesium can now be measured in the whole blood or serum using ion selective electrodes. However, its usefulness in routine clinical practice is not clear, particularly because significant differences have been reported among different analyzers.[28] Although free magnesium changes with pH in the same direction as calcium, the rate of change in ionized magnesium is less than that observed for calcium.[29] Measuring free magnesium may be useful when there are severe disturbances of acid–base balance, in critically ill patients, and during cardiopulmonary bypass, preeclampsia, neonatal distress, and administration of certain drugs.

In contrast to calcium and phosphate, magnesium shows little variability with the time of the day, in relationship to meals, between sexes, or in different ages.

REFERENCES

1. Endres D, Rude R 1999 Mineral and bone metabolism. In: Burtis C, Edward R (eds.) Tietz Textbook of Clinical Chemistry. W.B. Saunders, Philadelphia, PA, USA, pp. 1395–1456.
2. Glick MR, Ryder KW 1987 Analytical systems ranked by freedom from interferences. Clin Chem 33:1453–1458.
3. Bowers GN Jr, Brassard C, Sena SF 1986 Measurement of ionized calcium in serum with ion-selective electrodes: A mature technology that can meet the daily service needs. Clin Chem 32:1437–1447.
4. Boink AB, Buckley BM, Christiansen TF, Covington AK, Maas AH, Muller-Plathe O, Sachs C, Siggaard-Andersen O 1992 Recommendation on sampling, transport, and storage for the determination of the concentration of ionized calcium in whole blood, plasma, and serum. IFC Scientific Division, Working Group on Ion-Selective Electrodes (WGSE). J Int Fed Clin Chem 4:147–152.
5. Thode J 1990 Ionized calcium and cyclic AMP in plasma and urine. Biochemical evaluation in calcium metabolic disease. Scand J Clin Lab Invest Suppl 197:1–45.
6. Thode J, Holmegaard SN, Transbol I, Fogh-Andersen N, Siggaard-Andersen O 1990 Adjusted ionized calcium (at pH 7.4) and actual ionized calcium (at actual pH) in capillary blood compared for clinical evaluation of patients with disorders of calcium metabolism. Clin Chem 36:541–544.
7. Toffaletti JG, Wildermann RF 2001 The effects of heparin anticoagulants and fill volume in blood gas syringes on ionized calcium and magnesium measurements. Clin Chim Acta 304:147–151.
8. Renoe BW, McDonald JM, Ladenson JH 1980 The effects of stasis with and without exercise on free calcium, various cations, and related parameters. Clin Chim Acta 103:91–100.
9. Renoe BW, McDonald JM, Ladenson JH 1979 Influence of posture on free calcium and related variables. Clin Chem 25:1766–1769.
10. Buckley BM, Russell LJ 1988 The measurement of ionised calcium in blood plasma. Ann Clin Biochem 25:447–465.
11. Humphrey KR, Gruemer HD, Lott JA 1977 Impact of posture on the "reference range" for serum proteins and calcium. Clin Chem 23:1343–1346.
12. Pearce CJ, Hine TJ, Peek K 1991 Hypercalcaemia due to calcium binding by a polymeric IgA kappa-paraprotein. Ann Clin Biochem 28:229–234.
13. Rejnmark L, Lauridsen AL, Vestergaard P, Heickendorff L, Andreasen F, Mosekilde L 2002 Diurnal rhythm of plasma 1,25-dihydroxyvitamin D and vitamin D-binding protein in postmenopausal women: Relationship to plasma parathyroid hormone and calcium and phosphate metabolism. Eur J Endocrinol 146:635–642.
14. Calvo MS, Eastell R, Offord KP, Bergstralh EJ, Burritt MF 1991 Circadian variation in ionized calcium and intact parathyroid hormone: Evidence for sex differences in calcium homeostasis. J Clin Endocrinol Metab 72:69–76.
15. Keating FR Jr, Jones JD, Elveback LR, Randall RV 1969 The relation of age and sex to distribution of values in healthy adults of serum calcium, inorganic phosphorus, magnesium, alkaline phosphatase, total proteins, albumin, and blood urea. J Lab Clin Med 73:825–834.
16. Pitkin RM 1985 Calcium metabolism in pregnancy and the perinatal period: A review. Am J Obstet Gynecol 151:99–109.
17. Burritt MF, Slockbower JM, Forsman RW, Offord KP, Bergstralh EJ, Smithson WA 1990 Pediatric reference intervals for 19 biologic variables in healthy children. Mayo Clin Proc 65:329–336.
18. Lynch RE 1990 Ionized calcium: Pediatric perspective. Pediatr Clin North Am 37:373–389.
19. Gray TA, Paterson CR 1988 The clinical value of ionised calcium assays. Ann Clin Biochem 25:210–219.
20. Burritt MF, Pierides AM, Offord KP 1980 Comparative studies of total and ionized serum calcium values in normal subjects and patients with renal disorders. Mayo Clin Proc 55:606–613.
21. Wandrup J 1989 Critical analytical and clinical aspects of ionized calcium in neonates. Clin Chem 35:2027–2033.
22. Ladenson JH, Tsai LM, Michael JM, Kessler G, Joist JH 1974 Serum versus heparinized plasma for eighteen common chemistry tests: Is serum the appropriate specimen? Am J Clin Pathol 62:545–552.
23. Gomez P, Coca C, Vargas C, Acebillo J, Martinez A 1984 Normal reference-intervals for 20 biochemical variables in healthy infants, children, and adolescents. Clin Chem 30:407–412.
24. Sherman SS, Hollis BW, Tobin JD 1990 Vitamin D status and related parameters in a healthy population: The effects of age, sex, and season. J Clin Endocrinol Metab 71:405–413.
25. Portale AA, Halloran BP, Morris RC Jr, Lonergan ET 1996 Effect of aging on the metabolism of phosphorus and 1,25-dihydroxyvitamin D in healthy men. Am J Physiol 270:E483–E490.
26. Portale AA, Halloran BP, Morris RC Jr 1987 Dietary intake of phosphorus modulates the circadian rhythm in serum concentration of phosphorus. Implications for the renal production of 1,25-dihydroxyvitamin D. J Clin Invest 80:1147–1154.
27. Paleologos M, Stone E, Braude S 2000 Persistent, progressive hypophosphataemia after voluntary hyperventilation. Clin Sci (Lond) 98:619–625.
28. Hristova EN, Cecco S, Niemela JE, Rehak NN, Elin RJ 1995 Analyzer-dependent differences in results for ionized calcium, ionized magnesium, sodium, and pH. Clin Chem 41:1649–1653.
29. Wang S, McDonnell EH, Sedor FA, Toffaletti JG 2002 pH effects on measurements of ionized calcium and ionized magnesium in blood. Arch Pathol Lab Med 126:947–950.

Chapter 21.   Biochemical Markers of Bone Turnover

Pauline Camacho[1] and Michael Kleerekoper[2]

[1]Division of Endocrinology and Metabolism, Loyola University Medical Center, Maywood, Illinois; and [2]Wayne State University, Detroit, Michigan

INTRODUCTION

Throughout adult life, bone tissue is subject to a continuous process of turnover whereby old bone is removed and replaced by new bone by the coupled processes of bone resorption and bone formation. Moreover, most states of increased bone turnover, such as postmenopausal osteoporosis, are associated with a net increase in bone resorption over formation, resulting in bone loss. Thus, while measurement of BMD is critical in the clinical evaluation of the patient at risk for osteoporosis, BMD represents a static parameter, which provides no insight into the rate of bone turnover in a given patient. The ability to complement the static measurement of BMD with a dynamic assessment of bone turnover could, in principle, enhance the ability of BMD to predict the risk of subsequent fracture. While it has been possible to measure BMD at various skeletal sites for almost 20 years, bone turnover could only be assessed in the past by combined calcium balance and isotope kinetic studies (which are time consuming and enormously expensive)

The authors have reported no conflicts of interest.

Table 1. Currently Available Bone Biochemical Markers

A. Bone Formation Markers
  Serum
    Bone-specific alkaline phosphatase (BSALP)
    Osteocalcin (OC)
    Carboxyterminal propeptide of type I collagen (PICP)
    Aminoterminal propeptide of type I collagen (PINP)
B. Bone Resorption Markers
  Urine
    Free and total pyridinolines (Pyd)
    Free and total deoxypyridinolines (Dpd)
    N-telopeptide of collagen cross-links (NTx)
    C-telopeptide of collagen cross-links (CTx)
  Serum
    Cross-linked C-telopeptide of type I collagen (ICTP)
    Tartrate-resistant acid phosphatase 5b (TRACP5b)
    N-telopeptide of collagen cross-links (NTx)
    C-telopeptide of collagen cross-links (CTx)

or by tetracycline-based histomorphometry (which is invasive and expensive). Thus, the availability of biochemical markers for bone turnover represents a major methodological advance. These measurements are noninvasive, relatively inexpensive, generally available, can measure changes in bone turnover over short intervals of time, and can be assessed serially. However, where they fit into our clinical approach to patients with known or suspected osteoporosis is an evolving area. With this caveat in mind, this chapter reviews currently available biochemical markers for bone turnover and their potential clinical utility in the evaluation and management of patients with osteoporosis.

CURRENTLY AVAILABLE BIOCHEMICAL MARKERS OF BONE TURNOVER

Table 1 lists currently available bone turnover markers. Each of the markers represents a product released into the circulation during the process of bone formation or resorption. Hence, it is useful to discuss the markers in the context of these processes.

The major synthetic product of osteoblasts is type I collagen; however, osteoblasts also synthesize and secrete a variety of non-collagenous proteins, two of which are clinically useful markers of osteoblastic activity and, by inference, bone formation. Bone-specific alkaline phosphatase (BSALP) is an osteoblast product that is clearly essential for mineralization. A deficiency in BSALP in the disease hypophosphatasia, which is caused by a deactivating mutation of the *tissue nonspecific alkaline phosphatase (TNSALP)* gene leads to defective mineralization of bones and teeth.[1] The precise role of BSALP in the mineralization process, however, remains unclear. It may increase local concentrations of inorganic phosphate, destroy local inhibitors of mineral crystal growth, transport phosphate, or act as a calcium-binding protein or Ca^{2+}-ATPase.

Circulating ALP activity is derived from several tissues, including intestine, spleen, kidney, placenta (in pregnancy), liver, bone, or from various tumors. Thus, measurement of total ALP activity does not provide specific information on bone formation. However, because the two most common sources of elevated ALP levels are liver and bone, a number of techniques, including heat denaturation, chemical inhibition of selective activity, gel electrophoresis, and precipitation by wheat germ lectin have been used to distinguish the liver versus bone isoforms of the enzyme. Recent assays, however, have used tissue-specific monoclonal antibodies to measure the bone isoform that have 10–20% cross-reactivity with the liver isoform.

Osteocalcin (OC) is another non-collagenous protein secreted by osteoblasts and is widely accepted as a marker for osteoblastic activity, and hence, bone formation. However, it should be kept in mind that OC is incorporated into the matrix and is released into the circulation from the matrix during bone resorption, so the serum level at any one time has a component of both bone formation and resorption. Therefore, OC is more properly a marker of bone turnover rather than a specific marker of bone formation. It is a small protein of 49 amino acids, and in most species, contains three residues (at 17, 21, and 24) of γ-carboxyglutamic acid (Gla). The function of OC has not been identified, although its deposition in the bone matrix increases with hydroxyapatite deposition during skeletal growth. Studies suggest that OC may function to limit the process of mineralization and using OC "knockout" mice have found that these mice actually have increases in bone mass.

In the circulation, OC is present as the intact molecule and as a fragment or fragments of the intact molecule. It is unclear whether fragmentation of the intact molecule occurs in the blood, whether this occurs during bone resorption, or both. While older immunoassays that measured various OC fragments often gave widely discordant results even in the same individuals, newer assays measuring the major circulating forms of OC, which are either the intact molecule or a large N-terminal fragment spanning residues 1–43,[2] have shown much greater reliability as bone turnover markers. The role of vitamin K in bone metabolism has been increasingly recognized and is discussed in detail elsewhere. Because vitamin K plays a role in the γ-carboxylation of osteocalcin, in states of deficiency, levels of undercarboxylated osteocalcin are increased. Undercarboxylated osteocalcin may play a future role in the prediction of bone mass and fracture risk.[3,4] As noted earlier, the major synthetic product of osteoblasts is type I collagen so, in principle, indices of type I collagen synthesis would seem to be ideal bone formation markers. Several such assays have been developed, directed against either the carboxy- or amino-extension peptides of the procollagen molecule. These extension peptides (carboxyterminal propeptide of type I collagen [PICP] and aminoterminal propeptide of type I procollagen [PINP]) guide assembly of the collagen triple helix and are cleaved from the newly formed molecule in a stoichiometric relationship with collagen biosynthesis. However, because type I collagen is not unique to bone, these peptides are also produced by other tissues that synthesize type I collagen, including skin.

Several immunoassays for PICP and PINP have been developed; however, neither of these seems to be as useful as either BSALP or OC in terms of distinguishing normal from disease states. This may, in part, be caused by the inability of current assays to distinguish between bone and soft tissue contributions to the circulating levels of these peptides.

In contrast to the bone formation markers, where the non-collagenous proteins produced by osteoblasts seem to be the most useful markers, it is the collagen degradation products, rather than specific osteoclast proteins, that are most useful as markers of bone resorption. As the skeleton is resorbed, the collagen breakdown products are released into the circulation and ultimately cleared by the kidney. The development of rapid and relatively inexpensive immunoassays for various collagen breakdown products represents perhaps the major advance in this area and one that is likely to greatly increase the clinical use of the bone resorption markers. Collagen molecules in the bone matrix are staggered to form fibrils that are joined by covalent cross-links (Fig. 1).[5] These cross-links consist of hydroxylysyl-pyridinolines (pyridinolines [PYD]) and lysyl-pyridinolines (deoxypyridinolines [DPD]). PYD is present in the skeleton more abundantly than DPD, but DPD has greater

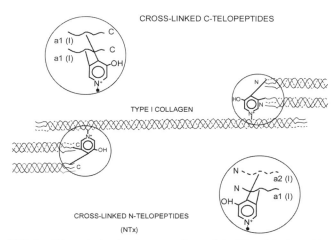

CROSS-LINKED C-TELOPEPTIDES

TYPE I COLLAGEN

CROSS-LINKED N-TELOPEPTIDES

(NTx)

FIG. 1. Schematic showing the source of cross-linked N- and C-telopeptides of type I collagen from bone. The amino- and carboxy-terminals of the collagen chains are linked to adjacent collagen chains by these cross-links. The telopeptides are the regions of the collagen chains where this cross-linking occurs; during the process of collagen breakdown, these telopeptides are released into the circulation and cleared by the kidney. (Adapted with permission from Calvo MS, Eyre DR, Gundberg CM 1996 Molecular basis and clinical application of biological markers of bone turnover. Endocr Rev **17:** 333–368. Copyright 1996, The Endocrine Society.)[5]

specificity because PYD is present to some extent in type II collagen of cartilage and other connective tissues. The PYD and DPD cross-links occur at two intermolecular sites in the collagen molecule: at or near residue 930, where two amino-telopeptides are linked to a helical site (N-telopeptide of collagen cross-links [NTX]), and at residue 87, where two carboxytelopeptides are linked to a helical site (C-telopeptide of collagen cross-links [CTX]; Fig. 1).

When osteoclasts resorb bone, they release a variety of collagen degradation products into the circulation that are metabolized further by the liver and the kidney. Thus, urine contains both free PYD and DPD (~40%) and peptide-bound PYD and DPD (~60%). The initial assays for PYD and DPD measured both free and, after acid hydrolysis of urine, total PYD and DPD by fluorometry after high-performance liquid chromatography.[6] While this likely remains the "gold standard" for measuring PYD and DPD in urine, it is relatively time-consuming and expensive, and there are now a number of immunoassays that can measure free PYD and DPD in urine.

In addition to the free PYD and DPD assays, immunoassays are also now available to measure the amino- and carboxy-terminal telopeptides released during bone resorption (NTX and CTX, respectively). There are, therefore, a number of rapid and relatively inexpensive methods for assessing urinary bone resorption markers, each with certain advantages and limitations. Moreover, assays have also been developed to measure DPD, NTX, and CTX in the circulation, which obviates the need for urine collections.

In addition to these assays, there has been another assay available for measuring cross-linked C-telopeptide of type I collagen (ICTP), which recognized an antigen in serum, but not in urine. While this assay has been available for several years, it has been relatively disappointing as a bone resorption marker,[7] and the peptides being recognized in serum have not been fully characterized.

Finally, the only osteoclast-specific product that has been evaluated to any extent as a bone resorption marker is TRACP5b. Acid phosphatase is a lysosomal enzyme that is present in a number of tissues, including bone, prostate, plate-

lets, erythrocytes, and the spleen. Osteoclasts contain TRACP that is released into the circulation. However, plasma TRACP is not entirely specific for the osteoclast, and the enzyme is relatively unstable in frozen samples. The development of immunoassays using monoclonal antibodies specifically directed against the bone isoenzyme of TRACP5b may improve its clinical use. However, in a study of clodronate-treated patients, TRACP5b was shown to be inferior to urinary NTX and serum PINP in detecting response to treatment.[8]

GENERAL CONSIDERATIONS IN THE USE OF BONE BIOCHEMICAL MARKERS

Before discussing the specific clinical settings in which bone biochemical markers might be useful, it is helpful to review certain general issues regarding the use of these markers. First, urinary resorption markers are generally reported after normalizing to creatinine excretion. This has certain limitations, including variability in the creatinine measurement that contributes to the overall variability in the measurement of the urinary markers, as well as potential artifactual changes in the urinary markers based on alterations in muscle mass. Thus, a more appropriate correction might be to express the urinary markers in terms of deciliter or liter of glomerular filtrate, although this is relatively cumbersome in the clinical setting. Nonetheless, this potential for artifact should be kept in mind when interpreting the urinary excretion markers. Serum and urine assays for NTX and CTX are now available commercially. These advances, particularly automation, have substantially reduced the "noise" in the assays, although it is still seems best to obtain a fasting blood specimen.

A second issue is that many of the bone turnover markers have circadian rhythms, so the timing of sampling is of some importance. Thus, both serum OC and PICP levels peak in the early morning hours (between 4:00 a.m. and 8:00 a.m.) and have nadirs in the mid- to late-afternoon.[9,10] BSALP, which has a long half-life in serum (1–2 days), however, does not show much circadian variability. All of the urinary and serum bone resorption markers also have significant circadian patterns, with peak levels occurring between 4:00 a.m. and 8:00 a.m.[11] (Fig. 2). For the urine markers, therefore, it is best to obtain either a 24-h urine collection which can conveniently be obtained when urinary calcium excretion is assessed or, alternatively, a second morning void sample can be used.

In adults, a third consideration is that most of the bone turnover markers tend to increase with age, except for a significant decline from adolescence to about age 25 years, as the phase of skeletal consolidation is completed.[9] Moreover, estrogen deficiency after menopause leads to a significant increase in bone turnover markers. This issue must be kept in mind in interpreting the results. Unlike the current WHO definitions for osteopenia and osteoporosis, there are currently no accepted criteria for defining "high" bone turnover. Most commercial laboratories report reference ranges based on menopausal state.

A fourth issue is the potential for differential changes in the various bone formation or resorption markers in different disease states or in response to different therapies. Thus, BSALP tends to show much larger increases in Paget's disease and osteomalacia than OC; conversely, glucocorticoid therapy is associated with larger decrements in OC levels as opposed to BSALP levels. In one study, OC was even inferior to serum total ALP in the diagnosis of osteomalacia.[12] Furthermore, the urinary excretion of free and peptide-bound fractions of PYD seems to be differently affected by bisphosphonate and estrogen therapy. Thus, bisphosphonate treatment has been reported to induce a specific decrease of cross-linked peptides without

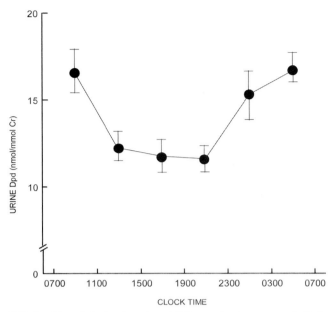

FIG. 2. Diurnal rhythm for urinary DPD excretion in a group of elderly women (71 ± 2 years). Note that urinary DPD excretion increases by ~50% between 9:00 p.m. and 7:00 a.m. (Adapted with permission from McKane WR, Khosla S, Egan KS, Robins SP, Burritt MF, Riggs BL 1996 Role of calcium intake in modulating age-related increases in parathyroid function and bone resorption. J Clin Endocrinol Metab **81:**1699–1703. Copyright 1996, The Endocrine Society.)[11]

any change in the excretion of free cross-links, whereas estrogen therapy decreases the urinary excretion of both forms of PYD and DPD.[13] Urinary markers of bone resorption have no role in metabolic bone disease work-up of patients with renal failure. BSALP may have some but limited use as a bone turnover marker among these individuals.[14]

Finally, one has to be aware of the potential variability (technical and biological) of the various bone turnover markers. BMD can be measured by DXA with an accuracy of >95% and a precision error for repeat measurements of between 0.5% and 2.5%. The technology needs to be this good because the rate of change in BMD is slow and, in many circumstances, the annual rate of change is less than the precision error of the measurement. In contrast, the biochemical markers of bone remodeling are subject to intra- and interassay variability (technical variability) as well as individual patient biological variability. As noted earlier, for the urine-based markers, this variability is compounded by the normalization to creatinine excretion, because there is considerable day-to-day variation of creatinine excretion in individual patients. In general, the long-term variability of the urine-based markers is in the order of 20–30%,[15] and the serum-based markers is in the order of 10–15%,[16] but this is improved to 3–5% with automated assays. This issue will be considered further below, because it is critical to keep this in mind when these markers are used in the clinical setting.

CURRENT AND POTENTIAL CLINICAL USES OF BONE BIOCHEMICAL MARKERS

Monitoring Effectiveness of Therapy

This represents perhaps the best-established clinical use of bone biochemical markers at present. Considerable data now indicate that, after initiation of antiresorptive therapy, there is a significant reduction in markers of bone resorption within 4–6 weeks,[7,17] and in markers of bone formation in 2–3 months.[7] Thus, bone turnover markers can be used to determine when therapy may be ineffective. Antiresorptive agents should produce a reduction in the markers of resorption of between 20% and 80%, depending on the agent and the markers. Thus, despite the potential technical and biological variability of the markers, changes of this magnitude should be clinically meaningful. For most treatments, the nadir will be reached between 2 and 3 months after initiation and will remain constant as long as the patient is on therapy.[18] Therefore, failure to show the expected reduction in resorption markers could indicate poor compliance to therapy or even improper administration of the oral bisphosphonates. BMD response to teriparatide therapy was recently shown to be predicted by the change in biochemical markers, specifically PICP and PINP, which had the highest sensitivities in predicting 18-month lumbar spine (LS) BMD change (59% and 69%, respectively).[19] This use of bone biochemical markers offers a marked advantage over using BMD to assess the effectiveness of therapy and to reassure patients, because the interval between serial measurements of BMD must be at least 12 (and possibly 24) months before significant changes in BMD can be documented or, more importantly, loss in BMD can be established with any certainty.

Prediction of Response to Therapy

Most recently, in several controlled clinical trials, baseline and/or changes in biochemical markers have been shown to be better predictors of antifracture efficacy than has been shown for DXA.[20–23] In a meta-analysis of 18 clinical trials, larger reductions in bone turnover markers were associated with larger reductions in nonvertebral fracture risk. A 70% reduction in bone resorption markers reduced risk by 40%, and a 50% reduction in bone formation markers reduced risk by 44%.[24] Furthermore, in a study of patients previously treated with alendronate and raloxifene, teriparatide use led to larger increases in bone markers and BMD in the raloxifene-treated group, which had significantly less suppression of bone resorption than the alendronate group. This was most pronounced in the first 6 months of therapy.[25]. The clinical application of this data, however, is not clear, because the study was not powered to detect differences in fracture protection between the two groups.

Prediction of Fracture Risk

This represents perhaps the most intriguing use of bone biochemical markers because, in principle; assessment of bone turnover may provide additional information on fracture risk beyond that provided by BMD. Several studies now do suggest that bone turnover may be an independent predictor of fracture risk.[26–28] Thus, in a prospective cohort study of elderly (age >75 years) French women, urinary CTX and free DPD excretion above the upper limit of the premenopausal range (i.e., mean + 2 SD) was associated with an increased risk of hip fracture (Fig. 3), even after adjusting for femoral neck BMD.[28] In population-based studies in women, bone resorption markers were negatively correlated with BMD of the hip, spine, and forearm, and women with osteoporosis were more likely to have high bone turnover.[26] Moreover, a history of osteoporotic fractures of the hip, spine, or distal forearm was associated with reduced hip BMD and with elevated biochemical markers of bone resorption.[26] The mechanisms by which increased bone turnover adversely affects fracture risk include exacerbation of rates of bone loss,[29] microarchitectural deterioration of the skeleton caused by perforation of trabeculae

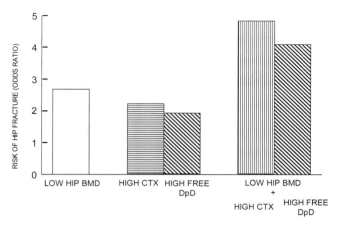

FIG. 3. Combination of BMD assessment and bone resorption rate to predict hip fracture risk in a cohort of elderly (mean age, 82.5 years) French women. Low BMD was defined by a value below 2.5 SD of the young adult mean and high bone resorption by urinary CTX or free DPD values above 2.0 SD of the young adult mean. (Adapted from J Bone Miner Res 11:1531–1538 with permission from the American Society for Bone and Mineral Research.)[28]

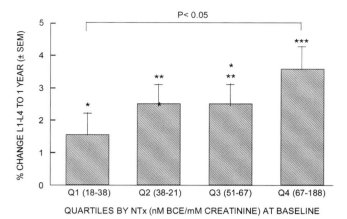

FIG. 5. Response to HT at the spine by quartiles of baseline NTX excretion in a group of early postmenopausal women (p values vs. baseline BMD: *$p < 0.05$; **$p < 0.001$; ***$p < 0.0001$). (Reprinted from Am J Med, vol. 102, Chestnut CH III, Bell NH, Clark GS, Drinkwater BL, English SC, Johnson CC Jr, Notelovitz M, Rosen C, Cain DF, Flessland KA, Mallinak NJ, Hormone replacement therapy in postmenopausal women: Urinary N-telopeptide of type I collagen monitors therapeutic effect and predicts response of bone mineral density, pp. 29–37, Copyright 1997, with permission from Excerpta Medica Inc.)[18]

and loss of structural elements of bone, or a reduction in bone strength caused by an enlarged remodeling space.[27] Thus, bone turnover, as assessed by biochemical markers, seems to have a significant impact on the risk of fracture independent of BMD. However, the exact use of biochemical markers in predicting absolute fracture risk alone or in combination with BMD and risk factor assessment has yet to be established.

Prediction of Bone Loss

Estrogen deficiency after menopause increases the rate of bone remodeling, which results in high turnover bone loss. This is reflected by a significant increase in the mean value of markers of resorption and formation from before to after menopause. Moreover, the individual variability in the bone turnover markers also increases after menopause, reflecting a variable skeletal response among different individuals to estrogen deficiency. This is also reflected in the variable rates of bone loss observed among women after menopause. Several studies now

indicate that, at least for groups of individuals, bone biochemical markers can be used to predict the rate of bone loss. Hansen et al.[30] measured the BMC of the forearm at baseline and 12 years later and attempted to predict the observed rate of bone loss by using a biochemical model that included fat mass, serum ALP activity, fasting urinary calcium to creatinine ratio, and fasting urinary hydroxyproline to creatinine ratio. Using these relatively crude bone turnover markers, they were able to predict the observed bone mass 12 years later with a high degree of accuracy. Thus, these and other data[31] suggest that

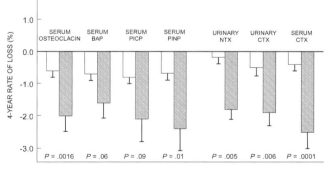

FIG. 4. Mid-radius BMD change over 4 years in 305 healthy postmenopausal women with low (open bars) and high (hatched bars) bone turnover at baseline. High turnover was defined as bone marker levels above the upper limit of the premenopausal range. P values refer to the difference in the rate of bone loss between the two groups of bone turnover. (Adapted from J Bone Miner Res **14:** 1614–1621 with permission from the American Society for Bone and Mineral Research.)[32]

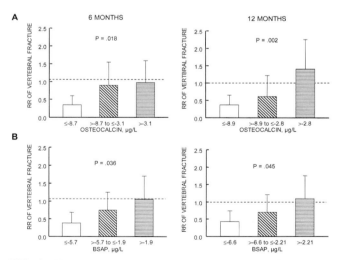

FIG. 6. The relative risk of new vertebral fractures (raloxifene vs. placebo) by tertiles of change in serum (A) OC and (B) BSALP after 6 and 12 months. The p values are for interaction and indicate the presence of a differential antifracture efficacy across tertiles for a model including tertile, therapy and tertile × therapy. (Adapted from Osteoporos Int, vol. 12, 2001, pp. 922–930, Six and twelve month changes in bone turnover are related to reduction in vertebral fracture risk during 3 years of raloxifene treatment in postmenopausal osteoporosis, Bjarnason NH, Sarkar S, Duong T, Mitlak B, Delmas PD, Christiansen C, Copyright 2001, with kind permission from Springer Science and Business Media.)[33]

bone turnover markers, either individually or in combination, may be able to predict rates of bone loss, thus complementing the static measurement of BMD. Recently, Garnero et al.[32] reported results of a 4-year prospective study of change in forearm BMD in early postmenopausal women as a function of bone turnover markers. Subjects were divided into those in whom the value for the marker being studied was within the reference interval for healthy premenopausal women (normal turnover group) or more than 2 SD above the mean value for premenopausal women (high turnover group). The study involved three markers of resorption and four formation markers. Women in the normal turnover group lost <1% of BMD over 4 years, whereas those in the high turnover group lost three to five times that amount of bone (Fig. 4).

Selection of Patients for Therapy

Several studies indicate that individuals with the highest levels of bone turnover seem to have the best response to antiresorptive therapy (i.e., with estrogen, calcitonin, or bisphosphonates). In a prospective 2-year study of hormone therapy (HT), Chesnut et al.[18] found that subjects in the highest quartiles for baseline urinary NTX excretion showed the greatest gain in BMD in response to HT (Fig. 5). In a study of postmenopausal women treated with 3 years of raloxifene, the changes in bone formation markers OC and BSALP were significant predictors of antifracture efficacy (Figs. 6A and 6B), whereas change in hip or spine BMD were not.[33] Changes in urinary CTX were also not predictors of antifracture effectiveness, and it remains to be seen whether this will change now that better assays for serum CTX, with less variability, are available.

Anabolic therapy data, however, seem to be different. It was previously postulated that patients with relatively lower bone turnover might respond better to teriparatide. However, recent posthoc analysis of the teriparatide data from the Fracture Prevention Study showed a strong positive correlation between baseline bone turnover markers; PINP, NTX, PICP, BSALP and DPD and subsequent increase in lumbar spine BMD at 18 months.[19] Thus, even patients with high rates of bone turnover at baseline seemed to have a robust BMD response to the drug.

Prediction of Bone Mass

Bone biochemical markers assess balance between resorption and formation, and although bone turnover markers are generally inversely correlated with BMD,[26] these correlations are not strong enough to have any value in terms of predicting bone mass for a given individual. Thus, these markers cannot and should not be used to diagnose osteoporosis or to predict bone mass; direct measurement of BMD is extremely effective at accomplishing this.

CONCLUSIONS

The availability of biochemical markers of bone formation and resorption that can be measured rapidly and relatively inexpensively represents a significant advance in the evaluation and treatment of patients at risk for or with osteoporosis. The markers provide a dynamic assessment of the skeleton that can potentially complement the static measurement of BMD. As with any new technology, however, one needs to understand their limitations and use them in the appropriate clinical setting. Table 2 summarizes the current and potential clinical use of these markers. Their use is likely to continue to increase with further clinical experience and technical refinements in the assays. This, in turn, has the potential for resulting in better selection of patients for therapy, tailoring specific therapies to

TABLE 2. Current and Potential Clinical Use of Biochemical Markers of Bone Remodeling

Clinical use	Quality of outcome
1. Monitor effectiveness of therapy	The most appropriate current use
2. Predict response to therapy	Potential use. Demonstrated in some studies
3. Monitor compliance and proper use of therapy	Potential use. Improper administration (such as intake with calcium supplements or food) of oral bisphosphonates can be detected
4. Select patients for therapy	Possibly useful, when used in conjunction with bone mass measurement, at segregating fast from slow losers. Without BMD, not until fracture prediction is better documented

different patients, and better monitoring of the effectiveness of therapy.

REFERENCES

1. Whyte MP 1994 Hypophosphatasia and the role of alkaline phosphatase in skeletal mineralization. Endocr Rev 15:439–461.
2. Deftos LJ, Wolfert RL, Hill CS, Burton DW 1992 Two-site assays of bone gla protein (osteocalcin) demonstrate immunochemical heterogeneity of the intact molecule. Clin Chem 38:2318–2321.
3. Booth SL, Broe KE, Peterson JW, Cheng DM, Dawson-Hughes B, Gundberg CM, Cupples LA, Wilson PW, Kiel DP 2004 Associations between vitamin K biochemical measures and bone mineral density in men and women. J Clin Endocrinol Metab 89:4904–4909.
4. Luukinen H, Kakonen SM, Pettersson K, Koski K, Laippala P, Lovgren T, Kivela SL, Vaananen HK 2000 Strong prediction of fractures among older adults by the ratio of carboxylated to total serum osteocalcin. J Bone Miner Res 15:2473–2478.
5. Calvo MS, Eyre DR, Gundberg CM 1996 Molecular basis and clinical application of biological markers of bone turnover. Endocr Rev 17:333–368.
6. Black D, Duncan A, Robins SP 1988 Quantitative analysis of the pyridinium crosslinks of collagen in urine using ion-paired reversed-phase high-performance liquid chromatography. Anal Biochem 169:197–203.
7. Garnero P, Shih WJ, Gineyts E, Karpf DB, Delmas PD 1994 Comparison of new biochemical markers of bone turnover in late postmenopausal osteoporotic women in response to alendronate treatment. J Clin Endocrinol Metab 79:1693–1700.
8. Tahtela R, Seppanen J, Laitinen K, Katajamaki A, Risteli J, Valimaki MJ 2005 Serum tartrate-resistant acid phosphatase 5b in monitoring bisphosphonate treatment with clodronate: A comparison with urinary N-terminal telopeptide of type I collagen and serum type I procollagen amino-terminal propeptide. Osteoporos Int 16:1109–1116.
9. Eastell R, Simmons PS, Colwell A, Assiri AM, Burritt MF, Russell RG, Riggs BL 1992 Nyctohemeral changes in bone turnover assessed by serum bone Gla-protein concentration and urinary deoxypyridinoline excretion: Effects of growth and ageing. Clin Sci 83:375–382.
10. Hassager C, Risteli J, Risteli L, Jensen SB, Christiansen C 1992 Diurnal variation in serum markers of type I collagen synthesis and degradation in healthy premenopausal women. J Bone Miner Res 7:1307–1311.
11. McKane WR, Khosla S, Egan KS, Robins SP, Burritt MF, Riggs BL 1996 Role of calcium intake in modulating age-related increases in parathyroid function and bone resorption. J Clin Endocrinol Metab 81:1699–1703.
12. Daniels ED, Pettifor JM, Moodley GP 2000 Serum osteocalcin has limited usefulness as a diagnostic marker for rickets. Eur J Pediatr 159:730–733.
13. Garnero P, Gineyts E, Arbault P, Christiansen C, Delmas PD 1995 Different effects of bisphosphonate and estrogen therapy on free and peptide-bound bone cross-links excretion. J Bone Miner Res 10:641–649.
14. Elder G 2002 Pathophysiology and recent advances in the management of renal osteodystrophy. J Bone Miner Res 17:2094–2105.
15. Gertz BJ, Shao P, Hanson DA, Quan H, Harris ST, Genant HK, Chesnut CH III, Eyre DR 1994 Monitoring bone resorption in early postmenopausal women by an immunoassay for cross-linked collagen peptides in urine. J Bone Miner Res 9:135–142.

16. Panteghini M, Pagani F 1995 Biological variation in bone-derived biochemical markers in serum. Scand J Clin Lab Invest **55**:609–616.
17. Prestwood KM, Pilbeam CC, Burleson JA, Woodiel FN, Delmas PD, Deftos LJ, Raisz LG 1994 The short-term effects of conjugated estrogen on bone turnover in older women. J Clin Endocrinol Metab **79**:366–371.
18. Chesnut CH III, Bell NH, Clark GS, Drinkwater BL, English SC, Johnson CC Jr, Notelovitz M, Rosen C, Cain DF, Flessland KA, Mallinak NJ 1997 Hormone replacement therapy in postmenopausal women: Urinary N-telopeptide of type I collagen monitors therapeutic effect and predicts response of bone mineral density. Am J Med **102**:29–37.
19. Chen P, Satterwhite JH, Licata AA, Lewiecki EM, Sipos AA, Misurski DM, Wagman RB 2005 Early changes in biochemical markers of bone formation predict BMD response to teriparatide in postmenopausal women with osteoporosis. J Bone Miner Res **20**:962–970.
20. Eastell R, Barton I, Hannon RA, Chines A, Garnero P, Delmas PD 2003 Relationship of early changes in bone resorption to the reduction in fracture risk with risedronate. J Bone Miner Res **18**:1051–1056.
21. Bauer DC, Black DM, Garnero P, Hochberg M, Ott S, Orloff J, Thompson DE, Ewing SK, Delmas PD 2004 Change in bone turnover and hip, non-spine, and vertebral fracture in alendronate-treated women: The fracture intervention trial. J Bone Miner Res **19**:1250–1258.
22. Reginster JY, Sarkar S, Zegels B, Henrotin Y, Bruyere O, Agnusdei D, Collette J 2004 Reduction in PINP, a marker of bone metabolism, with raloxifene treatment and its relationship with vertebral fracture risk. Bone **34**:344–351.
23. Sarkar S, Reginster JY, Crans GG, Diez-Perez A, Pinette KV, Delmas PD 2004 Relationship between changes in biochemical markers of bone turnover and BMD to predict vertebral fracture risk. J Bone Miner Res **19**:394–401.
24. Hochberg MC, Greenspan S, Wasnich RD, Miller P, Thompson DE, Ross PD 2002 Changes in bone density and turnover explain the reductions in incidence of nonvertebral fractures that occur during treatment with antiresorptive agents. J Clin Endocrinol Metab **87**:1586–1589.
25. Ettinger B, San Martin J, Crans G, Pavo I 2004 Differential effects of teriparatide on BMD after treatment with raloxifene or alendronate. J Bone Miner Res **19**:745–751.
26. Melton LJ III, Khosla S, Atkinson EJ, O'Fallon WM, Riggs BL 1997 Relationship of bone turnover to bone density and fractures. J Bone Miner Res **12**:1083–1091.
27. Riggs BL, Melton LJ III, O'Fallon WM 1996 Drug therapy for vertebral fractures in osteoporosis: Evidence that decreases in bone turnover and increases in bone mass both determine antifracture efficacy. Bone **18**(3 Suppl):197S–201S.
28. Garnero P, Hausherr E, Chapuy MC, Marcelli C, Grandjean H, Muller C, Cormier C, Breart G, Meunier PJ, Delmas PD 1996 Markers of bone resorption predict hip fracture in elderly women: The EPIDOS Prospective Study. J Bone Miner Res **11**:1531–1538.
29. Hansen MA, Overgaard K, Riis BJ, Christiansen C 1991 Role of peak bone mass and bone loss in postmenopausal osteoporosis: 12 year study. BMJ **303**:961–964.
30. Hansen MA, Overgaard K, Riis BJ, Christiansen C 1991 Role of peak bone mass and bone loss in postmenopausal osteoporosis: 12 year study. BMJ **303**:961–964.
31. Uebelhart D, Schlemmer A, Johansen JS, Gineyts E, Christiansen C, Delmas PD 1991 Effect of menopause and hormone replacement therapy on the urinary excretion of pyridinium cross-links. J Clin Endocrinol Metab **72**:367–373.
32. Garnero P, Sornay-Rendu E, Duboeuf F, Delmas PD 1999 Markers of bone turnover predict postmenopausal forearm bone loss over 4 years: The OFELY study. J Bone Miner Res **14**:1614–1621.
33. Bjarnason NH, Sarkar S, Duong T, Mitlak B, Delmas PD, Christiansen C 2001 Six and twelve month changes in bone turnover are related to reduction in vertebral fracture risk during 3 years of raloxifene treatment in postmenopausal osteoporosis. Osteoporos Int **12**:922–930.
34. Kleerekoper M 1996 Biochemical markers of bone remodeling. Am J Med Sci **312**:270–277.

Chapter 22.   Imaging in Children and Adults

Vicente Gilsanz

Childrens Hospital Los Angeles, Los Angeles, California

INTRODUCTION

The traditional evaluation of a patient includes a history and physical examination and a well-planned set of diagnostic tests, often including imaging. Imaging has changed dramatically in recent years. While conventional radiography continues to be the workhorse and the main diagnostic modality, advances in cross-sectional imaging and tissue characterization using computed tomography (CT), magnetic resonance imaging (MRI), and ultrasound (US) have provided accurate depictions of multiple structures other than bone, such as the cartilaginous epiphysis and physis, bone marrow, tendons, ligaments, and muscles.

The choice of modality to study a skeletal disorder is usually dictated by the clinical presentation and the availability of equipment. As a general rule, when confronted with reasonable alternatives, it is advisable to select the safest, the most comfortable, and the least expensive imaging examination first. Knowing which modality to choose is of paramount importance to ensure an accurate and timely diagnosis, with the least expense and detriment to the patient.[1] Currently, digital imaging is the most common way to obtain images, regardless of the modality used. The advantages of digital radiography include the ability to manipulate the images to enhance anatomical detail, to obtain quantitative data that may be useful to researchers, and to simultaneously display images at multiple locations, as well as to ease storage and retrieval. Images can also be made available in web browsers with secure techniques.[2,3]

Skeletal Radiography

Conventional radiographs represent basic and primary tools for the diagnosis of skeletal disorders and are commonly key in the diagnosis of many skeletal abnormalities. This is particularly important because the identification of a skeletal disease is often difficult by clinical and laboratory analysis alone. The radiologic diagnosis of many bone conditions, however, cannot be made solely based on recognizable radiographic patterns. Clinical data—the patient's age, sex, symptoms, history, and genetic and laboratory findings are also pertinent for the correct interpretation of radiographs.

Conventional radiographs distinguish differences in X-ray attenuation of four materials and tissues in the human body: air (no attenuation), fat (low attenuation), lean tissues and body fluids (intermediate attenuation), and bone (high attenuation). The mineral component of bone is easily depicted by radiography and allows information on bone production and destruction without the need for further contrast enhancement; a common requirement for other organ systems. This high resolution allows for outstanding depictions of trabecular and cortical bone detail. Moreover,

The author has reported no conflicts of interest.

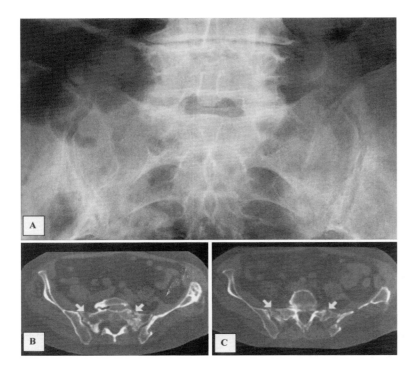

FIG. 1. A 75-year-old female with osteoporosis and bilateral insufficiency fractures of the sacrum and in the left ilium, (A) not recognized by conventional radiographs but (B and C) clearly depicted by CT [American College of Radiology. ACR Learning File® (Skeletal Edition)—1998. Reprinted with permission of the American College of Radiology. No other representation of this material is authorized without express, written permission from the American College of Radiology.]

when necessary, the resolution can be further enhanced using magnification techniques and film-screen combinations optimized for detail.[4] However, in comparison with CT and MRI, tissue contrast resolution in conventional radiographs is poor, and the various lean tissues cannot be differentiated. This limitation is especially noticeable when evaluating soft tissue lesions. Although conventional radiography is useful for assessing the effects of a soft tissue mass and for detecting calcification within soft tissue, other imaging techniques are needed when soft tissue imaging is required.

At least two views (anterioposterior and lateral) should be obtained, regardless of the location examined. The terms posterioanterior and anterioposterior refer to the direction of the X-ray beam from source to detector.[5] Each bone must be examined in its entirety, including the cortex, medullary canal, and articular ends. When disease is present, it is important to determine whether the process is limited to a single bone or multiple bones are involved. The presence and type of bone destruction (osteolytic) and bone production (osteoblastic), the appearance of the borders of the lesion, its size, shape, location, multiplicity, density, and the association of cortical expansion and periosteal reaction are characteristics that aid in the correct diagnosis.

Diagnoses may be conclusive in some instances; however, more frequently differential diagnoses are made because the exact condition cannot be determined. Many tumor-like lesions have distinct radiographic presentations that lead to unquestionable diagnoses on conventional studies and do not require biopsy confirmation. This is particularly true of a group of definitely benign lesions, which are commonly labeled "do not touch me lesions," such as bone islands, myositis ossificans, etc.[6] However, it is important to recognize the limits of noninvasive radiologic investigation in making the correct diagnosis and the need to know when to proceed with a bone biopsy.

Reaching the correct diagnosis is one of several ways radiologic investigations are used as outcomes. Frequently, the course of treatment often depends on the identification of distinguishing radiographic features for a particular disorder. For example, the diagnosis of Paget's disease, while important in the investigation, should be followed by the assessment of presence of malignant transformation. Similarly, localization and assessment of the extension and the sites for disease may be as important as the diagnosis itself; especially when studying the degree of metastatic bone disease.

Radiation exposure varies with location to be examined. While examination of the appendicular skeleton usually delivers a low radiation dose, studies of the axial skeleton, especially the lumbar spine, expose patients to higher radiation doses. Whenever possible, the gonads should not be exposed to X-rays, and stringent efforts should be taken to minimize radiation to children.

CT

Digital imaging started with CT in the 1970s, for the first time allowing the combination of true cross-sectional imaging and exquisite depiction of soft tissue density of <1% of the attenuation of water. When compared with routine skeletal radiography, the depiction of skeletal anatomy and the relationship of bones to contiguous structures by CT is superior; this is especially important in the evaluation of complex cross-sectional anatomy, which cannot be accurately assessed by projection techniques. Examples include insufficiency fractures not visible on plain radiographs (Fig. 1); sacroilitis, especially that of infectious origin; and articular collapse of the femoral head after osteonecrosis, indicating the need for joint replacement rather than a core procedure.[7] CT is also extremely useful in the evaluation of complex fractures and various bone and soft tissue tumors.[8] It allows for the accurate detection of small and displaced bony fragments after trauma. Because of its capability of providing a large cross-sectional field of view, CT is commonly used to provide guidance for biopsy or drainage procedures of bone or soft tissue lesions.

The spatial resolution of CT is, however, inferior to that of conventional radiography, but similar to that of MRI. Patient motion and metal instruments (prosthesis, rods,

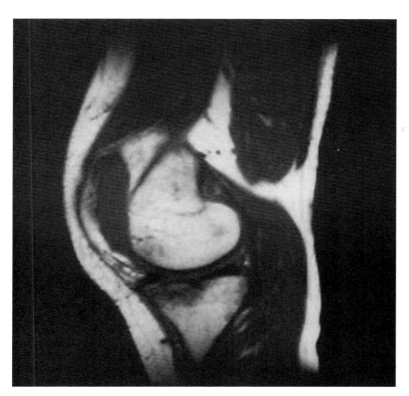

FIG. 2. Saggital MRI image of the knee depicting a bone bruise in the anteromedial tibia and joint effusion in an adolescent boy after trauma [American College of Radiology. ACR Learning File® (Skeletal Edition)—1998. Reprinted with permission of the American College of Radiology. No other representation of this material is authorized without express, written permission from the American College of Radiology.]

screws) produce significant artifacts, limiting the value of the examination. In contrast, CT shows soft tissue abnormalities (tissue contrast) better than does conventional radiography, but not as well as MRI. The radiation dose from CT is relatively high compared with plain radiographs. Although expensive, CT is less costly than MRI.

MRI

MRI brought huge advantages to musculoskeletal imaging because it provides images of soft tissue structures that are not visible by conventional radiography or CT.[9] MRI is based on the nuclear magnetic resonance phenomenon of atoms with an unpaired electron, principally hydrogen, that is ubiquitous within water molecules in biological tissues. It is a complex technique that involves changing the strength and timing of magnetic field gradients, as well as altering radiofrequency pulses and sampling the emitted energy.[10] By altering these factors appropriately, varying amounts of T1 and T2 weighting are imparted to the images to highlight different types of tissue and metabolic states. Altering these parameters can produce radically different images of the same anatomic site. This technology has the added advantage of displaying the anatomy in any plane.

Spatial resolution using the latest MRI equipment rivals that of CT, and contrast resolution in soft tissues is superior to that obtained by any other modality. In the skeleton, MRI is of great value in the evaluation of bone tumors, infection, and infarction. MRI is the study of choice for diagnosing osteonecrosis, which can mimic other causes of joint pain, especially in the hip. MRI can detect osteonecrosis early in the course of disease, when plain radiographs show no abnormalities. Because the image is dependent on the presence of hydrogen, it was initially thought that MRI would not be useful in the evaluation of bone. However, because of the abundance of hydrogen in the adjacent bone marrow, MRI is extremely sensitive to subtle bony abnormalities. Insufficiency fractures, although the cause of considerable pain, were extremely

difficult to diagnose before MRI.[11] Indeed, microfractures caused by trauma or stress, often referred to as bone bruises, essentially were unknown before MRI[12,13] (Fig. 2).

MRI is more expensive than most other imaging modalities, largely because of the cost of equipment and maintenance. This technique is free of the hazards of ionizing radiation and is presumed not to produce biologically harmful effects. The strong magnetic field can move metal objects such as surgically implanted vascular clips, cause pacemaker malfunction, and draw metal objects into the magnet.[14] Patients suffering from claustrophobia may not be able to tolerate the procedure.

Nuclear Medicine Imaging

Nuclear imaging is achieved by intravenously injecting radioactive isotopes, usually bound to an organic or biological molecular carrier. The carriers are designed to have an affinity for a particular tissue. In contradistinction to X-ray techniques, the body parts examined emit the radiation, rather than external radiation passing through the region examined. Cameras are designed to measure the amount of radiation emitted as a function of location and time.[10] These studies are similar in cost and radiation exposure to a CT scan.

Skeletal scintigraphy or bone scanning, a technique that detects the distribution of a radioactive agent in bone, is a valuable adjunct to standard radiography and has the advantage of offering an image of the entire skeleton at once. Scintigraphy after intravenous administration of agents such as 99m technetium methylene diphosphonate for bone scans, [99m]TC sulfur colloid for bone marrow scans, 67 gallium citrate, and leukocytes labeled with 111 indium are useful for evaluating a variety of skeletal disorders.[15,16] The ^{99m}Tc MDP triple-phase bone scan is the study most widely used for early detection of osteomyelitis. Images are obtained in the early vascular phase (during bolus injection of the radionuclide), intermediate blood-pool phase (5 minutes after injection), and late bone phase (3 hours after injection).

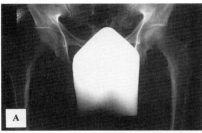
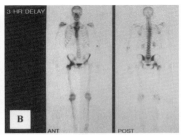
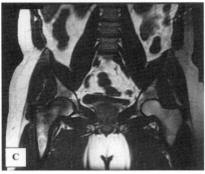

FIG. 3. (A) Conventional radiographs of the pelvis in a female patient with transient osteoporosis of the hip showing loss of cancellous bone in the right femoral neck. (B and C) Bone scans reveal increased radionuclide uptake and MR T1-weighted images depict increased signal in the femoral head and neck [American College of Radiology. ACR Learning File® (Skeletal Edition)—1998. Reprinted with permission of the American College of Radiology. No other representation of this material is authorized without express, written permission from the American College of Radiology.]

Bone-seeking radionuclides are taken up in areas of increased bone turnover and are quite sensitive for detecting many skeletal disorders.[17] While bone scanning can depict abnormalities that are not seen in plain radiography, this technique is nonspecific, and a number of different pathological processes may cause similar radionuclide accumulation. Hence, when areas of increased uptake are detected, additional studies such as MRI are frequently necessary to further define the type of abnormality (Fig. 3). Occasionally, depiction of the abnormality consists of decreased uptake of bone-seeking radiopharmaceuticals (for instance, in the early stages of osteonecrosis).[18] Bone scans are a reasonable alternative for early detection of osteonecrosis if MRI is not available.

The development of positron emission tomography (PET) yields extremely sensitive but not as specific images for evaluation of metastatic diseases.[19] PET using ^{18}F ion has been used to evaluate bone metabolic activity in patients with renal osteodystrophy and compared with histomorphometry. This technique can differentiate low turnover from high turnover lesions of renal osteodystrophy and provide quantitative estimates of bone cell activity that correlate with histomorphometric data.[20] Two limitations of this technology are its expense and the short half-life of the isotope, which requires proximity to a cyclotron where it is produced.

Ultrasonography

Ultrasound provides unique information by creating images based on the location of acoustic interfaces in tissue in any plane. This technology has no ionizing radiation, no contrast material to be administered, and no biologically harmful effects, and can be repeated as often as necessary. Moreover, the equipment is portable and relatively inexpensive. Spatial resolution is similar to CT and MRI, but the resolution depends on the transducer and is limited by the depth of tissue being studied; resolution is much higher for superficial structures. Unfortunately, ultrasonography is heavily operator-dependent, and it is not always possible for one investigator to reproduce or interpret the results of another. Moreover, although ultrasound has made an enormous impact in radiology, it is only rarely used in skeletal imaging.[21] Applications of ultrasound in orthopedics include evaluation of tendon injuries and soft tissue masses. Musculoskeletal ultrasonography is, how-

ever, very useful in pediatrics to examine (1) the extremities and spine of the fetus (Fig. 4); (2) developmental dysplasia of the hip; (3) joint effusions; (4) occult neonatal spinal dysraphism; (5) foreign bodies in soft tissues; and (6) popliteal cysts of the knee.[22]

Ultrasound has shown promise in evaluating osteoporosis. Sound transmission through bone provides some information about the microtrabecular structure, which relates to bone strength but cannot be assessed directly with radiographic techniques.[23] This information may prove to be complementary to information provided by BMD studies in evaluating a patient's fracture risk. Ultrasound also has been used to assess the surface properties of cartilage.[24]

SKELETAL DEVELOPMENT AND MATURITY

The axial skeleton consists primarily of the vertebrae, the ribs, and the sternum. The vertebrae are comprised of two main parts: vertebral bodies, composed primarily of cancellous bone, and the posterior elements (the pedicle, the transverse and articular processes, the lamina and the spinous process), which mainly constitute cortical bone. During growth, the circumference and the height of individual vertebral bodies enlarge by periosteal apposition and by endochondral ossification, respectively. The function of the cartilage in the end plates of the vertebrae is similar to that in any other growth plate.

The appendicular skeleton consists of long and short tubular bones, round bones in the wrists and ankles, and sesamoids, which are small bones found in muscles, tendons, and articular capsules. Tubular bones are comprised of three main parts: the diaphysis, the epiphysis, and the metaphysis, and an additional segment, the physis, or physeal plate, becomes apparent during adolescence, before skeletal maturity. Physeal plates are present at one end of tubular bones and at both ends of long bones and, during growth, the plates influence changes in the size and shape of the bone in response to mechanical stimulation. In contrast to epiphyses, which are bound by the physis and a joint, apophyses are outgrowths of bone that are also bound by a physis but are not in contact with the joint. The long bones are tubular structures that are loaded mainly in bending. The resistance of long bones to bending (i.e., bone strength) is represented by the cross-sectional

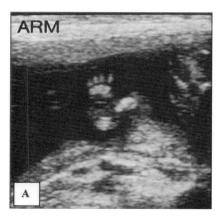
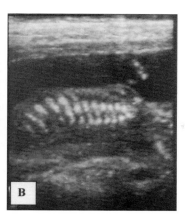
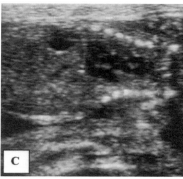

FIG. 4. (A) Second trimester ultrasound study showing markedly shortened, angulated and deformed upper extremity caused by multiple fractures in a fetus with type II osteogenesis imperfecta. (B) Parasaggital and (C) coronal scans of the thorax also showing multiple rib fractures and concavity of the chest [American College of Radiology. ACR Learning File® (Skeletal Edition)—1998. Reprinted with permission of the American College of Radiology. No other representation of this material is authorized without express, written permission from the American College of Radiology.]

moment of inertia (CSMI) $= \pi/4(R_p{}^4 - R_e{}^4)$; R_p and R_e indicate the periosteal radius and endosteal radius, respectively.

During the first two decades of life, the skeleton matures, and marked changes in size and structure occur. Cartilaginous tissues slowly grow and ossify, providing support and locomotion to our bodies, and the bone marrow, initially hematopoietic, is mostly transformed into fatty marrow. Using state-of-the-art imaging, the normal and abnormal aspects of these changes can be depicted accurately and noninvasively.

A series of recent CT and MRI studies clarified the distinction between increases in bone size and increases in volumetric BMD in the growing axial and appendicular skeletons, as well as the nature of ethnic and sex differences in bone geometry and BMD (Table 1). Trabecular BMD, as measured by QCT, does not increase before puberty,[25,26] but increases significantly during puberty, mainly because of thickening of the trabeculae.[27] The pubertal increases in BMD are comparable in girls and boys, but are significantly greater in black compared with white adolescents.[25,26,28]

Studies of cortical BMD and dimensions in the appendicular skeleton have produced conflicting results, potentially because of differences between the upper and lower extremities and differences in measurement techniques. Most studies reported significant increases in cortical BMD with age (reviewed by Hogler et al.[29]). A pQCT study reported greater cortical BMD in the radius in pubertal females compared with males,[30] whereas an MRI study did not detect sex differences.[29] An early study of cortical dimensions, based on 2-D radiogrammetry, concluded that the greater cortical bone mass in males was caused by sex differences in the rate of endosteal apposition and resorption.[31] Garn et al.[31] concluded that endosteal apposition began earlier and was in greater magnitude in girls than in boys as a result of the pubertal estrogen surge. The authors postulated that endosteal bone loss in menopause was a result of diminished estrogen levels and that endocortical bone had been accrued during puberty for that even-

tuality. Subsequent pQCT studies in the upper extremities also suggested sex differences in the endocortical surface, with constant dimensions with age in females, and increasing dimensions with age in males.[32] Furthermore, the timing of menarche in females is associated with radial endosteal dimensions in adulthood.[33] In contrast, studies in the weight-bearing femur[28,29] and tibia[34] failed to show sex differences in endocortical resorption.

Skeletal maturity is a measure of development incorporating the size, shape, and degree of mineralization of bone to define its proximity to full maturity. A single reading of skeletal age informs the clinician of the relative maturity of a patient at a particular time in his or her life, and, integrated with other clinical findings, separates the normal from the relatively advanced or retarded. Successive skeletal age readings indicate the direction of the child's development and/or show his or her progress under treatment. In normal subjects, bone age should be roughly within 10% of the chronological age. Greater discordance between skeletal age and chronological age occurs in children who are obese or who start puberty early, because their skeletal age is accelerated. There are two main applications for evaluations of skeletal maturation: the diagnosis of growth disorders and the prediction of final adult height.[35]

Osteoporosis

Bone is a composite material of approximately one-third organic (mostly collagen) and two-thirds inorganic components. The inorganic component consists of crystals of basic carbonate that contain a form of calcium phosphate called hydroxyapatite.[36] The mineral fraction possesses a higher attenuation coefficient, accounting for the depiction of bone on radiographs. To radiologists, the term "osteopenia" is a generic expression referring to a qualitative paucity of bone; it contributes no information about the etiology or pathogenesis of the condition that leads to this effect or about the status of bone matrix mineralization. In contrast to other

TABLE 1. CAUSES OF OSTEOPOROSIS

Disorders of multiple or uncertain etiology
    Involutional osteoporosis (postmenopausal and senile)
    Idiopathic male osteoporosis
    Juvenile osteoporosis
Secondary bone disorders
    Endocrine
        Cushing's disease
        Hypogonadism
        Pituitary
        Hypopituitarism
        Hyperthyroidism
        Hyperparathyroidism
    Marrow replacement and expansion
        Myeloma
        Leukemia
        Lymphoma
        Metastatic disease
        Gaucher's disease
        Anemias (sickle cell disease, thalassemia, hemophilia)
    Drugs and substances
        Steroids
        Heparin (osteoporosis)
        Anticonvulsants (osteomalacia)
        Immunosuppressants
        Alcohol
    Chronic disease
        Chronic renal disease
        Hepatic insufficiency
        Gastrointestinal malabsorption syndromes
        Chronic inflammatory polyarthropathies
        Chronic debility/immobilization
    Deficiency states
        Vitamin D (rickets/osteomalacia)
        Vitamin C (scurvy)

medical specialties, osteopenia, as referred to by the World Health Organization, refers to a loss of bone >1 but <2.5 SD below the mean reference values for the young adult population.[37]

A diminished mineral content (osteopenia) can result from many different conditions (Table 1). It is, however, generally the result of one of three major types of disorders: osteoporosis, rickets, or congenital/developmental diseases. Osteoporosis, a condition in which there is a parallel loss of bone mineral and matrix, is the most common cause, whereas rickets, a pathological loss of mineralized bone caused by a reduction in calcium-phosphate levels with resultant accumulation of nonmineralized matrix (osteoid), is less common. Last, defects in bone formation associated with congenital or developmental diseases, such as osteogenesis imperfecta (OI; Fig. 5), homocystinuria, galactosemia, or various chondrodysplasias, may lower BMC.[38] Through recent gains in our understanding of the molecular basis for these conditions, we are finding that many of these disorders are caused by mutations in collagen or fibroblast growth factor (FGF) receptors.

Senile osteoporosis, the result of bone mass decreasing with age, is the most common skeletal disorder in the world and is second only to arthritis as a leading cause of musculoskeletal morbidity in the elderly. Osteoporosis affects 20 million Americans and leads to ~1.3 million fractures in the United States each year; most notably of the vertebral body and proximal femur. Fractures of the hip are the most devastating of osteoporotic fractures. There are ~300,000 hip fractures each year in the United States in persons over the age of 65. During the course of their lifetime, approximately one third of all white women and one

sixth of all men will have a hip fracture. Fractures of the distal forearm (Colles' fractures) are also extremely common in women, but less frequent in men; the incidence in women rises sharply within 5–10 years of menopause (Fig. 6).[37]

The amount of bone that must be lost before osteopenia is radiographically detectable varies in different bones and in different parts of the same bone, depending on the structural composition of the region involved and on the diagnostic technique used. At all ages, however, conventional radiography allows for a rather limited evaluation of bone mineral in the skeleton, because bone mass may have already decreased 30–40% by the time osteoporosis is appreciated.[37] Therefore, more sensitive, noninvasive densitometric screening techniques are increasingly being used for early detection of osteopenia. Skeletal radiographs do, however, help to exclude obvious causes of back pain that are not related to osteopenia, especially in the elderly. They also aid in determining the pattern and extent of osteopenia (either focal or generalized) and in identifying the sites of compression fractures. Frequently, the detection of osteopenia on a plain radiograph directs the physician to investigate an underlying condition, particularly in a young or middle-aged patient. Because the various causes of osteopenia cannot be established by radiography alone, other tests are usually required for a definitive diagnosis.

Several quantitative assessments of skeletal morphometry have been described. Most evaluated the adult skeleton with grading systems relying on the appearance of the trabecular pattern in the vertebrae and the femur (Singh Index),[39,40] and of the cortical bone in the proximal femur. These techniques are, nevertheless, highly subjective, and have fallen into disuse with the possible exception of metacarpal radiogrammetry.

Osteoporosis usually manifests in the axial skeleton first, especially in the vertebral bodies, which contain a high proportion of metabolically active, high-turnover trabecular bone. The horizon-

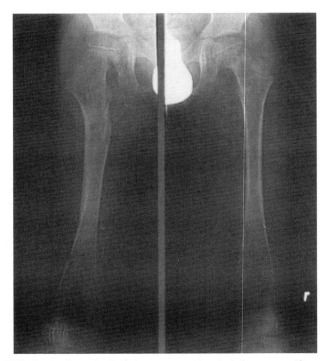

FIG. 5. Radiograph of the lower extremities depicting nonspecific osteoporosis in a child with osteogenesis imperfecta [American College of Radiology. ACR Learning File® (Skeletal Edition)—1998. Reprinted with permission of the American College of Radiology. No other representation of this material is authorized without express, written permission from the American College of Radiology.]

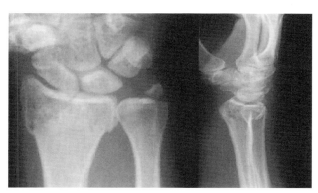

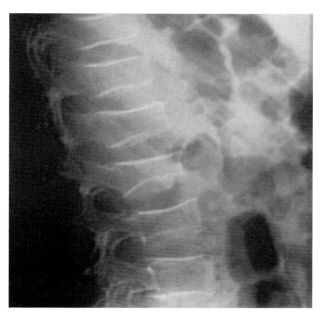

FIG. 6. Radiograph of the wrist and forearm of a 52-year-old female with Colles' fracture secondary to a fall on an outstretched hand. There is also an associated ulnar styloid fracture [American College of Radiology. ACR Learning File® (Skeletal Edition)—1998. Reprinted with permission of the American College of Radiology. No other representation of this material is authorized without express, written permission from the American College of Radiology.]

tal trabeculae are reabsorbed first, leading to an early accentuation of the vertical trabeculae. In more severe cases, thinning and loss of bone density give the vertebral column a washed-out appearance, followed by a collapse of the vertebral body (Fig. 7).

Lateral radiographs of the thoracic and lumbar spine should be obtained in any patient with a suspected compression fracture. A pathological compression fracture in a young or middle-aged patient or a fracture of the upper thoracic vertebra (T_5) in a patient of any age necessitates a thorough investigation to identify less common causes of osteopenia. The diagnosis of fractures in the appendicular skeleton is comparably simple, because cortical bone has eight times the density of cancellous bone and is easily recognized. In addition, cortical bone breaks are associated with pain, in contrast to vertebral fractures, which are commonly asymptomatic.

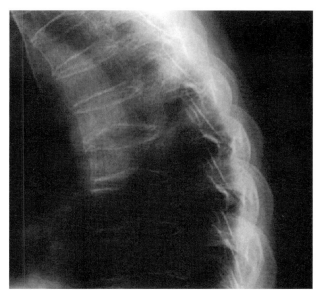

FIG. 7. Lateral radiograph of the spine in a postmenopausal woman showing loss of BMD mostly caused by resorption of the horizontal trabeculae and multiple compression fractures [American College of Radiology. ACR Learning File® (Skeletal Edition)—1998. Reprinted with permission of the American College of Radiology. No other representation of this material is authorized without express, written permission from the American College of Radiology.]

FIG. 8. Lateral spine radiograph of a 12-year-old with acute lymphoblastic leukemia and multiple thoracic and lumbar vertebral compression fractures.

In an effort to provide reproducible and objective methods to detect vertebral fractures, various quantitative morphometric approaches have recently been described, mainly intending to serve the assessment of fragility fractures in the adult population. The application and interpretation of these measures, however, have been complicated by the large differences observed from one technique to the next and by the lack of clear measures for defining fractures. Because there are no generally accepted guidelines to diagnose vertebral fractures, a common criteria for their identification is as follows: wedge fractures are identified by a reduction in anterior height compared with posterior height, central collapse fractures by a loss of height in the midportion of the vertebral body compared with either the anterior or posterior height, and crush fractures by a reduction in both the anterior and posterior height when compared with the closest adjacent intact vertebrae. On average, a reduction of 20–25% has also been proposed for the definition of an incident fracture.[41]

Vertebral fractures are far more common in the elderly than in the young. When occurring in children, vertebral fractures are usually the consequence of high impact trauma, leukemia, glucocorticosteroid excess, or OI (Fig. 8). In contrast to vertebral body fractures in the elderly, fractures in children (especially younger than 10 years of age) reconstitute completely with the process of continuous longitudinal growth; in older individuals, vertebral body fractures heal without regaining their original height. Regardless of age, a single vertebral compression fracture with no other radiographic signs of osteoporosis should encourage a search for other conditions, such as metastatic disease in the elderly or eosinophilic granuloma in the young.

Idiopathic juvenile osteoporosis (IJO) is a term reserved for acute osteoporosis with onset in the prepubertal or pubertal age. The initial complaint is pain in the extremities and difficulty walking, followed by multiple fractures of the spine and lower extremities. Radiologically, a severe generalized decrease in bone density is noted. Diagnosis of IJO is based on clinical radiographic studies and exclusion of other causes of osteoporosis, other diseases in bones, and renal, metabolic, and endocrine disorders (Fig. 9). Usually, the disease remits spontaneously after the onset of

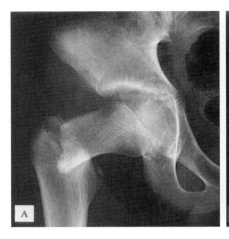 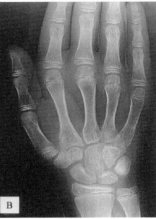

FIG. 9. Idiopathic juvenile osteoporosis in a 9-year-old boy with (A) a femoral neck fracture and (B) cortical thinning in the long bones of the left hand. This diagnosis should only be made after other conditions causing osteoporosis are excluded [American College of Radiology. ACR Learning File® (Skeletal Edition)—1998. Reprinted with permission of the American College of Radiology. No other representation of this material is authorized without express, written permission from the American College of Radiology.]

puberty. Milder forms of IJO may remain undiagnosed, because of the self-limited course and the similarities of pain associated with a variety of rheumatic disorders.

Transient osteoporosis of the hip is an uncommon condition characterized by pain and functional limitation, which may be related to the more general syndrome of regional migratory osteoporosis. Conventional radiographs may depict osteopenia with preservation of the articular space, while bone scans show increased uptake and MRI provides evidence of transitory edema. Clinical and radiographical features often overlap with trauma, reflex sympathetic dystrophy, transient bone marrow edema syndrome and avascular osteonecrosis.[42]

OI

OI causes a generalized decrease in bone mass (osteopenia) and makes the bone brittle. The disorder is frequently associated with blue sclerae, dental abnormalities (dentinogenesis imperfecta), progressive hearing loss, and a positive family history. The most common classification for OI includes four main types. The two principal forms are types I and IV, formerly known as OI tarda, and types II and III, formerly known as OI congenita. The inheritance is variable from type to type; some are autosomal dominant, others are recessive. Most patients with OI have mutations in one of the two genes that encode type I procollagen.[43]

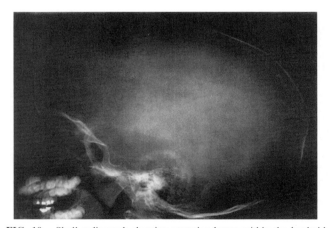

FIG. 10. Skull radiograph showing wormian bones within the lamboid structures of a child with osteogenesis imperfecta [American College of Radiology. ACR Learning File® (Skeletal Edition)—1998. Reprinted with permission of the American College of Radiology. No other representation of this material is authorized without express, written permission from the American College of Radiology.]

The bisphosphonate pamidronate has been reported to have a beneficial effect in children and adolescents with severe OI.[44]

In the congenital form, the disorder develops in utero and is usually diagnosed by US because of the angular deformities and multiple fractures in the long bones. It is the most common diagnosis of short, bent limbs in the second trimester (Fig. 4).[45] The tarda form of the disease is first noted during childhood because of the unusual tendency for fractures. The patients tend to have bluish sclera, laxity of the joints, deafness caused by otosclerosis, and discolored, fragile teeth. Radiographically, the long bones appear thin and gracile, with marked decrease of the cortical width and lack of trabeculae in the metaphyseal regions; the epiphyses are normal (Fig. 5). There is often extensive deformity owing to multiple fractures. Not uncommonly, fractures heal with exuberant callus.[46] In the skull, radiographic manifestions include multiple wormian bones, whereas in the spine, osteoporosis and multiple compression fractures are frequent (Fig. 10). Osteoporosis and secondary protrusio acetabuli are usual manifestations in the pelvis.[47,48]

Osteomalacia and Rickets

Osteomalacia is characterized by defective mineralization of osteoid in mature bone, whereas rickets is the term generally applied to a group of disorders that cause similar histological and radiological changes in the growing skeleton. Many disorders can alter the complex process involved in the mineralization of cartilage and bone, most resulting from a relative or absolute insufficient supply of vitamin D or its metabolites (Table 2).

Rickets is the most common metabolic bone disease in childhood. Regardless of the cause, the various types of rickets are associated histologically with osteomalacia and share common

TABLE 2. CAUSES OF IMPAIRED VITAMIN D ACTION

Vitamin D deficiency	Impaired 1 a-hydroxylation
Impaired cutaneous production	Hypoparathyroidism
Dietary absence	Renal failure
Malabsorption	Ketoconazole
Accelerated loss of vitamin D	1 α-hydroxylase mutation
Increased metabolism (barbiturates, phenytoin, rifampin)	Oncogenic osteomalacia
Impaired enterohepatic circulation	X-linked hypophosphatemic rickets
Impaired 25-hydroxylation	Target organ resistance
Liver disease	Vitamin D receptor mutation
Isoniazid	Phenytoin

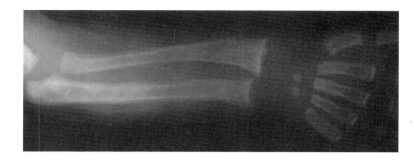

FIG. 11. Severe rickets in a 12-month-old girl with hepatic failure. Capping, widening, and irregularity of the distal metaphysis and prominent cortical thinning are present.

radiographic patterns and findings. The diagnosis of rickets may initially be made by a radiologist, but occasionally, the radiographic findings are absent or inconclusive while histological and biochemical changes are evident. The earliest radiographic manifestations are more prominent at the metaphyseal ends of fast growing tubular bones, such as the distal femur, proximal tibia, and distal ulna and radius; hence, the reason for requesting knee and wrist radiographs to evaluate this disorder. The principal radiographic feature is the indistinct demarcation of the zone of provisional calcification, which normally is depicted as a radiopaque fine line. In rickets, the sharply defined provisional zone of calcification fades out with the adjacent epiphyseal cartilage. Thereafter, the physis becomes thicker because of the accumulation of nonmineralized osteoid and cartilage, and the metaphysis becomes irregular, widened, and concave (Fig. 11). If not corrected, alterations are also seen in the diaphysis. The deficiency in mineral content at the shaft is manifested by thin cortices with coarse textures.

Quite often, bowing and deformities of the weakened bones are observed, most commonly manifesting in the lower limbs as knock-knees and bowlegs (genu varus and genu valgus; Fig. 12).[49] In advanced cases, insufficiency fractures may occur, which are usually bilateral and depicted as linear cortical lucencies. Occasionally, patients may present with florid pathological fractures, commonly through the femoral growth plate (slippage of the femoral head; Fig. 13). Healing and restoration of normal bone (the rule in dietary deficiency rickets) may be followed by sclerosis of the spongiosa for many years.

Rickets is occasionally suggested from chest radiographs by frayed, widened anterior rib ends (rachitic rosary), proximal humeral metaphyseal changes, and irregular concavity of the inferior scapular angle (Fig. 14). In skull radiographs, demineralization and, in the presence of concomitant secondary hyperparathyroidism, loss of the lamina dura around erupted and unerupted teeth, may be seen. Evidence of severe hyperparathyroidism, however, usually suggests renal osteodystrophy.

In contrast to rickets, the radiographic diagnosis of osteomalacia is difficult. In cancellous bone, the total number of trabeculae

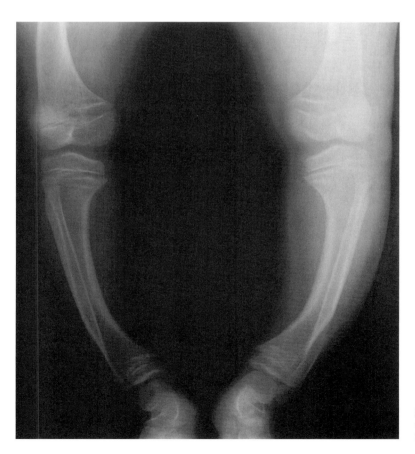

FIG. 12. Radiograph depicting bowlegs (genu varus) in a child with rickets. There is widening and irregularity of the metaphysis.

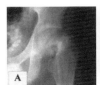
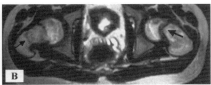

FIG. 13. (A) Left hip radiograph and (B) CT image showing slippage of the left femoral head (thick arrow) in a 14-year-old boy with rickets. An insufficiency fracture (Looser's zone) is also seen in the left femoral neck (thin arrow).

is decreased, but the remaining trabeculae remain prominent and project a "coarsened" radiographic pattern. Looser's zones, or pseudofractures, may precede other radiographic changes. These lucent areas are commonly perpendicular to the cortex, incompletely span the diameter of the bone, and are typically bilateral and symmetric. They tend to occur at the scapula, ribs, superior and inferior pubic rami, and at the proximal ends of the femora. Sclerosis and new bone often demarcate the intraosseous margins of pseudofractures. True fractures can occur through these weakened areas.

Looser's zones are considered to be a form of the insufficiency type of stress fracture, but, in contrast to fatigue type stress fractures, pseudofractures do not necessarily involve weight-bearing bones. In addition, Looser's zones appear without a preceding traumatic event as broad radiolucent bands perpendicular to the cortical surface and are usually associated with no callus. Radiolucent areas similar to pseudofractures may be found in bones affected by Paget's disease and fibrous dysplasia. The radiolucent zones in these diseases, however, are confined to the affected bone and, unlike pseudofractures, are not generalized.

Primary Hyperparathyroidism

Primary hyperparathyroidism (HPT) is caused by excessive production of PTH, usually because of either hyperplasia or adenoma of the parathyroid gland. Currently, the diagnosis of HPT is based on the incidental finding of a high blood calcium measurement, and most patients are asymptomatic at presentation. Today, imaging is mainly performed to localize parathyroid tumors and abnormal glands before surgery. US, CT, MRI, radionuclide scintigraphy and angiography, and venous sampling are all techniques that have been used to localize the adrenal gland. Parathyroid exploration is challenging and should only be undertaken by an experienced surgeon. In an increasing number of medical centers, a minimally invasive surgical approach using cervical block anesthesia, and guided by improved preoperative localization and intraoperative monitoring by PTH assays, is being performed on an outpatient basis. Preoperative ^{99m}Tc sestamibi scans with

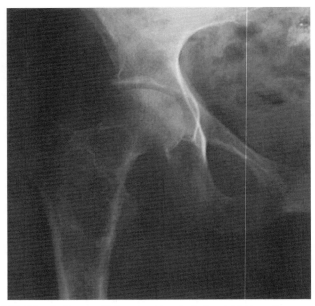

FIG. 15. A 63-year-old female with pain in the right hip and a nonaggressive cystic lesion in the intertrochanteric region, which turned out to be a brown tumor. Brown tumors are collections of osteoclasts, which typically have a nonaggressive appearance in a patient with primary or secondary HPT [American College of Radiology. ACR Learning File® (Skeletal Edition)—1998. Reprinted with permission of the American College of Radiology. No other representation of this material is authorized without express, written permission from the American College of Radiology.]

positron emission CT are used to predict the location of an abnormal gland, and intraoperative sampling of PTH before and at 5-minute intervals after removal of a suspected adenoma to confirm a rapid fall (>50%) to normal levels of PTH are obtained.

Detection of this osteopenia by noninvasive bone mineral measurements is important for early diagnosis because very few patients show the diagnostic radiographic features of HPT on clinical presentation. At very high levels, increased PTH production results in what is termed osteitis fibrosa cystica, which is radiographically depicted by bone resorption and eventually by marrow

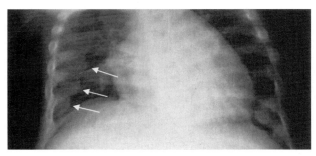

FIG. 14. AP chest radiograph depicting marked capping and widening of the anterior sternal ends of the ribs (arrows) giving the appearance commonly referred to as a rachitic rosary of a 9-month-old child with severe rickets.

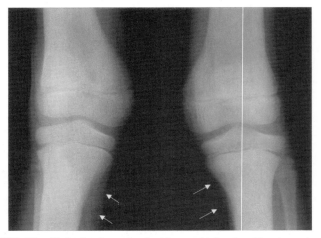

FIG. 16. Skeletal radiograph of a 10-year-old female with primary hyperparathyroidism shows changes of subperiosteal reabsorption (arrows) in the medial cortex of the proximal metaphysis of the tibia and osteosclerosis of the long bones, secondary to a parathyroid adenoma. Skeletal radiographs were normal 3 months after parathyroidectomy.

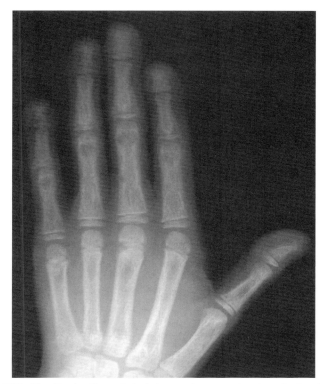

FIG. 17. Hand radiograph depicting patchy osteosclerosis and subperiosteal cortical resorption, most prominent in the middle phalanges and tufts of the distal phalanges in a 12-year-old boy with chronic renal disease. In the thumb, the cortical resorption is more prominent in the radial sides because of the strains associated with thumb apposition.

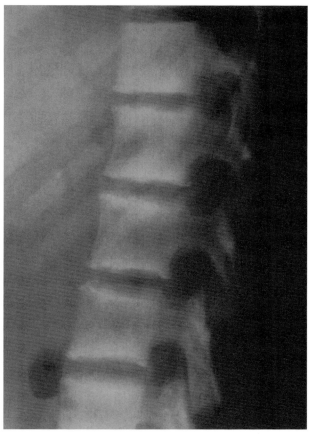

FIG. 18. Lateral spine radiograph of a 16-year-old male with chronic renal failure depicting sclerosis of the vertebral end plates and an appearance suggesting a "rugger jersey" spine.

fibrosis and cystic reparative bone lesions termed "brown tumors." Bone resorption is believed to result primarily from osteoclastic stimulation at many different sites: intracortical, endosteal, subchondral, subligamentous, and trabecular. Subperiosteal bone resorption, which is most characteristic of HPT, is seen in <10% of patients, most commonly along the radial aspect of the middle phalanges of the second and third digits. Other sites commonly affected include the phalangeal tufts and the medial metaphyses of the proximal humerus, femur, and tibia.

Cortical striations and intracortical tunneling caused by osteoclastic osteolysis may be seen in more than one half of patients. These findings are best detected in the tubular bones of the hands by using magnification techniques. Erosions involving the sacroiliac joints, the symphysis pubis, and the distal ends of the clavicle and the calcaneous may be attributed in part to subchondral resorption of ligamentous insertions at these sites. The skull may occasionally have a characteristic "pepperpot" pattern resulting from trabecular resorption and remodeling of the diploic space. In the majority of patients, the combined effect of all these patterns of bone resorption is osteopenia. Rarely, patients with primary HPT have diffuse osteosclerosis. The reason for this is not clear but may be because of the fact that, in addition to stimulating osteoclastic activity, PTH also stimulates osteoblastic activity.

Brown tumors (osteoclastomas) represent focal, bone-replacing lesions that occur most often in the metaphyses and diaphyses and tend to heal after treatment (Fig. 15). They contain collections of giant cells that are unusually responsive to PTH and may be solitary lesions or may involve multiple bones. Chondrocalcinosis (deposition of calcium pyrophosphate dihydrate crystals) occurs in 10–20% of patients with primary HPT, most frequently in the hyaline articular and fibrocartilage of the knee, symphysis pubis,

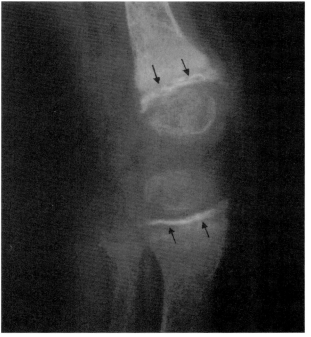

FIG. 19. Lateral knee radiograph of an 18-month-old boy with scurvy showing a transverse submetaphyseal lucent band in the distal femoral and proximal tibial metaphysis, commonly referred to as "scurvy lines" (arrows). There is also severe osteoporosis and marked cortical thinning.

© 2006 American Society for Bone and Mineral Research

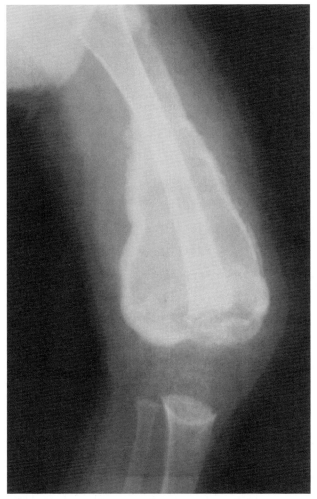

FIG. 20. Radiograph of the lower extremity of a 6-month-old infant with severe scurvy, fractures, and extensive calcified subperiosteal hematoma.

and triangular cartilage of the wrist. In contrast to adults, primary HPT is extremely rare in children, is usually characterized by severe bone disease, and is almost invariably caused by a parathyroid adenoma (Fig. 16).[50]

Renal Osteodystrophy

The term renal osteodystrophy refers to the metabolic bone abnormalities associated to chronic renal insufficiency. Radiographic findings include osteopenia and osteoporosis, patchy and generalized osteosclerosis, rickets, and secondary HPT. The pathognomonic finding of secondary HPT is also subperiosteal bone resorption. In children, subperiosteal resorption of cortical bone is most frequently seen in the femoral necks and proximal tibias, whereas in older children and adults, it is most commonly detected along the radial aspects of the middle and proximal phalanges of the second and third digits (Fig. 17). These sites are affected because of tendinous insertions and pulling during apposition of the second and third digits toward the thumb.[49,51] Osteosclerosis is commonly observed in the spine along the vertebral margins, giving the characteristic appearance of the "rugger jersey" spine (Fig. 18). There may also be epiphyseal separation, particularly involving the femoral head. Soft tissue calcifications occasionally develop in patients with secondary HPT; they may be subcutaneous, periarticular, visceral, or vascular.

Scurvy and Copper Deficiency

Ascorbic acid (vitamin C) and ascorbic acid oxydase, a copper-dependent enzyme, are needed for the synthesis of normal collagen, and their deficiency manifests with similar radiographic and clinical features. Scurvy, which, as a consequence of improved nutrition, is now extremely rare, occurs in children >6 months of age and is depicted radiographically by severe osteoporosis. Characteristically, there is atrophy of trabeculae just beneath a well-preserved zone of provisional calcification, leading to a lucent band, the "scurvy line" (Fig. 19). Pathological fractures through the metaphysis and extensive subperiosteal bleeding, frequently in the tibia, femur, and humerus, are also typical manifestations (Fig. 20).[49]

Copper deficiency is either the consequence of nutritional deficiency in premature infants, or of abnormal intestinal transport of copper, such as in Menkes disease (kinky hair syndrome). The skeletal radiographic findings are similar to those of scurvy (osteoporosis, prominent zones of provisional calcification, metaphyseal spurs), but the lucent band under the zone of provisional calcification is usually not present in copper deficiency. Copper deficiency and scurvy can mimic the metaphyseal fractures of battered child syndrome; however, the absence of severe osteoporosis aids in their differentiation.[49]

Hypothyroidism and Hyperthyroidism

Hypothyroidism in the newborn (cretinism) is usually detected by neonatal screening and is commonly caused by congenital absence or hypoplasia (often with ectopia) of the thyroid gland. The most striking clinical features include retarded growth, persistence of infantile proportions, lethargy, constipation, umbilical hernia, and macroglossia. Retarded skeletal maturation, usually >2 SD below the mean, is the main radiographic characteristic. In addition to the delayed appearance of the ossification centers, radiographs in hypothyroid children frequently depict fragmenta-

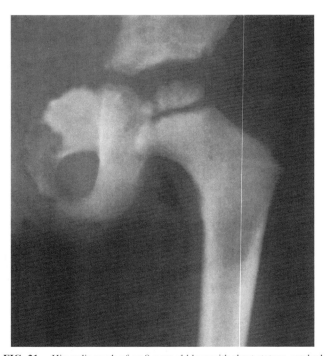

FIG. 21. Hip radiograph of an 8-year-old boy with short stature, marked delay in skeletal maturation, and hypothyroidism. There is epiphyseal dysgenesis (delayed maturation, irregularity, and fragmentation) of the femoral head.

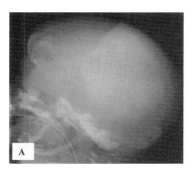
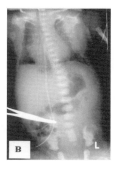

FIG. 22. (A) Radiographs of a newborn with perinatal (lethal) hypophosphatasia with a large anterior fontanel, large cranial sutures, and poor ossification of the membranous portion of the skull. (B) The vertebral bodies are dense, round, and flattened, while (C) the ribs and long bones are short and slender. There is metaphyseal capping and irregularity of the distal humerus, and the radius is extremely thin with minimal ossification.

tion and irregularity of the epiphysis. The ossification centers of the femoral epiphysis, instead of developing from a single focus and following uniform growth in all directions, develop from numerous small foci of ossification, which grow and coalesce to form an ossification of uneven density and irregular margins. This irregularity and fragmentation of the epiphysis is termed epiphyseal dysgenesis (Fig. 21). Skull radiographs usually show delayed closure of cranial structures and an increased number of wormian bones.[49]

Hyperthyroidism is uncommon in children. Its radiographic manifestations include accelerated skeletal maturation, premature sutural closure, osteopenia (hyperthyroid osteopathy), and thymomegaly. Early calcification of the costal cartilage may be observed in adolescents with hyperthyroidism. At any age, hyperthyroidism can result in severe osteoporosis, both in the appendicular and axial skeletons.

Hypophosphatasia and Hyperphosphatasemia

Hypophosphatasia (HP) is a rare inherited metabolic disease (incidence 1:100,000) characterized by reduced serum and tissue alkaline phosphatase and defective bone mineralization. HP affects all races, males and females equally, and all age groups; however, the severity of the disease differs with age. The childhood and adult forms of HP represent the clinical expressions of the heterozygous state, whereas homozygosity results in the clinically severe, autosomal recessive, infantile form. Radiographic manifestations of perinatal HP in the skull include very poor skeletal mineralization, large fontanelles, and wide cranial sutures. In the axial skeleton, the vertebral bodies are dense, round, or flattened with sagittal clefts; in the appendicular skeleton, shortening, bowing and frequent fractures of the long bones are common (Fig. 22).

During childhood, HP is characterized by metaphyseal rachitic changes; evidence of radiolucent projections from the epiphyseal plate into the metaphysis, which is not found in other types of rickets, is a hallmark of HP. Pseudofractures are commonly seen in the adult form of HP, often occurring in the lateral aspect of the proximal femur.[46,50] Girschick et al.[52] measured BMD by pQCT and DXA in six boys with childhood HP (age, 2–3 years). DXA

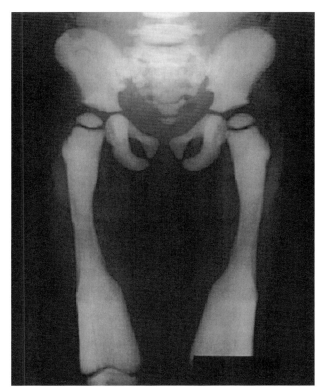

FIG. 23. Radiograph of a 7-year-old girl with osteopetrosis and marked cortical thickening, osteosclerosis of cancellous bone, and modeling defect of the metaphysis, called "Erlenmeyer flask" deformity [American College of Radiology. ACR Learning File® (Skeletal Edition)—1998. Reprinted with permission of the American College of Radiology. No other representation of this material is authorized without express, written permission from the American College of Radiology.]

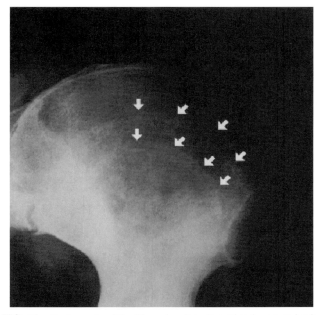

FIG. 24. Radiograph of the ilium showing alternating lucent and sclerotic bands in a patient with osteopetrosis [American College of Radiology. ACR Learning File® (Skeletal Edition)—1998. Reprinted with permission of the American College of Radiology. No other representation of this material is authorized without express, written permission from the American College of Radiology.]

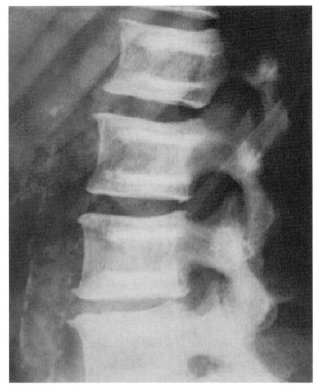

FIG. 25. Radiograph of an adult patient with osteopetrosis depicting a "bone in bone" appearance of the vertebral bodies [American College of Radiology. ACR Learning File® (Skeletal Edition)—1998. Reprinted with permission of the American College of Radiology. No other representation of this material is authorized without express, written permission from the American College of Radiology.]

values for total body and spinal BMD were in the lower normal range, wheras pQCT trabecular BMD of both radius and femur were grossly elevated. It was concluded that increased mineralization and sclerosis of trabecular bone might compensate for the mechanical incompetence associated with the impaired mineral-

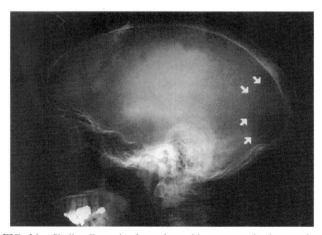

FIG. 26. Skull radiograph of a patient with osteoporosis circumscripta (arrows) representing the lytic phase of Paget's in the cranium [American College of Radiology. ACR Learning File® (Skeletal Edition)—1998. Reprinted with permission of the American College of Radiology. No other representation of this material is authorized without express, written permission from the American College of Radiology.]

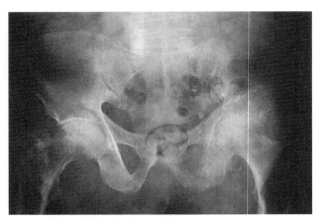

FIG. 27. Pelvic radiograph in a patient with Paget's disease depicting coarsened trabeculae and thickening of the left pubic bones, ischium, and ilium [American College of Radiology. ACR Learning File® (Skeletal Edition)—1998. Reprinted with permission of the American College of Radiology. No other representation of this material is authorized without express, written permission from the American College of Radiology.]

ization of cortical bone. Robinow[53] studied a patient with HP from age 20 months to 21 years. The skeletal deformities improved during childhood and puberty, but only minimal correction was observed in the osteopenia, indicating persistence in bone mineralization.

Congenital hyperphosphatasemia, or juvenile Paget's disease, is a rare disorder characterized by increased levels of serum alkaline phosphatase. Patients present with short stature, fragile bones with coarse trabeculations, cortical thickening, periosteal new bone formation, and bowing deformities.[49]

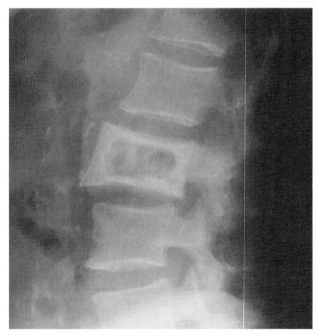

FIG. 28. Lateral spine radiograph depicting characteristic "picture frame" appearance because of the enlargement and lytic and sclerotic changes in the vertebral body in a patient with Paget's disease [American College of Radiology. ACR Learning File® (Skeletal Edition)—1998. Reprinted with permission of the American College of Radiology. No other representation of this material is authorized without express, written permission from the American College of Radiology.]

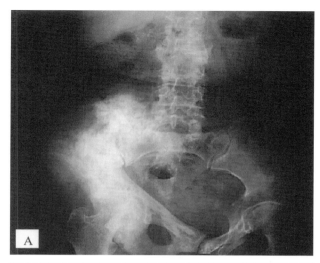

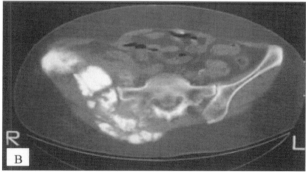

FIG. 29. Pelvic (A) radiograph and (B) CT scan showing malignant degeneration of Paget's disease to osteosarcoma in the left ilium. There is a large soft tissue component to the tumor with osteoid formation [American College of Radiology. ACR Learning File® (Skeletal Edition)—1998. Reprinted with permission of the American College of Radiology. No other representation of this material is authorized without express, written permission from the American College of Radiology.]

Hypervitaminoses

Prolonged feedings of excessive amounts of fat-soluble vitamins A and D lead to toxicity. Infants with vitamin A poisoning suffer from irritability and alopecia, and cortical hyperostoses of the long bones are apparent radiographically, usually in the clavicles and ulna. Histologically, an excess of normal subperiosteal bone is seen. Premature closure of the physeal plate causing growth arrest and cone epiphysis formation in the long bones is not uncommon. Similar changes can be seen with synthetic analoga of vitamin A (e.g., isotretinoin) used in the treatment of dermatological disorders.[49]

The radiographic findings of chronic vitamin D poisoning include vascular, renal, cardiac, pulmonary, gastrointestinal, and adrenal calcifications; renal US may show medullary nephrocalcinosis. In the long bones, the initial change is an increase in depth of the zones of provisional calcification, followed by cortical thickening and, later, osteoporosis. In the metaphysis, alternating bands of diminished (radiolucent) and increased (radioopaque) density are occasionally seen.[49]

Osteosclerosis and Hyperostosis

In contrast to the manifestations of most skeletal disorders, several pathological conditions are characterized by manifesting increased, not decreased, BMD. The term osteosclerosis is used to denote an increase in radiodensity of cancellous bone (usually caused by increased trabecular thickness), whereas hyperostosis describes an increase in cortical thickness. The conditions associated with osteosclerosis and hyperostosis include endocrine and metabolic disorders, infiltrative and neoplastic disorders of the bone, osteonecrosis, chronic healed osteomyelitis, and sclerosing bone dysplasias. Other causes of diffuse osteosclerosis are osteopetrosis, associated or not, to carbonic anhydrase II deficiency, pyknodysostosis, and idiopathic hypercalcemia (Williams syndrome).[51]

Osteopetrosis

Osteopetrosis (marble bone disease) occurs in two major clinical forms—the autosomal recessive or "malignant" type, which kills during infancy or early childhood, and the milder, adult form (Albers-Schonberg disease), also known as autosomal dominant osteopetrosis type II. Autosomal recessive carbonic anhydrase (CA) II deficiency produces osteopetrosis of intermediate severity associated with renal tubular acidosis and cerebral calcification.[54] During the past several years, molecular genetics studies have resulted in the identification of several disease-causing gene mutations. Thus far, all genes associated with human osteopetrosis encode proteins that participate in the functioning of the differentiation of the osteoclasts.[55] The loss of osteoclastic bone resorption and preservation of normal osteoblastic bone formation lead to osteopetrosis.

The radiographic hallmark of osteopetrosis is a generalized increase in bone density. The osteosclerosis depicted on skeletal

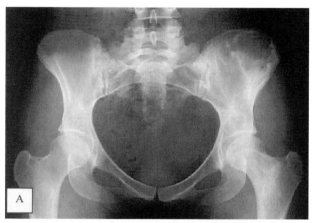

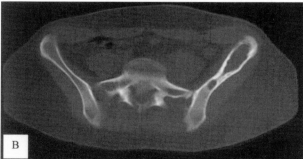

FIG. 30. Pelvic (A) radiograph and (B) CT scan in a 17-year-old female, depicting a lobulated, relatively well-defined lytic lesion with sclerotic borders in the left ilium. The appearance is characteristic of fibrous dysplasia [American College of Radiology. ACR Learning File® (Skeletal Edition)—1998. Reprinted with permission of the American College of Radiology. No other representation of this material is authorized without express, written permission from the American College of Radiology.]

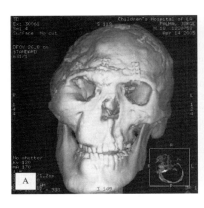 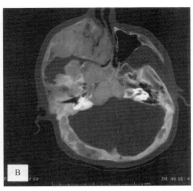

FIG. 31. (A) 3-D CT and (B) cross-sectional CT of a 20-year-old male with fibrous dysplasia involving the right mandible, maxilla, and malar bone. The maxilla is completely obliterated by the ossified fibrous tissue.

radiographs of patients with osteopetrosis results from an increase in the amount of bone, not from an increase in the degree of mineralization.[56] In the long bones, the medullary canal in the diaphysis and the trabeculae in the metaphysis are effaced because of the dense osteosclerosis. While the length of the bone is usually normal, modeling defects produce the "Erlenmeyer flask" deformity (Fig. 23). Alternating dense and lucent bands commonly occur in the metaphysis and pelvis (Fig. 24). The bones are brittle and fracture easily. The vertebrae are uniformly involved with sclerosis, depicting what has been termed "bone in bone" configuration or end-plate sclerosis crossing a "rugger jersey" appearance; similar, but better defined than the spinal sclerosis seen in patients with secondary hyperparathyroidism (Fig. 25). The base of the skull, best studied by CT, usually shows the most marked sclerosis and cranial nerve impingement because of the narrow cranial foramina. The use of MRI tends to be limited to imaging of the marrow in the severe recessive disease, which is usually fatal without marrow transplantation.[57]

Paget's Disease

Paget's disease is a focal bone disorder of unknown etiology, rare before middle age, and more often affecting men.[58] This condition is associated with increases in all elements of skeletal remodeling (resorption, formation, and mineralization) in one or multiple bones. Increased bone formation results in disorganized assembly of collagen, which gives rise to bony enlargement and deformity. A positive family history is present in ~10% of patients and the disease has a strong geographical variation, most commonly affecting whites.[59] In order of frequency, the following bones are affected: pelvis, vertebrae, femur, skull, tibia, clavicle, humerus, ribs, and, rarely, other bones.[60]

The radiographic appearance depends on the phase of the disease: lytic, reparative, or mixed; but most commonly a mixture of osteosclerosis and lysis is seen. The principal radiographic findings are thickening areas of lucency, patches of dense bone described as "cotton wool" or "cotton ball" and evidence of bone softening. In the skull, Paget's disease can manifest as a characteristic lytic lesion known as osteoporosis circumscripta (Fig. 26). Complications of Paget's disease include basilar invagination caused by softening of the bone in the skull base and narrowing of the cranial foramina, producing nerve entrapment.[61]

In the long bone, the process almost always involves the end of the bone extending into the diaphysis. In some cases, the entire shaft is involved. Mixed or sclerotic lesions are more common than osteolytic lesions. The cortices thicken and the overall diameters increase, while the intermedullary space is maintained. The thickened cortex suggests increased strength, although the bone is actually weakened, manifested by bowing of the long bones, usually more pronounced in the lower extremities. Pathological fractures are common and characteristically transverse rather than oblique or spiral, as in normal bone.[60,61]

In the pelvis, Paget's disease usually involves some portion of the acetabulum and the pubic bones, manifesting coarsening of the trabeculae and thickening of the cortex (Fig. 27). Because of bone softening, there may be intrapelvic protrusion of the bone acetabulum (protusio acetabuli). Healing of the lytic phase has been described as a result of treatment with diphosphonates and calcitonin.

In the spine, the disease usually affects the vertebral body more prominently. In the lateral view, because of cortical thickening, the vertebrae appear to be framed (picture frame vertebrae; Fig. 28). The trabecula within the vertebral body is also coarsened and occasionally the entire vertebrae is diffusely dense. The overall size of the vertebrae is increased, giving rise to spinal cord compression.[60,61]

Although rare, neoplasms arising from Pagetic bone are a complication; the incidence is ~1%.[62] Tumors are more frequent in the pelvis and long bones, and occur rarely in the vertebrae. The majority of the tumors are osteosarcomas, which usually present with new pain in a long-standing pagetic lesion (Fig. 29). Giant cell tumors have also been reported.

The bone affected by Paget's disease takes up all radionuclide bone scanning agents avidly; much more intensely than any other process. The diagnosis of Paget's disease can be made based on a bone scan because of this intense activity and the pattern of bone involvement—involvement of the end of the bone with variable extension into the shaft and often evidence of softening manifested by bowing of long bones and flattening of vertebrae.[63]

CT mirrors the findings on plain film radiography in Paget's disease: expansion, with cortical thickening, coarsening of the trabeculae, and focal sclerotic densities in intramedullary bone, the equivalent of "cotton balls." The osteolytic phase show considerable thinning of the cortex of long bones and tables of the skull. MRI displays similar osseous changes as low signals on both T1- and T2-weighted images. The marrow signal in the intramedullary and diploic spaces is variable, with high signal foci of fat seen on T1- and high-signal foci of fibrovascular marrow on T2-weighted images.[64]

Fibrous Dysplasia

Fibrous dysplasia usually begins during childhood and is characterized by the inability of mesenchymal cells to fully differentiate into osteoblasts and the replacement of bone by an abnormal proliferation of fibrous tissue. The disease may involve a single bone (monostotic) or, less frequently, may be widely distributed throughout the skeleton (polyostotic). The association of the polyostotic form with café-au-lait spots and hyperfunction of an endocrine system, such as pseudo-precocious puberty of ovarian origin, is known as McCune-Albright syndrome (MAS). Less commonly, there is pseudoprecocious puberty in boys or thyrotoxicosis, Cushing's disease, acromegaly, hyperprolactinemia, or hyperparathyroidism. In some patients, acquired renal phosphate wasting causes hypophosphatemic rickets or osteomalacia. Somatic mosaicism for an activating mutation in the gene that encodes the α subunit of the receptor/adenylate cyclase-coupling G protein causes fibrous dysplasia and the McCune-Albright Syndrome.[65]

Radiographically, the appearance of the lesions vary, but most are composed of sclerotic and lytic components. In long bones, the fibrous dysplastic lesions are typically well-defined, radiolucent areas with thin cortices and a ground-glass appearance. Lesions may be lobulated and may erode the cortex and produce local expansion (Fig. 30). Expanding bone lesions can cause deformity, and long-standing disease is usually associated with bowed and misshapen bone. The upper end of the femur characteristically has a "shepherd's crook" deformity and coxa vara, with lateral and anterior bowing of the shaft. Fractures are not uncommon and tend to heal with marked periosteal reaction. Sarcomatous degeneration has been reported but seems to be very uncommon.[66]

Involvement of facial bones usually presents as radiodense lesions, which may create leonine appearance (leontiasis osea) with frequent obliteration of the nasal cavities by abnormal proliferation of fibrous tissue. Expansile cranial lesions may narrow foramina and cause optic lesions, reduce hearing, and create other manifestations of cranial nerve compression.[67] The extent of craniofacial lesions are best depicted by CT (Fig. 31). Lesions of fibrous dysplasia are shown by MRI to be largely isointense with areas of hypointensity on T1-weighted images and appear heterogeneously hyperintense on T2-weighted images. The enhancement pattern can be patchy or homogeneous, reflecting the variable tissue components of this entity.[68]

REFERENCES

1. Cascade PN, Webster EW, Kazerooni EA 1998 Ineffective use of radiology: The hidden cost. AJR Am J Roentgenol 170:561–564.
2. Buckwalter KA, Braunstein EM 1992 Digital skeletal radiography. AJR Am J Roentgenol 158:1071–1080.
3. Murphey MD 1997 Computed radiography in musculoskeletal imaging. Semin Roentgenol 32:64–76.
4. Boudousq V, Goulart DM, Dinten JM, de Kerlen CC, Thomas E, Mares O, Kotzki PO 2005 Image resolution and magnification using a cone beam densitometer: Optimizing data acquisition for hip morphometric analysis. Osteoporos Int 16:813–822.
5. Meschan I, Farrer-Meschan RM 1987 Roentgen Signs in Diagnostic Imaging, vol. 4, 2nd ed. WB Saunders, Philadelphia, PA, USA.
6. Greenspan A 2000 Orthopedic Radiology: A Practical Approach, 3rd ed. Lippincott Williams & Wilkins, Philadelphia, PA, USA.
7. Wechsler RJ, Karasick D, Schweitzer ME 1992 Computed tomography of talocalcaneal coalition: Imaging techniques. Skeletal Radiol 21:353–358.
8. McEnery KW, Wilson AJ, Pilgram TK, Murphy WA Jr., Marushack MM 1994 Fractures of the tibial plateau: Value of spiral CT coronal plane reconstructions for detecting displacement in vitro. AJR Am J Roentgenol 163:1177–1181.
9. Levin DC, Spettell CM, Rao VM, Sunshine J, Bansal S, Bushee GR 1998 Impact of MR imaging on nationwide health care costs and comparison with other imaging procedures. AJR Am J Roentgenol 170:557–560.
10. Curry TS, Dowdey JE, Murry RC 1990 Christensen's Physics of Diagnostic Radiology, 4th ed. Lea & Febiger, Philadelphia, PA, USA.
11. Newhouse KE, el-Khoury GY, Buckwalter JA 1994 Occult sacral fractures in osteopenic patients. J Bone Joint Surg Am 74:1472–1477.
12. Anderson MW, Greenspan A 1996 Stress fractures. Radiology 199:1–12.
13. Kanberoglu K, Kantarci F, Cebi D, Yilmaz MH, Kurugoglu S, Bilici A, Koyuncu H 2005 Magnetic resonance imaging in osteomalacic insufficiency fractures of the pelvis. Clin Radiol 60:105–111.
14. Kanal E, Shellock FG, Talagala L 1990 Safety considerations in MR imaging. Radiology 176:593–606.
15. Schauwecker DS 1992 The scintigraphic diagnosis of osteomyelitis. AJR Am J Roentgenol 158:9–18.
16. Johnson RP 1997 The role of bone imaging in orthopedic practice. Semin Nucl Med 27:386–389.
17. Greenspan A, Stadalnik RC 1997 A musculoskeletal radiologist's view of nuclear medicine. Semin Nucl Med 27:372–385.
18. Stulberg BN, Davis AW, Bauer TW, Levine M, Easley K 1991 Osteonecrosis of the femoral head. A prospective randomized treatment protocol. Clin Orthop Relat Res 268:140–151.
19. Kumar R, Nadig MR, Chauhan A 2005 Positron emission tomography: Clinical applications in oncology. Part 1. Expert Rev Anticancer Ther 5:1079–1094.
20. Messa C, Goodman WG, Hoh CK, Choi Y, Nissenson AR, Salusky IB, Phelps ME, Hawkins RA 1993 Bone metabolic activity measured with positron emission tomography and [18F] fluoride ion in renal osteodystrophy: Correlation with bone histomorphometry. J Clin Endocrinol Metab 77:949–955.
21. Lund PJ, Nisbet JK, Valencia FG, Ruth JT 1996 Current sonographic applications in orthopedics. AJR Am J Roentgenol 166:889–895.
22. Gerscovich EO, Greenspan A, Cronan MS, Karol LA, McGahan JP 1994 Three-dimensional sonographic evaluation of developmental dysplasia of the hip: Preliminary findings. Radiology 190:407–410.
23. Herd RJ, Blake GM, Ramalingam T, Miller CG, Ryan PJ, Fogelman I 1993 Measurements of postmenopausal bone loss with a new contact ultrasound system. Calcif Tissue Int 53:153–157.
24. Adler RS, Dedrick DK, Laing TJ, Chiang EH, Meyer CR, Bland PH, Rubin JM 1992 Quantitative assessment of cartilage surface roughness in osteoarthritis using high frequency ultrasound. Ultrasound Med Biol 18:51–58.
25. Gilsanz V, Roe TF, Mora S, Costin G, Goodman WG 1991 Changes in vertebral bone density in black girls and white girls during childhood and puberty. N Engl J Med 325:1597–1600.
26. Gilsanz V, Kovanlikaya A, Costin G, Roe TF, Sayre J, Kaufman F 1997 Differential effect of gender on the sizes of the bones in the axial and appendicular skeletons. J Clin Endocrinol Metab 82:1603–1607.
27. Han ZH, Palnitkar S, Rao DS, Nelson D, Parfitt AM 1996 Effect of ethnicity and age or menopause on the structure and geometry of iliac bone. J Bone Miner Res 11:1967–1975.
28. Gilsanz V, Skaggs DL, Kovanlikaya A, Sayre J, Loro ML, Kaufman F, Korenman SG 1998 Differential effect of race on the axial and appendicular skeletons of children. J Clin Endocrinol Metab 83:1420–1427.
29. Hogler W, Blimkie CJ, Cowell CT, Kemp AF, Briody J, Wiebe P, Farpour-Lambert N, Duncan CS, Woodhead HJ 2003 A comparison of bone geometry and cortical density at the mid-femur between prepuberty and young adulthood using magnetic resonance imaging. Bone 33:771–778.
30. Schoenau E, Neu CM, Rauch F, Manz F 2002 Gender-specific pubertal changes in volumetric cortical bone mineral density at the proximal radius. Bone 31:110–113.
31. Garn SM, Frisancho AR, Sandusky ST, McCann MB 1972 Confirmation of the sex difference in continuing subperiosteal apposition. Am J Phys Anthropol 36:377–380.
32. Neu CM, Rauch F, Manz F, Schoenau E 2001 Modeling of cross-sectional bone size, mass and geometry at the proximal radius: A study of normal bone development using peripheral quantitative computed tomography. Osteoporos Int 12:538–547.
33. Rauch F, Neu C, Manz F, Schoenau E 2001 The development of metaphyseal cortex–implications for distal radius fractures during growth. J Bone Miner Res 16:1547–1555.
34. Kontulainen SA, Macdonald HM, Khan KM, McKay HA 2005 Examining bone surfaces across puberty: A 20-month pQCT trial. J Bone Miner Res 20:1202–1207.
35. Gilsanz V, Ratib O 2005 Hand Bone Age: A Digital Atlas of Skeletal Maturity. Springer-Verlag, Berlin, Germany.
36. Weiner S, Traub W 1992 Bone structure: From angstroms to microns. FASEB J 6:879–885.
37. Finkelstein JS 2004 Osteoporosis. In: Goldman L, Ausiello D (eds.) Cecil Textbook of Medicine. Saunders, Philadelphia, PA, USA, pp. 1547–1555.
38. Lachman E 1985 Osteoporosis: The potentialities and limitations of its radiologic diagnosis. AJR 4:712–717.
39. Aitken JM 1984 Relevance of osteoporosis in women with fracture of the femoral neck. BMJ (Clin Res Ed) 288:597–601.
40. Singh M, Nagrath AR, Maini PS 1970 Changes in trabecular pattern of the upper end of the femur as an index of osteoporosis. J Bone Joint Surg Am 52:457–467.
41. Black DM 1999 The role of clinical risk factors in the prediction of future risk. J Clin Densitom 2:361–362.
42. Toms AP, Marshall TJ, Becker E, Donell ST, Lobo-Mueller EM, Barker T 2005 Regional migratory osteoporosis: A review illustrated by five cases. Clin Radiol 60:425–438.

43. Prockip DJ 2004 Targeting gene therapy for osteogenesis imperfecta. N Engl J Med 350:2302–2304.
44. Rauch F, Munns C, Land C, Glorieux FH 2006 Pamidronate in children and adolescents with osteogenesis imperfecta: Effect of treatment discontinuation. J Clin Endocrinol Metab (in press).
45. Ruano R, Molho M, Roume J, Ville Y 2004 Prenatal diagnosis of fetal skeletal dysplasias by combining two-dimensional and three-dimensional ultrasound and intrauterine three-dimensional helical computer tomography. Ultrasound Obstet Gynecol 24:134–140.
46. Ramirez N, Vilella FE, Colon M, Flynn JM 2003 Osteogenesis imperfecta and hyperplastic callus formation in a family: A report of three cases and a review of the literature. J Pediatr Orthop B 12:88–96.
47. Shoenfeld Y 1975 Osteogenesis imperfecta. Review of the literature with presentation of 29 cases. Am J Dis Child 129:679–687.
48. Azouz EM, Karamitsos C, Reed MH, Baker L, Kozlowski K, Hoeffel JC 1993 Types and complications of femoral neck fractures in children. Pediatr Radiol 23:415–420.
49. Kottamasu SR 2004 Bone formation and metabolic bone disease. In: Kuhn JP, Slovis TL, Haller JO (eds.) Caffey's Pediatric Diagnostic Imaging, 10th ed., vol. 2. Elsevier, Philadelphia, PA, USA, pp. 2232–2268.
50. Boechat MI, Westra SJ, Van Dop C, Kaufman F, Gilsanz V, Roe TF 1996 Decreased cortical and increased cancellous bone in two children with primary hyperparathyroidism. Metabolism 45:76–81.
51. Laor T, Jaramillo D, Oestreich AE 1998 Musculoskeletal system. In: Kirks DR, Griscom NT (eds.) Practical Pediatric Imaging: Diagnostic Radiology of Infants and Children, 3rd ed. Lippincott-Raven Publishers, Philadelphia, PA, USA, pp. 327–510.
52. Girschick HJ, Schneider P, Kruse K, Huppertz HI 1999 Bone metabolism and bone mineral density in childhood hypophosphatasia. Bone 25:361–367.
53. Robinow M 1971 Twenty-year follow-up of a case of hypophosphatasia. Birth Defects Orig Artic Ser 7:86–93.
54. Lotan D, Eisenkraft A, Jacobsson JM, Bar-Yosef O, Kleta R, Gal N, Raviv-Zilka L, Gore H, Anikster Y 2006 Clinical and molecular findings in a family with the carbonic anhydrase II deficiency syndrome. Pediatr Nephrol 21:423–426.
55. Balemans W, Van Wesenbeeck L, Van Hul W 2005 A clinical and molecular overview of the human osteopetroses. Calcif Tissue Int 77:263–274.
56. Kovanlikaya A, Loro ML, Gilsanz V 1997 Pathogenesis of osteosclerosis in autosomal dominant osteopetrosis. AJR Am J Roentgenol 168:929–932.
57. Stoker DJ 2002 Osteopetrosis. Semin Musculoskelet Radiol 6:299–305.
58. Briesacher BA, Orwig D, Seton M, Omar M, Kahler KH 2005 Medical care costs of Paget's disease of bone in a privately insured population. Bone (in press).
59. Daroszewska A, Ralston SH 2005 Genetics of Paget's disease of bone. Clin Sci 109:257–263.
60. Resnick D 1998 Paget disease of bone: Current status and a look back to 1943 and earlier. AJR Am J Roentgenol 150:249–256.
61. Whitehouse RW 2002 Paget's disease of bone. Semin Musculoskelet Radiol 6:313–322.
62. Mankin HJ, Hornicek FJ 2005 Paget's sarcoma: A historical and outcome review. Clin Orthop Relat Res 438:97–102.
63. Scutellari PN, Giorgi A, De Sario V, Campanati P 2005 Correlation of multimodality imaging in Paget's disease of bone. Radiol Med (Torino) 110:603–615.
64. Vande Berg BC, Malghem J, Lecouvet FE, Maldague B 2001 Magnetic resonance appearance of uncomplicated Paget's disease of bone. Semin Musculoskelet Radiol 5:69–77.
65. DiCaprio MR, Enneking WF 2005 Fibrous dysplasia. Pathophysiology, evaluation, and treatment. J Bone Joint Surg Am 87:1848–1864.
66. Hudson TM, Stiles RG, Monson DK 1993 Fibrous lesions of bone. Radiol Clin North Am 31:279–297.
67. Gosain AK, Celik NK, Aydin MA 2004 Fibrous dysplasia of the face: Utility of three-dimensional modeling and ex situ malar recontouring. J Craniofac Surg 15:909–915.
68. Shah ZK, Peh WC, Koh WL, Shek TW 2005 Magnetic resonance imaging appearances of fibrous dysplasia. Br J Radiol 78:1104–1115.

Chapter 23.   Clinical Use of Bone Mass Measurements in Adults for the Assessment and Management of Osteoporosis

Paul D. Miller[1] and Mary B. Leonard[2]

[1]University of Colorado Health Sciences Center, Colorado Center for Bone Research, Lakewood, Colorado; and [2]Children's Hospital of Philadelphia, Philadelphia, Pennsylvania

INTRODUCTION

BMD measurements have provided the foundation for making the diagnosis of postmenopausal osteoporosis (PMO). BMD measurements have been the anchor for the prediction of fracture risk in the postmenopausal female and elderly male populations. In addition, it is used to monitor diseases that may negatively effect bone and the response to pharmacologic therapies for osteoporosis designed to increase skeletal strength. Finally, BMD is the measurement required by the Food and Drug Administration (FDA) for the randomization criteria in clinical trials designed for the registration of treatments for PMO.

BMD measurements, especially at the central sites (spine and hip) by DXA, are the pivotal measurements used by clinicians to make decisions regarding when to treat patients at risk for fragility fractures. BMD measurements, along with age, form the basis of the 10-year absolute global fracture risk model being developed by the World Health Organization (WHO), into which other risk factors are incorporated.

This chapter will examine the use of BMD in clinical practice.

CLINICAL USE OF BMD MEASUREMENTS

There are four fundamental applications of BMD measurements using central DXA for the management of PMO: (1) diagnosis of PMO using the WHO criteria; (2) prediction of fracture risk; (3) identification of prevalent vertebral fractures by vertebral fracture assessment (VFA); and (4) monitoring changes that might be caused by underlying disease or in response to pharmacologic therapies intended to stop bone loss and/or increase bone density.

Using DXA for the Diagnosis of Osteoporosis

The diagnosis of PMO can be made based on the presence of a fragility (low-trauma) fracture. Fractures that are predictive of a higher risk for future fracture in population studies as well

Dr. Miller has received scientific funding from Procter & Gamble, Aventis, Roche, Eli Lilly, Pharmacia, Merck & Co., Novartis, Pfizer, and Amgen and has served on speaker boards, advisory boards, and consulted for Procter & Gamble, Aventis, Merck & Co., Eli Lilly, Amgen, NPS, Novartis, Roche, and GlaxoSmithKline. Dr. Leonard has reported no conflicts of interest.

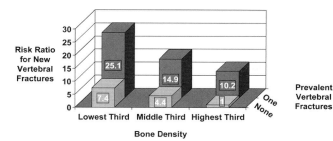

FIG. 1. The relationship between baseline BMD or prevalent vertebral fractures on future vertebral fracture risk. (Reproduced with permission from Ross PD, Davis JW, Epstein RS, Wasnich RD 1991 Pre-existing fractures and bone mass predict vertebral fracture incidence in women. Ann Intern Med **114:**919–923.)

as placebo arms of pharmacologic clinical trials are vertebral fractures (VCF), hip fractures, wrist and forearm fractures, humeral and shoulder fractures, other appendicular fractures, and rib fractures.[1–13] Fragility fractures at these sites are predictive of future fracture risk independent of the BMD.

It was recognized in 1991 that the presence of a VCF increased the risk of future fractures of the vertebrae independent of the baseline BMD, and the presence of an existing VCF in combination with low BMD increased the future fracture risk far more that the risk predicted by either a VCF or low BMD alone[14] (Fig. 1).

In 1992, a working group of the WHO met to attempt to use BMD measurements of the spine, hip, and forearm to define the prevalence of osteoporosis in the postmenopausal population of nations to address the potential economic burden of PMO worldwide. To provide a BMD threshold for the diagnosis of PMO, the WHO working group had to decide on a BMD value that was appropriate for the diagnosis of osteoporosis in the postmenopausal population. Data from the United Kingdom and the United States comparing population-based BMD to life-time fracture risk in white postmenopausal women age 50 and older was used. The WHO working group agreed on a BMD threshold that used the number of SDs below the young adult mean value (ultimately called a T score) of −2.5 for the diagnosis of PMO at the population level.[15] This value captured 30% of the postmenopausal population with a T score of −2.5 or below at the hip (femoral neck), anterior-posterior lumbar spine, or forearm that matched the lifetime risk for fracture at any of these three skeletal sites in these populations. In addition, examining the femoral neck alone, 16% of these populations were at or below −2.5, which also corresponded to the lifetime risk of hip fracture (16%). Hence, the prevalence of PMO created by the chosen threshold matched the observed lifetime fracture risk and thus the −2.5 threshold was chosen.

Obviously, the prevalence of osteoporosis can be influenced by the SD cut-point chosen. In 1992, the preliminary cut-point suggested was a T score of −2.0 for the diagnosis of PMO, and preliminary calculations of the prevalence of PMO were made.[16] In 1994, when the final cut-point of a T score of −2.5 was agreed on, the prevalence of PMO worldwide was recalculated.[17]

The T score, based on a SD value, was used rather than absolute BMD (g/cm²) because the different calibrations of devices from the three major manufacturers of central DXA machines would have required device-specific BMD values.

The substitution of the T score mitigated some, but not all, of the differences among DXA devices. Differences in T- scores may also exist in the same patient when calculated from different DXA machines even at the same skeletal site (e.g., spine), because the T score is dependent on the SD of the mean BMD of any given manufacturer's young-normal reference population.[18–21] The T score discrepancy among DXA manufacturers at the hip was removed when all manufacturers incorporated the only consistent

young-normal reference population database, the NHANES III (National Health and Nutrition Education Survey III).[22–24] There remains an approximate 0.5 SD difference among manufacturer T score calculations at the spine by central DXA and even larger differences at the forearm by central DXA or any peripheral BMD device or central QCT. This is caused, in large part, by inconsistent young-normal reference populations used by these otherwise accurate bone mass measuring devices[20,25–27] (Fig. 2).

Despite these limitations, the T score rapidly became the workhorse parameter for the clinical application of DXA for the diagnosis of PMO.[27–31] The T score provided the clinician with the ability and opportunity to diagnose osteoporosis before a fracture occurred, an important advance because of the exponential increase in subsequent fracture risk conferred by the first fracture, independent of the BMD. In this manner, the T score came to be used in patient management much as other surrogate markers for disease outcomes had been previously used in the management of otherwise asymptomatic patients such as the surrogate markers of blood pressure and cholesterol for the outcomes of stroke and myocardial infarction, respectively. If a postmenopausal woman was found to have a T score of −2.5 or poorer at the hip, spine, or forearm and the WHO criteria applied, a diagnosis of osteoporosis and subsequent management decisions could be made with the intention of preventing the first fracture. The recognition of the "T score" by international professional societies was followed by an increase in research funding for osteoporosis, the development of practice guidelines, and third party payer reimbursement for bone mass measurements. In 1997, in the United States, the Bone Mass Measurement Act formed the basis for Medicare reimbursement of bone mass measurements (BMMA/Screening). In 2004, the first U.S. Surgeon General's report on the status of America's skeletal health stressed BMD testing as a pivotal component in population screening and the assessment of the at-risk postmenopausal population (≥60 years).[32] There are other guidelines for the use of BMD in case finding strategies in the United States from different organizations for the entire postmenopausal population, even under the age of 60 years. The National Osteoporosis Foundation (NOF) guidelines for the postmenopausal population have been widely embraced: test all postmenopausal women ≥65 years of age regardless of risk factors and <65 years of age with additional risk factors.[33] The guidelines for BMD measurements in a variety of clinical circumstances have been provided by the International Society for Clinical Densitometry (ISCD) and are outlined in Table 1.[34,35]

The WHO working group on PMO also described a second diagnostic category, osteopenia. This category was defined as a T score of −1.0 to −2.5 measured at the spine, hip, or forearm. They justified the creation of this category between normal and osteopo-

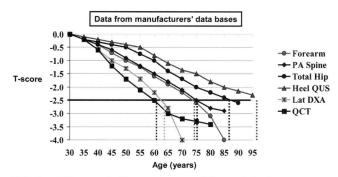

FIG. 2. Differences in T scores between different skeletal measurement technologies. (Reproduced with permission from Faulkner KG, von Stetten E, Miller P 1999 Discordance in patient classification using T-scores. J Clin Densit **2:**343–350.)

Table 1. Clinical Indications for Bone Mass Measurements Developed by the Position Development Conference of The International Society for Clinical Densitometry

Women aged 65 and older
Postmenopausal women under age 65 with risk factors
Men aged 70 and older
Adults with a fragility fracture
Adults with a disease or condition associated with low bone mass or bone loss
Adults taking medications associated with low bone mass or bone loss
Anyone being considered for pharmacologic therapy
Anyone being treated, to monitor treatment effect
Anyone not receiving therapy in whom evidence of bone loss would lead to treatment

Modified with permission from Leib E, Lewiecki M, Binkley N, Hamdy RC 2004 Official positions of the International Society for Clinical Densitometry. J Clin Densitom 7:1–6 and Binkley N, Bilezikian JP, Kendler DL, Leib ES, Lewiecki EM, Petak SM 2006 Official positions of the International Society for Clinical Densitometry and Executive Summary of the 2005 Position Development. J Clin Densitom (in press).

rosis to provide a clinical explanation of the fracture risk gradient. Data from population studies have consistently shown that more postmenopausal women and elderly men whose BMDs are in the osteopenic range have fragility fractures.[36–40] The results are probably because of the fact that many more people are osteopenic, and there are simply more fractures in this larger population.

The introduction of the label "osteopenia" has been criticized. The criticism is justified when the label of osteopenia is applied to low-risk postmenopausal women, who may be consequently over-treated with pharmacologic interventions, when evidence of a benefit/risk reduction is weaker than in postmenopausal women with osteoporosis. In addition, younger, low-risk "osteopenic" women are given a diagnostic label that may be detrimental to their quality of life and inhibit their ability to obtain health care coverage.

Despite the value of the WHO classifications to increase international awareness of PMO, there are acknowledged limitations: (1) the application of the WHO criteria to populations that were not used in the original data development, including men, nonwhite populations, premenopausal women, children, patients with glucocorticoid-induced bone loss, patients with renal osteodystrophy, etc. and (2) the assumption that the WHO criteria, which are diagnostic thresholds, are also intervention thresholds. It was never the intent of the WHO working group that their diagnostic criteria be used as thresholds for treatment intervention.

The ISCD held Position Development Conferences (PDCs) to address many of the issues facing clinicians related to the application of BMD measurements. The process of the ISCD-PDC and the results of that process have been published in *The Journal of Clinical Densitometry* and other peer-reviewed journals.[41,42]

Although the WHO population used for the criteria development was white and female, it is felt that the WHO criteria can be used for the diagnosis of osteoporosis in men ≥50 years of age. Justification for this recommendation is based on observations that men and women fracture at similar absolute femoral neck BMD and T scores. It is still recommended that T scores for men be calculated from a male young-normal reference database. Justification for this is that, although the similar fracture risk in men is seen when the T score is calculated from a female NHANES III reference population database, the prevalence of osteoporosis is underestimated.[43,44]

While there is increasing longitudinal data examining the relationship of BMD to fracture risk in men, there is very little data defining the relationship of low BMD to fracture risk with the intent of applying WHO diagnostic criteria to nonwhite populations. The ISCD has suggested the follow-ing[44,45]: the use of a uniform white (non–race-adjusted) female normative database for women of all ethnic groups and the use of a uniform white (non–race-adjusted) male normative database for men of all ethnic groups.

Although the central DXA machines have multiethnic reference population databases for calculation of T scores or Z scores (age-matched), there is paucity of data on the relationships between ethnic-specific derived T scores and lifetime fracture risk. In addition, at least for the U.S. population, there is only one head-to-head multiethnic fracture study that suggested the relative risk for fractures over 1 year was similar in whites, blacks, Hispanics, and Asian postmenopausal women when the T scores were calculated from a white reference population.[46] Absolute fracture rates were lower in Asians and blacks in the NORA study. Therefore, in parts of the world where gene pool mixing across multiethnic populations is common (e.g., United States), white reference population databases may be used for T score calculation in all ethnic groups. In an ideal world, nation-specific and ethnic-specific reference population databases would be created, and the nation- and ethnic-specific T scores would be linked to longitudinal fracture risk data. A carefully constructed analysis of this difficult issue states "Race/ethnicity is an ecosocial construct, not a biomedical entity, and is a proxy for other variables. Whether and how to use race/ethnicity in fracture assessment potentially places these two paradigms in opposition. The 'right' response goes far beyond simply addressing issues related to reference population data because this cannot resolve ethnic disparities in osteoporotic fracture rates."[47]

Use of BMD for Fracture Risk Assessment

Low BMD as measured by central or peripheral DXA, peripheral ultrasound, or spine QCT is predictive of an increased risk for fractures at any skeletal site.[48–58]

In addition, from individual longitudinal studies including population studies and from meta-analysis, all of these devices predict an increased risk of fracture in postmenopausal women, elderly men with an overlapping relative risk (RR) predictability: risk increases approximately two times for each 1.0 SD reduction in BMD calculated from T scores or the variance from the mean of an aged-matched population.[48]

However, fracture risk discrimination is quantified by the magnitude of the RR (e.g., the larger the value of RR, the more effective measurements are at identifying patients at increased risk of fracture). It has been suggested that the reason that all BMD measurements are capable of predicting similar RR for fracture, even at skeletal sites other than the measured site, is because of the high correlation coefficients among BMD technologies ($r = 0.55–0.65$).[58,59] If, however, there are unrecognized deviations from the published correlation coefficients among BMD technologies, there may be room for improvement in fracture prediction. In part, fracture risk prediction can be enhanced by incorporating additional risk factors into the assessment of fracture risk. The validation of how additional risk factors should be added to BMD to enhance risk prediction is important because the current DXA reports may be misleading in their subjective pronouncements of fracture risk.

It has been recognized since the forearm DXA studies of Hui et al.[60] that fracture risk is dependent on the age of the patient (Fig. 3). Any given patient's risk for fracture increases as age increases even at the same BMD or T score level.[60,61] Thus, DXA measurements capture an important, albeit fraction of the fracture risk. Understanding this fundamental point is pivotal to the proper interpretation of BMD values. The reason why risk is greater as age increases is not completely understood, but the higher risk for falls in the elderly may account for a portion of this age-related greater risk for fracture.[62] Older bone has less strength to resist fracture than younger bone at the same BMD or T score, and investigators dedicated to measuring bone quality are refining our understanding of these issues.[63–66] It is important to point out, however, that, although the absolute risk for fragility fracture increases at the same level of BMD or T score as age increases, fractures at both hip and nonhip skeletal sites are not infrequent in the younger (50–64 years) postmenopausal population. In the NORA study, nearly (37%) of all fractures occurred in this younger untreated postmenopausal group and was lower as the T score value lowered[67] (Table 2).

As previously mentioned, prior fracture in the postmenopausal population is an independent predictor of future fracture risk. Furthermore, combining a prevalent fracture (even asymptomatic vertebral fracture) and low BMD translates into a much greater risk for future fracture than what would be predicted by low BMD or prior fracture alone.[14] In 1993, data showed the interaction of risk factors captured in the Study of Osteoporotic Fractures (SOF) with low BMD to enhance fracture risk prediction for hip fractures[68] (Fig. 4). More recently, data from multiple population studies have documented the strong association between the presence of nonvertebral or nonhip fractures and fragility fractures of other skeletal sites including shoulder, wrist, and rib fractures.[10–14,69] Therefore, in the elderly population, any fragility fracture is symbolic of systemic skeletal fragility.

Clinicians should, therefore, incorporate BMD, age, and prior fracture in their assessment of fracture risk and patient management. Recent software upgrades in central DXA machine use these three risk factors to calculate fracture risk. Broad implementation of standardized DXA reports can only be realized when the independent risk factors for fragility fractures in the postmenopausal population are validated and endorsed at an international level.

The WHO absolute risk project is the large project assessing the long-term (10 year) risk for all fragility fractures as a function of validated risk factors from large international studies.[61] This work is still in progress and will require review and comment by the WHO per se before final publication and ultimate implementation.[70] Based on data that have been presented at many scientific meetings, there are eight validated risk factors for fracture risk. Those that may be included in the implementation of standardized DXA reports are BMD, prior fragility fracture, age, and family history, because beyond four or five risk factors, the absolute risk level increases only slightly. The combined risk increases according to the formula:

$$Combined\ risk\ =\ \sqrt{(RR1)^2 + (RR2)^2}$$

When implemented, it is hoped that absolute risk prediction calculation will facilitate intervention decisions for the post-

TABLE 2. THE RELATIONSHIP BETWEEN AGE AND FRACTURE RISK FROM THE NORA (NATIONAL OSTEOPOROSIS RISK ASSESSMENT POPULATION		
Age (years)	50–64	65+
Osteoporotic fracture		
No. fractures	905	1535
Fracture rate (95% CI)	8.4 (7.9, 9.0)	16.5 (15.6, 17.3)
Percent of fractures	37%	63%
Hip fractures		
No. fractures	86	354
Fracture rate (95% CI)	0.8 (0.6, 1.0)	3.8 (3.4, 4.2)
Percent fractures	20%	80%

menopausal population based on risk beyond T score alone. Risk stratification has been shown in previous models; however, they are either based on restricted population studies or use peripheral BMD technologies for risk assessment.[71,72] The WHO absolute risk study will link absolute risk for all fractures, calculated from validated population studies representing >90,000 postmenopausal women, to treatment intervention based on disuse costs of hip fracture using the current costs of drugs registered for the treatment of PMO:

- Hip fracture equivalents—weighting of fragility fractures* (asterisk never explained or defined) according to morbidity using disuse tables (one hip fracture in 50-year-old woman ~ two VF ~ four humerus fractures)
- Example (Sweden)—Treat a 65-year-old woman if 4% 10-year hip fracture risk equivalents, assuming therapy costs $500 per year, given for 5 years, results in 35% reduction in risk of any osteoporotic fracture, followed by waning of effect for 5 years, using cost-effectiveness threshold of $30,000 per QALY (Quality-Adjusted Life-Year) gained.

It is obvious that the government reimbursement plan will differ nation to nation by the gross domestic product (GDP) of a given nation. The WHO project does not include other risk factors that clinicians might reasonably use in counseling patients: nonclinical (morphometric) vertebral fractures, bone turnover markers, hip axis length, hip structural analysis, and other risk factors that might become identified in smaller, less well-validated multination population studies.[5,73–80] Morphometric vertebral fractures, however, will be acknowledged by the NOF clinical implementation of the WHO absolute risk analysis as being a strong risk factor for future fracture. In addition, the WHO absolute risk model will provide broad generalizations that will focus on intervention strategies, but it will not eliminate individual clinician decisions. Nevertheless, the WHO risk project will take the field of osteoporosis to a level comparable with the cardiovascular field regarding intervention decisions. In addition, the WHO absolute risk assessment may advocate treatment of women whose lower T scores or younger age might otherwise not have received treatment[61] (Fig. 5).

The WHO selected absolute risk rather than relative risk, although both calculations of risk have value. The power of any given BMD measurement device to predict risk is based on its ability to predict RR. However, RR does not incorporate other risk factors; it is the ratio of the absolute risk for the disease event in a target population to the absolute risk in a population not at risk for the disease event (BMD, smoking, etc.). Absolute risk incorporates the discovered cumulative risk factors into the prediction of the risk for fractures over a given period of time[59] (Table 3). As shown in Table 3, the RR risk for fracture per SD reduction in BMD is

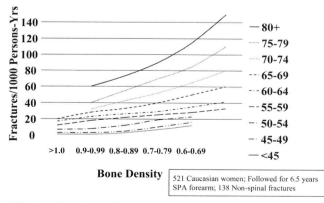

Bone Density | 521 Caucasian women; Followed for 6.5 years SPA forearm; 138 Non-spinal fractures

FIG. 3. The relationship between age, BMD, and risk for fracture. (Reproduced with permission from Hui SL, Slemenda CW, Johnston CC Jr 1988 Age and bone mass as predictors of fracture in a prospective study. J Clin Invest 81:1804–1809.)

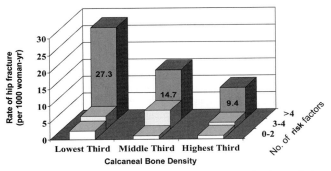

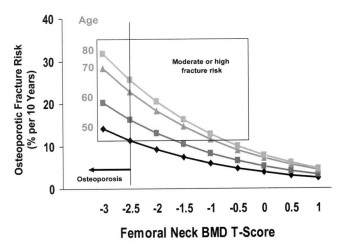

FIG. 4. The interaction between BMD and risk factors for the prediction of hip fracture risk from the Study of Osteoporotic Fractures. (Reproduced with permission from Cummings SR, Nevitt MC, Browner WS, Stone K, Fox KM, Ensrud KE, Cavley J, Black D, Vogt TM 1995 Risk factors for hip fracture in white women. Study of Osteoporotic Fractures Research Group. N Engl J Med **332:**767–773, Copyright © 1995 Massachusetts Medical Society. All rights reserved.)

FIG. 5. The potential impact of the WHO absolute fracture risk assessment on intervention thresholds in postmenopausal women. (Reproduced from J Bone Miner Res **16:**S194 with permission from the American Society for Bone and Mineral Research.)

constant over age, which is incorrect. Because other risk factors are included in this calculation, the absolute risk will increase with age.

Use of DXA for VFA

DXA is now a recognized technology for the identification of vertebral fractures. The presence of vertebral fractures, even if they are asymptomatic, is predictive of the risk for future (incident) vertebral fractures and nonvertebral fractures, independent of baseline BMD or T score. The majority of prevalent vertebral fractures are not recognized in postmenopausal women and elderly men. Population studies from the United States, Europe, Mexico, and Asia all suggest that vertebral fracture prevalence is similar across these ethnic groups and may be as high as 20–25% by the age of 65 years.[81–85] This suggests that osteoporosis is markedly underdiagnosed and that future fracture risk is markedly underestimated. Harry Genant has provided clinicians with a semiquantitative method for the identification of prevalent, as well as incident VCF, using either plain radiography or DXA-based VFA.[86] The VFA technology for prevalent VCF detection by DXA has progressed to the point that it is becoming a standard of care in the risk assessment of the postmenopausal population. The ISCD has provided guidelines for VFA determinations.[87] Table 4 outlines the ISCD indications for VFA by DXA.

If clinicians simply measure the height of their postmenopausal patients and perform a VFA assessment in those who have lost >1.5 in from their historical height, there is evidence that a large proportion of vertebral fractures will be detected.[88]

There are data to suggest that all "grades" of prevalent vertebral fractures are predictive of future fracture and that this risk is increased within 12 months of the detection—although the physician may not know when the prevalent vertebral fracture occurred.[5,75,89–92] The higher the grade (severity) of the existing vertebral fracture or the more vertebral fractures present (one, two, or three), the greater the risk for future fractures. Furthermore, because these vertebral fractures, even those that are asymptomatic, are associated with a high risk of fractures even at nonvertebral sites and are also associated with a higher morbidity and mortality compared with age-matched patients without vertebral fractures, the detection of VCF will not only establish a diagnosis of osteoporosis regardless of the prevailing T score[93] but also identify a high risk for fracture group that merits treatment.

Thus, the advancements in DXA technology that allow physicians to identify a prevalent VCF at the point of care when the BMD is done by DXA for diagnosis, risk assessment, or monitoring

has improved the management and assessment of the osteoporotic patient.

Use of DXA for Monitoring BMD

Central DXA has been the foundation for monitoring patients with osteoporosis. Monitoring is useful for following the effects of diseases that may negatively effect bone such as primary hyperparathyroidism, for following the effects of drugs that may negatively effect bone such as glucocorticoids, and for monitoring the effects of pharmacologic agents for the treatment of PMO.

While there has been widespread acceptance of the use of BMD for monitoring disease states,[94–96] there has been much debate regarding the use of BMD to monitor the pharmacologic response to osteoporosis therapies.[97–101] The debate has focused on the contribution that pharmacologically mediated changes in BMD account for the reduction in fracture risk. The use of the change in BMD as a surrogate marker for a change in bone strength is clouded by the fact that the change in BMD mediated by agents registered for the treatment of PMO is neither linear nor proportional and by the statistical methods applied to examine the relationship between BMD change and fracture risk reduction. Summary statistics (meta-analysis)[102–105] have suggested that this relationship is closer to

TABLE 3. RELATIONSHIP BETWEEN RELATIVE RISK VS. ABSOLUTE RISK FOR FRACTURE AND AGE

Age	T score	Relative risk	Absolute risk
50	0	1	0.2%
	−1	2	0.4%
	−2	4	1.1%
60	0	1	0.4%
	−1	2	1.0%
	−2	4	2.7%
70	0	1	0.7%
	−1	2	1.9%
	−2	4	5.3%

Reprinted with permission from Blake GM, Knapp KM, Fogelman I 2002 Absolute fracture risk varies with bone densitometry technique used. J Clin Densitom **5:**109–116.)

TABLE 4. INDICATIONS FOR VERTEBRAL FRACTURE ASSESSMENT (VFA)* FROM THE INTERNATIONAL SOCIETY FOR CLINICAL DENSITOMETRY

Age (women ≥65 and men ≥70)
Known height loss of ≥1.5 in (4 cm)
History of vertebral fracture with no documentation
Nonvertebral fragility fracture after age 45
BMD evidence of osteoporosis at hip or spine
Corticosteroid use (≥5 mg/day for ≥3 months)

Modified with permission from Vokes T, Bachman D, Baim S, Binkley N, Broy S, Ferrar L, Lewiecki EM, Richmond B, Schousboe J 2006 Vertebral fracture assessment: The 2005 ISCD official positions. J Clin Densitom (in press).
* VFA Task Force Recommendations Pending ISCD Position Development Conference.

being linear than the relationship defined by individual clinical trial analysis defined by Freedman and others.[106–108] In addition, the U.S. Surgeon General's report on America's bone health has stated that surrogate markers can be used within the context of clinical trials to reflect drug-induced improvements in bone strength. Finally, the FDA approval of intermittent bisphosphonate dosing intervals (weekly, monthly, quarterly) has been allowed based on the trust that changes in BMD reflect equal fracture risk reduction compared with the daily dosing regimens that were required to prove fracture reduction (bridging concept).[109–112] Nevertheless, other factors lead to fracture risk reduction mediated by osteoporosis-specific pharmacologic agents independent of change in BMD,[113–117] and head-to-head randomized studies comparing BMD changes with alendronate versus risedronate or alendronate versus teriparatide indicate that BMD change may reflect increased bone strength an assumption not founded on any prospective comparative fracture data.[118,119] Therefore, the debate continues regarding the value of measuring change in DXA-derived BMD as a surrogate marker for fracture risk. This debate, mostly driven by marketing, has clouded the value of BMD monitoring in patients being treated for osteoporosis. Without measuring BMD over time, patients would never receive any feedback to determine if their long-term therapy of an often asymptomatic condition is worth their commitment and expense. In addition, the discovery of a loss in BMD beyond the in vivo least significant change[120–122] should never become an acceptable standard of care in the management of the osteoporosis patient on treatment. A loss in BMD cannot be assumed to reflect a residual improvement in bone strength.[123,124] A loss of BMD may be caused by poor patient compliance or adherence to treatment or to previously unrecognized and possibly reversible secondary conditions that may be responsible for a loss of BMD (e.g., celiac disease). A loss in BMD may be reversed by providing an alternative route of administration (e.g., an intravenous or transdermal or subcutaneous route of administration) or a change in pharmacologic agents.[125–127]

A word should be said about monitoring the effect of teriparatide [recombinant human PTH(1-34)]. Teriparatide increases bone strength and reduces fracture risk in part by increasing periosteal bone formation.[128,129] Thus, teriparatide increases bone area. BMD as measured by DXA is a derived equation, $BMD = BMC\ (g)/bone\ area\ (cm^2)$, giving a 2D areal measurement (g/cm^2). It is possible that patients treated with teriparatide may have a drop in areal BMD yet have an increase in bone strength.[130,131] In cynomogolus monkeys treated with teriparatide, forearm BMD measured by DXA declined, yet volumetric BMD measured by pQCT increased and forearm bone strength increased as well.[132] The practical issue for patient management is that, if the clinician is convinced that the patient being treated with teriparatide is compliant and that secondary factors that might mitigate a pharmacologic response have been excluded, the patient on teriparatide needs reassurance and commitment to continuation of therapy.

QUANTITATIVE ASSESSMENT OF BONE IN CHILDREN

During the first two decades of life, the skeleton matures, and marked changes in size and structure occur. Cartilaginous tissues slowly grow and ossify, providing support and locomotion to our bodies, and the bone marrow, initially hematopoietic, is mostly transformed into fatty marrow. A series of recent CT and MR studies clarified the distinction between increases in bone size and increases in volumetric BMD in the growing axial and appendicular skeletons, as well as the nature of ethnic and sex differences in bone geometry and BMD (Table 5). Trabecular BMD, as measured by QCT, does not increase before puberty,[133,134] but increases significantly during puberty, mainly because of thickening of the trabeculae.[135] The pubertal increases in BMD are comparable in girls and boys but are significantly greater in black compared with white adolescents.[133,134,136]

Studies of cortical BMD and dimensions in the appendicular skeleton have produced conflicting results, potentially because of differences between the upper and lower extremities and differences in measurement techniques. Most studies reported significant increases in cortical BMD with age.[137] A pQCT study reported greater cortical BMD in the radius in pubertal females compared with males,[138] whereas an MR study did not detect sex differences.[137] An early study of cortical dimensions, based on 2D radiogrammetry, concluded that the greater cortical bone mass in males was caused by sex differences in the rate of endosteal apposition and resorption.[139] Garn et al.[139] concluded that endosteal apposition began earlier and was in greater magnitude in girls than in boys as a result of the pubertal estrogen surge. The authors postulated that endosteal bone loss in menopause was a result of diminished estrogen levels and that endocortical bone had been accrued during puberty for that eventuality. Subsequent pQCT studies in the

TABLE 5. BONE ACCRUAL DURING CHILDHOOD AND ADOLESCENCE

	Changes with growth	Effect of ethnicity
Trabecular bone		
BMD (mg/cm³)	Constant through Tanner stages I–II; then increases during puberty	No differences until puberty, when the increase in blacks is greater than whites
Cross-sectional area (cm²)	Increases with age	None
Cortical bone		
BMD (mg/cm³)	Increases with age	Uncertain
Cross-sectional area (cm²)	Cortical area increases proportionately greater than overall bone cross-sectional area. During puberty, males exhibit greater periosteal apposition. Gender differences in endosteal dimensions may be site-specific	Blacks have greater total cross-sectional area but similar cortical cross-sectional area

upper extremities also suggested sex differences in the endocortical surface, with constant dimensions with age in females and increasing dimensions with age in males.[140] Furthermore, the timing of menarche in females is associated with radius endosteal dimensions in adulthood.[141] In contrast, studies in the weight-bearing femur[136,137] and tibia[142] failed to show sex differences in endocortical resorption.

Skeletal maturity is a measure of development incorporating the size, shape, and degree of mineralization of bone to define its proximity to full maturity. A single reading of skeletal age informs the clinician of the relative maturity of a patient at a particular time in his or her life, and, integrated with other clinical findings, separates the normal from the relatively advanced or retarded. Successive skeletal age readings indicate the direction of the child's development and/or show his or her progress under treatment. In normal subjects, bone age should be roughly within 10% of the chronological age. Greater discordance between skeletal age and chronological age occurs in children who are obese or who start puberty early, because their skeletal age is accelerated. There are two main applications for evaluations of skeletal maturation: the diagnosis of growth disorders, and the prediction of final adult height.[143]

DXA

DXA has several pronounced limitations when used for pediatric assessments. These can be broadly classified as follows: (1) difficulties in scan acquisition because of limitations in the bone edge detection software in children with low bone mass; (2) inadequacy of pediatric reference data across varied maturation stages, ethnic groups, and sex groups; and (3) difficulties in the interpretation of DXA results in children with impaired growth, altered body composition, or delayed maturation caused by childhood illness.

Reference Data

DXA is widely accepted as a quantitative measurement technique for assessing skeletal status in postmenopausal women. The diagnosis of osteoporosis in adults is based on the comparison of a measured BMD result with the average BMD of young adults at the time of peak bone mass, defined as a T score.[15] T scores < -2.5 SD below the mean peak bone mass are associated with increased fracture risk and are used for the diagnosis of osteoporosis. While the T score is a standard component of DXA BMD results, it is clearly inappropriate to assess skeletal health in children through comparison with peak adult bone mass; T scores should not be used in children. At present, there are no evidence-based guidelines for classification of bone health in children. Despite the growing body of normative data, there is little agreement on the quantitative definition of osteopenia and osteoporosis in children.

Most BMD reference data sets in healthy children are based on chronologic age. A systematic comparison of published pediatric DXA BMD normative data in 1999 revealed differences in the age-specific means and SDs for BMD across five studies.[144–148] These differences had a significant impact on the diagnosis of osteopenia in children with chronic diseases.[149] Importantly, use of reference data that were not sex specific resulted in significantly greater misclassification of males as osteopenic.[149]

Substantial effort is needed to develop adequate reference data and validate classification schemes of bone health in children. In 2002, the National Institutes of Health initiated a prospective longitudinal study of DXA BMD in a multiethnic sample of 1500 children and adolescents to be enrolled at five pediatric centers across the country. DXA measures included whole body, anteroposterior spine, nondominant forearm, and left hip; data collection is underway. In 2005, both Hologic and Lunar (GE Healthcare) introduced FDA-approved, sex-specific pediatric reference data based on large numbers of children using newer automated analysis techniques.

Interpretation of DXA Results in Children

A significant limitation of DXA is the reliance on measurements of projected 2D measures of BMD. DXA calculates BMD as the amount of mineral (g) divided by the area scanned (cm^2), giving an "areal BMD" (g/cm^2). This is not a true volumetric density (g/cm^3) because the bone thickness in the direction of the beam is not measured. Bones of larger width and height also tend to be thicker. Because this third dimension is not factored into DXA estimates of areal BMD, DXA systematically underestimates the bone density of short people. This is especially important in the assessment of children with chronic diseases that are associated with poor growth. Poor growth may result in the appearance of decreasing areal BMD for age when the volumetric BMD has not changed.

The confounding effect of skeletal size on DXA measures is well recognized, and two analytic strategies have been proposed to estimate vertebral volumetric BMD from projected bone dimensions and BMC. The technique developed by Carter et al.[150] is based on the observation that vertebral BMC scaled proportionate to the projected bone area to the 1.5 power. Therefore, vertebral volume is estimated as (area)1.5, and bone mineral apparent density (BMAD) is defined as BMC/(area)1.5. DXA-derived volumetric BMD correlates moderately well with BMD based on MR-derived estimates of vertebral volume ($r = 0.665$). Although these methods provide estimates of vertebral volume, BMC includes the bone content of the superimposed cortical spinous processes. These two approaches have been used in numerous pediatric studies to assess the effects of puberty,[151,152] ethnicity,[153–155] gene polymorphisms,[156] and weight-bearing physical activity[157–159] on bone spine volumetric BMD in healthy children, to assess the effects of calcium deficiency and milk avoidance[160,161] and hypovitaminosis D[162] and to assess the effects of varied chronic disorders associated with poor growth, such as Turner syndrome,[163] cystic fibrosis,[164–166] hypogonadism,[167] growth hormone disorder,[168–170] prematurity,[171] Cushing syndrome,[172] thalassemia,[173] diabetes mellitus,[174] solid organ transplantation,[175] and childhood leukemia.[176,177] These approaches have also been used to assess the effects of bisphosphonates[178] and growth hormone therapy.[168,170]

DXA BMC is a more accurate and reliable measure than DXA BMD for assessing bone acquisition, particularly for prepubertal children and those in the early stages of sexual development. Use of DXA BMD would be reasonable if adjustments for body size, pubertal status, and skeletal maturity are made, but these additional assessments add significant complexity to research studies and to clinical interpretation.

Fracture studies in children have been largely limited to forearm fractures, the most common fracture site in childhood. Multiple studies in healthy children have reported that spine BMAD and areal BMD were lower in wrist and forearm fracture cases compared with controls.[179–181] Multiple sources of pediatric DXA reference data are now available for the calculation of whole body bone Z scores. These include sex-specific percentile curves, age- and height-specific means and SDs, and Z score prediction models.[147,182–188] In addition, the observed strong correlation between muscle mass and whole body BMC has prompted numerous investigators to advocate a multistage algorithm for the assessment of DXA bone data relative to muscle mass in children.[189–191]

Lunar (GE Healthcare) recently introduced pediatric software that will generate Z scores for whole body bone area for height and whole body BMC for bone area, whereas Hologic recently introduced reference data for whole body BMC relative to height.[192] Finally, the 2005 International Society of Clinical Densitometry

Official Positions Statement advises the following for the assessment of DXA results in individuals <20 years of age: spine and whole body are the preferred skeletal sites for measurement; T scores should not appear in reports or on DXA printouts in children; the diagnosis of osteoporosis in children should not be made on densitometric criteria alone; and there is no agreement on standards for adjusting BMD or BMC for factors such as bone size, pubertal stage, skeletal maturity, and body composition.

Comparison of DXA and QCT in Children

A recent study highlighted the differences between DXA and QCT results in children. DXA areal BMD and QCT volumetric BMD Z scores in the spine were compared in 200 healthy children and 200 chronically ill children.[193] The hypothesis of the study was that DXA results in the overdiagnosis of osteoporosis (defined as a Z score < −2.0) in children with poor growth. Consistent with this hypothesis, a significantly greater proportion of children were classified as osteopenic by DXA (76 of 400) compared with QCT (25 of 400), particularly among children below the fifth percentile for height and/or weight for age. Among 79 ill children with QCT Z scores greater than −2.0, 47 (26%) had DXA Z scores less than −2.0. These findings have important implications for the diagnosis of bone deficits in children with poor growth and are consistent with the findings by Gafni and Baron[194] that osteoporosis is overdiagnosed in children.

CONCLUSIONS

A BMD measurement by DXA is the most important clinical tool to allow the field of osteoporosis to move from theory to practical application. Proper interpretation of BMD results, including the proper use of T scores, fracture risk assessment, and monitoring BMD over time provides the clinician with the best clinical information to use in the management of the osteoporotic patient. Central DXA use requires strict quality control of the measurements performed by DXA technologists and well-educated physicians who interpret the results.[195] The trust a clinician and patient place on DXA measurements lies in the appropriate interpretation of the result. The implementation of the validated WHO absolute fracture risk project should facilitate decision making for management of the patient with postmenopausal osteoporosis.

ACKNOWLEDGMENTS

I would like to thank Sydney Bonnick, MD, of the Clinical Research Center of North Texas and Abby Erickson, BA, of the Colorado Center for Bone Research, for their valuable assistance.

REFERENCES

1. Kanis JA, Borgstrom F, De Laet C, Johansson H, Johnell O, Jonsson B, Oden A, Zethraeus N, Pfleger B, Khaltaev N 2005 Assessment of fracture risk. Osteoporos Int **16:**581–589.
2. Miller PD, Siris ES, Barrett-Connor E, Faulkner KG, Wehren LE, Abbott TA, Chen YT, Berger ML, Santora AC, Sherwood LA 2002 Prediction of fracture risk in postmenopausal white women with peripheral bone densitometry: Evidence from the National Osteoporosis Risk Assessment. J Bone Miner Res **17:**2222–2230.
3. Black DM, Arden NK, Palermo L, Pearson J, Cummings SR 1999 Prevalent vertebral deformities predict hip fractures and new vertebral deformities but not wrist fractures. Study of Osteoporotic Fractures Research Group. J Bone Miner Res **14:**821–828.
4. Melton LJ III, Atkinson EJ, Cooper C, O'Fallon WM, Riggs BL 1999 Vertebral fractures predict subsequent fractures. Osteoporos Int **10:**214–221.
5. Lindsay R, Silverman SL, Cooper C, Hanley DA, Barton I, Broy SB, Licata A, Benhamou L, Geusens P, Flowers K, Stracke H, Seeman E 2001 Risk of new vertebral fracture in the year following a fracture. JAMA **285:**320–323.
6. Ross PD, Genant HK, Davis JW, Miller PD, Wasnich RD 1993 Predicting vertebral fracture incidence from prevalent fractures and bone density among non-black, osteoporotic women. Osteoporos Int **3:**120–126.
7. Kotowicz MA, Melton LJ III, Cooper C, Atkinson EJ, O'Fallon WM, Riggs BL 1994 Risk of hip fracture in women with vertebral fracture. J Bone Miner Res **9:**599–605.
8. Schousboe JT, Fink HA, Taylor BC, Stone KL, Hillier TA, Nevitt MC, Ensrud KE 2005 Association between self-reported prior wrist fractures and risk of subsequent hip and radiographic vertebral fractures in older women: A prospective study. J Bone Miner Res **20:**100–106.
9. Papaioannou A, Joseph L, Ioannidis G, Berger C, Anastassiades T, Brown JP, Hanley DA, Hopman W, Josse RG, Kirkland S, Murray TM, Olszynski WP, Pickard L, Prior JC, Siminoski K, Adachi JD 2005 Risk factors associated with incident clinical vertebral and non-vertebral fractures in postmenopausal women: The Canadian Multicenter Osteoporosis Study (CaMos). Osteoporos Int **16:**568–578.
10. Klotzbuecher CM, Ross PD, Landsman PB, Abbott TA III, Berger M 2000 Patients with prior fractures have an increased risk of future fractures: A summary of the literature and statistical synthesis. J Bone Miner Res **15:**721–739.
11. Siris ES, Brenneman S, Barrett-Conner E, Miller PD, Sajjan S, Berger ML, Chen YT 2006 The effect of age and bone mineral density on the absolute, excess and relative risk of fracture in postmenopausal women age 50–99: Results from the National Osteoporosis Risk Assessment. Osteoporos Int (in press).
12. Johnell O, Kanis JA 2005 Epidemiology of osteoporotic fractures. Osteoporos Int **16**(Suppl 2)**:**S3–S7.
13. Kanis JA, Johnell O, De Laet C, Johansson H, Oden A, DelmasP, Eisman J, Fuliwara S, Garnero P, Kroger H, McCloskey EV, Mellstrom EV, Melton LJ III,Pols H, Reeve J, Silman A, Tenenhous A 2004 A meta-analysis of previous fracture and subsequent fracture risk. Bone **36:**375–382.
14. Ross PD, Davis JW, Epstein RS, Wasnich RD 1991 Pre-existing fractures and bone mass predict vertebral fracture incidence in women. Ann Intern Med **114:**919–923.
15. World Health Organization 1994 Assessment of Fracture Risk and Its Application to Screening for Postmenopausal Osteoporosis. Report of a WHO Study Group. World Health Organization, Geneva, Switzerland.
16. Melton JL III, Chrischilles EA, Cooper C, Lane AW, Riggs BL 2005 How many women have osteoporosis? JBMR Anniversary Classic. J Bone Miner Res **20:**886–892.
17. Melton LJ III 2004 How many women have osteoporosis now? J Bone Miner Res **10:**175–177.
18. Miller PD 2002 Controversial issues in bone densitometry. In: Bilezikian JP (ed.) Principles of Bone Biology. Academic Press, San Diego, CA, USA, pp. 1587–1597.
19. Miller PD 2000 Controversies in bone mineral density diagnostic classification. Calcif Tissue Int **66:**317–319.
20. Faulkner KG, von Stetten E, Miller P 1999 Discordance in patient classification using T-scores. J Clin Densit **2:**343–350.
21. Ahmed AIH, Blake GM, Rymer JM, Fogleman I 1997 Screening for osteopoenia and osteoporosis: Do the accepted normal ranges lead to overdiagnosis?. Osteoporos Int **7:**432–438.
22. Looker AC, Wahner HW, Dunn WL, Calvo MS, Harris TB, Heyse SP, Johnston CCJ, Lindsay R 1998 Updated data on proximal femur bone mineral levels of US adults. Osteoporos Int **8:**468–489.
23. Faulkner KG, Roberts L, McClung M 1996 Discrepancies in normative data between Lunar and Hologic DXA systems. Osteoporos Int **6:**432–436.
24. Binkley N, Kiebzak GM, Lewiecki EM, Krueger D, Gangnon KE, Miller PD, Shepherd JA, Drezner MF 2005 Recalculation of the NHANES database SD improves T-score agreement and reduces osteoporosis prevalence. J Bone Miner Res **20:**195–201.
25. Simmons A, Simpson DE, O'Doherty MJ, Barrington S, Coakley AJ 1997 The effects of standarization and reference values on patient classification for spine and femur dual-enegry X-ray absorptiometry. Osteoporos Int **7:**200–206.
26. McMahon K, Kalnins S, Freund J, Pocock N 2003 Discordance in lumbar spine T scores and non-standardization of standard deviations. J Clin Densitom **6:**1–6.
27. Miller PD, Bonnick SL, Rosen CJ 1996 Consensus of an international panel on the clinical utility of bone mass measurements in the detection of low bone mass in the adult population. Calcif Tissue Int **58:**207–214.
28. Miller PD, Bonnick SL 1999 Clinical application of bone densitometry. In: Favos MJ (ed.) Primer on the Metabolic Bone Diseases and Disorders of Mineral Metabolism, 4th ed. Lippincott Williams & Wilkins, Philadelphia, PA, USA, pp. 152–159.
29. Miller PD 2004 Pitfalls in bone mineral density measurements. Curr Osteoporos Rep **2:**59–64.

30. Miller PD 2003 Review: Bone mineral density—clinical use and application. Endocrinol Metab Clin North Am **32:**159–179.

31. Miller PD, Zapalowski C, Kulak CAM, Bilezikian JP 1999 Bone densitometry: The best way to detect osteoporosis and to monitor therapy. J Clin Endocrin Metab **84:**1867–1871.

32. U.S. Surgeon General's Report on America's Bone Health. 2004 Available at www.surgeongeneral.gov. Accessed April 6, 2005.

33. National Osteoporosis Foundation 1999 Physicians Guide to the Prevention and Treatment of Osteoporosis. National Osteoporosis Foundation, Washington, DC, USA.

34. Leib E, Lewiecki M, Binkley N, Hamdy RC 2004 Official positions of the International Society for Clinical Densitometry. J Clin Densitom **7:**1–6.

35. Binkley N, Bilezikian JP, Kendler DL, Leib ES, Lewiecki EM, Petak SM 2006 Official positions of the International Society for Clinical Densitometry and Executive Summary of the 2005 Position Development. J Clin Densitom (in press).

36. Siris E, Miller P, Barrett-Connor E, Faulkner K, Wehren L, Abbott T, Berger M, Santora A, Sherwood L 2001 Identification and fracture outcomes of undiagnosed low bone mineral density in postmenopausal women: Results from the National Osteoporosis Risk Assessment (NORA). JAMA **286:**2815–2822.

37. Siris ES, Chen Y-T, Abbott TA, Barrett-Connor E, Miller PD, Wehren L, Berger ML 2004 Bone mineral density thresholds for pharmacological intervention to prevent fractures. Arch Intern Med **164:**1108–1112.

38. De Laet CEDH, Van Hout BA, Burger H, Weel AEAM, Hofman R, Pols HAP 1998 Hip fracture prediction in the elderly men and women: Validation in the Rotterdam study. J Bone Miner Res **13:**1587–1593.

39. Schuit SC, van der Klift M, Weel AE, de Laet CE, Burger H, Seeman E, Hofman A, Utterlinden AG, Van Leeuwen JP, Pols HA 2004 Fracture incidence and association with bone mineral density in elderly men and women: The Rotterdam Study. Bone **34:**195-202.

40. Wainwright SA, Marshall LM, Ensrud KE, Cauley JA, Black DM, Hillier TA, Hochberg MC, Voght TM, Orwoll ES 2005 Hip fracture in women without osteoporosis. J Clin Endocrinol Metab **90:**2787–2793.

41. The Writing Group for the ISCD Position Development Conference 2004 2004 executive summary. J Clin Densitom **7:**7–12.

42. The Writing Group for the ISCD Position Development Conference 2004 Diagnosis of osteoporosis in men, premenopausal women and children. J Clin Densitom **7:**17–26.

43. Melton LJ III, Atkinson EJ, O'Conner MK, O'Fallon WM. Riggs BL 1998 Bone densitometry and fracture risk in men. J Bone Miner Res **13:**1915–1923.

44. Binkley NC, Schmeer P, Wasnich RD, Lenchik L 2002 What are the criteria by which a densitometric diagnosis of osteoporosis can be made in males and non-Caucasians? J Clin Densitom **5**(Suppl)**:**S19–S27.

45. Leslie WD, Adler RA, Fuleihan GEH, Hodsman A, Kendler DL, Miller PD,Watts N 2006 ,ztiApplication of the 1994 WHO classification to populations other than postmenopausal Caucasian women: The 2005 ISCD official positions. J Clin Densitom (in press).

46. Barrett-Connor E, Siris ES, Wehren LE, Miller PD, Abbott TA, Berger ML, Santora AC, Sherwood LM 2005 Osteoporosis and fracture risk in women of different ethnic groups. J Bone Miner Res **20:**185–194.

47. Leslie WD 2006 Race/ethnicity and fracture risk assessment: An issue that's more than skin deep (review). J Clin Densitom (in press).

48. Marshall D, Johnell O, Wedel H 1996 Meta-analysis of how well measurements of bone mineral density predict the occurrence of osteoporotic fractures. BMJ **312:**1254–1259.

49. Blake GM and Fogelman I 2001 Peripheral or Central Densitometry: Does it matter which technique we use. J Clin Densitom **4:**83–96.

50. Miller PD, Njeh C, Jankowski LG, Lenchik L 2002 What are the standards by which bone mass measurement at peripheral skeletal sites should be used in the diagnosis of osteoporosis?. J Clin Densitom **5:**S39–S45.

51. Greenspan SL, Cheng S, Miller PD, Orwoll ES for the QUS-2 PMA Trials Group 2001 Clinical performance of a highly portable, scanning calcaneal ultrasonometer. Osteoporos Int **12:**391–398.

52. Kanis JA, Gluer C-C, for the Committee of Scientific Advisors, International Osteoporosis Foundation 2000 An update on the diagnosis and assessment of osteoporosis with densitometry. Osteoporos Int **11:**92–202.

53. Gluer C-C, for the International Quantitative Ultrasound Consensus Group 1997 Quantitative ultrasound techniques for the assessment of osteoporosis: Expert agreement on current status. J Bone Miner Res **12:**1280–1288.

54. Baran DT, Faulkner KG, Genant HK, Miller PD, Pacifici R 1997 Diagnosis and management of osteoporosis: Guidelines for the utilization of bone densitometry. Calcif Tissue Int **61:**433–440.

55. Miller P, Siris E, Barrett-Connor E, Faulkner K, Abbott T, Berger M, Santora A, Sherwood L 2002 Prediction of fracture risk in postmenopausal white women with peripheral bone densitometry: Evidence from the National Osteoporosis Risk Assessment (NORA) program. J Bone Miner Res **17:**2222–2230.

56. Hans D, Dargent Molina P, Schott AM, Sebert JL, Cormier C, Kotzki PO, Delmas PD, Pouilles JM, Breart G, Meunier PJ 1996 Ultrasonographic heel measurements predict hip fracture in elderly women: The EPIDOS prospective study. Lancet **348:**511–514.

57. Hans D, Hartl F, Krieg MA 2003 Device-specific weighted T-score for two quantitative ultrasounds: Operational propositions for the management of osteoporosis for 65 years and older women in Switzerland. Osteoporos Int **14:**251–258.

58. Blake GM, Knapp KM, Spector TD, Fogelman I 2006 Predicting the risk of fracture at any site in the skeleton: Are all bone mineral density measurement sites equally effective?. Calcif Tissue Int **78:**9–17.

59. Blake GM, Knapp KM, Fogelman I 2002 Absolute fracture risk varies with bone densitometry technique used. J Clin Densitom **5:**109–116.

60. Hui SL, Slemenda CW, Johnston CC Jr 1988 Age and bone mass as predictors of fracture in a prospective study. J Clin Invest **81:**1804–1809.

61. Kanis JA, Johnell O, Oden A, Oglesby AK, De Laet CE 2001 Ten year probabilities of osteoporotic fractures according to BMD and diagnostic thresholds. J Bone Miner Res **16:**S194.

62. Dargent-Molina P, Favier F, Grandjean H, Baudoin C, Schott AM, Hausherr E, Meunier PJ, Breart G 1996 Fall-related factors and risk of hip fracture: The EPIDOS prospective study. Lancet **348:**145–149.

63. Riggs BL, Melton JL III, Robb RA, Camp JJ, Atkinson EL, Oberg AL, Rouleau PA, McCollough CH, Khosla S, Bouxsein ML 2006 Population-based analysis of the relationship of whole bone strength indices and fall-related loads to age- and sex-specific patterns of hip and wrist fractures. J Bone Miner Res **21:**315–323.

64. Bouxsein ML 2003 Bone quality: Where do we go from here? Osteoporos Int **14**(Suppl 5)**:**118–127.

65. Diab T, Condon KW, Burr DB, Vashishth D 2006 Age-related change in the damage morphology of human cortical bone and its role in bone fragility. Bone **38:**427–431.

66. Russo CR, Lauretani F, Seeman E, Bartali B, Band inelli S, Di Iorio A, Guralink J, Ferrucci L 2006 Structural adaptations to bone loss in aging men and women. Bone **38:**112–118.

67. Siris ES, Brenneman SK, Miller PD, Barrett-Connor E, Chen YT, Sherwood LM, Abbott TA 2004 Predictive value of low BMD for 1-year fracture outcomes is similar for postmenopausal women ages 50–64 and 65 and older: Results from the National Osteoporosis Risk Assessment (NORA). J Bone Miner Res **19:**1215–1220.

68. Cummings SR, Nevitt MC, Browner WS, Stone K, Fox KM, Ensrud KE, Cavley J, Black D, Vogt TM 1995 Risk factors for hip fracture in white women. Study of Osteoporotic Fractures Research Group. N Engl J Med **332:**767–773.

69. Haentjens P, Autier P, Collins J, Velkeniers B, Vanderschueren D, Boonen S 2003 Colles fracture, spine fracture, and subsequent risk of hip fracture in men and women: A meta-analysis. J Bone Joint Surg Am **85:**1936–1943.

70. Kanis J 2006 World Health Organization 10 Year Validated Absolute Fracture Risk Probabilities. International Osteoporosis Foundation, Toronto, Canada.

71. Black DM, Steinbuch M, Palmero L, Dargent-Molina P, Lindsay R, Hoseyni MS, Johnell O 2001 An assessment tool for predicting fracture risk in postmenopausal women. Osteoporos Int **12:**519–528.

72. Miller PD, Barlas SK, Brenneman SK, Abbott TA, Chen Y-T, Barrett-Connor E, Siris ES 2004 An approach to identifying osteopenic women at increased short-term risk of fracture. Arch Intern Med **164:**1113–1120.

73. Nevitt MC, Cummings SR, Stone KL, Palermo L, Black DM, Bauer DC, Genant HK, Hochberg MC, Ensrud KE, Hillier TA, Cauley JA 2005 Risk factors for a first-incident radiographic vertebral fracture in women > or = 65 years of age: The study of osteoporotic fractures. J Bone Miner Res **20:**131–140.

74. Papaioannou A, Joseph L, Ioannidis G, Berger C, Anastassiades T, Brown JP, Hanley DA, Hopman W, Josse RG, Kirkland S, Murray TM, Olszynski WP, Pickard L, Prior JC, Siminoski K, Adachi JD 2005 Risk factors associated with incident clinical vertebral and nonvertebral fractures in postmenopausal women: The Canadian Multicentre Osteoporosis Study (CaMos). Osteoporos Int **16:**568–578.

75. Gallagher JC, Genant HK, Crans GG, Vargas SJ, Krege JH 2005 Teriparatide reduces the fracture risk associated with increasing number and severity of osteoporotic fractures. J Clin Endocrinol Metab **90:**1583–1587.

76. Garnero P, Delmas P 2004 Contribution of bone mineral density and bone turnover markers to the estimation of risk of osteoporotic fracture in postmenopausal women. J Musculoskelet Neuronal Interact **4:**50–63.

77. Faulkner KG, Wacker WK, Barden HS, Simonelli C, Burke PK, Ragi S, Del Rio L 2005 Femur strength index predicts hip fracture independent of bone density and hip axis length. Osteoporos Int **31:**1–7.

78. Mayhew PM, Thomas CD, Clement JG, Loveridge N, Beck TJ, Bonfield W, Burgyone CJ, Reeve L 2005 Relation between age, femoral neck cortical stability, and hip fracture risk. Lancet **366:**129–135.

79. Uusi-Rasi K, Semanick LM, Zanchetta JR, Bogado CE, Eriksen EF, Sato M,

Beck T 2005 Effects of teriparatide [rhPTH (1–34)] treatment on structural geometry of the proximal femur in elderly osteoporotic women. Bone **36:** 948–958.

80. Khoo BC, Beck TJ, Qiao QH, Parakh P, Semanick L, Prince RL, Singer KP, Price RI 2005 In vivo short-term precision of hip structure analysis variables in comparison with bone mineral density using paired dual-energy X-ray absorptiometry scans from multi-center clinical trials. Bone **37:**112–121.

81. Melton LJ III, Lane AW, Cooper C, Eastell R, O'Fallon WM, Riggs BL 1993 Prevalence and incidence of vertebral deformities. Osteoporos Int **3:**113–119.

82. O'Neill TW, Felsenberg D, Varlow J, Cooper C, Kanis JA, Silman AJ 1996 The prevalence of vertebral deformity in european men and women: The European Vertebral Osteoporosis Study. J Bone Miner Res **11:**1010–1018.

83. Spector TD, McCloskey EV, Doyle DV, Kanis JA 1993 Prevalence of vertebral fracture in women and the relationship with bone density and symptoms: The Chingford Study. J Bone Miner Res **8:**817–822.

84. Ross PD, Fujiwara S, Huang C, Davis JW, Epstein RS, Wasnich RD, Kodama K, Melton LJ III 1995 Vertebral fracture prevalence in women in Hiroshima compared to Caucasians or Japanese in the US. Int J Epidemiol **24:**1171–1177.

85. Cooper C, O'Neill T, Silman A 1993 The epidemiology of vertebral fractures. European Vertebral Osteoporosis Study Group. Bone **14**(Suppl 1): S89–S97.

86. Genant HK, Li J, Wu CY, Shepherd JA 2000 Vertebral fractures in osteoporosis: A new method for clinical assessment. J Clin Densitom **3:**281–290.

87. Vokes T, Bachman D, Baim S, Binkley N, Broy S, Ferrar L, Lewiecki EM, Richmond B, Schousboe J 2006 Vertebral fracture assessment: The 2005 ISCD official positions. J Clin Densitom (in press).

88. Siminoski K, Warshawski RS, Jen H, Lee K 2006 The accuracy of historical height loss for the detection of vertebral fractures in postmenopausal women. Osteoporos Int **17:**290–296.

89. Seeman E, Crans GG, Diez-Perez A, Pinette KV, Delma P 2006 Anti-vertebral fracture efficacy of raloxifene: A meta-analysis. Osteoporos Int **17:**313–316.

90. Delmas P, Genant HK, Crans GG, Stock JL, Wong M, Siris E, Adachi JD 2003 Severity of prevalent vertebral fractures and the risk of subsequent vertebral and nonvertebral fractures: Results from the MORE trial. Bone **33:**522–532.

91. Lenchik L, Rogers LF, Delmas P, Genant HK 2004 Diagnosis of osteoporotic vertebral fractures: Importance of recognition and description by radiologists. AJR Am J Roentgenol **183:**949–958.

92. Duboeuf F, Bauer DC, Chapurlat RD, Dinten JM, Delmas P Assessment of vertebral fracture using densitometric morphometry. J Clin Densitom **8:**362–368.

93. Greenspan SL, von Stetten E, Emond SK, Jones L, Parker RA 2001 Instant vertebral assessment: A noninvasive dual X-ray absorptiometry technique to avoid misclassification and clinical mismanagement of osteoporosis. J Clin Densitom **4:**373–380.

94. Khosla S 2003 Surrogates for fracture end-points in clinical trials. J Bone Miner Res **18:**1146–1149.

95. Miller PD 2005 Bone density and markers of bone turnover in predicting fracture risk and how changes in these measures predict fracture risk reduction. Curr Osteoporos Rep **3:**103–110.

96. Miller PD, Bilezikian JP 2002 Bone densitometry in asymptomatic hyperparathyroidism. J Bone Miner Res **17:**S2;N98–N102.

97. Miller PD, Hochberg MC, Wehren LE, Ross P, Wasnich RD 2005 How useful are measures of BMD and bone turnover?. Clin Med Res Opin **4:**545–554.

98. Sarkar S, Reginster JY, Crans GG, Diez-Perez A, Pinette KV, Delmas PD 2004 Relationship between changes in biochemical markers of bone turnover and BMD to predict vertebral fracture risk. J Bone Miner Res **19:**394–401.

99. Delmas PD, Seeman E 2004 Changes in bone mineral density explain little of the reduction in vertebral or nonvertebral fracture risk with anti-resorptive therapy. Bone **34:**599–604.

100. Eastell R, Delmas PD 2005 How to interpret surrogate markers of efficacy in osteoporosis. J Bone Miner Res **20:**1261–1262.

101. Garnero P, Delmas PD 2004 Contribution of bone mineral density and bone turnover markers to the estimation of risk of osteoporotic fracture in postmenopausal women. J Musculoskelet Neuronal Interact **4:**50–63.

102. Hochberg M, Greenspan S, Wasnich R, Miller P, Thompson D, Ross P 2002 Changes in bone density and turnover explain the reductions in incidence of nonvertebral fractures that occur during treatment with antiresorptive agents. J Clin Endocrinol Metab **87:**1586–1592.

103. Wasnich RD, Miller PD 2000 Antifracture efficacy of antiresportive agents are related to changes in bone density. J Clin Endocrinol Metab **85:**1–6.

104. Cummings SR, Karpf DB, Harris F, Genant HK, Ensrud K, LaCroix HZ, Black DM 2002 Improvement in spine bone density and reduction in risk of vertebral fractures during treatment with anti-resorptive drugs. Am J Med **112:**281–289.

105. Delmas PD, Li Z, Cooper C 2004 Relationship between changes in bone mineral density and fracture risk reduction with antiresorptive drugs: Some issues with meta-analyses. J Bone Miner Res **19:**330–337.

106. Watts NB, Cooper C, Linday R, Eastell R, Manhart MD, Barton IP, Van Staa TP, Abachi JO 2004 Relationship between changes in bone mineral density and vertebral fracture risk associated with risedronate: Greater increases in bone mineral density do not relate to greater decreases in fracture risk. J Clin Densitom **7:**255–261.

107. Freedman LS, Graubard BI, Schatzkin A 1992 Statistical validation of intermediate endpoints for chronic diseases. Stat Med **11:**167–178.

108. Shih J, Bauer DC, Orloff J, Crepaldi G, Adami S, McClung M, Kiel D, Felsenberg D, Recker RR, Tonino RP, Roux C, Pinchera A, Foldes AJ, Greenspan SL, Levine MA, Emkey R, Santora AC 2nd, Faur A, Thompson DE, Yates J, Orloff JJ 2002 Proportion of fracture risk reduction explained by BMD changes using Freeman's analysis depends on choice of predictors. Osteoporos Int 13(Suppl 3):538–539.

109. Schnitzer T, Bone H, Crepasldi G, Adami S, McClung M, Kiel D, Felsenberg D, Recker RR, Tonino RP, Roux C, Pinchera A, Foldes AJ, Greenspan SL, Levine MA, Emkey R, Santora AC II, Kaur A, Thompson DE, Yates J, Orloff JJ 2000 Therapeutic equivalence of alendronate 70 mg once-weekly and alendronate 10 mg daily in the treatment of osteoporosis. Aging Clin Exp Res **12:**1–12.

110. Brown JP, Kendler DL, McClung MR 2002 The efficacy and tolerability of risedronate once a week for the treatment of postmenopausal osteoporosis. Calcif Tissue Int **71:**103–111.

111. Miller PD, McClung M, Macovei L, Stakkestad J, Luckey M, Bonvoisin B, Reginster J-Y, Recker R, Hughes C, Lewiecki M, Felsenberg D, Delmas P, Kendler D, Bolognese M, Mairon N, Cooper C 2005 Monthly oral ibandronate therapy in postmenopausal osteoporosis: One year results from the MOBILE study. J Bone Miner Res **20:**1315–1322.

112. Miller PD 2005 Optimizing the management of postmenopausal osteoporosis with bisphosphonates: The emerging role of intermittent therapy. Clin Therap **27:**1–16.

113. Russell RGG, Croucher PI, Rogers MJ 1999 Bisphosphonates: Pharmacology, mechanisms of action and clinical uses. Osteoporos Int **2:**S66–S80.

114. Borah B, Dufrense TE, Chmielewski PA, Gross GS, Prenger MC, Phipps AJ 2002 Risedronate preserves trabecular architecture and increases bone strength in vertebrae of oophorectomized minipigs as measured by 3-dimensional microcomputed tomography. J Bone Miner Res **17:**1139–1147.

115. Roschger P, Rinnerthaler S, Yates P, Rodan G, Klaushofer KJ, Fratel P 2001 Alendronate increases degree and uniformity of mineralization in cancellous bone and decreases the porosity in cortical bone of osteoporotic women. Bone **29:**185–191.

116. Eastell R, Barton I, Hannon RA, Chines A, Garner OP, Delmas PD 2003 Realtionship of early changes in bone resorption to the reduction in fracture risk with risedronate. J Bone Miner Res **18:**1051–1056.

117. Bauer DC, Black D, Garnero P, Hochberg M, Ott S, Orloff D, Thompson DE, Ewing SK, Delmas PD 2004 Reduction in bone turnover predicts hip, non-spine,and vertebral fracture in alendronate treated women: The Fracture Intervention Trial. J Bone Miner Res **19:**1250–1258.

118. Rosen CJ, Hochberg M, Bonnick S, McClung MR, Miller P, Broy S, Kagan R, Chene, Petruschke RA, Thompson DE, de Papp AE 2005 Treatment with once-weekly alendronate 70 mg compared to once-weekly risedronate 35 mg in women with postmenopausal osteoporosis: A randomized, double-blind study. J Bone Miner Res **20:**141–151.

119. McClung M, San Martin J, Miller PD, Ciretelli R, Bandeira F, Donley DW, Dalsky GP, Eriksen EF 2005 Teriparatide and alendronate increase bone mass by opposite effects on bone remodeling. Arch Int Med **165:**1762–1768.

120. Bonnick SL, Johnston CC Jr, Kleerekoper M, Lindsay R, Miller P, Siris E 2001 Importance of precision in bone density measurements. J Clin Densitom **4:**105–110.

121. Lenchick L, Leib ES, Hamdy RC, Binkley NC, Miller PD, Watts NB 2002 Executive summary International Society for Clinical Densitometry position development conference. J Clin Densitom **5**(S1):S1–S3.

122. Baim S, Wilson CR, Lewiecki EM, Luckey MM, Downs RW Jr, Lentle BC Precision assessment and radiation safety for dual-energy X-ray absorptiometry: Position paper of the International Society for Clinical Densitometry. J Clin Densitom **8:**371–378.

123. Chapurlat RD, Palmero L, Ramsay P, Cummongs SR 2005 Risk of fracture among women who lose bone density during treatment with alendronate. The Fracture Intervention Trial .Osteoporos Int **16:**842–848.

124. Watts NB, Geusens P, Barton IP, Felsenberg D 2005 Relationship between changes in BMD and nonvertebral fracture incidence associated with risedronate: Reduction in risk of nonvertebral fracture is not related to change in BMD. J Bone Miner Res **20:**2097–2104.

125. Lewiecki EM 2005 Review of guidelines for bone mineral density testing and treatment of osteoporosis. Curr Osteoporos Rep **3:**75–83.

126. Lewiecki EM 2003 Nonresponders to osteoporosis therapy. J Clin Densitom **6:**307–314.

127. Hodgson SF, Watts NB,Bilezikian JP, Clarke BL, Gray TK, Harris DW, Johnston CC Jr., Kleerkeeper M, Luckey MM, McClung MR, Nankin HP, Petak SM, Recker RR, Anderson RJ, Bergman DA, Bloomgarden ZT, Dickey RA, Palumbo PJ, Peters AL, Rettinger HI, Rodbard HW, Rubenstein HA, AACE Osteoporosis Task Force 2003 American Association of Clinical Endocrinologists medical guidelines for clinical practice for the prevention and treatment of postmenopausal osteoporosis: 2001 edition, with selected updates for 2003. Endocr Pract 9:544–564.

128. Misof BM, Roschger P, Cosman F, Kurland ES, Tesch W, Messmer P, Dempster DW, Nieves J, Shane E, Fratzl P, Klaushofer K, Bilezikian JP, Lindsay R 2003 Effects of intermittent parathyroid hormone administration on bone mineralization density in iliac crest biopsies from patients with osteoporosis: A paired study before and after treatment. J Clin Endocrinol Metab 88:1150–1156.

129. Zanchetta JR, Bogado CE, Ferretti JL, Wang O, Wilson MG, Sato M, Gaich G, Dalsky GP, Myers SL 2003 Effects of teriparatide [recombinant human parathyroid hormone (1–34)] on cortical bone in postmenopausal women with osteoporosis. J Bone Miner Res 18:539–543.

130. Miller PD, Bilezikian JP, Deal C, Harris ST, Pacifici R 2004 Clinical use of teriparatide in the real world: Initial insights. Endocr Prac 10:139–145.

131. Hodsman AB, Bauer DC, Dempster D, Dian L, Hanley DA, Harris ST, Kendler D, McClung MR, Miller PD, Olszynski WP, Orwoll E, Yuen CK 2005 Parathyroid hormone and teriparaide for the treatment of osteoporosis: A review of the evidence and suggested guidelines for it use. Endocr Rev 10:2004–2006.

132. Zanchetta J, Bogado C, Ferretti J, Wang O, Wilson M, Sato M, Gaich G, Dalsky G, Myers S 2003 Effects of teriparatide [recombinant human para-thyroid hormone (1–34)] on cortical bone in postmenopausal women with osteoporosis. J Bone Miner Res 18:539–543.

133. Gilsanz V, Roe TF, Mora S, Costin G, Goodman WG 1991 Changes in vertebral bone density in black girls and white girls during childhood and puberty. N Engl J Med 325:1597–1600.

134. Gilsanz V, Kovanlikaya A, Costin G, Roe TF, Sayre J, Kaufman F 1997 Differential effect of gender on the sizes of the bones in the axial and appendicular skeletons. J Clin Endocrinol Metab 82:1603–1607.

135. Han ZH, Palnitkar S, Rao DS, Nelson D, Parfitt AM 1996 Effect of ethnicity and age or menopause on the structure and geometry of iliac bone. J Bone Miner Res 11:1967–1975.

136. Gilsanz V, Skaggs DL, Kovanlikaya A, Sayre J, Loro ML, Kaufman F, Korenman SG 1998 Differential effect of race on the axial and appendicular skeletons of children. J Clin Endocrinol Metab 83:1420–1427.

137. Hogler W, Blimkie CJ, Cowell CT, Kemp AF, Briody J, Wiebe P, Farpour-Lambert N, Duncan CS, Woodhead HJ 2003 A comparison of bone geom-etry and cortical density at the mid-femur between prepuberty and young adulthood using magnetic resonance imaging. Bone 33:771–778.

138. Schoenau E, Neu CM, Rauch F, Manz F 2002 Gender-specific pubertal changes in volumetric cortical bone mineral density at the proximal radius. Bone 31:110–113.

139. Garn SM, Frisancho AR, Sandusky ST, McCann MB 1972 Confirmation of the sex difference in continuing subperiosteal apposition. Am J Phys An-thropol 36:377–380.

140. Neu CM, Rauch F, Manz F, Schoenau E 2001 Modeling of cross-sectional bone size, mass and geometry at the proximal radius: A study of normal bone development using peripheral quantitative computed tomography. Osteopo-ros Int 12:538–547.

141. Rauch F, Neu C, Manz F, Schoenau E 2001 The development of metaphyseal cortex—implications for distal radius fractures during growth. J Bone Miner Res 16:1547–1555.

142. Kontulainen SA, Macdonald HM, Khan KM, McKay HA 2005 Examining bone surfacesacross puberty: A 20-month pQCT trial. J Bone Miner Res 20:1202–1207.

143. Gilsanz V, Ratib O 2005 Hand Bone Age: A Digital Atlas of Skeletal Maturity. Springer-Verlag, New York, NY, USA.

144. Southard RN, Morris JD, Mahan JD, Hayes JR, Torch MA, Sommer A, Zipf WB 1991 Bone mass in healthy children: Measurement with quantitative DXA. Radiology 179:735–738.

145. Henderson RC, Madsen CD 1996 Bone density in children and adolescents with cystic fibrosis. J Pediatr 128:28–34.

146. Bonjour JP, Theintz G, Buchs B, Slosman D, Rizzoli R 1991 Critical years and stages of puberty for spinal and femoral bone mass accumulation during adolescence. J Clin Endocrinol Metab 73:555–563.

147. Faulkner RA, Bailey DA, Drinkwater DT, McKay HA, Arnold C, Wilkinson AA 1996 Bone densitometry in Canadian children 8–17 years of age. Calcif Tissue Int 59:344–351.

148. Glastre C, Braillon P, David L, Cochat P, Meunier PJ, Delmas PD 1990 Measurement of bone mineral content of the lumbar spine by dual energy x-ray absorptiometry in normal children: Correlations with growth parame-ters. J Clin Endocrinol Metab 70:1330–1333.

149. Leonard MB, Propert KJ, Zemel BS, Stallings VA, Feldman HI 1999 Discrepancies in pediatric bone mineral density reference data: Potential for misdiagnosis of osteopenia. J Pediatr 135:182–188.

150. Carter DR, Bouxsein ML, Marcus R 1992 New approaches for interpreting projected bone densitometry data. J Bone Miner Res 7:137–145.

151. Katzman DK, Bachrach LK, Carter DR, Marcus R 1991 Clinical and an-thropometric correlates of bone mineral acquisition in healthy adolescent girls. J Clin Endocrinol Metab 73:1332–1339.

152. Haapasalo H, Kannus P, Sievanen H, Pasanen M, Uusi-Rasi K, Heinonen A, Oja P, Vuori I 1996 Development of mass, density, and estimated mechanical characteristics of bones in Caucasian females. J Bone Miner Res 11:1751–1760.

153. Bachrach LK, Hastie T, Wang MC, Narasimhan B, Marcus R 1999 Bone mineral acquisition in healthy Asian, Hispanic, black, and Caucasian youth: A longitudinal study. J Clin Endocrinol Metab 84:4702–4712.

154. Bhudhikanok GS, Wang MC, Eckert K, Matkin C, Marcus R, Bachrach LK 1996 Differences in bone mineral in young Asian and Caucasian Americans may reflect differences in bone size. J Bone Miner Res 11:1545–1556.

155. Wang MC, Aguirre M, Bhudhikanok GS, Kendall CG, Kirsch S, Marcus R, Bachrach LK 1997 Bone mass and hip axis length in healthy Asian, black, Hispanic, and white American youths. J Bone Miner Res 12:1922–1935.

156. Boot AM, van der Sluis IM, de Muinck Keizer-Schrama SM, van Meurs JB, Krenning EP, Pols HA, Uitterlinden AG 2004 Estrogen receptor alpha gene polymorphisms and bone mineral density in healthy children and young adults. Calcif Tissue Int 74:495–500.

157. Ward KA, Roberts SA, Adams JE, Mughal MZ 2005 Bone geometry and density in the skeleton of pre-pubertal gymnasts and school children. Bone 36:1012–1018.

158. Dyson K, Blimkie CJ, Davison KS, Webber CE, Adachi JD 1997 Gymnastic training and bone density in pre-adolescent females. Med Sci Sports Exerc 29:443–450.

159. Morris FL, Naughton GA, Gibbs JL, Carlson JS, Wark JD 1997 Prospective ten-month exercise intervention in premenarcheal girls: Positive effects on bone and lean mass. J Bone Miner Res 12:1453–1462.

160. Pettifor JM, Moodley GP 1997 Appendicular bone mass in children with a high prevalence of low dietary calcium intakes. J Bone Miner Res 12:1824–1832.

161. Rockell JE, Williams SM, Taylor RW, Grant AM, Jones IE, Goulding A 2005 Two-year changes in bone and body composition in young children with a history of prolonged milk avoidance. Osteoporos Int 16:2016–2023.

162. Lehtonen-Veromaa MK, Mottonen TT, Nuotio IO, Irjala KM, Leino AE, Viikari JS 2002 Vitamin D and attainment of peak bone mass among peripubertal Finnish girls: A 3-year prospective study. Am J Clin Nutr 76:1446–1453.

163. Neely EK, Marcus R, Rosenfeld RG, Bachrach LK 1993 Turner syndrome adolescents receiving growth hormone are not osteopenic. J Clin Endocrinol Metab 76:861–866.

164. Bhudhikanok GS, Wang MC, Marcus R, Harkins A, Moss RB, Bachrach LK 1998 Bone acquisition and loss in children and adults with cystic fibrosis: A longitudinal study. J Pediatr 133:18–27.

165. Bhudhikanok GS, Lim J, Marcus R, Harkins A, Moss RB, Bachrach LK 1996 Correlates of osteopenia in patients with cystic fibrosis. Pediatrics 97:103–111.

166. Sood M, Hambleton G, Super M, Fraser WD, Adams JE, Mughal MZ 2001 Bone status in cystic fibrosis. Arch Dis Child 84:516–520.

167. Takahashi Y, Minamitani K, Kobayashi Y, Minagawa M, Yasuda T, Niimi H 1996 Spinal and femoral bone mass accumulation during normal adoles-cence: Comparison with female patients with sexual precocity and with hypogonadism. J Clin Endocrinol Metab 81:1248–1253.

168. Boot AM, Engels MA, Boerma GJ, Krenning EP, De Muinck Keizer-Schrama SM 1997 Changes in bone mineral density, body composition, and lipid metabolism during growth hormone (GH) treatment in children with GH deficiency. J Clin Endocrinol Metab 82:2423–2428.

169. Bachrach LK, Marcus R, Ott SM, Rosenbloom AL, Vasconez O, Martinez V, Martinez AL, Rosenfeld RG, Guevara-Aguirre J 1998 Bone mineral, histomorphometry, and body composition in adults with growth hormone receptor deficiency. J Bone Miner Res 13:415–421.

170. van der Sluis IM, Boot AM, Hop WC, De Rijke YB, Krenning EP, de Muinck Keizer-Schrama SM 2002 Long-term effects of growth hormone therapy on bone mineral density, body composition, and serum lipid levels in growth hormone deficient children: A 6-year follow-up study. Horm Res 58:207–214.

171. Backstrom MC, Kouri T, Kuusela AL, Sievanen H, Koivisto AM, Ikonen RS, Maki M 2000 Bone isoenzyme of serum alkaline phosphatase and serum inorganic phosphate in metabolic bone disease of prematurity. Acta Paediatr 89:867–873.

172. Abad V, Chrousos GP, Reynolds JC, Nieman LK, Hill SC, Weinstein RS, Leong GM 2001 Glucocorticoid excess during adolescence leads to a major persistent deficit in bone mass and an increase in central body fat. J Bone Miner Res 16:1879–1885.

173. Bielinski BK, Darbyshire P, Mathers L, Boivin CM, Shaw NJ 2001 Bone density in the Asian thalassaemic population: A cross-sectional review. Acta Paediatr 90:1262–1266.
174. Salvatoni A, Mancassola G, Biasoli R, Cardani R, Salvatore S, Broggini M, Nespoli L 2004 Bone mineral density in diabetic children and adolescents: A follow-up study. Bone 34:900–904.
175. Daniels MW, Wilson DM, Paguntalan HG, Hoffman AR, Bachrach LK 2003 Bone mineral density in pediatric transplant recipients. Transplantation 76:673–678.
176. van der Sluis IM, van den Heuvel-Eibrink MM, Hahlen K, Krenning EP, de Muinck Keizer-Schrama SM 2000 Bone mineral density, body composition, and height in long term survivors of acute lymphoblastic leukemia in childhood. Med Pediatr Oncol 35:415–420.
177. Lequin MH, van der Shuis IM, Van Rijn RR, Hop WC, van ven Huevel-Eibrink MM, MuinckKeizer-Schrama SM, van Kuijk C 2002 Bone mineral assessment with tibial ultrasonometry and dual-energy x-ray absorptiometry in long-term survivors of acute lymphoblastic leukemia in childhood. J Clin Densitom 5:167–173.
178. Gandrud LM, Cheung JC, Daniels MW, Bachrach LK 2003 Low-dose intravenous pamidronate reduces fractures in childhood osteoporosis. J Pediatr Endocrinol Metab 16:887–892.
179. Ma D, Jones G 2003 The association between bone mineral density, metacarpal morphometry, and upper limb fractures in children: A population-based case-control study. J Clin Endocrinol Metab 88:1486–1491.
180. Goulding A, Jones IE, Taylor RW, Williams SM, Manning PJ 2001 Bone mineral density and body composition in boys with distal forearm fractures: A dual-energy x-ray absorptiometry study. J Pediatr 139:509–515.
181. Goulding A, Jones IE, Taylor RW, Manning PJ, Williams SM 2000 More broken bones: A 4-year double cohort study of young girls with and without distal forearm fractures. J Bone Miner Res 15:2011–2018.
182. Ellis KJ, Shypailo RJ, Hardin DS, Perez MD, Motil KJ, Wong WW, Abrams SA 2001 Z score prediction model for assessment of bone mineral content in pediatric diseases. J Bone Miner Res 16:1658–1664.
183. Molgaard C, Thomsen BL, Prentice A, Cole TJ, Michaelsen KF 1997 Whole body bone mineral content in healthy children and adolescents. Arch Dis Child 76:9–15.
184. Binkley TL, Specker BL, Wittig TA 2002 Centile curves for bone densitometry measurements in healthy males and females ages 5–22 yr. J Clin Densitom 5:343–353.
185. Hannan WJ, Tothill P, Cowen SJ, Wrate RM 1998 Whole body bone mineral content in healthy children and adolescents. Arch Dis Child 78:396–397.
186. Maynard LM, Guo SS, Chumlea WC, Roche AF, Wisemandle WA, Zeller CM, Towne B, Siervogel RM 1998 Total-body and regional bone mineral content and areal bone mineral density in children aged 8–18 y: The Fels Longitudinal Study. Am J Clin Nutr 68:1111–1117.
187. van der Sluis IM, de Ridder MA, Boot AM, Krenning EP, de Muinck Keizer-Schrama SM 2002 Reference data for bone density and body composition measured with dual energy x-ray absorptiometry in white children and young adults. Arch Dis Child 87:341–347.
188. Horlick M, Wang J, Pierson RN Jr, Thornton JC 2004 Prediction models for evaluation of total-body bone mass with dual-energy x-ray absorptiometry among children and adolescents. Pediatrics 114:e337–e345.
189. Hogler W, Briody J, Woodhead HJ, Chan A, Cowell CT 2003 Importance of lean mass in the interpretation of total body densitometry in children and adolescents. J Pediatr 143:81–88.
190. Crabtree NJ, Kibirige MS, Fordham JN, Banks LM, Muntoni F, Chinn D, Boivin CM, Shaw NJ 2004 The relationship between lean body mass and bone mineral content in paediatric health and disease. Bone 35:965–972.
191. Schoenau E, Neu CM, Beck B, Manz F, Rauch F 2002 Bone mineral content per muscle cross-sectional area as an index of the functional muscle-bone unit. J Bone Miner Res 17:1095–1101.
192. Zemel BS, Leonard MB, Kalkwarf HJ, Specker BL, Moyer-Mileur LJ, Shepherd J, Cole TJ, Pan H, Kelly TL 2004 Reference data for the whole body, lumbar spine and proximal femur for American children relative to age, gender and body size. J Bone Miner Res.
193. Wren TA, Liu X, Pitukcheewanont P, Gilsanz V 2005 Bone densitometry in pediatric populations: Discrepancies in the diagnosis of osteoporosis by DXA and CT. J Pediatr 146:776–779.
194. Gafni RI, Baron J 2004 Overdiagnosis of osteoporosis in children due to misinterpretation of dual-energy x-ray absorptiometry (DEXA). J Pediatr 144:253–257.
195. Kahn AA, Bachrach L, Brown JP, Hanley DA, Josse RG, Kendler DL, Leib ES, Lentle BC, Leslie WD, Lewiecki EM, Miller PD 2004 Standards and guidelines for performing central dual-energy x-ray absorptiometry in pre-menopausal women, men, and children. J Clin Densitom 7:51–64.

Chapter 24. Bone Biopsy and Histomorphometry in Clinical Practice

Robert R. Recker and M. Janet Barger-Lux

Department of Medicine, Endocrinology Division, Osteoporosis Research Center, Creighton University Medical Center, Omaha, Nebraska

INTRODUCTION

Histological examination of undecalcified transilial bone biopsy specimens is a valuable and well-established clinical and research tool for studying the etiology, pathogenesis, and treatment of metabolic bone diseases. In this chapter, we will review the underlying organization and function of bone cells; identify a set of basic structural and kinetic histomorphometric variables; outline an approach to interpretation of findings, with examples from a range of metabolic bone diseases; describe techniques for obtaining, processing, and analyzing transilial biopsy specimens; identify clinical situations in which bone histomorphometry can be useful; and relate histomorphometric measures to data from other methods for assessing bone properties and bone physiology

Dr. Recker has received research funding from Merck, Roche, Eli Lilly, Amgen, Wyeth, and Procter & Gamble. Ms. Barger-Lux has reported no conflicts of interest.

ORGANIZATION AND FUNCTION OF BONE CELLS

Intermediary Organization of the Skeleton

In what he termed the intermediary organization (IO) of the skeleton, Frost[1] described four discrete functions of bone cells: growth, modeling, remodeling, and fracture repair. Although each involves the same osteoclasts and osteoblasts, the coordinated outcomes differ greatly. Growth elongates the skeleton; modeling shapes it during growth; remodeling removes and replaces bone tissue; and fracture repair heals sites of structural failure.

The remodeling IO, which predominates during adult life, is the focus of this chapter. Coordinated groups of bone cells (i.e., osteoclasts, osteoblasts, osteocytes, and lining cells) comprise the basic multicellular units (BMUs) that carry out bone remodeling. Basic structural units (BSUs) are the packets of new bone that BMUs form.[2] All adult metabolic bone disease involves derangement of the remodeling IO.

Bone Cells

Osteoclasts, large-to-giant cells that are typically multinucleated, resorb bone (both its matrix, or osteoid, and mineral). They excavate shallow pits on the surface of cancellous bone, and they appear at the leading edge of tunnels (cutting cones) in haversian bone. Light microscopy discloses an irregular cell shape, foamy, acidophilic cytoplasm, a striated perimeter zone of attachment to the bone (ruffled border), and positive staining for TRACP.

Osteoblasts form new bone at sites of resorption. They produce the collagenous and noncollagenous constituents of bone matrix and participate in mineralization.[3] Under light microscopy, they appear as plump cells lined up at the surface of unmineralized osteoid. As the site matures, the cells lose their plump appearance.

Osteocytes, derived from osteoblasts, remain at the remodeling site. They reside individually in small lacunae within the mineralized bone matrix. Their cytoplasmic processes extend through a fine network of narrow canaliculi to form an interconnected network that extends throughout living bone. This network may monitor the local strain environment and/or initiate organized bone cell work in response to changes in strain.

Lining cells, also of osteoblast origin, cover cancellous and endocortical bone surfaces. By light microscopy, they appear as elongated, flattened, darkly stained nuclei. The localization and initiation of remodeling probably involves these cells.

Bone Remodeling Process

Remodeling occurs on cancellous and haversian bone surfaces. The first step is activation of osteoclast precursors to form osteoclasts that begin to excavate a cavity. After removal of about 0.05 mm^3 of bone tissue, the site remains quiescent for a short time. Then, activation of osteoblast precursors occurs at the site, and the excavation is refilled. The average length of time required to complete the remodeling cycle is ~6 months[4]: about 4 weeks for resorption and the rest for formation.

The healthy bone remodeling system accesses the required building materials within a favorable physiologic milieu to replace fully a packet of aged, microdamaged bone tissue with new, mechanically competent bone. However, overuse can overwhelm the capacity of the system to repair microdamage (the stress fractures that occur in military recruits are an example). The healthy bone remodeling system modifies bone architecture to meet changing mechanical needs. However, the system also promptly reduces the mass of underused bone (the bone loss of extended bedrest, paralysis, or space travel are examples). All bone loss occurs through bone remodeling. The bone remodeling system responds to nutritional and humoral as well as mechanical influences. Among the effects of vitamin D deficiency in adults, for example, is impaired mineralization of bone matrix. Finally, as other chapters describe, bone remodeling involves complex signaling processes between and within bone cells, and metabolic bone diseases of genetic origin involve defects at this level. Figures 1–3 present representative photomicrographs from human transilial biopsy specimens. An extensive atlas has also been published.[5]

BASIC HISTOMORPHOMETRIC VARIABLES

Bone biopsy specimens for histomorphometric examination are ordinarily obtained at the transilial site and shipped to specialized laboratories for processing and microscopic analysis. Later sections of this chapter outline these procedures. Of the dozens of measurements and calculations that have been devised, we provide here descriptions of several frequently used variables. Together they describe a basic set of structural and kinetic features. Nomenclature is as approved by a committee of the American Society of Bone and Mineral Research.[6]

Structural Features

Core width (C.Wi) represents the thickness of the ilium (i.e., distance between periosteal surfaces, in mm) at the point of biopsy. Cortical width (Ct.Wi) is the combined thickness, in millimeters, of both cortices. Cortical porosity (Ct.Po) is the area of intracortical holes as percent of total cortical area.

Cancellous bone volume (BV/TV) is the percent of total marrow area (including trabeculae) occupied by cancellous bone. Wall thickness (W.Th) is the mean distance in micrometers between resting cancellous surfaces (i.e., surfaces without osteoid or Howship's lacunae) and corresponding cement lines.

Trabecular thickness (Tb.Th) is the mean distance across individual trabeculae, in micrometers, and trabecular separation (Tb.Sp) is the mean distance, also in micrometers, between trabeculae. Trabecular number (Tb.N) per millimeter is calculated as (BV/TV)/Tb.Th. These variables can be used to evaluate trabecular connectivity.[7] Other measures of trabecular connectivity include the ratio of nodes to free ends,[8] star volume,[9,10] and trabecular bone pattern factor (TBPf).[11]

Eroded surface (ES/BS) is the percent of cancellous surface occupied by Howship's lacunae, with and without osteoclasts. Osteoblast surface (Ob.S/BS) and osteoclast surface (Oc.S/BS) identify the percent of cancellous surface occupied by osteoblasts and osteoclasts, respectively. Osteoid surface (OS/BS) is the percent of cancellous surface with unmineralized osteoid, with and without osteoblasts. Osteoid thickness (O.Th) is the mean thickness, in micrometers of the osteoid on cancellous surfaces.

Kinetic Features

A fluorochrome labeling agent, taken orally on a strict schedule before biopsy, deposits a fluorescent double label at sites of active mineralization and allows rates of change to be determined.[12] Mineralizing surface (MS/BS) is the percent of cancellous surface that is mineralizing and thus labeled. The most accurate version of MS/BS includes surfaces with a double label plus one half of those with a single label. Clear definition of MS/BS is crucial, because it is used to calculate bone formation rates, bone formation periods, and mineralization lag time.

Mineral appositional rate (MAR), is the rate (μm/day) at which new bone mineral is being added to cancellous surfaces. MAR represents distance between labels at doubly labeled surfaces divided by the marker interval (span in days between the midpoints of each labeling period). This and all measurements of thickness must be corrected for obliquity (i.e., the randomness of the angle between the plane of the section and the plane of the cancellous surface) by use of a scaling factor.[13]

Activation frequency (Ac.f) is the probability that a new remodeling cycle will begin at any point on the cancellous bone surface. Bone formation rates (BFR/BV and BFR/BS) are estimates of cancellous bone volume (mm^3/mm^3/year) and cancellous bone surface (mm^3/mm^2/year), respectively, that are being replaced annually; BFR/BS = Ac.f × W.Th.[14] Formation period (FP) is the average time in years required to complete a new cancellous BSU. Mineralization lag time (Mlt) is the interval in days between osteoid formation and mineralization. The most accurate version of Mlt is calculated as O.Th/MAR × MS/OS.

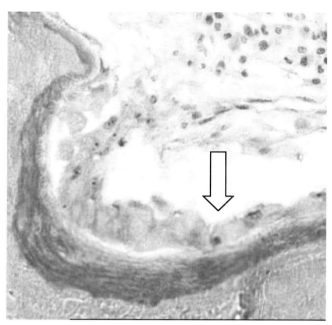

FIG. 1. A normal bone forming surface. Unmineralized osteoid is covered with plump osteoblasts, as identified by the arrow.

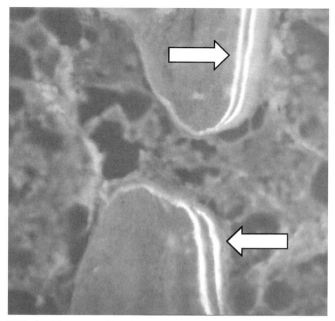

FIG. 3. The arrows identify two mineralizing surfaces with fluorescent double labels.

INTERPRETATION OF FINDINGS

Reference Data

In 1988, Recker et al.[4] published the results of a study to establish reference values for histomorphometric variables in postmenopausal white women. The 34 healthy subjects were evenly distributed into three age groups: 45–54, 55–64, and 65–74 years. They ranged broadly in age at menopause and in years past menopause at the time of biopsy. A comparative

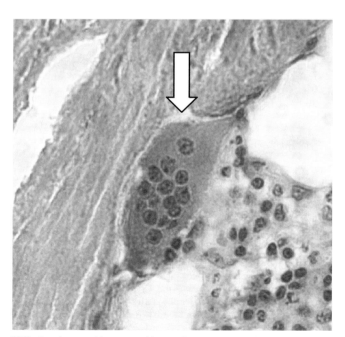

FIG. 2. A normal bone resorbing surface. The arrow locates a multinucleated osteoclast in a Howship's lacuna.

study of 12 blacks and 13 whites, 19–46 years of age, has also been published.[15]

In 2000, Glorieux et al.[16] reported histomorphometric data from 58 white subjects in each of five age groups: 1.5–6.9, 7.0–10.9, 11.0–13.9, 14.0–16.9, and 17.0–22.9 years. Biopsy specimens were obtained during corrective orthopedic surgeries, but the subjects had been ambulatory and otherwise healthy. The report includes within-subject CVs derived from analysis of adjacent duplicate biopsy specimens in eight subjects.

A recent paper from our center reported Ac.f in several sets of transilial biopsy specimens. In 50 paired transilial biopsy specimens taken during perimenopause and in early postmenopause, a year after last menses, median values for Ac.f increased from 0.13/year to 0.24/year, respectively ($p < 0.001$). Ac.f was higher still (median, 0.37; $p < 0.01$) in another group of ostensibly normal women who were postmenopausal by an average of 13 years.[17]

Replacement of Normal Marrow Elements

A variety of hematopoietic cells and a varying proportion of fat cells normally occupy the marrow space at the transilial biopsy site. If these normal marrow elements have been displaced by fibrous tissue (osteitis fibrosa), clumps of tumor cells, or sheets of abnormal hematopoietic cells, this change will be obvious to the histomorphometrist. The biopsy preparations described here preserve cellular detail, spatial relationships, and architectural features. However, this approach is unsuitable for hematologic diagnosis because of the time that histomorphometry laboratories require to generate a report (typically, at least 4 weeks).

Cortical Bone Deficit

Both the angle of the biopsy and site-to-site variation in cortical thickness at the biopsy site influence Ct.Wi. Nevertheless, low BMD at the lumbar spine and/or proximal femur is often reflected in low values for Ct.Wi.[18] Evidence of trabeculation of the cortex (i.e., formation of a transitional zone with characteristic coarse trabeculae) indicates that cortical bone, once present, has been lost.[19]

Cancellous Bone Deficit

Low BV/TV indicates a cancellous bone deficit. Generalized trabecular thinning (decreased Tb.Th) and/or complete loss of trabecular elements (poor trabecular connectivity) may contribute to this deficit. The latter finding (e.g., low Tb.N with high Tb.Sp) characterizes bone that is more fragile than its overall mass would suggest.

Altered Bone Remodeling

Ac.f is an indicator of overall level of remodeling activity in cancellous bone. In biopsy specimens from ostensibly healthy women, we have yet to see a case in which the subject had followed the fluorochrome labeling protocol but label could not be found in cancellous areas. However, a recent paper from our laboratory, cited earlier, reports three cases of no-label (i.e., zero Ac.f) among women with untreated postmenopausal osteoporosis.[17] Our physicians regularly determine bone-specific alkaline phosphatase (BSALP) before starting antiresorptive treatment.

Abnormal Osteoid Morphology

The characteristic arrangement of osteoid (collagen) fibers in lamellar and woven bone is readily apparent. Woven bone in transilial specimens is generally associated with either Paget's disease or renal osteodystrophy. It can also occur in osteitis fibrosa. In osteogenesis imperfecta, collagen abnormalities may be subtle enough to escape detection.

Accumulation of Unmineralized Osteoid

Parfitt has described the complex relationships between dynamic indices of bone formation and static indices of osteoid accumulation.[14] Increases in OS/BS, O.Th, and Mlt indicate failure of osteoid to mineralize normally. If mineralization is arrested completely, no double label will be seen, and Mlt is unmeasurable.[20]

FINDINGS IN METABOLIC BONE DISEASES

In Table 1, we identify key histomorphometric findings that characterize representative types of metabolic bone disease. For further information, we encourage the reader to consult disease-specific chapters in this volume and the current literature.

Postmenopausal Osteoporosis

Osteoporosis in postmenopausal women is characterized by a cortical bone deficit with trabeculation of endocortical bone and a cancellous bone deficit with poor trabecular connectivity. Decreases in Tb.Th are modest, and dynamic measures vary widely.[21,22] Median Ac.f remains high in specimens from women with postmenopausal osteoporosis, but values vary widely.[17]

Glucocorticoid-Induced Osteoporosis

Early in treatment, Ac.f is increased; later, Ac.f, MAR, and MS/BS are all decreased. In femoral specimens from patients with glucocorticoid-induced osteonecrosis, abundant apoptotic osteocytes and lining cells have been reported.[23]

Primary Hyperparathyroidism

Primary hyperparathyroidism leads to a cortical bone deficit, with increased Ct.Po and trabeculation of endocortical bone.[24] Ct.Po correlates positively with fasting serum PTH.[25] BV/TV is generally preserved, and normal cancellous bone architecture is maintained.[26,27] Osteoid with a woven appearance and peritrabecular fibrosis may also be seen.[28]

Hypogonadism

Hypogonadism in both women and men increases Ac.f and leads to deficits of both cortical bone and trabecular bone. At low levels of BV/TV and/or Tb.Th, loss of trabecular connectivity occurs.[29]

Hypovitaminosis D Osteopathy

Vitamin D depletion of any etiology leads to hypovitaminosis D osteopathy (HVO). Parfitt describes three stages. In HVOi (pre-osteomalacia), Ac.f and OS/BS are increased, but O.Th is not. Accumulation of unmineralized osteoid characterizes both HVOii and HVOiii (osteomalacia), with Mlt and O.Th clearly increased (i.e., Mlt >100 days and O.Th >12.5 μm after correction for obliquity).[20] Some double label can be seen in HVOii but not in HVOiii. A cortical bone deficit also characterizes advanced HVO; secondary hyperparathyroidism is usual, and fibrous tissue in the marrow spaces is frequently seen.

Low bone mass and bone disease with osteomalacic features does occur among patients treated with anti-epileptic drugs (AEDs).[30] Hepatic enzyme-inducing AEDs have been most clearly associated with these problems, but the newer AEDs cannot be exonerated at this time.[31]

Hypophosphatemic Osteopathy

Phosphate depletion of any etiology also leads to osteomalacia, with histomorphometric findings similar to those of advanced HVO.[20] These cases involve defects in renal tubular reabsorption of phosphate. Secondary hyperparathyroidism occurs variably. Transilial biopsy can be quite useful to assess the efficacy of treatment.

Gastrointestinal Bone Disease

Evidence of HVO has been reported in a variety of absorptive and digestive disorders.[32] However, these conditions also may promote deficiency of calcium and other nutrients. Malabsorption is not the only issue. For example, a calcium balance study of asymptomatic patients with celiac disease showed increased endogenous fecal calcium; the gut seemed to "weep" calcium into its lumen.[33] Bone histomorphometry may also reflect the results of treatment (i.e., corticosteroids or surgery). Parfitt described a histomorphometric profile of low bone turnover, often with evidence of HVO and secondary hyperparathyroidism, that represents the result of multiple insults to bone health in these patients.[20]

Renal Osteodystrophy

At least three patterns of histomorphometric findings have been described among patients with end-stage renal disease (ESRD): high bone turnover with osteitis fibrosa (hyperparathyroid bone disease); low bone turnover (including osteomalacic and adynamic subtypes); and mixed osteodystrophy with high bone turnover, altered bone formation, and accumulation of unmineralized osteoid.[34–37]

At this time, transilial bone biopsy remains a useful "gold standard" on which to base decisions about treatment of bone

Table 1. Patterns of Key Histomorphometric Findings That Characterize Several Types of Metabolic Bone Disease

	Marrow spaces	Cortical bone	Cancellous bone	Bone remodeling	Osteoid morphology	Osteoid mineralization
Postmenopausal osteoporosis	—	Cortical bone deficit with endocortical trabeculation	Cancellous bone deficit with poor trabecular connectivity	Ac.f generally increased, but values vary widely	—	—
Glucocorticoid-induced osteoporosis	—	Cortical bone deficit	Cancellous bone deficit	Early, increased Ac.f; later, decreased Ac.f	—	—
Primary hyperparathyroidism	Peritrabecular fibrosis may be seen	Cortical bone deficit, incr.Ct.Po, endocortical trabeculation	Typically unremarkable	—	Woven bone may be seen	—
Hypogonadism (males and females)	—	Cortical bone deficit	Cancellous bone deficit, sometimes with poor trabecular connectivity	Increased Ac.f	—	—
Hypovitaminosis D osteopathy	Fibrous tissue may be seen	—	—	Early, increased Ac.f	—	Early, increased OS/BS; later, incr. MLT and O.Th, double label may be absent
Hypophosphatemic osteopathy	Fibrous tissue may be seen	—	—	—	—	Increased MLT and O.Th; double label may be absent
Renal osteodystrophy (high turnover type)	Fibrous tissue may be seen	Endocortical trabeculation	Osteoblast, osteocyte, and trabecular abnormalities	Markedly increased remodeling activity	Woven bone may be seen	Increased OS/BS
Renal osteodystrophy (low turnover types)	—	—	—	Markedly decreased remodeling activity	—	Increased OS/BS (osteomalacic type); decreased OS/BS (adynamic type)
Renal osteodystrophy (mixed type)	Fibrous tissue may be seen	—	Variable BV/TV	Patchy remodeling activity	Irregular, woven bone and osteoid may be seen	Increased OS/BS and O.Th

disease in ESRD.[34] A dramatic example is the evaluation of bone pain and fractures in a chronic dialysis patient with hypercalcemia. If the biopsy shows high bone turnover and osteitis fibrosa, partial parathyroidectomy may be indicated. However, if the biopsy shows little turnover (little or no fluorochrome label), with or without extensive aluminum deposits, parathyroidectomy is contraindicated, and treatment with a chelating agent may be indicated. The same biopsy can also help determine the extent of vitamin D deprivation and indicate the adequacy of vitamin D treatment.

OBTAINING THE SPECIMEN

In this section, we outline the procedures for obtaining bone biopsy specimens, processing them, and carrying out histomorphometric analysis. For greater detail, we recommend another recent publication.[38]

Fluorochrome Labeling

In clinical settings, tetracycline antibiotics are the only suitable fluorochrome labeling agents.[12] Demeclocycline (150 mg, four times daily) or tetracycline hydrochloride (250 mg, four times daily) are commonly used. The double-labeling process involves two dosing periods, and close adherence to the dosing schedule is crucial. A schedule of 3 days on, 14 days off, 3 days on, and 5 days off before biopsy (abbreviated as 3-14-3:5) produces good results, with a marker interval of 17 days.[39] Tetracyclines must be taken on an empty stomach. Calcium interferes with tetracycline absorption; therefore, calcium-rich foods (e.g., dairy products), calcium-fortified foods, and calcium supplements must be avoided for at least 1 h before and after each dose.

Biopsy Instrument

Specimens for histomorphometric examination require use of a trephine with inner diameter of no less than 7.5 mm. The Rochester Bone Biopsy Trephine (Medical Innovations International, Rochester, MN, USA) is a suitable instrument. The needle should be sharpened (and reconditioned, if necessary) after every three to five procedures.

Biopsy Procedure

In our institution, transilial bone biopsy is an outpatient minor surgery, with the usual procedures (e.g., the surgeon scrubs and uses a cap, mask, gown, and gloves, and the site is prepared and draped) and precautions (e.g., pulse oximetry and blood pressure monitoring). For the procedure, the patient should be off aspirin for at least 3 days and have nothing orally for 4 h. If a second biopsy is done, it should always be on the side opposite the first; there is thus a practical limit of two transilial biopsy procedures per patient. The gowned patient lies in the supine position on the surgical table, and midazolam (2.5–5 mg) is given through a forearm intravenous catheter.

The biopsy site is about 2 cm posterior to the anterior–superior spine, which is about 2 cm inferior to the iliac crest. The skin and subcutaneous tissues on both sides of the ilium are infiltrated with local anesthetic. The periosteum is accessed by a 2-cm skin incision and blunt dissection. The trephine is inserted and advanced with steady, gentle pressure and a deliberate pace. The specimen—an intact, unfractured core with both cortices and the intervening cancellous bone—is transferred into a 20-ml screw-cap vial containing 70% ethanol. (Note that certain special procedures, presently used in research settings, require unfixed specimens.)

The bony defect is packed with Surgicel. After local pressure to facilitate hemostasis, the wound is closed with three to five stitches and covered by a pressure dressing. Follow-up care is specified clearly (i.e., dressing in place and absolutely dry for 48 h; then a daily shower is allowed; no bathing or strenuous physical activity until suture removal, 1 week after the procedure). The procedure produces localized aching for about 2 days and a small scar at the site.

Adverse Events

Patients typically describe feeling something "like a cramp" as the trephine advances, and the bone biopsy procedure described here rarely evokes pain. In the rare case in which the patient feels acute, sharp pain as the trephine passes through the marrow space, a small additional amount of intravenous midazolam can be given.

Although bleeding during the procedure is typically minimal, there is risk of bleeding in some situations (e.g., liver disease, hemodialysis, or medications that compromise hemostasis). Local bruising sometimes occurs, but hematoma is uncommon. In an early survey, physicians who were doing transilial biopsy specimens reported adverse events in 0.7% of 9131 biopsy procedures, that is, 22 with hematomas, 17 with pain for >7 days, 11 with transient neuropathy, 6 with wound infection, 2 with fracture, and 1 with osteomyelitis. No cases of death or permanent disability were reported.[40]

SPECIMEN PROCESSING AND ANALYSIS

Availability

Clinical pathology laboratories ordinarily do not handle undecalcified bone specimens or perform histomorphometry. However, processing and histomorphometric analysis of transilial bone biopsy specimens are available through several research laboratories that also handle clinical specimens. The specialized laboratory should be contacted before the procedure for explicit instructions on the fluorochrome labeling schedule, biopsy procedure, fixative, required patient information, shipping, etc. As noted earlier, most histomorphometry laboratories require, at minimum, 4 weeks to generate a report.

Specimen Handling and Processing

For routine histomorphometry, the bone biopsy specimen remains in 70% ethanol for at least 48 h for proper fixation. This solution is suitable for shipping and long-term storage at room temperature. The specimen vials should be filled to capacity with 70% ethanol for shipping, handling, and storage.

Steps in laboratory processing include dehydrating, defatting, embedding, sectioning, mounting, deplasticizing, staining, and microscopic examination.

The tissue block is sectioned parallel to the long axis of the biopsy core. Several sets of sections are obtained at 250- to 300-μm intervals, beginning 35–40% into the embedded specimen. Unstained sections 8–10 μm thick are used to examine osteoid morphology and to measure fluorochrome-labeled surfaces. Sections 5–7 μm thick stained with toluidine blue are used to measure wall thickness. Sections 5 μm thick with Goldner's stain[41] are used for other histomorphometric measurements.

Microscopy

The histomorphometric variables described earlier are derived from data gathered at the microscope. These data include the width of both cortices and—in defined sectors of cancellous bone—volumes of bone, osteoid, and marrow; total trabecular perimeter; perimeters with features of formation (see Fig. 1) or resorption (see Fig. 2); thickness of osteoid and osteon walls; and interlabel width. Methods have been described for unbiased sampling of microscopic features.[42]

Our histomorphometry laboratory uses an interactive image analysis system (BIOQUANT True Color for Windows; Bioquant R&M Biometrics, Nashville, TN, USA). A digital camera mounted on the microscope presents the microscopic images on-screen, and measurements are made using a mouse. Fluorescent light at a wavelength of 350 nm is used to examine fluorochrome labels (see Fig. 3).

INDICATIONS FOR BONE BIOPSY AND HISTOMORPHOMETRY

The purpose of bone histomorphometry in the clinical setting is to gather information (i.e., to establish a diagnosis, clarify a prognosis, or evaluate adherence or response to treatment) on which to base informed clinical decisions. As is the case for every invasive procedure, the risk, discomfort, and expense should be proportionate to the importance of the information to be gained. Given these caveats, the number of clinical indications for this procedure is limited.

TABLE 2. Examples of Clinical Situations in Which Bone Histomorphometry Can Provide Useful Information

1. When there is excessive skeletal fragility in unusual circumstances
2. When a mineralizing defect is suspected
3. To characterize the bone effects or evaluate adherence to treatment in celiac disease and similar disorders
4. To characterize the bone lesion in renal osteodystrophy
5. To diagnose or assess response to treatment in vitamin D-resistant osteomalacia and similar disorders
6. When a rare metabolic bone disease is suspected

Adapted from Recker RR, Barger-Lux MJ 2002 Transilial bone biopsy. In: Bilezikian JP, Raisz LG, Rodan GA (eds.) Principles of Bone Biology, 2nd ed. Academic Press, San Diego, CA, USA, pp. 1625–1634 with permission from Elsevier.

Clinicians can manage most metabolic bone diseases, including osteoporosis, without the aid of a bone biopsy. However, there are some situations in which bone biopsy after fluorochrome labeling is appropriate, as outlined in Table 2.

Bone histomorphometry has been, and remains, crucial for assessing the mechanisms of action, safety, and efficacy of new bone-active agents. Preclinical animal work includes serial biopsy specimens at multiple skeletal sites, using different colored fluorochrome labels (e.g., calcein or xylenol orange). Early testing of every new bone-active treatment should include bone biopsy in at least a subset of subjects. Some treatments can be predicted to fail based on the biopsy findings during treatment. An example would be continuous treatment with an agent that stops activation of remodeling and/or impairs bone formation significantly in those remodeling sites

undergoing formation at the time the agent was introduced. Such an agent might harm the mechanical strength of the skeleton in the long-term rather than improve it. This problem can be detected earlier by biopsy than with any other technology.

BONE HISTOMORPHOMETRY AND OTHER MEANS FOR ASSESSING BONE

Bone histomorphometry provides a method for examining both bone properties and bone physiology. Over the 30+ years that this technology has been in use, numerous other methods for examining bone have been introduced. This section places histomorphometric measures in the context of some of these other methods.

Bone Properties

Table 3 is a matrix in which information yielded by bone histomorphometry and other technologies is classified according to whether it describes bone mass, bone morphology, or material (i.e., physical or biomechanical) properties of bone. The material is further divided according to whether the data are derived from transilial bone biopsy specimens or direct testing of human subjects. In Tables 3 and 4, further consideration might be given to the level of organization (ultramicroscopic to total body) that each measure describes.

Bone Physiology

Table 4 is a second matrix in which information yielded by bone histomorphometry and other technologies is classified according to whether it describes mineral homeostasis, bone

TABLE 3. Relationships of Histomorphometric Measures and Data From Other Methods for Assessing Bone Properties

Mass	Morphology	Material/properties
Histomorphometric measures		
Core width (C.Wi); cortical width (Ct.Wi); cortical porosity (Ct.Po); cancellous bone volume (BV/TV)	Trabecular thickness (Tb.Th); trabecular spacing (Tb.Sp); trabecular number (Tb.N); wall thickness (W.Th)	—
Other in vitro measurements on transilial bone biopsies		
—	—	Collagen cross-link quality by Fourier transform infra-red imaging (FT-IRI)
—	Cancellous bone geometry by micro-computed tomography	Finite element analysis by micro-computed tomography
—	—	Site-specific degree of mineralization by quantitative micro-radiography
In vivo measurements		
Bone densitometry by DXA of total body and various regions	—	—
True volumetric bone density by quantitative computed tomography (QCT) at lumbar spine and proximal femur	—	—
Bone size and cortical area by standardized X-radiography with radiogrammetry at various sites		—
Speed of sound (SOS) or bone ultrasound attenuation (BUA) at calcaneus and patella		—
—	Assessment of vertebral body deformities by X-radiography and radiogrammetry	—
—	Trabecular connectivity by MRI at peripheral sites	—

Adapted with permission from tabular material published in Barger-Lux MJ, Recker RR 2005 Towards understanding bone quality: Transilial bone biopsy and bone histomorphometry. Clin Rev Bone Miner Metab (in press).

Table 4. Relationships of Histomorphometric Measures and Data From Other Methods for Assessing Bone Physiologic Processes

Mineral homeostasis	Bone formation	Bone resorption
Histomorphometric measures		
Osteoid surface (OS/BS); osteoid thickness (O.Th); mineralizing surface (MS/BS); mineral apposition rate (MAR); mineralization lag time (Mlt)		—
—	Osteoblast surface (Ob.S/BS)	Activation frequency (Ac.f); Osteoclast surface (Oc.S/BS)
In vitro measurements on serum or urine		
—	Bone formation markers	Bone resorption markers
PTH; 25-hydroxyvitamin D	—	—
Serum calcium; 2-h fasting urine calcium-to-creatinine ratio	—	—
Calcium absorption efficiency	—	—

Adapted with permission from tabular material published in Barger-Lux MJ, Recker RR 2005 Towards understanding bone quality: Transilial bone biopsy and bone histomorphometry. Clin Rev Bone Miner Metab (in press).

formation, or bone resorption. The material is further divided according to whether the data are derived from transilial bone biopsy specimens or testing of serum or urine.

ACKNOWLEDGMENTS

The authors thank Susan Bare and Toni Howard for assistance in describing technical methods and preparing digital photomicrographs.

REFERENCES

1. Frost HM 1986 Intermediary Organization of the Skeleton. CRC Press, Boca Raton, FL, USA.
2. Frost HM 1973 Bone Remodeling and Its Relationship to Metabolic Bone Diseases. Charles C. Thomas, Springfield, IL, USA.
3. Marotti G, Favia A, Zallone AZ 1972 Quantitative analysis on the rate of secondary bone mineralization. Calcif Tissue Res 10:67–81.
4. Recker RR, Kimmel DB, Parfitt AM, Davies KM, Keshawarz N, Hinders S 1988 Static and tetracycline-based bone histomorphometric data from 34 normal postmenopausal females. J Bone Miner Res 3:133–144.
5. Malluche HH, Faugere MC (eds.) 1986 Atlas of Mineralized Bone Histology. Karger, New York, NY, USA.
6. Parfitt AM, Drezner MK, Glorieux FH, Kanis JA, Malluche H, Meunier PJ, Ott SM, Recker RR 1987 Bone histomorphometry: Standardization of nomenclature, symbols, and units. J Bone Miner Res 2:595–610.
7. Parfitt AM 1983 The physiologic and clinical significance of bone histomorphometric data. In: Recker RR (ed.) Bone Histomorphometry: Techniques and Interpretation. CRC Press, Boca Raton, FL, USA, pp. 143–224.
8. Garrahan NJ, Mellish RW, Compstom JE 1986 A new method for the two-dimensional analysis of bone structure in human iliac crest biopsies. J Microsc 142:341–349.
9. Vesterby A, Gundersen HJG, Melsen F 1989 Star volume of marrow space and trabeculae of the first lumbar vertebra: Sampling efficiency and biological variation. Bone 10:7–13.
10. Vesterby A, Gundersen HJG, Melsen F, Mosekilde L 1991 Marrow space star volume in the iliac crest decreases in osteoporotic patients after continuous treatment with fluoride, calcium, and vitamin D2 for five years. Bone 12:33–37.
11. Hahn M, Vogel M, Pompesius-Kempa M, Delling G 1992 Trabecular bone pattern factor: A new parameter for simple quantification of bone microarchitecture. Bone 13:327–330.
12. Frost HM 1969 Measurement of human bone formation by means of tetracycline labeling. Can J Biochem Physiol 41:331–342.
13. Schwartz MP, Recker RR 1981 Comparison of surface density and volume of human iliac trabecular bone measured directly and by applied stereology. Calcif Tissue Int 33:561–565.
14. Parfitt AM 2002 Physiologic and pathogenetic significance of bone histomorphometric data. In: Coe FL, Favus MJ (eds.) Disorders of Bone Miner Metabolism, 2nd ed. Lippincott Williams & Wilkins, Philadelphia, PA, USA, pp. 469–485.
15. Weinstein RS, Bell NH 1988 Diminished rates of bone formation in normal black adults. N Engl J Med 319:1698–1701.
16. Glorieux FH, Travers R, Taylor A, Bowen JR, Rauch F, Norman M, Parfitt AM 2000 Normative data for iliac bone histomorphometry in growing children. Bone 26:103–109.
17. Recker RR, Lappe J, Davies KM, Heaney R 2004 Bone remodeling increases substantially in the years after menopause and remains increased in older osteoporosis patients. J Bone Miner Res 19:1628–1633.
18. Cosman F, Schnitzer MB, McCann PD, Parisien MV, Dempster DW, Lindsay R 1992 Relationships between quantitative histological measurements and noninvasive assessments of bone mass. Bone 13:237–242.
19. Keshawarz NM, Recker RR 1984 Expansion of the medullary cavity at the expense of cortex in postmenopausal osteoporosis. Metab Bone Dis Rel Res 5:223–228.
20. Parfitt AM 1998 Osteomalacia and related disorders. In: Avioli LV, Krane SM (eds.) Metabolic Bone Disease, 3rd ed. Academic Press, San Diego, CA, USA, pp. 327–386.
21. Kimmel DB, Recker RR, Gallagher JC, Ashok SV, Aloia JF 1990 A comparison of iliac bone histomorphometric data in post-menopausal osteoporotic and normal subjects. Bone Miner 11:217–235.
22. Recker RR, Barger-Lux MJ 2001 Bone remodeling findings in osteoporosis. In: Marcus R, Feldman D, Kelsey J (eds.) Osteoporosis, 2nd ed., vol. 2. Academic Press, San Diego, CA, USA, pp. 59–70.
23. Weinstein RS, Nicholas RW, Manolagas SC 2000 Apoptosis of osteocytes in glucocorticoid-induced osteonecrosis of the hip. J Clin Endocrinol Metab 85:2907–2912.
24. Eriksen EF 2002 Primary hyperparathyroidism: Lessons from bone histomorphometry. J Bone Miner Res 17:S2;N95–N97.
25. van Doorn L, Lips P, Netelenbos JC, Hackeng WH 1993 Bone histomorphometry and serum concentrations of intact parathyroid hormone (PTH 1–84) in patients with primary hyperparathyroidism. Bone Miner 23:233–242.
26. Parisien M, Mellish RW, Silverberg SJ, Shane E, Lindsay R, Bilezikian JP, Dempster DW 1992 Maintenance of cancellous bone connectivity in primary hyperparathyroidism: Trabecular strut analysis. J Bone Miner Res 7:913–919.
27. Uchiyama T, Tanizawa T, Ito A, Endo N, Takahashi HE 1999 Microstructure of the trabecula and cortex of iliac bone in primary hyperparathyroidism patients determined using histomorphometry and node-strut analysis. J Bone Miner Metab 17:283–288.
28. Monier-Faugere M-C, Langub MC, Malluche HH 1998 Bone biopsies: A modern approach. In: Avoli LV, Krane SM (eds.) Metabolic Bone Disease and Clinically Related Disorders, 3rd ed. Academic Press, San Diego, CA, USA, pp. 237–273.
29. Audran M, Chappard D, Legrand E, Libouban H, Baslé MF 2001 Bone microarchitecture and bone fragility in men: DXA and histomorphometry in humans and in the orchidectomized rat model. Calcif Tissue Int 69:214–217.
30. Pack AM, Morrell MJ 2004 Epilepsy and bone health in adults. Epilepsy Behav 5(Suppl 2):S24–S29.
31. Fitzpatrick LA 2004 Pathophysiology of bone loss in patients receiving anticonvulsant therapy. Epilepsy Behav 5(Suppl 2):S3–S15.
32. Arnala I, Kemppainen T, Kroger H, Janatuinen E, Alhava EM 2001 Bone histomorphometry in celiac disease. Ann Chir Gynaecol 90:100–104.
33. Ott SM, Tucci JR, Heaney RP, Marx SJ 1997 Hypocalciuria and abnormalities in mineral and skeletal homeostasis in patients with celiac sprue without intestinal symptoms. Endocrinol Metab 4:201–206.
34. Pecovnik Balon B, Bren A 2000 Bone histomorphometry is still the

golden standard for diagnosing renal osteodystrophy. Clin Nephrol **54:** 463–469.

35. Parker CR, Blackwell PJ, Freemont AJ, Hosking DJ 2002 Biochemical measurements in the prediction of histologic subtype of renal transplant bone disease in women. Am J Kidney Dis **40:**385–396.

36. Elder G 2002 Pathophysiology and recent advances in the management of renal osteodystrophy. J Bone Miner Res **17:**2094–2105.

37. Malluche HH, Langub MC, Monier-Faugere MC 1997 Pathogenesis and histology of renal osteodystrophy. Osteoporos Int **7**(Suppl 3)**:**S184–S187.

38. Recker RR, Barger-Lux MJ 2002 Transilial bone biopsy. In: Bilezikian JP, Raisz LG, Rodan GA (eds.) Principles of Bone Biology, 2nd ed. Academic Press, San Diego, CA, USA, pp. 1625–1634.

39. Schwartz MP, Recker RR 1982 The label escape error: Determination of

40. Rao DS, Matkovic V, Duncan H 1980 Transiliac bone biopsy: Complications and diagnostic value. Henry Ford Hosp Med J **28:**112–118.

41. Goldner J 1938 A modification of the Masson trichrome technique for routine laboratory purposes. Am J Pathol **14:**237–243.

42. Kimmel DB, Jee SS 1983 Measurements of area, perimeter, and distance: Details of data collection in bone histomorphometry. In: Recker RR (ed.) Bone Histomorphometry: Techniques and Interpretation. CRC Press, Boca Raton, FL, USA, pp. 80–108.

43. Barger-Lux MJ, Recker RR 2005 Towards understanding bone quality: Transilial bone biopsy and bone histomorphometry. Clin Rev Bone Miner Metab (in press).

the active bone-forming surface in histologic sections of bone measured by tetracycline double labels. Metab Bone Dis Rel Res **4:**237–241.

Chapter 25. Molecular Diagnosis of Bone and Mineral Disorders

Robert F. Gagel and Gilbert J. Cote

Department of Endocrine Neoplasia and Hormonal Disorders, University of Texas, MD Anderson Cancer Center, Houston, Texas

INTRODUCTION

With the complete sequencing of the human genome, we are moving from a period of progressive discovery to one where genetic analysis has become a common tool for the study of the molecular basis and clinical diagnosis of human disease. The past 20 years has seen exponential growth in the identification of genetic abnormalities that cause bone and mineral disorders. There are now specific genetic forms of osteoporosis and osteosclerosis; multiple causes of hypocalcemia, hypercalcemia, hypophosphatemia, hyperphosphatemia; and numerous examples of hereditary bone dysplasia. These observations have enriched our understanding of the hormonal and signal transduction pathways involved in bone formation, bone remodeling, and mineral homeostasis and have provided new therapeutic targets for treatment of a variety of bone disorders.

Diagnostic use of this type of information has quickly made its way into the clinical practice of medicine. For example, within 3 years after the description of missense mutations in the *RET* proto-oncogene in multiple endocrine neoplasia, type 2 (MEN2), genetic testing for these mutations has replaced prior nongenetic approaches. In addition, mutational analysis of the *MEN1* gene, *RET* gene (MEN2), *HPRT2* gene (*hyperparathyroidism-jaw tumor syndrome* gene, which is involved in some examples of familial isolated hyperparathyroidism), and the *CASR* gene (*calcium sensing receptor* gene) can be important for evaluation of hypercalcemia. This rapid acquisition of new information and its application to disease management underscores the importance of acquiring a fundamental knowledge of testing strategies and an understanding of the power and limitations of current approaches to genetic testing.

The single most important resource for up-to-date information related to specific genetic syndromes is provided by Online Mendelian Inheritance in Man (OMIM), available to all physicians without charge on the World Wide Web.[1] This concise but complete reference is an excellent starting point for genetic information relating to bone and mineral disorders and provides an intuitive, searchable textual database that is updated on a regular basis. For each genetic disorder, identifiable by a specific OMIM number, a detailed and well-referenced review discussing the mapping and identification of the causative gene, the spectrum of clinical presentation and management, molecular genetics, and specific animals models is available. Additional links provide a clinical synopsis, whether genetically related disorders exist, and a detailed description of the causative gene, including associated mutations. Because OMIM is incorporated into the National Center for Biotechnology Information (NCBI) website (www.ncbi.nlm.nih.gov), direct links to PubMed citations, genetic sequence, and expression profiles are easily accessed. Other databases provide specific information on the availability of genetic testing and individual gene mutations. The most widely used resource for information about genetic testing is available at www.genetests. org, a site that provides a searchable database of research and clinical sources for genetic testing and a variety of educational materials, including gene reviews and PowerPoint presentations.[2] Detailed information regarding the association of specific gene mutations with various disorders can be found at the Human Gene Mutation Database.[3] This site provides mutation data on >1800 genes and has direct links to several external websites including OMIM.

In the past 5–10 years, genetic testing for diagnosis has largely moved from individual research laboratories to large clinical laboratories that have been government certified to follow the Clinical Laboratory Improvement Amendments (CLIA; www.CMS.hhs.gov/clia) and mandated practices of quality assurance.[4] The CLIA program, originally put in place to ensure quality laboratory testing, has incorporated specific standards for genetic testing. With the widespread availability of genetic testing for use in the clinical setting, the goal of this chapter is to provide a basic overview of the primary techniques used to identify mutations and to briefly discuss the interpretations of test results.

PCR

A basic understanding of the principles underlying PCR is vital to molecular genetic diagnosis. The DNA used in diag-

Dr. Gagel is a consultant and member of the Speakers Bureau for Merck, Proctor & Gamble, Novartis, Eli-Lilly, Pfizer, and Astra Zeneca. Dr. Cote has reported no conflicts of interest.

Polymerase Chain Reaction (PCR)

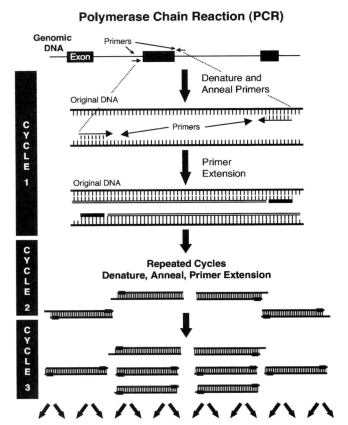

The Number of DNA Products = 2 ^{number of cycles}

FIG. 1. PCR. DNA from the patient to be tested is denatured by heating. Oligonucleotides, which complement a small sequence flanking the targeted piece of DNA, are added to the mixture. The oligonucleotides hybridize to the target DNA and serve as a template for extension of the DNA strand by a thermostabile polymerase. The DNA is again denatured by heating, followed by a new cycle of DNA synthesis (cycle 2). In subsequent cycles, there is a logarithmic increase in the number of copies of the targeted DNA. After 20–40 cycles, most of the DNA copies are of a single size.

nostic studies is most commonly extracted from peripheral white blood cells and occasionally from buccal smears or specific organs. It is important, if possible, to obtain blood from an affected family member as well as the patient at risk. Occasionally, a DNA copy of mRNA from a specific tissue can be made by a technique called reverse transcription. Either genomic DNA or the copy of the mRNA is used as a template for PCR, a method for amplification of a selected portion of a specific DNA sequence.[5]

The specific portion of the gene of interest to be copied is targeted using small single-stranded DNA fragments that are complementary to and flank the DNA sequence of interest (oligonucleotide primers). The addition of nucleotides and a thermostabile DNA polymerase, an enzyme that synthesizes new DNA, followed by heating and cooling through 20–40 cycles, results in the formation of millions of copies of the targeted DNA (Fig. 1). Copies will be made of both parental alleles of the target DNA sequence (one derived from each parent). The sensitivity of the PCR reaction is so great that appropriate controls must be included in each amplification experiment to exclude the possibility of external DNA contamination. The amplified DNA serves as the starting material for the majority of mutational analysis techniques.

GENERAL SCREENING TO DETECT MUTATIONS

This summary will focus only on the application of direct DNA sequencing for the detection of specific nucleotide mutations, small insertions, or small deletions (typically <50 base pairs). While it is possible to use sequencing to precisely map the DNA breakpoints of large insertions, deletions, or rearrangements, standard PCR approaches typically fail to identify these defects. For genetic disorders where DNA breakage is common, clinical laboratories will frequently supplement DNA sequence analysis with karyotype analysis, Southern blotting, or other newer approaches.[6] This is a particularly important consideration when interpreting negative results.

Over the years, several different strategies have been developed for identification of specific mutations. Cost, reproducibility, and specificity have typically been the driving factors in application of various methods to clinical testing. A benefit of the human genome project has been the continual reduction in the costs associated with direct DNA sequencing along with an accompanying increase in reliability. Direct DNA sequencing remains the "gold standard" for mutation detection. This has led most commercial laboratories to adopt automated PCR and DNA sequencing as the technique of choice. However, for genetic disorders with a limited and defined set of mutations, an array of equally reliable methodologies that allow high throughput analysis of DNA polymorphisms are also finding their way into clinical mutation screening applications. Many use capillary electrophoresis, high-performance liquid chromatography (HPLC), or mass spectrometry approaches to separate DNA fragments or techniques that rely on fluorescence-based imaging, such as DNA melting curve analysis or enzymatic detection of mismatches to define mutations.[6–11] Major factors for deciding which technique to use include the size of the DNA sequence to be examined, the spectrum of mutations that cause the disease, and access to newer equipment and technologies. For example, several disorders are known to result from mutations affecting collagen. Collagen genes are large and are comprised of numerous exons (>50), making it impractical to sequence the many exons of the many collagen genes. For Ehlers-Danlos syndrome, which involves mutations affecting type V collagen, one approach has been to perform initial biochemical analysis of proteins derived from cultured patient fibroblasts to determine whether a detailed genetic analysis is merited.[12] However, this type approach is limited to disorders where tissue or cells known to express the defective protein are available for analysis.

The remainder of this chapter will focus on a single technique, DNA sequencing, and interpretation of genetic results. As we move into the future, issues regarding the practical, ethical and clinical use of genetic testing will continue to evolve. Indeed, we continue to move closer to the day when newer technologies could lower the cost of whole genome sequencing to less than $1000.[13–15]

DIRECT DNA SEQUENCING

Direct DNA sequencing of PCR products is universally accepted as the most specific method for detection of genetic mutations.[6–11] Direct DNA sequencing of a PCR product derived from genomic DNA permits analysis of both alleles or copies of the gene and the identification of new or unreported mutations. The disadvantages of this method include its complexity, the requirement for expensive equipment, and the potential difficulties associated with analyzing >500–600 nucleotides in a single sequencing reaction. The process has been largely computer automated with an assembly line of robots coupling DNA isolation from blood, PCR amplification, sequencing, and output of results. Large clinical laboratories, with the means to invest in equipment, routinely use direct sequencing because it is more practical and cost effective, even for large genes. The methodology is based on the standard Sanger dideoxysequencing method.[16] PCR products are first typically enzymatically treated to remove unused oligonucleotide primers and to strip the deoxynucleotide triphosphates (dNTPs) of their phosphates. This step is required so that a new oligonucleotide primer can be added to direct the site-specific initiation of the sequencing reaction by DNA polymerase, similar to the annealing and elongation steps of PCR. Unlike PCR, however, the dNTP mixture includes fluorescently labeled dideoxynucleotides, which randomly terminate elongation when they become incorporated into the newly synthesized DNA strand (called "chain termination"). Each of the four dideoxynucleotides is labeled with a different color fluorescent label, which serves to identify the specific nucleotide ending the DNA chain. The mixture of end-labeled DNA fragments are separated based on their size by capillary electrophoresis. As individual end-labeled DNA fragments, which differ in size by a single nucleotide, pass by a laser detector, the fluorescent nucleotide is read. The DNA sequence is represented as a four-colored chromatograph with separate peaks representing individual nucleotides (Fig. 2). Single nucleotide mutations/polymorphisms are denoted by the presence of two nucleotides (peaks) migrating with the same apparent molecular weight. Insertions and deletions have a much more distinctive chromatograph pattern because the sequence frameshift results in an overlapping pattern of peaks from the point of the genetic defect (Fig. 2).

SOURCES OF ERROR IN GENETIC TESTING

It is important that clinicians be aware of the frequency and nature of genetic testing errors.[8,9,17] Both false-positive and negative results clearly have the potential to adversely impact outcome of patient care. Sample mix-up, especially in the setting of family screening where many family members share a common last name, may occur in up to 5% of analyses. These errors may occur at the time of blood drawing, during subsequent analysis or recording, or even at the clinical testing laboratory. A second potential source of error is contamination by DNA from individuals who harbor a disease causing mutation. The funneling of large numbers of samples to a few laboratories for analysis of a single disease further increases the chance of contamination. The extreme sensitivity of PCR analysis makes it possible that a positive result could occur as a result of airborne contamination of a reaction tube. This has become less of a concern at larger clinical laboratories that have taken specific measures to prevent sample mix-up and contamination through the use of automation and computerized coding.[9] A third source of error is the failure to amplify both alleles, thereby resulting in the possibility of a false-negative result because only the normal allele is included in the analysis. The most common explanation for amplification failure is a random polymorphism (DNA sequence change) acting to reduce oligonucleotide primer hybridization during the PCR reaction. Other causes for amplification failure include genetic defects involving insertion, deletion, or rearrangement of DNA sequence at the site of amplification. To help rule out these possibilities, it is always helpful to note whether an immediate family member or close relative has tested positive using the same PCR oligonucleotide primer set. Finally, despite the robust nature of PCR and DNA sequencing, the methodologies themselves are not error free.[9] Therefore, it is important to note whether DNA sequencing was performed on both the

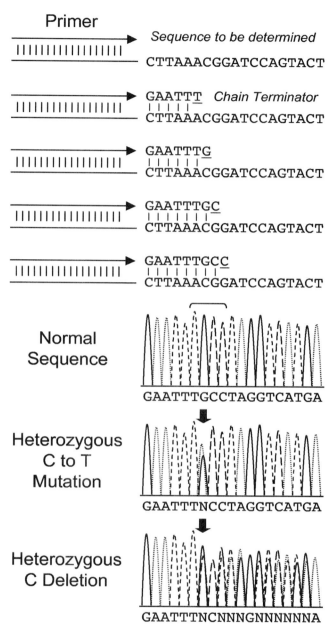

FIG. 2. DNA sequencing. Similar to the first step of PCR, an oligonucleotide primer is hybridized to a DNA target adjacent to the sequence to be determined and serves as a template for extension by a DNA polymerase. Unlike PCR, a precise mixture normal nucleotides with fluorescent dideoxynucleotides (underlined) causes the growth of the newly synthesized DNA strand to terminate selectively at each position. The mixture of newly synthesized DNA fragments is denatured and separated based on size by capillary electrophoresis, and the specific end-labeled nucleotide is detected by a laser scanner. The chromatograph simulates a representative sequencing output with the typical black (G), red (T), green (A), and blue (C) colors replaced by dotted and dashed lines. The bracketed region highlights the position of the four terminated DNA fragments shown above. Additional chromatographs provide examples of a heterozygous point mutation and a deletion. Arrow indicates the defect.

sense and antisense strands to safeguard against possible errors in sequencing.

Even under ideal conditions, mutation analysis errors will occur. Government-mandated standards and procedures in individual laboratories have reduced but not eliminated these errors completely.[4,9,12] If genetic testing is to be used as the sole determinant for decision-making in disease management, it is important for the clinician to be aware of the possibility of error and to take steps to minimize the impact on patient care. Many clinical testing laboratories and GeneTests.org provide estimates of the frequency of new mutation detection, the potential for large deletions or rearrangements, and the inherent error rate associated with the test results. Therefore, if not provided, the clinician should always request the gene-specific sensitivity and specificity that the clinical laboratory routinely observes. One simple approach that will eliminate the majority of these errors is to repeat each analysis, whether positive or negative, in a different laboratory on an independently obtained sample. This approach will eliminate most sample mix-up, DNA contamination, and technical errors. Sending the sample to a separate laboratory that uses a different primer set for PCR amplification will also reduce the likelihood of a single allele amplification error.

INTEGRATION OF GENETIC INFORMATION INTO CLINICAL MANAGEMENT

Genetic testing has several important clinical uses. Identification of a specific disease-causing mutation may clarify and simplify patient management. For example, the identification of a mutation of the CSR gene causative for familial hypercalcemic hypocalciuria in an individual with an atypical clinical presentation may prevent unnecessary parathyroid surgery. For other disorders, such as MEN2, the identification of a specific mutation may lead to a specific action (thyroidectomy) in a child.[8,17] However, genetic testing also imposes additional ethical and legal duties on the physician to ensure that the patient is properly counseled before testing and additionally when receiving their test results. Unlike most clinical testing, obtaining a blood sample for genetic testing requires informed patient consent. Unfortunately, a simple discussion of the use of testing in diagnosis and treatment is insufficient. The patient needs to be informed about the limitations of testing, genetic testing options, alternative tests, inheritance and risk models, genetic health risks to family members, and a wide variety of insurance and legal issues. In addition, the fear of genetic discrimination sometimes becomes a deterrent, preventing patients from seeking genetic testing. The complexity of these many issues, including state to state differences in the laws regarding the use of genetic information, make it advisable to involve a genetic counselor when possible (www.nsgc.org). In addition to dealing with issues surrounding consent, and disclosure of test results, a genetic counselor frequently can help the patient with many of the burdens associated with having a genetic disorder. For example, when caring for a patient with a hereditary cancer syndrome, the clinician has an ethical duty to warn the patient about genetic health risks to his or her family members. Genetic counselors can typically write a "family letter" to be offered to their family members as an educational tool and to relieve the patient from the burden of remembering a lot of technical information.

In other situations, the benefits of genetic screening may be more ambiguous. The identification of a mutation in an individual with a severe and fatal form of osteogenesis imperfecta may not alter therapy for the patient; however, detection of the mutation may make prenatal genetic screening possible. Identification and categorization of these mutations are also important because gene therapy strategies, especially for single gene defects, are evolving rapidly. The discovery that mutation of a single gene can be associated with multiple disease phenotypes has also led to a rethinking of how skeletal disorders should be classified. Three major classifications have emerged based primarily either on biochemical evidence, radiographic evidence, or genetic evidence.[18,19] Each classification group serves as a unique entry point in facilitating patient diagnosis and treatment. Included in the Appendix of this Primer is a table providing an extensive listing of serum mineral and skeletal disorders and their specific genetic defects. Information in this table was primarily obtained by a key word search of the OMIM website. We have grouped the disorders according to serum mineral findings and followed this list with disorders grouped according to a recent International Nosology and Classification of Constitutive Disorders of Bone consensus, which is a combination of morphological findings and molecular defects.[18] A classification of many of these disorders based on gene structure and function involved is also available.[19]

An evolving area of genetic research implicates subtle DNA differences in the pathogenesis of disease.[20] For example, genetic studies examining polymorphism have identified several candidate genes that may be involved in osteoporosis, including the *vitamin D receptor*, the *estrogen receptor*, and the *collagen type Iα1* genes, among others.[21] Although the role of these polymorphisms is currently controversial, there are examples in other systems that clearly point to population-based genetic differences that may influence disease expression, such as diabetes or hypertension.[20] Further characterization and clarification of the roles that these genetic polymorphisms play in disease genesis may permit us to identify high-risk populations for application of preventive strategies.

REFERENCES

1. John Hopkins University 2005 Online Mendelian inheritance in man, OMIM. Available online at http://www.ncbi.nlm.nih.gov/entrez/query.fcgi?db=OMIM. Accessed January 17, 2006.
2. University of Washington 2005 GeneTests: Medical genetics information resource. Available online at http://www.genetests.org. Accessed January 17, 2006.
3. Stenson PD, Ball EV, Mort M, Phillips AD, Shiel JA, Thomas NS, Abeysinghe S, Krawczak M, Cooper DN 2003 The human gene mutation database (HGMD): 2003 update. Hum Mutat 21:577–581.
4. Williams LO, Cole EC, Lubin IM, Iglesias NI, Jordan RL, Elliot LE 2003 Quality assurance in human molecular genetics testing. status and recommendations. Arch Pathol Lab Med 127:1353–1358.
5. Saiki RK, Gelfand DH, Stoffel S, Scharf SJ, Higuchi R, Horn GT, Mullis KB, Erlich HA 1988 Primer-directed enzymatic amplification of DNA with a thermostable DNA polymerase. Science 239:487–491.
6. Sellner LN, Taylor GR 2004 MLPA and MAPH: New techniques for detection of gene deletions. Hum Mutat 23:413–419.
7. Green ED, Klapholz S, Birren B 1998 Genome Analysis: A Laboratory Manual. Detecting Genes, vol. 2. Cold Spring Harbor Laboratory Press, New York, NY, USA.
8. Hoff AO, Cote GJ, Gagel RF 2002 Laboratory evaluation and screening of genetic endocrine diseases. In: Martini L, Baxter JD, Melmed S, New MI (eds.) Modern Endocrinology. Genetics in Endocrinology. Lippincott Williams & Wilkins, Philadelphia, PA, USA, pp. 189–220.
9. Strom CM 2005 Mutation detection, interpretation, and applications in the clinical laboratory setting. Mutat Res 573:160–167.
10. Tomita N, Oto M 2004 Molecular genetic diagnosis of familial tumors. Int J Clin Oncol 9:246–256.
11. Tost J, Gut IG 2005 Genotyping single nucleotide polymorphisms by MALDI mass spectrometry in clinical applications. Clin Biochem 38:335–350.
12. Ensenauer RE, Michels VV, Reinke SS 2005 Genetic testing: Practical, ethical, and counseling considerations. Mayo Clin Proc 80:63–73.
13. Shendure J, Mitra RD, Varma C, Church GM 2004 Advanced sequencing technologies: Methods and goals. Nat Rev Genet 5:335–344.
14. Hitt E 2005 DNA sequencing: A race toward the $1,000 genome. Available online at http://www.genpromag.com. Accessed January 17, 2006.
15. Spencer G 2005 NHGRI expands effort to revolutionize sequencing

technologies, grants awarded to develop faster, cheaper DNA sequencing. Available online at http://www.genome.gov/15015208. Accessed January 17, 2006.

16. Sanger F, Nicklen S, Coulson AR 1977 DNA sequencing with chain-terminating inhibitors. Proc Natl Acad Sci USA **74:**5463–5467.

17. Gagel RF, Cote GJ 2002 The role of the *RET* proto-oncogene in multiple endocrine neoplasia, type 2. In: Bilezikian JP, Raisz LG, Rodan GA (eds.) Principles of Bone Biology, 2nd ed. Academic Press. New York, NY, USA, pp. 1067–1078.

18. Hall CM 2002 International nosology and classification of constitutional disorders of bone. Am J Med Genet **113:**65–77.

19. Superti-Furga A, Bonafe L, Rimoin, DL 2001 Molecular-pathogenetic classification of genetic disorders of the skeleton. Am J Med Genet **106:**282–293.

20. Mayeux R 2005 Mapping the new frontier: Complex genetic disorders. J Clin Invest **115:**1404–1407.

21. Andrew T, Macgregor AJ 2004 Genes and osteoporosis. Curr Osteoporos Rep **2:**79–89.

SECTION V

Disorders of Serum Minerals
(Section Editors: Elizabeth Shane and Andrew F. Stewart)

Chapter 26. Hypercalcemia: Pathogenesis, Clinical Manifestations, Differential Diagnosis, and Management

Elizabeth Shane[1] and Dinaz Irani[2]

[1]Department of Medicine, Columbia University, College of Physicians and Surgeons, New York, New York; and [2]Metabolic Bone Disease Research Program, Columbia University Medical Center, New York, New York

INTRODUCTION

The clinical presentation of hypercalcemia varies from a mild, asymptomatic, biochemical abnormality detected during routine screening to a life-threatening medical emergency. In this chapter, pathogenesis, clinical manifestations, differential diagnosis, and management of hypercalcemia will be discussed.

PATHOGENESIS

The concentration of calcium in the extracellular fluid is critical for many physiologic processes. Under normal circumstances, the range is remarkably constant, between 8.5 and 10.5 mg/dl (2.1–2.5 mM). The exact normal range varies slightly, depending on the laboratory. Approximately one-half the total serum calcium is bound to plasma proteins, primarily albumin. A small component of the total calcium is complexed to anions such as citrate or sulfate. The remaining one-half circulates as the free calcium ion. It is only this ionized portion of the total serum calcium that is physiologically important, regulating neuromuscular contractility, the process of coagulation, and a variety of other cellular activities.

In a variety of chronic illnesses, there may be a substantial reduction in the serum albumin concentration. Under such circumstances, the total serum calcium concentration may be low, whereas ionized calcium concentrations remain normal. A simple correction for hypoalbuminemia may be made by adding 0.8 mg/dl to the total serum calcium concentration for every 1.0 g/dl by which the serum albumin concentration is lower than 4.0 g/dl. Thus, a patient with a total serum calcium of 10.5 mg/dl and a serum albumin level of 2.0 g/dl has a corrected total serum calcium of 12.1 mg/dl. Conversely, falsely elevated serum calcium levels may be observed, usually as the result of an elevation of the serum albumin because of dehydration or hemoconcentration during venipuncture. A similar maneuver can be performed to correct the serum calcium in this situation, except that the correction factor must be subtracted from the serum calcium level.

In contrast to changes in the serum albumin concentration, which affect the total but not the ionized calcium level, alterations in pH affect the ionized but not the total calcium concentration. Acidosis increases the ionized calcium by decreasing the binding of calcium ions to albumin, whereas alkalosis decreases the ionized calcium by enhancing binding of calcium ions to albumin. Measurement of total serum calcium, particularly if corrected for the serum albumin, is usually adequate for most situations. However in complex cases (changes in both albumin and pH), a direct measurement of the ionized calcium should be performed.

Under normal circumstances, the plasma calcium concentration reflects a balance between the flux of calcium into the extracellular fluid from the gastrointestinal (GI) tract, the skeleton, and the kidney, and the flux of calcium out of the extracellular fluid into the skeleton and the urine. Hypercalcemia develops when the rate of calcium entry into the blood compartment is greater than its rate of removal. This occurs most commonly when accelerated osteoclastic bone resorption or excessive GI calcium absorption delivers quantities of calcium into the blood that exceed the capac-

ities of the kidney to eliminate it and of the skeleton to reclaim it. Less commonly, normal rates of calcium entry into the extracellular fluid may result in hypercalcemia if the process of renal excretion or that of bone mineralization is impaired.

Accelerated bone resorption by multinucleated bone-resorbing osteoclasts is the primary pathogenetic mechanism in most instances of hypercalcemia.[1] Osteoclasts may be stimulated to resorb bone by PTH, PTH-related protein (PTHrP), and 1,25-dihydroxyvitamin D, all of which have been shown to cause hypercalcemia.[2,3] A number of cytokines (IL-1α, IL-1β, IL-6, TNF, lymphotoxin, and TGF-α) also stimulate osteoclastic bone resorption either alone or in concert with PTHrP.[4] Although low levels of PTHrP are expressed by many normal tissues, high levels may be secreted from some malignant tumors. Some cytokines have been linked to the development of hypercalcemia in human malignancy.[4] Excessive GI absorption of calcium is a much less common cause of hypercalcemia, although it may play a role in hypercalcemic states characterized by excess vitamin D, such as lymphoma or vitamin D intoxication. Whether the primary cause of the hypercalcemia is accelerated bone resorption or excessive GI tract absorption of calcium, the kidney is the primary defender against a rise in the serum calcium. Thus, hypercalcemia is usually preceded by hypercalciuria, and it is only when the capacity of the kidney to excrete calcium has been exceeded that the patient becomes hypercalcemic.[5]

Several other factors may contribute to the pathogenesis of hypercalcemia. In addition to stimulating osteoclast-mediated bone resorption, both PTH and PTHrP increase reabsorption of calcium from the distal tubule, thus interfering with the ability of the kidneys to clear the filtered calcium load. PTH and PTHrP also increase 1,25-dihydroxyvitamin D synthesis, further contributing to a hypercalcemic state.[6] Hypercalcemia interferes with the action of antidiuretic hormone on the distal tubule, causing a form of nephrogenic diabetes insipidus that results in polyuria. The thirst mechanism may not be fully operative because of the nausea and vomiting that frequently accompany hypercalcemia; thus, urinary fluid losses may not be replaced, and dehydration may ensue. The resulting reduction in the extracellular fluid volume and associated reduction in the glomerular filtration rate exacerbate the hypercalcemia. Finally, immobilization may also contribute to hypercalcemia by virtue of associated increases in bone resorption.

CLINICAL MANIFESTATIONS

The clinical presentation of the hypercalcemic patient[7] may involve any of several organ systems (see Table 1). The signs and symptoms tend to be similar regardless of the etiology of the hypercalcemia. Because an optimal extracellular calcium concentration is necessary for normal neurologic function, symptoms of neurologic dysfunction often predominate in hypercalcemic states. The patient (or family members) may notice subtle changes in the ability to concentrate or an increased sleep requirement. With increasing severity of the hypercalcemia, symptoms may gradually progress to depression, confusion, and even coma. Muscle weakness is common.

Gastrointestinal symptoms are often prominent, with constipation, anorexia, nausea, and vomiting present in varying degrees.

Dr. Shane has received research funding from Novartis, but not in the field of hypercalcemia. Dr. Irani has reported no conflicts of interest.

TABLE 1. CLINICAL MANIFESTATIONS OF HYPERCALCEMIA

Cardiovascular
  Shortened QT interval on ECG
  Arrhythmias (rare unless on digitalis)
  Bradycardia
  Hypertension
  Bundle branch/AV blocks
  Cardiac arrest (if severe)
Neuromuscular
  Emotional lability
  Confusion
  Delirium
  Psychosis
  Stupor
  Muscle weakness
  Headache
  Seizures (rare)
Renal
  Polyuria
  Polydispsia
  Nocturia
  Hypercalciuria
  Nephrolithiasis
  Nephrocalcinosis
  Renal failure
Gastrointestinal
  Nausea/vomiting
  Anorexia
  Constipation
  Abdominal pain
  Peptic ulcers
  Pancreatitis
Skeletal
  Bone pain/arthralgia
  Osteopenia/osteoporosis in cortical bone (often seen in wrist)
Other
  Shock
  Death

Pancreatitis and peptic ulcer disease are unusual but have been reported. They may be somewhat more common if the hypercalcemia is caused by primary hyperparathyroidism than other causes of hypercalcemia.

Polyuria, resulting from the impaired concentrating ability of the distal tubule, is common, particularly during the early phases. Polydipsia is also usually present. The combination of polyuria and diminished fluid intake caused by GI symptoms may lead to severe dehydration. Nephrolithiasis occurs in patients with primary hyperparathyroidism (15–20% in recent series), but along with nephrocalcinosis, it may also develop in patients with hypercalcemia because of other causes, particularly when the hypercalcemia is chronic.

Hypercalcemia increases the rate of cardiac repolarization. Thus, shortening of the Q-T interval is observed commonly on the electrocardiogram. Bradycardia and first-degree atrioventricular block, as well as other arrhythmias, may occur. Caution should be exercised when treating the hypercalcemic patient with digitalis, because increased sensitivity to this drug has been observed.

In general, the presence or absence of symptoms correlates both with the degree of elevation of the serum calcium and with the rapidity of its rise. Most patients do not begin to show clinical features of hypercalcemia until the total calcium concentration exceeds 12 mg/dl, and patients are almost invariably symptomatic at levels >14 mg/dl. However, there is much individual variation in this regard. Certain patients will be quite symptomatic with moderate hypercalcemia of 12.0–14.0 mg/dl, whereas others may show no overt symptomatology at a similar level. The latter situation occurs most often in the setting of chronic hypercalcemia. In other circumstances, the absence of symptoms in the severely hypercalcemic patient should prompt one to measure the ionized calcium level to be certain that hypercalcemia is not secondary to excessive binding of calcium to plasma proteins.

DIFFERENTIAL DIAGNOSIS

Detection of an elevated serum calcium requires that the etiology be established. The many causes of hypercalcemia are listed in Table 2, and most will be covered separately in subsequent chapters. However, certain general principles that apply to the differential diagnosis of hypercalcemia are covered here.

Malignancy and primary hyperparathyroidism are by far the most common causes of hypercalcemia, accounting for >90% of hypercalcemic patients.[7] Differentiating between these two diagnoses is generally not difficult on clinical grounds alone. The vast

TABLE 2. DIFFERENTIAL DIAGNOSIS OF HYPERCALCEMIA

Most common
  Primary hyperparathyroidism
  Malignant disease
    PTH-related protein (carcinoma of lung, esophagus, head and neck,
      renal cell, breast, ovary, and bladder)
    Ectopic production of 1,25-dihydroxyvitamin D (lymphoma)
    Lytic bone metastases (multiple myeloma, hematologic
      malignancies and breast carcinoma)
    Other factor(s) produced locally or ectopically
Uncommon
  Endocrine disorders
    Thyrotoxicosis
  Granulomatous diseases
    Sarcoidosis
    HIV
  Drug-induced
    Vitamin D
    Thiazide diuretics
    Lithium
    Estrogens and antiestrogens
    Androgens (breast cancer therapy)
    Aminophylline
    Vitamin A
    Aluminum intoxication (in chronic renal failure)
  Miscellaneous
    Immobilization
    Renal failure (acute and chronic)
    Total parenteral nutrition
Rare
  Endocrine disorders
    Pheochromocytoma
    Vasoactive intestinal polypeptide-producing tumor
    Familial hypocalciuric hypercalcemia
  Granulomatous diseases
    Tuberculosis
    Histoplasmosis
    Coccidioidomycosis
    Leprosy
  Miscellaneous
    Milk-alkali syndrome
    Hypophosphatasia
    William's syndrome
  Rhabdomyolysis (presentation is usually preceded by a hypocalcemic
    state)

majority of patients with primary hyperparathyroidism have relatively mild hypercalcemia, within 1.0 mg/dl above the upper limits of normal and usually <12.0 mg/dl. They are often asymptomatic. Review of past medical records may reveal that the hypercalcemia has been present for months to years. When symptoms of hypercalcemia are present, they tend to be chronic, such as nephrolithiasis. In contrast, patients with hypercalcemia of malignancy are usually overtly ill and are more likely to manifest the classic signs and symptoms of an elevated serum calcium. In general, the malignancy itself is readily apparent and presents little diagnostic challenge to the physician. Less commonly, occult malignancy may present with hypercalcemia, or the patient with primary hyperparathyroidism may present with moderate to severe elevation of the serum calcium that is associated with symptoms or with the acute onset of severe hypercalcemia (parathyroid crisis). Such cases pose a greater diagnostic problem.

The availability of reliable assays for intact PTH based on double antibody techniques (two-site, immunoradiometric, or chemiluminescent assays) has been of great diagnostic value in the evaluation of the hypercalcemic patient. The majority of patients with primary hyperparathyroidism have intact PTH levels that are frankly elevated. Patients with hypercalcemia of malignancy virtually always show suppressed or undetectable levels of intact PTH. It is distinctly unusual for a patient with malignancy (excepting parathyroid cancer) to show elevated levels of PTH. When this occurs, two possibilities exist: the patient may have concomitant primary hyperparathyroidism or the malignancy itself may be secreting PTH, an uncommon event.

In most patients with malignancy-associated hypercalcemia, the hypercalcemia is a result of secretion of PTHrP by the tumor.[2] Although elevated levels of PTHrP can prove helpful in the diagnosis of hypercalcemia of malignancy, a negative result does not exclude malignancy. Certain tumors cause hypercalcemia by mechanisms independent of PTHrP, such as secretion of other bone-resorbing cytokines or extrarenal conversion of 25-hydroxyvitamin D to 1,25-dihydroxyvitamin D. Local bone-resorbing effects of tumors such as breast cancer also may be involved.

Hypercalcemia from causes other than malignancy or primary hyperparathyroidism may also occur. A thorough history and physical examination are invaluable in arriving at the correct diagnosis. Each of the etiologies listed in Table 2 is covered in one of the other chapters in this section.

MANAGEMENT

The management of hypercalcemia rests on several principles. The underlying cause of the hypercalcemia should be elucidated, followed by maneuvers that reduce the serum calcium by expanding intravascular volume, increasing urinary calcium excretion and inhibiting bone resorption. The decision to institute therapy for the hypercalcemic patient depends on the level of the serum calcium and the presence or absence of clinical manifestations of an elevated serum calcium. In general, patients with mild hypercalcemia (<12.0 mg/dl) do not have symptoms of hypercalcemia and do not derive significant clinical benefit from normalization of their serum calcium. However, although immediate intervention is not usually necessary, such patients should be encouraged to increase oral fluid intake, avoid becoming dehydrated, eat a diet that is moderate in calcium content, and discontinue any drugs that might be contributing to the hypercalcemia (e.g., thiazide diuretics). In contrast, when the serum calcium is >14.0 mg/dl, more aggressive therapy should be initiated regardless of whether the patient has signs or symptoms of hypercalcemia. Moderate elevation of the serum calcium (12.0–14.0 mg/dl) should be treated aggressively if the patient shows clinical signs or symptoms consistent with hypercalcemia. However, if such a patient is asymp-

tomatic, a more conservative approach may be appropriate. It is also important to consider the underlying cause of the hypercalcemia when deciding whether therapy is necessary and the type of therapy to institute. For example, a patient with acute primary hyperparathyroidism, a completely curable condition, would warrant more aggressive treatment than a patient with diffuse metastatic cancer and a poor prognosis. Another difficult situation arises in the patient whose serum calcium is ~12.0 mg/dl, not within the range one would usually treat aggressively, yet who has an altered mental status or other symptoms that could conceivably be ascribed to a hypercalcemic state. In such situations, it is important to consider other potential causes for the symptoms.

The management of acute hypercalcemia is outlined in Table 3. When the serum calcium exceeds 12.0 mg/dl and signs and symptoms are present, a series of general measures should be instituted. Initial management should include the discontinuation of thiazides, parent vitamin D or vitamin D analog (e.g., calcitriol, paricalcitol), lithium, and sedatives because they may contribute to the hypercalcemic state. The patient should also be mobilized as soon as possible to prevent increased bone resorption.[8] Other therapeutic maneuvers tend to lower serum calcium by increasing urinary calcium excretion.[9,10] Dehydration, resulting from the pathophysiologic events induced by the hypercalcemia (anorexia, nausea, vomiting, defective urinary concentrating mechanism, and polyuria) is very common. Hydration with normal saline, to correct the extracellular fluid deficit, is central to the early management of hypercalcemia from any cause. Restoration of the volume deficit can usually be achieved by the continuous infusion of 3–6 liters of 0.9% sodium chloride over a 24- to 48-h period. This maneuver generally lowers the serum calcium by 1.0–3.0 mg/dl. Hydration with saline enhances urinary calcium excretion by increasing glomerular filtration of calcium and decreasing both proximal and distal tubular reabsorption of sodium and calcium. However, saline hydration alone does not usually establish normocalcemia unless the calcium concentration is only modestly elevated. Moreover, this form of therapy must be used with caution in elderly patients or in others with compromised cardiovascular, hepatic or renal function.

In severe cases of hypercalcemia, a loop diuretic, such as furosemide or ethacrynic acid, may be added to saline hydration in the therapy of hypercalcemia. Loop diuretics act on the thick ascending loop of Henle to inhibit both sodium and calcium reabsorption. Thus, the use of such agents enhances urinary calcium losses, increases the likelihood of normalization of the serum calcium level, and mitigates the dangers of hypernatremia and volume overload that may accompany the use of intravenous saline. However, loop diuretics are not necessary in most cases, should be initiated only after extracellular fluid volume has been replenished, and only in small doses (furosemide, 10–20 mg) as necessary to control clinical manifestations of volume excess. It is essential to monitor volume status and serum electrolytes closely if diuretics are necessary to control hypercalcemia. Overzealous use of loop diuretics before intravascular volume has been restored can worsen hypercalcemia by exacerbating volume depletion. Hypokalemia and other electrolyte abnormalities can ensue. Intensive therapy with large doses of furosemide (80–100 mg every 1–2 h) and replacement of fluid and electrolytes based on measured urinary losses is rarely indicated. It must be emphasized that thiazide diuretics are contraindicated in this setting because they decrease renal calcium excretion and may worsen hypercalcemia.

Dialysis, another general measure, is usually reserved for the severely hypercalcemic patient. Peritoneal dialysis or hemodialysis with a low or zero calcium dialysate will lower serum calcium rapidly in those patients who are refractory to other measures or who have renal insufficiency.

Specific approaches to the hypercalcemic patient are based on

TABLE 3. MANAGEMENT OF HYPERCALCEMIA

Intervention	Onset of action	Duration of action	Benefits	Risks
Normal saline 3–6 liters IV daily for 1–3 days	Hours	During infusion	Rehydration; enhanced filtration and excretion of calcium	Volume overload/congestive heart failure
Furosemide 10–20 mg IV (for use in severe cases, and ONLY after ECF volume is restored)	Hours	During treatment	Prevents volume overload; further increases urinary calcium excretion	Hypokalemia; dehydration (patient should be monitored closely)
Calcitonin 4–8 IU/kg IM injection every 6–8 h	Hours	2–3 days	Rapid onset	Limited effect; short duration of action, flushing, nausea, rebound increase in serum calcium
Zoledronic acid 4 mg IV over 15 minutes	1–3 days	Weeks	Most potent/effective bisphosphonate; long acting	Renal failure; transient fever, mild hypophosphatemia, asymptomatic hypocalcemia
Pamidronate 60–90 mg IV over 2–4 h	1–3 days	Weeks	Potent; less costly than zoledronic acid	Renal failure; transient fever, mild hypophosphatemia, asymptomatic hypocalcemia
Glucocorticoids 200–300 mg IV hydrocortisone (or equivalent) daily for 3–5 days	Days	Days to weeks	Useful in the setting of some hematological malignancies, vitamin D intoxication and sarcoidosis	Not useful in solid tumor malignancies or for hyperparathyroidism, immunosuppression, Cushing's syndrome
Dialysis	Hours	During use (~2 days)	Rapid onset, useful in renal failure patients	Invasive, complex procedure

General measures should include treatment of underlying causes, oral hydration, early mobilization, and discontinuation of medications that may cause or exacerbate hypercalcemia.

the underlying pathophysiology. Excessive mobilization of calcium from the skeleton resulting from an accelerated rate of bone resorption is the most important factor in the pathogenesis of hypercalcemia in the majority of patients. Numerous pharmacologic agents are available that specifically block osteoclast-mediated bone resorption and effectively lower serum calcium in most hypercalcemic patients (Table 3). In severely hypercalcemic patients, agents that specifically inhibit bone resorption are necessary to effect normalization of the serum calcium.

Bisphosphonates are bone-seeking compounds that bind to hydroxyapatite and prevent its dissolution. Osteoclast function is impaired after exposure to bisphosphonates, and these drugs have enjoyed increasing use in disorders characterized by excessive bone resorption. Intravenous administration is usually necessary when they are used to treat hypercalcemia. Bisphosphonates should be administered in large volumes of saline over 15 minutes to 4 h, depending on the bisphosphonate, to prevent nephrotoxicity caused by precipitation of calcium bisphosphonate. Three bisphosphonates, zoledronic acid, pamidronate, and etidronate, are currently approved for the treatment of hypercalcemia in the United States. Clodronate and ibandronate are also effective bisphosphonates that have enjoyed widespread use in Europe and the United Kingdom for the treatment of hypercalcemia.[11,12]

Zoledronic acid is currently the most potent bisphosphonate available for the treatment of hypercalcemia. The recommended dose is 4 mg administered intravenously over 15 minutes. The most common adverse event is transient fever (44.2%). Mild hypophosphatemia and asymptomatic hypocalcemia may also occur. The majority of patients will normalize serum calcium levels in <10 days.[13] Treatment with zoledronic acid may be repeated after at least 7 days if a complete response has not been achieved.

Pamidronate is also widely used for the treatment of hypercalcemia. Although a variety of regimens have been reported, the recommended dose is 60–90 mg administered intravenously as a single infusion over 2–4 h. Pamidronate may cause transient fever (33% of patients)[13] and myalgias during the day after the infusion. Preemptive treatment with acetaminophen ameliorates these side effects in the majority of patients. Occasionally, transient leukopenia may develop. Mild, usually asymptomatic, hypocalcemia and hypophosphatemia may occur in some patients, particularly with higher doses (90 mg). The 90-mg dose has also been associated with infusion reactions. The duration of the hypocalcemic effect of pamidronate is variable, ranging from several days to several weeks. The benefits of bisphosphonates reach beyond normalizing serum calcium levels in the setting of certain malignancies. Zoledronic acid, pamidronate, and clodronate are also beneficial in reducing the progression of skeletal metastases and preventing the onset of hypercalcemia in patients with breast and prostate cancer.[14–16] Additionally, monthly zoledronic acid and pamidronate infusions reduce the skeletal complications of multiple myeloma.[17,18] It is important to note that reversible decreases in renal function have been observed with the use of both zoledronic acid and pamidronate. Therefore, these agents should be used with caution in patients with impaired renal function. This risk is decreased when they are administered with adequate amounts of saline and over the appropriate amount of time (15 minutes for zoledronic acid and 2–4 h for pamidronate).[8]

A pooled analysis of two randomized, controlled clinical trials found zoledronic acid to be more effective and longer acting than pamidronate in the treatment of hypercalcemia. Zoledronic acid has the added benefit of a shorter infusion time (15 minutes versus 2–4 h). Adverse event profiles were similar in both groups. However, it should be noted that pamidronate is less costly and some argue the clinical significance of the difference in calcemic control between the two groups.[8]

Etidronate, a first-generation bisphosphonate, can also be administered through intravenous infusion for therapy of hypercalcemia.[14] However, the more potent bisphosphonates are associated with a more rapid onset of action, a larger decline in serum calcium, a longer duration of action, and less renal toxicity than a 3-day course of etidronate.[13,19] Therefore, zoledronic acid and pamidronate have largely replaced etidronate in the therapy of hypercalcemia.

Calcitonin is a polypeptide hormone that is secreted by the parafollicular C cells of the thyroid gland. Salmon calcitonin is the most potent and frequently used form of the drug. Calcitonin inhibits osteoclastic bone resorption, increases urinary calcium excretion, and is a very safe drug. Moreover, calcitonin has the most rapid onset of action of the available calcium-lowering drugs, causing the serum calcium to fall within 2–6 h of administration. The usual dose ranges from 4 to 8 IU/kg administered by intramuscular or subcutaneous injection every 6–8 h. Unfortunately, the hypocalcemic effect of calcitonin is transient, not as pronounced as the bisphosphonates, and rarely normalizes the serum calcium. The serum calcium concentration usually declines by a mean of 2 mg/dl and may begin to rise again within 24 h, despite continued therapy. Calcitonin given in combination with bisphosphonates seems to achieve a more rapid and greater decrease in the serum calcium than when either drug is administered by itself. Used in this way, calcitonin has a role at the outset of therapy in instances of severe hypercalcemia, when it is desirable to lower the serum calcium more rapidly than can be accomplished with a bisphosphonate alone.[9]

Plicamycin, previously called mithramycin, is a cytotoxic antibiotic that blocks RNA synthesis in osteoclasts and therefore inhibits bone resorption. Plicamycin has considerable toxicity (bone marrow, renal, hepatic), which limits its usefulness in the treatment of hypercalcemia. Bisphosphonates have replaced plicamycin as a less toxic first-line therapy in the severely hypercalcemic patient. Gallium nitrate, originally studied as a therapeutic agent for cancer, is also approved by the Food and Drug Administration for the therapy of hypercalcemia. The rate of fall of the serum calcium was rather slow, especially compared with calcitonin and the bisphosphonates. Gallium nitrate also has nephrotoxic effects and is contraindicated in renal failure. For these reasons, it is not the ideal agent for therapy of hypercalcemia and is not in common use.

Glucocorticoid therapy has been used for many years to treat hypercalcemia, particularly when caused by hematologic malignancies such as lymphoma and multiple myeloma. Glucocorticoids are also effective in situations such as vitamin D toxicity or granulomatous diseases in which the hypercalcemia is mediated by the actions of 1,25-dihydroxyvitamin D. Glucocorticoids are seldom effective in patients with solid tumors or primary hyperparathyroidism. The usual dose is 200–300 mg of intravenous hydrocortisone, or its equivalent, daily for 3–5 days.

Intravenous phosphate was used in the past to lower serum calcium in hypercalcemic patients. However, intravenous phosphate is accompanied by a substantial risk of precipitation of calcium–phosphate complexes, leading to severe organ damage and even death. This form of therapy is not recommended.

Therapy for the underlying cause of the hypercalcemia should not be neglected, because specific therapy may be the most effective approach to the problem. However, patients with widespread metastatic disease, in whom no further specific antitumor chemotherapy is to be given, may be approached with the realization that reduction of the serum calcium per se will achieve little in the long run. In these circumstances, sometimes the best approach is to resist specific measures to reduce the serum calcium and to make the patient as comfortable as possible.

REFERENCES

1. Attie MF 1989 Treatment of hypercalcemia. Endocrinol Metab Clin North Am **18:**807–828.
2. Halloran BP, Nissenson BA (eds.) 1992 Parathyroid Hormone-Related Protein: Normal Physiology and Its Role in Cancer. CRC Press, Boca Raton, FL, USA.
3. Adams JS, Fernandez M, Gacad MA, Gill PS, Endres DB, Rasheed S, Singer FR 1989 Vitamin-D metabolite-mediated hypercalcemia and hypercalciuria in patients with AIDS and non-AIDS associated lymphoma. Blood **73:**235–239.
4. Mundy GR 1996 Role of cytokines, parathyroid hormone and growth factors in malignancy. In: Bilezikian JP, Raisz LG, Rodan GA (eds.) Principles of Bone Biology. Academic Press, New York, NY, USA, pp. 827–836.
5. Harinck HIJ, Bijvoet OLM, Plantingh AS, Body JJ, Elte JW, Sleeboom HP, Wildiers J, Neijt JP 1987 Role of bone and kidney in tumor-induced hypercalcemia and its treatment with bisphosphonate and sodium chloride. Am J Med **82:**1133–1142.
6. Kremer R, Sebag M, Chapigny C, Meerovitch K, Hendy GN, White J, Goltzman D 1996 Identification and characterization of 1,25-dihydroxyvitamin D3-responsive repressor sequences in the rat parathyroid hormone-related peptide gene. J Biol Chem **271:**16310–16316.
7. Bilezikian JP, Singer FR 1994 Acute management of hypercalcemia due to parathyroid hormone and parathyroid hormone-related protein. In: Bilezikian JP, Marcus R, Levine MA (eds.) The Parathyroids. Raven Press, New York, NY, USA, pp. 359–372.
8. Stewart AF 2005 Hypercalcemia associated with cancer. N Engl J Med **352:**373–379.
9. Bilezikian JP 1992 Management of acute hypercalcemia. N Engl J Med **326:**1196–1203.
10. Grill V, Murray RM, Ho PW, Santamaria JD, Pitt P, Potts C, Jerums G, Martin TJ 1990 Circulating PTH and PTHrP levels before and after treatment of tumor induced hypercalcemia with pamidronate disodium. J Clin Endocrinol Metab **74:**1468–1470.
11. Pecherstorfer M, Steinhauer EU, Rizzoli R, Wetterwald M, Berstrom B 2003 Efficacy and safety of ibandronate in the treatment of hypercalcemia of malignancy: A randomized multicentric comparison to pamidronate. Support Care Cancer **11:**539–547.
12. Shah S, Hardy J, Rees E, Ling J, Gwilliam B, Davis C, Broadley K, A'Hern R 2002 Is there a dose response relationship for clodronate in the treatment of tumour induced hypercalcaemia?. Br J Cancer **86:**1235–1237.
13. Major P, Lortholary A, Hon J, Abodi E, Mills G, Menssen HD, Yunus F, Bell R, Body J, Quebe-Fehling E, Seaman J 2001 Zoledronic acid is superior to pamidronate in the treatment of hypercalcemia of malignancy: A pooled analysis of two randomized, controlled clinical trials. J Clin Oncol **19:**558–567.
14. Nussbaum SR 1993 Pathophysiology and management of severe hypercalcemia. Endocrinol Metab Clin North Am **22:**343–362.
15. Gordon DH 2005 Efficacy and safety of intravenous bisphosphonates for patients with breast cancer metastatic to bone: A review of randomized, double-blind, phase III trials. Clin Breast Cancer **6:**125–131.
16. Green JR 2005 Skeletal complications of prostate cancer: Pathophysiology and therapeutic potential of bisphosphonates. Acta Oncol **44:**282–292.
17. Jacobs TP, Gordon AC, Silverberg SJ, Shane E, Reich L, Clemens TL, Gundberg CM 1987 Neoplastic hypercalcemia: Physiologic response to intravenous etidronate disodium. Am J Med **82**(Suppl 2a)**:**42–50.
18. Berenson JR 2005 Myeloma bone disease. Best Prac Res Clin Haematol **18:**653–672.
19. Gucalp R, Ritch P, Wiernik PH, Sarma PR, Keller A, Richman SP, Tauer K, Neidhart J, Mallette LE, Siegel R 1992 Comparative study of pamidronate disodium and etidronate disodium in the treatment of cancer-related hypercalcemia. J Clin Oncol **10:**134–142.

Chapter 27. Primary Hyperparathyroidism

John P. Bilezikian[1] and Shonni J. Silverberg[2]

[1]Department of Medicine and Pharmacology and [2]Department of Medicine, College of Physicians and Surgeons, Columbia University, New York, New York

INTRODUCTION

Primary hyperparathyroidism is one of the two most common causes of hypercalcemia and thus ranks high as a key diagnostic possibility in anyone with an elevated serum calcium concentration. These two causes of hypercalcemia, primary hyperparathyroidism and malignancy, together account for >90% of all hypercalcemic patients. Other potential causes of hypercalcemia are considered after the first two are ruled out or if there is reason to believe that a different cause is likely. The differential diagnosis of hypercalcemia as well as features of hypercalcemia of malignancy are considered elsewhere in this primer. In this chapter, the clinical presentation, evaluation, and therapy of primary hyperparathyroidism are covered.

Primary hyperparathyroidism is a relatively common endocrine disease with an incidence as high as 1 in 500 to 1 in 1000. Among the endocrine diseases, perhaps only diabetes mellitus and hyperthyroidism are seen more frequently. The high visibility of primary hyperparathyroidism in the population today marks a dramatic change from several generations ago, when it was considered to be a rare disorder. A 4- to 5-fold increase in incidence was noted in the early 1970s, because of the widespread use of the autoanalyzer, which provided serum calcium determinations in patients being evaluated for a set of completely unrelated complaints. More recent data suggesting a decline in the incidence of primary hyperparathyroidism may be a local phenomenon or it may reflect a diminution of the "catch-up effect," because most cases of previously unrecognized asymptomatic disease have now been diagnosed. Primary hyperparathyroidism occurs at all ages but is most frequent in the sixth decade of life. Women are affected more often than men by a ratio of 3:1. The majority of individuals are postmenopausal women. When found in children, an unusual event, it might be a component of one of several endocrinopathies with a genetic basis, such as multiple endocrine neoplasia type I or II.

Primary hyperparathyroidism is a hypercalcemic state resulting from excessive secretion of PTH from one or more parathyroid glands. The disease is caused by a benign, solitary adenoma 80% of the time. A parathyroid adenoma is a collection of chief cells surrounded by a rim of normal tissue at the outer perimeter of the gland. In the patient with a parathyroid adenoma, the remaining three parathyroid glands are usually normal. Less commonly, primary hyperparathyroidism is caused by a pathological process characterized by hyperplasia of all four parathyroid glands. Four-gland parathyroid hyperplasia is seen in ~15–20% of patients with primary hyperparathyroidism. It may occur sporadically or in association with multiple endocrine neoplasia type I or II. A very rare presentation of primary hyperparathyroidism is parathyroid carcinoma, occurring in <0.5% of patients with hyperparathyroidism. Pathological examination of the malignant tissue might show mitoses, vascular or capsular invasion, and fibrous trabeculae, but it is often not definitive. Unless gross local or distant metastases are present, the diagnosis of parathyroid cancer can be exceedingly difficult to make.

The pathophysiology of primary hyperparathyroidism relates to the loss of normal feedback control of PTH by extracellular calcium. Under virtually all other hypercalcemic conditions, the parathyroid gland is suppressed, and PTH levels are low. Why the parathyroid cell loses its normal sensitivity to calcium is unknown, but in adenomas, this seems to be the major mechanism. In primary hyperparathyroidism due to hyperplasia of the parathyroid glands, the "setpoint" for calcium is not changed for a given parathyroid cell: it is the increase in the number of cells that gives rise to the hypercalcemia.

The underlying cause of primary hyperparathyroidism is not known. External neck irradiation in childhood, recognized in some patients, is unlikely to be causative in the majority of patients. The molecular basis for primary hyperparathyroidism continues to be elusive. The clonal origin of most parathyroid adenomas suggests a defect at the level of the gene controlling growth of the parathyroid cell or the expression of PTH. Patients with primary hyperparathyroidism have been discovered in whom the *PTH* gene is rearranged to a site adjacent to the *PRAD*-1 oncogene. This kind of gene rearrangement could be responsible for the altered growth properties of the abnormal parathyroid cell. Overexpression of cyclin D1, an important cell cycle regulator, is felt to have a role in the pathogenesis of some sporadic parathyroid adenomas. Loss of one copy of the *MEN1* tumor suppressor gene located on chromosome 11 has also been seen in sporadic parathyroid adenomas. Abnormalities in the *p53* tumor suppressor gene have not been described in primary hyperparathyroidism. Among other genes studied for a possible role in the development of sporadic parathyroid adenomas are the *calcium-sensing receptor* gene, the *vitamin D receptor* gene, and *RET*. To date, such studies have not been revealing.

SIGNS AND SYMPTOMS

Classical primary hyperparathyroidism is associated with skeletal and renal complications. The skeletal disease, described historically as *osteitis fibrosa cystica*, is characterized by subperiosteal resorption of the distal phalanges, tapering of the distal clavicles, a "salt and pepper" appearance of the skull, bone cysts, and brown tumors of the long bones. Overt hyperparathyroid bone disease is now seen in <5% of patients in the United States with primary hyperparathyroidism.

Like the skeleton, the kidney is also less commonly involved in primary hyperparathyroidism than before. The incidence of kidney stones has declined from ~33% in the 1960s to 20% now. Nephrolithiasis, nevertheless, is still the most common complication of the hyperparathyroid process. Other renal features of primary hyperparathyroidism include diffuse deposition of calcium–phosphate complexes in the parenchyma (nephrocalcinosis). Hypercalciuria (daily calcium excretion of >250 mg for women or >300 mg for men) is seen in 35–40% of patients. In the absence of any other cause, primary hyperparathyroidism may be associated with a reduction in creatinine clearance.

The classic neuromuscular syndrome of primary hyperparathyroidism included a definable myopathy that has virtually disappeared. In its place, however, is a less well-defined syndrome characterized by easy fatigue, a sense of weakness, and a feeling that the aging process is advancing faster than it

Dr. Silverberg received a research grant from Amgen. Dr. Bilezikian received a research grant from Amgen and is a consultant for Amgen and Merck.

should. This is sometimes accompanied by an intellectual weariness and a sense that cognitive faculties are less sharp. In some studies, psychodynamic evaluation has appeared to reveal a distinct psychiatric profile. Whether these nonspecific features of primary hyperparathyroidism are truly part and parcel of the disease process, reversible on successful parathyroid surgery, are issues that are under active investigation.

Gastrointestinal manifestations of primary hyperparathyroidism have classically included peptic ulcer disease and pancreatitis. Peptic ulcer disease is not likely to be linked in a pathophysiologic way to primary hyperparathyroidism unless type I multiple endocrine neoplasia is present. Pancreatitis is virtually never seen anymore as a complication of primary hyperparathyroidism because the hypercalcemia tends to be so mild. Like peptic ulcer disease, the association between primary hyperparathyroidism and hypertension is tenuous. Although there may be an increased incidence of hypertension in primary hyperparathyroidism, it is rarely corrected or improved after successful surgery. In classical primary hyperparathyroidism, cardiovascular features included myocardial, valvular, and vascular calcification, with subsequent increased cardiovascular mortality. Although such overt involvement is not seen in mild primary hyperparathyroidism today, studies into the presence of subtle cardiovascular manifestations of the disease are ongoing. Other potential organ systems that in the past were affected by the hyperparathyroid state are now relegated to being archival curiosities. These include gout and pseudogout, anemia, band keratopathy, and loose teeth.

CLINICAL FORMS OF PRIMARY HYPERPARATHYROIDISM

In the United States today, classical primary hyperparathyroidism is rarely seen. Instead, the most common clinical presentation of primary hyperparathyroidism is characterized by asymptomatic hypercalcemia with serum calcium levels within 1 mg/dl above the upper limits of normal. Most patients do not have specific complaints and do not show evidence for any target organ complications. They usually have been discovered accidentally in the course of a routine multichannel screening test. Rarely, a patient will show serum calcium levels in the life-threatening range, so-called acute primary hyperparathyroidism or parathyroid crisis. These patients are invariably symptomatic of hypercalcemia. Although this is an unusual presentation of primary hyperparathyroidism, it does occur and should always be considered in any patient who presents with acute hypercalcemia of unclear etiology.

The very earliest manifestation of primary hyperparathyroidism may present with isolated elevations in PTH levels, while serum calcium is still normal. This abnormality is generally recognized in patients undergoing evaluation for low BMD or in other individuals who are receiving comprehensive screening tests for their skeletal health. In such patients, causes of secondary hyperparathyroidism must be ruled out. It is particularly important to be sure that these individuals do not have vitamin D insufficiency, as defined by a 25-hydroxyvitamin D level of <30 ng/ml. Re-evaluation of these individuals after vitamin D repletion and/or after correction of other secondary causes of hyperparathyroidism is needed. Unusual clinical presentations of primary hyperparathyroidism include the multiple endocrine neoplasias types I and II, familial primary hyperparathyroidism not associated with any other endocrine disorder, familial cystic parathyroid adenomatosis, and neonatal primary hyperparathyroidism.

EVALUATION AND DIAGNOSIS OF PRIMARY HYPERPARATHYROIDISM

The history and the physical examination rarely give any clear indications of primary hyperparathyroidism but are helpful because of the paucity of specific manifestations of the disease. The diagnosis of primary hyperparathyroidism is established by laboratory tests. The two biochemical hallmarks of primary hyperparathyroidism are hypercalcemia and elevated levels of PTH. The serum phosphorus tends to be in the lower range of normal. In only approximately one third of patients is the serum phosphorus concentration frankly low. The serum alkaline phosphatase activity may be elevated when bone disease is present. More specific markers of bone formation (bone-specific alkaline phosphatase and osteocalcin) and bone resorption (urinary deoxypyridinoline and N-telopeptide of collagen) will be above normal when there is active bone involvement but otherwise tend to be in the upper range of normal. The actions of PTH to alter acid–base handling in the kidney will lead, in some patients, to a small increase in the serum chloride concentration and a concomitant decrease in the serum bicarbonate concentration. Urinary calcium excretion is elevated in 35–40% of patients. The circulating 1,25-dihydroxyvitamin D concentration is elevated in ~25% of patients with primary hyperparathyroidism, although it is of little diagnostic value because 1,25-dihydroxyvitamin D levels are increased in other hypercalcemic states, such as sarcoidosis, other granulomatous diseases, and some lymphomas. 25-Hydroxyvitamin D levels tend to be in the lower end of the normal range. Considering newer definitions of vitamin D insufficiency, most patients with primary hyperparathyroidism have levels that are below the defined cut-point (i.e., <30 ng/ml).

X-rays are not cost effective in the evaluation of the patient with primary hyperparathyroidism because the vast majority of patients lack specific radiologic manifestations. On the other hand, bone mineral densitometry has proved to be an essential component of the evaluation because of its great sensitivity to detect early changes in bone mass. Patients with primary hyperparathyroidism tend to show a pattern of bone involvement that preferentially affects the cortical as opposed to the cancellous skeleton. The typical pattern is a reduction in BMD of the distal third of the forearm, a site enriched in cortical bone, and relative preservation of the lumbar spine, a site enriched in cancellous bone. The hip region, best typified by the femoral neck, tends to show values intermediate between the distal radius and the lumbar spine because its composition is a more equal mixture of cortical and cancellous elements. A small subset of patients (~15%) present with an atypical BMD profile, characterized by vertebral osteopenia or osteoporosis. Other patients with primary hyperparathyroidism can show uniform reductions in BMD at all sites. Bone densitometry has become an invaluable aspect of the evaluation of primary hyperparathyroidism because it gives a more accurate assessment of the degree of involvement of the skeleton than any other approach at this time. This information is used to make recommendations for parathyroid surgery or for conservative medical observation (see following sections).

Measurement of the circulating PTH concentration is the most definitive way to make the diagnosis of primary hyperparathyroidism. In the presence of hypercalcemia, an elevated level of PTH virtually establishes the diagnosis. A PTH level in the mid- or upper end of the normal range in the face of hypercalcemia is also consistent with the diagnosis of primary hyperparathyroidism. The standard assay for measurement of PTH is the immunoradiometric (IRMA) or immunochemiluminometric (ICMA) assay that measures the "intact" molecule. This assay detects large carboxyterminal fragments [PTH(7-

84) is one such fragment] of PTH in addition to full-length PTH(1-84) and can therefore overestimate the amount of bioactive hormone in the serum. A newer assay, specific for PTH(1-84) only, is elevated somewhat more frequently in patients with primary hyperparathyroidism. Although this assay may offer increased diagnostic sensitivity in cases where the intact IRMA is within the normal range (albeit inappropriately), the intact IRMA currently remains the standard assay in the diagnosis of the disease. The clinical use of PTH measurements in the differential diagnosis of hypercalcemia is a result both of refinements in assay techniques and of the fact that the most common other cause of hypercalcemia, namely hypercalcemia of malignancy, is associated with suppressed levels of hormone. There is no cross-reactivity between PTH and PTH-related peptide (PTHrP; the major causative factor in humoral hypercalcemia of malignancy) in the immunoradiometric assays for PTH. The only hypercalcemic disorders in which the PTH concentration might be elevated are those related to lithium or thiazide diuretic use. It is relatively easy to exclude either of these two possibilities by the history. If it is conceivable that the patient has drug-related hypercalcemia, the only secure way to make the diagnosis of primary hyperparathyroidism is to withdraw the medication and to confirm persistent hypercalcemia and elevated PTH levels 2–3 months later.

TREATMENT OF PRIMARY HYPERPARATHYROIDISM

Surgery

Primary hyperparathyroidism is cured when the abnormal parathyroid tissue is removed. While it is clear that surgery is appropriate in patients with classical symptoms of primary hyperparathyroidism, there is considerable controversy concerning the need for intervention in patients who have no clear signs or symptoms of their disease. In 2002, a Workshop was conducted at the National Institutes of Health to review the available data on this group of patients. The results of that meeting have led to a revision of the guidelines for management of asymptomatic primary hyperparathyroidism that were first recommended by the 1990 Consensus Development Conference on this subject. Patients are always advised to have surgery if they have symptomatic disease, such as overt bone disease or kidney stones, or if they have survived an episode of acute primary hyperparathyroidism with life-threatening hypercalcemia. Asymptomatic patients are now advised to have surgery if the serum calcium is >1 mg/dl above the upper limit of normal. Marked hypercalciuria (>400 mg daily excretion) or significantly reduced creatinine clearance (>30% more than age- and sex-matched controls) is another general indication for surgery. If bone mass, as determined by bone densitometry, is more than 2.5 SD below young normal control subjects (T score < −2.5) at any site, surgery should be recommended. Finally, the patient with primary hyperparathyroidism who is <50 years old is at greater risk for progression of the hyperparathyroid disease process than older patients and should be advised to undergo parathyroidectomy.

Adherence to these guidelines for surgery, however, is dependent on both the physician and the patient. Some physicians will recommend surgery for all patients with primary hyperparathyroidism; other physicians will not recommend surgery unless clear-cut complications of primary hyperparathyroidism are present. Similarly, some patients cannot tolerate the idea of living with a curable disease and will seek surgery in the absence of the aforementioned guidelines. Other patients, with coexisting medical problems, may not wish to face the risks of surgery, although surgical indications are present.

Parathyroid surgery requires exceptional expertise and experience. The glands are notoriously variable in location, requiring the surgeon's knowledge of typical ectopic sites such as intrathyroidal, retroesophageal, the lateral neck, and the mediastinum. The surgeon must also be aware of the proper operation to perform. In the case of the adenoma, the other glands are ascertained to be normal and are not removed. More and more, expert parathyroid surgeons are performing this operation under local, as opposed to general, anesthesia. Recent advances in surgery have led to another approach to the patient with single gland disease. Minimally invasive parathyroidectomy (MIP) is an approach that takes advantage of successful preoperative localization by the most widely used localization modalities: technetium-99m-sestamibi and ultrasound. The surgeon limits the operative field only to the small region overlying the visualized adenoma. Within a few minutes after resection, a PTH level is obtained. If the PTH level falls by >50%, the adenoma that has been removed is considered to be the only source of abnormal glandular activity, and the operation is terminated. If the PTH level does not fall by >50%, the possibility of other overreactive parathyroid glands is considered, and the operation is converted to a more standardized approach. In the case of multiglandular disease, the approach is to remove all tissue except for a remnant that is left in situ or autotransplanted in the nondominant forearm. Postoperatively, the patient may experience a brief period of transient hypocalcemia, during which time the normal but suppressed parathyroid glands regain their sensitivity to calcium. This happens within the first few days after surgery, and it is usually not necessary to treat the postoperative patient aggressively with calcium when postoperative hypocalcemia is mild. Prolonged postoperative symptomatic hypocalcemia as a result of rapid deposition of calcium and phosphate into bone ("hungry bone" syndrome) is rarely seen today. Such patients may require parenteral calcium for symptomatic hypocalcemia. Permanent hypoparathyroidism is a potential complication of surgery in those who have had previous neck surgery or who undergo subtotal parathyroidectomy (for multiglandular disease). Another rare complication of parathyroid surgery is damage to the recurrent laryngeal nerve, which can lead to hoarseness and reduced voice volume.

A number of localization tests are available to define the site of abnormal parathyroid tissue preoperatively. Among the noninvasive tests, ultrasonography, CT, MRI, and scintigraphy are available. Radioisotopic imaging is now performed most commonly with technetium-99m-sestamibi. Sestamibi is taken up both by thyroid and parathyroid tissue but persists in the parathyroid glands. Parathyroid localization using scintigraphy offers important localization data that are mandatory before any planned minimally invasive surgery or for repeat parathyroid exploration. Parathyroid scintigraphy using Tc-99 alone may yield important information about the location of single parathyroid adenomata. Planar imaging may miss small or ectopic lesions. More precise localization is achieved by using single photon emission computed tomography (SPECT) as an adjunct to Sestamibi scanning. Use of iodine-123 along with Tc-99 may be helpful in distinguishing between thyroid and parathyroid tissue. It is important to note that these techniques are not particularly helpful in patients with primary hyperparathyroidism caused by hyperplasia. Invasive localization tests with arteriography and selective venous sampling for PTH in the draining thyroid veins are available when noninvasive studies have not been successful and it is deemed important to locate the abnormal parathyroid gland preoperatively.

The value of preoperative localization tests in patients about to undergo parathyroid surgery is controversial. In patients who have not had previous neck surgery, there is little evidence that such tests prevent failed operations or shorten operating time. An experienced parathyroid surgeon will find the abnormal parathyroid gland(s) >95% of the time in the patient who has not had previous neck surgery. Thus, it is hard to justify these tests in this group. On the other hand, these preoperative localization tests have become very popular and are now used routinely in the United States. In patients who are to undergo the MIP procedure, preoperative localization is mandatory.

In patients who have had prior neck surgery, preoperative localization tests should be done. The general approach is to use the noninvasive studies first. Ultrasound and radioisotope imaging are best for parathyroid tissue that is located in proximity to the thyroid, whereas CT and MRI testing are better for ectopically located parathyroid tissue. Arteriography and selective venous studies are reserved for those individuals in whom the noninvasive studies have not been successful.

In patients who undergo successful parathyroid surgery, the hyperparathyroid state is completely cured. Serum biochemistries normalize, and the PTH level returns to normal. In addition, bone mass improves substantially in the first 1–3 years after surgery. The increase is documented by bone densitometry. The cumulative increase in bone mass at the lumbar spine and femoral neck is ~12%, a rather impressive improvement, and is sustained for at least a decade after parathyroidectomy. It is particularly noteworthy that the lumbar spine, a site where PTH seems to protect from age-related and estrogen-deficiency bone loss, is a site of rapid and substantial improvement. Those patients who present with evidence of vertebral osteopenia or osteoporosis sustain an even more impressive improvement in spine BMD after cure and should therefore be routinely referred for surgery regardless of the severity of their hypercalcemia.

Medical Management

Patients who are not surgical candidates for parathyroidectomy seem to do very well when they are managed conservatively. Data on patients with primary hyperparathyroidism followed for up to a decade show that the biochemical indices of disease and BMD measures of bone mass remain remarkably stable. These include the serum calcium, phosphorus, PTH, 25-hydroxyvitamin D, 1,25-dihydroxyvitamin D, and urinary calcium excretion. More specific markers of bone formation and bone resorption also do not seem to change. There are several caveats to this statement, however. First, ~25% of patients with asymptomatic primary hyperparathyroidism will have biochemical or bone densitometric evidence of disease progression over a 10-year period. Second, those under the age of 50 years have a far higher incidence of progressive disease than do older patients (~65% versus 23%). This supports the notion that younger patients should be referred for parathyroidectomy. Finally, today, as in the day of classical primary hyperparathyroidism, patients with symptomatic disease do poorly when observed without surgery. Thus, the data support the safety of observation without surgery only in selected patients with asymptomatic primary hyperparathyroidism.

The longitudinal data on patients who do not have parathyroid surgery also support the need for medical monitoring. In those patients who do not undergo surgery, a set of general medical guidelines is recommended. Routine medical follow-up usually includes visits twice yearly with serum calcium determinations. Yearly assessment of serum creatinine and bone densitometry at the spine, hip, and distal one-third site of the forearm is also recommended. Adequate hydration and ambulation are always encouraged. Thiazide diuretics and lithium are to be avoided if possible, because they may lead to worsening hypercalcemia. Dietary intake of calcium should be moderate. There is no good evidence that patients with primary hyperparathyroidism show significant fluctuations of their serum calcium as a function of dietary calcium intake. High calcium intakes should be avoided, however, especially in patients whose 1,25-dihydroxyvitamin D level is elevated. Low calcium diets should also be avoided because they could theoretically lead to further stimulation of PTH secretion.

We still lack an effective and safe therapeutic agent approved for the medical management of primary hyperparathyroidism. Oral phosphate will lower the serum calcium in patients with primary hyperparathyroidism by ~0.5–1 mg/dl. Phosphate seems to act by three mechanisms: interference with absorption of dietary calcium, inhibition of bone resorption, and inhibition of renal production of 1,25-dihydroxyvitamin D. Phosphate, however, is not recommended as an approach to management, because of concerns related to ectopic calcification in soft tissues as a result of increasing the calcium–phosphate product. Moreover, oral phosphate may lead to an undesirable further elevation of PTH levels. Gastrointestinal tolerance is another limiting feature of this approach.

In postmenopausal women, estrogen therapy remains an option in those women desiring hormone replacement for treatment of symptoms of menopause. The rationale for estrogen use in primary hyperparathyroidism is based on the known antagonism by estrogen of PTH-mediated bone resorption. Although the serum calcium concentration does tend to decline after estrogen administration (by ~0.5 mg/dl), PTH levels and the serum phosphorous concentration do not change. Estrogen replacement may have a salutary effect on BMD in these patients as well. Preliminary data suggest that the selective estrogen receptor modulator, raloxifene, may have a similar effect on serum calcium levels in postmenopausal women with primary hyperparathyroidism.

Bisphosphonates have also been considered as a possible medical approach to primary hyperparathyroidism. Two of the original bisphosphonates, etidronate and dichloromethylene bisphosphonate (clodronate; which is not available in the United States), have been studied. Although etidronate is not effective, dichloromethylene bisphosphonate temporarily reduces the serum calcium in primary hyperparathyroidism. The use of pamidronate, available exclusively as an intravenous preparation, is restricted to acute hypercalcemic states associated with primary hyperparathyroidism. Alendronate improves vertebral BMD in patients with primary hyperparathyroidism who choose not to have surgery but does not affect the underlying disorder.

Finally, a more targeted approach to the medical therapy of primary hyperparathyroidism is to interfere specifically with the production of PTH. Calcimimetic agents that alter the function of the extracellular calcium-sensing receptor offer an exciting new approach to primary hyperparathyroidism. These agents increase the affinity of the parathyroid cell calcium receptor for extracellular calcium, leading to increased intracellular calcium, a subsequent reduction in PTH secretion, and ultimately a reduction in hypercalcemia. Clinical trials have shown normalization of serum calcium for up to 3 years. In this study, no change in BMD by DXA was documented. The effect of this agent on fracture incidence in patients with primary hyperparathyroidism is unknown.

ACKNOWLEDGMENTS

This work was supported in part by National Institutes of Health Grants DK32333 and DK66329.

SUGGESTED READING

1. Arnold A, Shattuck TM, Mallya SM, Krebs LJ, Costa J, Gallagher J, Wild Y, Saucier K 2002 Molecular pathogenesis of primary hyperparathyroidism. J Bone Miner Res **17:**N30–N36.
2. Bilezikian JP, Potts JT, El-Hajj Fuleihan G, Kleerekoper M, Neer R, Peacock M, Rastad J, Silverberg SJ, Udelsman R, Wells SA 2002 Summary statement from a workshop on asymptomatic primary hyperparathyroidism: A perspective for the 21st century. J Bone Miner Res **17:**S2; N2–N11.
3. Cetani F, Pinchera A, Pardi E, Cianferotti L, Vignali E, Picone A, Miccoli P, Viacava P, Marcocci C 1999 No evidence for mutations in the calcium-sensing receptor gene in sporadic parathyroid adenomas. J Bone Miner Res **14:**878–882.
4. Deftos LJ 2001 Immunoassays for PTH and PTHrP. In: Bilezikian JP, Marcus R, Levine MA (eds.) The Parathyroids, 2nd ed. Raven Press, New York, NY, USA, pp. 143–166.
5. Doppman JL 2001 Preoperative localization of parathyroid tissue in primary hyperparathyroidism. In: Bilezikian JP, Marcus R, Levine MA (eds.) The Parathyroids, 2nd ed. Raven Press, New York, NY, USA, pp. 475–486.
6. Fitzpatrick LA 2001 Acute primary hyperparathyroidism. In: Bilezikian JP, Marcus R, Levine MA (eds.) The Parathyroids, 2nd ed. Raven Press, New York, NY, USA, pp. 527–360.
7. Heath H III, Hodgson SF, Kennedy MA 1980 Primary hyperparathyroidism: Incidence, morbidity, and potential economic impact in a community. N Engl J Med **302:**189.
8. Kahn AA, Bilezikian JP, Kung A, Ahmed MM, Dubois SJ, Ho AYY, Schussheim DH, Rubin MR, Shaikh AM, Silverberg SJ, Standish TI, Syed Z, Syed ZA 2004 Alendronate in primary hyperparathyroidism: A double-blind, randomized, placebo-controlled trial. J Clin Endocrinol Metab **89:** 3319–3325.
9. Parisien MV, Silverberg SJ, Shane E, de la Cruz L, Lindasy R, Bilezikian JP, Dempster DW 1990 The histomorphometry of bone in primary hyperparathyroidism: Preservation of cancellous bone structure. J Clin Endocrinol Metab **70:**930–938.
10. Peacock M, Bilezikian JP, Klassen P, Guo, MD Turner SA, Shoback DS 2005 Cinacalcet HCl maintinas long normocalcemia in patients with primary hyperparathyroidism with. J Clin Endocrinol Metab **90:**135–141.
11. Rubin MR, Lee K, Silverberg SJ 2003 Raloxifene lowers serum calcium and markers of bone turnover in primary hyperparathyroidism. J Clin Endocrinol Metab **88:**1174–1178.
12. Shane E 2001 Parathyroid carcinoma. In: Bilezikian JP, Marcus R, Levine MA (eds.) The Parathyroids, 2nd ed. Raven Press, New York, NY, USA, pp. 515–526.
13. Silverberg SJ, Shane E, de la Cruz L, Dempster DW, Feldman F, Seldin D, Jacobs TP, Siris ES, Cafferty M, Parisien MV, Lindsay R, Clemens TL, Bilezikian JP 1989 Skeletal disease in primary hyperparathyroidism. J Bone Miner Res **4:**283–291.
14. Silverberg SJ, Locker FG, Bilezikian JP 1996 Vertebral osteopenia: A new indication for surgery in primary hyperparathyroidism. J Clin Endocrinol Metab **81:**4007–4012.
15. Silverberg SJ, Shane E, Dempster DW, Bilezikian JP 1999 Vitamin D Deficiency in primary hyperparathyroidism. Am J Med **107:**561–567.
16. Silverberg SJ, Shane E, Jacobs TP, Siris E, Bilezikian JP 1999 The natural history of treated and untreated asymptomatic primary hyperparathyroidism: A ten year prospective study. N Engl J Med **41:**1249–1255.
17. Silverberg SJ, Brown I, Bilezikian JP 2002 Youthfulness as a criterion for surgery in primary hyperparathyroidism. Am J Med **113:**681–684.
18. Silverberg SJ 2002 Non-classical target organs in primary hyperparathyroidism. J Bone Miner Res **17:**S2;N117–N125.
19. Silverberg SJ, Bilezikian JP 2003 "Incipient" primary hyperparathyroidism: A "forme fruste" of an old disease. J Clin Endocrinol Metab **88:** 5348–5352.
20. Silverberg SJ, Brown I, LoGerfo P, Gao P, Cantor T, Bilezikian JP 2003 Clinical utility of an immunoradiometric assay for whole PTH (1–84) in primary hyperparathyroidism. J Clin Endocrinol Metab **88:**4725–4730.
21. Silverberg SJ, Bilezikian JP 2006 Hyperparathyroidism. In: DeGroot LJ, Jameson JL (eds.) Endocrinology, 5th ed. JB Elsevier Saunders, Philadelphia, PA, USA, pp. 1533–1565.
22. Turken SA, Cafferty M, Silverberg SJ, de la Cruz L, Cimino C, Lange DJ, Lovelace RE, Bilezikian JP 1989 Neuromuscular involvement in mild, asymptomatic primary hyperparathyroidism. Am J Med **87:**553–557.
23. Udelsman R 2002 Surgery in primary hyperparathyroidism: The patient without previous neck surgery. J Bone Miner Res **17:**S2;N126–N132.
24. Wells SA, Doherty GM 2001 The surgical management of primary hyperparathyroidism. In: Bilezikian JP, Marcus R, Levine MA (eds.) The Parathyroids, 2nd ed. Raven Press, New York, NY, USA, pp. 487–498.
25. Wermers RA, Khosla S, Atkinson EJ, Grant CS, Hodgson SF, O'Fallon WM, Melton LJ III 1998 Survival after diagnosis of PHPT: A population based study. Am J Med **104:**115–122.

Chapter 28.   Familial Hyperparathyroid Syndromes

Andrew Arnold

Center for Molecular Medicine and Division of Endocrinology & Metabolism, University of Connecticut School of Medicine, Farmington, Connecticut

INTRODUCTION

Individuals with recognizable familial predispositions to the development of parathyroid tumors constitute a small and important minority of all patients with primary hyperparathyroidism (HPT). These familial syndromes have been recognized as exhibiting Mendelian inheritance patterns and have been genetically elucidated to a large extent. They include multiple endocrine neoplasia types 1 and 2A, hyperparathyroidism-jaw tumor syndrome, and familial isolated hyperparathyroidism. Familial (benign) hypocalciuric hypercalcemia (FHH, FBH, FBHH) and neonatal severe hyperparathyroidism (NSHPT) also fall into this category but are the subjects of a separate chapter. Extraparathyroid manifestations of some familial HPT syndromes will be mentioned but lie outside the focus of this chapter. It is worth noting that as more knowledge accumulates on genetic contributions to complex phenotypes, additional genetic loci may be identified as contributing to a less penetrant and more subtle predisposition to primary HPT in the general population.

MULTIPLE ENDOCRINE NEOPLASIA TYPE 1

Multiple endocrine neoplasia type 1 (MEN1) is a rare heritable disorder with an estimated prevalence of 2–3/100,000. It is classically defined as a predisposition to tumors of the parathyroids, anterior pituitary, and pancreatic islet cells, although affected patients are now known to be predisposed to many additional endocrine and nonendocrine tumors.[1,2] Primary HPT is the most penetrant component of MEN1, occurring in almost all affected individuals by age 50, and is the initial clinical manifestation of the disorder in most patients. Approximately 2% of all cases of primary HPT may be caused

---

The author has reported no conflicts of interest.

by MEN1. Some of the other types of tumors associated with MEN1 include duodenal gastrinomas, bronchial or thymic carcinoids, gastric enterochromaffin-like tumors, adrenocortical adenomas, lipomas, facial angiofibromas, and truncal collagenomas.[1]

The inheritance of MEN1 follows an autosomal dominant pattern, and the molecular genetic basis is an inactivating germline mutation of the *MEN1* tumor suppressor gene, located on chromosome band 11q13.[3] *MEN1* encodes a protein called menin, whose specific cellular functions have not been fully established but may involve transcriptional regulation of gene expression. Typically, patients with MEN1 have inherited one inactivated copy of the *MEN1* gene from an affected parent or may have a spontaneous new germline mutation. The outgrowth of a tumor requires the subsequent somatic (acquired) inactivation of the normal, remaining copy of the gene in one cell. Such a parathyroid cell, for example, would then be devoid of *MEN1*'s tumor suppressor function, contributing to a selective advantage over its neighbors and clonal proliferation.

Primary HPT in MEN1 has a number of different features from the common sporadic (nonfamilial) form of the disease. The male to female ratio is even in MEN1, in contrast to the female predominance of sporadic HPT. HPT in MEN1 typically presents in the second to fourth decade of life, and has been found as early as age 8. Multiple gland involvement is typical in MEN1, and in most patients, three to four tumors are evident on initial neck exploration. However, these multiple tumors may vary widely in size, with an average 10:1 ratio between the largest and smallest glands.[4] An inexorable drive to parathyroid tumorigenesis exists in MEN1, reflected by an impressively high rate of recurrent HPT after apparently successful subtotal parathyroidectomy (>50% after 12 years).[4] This high recurrence rate contrasts with the behavior of HPT in MEN2A or in sporadic primary parathyroid hyperplasia. As mentioned below, familial isolated hyperparathyroidism can manifest as an occult or variant presentation of *MEN1* mutation.

The biochemical diagnosis of primary HPT in known or suspected MEN1 is based on the finding of hypercalcemia with elevated (or inappropriately nonsuppressed) serum PTH levels. Once the biochemical diagnosis is established, the indications for surgical intervention are similar to those in patients with sporadic primary HPT and include symptomatic hypercalcemia, nephrolithiasis, fractures, and/or decreased bone mass, which has been observed in women with MEN1 at the age of 35.[2] Because hypercalcemia can worsen hypergastrinemia, another indication for parathyroidectomy in MEN1 is the presence of medically refractory symptoms of gastrinoma, an unusual situation given the success of pharmacotherapy for Zollinger-Ellison syndrome.

Because direct evidence is lacking, opinions differ as to the optimal timing of surgical treatment of HPT in MEN1. Early presymptomatic intervention might, on one hand, lead to better long-term bone health. On the other hand, because of the high rate of recurrent HPT, a policy of deferring surgery might decrease a patient's total number of operations and thereby decrease the risk of complications.

Preoperative localization studies are not generally indicated in unoperated patients because of the multiplicity of parathyroid tumors in MEN1, the need to identify all parathyroid glands at surgery, and the inability of imaging tools to reliably detect all hypercellular glands. For the same reasons, a suspected or firm preoperative diagnosis of MEN1 argues against performing minimally invasive parathyroidectomy. In the context of bilateral operations, however, intraoperative PTH measurement may be helpful.[4] In contrast, preoperative imaging/localization is useful before reoperation in patients with

recurrent or persistent disease. The initial operation most frequently performed in MEN1 patients is 3.5 gland subtotal parathyroidectomy with transcervical near-total thymectomy. A parathyroid remnant of ~50 mg is usually left in situ and may be marked with a metal clip, but alternatively the remnant can be autotransplanted[2] to the forearm after intentionally complete parathyroidectomy. The efficacy of thymectomy is unproven but seems reasonable because it may cure incipient thymic carcinoids or prevent their development; in addition, the thymus is a common site for parathyroid tumors in MEN1 patients with recurrent HPT. Involvement of a highly experienced parathyroid surgical team is crucial to optimal outcome.

Management of the pituitary, enteropancreatic, and other neoplastic manifestations of MEN1 are discussed in detail elsewhere.[2] It should be emphasized that MEN1-associated malignancies cause fully one third of the deaths in MEN1 patients, and for most of these cancers, no effective prevention or cure currently exists.

Direct genetic testing for germline *MEN1* mutations is commercially available, but the indications for such testing remain under discussion.[2,3] Genetic analyses, typically limited to the coding region, fail to detect *MEN1* mutation in ~30% of typical MEN1 kindreds.[3] In contrast to the clear clinical efficacy of testing for *RET* gene mutations in MEN2, presymptomatic genetic diagnosis has not been established to improve morbidity or mortality in MEN1, and biochemical screening with serum calcium and PTH provides a nongenetic alternative. Thus, DNA testing is not currently determinative of important clinical interventions in MEN1, and the rationale for its use is not as well established as in MEN2.[1-3] Similarly, periodic biochemical or anatomic screening for endocrine tumor manifestations in MEN1 patients, or in family members at risk, has not been proven to enhance clinical outcomes, and whether such testing is of incremental benefit compared with careful histories and physical examinations remains to be determined. Suggested protocols for use of pre-symptomatic testing are available.[2]

MULTIPLE ENDOCRINE NEOPLASIA TYPE 2A

MEN2 is subclassified into three major clinical syndromes: MEN2A, MEN2B, and familial medullary thyroid cancer (FMTC). Of these, MEN2A is the most common and the only one that manifests HPT.[1,2] MEN2A is a heritable predisposition to medullary thyroid cancer (MTC), pheochromocytoma, and primary HPT. The respective frequency of these tumors in MEN2A is >90% for MTC, 40–50% for pheochromocytoma, and 20% for HPT.[2] This low penetrance of HPT in MEN2A contrasts with the high penetrance found in all other familial hyperparathyroid syndromes.

MEN2A is inherited in an autosomal dominant pattern, with men and women affected in equal proportions. and the responsible genetic defect is germline mutation of the *RET* protooncogene on chromosome 10.[1,5] The RET protein is a receptor tyrosine kinase that normally transduces growth and differentiation signals in developing tissues including those derived from the neural crest. There are both differences and much overlap in the specific *RET* gene mutations underlying MEN2A and FMTC; in contrast, MEN2B is caused by entirely distinct *RET* mutations.[2,5] Why parathyroid disease fails to develop in FMTC patients who can bear identical *RET* mutations as found in MEN2A remains unclear. Unlike the numerous different inactivating mutations of *MEN1*, which are typical of a tumor suppressor mechanism, *RET* mutations in MEN2A are limited in number, reflecting the need for highly specific gain-of-function changes to activate this oncogene.[1,5] Germline *RET* mutation is detectable in >95% of MEN2A families. *RET* mutation at codon 634 seems to be highly associated with the expression of HPT in MEN2A.

HPT in MEN2A is often asymptomatic, and its biochemical diagnosis, as well as indications for surgical treatment, parallel those in sporadic primary HPT.[2] Evidence of pheochromocytoma should be sought before parathyroidectomy and, if present, the pheochromocytoma(s) should be removed before parathyroid surgery. Primary HPT in MEN2A is almost always multiglandular, but less than four overtly hypercellular glands may be present. Thus, bilateral neck exploration to identify all glands is advisable in known or suspected MEN2A, with resection of hypercellular parathyroid tissue (up to 3.5 glands) being the most common surgical approach. Issues of preoperative localization in unoperated patients are similar to MEN1. In contrast to MEN1, however, recurrent HPT is infrequent after apparently successful resection of enlarged glands, similar to the excellent long-term outcome of surgically treated patients with nonfamilial primary hyperplasia. The low penetrance of HPT in MEN2A and the success of its treatment argue against prophylactic total parathyroidectomy with forearm autotransplantation at the time of thyroidectomy for MTC, an approach carrying substantial risk of hypoparathyroidism.

The other major manifestations of MEN2A are MTC and pheochromocytoma. MTC, the major life-threatening manifestation of MEN2A, evolves from preexisting parafollicular C-cell hyperplasia, and its calcitonin production provides a useful marker for monitoring tumor burden. Despite the pharmacologic properties of calcitonin, mineral metabolism is generally normal in the setting of metastatic MTC and its often dramatic hypercalcitoninemia. DNA testing for germline *RET* mutations is central to clinical management and worthy of emphasis for its role in prevention of MTC. *RET* testing is superior to immunoassay for basal or stimulated calcitonin for diagnosis of MEN2A. Molecular diagnosis allows for prophylactic or curative thyroidectomy to be performed (i.e., sufficiently early in childhood as to minimize the likelihood that metastases will have occurred).[1,2,5]

Pheochromocytomas in MEN2A can be unilateral or bilateral. Extraadrenal or malignant pheochromocytomas are underrepresented in MEN2A patients compared with patients with sporadic pheochromocytoma. Because undiagnosed pheochromocytoma could cause substantial morbidity or even death during thyroid or parathyroid surgery in MEN2A patients, it is important to first screen for pheochromocytoma. Different approaches to screening exist; a consensus report suggested measurement of plasma metanephrines and 24-h urinary excretion of catecholamines and metanephrines on an annual basis and supplemented by periodic imaging studies.[1,2] Laparoscopic adrenalectomy has greatly improved the management of pheochromocytoma in MEN2A, and adrenal cortical-sparing surgery may be helpful in obviating the problem of adrenal insufficiency after treatment of bilateral pheochromocytoma.[5]

HYPERPARATHYROIDISM-JAW TUMOR SYNDROME

The hyperparathyroidism-jaw tumor syndrome (HPT-JT) is a rare, autosomal dominant predisposition to primary HPT, ossifying fibromas of the mandible and maxilla, renal manifestations including cysts, hamartomas, or Wilms tumors,[6,7] and uterine tumors.[8] In clinically ascertained "classical" HPT-JT kindreds, HPT is the most penetrant manifestation at 80% of adults, followed by 30% for ossifying fibromas, and lower for renal lesions. As mentioned below, familial isolated hyperparathyroidism and apparently sporadic parathyroid carcinoma can represent occult or allelic variant presentations of the molecular defect in HPT-JT.

Hyperparathyroidism in HPT-JT may develop as early as the first decade or two of life. Although all parathyroids are at risk, surgical exploration can reveal a solitary parathyroid tumor rather than multigland disease, in contrast to typical findings in MEN1 and MEN2A. Parathyroid neoplasms can be cystic, and whereas most tumors are classified as adenomas, the incidence of parathyroid carcinoma (15–20% of HPT) is markedly overrepresented in HPT-JT kindreds.[7] After a period of normocalcemia, treated patients may manifest recurrent HPT, and a solitary tumor asynchronously originating in a different parathyroid gland may prove responsible. The approach to monitoring and surgery in HPT-JT must take into account the predilection to parathyroid malignancy, and the finding of biochemical HPT should lead promptly to surgery. All parathyroids should be identified at operation, signs of malignancy sought, and appropriate resection of abnormal glands performed.[4] Because of malignant potential, consideration of prophylactic total parathyroidectomy has been raised as an alternative approach but is not favored by others in view of difficulties with lifelong management of surgical hypoparathyroidism, the incomplete penetrance of parathyroid cancer in the syndrome, and the plausible (albeit unproven) idea that close biochemical monitoring for recurrent HPT combined with early surgery will prevent metastatic disease.

Ossifying fibromas in HPT-JT may be large and destructive, but are often small, asymptomatic, and identified as incidental findings on dental radiographs. They are clearly distinct from the classic, osteoclast-rich "brown tumors" of severe hyperparathyroidism.

Germline mutation of the *HRPT2* gene, located on chromosome arm 1q, is responsible for HPT-JT.[9] The yield of *HRPT2* mutation detection in HPT-JT kindreds is ~60–70%[8,9]; the remaining kindreds most likely also have *HRPT2* mutations but evade detection because of their location outside the sequenced coding region. Mutations of *HRPT2* are predicted to inactivate or eliminate its protein product parafibromin, consistent with a classical "two-hit" tumor suppressor mechanism also shown in sporadic parathyroid carcinoma.[9,10] Parafibromin's normal cellular function may involve regulation of gene expression and chromatin modification.

Importantly, some patients with sporadic presentations of parathyroid carcinoma also harbor germline mutations in *HRPT2*, thus representing newly ascertained HPT-JT or a variant syndrome.[10] Recognition of *HRPT2*'s involvement in classic or variant HPT-JT has opened the door to DNA-based carrier identification in at-risk family members, aimed at preventing parathyroid malignancy.

FHH AND NSHPT

FHH and NSHPT are mentioned as a reminder of their inclusion in the category of familial hyperparathyroid syndromes, but are the subject of another chapter. Germline mutations in the *CASR* gene that cause partial or severe loss of function of its product, the extracellular G-protein–coupled calcium receptor, are a major cause of these syndromes. Genetic linkage analyses indicate that the FHH phenotype can also be caused by mutation of different genes, which have not yet been identified. As mentioned below, familial isolated hyperparathyroidism can manifest as an occult or variant presentation of *CASR* mutation.

FAMILIAL ISOLATED HYPERPARATHYROIDISM

Familial isolated primary hyperparathyroidism (FIHP) is a clinically defined entity, based on the absence of expression of the extraparathyroid manifestations that characterize other familial HPT syndromes. As such, a designation of FIHP can change with new findings in the family. Furthermore, FIHP is genetically heterogeneous and can be caused by variant expressions of germline mutations in *MEN1*, *HRPT2*, *CASR*, and probably other genes.[4,11,12] Clinical monitoring and management must take into consideration the possibility that additional features of a genetically defined HPT syndrome could emerge or become detectable. For example, the heightened risk of parathyroid carcinoma must be borne in mind in FIHP when the genetic basis is not established and occult *HRPT2* mutation is possible. DNA testing should be considered (e.g., when results might impact on the advisability of, or approach to, parathyroid surgery).

REFERENCES

1. Gagel RF, Marx SJ 2003 Multiple endocrine neoplasia. In: Larsen PR, Kronenberg HM, Melmed S, Polonsky K (eds.) Williams Textbook of Endocrinology, 10th ed. WB Saunders, Philadelphia, PA, USA, pp. 1717–1762.
2. Brandi ML, Gagel RF, Angeli A, Bilezikian JP, Beck-Peccoz P, Bordi C, Conte-Devolx B, Falchetti A, Gheri RG, Libroia A, Lips CJ, Lombardi G, Mannelli M, Pacini F, Ponder BA, Raue F, Skogseid B, Tamburrano G, Thakker RV, Thompson NW, Tomassetti P, Tonelli F, Wells SA Jr, Marx SJ 2001 Guidelines for diagnosis and therapy of MEN type 1 and type 2. J Clin Endocrinol Metab 86:5658–5671.
3. Marx SJ 2005 Molecular genetics of multiple endocrine neoplasia types 1 and 2. Nat Rev Cancer 5:367–375.
4. Marx SJ, Simonds WF, Agarwal SK, Burns AL, Weinstein LS, Cochran C, Skarulis MC, Spiegel AM, Libutti SK, Alexander HR Jr., Chen CC, Chang R, Chandrasekharappa SC, Collins FS 2002 Hyperparathyroidism in hereditary syndromes: Special expressions and special managements. J Bone Miner Res 17:S1:N37–N43.
5. Kouvaraki MA, Shapiro SE, Perrier ND, Cote GJ, Gagel RF, Hoff AO, Sherman SI, Lee JE, Evans DB 2005 RET proto-oncogene: A review and update of genotype-phenotype correlations in hereditary medullary thyroid cancer and associated endocrine tumors. Thyroid 15:531–544.
6. Jackson CE, Norum RA, Boyd SB, Talpos GB, Wilson SD, Taggart RT, Mallette LE 1990 Hereditary hyperparathyroidism and multiple ossifying jaw fibromas: A clinically and genetically distinct syndrome. Surgery 108:1006–1013.
7. Szabo J, Heath B, Hill VM, Jackson CE, Zarbo RJ, Mallette LE, Chew SL, Besser GM, Thakker RV, Huff V, Leppert MF, Heath H 1995 Hereditary hyperparathyroidism-jaw tumor syndrome: The endocrine tumor gene HRPT2 maps to chromosome 1q21–q31. Am J Hum Genet 56:944–950.
8. Bradley KJ, Hobbs MR, Buley ID, Carpten JD, Cavaco BM, Fares JE, Laidler P, Manek S, Robbins CM, Salti IS, Thompson NW, Jackson CE, Thakker RV 2005 Uterine tumours are a phenotypic manifestation of the hyperparathyroidism-jaw tumour syndrome. J Intern Med 257:18–26.
9. Carpten JD, Robbins CM, Villablanca A, Forsberg L, Presciuttini S, Bailey-Wilson J, Simonds WF, Gillanders EM, Kennedy AM, Chen JD, Agarwal SK, Sood R, Jones MP, Moses TY, Haven C, Petillo D, Leotlela PD, Harding B, Cameron D, Pannett AA, Hoog A, Heath H 3rd, James-Newton LA, Robinson B, Zarbo RJ, Cavaco BM, Wassif W, Perrier ND, Rosen IB, Kristofferson U, Turnpenny PD, Farnebo LO, Besser GM, Jackson CE, Morreau H, Trent JM, Thakker RV, Marx SJ, Teh BT, Larsson C, Hobbs MR 2002 HRPT2, encoding parafibromin, is mutated in hyperparathyroidism-jaw tumor syndrome. Nat Genet 32:676–680.
10. Shattuck TM, Valimaki S, Obara T, Gaz RD, Clark OH, Shoback D, Wierman ME, Tojo K, Robbins CM, Carpten JD, Farnebo LO, Larsson C, Arnold A 2003 Somatic and germ-line mutations of the HRPT2 gene in sporadic parathyroid carcinoma. N Engl J Med 349:1722–1729.
11. Simonds WF, James-Newton LA, Agarwal SK, Yang B, Skarulis MC, Hendy GN, Marx SJ 2002 Familial isolated hyperparathyroidism: Clinical and genetic characteristics of 36 kindreds. Medicine (Baltimore) 81:1–26.
12. Simonds WF, Robbins CM, Agarwal SK, Hendy GN, Carpten JD, Marx SJ 2004 Familial isolated hyperparathyroidism is rarely caused by germline mutation in HRPT2, the gene for the hyperparathyroidism-jaw tumor syndrome. J Clin Endocrinol Metab 89:96–102.

Chapter 29.   Familial Hypocalciuric Hypercalcemia

Stephen J. Marx

Genetics and Endocrinology Section, Metabolic Diseases Branch, National Institute of Diabetes and Digestive and Kidney Diseases, National Institutes of Health, Bethesda, Maryland

INTRODUCTION

Familial hypocalciuric hypercalcemia (FHH; also termed familial benign hypercalcemia or familial benign hypocalciuric hypercalcemia) is an autosomal dominant trait with lifelong high penetrance for both hypercalcemia and relative hypocalciuria.[1,2] The prevalence of FHH is similar to that for multiple endocrine neoplasia type 1; either accounts for ~2% of cases with asymptomatic hypercalcemia.

CLINICAL FEATURES

Symptoms and Signs

Patients with FHH are usually asymptomatic. Occasionally they note easy fatigue, weakness, thought disturbance, or polydipsia. These symptoms are less common and less severe than in typical primary hyperparathyroidism. There is a low but increased incidence of relapsing pancreatitis. The rate of peptic ulcer disease, nephrolithiasis, or even idiopathic hypercalciuria is the same as in a normal population.

Radiographs and Indices of Bone Function

Radiographs are usually normal. Nephrocalcinosis has the same incidence as in a normal population. There is an increased incidence of chondrocalcinosis (usually clinically silent) and premature vascular calcification. Bone turnover is mildly increased. Bone mass and susceptibility to fracture are normal.

Serum Electrolytes

Hypercalcemia has virtually 100% penetrance at all ages; its level is similar to that in typical primary hyperparathyroidism. Both free and bound calcium are increased, with a normal ratio of free to bound calcium. The degree of hypercalcemia clusters within kindreds, with several kindreds showing very modest hypercalcemia and several showing rather severe hypercalcemia (12.5–14 mg/dl).[1] Serum magnesium is typically in the high range of normal or modestly elevated, and serum phosphate is modestly depressed.

Urinary Calcium Excretion Indices

Creatinine clearance is generally normal. Urinary excretion of calcium is normal, with affected and unaffected family

---

The author has reported no conflicts of interest.

members showing a similar distribution of values. The normal urinary calcium in the face of hypercalcemia reflects increased renal tubular reabsorption of calcium (i.e., relative hypocalciuria). Because total urinary calcium excretion depends heavily on glomerular filtration rate, total calcium excretion is not a practical index to distinguish a case of FHH from typical primary hyperparathyroidism. The ratio of calcium clearance to creatinine clearance is calculated easily:

$$Ca_{Cl}/Cr_{Cl} = (Ca_u \times V/Ca_s)/$$
$$(Cr_u \times V/Cr_s) = (Ca_u \times Cr_s)/(Cr_u \times Ca_s)$$

It is an empirically chosen index that corrects for most of the variation from glomerular filtration rate. This clearance ratio in FHH is one third of that in typical primary hyperparathyroidism, and a cut-off value at 0.01 (note that all units cancel out) is imperfect but helpful for diagnosis, although only in a hypercalcemic patient.

Parathyroid Function and Surgery

Parathyroid function, including serum PTH and 1,25-dihydroxyvitamin D [1,25(OH)$_2$D], is usually normal, with modest elevations in 5–10% of cases.[3] Even the "normal" parathyroid function indices in the presence of lifelong hypercalcemia are inappropriate and reflect a specific role for the parathyroids in causing hypercalcemia. FHH cases often have mild enlargement of the parathyroid glands, evident only by careful measurement of gland size.[4,5] Most FHH cases are caused by heterozygous loss-of-function mutations in CASR, the gene that encodes the calcium sensing-receptor (Ca-S-R).[6,7] This explains the resistance of the parathyroid cell to suppression by hypercalcemia.

Standard subtotal parathyroidectomy in FHH results in only a very transient lowering of serum calcium, with restoration of hypercalcemia within a week. Total parathyroidectomy in FHH leads to low PTH, low 1,25(OH)$_2$D, and low calcium in blood, i.e., chronic hypoparathyroidism. However, attempted total parathyroidectomy can fail because a small remnant of parathyroid tissue is sufficient to sustain hypercalcemia in FHH.

BROAD SPECTRUM OF DISORDERS RELATED TO FHH

Making the Diagnosis of FHH

In the presence of hypercalcemia, a normal PTH, just like a low urine calcium, should raise the suspicion of FHH. Family screening for FHH can be valuable: first, to establish familial involvement (in the index case and in the family); second, to characterize a syndrome; and third, as a start toward avoiding failed parathyroidectomy. Because of high penetrance for hypercalcemia in FHH carriers, an accurate genetic assignment within a family can usually be made from one determination of total serum calcium (or preferably ionized or albumin-adjusted calcium). However, obtaining all the desired family data can take many months.

CASR mutation analysis (see below) also has an occasional role in diagnosis, particularly with an inconclusive clinical evaluation of the family or with an atypical presentation.[8] Failure to find mutation does not exclude this, because there may be a mutation outside the tested open reading frame (explaining 30% of false "normal" testing) or rarely in another FHH gene. Two unusual FHH kindreds not linked to the CASR locus at chromosome 3q, but linked to 19p or 19q, represent mutation in other unidentified genes.[9,10]

Disorders Resembling FHH

Typical Primary Hyperparathyroidism. The resemblance of typical primary hyperparathyroidism to FHH is evident and important; their distinction is the main topic of this chapter.

Autoimmune FHH. FHH has rarely been caused by autoantibodies against the Ca-S-R and associated with other autoimmune features (thyroiditis or sprue); there is no CASR mutation.[11]

CASR Loss-of-Function Mutation Without FHH. One large kindred with a germline missense mutation in the CASR had a hyperparathyroid syndrome unlike FHH. There was hypercalciuria, monoclonal parathyroid adenomas, and benefit from subtotal parathyroidectomy.[12] Several other small families with CASR loss-of-function mutations have contained some members with features partly resembling typical primary hyperparathyroidism.[8] Most are likely FHH kindreds with one affected member as outlier.

Neonatal Severe Primary Hyperparathyroidism

Neonatal severe primary hyperparathyroidism is an unusual state of life-threatening, severe hypercalcemia with massive hyperplasia of all parathyroid glands. Most cases reflect a double dose of FHH genes.[2,13] Urgent total parathyroidectomy can be life saving.

PATHOPHYSIOLOGY

FHH as an Atypical Form of Primary Hyperparathyroidism

The parathyroid gland functions abnormally in FHH. Even the surgically decreased gland mass can maintain the same high calcium level, necessarily by greatly increasing hormone secretion rate per unit mass of tissue. There is a selective and mild increase in glandular "set-point" for calcium suppression of PTH secretion. This is even more striking for the causally related neonatal severe primary hyperparathyroidism. FHH can therefore be labeled as a form of primary hyperparathyroidism, albeit atypical. However, some authorities prefer not to classify FHH as a form of primary hyperparathyroidism to emphasize its contrasting management needs.[14]

Independent Defect in the Kidneys

There also is a disturbance intrinsic to the kidneys. The tubular reabsorption of calcium, normally increased by PTH, is high and remains strikingly increased even after total parathyroidectomy in FHH.[15]

MANAGEMENT

Indications for Parathyroidectomy Are Rare

FHH is compatible with survival into the ninth decade. Because of the generally benign course and lack of response to subtotal parathyroidectomy, virtually all patients with FHH should be advised against parathyroidectomy. In rare situations, such as (1) life-threatening neonatal severe primary hyperparathyroidism, (2) an adult with relapsing pancreatitis, or (3) a child or an adult with serum calcium persistently above 14 mg/dl, parathyroidectomy may be necessary. Total parathyroidectomy should be attempted in these situations.

Pharmacologic Intervention in the Typical Case

Chronic hypercalcemia in FHH has been resistant to medications (diuretics, bisphosphonates, phosphates, and estrogens). Calcimimetic drugs, acting on the Ca-S-R, might change these considerations[16]; they have not yet been approved by the U.S. Food and Drug Administration for this indication or even reported in FHH.

Sporadic Hypocalciuric Hypercalcemia

Without a positive family history, the decision about management of sporadic hypocalciuric hypercalcemia is difficult. Because there is a wide range of urine calcium values in patients with FHH and with typical primary hyperparathyroidism, an occasional patient with parathyroid adenoma will show a very low calcium-to-creatinine clearance ratio. Moreover, occasionally a patient with FHH will show a high ratio. Sporadic hypocalciuric hypercalcemia should generally be managed as typical FHH. In time, the underlying diagnosis may become evident; low morbidity in such patients, even those with undiagnosed parathyroid adenoma, should be anticipated for the same reasons that the morbidity is low in FHH. Here, detection of a *CASR* mutation can be particularly helpful.

Near the Time of Pregnancy

Several pairings may cause antagonism of blood calcium regulation between fetus and mother. The affected offspring of a mother with FHH should show asymptomatic hypercalcemia. The unaffected offspring of a mother with FHH may show symptomatic hypocalcemia. The affected offspring of an unaffected mother may show transiently worsened neonatal hyperparathyroidism because of superimposed intrauterine secondary hyperparathyroidism.[13,17]

CONCLUSION

FHH is an important cause of asymptomatic hypercalcemia, with high representation in hypercalcemia at ages <20 years. The index case and sometimes relatives need appropriate assessments of serum calcium and PTH and a urinary calcium index. Subtotal parathyroidectomy virtually always results in persistent hypercalcemia. Although mild symptoms similar to those in typical primary hyperparathyroidism are common, almost no patients should have interventions.

REFERENCES

1. Marx SJ, Attie MF, Levine MA, Spiegel AM, Downs RW Jr, Lasker RD 1981 The hypocalciuric or benign variant of familial hypercalcemia: Clinical and biochemical features in fifteen kindreds. Medicine 60:397–412.
2. El-Hajj Fuleihan G, Brown EM, Heath H III 2002 Familial benign hypocalciuric hypercalcemia and neonatal primary hyperparathyroidism. In: Bilezikian JP, Raisz LG, Rodan GA (eds.) Principles of Bone Biology, 2nd ed. Academic Press, San Diego, CA, USA, pp. 1031–1045.
3. Firek AF, Kao PC, Heath H III 1991 Plasma intact parathyroid hormone (PTH) and PTH-related peptide in familial benign hypercalcemia: Greater responsiveness to endogenous PTH than in primary hyperparathyroidism. J Clin Endocrinol Metab 72:541–546.
4. Thorgeirsson U, Costa J, Marx SJ 1981 The parathyroid glands in familial hypocalciuric hypercalcemia. Hum Pathol 12:229–237.
5. Law WM Jr, Carney JA, Heath H III 1984 Parathyroid glands in familial bengn hypercalcemia (familial hypocalciuric hypercalcemia). Am J Med 76:1021–1026.
6. Tfelt-Hansen J, Brown EM 2005 The calcium-sensing receptor in normal physiology and pathophysiology: A review. Critic Rev Clin Lab Sci 42:35–70.
7. Pidasheva S, D'Souza-Li L, Canaff L, Cole DEC, Hendy GN 2004 CASRdb: Calcium-sensing receptor locus-specific database for mutations causing familial (Benign) hypocalciuric hypercalcemia, neonatal severe hyperparathyroidism, and autosomal dominant hypocalcemia. Hum Mutation 24:107–111.
8. Simonds WF, James-Newton LA, Agarwal SK, Yang B, Skarulis MC, Hendy GN, Marx SJ 2002 Familial isolated hyperparathyroidism: Clinical and genetic characteristics of thirty-six kindreds. Medicine 81:1–26.
9. Heath H III, Jackson CE, Otterud B, Leppert MF 1993 Genetic linkage analysis in familial benign (hypocalciuric) hypercalcemia: Evidence for locus heterogeneity. Am J Hum Genet 53:193–200.
10. Lloyd SE, Pannett AA, Dixon PH, Whyte MP, Thakker RV 1999 Localization of familial benign hypercalcemia, Oklahoma variant (FBHOk), to chromosome 19q13. Am J Hum Genet 64:189–195.
11. Pallais JC, Kifor O, Chen YB, Slovik D, Brown EM 2004 Brief report—acquired hypocalciuric hypercalcemia due to autoantibodies against the calcium-sensing receptor. N Engl J Med 351:362–369.
12. Szabo E, Carling T, Hessman O, Rastad J 2002 Loss of heterozygosity in parathyroid glands of familial hypercalcemia with hypercalciuria and point mutation in calcium receptor. J Clin Endocrinol Metab 87:3961–3965.
13. Marx SJ, Attie MF, Spiegel AM, Levine MA, Lasker RD, Fox M 1982 An association between neonatal severe primary hyperparathyroidism and familial hypocalciuric hypercalcemia in three kindreds. N Engl J Med 306:257–264.
14. Bilezikian JP, Potts JT Jr, El-Haj Fuleihan G, Kleerekoper M, Neer R, Peacock M, Rastad J, Silverberg SJ, Udelsman R, Wells SA Jr 2002 Summary statement from a workshop on asymptomatic primary hyperparathyroidism: A perspective for the 21st century. J Bone Miner Res 17:S2;N2–N12.
15. Attie MF, Gill RJ Jr, Stock JL, Spiegel AM, Downs RW Jr, Levine MA, Marx SJ 1983 Urinary calcium excretion in familial hypocalciuric hypercalcemia: Persistence of relative hypocalciuria after induction of hypoparathyroidism. J Clin Invest 72:667–676.
16. Peacock M, Bilezikian JP, Klassen PS, Guo MD, Turner SA, Shoback D 2005 Cinacalcet hydrochloride maintains long-term normocalcemia in patients with primary hyperparathyroidism. J Clin Endocrinol Metab 90:135–141.
17. Page LA, Haddow JE 1987 Self-limited neonatal hyperparathyroidism in familial hypocalciuric hypercalcemia. J Pediatr 111:261–264.

Chapter 30. Secondary and Tertiary Hyperparathyroidism

Richard L. Prince

School of Medicine and Pharmacology, University of Western Australia, Perth, Australia

INTRODUCTION

A detailed understanding of the physiological basis of the regulation of calcium homeostasis is central to the understanding of the causes of secondary hyperparathyroidism (HPT). It is failures in these systems that are detected biochemically as secondary HPT. PTH is the most important short-term endocrine initiator of defense against a reduction in the extracellular calcium concentration. Although magnesium, phosphate, and calcitriol also exert regulatory influences on PTH independent of the calcium level, the principal regulator of PTH secretion is

The author has reported no conflicts of interest.

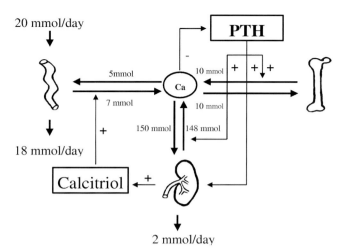

20 mmol/day

PTH

18 mmol/day

Calcitriol

2 mmol/day

FIG. 1. Physiology of calcium transport.

CONSEQUENCES OF SECONDARY HPT

Symptoms of hypocalcemia may occur if secondary HPT fails to maintain the extracellular calcium concentration, especially in children. The bone is a major "calcium sink" during skeletal growth and also during pregnancy and after cessation of lactation. If absorption of calcium from the intestine and reabsorption of filtered calcium from the renal tubule are ineffective in restoring the extracellular calcium concentration, the major alternate supply of calcium is resorption from the skeleton. Childhood and adolescence represent particularly important times when intestinal calcium absorption is important because there is a constant flux of calcium into the growing skeleton. At this time, dietary calcium deficiency can result in secondary HPT, and if persistent, rickets.[2] In adults, if intestinal calcium absorption consistently fails to replace calcium loss from the extracellular compartment, osteoporosis results.[3] Both osteoporosis and osteomalacia result in biomechanical insufficiency of bone; thus, persistent secondary HPT may result in bone pain, deformity, and minimal trauma fractures. It is of interest to note that under the influence of secondary HPT, bone is preferentially resorbed from the appendicular cortical skeleton[4] as opposed to estrogen deficiency, where axial trabecular bone is the first target.

INTESTINAL CAUSES OF SECONDARY HPT

The intestine is the only external source of calcium supply to the various body compartments. The sites of calcium loss that

the ionized calcium concentration. The sensing system uses the calcium sensing receptor located in the plasma membrane of the parathyroid gland.[1] When this system senses a calcium level below that considered physiological, increased PTH secretion occurs, termed secondary HPT. The raised level of PTH corrects the low calcium by actions on the bone and kidney, and indirectly the bowel, to correct the calcium level (Fig. 1). Thus, secondary HPT is a condition in which the parathyroid glands are responding appropriately to a low extracellular calcium concentration; this in general corrects the extracellular calcium. However, if the increased PTH secretion cannot correct the plasma calcium, either because of a disorder within those organs responsible for calcium transport or because of reduced availability of calcium, hypocalcemia can result. Thus, secondary HPT can be associated with calcium concentrations that are within or below the population reference range. It is the task of the clinician to determine the reason or reasons for the persistent error signal and correct them efficiently and effectively.

The three major regulated sources of calcium entry and exit into the extracellular compartment are the intestine, kidney, and bone. Perspiration is another small source of calcium loss to the extracellular compartment. Impairment in the balance between entry and exit of calcium from the intestine, bone, and kidney will induce secondary HPT when there is an overall inability of all the organs acting together to maintain a normal or reference range calcium concentration in the extracellular compartment. Thus, secondary HPT may be caused by a variety of disorders of the organs involved in maintenance of extracellular calcium concentrations (Table 1). In addition, calcium exchange occurs across all cell membranes under the influence of a variety of channels and transporters. In general, these fluxes of calcium have no net effect on extracellular calcium concentration because intracellular calcium concentrations are on the order of 100 nM, whereas extracellular calcium concentration is about 1.0 mM, a difference that is 10,000-fold greater in blood. As discussed below, there are a few pathological situations where this is not the case.

While it is true that high phosphate and low calcitriol levels may stimulate PTH secretion independently of the calcium level, they usually occur in the setting of chronic kidney disease, which is itself a low calcium state. One of the principal clinical effects of magnesium, in addition to impairing PTH action, is to reduce PTH secretion, thus counteracting secondary HPT.

TABLE 1. Differential Diagnosis of Secondary Hyperparathyroidism

Impaired intestinal calcium entry into the extracellular compartment
  Impaired dietary calcium intake
    Lactose intolerance
  Impaired dietary calcium absorption
    Pancreatic disease—fat malabsorption
    Damaged enterocytes—coeliac disease
    Calcium sequestration—phytates
  Deficiency of vitamin D
    Sunlight deprivation
    Intestinal vitamin D malabsorption (e.g., liver disease)
Loss of calcium from the extracellular compartment
  To the bone
    Growth
    Recovery postlactation
    Bisphosphonate treatment
      Pagets disease
      Osteoporosis
      Bone cancer
    "Hungry bone syndrome"
  To the urine
    Idiopathic hypercalciuria
    Increased sodium excretion
    Loop diuretics
  To soft tissue
    Rhabdomyolysis
    Sepsis
    Episodic oral phosphate for treatment of hypophosphatemia
Impaired PTH action
  Pseudo-hypoparathyroidism
    G protein deficiency
  Renal failure with impaired calcitriol formation and phosphate excretion
    Impaired gut calcium absorption
    Impaired parathyroid calcium sensing

intestinal calcium absorption must replace are the kidney, through a net obligatory renal calcium loss, the skeleton, as discussed above, and occasionally soft tissue.

Inadequate Dietary Calcium Intake

Reliable determination of dietary calcium deficiency based on dietary history is difficult. This is in part because the dietary calcium requirement depends on calcium handling in the kidney and bone. There are also great interindividual variations in the amount of dietary calcium required to achieve calcium balance. Thus, in practice, although it may be occasionally be possible to make a positive clinical diagnosis of a low calcium intake, it is usually a diagnosis of exclusion. It is appropriate to determine whether milk products cause abdominal symptoms because this may be an indicator of lactose intolerance, which reduces calcium intake associated with avoidance of milk products. In addition, in subjects with lactose intolerance lactose will itself induce calcium malabsorption. Interestingly, in normal subjects, lactose may increase calcium absorption. Lactose intolerance predicts development of osteoporosis and fracture.[5] The genetic polymorphism resulting in lactose intolerance has recently been described and presents a new diagnostic approach

Management of calcium deficiency in adults is discussed in elsewhere, but should include the use of calcium supplements in doses of at least 1200 mg of elemental calcium per day. Management of calcium deficiency in childhood is discussed elsewhere, but should include doses of calcium of at least 800 mg/day.

Dietary Calcium Malabsorption

Calcium soaps form in the intestinal lumen when free fatty acids are generated in the gut lumen but are not absorbed, and are therefore available to bind calcium and prevent its absorption. Formation of insoluble calcium soaps may occur in primary intestinal disorders such as celiac sprue and short bowel syndrome, but not in primary pancreatic disease where no lipase is produced.

Thus, secondary HPT, osteoporosis, and occasionally osteomalacia are common presenting features of celiac disease.[6]

Exocrine pancreatic failure may occur as a result of alcohol, biliary calculi, or cystic fibrosis, and results in fat malabsorption. This may promote the development of nonabsorbable calcium soaps within the bowel. Associated malabsorption of fat-soluble vitamins, particularly vitamin D, can induce calcium malabsorption caused by vitamin D deficiency.

Another minor cause of impaired calcium absorption is dietary fiber in the form of phytic acid that may bind calcium within the bowel, thus contributing to calcium malabsorption. Studies that have examined the effects of these diets on calcium absorption have not found any significant deleterious effects, at least at moderate consumption of these foods. However, at high fiber intakes, calcium retention can be reduced from 25% to 19%.[7]

Vitamin D Deficiency

The principal cause of vitamin D deficiency is lack of sunlight exposure preventing the formation of vitamin D in the skin. Patients at high risk of vitamin D are those with restricted sunlight exposure by reason of northern or southern latitude, lack of outdoor activity, clothing restrictions, or sunscreen use. The elderly are particularly at risk. Malabsorption and antiepileptic therapy may exacerbate the problem.

Secondary HPT and increased bone turnover markers such as alkaline phosphatase are common but not universal for reasons that remain somewhat unclear. Diagnosis is best estab-

lished by measuring the serum concentration of 25-hydroxyvitamin D. Renal calcium conservation manifest by hypocalciuria is usually present.

Therapy should include increased calcium intake and sunlight exposure where possible and the use of oral cholecalciferol or ergocalciferol in a dose of at least 10,000 U/week until healing has occurred. If there is impaired renal synthesis of calcitriol, a 1-hydroxylated derivative of vitamin D should be prescribed in addition to dietary calcium supplementation.

LOSS OF CALCIUM FROM THE EXTRACELLULAR COMPARTMENT AS A CAUSE OF SECONDARY HPT

A net loss of calcium from the extracellular compartment can occur into the skeleton, urine, breast milk during lactation, and the soft tissue of the body after ischemia. Under circumstances of extremely low calcium intake, there can be a net loss of calcium from the bowel because of calcium contained within pancreatic and intestinal secretions. This is called endogenous fecal calcium.

Entry of Calcium Into the Bone Compartment

A net flux of calcium into the skeletal compartment may be large enough to cause a decrease in the extracellular calcium concentration and the development of secondary HPT if intestinal calcium absorption and renal calcium reabsorption cannot maintain the calcium concentration. In childhood and adolescence, skeletal growth is the major cause of entry of calcium into the skeletal compartment. In adult life, the reformation of the skeleton after lactation-induced bone loss is the major physiological cause of entry of calcium into the skeletal compartment. Another cause of rapid entry of calcium into the skeleton may occur is bisphosphonate therapy for Paget's disease,[8] osteoporosis, or cancer. In the past, this phenomenon was observed with the use of estrogen in prostate cancer.[9] It may also occur after parathyroidectomy for severe primary HPT or tertiary HPT. The critical diagnostic factor in this setting is the low serum calcium concentration. Therapy is replacement of calcium and or vitamin D as discussed above.

Entry of Calcium Into Breast Milk

During lactation, skeletal calcium is released to provide calcium for the developing and growing infant. This process does not involve extra secretion of PTH and is thus not classified as a cause of secondary HPT, although there are many similarities. It has been suggested that PTH-related peptide secreted by the breast may be the etiological factor. At the end of lactation, the skeleton begins to regenerate, and secondary HPT may occur if dietary calcium intake is inadequate.[10]

Entry of Calcium Into the Urine

Primary renal calcium loss (renal hypercalciuria) is a hereditary disorder associated with renal stones, perhaps caused by defects in renal ion transport channels. It may also be caused by excessive salt intake[11] or loop diuretic therapy,[12] both of which increase calcium loss in the urine. If these losses are not matched by increased intestinal calcium absorption, secondary HPT and osteoporosis may occur. The diagnosis is supported by increased renal calcium excretion as assessed by an elevated 24 h and fasting urine calcium (Fig. 2).

Entry of Calcium Into Soft Tissue

Hypoxic tissue damage to muscle and other soft tissues may result in precipitation of calcium and phosphate as a result of

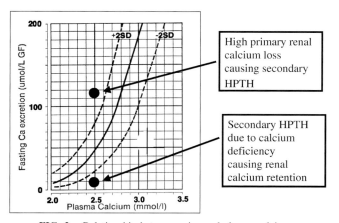

FIG. 2. Relationship between urine and plasma calcium.

the dramatic increases in the calcium × phosphate ion product that results from the release of large amounts of phosphate from damaged tissues as during crush injury and rhabdomyolysis or after chemotherapy. If rapid enough, this results in hypocalcemia and secondary HPT.[13] Rhabdomyolysis is associated with drugs or compartment syndromes and is best diagnosed by measurement of a raised creatine phosphokinase (CPK), myoglobinuria, and technetium diphosphonate isotope scan to detect the soft tissue uptake.[14] Therapy is supportive while muscle healing occurs.

IMPAIRED PTH ACTION ON KIDNEY AND BONE AS CAUSES OF SECONDARY HYPERPARATHYROIDISM

The bone and kidney are the two organs on which PTH exerts a direct action. Some of the conditions discussed above may in part result in impaired PTH action on the bone. However, the classical end organ resistance disease is pseudohypoparathyroidism. End organ damage to the kidney from any cause can result also result in secondary HPT from a complex set of pathophysiologic effects including resistance to PTH action because of reduced functional renal mass.

Impaired PTH Signal Transduction

Failure of PTH signal transduction in the bone and kidney caused by mutations in the G protein coupling system is an uncommon cause of secondary HPT, which is addressed elsewhere. The failure of PTH action on the bone and kidney results in hypocalcemia and appropriate secondary increases in HPT. One manifestation of this disorder, a syndrome first described by Fuller Albright in 1934 without the benefit of a PTH assay,[15] is associated with short stature, calcific deposits in soft tissue, and one or more short metacarpals or metatarsals. The defect in G protein signal transduction may be restricted to bone or kidney or may occur in both tissues. If there is loss of the effect of PTH on renal phosphate handling, a high plasma phosphate and renal phosphate threshold is present as opposed to a low phosphate and renal phosphate threshold found in other causes of secondary HPT. Management is aimed at correcting extracellular calcium, usually with the use of calcitriol and calcium.

Renal Failure

The role of PTH in the pathophysiology of renal failure is complex, but in essence could be considered a state of increased PTH action on the kidney and bone to compensate for inadequate production of calcitriol in the kidney. Secondary HPT appears early in the course of renal failure and may be evident before the appearance of phosphate retention[16] (when glomerular filtration rate [GFR] approaches 60 ml/minute). This is a treatable cause of progression of osteoporosis, especially frequent in elderly patients. Early in the course of development of renal failure, restoration of intestinal calcium absorption by increased dietary calcium and vitamin D intake either as calciferol or calcitriol should be undertaken. In addition, dietary calcium supplementation assists in the control of phosphate concentrations in the extracellular compartment by binding phosphate in the intestine. When serum phosphate concentrations rise, secondary HPT may develop by a direct stimulation of phosphate on PTH secretion[17] and by indirectly stimulating PTH secretion through lowering serum calcium by its complex with phosphate. Management includes a combination of dietary phosphorus restriction, phosphate binders, and dialysis to remove phosphate from the body.

TERTIARY HPT

The critical difference between secondary and tertiary HPT is that the plasma calcium is normal or low in secondary HPT but is elevated in tertiary HPT. Like primary HPT, the pathological problem in tertiary HPT is the development of adenoma or multigland hyperplasia. In addition, defective calcium-sensing receptor function may permit continued PTH secretion.

Tertiary HPT occurs after a prolonged period of secondary HPT. Indeed it has been argued that primary HPT may occur more commonly in populations with increased prevalence of calcium and vitamin D deficiency, perhaps causing subclinical stimulation of parathyroid cells eventually resulting in a clone of cells becoming hyperplastic.

A specific situation in which the term tertiary HPT is used is the hypercalcemic HPT that occurs after the prolonged secondary HPT of renal failure. This is caused by hyperplasia of one or more parathyroid glands. This term may also be used in the development of hypercalcemic HPT after the prolonged use of phosphate supplements in patients with hypophosphatemic rickets. In this situation, the episodic increase in plasma phosphate after ingestion of the supplement may induce transient hypocalcemia. Together with relative calcitriol deficiency, this results in parathyroid gland hyperplasia.[18] The diagnostic and therapeutic approach for tertiary HPT is similar to that used for primary HPT, which may be associated with four-gland hyperplasia or an enlarged single gland. The development of calcium mimetic drugs that activate the parathyroid calcium receptor, thus reducing tertiary HPT, is a promising new therapeutic approach. Currently, no calcimimetic agents have been approved by the Food and Drug Administration (FDA) for use in treatment of tertiary HPT.

BIOCHEMICAL DIAGNOSIS OF SECONDARY AND TERTIARY HPT

The diagnosis of secondary HPT is best made by the measurement of a PTH concentration above the reference range at the time that the measured plasma calcium is normal or low (Tables 1 and 2). As in primary HPT, the diagnosis of tertiary HPT is made by the measurement of a PTH concentration above the reference range at the time that the measured plasma calcium is high. These tests should be performed on a fasting resting venous blood sample taken without a tourniquet (because of its effects of increasing albumin concentrations and decreasing pH, both of which may inappropriately increase the measured calcium concentration).

The determination of the circulating calcium concentration

TABLE 2. CLINICAL HISTORY IN THE DIAGNOSIS OF THE CAUSE OF SECONDARY HYPERPARATHYROIDISM

Mechanism	Clinical history
Impaired intestinal calcium absorption	
Impaired dietary calcium intake	Low dairy product consumption
	Lactose intolerance
Impaired dietary calcium absorption	Pancreatic steatorrhoea
	Enterocyte failure
	Weight loss
	Diarrhea
	Iron or B_{12} deficiency
	High dietary fiber intake
Vitamin D deficiency	Extreme northern or southern latitudes
	Lack of outdoor exposure
	Lack of skin exposure (personal or religious preference)
	Use of sun screens (skin cancer protection, sun sensitivities)
Loss of calcium from the extracellular compartment	
To the bone	Growth
	Recent history of weaning
	Bisphosphonate treatment
To the urine	Kidney stones
	Family history
	Loop diuretic use
To soft tissue	Traumatic muscle damage
	Intensive care treatment
	Extensive burns
	Oral phosphate therapy
Impaired PTH action	
Renal failure	Pruritus
	Anemia
Pseudohypoparathyroidism	Albright phenotype
	Family history
	Tetany

should be undertaken by the use of an ionized calcium measurement corrected to a pH of 7.4, detected using a calcium-sensitive electrode. However, the albumin-corrected total calcium concentration is often used. It is especially important to definitively exclude hypercalcemia because, if present, the diagnosis is that of primary or tertiary HPT, diagnoses that require a radically different therapeutic approach. There are many excellent PTH assays now available that measure the full-length 1-84 molecule, although cross-reactivity with the 7-84 peptide may be a problem in chronic renal failure.

A good assay of circulating 25-hydroxyvitamin D, which measures both the cholecalciferol and ergocalciferol forms, is helpful for the diagnosis of vitamin D deficiency. Unfortunately, many current assays do not detect ergocalciferol with the same sensitivity as cholecalciferol. This may be a problem in patients who receive oral ergocalciferol as a vitamin D supplement because their vitamin D level may seem to be inappropriately low. Furthermore, there are substantial problems with cross-reactivity in many assays that do not use a vitamin D lipid extraction step, so that at high levels, they over-report but at low levels they under-report.

The diagnosis of increased end organ action on the kidney caused by secondary or tertiary HPT is facilitated by the use of the relation between plasma calcium and renal calcium excretion, first described by Nordin and Peacock.[19] In this test, the renal excretion of calcium per liter glomerular filtrate, easily calculated from the plasma and urine creatinine concentration and the urine calcium concentration, is plotted against the plasma calcium (Fig. 2). In secondary and tertiary HPT, the kidney conserves calcium by increasing renal calcium reab-sorption. This reabsorption may be stimulated by a variety of transporters in the distal tubule, including the sodium calcium co-transporter that is under the regulation of PTH.[20] Stimulation of renal transporters results in renal calcium conservation and a low urine calcium concentration. This is a sensitive measurement of parathyroid overactivity in calcium deficiency. It is detected by a low urine calcium excretion relative to the plasma calcium; when plotted, the patient's renal calcium excretion will be to the right of the reference data. The only exception is when the kidney is the primary source of loss of calcium from the body: so-called renal hypercalciuria. Under these circumstances, the renal calcium excretion is to the left of the reference curve. Another test of increased PTH activity on the kidney is that of a low renal phosphate threshold (Tm_p). This can be calculated from the measurement of plasma and urine creatinine concentration and the urine phosphate concentration and the use of a nomogram.[21] Finally, bone turnover markers are useful to identify increased bone resorption often associated with increased osteoblast activity associated with the skeletal response to secondary HPT.

The use of these measures on the same fasting blood and second urine sample after an overnight fast enables an efficient assessment of the function of the bone and kidney and indirectly the intestine under the action of PTH and usually allows a specific diagnosis that acts as the basis for treatment.

REFERENCES

1. Brown EM, MacLeod RJ 2001 Extracellular calcium sensing and extracellular calcium signaling. Physiol Rev 81:239–297.

2. Marie PJ, Pettifor JM, Ross FP, Glorieux FH 1982 Histological osteomalacia due to dietary calcium deficiency in children. N Engl J Med 307:584–588.
3. Prince RL, Dick IM, Lemmon J, Randell D 1997 The pathogenesis of age-related osteoporotic fracture: Effects of dietary calcium deprivation. J Clin Endocrinol Metab 82:260–264.
4. Price RI, Gutteridge DH, Stuckey BGA, Kent N, Retallack RW, Prince RL, Bhagat CI, Johnston CA, Nicholson GC, Stewart GO, 1993 Rapid, divergent changes in spinal and forearm bone density following short-term intravenous treatment of Paget's disease with pamidronate disodium. J Bone Miner Res 8:209–217.
5. Honkanen R, Koger H, Alhava E, Tuppurainen M, Saarikoski S 1997 Lactose intolerance associated with fractures of weight-bearing bones in Finnish women aged 38–57 years. Bone 21:473–477.
6. Selby PL, Davies M, Adams JE, Mawer EB 1999 Bone loss in celiac disease is related to secondary hyperparathyroidism. J Bone Miner Res 14:652–657.
7. Wisker E, Nagel R, Tanudjaja TK, Feldheim W 1991 Calcium, magnesium, zinc, and iron balances in young women: Effects of a low-phytate barley-fiber concentrate. Am J Clin Nutr 54:553–559.
8. Devlin RD, Retallack RW, Fenton AJ, Grill V, Gutteridge DH, Kent GN, Prince RL, Worth GK 1994 Long-term elevation of 1,25-dihydroxyvitamin D after short-term intravenous administration of pamidronate (aminohydroxypropylidene bisphosphonate, APD) in Paget's disease of bone. J Bone Miner Res 9:81–85.
9. Kukreja SC, Shanmugam A, Lad TE 1988 Hypocalcemia in patients with prostate cancer. Calcif. Tissue Int 43:340–345.
10. DeSantiago S, Alonso L, Halhali A, Larrea F, Isoard F, Bourges H 2002 Negative calcium balance during lactation in rural Mexican women. Am J Clin Nutr 76:845–851.
11. Devine A, Criddle RA, Dick IM, Kerr DA, Prince RL 1995 A longitudinal study of the effect of sodium and calcium intakes on regional bone density in postmenopausal women. Am J Clin Nutr 62:740–745.
12. Stein MS, Scherer SC, Walton SL, Gilbert RE, Ebeling PR, Flicker L, Wark JD 1996 Risk factors for secondary hyperparathyroidism in a nursing home population. Clin Endocrinol (Oxf) 44:375–383.
13. Llach F, Felsenfeld AJ, Haussler MR 1981 The pathophysiology of altered calcium metabolism in rhabdomyolysis-induced acute renal failure. Interactions of parathyroid hormone, 25-hydroxycholecalciferol, and 1,25-dihydroxycholecalciferol. N Engl J Med 305:117–123.
14. Prince RL, Eisman JA, Simpson RW 1983 Hypercalcaemia in association with renal failure: The role of immobilisation. Aust NZ J Med 13:8–10.
15. Albright F BC, Smith OH 1942 Pseudohypoparathyroidism: An example of "Seabright Bantam" syndrome. Endocrinology 30:922–932.
16. St. John A, Thomas MB, Davies CP, Mullan B, Dick I, Hutchison B, van der Schaff A, Prince RL 1992 Determinants of intact parathyroid hormone and free 1,25-dihydroxyvitamin D levels in mild and moderate renal failure. Nephron 61:422–427.
17. Estepa JC, Aguilera-Tejero E, Lopez I, Almaden Y, Rodriguez M, Felsenfeld AJ 1999 Effect of phosphate on parathyroid hormone secretion in vivo. J Bone Miner Res 14:1848–1854.
18. Makitie O, Kooh SW, Sochett E 2003 Prolonged high-dose phosphate treatment: A risk factor for tertiary hyperparathyroidism in X-linked hypophosphatemic rickets. Clin Endocrinol (Oxf) 58:163–168.
19. Nordin BE, Peacock M 1969 Role of kidney in regulation of plasma-calcium. Lancet 2:1280–1283.
20. Khundmiri SJ, Dean WL, McLeish KR, Lederer ED 2005 Parathyroid hormone-mediated regulation of Na+-K+-ATPase requires ERK-dependent translocation of protein kinase C alpha. J Biol Chem 280:8705–8713.
21. Walton RJ, Bijvoet OLM 1975 Nomogram for derivation of renal threshold phosphate concentration. Lancet 1:309–310.

Chapter 31.   Hypercalcemia Associated With Malignancy

Mara J. Horwitz and Andrew F. Stewart

Division of Endocrinology, University of Pittsburgh School of Medicine, Pittsburgh, Pennsylvania

INTRODUCTION

Malignancy-associated hypercalcemia (MAHC) was first reported to occur simultaneously with the deployment of clinical serum calcium measurements in the early 1920s. It is by far the most common cause of hypercalcemia among hospitalized patients and is a frequent cause of death among patients with cancer. It is also a serious, life-threatening complication of cancer and forecasts a grave prognosis: it has reported that the 50% survival among patients with MAHC, regardless of treatment, is 30 days.

The first clinical series included patients with extensive skeletal involvement caused by multiple myeloma and breast cancer, a syndrome called "local osteolytic hypercalcemia" (LOH). By the 1940s and 1950s, it was apparent that many patients with MAHC had limited or no skeletal involvement and had different tumor types than those with LOH. These patients are now referred to as having "humoral hypercalcemia of malignancy" (HHM). In the 1980s, occasional patients with lymphoma and MAHC were described in whom hypercalcemia resulted from production by tumors of the active from of vitamin D, 1,25(OH)$_2$D, also called calcitriol. Most recently, beginning in the 1990s, rare but convincing cases of authentic ectopic secretion of PTH have been described. The salient features of these four mechanistic subtypes of MAHC are summarized in Table 1. Each is discussed in more detail below. Therapy of HHM is discussed in more detail elsewhere and should include measures aimed at (1) reducing the tumor burden; (2) reducing osteoclastic bone resorption; and (3) augmenting renal calcium clearance.

Finally, it is important to emphasize that patients with cancer may develop hypercalcemia as a result of other coexisting conditions, such as primary hyperparathyroidism (HPT), tuberculosis, sarcoidosis, immobilization, and use of calcium-containing hyperalimentation solutions. These causes are summarized elsewhere and should be actively sought and corrected because they are easier to treat and have a more optimistic prognosis than MAHC.

LOH

In large series of unselected patients with MAHC, LOH accounts for ~20% of cases. Skeletal involvement is extensive, as assessed by bone or bone marrow biopsy, bone scintigraphic scanning, and/or autopsy. Biochemically (Figs. 1–3; Table 2), LOH is characterized by hypercalcemia, normal or high serum phosphorus levels, suppression of PTH secretion with reductions in nephrogenous cyclic AMP excretion, an increase in fractional and 24-h calcium excretion, a reduction in serum 1,25(OH)$_2$D, and increased markers of bone resorption (e.g.,

Dr. Stewart is a consultant for Wyeth, Eli Lilly, Proctor & Gamble, and Amgen and owns stock in Osteotrophin. Dr. Horwitz has reported no conflicts of interest.

TABLE 1. MECHANISTIC CATEGORIES OF MAHC

LOH
  20% of patients with MAHC
  Extensive skeletal tumor involvement
  Types of tumors
    Breast cancer
    Multiple myeloma
    Lymphoma
    Leukemia
HHM
  80% of patients with MAHC
  Limited or no skeletal tumor involvement
  Types of tumors
    Squamous carcinoma, any organ
    Renal carcinoma
    Bladder carcinoma
    Ovarian carcinoma
    Endometrial carcinoma
    HTLV-1 lymphoma
    Breast cancer
$1,25(OH)_2$ Vitamin D–mediated hypercalcemia
  Rare (~50 cases)
  Variable skeletal tumor involvement
  Types of tumors
    Lymphoma
    Ovarian dysgerminoma
Authentic ectopic hyperparathyroidism
  Rare (~9 cases)
  Variable skeletal involvement
  Types of tumors: variable

serum N-telopeptide). Two general tumor types are typical: breast cancer and hematologic malignancies.

Breast Cancer

Whereas many types of solid tumors metastasize to bone, among solid tumors, breast cancer is by far the most com-
mon cause of LOH. To be sure, prostate cancer and small cell cancer frequently metastasize to the skeleton, but they rarely cause hypercalcemia. Squamous carcinoma of the lung frequently causes hypercalcemia, but typically through HHM. Breast cancer cells seem to have a particular trophism for bone, and it is now well established that breast cancer cells within the skeleton are particularly likely to produce PTH-related protein (PTHrP) and that local PTHrP production by breast cancers is augmented by the resultant release of bone-derived cytokines such as TGF-β. Thus, a vicious cycle develops in which PTHrP leads to increasing skeletal resorption by osteoclasts, which in turn release local cytokines that augment PTHrP secretion by the breast cancer metastases. These mechanisms are described in further detail elsewhere.

Hematologic Malignancies

Multiple myeloma (MM) remains the hematologic malignancy most commonly associated with hypercalcemia: up to 30% of patients with multiple myeloma may develop hypercalcemia. Histologically, myeloma is characterized by purely lytic or osteoclastic bone resorption, with absent bone formation. Hypercalcemia is most likely to occur in patients with renal insufficiency, who combine increases in bone resorption with reduced calcium clearance. Hypercalcemia of this type is also associated with other hematologic malignancies, particularly lymphomas of all histologies. Chronic lymphocytic leukemia, acute lymphoblastic leukemia, chronic myelocytic leukemia, and acute myeloblastic leukemia have all been reported to cause hypercalcemia, but this is uncommon. The mechanisms responsible for increased osteoclastic activity and bone destruction in hematologic malignancies include local production by tumor cells within the marrow compartment of specific osteoclast-activating cytokines, including macrophage inflammatory protein-1α, interleukins-1 and -6, PTHrP, RANKL, and others. These are discussed in detail elsewhere.

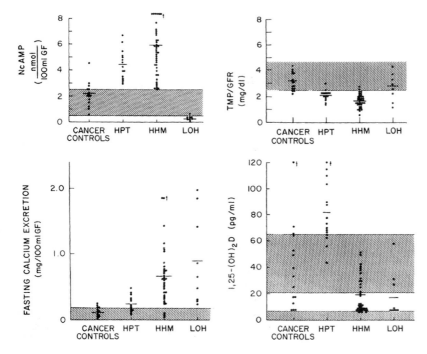

FIG. 1. Nephrogenous cyclic adenosine monophosphate excretion (NcAMP), renal tubular maximum for phosphorus (TmP/GFR), fasting calcium excretion, and plasma 1,25-dihydroxyvitamin D values in normocalcemic patients with cancer (cancer controls) and in patients with primary HPT, HHM, and hypercalcemia caused by bone metastases or local osteolytic hypercalcemia (LOH). (Adapted with permission from Stewart AF, Horst R, Deftos LJ, Cadman EC, Lang R, Broadus AE 1980 Biochemical evaluation of patients with cancer-associated hypercalcemia: Evidence for humoral and non-humoral groups. N Engl J Med **303**:1377–1383.) Copyright © 1980 Massachusetts Medical Society. All rights reserved. Adapted with permission, 2006.

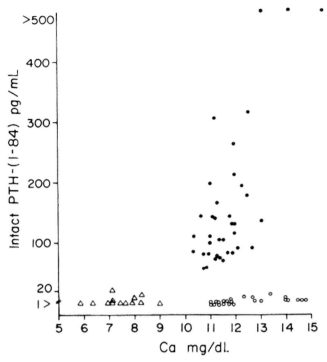

FIG. 2. Immunoreactive PTH concentration of PTH by using a two-site immunoradiometric assay for PTH(1-84) in patients with primary HPT (●), hypoparathyroidism (△), and hypercalcemia of malignancy (○). (Reprinted with permission from Nussbaum S, Zahradnik RJ, Lavigne JR, et al. 1987 Highly sensitive two-site immunoradiometric assay of parathyrin and its clinical utility in evaluating patients with hypercalcemia. Clin Chem 33:1364–1367.)

HHM

The term "humoral hypercalcemia of malignancy" describes a clinical syndrome that results from the production of PTHrP. The syndrome was first described in 1941 in a patient with renal carcinoma and a solitary skeletal metastasis. Reports in the 1950s and 1960s documented the humoral nature of the syndrome by showing that (1) typical patients had little or no skeletal tumor involvement and (2) the hypercalcemia and other biochemical abnormalities reversed when the tumor was resected or treated. Evidence from the 1960s and 1970s suggested that the responsible factor was either prostaglandin E_2, a vitamin D–like sterol, or PTH. It is now clear that none of these is responsible.

Large clinical series show that HHM accounts for up to 80% of patients with MAHC. From a clinical standpoint, patients with HHM have advanced disease with tumors that are usually large, obvious clinically and with a poor prognosis. In contrast to the typical tumor types associated with LOH, patients with HHM most often have squamous carcinomas (involving lung, esophagus, head and neck, cervix, vulva, skin, etc.; Table 1). Other tumor types commonly associated with HHM are renal, bladder, and ovarian carcinomas. Breast carcinoma may cause typical HHM or may lead to hypercalcemia through skeletal metastatic involvement. Finally, the subset of hypercalcemic patients with lymphomas caused by human T-cell leukemia virus-I seems to have classic PTHrP-mediated HHM, although, others have suggested that macrophage inflammatory protein-1α may also contribute to the syndrome.

Biochemically and histologically, patients with HHM share certain features with patients with primary HPT and differ in

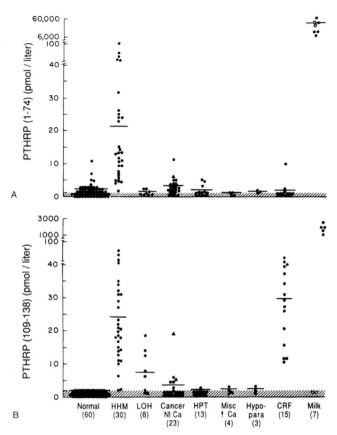

FIG. 3. Immunoreactive PTHrP values in patients with HHM and in various control groups. PTHrP values shown were obtained by using a two-site immunoradiometric assay (IRMA) directed against PTHrP(1-74). (Reprinted with permission from Burtis WJ, Brady TG, Orloff JJ, et al. 1980 Immunochemical characterization of circulating PTH-related protein in patients with humoral hypercalcemia of malignancy. N Engl J Med 322:1106–1112.) Copyright © 1980 Massachusetts Medical Society. All rights reserved.

other respects (Table 2; Figs. 1–4). Both groups of patients have a humoral syndrome, both are hypercalcemic, and both are hypophosphatemic and display reductions in the renal tubular phosphorus threshold. Both groups display increased

TABLE 2. SIMILARITIES AND DIFFERENCES BETWEEN PATIENTS WITH PRIMARY HPT AND HHM

	HPT	HHM	LOH
Humorally mediated hypercalcemia	+	+	−
Increased osteoclastic bone resorption	+	+	+
Increased renal calcium reabsorption	+	+	−
Hypophosphatemia	+	+	−
Phosphaturia	+	+	−
Nephrogenous cAMP elevation	+	+	−
Increased plasma 1,25(OH)$_2$D	+	−	−
Increased osteoblastic bone formation	+	−	±
Increased circulating immunoreactive PTH	+	−	−
Increased circulating immunoreactive PTHrP	−	+	−
Hypercalcemia due primarily to effects on kidney and GI tract	+	−	−
Hypercalcemia due to combined effects on kidney and bone	−	+	−
Hypercalcemia due primarily to effects on bone	−	−	+

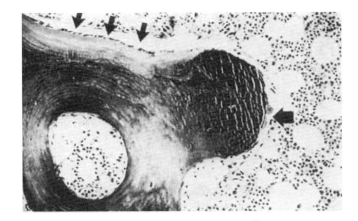

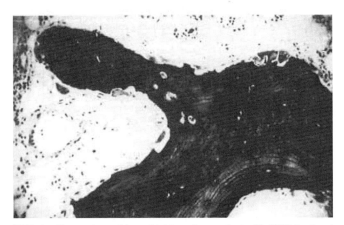

FIG. 4. Comparison of bone histology in a patient with HPT (top) and HHM (bottom). In both groups, osteoclastic activity is accelerated, although it is higher in HHM than in HPT. In HPT, osteoblastic activity and osteoid are increased, but both are markedly decreased in HHM. This uncoupling of formation from resorption in HHM plays the major rule in causing hypercalcemia. (Reprinted with permission from Stewart AF, Vignery A, Silvergate A, et al. 1982 Quantitative bone histomorphometry in humoral hypercalcemia of malignancy: Uncoupling of bone cell activity. J Clin Endocrinol Metab **55**:219–227.) Copyright © 1982, The Endocrine Society.

nephrogenous or urinary cAMP excretion, indicating an interaction of the respective humoral mediator with proximal tubular PTH receptors. Both groups display increases in osteoclastic bone resorption histologically (Fig. 4) and using bone resorption markers. Hypercalcemia in both groups result, in part, from increased distal tubular calcium reabsorption mediated by PTH and PTHrP.

In contrast, patients with HHM differ from those with HPT in two important respects (Table 2). First, because PTH is a potent stimulus for the renal production of $1,25(OH)_2D$, patients with HPT typically show increases in circulating $1,25(OH)_2D$ (Fig. 1) and a resultant increase in calcium absorption by the intestine. In contrast, patients with HHM display reductions in serum $1,25(OH)_2D$ values and in intestinal calcium absorption. The pathophysiology underlying this observation is uncertain, but PTHrP seems to be a poor agonist for $1,25(OH)_2D$ production in humans. Second, in patients with HPT, osteoblastic bone formation is increased and coupled to the increased bone resorption rate (Fig. 4). In patients with HHM, however, osteoblastic bone formation is reduced and is therefore dissociated or uncoupled from the increased osteoclastic bone resorption. This is apparent both histologically as

well as by measurement of biochemical markers of bone formation. The reasons for this uncoupling are also unclear. Of course, PTH concentrations in plasma are elevated in patients with HPT, but they are suppressed in patients with HHM (Fig. 2). Conversely, PTHrP values are elevated in HHM, but they are normal in patients with HPT (Fig. 3). Preliminary studies suggest that the PTHrP concentration may be useful in monitoring responses to surgery, chemotherapy, or radiotherapy in patients in whom levels are elevated before therapy.

Hypercalcemia in patients with HHM has both skeletal and renal components. The skeletal component, as noted earlier, reflects increased osteoclast activity and uncoupling of osteoblasts from osteoclasts. The renal component reflects PTHrP-mediated increases in distal tubular calcium reabsorption. In addition, patients with HHM are usually volume depleted, partly as a result of their hypercalcemia, with resultant inability to concentrate the urine, and partly as a result of poor oral fluid intake. The volume depletion leads to a reduction in the filtered load of calcium and a reduction in the fractional excretion of calcium.

$1,25(OH)_2D$-MEDIATED HYPERCALCEMIA

In the 1980s, six patients were described with malignant lymphomas in whom circulating concentrations of $1,25(OH)_2D$ were found to be elevated, in some cases strikingly so. More cases were added in 1994, and additional cases have been reported subsequently. The elevation of plasma $1,25(OH)_2D$ contrasts with findings in other types of malignancy-associated hypercalcemia (Fig. 1). No evidence for a role for either PTH or PTHrP has been found. Resection or medical therapy of the lymphomas reverses the hypercalcemia and reverses the elevations of $1,25(OH)_2D$ in plasma. No unifying histological theme is present among the lymphomas. Rather, lymphomas of several different subcategories are included in this group. The $1,25(OH)_2D$ elevations and hypercalcemia are corrected with glucocorticoid therapy. This syndrome seems to be the malignant counterpart of sarcoidosis, with malignant lymphocytes, macrophages, or both converting diet- and sun-derived $25(OH)D$ to $1,25(OH)_2D$. In addition to lymphomas, dysgerminomas of the ovary have also been associated with hypercalcemia caused by elevated serum $1,25(OH)_2D$. It is thought that the local inflammatory response to the dysgerminoma stimulates the expression and activity of 1α-hydroxylase. This in turn leads to the increased levels of circulating $1,25(OH)_2D$.

AUTHENTIC ECTOPIC HYPERPARATHYROIDISM

From the 1940s through the 1970s, what is now called HHM was widely attributed to ectopic secretion of PTH by malignant tumors. Terms such as "ectopic hyperparathyroidism" and "pseudohyperparathyroidism" were in common use. By the 1980s, it was clear that the vast majority of cases of HHM were caused by PTHrP, and it was questioned whether "ectopic secretion of PTH" even existed. In the 1990s, this question was clearly answered by the unequivocal demonstration that tumors can express the *PTH* gene and thereby cause hypercalcemia. At the time of this writing, nine cases of what can be described as "authentic ectopic hyperparathyroidism" have been reported. These tumors included three small-cell carcinomas (two of the lung and one of the ovary), a squamous carcinoma of the lung, an adenocarcinoma of the ovary, a thymoma, an undifferentiated neuroendocrine tumor, and a papillary carcinoma of the thyroid. Immunoreactive PTH was found to be elevated in state-of-the-art PTH two-site assays and declined with the hypercalcemia after tumor resection. In most cases, PTH was present immunohistochemically; the tumors secreted PTH, but not PTHrP, into their culture medium in vitro; the tumors contained PTH, but not PTHrP, mRNA. In one case, PTH overexpression by an ovarian tumor resulted from a rearrangement of the *PTH* gene, which placed it under the control of an ovarian promoter. These findings make it clear that authentic ectopic secretion of PTH, although exceedingly rare, can occur. This entity should be considered in the diagnosis of patients with hypercalcemia and increased concentrations of PTH.

UNUSUAL FORMS OF HUMORAL HYPERCALCEMIA

The four broad categories of malignancy-associated hypercalcemia described in Table 1 comprise the vast majority of patients with cancer and hypercalcemia. It should, however, be clear that other mechanisms, although uncommon, may be encountered. For example, patients who clearly display humorally mediated hypercalcemic syndromes (i.e., hypercalcemia that is reversed by tumor resection) have been reported who do not fit into the HHM biochemical categorization described. The humoral mediator in these patients is unknown. Rare patients with renal carcinomas have been described who seem to have bona fide tumor secretion of prostaglandin E_2 as a cause.

SUGGESTED READING

1. Stewart AF, Broadus AE 2006 Malignancy-associated hypercalcemia. In: DeGroot L, Jameson LJ (eds.) Endocrinology, 5th ed. W.B. Saunders, Philadelphia, PA, USA, pp. 1555–1565.
2. Stewart AF 2005 Hypercalcemia associated with cancer. N Engl J Med **352:**373–379.
3. Perry CM, Figgitt DP 2004 Zoledronic acid: A review of its use in patients with advanced cancer. Drugs **64:**1197–1211.
4. Major P, Lortholary A, Hon J, Abdi E, Mills G, Menssen HD, Yunus F, Bell R, Body J, Quebe-Fehling E, Seaman J 2001 Zoledronic acid is superior to pamidronate in the treatment of hypercalcemia of malignancy: A pooled analysis of two randomized, controlled clinical trials. J Clin Oncol **19:**558–567.
5. Ralson SH, Gallagher SJ, Patel U, Campbell J, Boyle IT 1990 Cancer-associated hypercalcemia: Morbidity and mortality. Ann Intern Med **112:**499–504.
6. Nakayama K, Fukumoto S, Takeda S, Takeuchi Y, Ishikawa T, Miura M, Hata K, Hane M, Tamura Y, Tanaka Y, Kitaoka M, Obara T, Ogata E, Matsumoto T 1996 Differences in bone and vitamin D metabolism between primary hyperparathyroidism and malignancy-associated hypercalcemia. J Clin Endocrinol Metab **81:**607–611.
7. Guise TA, Yin JJ, Taylor SD 1996 Evidence for a causal role of parathyroid hormone–related protein in the pathogenesis of human breast cancer–mediated osteolysis. J Clin Invest **98:**1544.
8. Anderson KC, Shaughnessy JD, Barlogie B, Harousseau JL, Roodman GD 2002 Multiple Myeloma. American Society of Hematology, Washington, DC, USA.
9. Kakonen SM, Mundy GR 2003 Mechanisms of osteolytic bone metastases in breast carcinoma. Cancer **97**(3 Suppl):834–839.
10. Roodman GD 2004 Mechanisms of bone metastasis. N Engl J Med **350:**1655–1664.
11. Stewart AF, Horst R, Deftos LJ, Cadman EC, Lang R, Broadus AE 1980 Biochemical evaluation of patients with cancer-associated hypercalcemia: Evidence for humoral and non-humoral groups. N Engl J Med **303:**1377–1383.
12. Stewart AF, Vignery A, Silvergate A, Ravin ND, LiVolsi V, Broadus AE, Baron R 1982 Quantitative bone histomorphometry in humoral hypercalcemia of malignancy: Uncoupling of bone cell activity. J Clin Endocrinol Metab **55:**219–227.
13. Burtis WJ, Brady TG, Orloff JJ, Ersbak JB, Warrell RP, Olson BR, Wu TL, Mitnick, MA, Broadus AE, Stewart AF 1990 Immunochemical characterization of circulating parathyroid hormone-related protein in patients with humoral hypercalcemia of malignancy. N Engl J Med **322:**1106–1112.
14. Motokura T, Fukomoto S, Matsumoto T, Takahashi S, Fujita A, Yamashita T, Igarashi T, Ogata E 1989 Parathyroid hormone-related protein in adult T-cell leukemia-lymphoma. Ann Intern Med **111:**484–488.
15. Grill V, Ho P, Body JJ, Johanson N, Lee SC, Kukreja SC, Moseley JM, Martin TJ 1991 Parathyroid hormone-related protein: Elevated levels in both humoral hypercalcemia of malignancy and hypercalcemia complicating metastatic breast cancer. J Clin Endocrinol Metab **73:**1309–1315.
16. Ikeda K, Ohno H, Hane M, Yokoi H, Okada M, Honma T, Yamada A, Tatsumi Y, Tanaka T, Saitoh T 1994 Development of a sensitive two-site immunoradiometric assay for parathyroid hormone-related peptide: Evidence for elevated levels in plasma from patients with adult T-cell leukemia/lymphoma and B-cell lymphoma. J Clin Endocrinol Metab **79:**1322–1327.
17. Horwitz MJ, Tedesco MB, Sereika S, Hollis B, Garcia-Ocaña A, Stewart AF 2003 Direct comparison of sustained infusion of hPTHrP(1–36) versus hPTH(1–34) on serum calcium, plasma 1,25(OH)$_2$ vitamin D concentrations and fractional calcium excretion in healthy human volunteers. J Clin Endocrinol Metab **88:**1603–1609.
18. Okada Y, Tsukda J, Nakano K, Tonai S, Mine S, Tanaka Y 2004 Macrophage inflammatory protein-1α induces hypercalcemia in adult T-cell leukemia. J Bone Miner Res **19:**1105–1113.
19. Horwitz MJ, Tedesco MB, Sereika SM, Syed MA, Garcia-Ocaña A, Bisello A, Hollis BW, Rosen CJ, Wysolmerski JJ, Dann P, Gundberg CM, Stewart AF 2005 Continuous infusion of parathyroid hormone versus parathyroid hormone-related protein in humans: Discordant effects on 1,25(OH)$_2$ vitamin D and prolonged suppression of bone formation. J Bone Miner Res **20:**1792–1803.
20. Breslau NA, McGuire JL, Zerwekh JR, Frenkel EP, Pak CYC 1984 Hypercalcemia associated with increased serum calcitrion levels in three patients with lymphoma. Ann Intern Med **100:**1–7.
21. Rosenthal NR, Insogna KL, Godsall JW, Smaldone L, Waldron JW, Stewart AF 1985 1,25 dihydroxyvitamin D-mediated humoral hypercalcemia in malignant lymphoma. J Clin Endocrinol Metab **60:**29–33.
22. Seymour JF, Gagel RF, Hagemeister FB, Dimopoulos MA, Cabanillas F 1994 Calcitriol production in hypercalcemia and normocalcemic patients with non-Hodgkin lymphoma. Ann Intern Med **121:**633–640.
23. Evans KN, Taylor H, Zehnder D, Kilby MD, Bulmer JN, Shah F, Adams JS, Hewison M 2004 Increased expression of 25-hydroxyvitamin D-1alpha-hydroxylase in dysgerminomas: A novel form of humoral hypercalcemia of malignancy. Am J Pathol **165:**807–813.
24. Nussbaum SR, Gaz RD, Arnold A 1990 Hypercalcemia and ectopic secretion of PTH by an ovarian carcinoma with rearrangement of the gene for PTH. N Engl J Med **323:**1324–1328.
25. Iguchi H, Miyagi C, Tomita K, Kawauchi S, Nozuka Y, Tsuneyoshi M, Wakasugi H 1998 Hypercalcemia caused by ectopic production of parathyroid hormone in a patient with papillary adenocarcinoma of the thyroid gland. J Clin Endocrinol Metab **83:**2653–2657.
26. Eid W, Wheeler TM, Sharma MD 2004 Recurrent hypercalcemia due to ectopic production of parathyroid hormone-related protein and intact parathyroid hormone is a single patient with multiple malignancies. Endoc Pract **10:**125–128.

Chapter 32. Hypercalcemia Caused by Granuloma-Forming Disorders

John S. Adams and Martin Hewison

Division of Endocrinology, Diabetes and Metabolism, Burns and Allen Research Institute, Cedars-Sinai Medical Center, Los Angeles, California

PATHOGENESIS

The association of dysregulated calcium homeostasis and granuloma-forming disease was established in 1939 by the work of Harrell and Fisher.[1] With the advent of automated serum chemistry testing, more recent studies indicate that mild to severe hypercalcemia is detected in 10% of patients with sarcoidosis, and up to 50% of patients will become hypercalciuric at some time during the course of their disease.[2] Vitamin D was implicated in the pathogenesis of abnormal calcium metabolism after it was appreciated that patients with sarcoidosis who had hypercalcemia or hypercalciuria (or both) absorbed high amounts of dietary calcium and that normocalcemic patients were prone to hypercalcemia after receiving small amounts of vitamin D or UV light.[3] It has been proposed that bone resorption is also an important contributor to the pathogenesis of hypercalciuria and hypercalcemia,[4] based on the observations that a diet low in calcium seldom induces a normocalcemic state in sarcoidosis patients with moderate to severe hypercalcemia and that urinary calcium excretion often exceeds dietary calcium intake. More recent studies have shown that generalized, accelerated trabecular bone loss occurs in patients with sarcoidosis before institution of steroid therapy. Rizzato et al.[5] showed that (1) bone mass was significantly decreased in patients with active sarcoidosis, (2) bone loss was most marked in patients with hypercalcemia and/or hypercalciuria, and (3) bone loss was most prominent in postmenopausal women with long-standing disease.

For many years, these and similar clinical observations suggested that hypercalcemia and/or hypercalciuria in patients with sarcoidosis resulted from a heightened sensitivity to the biological effects of vitamin D. However, the discovery that a high proportion of these patients had elevated circulating concentrations of 1,25-dihydroxyvitamin D [1,25(OH)$_2$D] indicated that the endogenous overproduction of an active vitamin D metabolite was the etiology of disordered calcium regulation in this disease. High serum 1,25(OH)$_2$D concentrations have been reported in hypercalcemic patients with other granuloma-forming diseases and in patients harboring lymphoproliferative neoplasms (Table 1). In all of these disorders, there is a presumed extrarenal source for 1,25(OH)$_2$D.[6–23]

CELLULAR SOURCE OF ACTIVE VITAMIN D METABOLITES

The experiments of Barbour et al.[24] proved that in sarcoidosis the source of 1,25(OH)$_2$D is extrarenal. These investigators described an anephric patient with sarcoidosis, hypercalcemia, and a high serum 1,25(OH)$_2$D concentration. Subsequent studies showed that the elevated level of 1,25(OH)$_2$D in patients with sarcoidosis was caused by increased production of the steroid hormone by macrophages,[6] which make up a significant proportion of the cell population in sarcoid granulomata. More recent work has revealed that macrophage synthesis of 1,25(OH)$_2$D is also be a feature of lymphomas and other malignancies. Immunohistochemical analysis of the enzyme 1α-hydroxylase in a B-cell lymphoma associated with hypercalcemia and raised circu-

TABLE 1. HUMAN DISEASE ASSOCIATED WITH 1,25-DIHYDROXYVITAMIN D–MEDIATED HYPERCALCEMIA/HYPERCALCIURIA

Granuloma-forming diseases	
Noninfectious	
Sarcoidosis	Adams et al. (6)
Silicone-induced granulomatosis	Kozeny et al. (7)
Paraffin-induced granulomatosis	Albitar et al. (8)
Berylliosis	Stoeckle et al. (9)
Wegener's granulomatosis	Edelson et al. (10)
Eosinophilic granuloma	Jurney (11)
Infantile fat necrosis	Cook et al. (12)
Crohn's disease	Abreu et al. (13)
Infectious	
Tuberculosis	Gkonos et al. (14)
Candidiasis	Kantarijian et al. (15)
Leprosy	Hoffman and Korzeniowski (16)
Histoplasmosis	Walker et al. (17)
Coccidiodmycosis	Parker et al. (18)
Cat-scratch disease	Bosch (19)
Malignant lymphoproliferative disease	
B-cell lymphoma	Adams et al. (20)
Hodgkin's disease	Seymor and Gagel (21)
Lymphomatoid granulomatosis	Schienman et al. (22)
Dysgerminoma/seminoma	Evans et al. (23)

lating levels of 1,25(OH)$_2$D suggests that the tumor itself is not a source of the steroid hormone. Rather, macrophages adjacent to the tumor are likely to be the major site of 1,25(OH)$_2$D synthesis.[25] Similar observations have been made for other tumors, such as dysgerminomas, which are also known to be associated with hypercalcemia.[23] However, the situation with more common malignancies is less clear. Breast tumors show elevated levels of 1α-hydroxylase expression, but this seems to involve expression of the enzyme by both malignant cells and leukocytes from the associated immune infiltrate.[26] Furthermore, it is not immediately apparent that the increased expression of extrarenal 1α-hydroxylase seen in breast cancer is a cause of elevated serum 1,25(OH)$_2$D. This seems be caused by coincident expression of the vitamin D catabolic enzyme 24-hydroxylase, which attenuates accumulation of 1,25(OH)$_2$D by catalyzing its conversion to less active metabolites such as 1,24,25-trihydroxyvitamin D.[26] In view of this, it is possible to speculate that there are two forms of humoral hypercalcemia of malignancy. In common neoplasms such as breast cancer, which have relatively normal circulating levels of 1,25(OH)$_2$D, the underlying cause of hypercalcemia seems to be PTH-related peptide. In contrast, in tumors such as lymphomas or dysgerminomas, the apparent cause of hypercalcemia is extrarenal 1α-hydroxylase activity associated with raised circulating levels of 1,25(OH)$_2$D.

REGULATION OF EXTRARENAL 1α-HYDROXYLASE ACTIVITY

Recent RNA and protein analyses have confirmed that the enzyme 1α-hydroxylase is overexpressed in affected tissues from patients with granulomatous diseases. However, this alone does not seem to account for the high levels of local 1,25(OH)$_2$D

The authors have reported no conflicts of interest.

production required to raise circulating levels of the hormone. Indeed, four major lines of clinical evidence suggest that the endogenous extrarenal synthesis of $1,25(OH)_2D$ in hypercalcemic/hypercalciuric patients with granulomatous disease or lymphoma is not subject to normal, physiologic regulatory influences.[27–29] First, hypercalcemic patients possess high or inappropriately elevated serum $1,25(OH)_2D$ concentrations, although serum immunoreactive PTH levels are suppressed and serum phosphorus concentrations are relatively elevated. If $1,25(OH)_2D$ synthesis were under the trophic control of PTH and phosphorus, $1,25(OH)_2D$ concentrations would be low. Second, in normal individuals, serum $1,25(OH)_2D$ concentrations are not influenced by small to moderate increments of circulating 25-hydroxyvitamin D [25(OH)D] concentrations. In contrast, in patients with active sarcoidosis who have widespread disease and high serum angiotensin-converting enzyme activity, small to moderate changes in 25(OH)D are associated with increases in $1,25(OH)_2D$ that are, in turn, likely to cause hypercalciuria or hypercalcemia. Third, serum calcium and $1,25(OH)_2D$ concentrations are positively correlated to indices of disease activity; patients with sarcoidosis who have widespread disease and high serum angiotensin-converting enzyme activity are more likely to hypercalciuric or hypercalcemic. Finally, the rate of endogenous $1,25(OH)_2D$ production, which is significantly increased in patients with sarcoidosis, is unusually sensitive to inhibition by factors (e.g., glucocorticoids) that do not directly influence the renal 1α-hydroxylase enzyme that catalyzes synthesis of $1,25(OH)_2D$.

Although substrate specificity and enzyme kinetics for the 1α-hydroxylase reaction seems to be the same for both kidney cells and macrophages,[30] the regulation of $1,25(OH)_2D$ synthesis at these sites seems to be very different. For example, the macrophage 1α-hydroxylation reaction is not induced by PTH, but it is very sensitive to stimulation by immunoactivators such as lipopolysaccharide[30] and cytokines such as interferon-γ (IFN-γ).[31] Macrophage synthesis of $1,25(OH)_2D$ is very sensitive to inhibition by glucocorticoids,[31] chloroquine and related analogs,[32] and the cytochrome P-450 inhibitor ketoconazole,[33] but it is refractory to inhibition by $1,25(OH)_2D$.[31] The renal enzyme, on the other hand, is relatively insensitive to inhibition by glucocorticoids and is downregulated by $1,25(OH)_2D$. These differences in the regulation of 1α-hydroxylase activity in the kidney and macrophages do not seem to be caused by the expression of two different gene products. Analysis of mRNA for 1α-hydroxylase in extrarenal tissues including macrophages and keratinocytes has revealed identity with the renal gene sequence.[34,35] Rather, it is likely that there is differential regulation of the 1α-hydroxylase gene in different cell types.[36] Renal 1α-hydroxylase is upregulated at the level of transcription by calciotropic hormones such as PTH and calcitonin and is also subject to exquisite autoregulation by $1,25(OH)_2D$ itself.[37] In contrast, macrophage 1α-hydroxylase mRNA expression is potently stimulated by inflammatory agents such as IFN-γ and shows no feedback control in response to $1,25(OH)_2D$.[38] The precise molecular mechanism for this remains unclear and may involve differential induction of the catabolic enzyme 24-hydroxylase.

IMMUNOACTIVITY OF $1,25(OH)_2D$

Studies over the last 25 years have shown very clearly that vitamin D can exert effects that extend far beyond its established role in calcium homeostasis and bone metabolism. For example, the antiproliferative properties of $1,25(OH)_2D$ have promoted its potential use in the treatment of cancer and psoriasis and has led in turn to the development of synthetic analogs of $1,25(OH)_2D$ to limit calcemic side effects.[39] Stud-

ies in vitro suggest that $1,25(OH)_2D$ is also a potent immunomodulatory steroid capable of suppressing lymphocyte proliferation, lymphokine production, and immunoglobulin synthesis.[39] While this represents another potential therapeutic target for vitamin D analogs, it has become apparent that $1,25(OH)_2D$ may play a role as an endogenous modulator of normal immune responses. In particular, it has been suggested that $1,25(OH)_2D$ produced by the macrophage in granulomatous diseases fulfills a paracrine immunoinhibitory function by modulating the proliferation and cytokine profile of neighboring, activated lymphocytes that express receptors for the hormone. In this way, locally synthesized $1,25(OH)_2D$ may act to slow an otherwise "overzealous" immune response that may be detrimental to the host.[40] The physiological significance of this has been highlighted by the recent development of 1α-hydroxylase knockout mouse models,[41,42] which presented with multiple enlarged lymph nodes.

TREATMENT OF HYPERCALCEMIA/HYPERCALCIURIA ASSOCIATED WITH SARCOIDOSIS

The most important factor in the successful management of disordered vitamin D metabolism of sarcoidosis is recognition of patients at risk. Those at risk include patients with (1) indices of active, widespread disease (i.e., elevated serum angiotensin-converting enzyme levels, diffuse infiltrative pulmonary disease); (2) preexistent hypercalciuria; (3) a previous history of hypercalcemia or hypercalciuria; (4) a diet enriched in vitamin D and calcium; and (5) a recent history of sunlight exposure or treatment with vitamin D. All patients with active sarcoidosis should be screened for hypercalciuria. In a timed, fasting urine collection, a fractional urinary calcium excretion rate exceeding 0.16 mg calcium/100 ml glomerular filtrate is considered hypercalciuria. Alternatively, 24-h urinary calcium excretion values greater than the usual normal limits for men (300 mg) and women (250 mg) are also indicative of hypercalcuria, based on a complete sample collection containing between 1.0 and 2.0 g creatinine. If the urinary calcium excretion is elevated, serum 25(OH)D and $1,25(OH)_2D$ concentrations should be determined as a disease marker and to judge the efficacy of therapy. Because hypercalciuria frequently precedes the development of overt hypercalcemia, the occurrence of either is an indication for therapy.

Glucocorticoids (40–60 mg prednisone or equivalent daily) are the mainstay of therapy of disordered calcium homeostasis resulting from the endogenous overproduction of active vitamin D metabolites. Institution of glucocorticoid therapy results in a prompt decrease in the circulating $1,25(OH)_2D$ concentration (within 3 days), presumably by inhibition of macrophage 1α-hydroxylase activity. Normalization of the serum or urine calcium usually occurs within a matter of days.[28] Failure to normalize the serum calcium after 10 days of therapy suggests the coexistence of another hypercalcemic process (e.g., hyperparathyroidism or humoral hypercalcemia of malignancy). The dietary intake of calcium and vitamin D should be limited in such patients, as should sunlight (UV light) exposure. After a hypercalcemic episode, urinary calcium excretion rates should be monitored intermittently to detect recurrence.

TREATMENT OF HYPERCALCEMIA/HYPERCALCIURIA IN OTHER DISORDERS ASSOCIATED WITH OVERPRODUCTION OF $1,25(OH)_2D$

Glucocorticoids may also be effective in the management of vitamin D–mediated hypercalcemia or hypercalciuria associated with lymphoma or granuloma-forming diseases other than sarcoidosis. However, steroid therapy may not always be appropriate for these diseases, and consequently, alternative treatments may be necessary. Chloroquine [32,43] or hydroxychloroquine[44] and ketoconazole[33] are also capable of reducing the serum $1,25(OH)_2D$ and calcium concentrations, although chloroquine and its analogs do not seem to be effective in lymphoma patients.[44] Because of the limited experience with these drugs as antihypercalcemic agents, they should be restricted to patients in whom steroid therapy is unsuccessful or contraindicated. The theoretic advantage of these agents over glucocorticoids is that correction of the serum $1,25(OH)_2D$ concentration should result in rapid recovery of at least some of the BMD lost to the disease.[45] The use of the newer bisphosphonates in blocking bone resorption in hypercalcemic/hypercalciuric patients with sarcoidosis is still unknown.

REFERENCES

1. Harrell GT, Fisher S 1939 Blood chemical changes in Boeck's sarcoid with particular reference to protein, calcium and phosphates values. J Clin Invest 18:687–693.
2. Studdy PR, Bird R, Neville E, James DG 1980 Biochemical findings in sarcoidosis. J Clin Pathol 33:528–533.
3. Bell NH, Gill JR Jr, Bartter FC 1964 On the abnormal calcium absorption in sarcoidosis: Evidence for increased sensitivity to vitamin D. Am J Med 36:500–513.
4. Fallon MD, Perry HM 3rd, Teitelbaum SL 1981 Skeletal sarcoidosis with osteopenia. Metab Bone Dis Relat Res 3:171–174.
5. Rizzato GL, Montemurro L, Fraioli P 1992 Bone mineral content in sarcoidosis. Semin Resp Med 13:411–423.
6. Adams JS, Singer FR, Gacad MA, Sharma OP, Hayes MJ, Vouros P, Holick MF 1985 Isolation and structural identification of 1,25-dihydroxyvitamin D3 produced by cultured alveolar macrophages in sarcoidosis. J Clin Endocrinol Metab 60:960–966.
7. Kozeny GA, Barbato AL, Bansal VK, Vertuno LL, Hano JE 1984 Hypercalcemia associated with silicone-induced granulomas. N Engl J Med 311:1103–1105.
8. Albitar S, Genin R, Fen-Chong M, Schohn D, Riviere JP, Serveaux MO, Chuet C, Bourgeon B 1997 Multisystem granulomatous injuries 28 years after paraffin injections. Nephrol Dial Transplant 12:1974–1976.
9. Stoeckle JD, Hardy HL, Weber AL 1969 Chronic beryllium disease. Long-term follow-up of sixty cases and selective review of the literature. Am J Med 46:545–561.
10. Edelson GW, Talpos GB, Bone HG III 1993 Hypercalcemia associated with Wegener's granulomatosis and hyperparathyroidism: Etiology and management. Am J Nephrol 13:275–277.
11. Jurney TH 1984 Hypercalcemia in a patient with eosinophilic granuloma. Am J Med 76:527–528.
12. Cook JS, Stone MS, Hansen JR 1992 Hypercalcemia in association with subcutaneous fat necrosis of the newborn: Studies of calcium-regulating hormones. Pediatrics 90:93–96.
13. Abreu MT, Kantorovich V, Vasiliauskas EA, Gruntmanis U, Matuk R, Daigle K, Thomas LS, Chen S, Zehnder D, Lin Y, Yang H, Hewison M, Adams JS 2004 Measurement of vitamin D levels in inflammatory bodel Disease (IBD) patients reveals a subset of Crohn's disease patients with elevated 1,25-dihydroxyvitamin D and low bone mineral density. Gut 53:1129–1136.
14. Gkonos PJ, London R, Hendler ED 1984 Hypercalcemia and elevated 1,25-dihydroxyvitamin D levels in a patient with end-stage renal disease and active tuberculosis. N Engl J Med 311:1683–1685.
15. Kantarjian HM, Saad MF, Estey EH, Sellin RV, Samaan NA 1983 Hypercalcemia in disseminated candidiasis. Am J Med 74:721–724.
16. Hoffman VN, Korzeniowski OM 1986 Leprosy, hypercalcemia, and elevated serum calcitriol levels. Ann Intern Med 105:890–891.
17. Walker JV, Baran D, Yakub N, Freeman RB 1977 Histoplasmosis with hypercalcemia, renal failure, and papillary necrosis. Confusion with sarcoidosis. Jama 237:1350–1352.
18. Parker MS, Dokoh S, Woolfenden JM, Buchsbaum HW 1984 Hypercalcemia in coccidioidomycosis. Am J Med 76:341–344.
19. Bosch X 1988 Hypercalcemia due to endogenous overproduction of active vitamin D in identical twins with cat-scratch disease. Jama 279:532–534.
20. Adams JS, Fernandez M, Gacad MA, Gill PS, Endres DB, Rasheed S, Singer FR 1989 Vitamin D metabolite-mediated hypercalcemia and hypercalciuria patients with AIDS- and non-AIDS-associated lymphoma. Blood 73:235–239.
21. Seymour JF, Gagel RF 1993 Calcitriol: The major humoral mediator of hypercalcemia in Hodgkin's disease and non-Hodgkin's lymphomas. Blood 82:1383–1394.
22. Scheinman SJ, Kelberman MW, Tatum AH, Zamkoff KW 1991 Hypercalcemia with excess serum 1,25 dihydroxyvitamin D in lymphomatoid granulomatosis/angiocentric lymphoma. Am J Med Sci 301:178–181.
23. Evans KN, Shah F, Innes BA, Bulmer JN, Adams JS, Taylor H, Kilby MD, Hewison M 2004 Increased expression of 25-hydroxyvitamin D-1α-hydroxylase in dysgerminomas: A novel form of humoral hypercalcemia of malignancy. Am J Pathol 165:807–813.
24. Barbour GL, Coburn JW, Slatopolsky E, Norman AW, Horst RL 1981 Hypercalcemia in an anephric patient with sarcoidosis: Evidence for extrarenal generation of 1,25-dihydroxyvitamin D. N Engl J Med 305:440–443.
25. Hewison M, Kantorovich V, Van Herle AJ, Cohan P, Zehnder D, Adams JS 2003 Vitamin D-mediated hypercalcemia in lymphoma: Evidence for hormone production by tumor-adjacent macrophages. J Bone Miner Res 18:579–582.
26. Townsend K, Banwell CM, Guy M, Colston KW, Mansi JL, Stewart PM, Campbell MJ, Hewison M 2005 Autocrine metabolism of vitamin D in normal and malignant breast tissue. Clin Cancer Res 11:3579–3586.
27. Sandler LM, Winearls CJ, Fraher LJ, Clemens TL, Smith R, O'Riordan JLH 1984 Studies of the hypercalcaemia of sarcoidosis: Effect of steroids and exogenous vitamin D3 on the circulating concentrations of 1,25-dihydroxy vitamin D3. Q J Med 53:165–180.
28. Meyrier A, Valeyre D, Bouillon R, Paillard F, Battesti JP, Georges R 1985 Resorptive versus absorptive hypercalciuria: Correlations with 25-hydroxy vitamin D3 and 1,25-dihydroxy vitamin D3 and parameters of disease activity. Q J Med 54:269–281.
29. Insogna KL, Dreyer BE, Mitnick M, Ellison AF, Broadus AE 1988 Enhanced production rate of 1,25-dihydroxyvitamin D in sarcoidosis. J Clin Endocrinol Metab 66:72–75.
30. Reichel H, Koeffler HP, Bishop JE, Norman AW 1987 25-Hydroxyvitamin D3 metabolism by lipopolysaccharide-stimulated normal human macrophages. J Clin Endocrinol Metab 64:1–9.
31. Adams JS, Gacad MA 1985 Characterization of 1 alpha-hydroxylation of vitamin D3 sterols by cultured alveolar macrophages from patients with sarcoidosis. J Exp Med 161:755–765.
32. Adams JS, Diz MM, Sharma OP 1989 Effective reduction in the serum 1,25-dihydroxyvitamin D and calcium concentration in sarcoidosis-associated hypercalcemia with short-course chloroquine therapy. Ann Intern Med 111:437–438.
33. Adams JS, Sharma OP, Diz MM, Endres DB 1990 Ketoconazole decreases the serum 1,25-dihydroxyvitamin D and calcium concentration in sarcoidosis-associated hypercalcemia. J Clin Endocrinol Metab 70:1090–1095.
34. Fu GK, Lin D, Zhang MY, Bikle DD, Shackleton CH, Miller WL, Portale AA 1997 Cloning of human 25-hydroxyvitamin D-1α-hydroxylase and mutations causing vitamin D-dependent rickets type 1. Mol Endocrinol 11:1961–1970.
35. Smith SJ, Rucka AK, Berry JL, Davies M, Mylchreest S, Paterson CR, Heath DA, Tassabehji M, Read AP, Mee AP, Mawer EB 1999 Novel mutations in the 1alpha-hydroxylase (P450c1) gene in three families with pseudovitamin D-deficiency rickets resulting in loss of functional enzyme activity in blood-derived macrophages. J Bone Miner Res 14:730–739.
36. Hewison M, Bland R, Zehnder D, Stewart PM 2000 1α-hydroxylase and the action of vitamin D. J Mol Endo 25:141–148.
37. Kong XF, Zhu XH, Pei YL, Jackson DM, Holick MF 1999 Molecular cloning, characterization, and promoter analysis of the human 25-hydroxyvitamin D3-1alpha-hydroxylase gene. Proc Natl Acad Sci USA 96:6988–6993.
38. Monkawa T, Yoshida T, Hayashi M, Saruta T 2000 Identification of 25-hydroxyvitamin D3 1α-hydroxylase gene expression in macrophages. Kidney Int 58:559–568.
39. Nagpal S, Na S, Rathnachalam R 2005 Noncalcemic actions of vitamin D receptor ligands. Endocr Rev 26:662–687.
40. Lemire JM 1995 Immunomodulatory actions of 1,25-dihydroxyvitamin D3. J Steroid Biochem Mol Biol 53:599–602.
41. Panda DK, Miao D, Tremblay ML, Sirois J, Farookhi R, Hendy GN, Goltzman D 2001 Targeted ablation of the 25-hydroxyvitamin D 1alpha-hydroxylase enzyme: Evidence for skeletal, reproductive, and immune dysfunction. Proc Natl Acad Sci USA 98:7498–7503.
42. Dardenne O, Prud'homme J, Arabian A, Glorieux FH, St-Arnaud R 2001 Targeted inactivation of the 25-hydroxyvitamin D3-1alpha-hydroxylase gene (CYP27B1) creates an animal model of pseudovitamin D-deficiency rickets. Endocrinology 142:3135–3141.
43. O'Leary TJ, Jones G, Yip A, Lohnes D, Cohanim M, Yendt ER 1986 The effects of chloroquine on serum 1,25-dihydroxyvitamin D and calcium metabolism in sarcoidosis. N Engl J Med 315:727–730.
44. Adams JS, Kantorovich V 1999 Inability of short-term, low dose hydroxychloroquine to resolve vitamin D-mediated hypercalcemia in patients with B-cell lymphoma. J Clin Endocrinol Metab 84:799–801.
45. Adams JS, Lee G 1997 Recovery of bone mineral density with resolution of exogenous vitamin D intoxication. Ann Intern Med 127:203–206.

Chapter 33. Miscellaneous Causes of Hypercalcemia

John J. Wysolmerski

Section of Endocrinology and Metabolism, Department of Internal Medicine, Yale University School of Medicine, New Haven, Connecticut

INTRODUCTION

The majority of cases of hypercalcemia are caused by disorders of PTH secretion, by malignancy or by granulomatous disorders. Each of these situations has been discussed separately in other chapters. This chapter will discuss less common causes of hypercalcemia.

PSEUDOHYPERCALCEMIA

Pseudohypercalcemia refers to instances in which the measured total serum calcium is elevated, but the patient is not truly hypercalcemic. This has been described in three settings: hyperalbuminemia, increased circulating levels of an abnormal, calcium-binding immunoglobulin, and pronounced thrombocytosis.

Albumin is the primary binding protein for circulating calcium ions. Therefore, abnormalities in the concentration of albumin can lead to abnormalities in the total concentration of calcium measured in the bloodstream. Although it is widely recognized that hypoalbuminemia can lead to hypocalcemia on this basis, it is less appreciated that hyperalbuminemia can result in hypercalcemia. Hyperalbuminemia principally occurs in the setting of volume contraction, and although the total calcium is elevated, the ionized calcium level is normal. Therefore, symptoms and signs of hypercalcemia are absent. Formulae have been developed to correct the calcium concentration for elevations or reductions in serum albumin, but these are not fully reliable. This is especially true in critically ill patients, and recent studies have suggested that the usual correction formulas systematically overestimate the incidence of hypercalcemia in intensive care units.[1] If knowing the true calcium concentration is important clinically, an ionized calcium level should be determined.

Abnormalities in calcium binding in the circulation have also been reported in multiple myeloma and Waldenstrom's macroglobulinemia.[2,3] These patients have an abnormal circulating immunoglobulin that binds calcium ions. In this setting, the globulin fraction, the total protein, and the total calcium levels are all elevated, but the ionized calcium level is normal. A similar situation has been reported when elevated immunoglobulins interfere with the total calcium determination by autoanalyzer. In this instance, the total calcium performed by autoanalyzer is elevated. However, both the total calcium level performed by atomic absorption and the ionized calcium level are normal. Because true hypercalcemia can complicate multiple myeloma, and because hyperparathyroidism has been reported to be associated with monoclonal gammopathy, care must be taken not to confuse pseudohypercalcemia and true hypercalcemia in these settings. As before, the absence of all signs and symptoms of hypercalcemia coupled with a normal ionized calcium level should allow for the discrimination between these possibilities and prevent inappropriate therapy directed at pseudohypercalcemia.

The third and final situation in which pseudohypercalcemia has been described is in patients with essential thrombocythemia and platelet counts >700,000.[4] One study reported that 15% of these patients had frank hypercalcemia when total calcium levels were measured. Ionized calcium levels were also elevated, and PTH levels were normal (not suppressed). Signs and symptoms of hypercalcemia were absent. The hypercalcemia was accompanied by hyperkalemia and resolved when platelet counts were normalized. It is thought that the hypercalcemia and hyperkalemia result from the secretion of these ions from the large number of abnormally activated platelets within the specimen tube as a clot is formed. Consistent with this thought, calcium and potassium levels have been found to improve if plasma samples are analyzed instead of serum samples. As in the previous two disorders, the elevation in serum calcium is an artifact that does not warrant specific therapy.

ENDOCRINE CAUSES OF HYPERCALCEMIA OTHER THAN HYPERPARATHYROIDISM

Thyrotoxicosis

Patients with thyrotoxicosis frequently manifest mild degrees of hypercalcemia.[5–9] It has been reported that the average calcium level rises in patients with hyperthyroidism, and up to 50% of patients with thyrotoxicosis present with serum calciums in the range of 10.5–11.5 mg/dl. A number of cases of coexistent Graves disease and hyperparathyroidism have also been reported. In this instance, the hyperthyroidism can exacerbate the degree of hypercalcemia and actually suppress the PTH values toward the normal range. However, thyrotoxicosis alone can clearly result in elevations of serum calcium, which can be severe. Thyroid hormone has been shown to exert direct effects on bone turnover, increasing bone resorption rates. In addition, recent studies have suggested that thyroid-stimulating hormone (TSH) may directly suppress bone resorption. Perhaps because of a combination of these factors, thyrotoxicosis leads to excess bone resorption, which releases calcium into the circulation and suppresses PTH levels. Therefore, patients with hyperthyroidism as a sole cause of their hypercalcemia should have low PTH and 1,25-dihydroxyvitamin D [1,25(OH)$_2$D] levels with reduced renal reabsorption of calcium. Hypercalcemia may respond to β-adrenergic blockade and is fully reversible on correction of the thyrotoxicosis.

Pheochromocytoma

Hypercalcemia can occur in patients with pheochromocytoma for two reasons.[10,11] Most commonly, the hypercalcemia is a reflection of coexistent primary hyperparathyroidism in patients with multiple endocrine neoplasia (MEN)IIa. The diagnosis of pheochromocytoma should be considered before parathyroidectomy in all hypertensive patients with hyperparathyroidism. However, hypercalcemia that resolves after adrenalectomy has also been reported in sporadic cases of pheochromocytoma, suggesting that elevations in calcium can result from factors secreted by the tumor itself. There is some evidence that catecholamines can directly affect bone turnover and thus might be the cause of hypercalcemia. However, recent experience has shown that, like many other tumors of neuroendocrine origin, pheochromocytomas can secrete PTH-related protein (PTHrP) and produce hypercalcemia in a fashion identical to many carcinomas.

Dr. Wysolmerski has been a consultant for and received funding from Procter and Gamble Pharmaceuticals.

Adrenal Insufficiency

Hypercalcemia has been associated with adrenal insufficiency, especially in patients presenting with Addisonian crisis.[12–14] It has been seen both in patients with primary as well as secondary adrenal insufficiency. The pathophysiology is unclear. Hypercalcemia may result in part from hemoconcentration and hypovolemia, but some reports have noted increases in ionized as well as total calcium. More recent reports have described suppressed values for PTH and $1,25(OH)_2D$. It is interesting that the human homolog of stanniocalcin, a calcium-lowering agent in fish, has recently been shown to be expressed in the adrenal gland.[15] It is not yet clear if this hormone has any effects on systemic calcium metabolism in humans. Hypercalcemia responds to intravenous fluids and glucocorticoid replacement.

Islet Cell Tumors of the Pancreas/Vasoactive Intestinal Polypeptideomas

Islet cell tumors can be associated with hypercalcemia caused by MEN1 syndrome and coexistent primary hyperparathyroidism. They have also been found to secrete PTHrP and mimic humoral hypercalcemia of malignancy (HHM) syndrome.[16] In addition, up to 90% of patients with islet cell tumors producing vasoactive intestinal polypeptide (VIP) develop hypercalcemia.[17–19] These patients typically present with the syndrome of watery diarrhea, hypokalemia, and achlorhydria. The pathophysiology of the hypercalcemia in this syndrome has not been fully defined. However, recent studies have shown that PTH levels are suppressed during hypercalcemia, suggesting a PTH-independent mechanism. Furthermore, VIP and VIP receptors have been shown to be present in bone cells and exert effects on bone turnover in cell culture systems. Therefore, it is likely that the hypercalcemia is caused by direct effects of VIP acting on the skeleton.

MILK-ALKALI SYNDROME

The milk-alkali syndrome results from the ingestion of large amounts of calcium and absorbable alkali.[20–22] It was first described in the 1930s as a complication of ulcer therapy, which, at the time, required the ingestion of large quantities of milk together with sodium bicarbonate. It continued to be seen commonly in the era before the introduction of H_2-blockers when peptic ulcer disease was often treated with up to 20–60 g of calcium carbonate per day. With the introduction of nonabsorbable antacids and then H_2-blockers and proton pump inhibitors, this syndrome became rare. However, in recent years, it has become more common again because of the widespread use of calcium carbonate to treat or prevent osteoporosis. The syndrome has also been documented in betel-nut users, who sometimes mix the nuts with oyster shell calcium and alkali. One series from the University of Oklahoma reported that milk-alkali syndrome caused by calcium carbonate ingestion had become the third most common cause of hypercalcemia in hospitalized patients, representing 16% of hospital admissions for hypercalcemia over a 3-year survey.

Milk-alkali syndrome is classically defined as the triad of hypercalcemia, systemic alkalosis, and renal insufficiency. Hypercalcemia is often severe and symptomatic, with presenting values commonly between 15 and 20 mg/dl. Renal dysfunction can vary from mild to severe, and nephrocalcinosis often exists if the syndrome has been present for some time. Other sites of soft tissue calcification, as evidenced by band keratopathy, are common as well. In the older literature, patients were generally reported to be hyperphosphatemic, but in more recent series, phosphate levels have been reported to be normal or low. This most likely reflects the shift from milk, which has a high phosphate content, as a source of calcium to calcium carbonate, which does not. Although some confusion existed in the original literature, recent measurements using modern assays have documented that PTH levels are suppressed. The diagnosis of the syndrome requires a careful history especially of over-the-counter medication use.

The pathophysiology of milk-alkali syndrome is not fully understood, but most likely represents a viscous cycle set up by the ingestion of large amounts of calcium in the setting of volume contraction, systemic alkalosis, and progressive renal insufficiency. It is unclear what the threshold for the induction of hypercalcemia from oral calcium is, but it may be as low as 2 g of calcium daily. This varies with renal function and also between different subjects. By suppressing PTH and leading to volume contraction, hypercalcemia can limit the kidney's ability to excrete bicarbonate. There may also be direct tubular effects of calcium in this regard. In turn, systemic alkalosis can impair the renal excretion of calcium, and it also favors the precipitation of calcium phosphate in the kidney and other soft tissues. The development of nephrocalcinosis leads to progressive renal dysfunction which, in turn, contributes to the inability to excrete calcium and bicarbonate. Vomiting can precipitate the syndrome by causing volume contraction and the induction of systemic alkalosis. Likewise, the use of thiazide diuretics is a risk factor caused by these drugs' ability to interfere with calcium excretion and to cause volume contraction. The biochemical abnormalities are usually reversible with the discontinuation of oral calcium and alkali and with rehydration followed by forced saline diuresis. If renal failure is severe, making vigorous hydration difficult, hemodialysis against a low calcium bath has also been shown to be effective in lowering calcium levels. If the syndrome is acute, hypercalcemia and renal dysfunction resolve promptly and completely. In this setting, there can be rebound hypocalcemia and secondary hyperparathyroidism. In more chronic cases, especially if severe nephrocalcinosis is present, recovery takes longer and renal function may not completely normalize.

IMMOBILIZATION

The skeleton has the ability to sense mechanical stress and adjust bone mass to meet the physical load placed on it. Although the mechanisms underlying this skeletal "mechanosensing" are not fully understood, it seems that the coupling of loading and bone turnover is accomplished primarily through the actions of osteocytes and osteoblasts. One pathological consequence of the active adjustment of bone mass to mechanical demands is that unloading of the skeleton, as happens during the weightlessness of space flight or during prolonged and complete bed rest after orthopedic or neurologic injury, leads to reductions in bone mass.[23–27] In this setting, bone loss occurs because of an uncoupling of bone turnover; one sees a simultaneous reduction in the rate of bone formation and an increase in the rate of bone resorption. This, in turn, leads to the rapid efflux of calcium from skeletal stores, the suppression of PTH and $1,25(OH)_2D$ levels, and the development of hypercalciuria. If the amount of calcium released from the skeleton exceeds the amount of calcium that can be excreted by the kidney, hypercalcemia ensues. The two main risk factors for the development of hypercalcemia during immobilization seem to be (1) an impairment in renal function and (2) an antecedent elevation in bone turnover. Possible reasons for an increased baseline rate of bone turnover include a growing skeleton as seen in children, adolescents, and young adults, hyperparathyroidism, Paget's disease of bone, and "subclinical" or mild malignancy-associated hypercalcemia. For example, 25% of children or young adults with spinal cord injury develop hypercalcemia, whereas it is unusual in middle-aged patients with normal renal function, despite similar degrees of immobility. Although the classic presentation is in a child or young adult with spinal cord injury, recent reports have suggested that hypercalcemia is a more common complication of stroke and hip fracture than was previously appreciated. This may be a consequence of the age-related decline of renal function in these generally older populations. Another population reported to be at risk are those suffering serious complications after bariatric surgery.[28] Special care needs to be taken in the management of patients with hyperparathyroidism or Paget's disease who are put at bed rest, because severe elevations in serum calcium levels can occur. Hypercalcemia, if it is to occur, develops within days to weeks of complete bed rest and, if immobilization is prolonged, it can be associated with the development of upper and lower tract nephrolithiasis and osteopenia. The best treatment is the restoration of weight bearing, which normalizes calcium levels and bone turnover parameters. Passive range-of-motion exercises are not effective. If weight bearing is not possible, hydration, forced saline diuresis, and bisphosphonates have been shown to be effective at lowering calcium levels.

TOTAL PARENTERAL NUTRITION

Hypercalcemia has been reported in patients receiving total parenteral nutrition (TPN) for two reasons.[29–31] The first involves the addition of excessive amounts of calcium and/or vitamin D to the hyperalimentation fluid. This usually occurs early in the course of therapy (days to weeks) and resolves with the reduction of the amount of calcium in the TPN formula. However, there has also been at least one case report of nephrocalcinosis and hypercalcemia developing after several years of continuous TPN that responded to a reduction of the calcium content of the TPN. The second involves inadvertent aluminum toxicity derived from amino acid hydrolysates added to the hyperalimentation fluid. These patients presented after having been on TPN for months to years and were found to have hypercalcemia and low turnover osteomalacia, characteristic of aluminum bone disease. Now that aluminum has been removed from the TPN formulations, this syndrome has disappeared.

HYPERCALCEMIA SECONDARY TO MEDICATIONS

Vitamin D and Its Analogs

Hypercalcemia is a common complication of therapy with vitamin D preparations.[32–36] Vitamin D exerts effects on the intestine, skeleton, and kidney, and the hypercalcemia of vitamin D intoxication seems to be multifactorial, resulting primarily from a combination of increased gastrointestinal absorption of calcium and increased bone resorption. In the kidney, vitamin D primarily regulates the production and metabolism of calcitriol, although it has also been suggested to affect renal tubular calcium handling. Classically, patients with vitamin D intoxication present with hypercalcemia, hyperphosphatemia, and markedly elevated levels of 25-hydroxyvitamin D. Because PTH levels are appropriately suppressed, and because vitamin D and hypercalcemia both exert negative feedback on 1α-hydroxylase in the proximal tubules, $1,25(OH)_2D$ levels are usually either normal or only slightly elevated. The recommended daily allowance for vitamin D is 400–800 IU/day. The amount of vitamin D required to produce hypercalcemia has been estimated to be in excess of 25,000–50,000 IU/week. Therefore, it is unusual to see vitamin D intoxication from

over-the-counter nutritional supplements. However, there have been reports of hypercalcemia caused by poor quality control in the manufacture of these supplements. In these cases, the actual vitamin D content of the supplements was much higher than what was listed on the labels. There have also been outbreaks of vitamin D intoxication resulting from the accidental over-supplementation of vitamin D into cow's milk by commercial dairies. Nevertheless, the majority of cases of hypercalcemia occur in patients treated with pharmacologic doses of vitamin D or its analogs for the therapy of hypoparathyroidism, malabsorption, or renal osteodystrophy. Potent vitamin D analogs have also been used in topical preparations for the treatment of psoriasis and for the treatment of advanced prostate cancer. The most frequent setting in which vitamin D use leads to hypercalcemia remains the treatment of secondary hyperparathyroidism complicating renal osteodystrophy. However, newer analogs of vitamin D, such as 1α-hydroxy vitamin D_2 (Hectorol; Bone Care International, Middleton, WI, USA) and paricalcitol (Zemplar; Abbot Laboratories, North Chicago, IL, USA) seem to have less of a tendency to produce hypercalcemia. Treatment of vitamin D intoxication involves discontinuation of the vitamin D compound, volume expansion, and calciuresis. If hypercalcemia is severe or refractory to the above, treatment with glucocorticoids and/or bisphosphonates may be necessary. The duration of hypercalcemia after the withdrawal of the vitamin D source depends on the biological half-life of the compound used.

PTH

It has been known for some time that while continuous exposure to excess PTH leads to high bone turnover and bone loss, exposure to intermittent elevations in PTH lead to high bone turnover and an increase in bone mass.[37,38] These observations have now led to the therapeutic use of once daily injections of PTH(1–34) (teriparatide) for the treatment of osteoporosis. PTH(1–84) is currently being evaluated by the Food and Drug Administration for use in osteoporosis as well. Hypercalcemia was reported to occur in ~10% of patients in trials with teriparatide. The degree of hypercalcemia was generally mild, and it was usually transient. Sustained hypercalcemia responded to withholding the drug and/or reductions in the dose of teriparatide. Mechanistically, this is a form of drug-induced, iatrogenic hyperparathyroidism.

Vitamin A and Related Compounds

Vitamin A activates osteoclast-mediated bone resorption through mechanisms not well understood. The use of supplements containing vitamin A has been associated with low bone mass and fractures, and the ingestion of large doses (>50,000 IU/day) has been associated with hypercalcemia.[39–42] Like other types of "resorptive" hypercalcemia, PTH and $1,25(OH)_2D$ levels are suppressed in vitamin A intoxication. In the past, this disorder was only seen as the result of drug overdoses and in the exotic setting of arctic explorers consuming polar bear or sled-dog liver. However, more recently, hypercalcemia has been associated with the use of Vitamin A analogs, such as cis-retinoic acid and all trans-retinoic acid for the treatment of dermatologic conditions and for the therapy of neuroblastoma and hematologic malignancies.

Lithium

There have been many reports of hypercalcemia in patients receiving lithium carbonate.[43–45] The true prevalence of this disorder is uncertain, but retrospective series have suggested that hypercalcemia can occur in 5–40% of patients on the drug.

Prospective studies have documented that the average serum calcium level rises in patients started on lithium. The classic presentation resembles familial hypocalciuric hypercalcemia (FHH), with elevations in calcium and PTH levels and reductions in renal calcium excretion. In fact, studies in vitro and in vivo have shown that, just like FHH, the set point for calcium-regulated PTH release is shifted to the right in patients taking lithium. That is, there is an impairment of the ability of elevated calcium levels to suppress PTH release from the parathyroids. The mechanisms for this shift in Ca-PTH set-point are not completely understood, but these observations suggest that lithium may somehow modulate the function of the extracellular calcium-sensing receptor (CaR). There are also reports of an association between lithium use and the development of parathyroid adenomas. However, many of these cases are likely to be patients with previously mild or subclinical primary hyperparathyroidism whose hypercalcemia was worsened by the initiation of therapy with lithium. Hypercalcemia should resolve completely after the discontinuation of lithium.

Estrogens and Antiestrogens

The initiation of antiestrogens (or estrogens) has been shown to produce hypercalcemia in ~30% of patients with breast cancer metastatic to the skeleton.[46,47] This estrogen, or antiestrogen, flare is often associated with an increase in bone pain and seems to be related to transient increases in rates of bone resorption surrounding tumor deposits in the skeleton. The mechanisms leading to this flare are not fully understood, although recent work has suggested that estrogens and antiestrogens may modulate the production of PTHrP by breast tumors. The hypercalcemia can be treated with hydration, glucocorticoids, and bisphosphonates and is self-limiting. The occurrence of this flare has been shown to be a good prognostic sign and may be associated with subsequent tumor regression.

Thiazide Diuretics

Thiazide diuretics enhance calcium reabsorption in the distal tubule.[48] This effect on the kidney is used therapeutically to limit urinary calcium excretion in patients with hypoparathyroidism and nephrolithiasis caused by renal calcium wasting. However, in some patients, it can produce hypercalcemia. Other mechanisms may also contribute to the development of hypercalcemia; it has been reported in anephric patients on thiazides as well. The degree of hypercalcemia is usually mild and it resolves rapidly on discontinuation of the drug.

Aminophylline

Mild hypercalcemia has been reported in association with the use of aminophylline and theophylline.[49] This has been observed in the setting of acute loading doses that result in drug levels that exceed the therapeutic range. It has uniformly resolved when patients are placed on maintenance therapy and levels are kept within the therapeutic range. The mechanisms causing the hypercalcemia are unknown.

Growth Hormone

Growth hormone has been used in patients with AIDS, in burn patients, and in patients in surgical intensive care units to try to reverse the catabolic state of severe illness. The use of growth hormone in this way has been reported to cause moderate degrees of hypercalcemia with serum calcium values between 11.5 and 13.5 mg/dl. The mechanisms leading to the hypercalcemia are not well defined, but serum PTH and $1,25(OH)_2D$ levels have been reported to be low.[50,51]

8-Chloro-cAMP

8-Chloro-cAMP is a protein kinase A modulator developed as an anti-neoplastic agent. In phase I trials, hypercalcemia was a dose-limiting toxicity. It seems that the hypercalcemia occurs, in part, because of a PTH-like induction of renal $1,25(OH)_2D$ production.[52]

Foscarnet

Foscarnet is an antiviral agent used in the treatment of patients with AIDS. It has been reported to cause both hypocalcemia and hypercalcemia through unknown mechanisms.[53]

Fibrin Glue

Fibrin glue is a biological adhesive that contains fibrinogen, factor XIII, thrombin, and calcium and forms a fibrin clot on activation. Use of fibrin glue in the treatment of persistent pneumothorax in neonates was reported to cause hypercalcemia in 25% of patients in one report.[54] The mechanism of the hypercalcemia was not studied, but it was speculated to be related to the large amounts of calcium contained within the fibrin glue.

INFLAMMATORY DISEASES

As reviewed in another chapter, granulomatous disorders such as sarcoidosis and tuberculosis can lead to hypercalcemia because of the unregulated production of $1,25(OH)_2D$ by activated macrophages. In addition, several other inflammatory conditions such as systemic lupus erythematosus, juvenile rheumatoid arthritis, and recent hepatitis B vaccination have also been reported to cause hypercalcemia.[55–57] In patients with lupus, hypercalcemia has been reported together with lymphadenopathy and pleuritis. This so-called "hypercalcemia-lymphoedema" syndrome has sometimes been associated with elevated circulating levels of PTHrP. It has also been suggested that these patients might have circulating antibodies that activate the PTH receptor. In general, the mechanisms for hypercalcemia in patients with these inflammatory disorders are ill defined.

AIDS

AIDS patients can develop hypercalcemia for a variety of reasons. As already discussed, hypoadrenalism caused by infections, granulomatous disorders such as typical and atypical mycobacterial infections, and malignancy-associated hypercalcemia caused by lymphomas can all occur. In addition, skeletal infection with HIV, HTLV-III, and/or cytomegalovirus has been reported to lead to bone resorption and hypercalcemia.[58]

RENAL FAILURE

Hypercalcemia is a common occurrence in patients with chronic renal failure on hemodialysis and can result from hyperparathyroidism, vitamin D intoxication, calcium antacid overingestion, immobilization, aluminum toxicity, or combinations of these factors. In addition, hypercalcemia is particularly common in the first year after renal transplantation. Renal bone disease and related disorders of mineral homeostasis are discussed in greater detail elsewhere.

Hypercalcemia can also occur in acute renal failure.[59] This has classically been described during the recovery phase from acute tubular necrosis caused by rhabdomyolysis. It has been postulated that the severe hyperphosphatemia that accompanies this syndrome leads to the deposition of calcium phosphate in soft tissues and causes hypocalcemia and secondary hyperparathyroidism. When renal function recovers, soft tissue calcium is mobilized and there is a lag in the return of parathyroid function to normal. The combination of these two phenomena leads to transient hypercalcemia. Hypercalcemia has also been associated with granulomatous forms of interstitial nephritis caused by drug allergy.[60]

Continuous renal replacement therapy (CRRT) is a common therapy for the treatment of acute renal failure in critically ill patients. Systemic anticoagulation of this patient population with heparin is often associated with bleeding complications. Therefore, an increasingly common alternative for CRRT is regional citrate anticoagulation. This is involves the infusion of citrate and calcium and has been reported to lead to either hypocalcemia or hypercalcemia. Patients with liver dysfunction seem to be at increased risk for the development of hypercalcemia with these regimens.[61]

MAMMARY HYPERPLASIA

PTHrP is produced by mammary epithelial cells during lactation and it participates in the regulation of maternal calcium metabolism during this time. There have been several reports of hypercalcemia caused by elevated circulating levels of PTHrP associated with the development of significant mammary hyperplasia in pregnant or lactating women.[62] This has also occurred in the setting of breast hyperplasia and inflammation caused by cyclosporin use after organ transplantation. The hypercalcemia has resolved with the resolution of the breast hyperplasia or on reduction mammoplasty.

GAUCHER'S DISEASE

One case of hypercalcemia in a patient with Gaucher's disease and acute pneumonia has been reported.[63] This patient had a normal calcium before developing pneumonia, and the mechanisms of the elevation in calcium are unknown.

MANGANESE INTOXICATION

Workers exposed to toxic concentrations of manganese in contaminated workplaces or wells can develop severe hypercalcemia.[64] The mechanisms by which manganese exposure causes hypercalcemia are unknown.

END-STAGE LIVER DISEASE

Patients with end-stage chronic liver disease awaiting liver transplantation have been reported to develop hypercalcemia.[65] The mechanisms underlying the elevations in calcium are not known, but are likely to be multifactorial.

PRIMARY OXALOSIS

Adults with primary oxalosis have been reported to develop severe hypercalcemia.[66] There seems to be increased bone resorption, perhaps caused by the formation of oxalate-induced granulomas in the bone marrow. This would be consistent with the observation that PTH and $1,25(OH)_2D$ levels are low. However, the mechanisms underlying the development of hypercalcemia are not completely understood.

ACKNOWLEDGMENTS

This work was supported by National Institutes of Health Grants DK55501, DK069542, and CA094175.

REFERENCES

1. Slomp J, van der Voort PHJ, Gerritsen RT, Berk JAM, Bakker AJ 2003 Albumin-adjusted calcium is not suitable for diagnosis of hyper- and hypocalcemia in the critically ill. Crit Care Med 31:1389–1393.
2. Merlini G, Fitzpatrick LA, Siris ES, Bilezikian JP, Birken S, Beychok S, Osserman EF 1984 A human myeloma immunoglobulin G binding four moles of calcium associated with asymptomatic hypercalcemia. J Clin Immunol 4:185–196.
3. John R, Oleesky D, Issa B, Scanlon MF, Williams CP, Harrison CB, Child DF 1997 Pseudohypercalcemia in two patients with IgM paraproteinemia. Ann Clin Biochem 34:694–696.
4. Howard MR, Ashwell S, Bond LR, Holbrook I 2000 Artefactual serum hyperkalaemia and hypercalcaemia in essential thrombocythaemia. J Clin Path 53:105–109.
5. Burman KD, Monchick JM, Earll JM, Wartofski L 1976 Ionized and total serum calcium and parathyroid hormone in hyperthyroidism. Ann Intern Med 84:668–671.
6. Britto JM, Fenton AJ, Holloway WR, Nicholson GC 1994 Osteoblasts mediate thyroid hormone stimulation of osteoclastic bone resorption. Endocrinology 123:169–176.
7. Rude RK, Oldham SB, Singer FR, Nicoloff JT 1976 Treatment of thyrotoxic hypercalcemia with propranolol. N Engl J Med 294:431–433.
8. Xiao H, Yu B, Wang S, Chen G 2002 Concomitant Graves disease and primary hyperparathyroidism: The first case report in mainland of China and literature review. Chinese Med J 115:939–941.
9. Abe E, Marians RC, Yu W, Wu XB, Ando T, Li Y, Iqbal J, Eldeiry L, Rajendren G, Blair HC, Davies TF, Zaidi M 2003 TSH is a negative regulator of skeletal remodeling. Cell 115:151–162.
10. Mune T, Katakami H, Kato Y, Yasuda K, Matsukura S, Miura K 1993 Production and secretion of parathyroid hormone-related protein in pheochromocytoma: A participation of an α-adrenergic mechanism. J Clin Endocrinol Metab 76:757–762.
11. Taleda S, Elefteriou F, Levasseur R, Liu X, Zhao L, Parker KL, Armstrong D, Ducy P, Karsenty G 2002 Leptin regulates bone formation via the sympathetic nervous system. Cell 111:305–317.
12. Muls E, Bouillon R, Boelaert J, Lamberigts G, Van Imschoot S, Daneels R, De Moor P 1982 Etiology of hypercalcemia in a patient with Addison's disease. Calcif Tissue Int 34:523–526.
13. Vasikaran SD, Tallis GA, Braund WJ 1994 Secondary hypoadrenalism presenting with hypercalcaemia. Clin Endocrinol (Oxf) 41:261–265.
14. Wong RK, Gregory R, Lo TC 2000 A case of isolated ACTH deficiency presenting with hypercalcemia. Int J Clin Practice 54:623–624.
15. Miura W, Mizunashi K, Kimura N, Koide Y, Noshiro T, Miura Y, Furukawa Y, Nagura H 2000 Expression of stanniocalcin in zona glomerulosa and medulla of normal human adrenal glands, and some adrenal tumors and cell lines. Acta Pathol Microbiol Immunol Scand 108:367–372.
16. Asa SL, Henderson J, Goltzman D, Drucker DJ 1990 Parathyroid hormone-like peptide in normal and neoplastic human endocrine tissues. J Clin Endocrinol Metab 71:1112–1118.
17. Holdaway IM, Evans MC, Clarke ED 1977 Watery diarrhoea syndrome with episodic hypercalcaemia. Aust N Z J Med 7:63–65.
18. Lundgren P, Lundgren I, Mukohyama H, Lehenkari PP, Horton MA, Lerner UH 2001 Vasoactive intestinal peptide (VIP)/pituitary adenylate cyclase-activating peptide receptor subtypes in mouse calvarial osteoblasts: Presence of VIP-2 receptors and differentiation-induced expression of VIP-1 receptors. Endocrinology 142:339–347.
19. Lundberg P, Lie A, Bjurholm A, Lehenkari PP, Horton MA, Lerner UH, Ransjo M 2000 Vasoactive intestinal peptide regulates osteoclast activity via specific binding sites on both osteoclasts and osteoblasts. Bone 27:803–810.
20. Beall DP, Scofield RH 1995 Milk-alkali syndrome associated with calcium carbonate consumption. Medicine 74:89–96.
21. Fiorino AS 1996 Hypercalcemia and alkalosis due to the milk-alkali syndrome: A case report and review. Yale J Biol Med 69:517–523.
22. Wu KD, Chuang RB, Wu FL, Hsu WA, Jan IS, Tsai KS 1996 The milk-alkali syndrome caused by betelnuts in oyster shell paste. J Toxicol 34:741–745.
23. Stewart AF, Adler M, Byers CM, Segre GV, Broadus AE 1982 Calcium homestasis in immobilization: An example of resorptive hypercalciuria. N Engl J Med 306:1136–1140.
24. Roberts D, Lee W, Cuneo RC, Wittmann J, Ward G, Flatman R, McWhinney B, Hickman PE 1998 Longitudinal study of bone turnover after acute spinal cord injury. J Clin Endocrinol Metab 83:415–42.
25. Sato Y, Kaji M, Higuchi F, Yanagida I, Oishi K, Oizumi K 2001 Changes in bone and calcium metabolism following hip fracture in elderly patients. Osteopor Int 12:445–449.

26. Sato Y 2000 Abnormal bone and calcium metabolism in patients after stroke. Arch Phys Med Rehab **81:**117–121.
27. Massagli TL, Cardenas DD 1999 Immobilization hypercalcemia treatment with pamidronate disodium after spinal cord injury. Arch Phys Med Rehab **80:**998–1000.
28. Alborzi F, Leibowitz AB 2002 Immobilization hypercalcemia in critical illness following bariatric surgery. Obes Surg **12:**871–873.
29. Ott SM, Maloney NA, Klein GL, Alfrey AC, Ament ME, Coburn JW, Sherrard DJ 1983 Aluminum is associated with low bone formation in patients receiving chronic parenteral nutrition. Ann Intern Med **96:**910–914.
30. Shike M, Sturtridge WC, Tam CS, Harrison JE, Jones G, Murray TM, Husdan H, Whitwell J, Wilson DR, Jeejeebhoy KN 1981 A possible role of vitamin D in the genesis of parenteral-nutrition-induced metabolic bone disease. Ann Intern Med **95:**560–568.
31. Ikema S, Horikawa R, Nakano M, Yokouchi K, Yamazaki H, Tanaka T, Tanae A. 2000 Growth and metabolic disturbances in a patient with total parenteral nutrition: A case of hypercalciuric hypercalcemia. Endocrine J **47**(Suppl):S137–S140.
32. Holick MF, Shao Q, Liu WW, Chen TC 1992 The vitamin D content of fortified milk and infant formula. N Engl J Med **326:**1178–1181.
33. Jacobus CH, Holick MF, Shao Q, Chen TC, Holm IA, Kolodny JM, Fuleihan GE, Seely EW 1992 Hypervitaminosis D associated with drinking milk. N Engl J Med **326:**1173–1177.
34. Pettifor JM, Bikle DD, Cavalerso M, Zachen D, Kamdar MC, Ross FP 1995 Serum levels of free 1,25-dihydroxyvitamin D in vitamin D toxicity. Ann Intern Med **122:**511–513.
35. Martin KJ, Gonzalez E, Lindberg JS, Taccetta C, Amdahl M, Malhotra K, Llach F 2001 Paricalcitol dosing according to body weight or severity of hyperparathyroidism: A double-blind, multicenter, randomized study. Am J Kid Dis **38**(Suppl 5):S57–S63.
36. Koutkia P, Chen TC, Holick MF 2001 Vitamin D intoxication associated with an over-the-counter supplement. N Engl J Med **345:**66–67.
37. Cappuzzo KA, Delafuente JC 2004 Teriparatide for severe osteoporosis. Ann Pharmacother **38:**294–302.
38. Neer RM, Arnaud CD, Zanchetta JR, Prince R, Gaich GA, Reginster JY, Hodsman AB, Eriksen EF, Ish-Shalom S, Genant HK, Wang O, Mitlak BH 2001 Effect of parathyroid hormone (1–34) on fractures and bone mineral density in postmenopausal women with osteoporosis. N Engl J Med **344:**1434–1441.
39. Valente JD, Elias AN, Weinstein GD 1983 Hypercalcemia associated with oral isotretinoin in the treatment of severe acne. JAMA **250:**1899.
40. Suzumiya J, Asahara F, Katakami H, Kimuran N, Hisano S, Okumura M, Ohno R 1994 Hypercalcaemia caused by all-trans retinoic acid treatment of acute promyelocytic leukaemia: Case report. Eur J Haematol **53:**126–127.
41. Villablanca JG, Khan AA, Avramis VI, Seeger RC, Matthay KK, Ramsay NK, Reynolds CP 1995 Phase I trial of 13-cis-retinoic acid in children with neuroblastoma following bone marrow transplantation. J Clin Oncol **13:**894–901.
42. Michaëlsson K, Lithell H, Vessby B, Melhus H 2003 Serum retinal levels and the risk of fracture. N Engl J Med **348:**287–294.
43. Haden ST, Stoll AL, McCormick S, Scott J, Fuleihan GE 1979 Alterations in parathyroid dynamics in lithium-treated subjects. J Clin Endocrinol Metab **82:**2844–2848.
44. Rifal MA, Moles K, Harrington DP 2001 Lithium-induced hypercalcemia and parathyroid dysfunction. Psychosomatics **42:**359–361.
45. Dwight T, Kytola S, The BT, Theodosopoulos G, Richardson AL, Philips J, Twigg S, Delbridge L, Marsh DJ, Nelson AE, Larrson C, Robinson BG 2002 Genetic analysis of lithium-associated parathyroid tumors. Euro J Endocrin **146:**619–627.
46. Legha SS, Powell K, Buzdar AU, Blumen-Schein GR 1981 Tamoxifen-induced hypercalcemia in breast cancer. Cancer **47:**2803.
47. Funk JL, Wei H 1998 Regulation of parathyroid hormone-related protein expression of MCF-7 breast carcinoma cells by estrogen and antiestrogens. Bio Biophy Res Comm **251:**849–854.
48. Porter RH, Cox BG, Heaney D, Hostetter TH, Stinebaugh BJ, Suki WN 1978 Treatment of hypoparathyroid patients with chlorthalidone. N Engl J Med **298:**577.
49. McPherson ML, Prince SR, Atamer E, Maxwell DB, Ross-Clunis H, Estep H 1986 Theophylline-induced hypercalcemia. Ann Intern Med **105:**52–54.
50. Knox JB, Demling RH, Wilmore DW, Sarraf P, Santos AA 1995 Hypercalcemia associated with the use of human growth hormone in an adult surgical intensive care unit. Arch Surg **130:**442–445.
51. Sakoulas G, Tritos NA, Lally M, Wanke C, Hartzband P 1977 Hypercalcemia in an AIDS patient treated with growth hormone. AIDS **11:**1353–1356.
52. Saunders MP, Salisbury AJ, O'Byrne KJ, Long L, Whitehouse RM, Talbot DC, Mawer EB, Harris AL 1997 A novel cyclic adenosine monophosphate analog induces hypercalcemia via production of 1,25-dihydroxyvitamin D in patients with solid tumors. J Clin Endocrinol Metab **83:**4044–4048.
53. Gayet S, Ville E, Durand JM, Mars ME, Morange S, Kaplanski G, Gallais H, Soubeyrand J 1997 Foscarnet-induced hypercalcemia in AIDS. AIDS **11:**1068–1070.
54. Sarkar S, Hussain N, Herson V 2003 Fibrin glue for persistent pneumothorax in neonates. J Perinatology **23:**82–84.
55. Schurman SJ, Bergstrom WH, Root AW, Souid AK, Hannah WP 1998 Interlukin 1 beta-mediated calcitropic activity in serum of children with juvenile rheumatoid arthritis. J Rheumatol **25:**161–165.
56. Cathebras P, Cartry O, Lafage-Proust MH, Lauwers A, Acquart S, Thomas T, Rousset H 1996 Arthritis, hypercalcemia and lytic bone lesions after hepatitis B vaccination. J Rheumatol **23:**558–560.
57. Berar-Yanay N, Weiner P, Magadle R 2001 Hypercalcaemia in systemic lupus erythematosus. Clin Rheumatol **20:**147–149.
58. Zaloga GP, Chernow B, Eil C 1985 Hypercalcemia and disseminated cytomegalovirus infection in the acquired immunodeficiency syndrome. Ann Intern Med **102:**331–333.
59. Llach F, Felsenfeld AJ, Haussler MR 1981 The pathophysiology of altered calcium metabolism in rhabdomyolysis-induced acute renal failure. N Engl J Med **305:**117–123.
60. Wall CA, Gaffney EF, Mellotte GJ 2000 Hypercalcaemia and acute interstitial nephritis associated with omeprazole therapy. Nephrol Dial Transplant **15:**1450–1452.
61. Morgera S, Scholle C, Voss M, Haase M, Vargas-Hein O, Krausch D, Melzer C, Rosseau S, Zuckermann-Becker H, Neumayer HH 2004 Metabolic complications during regional citrate anticoagulation in continuous venous hemodialysis: Single-center experience. Nephron Clin Pract **97:**c131–c136.
62. Khosla S, van Heerden JA, Gharib H, Jackson IT, Danks J, Hayman JA, Martin TJ 1990 Parathyroid hormone-related protein and hypercalcemia secondary to massive mammary hyperplasia. N Engl J Med **322:**1157.
63. Bryne CD, Bermann L, Cox TM 1997 Pathologic bone fractures preceded by sustained hypercalcemia in Gaucher disease. J Inherit Metab Dis **20:**709–710.
64. Chandra SV, Seth PK, Mankeshwar JK 1974 Manganese poisoning: Clinical and biochemical observations. Environ Res **7:**374–380.
65. Gerhardt A, Greenberg A, Reilly JJ, Van Thiel DH 1987 Hypercalcemia, a complication of advanced chronic liver disease. Arch Intern Med **147:**274–277.
66. Yamaguchi K, Grant J, Noble-Jamieson G, Jamieson N, Barnes ND, Compston JE 1995 Hypercalcemia in primary oxalosis: Role of increased bone resorption and effects of treatment with pamidronate. Bone **16:**61–67.

Chapter 34. Hypercalcemic Syndromes in Infants and Children

Craig B. Langman

Department of Pediatrics, Feinberg School of Medicine, Northwestern University, and Kidney Diseases Department, Children's Memorial Hospital, Chicago, Illinois

INTRODUCTION

Blood ionized calcium levels in normal infants and young children are similar to those of adults, with a mean $\pm$ -2 SD $=$ 1.21 ± -0.13 mM. In neonates, the normal blood ionized calcium level is dependent on postnatal age.[1] In the first 72 h after birth, there is a significant decrease in the blood ionized calcium level in term newborns, from 1.4 to 1.2 mM; the decrease is exaggerated in preterm neonates. Levels of total calcium vary in parallel with the ionized calcium values, but additionally, are dependent on the level of serum albumin. Hypercalcemia is defined by a total blood calcium level >10.8 mg/dl.

Chronic hypercalcemia in young infants and children may not be associated with the usual signs and symptoms described elsewhere. Rather, the predominant manifestation of hypercalcemia is "failure to thrive," in which linear growth is arrested, and there is lack of appropriate weight gain. Additional features of chronic hypercalcemia in children include nonspecific symptoms of irritability, gastrointestinal reflux, abdominal pain, and anorexia. Acute hypercalcemia is very uncommon in infants and children; when it occurs, its manifestations are similar to those of older children and adults, with potential alterations in the nervous system, the conduction system of the heart, and kidney glomerular and tubular functions.

WILLIAMS SYNDROME

Williams et al.[2] described a syndrome in infants with supravalvular aortic stenosis and peculiar (elfin-like) facies; hypercalcemia during the first year of life also was noted.[3] However, the severe elevations in serum calcium initially described failed to appear with equal frequency in subsequent series of such infants. Other series of children with the cardiac lesion failed to show the associated facial dysmorphism. It is thought that there exists a spectrum of infants with some or all of these abnormalities, and a scoring system has been described to assign suspected infants as lying within or outside of the syndrome classification.[4]

Two thirds of infants with Williams syndrome are small for their gestational age, and many are born past their expected date of birth. The facial abnormalities consist of structural asymmetry, temporal depression, flat malae with full cheeks, microcephaly, epicanthal folds, lacy or stellate irises, a short nose, long philtrum, arched upper lip with full lower lip, and small, maloccluded teeth. The vocal tone is often hoarse. Neurologic manifestations include hypotonia, hyperreflexia, and mild-to-moderate motor retardation. The personality of affected children has been described as "cocktail party," in that they are unusually friendly to strangers. Other vascular abnormalities have been described in addition to supravalvular aortic stenosis, including other congenital heart defects and many peripheral organ arterial stenoses (renal, mesenteric, and celiac).

Hypercalcemia, if initially present, rarely persists to the end of the first year of life and generally disappears spontaneously.

Despite the rarity of chronic hypercalcemia, persistent hypercalciuria is not uncommon. Additionally, many of the signs and symptoms of hypercalcemia mentioned previously and in the introduction to this section have been noted in these infants. The long-term prognosis for patients with Williams syndrome seems to depend on features other than the level of blood calcium, such as the level of mental retardation and the clinical significance of the cardiovascular abnormalities. Approximately 25% of patients may have radioulnar synostosis, which may impede normal developmental milestones of fine motor activities of the upper extremities if not recognized.[5]

A search for the gene(s) responsible for Williams syndrome localized the cardiac component, supravalvular aortic stenosis, the long arm of chromosome 7.[6] It seems that translocations of the elastin gene may be responsible for isolated or familial supravalvular aortic stenosis,[7,8] whereas a heterozygous microdeletion of chromosome 7q11.23, which encompasses the elastin gene,[9] produces Williams syndrome. Rarely it may involve a defect of chromosome 11 [del(11)(q13.5q14.2)] or 22 [r(22)(p11→q13)].[10]

Despite the potential localization of the disorder of the deletion of the elastin locus on chromosome 7, the pathogenesis of the disorder remains unknown, although many studies focused on disordered control of vitamin D metabolism. Previous studies of affected children showed increased circulating levels of 25-hydroxyvitamin D after vitamin D administration,[11] increased levels of calcitriol {1,25-dihydroxyvitamin D [1,25(OH)$_2$D] } during periods of hypercalcemia[12] but not during normocalcemia,[13,14] or diminished levels of calcitonin during calcium infusion.[15] Although excess administration of vitamin D to pregnant rabbits may produce an experimental picture not dissimilar to that in humans with Williams syndrome, the overwhelming majority of children with Williams syndrome are not the result of maternal vitamin D intoxication.

IDIOPATHIC INFANTILE HYPERCALCEMIA

In the early 1950s in England, Lightwood[16] reported a series of infants with severe hypercalcemia. Epidemiologic studies revealed that the majority of affected infants were born to mothers ingesting foods heavily fortified with vitamin D. The incidence of the disease declined dramatically with reduction of vitamin D supplementation. Other cases have been described without previous exposure to excessive maternal vitamin D intake, and the incidence of idiopathic infantile hypercalcemia (IIH) has remained fixed over the past 20 years. Affected infants have polyuria, increased thirst, and the general manifestations of hypercalcemia previously noted. Severely affected neonates may have cardiac lesions similar to those seen in Williams syndrome and may even manifest the dysmorphic features of those infants and children. The distinction between the two syndromes remains problematic.[17] Other clinical manifestations include chronic arterial hypertension, strabismus, inguinal hernias, musculoskeletal abnormalities (disordered posture and mild kyphosis), and bony abnormalities (radioulnar synostosis and dislocated patella). Hyperacusis is present in the majority of affected children with IIH, but not Williams syndrome, and it is persistent.

As in Williams syndrome, disordered vitamin D metabolism

The author has reported no conflicts of interest.

with increased vitamin D sensitivity with respect to gastrointestinal transport of calcium has been posited as the cause of this disorder,[18] although the data are conflicting. We identified seven consecutive children with IIH in whom the presence of an elevated level of N-terminal PTH-related peptide (PTHrP) was shown at the time of hypercalcemia.[19] Its familial occurrence has been described.[20] Furthermore, in five of these children who achieved normocalcemia, the levels of PTHrP normalized or were unmeasurably low, and in one child with persistent hypercalcemia, the level of PTHrP remained elevated. No other nonmalignant disorder of childhood that we have examined, including two children with hypercalcemia from Williams syndrome, has had elevated levels of PTHrP, although a report of an infantile fibrosarcoma and hypercalcemia showed PTHrP production from the soft tissue tumor.[21] In contrast to the hypercalcemia of Williams syndrome, the level of blood calcium in IIH remains elevated for a prolonged period in the most severely affected children. After relief of the hypercalcemia, persistent hypercalciuria has been noted.[22] Therapy includes the use of glucocorticoids to reduce gastrointestinal absorption of calcium, as well as the avoidance of vitamin D and excess dietary calcium.

FAMILIAL HYPOCALCIURIC HYPERCALCEMIA

This disorder also is called familial benign hypercalcemia and has been recognized since 1972[23] as a cause of elevated total and serum ionized calcium. The onset of the change in calcium is commonly before 10 years of age and was described in newborns.[24]

NEONATAL PRIMARY HYPERPARATHYROIDISM

Primary hyperparathyroidism is uncommon in neonates and children,[25] with <100 cases reported. Additionally, only 20% of those reported cases occur in children younger than 10 years of age. Hypercalcemia in the first decade of life may more likely be caused by the other disorders discussed in this chapter. The presenting clinical manifestations are weakness, anorexia, and irritability, which are seen in a multitude of pediatric disorders. The association with other endocrine disorders occurs with decreased frequency in young children with primary hyperparathyroidism. Histological examination of the parathyroid glands show that 20–40% of affected children may have hyperplasia rather than the more typical adenoma in older individuals.

However, the neonate may show one unusual form of hyperparathyroidism. Neonatal severe primary hyperparathyroidism is now known to result from inheritance of two mutant alleles associated with the calcium-sensing receptor gene on chromosome 3.[26] Extreme elevations of serum calcium (total calcium ≥ 20 mg/dl; blood ionized calcium levels ≥ 3 mM) is a hallmark of the disorder, and emergency total surgical parathyroidectomy is required for life-saving reasons. An attempt to salvage one of the parathyroid glands and perform autotransplantation is suggested for such infants. Certain heterozygous inactivating mutations in the extracellular calcium receptor gene may still produce neonatal hypercalcemia,[27] leading to the conclusion that even the heterozygous state has important clinical implications for the neonate.

JANSEN SYNDROME

Jansen syndrome[28–31] presents in neonates with hypercalcemia and skeletal radiographs that resemble a rachitic condition. It is a form of metaphyseal dysplasia, and after infancy, the radiographic condition evolves into a more typical picture,

with resultant mottled calcifications in the distal end of the long bones (Fig. 1). These areas represent patches of partially calcified cartilage protruding into the diaphyseal portion of bone. The skull and spine may be affected also. The hypercalcemia seems to be lifelong. The life span of patients with Jansen syndrome remains uncertain, but there are several adult survivors with the syndrome.

Biochemical findings in patients with Jansen syndrome are consistent with primary hyperparathyroidism, but there are no measurable levels of PTH or PTHrP. The disorder results from a defect in the gene for the PTH/PTHrP receptor. One of three different amino acid substitutions produces a mutant receptor that is capable of autoactivation in the absence of ligand. This produces unopposed PTH/PTHrP actions in such patients and thereby explains the absence of circulating levels of either hormone. Such patients seem to be at risk for the development of the complications of hyperparathyroidism in the adult years. However, other patients have been given the diagnosis of Jansen syndrome without either hypercalcemia or the finding of a mutation in the gene for the PTH/PTHrP receptor.

MISCELLANEOUS DISORDERS

Subcutaneous Fat Necrosis

Michael et al.[32] reported the association of significant birth trauma with fat necrosis in two small-for-gestational-age infants who subsequently developed severe hypercalcemia (serum calcium > 15 mg/dl) and violaceous discolorations at pressure sites. Histological examination of the affected pressure sites in such patients showed both an inflammatory, mononuclear cell infiltrate and crystals that contain calcium. We also noted hypercalcemia in several children with subcutaneous fat necrosis associated with major trauma or disseminated varicella. The mechanism of the hypercalcemia is unknown, but it may be related to mildly elevated levels of $1,25(OH)_2D$[33] or excess prostaglandin E production.[34] The prognosis for infants and children with subcutaneous fat necrosis depends on the duration of the hypercalcemia. Reductions in serum calcium have been noted with the use of exogenous corticosteroids, saline, and furosemide diuresis and the avoidance of excess dietary calcium and vitamin D. Recurrence of hypercalcemia has not been seen.

Hypophosphatasia

This disorder is discussed in detail elsewhere in this book and is mentioned here only for completeness. Severe infantile hypophosphatasia is associated with markedly elevated serum calcium levels and a reduction in circulating alkaline phosphatase, increase in urinary phosphoethanolamine, and elevated serum pyridoxal-5-phosphate concentrations. The use of calcitonin in a neonate with hypercalcemia was reported as beneficial to long-term outcome.[35]

Sarcoidosis and Other Granulomatous Disorders of Childhood

Thirty percent to 50% of children with the autoimmune disorder sarcoidosis[36] manifest hypercalcemia, and an additional 20–30% show hypercalciuria with normocalcemia. Many of the presenting manifestations of children with sarcoidosis may be related to the presence of hypercalcemia. A recent report of hypercalcemia in twin children with cat-scratch disease,[37] a granulomatous disorder resulting from infection with *Bartonella henselae*, showed that the granuloma may represent a source of $1,25(OH)_2D$ production that leads to the

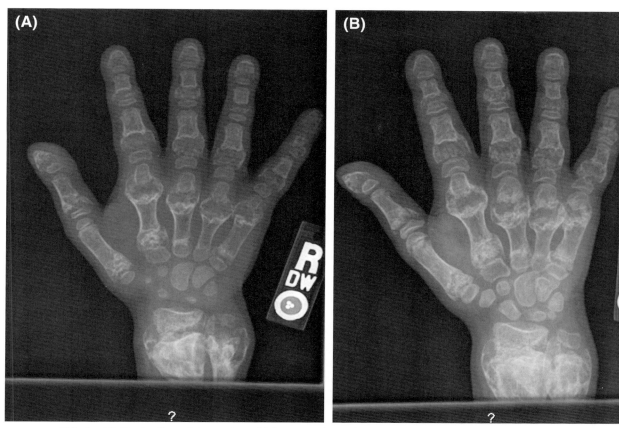

FIG. 1. (A) Hand radiograph in a patient with Jansen syndrome, 8 years of age. (B) The same patient at 12 years of age.

hypercalcemia. Successful therapy of these disorders reduces the circulating levels of that hormone to normal.

Limb Fracture

Isolated weight-bearing limb fracture[38] that requires immobilization for even several days may be associated with elevated blood ionized calcium levels and hypercalciuria in young children and adolescents. Although prolonged immobilization itself commonly produces hypercalcemia and hypercalciuria, the occurrence after short-term bed rest in children probably reflects their more rapid skeletal turnover.

Vitamin D (or Vitamin D Metabolite)

Hypervitaminosis D (vitamin D intoxication) produces symptomatic hypercalcemia. In childhood, vitamin D intoxication has been seen after excessively prolonged feeding of premature infants with a vitamin D–fortified formula,[39] after ingestion of improperly fortified dairy milk,[40,41] and in children receiving therapeutic vitamin D or vitamin D metabolites.[42]

An outbreak of hypercalcemia in eight patients was reported from the incorrect dosing of dairy milk with vitamin D,[40] and in addition, a defect was found in the concentrate used to fortify the milk (containing cholecalciferol rather than the expected ergocalciferol). These same investigators extended their measurements of the vitamin D content to both commercial dairy milks and fortified infant formulas, and they found that only 29% of the milks and formulas contained a vitamin D content within 20% of the stated amount.[41] These studies suggest that improved monitoring of the fortification process is

mandatory and may explain the rare finding of clinical vitamin D deficiency in children drinking fortified milk.

Children with renal osteodystrophy are commonly treated with 1,25-dihydroxyvitamin D_3 [$1,25(OH)_2D_3$] and develop hypercalcemia once every 12–15 treatment months, whereas the use of 25-hydroxyvitamin D_3 is associated with a lower incidence of hypercalcemia. Children with frank hypocalcemic disorders treated with $1,25(OH)_2D_3$ develop hypercalcemia at one third the frequency of children with renal osteodystrophy treated with any vitamin D metabolite.[42] Treatment with the parent vitamin D compound is associated with the production of hypercalcemia similar to the rate produced with calcitriol. However, the hypercalcemia associated with vitamin D is prolonged 4- to 6-fold in comparison with hypercalcemia with metabolite therapy because of retention in body fat stores.

Prostaglandin E

Bartter syndrome may result from one of several mutations in the genes for various sodium-linked chloride transporters.[43] A neonatal form may produce a marked increase in prostaglandin E production and lead to hypercalcemia, in part, from excessive bone resorption.[44] Such a disturbance in bone also may contribute to the hypercalcemia seen in neonates who receive prostaglandin E infusions for congenital cardiovascular diseases that mandate patency of the fetal ductus arteriosus.

Congenital Lactase Deficiency

In one study it was noted that 7 of 10 infants with congenital lactase deficiency manifested hypercalcemia within the first 3 months of life, and this was associated with renal medullary nephrocalcinosis.[45] A lactose-free diet was associated with return of elevated serum calcium levels to normal. The mechanism of the hypercalcemia remains unclear but may reflect the known effects of lactose to promote direct calcium absorption through the intestine.

Extremely Rare Reported Causes

Hypercalcemia has been reported twice in Down syndrome, once in infantile hypothyroidism, and once in oxalosis.[46]

REFERENCES

1. Specker BL, Lichtenstein P, Mimouni F, Gormley C, Tsang RC 1986 Calcium-regulating hormones and minerals from birth to 18 months of age: A cross-sectional study. II. Effects of sex, rage, age, season and diet on serum minerals, parathyroid hormone and calcitonin. Pediatrics 77:891–896.
2. Williams JCP, Barratt-Boyes BG, Lower JB 1961 Supravalvular aortic stenosis. Circulation 24:1311–1316.
3. Black JA, Bonham Carter RE 1984 Association between aortic stenosis and facies of severe infantile hypercalcemia. Lancet 2:745–748.
4. Preus M 1984 The Williams syndrome: Objective definition and diagnosis. Clin Genet 25:422–428.
5. Charvat KA, Hornstein L, Oestreich AE 1991 Radio-ulnarsynostosis in Williams syndrome: A frequently associated anomaly. Pediatr Radiol 21:508–510.
6. Ewart AK, Morris CA, Ensing GJ, Loker J, Moore C, Leppert M, Keating M 1993 A human vascular disorder, supravalvular aortic stenosis, maps to chromosome 7. Proc Natl Acad Sci USA 90:3226–3230.
7. Curran ME, Atkinson DL, Ewart AK, Morris CA, Keppert MF, Keating MT 1993 The elastin gene is disrupted by a translocation associated with supravalvular aortic stenosis. Cell 73:159–168.
8. Ewart AK, Jin W, Atkinson D, Morris CA, Keating MT 1994 Supravalvular aortic stenosis associated with a deletion disrupting the elastin gene. J Clin Invest 93:1071–1077.
9. Perez Jurado LA, Peoples R, Kaplan P, Hamel BC, Francke U 1996 Molecular definition of the chromosome 7 deletion in Williams syndrome and parent-of-origin effects on growth. Am J Hum Genet 59:781–792.
10. Joyce CA, Zorich B, Pike SJ, Barber JC, Dennis NR 1996 Williams-Beuren syndrome: Phenotypic variability and deletions of chromosomes 7, 11 and 22 in a series of 52 patients. J Med Genet 33:986–992.
11. Taylor AB, Stern PH, Bell NH 1982 Abnormal regulation of circulating 25OHD in the Williams syndrome. N Engl J Med 306:972–975.
12. Garabedian M, Jacqz E, Guillozo H, Grimberg R, Guillot M, Gagnadoux MF, Broyer M, Lenoir G, Balsan S 1985 Elevated plasma 1,25(OH)$_2$D$_3$ concentrations in infants with hypercalcemia and an elfin facies. N Engl J Med 312:948–952.
13. Martin NDT, Snodgrass GJAI, Makin HLJ, Cohen RD 1985 Letter. N Engl J Med 313:889–890.
14. Chesney RW, DeLuca HF, Gertner JM, Genel M 1985 Letter. N Engl J Med 313:889–890.
15. Culler FL, Jones KL, Deftos LJ 1985 Impaired calcitonin secretion in patients with Williams syndrome. J Pediatr 107:720–723.
16. Lightwood RL 1952 Idiopathic hypercalcemia with failure to thrive. Arch Dis Child 27:302–303.
17. Martin NDT, Snodgras GJAI, Cohen RD 1984 Idiopathic infantile hypercalcemia: A continuing enigma. Arch Dis Child 59:605–613.
18. Aarskog D, Asknes L, Markstead T 1981 Vitamin D metabolism in idiopathic infantile hypercalcemia. Am J Dis Child 135:1021–1025.
19. Langman CB, Budayr AA, Sailer DE, Strewler GJ 1992 Nonmalignant expression of parathyroid hormone-related protein is responsible for idiopathic infantile hypercalcemia. J Bone Miner Res 7:593S.
20. McTaggart SJ, Craig J, MacMillan J, Burke JR 1999 Familial occurrence of idiopathic infantile hypercalcemia. Pediatr Nephrol 13:668–671.
21. Michigami T, Yamato H, Mushiake S, Nakayama M, Yoneda A, Satomura K, Imura K, Ozono K 1996 Hypercalcemia associated with infantile fibrosarcoma producing parathyroid hormone-related protein. J Clin Endocrinol Metab 81:1090–1095.
22. Pronicka E, Rowinska E, Kulzycka H, Lukaszkiewicz J, Lorenc R, Janas R 1997 Persistent hypercalciuria and elevated 25-hydroxy-vitamin D$_3$ in children with infantile hypercalcemia. Pediatr Nephrol 11:2–6.
23. Foley TP Jr, Jarrison HC, Arnaud CD, Harrison HE 1972 Familial benign hypercalcemia. J Pediatr 81:1060–1067.
24. Marx SJ, Attie MF, Spiegel AM, Levine MA, Lasker RD, Fox M 1982 An association between neonatal severe primary hyperparathyroidism and familial hypocalciuric hypercalcemia. N Engl J Med 306:257–264.
25. Bernulf J, Hall K, Sjogren I, Werner I 1970 Primary hyperparathyroidism in children. Acta Pediatr Scand 59:249–258.
26. Pollak MR, Chou YH, Marx SJ, Steinmann B, Cole DE, Brandi ML, Papapoulos SE, Menko FH, Hendy GN, Brown EM 1994 Familial hypocalciuric hypercalcemia and neonatal severe hyperparathyroidism: Effects of mutant gene dosage on phenotype J Clin Invest 93:1108–1112.
27. Cole DE, Janicic N, Salisbury SR, Hendy GN 1997 Neonatal severe hyperparathyroidism, secondary hyperparathyroidism and familial hypocalciuric hypercalcemia: Multiple different phenotypes associated with an inactivating Alu insertion mutation of the calcium-sensing receptor gene. Am J Hum Genet 71:202–210.
28. Frame B, Poznanski AK 1980 Conditions that may be confused with rickets. In: Deluca HR, Anast CN (eds.) Pediatric Diseases Related to Calcium. Elsevier, New York, NY, USA, pp. 269–289.
29. Schipani E, Kruse K, Jüppner H 1995 A constitutively active mutant PTH-PTHrp receptor in Jansen-type metaphyseal chondrodysplasia Science 268:98–100.
30. Schipani E, Langman CB, Parfitt AM, Jensen GS, Kikuchi S, Kooh SW, Cole WG, Juppner H 1996 Two different constitutively active PTH/PTHrP receptor mutations cause Jansen-type metaphyseal chondrodysplasia. N Engl J Med 335:708–714.
31. Schipani E, Langman C, Hunzelman J, Le Merrer M, Loke KY, Dillon MJ, Silve C, Jüppner H 1999 A novel parathyroid hormone (PTH)/PTH-related peptide receptor mutation in Jansen's metaphyseal chondrodysplasia. J Clin Endocrinol Metab 84:3052–3057.
32. Michael AF, Hong R, West CD 1962 Hypercalcemia in infancy. Am J Dis Child 104:235–244.
33. Sharata H, Postellon DC, Hashimoto K 1995 Subcutaneous fat necrosis, hypercalcemia and prostaglandin E. Pediatr Dermatol 12:43–47.
34. Kruse K, Irle U, Uhlig R 1993 Elevated 1,25-dihydroxyvitamin D serum concentrations in infants with subcutaneous fat necrosis. J Pediatr 122:460–463.
35. Barcia JP, Strife CF, Langman CB 1997 Infantile hypophosphatasia: Treatment options to control acute hypercalcemia and chronic bone demineralization. J Pediatr 130:825–828.
36. Jasper PL, Denny FW 1968 Sarcoidosis in children. J Pediatr 73:499–512.
37. Bosch X 1998 Hypercalcemia due to endogenous overproduction of vitamin D in identical twins with cat-scratch disease. JAMA 279:532–534.
38. Rosen JF, Wolin DA, Finberg L 1978 Immobilization hypercalcemia after single limb fractures in children and adolescents. Am J Dis Child 132:560–564.
39. Nako Y, Fukushima N, Tomomasa T, Nagashima K, Kuroume T 1993 Hypervitaminosis D after prolonged feeding with a premature formula. Pediatrics 92:862–864.
40. Jacobus CH, Holick MF, Shao Q, Chen TC, Holm IA, Kolodny JM, Fuleihan GE, Seely EW 1992 Hypervitaminosis D associated with drinking milk. N Engl J Med 326:1173–1177.
41. Holick MF, Shao Q, Liu WW, Chen TC 1992 The vitamin D content of fortified milk and infant formula. N Engl J Med 326:1178–1181,.
42. Chan JCM, Young RB, Alon U, Manunes P 1983 Hypercalcemia in children with disorders of calcium and phosphate metabolism during long-term treatment with 1,25(OH)$_2$D. Pediatrics 72:225–233.
43. Karolyi L, Koch MC, Grzeschik KH, Seyberth HW 1998 The molecular genetic approach to Bartter's syndrome. J Mol Med 76:317–325.
44. Welch TR 1997 The hyperprostaglandin E syndrome: A hypercalciuric variation of Bartter syndrome. J Bone Miner Res 12:1753–1754.
45. Saarela T, Simila S, Koivisto M 1995 Hypercalcemia and nephrocalcinosis in patients with congenital lactase deficiency. J Pediatr 127:920–923.
46. Jacobs TB, Bilezikian JP 2005 Rare causes of hypercalcemia. J Clin Endocrinol Metab 90:6316–6322.

Chapter 35. Hypocalcemia: Pathogenesis, Differential Diagnosis, and Management

Rajesh V. Thakker

Nuffield Department of Clinical Medicine, Oxford Centre for Diabetes, Endocrinology and Metabolism, Churchill Hospital, University of Oxford, Headington, Oxford, United Kingdom.

INTRODUCTION

Hypocalcemia, which is frequently encountered in adult and pediatric medicine, has many causes (Table 1) that can be broadly subdivided into two groups according to whether the hypocalcemia is associated with low serum PTH concentrations (i.e., hypoparathyroidism) or with high PTH concentrations (i.e., secondary hyperparathyroidism). These hypocalcemic diseases are considered separately in subsequent chapters, and this chapter will review the general principles that determine calcium homeostasis and apply to the differential diagnosis and management of hypocalcemia.

CALCIUM HOMEOSTASIS, PATHOGENESIS, AND DIFFERENTIAL DIAGNOSIS OF HYPOCALCEMIA

The total body content of calcium in a normal adult is 1000 g; >99% of this is within the crystal structure of bone mineral and <1% is in the soluble form in the extracellular and intracellular fluid compartments. In the extracellular fluid (ECF) compartment, ~50% of the total calcium is ionized, and the rest is principally bound to albumin or complexed with counter-ions. The ionized calcium concentrations range from 1.00 to 1.25 mM, and the total serum calcium concentration ranges from 2.20 to 2.60 mM (8.8–10.2 mg/dl), depending on the laboratory. Measurements of ionized calcium, which has the main regulatory role, are not often undertaken because the methods are difficult and variable; thus, a total serum calcium concentration is the usual estimation. However, the usual 2:1 ratio of total to ionized calcium may be disturbed by disorders such as metabolic acidosis, which reduces calcium binding by proteins; metabolic alkalosis, which increases calcium binding by proteins; or by changes in protein concentration (e.g., starvation, cirrhosis, dehydration, venous stasis, or multiple myeloma). In view of this, total serum calcium concentrations are adjusted, or "corrected," to a reference albumin concentration; thus, the corrected serum calcium may be expressed to a reference albumin concentration of 41 g/liter (4.1 g/dl), and for every 1 g/liter (1.0 g/dl) of albumin above or below the reference value, the calcium is adjusted by ±0.016 mM (0.064 mg/dl), respectively. For example, a total serum calcium of 2.10 mM (8.4 mg/dl) with an albumin concentration of 35 g/liter (3.5 g/dl) would be would be equivalent to a corrected serum calcium of 2.20 mM (8.8 mg/dl), thereby correcting the initial apparent hypocalcemic value to a normal value.

The extracellular concentration of calcium is closely regulated within the narrow physiological range that is optimal for the normal cellular functions affected by calcium in many tissues. This regulation of extracellular calcium takes place through complex interactions (Fig. 1) at the target organs of the major calcium regulating hormone (PTH) and vitamin D and its active metabolites [e.g., 1,25-dihydroxy (1,25(OH)$_2$] vitamin D. The parathyroid glands secrete PTH at a rate that is appropriate to, and dependent on, the prevailing extracellular calcium ion concentration. Thus, hypocalcemic diseases may arise because of a destruction of the parathyroids or from a failure of parathyroid gland development, PTH secretion, or PTH-mediated actions in target tissues. These diseases may therefore be classified as being caused by a deficiency of PTH, a defect in the PTH receptor (i.e., the PTH/PTH-related protein [PTHrP] receptor), or an insensitivity to PTH caused by defects downstream of the PTH-PTHrP receptor (Fig. 1). The diseases may be inherited, and molecular genetic studies have identified many of the underlying genetic abnormalities (Table 2).

CLINICAL FEATURES AND INVESTIGATIONS

The clinical presentation of hypocalcemia (serum calcium < 2.20 mM or 8.8 mg/dl) ranges from an asymptomatic biochemical abnormality to a severe, life-threatening condition. In mild hypocalcemia (serum calcium = 2.00–2.20 mM or 8.0–8.8 mg/dl), patients may be asymptomatic. Those with more severe (serum calcium < 1.9 mM or 7.6 mg/dl) and long-term hypocalcemia may develop acute symptoms of neuromuscular irritability (Table 3); ectopic calcification (e.g., in the basal ganglia, which may be associated with extrapyramidal neurological symptoms); subcapsular cataracts; papilledema; or abnormal dentition. Studies should be directed at confirming the presence of hypocalcemia and establishing the cause.

The causes of hypocalcemia (Table 1) can be classified according to whether serum PTH concentrations are low (i.e., hypoparathyroid disorders) or high (i.e., disorders associated with secondary hyperparathyroidism). The most common causes of hypocalcemia are hypoparathyroidism, a deficiency or abnormal metabolism of vitamin D, acute or chronic renal failure, and hypomagnesemia. In hypoparathyroidism, serum calcium is low, phosphate is high, and PTH is undetectable; renal function and concentrations of the 25-hydroxy and 1,25-dihydroxy metabolites of vitamin D are usually normal. The features of pseudohypoparathyroidism are similar to those of hypoparathyroidism except for PTH, which is markedly increased. In chronic renal failure, which is the most common cause of hypocalcemia, phosphate is high, and alkaline phosphatase, creatinine, and PTH are elevated; 25-hydroxyvitamin D$_3$ is normal and 1,25-dihydroxyvitamin D$_3$ is low. In vitamin D deficiency osteomalacia, serum calcium and phosphate are low, alkaline phosphatase and PTH are elevated, renal function is normal, and 25-hydroxy vitamin D$_3$ is low. The most common artifactual cause of hypocalcemia is hypoalbuminemia, such as occurs in liver disease.

MANAGEMENT OF ACUTE HYPOCALCEMIA

The management of acute hypocalcemia depends on the severity of the hypocalcemia, the rapidity with which it developed, and the degree of neuromuscular irritability (Table 3). Treatment should be given to symptomatic patients (e.g., with seizures or tetany) and asymptomatic patients with a serum calcium of <1.90 mM (7.6 mg/dl) who may be at high risk of developing complications. The preferred treatment for acute symptomatic hypocalcemia is calcium gluconate, 10 ml 10% wt/vol (2.20 mmol or 90 mg of calcium) intravenously, diluted in 50 ml of 5% dextrose or 0.9% sodium chloride and given by slow injection (>5 minutes); this can be repeated as required to control symptoms. Serum calcium should be assessed regu-

---

The author has reported no conflicts of interest.

TABLE 1. CAUSES OF HYPOCALCEMIA

Low PTH levels (hypoparathyroidism)
- Parathyroid agenesis
  - Isolated or part of complex developmental anomaly (e.g., Di George syndrome)
- Parathyroid destruction
  - Surgery*
  - Radiation
  - Infiltration by metastases or systemic disease (e.g., hemochromatosis, amyloidosis, sarcoidosis, Wilson's disease, thalassemia)
- Autoimmune
  - Isolated
  - Polyglandular (type 1)*
- Reduced parathyroid function (i.e., PTH secretion)
  - PTH gene defects
  - Hypomagnesaemia*
  - Neonatal hypocalcemia (may be associated with maternal hypercalcemia)
  - Hungry bone disease (post-parathyroidectomy)
  - Calcium-sensing receptor mutations
High PTH levels (secondary hyperparathyroidism)
- Vitamin D deficiency*
  As a result of nutritional lack,* lack of sunlight,* malabsorption,* liver disease, or acute or chronic renal failure.*
- Vitamin D resistance (rickets)
  As a result of renal tubular dysfunction (Fanconi's syndrome), or vitamin D receptor defects
- PTH resistance (e.g., pseudohypoparathyroidism, hypomagnesaemia)
- Drugs
  - Calcium chelators (e.g., citrated blood transfusions, phosphate, cow's milk is rich in phosphate)
  - Inhibitors of bone resorption (e.g., bisphosphonate, calcitonin, plicamycin, gallium nitrate, cisplatinum, doxorubicin)
  - Altered vitamin D metabolism (e.g., phenytoin, ketaconazole)
  - Foscarnet
- Miscellaneous
  - Acute pancreatitis
  - Acute rhabdomyolysis
  - Massive tumour lysis
  - Osteoblastic metastases (e.g., from prostate or breast carcinoma)
  - Toxic shock syndrome
  - Hyperventilation
  - Acute severe illness

* Most common causes.

larly. Continuing hypocalcemia may be managed acutely by administration of a calcium gluconate infusion; for example, dilute 10 ampoules of calcium gluconate, 10 ml 10% wt/vol (22.0 mmol or 900 mg of calcium), in 1 liter of 5% dextrose or 0.9% sodium chloride, start infusion at 50 ml/h, and titrate to maintain serum calcium in the low normal range. Generally, 0.30–0.40 mmol/kg or 15 mg/kg of elemental calcium infused over 4–6 h increases serum calcium by 0.5–0.75 mM (2–3 mg/dl). If hypocalcemia is likely to persist, oral vitamin D therapy should also be started. It is important to note that, in hypocalcemic patients who are also hypomagnesemic, the hypomagnesemia must be corrected before the hypocalcemia will resolve. This may occur in the post-parathyroidectomy period or in those with alcoholism or severe malabsorption. While acute hypocalcemia is being treated, studies to establish the underlying cause (Table 1) should be undertaken, and appropriate treatment should be initiated.

MANAGEMENT OF PERSISTENT HYPOCALCEMIA

The two major groups of drugs available for the treatment of hypocalcemia are supplemental calcium, ~10–20 mmol (400–800 mg) calcium every 6–12 h, and vitamin D preparations. Patients with hypoparathyroidism seldom require calcium supplements after the early stages of stabilization on vitamin D. A variety of vitamin D preparations have been used. These include vitamin D_3 (cholecalciferol) or vitamin D_2 (ergocalciferol), 40,000–100,000 U (1.0–2.5 mg/day); dihydrotachysterol (now seldom used), 0.25–1.25 mg/day; alfacalcidol (1α-hydroxycholecalciferol), 0.25–1.0 μg/day; and calcitriol (1,25-dihydroxycholecalciferol), 0.25–2.0 μg/day. In children, these preparations are prescribed in doses based on body weight. Cholecalciferol and ergocalciferol are the least expensive preparations but have the longest durations of action and may result in prolonged toxicity. The other preparations, which do not require renal 1α-hydroxylation, have the advantage of shorter half-lives and thereby minimize the risk of prolonged toxicity.

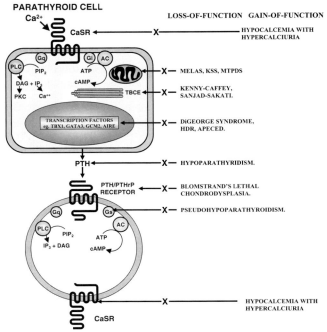

FIG. 1. Schematic representation of some of the components involved in calcium homeostasis. Alterations in extracellular calcium are detected by the calcium-sensing receptor (CaSR), which is a 1078 amino acid G protein–coupled receptor. The PTH/PTHrP receptor, which mediates the actions of PTH and PTHrP, is also a G protein–coupled receptor. Thus, Ca^{2+}, PTH, and PTHrP involve G protein–coupled signaling pathways, and interaction with their specific receptors can lead to activation of Gs, Gi, and Gq, respectively. Gs stimulates adenylyl cyclase (AC), which catalyzes the formation of cAMP from ATP. Gi inhibits AC activity. cAMP stimulates protein kinase A (PKA), which phosphorylates cell-specific substrates. Activation of Gq stimulates phospholipase C (PLC), which catalyzes the hydrolysis of the phosphoinositide (PIP_2) to inositol triphosphate (IP_3), which increases intracellular calcium, and diacylglycerol (DAG), which activates protein kinase C (PKC). These proximal signals modulate downstream pathways, which result in specific physiological effects. Abnormalities in several genes, which lead to mutations in proteins in these pathways, have been identified in specific disorders of calcium homeostasis (Table 2). (Adapted from Thakker RV 2000 Parathyroid disorders, molecular genetics and histology. In: Morris PJ, Wood WC (eds.) Oxford Textbook of Surgery. Oxford University Press, Oxford, UK, pp. 1121–1129.)

TABLE 2. HYPOPARATHYROID DISEASES AND THEIR CHROMOSOMAL LOCATIONS

Disease	Inheritance	Gene product	Chromosomal location
Isolated hypoparathyroidism	Autosomal dominant	PTH	11p15*
	Autosomal recessive	PTH, GCMB	11p15*, 6p23–24*
	X-linked recessive	SOX3	Xq26–27
Hypocalcemic hypercalciuria	Autosomal dominant	CaSR	3q21.1
Hypoparathyroidism associated with polyglandular autoimmune syndrome (APECED)	Autosomal recessive	AIRE-1	21q22.3
Hypoparathyroidism associated with KSS, MELAS and MTPDS	Maternal	Mitochondrial genome	
Hypoparathyroidism associated with complex congenital syndromes			
DiGeorge	Autosomal dominant	TBX1	22q11.12/10p
HDR syndrome	Autosomal dominant	GATA3	10p13–14
Blomstrand lethal chondrodysplasia	Autosomal recessive	PTH/PTHrPR	3p21.1-p22
Kenney-Caffey, Sanjad-Sakati	Autosomal recessive	TBCE	1q43–44
Barakat	Autosomal recessive†	Unknown	?
Lymphoedema	Autosomal recessive	Unknown	?
Nephropathy, nerve deafness	Autosomal dominant†	Unknown	?
Nerve deafness without renal dysplasia	Autosomal dominant	Unknown	?
Pseudohypoparathyroidism (type Ia)	Autosomal dominant parentally imprinted	GNAS1 exons 1–13	20q13.3
Pseudohypoparathyroidism (type Ib)	Autosomal dominant parentally imprinted	GNAS1—deletions within or upstream of locus	20q13.3

* Mutations identified only in some families.
† Most likely inheritance shown.
? Location not known.

KSS, Kearns Sayre syndrome; MELAS, mitochondrial encephalopathy, lactic acidosis, and stroke-like episodes; MTPDS, mitochondrial trifunctional protein deficiency syndrome; AIRE-1, autoimmune regulator 1; HDR, hypoparathyroidism, deafness, renal dysplasia; GCMB, glial cells missing B; GATA3, third member of family of transcriptional factors that bind to DNA sequence motif GATA; TBCE, tubulin-specific chaperone E.

Calcitriol is probably the drug of choice because it is the active metabolite and, unlike alfacalcidol, does not require hepatic 25-hydroxylation. However, in patients with low serum 25-hydroxy vitamin D concentrations because of vitamin D deficiency, the treatment of choice is a parent vitamin D compound such as cholecalciferol or ergocalciferol. Close monitoring of the patient's serum and urine calcium are required initially at ~1- to 2-week intervals, and at 3- to 6-month intervals once stabilization is achieved. The aim is to avoid hypercalcemia, hypercalciuria, nephrolithiasis, and renal failure. It should be noted that hypercalciuria may occur in the absence of hypercalcemia.

TABLE 3. HYPOCALCEMIC CLINICAL FEATURES OF
NEUROMUSCULAR IRRITABILITY

Paraesthesia, usually of fingers, toes, and circumoral regions
Tetany, carpopedal spasm, muscle cramps
Chvostek's sign*
Trousseau's sign†
Seizures of all types (i.e., focal or petit mal, grand mal, or syncope)
Prolonged QT interval on ECG
Laryngospasm
Bronchospasm

* Chvostek's sign is twitching of the circumoral muscles in response to gentle tapping of the facial nerve just anterior to the ear; it may be present in 10% of normal individuals.
† Trousseau's sign is carpal spasm elicited by inflation of a blood pressure cuff to 20 mmHg above the patient's systolic blood pressure for 3 minutes.

SUGGESTED READING

1. Thakker RV 2004 Genetics of endocrine and metabolic disorders: parathyroid. Rev Endocr Metab Dis **5:**37–57.
2. Deftos LJ 1998 Clinical Essentials of Calcium and Skeletal Disorders, 1st ed. Professional Communications, Caddo, OK, USA.
3. Thakker RV, Juppner H 2001 Genetic disorders of calcium homeostasis caused by abnormal regulation of parathyroid hormone secretion or responsiveness. In: DeGroot LJ, Jameson JL (eds.) Endocrinology, 4th ed. WB Saunders Company, Philadelphia, PA, USA, pp. 1062–1074.
4. Marx SJ 2000 Hyperparathyroid and hypoparathyroid disorders. N Engl J Med **343:**1803–1875.
5. Thakker RV 2000 Parathyroid disorders. Molecular genetics and physiology. In: Morris PJ, Wood WC (eds.) Oxford Textbook of Surgery. Oxford University Press, Oxford, UK, pp. 1121–1129.

Chapter 36. Hypoparathyroidism

David Goltzman[1] and David E. C. Cole[2]

[1]*Department of Medicine, McGill University and McGill University Health Centre, Montreal, Quebec, Canada; and* [2]*Departments of Laboratory Medicine and Pathobiology, Medicine, and Paediatrics (Genetics), University of Toronto, Toronto, Ontario, Canada*

INTRODUCTION

Hypoparathyroidism is a clinical disorder that manifests when the PTH produced by the parathyroid gland is insufficient to maintain extracellular fluid (ECF) calcium in the normal range or when adequate circulating concentrations of PTH are unable to function optimally in target tissues to maintain normal ECF calcium levels. The causes of hypoparathyroidism (Table 1) can be classified broadly as (1) failure of parathyroid gland development, (2) destruction of the parathyroid glands, (3) reduced parathyroid gland function caused by altered PTH production or secretion, and (4) impaired PTH action. The common aspect of these conditions is the presence of reduced, biologically active PTH. This results in characteristic clinical and laboratory features, which may be influenced, however, by the specific pathogenetic mechanism.

CLINICAL MANIFESTATIONS

The acute clinical signs and symptoms of hypoparathyroidism of any etiology include evidence of latent or overt increased neuromuscular irritability caused by hypocalcemia. The acute symptoms are more likely to occur during times of increased demand on the calcium homeostatic system (pregnancy and lactation, the menstrual cycle, and states of alkalosis). Chronically, patients may manifest muscle cramps, pseudopapilledema, extrapyramidal signs, mental retardation, and personality disturbances, as well as cataracts, dry rough skin, coarse brittle hair, alopecia, and abnormal dentition. The dental abnormalities may include defects caused by enamel hypoplasia, defects in dentin, shortened premolar roots, thickened lamina dura, delayed tooth eruption, and increased frequency of dental caries. Occasionally, patients may be edentulous. Finally, some patients may be diagnosed only after a low serum calcium is detected on routine blood screening.

LABORATORY ABNORMALITIES

The biochemical hallmarks of hypoparathyroidism are hypocalcemia and hyperphosphatemia in the presence of normal renal function. Serum calcium concentrations are often 6–7 mg/dl (1.50–1.75 mM) and serum phosphorus levels 6–9 mg/dl (1.93–2.90 mM). In most instances, an ionized calcium concentration of <4 mg/liter (1.0 mM) is also observed. Serum concentrations of immunoreactive PTH are low or undetectable except in cases of PTH resistance, where they are elevated or high normal. Serum concentrations of $1,25(OH)_2D$ are usually low or low normal, but alkaline phosphatase activity is unchanged. The 24-h urinary excretion of calcium is reduced, despite the fact that the fractional excretion of calcium is increased because the filtered load is low, caused by the hypocalcemia induced by decreased intestinal calcium absorption and diminished bone resorption. Nephrogenous cAMP excretion is low, and renal tubular reabsorption of phosphorus is elevated. Urinary cAMP and phosphorus excretion both increase markedly after administration of exogenous bioactive PTH except in PTH-resistant states. If hypoparathyroidism presenting at birth or in early childhood is not otherwise explained, serum magnesium should be measured. If serum magnesium is low, a more complete assessment of magnesium metabolism is warranted.

Calcification of the basal ganglia or other intracranial structures may be detected on routine radiographs or by enhanced imaging (CT scan or MRI), and electroencephalographic changes may be present. These are occasionally the only clinical evidence of disease. Detection of limited parathyroid gland reserve may rarely require an EDTA or citrate infusion study, which should only be conducted under close supervision.

CAUSES OF HYPOPARATHYROIDISM

Abnormal Parathyroid Gland Development

Congenital agenesis or hypoplasia of the parathyroid glands can produce hypoparathyroidism that manifests in the newborn period. Most often, this occurs as isolated or sporadic hypoparathyroidism and would have previously been considered idiopathic. There is now evidence that de novo activating mutations of the calcium-sensing receptor gene account for a number of these cases.

Familial isolated hypoparathyroidism may show autosomal recessive or X-linked inheritance patterns. Examples of the latter are rare. However, linkage analysis of the few affected families has narrowed the X chromosome locus to the Xq26–27 region. Recently, an autosomal recessive form of familial isolated hypoparathyroidism has been attributed to mutations of the *GCMB* (*glial cells missing B*) gene, which encodes a nuclear transcription factor that is predominantly expressed in the parathyroid gland and is critical for its development.

Maldevelopment of the parathyroid gland more often occurs as a feature of various multiple malformation syndromes. When other structures derived from the third and fourth branchial pouches are involved, thymic aplasia with immunodeficiency and congenital conotruncal cardiac anomalies are typically present. Originally called DiGeorge syndrome, this phenotype is now known to include a wide range of congenital anomalies, including distinctive facial features, cleft lip/palate, oropharyngeal anomalies, and other forms of congenital heart disease. In most cases, a microdeletion of chromosome 22 in the region of 22q11.21-q11.23 is the cause. Detection of the microdeletion by fluorescence in situ hybridization (FISH) is diagnostic, but a negative result does not exclude the possibility of a 22q abnormality. Individuals with the velocardiofacial (VCF or Schprintzen) syndrome also have microdeletions of 22q, and the two conditions overlap. Haploinsufficiency of a transcription factor gene, *Tbx1*, has been implicated as the common molecular defect, but there are no human examples to date of specific *Tbx1* mutations causing the DiGeorge phenotype. The possibility that other candidate genes or modifiers may be important is being pursued.

The clinical overlap has led to increasing use of the term, 22q11 syndrome, to include the varying phenotypes associated with the chromosomal microdeletion. In the VCF subgroup, anatomical anomalies of the pharynx are prominent, and hypernasal speech caused by abnormal pharyngeal musculature with or without cleft palate is typical. In most patients, some degree of intellectual deficit is present, and there is strong predisposition to psychotic illness (schizophrenia or bipolar disorder) in adolescents and adults. A number of web sites (http://www.vcfsef.org/ or http://www.geneclinics.org/profiles/22q11deletion/details.html) provide regularly updated information on this common and complex group of disorders.

Hypoparathyroidism is a part of the Barakat or HDR (hypoparathyroidism, nerve deafness, and renal dysplasia) syndrome. De-

---

The authors have reported no conflicts of interest.

TABLE 1. PATHOGENETIC CLASSIFICATION OF HYPOPARATHYROIDISM

I. Abnormal parathyroid gland development
  Isolated hypoparathyroidism
    X-linked (307700)*
    Autosomal recessive (241400)
      GCMB mutation (603716)
  DiGeorge syndrome (188400)
    Velocardiofacial (VCF) syndrome (192430)
      DiGeorge critical region 1—22q11.2 (602054)
    Barakat (HDR) syndrome—10p (146255 and 256340)
      DiGeorge critical region 2—10p13–14 (601362)
        GATA3 haploinsufficiency (131320)
  Hypoparathyroidism with short stature, mental retardation, and
  seizures
    Sanjat-Sakati syndrome (241410)
    Kenny-Caffey syndrome Type I (244460)
      TBCE mutations (604934)
  Mitochondrial neuromyopathies
    Kearns-Sayre syndrome (530000)
    Pearson syndrome (557000)
    tRNA-Leu mutations (590050)
  Long-chain hydroxyacyl-CoA dehydrogenase deficiency (600890)
II. Destruction of the parathyroid glands
  Surgical
  Autoimmune disease
    Polyglandular autoimmune disease (APECED) (240300)
      AIRE mutations (607358)
  Radiation
  Metal overload (iron, copper)
  Granulomatous infiltration
  Neoplastic invasion
III. Decreased parathyroid gland function caused by altered PTH
    production or secretion
  Primary
    Autosomal dominant (146200)
      Calcium-sensing receptor mutations (145980)†
      PTH mutation (168450.0001)
    Autosomal recessive
      PTH mutation (168450.0002)
  Secondary
    Activating antibodies to CASR
    Maternal hyperparathyroidism
    Hypomagnesemia
IV. Impaired PTH action
  Hypomagnesemia
  Pseudohypoparathyroidism

* Numbers from Online Mendelian Inheritance in Man'. (http://www.ncbi.nlm.nih.gov/entrez/query.fcgi?db=OMIM), accessible by browsing the Internet using the search term "OMIM."
† De novo mutations are common in sporadic hypoparathyroidism.

letions of two nonoverlapping regions of chromosome 10p contribute to a DiGeorge-like phenotype (the DiGeorge critical region II on 10p13–14 and the HDR syndrome (10p14–10pter). Deletion mapping studies in HDR patients defined a region containing the GATA3 gene that encodes a zinc finger transcription factor involved in vertebrate embryonic development. Microdeletions leading to GATA3 haploinsufficiency and point mutations in the gene itself have been identified in various HDR kindreds. Thus, GATA3 seems essential for normal embryonic development of the parathyroids, auditory system, and kidney.

All patients with otherwise unexplained persistent hypoparathyroidism in childhood should be karyotyped (±FISH for 22q11 or 10p microdeletions) and evaluated for other occult anomalies, including subclinical cardiac disease, renal dysplasia, hearing abnormalities, and gastrointestinal maldevelopment. Conversely, because the hypoparathyroidism may be very mild, transient, or greatly delayed in onset, demonstration of decreased parathyroid reserve in an otherwise healthy individual with a suspected syndrome may require provocative testing. Evidence of dominant inheritance may depend on detailed examination to identify other features (conotruncal cardiac anomalies, renal dysplasia, decreased cell-mediated immunity, etc.) in first degree relatives of the index case. Although many cases with the DiGeorge phenotype are the result of de novo deletions, autosomal dominant inheritance is not uncommon, and such families require detailed genetic counseling and follow-up. Other karyotypic abnormalities have been reported occasionally in patients with the DiGeorge phenotype, raising the possibility that other genetic loci are yet to be identified.

The Sanjat-Sakati syndrome is an autosomal recessive disorder of congenital hypoparathyroidism associated with short stature, mental retardation, and seizures. Distinctive dysmorphic features include deep-set eyes, depressed nasal bridge with beaked nose, long philtrum, thin upper lip, micrognathia, and large floppy ears. Described in Middle Eastern kindreds, it has been localized to chromosome 1q43–44 along with a recessive form of Kenny-Caffey syndrome, a condition dominated by radiologic findings that include calvarial hyperostosis and marked tubular stenosis of the long bones. The relationship between mutations of the TBCE (tubulin-specific chaperone E) gene, which encodes a protein required for folding of α-tubulin and its heterodimerization with β-tubulin, and hypoparathyroidism is unexpected, and further studies will undoubtedly offer new insights into parathyroid gland biology.

Hypoparathyroidism is also a variable component of the neuromyopathies caused by mitochondrial gene defects. Among the clinical conditions are the Kearns-Sayre syndrome (ophthalmoplegia, retinal degeneration, and cardiac conduction defects), the Pearson marrow pancreas syndrome (lactic acidosis, neutropenia, sideroblastic anemia, and pancreatic exocrine dysfunction), and mitochondrial encephalomyopathy. The molecular defects range from large deletions of the mitochondrial genomes in an extensive range of tissues (Pearson syndrome) to single base pair mutations in one of the transfer RNA genes found only in a restricted range of cell types (mitochondrial encephalomyopathy). Because renal magnesium wasting is frequently seen in these conditions, a readily reversible form of hypocalcemic hypoparathyroidism caused by hypomagnesemia should also be considered.

Another unusual myopathy associated with an inborn error of fatty acid oxidation (long-chain hydroxyacyl CoA dehydrogenase deficiency or LCHAD) may also be accompanied by hypoparathyroidism. This condition manifests as nonketotic hypoglycemia, cardiomyopathy, hepatic dysfunction, and developmental delay and is associated with maternal fatty liver of pregnancy.

Destruction of the Parathyroid Glands

The most common cause of hypoparathyroidism in adults is surgical excision of or damage to the parathyroid glands as a result of total thyroidectomy for thyroid cancer, radical neck dissection for other cancers, or repeated operations for primary hyperparathyroidism. Transient and reversible hypocalcemia after parathyroid surgery may be caused by (1) edema or hemorrhage into the parathyroids, (2) "hungry bone syndrome" caused by severe hyperparathyroidism, or (3) postoperative hypomagnesemia. Prolonged hypocalcemia, which may develop immediately or weeks to years after neck surgery, suggests permanent hypoparathyroidism. The incidence of this condition after neck exploration for primary hyperparathyroidism is usually <5%. In patients with a higher risk of developing permanent hypoparathyroidism, such as those with primary parathyroid hyperplasia or with repeated neck explorations required to identify an adenoma, parathyroid tissue may be autotransplanted into the brachioradialis or sternocleidomastoid muscle at the time of parathyroidectomy or cryopreserved for subsequent transplantation as necessary.

Rarely, hypoparathyroidism has also been described in a small number of patients who receive extensive radiation to the neck and mediastinum. It is also reported in metal overload diseases such as hemochromatosis (iron), thalassemia (iron), and Wilson's disease (copper), and in neoplastic or granulomatous infiltration of the parathyroid glands. In view of the fact that permanent hypoparathyroidism will only occur if all four parathyroid glands are affected, these are unusual causes of hypoparathyroidism.

Hypoparathyroidism may also occur as a presumed autoimmune disorder either alone or in association with other endocrine deficiency states. Antibodies directed against parathyroid tissue can be detected in 33% of patients with isolated disease and 41% of patients with hypoparathyroidism and other endocrine deficiencies. The genetic etiology of the autosomal recessive polyglandular disorder, APECED (autoimmune polyglandular candidiasis ectodermal dystrophy syndrome)—also known as APS1 (autoimmune polyglandular syndrome, type 1)—has been traced to mutations of the *autoimmune regulator* (*AIRE*) gene on chromosome 21q22.3, which encodes a unique protein with characteristics of a transcription factor. Showing either sporadic or autosomal-recessive inheritance, APECED has been associated with >40 different mutations of the AIRE gene, and updates can be found in the online mutation database (http://bioinf.uta.fi/AIREbase/).

This protein is expressed predominantly in immunologically related tissues, especially the thymus, and functional loss leads to breakdown of immune tolerance to organ-specific self-antigens. Clinically, the most common associated manifestations are hypoparathyroidism with mucocutaneous candidiasis and Addison's disease. Additional associations include insulin-dependent diabetes mellitus, primary hypogonadism, and autoimmune thyroiditis, as well as ectodermal dysplasia, keratoconjunctivitis, pernicious anemia, chronic active hepatitis, steatorrhea (malabsorption resembling celiac disease), alopecia (totalis or areata), and vitiligo.

The phenotype is quite variable, and patients may not express all elements of the basic triad, leading to the suggestion that the criteria used for deciding whether to screen for mutations be relaxed. Typically, however, the disease usually presents in infancy with candidiasis, followed by hypoparathyroidism in the first decade, and adrenocortical failure in the third decade. The hypoparathyroidism may present between 6 months and 20 years of age (average age, 7–8 years). Candidiasis may affect the skin, nails and mucous membranes of the mouth and vagina and is often intractable. Addison's disease can mask the presence of hypoparathyroidism or may manifest only in improvement of the hypoparathyroidism with a reduced requirement for calcium and vitamin D. By diminishing gastrointestinal absorption of calcium and increasing renal calcium excretion, glucocorticoid therapy for the adrenal insufficiency may exacerbate the hypocalcemia and could cause complications if introduced before the hypoparathyroidism is recognized.

The antibody epitopes responsible for the hypoparathyroidism are not well understood, but these are presumably not directed to epitopes in the calcium-sensing receptor (CaSR) and presumably initiate destruction of parathyroid tissue. Nondestructive antibodies to CaSR have also been described.

Reduced Parathyroid Gland Function Because of Altered Regulation

Altered regulation of parathyroid gland function may be primary or secondary. Primary alterations of parathyroid gland secretion are most commonly caused by activating mutations of the *CaSR* gene on chromosome 3q13.3-q21. These mutations, which decrease the set-point for calcium or otherwise increase the sensitivity to ECF calcium concentrations, cause a functional hypoparathyroid state with hypocalcemia and hypercalciuria (online CaSR database: http://www.casrdb.mcgill.ca/). When the mutations are transmitted through several generations, the clinical picture is one of familial isolated autosomal dominant hypocalcemia. Not infrequently, however, sporadic disease has been shown to arise from de novo activating mutations. The consequence of the activated parathyroid gland CaSR is chronic suppression of PTH secretion, whereas the activated CaSR receptor in kidney induces hypercalciuria that exacerbates the hypocalcemia. In many instances, however, the degree of hypocalcemia and hypercalciuria may be mild and well-tolerated. For subjects without symptoms, the greatest threat can be excessive intervention with vitamin D. However, individuals who are aware of the condition are more likely to identify early, nonspecific signs and symptoms of hypocalcemia and can avert the sudden, unexpected onset of more serious manifestations, such as tetany and seizures. Because of the therapeutic implications, molecular studies to identify *CaSR* mutations are now recommended for all cases of sporadic isolated hypoparathyroidism.

Isolated hypoparathyroidism has also been found with a single base substitution in exon 2 of the *PTH* gene. This mutation in the signal sequence of PTH apparently impedes conversion of pre-pro-PTH to pro-PTH, thereby reducing normal production of the mature hormone. In another family with autosomal recessive isolated hypoparathyroidism, the entire exon 2 of the *PTH* gene was deleted. This exon contains the initiation codon and a portion of the signal sequence required for peptide translocation at the endoplasmic reticulum in the process of generating a mature secretory peptide.

Secondary alterations in parathyroid regulation may occur as a result of activating autoantibodies to CaSR. These may occur in association with other autoimmune disorders such as Graves disease and Addison's disease and are generally not destructive to the gland. They do, however, inhibit PTH release and may cause hypercalciuria. The spectrum of epitopes responsible for the hypoparathyroidism is not well understood, but antibodies directed against the extracellular domain of CaSR have been found in more than one-half of patients with APS-1 and hypoparathyroidism with autoimmune hypothyroid disease. Although some studies have found a similarly high rate in patients with isolated acquired hypoparathyroidism, the positive rate in controls may be >10%. Some have argued that CaSR antibody assays are clinically indicated in acquired isolated hypoparathyroidism, whereas others urge caution, at least until better assay standardization has been achieved.

Secondary causes of parathyroid gland suppression include maternal hyperparathyroidism and hypomagnesemia. The infant of a mother with primary hyperparathyroidism generally develops hypocalcemia within the first 3 weeks of life, but it may occur up to a year after birth. Although therapy may be required acutely, the disorder is usually self-limited. Hypomagnesemia caused by defective intestinal absorption or renal tubular reabsorption of magnesium may impair secretion of PTH and in this way contribute to hypoparathyroidism. Magnesium replacement will correct the hypoparathyroidism.

Impaired PTH Action

Although, in theory, a bioinactive form of PTH could be synthesized and secreted by the parathyroid gland, this has not been documented. Rather, ineffective PTH action seems to be caused by peripheral resistance to the hormone's effects. Such resistance may occur secondary to hypomagnesemia or as a primary disorder (pseudohypoparathyroidism and its variants).

PATHOPHYSIOLOGY

Recently the availability of murine models of hypoparathyroidism has shed new light on the pathophysiology of this disorder. Hypoparathyroidism has generally been reported to be characterized by increased bone mass associated with decreased bone turnover caused by diminished circulating PTH. Analysis of mouse fetuses and neonates with targeted deletion of the *PTH* gene has shown reduced trabecular bone volume, reflecting the deficient anabolic action of endogenous PTH. With increasing age, however, bone mass in these animals increases, reflecting the deficient catabolic actions of the PTH, but even this change in bone mass in hypoparathyroid animals may be modified by dietary calcium intake. Furthermore, adult mice expressing the PTH null allele who are also lacking one allele encoding PTHrP exhibited reduced rather than increased trabecular bone. The increased trabecular bone volume in PTH deficiency therefore seems to be caused by diminished PTH-induced osteoclastic bone resorption coupled with persistent PTHrP-stimulated osteoblastic bone formation. These observations in mice may provide new insight into the complexity of both the hypoparathyroid state and of PTH action during development in humans and rodents, but confirmation in humans will be required.

THERAPY

The major goal of therapy in all hypoparathyroid states is to restore serum calcium and phosphorus as close to normal as possible. The main pharmacologic agents available are supplemental calcium and vitamin D preparations. Phosphate binders and thiazide diuretics may be useful ancillary agents. The major impediment to restoration of normocalcemia is the development of hypercalciuria with a resulting predilection for renal stone formation. With the loss of the renal calcium-retaining effect of PTH, the enhanced calcium absorption of the gut induced by vitamin D therapy results in an increased filtered load of calcium that is readily cleared through the kidney. Consequently, urinary calcium excretion frequently increases in response to vitamin D supplementation well before serum calcium is normalized. It is often necessary, or even desirable, to aim for a low normal serum calcium concentration to prevent chronic hypercalciuria. Avoidance of hypercalciuria is probably most important for patients with hypercalciuric hypocalcemia caused by activating mutations of the *CaSR* gene, and thiazides may be the preferred treatment. Hydrochlorothiazide therapy (25–100 mg/day in adults to 0.5–2.0 mg/kg/day in children) have been effective in reducing the vitamin D requirement, but potassium supplementation is necessary to offset the thiazide-induced hypokalemia. Recombinant human PTH (rhPTH or teriparatide) has recently become available, and it offers considerable promise as a long-term alternative in patients who do not respond to vitamin D and/or thiazide therapy. Furthermore, in the future, it is possible that calcilytics (small molecule inhibitors of CaSR function) may be of therapeutic use in some patients with autoimmune hypoparathyroidism caused by activating CaSR antibodies.

If serum calcium is normalized, and serum phosphorus remains >6 mg/dl (1.93 mM), a nonabsorbable antacid may be added to reduce the hyperphosphatemia and prevent metastatic calcification. Dairy products, which are high in phosphate, should be avoided, and calcium should be administered in the form of supplements. Generally, at least 1 g/day of elemental calcium is required.

A variety of vitamin D preparations may be used including (1) vitamin D_3 or D_2, 25,000–100,000 IU (1.25–5 mg) per day; (2) dihydrotachysterol, 0.2–1.2 mg/day; (3) 1α-hydroxyvitamin D_3, 0.5–2.0 μg/day; or intravenous calcitriol $[1,25(OH)_2D_3]$, 0.25–1.0 μg/day. Although vitamin D_3 and D_2 are the least expensive forms of therapy, they have the longest duration of action and can result in prolonged toxicity. Vitamin D_3 is generally of more reliable potency and is to be preferred. The other preparations listed above all have the advantage of shorter half-lives and no requirement for renal 1α-hydroxylation, which is impaired in hypoparathyroidism. Dihydrotachysterol is rarely used today, however, and calcitriol is probably the treatment of choice. In children, these preparations should be prescribed on a body weight basis. Close monitoring of urine calcium, serum calcium, and serum phosphate are required in the first month or so, but follow-up at 3- to 6-month intervals may be adequate once stable laboratory values are reached.

SUGGESTED READING

1. Daw SC, Taylor C, Kraman M, Call K, Mao J, Schuffenhauer S, Meitinger T, Lipson T, Goodship J, Scambler P 1996 A common region of 10p deleted in diGeorge and velocardiofacial syndromes. Nature Genet **13**:458–460.
2. Ding C, Buckingham B, Levine MA 2001 Familial isolated hypoparathyroidism caused by a mutation in the gene for the transcription factor GCMB. J Clin Invest **108**:1215–1220.
3. Eisenbarth GS, Gottlieb PA 2004 Autoimmune polyendocrine syndromes. N Engl J Med **350**:2068–2079.
4. Gidding SS, Minciotti AL, Langman CB 1988 Unmasking of hypoparathyroidism in familial partial DiGeorge syndrome by challenge with disodium edetate. N Engl J Med **319**:1589–1591.
5. Harvey JN, Barnett D 1992 Endocrine dysfunction in Kearns-Sayre syndrome. Clin Endocrinol (Oxf) **37**:97–103.
6. HRD/Autosomal Recessive Kenny-Caffey Syndrome Consortium 2002 Mutation of *TBCE* causes hypoparathyroidism retardation dysmorphism and autosomal recessive Kenny-Caffey syndrome. Nature Genet **32**:448–452.
7. Kifor O, McElduff A, LeBoff MS, Moore FD Jr, Butters R, Gao P, Cantor TL, Kifor I, Brown EM 2004 Activating antibodies to the calcium-sensing receptor in two patients with autoimmune hypoparathyroidism. J Clin Endocrinol Metab **89**:548–556.
8. Lienhardt A, Bai M, Lagarde JP, Rigaud M, Zhang Z, Jiang Y, Kottler ML, Brown EM, Garabedian M 2001 Activating mutations of the calcium-sensing receptor: Management of hypocalcemia. J Clin Endocrinol Metab **86**:5313–5323.
9. Miao D, He B, Karaplis AC, Goltzman D 2002 Parathyroid hormone is essential for normal fetal bone formation. J Clin Invest **109**:1173–1182.
10. Miao D, Li J, Xue Y, Su H, Karaplis AC, Goltzman D 2004 Parathyroid hormone-related peptide is required for increased trabecular bone volume in parathyroid hormone-null mice. Endocrinology **145**:3554–3562.
11. Xue Y, Karaplis AC, Hendy GN, Goltzman D, Miao D 2005 Genetic models show that parathyroid hormone and 1,25-dihydroxyvitamin D3 play distinct and synergistic roles in postnatal mineral ion homeostasis and skeletal development. Hum Mol Genet **14**:1515–1528.
12. Muroya K, Hasegawa T, Ito Y, Nagai T, Isotani H, Iwata Y, Yamamoto K, Fujimoto S, Seishu S, Fukushima Y, Hasegawa Y, Ogata T 2001 GATA3 abnormalities and the phenotypic spectrum of HDR syndrome. J Med Genet **38**:374–380.
13. Okano O, Furukawa Y, Morii H, Fujita T 1982 Comparative efficacy of various vitamin D metabolites in the treatment of various types of hypoparathyroidism. J Clin Endocrinol Metab **55**:238–243.
14. Pollak MR, Brown EM, Estep HL, McLaine PN, Kifor O, Park J, Hebert SC, Seidman CE, Seidman JG 1994 Autosomal dominant hypocalcemia caused by a Ca^{2+}-sensing receptor gene mutation. Nature Genet **8**:303–307.
15. Sato K, Hasegawa Y, Nakae J, Nanao K, Takahashi I, Tajima T, Shinohara N, Fujieda K 2002 Hydrochlorothiazide effectively reduces urinary calcium excretion in two Japanese patients with gain-of-function mutations of the calcium-sensing receptor gene. J Clin Endocrinol Metab **87**:3068–3073.
16. Seneca S, DeMeirleir L, DeSchepper J, Balduck N, Jochmans K, Liebaers I, Lissens W 1997 Pearson marrow pancreas syndrome: A molecular study and clinical management. Clin Genet **51**:338–342.
17. Sherwood LM, Santora AC 1994 Hypoparathyroid states in the differential diagnosis of hypocalcemia. In: Bilezikian JP, Marcus R, Levine MA (eds.) The Parathyroids. Raven Press, New York, NY, USA, pp. 747–752.
18. Stewart AF 2004 Translational implications of the parathyroid calcium receptor. N Engl J Med **351**:324–632.
19. Thakker RV 2001 Genetic developments in hypoparathyroidism. Lancet **357**:974–976.
20. Winer KK, Ko CW, Reynolds JC, Dowdy K, Keil M, Peterson D, Gerber LH, McGarvey C, Cutler GB Jr 2003 Long-term treatment of hypoparathyroidism: A randomized controlled study comparing parathyroid hormone-(1–34) versus calcitriol and calcium. J Clin Endocrinol Metab **88**:4214–4220.

Chapter 37. Parathyroid Hormone Resistance Syndromes

Michael A. Levine

Children's Hospital, Cleveland Clinic and Department of Pediatrics, Cleveland Clinic Lerner College of Medicine, Case Western Reserve University, Cleveland, Ohio

INTRODUCTION

The term pseudohypoparathyroidism (PHP) describes a group of disorders characterized by biochemical hypoparathyroidism (i.e., hypocalcemia and hyperphosphatemia), increased secretion of PTH, and target tissue unresponsiveness to the biological actions of PTH.

In the initial description of PHP, Albright et al.[1] focused on the failure of patients with this syndrome to show either a calcemic or a phosphaturic response to administered parathyroid extract. These observations provided the basis for the hypothesis that PHP was not caused by a deficiency of PTH but rather to resistance of the target organs, bone and kidney, to the biological actions of PTH. Thus, the pathophysiology of PHP differs fundamentally from true hypoparathyroidism, in which PTH secretion rather than PTH responsiveness is defective.

The initial event in PTH action is binding of the hormone to specific G protein–coupled receptors that are embedded in the plasma membrane of target cells. The primary receptor for PTH also binds PTH-related protein (PTHrP) with equivalent affinity, and thus is termed the PTH/PTHrP or PTH1 receptor. The PTH1 receptor is a member of a superfamily of receptors that are coupled by heterotrimeric (α, β, γ) guanine nucleotide binding regulatory proteins (G proteins) to signal effector molecules that are localized to the inner surface of the plasma membrane. PTH binding leads to generation of a variety of second messengers, including cAMP, inositol 1,4,5-trisphosphate, and diacylglycerol, and cytosolic calcium, consistent with evidence that the PTH1 receptor can couple not only to G_s to stimulate adenylyl cyclase but also to G_q and G_{11}, albeit with lesser affinity, to stimulate phospholipase C. The best-characterized mediator of PTH action is cAMP, which rapidly activates protein kinase A. The relevant target proteins that are phosphorylated by protein kinase A and the precise actions of these proteins have not yet been fully characterized, but include enzymes, ion channels, and proteins that regulate gene expression. In contrast to the well-recognized effects of the second messenger cAMP in bone and kidney cells, the physiological importance of the phospholipase C signaling pathway in these PTH target tissues has not yet been established.

PATHOGENESIS OF PSEUDOHYPOPARATHYROIDISM

The PTH infusion test facilitates the diagnosis of PHP and enables distinction between the several variants of the syndrome (Fig. 1). Thus, patients with PHP type 1 fail to show an appropriate increase in urinary excretion of both cAMP and phosphate, whereas subjects with the less common type 2 form show a normal increase in urinary cAMP excretion but do not manifest a phosphaturic response.

Pseudohypoparathyroidism Type 1

The blunted nephrogenous cAMP response to PTH in subjects with PHP type 1 is caused by a deficiency of the alpha subunit of Gs ($G\alpha_s$), the signaling protein that couples PTH1 receptors to stimulation of adenylyl cyclase. Studies of $G\alpha_s$ expression in membranes from a variety of accessible cell types, including erythrocytes and cultured fibroblasts, have provided a basis for distinguishing two groups of patients with PHP type 1: patients with generalized $G\alpha_s$ deficiency are classified as PHP type 1a, whereas patients with tissue-specific deficiency of $G\alpha_s$ are classified as PHP type 1b. Comprehensive studies of endocrine function in patients with PHP type 1a have shown that these patients have resistance not only to PTH, but also to additional hormones, including thyroid-stimulating hormone (TSH), gonadotropins, glucagon, calcitonin, and growth hormone releasing hormone, whose receptors interact with Gs to stimulate adenylyl cyclase. In contrast, subjects with PHP type 1b show hormone resistance that is principally to PTH.

Albright Hereditary Osteodystrophy

In addition to hormone resistance, patients with PHP type 1a (OMIM 30080, 103580) also manifest a constellation of developmental and somatic defects that are collectively termed Albright's hereditary osteodystrophy (AHO). The AHO phenotype consists of short stature, round faces, obesity, brachydactyly, and subcutaneous ossifications (Fig. 1), but dental defects and sensory-neural abnormalities may also be present. Some individuals with AHO have normal hormone responsiveness, a condition that is termed pseudopseudohypoparathyroidism (pseudo-PHP). Subjects with pseudo-PHP have a normal urinary cAMP response to PTH, which distinguishes them from occasional patients with PHP type 1a who maintain normal serum calcium levels without treatment. Pseudo-PHP is genetically related to PHP type 1a, and within a given kindred, some affected members will have only AHO (i.e., pseudo-PHP), whereas others will have hormone resistance as well (i.e., PHP type 1a), despite equivalent functional deficiency of $G\alpha_s$ in tissues that have been analyzed.

$G\alpha_s$ deficiency in patients with AHO results from heterozygous inactivating mutations in the *GNAS* gene that account for autosomal dominant inheritance of the disorder. AHO patients with *GNAS* mutations on maternally inherited alleles develop hormone resistance. In contrast, AHO patients with *GNAS* mutations on paternally inherited alleles have only the phenotypic features of AHO without hormonal resistance (i.e., pseudo-PHP). This unusual inheritance pattern was first observed clinically by inspection of published pedigrees and was subsequently ascribed to genomic imprinting of the *GNAS* gene.

The *GNAS* locus on chromosome 20q13.2 in humans and the syntenic mouse *Gnas* locus on chromosome 2 consist of 13 exons that encode $G\alpha_s$ (Fig. 2). Upstream of exon 1 are three alternative first exons that each splice onto exons 2–13 to create novel transcripts. These include XL, which is expressed only from the paternal allele and which generates a transcript with overlapping open reading frames that encode XLαs and ALEX, (the alternative gene product encoded by the XL-exon). The two proteins are interacting cofactors and are specifically expressed in neuroendocrine cells. XLαs is a much larger signaling protein than $G\alpha_s$ ($\approx$78 versus 45–52 kDa) and is able to interact with $\beta\gamma$ chains through sequences in the carboxy-terminal region of the XL domain, which shows high homology to the exon 1–encoded portion of $G\alpha_s$ that promotes

The author has reported no conflicts of interest.

binding to $\beta\gamma$ dimers. XLαs is targeted to the plasma membrane and can activate adenylyl cyclase. Although recombinant XLαs can interact with receptors for PTH and a variety of other hormones in vitro, the native receptors that interact with XLαs in vivo are presently unknown. A second alternative promoter encodes the secretory protein Nesp55, which is expressed only from the maternal allele and shares no protein homology with Gα_s. An exon 1A (associated first exon) transcript is derived only from the paternal allele and does not encode a known protein. These alternative first exons are reciprocally imprinted and are associated with promoters that contain differentially methylated regions (DMRs) that are methylated on the nonexpressed allele (Fig. 2). In contrast, the promoter for exon 1 is within a CpG island but is unmethylated on both alleles in all tissues. Imprinting of *GNAS* is controlled by at least two primary maternal imprint marks that are established during oogenesis and that control independent imprinting domains (NESP/XL and exon 1A/Gα_s).

Pseudohypoparathyroidism Type 1a

PHP type 1a is characterized by resistance to multiple hormones whose receptors require Gα_s for activation of adenylyl cyclase. Gα_s is biallelically transcribed in most tissues, so a heterozygous mutation would be expected to reduce Gα_s expression to 50% of normal, certainly an adequate level to permit normal hormone signaling. However, expression of the paternal Gα_s allele is naturally suppressed in some tissues, including the renal proximal tubule cells, human pituitary, human thyroid, and human ovary. Thus, inactivating germline mutations on the maternal *GNAS* allele will lead to expression of little or no Gα_s protein only in these imprinted tissues, which accounts for the characteristic pattern of hormone resistance found in patients with PHP type 1a and in murine models of AHO in which the maternal *Gnas* allele has been disrupted. The *cis*-acting elements that control tissue-specific paternal imprinting of Gα_s seem to be located within the primary imprint region in exon 1A, because paternal deletion of the

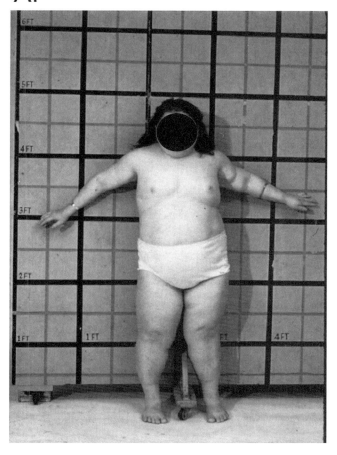

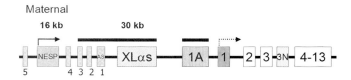
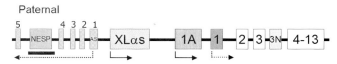

FIG. 2. General organization of the *GNAS* gene complex. The *GNAS* gene complex consists of 13 exons that encode the signaling protein Gα_s. Upstream of exon 1 are three alternative first exons that are labeled exon 1A, XLαs, and Nesp55; exons 1–5 for the NESP antisense transcript (AS) are also depicted. The three alternative exons are spliced to exons 2–13 to produce unique transcripts. The DMRs are denoted above the respective promoters, and arrows denote the direction of transcription. Nesp55 is transcribed exclusively from the maternal allele; XLαs and exon 1A are transcribed exclusively from the paternal allele. Nesp AS (antisense) and exon 1a transcripts produce noncoding RNA. Gα_s transcripts are biallelically expressed except in a small number of tissues, such as the renal proximal tubules, thyroid, gonads, and pituitary somatotrophs, where expression is preferentially from the maternal allele.

FIG. 1. (A) Typical features of AHO. The female in the picture show short stature, obesity, sexual immaturity, and brachydactyly. (B) cAMP excretion in urine in response to intravenous administration of bovine parathyroid extract (300 USP units) from 9:00 a.m. to 9:15 a.m. The peak response in normals (▲) is 50- to 100-fold times basal; patients with PHP type Ia (●) or PHP type Ib (○) show only a 2- to 5-fold response.

exon 1A DMR in mice is associated with increased $G\alpha_s$ expression.

Although at least three unique proteins are produced from the *GNAS* gene, it seems as if loss of $G\alpha_s$ is sufficient to explain the PHP type 1a phenotype. In contrast, generation of knockout mice that specifically lack XLαs or Nesp55 manifest unique characteristics that implicate these proteins in a variety of other postnatal adaptations. Similarly, patients with paternal deletion of the *GNAS* imprinted locus, and consequent deficiency of XLαs, have severe pre- and postnatal growth retardation intractable feeding difficulties and abnormal adipose tissue and other neurocognitive defects. Thus, loss of these additional proteins can explain the unusual body habitus, poor suckling behavior, and high perinatal mortality of knockout mice that lack exon 2 of *Gnas*.

Private mutations have been found in nearly all of the AHO kindreds studied, although a four-base deletion in exon 7 has been detected in multiple families, and an unusual missense mutation in exon 13 (A366S) has been identified in two unrelated young boys suggesting that these two regions may be genetic "hot spots." Small deletions or point mutations can be identified in ~80% of AHO patients using PCR-based techniques, and larger genomic rearrangements or uniparental disomy may account for AHO in other patients.

Postzygotic somatic mutations in the *GNAS* gene that enhance activity of the protein are found in many autonomous endocrine tumors and affected tissues of patients with the McCune-Albright syndrome. These mutations lead to constitutive activation of adenylyl cyclase, and result in proliferation and autonomous hyperfunction of hormonally responsive cells. Clinically significant effects are more likely to ensue when *GNAS* activating mutations occur on the maternally derived allele, which is preferentially expressed in imprinted tissues. The clinical significance of $G\alpha_s$ activity as a determinant of hormone action is further emphasized by the description by Iiri et al. of two unrelated males with both precocious puberty and PHP type 1a. These two subjects had identical *GNAS* mutations in exon 13 (A366S) that resulted in a temperature-sensitive form of $G\alpha_s$. This $G\alpha_s$ is constitutively active in the cooler environment of the testis, while being rapidly degraded in other tissues at normal body temperature. Thus, different tissues in these two individuals could show hormone resistance (to PTH and TSH), hormone responsiveness (to adrenocorticotropic hormone [ACTH]), or hormone independent activation (to lutineinizing hormone [LH]).

Pseudohypoparathyroidism Type 1b

The characteristics of PHP type 1a contrast sharply with those of PHP type 1b (OMIM 603233). Although most cases of PHP type 1b are sporadic, the disorder may be transmitted in an autosomal dominant manner with phenotypic expression dependent on genomic imprinting. Subjects with PHP type 1b lack features of AHO, show decreased responsiveness to PTH as the principal manifestation of hormone resistance, and have normal $G\alpha_s$ activity in accessible tissues. Despite renal resistance to PTH, subjects with PHP type 1b who have elevated levels of PTH often manifest skeletal lesions similar to those that occur in patients with hyperparathyroidism.

Specific resistance of target tissues to PTH, and normal activity of $G\alpha_s$, first suggested decreased expression or function of the PTH/PTHrP receptor as the cause for hormone resistance in PHP type 1b. However, a variety of genetic studies failed to disclose mutations in the coding exons and promoter regions of the PTH/PTHrP receptor gene or its mRNA, and mice and humans that are heterozygous for inactivation of the gene encoding the PTH/PTHrP receptor do not

manifest PTH resistance or hypocalcemia. In contrast, genetic linkage analyses of PHP type 1b kindreds have mapped PHP type 1b to the *GNAS* locus. The nucleotide sequence of the coding exons and flanking intron-exon boundaries of the *GNAS* gene is normal in patients with PHP type 1b, but an epigenetic defect that results in switching of the maternal *GNAS* allele to a paternal pattern of methylation (i.e., paternal epigenotype) is a consistent finding in sporadic and familial PHP type 1b. Mutations have been described in familial but not sporadic forms of PHP type 1b, including two microdeletions in the *STX16* gene located ~220 kb centromeric of *GNAS* exon 1A and deletions that remove the DMR encompassing exon NESP55 and exons 3 and 4 of the antisense transcript (Fig. 2). In each case, inheritance of the mutation from a female abolishes the maternal *GNAS* epigenotype and results in PTH resistance.

It is conceivable that the conversion of the maternal *GNAS* allele to a "paternal" epigenotype in PHP type 1b leads to transcriptional silencing of the $G\alpha_s$ promoter in imprinted tissues, with the result that little or no $G\alpha_s$ is expressed from either *GNAS* allele in these tissues. A similar mechanism has been invoked to explain the development of $G\alpha_s$ deficiency in one patient with an unusual form of PHP type 1b, in whom molecular genetic studies showed paternal uniparental disomy of *GNAS*. This mechanism would explain severe deficiency of functional $G\alpha_s$ in some imprinted tissues (e.g., the renal proximal tubules) and normal expression of $G\alpha_s$ in nonimprinted tissues (e.g., erythrocytes).

Pseudohypoparathyroidism Type 1c

In rare instances, patients with PHP type 1 and features of AHO show resistance to multiple hormones in the absence of a demonstrable biochemical defect in G_s or G_i. Recent molecular studies now suggest that these patients have *GNAS* mutations that result in functional defects of $G\alpha_s$ that are not apparent in current in vitro assays.

Pseudohypoparathyroidism Type 2

Pseudohypoparathyroidism type 2 lacks a clear genetic or familial basis. PTH resistance is manifested by a reduced phosphaturic response to administration of PTH, despite a normal increase in urinary cAMP excretion. These observations have suggested that the PTH receptor–adenylyl cyclase complex functions normally to increase nephrogenous cAMP in response to PTH and are consistent with a model in which PTH resistance arises from an inability of intracellular cAMP to activate downstream targets. A similar clinical and biochemical picture occurs in patients with severe deficiency of vitamin D, which raises the possibility that most cases of PHP type 2 are actually examples of unsuspected vitamin D deficiency.

Osteoma Cutis and Progressive Osseous Heteroplasia

Some patients with isolated ectopic ossification have heterozygous *GNAS* mutations that are identical to those that occur in patients with AHO. The ossification occurs in the absence of a preexisting or associated lesion, as opposed to secondary types of cutaneous ossification that occur by metaplastic reaction to inflammatory, traumatic, and neoplastic processes. Osteoma cutis refers to the development of membranous ossification that is limited to the superficial skin. Progressive osseous heteroplasia (POH) is a more disabling disorder, in which extensive dermal ossification occurs during childhood, followed by widespread ossification of skeletal muscle and deep connective tissue. Heterozygous inactivating *GNAS* mutations have been identified in many patients with

POH, and in each case, the defective allele was paternally inherited. Remarkably, although these patients lack other features of AHO, when POH females transmit the defective *GNAS* allele, their affected children manifest the complete PHP type 1a phenotype. The development of ectopic ossification in patients with haploinsufficiency of *GNAS* is consistent with the role of $G\alpha_s$ and cAMP as negative regulators of osteogenic commitment.

Circulating Inhibitors as a Cause of PTH Resistance

Several studies have reported an apparent dissociation between circulating levels of immunoreactive and bioactive PTH in patients with PHP type 1, and plasma from many of these patients had been shown to diminish the biological activity of exogenous PTH in in vitro cytochemical bioassays. Although the identity of this putative inhibitor or antagonist is unknown, one potential candidate is the N-terminally truncated PTH fragment, hPTH(7-84), which can inhibit the calcemic actions of hPTH(1-34) or hPTH(1-84) through a nonclassical PTH receptor. Circulating levels of PTH(7-84 immunoreactivity are elevated in patients with PHP type 1a and 1b, and the proportion of PTH(7-84)-like fragments to biologically active PTH(1-84) is increased. Although it is conceivable that circulating hPTH(7-84)-like fragments may contribute to PTH resistance in some patients with PHP, it is likely that these circulating antagonists arise as a consequence of sustained secondary hyperparathyroidism and do not have a significant role in the primary pathophysiology of the disorder.

DIAGNOSIS OF PSEUDOHYPOPARATHYROIDISM

PHP should be considered in any patient with functional hypoparathyroidism (i.e., hypocalcemia and hyperphosphatemia) and an elevated plasma concentration of PTH. Hypomagnesemia and severe vitamin D deficiency can produce biochemical features of PTH resistance in some patients, and thus plasma concentrations of magnesium and 25(OH)D must be measured. Unusual initial manifestations of PHP include neonatal hypothyroidism, unexplained cardiac failure, seizures, intracerebral calcification of basal ganglia and frontal lobes, dyskinesia and other movement disorders, and spinal cord compression.

PHP or pseudo-PHP may be suspected in patients who present with somatic features of AHO. However, several aspects of AHO, such as obesity, round face, brachydactyly, and mental retardation, also occur in other congenital disorders (e.g., Prader-Willi syndrome, acrodysostosis, Ullrich-Turner syndrome). An interesting phenocopy of AHO occurs in subjects who have small terminal deletions of chromosome 2q37 [del(2)(q37.3)]. These patients have normal endocrine function and normal $G\alpha_s$ activity.

The classical tests for PHP, the Ellsworth-Howard test and later modifications by Chase et al., involved the administration of 200–300 USP units of purified bovine PTH or parathyroid extract. Although these preparations are no longer available, the synthetic hPTH(1-34) peptide has been approved for human use, and several protocols for its use in the differential diagnosis of hypoparathyroidism have been developed. These protocols are based on intravenous infusion of the peptide, but similar results may be obtained after subcutaneous injection of hPTH(1-34) or hPTH(1-84), albeit requiring administration of higher doses of peptide. The patient should be fasting except for fluids (250 ml of water hourly from 6:00 a.m. to 12:00 a.m.). Two control urine specimens are collected before 9:00 a.m. Synthetic human PTH(1-34) peptide (0.625 μg/kg body weight to a maximum of 25 μg for intravenous use and 40 μg for subcutaneous use) is administered at 9:00 a.m. either by subcutaneous injection or intravenous infusion over 15

minutes, and experimental urine specimens are collected from 9:00 a.m. to 9:30 a.m., 9:30 a.m. to 10:00 a.m., 10:00 a.m. to 11:00 a.m., and 11:00 a.m. to 12:00 a.m. Blood samples should be obtained at 9:00 a.m. and 11:00 a.m. for measurement of serum creatinine and phosphorous concentrations. Urine samples are analyzed for cAMP, phosphorous, and creatinine concentrations, and results are expressed as nanomoles of cAMP per 100 ml glomerular filtrate (GF) and TmP/GFR. Normal subjects and patients with hormonopenic hypoparathyroidism usually display a 10- to 20-fold increase in urinary cAMP excretion, whereas patients with PHP type 1 (type 1a and type 1b), regardless of their serum calcium concentration, will show a markedly blunted response (Fig. 1). Thus, this test can distinguish patients with so-called "normocalcemic" PHP (i.e., patients with PTH resistance who are able to maintain normal serum calcium levels without treatment) from subjects with pseudo-PHP (who will have a normal urinary cAMP response to PTH. Recent studies indicate that measurement of plasma cAMP or plasma 1,25-dihydroxyvitamin D after infusion of hPTH(1-34) may also differentiate PHP type 1 from other causes of hypoparathyroidism.

Mutational analysis of the *GNAS* gene is now available as an approved test by several clinical laboratories. In contrast, genetic testing for PHP type 1b is still considered a research test.

The diagnosis of PHP type 2 requires exclusion of magnesium depletion or vitamin D deficiency. Documentation of elevated serum PTH and nephrogenous cAMP is a prerequisite for a definitive diagnosis of PHP type 2. These subjects have a normal urinary cAMP response to infusion of PTH but characteristically fail to show a phosphaturic response. Unfortunately, interpretation of the phosphaturic response to PTH is often complicated by random variations in phosphate clearance, and it is sometimes not possible to classify a phosphaturic response as normal or subnormal regardless of the criteria used.

TREATMENT

Treatment of hypocalcemia in PHP is directed at maintaining a low- to mid-normal serum calcium concentration to relieve symptoms of tetany while avoiding hypercalciuria. Activated forms of vitamin D (e.g., calcitriol) provide the advantage of rapid onset (and offset) of action, but their corresponding short half-lives necessitate multiple daily doses. Patients with PHP require lower doses of vitamin D and have less risk of treatment-related hypercalciuria than patients with hormonopenic forms of hypoparathyroidism. All patients with hypocalcemia should receive treatment, and it is the author's practice to initiate vitamin D therapy even in normocalcemic patients when the serum concentration of PTH exceeds the upper limit of normal to prevent adverse effects of hyperparathyroidism on the skeleton. Treatment with calcium and vitamin D usually decreases the elevated serum phosphate to a high normal level because of a favorable balance between increased urinary phosphate excretion and decreased intestinal phosphate absorption. In some cases, short-term use of phosphate-binding gels such as aluminum hydroxide may be helpful, but these agents are typically not required for maintenance therapy.

Estrogen therapy and pregnancy have particularly interesting effects on the maintenance of normocalcemia in patients with PHP. Estrogen therapy may reduce serum levels of calcium in women with PHP or hypoparathyroidism. In addition, symptomatic hypocalcemia may also occur in some women at the time of the menses, when estrogen levels are low, with the cause remaining unknown. Paradoxically, during the high estrogen state of pregnancy, some patients with PHP have required less, or no, vitamin D to maintain normal serum concentrations of calcium owing to physiological increases in serum concentration of $1,25(OH)_2D_3$. After delivery, serum calcium and $1,25(OH)_2D_3$ levels typically decrease and PTH rises. Because placental synthesis of $1,25(OH)_2D_3$ is not compromised in patients with PHP, it seems that the placenta may contribute to the maintenance of normocalcemia during pregnancy. In contrast, patients with hypoparathyroidism may require treatment with larger amounts of vitamin D and calcium in the latter half of pregnancy.

Patients with PHP type 1a will frequently manifest resistance to other hormones in addition to PTH and may display clinical evidence of hypothyroidism, gonadal dysfunction, or growth hormone deficiency. The basic principles used in the diagnosis and treatment of these additional endocrine defects apply to patients with PHP type 1a.

SUGGESTED READING

1. Albright F, Burnett CH, Smith PH 1942 Pseudohypoparathyroidism: An example of "Seabright-Bantam syndrome." Endocrinology **30:**922–932.
2. Bastepe M, Frohlich LF, Hendy GN, Indridason OS, Josse RG, Koshiyama H, Korkko J, Nakamoto JM, Rosenbloom AL, Slyper AH, Sugimoto T, Tsatsoulis A, Crawford JD, Juppner H 2003 Autosomal dominant pseudohypoparathyroidism type Ib is associated with a heterozygous microdeletion that likely disrupts a putative imprinting control element of GNAS. J Clin Invest **112:**1255–1263.
3. Bastepe M, Frohlich LF, Linglart A, Abu-Zahra HS, Tojo K, Ward LM, Juppner H 2005 Deletion of the NESP55 differentially methylated region causes loss of maternal GNAS imprints and pseudohypoparathyroidism type Ib. Nat Genet **37:**25–27.
4. Drezner MK, Neelon FA, Lebovitz HE 1973 Pseudohypoparathyroidism type II: A possible defect in the reception of the cyclic AMP signal. N Engl J Med **280:**1056–1060.
5. Germain-Lee EL, Schwindinger W, Crane JL, Zewdu R, Zweifel LS, Wand G, Huso DL, Saji M, Ringel MD, Levine MA 2005 A mouse model of Albright hereditary osteodystrophy generated by targeted disruption of exon 1 of the Gnas gene. Endocrinology **146:**4697–4709.
6. Hayward BE, Moran V, Strain L, Bonthron DT 1998 Bidirectional imprinting of a single gene: GNAS1 encodes maternally, paternally, and biallelically derived proteins. Proc Natl Acad Sci USA **95:**15475–15480.
7. Levine MA, Zapalowski C, Kappy MS 2005 Disorders of calcium, phosphate, parathyroid hormone and vitamin D. In: Kappy MS, Allen DB, Geffner ME (eds.) Principles and Practice of Pediatric Endocrinology. Charles C. Thomas, Springfield, IL, USA, pp. 695–814.
8. Linglart A, Gensure RC, Olney RC, Juppner H, Bastepe M 2005 A novel STX16 deletion in autosomal dominant pseudohypoparathyroidism type Ib redefines the boundaries of a cis-acting imprinting control element of GNAS. Am J Hum Genet **76:**804–814.
9. Liu J, Chen M, Deng C, Bourc'his D, Nealon JG, Erlichman B, Bestor TH, Weinstein LS 2005 Identification of the control region for tissue-specific imprinting of the stimulatory G protein alpha-subunit. Proc Natl Acad Sci USA **102:**5513–5518.
10. Liu J, Litman D, Rosenberg MJ, Yu S, Biesecker LG, Weinstein LS 2000 A GNAS1 imprinting defect in pseudohypoparathyroidism type IB. J Clin Invest **106:**1167–1174.
11. Rao DS, Parfitt AM, Kleerekoper M, Pumo BS, Frame B 1985 Dissociation between the effects of endogenous parathyroid hormone on adenosine 3',5'-monophosphate generation and phosphate reabsorption in hypocalcemia due to vitamin D depletion: An acquired disorder resembling pseudohypoparathyroidism type II. J Clin Endocrinol Metab **61:**285–290.
12. Shore EM, Ahn J, Jan de Beur SM, Li M, Xu M, Gardner RJ, Zasloff MA, Whyte MP, Levine MA, Kaplan FS 2002 Paternally inherited inactivating mutations of the GNAS1 gene in progressive osseous heteroplasia. N Engl J Med **346:**99–106.
13. Yu S, Yu D, Lee E, Eckhaus M, Lee R, Corria Z, Accili D, Westphal H, Weinstein LS 1998 Variable and tissue-specific hormone resistance in heterotrimeric Gs protein alpha-subunit (Gsalpha) knockout mice is due to tissue-specific imprinting of the gsalpha gene. Proc Natl Acad Sci USA **95:**8715–8720.

Chapter 38. Neonatal Hypocalcemia

Thomas O. Carpenter

Department of Pediatrics, Yale University School of Medicine, New Haven, Connecticut

CALCIUM METABOLISM IN THE PERINATAL PERIOD

Mineralization of the fetal skeleton is provided for by active calcium (Ca) transport from mother to fetus across the placenta, such that the fetus is relatively hypercalcemic compared with the mother. The rate-limiting step in Ca transport is thought to be a Ca pump in the basal membrane (fetus-directed side) of the trophoblast. The net effect of this system is to maintain a 1:1.4 (mother:fetus) Ca gradient throughout gestation,[1] providing ample mineral for the demands of mineralization of the skeleton. Although there seems to be little Ca flux in early gestation, this becomes considerable in the third trimester. Both PTH-related protein (PTHrP) and PTH are thought to contribute to the regulation of transplacental Ca transport. At term, the fetus is hypercalcemic and has low levels of PTH compared with the maternal circulation. An abrupt transition to autonomous regulation of mineral homeostasis occurs at partum. With removal of the abundant placental supply of Ca, circulating Ca level decreases, reaching a nadir within the first 3–4 days of life, subsequently rising to normal adult levels in the second week of life. This decrease in ionized Ca levels postpartum provides the initial stimulus for extrauterine PTH secretion.

HYPOCALCEMIC SYNDROMES IN THE NEWBORN PERIOD

Manifestations of neonatal hypocalcemia are variable and may not correlate with the magnitude of depression in the circulating ionized Ca level. As in older people, increased neuromuscular excitability (tetany) is a cardinal feature of newborn hypocalcemia. Generalized or focal clonic seizures, jitteriness, irritability, and frequent twitches or jerking of limbs are seen. Hyperacusis and laryngospasm may occur. Nonspecific signs include apnea, tachycardia, tachypnea, cyanosis, and edema; vomiting has also been reported. Neonatal hypocalcemia is traditionally classified by its time of onset; differences in etiology are suggested by "early" occurring hypocalcemia versus that occurring "late."[2]

Early Neonatal Hypocalcemia

Early neonatal hypocalcemia occurs during the first 3 days of life, usually between 24 and 48 h, and characteristically is seen in premature infants, infants of diabetic mothers, and asphyxiated infants. The premature infant normally has an exaggerated postnatal depression in circulating Ca, dropping lower and

---

The author has reported no conflicts of interest.

TABLE 1. NEONATAL HYPOCALCEMIA

	Characteristics	Mechanism
Early	Onset within first 3–4 days of life; seen in infants of diabetic mother, perinatal asphyxia, pre-eclampsia	Likely decrease in parathyroid response possible exaggerated postnatal calcitonin surge
Late	Onset days 5–10 of life, more common in winter, in infants of mother with marginal vitamin D intake; associated with dietary phosphate load	Possible transient parathyroid dysfunction; hypomagnesemia in some cases; calcium malabsorption

Congenital hypoparathyroidism	Usually present after first 5 days of life with overt tetany
"Late-late" hypocalcemia	Presents in premature at 2–4 months; associated with skeletal hypomineralization and inadequate dietary mineral or vitamin D intake
Infants of hyperparathyroid mothers	May present as late as 1 year of age; mother possibly undiagnosed
Ionized hypocalcemia (with normal total calcium)	In exchange transfusion with citrated blood produces, lipid infusions, or alkalosis
Phosphate load	Can be severe after administration of phosphate enemas
Osteopetrosis	Defective mobilization of skeletal calcium due to severe osteoclast defects
Magnesium-wasting	Familial disorders of renal Mg wasting may result in refractory hypocalcemia in infancy

earlier than in the term infant. Total Ca levels may drop below 7.0 mg/dl, but the proportional drop in ionized Ca is less and may explain the lack of symptoms in many premature infants with total Ca in this range.

PTH secretion in response to low serum Ca is often insufficient in premature infants, and the transition to a normal response to hypocalcemia is prolonged. A several-day delay in the phosphaturic effect of PTH in term and preterm infants has been described; resultant hyperphosphatemia may decrease serum Ca. The premature infant's exaggerated rise in calcitonin may provoke hypocalcemia. A role for vitamin D and its metabolites in early neonatal hypocalcemia has been suggested in the setting of severe maternal vitamin D deficiency.

The infant of the diabetic mother (IDM) shows an exaggerated postnatal decrease in circulating Ca compared with other infants of comparable maturity. The pregnant diabetic tends to have lower circulating PTH and magnesium levels; the IDM has lower circulating magnesium and PTH, but normal calcitonin. Abnormalities in vitamin D metabolism do not seem to play a role in the development of hypocalcemia in the IDM. IDMs who maintain optimal glycemic control during pregnancy have a decreased incidence of hypocalcemia compared with infants of diabetic mothers with less regulated blood sugar levels; however, the incidence of hypocalcemia, even with optimal maternal glycemic control, is greater than control infants of mothers without diabetes.[3] One preventative strategy, administration of intramuscular magnesium to IDMs, failed to show a reduction in the incidence of hypocalcemia.[4]

Early hypocalcemia occurs in asphyxiated infants; calcitonin response is augmented, and PTH levels are elevated. Infants of pre-eclamptic mothers and postmature infants with growth retardation develop early hypocalcemia and are prone to hypomagnesemia.

Late Neonatal Hypocalcemia

The presentation of hypocalcemic tetany between 5 and 10 days of life is termed "late" neonatal hypocalcemia and occurs more frequently in term infants that in premature infants. It is not correlated with birth trauma or asphyxia. Affected children may have received cow's milk or cow's milk formula, which may have considerably more phosphate than human milk. Hyperphosphatemia is associated with late neonatal hypocalcemia and may reflect (1) inability of the immature kidney to efficiently excrete phosphate; (2) dietary phosphate load; or (3)

transiently low levels of circulating PTH. Others have noted an association between late neonatal hypocalcemia and modest maternal vitamin D insufficiency. An increased occurrence of late neonatal hypocalcemia in winter has also been noted.

Hypocalcemia associated with magnesium deficiency may present as late neonatal hypocalcemia. Severe hypomagnesemia (circulating levels < 0.8 mg/dl) may occur in congenital defects of intestinal magnesium absorption or renal tubular reabsorption. Transient hypomagnesemia of unknown etiology is associated with a less severe decrease in circulating magnesium (between 0.8 and 1.4 mg/dl). Hypocalcemia frequently complicates hypomagnesemic states because of impaired secretion of PTH. Impaired PTH responsiveness has also been shown as an inconsistent finding in magnesium deficiency. Hypomagnesemia with secondary hypocalcemia (and hypocalciuria) has been recently identified to be caused by homozygous mutations in TRPM6, a bifunctional protein found in renal and intestinal epithelia.[5] The protein acts as a divalent cation channel and has receptor-like protein kinase activity. Hypocalcemia in this setting is refractory to therapy unless correction of magnesium levels is attained and usually presents at several weeks of age. Mutations in a renal tubular paracellular transport protein, CLDN16, also can cause hypomagnesemia and hypocalcemia associated with hypercalciuria.[6]

Other Causes of Neonatal Hypocalcemia

Symptomatic neonatal hypocalcemia may occur within the first 3 weeks of life in infants born to mothers with hyperparathyroidism. Presentation at 1 year of age has also been reported. Serum phosphate is often >8 mg/dl; symptoms may be exacerbated by feeding cow's milk or other high phosphate formulas. The proposed mechanism for the development of neonatal hypocalcemia in the infant of the hyperparathyroid mother is as follows: maternal hypercalcemia occurs secondary to hyperparathyroidism, resulting in increased Ca delivery to the fetus and fetal hypercalcemia, which inhibits fetal parathyroid secretion. The infant's oversuppressed parathyroid is not able to maintain normal Ca levels postpartum. Hypomagnesemia may be observed in the infant of the hyperparathyroid mother. Maternal hyperparathyroidism has been diagnosed after hypocalcemic infants have been identified.

"Late-late" neonatal hypocalcemia has been used in reference to premature infants who develop hypocalcemia with poor bone mineralization within the first 3–4 months of life. These infants tend to have an inadequate dietary supply of mineral and/or vitamin D.

The previously discussed forms of neonatal hypocalcemia are generally found to be of a transient nature. More rarely, hypocalcemia that is permanent is detected in the newborn periods and caused by congenital hypoparathyroidism. Isolated absence of the parathyroids may be inherited in X-linked recessive or autosomal dominant or recessive fashion. Mutations in genes involved in parathyroid gland development, PTH processing, PTH secretion (CaSR),[7] PTH structure, and PTH action (PTH receptor, Gsα) have been identified. The most frequently identified defect of parathyroid gland development is the DiGeorge anomaly: the triad of hypoparathyroidism, T-cell incompetence caused by a partial or absent thymus, and conotruncal heart defects (e.g., tetralogy of Fallot, truncus arteriosus) or aortic arch abnormalities. These structures are derived from the embryologic third and fourth pharyngeal pouches; the usual sporadic occurrence reflects developmental abnormalities of these structures, which can be seen in association with microdeletions of chromosome 22q11.2.[8] Other defects may variably occur in this broad spectrum field defect, including other midline anomalies such as cleft palate and facial dysmorphism or the velo-cardio-facial syndrome. Individuals with various phenotypic features of this syndrome have come to attention in late childhood or in adolescence with the onset of symptomatic hypocalcemia.[9] Presumably "partial" hypoparathyroidism in these individuals was not apparent early in life because of the mild nature of the defect. Deletion of the gene encoding the T-box transcription factor *TBX1* has recently been identified as sufficient to cause the cardiac, parathyroid, thymic, facial, and velopharyngeal features of DiGeorge syndrome.[10] Other known causes of heritable hypoparathyroidism[11] evident in the newborn period are discussed in greater detail elsewhere.

Severe hypocalcemia has been induced in the newborn period when phosphate enema preparations have been administered.[12] The phosphate load resulting from this inappropriate measure can result in extreme hyperphosphatemia, life-threatening hypocalcemia, and hypomagnesemia. Such preparations should never be administered to infants <2 years of age. Rotavirus infections in newborns frequently result in hypocalcemia,[13] because of the malabsorption that accompanies markedly increased intestinal transit time with severe diarrhea.

Hypocalcemia in the newborn period may be the presenting manifestation of malignant infantile osteopetrosis, in which resorption of bone is defective, thereby compromising the maintenance of normal serum Ca levels. Resistance to PTH in infancy has also been described in association with propionic acidemia.[14]

Decreases in the ionized fraction of the circulating Ca occur in infants undergoing exchange transfusions with citrated blood products or receiving lipid infusions. Citrate and fatty acids form complexes with ionized Ca, reducing the free Ca compartment. Alkalosis secondary to adjustments in ventilatory assistance may provoke a shift of ionized Ca to the protein-bound compartment. It should be pointed out that appropriate collection of sample for performance of ionized Ca levels may require collection of blood with no exposure to air (thus filling collection tubes completely) and without a tourniquet. Additionally, prompt sample handling is usually important for accurate results. Given all of these conditions, the measurement of ionized Ca may be difficult to obtain under routine circumstances in small children.

TREATMENT OF NEONATAL HYPOCALCEMIA

Early neonatal hypocalcemia may be asymptomatic, and the necessity of therapy may be questioned in such infants. Most authors recommend that early neonatal hypocalcemia be treated when the circulating concentration of total serum Ca is <5–6 mg/dl (1.25–1.50 mM; or of ionized Ca <2.5–3 mg/dl, 0.62–0.72 mM) in the premature infant and when total serum Ca is <6–7 mg/dl (1.50–1.75 mM) in the term infant. Emergency therapy of acute tetany consists of intravenous (never intramuscular) Ca gluconate (10% solution) given slowly (<1 ml/minute). A dose of 1–3 ml will usually arrest convulsions. Doses should generally not exceed 20 mg of elemental Ca/kg body weight and may be repeated up to four times per 24 h. After successful management of acute emergencies, maintenance therapy may be achieved by intravenous administration of 20–50 mg elemental Ca/kg body weight/24 h. Ca glubionate is a commonly used oral supplement. Management of late neonatal tetany should include a low phosphate formula such as Similac PM 60/40 (Ross Products, Abbott Laboratories, Abbott Park, IL, USA) in addition to Ca supplements. A Ca:phosphate ratio of 4:1 has been recommended. Monitoring generally reveals that therapy can be discontinued after several weeks.

When hypomagnesemia is a causal feature of hypocalcemia, magnesium administration may be indicated. Magnesium sulfate is given intravenously using cardiac monitoring or intramuscularly as a 50% solution at a dose of 0.1–0.2 ml/kg. One or two doses may treat transient hypomagnesemia: a dose may be repeated after 12–24 h. Patients with primary defects in magnesium metabolism require long-term oral magnesium supplements.

The place of vitamin D in the management of transient hypocalcemia is less clear. A significant portion of intestinal calcium absorption in newborns occurs by facilitated diffusion and is not vitamin D dependent. Thus, pharmacologic use of active metabolites may not be as useful for the short-term management of transient hypocalcemia as the provision of added calcium. Nevertheless, the recent rise in reported cases of vitamin D deficiency has resulted in the suggestion that all premature infants receive daily supplementation of 400–800 U of vitamin D as a preventative measure. Those patients with no evidence of generalized intestinal malabsorption who develop "late-late" hypocalcemia with vitamin D deficiency rickets should respond within 4 weeks to 1000–2000 U of daily oral vitamin D. Such patients should receive a total of at least 40 mg of elemental Ca/kg body weight/day. In the various forms of persistent congenital hypoparathyroidism, long-term treatment with vitamin D (or its therapeutic metabolites) are used; the preferred agent is calcitriol for these purposes at our center.

REFERENCES

1. Kohlmeier L, Marcus R 1995 Calcium disorders of pregnancy. Endocrinol Metab Clin North Am **24:**15–39.
2. Hillman LS, Haddad JG 1982 Hypocalcemia and other abnormalities of mineral homeostasis during the neonatal period. In: Heath DA, Marx SJ (eds.) Calcium Disorders. Butterworths International Medical Reviews, Butterworths, London, UK, pp. 248–276.
3. Jimenez-Moleon JJ, Bueno-Cavanillas A, Luna-del-Castillo Jde D, Garcia-Martin M, Lardelli-Claret P, Galvez-Vargas R 2002 Impact of different levels of carbohydrate intolerance on neonatal outcomes classically associated with gestational diabetes mellitus. Eur J Obstet Gyn Reprod Biol **102:**36–41.
4. Mehta KC, Kalkwarf HJ, Mimouni F, Khoury J, Tsang RC 1998 Randomized trial of magnesium administration to prevent hypocalcemia in infants of diabetic mothers. J Perinatol **18:**352–356.
5. Schlingmann KP, Weber S, Peters M, Niemann Nejsum L, Vitzhum H, Klingel K, Kratz M, Haddad E, Ristoff E, Dinour D, Syrrou M, Nielsen S, Sassen M, Waldegger S, Seyberth HW, Konrad M 2002 Hypomagnesemia with secondary hypocalcemia is caused by mutations in *TRPM6*, a new member of the TRPM gene family. Nat Genet **31:**166–170.
6. Simon DB, Lu Y, Choate KA, Velazquez H, Al-Sabban E, Praga M, Casari G, Bettinelli A, Colussi G, Rodriguez-Soriano J, McCredie D, Milford D, Sanjad S, Lifton RP 1999 Paracellin-1, a renal tight junction protein required for paracellular Mg²⁺ resorption. Science **285:**103–106.

7. Watanabe T, Bai M, Lane CR, Matsumoto S, Minamatani K, Minagawa M, Niimi H, Brown EM, Yasuda T 1998 Familial hypoparathyroidism: Identification of a novel gain of function mutation in transmembrane domain 5 of the calcium-sensing receptor. J Clin Endocrinol Metab **83:**2497–2502.
8. Webber SA, Hatchwell E, Barber JC, Daubeney PE, Crolla JA, Salmon AP, Keeton BR, Temple IK, Dennis NR 1996 Importance of microdeletions of chromosomal region 22q11 as a cause of selected malformations of the ventricular outflow tracts and aortic arch: A three-year prospective study. J Pediatr **129:**26–32.
9. Sykes KS, Bachrach LK, Siegel-Bartelt J, Ipp M, Kooh SW, Cytrynbaum C 1997 Velocardiofacial syndrome presenting as hypocalcemia in early adolescence. Archiv Pediatr Adolescent Med **151:**745–747.
10. Thakker RV 2004 Genetics of endocrine and metabolic disorders: Parathyroid. Revs Endocr Metabol Disorders **5:**37–51.
11. Hsu SC, Levine MA 2004 Perinatal calcium metabolism: Physiology and pathophysiology. Sem Neonatol **9:**23–36.
12. Walton DM, Thomas DC, Aly HZ, Short BL 2000 Morbid hypocalcemia associated with phosphate enema in a six-week-old infant. Pediatrics **106:**E37.
13. Foldenauer A, Vossbeck S, Pohlandt F 1998 Neonatal hypocalcaemia associated with rotavirus diarrhoea. Eur J Pediatr **157:**838–842.
14. Griffin TA, Hostoffer RW, Tserng KY, Lebovitz DJ, Hoppel CL, Mosser JL, Kaplan D, Kerr DS 1996 Parathyroid hormone resistance and B cell lymphopenia in propionic acidemia. Acta Paediatr **85:**875–878.

Chapter 39.   Miscellaneous Causes of Hypocalcemia

Robert W. Downs, Jr.

Division of Endocrinology and Metabolism, Department of Internal Medicine, Virginia Commonwealth University School of Medicine, Richmond, Virginia

INTRODUCTION

The complete differential diagnosis of hypocalcemic disorders is extensive and is reviewed in a previous chapter. Other chapters in this text have covered in detail the important aspects of hypoparathyroidism, pseudohypoparathyroidism, disorders of vitamin D deficiency, and vitamin D metabolism, and special consideration has been given to neonatal hypocalcemia and magnesium depletion as causes of hypocalcemia.

This chapter will deal with other "miscellaneous," but not necessarily less common, causes of hypocalcemia

HYPOALBUMINEMIA

The ionized or free fraction of serum calcium is physiologically important for cellular function, and low ionized calcium is responsible for the symptoms of hypocalcemia. However, we most often measure total serum calcium, of which about one half is bound to proteins, mostly to albumin. Significant changes in serum protein concentrations can sometimes cause large changes in total serum calcium concentration without affecting the important ionized calcium fraction. Thus, in malnourished and ill individuals, hypoalbuminemia is the most common cause of a low total serum calcium measurement, and such patients do not have symptoms or clinical signs of ionized hypocalcemia (see other chapters for review of the effect of albumin on calcium concentration in hypercalcemia).

There are a number of "rule of thumb" correction formulas that can be used to estimate whether low total serum calcium can be attributed simply to low albumin or serum protein. The most widely used is based on the fact that, at normal pH, each gram of albumin is capable of binding ~0.8 mg of calcium:

"Corrected Calcium" = Measured Total Calcium

$$+ [0.8 \times (4.0 - \text{Measured Albumin})]$$

None of these formulas are entirely satisfactory, however.[1] Low sensitivity for the accurate diagnosis of hypocalcemia has been well documented, particularly in severely ill patients.[2]

Dr. Downs has been a consultant for and received research support from Merck, Novartis, Roche and GlaxoSmithKline.

Therefore, in severely ill patients or when there are symptoms or signs that could be caused by hypocalcemia, it is preferable to obtain direct measurement of ionized calcium performed in a reliable laboratory.

LABORATORY ERROR

It should be obvious that laboratory test results suggesting hypocalcemia can only be dependable if sample collection and handling is correct. Nevertheless, it is worth emphasizing that if the serum calcium is significantly abnormal in a patient who is asymptomatic, the laboratory findings should be confirmed. There have been reports of apparently "severe" hypocalcemia in cases in which blood is mistakenly collected in tubes containing EDTA.[3] Recently two gadolinium chelates, gadodiamide and gadoversetamide, have been reported to interfere with the commonly used colorimetric assay of calcium, but other gadolinium containing contrast agents do not show this interference.[4,5]

ALTERATIONS IN BOUND CALCIUM

In addition to the binding of calcium to albumin and plasma proteins, ~5% of circulating calcium is complexed with inorganic anions. There are a number of situations in which increases in the concentration of anions or changes in pH will result in a shift between bound and ionized calcium.

Hyperphosphatemia is a common cause of hypocalcemia. Rapid increases in serum phosphorus concentrations can occur in the setting of exogenous phosphate administration by oral, rectal, or intravenous routes. Hypocalcemia has been reported after phosphate enemas, particularly in children.[6] Even short courses of oral sodium phosphate can cause symptomatic hypocalcemia in adults who may have underlying asymptomatic vitamin D deficiency, magnesium depletion, or significant renal insufficiency preventing normal elimination of phosphorus.[7] Patients who have impaired ability to mobilize calcium from skeletal stores because of bisphosphonate therapy may also be at increased risk for the development of hypocalcemia after phosphate administration.[8] Hyperphosphatemia can also cause hypocalcemia as a result of release of phosphate from endogenous tissue stores in patients who have rhabdomyolysis and the tumor lysis syndrome.[9] The causes of hyperphosphatemia and its management are reviewed in detail elsewhere in this volume.

Infusion of citrate will complex calcium and lead to acute decreases in ionized calcium concentrations. This is well recognized for massive transfusion with citrated blood products, particularly in the setting of liver transplantation, in which the citrate may not be readily metabolized.[10] Citrate is also used during plasma exchange and during apheresis, and monitoring of citrate delivery and steps to prevent hypocalcemic toxicity during plasmapheresis are important.[11] Mild hypocalcemia without serious symptoms can even occur during simple automated plateletpheresis in normal blood donors.[12] Interestingly, small volume blood transfusion has been associated with the precipitation of hypocalcemic symptoms in patients with pre-existing untreated asymptomatic hypocalcemia.[13]

Other calcium chelators can also cause hypocalcemia. A review of the effects of EDTA chelation therapy for cardiovascular disease emphasizes that hypocalcemia may occur as an adverse event during such treatment.[14]

Because albumin binds calcium, it is possible that infusion of albumin could lower ionized calcium. This is generally not a problem for the small 100-ml volumes of 25% albumin administered to patients on medical wards, but can be a problem during infusion of larger volumes of colloid during therapeutic plasma exchange, a problem that can be ameliorated by use of an alternate non–calcium-binding colloid.[11]

INCREASED OSTEOBLASTIC ACTIVITY

Bone formation and resorption are usually tightly coupled, but in certain circumstances, osteoblastic activity may be so great that hypocalcemia occurs. Two situations in which this occurs are during healing of bone disease after parathyroidectomy (hungry-bones syndrome) and in the presence of widespread osteoblastic metastases.

In most patients with relatively mild hyperparathyroidism, surgical removal of an abnormal parathyroid gland results in mild transient hypocalcemia caused by suppression of the remaining normal parathyroid glands, but prompt recovery to normal serum calcium concentrations is expected. In other patients with more severe hyperparathyroidism who have evidence for significant bone disease, hypocalcemia and hypophosphatemia persist despite recovery of PTH secretion from the remaining normal glands. The distinction between hungry bones and postoperative hypoparathyroidism is based on the persistently low serum phosphorus concentration in patients with hungry bones and on normal or even high concentrations of PTH. Individuals with pre-existing vitamin D deficiency accompanying their primary hyperparathyroidism seem to be at greater risk for hungry bones. Patients may require treatment with calcium and vitamin D to enhance intestinal calcium absorption for weeks and even months, until the bone heals.[15,16]

Avid uptake of calcium by osteoblastic metastatic lesions can also cause hypocalcemia. Prostate cancer metastases are commonly osteoblastic and are frequently associated with this syndrome, but other cancers can also cause hypocalcemia by this mechanism.[17] A prospective study of patients with advanced prostate cancer found that 57% of patients with proven bone metastases had elevated circulating concentrations of PTH, suggesting that mild secondary hyperparathyroidism caused by osteoblastic metastases could be more common than generally recognized.[18]

ACUTE ILLNESS

Hypocalcemia is quite common in severely ill patients.[19] In some patients, changes in serum proteins are responsible for the majority of the change in serum calcium, and ionized calcium remains normal. This seems to be the case for much of the mild hypocalcemia that often accompanies surgical procedures.[20] However, most patients develop some ionized hypocalcemia during severe acute illness, and in some patients, the degree of hypocalcemia is clinically significant. Because serum proteins are often abnormal in these patients, ionized calcium determination is required in severely ill individuals for appropriately diagnosis and treatment.

Hypocalcemia is common in acute pancreatitis and is one of the prognostic signs indicative of overall poor outcome. Free fatty acids are generated by the actions of pancreatic enzymes, and these complex with calcium to form insoluble soaps. In addition, the inflammatory process may be associated with other systemic mediators, although it is not clear whether elevations of these mediators are causally related to the hypocalcemia. Patients with acute pancreatitis may often have other factors contributing to the development of hypocalcemia, such as hypomagnesemia, malabsorption with vitamin D deficiency, and hypoalbuminemia.[21]

Hypocalcemia in the setting of other acute illnesses, particularly bacterial sepsis, is a very poor prognostic sign. The mechanism of hypocalcemia in sepsis remains unclear. PTH secretion seems to be appropriately increased, but the degree of hypocalcemia is inversely correlated with TNF-α and interleukin-6 (IL-6) activity, so it is likely that circulating cytokines play a role in the development of the hypocalcemia.[22] Patients with AIDS and hypocalcemia may have a distinct pathophysiology. After adjusting for hypoalbuminemia, hypocalcemia is present in AIDS patients more commonly than in control hospital outpatients (6.5% versus 1.1% in one study). AIDS patients may have concomitant vitamin D deficiency or hypomagnesemia and may not have an entirely normal parathyroid hormone secretory response for the degree of hypocalcemia.[23] CD4 is expressed in parathyroid glands, so there is the possibility that a lack of parathyroid hormone reserve could be related to HIV infection of parathyroid cells.[24]

MEDICATIONS

In patients who seem to have drug-related hypocalcemia, the presence of symptomatic hypocalcemia should prompt a complete evaluation for other underlying abnormalities of calcium regulatory hormones. A common theme that runs through many of the case reports of patients who have symptomatic hypocalcemia induced by medications and during acute illness is that the development of hypocalcemia often leads to the discovery of previously unrecognized vitamin D deficiency or hypoparathyroidism.

During aggressive treatment of patients who have hypercalcemia, potent antiresorptive medications that interfere with mobilization of calcium from skeletal stores can cause hypocalcemia. Even when care is used, there may be a brief phase of transient hypocalcemia after successful reduction of the serum calcium until PTH secretion recovers from suppression. If treatment is particularly zealous, osteoclastic activity may be more profoundly decreased, and hypocalcemia can be longlasting. In addition, patients with malignancy may have other problems, such as hypomagnesemia or vitamin D deficiency, which can be unmasked during aggressive intravenous bisphosphonate treatment.[25]

Mild asymptomatic hypocalcemia occurs occasionally in patients with osteoporosis, Paget's disease, or metastatic bone disease who are treated with oral or intravenous bisphosphonates, and this is not usually a clinical problem. However, patients who have unrecognized hypoparathyroidism or vitamin D deficiency can develop more severe and prolonged symptomatic hypocalcemia during bisphosphonate therapy.[26,27]

Long-term anticonvulsant therapy with phenytoin or phenobarbital is associated with an increased risk for osteomalacia and hypocalcemia. Institutionalized patients seem most likely to be affected,[28] and ambulatory outpatients who have adequate calcium and vitamin D intake have a fairly low risk for this complication.

Medications that cause hypomagnesemia, such as amphotericin B, furosemide, cyclosporine, and cisplatin, can provoke hypocalcemia.[29] Medications that contain calcium-binding properties can precipitate hypocalcemia. Fosphenytoin provides a large phosphate load.[30] Foscarnet, an antiviral antibiotic used primarily in patients with AIDS, is a pyrophosphate analog that complexes calcium and magnesium.[31] Intravenous contrast agents containing EDTA were previously reported to cause hypocalcemia and are not used commonly, but EDTA chelation therapy is associated with the development of hypocalcemia in some patients.[14]

Antineoplastic agents seem capable of causing hypocalcemia in some patients, even when a tumor lysis syndrome does not occur. It may be that effective treatment of patients who have bone lesions allows healing of bones with a hungry-bones effect, and this has been reported in several patients who have prostate cancer treated with estramustine.[32]

Finally, symptomatic hypocalcemia has been reported in patients receiving magnesium as tocolytic therapy for premature labor.[33] Increases in magnesium are known to suppress PTH secretion, probably through effects on the calcium-sensing receptor, but it is not clear why some patients are more susceptible to this complication.

REFERENCES

1. Ladenson JH, Lewis JW, Boyd JC 1978 Failure of total calcium corrected for protein, albumin, and pH to correctly assess free calcium status. J Clin Endocrinol Metab **46:**986–993.
2. Dickerson RN, Alexander KH, Minard G, Croce MA, Brown RO 2004 Accuracy of methods to estimate ionized and "corrected" serum calcium concentrations in critically ill multiple trauma patients receiving specialized nutrition support. J Parenter Enteral Nutr **28:**133–141.
3. Naguib MT, Evans N 2002 Combined false hyperkalemia and hypocalcemia due to specimen contamination during routine phlebotomy. South Med J **95:**18–20.
4. Lowe A, Balzer T, Hirt U 2005 Interference of gadolinium-containing contrast-enhancing agents with colorimetric calcium laboratory testing. Invest Radiol **40:**521–525.
5. Prince MR 2004 More on pseudohypocalcemia and gadolinium-enhanced MRI. N Engl J Med **350:**87–88.
6. Helikson MA, Parham WA, Tobias JD 1997 Hypocalcemia and hyperphosphatemia after phosphate enema use in a child. J Pediatr Surg **32:**1244–1246.
7. Boivin MA, Kahn SR 1998 Symptomatic hypocalcemia from oral sodium phosphate: A report of two cases. Am J Gastroenterol **93:**2577–2579.
8. Campisi P, Badhwar V, Morin S, Trudel JL 1999 Postoperative hypocalcemic tetany caused by fleet phosphosoda preparation in patient taking alendronate sodium: Report of a case. Dis Colon Rectum **42:**1499–1501.
9. Akmal M, Bishop JE, Telfer N, Norman AW, Massry SG 1986 Hypocalcemia and hypercalcemia in patients with rhabdomyolysis with and without acute renal failure. J Clin Endocrinol Metab **63:**137–142.
10. Wu AH, Bracey A, Bryan-Brown CW, Harper JV, Burritt MF 1987 Ionized calcium monitoring during liver transplantation. Arch Pathol Lab Med **111:**935–938.
11. Weinstein R 2001 Hypocalcemic toxicity and atypical reactions in therapeutic plasma exchange. J Clin Apheresis **16:**210–211.
12. Das SS, Chaudhary R, Khetan D, Shukla JS, Agarwal P, Mishra RB 2005 Calcium and magnesium levels during automated plateletpheresis in normal donors. Transfus Med **15:**233–236.
13. Niven MJ, Zohar M, Shimoni Z, Glick J 1998 Symptomatic hypocalcemia precipitated by small-volume blood transfusion. Ann Emerg Med **32:**498–501.
14. Seely DM, Wu P, Mills EJ 2005 EDTA chelation therapy for cardiovascular disease: A systematic review. BMC Cardiovasc Disord **5:**32.
15. Brasier AR, Nussbaum SR 1988 Hungry bone syndrome: Clinical and biochemical predictors of its occurrence after parathyroid surgery. Am J Med **84:**654–660.
16. Savazzi GM, Allegri L 1993 The hungry bone syndrome: Clinical problems and therapeutic approaches following parathyroidectomy. Eur J Med **2:**363–368.
17. Riancho JA, Arjona R, Valle R, Sanz J, Gonzalez-Macias J 1989 The clinical spectrum of hypocalcemia associated with bone metastases. J Intern Med **226:**449–452.
18. Murray RML, Grill V, Crinis N, Ho PWM, Davison J, Pitt P 2001 Hypocalcemia and normocalcemic hyperparathyroidism in patients with advanced prostate cancer. J Clin Endocrinol Metab **86:**4133–4138.
19. Vivien B, Langeron O, Morell E, Devilliers C, Carli PA, Coriat P, Riou B 2005 Early hypocalcemia in severe trauma. Crit Care Med **33:**1946–1952.
20. Lepage R, Legare G, Racicot C, Brossard J-H, Lapointe R, Dagenais M, D'Amour P 1999 Hypocalcemia induced during major and minor abdominal surgery in humans. J Clin Endocrinol Metab **84:**2654–2658.
21. Ammori BJ, Barclay GR, Larvin M, McMahon MJ 2003 Hypocalcemia in patients with acute pancreatitis: A putative role for systemic endotoxin exposure. Pancreas **26:**213–217.
22. Lind L, Carlstedt F, Rastad J, Stiernstrom H, Stridsberg M, Ljunggren O, Wide L, Larsson A, Hellman P, Ljunghall S 2000 Hypocalcemia and parathyroid hormone secretion in critically ill patients. Crit Care Med **28:**93–99.
23. Kuehn EW, Anders HJ, Bogner JR, Obermaier J, Goebel FD, Schlondorff D 1999 Hypocalcemia in HIV infection and AIDS. J Intern Med **245:**69–73.
24. Hellman P, Karlsson PA, Klareskog L, Ridefelt P, Bjerneroth G, Rastad J 1996 Expression and function of a CD-4 like molecule in parathyroid tissue. Surgery **120:**985–992.
25. Champallou C, Basuyau JP, Veyret C, Chinet P, Debled M, Chevrier A, Grongnet MH, Brunelle P 2003 Hypocalcemia following pamidronate administration for bone metastases of solid tumor: Three clinical case reports. J Pain Symptom Manage **25:**185–190.
26. Breen TL, Shane E 2004 Prolonged hypocalcemia after treatment with zoledronic acid in a patient with prostate cancer and vitamin D deficiency. J Clin Oncol **22:**1531–1532.
27. Schussheim DH, Jacobs TP, Silverberg SJ 1999 Hypocalcemia associated with alendronate. Ann Intern Med **130:**329.
28. Schmitt BP, Nordlund DJ, Rodgers LA 1984 Prevalence of hypocalcemia and elevated serum alkaline phosphatase in patients receiving chronic anticonvulsant therapy. J Fam Pract **18:**873–877.
29. Atsmon J, Dolev E 2005 Drug-induced hypomagnesaemia: Scope and management. Drug Saf **28:**763–788.
30. Keegan MT, Bondy LR, Blackshear JL, Lanier WL 2002 Hypocalcemia-like electrocardiographic changes after administration of fosphenytoin. Mayo Clin Proc **77:**584–586.
31. Huycke MM, Naguib MT, Stroemmel MM, Blick K, Monti K, Martin-Munley S, Kaufman C 2000 A double-blind placebo-controlled crossover trial of intravenous magnesium sulfate for foscarnet-induced ionized hypocalcemia and hypomagnesemia in patients with AIDS and cytomegalovirus infection. Antimicrob Agents Chemother **44:**2143–2148.
32. Park DS, Sellin RV, Tu SM 2001 Estramustine-related hypocalcemia in patients with prostate carcinoma and osteoblastic metastases. Urology **58:**105xii–105xv.
33. Koontz SL, Friedman SA, Schwartz ML 2004 Symptomatic hypocalcemia after tocolytic therapy with magnesium sulfate and nifedipine. Am J Obstet Gynecol **190:**1773–1776.

Chapter 40.   Magnesium Depletion and Hypermagnesemia

Division of Endocrinology, Keck School of Medicine, University of Southern California, Los Angeles, California

HYPOMAGNESEMIA/MAGNESIUM DEPLETION

Magnesium (Mg) depletion, as determined by low serum Mg levels, is present in ~10% of patients admitted to city hospitals and as many as 65% of patients in intensive care units. Hypomagnesemia and/or Mg depletion is usually caused by losses of Mg from either the gastrointestinal tract or the kidney, as outlined in Table 1.

Causes of Magnesium Depletion

The Mg content of upper intestinal tract fluids is ~1 mEq/liter; therefore, vomiting and nasogastric suction may contribute to Mg depletion. The Mg content of diarrheal fluids and fistulous drainage are much higher (up to 15 mEq/liter), and consequently, Mg depletion is common in acute and chronic diarrhea, regional enteritis, ulcerative colitis, and intestinal and biliary fistulas. Malabsorption syndromes may also result in Mg deficiency. Steatorrhea and resection or bypass of the small bowel, particularly the ileum, often results in intestinal Mg malabsorption. Last, acute severe pancreatitis is associated with hypomagnesemia, which may be caused by a clinical problem, such as alcoholism, or to saponification of Mg in necrotic parapancreatic fat. A primary defect in intestinal Mg absorption, which presents early in life with hypomagnesemia, hypocalcemia, and seizures, has been described as an autosomal recessive disorder linked to chromosome 9q22. This disorder seems to be caused by mutations in *TRPM6*, which expresses a protein involved with active intestinal Mg transport.

Excessive excretion of Mg into the urine may be the basis of Mg depletion. Renal Mg reabsorption is proportional to tubular fluid flow as well as to sodium and calcium excretion. Chronic parenteral fluid therapy, particularly with saline, and volume expansion states such as primary aldosteronism may result in Mg depletion. Hypercalciuric states may also cause renal Mg wasting. Hypercalcemia has been shown to decrease renal Mg reabsorption, probably mediated by calcium binding to the calcium-sensing receptor in the thick ascending limb of Henle and decreasing transepithelial voltage, and hence a decrease in paracellular absorption of both calcium and Mg. This is probably the cause of renal Mg wasting and hypomagnesemia observed in many hypercalcemic states. Osmotic diuresis caused by glucosuria will result in urinary Mg wasting. Diabetes mellitus is probably the most common clinical disorder associated with Mg depletion.

An increasing list of drugs is becoming recognized as causing renal Mg wasting and Mg depletion. The major site of renal Mg reabsorption is at the loop of Henle; therefore, diuretics such as furosemide have been shown to result in marked Mg wasting. Aminoglycosides have been shown to cause a reversible renal lesion that results in hypermagnesuria and hypomagnesemia. Similarly, amphotericin B therapy has been reported to result in renal Mg wasting. Other renal Mg-wasting agents include cisplatin, cyclosporin, tacrolimus, and pentamidine. A rising blood alcohol level is associated with hypermagnesuria and is one factor contributing to Mg depletion in chronic alcoholism. Metabolic acidosis caused by diabetic ketoacido-

sis, starvation, or alcoholism may also result in renal Mg wasting.

Several renal Mg wasting disorders have been described that may be genetic or sporadic. One form, which is autosomal recessive, results from mutations in the *paracellin-1* gene on chromosome 3. This disorder is characterized by low serum Mg, hypercalciuria, and nephrocalcinosis. Another autosomal dominant form of isolated renal Mg wasting and hypomagnesemia has been linked to chromosome 11q23 and identified as a mutation on the Na^+,K^+-ATPase γ-subunit of the *FXYD2* gene. Gitelman syndrome (familial hypokalemia-hypomagnesemia syndrome) is an autosomal recessive disorder caused by a genetic defect of the thiazide-sensitive NaCl cotransporter gene on chromosome 16.

Hypomagnesemia may accompany a number of other disorders. Phosphate depletion has been shown experimentally to result in urinary Mg wasting and hypomagnesemia. Hypomagnesemia may also accompany the "hungry bone" syndrome, a phase of rapid bone mineral accretion in subjects with hyperparathyroidism or hyperthyroidism after surgical treatment. Finally, chronic renal tubular, glomerular, or interstitial diseases may be associated with renal Mg wasting. Rarely excessive lactation may result in hypomagnesemia.

TABLE 1. CAUSES OF MG DEFICIENCY

Gastrointestinal disorders
   Prolonged nasogastric suction/vomiting
   Acute and chronic diarrhea
   Intestinal and biliary fistulas
   Malabsorption syndromes
   Extensive bowel resection or bypass
   Acute hemorrhagic pancreatitis
   Protein-calorie malnutrition
   Primary intestinal hypomagnesemia
Renal loss
   Chronic parenteral fluid therapy
   Osmotic diuresis (glucose, urea, manitol)
   Hypercalcemia
   Alcohol
   Diuretics (eg. furosemide)
   Aminoglycosides
   Cisplatin
   Cyclosporin
   Amphotericin B
   Pentamidine
   Tacrolimus
   Metabolic acidosis
   Chronic renal disorders with Mg wasting
   Primary renal hypomagnesemia
Endocrine and metabolic disorders
   Diabetes mellitus (glycosuria)
   Phosphate depletion
   Primary hyperparathyroidism (hypercalcemia)
   Hypoparathyroidism (hypercalciuria, hypercalcemia due to overtreatment with vitamin D)
   Primary aldosteronism
   Hungry bone syndrome
   Excessive lactation

Dr. Rude has been a consultant for Blaine Pharmaceuticals.

© 2006 American Society for Bone and Mineral Research

Manifestations of Magnesium Depletion

Because Mg depletion is usually secondary to another disease process or to a therapeutic agent, the features of the primary disease process may complicate or mask Mg depletion. A high index of suspicion is therefore warranted.

Neuromuscular hyperexcitability may be the presenting complaint. Latent tetany, as elicited by positive Chvostek's and Trousseau's signs, or spontaneous carpal-pedal spasm may be present. Frank generalized seizures may also occur. Although hypocalcemia often contributes to the neurological signs, hypomagnesemia without hypocalcemia has been reported to result in neuromuscular hyperexcitability. Other signs may include vertigo, ataxia, nystagmus, and athetoid and choreiform movements as well as muscular tremor, fasciculation, wasting, and weakness.

Electrocardiographic abnormalities of Mg depletion in humans include prolonged P-R interval and Q-T interval. Mg depletion may also result in cardiac arrhythmias. Supraventricular arrhythmias including premature atrial complexes, atrial tachycardia, atrial fibrillation, and junctional arrhythmias have been described. Ventricular premature complexes, ventricular tachycardia, and ventricular fibrillation are more serious complications. Mg administration to patients with acute myocardial infarction may decrease the mortality rate.

A common laboratory feature of Mg depletion is hypokalemia. During Mg depletion, there is loss of potassium from the cell with intracellular potassium depletion as well as an inability of the kidney to conserve potassium. Attempts to replete the potassium deficit with potassium therapy alone are not successful without simultaneous Mg therapy. This biochemical feature may be a contributing cause of the electrocardiologic findings and cardiac arrhythmias discussed above.

Hypocalcemia is a common manifestation of moderate to severe Mg depletion. The hypocalcemia may be a major contributing factor to the increased neuromuscular excitability often present in Mg-depleted patients. The pathogenesis of hypocalcemia is multifactorial. In normal subjects, acute changes in the serum Mg concentration will influence PTH secretion in a manner similar to calcium through binding to the calcium-sensing receptor. An acute fall in serum Mg stimulates PTH secretion, whereas hypermagnesemia inhibits PTH secretion. During chronic and severe Mg depletion, however, PTH secretion is impaired. Most patients will have serum PTH concentrations that are undetectable or inappropriately normal for the degree of hypocalcemia. Some patients, however, may have serum PTH levels above the normal range that may reflect early magnesium depletion. Regardless of the basal circulating PTH concentration in a Mg-deficient patient, an acute injection of Mg stimulates PTH secretion as shown in Fig. 1. Impaired PTH secretion therefore seems to be a major factor in hypomagnesemia-induced hypocalcemia. Hypocalcemia in the presence of normal or elevated serum PTH concentrations also suggests end-organ resistance to PTH. Patients with hypocalcemia caused by Mg depletion have both renal and skeletal resistance to exogenously administered PTH as manifested by subnormal urinary cyclic adenosine monophosphate (cAMP) and phosphate excretion and diminished calcemic response. This renal and skeletal resistance to PTH is reversed after several days of Mg therapy. The basis for the defect in PTH secretion and PTH end-organ resistance is unclear but may be caused by a defect in the adenylate cyclase and/or phospholipase C second messenger systems, because they are important in PTH secretion and mediating PTH effects in kidney and bone. Magnesium is necessary for the activity of the G-proteins in both enzyme systems. Magnesium is also necessary for substrate formation (MgATP) as well as being an allosteric

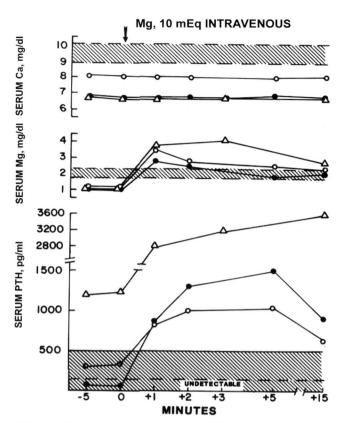

FIG. 1. Effect of an intravenous injection of 10 mEq magnesium on the serum concentration of calcium, magnesium, and PTH in hypocalcemic magnesium-deficient patients with undetectable (●), normal (○), or elevated (△) levels of PTH. Shaded area represents the range of normal for assay. Broken line for the PTH assay represents the level of detection. The magnesium injection resulted in a marked rise in PTH secretion within 1 minute in all three patients.

activator of adenylate cyclase. Recent data suggest that Mg deficiency disinhibits Gα subunits and mimics activation of the calcium-sensing receptor.

Clinically, patients with hypocalcemia caused by Mg depletion are resistant not only to PTH, but also to calcium and vitamin D therapy. The vitamin D resistance may be caused by impaired metabolism of vitamin D, because serum concentrations of 1,25-dihydroxyvitamin D are low.

Diagnosis of Magnesium Depletion

Measurement of the serum Mg concentration is the most commonly used test to assess Mg status. The normal serum Mg concentration ranges from 1.5 to 1.9 mEq/liter (1.8–2.2 mg/dl) and a value <1.5 mEq/liter usually indicates Mg depletion. Mg is principally an intracellular cation and only ~1% of the body Mg content is in the extracellular fluid compartments. The serum Mg concentration therefore may not reflect the intracellular Mg content. Ion selective electrodes for Mg are now available; however, different instruments between manufacturers differ in accuracy from each other and may give misleading results in sera with low Mg levels. Because vitamin D and calcium therapy are relatively ineffective in correcting the hypocalcemia, there must be a high index of suspicion for the presence of Mg depletion. Patients with Mg depletion severe enough to result in hypocalcemia are usually significantly hypomagnesemic. However, occasionally, patients may have

TABLE 2. SUGGESTED PROTOCOL FOR USE OF MAGNESIUM
TOLERANCE TEST

I.	Collect baseline 24-h urine for magnesium/creatinine ratio.*
II.	Infuse 0.2 mEq (2.4 mg) elemental magnesium per kilogram lean body weight in 50 ml 5% dextrose over 4 h.
III.	Collect urine (starting with infusion) for magnesium and creatinine for 24 h.
IV.	Percentage magnesium retained is calculated by the following formula:

$$\%Mg\ retained = 1 - \frac{[\text{Postinfusion 24-h urine Mg} - \text{Preinfusion urine Mg}/\text{creatinine} \times \text{Postinfusion urine creatinine}]}{\text{Total elemental Mg infused}} \times 100$$

V.	Criteria for Mg deficiency: >50% retention at 24 h = definite deficiency >25% retention at 24 h = probable deficiency

* A fasting shorter timed-urine (2-h spot) may be used.

normal serum Mg concentrations. Magnesium deficiency in the presence of a normal serum Mg concentration has been shown by measuring intracellular Mg or by whole body retention of infused Mg. Therefore, hypocalcemic patients who are at risk for Mg depletion but who have normal serum Mg levels should receive a trial of Mg therapy. The Mg tolerance test (or retention test) seems to be an accurate means of assessing Mg status. Correlations with skeletal muscle Mg content and Mg balance studies have been shown. This test seems to be discriminatory in patients with normal renal function; however, its usefulness may be limited if the patient has a renal Mg wasting disorder or is on a medication that induces renal Mg wasting. A suggested protocol for the Mg tolerance test is shown in Table 2.

Therapy

Patients who present with signs and symptoms of Mg depletion should be treated with Mg. These patients will usually be hypomagnesemic and/or have an abnormal Mg tolerance test. The extent of the total body Mg deficit is impossible to predict, but it may be as high as 200–400 mEq. Under these circumstances, parenteral Mg administration is usually indicated. An effective treatment regimen is the administration of 2 g $MgSO_4 \cdot 7\,H_2O$ (16.2 mEq Mg) as a 50% solution every 8 h intramuscularly. Because these injections are painful, a continuous intravenous infusion of 48 mEq over 24 h may be preferred. Either regimen will usually result in a normal to slightly elevated serum Mg concentration. Despite the fact that PTH secretion increases within minutes after beginning Mg administration, the serum calcium concentration may not return to normal for 3–7 days. This probably reflects slow restoration of intracellular Mg. During this period of therapy, serum Mg concentration may be normal, but the total body deficit may not yet be corrected. Magnesium should be continued until the clinical and biochemical manifestations (hypocalcemia and hypokalemia) of Mg depletion are resolved.

Patients who are hypomagnesemic and have seizures or an acute arrhythmia may be given 8–16 mEq of Mg as an intravenous injection over 5–10 minutes followed by 48 mEq IV/day. Ongoing Mg losses should be monitored during therapy. If the patient continues to lose Mg from the intestine or kidney, therapy may have to be continued for a longer duration. Once repletion has been accomplished, patients usually can maintain a normal Mg status on a regular diet. If repletion is accom-plished and the patient cannot eat, a maintenance dose of 8 mEq should be given daily. Patients who have chronic Mg loss from the intestine or kidney may require continued oral Mg supplementation. A daily dose of 300–600 mg of elemental Mg may be given, but these should be in divided doses to avoid the cathartic effect of Mg.

Caution should be taken during Mg therapy in patients with any degree of renal failure. If a decrease in glomerular filtration rate exists, the dose of Mg should be halved, and the serum Mg concentration must be monitored daily. If hypermagnesemia ensues, therapy must be stopped.

HYPERMAGNESEMIA

Magnesium intoxication is not a frequently encountered clinical problem, although mild to moderate elevations in the serum Mg concentration may be seen in as many as 12% of hospitalized patients.

Symptomatic hypermagnesemia is virtually always caused by excessive intake or administration of Mg salts. The majority of patients with hypermagnesemia have concomitant renal failure. Hypermagnesemia is usually seen in patients with renal failure who are receiving Mg as an antacid, enema, or infusion. Hypermagnesemia is also sometimes seen in acute renal failure in the setting of rhabdomyolysis.

Large amounts of oral Mg have rarely been reported to cause symptomatic hypermagnesemia in patients with normal renal function. The rectal administration of Mg for purgation may result in hypermagnesemia. Mg is a standard form of therapy for pregnancy-induced hypertension (preeclampsia and eclampsia) and may cause Mg intoxication in the mother as well as in the neonate. Ureteral irrigation with hemiacidrin (Renacidin) has been reported to cause symptomatic hypermagnesemia in patients with and without renal failure. Modest elevations in the serum Mg concentration may be seen in familial hypocalciuric hypercalcemia, lithium ingestion, and during volume depletion.

Signs and Symptoms

Neuromuscular symptoms are the most common presenting problem of Mg intoxication. One of the earliest shown effects of hypermagnesemia is the disappearance of the deep tendon reflexes. This is reached at serum Mg concentrations of 4–7 mEq/liter. Depressed respiration and apnea caused by paralysis of the voluntary musculature may be seen at serum Mg concentrations in excess of 8–10 mEq/liter. Somnolence may be observed at levels as low as 3 mEq/liter and above.

Moderate elevations in the serum Mg concentration of 3–5 mEq/liter result in a mild reduction in blood pressure. High concentrations may result in severe symptomatic hypotension. Mg can also be cardiotoxic. At serum Mg concentrations >5 mEq/liter, electrocardiographic findings of prolonged P-R intervals as well as increased QRS duration and QT interval are seen. Complete heart block, as well as cardiac arrest, may occur at concentrations >15 mEq/liter.

Hypermagnesemia causes a fall in the serum calcium concentration. The hypocalcemia may be related to the suppressive effect of hypermagnesemia on PTH secretion or to hypermagnesemia-induced PTH end-organ resistance. A direct effect of Mg on decreasing the serum calcium is suggested by the observation that hypermagnesemia causes hypocalcemia in hypoparathyroid subjects as well.

Other nonspecific manifestations of Mg intoxication include nausea, vomiting, and cutaneous flushing at serum levels of 3–9 mEq/liter.

Therapy

The possibility of Mg intoxication should be anticipated in any patient receiving Mg, especially if the patient has a reduction in renal function. Mg therapy should merely be discontinued in patients with mild to moderate elevations in the serum Mg level. Excess Mg will be excreted by the kidney, and any symptoms or signs of Mg intoxication will resolve. Patients with severe Mg intoxication may be treated with intravenous calcium. Calcium will antagonize the toxic effects of Mg. This antagonism is immediate but transient. The usual dose is an infusion of 100–200 mg of elemental calcium over 5–10 minutes. If the patient is in renal failure, peritoneal dialysis or hemodialysis against a low dialysis Mg bath will rapidly and effectively lower the serum Mg concentration.

SUGGESTED READING

1. Cholst IN, Steinberg SF, Trooper PJ, Fox HE, Segre GV, Bilezikian JP 1984 The influence of hypermagnesemia on serum calcium and parathyroid hormone levels in human subjects. N Engl J Med **310:**1221–1225.
2. Fassler CA, Rodriguez RM, Badesch DB, Stone WJ, Marini JJ 1985 Magnesium toxicity as a cause of hypotension and hypoventilation: Occurrence in patients with normal renal function. Arch Intern Med **145:**1604–1606.
3. Quamme GA 1997 Renal magnesium handling: New insights in understanding old problems. Kidney Int **52:**1180–1195.
4. Rude RK 1998 Magnesium deficiency: A heterogeneous cause of disease in humans. J Bone Miner Res **13:**749–758.
5. Brown EM, MacLeod RJ 2001 Extracellular calcium sensing and extracellular calcium signaling. Physiol Rev **81:**239–297.
6. Quitterer U, Hoffmann M, Freichel M, Lohse MJ 2001 Paradoxical block of parathormone secretion is mediated by increased activity of G alpha subunits. J Biol Chem **276:**6763–6769.
7. Rude RK 2001 Magnesium deficiency in parathyroid function. In: Bilezikian JP (ed.) The Parathyroids. Raven Press, New York, NY, USA, pp. 763–777.
8. Magnesium in Coronaries (MAGIC) Trial Investigators 2002 Early administration of intravenous magnesium to high-risk patients with acute myocardial infarction in the magnesium coronaries (MAGIC) trial: A randomized controlled trial. Lancet **360:**1189–1196.
9. Vetter T, Lohse MJ 2002 Magnesium and the parathyroid. Curr Opin Nephrol Hypertens **11:**403–410.
10. Kondrad M, Weber S 2003 Recent advances in molecular genetics of hereditary magnesium-losing disorders. J Am Soc Nephrol **14:**249–260.
11. Rude RK, Gruber HE 2004 Magnesium deficiency and osteoporosis: Animal and human observations. J Nutr Biochem **15:**710–716.
12. Silver BB 2004 Development of cellular magnesium nano-analysis in treatment of clinical magnesium deficiency. J Am Coll Nutr **23:**732S–737S.
13. Rude RK 2005 Magnesium. In: Coates P, Blackman MR, Cragg G, Levine M, Moss J, White J (eds.) Encyclopedia of Dietary Supplements. Marcel Dekker, New York, NY, USA, pp. 445–455.
14. Tong GM, Rude RK 2005 Magnesium deficiency in critical illness. J Intensive Care Med **20:**3–17.

Chapter 41. Hyperphosphatemia and Hypophosphatemia

Keith A. Hruska

Departments of Pediatrics, Medicine, and Cell Biology, Washington University School of Medicine, St. Louis, Missouri

INTRODUCTION

New data show that serum phosphate, similar to serum calcium, is a signaling molecule and this chapter begins to consider the serum phosphorus in a greater arena than one limited to mineral homeostasis. The mechanisms for sensing serum phosphate and stimulating signal transduction are not understood. The bulk of total body phosphate (85%) is in the bone as part of the mineralized extracellular matrix. This phosphate pool is accessible, albeit in a limited fashion through bone resorption. Phosphate is a predominantly intracellular anion with an estimated concentration of ~100 mM, most of which is either complexed or bound to proteins or lipids. Serum phosphorus concentration varies with age, time of day, fasting state, and season. It is higher in children than adults. Phosphorus levels exhibit a diurnal variation, with the lowest phosphate level occurring near noon. Serum phosphorus concentration is regulated by diet, hormones, and physical factors such as pH and changes in intestinal, kidney, and skeletal function. Importantly, because phosphate moves in and out of cells under several influences, the serum concentration of phosphorus may not reflect phosphate stores.

HYPERPHOSPHATEMIA

Serum inorganic phosphorus (Pi) concentrations are generally maintained at 2.5–4.5 mg/dl or 0.75–1.45 mM in adults. In children, normal serum Pi levels are 6–7 mg/dl at <2 years of age. Hyperphosphatemia may be the consequence of an increased intake of Pi, a decreased excretion of Pi, or translocation of Pi from tissue breakdown into the extracellular fluid[1] (Table 1). Because the kidneys are able to excrete phosphate very efficiently over a wide range of dietary intakes, hyperphosphatemia most frequently results from renal insufficiency and the attendant inability to excrete Pi. However, in metabolic bone disorders such as osteoporosis and renal osteodystrophy, the skeleton is a poorly recognized contributor to the serum phosphorus.

Etiology and Pathogenesis

Increased Intake. Hyperphosphatemia may be caused by an increased dietary intake or the administration of Pi. Intravenous administration of Pi during parenteral nutrition, the treatment of Pi depletion, or hypercalcemia can cause hyperphosphatemia, especially in patients with underlying renal insufficiency. Hyperphosphatemia may also result from overzealous use of oral phosphates or of phosphate-containing enemas, because phosphate can be absorbed passively from the colon through paracellular pathways. Administration of vitamin D and its metabolites in pharmacologic doses may be responsible for the development of hyperphosphatemia, although suppression of PTH and hypercalcemia-induced renal failure are important pathogenetic co-factors in this setting.

Decreased Renal Excretion. Clinically, hyperphosphatemia is most often caused by impaired excretion because of kidney failure. During stages II and III of chronic kidney diseases (CKDs), phosphate balance is maintained by a progressive

The author has reported no conflicts of interest.

Table 1. Causes of Hyperphosphatemia

Increased intake
    Intravenous—sodium or potassium phosphate
    Oral administration—NeutraPhos
    Rectal—Fleets phosphosoda enemas
Decreased renal excretion
    Renal insufficiency/failure—acute or chronic
    Pseudohypoparathyroidism
    Tumoral calcinosis
    Hypoparathyroidism
    Acromegaly
    Bisphosphonates
    Childhood
Excess bone resorption
    Transcellular shift from intracellular to extracellular spaces
    Catabolic states
    Fulminant hepatitis
    Hyperthermia
    Rhabdomyolysis—crush injuries or nontraumatic
    Cytotoxic therapy—tumor lysis
    Acute leukemia
    Diabetic ketoacidosis
    Hemolytic anemia
    Acidosis—metabolic or respiratory
Artifactual

reduction in the fraction of filtered phosphate resorbed by the tubules, leading to increased Pi excretion by the remaining nephrons and a maintenance of normal renal Pi clearance.[2] In advanced kidney failure, the fractional excretion of Pi may be as high as 60–90% of the filtered load of phosphate. However, when the number of functional nephrons becomes too diminished (glomerular filtration rate usually <20 ml/minute) and dietary intake is constant, Pi balance can no longer be maintained by reductions of tubular reabsorption, and hyperphosphatemia develops.[2] When hyperphosphatemia develops, the filtered load of Pi per nephron increases, and Pi excretion rises. As a result, Pi balance and renal excretory rate is re-established but at a higher serum Pi level (hyperphosphatemia).

Defects in renal excretion of Pi in the absence of renal failure may be primary, as in pseudohypoparathyroidism (PHP). PHP is a term for a group of disorders characterized by hypocalcemia and hyperphosphatemia caused by resistance to the renal tubular actions of PTH.[3] PHP1a is caused by mutations in the heterotrimeric G protein, $G_s\alpha$, whereas the molecular pathogenesis of PHP1b seems to be related to abnormalities in epigenetic imprinting of maternal $G_s\alpha$ alleles[4] and that of PHP2 is unknown. As a result of the molecular abnormalities in PHP, PTH does not decrease proximal renal tubular phosphate transport causing hyperphosphatemia.

A second primary defect in renal Pi excretion is tumoral calcinosis.[5] This is usually seen in young black males with ectopic calcification around large joints and is characterized by increased tubular reabsorption of calcium and Pi and normal responses to PTH. Familial forms of tumoral calcinosis are caused by mutations in the UDP-N-acetyl-α-D-galactosamine: polypeptide N-acetylgalactosaminyltransferase 3 (GALNT3) gene[6] and missense mutations in fibroblast growth factor (FGF)-23.[7,8] These studies show that, besides PTH, FGF23 is a second hormonal regulator of renal phosphate transport in physiologic conditions.

Secondary tubular defects in phosphate transport include hypoparathyroidism[9] and high blood levels of growth hormone in acromegaly. Finally, bisphosphonates such as Didronel (disodium etidronate), pamidronate, or alendronate

may cause hyperphosphatemia. The mechanisms of action are unclear, but they may involve cellular phosphate redistribution and decreased renal excretion.[10]

Excess Bone Resorption. Clinical and translational studies show that excess bone resorption contributes to the level of serum phosphorus that is poorly appreciated. Even in clinical situations where bone formation is decreased (adynamic) such as osteoporosis, a variability in the serum phosphorus is produced when bone formation is stimulated (Fig. 1).[11,12] For instance, in low turnover osteodystrophy treated with a skeletal anabolic agent, if phosphorus intake is constant, the serum phosphorus falls despite no change or a decrease in phosphate excretion[12] (Fig. 1B).

Transcellular Shift. Transcellular shift of Pi from cells into the extracellular fluid compartment may lead to hyperphosphatemia, as seen in conditions associated with increased catabolism or tissue destruction (e.g., systemic infections, fulminant hepatitis, severe hyperthermia, crush injuries, nontraumatic rhabdomyolysis, and cytotoxic therapy for hematologic malignancies such as acute lymphoblastic leukemia and Burkitt's lymphoma).[13,1] In the "tumor lysis syndrome," serum Pi levels typically rise because of release from dying cells within 12 days after initiation of treatment. The rising serum Pi concentration often is accompanied by hypocalcemia, hyperuricemia, hyperkalemia, and renal failure. Patients with diabetic ketoacidosis commonly have hyperphosphatemia at the time of presentation despite total body Pi depletion. Insulin, fluid, and acid–base therapy are accompanied by a shift of Pi back into cells and the development of hypophosphatemia. In lactic acidosis, hyperphosphatemia likely results from tissue hypoxia with a breakdown of ATP to AMP and Pi.

Artifactual. Hyperphosphatemia may be artifactual when hemolysis occurs during the collection, storage, or processing of blood samples.

Clinical Consequences of Hyperphosphatemia

The most important short-term consequences of hyperphosphatemia are hypocalcemia and tetany, which occur most commonly in patients with an increased Pi load from any source, exogenous or endogenous. In contrast, soft tissue calcification and secondary hyperparathyroidism are long-term consequences of hyperphosphatemia that occur mainly in patients with renal insufficiency and decreased renal Pi excretion.

Hypocalcemia and Tetany. With rapid elevations of serum Pi, hypocalcemia and tetany may occur with serum Pi concentrations as low as 6 mg/dl, a level that, if reached more slowly, has no detectable effect on serum calcium. Hyperphosphatemia, in addition to its effect on the calcium × phosphate ion product with resultant calcium deposition in soft tissues, also inhibits the activity of 1α-hydroxylase in the kidney, resulting in a lower circulating level of 1,25-dihydroxyvitamin D_3. This further aggravates hypocalcemia by impairing intestinal absorption of calcium and inducing a state of skeletal resistance to the action of PTH.

Phosphate-induced hypocalcemia is common in patients with acute or chronic renal failure and usually develops slowly. Tetany is uncommon unless a superimposed acid–base disorder produces an abrupt rise in plasma pH that acutely lowers the serum ionized calcium concentration. Profound hypocalcemia and tetany are occasionally observed during the early phase of the "tumor lysis" syndrome and rhabdomyolysis.

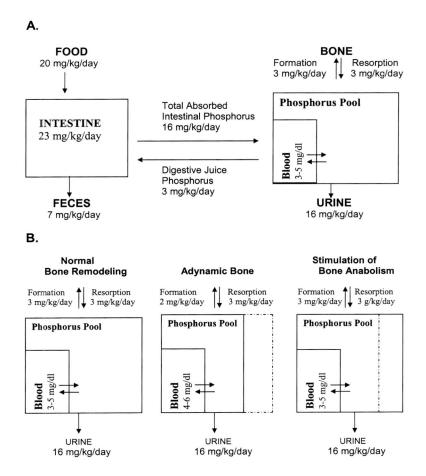

FIG. 1. Skeletal remodeling contributes to phosphate balance and serum phosphorus levels. (A) The phosphate balance diagram is amplified to show that serum phosphorus is a small component of a rapidly exchangeable phosphorus pool comprised of cellular phosphorus and the bone mineralization front. (B) When bone formation is decreased (adynamic bone disorders), the exchangeable pool size is diminished, and intestinal absorption from food intake will produce larger fluctuations in the serum phosphorus. These fluctuations are sufficient to activate the signaling actions of the serum Pi, although the fasting serum Pi is normal. Stimulation of bone anabolism increases the exchangeable phosphorus pool size and decreases serum phosphorus fluctuations. In end-stage kidney disease, treatment of secondary hyperparathyroidism with a calcimimetic that does not affect phosphate absorption decreases the serum phosphate, showing the role of the skeleton in hyperphosphatemia.

Soft Tissue Calcification. Extraskeletal calcification associated with hyperphosphatemia is usually seen in patients with CKD, diabetes, severe atherosclerosis, and aging. Recent basic, translational, and clinical research studies have led to new theories concerning the pathogenesis and the consequences of this phenomenon.[14–16] Several inhibitors of vascular calcification have been discovered, including osteoprotegerin,[17] osteopontin,[18,19] matrix Gla protein,[20] the klotho gene product,[21] and Smad 6[22] through phenotyping transgenic knockout mice. These substances constitute an inherent defense against heterotopic mineralization that is breached in the disease environment. In the setting of CKD, hyperphosphatemia has been identified as a major factor contributing to the forces favoring mineralization.[23] In contrast to the breach of defense theory of vascular calcification, there is significant evidence that vascular cells undergo osteogenic differentiation including expression of the osteoblast-specific transcription factors RUNX2/Cbfal, osterix, MSX2, and DlX5. As a result, the osteoblastic transcriptosome, including the marker protein osteocalcin, and vascular mineralization is observed.[14–16] Experimental models have shown that elevated phosphate is a direct stimulus of this transformation.[11,24,25] The finding of vascular calcification and the role of hyperphosphatemia has more than academic significance. Calcification of the neointima or the tunica media including the large blood vessels, coronary arteries, and heart valves in renal failure patients and diabetic subjects is associated with a high morbidity and mortality from systolic hypertension, congestive heart failure, coronary artery disease, and myocardial infarction.[26–28] Another manifestation of vascular calcification in more peripheral arteries, calciphylaxis, is also associated with hyperphosphatemia and carries a poor prognosis.[29,30] As a result, both vascular calcification and hyperphosphatemia are independent risk factors for cardiovascular disease and mortality.

Occasionally, an acute rise in serum Pi (e.g., during Pi treatment for hypercalcemia or vitamin D intoxication) may lead to soft tissue calcification in clinical settings besides those mentioned in the preceding paragraph. The blood vessels, skin, cornea (band keratopathy), and periarticular tissues are common sites of calcium phosphate deposition.

Secondary Hyperparathyroidism and Renal Osteodystrophy. Hyperphosphatemia caused by renal failure also plays a critical role in development of secondary hyperparathyroidism, renal osteodystrophy, and mortality.[11,23,31,32] Several mechanisms contribute to these complications including hyperphosphatemia-induced hypocalcemia through physical–chemical interactions, expression of TGFα and the epidermal growth factor receptor (EGFR) in parathyroid chief cells leading to hyperplasia and increased PTH secretion,[33,34] and inhibition of vitamin D synthesis and hyperphosphatemia-stimulated vascular calcification.[11] In patients with advanced renal failure, the enhanced phosphate load from PTH-mediated osteolysis may ultimately become the dominant influence on serum phosphorus levels (Fig. 1B). This phenomenon may account for the correlation between serum phosphorus levels and the severity of osteitis fibrosa cystica in patients maintained on chronic hemodialysis. Hyperphosphatemia also plays a critical role in the development of vascular calcification as discussed above.[11,25] There is a direct relationship between defective orthotopic mineralization (bone formation) in CKD and increased heterotopic mineralization.[11,17,24,35] Our data[11] and that of Price et al.[36] and Morshita et al.[24] show that increasing bone formation will lower phosphate levels and diminish vascular calcification in CKD.

Treatment

Correction of the pathogenetic defect should be the primary aim in the treatment of hyperphosphatemia. When hyperphosphatemia is due solely to increased intake, discontinuation of supplemental phosphate and maintenance of adequate volume for diuresis is generally sufficient because the kidneys will promptly excrete the excess. In the uncommon circumstance of significant hyperphosphatemia caused by transcellular shift, treatment should be dictated by the underlying cause. For example, hyperphosphatemia that accompanies diabetic ketoacidosis will resolve with insulin therapy, because insulin stimulates cellular uptake of phosphate. On the other hand, hyperphosphatemia seen with tumor lysis, rhabdomyolysis, or other conditions characterized by massive cell death or injury should be treated as an excess phosphate load, albeit endogenous instead of exogenous. Limitation of phosphate intake and enhanced diuresis will generally resolve this cause of hyperphosphatemia, provided renal function is adequate.

When renal insufficiency is present, however, the most effective way to treat hyperphosphatemia is to reduce dietary Pi intake and to add phosphate- binding agents. Because Pi is present in almost all foodstuffs, rigid dietary phosphate restriction requires a barely palatable diet that few patients can accept. However, dietary Pi can be reduced to 800-1000 mg/day with modest protein restriction. A predialysis level of 4.5–5.0 mg/dl is reasonable and allows some room for removal of phosphorus with dialysis while avoiding severe postdialysis hypophosphatemia. To achieve this, the addition of phosphate binders to reduce intestinal absorption of dietary Pi is required. Calcium salts and Sevelamer have replaced aluminum salts as first-line Pi binders.[37,38] However, calcium salts contribute to the calcium phosphate ion product, and massive calcium intake is often required to maintain serum phosphorus in the target range. Elevated calcium phosphorus products and the calcium load induced increase in the serum calcium contribute to the development of vascular calcification.[39,40] Therefore, newer Pi binders have been introduced such as sevelamer hydrochloride and lanthanum carbonate. Sevelamer has an improved safety profile over calcium salts, and as a binding resin, it also binds cholesterol and low-density lipoproteins (LDLs), leading to improved lipid profiles in patients with end-stage kidney disease (ESKD).[38] Calcium acetate and lanthanum carbonate bind more Pi than equivalent amounts of calcium carbonate or citrate. Sevelamer binds calcium equally to calcium carbonate, but the large doses required to maintain serum phosphorus, the pill sizes, and gastrointestinal side effects make compliance a difficult issue with the sole use of sevelamer. In addition, the cost of new agents have limited coverage in some instances. Therefore, the prescription of an effective Pi-binding regimen is a complex issue for patients with ESKD.

New treatments for secondary hyperparathyroidism of kidney failure besides phosphate binders discussed above and vitamin D analogs that suppress PTH gene transcription but increase intestinal Pi absorption are calcimimetics, which activate the Ca sensor of the PTH gland. A calcimimetic (cinacalcet), when used in dialysis patients, decreases serum phosphorus, showing the role of the skeleton in the hyperphosphatemia of ESKD.

The treatment of chronic hyperphosphatemia secondary to

TABLE 2. CAUSES OF MODERATE HYPOPHOSPHATEMIA AND/OR PHOSPHATE DEPLETION

Decreased intestinal absorption
  Abnormalities of vitamin D metabolism
  Antacid abuse
  Malabsorption
  Alcoholism
  Starvation—famine, anorexia nervosa, alcoholism
Increased urinary losses
  Alcoholism
  Hyperparathyroidism
  Renal tubular defects—Fanconi, Dent's, post transplant, hypomagnesemia, fructose intolerance
  X-linked hypophosphatemia, autosomal dominant hypophosphatemia
  Oncogenic osteomalacia
  McCune-Albright syndrome (MAS) and fibrous dysplasia (FD)
  Diabetic ketoacidosis
  Metabolic or respiratory acidosis
  Respiratory alkalosis
  Drugs: calcitonin, diuretics, glucocorticoids, bicarbonate, agonists
  Extracellular fluid volume expansion
Transcellular shift from the extracellular to the intracellular space
  Respiratory alkalosis
  Leukemia (Blast Crisis)
  Recovery from metabolic acidosis, commonly diabetic ketoacidosis
  Recovery from hypothermia
  Nutritional repletion—refeeding syndrome
  Sepsis, especially gram negative bacteremia
  Salicylate intoxication
  Sugars—glucose, fructose, glycerol
  Insulin therapy
  "Hungry-bone" syndrome after parathyroidectomy

hypoparathyroidism occasionally requires that phosphate binders be added to the other therapeutic agents.

HYPOPHOSPHATEMIA

Hypophosphatemia is defined as an abnormally low concentration of inorganic phosphate in serum or plasma. Hypophosphatemia does not necessarily indicate total body Pi depletion, because only 1% of the total body Pi is found in extracellular fluids. Conversely, serious Pi depletion may exist in the presence of a normal or even elevated serum Pi concentration. Moderate hypophosphatemia, defined as a serum Pi concentration between 2.5 and 1 mg/dl, is not uncommon, and is usually not associated with signs or symptoms.[1] Severe hypophosphatemia, defined as serum phosphorus levels <1.0 mg/dl, is often associated with clinical signs and symptoms that require therapy. Approximately 2% of hospital patients have levels of serum Pi <2 mg/dl according to some estimates. Hypophosphatemia is encountered more frequently among alcoholic patients, and up to 10% of patients admitted to hospitals because of chronic alcoholism are hypophosphatemic.

Etiology and Pathogenesis

Three types of pathophysiologic abnormalities can cause hypophosphatemia and total body Pi depletion: decreased intestinal absorption of Pi, increased urinary losses of this ion, and a shift of Pi from extracellular to intracellular compartments (Table 2). Combinations of these disturbances are common. The causes and mechanisms of moderate hypophosphatemia are shown in Table 2; the clinical conditions associated with severe hypophosphatemia are shown in Table 3.

TABLE 3. RISK FACTORS FOR SEVERE HYPOPHOSPHATEMIA AND/OR PHOSPHATE DEPLETION

Alcohol withdrawal
Nutritional repletion in at risk patients
   Anorexia nervosa and other eating disorders
   Starvation due to famine, neglect, alcoholism, malabsorption, prisoners of war
   AIDS and other chronic infections
   Massive weight loss for morbid obesity
Treatment of diabetic ketoacidosis
Critical illness
   Sepsis
   Posttrauma
   Extensive burns

Decreased Intestinal Absorption

Vitamin D Deficiency. Diets deficient in vitamin D lead to the metabolic disorder known as rickets in children or osteomalacia when it appears in adults.[41] Rickets result in severe deformities of bone because of rapid growth. These deformities are characterized by soft loose areas in the skull known as craniotabes and costochondral swelling or bending (known as rachitic rosary). The chest usually becomes flattened, and the sternum may be pushed forward to form the so-called pigeon chest. Thoracic expansion may be greatly reduced with impairment of respiratory function. Kyphosis is a common finding. There is remarkable swelling of the joints, particularly the wrists and ankles, with characteristic anterior bowing of the legs, and fractures of the "greenstick" variety may also be seen. In adults, the symptoms are not as striking and are usually characterized by bone pain, weakness, radiolucent areas, and pseudofractures. Pseudofractures represent stress fractures in which the normal process of healing is impaired because of a mineralization defect. Mild hypocalcemia may be present; however, hypophosphatemia is the most frequent biochemical alteration. This metabolic abnormality responds well to administration of small amounts of vitamin D.

Vitamin D–Resistant Rickets. These are recessively inherited forms of vitamin D refractory rickets. The conditions are characterized by hypophosphatemia, hypocalcemia, elevated levels of serum alkaline phosphatase, and sometimes, generalized aminoaciduria and severe bone lesions. Two main forms of vitamin D–dependent rickets have been characterized. The serum concentrations of 1,25-dihydroxycholecalciferol serves to differentiate the two types of vitamin D–dependent rickets. Type I is caused by a mutation in the gene converting 25(OH)D to 1,25-dihydroxycholecalciferol, the renal 1α-hydroxylase enzyme.[42] This condition responds to very large doses of vitamin D_2 and D_3 (100–300 times the normal requirement of physiologic doses; 0.5–1.0 μg/day of 1,25-dihydroxycholecalciferol). Type II is characterized by an end-organ resistance to 1,25-dihydroxycholecalciferol. Plasma levels of 1,25-dihydroxycholecalciferol are elevated. This finding, in association with radiographic and biochemical signs of rickets, implies resistance to the target tissue to 1,25-dihydroxycholecalciferol. Cellular defects found in patients with Vitamin D–resistant rickets type II are heterogeneous, providing in part an explanation for the different clinical manifestations of this disorder.

Numerous studies[43] have shown that hereditary type II vitamin D–resistant rickets is a genetic disease affecting the vitamin D receptor (VDR). The treatment of this condition requires large pharmacologic doses of calcium, which over-come the receptor defects and maintain bone remodeling.[43] Studies in mice with targeted disruption of the *VDR* gene, an animal model of vitamin D–resistant rickets type II, confirm that many aspects of the clinical phenotype are caused by decreased intestinal ion transport and can be overcome by adjustments of dietary intake.[44]

Antacid Abuse and Malabsorption. Severe hypophosphatemia and phosphate depletion may result from vigorous use of oral antacids, which bind phosphate, usually for peptic ulcer disease.[45] Patients so treated may develop osteomalacia and severe skeletal symptoms caused by phosphorus deficiency. Intestinal malabsorption can cause hypophosphatemia and phosphate depletion through malabsorption of Pi and vitamin D and through increased urinary Pi losses resulting from secondary hyperparathyroidism induced by calcium malabsorption.

Alcohol and Alcohol Withdrawal. Alcohol abuse is a common cause of hypophosphatemia, which may be severe (Table 2),[46,47] due to both poor intake and excessive losses. Poor intake results from dietary deficiencies, the use of antacids, and vomiting. Patients with alcoholism have also been shown to have a variety of defects in renal tubular function, including a decrease in threshold for phosphate excretion, which are reversible with abstinence. Ethanol enhances urinary Pi excretion, and marked phosphaturia tends to occur during episodes of alcoholic ketoacidosis. Because such patients often eat poorly, ketonuria is common. Repeated episodes of ketoacidosis catabolize organic phosphates within cells and cause phosphaturia by mechanisms analogous to those seen in diabetic ketoacidosis. Chronic alcoholism may also cause magnesium deficiency and hypomagnesemia, which may, in turn, cause phosphaturia and Pi depletion, especially in skeletal muscle.

Nutritional Repletion: Oral, Enteral, and Parenteral Nutrition. Nutritional repletion of the malnourished patient implies the provision of sufficient calories, protein, and other nutrients to allow accelerated tissue accretion. In the course of this process, cellular uptake and use of Pi increase. When insufficient amounts of Pi are provided, an acute state of severe hypophosphatemia and intracellular Pi depletion with serious clinical and metabolic consequences can occur.[48,49] This type of hypophosphatemia has been observed in malnourished patients receiving parenteral nutrition and after refeeding of prisoners of war.

Increased Urinary Losses

Hyperparathyroidism. Primary hyperparathyroidism (Table 2) is a common entity in clinical medicine. PTH is secreted in excess of the physiologic needs for mineral homeostasis owing either to adenoma or hyperplasia of the parathyroid glands. This results in decreased phosphorus reabsorption by the kidney, and the urinary losses of phosphorus result in hypophosphatemia. The degree of hypophosphatemia varies considerably because mobilization of phosphorus from stimulation of skeletal remodeling in part mitigates the hypophosphatemia. Secondary hyperparathyroidism associated with normal renal function has been observed in patients with gastrointestinal abnormalities resulting in calcium malabsorption. Such patients may have low levels of serum calcium and phosphorus. In these patients, the hypocalcemia is responsible for increased release of PTH. Decreased intestinal absorption of phosphorus as a result of the primary gastrointestinal disease may contribute to the decrement in the levels of the serum phosphorus. In general, these patients have urinary losses of phosphorus that are out of proportion to the hypophosphatemia in contrast to patients with predominant phosphorus malabsorption and no secondary hyperparathyroidism in whom urinary excretion of phosphorus is low.

Renal Tubular Defects. Several conditions characterized by either single or multiple tubular ion transport defects have been characterized in which phosphorus reabsorption is decreased. In Fanconi syndrome, patients excrete not only an increased amount of phosphorus in the urine but also increased quantities of amino acids, uric acid, and glucose, resulting in hypouricemia and hypophosphatemia.[50] In Dent's disease, a proximal tubular trafficking vesicle chloride channel, CLCN5,[51,52] is mutated. This leads to hypercalciuria and hypophosphatemia.[53] There are other conditions in which an isolated defect in the renal tubular transport of phosphorus has been found (e.g., in fructose intolerance, an autosomal recessive disorder). After renal transplantation, an acquired renal tubular defect is responsible for the persistence of hypophosphatemia in some patients. Studies in patients after transplantation[54,55] show that a phosphatonin-like substance is responsible for posttransplant hypophosphatemia. The hypophosphatemia is important because recent studies implicate it in the osteoblast failure contributing to the development of osteoporosis.[56] The known phosphatonins, FGF23, secreted Frizzled related protein 4 (sFRP4), and matrix extracellular phosphoglycoprotein expression (MEPE) have been studied and found not to be the basis for posttransplant hypophosphatemia.[1,55]

X-Linked Hypophosphatemic Rickets and Autosomal Dominant Hypophosphatemic Rickets. These hereditary disorders are characterized by hypophosphatemia, decreased reabsorption of phosphorus by the renal tubule, decreased absorption of calcium and phosphorus from the gastrointestinal tract, and varying degrees of rickets or osteomalacia.[57] Patients with the disorders exhibit normal or reduced levels of 1,25-dihydroxycholecalciferol (which should be elevated because of the hypophosphatemia) and reduced Na-phosphate transport in the proximal tubule in the face of severe hypophosphatemia. The gene for X-linked hypophosphatemia (XLH) is not the Pi transport protein itself,[58] but a gene termed *PHEX*,[59] which encodes for a neutral endopeptidase presumed to be responsible for degradation of a group of new hormones identified as systemic phosphaturic factors, "phosphatonins."[60–62] The defective *PHEX* gene product in XLH rickets permits a phosphatonin, most likely FGF23, to inhibit renal phosphate absorption, despite persistent hypophosphatemia.[63] Studies have shown that FGF23 levels are elevated in many, but not all, patients with XLH.[64] A substance that stimulates FGF23 expression and is not appropriately processed by the mutated PHEX seems to be the pathogenesis of XLH.[65,66]

Oncogenic Osteomalacia. This entity is characterized by hypophosphatemia in association with mesenchymal tumors. The patients exhibit osteomalacia on histomorphologic examination of bone biopsy specimens, renal wasting of phosphorus, and markedly reduced levels of 1,25-dihydroxyvitamin D_3. The existence of a possible circulating humoral factor has long been suspected and is supported by the identification of tumor products from patients with hemangiopericytomas that inhibit renal phosphate transport[67] and recent genetic screens of tumors associated with hypophosphatemia compared with those without.[68–70] Three novel new hormones have been discovered by these studies. The first, FGF23, is the etiologic agent in XLH and autosomal dominant hypophosphatemic rickets (ADHR) discussed above. Physiologic secretion of FGF23 by osteoblasts is low because of the function of *PHEX*. Overpro-

duction of FGF23 by the oncogenic osteomalacic tumors leads to the syndrome. Thus, FGF23 is the first hormone discovered that is produced in the bone and functions to regulate renal and intestinal phosphate transport.

The second new hormone regulating phosphate transport in the kidney is a member of the secreted frizzled related protein (sFRP) family, decoy receptors involved in Wnt signaling.[71] Recent studies have shown that sFrp4 is a phosphatonin in some cases of oncogenic osteomalacia.[69] The frizzled proteins are the receptors for the Wnt family of developmental morphogens along with the co-receptor, low-density lipoprotein receptor–related protein 5 (Lrp5).[72] Lrp5 is a member of the Lrp family, which are promiscuous endocytic receptors.[73] Lrp2 is megalin, which is involved in endocytosis of the vitamin D–binding protein in the proximal tubule and delivery of 25(OH)D_3 for production of calcitriol.[74] Lrp5 is a divergent family member and its main function seems to be as the co-receptor with the frizzled family for the Wnts.[75] Lrp5 has been identified as the nonsyndromic high bone mass gene,[76] showing the critical nature of Wnt signaling in bone anabolism and setting the pathophysiologic stage for interference with Wnt signaling by sFrp4 to decrease bone formation and as a phosphatonin to increase Pi excretion. SFrp4 is widely expressed, including in the kidney, and disease states increase its production,[77] potentially leading to a mechanism whereby CKD inhibits bone formation and contributes to renal osteodystrophy.

The third phosphatonin is MEPE, which is expressed in osteoblasts and is upregulated in murine XLH (Hyp).[78–80] Processing of MEPE yields an acidic serine-aspartate rich motif (ASARM) peptide that plays a role in mineralization (Minhibin). *PHEX* prevents proteolysis of MEPE and release of ASARM.[81] Disruption of the *MEPE* gene results in increased bone formation and mass,[82] but the mice have normal Pi levels.

McCune-Albright Syndrome/Fibrous Dysplasia. McCune-Albright Syndrome (MAS) is a triad of polyostotic fibrous dysplasia (FD), café au lait skin pigmentation, and endocrine disorders mediated by activating mutations in the receptor associated heterotrimeric G protein, $G_s\alpha$.[83] The effects of the $G_s\alpha$ mutation, increased cAMP, may lead to rickets and osteomalacia because of hyperphosphaturic hypophosphatemia.[84,85]

Diabetic Ketoacidosis. Patients with well-controlled diabetes mellitus do not have excessive losses of phosphate. However, in the presence of hyperglycemia, polyuria, and acidosis, Pi is lost through the urine in excessive amounts. In ketoacidosis, intracellular organic components tend to be broken down, releasing a large amount of Pi into the plasma, which is subsequently lost in the urine. This process, combined with the enhanced osmotic Pi diuresis secondary to glycosuria, ketonuria, and polyuria, may cause large urinary losses of Pi and subsequent depletion. The plasma Pi is usually normal or slightly elevated in the ketotic patient despite the excessive urinary losses because of the continuous large shift of Pi from the cells into the plasma. With insulin, fluids, and correction of the ketoacidosis, however, serum and urine Pi may fall sharply. Despite the appearance of hypophosphatemia during treatment, previously well-controlled patients with diabetic ketoacidosis of only a few days duration almost never have serious phosphorus deficiency. Serum Pi rarely falls below 1.0 mg/dl in these patients. Administration of Pi-containing salts does not improve glucose use, nor does it reduce insulin requirements or the time for recovery from ketoacidosis. Thus, Pi therapy should be reserved for patients with serum Pi concentration <1.0 mg/dl.

TABLE 4. CONSEQUENCES OF SEVERE HYPOPHOSPHATEMIA

CNS dysfunction—encephalopathy, seizures, delirium, coma, paresthesias
Red blood cell dysfunction—hemolysis, tissue hypoxia
Leukocyte dysfunction—increased susceptibility to infectin
Platelet dysfunction—thrombocytopenia, hemorrhage
Skeletal muscle dysfunction—weakness, respiratory failure, rhabdomyolysis
Cardiac muscle dysfunction—cardiomyopathy, congestive heart failure
Bone disease—osteomalacia/rickets
Metabolic acidosis

Miscellaneous Urinary Losses. Abnormalities in tubular handling of phosphate have also been implicated in the genesis of severe hypophosphatemia induced by systemic acidosis, hypokalemia, hypomagnesemia, hypothyroidism, and humoral hypercalcemia of malignancy. During the recovery phase from severe burns (Table 3), hypophosphatemia may occur secondary to massive diuresis with phosphaturia.

Transcellular Shift

Respiratory Alkalosis. Intense hyperventilation for prolonged periods may depress serum Pi to values <1.0 mg/dl.[86] This is important in patients with alcoholic withdrawal who have attendant hyperventilation and Pi depletion. A similar degree of alkalemia induced by infusion of bicarbonate depresses Pi concentration only mildly. The combined hypophosphatemic effects of respiratory and metabolic alkalosis may be pronounced.

Severe hypophosphatemia is common in patients with extensive burns (Table 3). It usually appears within several days after the injury. Phosphorus is virtually undetectable in the urine. Hypophosphatemia may result from transductive losses, respiratory alkalosis, or other factors.

Leukemia (Blast Crisis). Advanced leukemia that is markedly proliferative (blast crisis) with total leukocyte counts >100,000 has been associated with severe hypophosphatemia. This would seem to result from excessive phosphorus uptake into rapidly multiplying cells.[87]

Clinical Consequences of Severe Hypophosphatemia

Severe hypophosphatemia with phosphorus deficiency may cause widespread disturbances. There are at least eight well-established effects of severe hypophosphatemia (Table 4). The signs and symptoms of severe hypophosphatemia may be related to a decrease in 2,3-diphosphoglycerate in the red cell. This change is associated with increased affinity of hemoglobin for oxygen and therefore tissue hypoxia. There is also a decrease in tissue content of ATP and, consequently, a decrease in the availability of energy-rich phosphate compounds for cell function.

Central Nervous System

Some patients with severe hypophosphatemia display symptoms compatible with metabolic encephalopathy.[88–90] They may display, in sequence, irritability, apprehension, weakness, numbness, paresthesias, dysarthria, confusion, obtundation, seizures, and coma. In contrast to delirium tremens, the syndrome does not include hallucinations. Patients with very severe hypophosphatemia may show diffuse slowing of their electroencephalogram.

Hematopoietic System

A decrease in the red cell content of 2,3-diphosphoglycerate and ATP leads to increased rigidity and, in rare instances, hemolysis.[91] Hemolysis is usually provoked by unusual stress on the metabolic requirements of the red cell, such as severe metabolic acidosis or infection. When hemolysis has occurred, ATP content has invariably been reduced. Leukocyte/macrophage dysfunction can be shown in vitro using Pi-depleted cells.[92] The suggestion that a predisposition to infection commonly seen in patients on intravenous hyperalimentation may be partly related to hypophosphatemia remains to be proven. Hypophosphatemia impairs granulocyte function by interfering with ATP synthesis. In experimental hypophosphatemia there is an increase in platelet diameter, suggesting shortened platelet survival and also a marked acceleration of platelet disappearance from the blood. These lead to thrombocytopenia and a reactive megakaryocytosis. In addition, there is an impairment of clot retraction and a hemorrhagic tendency, especially involving gut and skin.

Musculoskeletal System

Myopathy and Rhabdomyolysis. Muscle tissue requires large amounts of high-energy bonds (ATP, creatine phosphate) and oxygen for contraction for maintenance of membrane potential and for other functions. Pi deprivation induces muscle cell injury characterized by a decrease in intracellular Pi and an increase in water, sodium, and chloride. An apparent relationship between hypophosphatemia and alcoholic myopathy has been observed in chronic alcoholism.[93] The muscular clinical manifestations of Pi deficiency syndrome include myalgia, objective weakness, and myopathy with pathological findings of intracellular edema and a subnormal resting muscle membrane potential on electromyography. In patients with pre-existing Pi deficiency who develop acute hypophosphatemia, rhabdomyolysis might occur.[94] Hypophosphatemia and phosphate deficiency may be associated with creatine phosphokinase elevations in blood.

Bone. Skeletal defects have been reported in association with Pi depletion of different causes. These are discussed in detail elsewhere. Suffice it to say here that phosphate depletion is associated with rickets in children and osteomalacia in adults. However, the discovery of the phosphatonins, especially FGF23, shows that osteomalacia is more just hypophosphatemia decreasing mineralization, but rather impaired osteoblast function caused by the actions of FGF23 or the inhibition of Wnt signaling by sFrp4 that contribute directly to impaired mineralization.

Cardiovascular System

Severe hypophosphatemia has been associated with a cardiomyopathy characterized by a low cardiac output, a decreased ventricular ejection velocity, and an elevated left ventricular end diastolic pressure.[95] A decrease in myocardial content of inorganic phosphorus, ATP, and creatinine phosphate seems to underlie the impairment in myocardial contractibility.[96] During phosphorus depletion, blood pressure may be low, and the pressor response to naturally occurring vasoconstrictor agonists such as norepinephrine or angiotensin II is reduced.

Renal Effects of Hypophosphatemia and Phosphate Depletion

Severe hypophosphatemia and phosphate depletion affect the balance and serum concentrations of various electrolytes.[1]

TABLE 5. RENAL EFFECTS OF HYPOPHOSPHATEMIA

Decreased glomerular filtration rate
Metabolic abnormalities
    Decreased gluconeogenesis
    Insulin resistance
    Hypoparathyroidism, reduced urinary cAMP
    Increased production of 1,25 dihydroxyvitamin D_3
Transport abnormalities
    Hypercalciuria
    Decreased proximal tubular sodium transport
    Hypermagnesiuria
    Hypophosphaturia
    Bicarbonaturia
    Glycosuria

It may produce changes in cardiovascular function as described above; renal hemodynamics affect renal tubular transport processes and induce marked changes in renal cell metabolism. These disturbances are listed in Table 5.

Tubular Transport

Calcium. A marked increase in urinary calcium excretion occurs during phosphate depletion proportional to the severity of phosphate depletion and the degree of hypophosphatemia.[97]

Phosphate. Dietary Pi restriction and Pi depletion is associated with enhanced renal tubular reabsorption of Pi.[89,98] Urinary excretion of Pi declines within hours after the reduction in its dietary intake, and Pi virtually disappears from the urine within 12 days. The changes in renal tubular reabsorption of Pi occur before detectable falls in the serum Pi. The adaptation to a reduction in Pi supply is a direct response of the proximal tubule, rendering this nephron segment resistant to most phosphaturic stimuli, including PTH.[98] Acutely, Pi depletion causes an increase in the apical membrane expression of sodium–phosphate co-transporters likely by insertion of pre-existing transporter proteins from an endosomal pool.[1] Chronically, the increase in transporter expression is also accomplished by the synthesis of new transporter proteins. The adaptation to reduced Pi supply is independent of cellular responses to PTH. The signaling mechanisms responsible for adaptation are unknown.

Metabolic Acidosis. Severe hypophosphatemia with Pi deficiency may result in metabolic acidosis through three mechanisms.[99,100] First, severe hypophosphatemia is generally associated with a proportionate reduction of Pi excretion in the urine, thereby limiting hydrogen excretion as a titratable acid. Second, if Pi buffer is inadequate, acid secretion depends on production of ammonia and its conversion to ammonium ion. Ammonia production is severely depressed in Pi deficiency. The third mechanism is that of decreased renal tubular reabsorption of bicarbonate.

Treatment

The appropriate management of hypophosphatemia and Pi depletion requires identification of the underlying causes, treatment with supplemental Pi when necessary, and prevention of recurrence of the problem by correcting the underlying causes. The symptoms and signs of Pi depletion can vary, are nonspecific, and are usually seen in patients with multiple problems such as those encountered in intensive care unit settings. This makes it difficult to identify Pi depletion as the cause of clinical manifestations and Pi depletion is frequently overlooked.

Mild hypophosphatemia secondary to redistribution, with plasma Pi levels >2 mg/dl, is transient and requires no treatment. In cases of moderate hypophosphatemia, associated with Pi depletion (serum Pi >1.0 mg/dl in adults or 2.0 mg/dl in children), Pi supplementation should be administered in addition to treating the cause of hypophosphatemia. Milk is an excellent source of phosphorus, containing 1 g (33 mM) of inorganic phosphorus per liter. Skimmed milk may be better tolerated than whole milk, especially in children and malnourished patients because of concomitant lactose or fat intolerance. Alternatively, Neutraphos tablets (which contain 250 mg of Pi per tablet as a sodium or potassium salt) may be given. Oral Pi can be given in a dose up to 3 g/day (i.e., 3 tablets of Neutraphos every 6 h). The serum Pi level rises by as much as 1.5 mg/dl, 60–120 minutes after ingestion of 1000 mg of Pi. A phosphosoda enema solution, composed of buffered sodium phosphate, may also be used in a dose of 15–30 ml three or four times daily.

Severe hypophosphatemia with serum levels <0.5 mg/dl occurs only when there is cumulative net loss of >3.3 g of Pi. If asymptomatic, oral replacement with a total of 6–10 g of Pi (1–3 g Pi/day) over a few days is usually sufficient. Symptomatic hypophosphatemia indicates that net Pi deficit exceeds 10 g. In these cases, 20 g of Pi is given spread over 1 week (up to 3 g/day). Patients with Pi deficiency tolerate substantially larger doses of oral Pi without side effects, such as diarrhea, than do normal subjects. However, patients with severe symptomatic hypophosphatemia who are unable to eat may be safely treated intravenously with 1 g of Pi delivered in 1 liter of fluid over 8–12 h. This is usually sufficient to raise serum Pi level to 1.0 mg/dl. It is unusual for hypophosphatemia to cause metabolic disturbances at serum Pi >1.0 mg/dl, so that full parenteral replacement is neither necessary nor desirable.

Treatment with phosphate can result in diarrhea, hyperphosphatemia, hypocalcemia, and hyperkalemia. These side effects can be prevented by paying careful attention to phosphorus dosages.

Prevention

The most effective approach to hypophosphatemia is prevention of predisposing conditions. Patients on total parenteral nutrition should receive a daily maintenance dose of Pi amounting to 1000 mg in 24 h, with increases as required by the clinical and metabolic states. Alcoholic patients and malnourished patients receiving intravenous fluids, particularly those containing glucose, should receive Pi supplementation, particularly if hypophosphatemia is observed.

ACKNOWLEDGMENTS

This work was supported by National Institutes of Health Grants DK59602, AR41677, and DK09976 and a grant from Johnson and Johnson.

REFERENCES

1. Hruska KA, Levi M, Slatopolsky E 2006 Disorders of phosphorus, calcium, and magnesium metabolism. In: Schrier RW (ed.) Diseases of the Kidney and Urinary Tract, 8th ed. Lippincott Williams & Wilkins, Philadelphia, USA (in press).
2. Slatopolsky E, Robson AM, Elkan I, Bricker NS 1968 Control of phosphate excretion in uremic man. J Clin Invest **47:**1865–1874.
3. Weinstein LS, Liu J, Sakamoto A, Xie T, Chen M 2004 Minireview: GNAS: Normal and abnormal functions. Endocrinology **145:**5459–5464.
4. Bastepe M, Frohlich LF, Linglart A, Abu-Zahra HS, Tojo K, Ward LM, Juppner H 2005 Deletion of the NESP55 differentially methylated region

causes loss of maternal GNAS imprints and pseudohypoparathyroidism type Ib. Nat Genet **37:**25–27.

5. Mitnick PD, Goldbarb S, Slatopolsky E, Lemann JJ, Gray RW, Agus ZS 1980 Calcium and phosphate metabolism in tumoral calcinosis. Ann Intern Med **92:**482–487.

6. Ichikawa S, Lyles KW, Econs MJ 2005 A novel GALNT3 mutation in a pseudoautosomal dominant form of tumoral calcinosis: Evidence that the disorder is autosomal recessive. J Clin Endocrinol Metab **90:**2420–2423.

7. Benet-Pages A, Orlik P, Strom TM, Lorenz-Depiereux B 2005 An FGF23 missense mutation causes familial tumoral calcinosis with hyperphosphatemia. Hum Mol Genet **14:**385–390.

8. Larsson T, Yu X, Davis SI, Draman MS, Mooney SD, Cullen MJ, White KE 2005 A novel recessive mutation in fibroblast growth factor-23 causes familial tumoral calcinosis. J Clin Endocrinol Metab **90:**2424–2427.

9. Parfitt AJ 1972 The spectrum of hypoparathyroidism. J Clin Endocrinol Metab **34:**152.

10. Walton RJ, Russell RG, Smith R 1975 Changes in the renal and extra-renal handling of phosphate induced by disodium etidronate (EHDP) in man. Clin Sci Mol Med **49:**45–56.

11. Davies MR, Lund RJ, Mathew S, Hruska KA 2005 Low turnover osteodystrophy and vascular calcification are amenable to skeletal anabolism in an animal model of chronic kidney disease and the metabolic syndrome. J Am Soc Nephrol **16:**917–928.

12. Lund RJ, Davies MR, Brown AJ, Hruska KA 2004 Successful treatment of an adynamic bone disorder with bone morphogenetic protein-7 in a renal ablation model. J Am Soc Nephrol **15:**359–369.

13. Cohen LF, Balow JE, Magrath IT, Poplack DG, Ziegler JL 1980 Acute tumor lysis syndrome. A review of 37 patients with Burkitt's lymphoma. Am J Med **68:**486–491.

14. Hruska KA, Mathew S, Saab G 2005 Bone morphogenetic proteins in vascular calcification. Circ Res **97:**105–114.

15. Doherty TM, Asotra K, Fitzpatrick LA, Qiao J, Wilkin DJ, Detrano RC, Dunstan CR, Shah PK, Rajavashisth TB 2004 Calcification in atherosclerosis: Bone biology and chronic inflammation at the arterial crossroads. Proc Natl Acad Sci USA **100:**11201–11206.

16. Vattikuti R, Towler DA 2004 Osteogenic regulation of vascular calcification: An early perspective. Am J Physiol Endocrinol Metab **286:**E686–E696.

17. Bucay N, Sarosi I, Dunstan CR, Morony S, Tarpleyl J, Capparelli C, Scully S, Tan HL, Xu W, Lacey DL, Boyle WJ, Simonet WS 1998 Osteoprotegerin-deficient mice develop early onset osteoporosis and arterial calcification. Genes Dev **12:**1260–1268.

18. Jono S, Peinado C, Giachelli CM 2000 Phosphorylation of osteopontin is required for inhibition of vascular smooth muscle cell calcification. J Biol Chem **275:**20197–20203.

19. Demer LL, Tintut Y 1999 Osteopontin: Between a rock and a hard plaque. Circ Res **84:**250–252.

20. Luo G, Ducy P, McKee MD, Pinero GJ, Loyer E, Behringer RR, Karsenty G 1997 Spontaneous calcification of arteries and cartilage in mice lacking matrix GLA protein. Nature **386:**78–81.

21. Kawaguchi H, Manabe N, Miyaura C, Chikuda H, Nakamura K, Kuro-o M 1999 Independent impairment of osteoblast and osteoclast differentiation in klotho mouse exhibiting low-turnover osteopenia. J Clin Invest **104:**229–237.

22. Galvin KM, Donovan MJ, Lynch CA, Meyer RI, Paul RJ, Lorenz JN, Fairchild-Huntress V, Dixon KL, Dunmore JH, Gimbrone MA Jr, Falb D, Huszar D 2000 A role for Smad6 in development and homeostasis of the cardiovascular system. Nat Genet **24:**171–174.

23. Block GA, Port FK 2000 Re-evaluation of risks associated with hyperphosphatemia and hyperparathyroidism in dialysis patients: Recommendations for a change in management. Am J Kidney Dis **35:**1226–1237.

24. Morishita K, Shirai A, Kubota M, Katakura Y, Nabeshima Y, Takeshige K, Kamiya T 2001 The progression of aging in klotho mutant mice can be modified by dietary phosphorus and zinc. J Nutr **131:**3182–3188.

25. Jono S, McKee MD, Murry CE, Shioi A, Nishizawa Y, Mori K, Morii H, Giachelli CM 2000 Phosphate regulation of vascular smooth muscle cell calcification. Circ Res **87:**e10–e17, 2000.

26. Blacher J, Guerin AP, Pannier B, Marchais SJ, London GM 2001 Arterial calcifications, arterial stiffness, and cardiovascular risk in end-stage renal disease. Hypertension **38:**938–942.

27. Iribarren C, Sidney S, Sternfeld B, Browner WS 2000 Calcification of the aortic arch: Risk factors and association with coronary heart disease, stroke, and peripheral vascular disease. JAMA **283:**2810–2815.

28. Newman AB, Naydeck BL, Sutton-Tyrrell K, Edmmundowicz D, O'Leary D, Kronmal R, Burke GL, Kuller LH 2002 Relationship between coronary artery calcification and other measures of subclinical cardiovascular disease in older adults. Arterioscler Thromb Vasc Biol **22:**1674–1679.

29. Ahmed S, O'Neill KD, Hood AF, Evan AP, Moe SM 2001 Calciphylaxis is associated with hyperphosphatemia and increased osteopontin expression by vascular smooth muscle cells. Am J Kid Dis **37:**1267–1276.

30. Wilmer WA, Magro CM 2002 Calciphylaxis: Emerging concepts in prevention, diagnosis, and treatment. Semin Dial **15:**172–186.

31. Slatopolsky E, Finch J, Denda M, Ritter C, Zhong M, Dusso A, MacDonald PNBAJ 1996 Phosphorus restriction prevents parathyroid gland growth. High phosphorus directly stimulates PTH secretion in vitro. J Clin Invest **97:**2534–2540.

32. Fatica RA, Dennis VW 2002 Cardiovascular mortality in chronic renal failure: Hyperphosphatemia, coronary calcification, and the role of phosphate binders. Cleve Clin J Med **69:**S21–S27.

33. Cozzolino M, Lu Y, Sato T, Yang J, Suarez IG, Brancaccio D, Slatopolsky E, Dusso ASA 2005 Critical role for enhanced-TGF-alpha and EGFR expression in the initiation of parathyroid hyperplasia in experimental kidney disease. Am J Physiol Renal Physiol **20:**F1096–F1102.

34. Martin DR, Ritter CS, Slatopolsky E, Brown AJ 2005 Acute regulation of parathyroid hormone by dietary phosphate. Endocrinol Metab **289:**E729–E734.

35. Hak AE, Pols HAP, van Hemert AM, Hofman A, Witteman JCM 2000 Progression of aortic calcification is associated with metacarpal bone loss during menopause. A population-based longitudinal study. Arterio Thromb Vasc Biol **20:**1926–1931.

36. Price PA, June HH, Buckley JR, Williamson MK 2001 Osteoprotegerin inhibits artery calcification induced by warfarin and by vitamin D. Arterioscler Thromb Vasc Biol **21:**1610–1616.

37. Slatopolsky E, Weerts C, Lopez S 1986 Calcium carbonate is an effective phosphate binder in dialysis patients. N Engl J Med **315:**157.

38. Slatopolsky E, Burke SK, Dillon MA 1999 RenaGel, a nonabsorbed calcium and aluminum-free phosphate-binder, lowers serum phosphorus and parathyroid hormone. Kidney Int **55:**299–307.

39. Chertow GM, Burke SK, Raggi P 2002 Sevelamer attenuates the progression of coronary and aortic calcification in hemodialysis patients. Kidney Int **62:**245–252.

40. Chertow GM, Burke SK, Dillon MA, Slatopolsky E 1999 Long-term effects of sevelamer hydrochloride on the calcium x phosphate product and lipid profile of haemodialysis patients. Nephrol Dialysis Transplant **14:**2907–2914.

41. Frame B, Parfitt AM 1978 Osteomalacia current concepts. Ann Intern Med **89:**966–982.

42. Fu GK, Lin D, Zhang MY, Bikle DD, Shackleton CH, Miller WL, Portale AA 1997 Cloning of human 25-hydroxyvitamin D-1 alpha-hydroxylase and mutations causing vitamin D-dependent rickets type 1. Molec Endocrinol **11:**1961–1970.

43. Hochberg Z, Weisman Y 1995 Calcitriol-resistant rickets due to vitamin D receptor defects. Trends Endocrinol Metab **6:**216–220.

44. Li YC, Amling M, Pirro AE, Priemel M, Meuse J, Baron R, Delling G, Demay MB 1998 Normalization of mineral ion homeostasis by dietary means prevents hyperparathyroidism, rickets, and osteomalacia, but not alopecia in vitamin D receptor-ablated mice. Endocrinology **139:**4391–4396.

45. Shields HM 1978 Rapid fall of serum phosphorus secondary to antacid therapy. Gastroenterology **75:**1137–1141.

46. Larsson L, Rebel K, Sorbo B 1983 Severe hypophosphatemia—a hospital survey. Acta Med Scand **214:**221–223.

47. Ryback RS, Eckardt MJ, Pautler CP 1980 Clinical relationships between serum phosphorus and other blood chemistry values in alcoholics. Arch Intern Med **140:**673–677.

48. Juan D, Elrazak MA 1979 Hypophosphatemia in hospitalized patients. JAMA **242:**163–164.

49. Betro MG, Pain RW 1972 Hypophosphatemia and hyperphosphatemia in a hospital population. BMJ **1:**273–276.

50. Roth KS, Foreman JW, Segal S 1981 The Faconi syndrome and mechanisms of tubular dysfunction. Kidney Int **20:**705–716.

51. Lloyd SE, Pearce SHS, Fisher SE, Steinmeyer K, Schwappach B, Scheinman SJ, Harding B, Bolino A, Devoto M, Goodyer P, Rigden SPA, Wrong O, Jentsch TJ, Craig IW, Thakker RV 1996 A common molecular basis for three inherited kidney stone diseases. Nature **379:**445–449.

52. Scheinman SJ 1998 X-linked hypercalciuric nephrolithiasis: Clinical syndromes and chloride channel mutations. Kidney Int **53:**3–17.

53. Jentsch TJ, Poet M, Fuhrmann JC, Zdebik AA 2005 Physiological functions of CLC Cl⁻ channels gleaned from human genetic disease and mouse models. Annu Rev Physiol **67:**779–807.

54. Rosenbaum RW, Hruska KA, Korkor A, Anderson C, Slatopolsky E 1981 Decreased phosphate reabsorption after renal transplantation: Evi-

dence for a mechanism independent of calcium and parathyroid hormone. Kidney Int **19**:568–578.

55. Green J, Debby H, Lederer E, Levi M, Zajicek HK, Bick T 2001 Evidence for a PTH-independent humoral mechanism in post-transplant hypophosphatemia and phosphaturia. Kidney Int **60**:1182–1196.

56. Rojas E, Carlini RG, Clesca P, Arminio A , Zuniaga O, de Elguezabal K, Weisinger JR, Hruska KA, Bellorin-Font E 2003 The pathogenesis of post-transplant osteodystrophy as detected by early alterations in bone remodeling. Kidney Int **63**:1915–1923.

57. Econs MJ, Francis F 1997 Positional cloning of the PEX gene: New insights into the pathophysiology of X-linked hypophosphatemic rickets. Am J Physiol **273**:F489–F498.

58. Tenenhouse HS 2005 Regulation of phosphorus homeostasis by the type IIa Na/phosphate cotransporter. Annu Rev Nutr **25**:10.1–10.18.

59. The Hyp Consortium 1995 A gene (PEX) with homologies to endopeptidases is mutated in patients with X-linked hypophosphatemic rickets. Nat Genet **11**:130–136.

60. Econs MJ, Drezner MK 1994 Tumor-induced osteomalacia: Unveiling a new hormone. N Engl J Med **330**:1645–1649.

61. Schiavi SC, Kumar R 2004 The phosphatonin pathway: New insights in phosphate homeostasis. Kidney Int **65**:1–14.

62. Quarles LD 2003 FGF23, PHEX, and MEPE regulation of phosphate homeostasis and skeletal mineralization. Am J Physiol Endocrinol Metab **285**:1–9.

63. The ADHR consortium, Group 1: White KE, Evans WE, O'Riordan JLH, Speer MC, Econs JJ, Groups 2: Lorenz-Depiereux B, Grabowski M, Meitinger T, Strom TM 2000 Autosomal dominant hypophosphatemic rickets is associated with mutations in FGF23. Nat Genet **26**:345–348.

64. Yamazaki Y, Okazaki R, Shibata M, Hasegawa Y, Satoh K, Tajima T, Takeuchi Y, Fujita T, Nakahara K, Yamashita T, Fukumoto S 2002 Increased circulatory level of biologically active full-length FGF-23 in patients with hypophosphatemic rickets/osteomalacia. J Clin Endocrinol Metab **87**:4957–4960.

65. Liu S, Guo R, Simpson LG, Xiao ZS, Burnham CE, Quarles LD 2003 Regulation of fibroblastic growth factor 23 expression but not degradation by PHEX131. J Biol Chem **278**:37419–37426.

66. Shimada T, Urakawa I, Yamazaki Y, Hasegawa H, Hino R, Yoneya T, Takeuchi Y, Fujita T, Fukumoto S, Yamashita T 2004 FGF-23 transgenic mice demonstrate hypophosphatemic rickets with reduced expression of sodium phosphate cotransporter type IIa. Biochem Biophys Res Com **314**:409–414.

67. Cai Q, Hodgson SF, Kao PC, Lennon VA, Klee GG, Zinsmeister AR, Kumar R 1994 Brief report: Inhibition of renal phosphate transport by a tumor product in a patient with oncogenic osteomalacia. N Engl J Med **330**:1645–1649.

68. Shimada T, Mizutani S, Muto T, Yoneya T, Hino R, Takeda S, Takeuchi Y, Fujita T, Fukumoto S, Yamashita T 2001 Cloning and characterization of FGF23 as a causative factor of tumor-induced osteomalacia. Proc Natl Acad Sci USA **98**:6500–6505.

69. Kumar R 2002 New insights into phosphate homeostasis: Fibroblast growth factor 23 and frizzled-related protein-4 are phosphaturic factors derived from tumors associated with osteomalacia. Curr Opin Nephrol Hypertens **11**:547–553.

70. Rowe PS, de Zoysa PA, Dong R, Wang HR, White KE, Econs MJ, Oudet CL 2000 MEPE, a new gene expressed in bone marrow and tumors causing osteomalacia. Genomics **67**:54–68.

71. Berndt T, Craig TA, Bowe AE, Vassiliadis J, Reczek D, Finnegan R, Jan de Beur SM, Schiavi SC, Kumar R 2003 Secreted frizzled-related protein 4 is a potent tumor-derived phosphaturic agent. J Clin Invest **112**:785–94.

72. Hey PJ, Twells RCJ, Phillips MS, Nakagawa Y, Brown SD, Kawaguchi Y, Cox R, Xie G, Dugan V, Hammond H, Metzker ML, Todd JA, Hess JF 1998 Cloning of a novel member of the low-density lipoprotein receptor family. Gene **216**:103–111.

73. Schneider WJ, Nimpf J 2003 LDL receptor relatives at the crossroad of endocytosis and signaling. Cell Mol Life Sci **60**:903.

74. Leheste JR, Melsen F, Wellner M, Jansen P, Schlichting U, Renner-Müller I, Andreassen TT, Wolf E , Bachmann S, Nykjaer A, Willnow TE 2002 Hypocalcemia and osteopathy in mice with kidney-specific megalin gene defect. FASEB J **17**:247–249.

75. He X, Semenov M, Tamai K, Zeng X 2004 LDL receptor-related proteins 5 and 6 in Wnt/β-catenin signaling: Arrows point the way. Development **131**:1663–1667.

76. Little RD, Carulli JP, DelMastro RG, Dupuis J, Osborne M, Folz C, Manning SP, Swain PM, Zhao S-C, Eustace B, Lappe MM, Spitzer L, Zweier S, Braunschweiger K, Benchekroun Y, Hu X, Adair R, Chee L, Fitzgerald MG, Tulig C, Caruso A, Tzellas N, Bawa A, Franklin B,

McGuire S, Nogues X, Gong G, Allen KM, Anisowicz A , Morales AJ, Lomedico PT, Recker SM, Van Eerdewegh P, Recker RR, Johnson ML 2002 A mutation in the LDL receptor-related protein 5 gene results in the autosomal dominant high-bone-mass trait. Am J Hum Genet **70**:11–19.

77. Surendran K, Schiavi S, Hruska KA 2005 Wnt-dependent-β-catenin signaling is activated after unilateral ureteral obstruction, and recombinant secreted frizzled-related protein 4 alters the progression of renal fibrosis. J Am Soc Neph **16**:2373–2384.

78. Argiro L, Desbarats M, Glorieux FH, Ecarot B 2001 Mepe, the gene encoding a tumor-secreted protein in oncogenic hypophosphatemic osteomalacia, is expressed in bone. Genomics **74**:342–351.

79. Bresler D, Bruder J, Mohnike K, Fraser WD, Rowe PS 2004 Serum MEPE-ASARM-peptides are elevated in X-linked rickets (HYP): Implications for phosphaturia and rickets. J Endocrinol **183**:1–9.

80. Rowe PS, Kumagai Y, Gutierrez G, Garrett IR, Blacher R, Rosen D, Cundy J, Navvab S, Chen D, Drezner MK, Quarles LD, Mundy GR 2004 MEPE has the properties of an osteoblastic phosphatonin and minhibin. Bone **34**:303–19.

81. Rowe PS, Garrett IR, Schwarz PM, Carnes DL, Lafer EM, Mundy GR, Gutierrez GE 2005 Surface plasmon resonance (SPR) confirms that MEPE binds to PHEX via the MEPE-ASARM motif: A model for impaired mineralization in X-linked rickets (HYP). Bone **36**:33–46.

82. Gowen LC, Petersen DN, Mansolf AL, Qi H, Stock JL, Tkalcevic GT, Simmons HA, Crawford DT, Chidsey-Frink KL, Ke HZ, McNeish JD, Brown TA 2003 Targeted disruption of the osteoblast/osteocyte factor 45 gene (OF45) results in increased bone formation and bone mass. J Biol Chem **278**:1998–2007.

83. Weinstein LS, Shenker A, Gejman PV, Merino MJ, Friedman E, Spiegel AM 1991 Activating mutations of the stimulatory G protein in the McCune-Albright syndrome. N Engl J Med **325**:1688–1695.

84. Collins MT, Chebli C, Jones J, Kushner H , Consugar M, Rinaldo P, Wientroub S, Bianco P, Robey PG 2001 Renal phosphate wasting in fibrous dysplasia of bone is part of a generalized renal tubular dysfunction similar to that seen in tumor-induced osteomalacia167. J Bone Miner Res **16**:806–813.

85. Corsi A, Collins MT, Riminucci M, Howell PG, Boyde A, Robey PG, Bianco P 2003 Osteomalacic and hyperparathyroid changes in fibrous dysplasia of bone: Core biopsy studies and clinical correlations. J Bone Miner Res **18**:1235–1246.

86. Mostellar ME, Tuttle EPJ 1964 Effects of alkalosis on plasma concentration and urinary excretion of urinary phosphate in man. J Clin Invest **43**:138–149.

87. Zamkoff KW, Kirshner JJ 1980 Marked hypophosphatemia associated with acute myelomonocytic leukemia: Indirect evidence of phosphorus uptake by leukemic cells. Arch Intern Med **140**:1523–1524.

88. Lotz M, Ney R, Bartter FC 1964 Osteomalacia and debility resulting from phosphorus depletion. Trans Assoc Am Physicians **77**:281–295.

89. Lotz M, Zisman E, Bartter FC 1968 Evidence for a phosphorus-depletion syndrome in man. N Engl J Med **278**:409–415.

90. Prins JG, Schrijver H, Staghouwer JM 1973 Hyperalimentation, hypophosphatemia and coma. Lancet **1**:1253–1254.

91. Jacob HS, Amsden T 1971 Acute hemolytic anemia and rigid red cells in hypophosphatemia. N Engl J Med **285**:1446–1450.

92. Craddock PR, Yawata Y, Van Santen L, Gilberstadt S, Silvis S, Jacob HS 1974 Acquired phagocyte dysfunction: A complication of the hypophosphatemia of parental hyperalimentation. N Engl J Med **290**:1403–1407.

93. Knochel JP, Bilbrey GL, Fuller TJ 1975 The muscle cell in chronic alcoholism: The possible role of phosphate depletion in alcoholic myopathy. Ann NY Acad Sci **252**:274–286.

94. Knochel JP, Barcenas C, Cotton JR, Fuller TJ, Haller R, Carter NW 1978 Hypophosphatemia and rhabdomyolysis. J Clin Invest **62**:1240–1246.

95. Zazzo J-F, Troche G, Ruel P, Maintenant J 1995 High incidence of hypophosphatemia in surgical intensive care patients: Efficacy of phosphorus therapy on myocardial function . Intensive Care Med **21**:826–831.

96. Fuller TJ, Nichols WW, Brenner BJ, Peterson JC 1978 Reversible depression in myocardial performance in dogs with experimental phosphorus deficiency. J Clin Invest **62**:1194–1190.

97. Coburn JW, Massry SG 1970 Changes in serum and urinary calcium during phosphate depletion: Studies on mechanisms. J Clin Invest **49**:1073–1087.

98. Steele TH, Stromberg BA, Larmore CA 1976 Renal resistance to parathyroid hormone during phosphorus deprivation. J Clin Invest **58**:1461–1464.

99. Dominguez JH, Gray RW, Lemann JJ 1976 Dietary phosphate deprivation in women and men: Effects on mineral and acid balances, parathyroid hormone and the metabolism of 25-OH-vitamin D. J Clin Endocrinol Metab **43**:1056–1068.

100. O'Donovan DJ, Lotspeich WD 1966 Activation of kidney mitochondrial glutaminase by inorganic phosphate and organic acids. Nature **212**:930–932.

Osteoporosis
(Section Editors: Michael Kleerekoper and Nancy Lane)

Chapter 42.   Epidemiology of Osteoporotic Fractures

Nicholas Harvey, Susannah Earl, and Cyrus Cooper

MRC Epidemiology Resource Centre, University of Southampton, Southampton General Hospital, Southampton, United Kingdom

INTRODUCTION

Osteoporosis is a skeletal disease characterized by low bone mass and microarchitectural deterioration of bone tissue with a consequent increase in bone fragility and susceptibility to fracture.[1] The term osteoporosis was first introduced in France and Germany during the last century. It means "porous bone," and initially implied a histological diagnosis, but was later refined to mean bone that was normally mineralized but reduced in quantity. Historically, the definition of osteoporosis has been difficult. A definition based on BMD may not encompass all the risk factors for fracture, whereas a fracture-based definition will not enable identification of at risk populations. In 1994, the World Health Organization (WHO)[2] convened to resolve this issue, defining osteoporosis in terms of BMD and previous fracture, as shown in Table 1. Thus, the WHO definition does not take into account microarchitectural changes that may weaken bone independently of any effect on BMD.[2]

More recently, there has been a move toward assessment of individualized 5- or 10-year absolute risk.[3] This has the advantage of incorporating risk factors that are partly independent of BMD, such as age and previous fracture, and thus allows decisions regarding commencement of therapy to be made more readily. Osteoporotic fracture has a huge impact economically, in addition to its effect on health: Osteoporotic fractures cost the United States around $17.9 billion per annum, with the cost in the United Kingdom being £1.7 billion (Table 2).[4] Hip fractures contribute most to these figures.[40]

FRACTURE EPIDEMIOLOGY

Incidence and Prevalence

The recent report from the U.S. Surgeon General highlighted the enormous burden of osteoporosis-related fractures (Fig. 1).[5–7] An estimated 10 million Americans >50 years old have osteoporosis, and there are ~1.5 million fragility fractures each year. Another 34 million Americans are at risk of the disease. A study of British fracture occurrence indicates that population risk is similar in the United Kingdom.[5] Thus, one in two women that are 50 years of age will have an osteoporotic fracture in their remaining lifetime; the figure for men is one in five.

Fracture incidence in the community is bimodal, showing peaks in youth and in the very elderly. In young people, fractures of long bones predominate, usually after substantial trauma, and are more frequent in males than females. In this group, the question of bone strength rarely arises, although there are now data suggesting that this may not be entirely irrelevant as a risk factor.[8] Over the age of 35 years, fracture incidence in women climbs steeply, so that rates become twice those in men. Before studies ascertaining vertebral deformities radiographically, rather than by clinical presentation, this peak was thought to be mainly caused by hip and distal forearm fracture, but as Fig. 1 shows, vertebral fracture can now be shown to make a significant contribution.

Hip Fracture. In most populations, hip fracture incidence increases exponentially with age (Fig. 1). Above 50 years of age, there is a female to male incidence ratio of around two to one.[9] Overall, ~98% of hip fractures occur among people ≥35 years of age, and 80% occur in women (because there are more elderly women than men). Worldwide there were an estimated 1.66 million hip fractures in 1990[10]; about 1.19 million in women and 463,00 in men. The majority occur after a fall from standing height or less; 90% occur in people >50 years old, and 80% are in women.[11] Recent work has characterized the age- and sex-specific incidence in the UK population, using the General Practice Research Database (GPRD, which includes 6% of the UK population). Thus, the lifetime risk of hip fracture for 50 year olds in the United Kingdom is 11.4% and 3.1% for women and men, respectively.[5] Most of this increased risk is accrued in old age, such that a 50-year-old woman's 10-year risk of hip fracture is 0.3%, rising to 8.7% when she is 80 years old.[5] The corresponding figures for men are 0.2% and 2.9%, respectively. Hip fractures are seasonal, with an increase in winter in temperate countries, but occur mainly indoors; therefore, the increase is not caused by slipping on icy pavements. It may be related to slowed neuromuscular reflexes and lower light in winter weather. The direction of falling is important, and a fall directly onto the hip (sideways) is more likely to cause a fracture than falling forward.[12]

Incidence rates vary substantially from one population to another, and incidence is usually greater in whites than nonwhites, although there are differences within populations of a given sex or race. In Europe, hip fracture rates vary 7-fold between countries.[13] These findings suggest an important role for environmental factors in the etiology of hip fracture, but factors studied thus far, such as smoking, alcohol consumption, activity levels, obesity, and migration status, have not explained these trends. Further research is needed to explain these important environmental factors.

Vertebral Fracture. Many vertebral fractures are asymptomatic, and there is disagreement about the radiographic definition of deformities in those patients who do present. Thus, in studies using radiographic screening of populations, the incidence of all vertebral deformities has been estimated to be three times that of hip fracture, with only one third of these coming to medical attention.[14] Recently, data from the prospective European Vertebral Osteoporosis Study (EVOS) have allowed accurate assessment of radiographically determined vertebral fractures in a large population. At the age of 75–79 years, the incidence of vertebral fractures so-defined was 13.6/1000 person-years for men and 29.3/1000 person-years for women.[6] This compares with 0.2/1000 person-years for men and

TABLE 1. DIAGNOSTIC CATEGORIES FOR OSTEOPOROSIS BASED ON WHO CRITERIA

Category	Definition by BMD
Normal	A value for BMD that is not more than 1 SD below the young adult mean value
Low bone mass (Osteopenia)	A value for BMD that lies between 1 and 2.5 SD below the young adult mean value
Osteoporosis	A value for BMD that is more than 2.5 SD below the young adult mean value

World Health Organization 1994.

The authors have reported no conflicts of interest.

TABLE 2. Impact of Osteoporosis-Related Fractures[40]

	Hip	Spine	Wrist
Lifetime risk (%)			
Women	14	28	13
Men	3	12	2
Cases/year	70,000	120,000	50,000
Hospitalization (%)	100	2–10	5
Relative survival	0.83	0.82	1.00

Costs: all sites combined ~£1.7 billion.

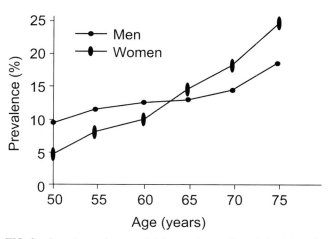

FIG. 2. Prevalence of vertebral deformity by sex. Data derived from the European Vertebral Osteoporosis Survey. (Reproduced from J Bone Miner Res 1996:**11**:1011–1019 with permission of the American Society for Bone and Mineral Research.)

9.8/1000 person-years in 75–84 year olds, where the fractures were defined by clinical presentation in an earlier study from Rochester, Minnesota.[14] The overall age-standardized incidence in EVOS was 10.7/1000 person-years in women and 5.7/1000 person-years in men. The age-standardized population prevalence across Europe was 12.2% for men and 12.0% for women 50–79 years of age.[15] Figure 2 shows the prevalence by age and sex in this population. Historically, it was believed that vertebral fractures were more common in women than men, but the EVOS data suggest that this is not the case at younger ages, such that the prevalence of deformities in 50–60 year olds is similar, if not higher in men, possibly because of a higher incidence of trauma.[15] The majority of vertebral fractures in elderly women occur through normal activities such as lifting, rather than through falling (Fig. 2).

Distal Forearm Fracture. Wrist fractures show a different pattern of occurrence to hip and vertebral fractures. There is an increase in incidence in white women between the ages of 45 and 60 years, followed by a plateau.[16] This may relate to altered neuromuscular reflexes with aging, and as a result, a tendency to fall sideways or backward, and thus not to break the fall with an outstretched arm. Most wrist fractures occur in women, and 50% occur in women >65 years old. Data from the GPRD show that a woman's lifetime risk of wrist fracture at 50 years old is 16.6% and falls to 10.4% at 70 years. The incidence in men is low and does not rise much with aging (lifetime risk, 2.9% at the age of 50 years and 1.4% at the age of 70 years).[5]

Clustering of Fractures in Individuals

Epidemiological studies suggest that patients with different types of fragility fractures are at increased risk of developing other types of fracture. For example, the presence of a previous vertebral deformity leads to a 7- to 10-fold increase in the risk of subsequent vertebral deformities.[17] This is a comparable level of increased risk to that seen for individuals who have sustained one hip fracture to then sustain a second. Furthermore, data from Rochester, Minnesota, suggest that the risk of a hip fracture is increased 1.4-fold in women and 2.7-fold in men after the occurrence of a distal forearm fracture.[18] The corresponding figures for subsequent vertebral fracture are 5.2 and 10.7. Data from EVOS show that prevalent vertebral deformity predicts incident hip fracture with a rate ratio of 2.8–4.5, and this increases with the number of vertebral deformities.[19] The number and morphometry of baseline vertebral deformities also predicts incident vertebral fracture.[20] The incidence of new vertebral fracture within a year of an incident vertebral fracture is 19.2%,[21] and in Rochester, the cumulative incidence of any fracture 10 years after baseline event was

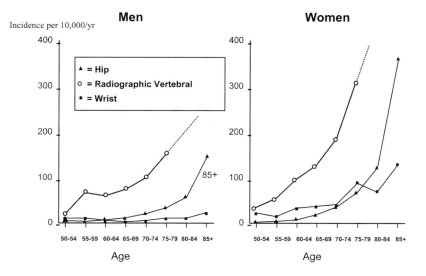

FIG. 1. Radiographic vertebral, hip, and wrist fracture incidence by age and sex.[5,6] (Modified from Bone, vol. 29, van Staa TP, Dennison EM, Leufkens HG, Cooper C, Epidemiology of fractures in England and Wales, pp. 517–522, Copyright 2001, with permission from Elsevier, and from J Bone Miner Res 2002:**17**:716–724 with permission of the American Society for Bone and Mineral Research.)

70%; these data emphasize the importance of prompt therapeutic action on discovering vertebral deformities.

Time Trends and Future Projections

Life expectancy is increasing around the globe, and the number of elderly individuals is rising in every geographic region. The world population is expected to rise from the current 323 million individuals ≥65 years of age to 1555 million by the year 2050. These demographic changes alone can be expected to increase the number of hip fractures occurring among people ≥35 years of age worldwide: the incidence is estimated to rise from 1.66 million in 1990 to 6.26 million in 2050. Assuming a constant age-specific rate of fracture, as the number of those >65 years of age increases from 32 million in 1990 to 69 million in 2050, the number of hip fractures in the United States will increase 3-fold.[22] In the United Kingdom, the number of hip fractures may increase from 46,000 in 1985 to 117,000 in 2016.[23]

An increasingly elderly population in Latin America and Asia could lead to a shift in the geographical distribution of hip fractures, with only a quarter occurring in Europe and North America (Fig. 3).[22]

Such projections are almost certainly optimistic considering that increases in the incidence of hip fractures have been observed even after adjusting for the growth in the elderly population. Although the age-adjusted rate of hip fracture seems to have leveled off in the northern regions of the United States, in parts of Sweden, and the United Kingdom, the rates in Hong Kong rose substantially between 1966 and 1985. Thus, the above figures potentially represent a significant underestimate of the number of hip fractures in the next one-half century.

Geography

There is variation in the incidence of hip fracture within populations of a given race and sex (Fig. 4).[13,24,25] Thus, age-adjusted hip fracture incidence rates are higher among white residents of Scandinavia than comparable subjects in the United States or Oceania. Within Europe, the range of variation was ~11-fold.[24] These differences were not explained by variation in activity levels, smoking, obesity, alcohol consump-

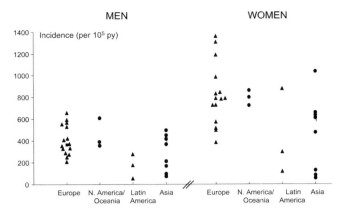

FIG. 4. Geographic variation in hip fracture incidence. (Adapted from J Bone Miner Res 2002;**17**:1237–1244 with permission of the American Society for Bone and Mineral Research.)

tion, or migration status.[13] The EVOS study showed a 3-fold difference in the prevalence of vertebral deformities between countries, with the highest rates in Scandinavia. The prevalence range between centers was 7.5–19.8% for men and 6.2–20.7% for women. The differences were not as great as those seen for hip fracture in Europe, and some of the differences could be explained by levels of physical activity and body mass index (BMI).[26]

MORTALITY AND MORBIDITY

Mortality

Mortality patterns have been studied for the three most frequent osteoporotic fractures. Survival rates 5 years after hip and vertebral fractures were found in Rochester, Minnesota, to be ~80% of those expected for men and women of similar age without fractures (Fig. 5).[26]

Hip Fracture. Hip fracture mortality is higher in men than women, increases with age,[26] and is greater for those with co-existing illnesses and poor prefracture functional status. There are ~31,000 excess deaths within 6 months of the ~300,000 hip fractures that occur annually in the United States. About 8% of men and 3% of women >50 years of age die while hospitalized for their fracture. In the United Kingdom, the 12-month survival after hip fracture for men is 63.3% versus 90.0% expected, and for women, 74.9% versus 91.1% expected.[5] The risk of death is greatest immediately after the fracture and decreases gradually over time. The cause of death is not usually directly attributable to the fracture itself but to other chronic diseases, which lead both to the fracture and to the reduced life expectancy.

Vertebral Fracture. In contrast to this pattern, vertebral fractures are associated with increased mortality well after a year after fracture.[26] Again, it seems that it is comorbid conditions that are responsible. The impairment of survival after vertebral fracture also markedly worsens as time from diagnosis of the fracture increases. This is in contrast to the pattern of survival for hip fractures. In the UK GPRD study, the observed survival in women 12 months after vertebral fracture was 86.5% versus 93.6% expected. At 5-year survival it was 56.5% observed and 69.9% expected.[5]

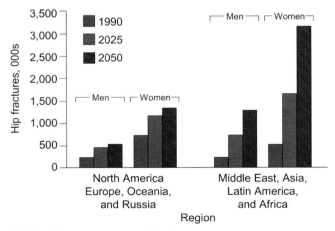

FIG. 3. Estimated numbers of hip fractures among men and women in different regions of the world in 1990 and 2050.[22] (Modified from Osteoporosis Int, vol. 2, 1992, pp. 285–289, Hip fractures in the elderly: A world-wide projection, Cooper C, Campion G, Melton LJ, with kind permission from Springer Science and Business Media.)

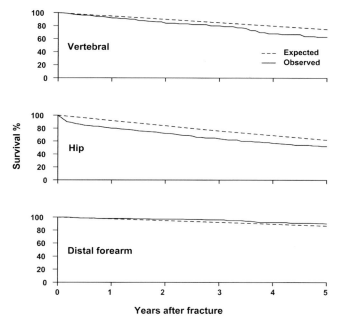

FIG. 5. Five-year survival after a clinically diagnosed hip, vertebral, or distal forearm fracture in Rochester, MN, 1985–1989.[26] (Modified from Cooper C, Atkinson EJ, Jacobsen SJ, O'Fallon WM, Melton LJ, Population-based study of survival after osteoporotic fractures, Am J Epidemiol, 1993, vol. 137, pp. 1001–1005, by permission of Oxford University Press.)

Morbidity

In the United States, 7% of survivors of all types of fracture have some degree of permanent disability, and 8% require long-term nursing home care. Overall, a 50-year old-white American woman has a 13% chance of experiencing functional decline after any fracture.[27]

Hip Fracture. As with mortality, hip fractures contribute most to osteoporosis-associated disability. Patients are prone to developing acute complications such as pressure sores, bronchopneumonia, and urinary tract infections. Perhaps the most important long-term outcome is impairment of the ability to walk. Fifty percent of those ambulatory before the fracture are unable to walk independently afterward. Age is an important determinant of outcome, with 14% of 50- to 55-year-old hip fracture victims being discharged to nursing homes versus 55% of those >90 years old.[27]

Vertebral Fracture. Despite only a minority of vertebral fractures coming to clinical attention, they account for 52,000 hospital admissions in the United States and 2188 in England and Wales each year in patients ≥45 years of age. The major clinical consequences of vertebral fracture are back pain, kyphosis, and height loss. Quality of life (QUALEFFO) scores decrease as number of vertebral fractures increases.[28]

Distal Forearm Fracture. Wrist fractures do not seem to increase mortality.[5] These trends are shown in Fig. 5. Although wrist fractures may impact on some activities such as writing or meal preparation, overall, few patients are completely disabled, despite over one half reporting only fair to poor function at 6 months.[27]

Low Bone Mass in Children

There has been considerably less study of the role of bone fragility in childhood fractures, probably because of the perception that the primary determinant of fracture in this age group is trauma. There are also considerable difficulties in reaching a definition of "osteoporosis" in a growing skeleton, when there is no straightforward relationship between BMD and fracture risk. Thus, the consensus view is that the term "low bone mass for age (with or without fractures)" is used rather than "osteoporosis." Most evidence comes from two large studies, based in the United Kingdom and Sweden, which describe the epidemiology of fractures in childhood.[29–31] In Malmo, Sweden, the overall incidence of fracture was 212/10,000 girls and 257/10,000 boys, with 27% of girls and 42% of boys sustaining a fracture between birth and 16 years of age. Fractures of the distal radius occurred most commonly, followed by fractures of the phalanges of the hand.[30] A follow-up study in Malmo between 1993–1994 found the incidence of fracture had decreased by almost 10% since the original study.[32]

A similar pattern was found in the UK GPRD.[29] The overall incidence of fracture was 133.1/10,000 children, with fractures being more common in boys than girls with an incidence of 161.6/10,000 and 102.9/10,000, respectively. Again the most common fracture site in both sexes was the radius/ulna with a total of 39.3/10,000 per year. Historically most work has focused on the impact of trauma in the etiology of childhood fractures, contrasting with the role of bone fragility in the elderly. However, several recent studies have documented lower areal and volumetric BMD in children with distal forearm fractures than age- and sex-matched controls.[33] The age and sex distribution of fractures may also suggest an influence of bone fragility. In the GPRD, fracture incidence peaked at 14 years in boys and 11 years in girls. Thus, peak fracture rate was found to be highest in both sexes at the start of puberty, when the discordance between height gain and accrual of volumetric bone density is greatest.[29]

Early Life Influences on Adult Fragility Fracture

The importance of achievement of adequate peak bone mass (PBM) in early adulthood has been emphasized in recent work, showing that PBM is a major determinant osteoporosis risk in later life. Thus, bone mass in childhood, and subsequent fractures may well have implications for risk for later life. Over the last 20 years, evidence has accrued that the early environment may have long-term influences on future bone health. This phenomenon of "developmental plasticity," whereby a single genotype may lead to different phenotypes, dependent on the prevailing environmental milieu, is well established in the natural world. There is a growing body of epidemiological evidence that a poor intrauterine environment leads to lower bone mass in adult life, both in third and sixth/seventh decades.[34–36] Additionally work in Finland has demonstrated as association between poor infant and childhood growth and increased risk of hip fractures even decades later.[37,38] Physiological studies have implicated the PTH/vitamin D axis in mechanisms underlying this phenomenon, such that mothers who are deficient in vitamin D in late pregnancy have children with decreased bone mass in childhood.[39] This novel area of research may lead ultimately to innovative strategies to improve bone health in children, with a subsequent reduction in the burden of osteoporotic fracture in future generations.

CONCLUSION

Osteoporosis is therefore a disease that has a huge effect on public health. The impact of osteoporotic fracture is massive, not just for individuals, but for the health service, economy, and population as a whole. The characterization of some of the risk factors for inadequate peak bone mass, involutional loss, and fracture have been elucidated and coupled with new pharmacologic therapies, we are now in a position to develop novel preventative and therapeutic strategies, both for the entire population and those at highest risk.

REFERENCES

1. Anonymous 1993 Consensus development conference: Diagnosis, prophylaxis and treatment of osteoporosis. Am J Med 941:646–650.
2. World Health Organization Study Group 1994 Assessment of fracture risk and its application to screening for postmenopausal osteoporosis. World Health Organization, Geneva, Switzerland.
3. Kanis JA, Johnell O, Oden A, Dawson A, De Laet C, Jonsson B 2001 Ten year probabilities of osteoporotic fractures according to BMD and diagnostic thresholds. Osteoporos Int 12:989–995.
4. Department of Health 1994 Advisory Group on Osteoporosis. Department of Health, London, UK.
5. van Staa TP, Dennison EM, Leufkens HG, Cooper C 2001 Epidemiology of fractures in England and Wales. Bone 29:517–522.
6. The European Prospective Osteoporosis Study (EPOS) Group 2002 Incidence of vertebral fracture in Europe: Results from the European Prospective Osteoporosis Study (EPOS). J Bone Miner Res 17:716–724.
7. U.S. Department of Health and Human Services 2004 Bone Health and Osteoporosis: A Report of the Surgeon General. U.S. Department of Health and Human Services, Rockville, MD.
8. Goulding A, Jones IE, Taylor RW, Manning PJ, Williams SM 2000 More broken bones: A 4-year double cohort study of young girls with and without distal forearm fractures. J Bone Miner Res 15:2011–2018.
9. Melton LJ III 1988 Epidemiology of Fractures. In: Riggs BL, Melton LJ III (eds.) Osteoporosis: Etiology, Diagnosis and Management. Raven Press, New York, NY, USA, pp. 133–154.
10. Cooper C, Melton LJ 1992 Epidemiology of osteoporosis. Trends Endocrinol Metab 314:224–229.
11. Gallagher JC, Melton LJ, Riggs BL, Bergstrath E 1980 Epidemiology of fractures of the proximal femur in Rochester, Minnesota. Clin Orthop 150:163–171.
12. Nevitt MC, Cummings SR 1993 Type of fall and risk of hip and wrist fractures: The study of osteoporotic fractures. The Study of Osteoporotic Fractures Research Group. J Am Geriatr Soc 41:1226–1234.
13. Johnell O, Gullberg B, Allander E, Kanis JA 1992 The apparent incidence of hip fracture in Europe: A study of national register sources. MEDOS Study Group. Osteoporos Int 2:298–302.
14. Cooper C, Atkinson EJ, O'Fallon WM, Melton LJ III 1992 Incidence of clinically diagnosed vertebral fractures: A population-based study in Rochester, Minnesota, 1985–1989. J Bone Miner Res 7:221–227.
15. O'Neill TW, Felsenberg D, Varlow J, Cooper C, Kanis JA, Silman AJ 1996 The prevalence of vertebral deformity in European men and women: The European Vertebral Osteoporosis Study. J Bone Miner Res 11:1010–1018.
16. Melton LJ, Cooper C 2001 Magnitude and impact of osteoporosis and fractures. In: Marcus R, Feldman D, Kelsey J (eds.) Osteoporosis, 2nd ed., vol 1. Academic Press, San Diego, CA, USA, pp. 557–567.
17. Ross PD, Davis JW, Epstein RS, Wasnich RD 1991 Pre-existing fractures and bone mass predict vertebral fracture incidence in women. Ann Intern Med 114:919–923.
18. Cuddihy MT, Gabriel SE, Crowson CS, O'Fallon WM, Melton LJ 1999 Forearm fractures as predictors of subsequent osteoporotic fractures. Osteoporos Int 9:469–475.
19. Ismail AA, Cockerill W, Cooper C, Finn JD, Abendroth K, Parisi G, Banzer D, Benevolenskaya LI, Bhalla AK, Bruges Armas J, Cannata JB, Delmas PD, Dequeker J, Dilsen G, Eastell R, Ershova O, Falch JA, Belsch B, Havelka S, Hoszowski K, Jajic I, Kragl U, Johnell O, Lopez Vaz A, Lorenc R, Lyritis G, Marchand F, Masaryk P, Matthis C, Miazgowski T, Pols HAP, Poor G, Rapado A, Raspe HH, Reid DM, Reisinger W, Janott J, Scheidt-Nave C, Stepan J, Todd C, Weber K, Woolf AD, Ambrecht G, Gowin W, Felsenberg D, Lunt M, Kanis JA, Reeve J, Silman AJ, O'Neill TW 2001 Prevalent vertebral deformity predicts incident hip though not distal forearm fracture: Results from the European Prospective Osteoporosis Study. Osteoporos Int 12:85–90.
20. Lunt M, O'Neill T, Armbrecht G, Reeve J, Felsenberg D, Cooper C 2002 Characteristics of prevalent vertebral deformity and the risk of incident vertebral fracture. Rheumatology 41(Suppl 1):101–102.
21. Lindsay R, Silverman SL, Cooper C, Hanley DA, Barton I, Broy SB Licata A, Benhamou L, Geusens P, Flowers K, Stracke H, Seeman E 2001 Risk of new vertebral fracture in the year following a fracture. JAMA 285:320–323.
22. Cooper C, Campion G, Melton LJ 1992 Hip fractures in the elderly: A world-wide projection. Osteoporos Int 2:285–289.
23. Royal College of Physicians 1989 Fractured neck of femur: Prevention and management. Summary and report of the Royal College of Physicians. J R Coll Physicians Lond 23:8–12.
24. Elffors I, Allander E, Kanis JA, Gullberg B, Johnell O, Dequeker J, Dilsen G, Gennari C, Lopes Vaz AA, Lyritis G 1994 The variable incidence of hip fracture in southern Europe: The MEDOS Study. Osteoporos Int 4:253–263.
25. Nagant dD, Devogelaer JP 1988 Increase in the incidence of hip fractures and of the ratio of trochanteric to cervical hip fractures in Belgium. Calcif Tissue Int 42:201–203.
26. Cooper C, Atkinson EJ, Jacobsen SJ, O'Fallon WM, Melton LJ 1993 Population-based study of survival after osteoporotic fractures. Am J Epidemiol 137:1001–1005.
27. Chrischilles EA, Butler CD, Davis CS, Wallace RB 1991 A model of lifetime osteoporosis impact. Arch Intern Med 151:2026–2032.
28. Oleksik A, Lips P, Dawson A, Minshall ME, Shen W, Cooper C, Kanis J 2000 Health-related quality of life in postmenopausal women with low BMD with or without prevalent vertebral fractures. J Bone Miner Res 15:1384–1392.
29. Cooper C, Dennison EM, Leufkens HG, Bishop N, van Staa TP 2004 Epidemiology of childhood fractures in Britain: A study using the General Practice Research Database. J Bone Miner Res 19:1976–1981.
30. Landin LA 1997 Epidemiology of children's fractures. J Pediatr Orthop B 6:79–83.
31. Landin LA 1983 Fracture patterns in children. Analysis of 8,682 fractures with special reference to incidence, etiology and secular changes in a Swedish urban population 1950–1979. Acta Orthop Scand Suppl 202:1–109.
32. Tiderius CJ, Landin L, Duppe H 1999 Decreasing incidence of fractures in children: An epidemiological analysis of 1,673 fractures in Malmo, Sweden, 1993–1994. Acta Orthop Scand 70:622–626.
33. Jones IE, Taylor RW, Williams SM, Manning PJ, Goulding A 2002 Four-year gain in bone mineral in girls with and without past forearm fractures: A DXA study. J Bone Miner Res 17:1065–1072.
34. Cooper C, Cawley M, Bhalla A, Egger P, Ring F, Morton L, Barker D 1995 Childhood growth, physical activity, and peak bone mass in women. J Bone Miner Res 10:940–947.
35. Gale CR, Martyn CN, Kellingray S, Eastell R, Cooper C 2001 Intrauterine programming of adult body composition. J Clin Endocrinol (Oxf) Metab 86:267–272.
36. Cooper C, Fall C, Egger P, Hobbs R, Eastell R, Barker D 1997 Growth in infancy and bone mass in later life. Ann Rheum Dis 56:17–21.
37. Javaid MK, Eriksson JG, Valimaki MJ, Forsen T, Osmond C, Barker DJ, Cooper C 2005 Growth in infancy and childhood predicts hip fracture risk in late adulthood. Bone 36(Suppl 1):S38.
38. Cooper C, Eriksson JG, Forsen T, Osmond C, Tuomilehto J, Barker DJ 2001 Maternal height, childhood growth and risk of hip fracture in later life: A longitudinal study. Osteoporos Int 12:623–629.
39. Javaid M, Crozier S, Harvey N, Gale C, Dennison E, Bracher G, Arden N, Godfrey JE, Cooper C, and the Princess Anne Hospital Study Group 2006 Maternal vitamin D status during pregnancy and childhood bone mass at age 9 years: A longitudinal study. Lancet 367:36–43.
40. Cooper C 1999 Epidemiology of osteoporosis. Osteoporos Int 9(Suppl 2):S2–S8.

Chapter 43.   Genetics of Osteoporosis

John A. Eisman

Bone and Mineral Research Program, Garvan Institute of Medical Research, University of New South Wales, and St. Vincent's Hospital Campus, Sydney, New South Wales, Australia

INTRODUCTION

In the field of osteoporosis, the fundamental questions in genetics relate to what insight genetic studies have currently provided and how genetic information might be used in clinical and basic studies of bone biology in the future. More than 25 years ago, it was recognized that a high proportion of measures of bone mass and structure, such as bone density, were more highly similar between identical (monozygotic) twins than between dizygotic (fraternal) twins.[1–3] These differences in concordance indicated a high level of heritability for such predictors of osteoporotic fracture risk. These studies confirmed individual patient's concerns that osteoporosis seemed to run in their family. Subsequently a variety of related bone parameters, such as bone turnover markers and bone geometric parameters, have also been shown to be highly heritable. Each of these parameters has also been associated with osteoporotic fracture risk. There have also been some studies showing clear, if modest, heritability of fracture risk.

The significance of these heritable effects generated considerable interest, although it was realized early that any genotype-phenotype relationships were likely to be complex. These human studies also gave impetus to animal studies where sophisticated breeding and congenic studies have allowed rapid progress. This intense interest has also been translated into a range of human studies including linkage studies in small families with extreme phenotype and in nuclear families as well as association studies in increasingly larger population sets. For various reasons, some obvious, these studies have not always been very productive of novel biological insights or identified novel pathways. However, there is clear potential for genetic studies in identifying novel biological pathways affecting bone as well as for developing new paradigms for assessment of risk for fracture and likelihood of response to treatment and potentially even for adverse effects. Many of these studies have suffered from limitations related to focusing on existing knowledge and on animal models as well as major limitations related to sample size and other statistical issues.

This chapter will not catalog the wide range of genes and genetic loci that have now been associated with bone biology and pathology; rather, it will consider the genetics of osteoporosis under the general headings of what can/should be measured, genome-wide scans and accidents of nature versus investigation of a priori selected loci, gender specificity, and statistical issues.

WHAT CAN/SHOULD BE MEASURED?

Although any bone can and will fracture if sufficient force is applied to it, when considering osteoporosis, the event of major clinical importance is a fracture after minimal trauma. These fractures are associated with significant morbidity, mortality, and costs to the individual and to the community. Understanding the biology of bone weakness that predisposes to such fractures has been very productive in recent decades. A number of other indicators ranging from body weight to family history

and ethnicity to hair color (gray) have been associated with osteoporosis and/or fracture risk. However, because these are unlikely to be directly related to bone fragility or fracture, they do not seem particularly useful parameters to pursue as primary endpoints in genetic studies. In fact, any parameter identified should only be considered as providing some insight and opening the way to more in-depth biological or target development studies.

Few twin and family analyses of heritability of osteoporotic fracture per se have been conducted; however, heritability has been shown in three large-scale studies. The risk of wrist fractures were shown to have significant heritability among nearly 2500 Midwestern U.S. women[4] and in a study of >6500 twins.[5] In these two studies, the heritable contribution (h^2), with a potential maximum of 1.0, was estimated at 0.25 and 0.48, respectively. The liability to osteoporotic fractures was also shown to have significant heritability (any, $h^2 = 0.27$; hip, $h^2 = 0.48$) in the large Swedish twin registry on >33,000 twins born before 1944.[6] Similar findings have been reported from a range of family-based studies.[7–11] In a meta-analysis of epidemiologic data from seven European, UK, Canadian, and Australian cohorts comprising nearly 35,000 men and women, family history of osteoporotic fracture was associated with an increase risk of any osteoporotic fracture (RR = 1.18) and particularly for hip fracture (RR = 1.49). A family history of hip fracture was associated with a higher risk of any osteoporotic fracture (RR = 1.54) and again particularly of hip fracture (RR = 2.27).[12] Although fracture is the ultimate outcome of concern in osteoporosis, a fundamental difficulty with fracture-focused studies is the large sample size required and the inherently limited mechanistic insights that can be drawn from them.

Before these fracture-oriented studies, several key twin-based studies looked at BMD as a surrogate marker for bone fragility. In each of these, BMD was found to be highly heritable, with genetic factor accounting for around 66–75% of the variability in BMD among individuals (equivalent to a h^2 value of 0.66–0.75) in multiple skeletal sites in the peripheral and axial skeleton.[1–3] It was also shown that relatives of individuals with osteoporotic fractures also had lower BMD than their age- and sex-adjusted reference values.[13,14]

Despite these studies all setting the scene for identifying possible "osteoporosis" genes, osteoporosis was considered to be a complex multifactorial genetic disorder that, by implication, meant it was not amenable to further genetic dissection. That position changed after the initial reports of association of bone turnover and BMD to polymorphic markers in the vitamin D receptor (*VDR*) gene.[15,16] Although there were some errors in genotyping in the second report and, despite variable results in other samples, these polymorphisms have been reported to be associated with fracture in different populations.[17–19] Subsequent to this first report, a range of genetic loci have been identified; of these, the next and perhaps most robust in different studies has been a Sp1 polymorphic site in the promoter of the collagen Iα1 (*COL1A1*) gene.[20] Although identified in relation to BMD as for the *VDR* polymorphisms, the *COL1A1* polymorphism has also been shown to associated with fracture risk and again independent of BMD.[21,22]

Interestingly, in each of these studies, the effect size was small. This is relevant to a later question of the importance of any single genetic factor in risk assessment. As well as genetic

Dr. Eisman has provided consultation to Amgen, deCode, Eli Lilly, GE-Lunar, Merck Sharp & Dohme, Novartis, Organon, Pfizer, Roche-GSK, Sanofi-Aventis, and Servier.

studies based on BMD, other studies have examined parameters of bone geometry, which is itself an important aspect of bone strength that has been shown to be associated with fracture.[23–25] The examination of BMD and structure is complicated by the inter-relationships between these parameters. Various reports have found heritability to differ between cortical and trabecular bone sites and between various geometric bone measures.[7,23–31]

These parameters are important because the strength of any bone relates to the structure of both cortical and trabecular components and a trade-off between increasing mineralization that gives greater stiffness at the same time as it leads to greater brittleness.[32] The implications of this "conflict" can be seen in animal models; for example, between the two mouse strains C3H and B6, where higher bone mass in one region (cortical bone) is balanced by lesser bone mass in another (trabecular bone) with subtle differences in measured bone strength.[33,34] Using these two mouse strains and examining cortical bone clearly could help identify specific genetic loci: However, given the differences between the cortical and trabecular bone sites, if the same studies were performed examining trabecular bone sites, quite different loci could be expected to be identified. In this regard, it is of interest that several genetic markers initially identified as associated or linked with BMD have now been reported to be associated with fracture risk independent of BMD.[18,19,22] These reports indicate that, while using a single specific trait such as BMD or geometry may be a reasonable starting point for initial studies, they are unlikely to be sufficient in studies of genetic components of bone biology. Hence, it could be argued that optimal studies in human and animal models of the genetics of osteoporosis should encompass multiple phenotypes including BMD, bone size, and bone shape by pQCT and markers of bone remodeling and such tests of bone quality and structure, as become available. The contrary argument comes from the statistical issue of multiple testing and the effect this has on increasing the required sample size, although multivariate analyses can help with this problem. While it is clear that this is currently not being dealt with in an ideal manner at present, a reasonable solution to this dilemma will probably come from using an initial set of major criteria or factors followed by exploratory evaluations of minor, contributory or even deterministic factors.

ACCIDENTS OF NATURE

Accidents of nature have often provided invaluable insight into human biology and disease. For osteoporosis, the obvious example is osteogenesis imperfecta. In most individuals, this is caused by mutation in one of the collagen I genes. Interestingly, complete failure to produce one copy of either collagen chain generally results in less severe disease than production of an abnormal peptide that cannot form the normal heterotrimer of two α1 and one α2 peptide chains. Unbalanced expression of the COL1A1 and COL1A2 mRNA, and thus unbalanced levels of the collagen type α1 (I) and α2 (I) gene products, may be the explanation for the effects reported with the polymorphic Sp1 binding site.[21] These collagen studies were perhaps not surprising given the known contribution of collagen type I as the major protein in bone.

On the other hand, the unexpected findings in the osteoporosis-pseudoglioma and high bone mass families lead to the identification of the novel low-density lipoprotein receptor–related protein 5 (LRP5) and the role of the entire Wnt pathway in bone biology.[35,36] Following on these identifications of this pathway, there have been several studies supporting the use of single nucleotide polymorphisms (SNPs) or polymorphisms in this gene as markers for osteoporosis risk.[37–42]

The collagen or vitamin D receptor polymorphisms on the one hand and the LRP5 types of studies on the other emphasize the difference between the concept of exploiting known genes in relation to bone biology and taking a more open exploratory approach that can identify novel genes involved. Although the former approach in many studies has confirmed the role of polymorphisms or SNPs of known bone biology–related genes in association with differences in BMD and other phenotypes in many different populations, these studies have often been marred by small sample sizes and by limited reproducibility in combination with modest effect size in extended populations.

GENOME-WIDE SCANS

The alternate approach to the known gene or accident of nature approaches is the genome-wide scan in selected populations and families. These studies do not depend on any a priori assumption of mechanism involved. This has led to some confusion about "fishing expeditions" versus "hypothesis-based" science. However, these studies are based on the explicit or implicit assumption that one or more gene variants is common enough in the sample to be statistically associated or linked with a phenotypic difference of interest in the selected population. This approach has been used with some effect in the large Icelandic sample, leading to the identification of the BMP2 gene, perhaps unsurprisingly, as a contributor to osteoporosis in a population at large.[43] This success can be seen as proof-of-principle for such studies. However, the sample size and resources involved are not trivial. An alternate approach is studies within single large extended or multiple nuclear families. These studies often depend on enrichment of the sample with probands with an extreme bone phenotype; the osteoporosis pseudoglioma and high bone mass family studies are extreme examples of this approach. These studies in multiple nuclear families have led to suggestions of other genetic loci, although following these to any specific gene has been more difficult.[28,29,44–50]

The genome-wide scan approach can be particularly well applied to rodent studies. These essentially depend on identification of strains that seem to have high or low bone mass at some site or other. These are crossbred and selectively backcrossed on to one parental strain until the phenotype of one strain has effectively between transferred onto a nearly pure background of the alternate mouse strain. Genetic analysis can allow the identification of the transferred locus relatively straightforwardly. However, even these studies are complicated by the presence of competing genetic effectors in the parental strains (i.e., each strain carries some loci that dispose to both higher and lower bone mass as well as divergence in other structural measures).[51–53] Identification of any particular locus can be relatively rapidly compared with human studies by synteny and of course by comparison of genes identified from the various animal genomes. This process led to the highly successful approach of identifying the role of ALOX15 from mouse crosses.[54] Studies in primates have also been informative in this regard.[55,56]

These animal crossing studies, as for family-based human studies, suffer from one major and self-evident but often ignored limitation: Such analyses, even if fully successful, can only identify genetic loci that differ among those selected individuals or families. An example of this relates to variants of the alkaline phosphatase gene that were associated with peak bone mass in one set of studies but not in another. This was simply because the two strains used in one study carried the same variant at the site in question that differed between strains in the other study.[57,58] This limitation merely means that lack of reproducibility of a study between strains of animals or between human populations may reflect inherent differences between the samples/strains studied rather than lack of effect of a gene variant per se.

Animal models are powerful tools to examine the role of genes identified by the "simple" approaches of knockout and knockin models. However, these essentially identify a role in normal physiology rather than a role in normal physiological variability (i.e., a permissive role rather than a regulatory effect).[59] In fact, such regulatory factors or pathways should be a focus of future studies.

GENDER SPECIFICITY

Gender specificity has now been described in a variety of human and animal studies. Clearly osteoporosis, as measured by BMD and as seen by fracture outcomes, is more common and occurs at younger ages in women than men. However, the adverse outcomes including mortality are arguably worse in men than women.[60]

In some cases the observation of gender specificity makes sense, for example, in differences related to sex hormone synthesis and sex hormone receptors.[61–72] However, in many cases, it is not clear whether there is a real difference, an apparent difference related to different sample sizes studied for men and women, or an artifact related to multiple testing. For example, in the methylenetetrahydrofolate reductase (*MTHFR*) gene, one allelic variant at a single locus was associated with increased fracture risk in women (RR = 1.93; 95% CI, 1.03–3.61) but reduced risk in a smaller sample of men (RR = 0.12; 95% CI, 0.01–0.96).[73] Similarly, polymorphisms of the *LRP5* gene have been reported to be associated with vertebral bone mass and size in men but not in women from the same population.[41] Taken at face value, these studies suggest there may be distinct gender-specific loci that determine aspects of bone size, shape, and/or strength in both human and animal studies.[45,74,75] This issue requires continuing analysis and study designs to minimize confounding by small sample sizes and other limitations.

STATISTICAL ISSUES

Statistical issues are a major concern in all genetic studies on a number of different levels including randomization, genetic background and stratification, sample size, reproducibility across samples, and effect size versus frequency of a genetic contribution.

The standard approach of randomized controlled trials and similar experimental models are difficult to implement in genetic models because the sample has its own genetic background that cannot be altered and must be taken into account. In animal studies, it is of course possible to select genetically similar animals and introduce a specific genetic change (e.g., by knockout or knockin). However, as noted above, while this approach can determine a "permissive" role, it seldom allows study of a regulatory role. In contrast, in human studies, genetic background can seldom be selected or precisely controlled. Population admixture is common in most human samples and stratification of ethnic backgrounds can readily confound genotype–phenotype analyses.[76] Differences in frequency of common polymorphisms between human populations are well recognized and can confound reproducibility studies. Simulations based on known ethnic differences between BMD and polymorphic marker frequency between white and black women produced false-positive associations with admixtures of as little as 5%.[76] Other studies have noted major differences in polymorphism frequencies between samples and have suggested that these may explain reported differences in bone phenotypes and even to reported differences in response to therapy.[72,77–84] The latter may give some insight into pharmacogenetics but have generally been posthoc analyses rather than a priori studies. Thus, as with understanding related to gender-specific effects, specifically designed randomized controlled trials are required to evaluate response to therapies based on preselected polymorphisms.

Another set of issues, addressed in many studies of osteoporosis genetics, is focused on fracture prediction by genetic markers. An interesting editorial related to a genetic marker of cardiovascular risk suggested that, to achieve medical usefulness or relevance, any polymorphism had to meet certain criteria.[85] These included two groups of requirements: First, the "effect" allele should be associated with a clear alteration in function or level of an effector protein, and there should be a plausible mechanism of effect. Second, the effect should be supported by a large enough number of cases associated with an allele to be convincing and have a clear-cut clinical difference.[85] These seem like reasonable requirements but do contain inherent limitations and contradictions. The inherent limitation of the first requirement is that a novel effect is likely to be complex and its mechanism unclear, at least initially. Fulfilling this requirement would have delayed the LRP5 studies until further revelations and understanding of the Wnt/LRP5/β-catenin pathway.[86,87] The second requirement could be restated as the effect should be both large enough to be clinically important and frequent enough to be clinically meaningful: This holds within it the real contradiction that if an effect is both large and common, it would shift the population mean or even produce a bimodal distribution. In contrast, the genetic loci associated with fractures have usually been reported to have a 1.5- to 2-fold increase in risk for a relatively uncommon allele present in 5–20% of the population.[20,69,88–98] Although the "perverse polymorphisms" editorial did not set out precisely what the criteria for medical usefulness might be quantitatively, it seems likely that all of these fracture-associated loci could fail to meet it. Interestingly, within a sample where a minor allele at more than one site in the same gene had an association with fracture, the higher its frequency, the smaller its apparent effect size.[99] This relationship is also seen across studies with different genetic loci (i.e., large effect sizes are only reported with uncommon variants). Also, large, more statistically robust, studies have generally been associated with smaller effect sizes (Fig. 1). It is not clear whether these findings reflect artifacts of modest sample size and/or multiple testing or the mathematical requirement that a locus cannot have both a large effect and be common in a single sample simultaneously.

It may be useful to think about this concept with a simple mathematical simulation. For this simulation, it is necessary to ignore the possibility that genetic loci may interact, such that the presence of two loci may have a much larger effect than either alone or that even could cancel each other. Let there be six risk genes where each risk allele is present in 10% of the population, each causes a 2-fold increase in risk, and each contributes independently of the other loci considered. If any one individual had all six risk alleles, they would have a 2^6 relative risk (i.e., a 64-fold risk). Clearly a clinically massive effect but very uncommon in the population, because the risk of having all six would be 0.1^6 (i.e., literally one in a million)! This might lead to the suggestion that these risk alleles are unlikely to be clinically useful, because the person suffering a large effect would have to be very, very rare. However, the likelihood of any person having any three of these six hypothetical alleles is $6/10 \times 5/10 \times 4/10$ (i.e., in 12% of this

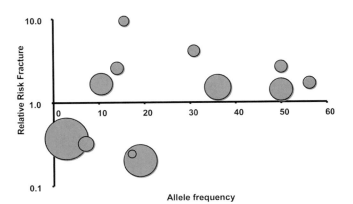

FIG. 1. Allele frequency vs. effect size for genetic loci associated with osteoporotic fracture risk. Larger studies (bubble size) generally report smaller effects and tighter confidence limits. Similar relationships are observed with the even larger numbers of studies looking at quantitative variables, such as BMD, BMC, geometric parameters, and ultrasound measurements. In each case, large effect size and high frequency are mutually exclusive; particularly in studies of sufficient size to provide reasonable confidence in the estimated effect size (see Refs. 38, 69, 70, 73, 88, 90–97, and 99–103).

hypothetical population) and that would indicate a relative risk of 2^3, conferring a very respectable 8-fold relative risk, somewhat greater than any other currently used clinical risk factor including prior fractures. Of course, this is hypothetical and does not take into account the potential effect of gene–gene interaction, but it does indicate the ways in which known genetics markers could be used to understand and identity risk in osteoporosis.

In summary, it is clear that genetic factors play a major role in the determination of bone mass, size, and structure and that many of these genetic pathways vary between individuals and can have clinically discernible and relevant effects in humans. Human linkage studies and animal models continue to identify novel pathways that contribute to our understanding of bone biology and to the complex determination of bone phenotypes including sensitivity to humeral, life style, and environmental factors. To some extent, the door to this complex area of bone biology is just opening and there needs to be new approaches and study designs to ask the questions that have most clinical and biological relevance. It is likely that genetic factors will eventually be standard contributors in ascertainment of risk, selection of appropriate therapy, and even to understanding the occurrence of adverse events. Given that this scientific development is still at the beginning, its scope and potential for contributing to improved osteoporosis care are outstanding.

ACKNOWLEDGMENTS

This study was supported by Amgen, deCode, Eli Lilly, GE-Lunar, Merck Sharp & Dohme, Novartis, Organon, Pfizer, Roche-GSK, Sanofi-Aventis, and Servier.

REFERENCES

1. Dequeker J, Nijs J, Verstraeten A, Geusens P, Gevers G 1987 Genetic determinants of bone mineral content at the spine and radius: A twin study. Bone **8:**207–209.
2. Pocock NA, Eisman JA, Hopper JL, Yeates MG, Sambrook PN, Eberl S 1987 Genetic determinants of bone mass in adults. A twin study. J Clin Invest **80:**706–710.
3. Smith DM, Nance WE, Kang KW, Christian JC, Johnston CC Jr 1973 Genetic factors in determining bone mass. J Clin Invest **52:**2800–2808.
4. Deng HW, Chen WM, Recker S, Stegman MR, Li JL, Davies KM, Zhou Y, Deng H, Heaney R, Recker RR 2000 Genetic determination of Colles' fracture and differential bone mass in women with and without Colles' fracture. J Bone Miner Res **15:**1243–1252.
5. Andrew T, Antioniades L, Scurrah KJ, Macgregor AJ, Spector TD 2005 Risk of wrist fracture in women is heritable and is influenced by genes that are largely independent of those influencing BMD. J Bone Miner Res **20:**67–74.
6. Michaelsson K, Melhus H, Ferm H, Ahlbom A, Pedersen NL 2005 Genetic liability to fractures in the elderly. Arch Intern Med **165:**1825–1830.
7. Deng HW, Stegman MR, Davies KM, Conway T, Recker RR 1999 Genetic determination of variation and covariation of peak bone mass at the hip and spine. J Clin Densitom **2:**251–263.
8. Keen RW, Hart DJ, Arden NK, Doyle DV, Spector TD 1999 Family history of appendicular fracture and risk of osteoporosis: A population-based study. Osteoporos Int **10:**161–166.
9. Danielson ME, Cauley JA, Baker CE, Newman AB, Dorman JS, Towers JD, Kuller LH 1999 Familial resemblance of bone mineral density (BMD) and calcaneal ultrasound attenuation: The BMD in mothers and daughters study. J Bone Miner Res **14:**102–110.
10. Cohen-Solal ME, Baudoin C, Omouri M, Kuntz D, De Vernejoul MC 1998 Bone mass in middle-aged osteoporotic men and their relatives: Familial effect. J Bone Miner Res **13:**1909–1914.
11. Sowers MR, Burns TL, Wallace RB 1986 Familial resemblance of bone mass in adult women. Genet Epidemiol **3:**85–93.
12. Kanis JA, Johansson H, Oden A, Johnell O, De Laet C, Eisman JA, McCloskey EV, Mellstrom D, Melton LJ III, Pols HA, Reeve J, Silman AJ, Tenenhouse A 2004 A family history of fracture and fracture risk: A meta-analysis. Bone **35:**1029–1037.
13. Seeman E, Hopper JL, Bach LA, Cooper ME, Parkinson E, McKay J, Jerums G 1989 Reduced bone mass in daughters of women with osteoporosis. N Engl J Med **320:**554–558.
14. Evans RA, Marel GM, Lancaster EK, Kos S, Evans M, Wong SY 1988 Bone mass is low in relatives of osteoporotic patients. Ann Intern Med **109:**870–873.
15. Morrison NA, Qi JC, Tokita A, Kelly PJ, Crofts L, Nguyen TV, Sambrook PN, Eisman JA 1994 Prediction of bone density from vitamin D receptor alleles. Nature **367:**284–287.
16. Morrison NA, Yeoman R, Kelly PJ, Eisman JA 1992 Contribution of trans-acting factor alleles to normal physiological variability: Vitamin D receptor gene polymorphism and circulating osteocalcin. Proc Natl Acad Sci USA **89:**6665–6669.
17. Uitterlinden AG, Burger H, Huang Q, Odding E, Duijn CM, Hofman A, Birkenhager JC, van Leeuwen JP, Pols HA 1997 Vitamin D receptor genotype is associated with radiographic osteoarthritis at the knee. J Clin Invest **100:**259–263.
18. Nguyen TV, Esteban LM, White CP, Grant SF, Center JR, Gardiner EM, Eisman JA 2005 Contribution of the collagen I alpha1 and vitamin D receptor genes to the risk of hip fracture in elderly women. J Clin Endocrinol Metab **90:**6575–6579.
19. Garnero P, Munoz F, Borel O, Sornay-Rendu E, Delmas PD 2005 Vitamin D receptor gene polymorphisms are associated with the risk of fractures in postmenopausal women, independently of bone mineral density. J Clin Endocrinol Metab **90:**4829–4835.
20. Grant SF, Reid DM, Blake G, Herd R, Fogelman I, Ralston SH 1996 Reduced bone density and osteoporosis associated with a polymorphic Sp1 binding site in the collagen type I alpha 1 gene. Nat Genet **14:**203–205.
21. Mann V, Hobson EE, Li B, Stewart TL, Grant SF, Robins SP, Aspden RM, Ralston SH 2001 A COL1A1 Sp1 binding site polymorphism predisposes to osteoporotic fracture by affecting bone density and quality. J Clin Invest **107:**899–907.
22. Mann V, Ralston SH 2003 Meta-analysis of COL1A1 Sp1 polymorphism in relation to bone mineral density and osteoporotic fracture. Bone **32:**711–717.
23. Flicker L, Faulkner KG, Hopper JL, Green RM, Kaymacki B, Nowson CA, Young D, Wark JD 1996 Determinants of hip axis length in women aged 10–89 years: A twin study. Bone **18:**41–45.
24. Livshits G, Yakovenko K, Kobyliansky E 2003 Quantitative genetic study of radiographic hand bone size and geometry. Bone **32:**191–198.
25. Slemenda CW, Turner CH, Peacock M, Christian JC, Sorbel J, Hui SL, Johnston CC 1996 The genetics of proximal femur geometry, distribution of bone mass and bone mineral density. Osteoporos Int **6:**178–182.
26. Lee M, Czerwinski SA, Choh AC, Towne B, Demerath EW, Chumlea WC, Sun SS, Siervogel RM 2004 Heritability of calcaneal quantitative

ultrasound measures in healthy adults from the Fels Longitudinal Study. Bone **35**:1157–1163.

27. Albagha OM, Ralston SH 2003 Genetic determinants of susceptibility to osteoporosis. Endocrinol Metab Clin North Am **32**:65–81.

28. Karasik D, Myers RH, Hannan MT, Gagnon D, McLean RR, Cupples LA, Kiel DP 2002 Mapping of quantitative ultrasound of the calcaneus bone to chromosome 1 by genome-wide linkage analysis. Osteoporos Int **13**:796–802.

29. Nguyen TV, Blangero J, Eisman JA 2000 Genetic epidemiological approaches to the search for osteoporosis genes. J Bone Miner Res **15**:392–401.

30. Eisman JA 1999 Genetics of osteoporosis. Endocr Rev **20**:788–804.

31. Arden NK, Baker J, Hogg C, Baan K, Spector TD 1996 The heritability of bone mineral density, ultrasound of the calcaneus and hip axis length: A study of postmenopausal twins. J Bone Miner Res **11**:530–534.

32. Currey JD 2005 Bone architecture and fracture. Curr Osteoporos Rep **3**:52–56.

33. Turner CH, Hsieh YF, Muller R, Bouxsein ML, Rosen CJ, McCrann ME, Donahue LR, Beamer WG 2001 Variation in bone biomechanical properties, microstructure, and density in BXH recombinant inbred mice. J Bone Miner Res **16**:206–213.

34. Turner CH, Hsieh YF, Muller R, Bouxsein ML, Baylink DJ, Rosen CJ, Grynpas MD, Donahue LR, Beamer WG 2000 Genetic regulation of cortical and trabecular bone strength and microstructure in inbred strains of mice. J Bone Miner Res **15**:1126–1131.

35. Little RD, Carulli JP, Del Mastro RG, Dupuis J, Osborne M, Folz C, Manning SP, Swain PM, Zhao SC, Eustace B, Lappe MM, Spitzer L, Zweier S, Braunschweiger K, Benchekroun Y, Hu X, Adair R, Chee L, FitzGerald MG, Tulig C, Caruso A, Tzellas N, Bawa A, Franklin B, McGuire S, Nogues X, Gong G, Allen KM, Anisowicz A, Morales AJ, Lomedico PT, Recker SM, Van Eerdewegh P, Recker RR, Johnson ML 2002 A mutation in the LDL receptor-related protein 5 gene results in the autosomal dominant high-bone-mass trait. Am J Hum Genet **70**:11–19.

36. Gong Y, Slee RB, Fukai N, Rawadi G, Roman-Roman S, Reginato AM, Wang H, Cundy T, Glorieux FH, Lev D, Zacharin M, Oexle K, Marcelino J, Suwairi W, Heeger S, Sabatakos G, Apte S, Adkins WN, Allgrove J, Arslan-Kirchner M, Batch JA, Beighton P, Black GC, Boles RG, Boon LM, Borrone C, Brunner HG, Carle GF, Dallapiccola B, De Paepe A, Floege B, Halfhide ML, Hall B, Hennekam RC, Hirose T, Jans A, Juppner H, Kim CA, Keppler-Noreuil K, Kohlschuetter A, LaCombe D, Lambert M, Lemyre E, Letteboer T, Peltonen L, Ramesar RS, Romanengo M, Somer H, Steichen-Gersdorf E, Steinmann B, Sullivan B, Superti-Furga A, Swoboda W, van den Boogaard MJ, Van Hul W, Vikkula M, Votruba M, Zabel B, Garcia T, Baron R, Olsen BR, Warman ML 2001 LDL receptor-related protein 5 (LRP5) affects bone accrual and eye development. Cell **107**:513–523.

37. Ferrari SL, Rizzoli R 2005 Gene variants for osteoporosis and their pleiotropic effects in aging. Mol Aspects Med **26**:145–167.

38. Bollerslev J, Wilson SG, Dick IM, Islam FM, Ueland T, Palmer L, Devine A, Prince RL 2005 LRP5 gene polymorphisms predict bone mass and incident fractures in elderly Australian women. Bone **36**:599–606.

39. Koay MA, Brown MA 2005 Genetic disorders of the LRP5-Wnt signalling pathway affecting the skeleton. Trends Mol Med **11**:129–137.

40. Koller DL, Ichikawa S, Johnson ML, Lai D, Xuei X, Edenberg HJ, Conneally PM, Hui SL, Johnston CC, Peacock M, Foroud T, Econs MJ 2005 Contribution of the LRP5 gene to normal variation in peak BMD in women. J Bone Miner Res **20**:75–80.

41. Ferrari SL, Deutsch S, Choudhury U, Chevalley T, Bonjour JP, Dermitzakis ET, Rizzoli R, Antonarakis SE 2004 Polymorphisms in the low-density lipoprotein receptor-related protein 5 (LRP5) gene are associated with variation in vertebral bone mass, vertebral bone size, and stature in whites. Am J Hum Genet **74**:866–875.

42. Lev D, Binson I, Foldes AJ, Watemberg N, Lerman-Sagie T 2003 Decreased bone density in carriers and patients of an Israeli family with the osteoporosis-pseudoglioma syndrome. Isr Med Assoc J **5**:419–421.

43. Styrkarsdottir U, Cazier JB, Kong A, Rolfsson O, Larsen H, Bjarnadottir E, Johannsdottir VD, Sigurdardottir MS, Bagger Y, Christiansen C, Reynisdottir I, Grant SF, Jonasson K, Frigge ML, Gulcher JR, Sigurdsson G, Stefansson K 2003 Linkage of osteoporosis to chromosome 20p12 and association to BMP2. PLoS Biol **1**:E69.

44. Devoto M, Spotila LD, Stabley DL, Wharton GN, Rydbeck H, Korkko J, Kosich R, Prockop D, Tenenhouse A, Sol-Church K 2005 Univariate and bivariate variance component linkage analysis of a whole-genome scan for loci contributing to bone mineral density. Eur J Hum Genet **13**:781–788.

45. Ralston SH, Galwey N, MacKay I, Albagha OM, Cardon L, Compston JE, Cooper C, Duncan E, Keen R, Langdahl B, McLellan A, O'Riordan J, Pols HA, Reid DM, Uitterlinden AG, Wass J, Bennett ST 2005 Loci

for regulation of bone mineral density in men and women identified by genome wide linkage scan: The FAMOS study. Hum Mol Genet **14**:943–951.

46. Xu FH, Liu YJ, Deng H, Huang QY, Zhao LJ, Shen H, Liu YZ, Dvornyk V, Conway T, Li JL, Davies KM, Recker RR, Deng HW 2004 A follow-up linkage study for bone size variation in an extended sample. Bone **35**:777–784.

47. Peacock M, Koller DL, Hui S, Johnston CC, Foroud T, Econs MJ 2004 Peak bone mineral density at the hip is linked to chromosomes 14q and 15q. Osteoporos Int **15**:489–496.

48. Huang QY, Recker RR, Deng HW 2003 Searching for osteoporosis genes in the post-genome era: Progress and challenges. Osteoporos Int **14**:701–715.

49. Devoto M, Specchia C, Li HH, Caminis J, Tenenhouse A, Rodriguez H, Spotila LD 2001 Variance component linkage analysis indicates a QTL for femoral neck bone mineral density on chromosome 1p36. Hum Mol Genet **10**:2447–2452.

50. Koller DL, Liu G, Econs MJ, Hui SL, Morin PA, Joslyn G, Rodriguez LA, Conneally PM, Christian JC, Johnston CC, Jr., Foroud T, Peacock M 2001 Genome screen for quantitative trait loci underlying normal variation in femoral structure. J Bone Miner Res **16**:985–991.

51. Klein RF, Mitchell SR, Phillips TJ, Belknap JK, Orwoll ES 1998 Quantitative trait loci affecting peak bone mineral density in mice. J Bone Miner Res **13**:1648–1656.

52. Bouxsein ML, Uchiyama T, Rosen CJ, Shultz KL, Donahue LR, Turner CH, Sen S, Churchill GA, Muller R, Beamer WG 2004 Mapping quantitative trait loci for vertebral trabecular bone volume fraction and microarchitecture in mice. J Bone Miner Res **19**:587–599.

53. Jepsen KJ, Akkus OJ, Majeska RJ, Nadeau JH 2003 Hierarchical relationship between bone traits and mechanical properties in inbred mice. Mamm Genome **14**:97–104.

54. Klein RF, Allard J, Avnur Z, Nikolcheva T, Rotstein D, Carlos AS, Shea M, Waters RV, Belknap JK, Peltz G, Orwoll ES 2004 Regulation of bone mass in mice by the lipoxygenase gene Alox15. Science **303**:229–232.

55. Havill LM, Cox LA, Rogers J, Mahaney MC 2005 Cross-species replication of a serum osteocalcin quantitative trait locus on human chromosome 16q in pedigreed baboons. Calcif Tissue Int **77**:205–211.

56. Havill LM, Mahaney MC, Cox LA, Morin PA, Joslyn G, Rogers J 2005 A quantitative trait locus for normal variation in forearm bone mineral density in pedigreed baboons maps to the ortholog of human chromosome 11q. J Clin Endocrinol Metab **90**:3638–3645.

57. Foreman JE, Blizard DA, Gerhard G, Mack HA, Lang DH, Van Nimwegen KL, Vogler GP, Stout JT, Shihabi ZK, Griffith JW, Lakoski JM, McClearn GE, Vandenbergh DJ 2005 Serum alkaline phosphatase activity is regulated by a chromosomal region containing the alkaline phosphatase 2 gene (Akp2) in C57BL/6J and DBA/2J mice. Physiol Genom **23**:295–303.

58. Klein R, Carlos A, Kansagor J, OLsen D, Wagoner W, EA L, Dinulescu D, Munsey T, Vanek C, Madisin D, Lundblad J, Belknap J, Orwoll E 2005 Identification of Akp2 as a gene that regualtes peak bone mass in mice. J Bone Miner Res **20**(Suppl 1):S9.

59. Parfitt A 2006 Regulation or permission? J Bone Miner Res **21**:659–660.

60. Center JR, Nguyen TV, Schneider D, Sambrook PN, Eisman JA 1999 Mortality after all major types of osteoporotic fracture in men and women: An observational study. Lancet **353**:878–882.

61. Gennari L, Masi L, Merlotti D, Picariello L, Falchetti A, Tanini A, Mavilia C, Del Monte F, Gonnelli S, Lucani B, Gennari C, Brandi ML 2004 A polymorphic CYP19 TTTA repeat influences aromatase activity and estrogen levels in elderly men: Effects on bone metabolism. J Clin Endocrinol Metab **89**:2803–2810.

62. Zarrabeitia MT, Hernandez JL, Valero C, Zarrabeitia AL, Garcia-Unzueta M, Amado JA, Gonzalez-Macias J, Riancho JA 2004 A common polymorphism in the 5′-untranslated region of the aromatase gene influences bone mass and fracture risk. Eur J Endocrinol **150**:699–704.

63. Shearman AM, Karasik D, Gruenthal KM, Demissie S, Cupples LA, Housman DE, Kiel DP 2004 Estrogen receptor beta polymorphisms are associated with bone mass in women and men: The Framingham Study. J Bone Miner Res **19**:773–781.

64. van Meurs JB, Schuit SC, Weel AE, van der Klift M, Bergink AP, Arp PP, Colin EM, Fang Y, Hofman A, van Duijn CM, van Leeuwen JP, Pols HA, Uitterlinden AG 2003 Association of 5′ estrogen receptor alpha gene polymorphisms with bone mineral density, vertebral bone area and fracture risk. Hum Mol Genet **12**:1745–1754.

65. Ioannidis JP, Stavrou I, Trikalinos TA, Zois C, Brandi ML, Gennari L, Albagha O, Ralston SH, Tsatsoulis A 2002 Association of polymorphisms of the estrogen receptor alpha gene with bone mineral density and fracture risk in women: A meta-analysis. J Bone Miner Res **17**:2048–2060.

66. Salmen T, Heikkinen AM, Mahonen A, Kroger H, Komulainen M, Saarikoski S, Honkanen R, Partanen J, Maenpaa PH 2002 Relation of estrogen receptor-alpha gene polymorphism and hormone replacement therapy to fall risk and muscle strength in early postmenopausal women. Ann Med 34:64–72.

67. Kobayashi N, Fujino T, Shirogane T, Furuta I, Kobamatsu Y, Yaegashi M, Sakuragi N, Fujimoto S 2002 Estrogen receptor alpha polymorphism as a genetic marker for bone loss, vertebral fractures and susceptibility to estrogen. Maturitas 41:193–201.

68. Simpson ER, Davis SR 2001 Minireview: Aromatase and the regulation of estrogen biosynthesis—some new perspectives. Endocrinology 142:4589–4594.

69. Salmen T, Heikkinen AM, Mahonen A, Kroger H, Komulainen M, Saarikoski S, Honkanen R, Maenpaa PH 2000 The protective effect of hormone-replacement therapy on fracture risk is modulated by estrogen receptor alpha genotype in early postmenopausal women. J Bone Miner Res 15:2479–2486.

70. Langdahl BL, Lokke E, Carstens M, Stenkjaer LL, Eriksen EF 2000 A TA repeat polymorphism in the estrogen receptor gene is associated with osteoporotic fractures but polymorphisms in the first exon and intron are not. J Bone Miner Res 15:2222–2230.

71. Giguere Y, Dodin S, Blanchet C, Morgan K, Rousseau F 2000 The association between heel ultrasound and hormone replacement therapy is modulated by a two-locus vitamin D and estrogen receptor genotype. J Bone Miner Res 15:1076–1084.

72. Kurabayashi T, Tomita M, Matsushita H, Yahata T, Honda A, Takakuwa K, Tanaka K 1999 Association of vitamin D and estrogen receptor gene polymorphism with the effect of hormone replacement therapy on bone mineral density in Japanese women. Am J Obstet Gynecol 180:1115–1120.

73. Villadsen MM, Bunger MH, Carstens M, Stenkjaer L, Langdahl BL 2005 Methylenetetrahydrofolate reductase (MTHFR) C677T polymorphism is associated with osteoporotic vertebral fractures, but is a weak predictor of BMD. Osteoporos Int 16:411–416.

74. Peacock M, Koller DL, Fishburn T, Krishnan S, Lai D, Hui S, Johnston CC, Foroud T, Econs MJ 2005 Sex-specific and non-sex-specific quantitative trait loci contribute to normal variation in bone mineral density in men. J Clin Endocrinol Metab 90:3060–3066.

75. Turner CH, Sun Q, Schriefer J, Pitner N, Price R, Bouxsein ML, Rosen CJ, Donahue LR, Shultz KL, Beamer WG 2003 Congenic mice reveal sex-specific genetic regulation of femoral structure and strength. Calcif Tissue Int 73:297–303.

76. Koller DL, Peacock M, Lai D, Foroud T, Econs MJ 2004 False positive rates in association studies as a function of degree of stratification. J Bone Miner Res 19:1291–1295.

77. Qureshi AM, Herd RJ, Blake GM, Fogelman I, Ralston SH 2002 COLIA1 Sp1 polymorphism predicts response of femoral neck bone density to cyclical etidronate therapy. Calcif Tissue Int 70:158–163.

78. Morrison NA, George PM, Vaughan T, Tilyard MW, Frampton CM, Gilchrist NL 2005 Vitamin D receptor genotypes influence the success of calcitriol therapy for recurrent vertebral fracture in osteoporosis. Pharmacogenet Genomics 15:127–135.

79. Kurabayashi T, Matsushita H, Kato N, Nagata H, Kikuchi M, Tomita M, Yahata T, Honda A, Tanaka K 2004 Effect of vitamin D receptor and estrogen receptor gene polymorphism on the relationship between dietary calcium and bone mineral density in Japanese women. J Bone Miner Metab 22:139–147.

80. Eisman JA 2001 Pharmacogenetics of the vitamin D receptor and osteoporosis. Drug Metab Dispos 29:505–212.

81. Ho YV, Briganti EM, Duan Y, Buchanan R, Hall S, Seeman E 1999 Polymorphism of the vitamin D receptor gene and corticosteroid-related osteoporosis. Osteoporos Int 9:134–138.

82. MacDonald HM, McGuigan FA, New SA, Campbell MK, Golden MH, Ralston SH, Reid DM 2001 COL1A1 Sp1 polymorphism predicts perimenopausal and early postmenopausal spinal bone loss. J Bone Miner Res 16:1634–1641.

83. Altun B, Kiykim AA, Seyrantepe V, Usalan C, Arici M, Caglar M, Erdem Y, Yasavul U, Turgan C, Caglar S 2004 Association between activated renin angiotensin system and bone formation in hemodialysis patients: Is the bone mass genetically determined by ACE gene polymorphism?. Ren Fail 26:425–431.

84. Ferrari S, Rizzoli R, Chevalley T, Slosman D, Eisman JA, Bonjour JP 1995 Vitamin-D-receptor-gene polymorphisms and change in lumbar-spine bone mineral density. Lancet 345:423–424.

85. Rosenthal N, Schwartz RS 1998 In search of perverse polymorphisms. N Engl J Med 338:122–124.

86. Johnson ML, Harnish K, Nusse R, Van Hul W 2004 LRP5 and Wnt signaling: A union made for bone. J Bone Miner Res 19:1749–1757.

87. Zorn AM 2001 Wnt signalling: Antagonistic Dickkopfs. Curr Biol 11:R592–R595.

88. Moffett SP, Zmuda JM, Oakley JI, Beck TJ, Cauley JA, Stone KL, Lui LY, Ensrud KE, Hillier TA, Hochberg MC, Morin P, Peltz G, Greene D, Cummings SR 2005 Tumor necrosis factor-alpha polymorphism, bone strength phenotypes, and the risk of fracture in older women. J Clin Endocrinol Metab 90:3491–3497.

89. Schoofs MW, van der Klift M, Hofman A, van Duijn CM, Stricker BH, Pols HA, Uitterlinden AG 2004 ApoE gene polymorphisms, BMD, and fracture risk in elderly men and women: The Rotterdam study. J Bone Miner Res 19:1490–1496.

90. Lauridsen AL, Vestergaard P, Hermann AP, Moller HJ, Mosekilde L, Nexo E 2004 Female premenopausal fracture risk is associated with gc phenotype. J Bone Miner Res 19:875–881.

91. Dick IM, Devine A, Li S, Dhaliwal SS, Prince RL 2003 The T869C TGF beta polymorphism is associated with fracture, bone mineral density, and calcaneal quantitative ultrasound in elderly women. Bone 33:335–341.

92. Fang Y, van Meurs JB, Bergink AP, Hofman A, van Duijn CM, van Leeuwen JP, Pols HA, Uitterlinden AG 2003 Cdx-2 polymorphism in the promoter region of the human vitamin D receptor gene determines susceptibility to fracture in the elderly. J Bone Miner Res 18:1632–1641.

93. Suuriniemi M, Mahonen A, Kovanen V, Alen M, Cheng S 2003 Relation of PvuII site polymorphism in the COL1A2 gene to the risk of fractures in prepubertal Finnish girls. Physiol Genom 14:217–224.

94. Masi L, Becherini L, Gennari L, Amedei A, Colli E, Falchetti A, Farci M, Silvestri S, Gonnelli S, Brandi ML 2001 Polymorphism of the aromatase gene in postmenopausal Italian women: Distribution and correlation with bone mass and fracture risk. J Clin Endocrinol Metab 86:2263–2269.

95. Langdahl BL, Lokke E, Carstens M, Stenkjaer LL, Eriksen EF 2000 Osteoporotic fractures are associated with an 86-base pair repeat polymorphism in the interleukin-1–receptor antagonist gene but not with polymorphisms in the interleukin-1beta gene. J Bone Miner Res 15:402–414.

96. Gennari L, Becherini L, Mansani R, Masi L, Falchetti A, Morelli A, Colli E, Gonnelli S, Cepollaro C, Brandi ML 1999 FokI polymorphism at translation initiation site of the vitamin D receptor gene predicts bone mineral density and vertebral fractures in postmenopausal Italian women. J Bone Miner Res 14:1379–1386.

97. Uitterlinden AG, Burger H, Huang Q, Yue F, McGuigan FE, Grant SF, Hofman A, van Leeuwen JP, Pols HA, Ralston SH 1998 Relation of alleles of the collagen type Ialpha1 gene to bone density and the risk of osteoporotic fractures in postmenopausal women. N Engl J Med 338:1016–1021.

98. Vogt MT, Cauley JA, Kuller LH 1997 Apolipoprotein E phenotype, arterial disease, and mortality among older women: The study of osteoporotic fractures. Genet Epidemiol 14:147–156.

99. Langdahl BL, Carstens M, Stenkjaer L, Eriksen EF 2002 Polymorphisms in the osteoprotegerin gene are associated with osteoporotic fractures. J Bone Miner Res 17:1245–1255.

100. Langdahl BL, Stenkjaer L, Carstens M, Tofteng CL, Eriksen EF 2003 A CAG repeat polymorphism in the androgen receptor gene is associated with reduced bone mass and increased risk of osteoporotic fractures. Calcif Tissue Int 73:237–243.

101. Langdahl BL, Ralston SH, Grant SF, Eriksen EF 1998 An Sp1 binding site polymorphism in the COLIA1 gene predicts osteoporotic fractures in both men and women. J Bone Miner Res 13:1384–1389.

102. Langdahl BL, Knudsen JY, Jensen HK, Gregersen N, Eriksen EF 1997 A sequence variation: 713–8delC in the transforming growth factor-beta 1 gene has higher prevalence in osteoporotic women than in normal women and is associated with very low bone mass in osteoporotic women and increased bone turnover in both osteoporotic and normal women. Bone 20:289–294.

103. Ioannidis JP, Ralston SH, Bennett ST, Brandi ML, Grinberg D, Karassa FB, Langdahl B, van Meurs JB, Mosekilde L, Scollen S, Albagha OM, Bustamante M, Carey AH, Dunning AM, Enjuanes A, van Leeuwen JP, Mavilia C, Masi L, McGuigan FE, Nogues X, Pols HA, Reid DM, Schuit SC, Sherlock RE, Uitterlinden AG 2004 Differential genetic effects of ESR1 gene polymorphisms on osteoporosis outcomes. JAMA 292:2105–2114.

Chapter 44. Nutrition and Osteoporosis

Robert P. Heaney

Creighton University, Omaha, Nebraska

INTRODUCTION

Nutrition plays a role in the pathogenesis, prevention, and treatment of osteoporosis.[1] Bone cells are as dependent on total nutrition as are all other cells and tissues. However, current bone mass and bone strength are dependent on cell activity extending back in time over a many-year period. Therefore, acute nutrient deficiencies, while undoubtedly impairing current cellular competence, tend to have less effect on overall bone strength, which is the main concern relative to osteoporosis. The major exceptions to this generalization are the following nutrients: calcium, vitamin D, and protein. Phosphorus, certain trace minerals (manganese, copper, and zinc), and vitamins C and K, while involved in bone health generally, are less certainly involved in osteoporosis.

CALCIUM

Calcium is the principal cation of bone mineral. Bone constitutes a very large nutrient reserve for calcium that, over the course of evolution, acquired a secondary, structural function that is responsible for its importance for osteoporosis. Bone strength varies as the approximate second power of bone structural density. Accordingly, any decrease in bone mass produces a corresponding decrease in bone strength. While reserves are designed to be used in times of need, such use would normally be temporary. Sustained, unbalanced withdrawals deplete the reserves and thereby reduce bone strength.

Bone mass is ultimately determined by the genetic program as modified by current and past mechanical loading and limited or permitted by nutrition. The genetic potential cannot be reached or maintained if dietary calcium intake and absorption are insufficient. The aggregate total of bone resorptive activity is controlled systemically by PTH, which in turn responds to the demands of extracellular fluid calcium ion homeostasis, not to structural need for bone mass. Whenever absorbed calcium intake is insufficient to meet the demands of growth and/or the drain of cutaneous and excretory losses, resorption will be stimulated, and bone mass will be reduced. In addition to depleting or limiting bone mass, low calcium intakes directly cause fragility through this PTH-stimulated increase in bone remodeling. Resorption pits on trabeculae cause applied loads to shift to adjacent bone, leading to increased strain locally. In this way, excessive remodeling is itself a fragility factor, altogether apart from its effect on bone mass. When adequate calcium is absorbed, PTH-stimulated remodeling decreases immediately.[2] Fracture rate responses in the major treatment trials show the predicted prompt reduction in fracture risk.[3,4]

The intake of calcium that is optimal for growth and adult maintenance has been estimated by both the National Institutes of Health[5] and the Institute of Medicine.[6] Harmonizing these two sets of recommendations results in the following composite RDA estimates for various ages and states: ages 1–3: 600 mg/day; 4–8: 1000 mg/day; 9–18: 1600 mg/day; 19–50: 1200 mg/day; 50+: 1400 mg/day; pregnancy and lactation in women over age 19: 1200 mg/day.

The specific applicability of these values to North America reflects to some extent the effect of other nutrients on the calcium requirement, and therefore is a function of the total diet of the North American population. Diets high in protein and sodium and low in potassium, such as are typical of the developed nations, can increase urinary calcium loss and thereby increase the calcium intake required for bone balance. On low intakes of sodium and with small body size, such as might be found in certain Third World environments, the adult calcium requirement for bone maintenance can be <500 mg/day. This is part of the reason why requirements seem to vary across countries and cultures.

Low calcium intakes early in life not only predispose to osteoporosis late in life, but make bones more fragile in childhood and adolescence as well.[1,7–9] Calcium intakes are positively correlated with bone mass at all ages, but most especially at old age, when the requirement rises and the calcium intake tends to drop (thereby widening the gap between need and supply). Calcium supplementation reduces both bone loss and fracture rate in the elderly.[3,4,10–13] Only in the few years immediately after estrogen withdrawal at menopause is calcium without much effect.[14] This is largely because bone loss then is caused mainly by estrogen deficiency and not by nutrient deficiency. Even then, calcium greatly augments the bone-sparing effect of estrogen replacement.[15] The abnormal parathyroid secretory physiology, high circulating PTH levels, and elevated biomarkers for bone resorption typical of the elderly are all reversible with a high calcium intake.[16] These hallmarks of the calcium economy in the elderly, once considered to be caused by aging itself, are now recognized as manifestations of calcium privation. It is in these ways that low calcium intakes contribute to the pathogenesis of osteoporosis.

Optimal prophylaxis is provided by meeting the National Institutes of Health/Institute of Medicine calcium intake recommendations, either with natural foods (principally dairy products, calcium-set tofu, a few greens and nuts, and a few crustaceans) or with such calcium-fortified foods that may be available locally (e.g., fortified fruit juices, bread, breakfast cereals). Calcium-rich foods, especially milk, tend to be less expensive per calorie than the calcium-poor foods they would displace in the total diet. For this reason, dairy calcium has a negative cost, and therefore a high dairy diet exhibits a very favorable cost–benefit relationship as a stratagem in fracture prevention.

Supplements may also be indicated. Most calcium salts exhibit similar bioavailability.[17–19] Calcium carbonate is the salt most widely used in the United States. Like all calcium sources (including food), supplements should be taken with meals to ensure optimal absorption. Even for relatively less soluble salts such as the carbonate or phosphate, gastric acid is not necessary if the supplement is taken with food. Brand name or chewable products have been shown over the years to be the most reliable.

Calcium is also of critical importance as co-therapy in the prevention and treatment of established osteoporosis. Estrogen prophylaxis exhibits a two to three times larger protective effect when taken with supplemental calcium than when administered alone.[15,20] Agents capable of substantially increasing bone mass (such as teriparatide and fluoride) cannot achieve their full effect if absorbed calcium intake is limiting. Agents with a preferential trophic effect for axial cancellous bone will actually take bone from other regions of the skeleton to meet the needs of new bone formation in the central skeleton when ingested calcium is not adequate. Because of reduced

---

The author has reported no conflicts of interest.

absorption efficiency common in the elderly and in many patients with osteoporosis, therapeutic calcium intakes may need to be above the maintenance figure for older adults of 1400 mg/day, possibly 2000–2500 mg/day. Unless the number and variety of available calcium-fortified foods increases substantially, supplements will be the obvious choice.

VITAMIN D

Vitamin D is important for bone, certainly for its role in facilitating calcium absorption and osteoclastic resorption, but probably for other reasons as well. Serum 25(OH)D levels, which are the best clinical indicators of vitamin D nutritional status, decline with age. This is caused mainly by decreased solar exposure and decreased efficiency of vitamin D synthesis in skin. Best current estimates of the lower limit of the healthy range for serum 25(OH)D are 30–32 ng/ml (75–80 nM),[21] which are substantially higher than recent laboratory reference ranges have suggested.

The 1997 recommendations for oral intake of vitamin D are 200 IU up to age 50, 400 IU up to age 70, and 600–800 above age 70.[6] However, the current best estimate of 75–80 nM for serum 25(OH)D means that, without extensive sun exposure, current recommended intakes will not suffice. Oral intakes are typically much less than even the current, low recommendations. Because solar exposure tends to be limited, suboptimal 25(OH)D levels are found in a majority of adults living in North America and Northern Europe.[22–24] It may be noted that, if individuals succeed in raising their calcium intakes through increased milk consumption, they will at the same time improve their vitamin D status, because fluid milks in the United States and Canada are fortified with vitamin D at a level of 100 IU per serving.

Vitamin D supplementation in the elderly, raising serum 25(OH)D to 80 nM or above, improves calcium absorption substantially,[25] reduces fractures of all types,[3,4,26,27] and reduces fall frequency by about one-half.[28,29] It is common experience that patients with osteoporosis require 1000–2000 IU/day. As a rough approximation, one can estimate that steady-state serum 25(OH)D will rise by about 1 nM for every microgram (40 IU) of cholecalciferol taken daily.[30] Thus, for example, a patient with a starting value of 50 nM will typically require 30 μg/day (1200 IU) to reach and sustain 80 nM. It should also be noted that vitamin D_2 (ergocalciferol) has a very different profile of activity from vitamin D_3 (cholecalciferol). With single doses of 50,000 IU, AUC for the evoked rise in 25(OH)D is more than four times greater for cholecalciferol than for ergocalciferol.[31]

PROTEIN

About one-half the volume of the extracellular material of bone consists of protein. Because of cross-links and other post-translational modifications, many of the constituent amino acids of bone matrix protein cannot be recycled when bone turns over. Hence, bone remodeling requires a continuing input of fresh dietary protein. Protein, once considered harmful for bone because of reported increases in urinary calcium, is now recognized as an important cofactor for bone health along with calcium. In the Framingham cohort, for example, age-related bone loss was inversely related to protein intake,[32] and in a calcium intervention trial, bone gain occurred only in subjects with the highest protein intake.[33] In both studies, animal products were the principal source of dietary protein. Finally, adequacy of protein intake ($\sim$1 g protein/kg body weight/day) substantially improves outcome after hip fracture.[34] Patients with hip fracture are commonly malnourished, enter the hos-

pital with low serum albumin levels, and typically become more severely hypoproteinemic during hospitalization. Serum albumin levels are the single best predictor of survival or death after fracture.[35] Protein supplementation of hip fracture patients has been shown to improve outcome dramatically (fewer deaths, less permanent institutionalization, more return to independent living).[34,36] Unfortunately, most hospital standards of care for hip fracture patients lack a nutritional component.

REFERENCES

1. Heaney RP 2001 Nutrition and risk for osteoporosis. In: Marcus R, Feldman D, Kelsey J (eds.) Osteoporosis, 2nd ed., vol. 2. Academic Press, San Diego, CA, USA, pp. 513–5321.
2. Wastney ME, Martin BR, Peacock M, Smith D, Jiang XY, Jackman LA, Weaver CM 2000 Changes in calcium kinetics in adolescent girls induced by high calcium intake. J Clin Endocrinol Metab 85:4470–4475.
3. Chapuy MC, Arlot ME, Duboeuf F, Brun J, Crouzet B, Arnaud S, Delmas PD, Meunier PJ 1992 Vitamin D_3 and calcium to prevent hip fractures in elderly women. N Engl J Med 327:1637–1642.
4. Dawson-Hughes B, Harris SS, Krall EA, Dallal GE 1997 Effect of calcium and vitamin D supplementation on bone density in men and women 65 years of age or older. N Engl J Med 337:670–676.
5. NIH Consensus Conference 1994 Optimal calcium intake. JAMA 272: 1942–1948.
6. Food and Nutrition Board 1997 Dietary Reference Intakes for Calcium, Magnesium, Phosphorus, Vitamin D, and Fluoride. Institute of Medicine, National Academy Press, Washington, DC, USA.
7. Chan GM, Hess M, Hollis J, Book LS 1984 Bone mineral status in childhood accidental fractures. Am J Dis Child 138:569–570.
8. Goulding A, Cannan R, Williams SM, Gold EJ, Taylor RW, Lewis-Barned NJ 1998 Bone mineral density in girls with forearm fractures. J Bone Miner Res 13:143–148.
9. Goulding A, Rockell JEP, Black RE, Grant AM, Jones IE, Williams SM 2004 Children who avoid drinking cow's milk are at increased risk for prepubertal bone fractures. J Am Diet Assoc 104:250–253.
10. Chevalley T, Rizzoli R, Nydegger V, Slosman D, Rapin C-H, Michel J-P, Vasey H, Bonjour J-P 1994 Effects of calcium supplements on femoral bone mineral density and vertebral fracture rate in vitamin D-replete elderly patients. Osteoporos Int 4:245–252.
11. Recker RR, Hinders S, Davies KM, Heaney RP, Stegman MR, Kimmel DB, Lappe JM 1996 Correcting calcium nutritional deficiency prevents spine fractures in elderly women. J Bone Miner Res 11:1961–1966.
12. Reid IR, Ames RW, Evans MC, Gamble GD, Sharpe SJ 1993 Effect of calcium supplementation on bone loss in postmenopausal women. N Engl J Med 328:460–464.
13. Aloia JF, Vaswani A, Yeh JK, Ross PL, Flaster E, Dilmanian FA 1994 Calcium supplementation with and without hormone replacement therapy to prevent postmenopausal bone loss. Ann Intern Med 120:97–103.
14. Dawson-Hughes B, Dallal GE, Krall EA, Sadowski L, Sahyoun N, Tannenbaum S 1990 A controlled trial of the effect of calcium supplementation on bone density in postmenopausal women. N Engl J Med 323:878–883.
15. Nieves JW, Komar L, Cosman F, Lindsay R 1998 Calcium potentiates the effect of estrogen and calcitonin on bone mass: Review and analysis. Am J Clin Nutr 67:18–24.
16. McKane WR, Khosla S, O'Fallon WM, Robins SP, Burritt MF, Riggs BL 1996 Role of calcium intake in modulating age-related increases in parathyroid function and bone resorption. J Clin Endocrinol Metab 81:1699–1703.
17. Heaney RP, Recker RR, Weaver CM 1990 Absorbability of calcium sources: The limited role of solubility. Calcif Tissue Int 46:300–304.
18. Heaney RP, Dowell MS, Barger-Lux MJ 1999 Absorption of calcium as the carbonate and citrate salts, with some observations on method. Osteoporos Int 9:19–23.
19. Heaney RP, Dowell MS, Bierman J, Hale CA, Bendich A 2001 Absorbability and cost effectiveness in calcium supplementation. J Am Coll Nutr 20:239–246.
20. Davis JW, Ross, PD, Johnson NE, Wasnich RD 1995 Estrogen and calcium supplement use among Japanese-American women: Effects upon bone loss when used singly and in combination. Bone 17:369–373.
21. Dawson-Hughes B, Heaney RP, Holick MF, Lips P, Meunier PJ, Vieth R 2005 Estimates of optimal vitamin D status. Osteoporos Int 16:713–716.
22. Chapuy M-C, Preziosi P, Maamer M, Arnaud S, Galan P, Hercberg S, Meunier PJ 1997 Prevalence of vitamin D insufficiency in an adult normal population. Osteoporos Int 7:439–443.

23. Looker AC, Dawson-Hughes B, Calvo MS, Gunter EW, Sahyoun NR 2002 Serum 25-hydroxyvitamin D status of adolescents and adults in two seasonal subpopulations from NHANES III. Bone **30**:771–777.
24. Thomas MK, Lloyd-Jones DM, Thadhani RI, Shaw AC, Deraska DJ, Kitch BT, Vamvakas EC, Dick IM, Prince RL, Finkelstein JS 1998 Hypovitaminosis D in medical inpatients. N Engl J Med **338**:777–783.
25. Heaney RP, Dowell MS, Hale CA, Bendich A 2003 Calcium absorption varies within the reference range for serum 25-hydroxyvitamin D. J Am Coll Nutr **22**:142–146.
26. Heikinheimo RJ, Inkovaara JA, Harju EJ, Haavisto MV, Kaarela RH, Kataja JM, Kokko AM-L, Kolho LA, Rajala SA 1992 Annual injection of vitamin D and fractures of aged bones. Calcif Tissue Int **51**:105–110.
27. Bischoff-Ferrari HA, Willett WC, Wong JB, Giovannucci E, Dietrich T, Dawson-Hughes B 2005 Fracture prevention with vitamin D supplementation. JAMA **293**:2257–2264.
28. Bischoff HA, Stähelin HB, Dick W, Akos R, Knecht M, Salis C, Nebiker M, Theiler R, Pfeifer M, Begerow B, Lew RA, Conzelmann M 2003 Effects of vitamin D and calcium supplementation on falls: A randomized controlled trial. J Bone Miner Res **18**:343–351.
29. Bischoff-Ferrari HA, Dawson-Hughes B, Willett WC, Stähelin HB, Bazemore MG, Zee RY, Wong JB 2004 Effect of vitamin D on falls. JAMA **291**:1999–2006.
30. Heaney RP, Davies KM, Chen TC, Holick MF, Barger-Lux MJ 2003 Human serum 25-hydroxy-cholecalciferol response to extended oral dosing with cholecalciferol. Am J Clin Nutr **77**:204–210.
31. Armas LAG, Hollis BW, Heaney RP 2004 Vitamin D₂ is much less effective than vitamin D₃ in humans. J Clin Endocrinol Metab **89**:5387–5391.
32. Hannan MT, Tucker KL, Dawson-Hughes B, Cupples LA, Felson DT, Kiel DP 2000 Effect of dietary protein on bone loss in elderly men and women: The Framingham Osteoporosis Study. J Bone Miner Res **15**:2504–2512.
33. Dawson-Hughes B, Harris SS 2002 Calcium intake influences the association of protein intake with rates of bone loss in elderly men and women. Am J Clin Nutr **75**:773–779.
34. Delmi M, Rapin CH, Bengoa JM, Delmas PD, Vasey H, Bonjour JP 1990 Dietary supplementation in elderly patients with fractured neck of the femur. Lancet **335**:1013–1016.
35. Rico H, Revilla M, Villa LF, Hernandez ER, Fernandez JP 1992 Crush fracture syndrome in senile osteoporosis: A nutritional consequence. J Bone Miner Res **7**:317–319.
36. Bastow MD, Rawlings J, Allison SP 1983 Benefits of supplementary tube feeding after fractured neck of femur. BMJ **287**:1589–1592.

Chapter 45.   Calcium and Vitamin D

Bess Dawson-Hughes

Jean Mayer USDA Human Nutrition Research Center on Aging at Tufts University, Boston, Massachusetts

INTRODUCTION

Calcium is required for the bone formation phase of bone remodeling. Typically, about 5 nmol (200 mg) of calcium is removed from the adult skeleton and replaced each day. To supply this amount, one would need to consume about 600 mg of calcium, because calcium is not very efficiently absorbed. Calcium also affects bone mass through its impact on the remodeling rate. An inadequate intake of calcium results in reduced calcium absorption, a lower circulating ionized calcium concentration, and an increased secretion of PTH, a potent bone-resorbing agent. A high remodeling rate leads to bone loss; it is also an independent risk factor for fracture. Dietary calcium at sufficiently high levels, usually 1000 mg/day or more, lowers the bone remodeling rate by ~10–20% in older men and women, and the degree of suppression seems to be dose related.[1] The reduction in remodeling rate accounts for the increase in BMD that occurs in the first 12–18 months of treatment with calcium.

With aging, there is a decline in calcium absorption efficiency in men and women. This may be related to loss of intestinal vitamin D receptors or resistance of these receptors to the action of 1,25(OH)₂D. Diet composition, season, and race also influence calcium absorption efficiency.

Vitamin D is acquired from the diet and from skin synthesis on exposure to UV B rays. The best clinical indicator of vitamin D status is the serum 25-hydroxyvitamin D [25(OH)D] level. Serum 25(OH)D levels are lower in individuals using sunscreens and in those with more pigmented skin. Season is an important determinant of vitamin D levels. In much of the temperate zone, skin synthesis of vitamin D does not occur during the winter. Consequently, 25(OH)D levels fall in the winter and early spring. Serum PTH levels vary inversely with 25(OH)D levels. These cyclic changes are not benign. Bone loss is greater in the winter/spring when 25(OH)D levels are lowest (and PTH levels are highest) than in the summer/fall when 25(OH)D levels are highest (and PTH levels are lowest).

Serum 25(OH)D levels decline with aging for several reasons. There is less efficient skin synthesis of vitamin D with aging as a result of an age-related decline in the amount of 7-dehydrocholesterol, the precursor to vitamin D, in the epidermal layer of skin.[2] Also, older individuals as a group spend less time outdoors. There does not seem to be an impairment in the intestinal absorption of vitamin D with aging.[3]

IMPACT ON BMD

Calcium and vitamin D support bone growth in children and adolescents and lower rates of bone loss in adults and the elderly. A recent meta-analysis of 15 trials found that calcium alone in adults caused positive mean percentage BMD changes from baseline of 1.7% at lumbar spine, 1.6% at the hip, and 1.9% at the distal radius.[4] In one trial, the effects of calcium from food (milk powder) and supplement sources on changes in BMD in older postmenopausal women were compared and found to be similar.[5]

Higher serum 25(OH)D levels have been associated with higher BMD of the hip in young and older adult men and women in the National Health and Nutrition Evaluation Survey III (NHANES III).[6] This association was present at 25(OH)D levels up through the upper end of the reference range (92 nM or 36.8 ng/ml). Supplementation with vitamin D also reduces rates of bone loss in older adults.[7] To sustain the reduced turnover rate and higher bone mass induced by increased calcium and vitamin D intakes, the higher intakes need to be maintained.

IMPACT ON MUSCLE STRENGTH AND FALLING

In HANES III women ≥60 years of age, higher 25(OH)D levels were associated with improved lower extremity function

---

The author has reported no conflicts of interest.

(faster walking and sit-to-stand speeds).[8] A meta-analysis of five randomized placebo-controlled vitamin D intervention trials revealed that supplementation lowered risk of falling by 22%.[9] The trials in which the effect was most apparent used doses of 20 μg (800 IU)/day. The mechanism(s) by which vitamin D influences muscle performance/strength are not well established but are likely to involve the vitamin D receptors known to be present in muscle.

IMPACT ON FRACTURE RATES

Several small studies have examined the impact of calcium on fracture rates. The Shea meta-analysis of these studies[4] found that calcium alone (versus placebo) tended to lower risk of vertebral fractures (relative risk [RR] = 0.77; 95%CI, 0.54–1.09) but not nonvertebral fractures (RR = 0.86; 95% CI, 0.43–1.72). The studies in this analysis ranged from 18 months to 4 years in duration. The recent RECORD trial in older people with a prior fracture revealed that supplementation with 1000 mg/day of calcium did not lower fracture risk over 45 months.[10] Poor compliance may have contributed. At 24 months, 54.5% of subjects were still taking pills.

The effect of supplemental vitamin D on fracture incidence has been examined in several randomized controlled trials. A recent meta-analysis of randomized controlled trials revealed that supplementation with vitamin D lowers risk of hip fracture by 26% and any nonvertebral fracture by 23%.[11] The trials using doses of 17.5–20 μg (700–800 IU)/day were positive and those using 10 μg (400 IU)/day were neutral.

Serum 25(OH)D levels were measured in most of these trials, and fracture risk reduction was inversely related to the serum 25(OH)D level achieved with supplementation.[11] Two large trials published more recently showed no positive effect of vitamin D on fracture rates.[10,12] In a secondary prevention study, the RECORD trial, 20 μg (800 IU)/day of vitamin D with and without 1000 mg of supplemental calcium did not lower fracture risk over a 45-month period in people ≥70 years of age.[10] A small nonrandom subset of participants had 25(OH)D levels measured, and the mean value during supplementation was 62 nM (24.8 ng/ml), which is in the range of other negative studies. This relatively low value is a reflection of poor compliance. As indicated earlier, only 54.5% of the overall sample was taking the supplements at 24 months.

The other recent negative trial was an open trial of 20 μg (800 IU) of vitamin D plus 1000 mg of calcium versus no treatment for an average of 25 months in 3314 women ≥70 years of age. Serum 25(OH)D levels were not measured. Compliance may have been a factor in this trial also. Only 60% of subjects were still taking any pills at 12 months.

From the available evidence, it seems that a serum 25(OH)D level of about 80 nM (32.5 ng/ml) or above is needed to lower risk of fracture. The reduced risk of fracture seems to result from effects of vitamin D on both muscle and bone metabolism.

ROLE IN PHARMACOTHERAPY

In recent randomized, controlled trials testing the antifracture efficacy of the antiresorptive therapies alendronate, risedronate, raloxifene, and calcitonin and the anabolic drug, PTH(1-34), calcium and vitamin D have been given to both the control and intervention groups. This allows one to define the impact of these drugs in calcium- and vitamin D–replete patients and to conclude that any efficacy of the drugs is beyond that associated with calcium and vitamin D alone. Based on the evidence that follows, however, one can't conclude that these drugs would have the same efficacy in calcium- and vitamin

D–deficient patients. In a comparative analysis of the impact of estrogen on BMD in early postmenopausal women who did and did not take calcium supplements, Nieves et al.[13] found that the BMD gains at the spine, hip, and forearm were several-fold greater in the women who increased their calcium intakes than in those who took estrogen without added calcium. From this, it seems that calcium enables estrogen to be more effective in building BMD. In the Mediterranean Osteoporosis Study (MEDOS) in southern Europe,[14] use of nasal calcitonin was associated with a nonsignificant decrease in vertebral fracture risk (RR = 0.78) as was use of calcium alone (RR = 0.82). Use of calcitonin and calcium together, however, was associated with a significant reduction in vertebral fracture risk (RR = 0.63), suggesting that the effects of calcium and this antiresorptive therapy are additive. Little information is available on a potential interaction of other osteoporosis treatments with calcium intake. One can certainly infer that an adequate calcium intake is essential for an optimal response to treatment with the bone-building drug, PTH(1-34). Little direct evidence is available for an interaction of vitamin D with pharmacotherapy, but because vitamin D works in concert with calcium, adequate vitamin D status is very likely to be an important component of the therapy.

INTAKE REQUIREMENTS

Calcium intake recommendations vary enormously worldwide. Recommendations by the U.S. National Academy of Sciences (NAS) are among the highest. The NAS recommended intakes of calcium are as follows: ages 1–3 years, 500 mg/day; 4 -8 years, 800 mg/day; 9–18 years, 1300 mg/day; 19–50 years, 1000 mg/day; 51+ years, 1200 mg/day.[15] Lower calcium intakes would likely be adequate for populations with lower intakes of salt and protein.

Among females in the United States, fewer than 1 in 10 up to age 70 years and fewer than 1 in 100 over that age meet the calcium requirement through their diets. Among males, no more than 25% in any age group has an adequate calcium intake from the diet. Without major dietary changes, most of the American population will need to rely on fortified foods and supplements to meet calcium requirements. Calcium from calcium carbonate, the most commonly used supplement, is better absorbed when taken with a meal.[16,17] Absorption from all supplements is more efficient in single doses of 500 mg or less.[18] Thus, individuals requiring >500 mg/day from supplements should take it in divided doses. The safe upper limit for calcium set by the NAS is 2500 mg/day.[15]

The vitamin D intake recommendations of the NAS, made in 1997, are as follows: for adult men and women up to age 50 years, 5 μg (200 IU)/day; 51–70 years, 10 mg (400 IU)/day; and 71+ years, 15 μg (600 IU)/day.[15] These recommendations are based on the amount of vitamin D needed to maximally suppress PTH secretion. However, for reasons that are not entirely clear, variability in this endpoint is large across study populations. Several studies have placed the 25(OH)D level needed for maximal PTH suppression in the range of 75–110 nM (30–44 ng/ml), whereas another places it as low as 25 nM (10 ng/ml).[19] The currently recommended vitamin D intake of 600 IU (15 μg)/day for men and women ≥71 years of age is not adequate to bring most of the elderly population to 25(OH)D levels of 75–80 nM (30–32 ng/ml), the level apparently needed to lower fracture risk.

The increase in 25(OH)D with supplementation is inversely related to the starting level. At low starting levels, 1 μg (40 IU) of vitamin D will increase serum 25(OH)D by 1.2 nM (0.48 ng/ml); at a higher starting level of 70 nM (28 ng/ml), the increase from this dose would be only about 0.7 nM (0.28

ng/ml).[20,21] The average older man and woman will need an intake of at least 20–25 μg (800–1000 IU)/day to reach a serum 25(OH)D level of 75 nM (30 ng/ml).[19] The NAS has placed the safe upper limit for vitamin D at 50 μg (2000 IU)/day.[15]

Vitamin D is available in two forms: the plant-derived ergocalciferol (D_2) and cholecalciferol (D_3), which is of animal origin. For years these forms were considered to be equipotent in humans. Recent evidence suggests that vitamin D_2 gives a smaller increment in serum 25(OH)D (0.3 nM for every μg or 0.3 ng/ml for every 100 IU) than vitamin D_3 ($\geq$0.7 nM for every μg or 0.7 ng/ml for every 100 IU).

In conclusion, adequate intakes of calcium and vitamin D are essential preventative measures and essential components of any therapeutic regimen for osteoporosis. Many men and women will need supplements to meet the intake requirements. Current evidence suggests that a 25(OH)D level of 75 nM (30 ng/ml) or higher is needed to lower fracture risk. The average older person will need 20–25 μg (800–1000 IU) per day of vitamin D_3 to reach this level.

REFERENCES

1. Elders PJ, Netelenbos JC, Lips P, van Ginkel FC, Khoe E, Leeuwenkamp OR, Hackeng WH, van der Stelt PF 1991 Calcium supplementation reduces vertebral bone loss in perimenopausal women: A controlled trial in 248 women between 46 and 55 years of age. J Clin Endocrinol Metab **73:**533–540.
2. MacLaughlin J, Holick MF 1985 Aging decreases the capacity of human skin to produce vitamin D_3. J Clin Invest **76:**1536–1538.
3. Harris SS, Dawson-Hughes B 2002 Plasma vitamin D and 25OHD responses of young and old men to supplementation with vitamin D_3. J Am Coll Nutr **21:**357–362.
4. Shea B, Wells G, Cranney A, Zytaruk N, Robinson V, Griffith L, Ortiz Z, Peterson J, Adachi J, Tugwell P, Guyatt G 2002 VII. Meta-analysis of calcium supplementation for the prevention of postmenopausal osteoporosis. Endocr Rev **23:**552–559.
5. Prince R, Devine A, Dick I, Criddle A, Kerr D, Kent N, Price R, Randell A 1995 The effects of calcium supplementation (milk powder or tablets) and exercise on bone density in postmenopausal women. J Bone Miner Res **10:**1068–1075.
6. Bischoff-Ferrari HA, Dietrich T, Orav EJ, Dawson-Hughes B 2004 Positive association between 25-hydroxy vitamin D levels and bone mineral density: A population-based study of younger and older adults. Am J Med **116:**634–639.
7. Ooms ME, Roos JC, Bezemer PD, van der Vijgh WJ, Bouter LM, Lips P 1995 Prevention of bone loss by vitamin D supplementation in elderly women: A randomized double-blind trial. J Clin Endocrinol Metab **80:** 1052–1058.
8. Bischoff-Ferrari HA, Dietrich T, Orav EJ, Zhang Y, Karlson EW, Dawson-Hughes B 2004 Higher 25-hydroxyvitamin D levels are associated with better lower extremity function in both active and inactive adults 60+ years of age. Am J Clin Nutr **80:**752–758.
9. Bischoff-Ferrari HA, Dawson-Hughes B, Willett WC, Staehlin HB, Bazemore MG, Zee RY, Wong JB 2004 Effect of vitamin D on falls —a meta-analysis. J Am Med Assoc **291:**1999–2006.
10. Grant AM, Avenell A, Campbell MK, McDonald AM, MacLennan GS, McPherson GC, Anderson FH, Cooper C, Francis RM, Donaldson C, Gillespie WJ, Robinson CM, Torgerson DJ, Wallace WA, RECORD Trial Group 2005 Oral vitamin D3 and calcium for secondary prevention of low-trauma fractures in elderly people (Randomised Evaluation of Calcium Or vitamin D, RECORD): A randomised placebo-controlled trial. Lancet **365:**1621–1628.
11. Bischoff-Ferrari HA, Willett W, Wong JB, Giovannucci E, Dietrich T, Dawson-Hughes B 2005 Fracture prevention by vitamin D supplementation: A meta-analysis of randomized controlled trials. JAMA **293:**2257–2264.
12. Porthouse J, Cockayne S, King C, Saxon L, Steele E, Aspray T, Baverstock M, Birks Y, Dumville J, Francis R, Iglesias C, Puffer S, Sutcliffe A, Watt I, Torgerson DJ 2005 Randomised controlled trial of calcium and supplementation with cholecalciferol (vitamin D3) for prevention of fractures in primary care. BMJ **330:**1003–1008.
13. Nieves JW, Komar L, Cosman F, Lindsay R 1998 Calcium potentiates the effect of estrogen and calcitonin on bone mass: Review and analysis. Am J Clin Nutr **67:**18–24.
14. Johnell O, Gullberg B, Kanis JA, Allander E, Elffors L, Dequeker J, Dilsen G, Gennari C, Lopes VA, Lyritis G 1995 Risk factors for hip fracture in European women: The MEDOS Study. Mediterranean Osteoporosis Study. J Bone Miner Res **10:**1802–1815.
15. Anonymous 1997 Dietary Reference Intakes: Calcium, Phosphorus, Magnesium, Vitamin D, and Fluoride. National Academy Press, Washington, DC, USA.
16. Heaney RP, Smith KT, Recker RR, Hinders SM 1989 Meal effects on calcium absorption. Am J Clin Nutr **49:**372–376.
17. Recker RR 1985 Calcium absorption and achlorhydria. N Engl J Med **313:**70–73.
18. Harvey JA, Zobitz MM, Pak CY 1988 Dose dependency of calcium absorption: A comparison of calcium carbonate and calcium citrate. J Bone Miner Res **3:**253–258.
19. Dawson-Hughes B, Heaney RP, Holick MF, Lips P, Meunier PJ, Vieth R 2005 Estimates of optimal vitamin D status. Osteoporos Int **16:**713–716.
20. Vieth R, Ladak Y, Walfish PG 2003 Age-related changes in the 25-hydroxyvitamin D versus parathyroid hormone relationship suggest a different reason why older adults require more vitamin D. J Clin Endocrinol Metab **88:**185–191.
21. Heaney RP, Davies KM, Chen TC, Holick MF, Barger-Lux MJ 2003 Human serum 25-hydroxycholecalciferol response to extended oral dosing with cholecalciferol. Am J Clin Nutr **77:**204–210.

Chapter 46.   Pathogenesis of Postmenopausal Osteoporosis

Richard Eastell

Academic Unit of Bone Metabolism, Section of Human Metabolism, Division of Clinical Sciences (North), University of Sheffield, Sheffield, United Kingdom

INTRODUCTION

Osteoporosis-related fractures result from a combination of decreased BMD and a deterioration in bone microarchitecture. A BMD below average for age can be considered a consequence of inadequate accumulation of bone in young adult life (low peak bone mass) or of excessive rates of bone loss. The microarchitectural changes occur with the bone loss but will be considered separately.

DETERMINANTS OF PEAK BONE MASS

The increase in bone mass that occurs during childhood and puberty results from a combination of growth of bone at the endplates (endochondral bone formation) and of change in bone shape (modeling). The rapid increase in bone mass at puberty is associated with an increase in sex hormone levels

The author has reported no conflicts of interest.

and the closure of the growth plates. Within 3 years of menarche, there is little further increase in bone mass. The small increase in BMD over the next 5–15 years is a consequence of periosteal apposition (modeling). The resulting peak bone mass is achieved by 20–30 years of age.

Genetic factors are the main determinants of peak bone mass.[1] This has been shown by studies made on twins or on mother-daughter pairs. Hereditability seems to account for ~50–85% of the variance in bone mass, depending on the skeletal site. It is likely that several genes regulate bone mass, each with a modest effect, and likely candidates include the genes for type I collagen (COL1A1), LRP5, and the vitamin D receptor. The nongenetic factors include low calcium intake during childhood, low body weight at maturity and at 1 year of life, sedentary lifestyle, and delayed puberty. Each of these results in decreased bone mass.

BONE LOSS

Mechanisms

Bone loss occurs in the postmenopausal woman as a result of an increase in the rate of bone remodeling and an imbalance between the activity of osteoclasts and osteoblasts. Bone remodeling occurs at discrete sites within the skeleton and proceeds in an orderly fashion with bone resorption always being followed by bone formation, a phenomenon referred to as "coupling." In cortical and cancellous bone, the sequence of bone remodeling is similar.[2] The quiescent bone surface is converted to activity (origination), and the osteoclasts resorb bone (progression) forming a cutting cone (cortical bone) or a trench (cancellous bone). The osteoblasts synthesize bone matrix that subsequently mineralizes. The sequence takes up to 8 months. If the processes of bone resorption and bone formation are not matched, a remodeling imbalance results. In postmenopausal women, this imbalance is magnified by the increase in the rate of initiation of new bone remodeling cycles (activation frequency). In women with postmenopausal osteoporosis, there is a further increase in activation frequency, and yet the duration of the remodeling cycle may be longer than in young women.

Remodeling imbalance results in irreversible bone loss. There are two other causes of irreversible bone loss, referred to as "remodeling errors." First is excavation of overlarge haversian spaces in cortical bone.[3] Radial infilling is regulated by signals from the outermost osteocytes and is generally no more than 90 mm. Hence, large external diameters, which may simply occur randomly, lead to large central haversian canals, which accumulate with age, leading to increased cortical porosity.[4] In a similar way, osteoclast penetration of trabecular plates, or severing of trabecular beams, removes the scaffolding needed for osteoblastic replacement of resorbed bone. In both ways, random remodeling errors tend to reduce both cancellous and cortical BMD and structural integrity.

Causes

Estrogen deficiency. Bone loss in the postmenopausal woman occurs in two phases.[5] There is a phase of rapid bone loss that lasts for 5 years (~3%/year in the spine). Subsequently, there is lower bone loss that is more generalized (~0.5%/year at many sites). This slower phase of bone loss affects men, starting at about age 55 years.

The major mechanism of the rapid phase of bone loss in women is estrogen deficiency. The circulating level of estradiol decreases by 90% at the time of menopause. This bone loss can be prevented by the administration of estrogen

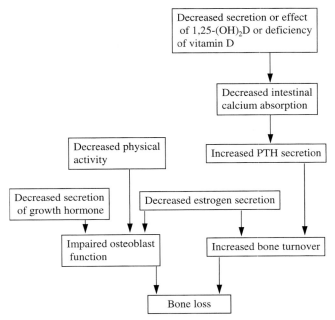

FIG. 1. Proposed mechanism for age-related bone loss in women.[5] Note how estrogen deficiency probably results in both increased bone turnover and remodeling imbalance.[4]

and progestins to the postmenopausal woman. It has been estimated that this rapid phase of bone loss contributes 50% to the spinal bone loss across the life in women.[5] The residual level of estrogen in a postmenopausal woman is important in regulating bone turnover and low levels, such as the levels attained during treatment with aromatase inhibitors, predispose to fractures.[6]

The major effect of estrogen deficiency is on bone, where it increases activation frequency and may contribute to the remodeling imbalance. Much has been learned about the role of estrogen in bone loss, but there are still significant gaps in our knowledge.[5] Estrogen may act partly through the osteoblast (e.g., increased synthesis of IGF-I, osteoprotegerin, and TGF-β and decreased synthesis of RANKL) and partly through monocytes in the bone marrow environment (e.g., decreased synthesis of IL-1, IL-6, and TNF-α).[7] This modulation of locally active growth factors and cytokines mediates the effects of estrogen on osteoblasts and osteoclasts. Thus, a greater increase in cytokines (e.g., IL-1) in response to estrogen deficiency may account for the more rapid bone loss in some women.

Estrogen deficiency may be a determinant of bone loss in men.[5] Decreased BMD has been reported in men with an inactivating mutation of the genes for the estrogen receptor[8] or for aromatase (the enzyme that converts androgens to estrogens).[9] In older men, estrogen levels correlate more closely with BMD than testosterone levels. In men with osteoporosis, estradiol (but not testosterone) levels have been reported to be decreased.[10]

Aging. The slow phase of bone loss is attributed to age-related factors such as an increase in PTH levels and to osteoblast senescence (Fig. 1). An increase in PTH levels (and action) occurs in both men and women with aging.[11] PTH levels correlate with biochemical markers of bone turnover and both may be returned to levels found in young adults by the intravenous infusion of calcium. The increase in PTH results from decreased renal calcium reabsorption and decreased intestinal

Causes of Low Bone Mass

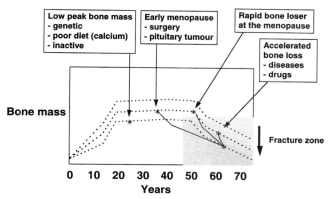

FIG. 2. Causes of low BMD in postmenopausal women. BMD reaches a peak between ages 20 and 30 and is followed by a rapid phase of bone loss at menopause lasting 5 years followed by a slower phase of bone loss. Bone loss in a 65-year-old woman may have a single cause (as shown here) or there may be several causes contributing to the low BMD.

calcium absorption. The latter may result from vitamin D deficiency (e.g., in the housebound elderly), decreased 1α-hydroxylase activity in the kidney, resulting in decreased synthesis of $1,25(OH)_2$ vitamin D, or resistance to vitamin D. Whatever the cause, a diet high in calcium returns both PTH and bone turnover markers to levels found in healthy young adults.[12]

It has been proposed that the age-related increase in PTH could result from indirect effects of estrogen deficiency.[5] This proposal is based on the following evidence. In older women treated with estrogen, (1) there is a decrease in bone turnover markers and PTH levels, (2) there is an increase in calcium absorption, possibly mediated by an increase in $1,25(OH)_2$ vitamin D, (3) there is an increase in the PTH-independent calcium reabsorption in the kidney, and (4) there is a decrease in the parathyroid secretory reserve.

Accelerating factors. A number of diseases and drugs are clearly related to accelerated bone loss, and these are described elsewhere. Their effects are superimposed on those described above. Thus, a patient starting on corticosteroid therapy is more likely to have an osteoporosis-related fracture if she has low BMD resulting from low peak bone mass and the accelerated bone loss of the menopause.

Identification of Mechanism of Bone Loss in an Individual

In a woman presenting with osteoporosis at the age of 65 years, it is often possible to identify several reasons for low BMD (Fig. 2). Some of these may be identified from history-taking (early menopause, drugs that accelerate bone loss), but some cannot be identified in retrospect (low peak bone mass, rapid losers).

OTHER DETERMINANTS OF BONE STRENGTH

Bone Geometry

Bone geometry has a major effect on fracture risk.[3] One example is hip axis length, the distance from the lateral surface of the trochanter to the inner surface of the pelvis, along the axis of the femoral neck. Short hip axis length results in an architecturally stronger structure for any given BMD. This is

probably the reason why Japanese and other Asians have about one half the hip fracture rate of whites, despite similar BMD values. Likewise, large vertebral body endplate areas result in lower spine compression force for individuals of the same body size. Those with small vertebral bodies are thus more likely to fracture. Such geometric factors both contribute to individual fracture risk and explain a substantial portion of the population-level variance in fracture rate. In each situation, however, the ultimate pathogenesis of the fracture is the fall and the force sustained by the bone on impact.

Fatigue Damage

Fatigue damage consists of ultramicroscopic rents in the basic bony material, resulting from the inevitable bending that occurs when a structural member is loaded.[3] Fatigue damage is the principal cause of failure in mechanical engineering structures; its prevention is the responsibility of the remodeling apparatus, which detects and removes fatigue-damaged bone. Fractures related to fatigue damage occur whenever the damage occurs faster than remodeling can repair it or whenever the remodeling apparatus is defective. March fractures and the fractures of radiation necrosis are well-recognized examples of fractures caused by these two mechanisms. Fatigue damage definitely occurs in normal bone, under ordinary use, although it is less certain as to precisely what role it may play in predisposing to osteoporotic fracture. Furthermore, there is suggestive evidence for certain fractures (notably hip) that remodeling repair may be defective specifically at the site that ultimately fractures. Why remodeling surveillance or effectiveness might fail locally is not known. Nevertheless, it is clear that such failure would lead to accumulation of fatigue damage and, therefore, to local weakening of bone.[13]

Loss of Trabecular Connectivity

Bone structures loaded vertically, such as the vertebral bodies and femoral and tibial metaphyses, derive a substantial portion of their structural strength from a system of horizontal, cross-bracing trabeculae, which support the vertical elements and limit lateral bowing and consequent snapping under vertical loading.[3] Severance of such trabecular connections is known to occur preferentially in postmenopausal women and is considered to be a major reason for the large female/male preponderance of vertebral osteoporosis. That long, unsupported vertical trabeculae are susceptible to fracture is reflected in the extraordinarily high prevalence of trabecular fracture callus sites in vertebral bodies examined at autopsy, typically 200–450 healing or healed fractures per vertebral body. While many of these will be well enough healed at any given time to be structurally competent, others will be fresh and structurally weak. Such fractures are asymptomatic, and their accumulation both reflects the impact of lost trabecular connections and greatly weakens the cancellous structure of the vertebral body. The incident fracture prediction ability of prior vertebral fractures is probably caused in part by the presence of such otherwise undetected trabecular defects. That is why prior fracture seems to predict future fracture even when BMD is relatively high. The reason for preferential osteoclastic severance of horizontal trabeculae is not known. It is sometimes attributed to overaggressive osteoclastic resorption but that seems more descriptive than explanatory.

REFERENCES

1. Jin H, Ralston SH 2005 Genetics of osteoporosis. Curr Rheumatol Rep 7:66–70.
2. Parfitt AM, Mundy GR, Roodman GD, Hughes DE, Boyce BF 1996 A

new model for the regulation of bone resorption, with particular reference to the effects of bisphosphonates. J Bone Miner Res **11**:150–159.

3. Seeman E 2002 Pathogenesis of bone fragility in women and men. Lancet **359**:1841–1850.
4. Bell KL, Loveridge N, Jordan GR, Power J, Constant CR, Reeve J 2000 A novel mechanism for induction of increased cortical porosity in cases of intracapsular hip fracture. Bone **27**:297–304.
5. Riggs BL, Khosla S, Melton LJ III 2002 Sex steroids and the construction and conservation of the adult skeleton. Endocr Rev **23**:279–302.
6. Eastell R, Hannon R 2005 Long-term effects of aromatase inhibitors on bone. J Steroid Biochem Mol Biol **95**:151–154.
7. Rogers A, Eastell R 2005 Circulating osteoprotegerin (OPG) and receptor activator for NF{kappa}B ligand (RANKL): Clinical utility in metabolic bone disease assessment. J Clin Endocrinol Metab **90**:6323–6331.
8. Smith EP, Boyd J, Frank GR, Takahashi H, Cohen RM, Specker B, Williams TC, Lubahn DB, Korach KS 1994 Estrogen resistance caused by a mutation in the estrogen-receptor gene in a man. N Engl J Med **331**:1056–1061.
9. Bilezikian JP, Morishima A, Bell J, Grumbach MM 1998 Increased bone mass as a result of estrogen therapy in a man with aromatase deficiency. N Engl J Med **339**:599–603.
10. Carlsen CG, Soerensen TH, Eriksen EF 2000 Prevalence of low serum estradiol levels in male osteoporosis. Osteoporos Int **11**:697–701.
11. Fatayerji D, Mawer EB, Eastell R 2000 The role of insulin-like growth factor I in age-related changes in calcium homeostasis in men. J Clin Endocrinol Metab **85**:4657–4662.
12. Riggs BL, O'Fallon WM, Muhs J, O'Connor MK, Kumar R, Melton LJ III 1998 Long-term effects of calcium supplementation on serum parathyroid hormone level, bone turnover, and bone loss in elderly women. J Bone Miner Res **13**:168–174.
13. Frost HM 2000 Does bone design intend to minimize fatigue failures? A case for the affirmative. J Bone Miner Metab **18**:278–282.

Chapter 47. Assessing Fracture Risk: Who Should be Screened?

John T. Schousboe,[1] Brent C. Taylor,[2] and Kristine E. Ensrud[2,3]

[1]Park Nicollet Health Services, Minneapolis, Minnesota and Division of Health Services Research and Policy, School of Public Health, University of Minnesota, Minneapolis, Minnesota; [2]Center for Chronic Disease Outcomes Research, Veterans Affairs Medical Center, Minneapolis, Minnesota; and [3]Department of Medicine and Division of Epidemiology and Community Health, School of Public Health, University of Minnesota, Minneapolis, Minnesota

OSTEOPOROSIS: WHO SHOULD BE SCREENED?

Osteoporosis has now been broadly defined for more than a decade as a metabolic bone disease characterized by low bone mass and microarchitectural deterioration of bone, leading to enhanced bone fragility and increased fracture risk. Implicit in that definition are three elements: low bone mass, microarchitectural deterioration, and fracture risk.

Screening generally refers to application of a test or procedure to large segments of the population at large to establish the presence or absence of a disease or condition. Such tests can be as simple as queries regarding personal and family characteristics and history (through interview or self-administered questionnaires) or involve technologically based diagnostic procedures. Given that low bone mass is one of the strongest predictors of fracture, the topic of screening for osteoporosis could be narrowly construed as a discussion of who is at risk for low bone mass and should undergo bone densitometry. Ultimately, however, the purpose of any screening program for osteoporosis is to identify those at high risk of fracture (and for whom, therefore, specific interventions are indicated). Consequently, the issue of screening for osteoporosis involves two closely related but distinct questions: who is at risk for low bone mass (and should undergo bone densitometry) and who is at risk for fracture.

In this chapter, we will first address the issue of screening for fracture risk in three steps. The first step is determining who, based on clinical risk factors, is or may be at high risk for fracture, and therefore should have bone densitometry to refine the assessment of their fracture risk. The second step is determining if fracture risk assessment would benefit further from additional assessment methods, such as spinal imaging (vertebral fracture assessment) and/or measurement of markers of bone metabolism. The third step is assessing fracture risk based on the combined effect of BMD, clinical risk factors, and additional diagnostic studies that may have been performed.

Implicit in this discussion is that one of the primary purposes of such a screening cascade is to identify individuals who are candidates for some intervention, such as medical. Preventive measures such as ensuring adequate calcium and vitamin D intake and weight-bearing exercise arguably should be recommended regardless of the presence or absence of additional fracture risk factors such as low BMD.

CLINICAL RISK FACTORS

Table 1 lists the most important clinical risk factors for fracture. Increasing age and female gender are strongly associated with fracture. Race is also an important clinical risk factor. For example, in the United States, whites have a significantly higher age-adjusted risk of fracture compared with blacks.[1] Prior clinical fractures are a strong risk factor for subsequent fractures.[2] In particular, prior clinical vertebral fractures are a particularly powerful risk factor for subsequent vertebral fractures.[3] The presence of prevalent radiographic vertebral fracture (whether clinically recognized or not) in general are also strongly associated with incident radiographic vertebral fracture, and to a lesser degree with incident nonvertebral fracture.[4] Family history of fracture in a first degree relative is also associated with incident hip and other nonvertebral fractures.[5]

Perhaps the best documented anthropometric risk factor for both vertebral[6] and nonvertebral fractures[7] is low body weight. Weight loss is also an important risk factor for nonspine fractures in general,[8] and hip fracture in particular,[9] independent of current body weight. Height is also a modest risk factor for hip fracture, presumably because of the greater force applied to the trochanter of the hip when falling from even a slightly greater height.[10]

The authors have reported no conflicts of interest.

TABLE 1. CLINICAL RISK FACTORS FOR FRACTURE

Factor

Advanced age
Female gender
White race
Prior fracture
Maternal or paternal history of hip fracture
  Maternal history of any clinical fracture
Anthropometric measures
  Low body weight or body mass index
  Weight loss
  Greater height
Lifestyle factors
  Cigarette smoking
  Protein/calorie intake
  Low physical activity
Health status
  Self reported poor general health
  High pulse rate (age 65 and older)
  Poor vision
  Impaired neuromuscular function
  Falls
Medications
  Glucocorticoids
  Anti-convulsants
  Benzodiazepines
  Anti-depressants
Other medical conditions
  Eating disorders
  Hyperparathyroidism
  Hyperthyroidism
  Hypercortisolism
  Gonadal hormone deficiency
  Autoimmune diseases
  Chronic lung disease
  Parkinson's disease
  Diabetes mellitus

Factors in bold have also been shown to be at least moderately predictive of incident fracture (risk >1.5 in those with relative to those without the factor) independent of BMD.

Several lifestyle factors are associated with fracture risk. Cigarette smoking is moderately associated with fracture.[11] Protein calorie malnutrition is associated with incident fractures, both among younger women with eating disorders[12] and among the elderly.[13] While current calcium intake has been shown to be associated only weakly with fracture, other studies have found a stronger association between calcium intake as a teenager or during pregnancy and fracture risk as an older adult.[14] Vitamin D intake has been shown in some studies to also be a fracture risk factor, at least for hip fracture.[15] A sedentary lifestyle, assessed as either being on one's feet <4 h/day[10] or as walking very little and performing little housework,[6] is also associated with a higher risk of fracture.

More than 90% of nonvertebral fractures occur with a fall, and the self-reported number of falls during the prior year are associated with an increased risk of nonvertebral fractures,[10] and in one study, with an increased risk of vertebral fractures.[6] Not surprisingly, many other factors that may well increase the risk of falls such as poor vision[10] and use of medications that may impair balance such as benzodiazepines and anti-convulsants are also associated with an increased risk of fracture.[10] Impaired neuromuscular function, such as inability to rise from a chair,[16] and low grip strength are also strongly

associated with incident fractures. In addition, use of systemic glucocorticoids are associated with a higher risk of vertebral and nonvertebral fractures.[17]

Self-reported poor health status is associated with an increased risk of incident vertebral and nonvertebral fractures.[10,18] Many medical conditions are associated with an increased fracture risk. Endocrine conditions most notably linked to increased fracture risk are hyperparathyroidism, hyperthyroidism, hypercortisolism, and premature menopause.[12] There is some evidence that testosterone deficiency in men is associated with an increased risk of hip fracture, but not with a higher risk of vertebral fracture.[19] Autoimmune disorders associated with an increased risk of fracture include systemic lupus erythematosus,[20] rheumatoid arthritis,[21] and ankylosing spondylitis. While glucocorticoid treatment for these conditions accounts in part for these associations with fracture, the underlying diseases themselves constitute risk factors for fracture. Finally, additional medical conditions including chronic obstructive pulmonary disease (COPD), diabetes mellitus, Parkinson's disease, liver failure, and end-stage renal disease are all associated with increased fracture risks.[12]

USE OF BONE DENSITOMETRY TO REFINE ASSESSMENT OF FRACTURE RISK

BMD is one of the key determinants of bone strength and can be assessed at a variety of skeletal sites using DXA, single energy X-ray absorptiometry, or single energy X-ray. BMD of the distal or proximal radius, calcaneus, spine, and hip is associated with fractures at all of the major skeletal sites (hip, pelvis, spine, distal forearm, and proximal humerus) of osteoporotic fractures.[22] Measurement of BMD specifically at the spine and hip, however, tend to be most predictive of spine and hip fractures, respectively (Table 2), at least among postmenopausal women ≥65 years of age.[23]

Relationship of Clinical Risk Factors to and Their Independence of BMD

Many of the aforementioned clinical risk factors are associated with BMD. Age and sex are strongly associated with BMD. In the United States, black race is associated with higher BMD relative to whites and Hispanics. Low body weight is strongly associated with BMD, so much that, at least among white and Asian postmenopausal women, the combination of age and body weight together are moderately predictive of BMD.[24] At present, no combination of risk factors broadly predicts which individuals have BMD below a specific threshold (such as a T score ≤ −2.5) with high sensitivity and specificity.

Because several of the clinical factors discussed previously are associated with fracture by virtue of their relationship with low BMD, their relationship with incident fracture

TABLE 2. RELATIVE RISKS OF FRACTURE FOR 1 SD DECREASE IN BMD, ACCORDING TO SKELETAL SITE OF BMD MEASUREMENT AND SKELETAL SITE OF FRACTURE*

	Incident fracture site			
BMD site	*Forearm*	*Hip*	*Vertebra*	*All*
Forearm	1.7	1.8	1.7	1.4
Femoral neck	1.4	2.6	1.8	1.6
Lumbar spine	1.5	1.6	2.3	1.5

* From Marshall D, et al. 1996 BMJ **312**:1254–1259. Reproduced with permission from the BMJ Publishing Group.

is either strongly attenuated or disappears when adjusted for BMD (Table 1). For example, the relationship between body weight and fracture disappears when adjusted for BMD.[7] A recent meta-analysis of several large observational studies, however, did find that body mass index (BMI; weight/height^2) is associated with incident hip fracture, independent of BMD.[7] Moreover, the association between weight loss and incident hip fracture is independent of hip BMD.[9] Age, chronic systemic glucocorticoid use, prevalent radiographic vertebral fracture, and recent prior clinical fracture[25] are additional clinical risk factors that are strongly associated with incident fractures even after adjustment for BMD. In the United States, black postmenopausal women have a relative age- and BMD-adjusted risk for incident nonspine fractures of 0.5 relative to white women.[1] Asian women residing in their native countries also seem to have a lower age- and BMD-adjusted risk of hip and other nonvertebral fractures,[26] relative to white women. Maternal and paternal history of hip fracture is a moderate risk factor for hip fracture independent of BMD,[6,10] but maternal history of any fracture is a weaker risk factor for any nonspine fracture.[5] Physical activity,[6] impaired neuromuscular function,[16] and menopause before age 45 retain a moderate relationship with incident fracture,[12] even after adjustment for BMD. Fall risk factors and other measures of physical frailty such as poor vision, impaired neuromuscular function, and elevated pulse rate are all weak to moderate predictors of fracture after adjustment for BMD. Cigarette smoking is only a weak fracture risk factor after adjustment for body weight and BMD.[11]

Who Should Undergo Bone Densitometry?

Bone densitometry in general should be done for those individuals for whom the results are likely to alter patient management. In a clinical setting, the typical patient management decision under consideration is whether or not to recommend pharmacologic therapy to prevent osteoporotic fractures. In other words, densitometry is indicated if there is a reasonable pretest probability of finding BMD at or below a value that represents a reasonable intervention threshold.

By these criteria, bone densitometry is indicated for those who have a prevalent radiographic vertebral fracture, have had a prior clinical fracture with minor trauma, are on chronic glucocorticoid therapy, or have other chronic illnesses that are strongly associated with osteoporosis and fracture (Fig. 1). Bone densitometry is now recommended as a screening test for women age 65 or older, because for this segment of the population, there is a reasonable likelihood of BMD being at or below a treatment threshold.[27] For postmenopausal women <65 years of age, bone densitometry is also appropriate if they have other BMD-independent fracture risk factors (Fig. 1). In the absence of additional BMD-independent fracture risk factors, BMD is most strongly associated with age and weight, and the decision whether or not bone densitometry should be done can be decided primarily based on those two factors (Fig. 2). For example, an Osteoporosis Self-Assessment Tool (OST) score of 1 or less has a sensitivity of 88–91% and a specificity of 45–52% for postmenopausal women with a lumbar spine or femoral neck T score of −2.5 or worse.[24] This performs as well as and is simpler than other risk indices (such as the Osteoporosis Risk Assessment Index [ORAI]), which include additional risk factors for low BMD such as use of hormone replacement and personal history of prior fractures.[24]

If there is no intention to assess the results of drug therapy with serial bone densitometry, bone densitometry arguably would not be necessary in those for whom drug therapy is

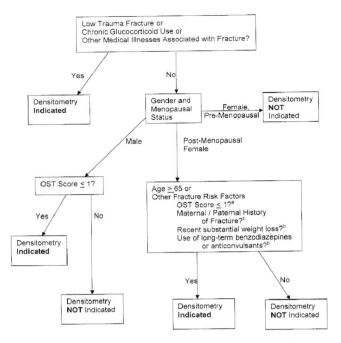

FIG. 1. Algorithm to guide use of bone densitometry.

indicated regardless of BMD, or who, based on clinical risk factors, are highly likely to have BMD below the appropriate treatment threshold (such as an older person with a recent clinical vertebral or hip fracture).[28]

For elderly men, it is unclear at this point if there should be any universal screening above a certain age. Some have suggested that bone densitometry may be reasonable for all men >70 or 75 years of age,[29] but the cost effectiveness of this has yet to be shown, and such recommendations at the moment may be premature. Clearly, bone densitometry would be appropriate in those elderly men on long-term glucocorticoid therapy or with a history of fracture. Otherwise, weight and age are strongly associated with BMD in men, and the OST can be used in men to help decide whether or not bone densitometry is indicated.[30] In two large observational cohorts of elderly men, an OST score of 2 or less had specificities of 32% and 51% and sensitivities of 88% and 79% for men with a sex-specific femoral neck T score of −2.5 or less.[30] If, however, young female norms are used to establish T scores in men (as is currently recommended by the International Society for Clinical Densitometry), an OST score of 2 or less would have higher sensitivity but lower specificity for a T score of −2.5 in men than the study of Hochberg et al. suggests. Therefore, in the absence of prior fracture, current glucocorticoid therapy, or other chronic conditions strongly associated with risk of fracture, based on currently available data, we believe that bone densitometry is reasonable in elderly men with an OST score of 1 or less. This is the same threshold value that has been recommended for performing bone densitometry in elderly women.[24]

Bone densitometry is otherwise not indicated for premenopausal women or men with no fragility fracture history, no prevalent radiographic vertebral fracture, who are not on

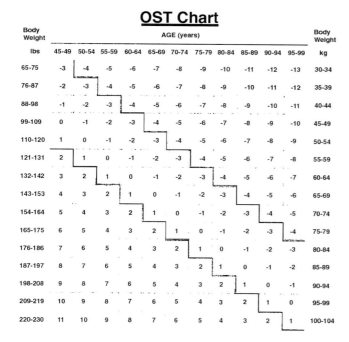

OST Chart

Body Weight lbs	AGE (years) 45-49	50-54	55-59	60-64	65-69	70-74	75-79	80-84	85-89	90-94	95-99	Body Weight kg
65-75	-3	-4	-5	-6	-7	-8	-9	-10	-11	-12	-13	30-34
76-87	-2	-3	-4	-5	-6	-7	-8	-9	-10	-11	-12	35-39
88-98	-1	-2	-3	-4	-5	-6	-7	-8	-9	-10	-11	40-44
99-109	0	-1	-2	-3	-4	-5	-6	-7	-8	-9	-10	45-49
110-120	1	0	-1	-2	-3	-4	-5	-6	-7	-8	-9	50-54
121-131	2	1	0	-1	-2	-3	-4	-5	-6	-7	-8	55-59
132-142	3	2	1	0	-1	-2	-3	-4	-5	-6	-7	60-64
143-153	4	3	2	1	0	-1	-2	-3	-4	-5	-6	65-69
154-164	5	4	3	2	1	0	-1	-2	-3	-4	-5	70-74
165-175	6	5	4	3	2	1	0	-1	-2	-3	-4	75-79
176-186	7	6	5	4	3	2	1	0	-1	-2	-3	80-84
187-197	8	7	6	5	4	3	2	1	0	-1	-2	85-89
198-208	9	8	7	6	5	4	3	2	1	0	-1	90-94
209-219	10	9	8	7	6	5	4	3	2	1	0	95-99
220-230	11	10	9	8	7	6	5	4	3	2	1	100-104

Osteoporosis Self-Assessment Tool (OST) showing combinations of age and weight indicating high risk of osteoporosis (OST score ≤ -4), low risk of osteoporosis (OST score ≥ 2), and indeterminate risk of osteoporosis (OST score between -3 and 1)

From Cadarette SM, et. al. *Osteoporos Int.* May 2004;15(5):361-366. Copyright 2004, with kind permission from Springer Science and Business Media.

FIG. 2. Risk of osteoporosis (T score ≤ −2.5) among white postmenopausal women according to age and body weight.

chronic glucocorticoid therapy, and do not have other medical conditions associated with osteoporosis and incident fracture.

SPINAL IMAGING TO DETECT PREVALENT RADIOGRAPHIC VERTEBRAL DEFORMITY

Prevalent radiographic vertebral deformity is strongly associated with subsequent incident vertebral fracture and moderately associated with incident nonvertebral fracture, independent of BMD.[4] Vertebral deformities are increasingly prevalent with increasing age, especially over age 65,[31] and also among those who have had 4 cm or more height loss compared with their recalled young adult height, or with incident height loss of 2 cm or more.[32] Spinal imaging with either standard radiographs or absorptiometry to identify those who have one or more prevalent radiographic vertebral fractures may therefore impact assessment of fracture risk to an extent that decisions regarding pharmacologic therapy to prevent therapy are altered. For example, for postmenopausal women 60–80 years of age with osteopenia (T score between −1.5 and −2.4), the presence of one or more vertebral deformities may nonetheless indicate sufficient incident fracture risk to justify pharmacologic intervention.[33] Antiresorptive drug therapy reduces the risk of incident vertebral fracture in those with prevalent vertebral deformity, even when BMD T scores are greater than −2.5.[28] Spine imaging using DXA can now detect prevalent vertebral deformity with nearly the accuracy of standard radiography and can be done easily at the time of bone densitometry to further refine assessment of fracture risk.[34]

MARKERS OF BONE METABOLISM

Serum and urine markers of bone metabolism are additional screening tests that may further refine assessment of fracture risk. Those with high bone turnover may have an elevated risk of fracture relative to those with low bone turnover, independent of BMD. However, use of these markers in the clinical setting continues to be hampered by their biological variability and poor precision. This may account for the fact that prospective studies done to date disagree on which markers of bone metabolism are associated with incident fracture. Newer markers such as serum RANKL[35] and TRACP5b[36] show significant promise as indicators of high fracture risk, but confirmatory prospective studies of their predictive value for incident fracture independent of BMD have not been reported. For any bone marker, further research showing consistent identification of individuals at higher risk of fracture independent of BMD is needed before routine use of the marker in clinical practice to assess fracture risk can be recommended.

ADDITIONAL SCREENING PROCEDURES

Heel ultrasound seems to assess aspects of bone quality different than BMD per se. Transmission ultrasound of the calcaneus yields two parameters of bone (speed of ultrasound transmission through bone and broadband ultrasound attenuation) that can be combined into a stiffness index or estimated heel BMD. Broadband ultrasound attenuation and stiffness index are as strongly associated with incident nonvertebral fracture as BMD, and nearly as predictive of incident hip fracture as femoral neck BMD.[37] Moreover, even after adjustment for BMD, ultrasound parameters are still modestly associated with incident hip fracture. Nonetheless, use of both ultrasound and BMD together does not seem to predict incident fracture any better than either technology alone.[37] Ultrasound can be used in place of DXA to define fracture risk, but there does not seem to be any clear advantage to using both together. An important advantage of DXA over ultrasound is that, in clinical trials establishing the effectiveness of antiresorptive agents, DXA has been used to define the study populations. It is not clear at this time how effectively pharmacologic agents prevent fractures in populations defined by ultrasound.

Heel ultrasound has been proposed as a prescreening tool to select postmenopausal women for bone densitometry using central (hip and spine) DXA, but may not identify those who are likely to have a T score ≤ -2.5 at the femoral neck any more accurately than clinical risk factors.[38] Although a screening program for osteoporosis incorporating heel ultrasound would reduce the number of DXA tests required for each case of osteoporosis detected, a screening strategy of heel ultrasound combined with central DXA may be no more cost effective than a strategy of DXA alone, because the cost savings from reduced use of DXA may be counterbalanced by the costs of heel ultrasound.[39] Further studies of the use of using heel ultrasound with selected use of DXA are needed.[40]

With respect to hip fracture, structural variables such as femoral neck width and hip axis length seem to be predictors of incident hip fracture independent of BMD,[41] and can be measured on DXA images of the hip. Further research into how best to incorporate these and other measures of bone structural parameters into overall assessment of hip fracture risk are needed, especially in the presence or absence of other clinical risk factors.

ESTIMATING RISK OF FRACTURE COMBINING BONE DENSITY AND BMD-INDEPENDENT CLINICAL FRACTURE RISK FACTORS

The advantage of combining multiple independent risk factors for fracture together, as opposed to simply one such as BMD, is that the combination reveals a stronger gradient of risk, such that a smaller proportion of the whole population in whom the majority of fractures occur can be identified.[42] One can consider an individual's risk of fracture integrating BMD and the presence of additional BMD-independent fracture risk factors either by comparison of that person's aggregate risk relative to a specific standard or in terms of absolute fracture risk over a specific future time period.

An example of this type of approach would be to use estimates of 10-year absolute fracture risk, considering all factors that independently confer risk for incident fracture. For example, Kanis et al.[43] have published 10-year estimates of absolute fracture risk for the population of Sweden based on both age and femoral neck BMD. These estimates can be adjusted for the presence or absence of additional BMD-independent risk factors, using the relative risks of incident fracture in those with compared with those without the risk factor and the prevalence of the risk factor within the population.

Consider, for example, a population with a 10-year risk of incident vertebral fracture of 10% and an additional risk factor that confers a specific relative risk of incident fracture in those with compared with those without the risk factor ($RR_{with\ versus\ without}$). The relative risk for incident fracture in the subset with the risk factor relative to that whole population ($RR_{with\ versus\ whole}$) is given by the following formula[44]

$$RR^{with\ vs\ whole} =$$

$$RR^{with\ vs\ without}/[1 + (RR^{with\ vs\ without} - 1) \times prev]$$

where prev is the prevalence of the risk factor in the population. Those who have a baseline prevalent vertebral deformity have a relative risk of 4.0 for incident vertebral fracture com-

pared with those without baseline vertebral deformity. Therefore, if the prevalence of baseline vertebral deformity is 25% in this hypothetical population, the relative risk of incident vertebral fracture for those with baseline vertebral deformity compared with the whole population is

$$4.0/[1 + (4.0 - 1) \times prevalence_{deformity}] =$$

$$4/(1 + 3 \times 0.25) = 4/1.75 = 2.3$$

Therefore, the absolute 10-year fracture risk for those within this population with one or more baseline vertebral deformities is estimated to be $0.1 \times 2.3 = 0.23$.

Composing comprehensive 10-year fracture risks based on multiple such risk factors is obviously a challenging mathematical chore. Such comprehensive absolute 10-year fracture estimates incorporating many additional fracture risk factors are currently being developed by the World Health Organization.

For individual patients, screening for fracture risk has only modest use to predict whether or not they will or will not suffer a fracture in the future, even considering BMD and additional fracture risk factors jointly. At the population level, however, there is good evidence that targeted screening programs such as that outlined in this chapter are as cost effective (or more so)[33,45,46] as screening programs for breast cancer using mammography[47] or colon cancer using colonoscopy.[48]

CONCLUSION

Osteoporosis and related fractures are common, debilitating, and to some degree, preventable. Therefore, targeted screening procedures to identify those subsets at high risk of fracture are justified. Bone densitometry is the primary diagnostic test used to assess fracture risk, and its primary purpose is to aid identification of those for whom intervention to reduce the risk of fracture might be indicated. The relationship between BMD and incident fracture is not so strong, however, that universal screening of the population as a whole is justified. Rather, a step-wise targeted case-finding strategy is recommended. The first step involves an initial assessment of fracture risk based on evident clinical risk factors, and the second involves targeted use of bone densitometry in those who based on their clinical risk factors have a reasonable likelihood of having bone density below a target threshold. A judgment can be made as to whether or not additional tests such as spinal imaging may be worthwhile to further refine fracture risk. Efforts are currently underway to establish age- and sex-specific estimates of 10-year fracture risks based on the presence or absence of multiple risk factors.

REFERENCES

1. Cauley JA, Lui LY, Ensrud KE, Zmuda JM, Stone KL, Hochberg MC, Cummings SR 2005 Bone mineral density and the risk of incident nonspinal fractures in black and white women. JAMA 293:2102–2108.
2. Klotzbuecher CM, Ross PD, Landsman PB, Abbott TA III, Berger M 2000 Patients with prior fractures have an increased risk of future fractures: A summary of the literature and statistical synthesis. J Bone Miner Res 15:721–739.
3. Melton LJ III, Atkinson EJ, Cooper C, O'Fallon WM, Riggs BL 1999 Vertebral fractures predict subsequent fractures. Osteoporos Int 10:214–221.
4. Black DM, Arden NK, Palermo L, Pearson J, Cummings SR 1999 Prevalent vertebral deformities predict hip fractures and new vertebral deformities but not wrist fractures. Study of Osteoporotic Fractures Research Group. J Bone Miner Res 14:821–828.
5. Siris ES, Miller PD, Barrett-Connor E, Faulkner KG, Wehren LE, Abbott TA, Berger ML, Santora AC, Sherwood LM 2001 Identification and fracture outcomes of undiagnosed low bone mineral density in postmenopausal women: Results from the National Osteoporosis Risk Assessment. JAMA 286:2815–2822.

6. Nevitt MC, Cummings SR, Stone KL, Palermo L, Black DM, Bauer DC, Genant HK, Hochberg MC, Ensrud KE, Hillier TA, Cauley JA 2005 Risk factors for a first-incident radiographic vertebral fracture in women > or = 65 years of age: The study of osteoporotic fractures. J Bone Miner Res 20:131–140.

7. Margolis KL, Ensrud KE, Schreiner PJ, Tabor HK 2000 Body size and risk for clinical fractures in older women. Study of Osteoporotic Fractures Research Group. Ann Intern Med 133:123–127.

8. Ensrud KE, Cauley J, Lipschutz R, Cummings SR 1997 Weight change and fractures in older women. Study of Osteoporotic Fractures Research Group. Arch Intern Med 157:857–863.

9. Ensrud KE, Ewing SK, Stone KL, Cauley JA, Bowman PJ, Cummings SR 2003 Intentional and unintentional weight loss increase bone loss and hip fracture risk in older women. J Am Geriatr Soc 51:1740–1747.

10. Cummings SR, Nevitt MC, Browner WS, Stone K, Fox KM, Ensrud KE, Cauley J, Black D, Vogt M 1995 Risk factors for hip fracture in white women. Study of Osteoporotic Fractures Research Group. N Engl J Med 332:767–773.

11. Kanis JA, Johnell O, Oden A, Johansson H, De Laet C, Eisman JA, Fujiwara S, Kroger H, McCloskey EV, Mellstrom D, Melton LJ, Pols H, Reeve J, Silman A, Tenenhouse A 2005 Smoking and fracture risk: A meta-analysis. Osteoporos Int 16:155–162.

12. Fitzpatrick LA 2002 Secondary causes of osteoporosis. Mayo Clin Proc 77:453–468.

13. Wengreen HJ, Munger RG, West NA, Cutler DR, Corcoran CD, Zhang J, Sassano NE 2004 Dietary protein intake and risk of osteoporotic hip fracture in elderly residents of Utah. J Bone Miner Res 19:537–545.

14. Kalkwarf HJ, Khoury JC, Lanphear BP 2003 Milk intake during childhood and adolescence, adult bone density, and osteoporotic fractures in US women. Am J Clin Nutr 77:257–265.

15. Dawson-Hughes B, Harris SS, Krall EA, Dallal GE 1997 Effect of calcium and vitamin D supplementation on bone density in men and women 65 years of age or older. N Engl J Med 337:670–676.

16. Taylor BC, Schreiner PJ, Stone KL, Fink HA, Cummings SR, Nevitt MC, Bowman PJ, Ensrud KE 2004 Long-term prediction of incident hip fracture risk in elderly white women: Study of osteoporotic fractures. J Am Geriatr Soc 52:1479–1486.

17. Johnell O, Kanis JA, Black DM, Balogh A, Poor G, Sarkar S, Zhou C, Pavo I 2004 Associations between baseline risk factors and vertebral fracture risk in the Multiple Outcomes of Raloxifene Evaluation (MORE) Study. J Bone Miner Res 19:764–772.

18. Papaioannou A, Joseph L, Ioannidis G, Berger C, Anastassiades T, Brown JP, Hanley DA, Hopman W, Josse RG, Kirkland S, Murray TM, Olszynski WP, Pickard L, Prior JC, Siminoski K, Adachi JD 2005 Risk factors associated with incident clinical vertebral and nonvertebral fractures in postmenopausal women: The Canadian Multicentre Osteoporosis Study (CaMos). Osteoporos Int 16:568–578.

19. Goderie-Plomp HW, van der Klift M, de Ronde W, Hofman A, de Jong FH, Pols HA 2004 Endogenous sex hormones, sex hormone-binding globulin, and the risk of incident vertebral fractures in elderly men and women: The Rotterdam Study. J Clin Endocrinol Metab 89:3261–3269.

20. Ramsey-Goldman R, Dunn JE, Huang CF, Dunlop D, Rairie JE, Fitzgerald S, Manzi S 1999 Frequency of fractures in women with systemic lupus erythematosus: Comparison with United States population data. Arthritis Rheum 42:882–890.

21. Sinigaglia L, Nervetti A, Mela Q, Bianchi G, Del Puente A, DiMunno O, Frediani B, Cantatore F, Pellerito R, Bartolone S, La Montagna G, Adami S 2000 A multicenter cross sectional study on bone mineral density in rheumatoid arthritis. Italian Study Group on Bone Mass in Rheumatoid Arthritis. J Rheumatol 27:2582–2589.

22. Stone KL, Seeley DG, Lui LY, Cauley JA, Ensrud K, Browner WS, Nevitt MC, Cummings SR 2003 BMD at multiple sites and risk of fracture of multiple types: Long-term results from the Study of Osteoporotic Fractures. J Bone Miner Res 18:1947–1954.

23. Marshall D, Johnell O, Wedel H 1996 Meta-analysis of how well measures of bone mineral density predict occurrence of osteoporotic fractures. BMJ 312:1254–1259.

24. Cadarette SM, McIsaac WJ, Hawker GA, Jaakkimainen L, Culbert A, Zarifa G, Ola E, Jaglal SB 2004 The validity of decision rules for selecting women with primary osteoporosis for bone mineral density testing. Osteoporos Int 15:361–366.

25. Johnell O, Kanis JA, Oden A, Sernbo I, Redlund-Johnell I, Petterson C, De Laet C, Jonsson B 2004 Fracture risk following an osteoporotic fracture. Osteoporos Int 15:175–179.

26. Barrett-Connor E, Siris ES, Wehren LE, Millar PD, Abbott TA, Berger ML, Santora AC, Sherwood LM 2005 Osteoporosis and fracture risk in women of different ethnic groups. J Bone Miner Res 20:185–194.

27. U.S. Preventive Services Task Forces 2002 Screening for osteoporosis in postmenopausal women: Recommendations and rationale. Ann Intern Med 137:526–528.

28. Kanis JA, Barton IP, Johnell O 2005 Risedronate decreases fracture risk in patients selected solely on the basis of prior vertebral fracture. Osteoporos Int 16:475–482.

29. Khan AA, Bachrach L, Brown JP, Hanley DA, Josse RG, Kendler DL, Leib ES, Lentle BC, Leslie WD, Lewiecki EM, Miller PD, Nicholson RL, O'Brien C, Olszynski WP, Theriault MY, Watts NB 2004 Standards and guidelines for performing central dual-energy x-ray absorptiometry in premenopausal women, men, and children. J Clin Densitom 7:51–64.

30. Hochberg MC, Tracy JK, van der Klift M, Pols H 2002 Validation of a risk index to identify men with an increased likelihood of osteoporosis. J Bone Miner Res 17:S1;S231.

31. Melton LJ III, Lane AW, Cooper C, Eastell R, O'Fallon WM, Riggs BL 1993 Prevalence and incidence of vertebral deformities. Osteoporos Int 3:113–119.

32. Siminoski K, Jiang G, Adachi JD, Hanley DA, Cline G, Ioannidis G, Hodsman A, Josse RG, Kendler D, Olszynski WP, Ste Marie LG, Eastell R 2005 Accuracy of height loss during prospective monitoring for detection of incident vertebral fractures. Osteoporos Int 16:403–410.

33. Schousboe JT, Ensrud KE, Nyman JA, Kane RL, Melton LJ III 2005 Potential cost-effective use of spine radiographs to detect vertebral deformity and select osteopenic post-menopausal women for amino-bisphosphonate therapy. Osteoporos Int 16:1883–1893.

34. Vokes TJ, Dixon LB, Favus MJ 2003 Clinical utility of dual-energy vertebral assessment (DVA). Osteoporos Int 14:871–878.

35. Schett G, Kiechl S, Redlich K, Oberhollenzer F, Weger S, Egger G, Mayr A, Jocher J, Xu Q, Pietschmann P, Teitelbaum S, Smolen J, Willeit J 2004 Soluble RANKL and risk of nontraumatic fracture. JAMA 291:1108–1113.

36. Gerdhem P, Ivaska KK, Alatalo SL, Halleen JM, Hellman J, Isaksson A, Pettersson K, Vaananen HK, Akesson K, Obrant KJ 2004 Biochemical markers of bone metabolism and prediction of fracture in elderly women. J Bone Miner Res 19:386–393.

37. Bauer DC, Gluer CC, Cauley JA, Vogt TM, Ensrud KE, Genant HK, Black DM 1997 Broadband ultrasound attenuation predicts fractures strongly and independently of densitometry in older women. A prospective study. Study of Osteoporotic Fractures Research Group. Arch Intern Med 157:629–634.

38. Kung AW, Ho AY, Sedrine WB, Reginster JY, Ross PD 2003 Comparison of a simple clinical risk index and quantitative bone ultrasound for identifying women at increased risk of osteoporosis. Osteoporos Int 14:716–721.

39. Sim MF, Stone M, Johansen A, Evans W 2000 Cost effectiveness analysis of BMD referral for DXA using ultrasound as a selective pre-screen in a group of women with low trauma Colles' fractures. Technol Health Care 8:277–284.

40. Kraemer DF, Nelson HD, Bauer DC, Helfand M 2006 Economic comparison of diagnostic approaches for evaluating osteoporosis in older women. Osteoporos Int 17:68–76.

41. Cummings SR, Cauley JA, Palermo L, Ross PD, Wasnich RD, Black D, Faulkner KG 1994 Racial differences in hip axis lengths might explain racial differences in rates of hip fracture. Study of Osteoporotic Fractures Research Group. Osteoporos Int 4:226–229.

42. De Laet C, Oden A, Johansson H, Johnell O, Jonsson B, Kanis JA 2005 The impact of the use of multiple risk indicators for fracture on case-finding strategies: A mathematical approach. Osteoporos Int 16:313–318.

43. Kanis JA, Johnell O, Oden A, De Laet C, Jonsson B, Dawson A 2002 Ten-year risk of osteoporotic fracture and the effect of risk factors on screening strategies. Bone 30:251–258.

44. Kanis JA, Johnell O, Oden A, Jonsson B, Dawson A, Dere W 2000 Risk of hip fracture derived from relative risks: An analysis applied to the population of Sweden. Osteoporos Int 11:120–127.

45. Kanis JA, Dawson A, Oden A, Johnell O, de Laet C, Jonsson B 2001 Cost-effectiveness of preventing hip fracture in the general female population. Osteoporos Int 12:356–361.

46. Schousboe JT, Ensrud KE, Nyman JA, Melton LJ III, Kane RL 2005 Universal bone densitometry screening combined with alendronate therapy for those diagnosed with osteoporosis is highly cost-effective for elderly women. J Am Geriatr Soc 53:1697–1704.

47. Mandelblatt J, Saha S, Teutsch S, Hoerger T, Siu AL, Atkins D, Klein J, Helfand M 2003 The cost-effectiveness of screening mammography beyond age 65 years: A systematic review for the U.S. Preventive Services Task Force. Ann Intern Med 139:835–842.

48. Pignone M, Saha S, Hoerger T, Mandelblatt J 2002 Cost-effectiveness analyses of colorectal cancer screening: A systematic review for the U.S. Preventive Services Task Force. Ann Intern Med 137:96–104.

Chapter 48.   Evaluation of Postmenopausal Osteoporosis

Susan L. Greenspan and Marjorie M. Luckey

Division of Endocrinology, University of Pittsburgh, Pittsburgh, Pennsylvania

INTRODUCTION

Osteoporosis is the most common disorder of bone mineral metabolism and affects up to 40% of postmenopausal women. It is considered a silent disease because bone loss occurs without signs or symptoms, and approximately two-thirds of vertebral fractures are asymptomatic.[1,2] By the time a woman has her first osteoporotic fracture, she may have already lost 30% of her bone mass. Therefore, the goal in evaluating postmenopausal women is to identify those who are at risk for an osteoporotic fracture, to classify the degree of bone loss, and to exclude secondary causes of bone loss.[3] For those who are diagnosed with this disease, preventive measures are recommended, and therapeutic alternatives are prescribed if clinically indicated.

PEAK BONE MASS AND BONE LOSS

The bone mass of a postmenopausal woman is determined by the development of her peak bone mass and the presence of factors causing bone loss in adulthood.[4] Peak bone mass is usually achieved between 25 and 30 years of age for women and is primarily determined by genetic factors. For instance, black and Hispanic women have a higher peak bone mass than white or Asian women. Men have a higher peak bone mass than women. Multiple genes, such as the vitamin D receptor allele, estrogen receptor genes, collagen receptor genes, and the high bone mass gene *LRP5*, may be associated with development of peak bone mass. Additional factors such as gonadal steroids, timing of puberty, growth hormone, calcium intake, and exercise are important in the development of peak bone mass.

The causes of bone loss in adult women are multifactorial, because bone mass is influenced by calcium intake, vitamin D, physical activity, and body weight. During the first 10 years of menopause, estrogen deficiency may cause losses of 20–30% in cancellous bone and 5–10% in cortical bone.[5] However, women continue to lose bone throughout the remainder of their lives, and bone loss is often accelerated after the mid-seventies. In addition, a variety of conditions and medications may precipitate or accelerate bone loss.

RISK FACTORS FOR OSTEOPOROSIS AND FRACTURES

Epidemiologic studies have examined the risk factors that are associated with low bone mass and hip fractures. As outlined by the National Osteoporosis Foundation, major risk factors for osteoporosis and related fractures include a personal history of fracture as an adult, a history of fragility fracture in a first degree relative, low body weight, current smoking, and use of oral corticosteroid therapy (Table 1).[6] Risk factors for hip fracture were examined by the Study of Osteoporotic Fractures, which followed 9704 postmenopausal women >65 years of age (Table 2).[7] The investigators determined that many factors, in addition to low BMD, contribute independently to the risk of fracture, including age, history of maternal hip fracture, low body weight, height, poor health, previous hyperthyroidism, poor depth perception, tachycardia, previous fracture, and benzodiazepines (Table 2). Other studies have found that a sideways fall, low bone mass, and increased biochemical markers of bone turnover are independent contributors to the risk of hip fracture.[8,9] Preexisting fractures double to quadruple the risk of a subsequent osteoporotic fracture.

BONE MINERAL DENSITY

BMD is the single best predictor of osteoporotic fracture risk. Prospective studies suggest that a decrease of 1 SD in bone mass at the spine, hip, or wrist is associated with an approximate doubling of fracture risk (Table 3).[10] BMD can be assessed with a variety of techniques, including DXA, single X-ray absorptiometry (SXA), QCT, and calcaneal ultrasonometry.[3] The International Society for Clinical Densitometry (ISCD) recommends measurements at the spine (L_1–L_4) and the hip (femoral neck, total hip, and trochanter). In patients with hyperparathyroidism, a measurement of the radius (at the one-third site) is also recommended to better assess cortical bone.[11] Bone mass measurements in postmenopausal women can be classified according to World Health Organization (WHO) criteria.[12,13] Women with a BMD T score lower than −2.5 SD are classified as osteoporotic. If the T score is ≥ −1.0 SD, BMD is normal. Those women with a BMD T score between −1.0 and −2.5 SD are classified as osteopenic (low bone mass). Although the WHO guidelines were based on BMD data from postmenopausal white women, these cut-off values are also commonly used for postmenopausal Hispanic and black women, but should not be used for children or premenopausal women. The WHO T score criteria are also only applicable to measurements by DXA and cannot be applied to "peripheral devices" (equipment that assesses bone mass of the finger or heel) or to QCT measurements.

Clinicians should base their management not only on bone mass, but other risk factors. The risk of fracture increases significantly with the cumulative effect of multiple risk factors (Fig. 1). For example, women with very low bone mass and multiple risk factors are at significantly higher risk of fracture than those with low bone mass and no risk factors. In addition to bone mass, there are several clinical risk factor algorithms available to predict which patients have osteoporosis or are at

TABLE 1. MAJOR RISK FACTORS FOR OSTEOPOROSIS

Major risk factors for osteoporosis and related fractures in postmenopausal women
- Personal history of fracture as an adult
- History of fragility fracture in a first degree relative
- Low body weight (less than ~127 lb)
- Current smoking
- Use of oral corticosteroid therapy for >3 months

Additional risk factors
- Impaired vision
- Estrogen deficiency (early menopause [<age 45]) or bilateral ovariectomy; prolonged premenopausal amenorrhea [>1 year])
- Dementia
- Poor health/frailty
- Recent falls
- Low calcium intake (lifelong)
- Low physical activity
- Alcohol in amounts >2 drinks per day

Information from the National Osteoporosis Foundation.[6]

The authors have reported no conflicts of interest.

TABLE 2. MAJOR RISK FACTORS FOR HIP FRACTURES[7–9]

Risk factors for hip fracture
- Age
- Maternal history of hip fracture
- Weight loss
- Tall height at age 25
- Poor health
- Previous hyperthyroidism
- Use of long-acting benzodiazepines
- Use of anticonvulsants
- Current caffeine intake (per 190 mg/day)
- Inability to rise from a chair
- Poor depth perception
- Poor contrast sensitivity (vision)
- Pulse >80 beats per minute
- Previous fracture since age 50
- Sideways fall
- Low bone mass
- Low body mass index
- Increased markers of bone resorption

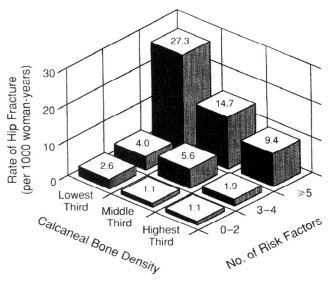

FIG. 1. Annual risk of hip fracture according to the number of risk factors and the age-specific calcaneal BMD. The risk factors are as follows: age ≥80 years; maternal history of hip fracture; any fracture (except hip fracture) since the age of 50; fair, poor, or very poor health; previous hyperthyroidism; anticonvulsant therapy; current long-acting benzodiazepine therapy; current weight less than at the age of 25; height at the age of 25 ≥168 cm; caffeine intake more than the equivalent of 2 cups of coffee per day; on feet ≤4 h/day; no walking for exercise; inability to rise from chair without using arms; lowest quartile (SD > 2.44) of depth perception; lowest quartile (≤0.70 U) of contrast sensitivity; and pulse rate >80/minute. (Reprinted with permission from Cummings SR, Nevitt MC, Browner WS, et al. 1995 Risk factors for hip fracture in white women. N Engl J Med **332:**767–773.) (Copyright © 1995 Massachusetts Medical Society. All rights reserved.)

risk of fracture. Algorithms are being developed by the WHO that predict 10-year risk of fracture based on clinical risk factors alone or in combination with BMD.

WHO SHOULD BE MEASURED

Guidelines established by the National Osteoporosis Foundation (NOF) suggest that all women over the age of 65 have bone mass assessments, because the rate of fracture and prevalence of osteoporosis in this age group are significant.[6] The NOF also suggests that bone mass be measured in postmenopausal women up to 65 years who have one or more risk factors (Table 4). In addition, women should be assessed if they are considering therapy for osteoporosis or if they present with fractures (to confirm the diagnosis).

In 2002, the U.S. Preventive Health Task Force issued recommendations for bone mass testing (Table 4).[14] The panel suggested that all women >65 years and women between 60 and 65 years who have risk factors should have BMD assessments. They did not make recommendations for or against testing in postmenopausal women <60 years of age.

Currently, Medicare (applicable only in the United States) covers BMD testing for individuals 65 years and older with estrogen deficiency, individuals with vertebral abnormalities, those who are on or are planning to initiate long-term glucocorticoid therapy, patients with primary hyperparathyroidism, and patients who are being monitored to assess the efficacy of an approved osteoporosis therapy (Table 4).[15]

The current recommendation of the ISCD is to consider

monitoring therapy with bone mass measurements every 1–2 years at the same facility with the same device that was previously used. The Bone Mass Measurement Act covers follow-up after a 2-year interval for Medicare patients.

TABLE 4. WHO SHOULD BE TESTED

National Osteoporosis Foundation[6]
1. All women age 65 and older regardless of risk factors
2. All postmenopausal women under age 65 years who have one or more risk factors for osteoporotic fracture (other than being white, postmenopausal, and female)
3. Postmenopausal women who are considering therapy for osteoporosis, if BMD testing would facilitate the decision
4. Postmenopausal women who present with fractures (to confirm the diagnosis and determine disease severity

U.S. Preventive Services Task Force[14]
1. Postmenopausal women age 65 years and older
2. Postmenopausal women age 60 to 64 years with a risk factor (weight <70 kg; estrogen deficiency)

Medicare Coverage for BMD—Bone Mass Act*
1. Estrogen deficient women at clinical risk for osteoporosis
2. Individuals with vertebral abnormalities
3. Individuals receiving, or planning to receive, long-term corticosteroid therapy
4. Individuals with primary hyperparathyroidism
5. Individuals being monitored to assess the response or efficacy of an approved osteoporosis drug therapy

* Applies only to the United States.

TABLE 3. RELATIVE RISK OF FRACTURE FOR 1 SD
DECREASE IN BMD*[10]

Site	Hip fracture	Vertebral fracture
Distal radius	1.8	1.7
Proximal radius	2.1	2.2
Calcaneus	2.0	2.4
Spine	1.6	2.3
Femoral neck	2.6	1.8

* Meta-analysis of 11 prospective cohort studies, with 90,000 person-years observation and >2000 fractures.

SECONDARY CAUSES OF BONE LOSS

The diagnosis of osteoporosis can be made with a BMD test or after an acute clinical fracture. However, secondary causes of bone loss need to be evaluated. The true prevalence of secondary osteoporosis in women is unknown. In published studies from referral centers, ~50% of women with low BMD have a history of other disorders or medications known to cause bone loss.[16–18] In addition, these studies report that 20–64% of women who present with osteoporosis have an occult secondary cause of bone loss that was identified only by laboratory testing.[16–21] The list of secondary causes of osteoporosis can be separated into (1) endocrine disorders, (2) gastrointestinal disorders, (3) bone marrow and connective tissue disorders, (4) renal disorders, (5) miscellaneous disorders, and (6) medications associated with bone loss (Table 5).

Endocrine Disorders

The most common endocrine disorders that cause bone loss include hyperparathyroidism and hyperthyroidism. Both conditions are more common in elderly women than young women. Hyperparathyroidism has been shown to be associated with significant bone loss at cortical sites, such as the forearm and hip, but also causes trabecular bone loss in a small subset of women with this disease. Excessive production of PTH causes increased bone resorption and turnover in addition to hypercalcemia. After treatment of hyperparathyroidism, vertebral bone mass improves significantly. Patients can be screened with serum calcium and PTH to exclude hyperparathyroidism. Grave's disease and other causes of hyperthyroidism have been associated with fractures and bone loss, especially at sites of cortical bone. The etiology of this bone loss is caused by an increase in bone resorption. Serum thyroid stimulating hormone is the single best test to exclude hyperthyroidism, which can present silently in older women.

Other endocrine disorders that can cause secondary bone loss are conditions that lead to hypogonadism (such as hyperprolactinemia, female athlete triad, etc.), acromegaly, Cushing's syndrome, eating disorders (anorexia and bulimia if the latter is associated with low body mass index [BMI]), and type 1 diabetes. Vitamin D insufficiency and deficiency are common causes of low bone mass, with a reported prevalence of 16–50% in women presenting with low BMD or fractures.[20–23] Without vitamin D, osteoid cannot be mineralized and calcium absorption is decreased. Patients with vitamin D deficiency (25-hydroxyvitamin D < 20 ng/dl) may present with normal levels of calcium and increased serum PTH and hypocalciuria. The most reliable test for vitamin D deficiency is a 25-hydroxyvitamin D level. A bone biopsy is rarely indicated to exclude osteomalacia.

Gastrointestinal Disorders

Gastrointestinal disorders can cause bone loss through malabsorption or liver disease. Such conditions include subtotal gastrectomy, bariatric surgery, malabsorption syndromes (e.g., celiac disease, ulcerative colitis, Crohn's disease), primary biliary cirrhosis, other types of cirrhosis, chronic obstructive jaundice, and hepatitis. Liver function tests are needed to evaluate hepatic status. A low albumin level may be seen with malabsorption, coupled with hypocalciuria. Celiac disease may be subtle, leading to calcium malabsorption, often without other symptoms or findings associated with generalized malabsorption. The only indication of its presence may be hypocalciuria in association with elevated levels of serum tissue transglutaminase. A small bowel biopsy may be needed for verification.

TABLE 5. SECONDARY CAUSES OF LOW BONE MASS

Endocrine disorders
  Acromegaly
  Diabetes mellitus type 1
  Female hypogonadism
    Hyperprolactinemia
    Hypothalamic amenorrhea
    Female athlete triad
    Anorexia nervosa
    Premature and primary ovarian failure
  Hyperthyroidism
  Hyperparathyroidism
  Hypercortisolism
  Vitamin D insufficiency, deficiency, resistance
Gastrointestinal disorders
  Bariatric surgery
  Chronic obstructive jaundice
  Hemochromatosis
  Malabsorption syndromes
    Celiac disease
    Inflammatory bowel disease
  Other cirrhoses
  Primary biliary cirrhosis
  Subtotal gastrectomy
Bone marrow disorders
  AIDS/HIV
  Gaucher's disease
  Hemophilia
  Hemochromatosis
  Leukemia and lymphoma
  Metastatic carcinoma
  Multiple myeloma
  Systemic mastocytosis
  Thalassemia
Connective tissue disorders
  Ankylosing spondylitis
  Ehler-Danlos syndrome
  Homocystinuria
  Marfan's syndrome
  Osteogenesis imperfecta
  Rheumatoid arthritis
Renal disorders
  Hypercalciuria
  Renal osteodystrophy
  Renal tubular acidosis
Miscellaneous disorders
  Amyloidosis
  Idiopathic scoliosis
  Immobilization
  Multiple sclerosis
  Porphyria
  Weight loss
Medications associated with low bone mass
  Alcohol
  Aluminum
  Aromatase inhibitors
  Antiepileptics
  Chemotherapy/immunosuppressive agents
  Corticosteroids
  Cyclosporine
  Excess thyroid hormone
  Gonadotropin-releasing hormone agonists
  Heparin
  Lithium
  Smoking
  Tamoxifen (premenopausal women)
  Total parenteral nutrition

Bone Marrow and Connective Tissue Disorders

Bone marrow disorders can mimic osteoporotic bone loss and result in fractures. Elderly patients with anemia who present with height loss or a fracture should have a clinical and laboratory evaluation for multiple myeloma, lymphoma, and leukemia. Elderly patients can be screened for myeloma with a urine or serum protein electrophoresis. In addition, patients with metastatic cancer can present with an osteoporotic fracture. Infiltrative disorders include systemic mastocytosis (generally presenting with pruritus, flushing, urticaria, and hypotension), which can be identified with focal radiologic abnormalities; a small number of patients present with generalized osteopenia. Histocytosis generally presents in childhood with focal radiologic abnormalities. Connective tissue diseases, including osteogenesis imperfecta, Ehler-Danlos syndrome, Marfan's syndrome, and homocystinuria, can present with low bone mass. Autoimmune-related disorders that are associated with low bone mass include rheumatoid arthritis and ankylosing spondylitis.

Renal Disorders

Significant renal disease can lead to renal osteodystrophy. In addition, idiopathic hypercalciuria and renal tubular acidosis are associated with increased bone loss and osteoporosis. Patients with renal tubular acidosis have a metabolic acidosis and hypercalciuria.

Miscellaneous Disorders

Immobilization and weight loss are associated with loss of bone mass. Furthermore, patients undergoing bone marrow, heart, liver, kidney, or lung transplantation have significant bone loss caused by corticosteroid therapy, immobilization, immunosuppressive agents, and poor nutritional status.

Drugs Associated With Bone Loss

The list of medications associated with bone loss is extensive (Table 5). Corticosteroids are well known to cause bone loss because of suppression of osteoblastic function, increased osteoclast-mediated bone loss, inhibition of intestinal calcium absorption, and increased renal calcium excretion. In addition, excess use of corticosteroids may cause hypogonadism, which may accelerate bone loss. Studies have shown that as little as 2.5 mg of oral prednisone per day can produce bone loss, but a minimum dose has not been established. It is clear that the higher the dose and the greater the duration of treatment, the greater the bone loss. Some studies suggest that even inhaled glucocorticoids may be associated with bone loss.

Anticonvulsants have also been associated with high turnover osteoporosis. Phenobarbital, phenytoin, primidone, valproate, and carbamazepine are the most commonly used antiepileptics associated with low BMD. The mechanisms by which these medications can increase bone loss include vitamin D deficiency (because of increased metabolism and clearance of vitamin D) as well as vitamin D–independent mechanisms such as impaired calcium absorption, resistance to PTH, and sex steroid deficiency.

Excess thyroid hormone has been shown to cause bone loss. Thyroid hormone replacement is common in postmenopausal women. Up to 10% of elderly women may be on thyroid hormone replacement. However, only excess use of thyroid hormone has been associated with significant bone loss in postmenopausal, but not in premenopausal, women.

Other medications that contribute to bone loss include aromatase inhibitors, aluminum, cyclosporine, excess vitamin A, gonadotropin releasing hormone agonists, heparin, and lithium.

Tamoxifen, a selective estrogen receptor modulator, leads to bone loss only in premenopausal women.

Alcoholism and smoking also contribute to bone loss.

WORK-UP FOR SECONDARY CAUSES OF BONE LOSS

Although many secondary causes of osteoporosis can be identified in the medical history, others will remain undetected without laboratory testing. The reported prevalence of occult disorders ranges from 5% to 63%, depending, in part, on the extent of the laboratory evaluation.[16,17,20,24,25] There are currently no established guidelines for the most cost-effective evaluation to exclude secondary causes of bone loss in patients without an obvious etiology. A recent study examined 173 postmenopausal osteoporotic women without a history of diseases or medications known to affect bone mineral metabolism.[17,22] Evaluation in this study included a complete blood count, chemistry profile, 24-h urinary calcium, serum 25-hydroxyvitamin D, and serum PTH as well as thyroid-stimulating hormone (TSH), serum protein electrophoresis, and urinary cortisol in most subjects. More than 40% of women were discovered to have previously unsuspected disorders of bone and mineral metabolism when the current definition of vitamin D deficiency (25-hydroxyvitamin D < 20 ng/ml) was used (M.M. Luckey, personal communication, 2005). In this reanalysis, 20% of these osteoporotic women were vitamin D deficient.[22] Hypercalciuria was found in 10%, malabsorption in 7%, and primary or secondary hyperparathyroidism in 3%. Among osteoporotic women on thyroid replacement, 29% had a suppressed TSH. Unfortunately, no clinical factors (including age or the severity of osteoporosis) helped to identify which patients were more likely to have an underlying disorder. The reanalyzed data from this study, however, identified a simplified laboratory testing strategy, which included measurements of serum calcium, 25-hydroxyvitamin D, and 24-h urinary calcium for all women and TSH for women on thyroid hormone replacement, which correctly identify 92% of the cases of secondary osteoporosis. Although a 24-h urine collection may seem onerous to some patients, and the results are influenced by incomplete collection and variations in dietary sodium and protein intake, 34% of the occult disorders identified in the above study would have been missed without this measurement.

In bone mineral densitometry, the Z score represents the SD from the mean for individuals of the same age and sex. Although secondary causes of osteoporosis often accelerate bone loss, the Z score does not reliably predict which osteoporotic patients have an underlying disorder.[16,17] Thus, some laboratory testing is needed even in patients with a Z score within the normal range. A very low Z score (≤ -2.0) should prompt a thorough evaluation for secondary causes of bone loss. In addition to a careful history and physical examination, the routine laboratory evaluation discussed above may be augmented with a serum or urine protein electrophoresis (SPEP or UPEP) to rule out multiple myeloma, and a tissue transglutaminase may be needed to exclude celiac disease. In some patients, a 24-h urinary free cortisol should be collected to assess the possibility of Cushing's syndrome.

Bone biopsy is rarely indicated, except for a formal evaluation for osteomalacia. Patients who present with back pain should be considered for vertebral X-rays to assess for an osteoporotic versus a pathological fracture. Bone mineral densitometry software is available to assess vertebral fractures through a technique known as Instant Vertebral Assessment.[26] While this is not as sensitive as an X-ray, it can examine vertebral compression fractures without the radiation exposure of a standard X-ray.

BIOCHEMICAL INDICES OF BONE MINERAL METABOLISM

In addition to bone mass, the rate of bone turnover may be assessed with biochemical markers of bone turnover.[27] They provide a dynamic assessment of skeletal activity but do not provide information on the density of the skeleton. Osteoclast function can be assessed with markers of bone resorption, including N-telopeptide crosslinked collagen type 1 (NTx), deoxypyridinoline (Dpd), and C-telopeptide crosslinked collagen type 1 (CTx). Osteoblastic activity can be assessed through a variety of markers, including osteocalcin, bone-specific alkaline phosphatase (BSALP), and amino-terminal propeptide of type 1 collagen (P1NP). While many of these assessments are measured in clinical research studies, they are still under evaluation for use in clinical practice. High bone turnover has been shown to be an independent risk factor for fracture. Patients with a normal BMD and a high rate of resorption are at risk for fracture. However, resorption markers are more often used to assess medication compliance. A decrease in resorption markers should occur ~3 months after initiation of therapy.

SUMMARY

The evaluation of postmenopausal osteoporosis includes an assessment of risk factors for fractures and determination of bone mass measurements of the hip and spine. Patients without an obvious secondary cause of bone loss should have a general evaluation, including serum calcium, serum 25-hydroxyvitamin D, and 24-h urinary calcium and serum TSH if they are on thyroid hormone replacement. However, patients who have a Z score that is $\geq$2 SD below the age-matched mean should have a more comprehensive evaluation for a secondary and potentially reversible cause of bone loss.

REFERENCES

1. Ray N, Chan J, Melton L 1997 Medical expenditures of the treatment of osteoporotic fractures in the United States in 1995: Report from the National Osteoporosis Foundation. J Bone Miner Res 12:24–35.
2. Cooper C, Atkinson EJ, O'Fallon WM, Melton LJ III 1992 Incidence of clinically diagnosed vertebral fractures: A population-based study in Rochester, Minnesota, 1985–1989. J Bone Miner Res 7:221–227.
3. U.S. Department of Health and Human Services 2004 Bone Health and Osteoporosis: A Report of the Surgeon General. U.S. Department of Health and Human Services, Office of the Surgeon General, Rockville, MD, USA.
4. Seeman E 2002 Pathogenesis of bone fragility in women and men. Lancet 359:1841–1850.
5. Riggs BL, Khosla S, Melton LJ III 1998 A unitary model for involutional osteoporosis: Estrogen deficiency causes both type I and type II osteoporosis in postmenopausal women and contributes to bone loss in aging men. J Bone Miner Res 13:763–773.
6. National Osteoporosis Foundation 2003 Physician's Guide to Prevention and Treatment of Osteoporosis. Excerpta Medica, Belle Mead, NJ, USA.
7. Cummings SR, Nevitt MC, Browner WS, Stone K, Fox KM, Ensrud KE, Cauley J, Black D, Vogt TM 1995 Risk factors for hip fractures in white women. N Engl J Med 332:767–773.
8. Greenspan SL, Myers ER, Maitland LA, Resnick NM, Hayes WC 1994 Fall severity and bone mineral density as risk factors for hip fracture in ambulatory elderly. JAMA 271:128–133.
9. Garnero P, Hausherr E, Chapuy MC, Marcelli C, Grandjean H, Muller C, Cormier C, Breart G, Meunier PJ, Delmas PD 1996 Markers of bone resorption predict hip fracture in elderly women: The EPIDOS Prospective Study. J Bone Miner Res 11:1531–1538.
10. Marshall D, Johnell O, Wedel H 1996 Meta-analysis of how well measures of bone mineral density predict occurrence of osteoporotic fractures. BMJ 312:1254–1259.
11. Hamdy RC, Petak SM, Lenchik L 2002 Which central dual X-ray absorptiometry skeletal sites and regions of interest should be used to determine the diagnosis of osteoporosis? J Clin Densitom 5(Suppl):S11–S17.
12. Kanis JA for the WHO Study Group 1994 Assessment of fracture risk and its application to screening for postmenopausal osteoporosis: Synopsis of a WHO report. Osteoporos Int 4:368–381.
13. Kanis JA 2003 Diagnosis of osteoporosis and assessment of fracture risk. Lancet 359:1929–1936.
14. U.S. Preventive Services Task Force 2002 Screening for osteoporosis in postmenopausal women: Recommendations and rationale. Ann Intern Med 137:526–528.
15. Anonymous 1998 Medicare coverage of and payments for bone mass measurements. Fed Regist 63:34320–34328.
16. Deutschmann HA, Weger M, Weger W, Kotanko P, Deutschmann MJ, Skrabal F 2002 Search for occult secondary osteoporosis: Impact of identified possible risk factors on bone mineral density. J Intern Med 252:389–397.
17. Tannenbaum C, Clark J, Schwartzman K, Wallenstein S, Lapinski R, Meier D, Luckey M 2002 Yield of laboratory testing to identify secondary contributors to osteoporosis in otherwise healthy women. J Clin Endocrinol Metab 87:4431–4437.
18. Fitzpatrick LA 2002 Secondary causes of osteoporosis. Mayo Clin Proc 77:453–468.
19. Caplan GA, Scane AC, Francis RM 1994 Pathogenesis of vertebral crush fractures in women. J R Soc Med 87:200–202.
20. Freitag A, Barzel U 2002 Differential diagnosis of osteoporosis. Gerontology 48:98–102.
21. Haden ST, Fuleihan GE, Angell JE, Cotran NM, LeBoff MS 1999 Calcidiol and PTH levels in women attending an osteoporosis program. Calcif Tissue Int 64:275–279.
22. Luckey MM, Tannenbaum C 2003 Authors' response: Recommended testing in patients with low bone density. J Clin Endocrinol Metab 88:1405.
23. LeBoff MS, Kohlmeier L, Hurwitz S, Franklin J, Wright J, Glowacki J 1999 Occult vitamin D deficiency in postmenopausal US women with acute hip fracture. JAMA 281:1505–1511.
24. Heaney RP 2000 Vitamin D: How much do we need, and how much is too much?. Osteoporos Int 11:553–555.
25. Jamal SA, Leiter RE, Bayoumi AM, Bauer DC, Cummings SR 2005 Clinical utility of laboratory testing in women with osteoporosis. Osteoporos Int 16:534–540.
26. Greenspan SL, von Stetten E, Emond SK, Jones L, Parker RA 2001 Instant vertebral assessment: A noninvasive DXA technique to avoid misclassification and clinical mismanagement of osteoporosis. J Clin Densitom 4:373–380.
27. Miller PD, Baran DT, Bilezikian JP, Greenspan SL, Lindsay R, Riggs BL, Rosen CJ, Watts NB 1999 Practical clinical application of biochemical markers of bone turnover: Consensus of an expert panel. J Clin Densitom 2:323–342.

Chapter 49.   Effect of Estrogen Intervention on the Skeleton

Robert Lindsay and Felicia Cosman

Department of Clinical Medicine, Columbia University, New York, New York

INTRODUCTION

In his original observations in 1947, Fuller Albright showed that estrogens reversed the calcium loss (negative calcium balance) observed in postmenopausal women with osteoporosis-related fractures.[1,2] Henneman and Wallach, in a review of the patients with osteoporosis originally treated by Albright, showed that height loss, a surrogate for vertebral fracture, was unusual in estrogen-treated patients while untreated individuals with osteoporosis continued to have sporadic height reduction.[3] Since the early 1970s, overwhelming data from controlled clinical trials have shown that estrogen intervention prevents bone loss among estrogen-deficient women.[4–17] Estrogen, or estrogen plus progestin treatment, in traditional doses (0.626 mg conjugated equine estrogens per day or equivalent), returns bone remodeling to premenopausal levels. Data from three small controlled studies showed reduction in fracture risk with estrogen intervention.[6–8] One involved transdermal estrogen in patients with osteoporosis, and showed a 50% reduction in the risk of vertebral fracture over 1–2 years.[8] The other randomized studies, which involved oral estrogen over 9–10 years of observation, showed a reduction in radiological vertebral fracture rate,[6] as well as a reduction in clinical fractures.[7] Over the same period, several large epidemiological studies also suggested that estrogens reduce the risk of clinical fractures including fractures of the hip and other nonvertebral fractures.[18–30] The concern was raised, however, that these results were caused by a healthy user effect, similar to that suggested for the effect of estrogen on cardiovascular disease seen in epidemiological studies; women who used hormones were healthier and exhibited more health-seeking behaviors than those who did not.[31] Additional randomized controlled trials were required to confirm the effect of estrogen and hormone therapy against osteoporosis and related fractures.

Two more recent European clinical trials have indicated that intervention with estrogen and progestin in the early years after menopause reduces the risk of Colles' fracture and other clinical nonvertebral fractures.[32,33] In the United States, two separate National Institutes of Health–supported efforts evaluated the effects of standard doses of estrogen with or without a progestin on BMD in women[34] and on clinical fractures.[35–37] The first of these studies, the PEPI (Postmenopausal Estrogen/Progestin Intervention) study, had BMD as the primary outcome. That study of ~800 early postmenopausal women extended the results of other published clinical trials showing that 0.625 mg of conjugated equine estrogen (CEE) daily over 3 years prevented bone loss and that the addition of medroxyprogesterone acetate (MPA) or micronized progesterone to this dose of estrogen had no measurable effect on the skeletal outcome. Furthermore, the study confirmed that >90% of women who took the drug did not lose bone and that when treatment was stopped, bone loss recurred.[38] Despite these positive findings, a study undertaken in women with overt cardiovascular disease, the Heart and Estrogen/Progestin Replacement Study (HERS), failed to show a positive effect on fractures or on heart disease outcomes.[39] The HERS study is the only large randomized controlled trial of estrogen that did not show an effect of estrogen against osteoporosis-related fractures.

The Women's Health Initiative (WHI) evaluated the effect of hormones (CEE or CEE with MPA) on fractures in a fairly healthy population of postmenopausal women of average age 62 years. This study has resulted in a number of publications, which have raised interesting questions about endpoint(s) other than the skeleton. The fracture data, however, are solid and consistent, and in agreement with prior observational and randomized controlled trials of the effect of estrogen intervention on the skeleton, both with regard to surrogate markers (bone mass and bone turnover) and fracture outcomes.[35–37] WHI consisted of two cohorts of women between the ages of 50 and 79 years of age. The larger cohort of ~16,000 relatively healthy, naturally postmenopausal women were enrolled in a controlled clinical trial of CEE (0.625 mg/day) plus MPA (2.5 mg/day) for an intended 8 years of observation. This study was halted after a median observation period of 5.2 years because the Data Safety Monitoring Board perceived excess harm with hormone therapy use, based on a global index, originally designed to show the overall benefit that was anticipated with hormone therapy. The second study involved ~10,000 women who had had hysterectomies enrolled in a study of CEE (0.625 mg/day) alone. This study was discontinued after a median observation period of 6.2 years, because of an increased risk of stroke, although little further might have been gained by continuing the study, because >50% of the subjects had discontinued or been lost to follow-up. Clinical fractures (both spine and nonspine) were a secondary outcome of both studies, but unlike other osteoporosis studies, subjects were not recruited based on BMD or prior fractures. BMD was done on a subpopulation of ~10% in the combination study, and in that sample, only ~9% had osteoporosis by BMD measurement. In both studies, there were a large number of incident clinical fractures, documented by radiographs and confirmed centrally. In each study, overall fracture risk was reduced by 24% in the hormone or estrogen intervention group (Fig. 1). In this relatively young, low-risk population, the risk of hip fracture was also reduced by ~30% ($p < 0.05$ using nominal confidence limits), and clinically apparent vertebral fractures were reduced by a similar amount. Thus, as a result of these two studies, there is now robust evidence that estrogen, in a standard dose, reduces the risk of fractures in postmenopausal women. The data are particularly impressive because they have been obtained in women at relatively low risk of fracture (low frequency of osteoporosis, relatively young, high prevalence of overweight, and high frequency of smoking, which might attenuate the effects of estrogen on the skeleton). Fracture reduction at nonspine sites has been a difficult endpoint to achieve with other bone active agents, such as the bisphosphonates, in individuals with BMD within the normal premenopausal range, where the clear fracture benefits have been seen primarily in women with osteoporosis at higher risk of fracture.[40,41] WHI has no measure of morphometric vertebral fractures that make up about two thirds of the vertebral fracture

---

Dr. Lindsay has been a consultant for Procter and Gamble, NPS, Sanofi-Aventis, GlaxoSmithKline, Roche, Novartis, and Wyeth. Dr. Cosman has been a consultant for Merck, Lilly, Wyeth, NPS, Roche, Novartis, and GlaxoSmithKline.

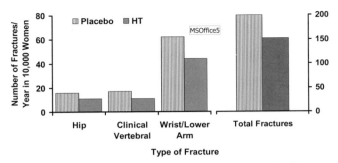

FIG. 1. WHI results: effect of hormone therapy in preventing fractures.

load, but there is little reason to believe that the effect would be different than that seen for clinical vertebral fractures.

The WHI fracture data confirm the previous smaller controlled clinical trials, the epidemiological data, and the large number of positive BMD studies on estrogens. WHI is also in agreement with the known pathophysiology of osteoporosis in postmenopausal women. Estrogen intervention, with or without a progestin, reduces the risk of fractures among postmenopausal women. The problems with the use of hormone and estrogen therapy for this purpose relates to the other clinical outcomes observed in WHI (Fig. 2). Hormone therapy was associated with an increased risk of deep venous thrombosis, pulmonary embolism, stroke, myocardial infarction, and breast cancer, although not all were statistically significant, and estrogen therapy was associated with an increase in the risk of deep venous thrombosis, pulmonary embolism, and stroke. For hormone therapy, there was a reduction in the risk of colon cancer, which was not seen in the estrogen-only arm of the study.

MECHANISM OF FRACTURE RISK REDUCTION

In the past, it has been assumed that antiresorptive drugs, such as estrogens, reduce fracture risk by increasing BMD. Recently, that conclusion has been challenged. There is, in fact, only a weak relationship between the change in BMD and fracture risk reduction, and it seems that much of the BMD effect is related to greater accumulation of mineral into already existing bone tissue. Meta-analyses have suggested that <20% of the fracture effect can be accounted for by the BMD change.[42–44] Additionally, the fracture effects begin to appears fairly soon after drug treatment has begun (within a few months) and well before the effects on BMD have fully materialized. The reduction in fracture occurrence is temporally related to the decline in bone remodeling, suggesting that the decline in remodeling is a major factor responsible for fracture risk decline.[45] In the large clinical trials, there is a relationship between reduction in remodeling and fracture risk reduction.[46]

In epidemiological studies, high bone remodeling rates are themselves risk factors for bone loss and fractures, independent of BMD.[47] Increased activation of remodeling increases the chance of trabecular penetration, leading to disconnections among trabeculae and creating disordered trabecular architecture, a main feature of osteoporosis. If indeed it is the increased remodeling that is primarily responsible for the architectural changes, the logic follows that antiresorptive drugs might effectively reduce fracture risk, not by increasing BMD, but by simply reducing bone remodeling to more normal premenopausal levels. This has been clearly shown for the bisphosphonates.[46]

EFFECTS OF LOWER DOSES OF HORMONE THERAPY

For the past 20 years, data from two studies performed in the early 1980s were interpreted as showing that lower doses of estrogen would not provide sufficient protection against bone loss to produce a fracture benefit.[13,48] In each case, the outcome measure was BMD, measured peripherally in both and centrally by QCT in one. Both were relatively small studies, but close review of the data suggests that there was some effect of a lower dose of CEE (0.3 mg daily), except for QCT measurements of the spine. Recently, low doses of hormone therapy (lower than those previously considered to be standard) have been introduced in the United States. While fracture studies have not been performed with these lower doses, there is some evidence to support the concept that these doses will have fracture benefits.

Recent data have suggested that even the relatively small amount of estrogen produced by postmenopausal women has skeletal effects.[49,50] In a population-based study of women >65 years of age, Cummings et al.[51] showed that women with estradiol levels between 10 and 15 pg/ml had higher bone mass that those with estradiol levels <5 pg/ml. In a logical extension of these data, it was shown that women with the lowest estradiol levels had the highest risk of vertebral and hip fractures and that this risk further increased in women with high levels of sex hormone–binding globulin, which would be expected to lower the biologically active estradiol further.

Evaluation of low-dose estrogen administration has also shown biological effects on bone.[52–55] In a multidose study, we showed reductions in bone remodeling at all doses of conjugated equine estrogens administered with and without the addition of a progestin. Biochemical markers of remodeling were only slightly less suppressed at 0.3 mg/day CEE than at 0.625 mg/day, with little noted effect of the progestin (MPA). In this study, bone mass increased at all doses, and >90% of individuals responded to treatment by either maintaining or gaining bone mass at spine or hip. Other studies of relatively low doses of hormone therapy confirm these findings. A recent study of what has been called ultra-low dose (transdermal delivery of 0.014 mg estradiol) again confirms reduction in remodeling and preservation of bone mass.[56] These doses of estrogen all provide increases in circulating estrogens that would at least raise circulating estradiol levels to those suggested to be biologically active in untreated older women. CEE will, of course, provide other estrogens in addition. The reductions in turnover are similar to those seen with other antiresorptive agents, suggesting that fracture studies might yield

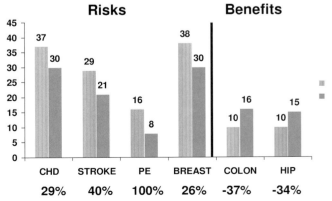

FIG. 2. Events per 10,000 women per year as reported by the Hormone Therapy arm of the WHI.

positive results, if indeed as argued above, it is the reduction in bone remodeling rate that is the principal mechanism of the antifracture efficacy.

EFFECTS OF DISCONTINUING HORMONES

It is clear that discontinuing hormone therapy results in bone loss, which begins immediately on stopping therapy.[38,57,58] However, what is not clear is whether there is accelerated rate of loss comparable with that seen after ovariectomy. Some data suggest that there is an immediate increase in risk of fracture after stopping, whereas other studies suggest that more prolonged reduction in risk occurs even when treatment is discontinued.[59,60] In general, the impression from all the data available is that to obtain the fracture benefit, continued therapy is necessary.

CLINICAL USE OF HORMONE THERAPY FOR OSTEOPOROSIS

For many years, therapy with estrogen, with or without a progestin, was the only pharmacologic approach to osteoporosis. Today several agents are approved for the prevention or treatment of osteoporosis, including bisphosphonates, calcitonin, and as of now, one selective estrogen receptor modulator (SERM) (raloxifene). Since the publication of WHI, several organizations have provided guidance to physicians about the use of hormone therapy in the postmenopausal population. In general, these statements recommend that hormones be used primarily for treatment of menopausal symptoms and for the shortest period of time compatible with obtaining symptom relief. Hormones, it is argued, should only be used for osteoporosis after all other treatments have been considered and when all the risks and benefits are carefully explained to the patient. However, the hormone studies have more substantial and robust fracture data in a non-osteoporosis population than any other agent. Furthermore, in the early postmenopausal population, and especially after hysterectomy, where estrogen can be used in the absence of a progestin, the risk benefit equation for the use of hormones may be quite different than that seen in the WHI population overall. Detailed analyses of WHI may inform clinicians about such differences and there may indeed be populations for whom hormones can still be recommended as first-line treatment. The risk benefit equation might be considerably different for estrogens other than CEE and MPA and indeed for the lower doses that seem to have beneficial effects on bone remodeling. Clearly those issues require further study. Like any good study, WHI raises more questions than it provides answers. Unfortunately, for clinicians and their patients, these questions will be difficult to address in appropriate clinical studies.

REFERENCES

1. Albright F, Bloomburg E, Smith PH 1940 Postmenopausal Osteoporosis. Trans Assoc Am Phys 55:298–305.
2. Albright F 1947 The effect of hormones on osteoporosis in man. Rec Prog Hormone Res 1:293–353.
3. Henneman PH, Wallach S 1957 A review of the prolonged life of estrogens and androgens in postmenopausal and senile osteoporosis. Arch J Med 100:715–723.
4. Aitken JM 1973 Hart DM, Lindsay R, Oestrogen replacement therapy for prevention of osteoporosis after oopharectomy. BMJ 3:515–518.
5. Lindsay R, Hart DM, Forrest C, Baird C 1976 Long-term prevention of postmenopausal osteoporosis by estrogen. Lancet 1976:1038–1041.
6. Lindsay R, Hart DM, Forrest C, Baud C 1980 Prevention of Spinal Osteoporosis in oopharectomized Women. Lancet 2:1151–1153.
7. Nachtigall LE, Nachtigall RH, Nachtigall RD, Beckman EM 1979 Estrogen replacement therapy I. A 10-year prospective study in the relationship to osteoporosis. Obstet Gynecol 53:277–281.
8. Lufkin EG, Wahner HW, O'Fallon WM, Hodgson SF, Kotowicz MA, Lane AW, Judd HL, Caplan RH, Riggs BL 1992 Treatment of postmenopausal osteoporosis with transdermal estrogen. Ann Intern Med 117:1–9.
9. Al-Azzawi F, Hart DM, Lindsay R 1987 Long-term effect of oestrogen replacement therapy on bone mass as measured by dual photon absorptiometry. BMJ 294:1261–1262.
10. Horsman A, Gallagher JC, Simpson J, Nordin BEC 1977 Prospective trial of oestrogen and calcium in postmenopausal women. BMJ 2:789–792.
11. Recker RR, Saville PD, Heaney RP 1977 Effects of estrogens and calcium carbonate on bone loss in postmenopausal women. Ann Intern Med 87:649–655.
12. Christiansen C, Christensen S, McNair P, Hagen C, Stocklund KE, Transbol I 1980 Prevention of early postmenopausal bone loss: Controlled 2 year study in 315 normal females. Eur J Clin Invest 10:273–279.
13. Genant HK, Cann CE, Ettinger B, Gordan GS 1982 Quantitative computed tomography of vertebral spongiosa: A sensitive method for detecting early bone loss after oophorectomy. Ann Intern Med 97:699–705.
14. Munk-Jensen N, Nielsen SP, Obel EB, Eriksen PB 1988 Reversal of postmenopausal vertebral bone loss by oestrogen, and progestogen: A double blind placebo controlled study. BMJ 296:1150–1152.
15. Gallagher JC, Kable WT, Goldgar D 1991 Effect of progestin therapy on cortical and trabecular bone: Comparison with estrogen. Am J Med 90:171–178.
16. Christiansen C, Riis BJ 1990 17 beta-estradiol and continuous noethisterone: A unique treatment for established osteoporosis in elderly women. J Clin Endocrinol Metab 71:836–841.
17. Greendale G, Causley J. 2002 Estrogens in osteoporosis. In: Cummings SR, Cosman F, Jamal SA (eds.) Osteoporosis: An Evidence-Based Guide To Prevention and Management. American College of Physicians, Philadelphia, PA, USA, pp. 127–150.
18. Cauley JA, Seeley DG, Ensrud K, Ettinger B, Black D, Cummings SR 1995 Estrogen replacement therapy and fractures in older women. Ann Intern Med 122:9–16.
19. Naessen T, Persson I, Adami HO, Bergstrom R, Bergkvist L 1990 Hormone replacement therapy and the risk for the first hip fracture. A prospective, population-based cohort study. Ann Intern Med 133:95–103.
20. Maxim P, Ettinger B, Spitalny GM 1995 Fracture protection provided by long-term estrogen treatment. Osteoporos Int 5:23–29.
21. Weiss NS, Ure CL, Ballard JH, Williams AR, Daling JR 1980 Decreased risk of fractures of hip and lower forearm with postmenopausal use of estrogen. N Engl J Med 303:1195–1198.
22. Kiel DP, Felson DT, Anderson JJ, Wilson PW, Moskowitz MA 1987 Hip fracture and the use of estrogens in postmenopausal women. The Framingham Study. N Engl J Med 317:1169–1174.
23. Paganini-Hill A, Ross RK, Gerkins VR, Henderson BE, Arthur M, Mack TM 1981 Menopausal estrogen therapy and hip fractures. Ann Intern Med 95:28–31.
24. Michaëlsson K, Baron JA, Farahmand BY, Johnell O, Magnusson C, Persson PG, Persson I, Ljunghall S 1988 Hormone replacement therapy and risk of hip fracture: Population based case-control study. BMJ 316:1858–1863.
25. Krieger N, Kelsey JL, Holford TR, O'Connor T 1982 An epidemiologic study of hip fracture in postmenopausal women. Am J Epidemiol 116:114–118.
26. Ettinger B, Genant HK, Cann CE 1985 Long-term estrogen replacement therapy prevents bone loss and fractures. Ann Intern Med 102:319–324.
27. Gordon GS, Picchi J and Roof BS 1973 Antifracture efficacy of long-term estrogens for osteoporosis. Trans Assoc Am Physicians 86:326–332.
28. Hutchinson TA, Polansky SMN, Feinstein AR 1979 Postmenopausal oestrogens protect against fractures of hip and distal radius. Lancet 2:706–710.
29. Johnson ER, Specht EE 1981 The risk of hip fracture in postmenopausal females with and without estrogen drug exposure. Am J Public Health 71:138–144.
30. Williams AR, Weiss NS, Ure CL, Ballard J, Daling JR 1982 Effect of weight, smoking and estrogen use of the risk of hip and forearm fractures in postmenopausal women. Obstet Gynecol 60:695–699.
31. Barrett-Conner E 1991 Postmenopausal estrogen and prevention bias. Ann Intern Med 115:455–456.
32. Komulainen MH, Kroger H, Tuppurainen MT, Heikkinen AM, Alhava E, Honkanen R, Saarikoski S 1998 HRT and Vitamin D in prevention of non-vertebral fractures in postmenopausal women. A 5 year randomized trail. Maturitas 31:45–54.
33. Mosekilde L, Beck-Nielsen H, Sorensen OH, Nielsen SP, Charles P, Vestergaard P, Hermann AP, Gram J, Hansen TB, Abrahamsen B, Ebbesen EN, Stilgren L, Jensen LB, Brot C, Hansen B, Tofteng CL,

Eiken P, Kolthoff N 2000 Hormonal replacement therapy reduces forearm fracture incidence in recent postmenopausal women. Results of the Danish Osteoporosis Prevention Study. Maturitas 36:181–193.

34. Writing Group for the PEPI 1996 for the PEPI writing group. Effects of hormone therapy on bone mineral density: Results from the postmenopausal estrogen/piogestin interventions (PEPI) trial. JAMA 276:1389–1396.

35. Rossouw JE, Anderson GL, Prentice RL, LaCroix AZ, Kooperberg C, Stefanick ML, Jackson RD, Beresford SA, Howard BV, Johnson KC, Kotchen JM, Ockene J, Writing Group for the Women's Health Initiative Investigators 2002 Risks and benefits of estrogen plus progestin in healthy postmenopausal women: Principal results from the Women's Health Initiative randomized controlled trial. JAMA 288:321–333.

36. Cauley JA, Robbins J, Chen Z, Cummings SR, Jackson RD, LaCroix AZ, LeBoff M, Lewis CE, McGowan J, Neuner J, Pettinger M, Stefanick ML, Wactawski-Wende J, Watts NB, Women's Health Initiative Investigators 2003 Effects of estrogen plus progesterone on the risk of fractures and bone mineral density. The Women's Health Initiative Randomized Trial. JAMA 290:1729–1738.

37. Anderson GL, Limacher M, Assaf AR, Bassford T, Beresford SA, Black H, Bonds D, Brunner R, Brzyski R, Caan B, Chlebowski R, Curb D, Gass M, Hays J, Heiss G, Hendrix S, Howard BV, Hsia J, Hubbell A, Jackson R, Johnson KC, Judd H, Kotchen JM, Kuller L, LaCroix AZ, Lane D, Langer RD, Lasser N, Lewis CE, Manson J, Margolis K, Ockene J, O'Sullivan MJ, Phillips L, Prentice RL, Ritenbaugh C, Robbins J, Rossouw JE, Sarto G, Stefanick ML, Van Horn L, Wactawski-Wende J, Wallace R, Wassertheil-Smoller S, Women's Health Initiative Steering Committee 2004 Effects of conjugated equine estrogen in postmenopausal women with hysterectomy: The Women's Health Initiative randomized controlled trial. JAMA 291:1701–1712.

38. Greendale GA, Espeland ME, Slone S, Marcus R, Barrett-Connor E, PEPI Safety Follow-Up Study (PSFS) Investigators 2002 Bone mass response to discontinuation or long-term use of hormone replacement therapy: Results from the Postmenopausal Estrogen/Progestin Inverventions (PEPI) Safety Follow-up Study. Arch Intern Med 162:665–676.

39. Cauley JA, Black DM, Barrett-Connor E, Harris F, Shields K, Applegate W, Cummings SR 2001 Effects of hormone replacement therapy on clinical fractures and height loss. The Heart and Estrogen/Progestin Replacement Study (HERS). Am J Med 110:442–450.

40. Hochberg MC 1998 Bisphosphonates. In: Cummings SR, Cosman F, Jamal SA (eds.) Osteoporosis: An Evidence-Based Guide To Prevention and Management. American College of Physicians, Philadelphia, PA, USA, pp. 181–195.

41. Hosking D, Chilvers CE, Christiansen C, Ravn P, Wasnich R, Ross P, McClung M, Balske A, Thompson D, Daley M, Yates AJ 1998 Prevention of bone loss with alendronate in postmenopausal women under 60 years of age. Early Postmenopausl Intervention Cohort Study. N Engl J Med 338:485–489.

42. Cummings SR, Karpf DB, Harris F, Genant HK, Ensrud K, LaCroix AZ, Black DM 2002 Improvement in spine bone density and reduction in risk of vertebral fractures during treatment with antiresorptive drugs. Am J Med 112:281–289.

43. Sarkar S, Mitlak B, Wong M, Stock JL, Black DM, Harper KD 2002 Relationships between bone mineral density and incident vertebral fracture risk with raloxifene therapy. J Bone Miner Res 17:1–10.

44. Li Z, Meredith MP, Hoseyni MS 2001 A method to assess the proportion of treatment effect explained by a surrogate endpoint. Stats Med 20:3175–3188.

45. Delmas PD 2002 Treatment of postmenopausal osteoporosis. Lancet 359:2018–2026.

46. Eastell R, Barton I, Hannon RA, Chines A, Garnero P, Delmas PD 2003 Relationship of early changes in bone resorption to the reduction in fracture risk with risedronate. J Bone Miner Res 18:1051–1056.

47. Garnero P, Sornay-Rendu E, Chapuy MC, Delmas PD 1996 Increased bone turnover in late postmenopausal women is a major determinant of osteoporosis. J Bone Miner Res 11:337–349.

48. Lindsay R, Hart DM, Clarie AC 1986 The minimum effective dose of estrogen for prevention of postmenopausal bone loss. Obstet Gynecol 63:759–763.

49. Greendale GA, Espeland M, Slone S, Marcus R, Barrett-Connor E 2002 PEPI Safety Follow-Up Study (PSFS) Investigators. Bone mass response to discontinuation of long-term hormone replacement therapy: Results from the Postmenopausal Estrogen/Progestin Intervention (PEPI) Safety Follow-up Study. Arch Intern Med 162:665–672.

50. Greendale GA, Edelstein S, Barrett-Connor E 1997 Endogenous sex steroids and bone mineral density in older women and men: The Rancho Bernardo Study. J Bone Miner Res 12:1833–1843.

51. Cummings SR, Browne WS, Bauer D, Stone K, Ensrud K, Jamal S, Ettinger B 1998 Endogenous hormones and the risk of hip and vertebral fractures. N Engl J Med 339:733–738.

52. Weiss SR, Ellman H, Dolker M 1999 A randomized controlled trial of four doses of transdermal estradiol for preventing postmenopausal bone loss. Obstet Gynecol 94:330–336.

53. Prestwood KM, Kenny AM, Unson C, Kulldorff M 2000 The effect of low dose micronized 17β-estradiol on bone turnover, sex hormone levels, and side effects in older women: A randomized, double blind, placebo controlled study. J Clin Endocrinol Metab 85:4462–4469.

54. Lindsay R, Gallagher JC, Kleeerekoper M, Pickar JH 2002 Effect of lower doses of conjugated equine estrogens with and without medroxyprogesterone acetate on bone in early postmenopausal women. JAMA 287:2668–2676.

55. Recker RR, Davies KM, Dowd RM, Heaney R 1999 The effect of low-dose continuous estrogen and progesterone therapy with calcium and vitamin D on bone in elderly women: A randomized, controlled trial. Ann Intern Med 130:897–904.

56. Cummings SR, Yankov V, Ensrud K, Ettinger BE, Wallace R, Johnson K, Maer J, Vittinghoff E, Grady D 2003 Ultra low estradiol increases BMD and decreases bone turnover in older women, particularly those with undetectable estradiol: The Ultra Trial. J Bone Miner Res 18:S2;1207.

57. Lindsay R, Hart DM, MacLean A, Clark AC, Kraszewski A, Garwood J 1978 Bone response to termination of oestrogen treatment. Lancet 1:1325–1327.

58. Christiansen C, Christiansen MS, Transbol I 1981 Bone mass in postmenopausal women after withdrawal of estrogen/gestagen replacement therapy. Lancet 1:459–461.

59. Felson DT, Zhang Y, Hannan MT, Kiel DP, Wilson PW, Anderson JJ 1993 The effect of postmenopausal estrogen therapy on bone density in elderly women. N Engl J Med 329:1141–1146.

60. Yates J, Barrett-Connor E, Barias S, Cheny J, Miller PD, Siris E 2002 Rapid loss of hip fracture protection after estrogen cessation: Evidence from National Osteoporosis Risk Assessment. Obstet Gynecol 103:440–446.

Chapter 50. Bisphosphonates for the Prevention and Treatment of Osteoporosis

Dennis Black[1] and Cliff J. Rosen[2]

[1]Department of Epidemiology and Biostatistics, University of California San Francisco, San Francisco, California; and [2]St. Joseph Hospital, Maine Center for Osteoporosis Research and Education, Bangor, Maine

INTRODUCTION

Bisphosphonates belong to a class of agents with a relatively simple core structure composed of two phosphate molecules joined to a central carbon atom (i.e., P-C-P). Several of these compounds have been known for more than a century and have been used to soften hard water or used in toothpaste. The bisphosphonates are produced from an identical phosphate-carbon-phosphate (P-C-P) core, but differ structurally in the two side chains, designated R^1 and R^2 (Fig. 1). The phosphate ends of the P-C-P bind avidly to calcium hydroxyapatite, thereby anchoring the bisphosphonates to the bone surface where they can be incorporated during remodeling. The duration of bisphosphonate residency within the skeleton, which is important for its biological actions, is determined by several critical factors. One factor is the rate of bone remodeling in the host (i.e., faster remodeling leads to a shorter skeletal half-life). A second factor is the side chain, which can alter the extent of bisphosphonate binding in either direction in certain circumstances and can be used to tailor "designer" bisphosphonates. A third determinant is the amount of drug that reaches the bone. For example, intravenous bisphosphonates rapidly go either to the skeleton or to the kidney for clearance. On the other hand, oral bisphosphonates must pass through the stomach and intestine to be absorbed. In general, absorption is very low: <5% of the administered oral dose of bisphosphonate is bioavailable.[1] Hence, the timing of administration and the extent of other nutrients ingested help define bioavailability.

The R^1 side chain determines the binding affinity of the compound. Hence, affinities for the skeleton may differ widely within this class of drugs. The R^2 side chain determines the antiresorptive potency of the agent, and once again, modifications in these molecules, particularly with nitrogen-containing compounds, can result in a wide range of antiresorptive activity. This is clinically relevant in respect to change in BMD, as well as antifracture efficacy for a particular compound (Table 1). It is important to note that, because of their strong affinity for the skeleton, absence of hepatic metabolism, clearance through the kidney, and lack of activity in other tissues, bisphosphonates are used as therapeutic agents in a variety of skeletal diseases besides osteoporosis. These include disorders characterized by increased bone remodeling, such as heterotopic ossification, fibrous dysplasia, osteogenesis imperfecta, Paget's disease of bone, hypercalcemia due to a variety of causes, bone loss due to a variety of causes, destructive arthropathy, and skeletal involvement with metastatic cancer or multiple myeloma. Dose and frequency of bisphosphonate administration in these other disorders often differ from those used in the management of osteoporosis because high rates of remodeling allow for more exposure and binding of these agents, but also greater clearance from the skeleton.

MECHANISMS OF ACTION

Bisphosphonates reduce osteoclast-mediated bone resorption by enhancing programmed cell death and inhibiting enzymes in the cholesterol biosynthetic pathway. This feature can be shown on bone biopsy where less eroded surfaces and the number of osteoclasts are markedly reduced. Although often postulated to have an effect on bone formation, there is little supporting evidence for this in preclinical and clinical studies. Overall, this class of agents works to slow bone turnover. Because the remodeling units persist for a longer time period, the degree of mineralization is enhanced by these drugs. This seems to be the most likely mechanism for progressive increases in BMD seen in all trials with this class of agents.

Non–nitrogen-containing bisphosphonates (e.g., etidronate, clodronate; see Table 1) inhibit bone resorption by producing toxic analogs of ATP that cause premature death in osteoclasts.[2] Nitrogen-containing compounds (e.g., alendronate, risedronate, and others; see Table 1) interfere with protein prenylation by inhibiting farnesyl pyrophosphatase, an enzyme in the HMG-CoA reductase pathway.[3] Inhibition of this enzyme prevents post-translational prenylation of guanosine triphosphate (GTP)-binding proteins, which leads to reduced resorptive activity of osteoclasts and accelerated apoptosis (programmed cell death).[4]

Bisphosphonates have proven efficacy for prevention of bone loss caused by aging, estrogen deficiency, and glucocorticoid use and for prevention of fractures in women with postmenopausal osteoporosis and in women and men with glucocorticoid-induced osteoporosis. Three bisphosphates, alendronate, risedronate, and ibandronate, are currently approved by the U.S. Food and Drug Administration (FDA) for the prevention and treatment of osteoporosis.[5] Several bisphosphonates are approved for other indications, most often for the treatment or prevention of metastatic bone disease.

SPECIFIC ORAL BISPHOSPHONATES CURRENTLY APPROVED FOR USE FOR OSTEOPOROSIS

Alendronate

Alendronate is a nitrogen-containing bisphosphonate (Table 1). It was approved in 1995 and was the first bisphosphonate ap-

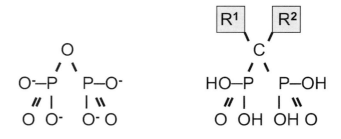

PYROPHOSPHATE   BISPHOSPHONATE

FIG. 1.   Structure of pyrophosphate and geminal bisphosphonates. (Reprinted from Avioli L 2000 Bisphosphonate therapy for postmenopausal osteoporosis. The Osteoporotic Syndrome. pp. 121–132 with permission from Elsevier.)

Dr. Black has received grants from Novartis, has been a speaker for Merck, and has been a consultant for NPS and Roche. Dr. Rosen is a principal investigator for Wyeth, Merck, Aventis, Lilly, NPS, Novartis, Allelix, and GSK.

TABLE 1. STRUCTURES OF BISPHOSPHONATES IN GENERAL CLINICAL USE
IN NORTH AMERICA

	R^1	R^2
Non–nitrogen-containing compounds		
Etidronate	OH	CH_3
Clodronate	Cl	Cl
Tiludronate	H	SC_6H_3Cl
Nitrogen-containing compounds		
Pamidronate	OH	$CH_2CH_2NH_2$
Alendronate	OH	$CH_2CH_2CH_2NH_2$
Risedronate	OH	CH_2-3-pyridinyl
Zoledronate	OH	$CH_2C_3N_2H_3$

Reprinted from Clinics in Geriatric Medicine, Siris E 2003. Bisphosphonate treatment for osteoporosis, pp. 395–414 with permission from Elsevier.

proved for the treatment of osteoporosis. The pivotal phase III study[6] included ~530 postmenopausal women (on either placebo or 10 mg/day) with low BMD and showed that alendronate increased BMD in the hip and spine: 10 mg/day (which seems to be the optimal dose) increases spine BMD by ~9% and femoral neck hip BMD by ~6% versus placebo over 3 years (Fig. 2). Studies with continued alendronate for as long as 10 years show that BMD increases are maintained for at least that long.[7,8] Alendronate reduces bone turnover markers by 50–70%, and these decreases are maintained as long as treatment is continued. BMD and bone turnover effects of 10 mg/day are similar to those for 70 mg/week,[9] and based on these results, the weekly dose was approved in 2000.

The Vertebral Fracture Arm of the Fracture Intervention Trial (FIT) was the first randomized trial to show a reduction in fractures with any agent. Two thousand twenty-seven women with prevalent vertebral fractures received either alendronate (5 mg/day for 2 years, 10 mg/day for 1 year) or placebo. The incidence of new fractures was reduced by ~50% with alendronate treatment compared with placebo (47%, 48%, and 51% for radiographic, wrist fractures, and hip fractures, respectively; Fig. 3).[10] In the Clinical Fracture Arm of FIT, 4432 women without prevalent vertebral fractures showed a decrease of ~50% in the first incident vertebral fracture and a 12% reduction (nonsignificant, $p = 0.07$) in nonvertebral fracture.[11] However, both nonvertebral and hip fractures were significantly reduced in those (~33%) with a hip BMD T score below −2.5 (36% reduction in nonvertebral fracture, $p < 0.001$). Several studies have suggested reductions in fractures within 1 year of alendronate treatment.[12,13] In addition to reducing fracture risk, therapy with alendronate has been shown to reduce days of decreased activity, days in bed, and use of hospital services.[14]

Five milligrams per day of alendronate in early postmenopausal women has been shown to prevent bone loss for at least 5 years of treatment.[15] In men followed for 2 years, BMD increases with alendronate (10 mg/day) were similar to those in women, and there was a suggestion of a vertebral fracture reduction.[16] In a study of 477 men and women receiving corticosteroid therapy, alendronate significantly improved spine and hip BMD over 48 weeks.[17]

For treatment of postmenopausal osteoporosis, the recommended dose is 10 mg/day or 70 mg weekly, and for prevention, the recommended dose is 5 mg/day (or 35 mg given once weekly). For treatment of corticosteroid-induced osteoporosis, the indicated dose is 5 mg daily for men and estrogen-replete women and 10 mg daily for postmenopausal women who are not taking estrogen. "Off label" use for prevention of corticosteroid-induced osteoporosis and for prevention and treatment of various secondary forms of osteoporosis is common.

Risedronate

Risedronate has a nitrogen molecule in a pyridinyl ring in the R^2 position (Table 1). Risedronate (5 mg/day) increases spine BMD by 4–5% and hip BMD by ~2–4% versus placebo over 3 years.[19] It reduces bone turnover markers by 40–60%. A weekly dose of risedronate (35 mg) was shown to have a similar effect on BMD and bone turnover, and this was approved in 2003.[18]

Risedronate (5 mg/day) was shown to reduce vertebral fractures by 40–50% in two 3-year studies that included ~3600 women with prevalent vertebral fractures[19,20] (Fig. 4). The reduction was evident as early as 1 year. Osteoporotic nonvertebral fractures were reduced by 39% in one of these.[19] The Hip Intervention Program Risedronate (HIP; 2.5 and 5 mg/day versus placebo) studied 9331 women >70 years of age at high risk of hip fracture and showed a 30% overall reduction in hip fractures[21] in the combined doses versus placebo. In the subset of women 70–79 years of age with very low BMD (hip T score below −3 or −4 with a risk factor), there was a 40% reduction. However, among those >80 years of age who were enrolled with at least one risk factor (but no necessarily low bone mass), there was not a significant reduction in hip fracture risk.

Risedronate has been shown to prevent bone loss in recently menopausal women.[22] It has also been shown to prevent corticosteroid-induced bone loss in patients beginning corticosteroid therapy[23] and to increase BMD in patients who have been

(A)

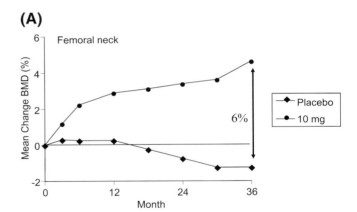

(B)

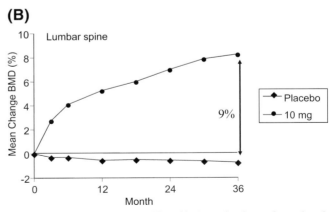

FIG. 2. Effect of alendronate (10 mg/day) vs. placebo on femoral neck and lumbar spine BMD over 3 years. (Adapted with permission from Liberman UA, Weiss SR, Broll J, Minne HW, Quan H, Bell NH, Rodriguez-Portales J, Downs RW Jr., Dequeker J, Favus M 1995 Effect of oral alendronate on bone mineral density and the incidence of fractures in postmenopausal osteoporosis. The Alendronate Phase III Osteoporosis Treatment Study Group. N Engl J Med **333:**1437–1443. Copyright © 1995 Massachusetts Medical Society. All rights reserved.)

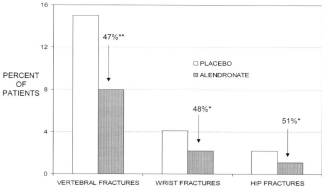

FIG. 3. Percent of placebo patients (open bars) and alendronate-treated patients (shaded bars) in the Vertebral Fracture Arm of the FIT having new fractures after 3 years of treatment. **$p < 0.001$, *$p < 0.05$. (Adapted from Black DM, Cummings SR, Karpf DB, Cauley JA, Thompson DE, Nevitt MC, Bauer DC, Genant HK, Haskell WL, Marcus R, Ott SM, Torner JC, Quandt SA, Reiss TF, Ensrud KE 1996 Randomized trial of effect of alendronate on risk of fracture in women with existing vertebral fractures. Fracture Intervention Trial Research Group. Lancet **348**:1535–1541 with permission from Elsevier.)

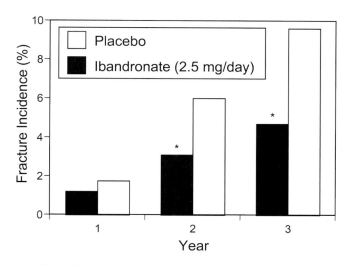

* P < 0.001 versus placebo

FIG. 5. Cumulative effect of oral daily ibandronate (2.5 mg/day) vs. placebo on new vertebral fractures during each year of study. (Adapted with permission from J Bone Miner Res 2004 **19**:1241–1249 with permission of the American Society for Bone and Mineral Research.)

previously treated with glucocorticoids for a mean of 5 years.[24] Risedronate is approved by the FDA for the prevention and treatment of both postmenopausal osteoporosis and corticosteroid-induced osteoporosis.

Ibandronate

Ibandronate has a nitrogen molecule in the middle part of the P-C-P structure and a hydroxyl group in the R^1 side chain (Table 1). Given as a daily dose of 2.5 mg/day, it has been shown to increase spine BMD by 5% and hip BMD by 3–4% over 3 years.[25] It also decreases bone turnover markers by ~40–60%.[26] A trial comparing 2.5 mg/day to 100 and 150 mg once per month showed similar or better BMD gains for the monthly formulations,[27] and the once-monthly formulation (150 mg) was approved in 2005. Trials in men and early postmenopausal women show similar changes in bone turnover markers, although most of these studies were small and limited in scope.

In the BONE trial, 1964 women with prevalent vertebral fractures showed a reduction in new vertebral fractures by 50% ($p < 0.001$) over 3 years on 2.5 mg/day (Fig. 5).[25] In this trial, there was no overall reduction in nonvertebral fractures, although in a

posthoc analysis, there was a reduction of 69% in nonvertebral fractures in those with femoral neck BMD T scores < -3 (~15% of the study population).

OTHER ORAL BISPHOSPHONATES IN CLINICAL USE

Etidronate

Etidronate was the first bisphosphonate to be studied in osteoporosis. Etidronate may impair mineralization of new bone if given continuously, so an intermittent cyclical regimen (400 mg daily for 14 days every 3 months) has been used for treatment of osteoporosis. The studies with cyclical etidronate in women with postmenopausal osteoporosis showed an increase in BMD but were not powered to show a benefit on fracture.[28,29] However, they suggested a decrease in the risk of vertebral fractures, especially among high-risk patients, that has been reinforced by post-marketing data.[30] Treatment with intermittent cyclical etidronate therapy has been shown to prevent bone loss in recently menopausal women[31] and glucocorticoid-induced osteoporosis.[32] A small, open study has shown increases in BMD in osteoporotic men treated with etidronate. Etidronate is generally well tolerated and seems safe through at least 7 years of treatment.[33] Etidronate is not approved in the United States for use in osteoporosis but is approved in Canada and many European countries. It is available in the United States for other indications. Because of its good tolerability and relatively low cost, etidronate is sometimes used "off label" in the United States for patients who cannot tolerate other oral bisphosphonates.

Other Oral Bisphosphonates

There have been some small trials of clodronate for treatment of osteoporosis, but there is not enough data to judge its effectiveness. Clodronate is not available in the United States. In Europe and Canada, where it is available, clodronate is used mainly for treatment of hypercalcemia of malignancy. Tiludronate (given orally) failed to show a fracture benefit in large trials, perhaps because the doses chosen were not optimal. Tiludronate is approved by the FDA for treatment of Paget's disease.

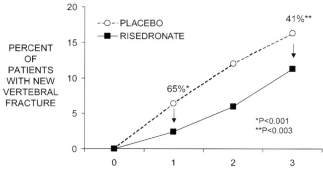

FIG. 4. Percent of placebo patients (○, dashed line) and risedronate 5 mg patients (■, solid line) in the North American Vertebral Effectiveness of Risedronate Therapy (VERT) study having new vertebral fractures. *p < 0,001, **p < 0.003. (Reprinted with permission from JAMA 1999 **282**: 1344–1352. Copyright © 1999, American Medical Association. All rights reserved.)

INTRAVENOUS BISPHOSPHONATES

Pamidronate

Pamidronate (sometimes called APD, for aminopropylidene diphosphonate) is approved by the FDA for treatment of hypercalcemia of malignancy and Paget's disease of bone. Pamidronate administered intravenously has been shown to increase BMD or prevent bone loss in patients with postmenopausal osteoporosis,[34] in recently menopausal women, and in patients with corticosteroid-induced osteoporosis.[35] A typical regimen is an initial dose of pamidronate 90 mg intravenously with subsequent doses of 30 mg every third month. The 30-mg dose can be infused over a minimum of 2 h.[36] Pamidronate is not approved in the United States for use in osteoporosis. It is used "off label" for patients who cannot tolerate or cannot absorb oral bisphosphonates.

Ibandronate

A recent trial compared 3 mg of ibandronate given every 3 months to oral ibandronate (2.5 mg/day) and found equivalent gains in BMD and similar suppression in bone turnover that lasted up to 3 months.[37] Intravenous ibandronate was recently approved based on this equivalence. However, there are no trials showing fracture efficacy for intravenous bisphosphonates. An earlier study of a lower dose (1 mg every 3 months) of ibandronate with an endpoint of vertebral fracture showed an increase of 2.8% in spine BMD but did not show a decrease in vertebral fractures. It has been hypothesized that the lack of fracture efficacy in this trial was caused by the fact that bone remodeling did not remain fully suppressed between doses.

Zoledronic Acid

Zoledronic acid contains two nitrogens in the R^2 position and is the most potent bisphosphonate currently available. It is approved by the FDA (at a dose of 4 mg) for treatment of malignant hypercalcemia and prevention and treatment of bone metastasis. In a phase II trial of women with postmenopausal osteoporosis, a single intravenous 4-mg dose of zoledronate increased bone mass and resulted in a sustained reduction in bone turnover that lasted at least 12 months.[38] It is not currently approved for osteoporosis, but is used "off label." Large-scale phase III trials of 5 mg given annually to evaluate the antifracture effect of intravenous zoledronate are currently under way.

DOSING, SIDE EFFECTS, AND SAFETY ISSUES

Bisphosphonates taken orally are very poorly absorbed under ideal conditions. Absorption is completely abolished in the presence of divalent cations and dairy products. All bisphosphonates must be taken in the fasting state; for most, a prolonged fast is required (generally an overnight fast), with nothing but water orally for at least 30 minutes after ingestion. To minimize the chance of esophageal irritation, the tablet should be taken with 8 oz of water (to be certain the tablet passes through the esophagus), and the patient should remain upright (seated or standing) until after eating (to avoid reflux of drug into the esophagus). Patients who cannot remain upright, who have active upper gastrointestinal symptoms, or who have delayed esophageal emptying (e.g., strictures, achalasia, or severe dysmotility) should use extreme caution when taking any nitrogen-containing bisphosphonates.

Etidronate does not seem to cause the same upper gastrointestinal symptoms that occur with nitrogen-containing bisphosphonates. Occasionally, etidronate causes diarrhea, which, if it occurs, is typically mild. As is true for other bisphosphonates, etidronate must be taken on an empty stomach (with water only). However, etidronate can be taken between meals (2 h before and 2 h after eating) or during the night.

A significant proportion (10–30%) of patients receiving their first intravenous dose of nitrogen-containing bisphosphonate experience acute phase reactions (fever, myalgias, lymphopenia, etc.),[39–41] but these rarely recur with repeated administration. Pretreatment with histamine blockers, antipyretics, or corticosteroids may reduce these symptoms. The only route of elimination of bisphosphonates is renal excretion, but little information is available on dosing in patients who have impaired renal function. Renal toxicity may occur with rapid intravenous administration such that 15 minutes is the suggested time of administration for an agent, such as zoledronic acid. Other side effects include eye reactions (uveitis, scleritis, episcleritis, and conjunctivitis), which have been reported with a frequency of about 1:1000, mainly with intravenous pamidronate. With rapid parenteral administration of bisphosphonates, hypocalcemia may occur; however, it is infrequent and usually mild. Pancreatitis has been reported with alendronate.[42] There have been some recent reports of osteonecrosis of the jaw associated with bisphosphonate use, but these have been primarily confined to oncology patients, receiving frequent doses of intravenous bisphosphonates.

Optimal effectiveness of bisphosphonates requires that patients engage in weight-bearing exercise and have adequate calcium and vitamin D nutrition. Bisphosphonates are contraindicated in patients with hypocalcemia and should be used with caution in those individuals with low serum 25-hydroxyvitamin D because this can prompt severe hypocalcemia.[43]

There has also been concern that potent antiresorptive agents, such as bisphosphonates, might turn off remodeling completely, leading to "frozen bone" and eventual increased bone fragility. There is no evidence that this actually occurs with the doses used clinically. Some studies in dogs have shown that treatment with very high doses of bisphosphonates have shown increased microcracks.[44] However, biomechanical and bone strength were preserved, so the relevance of the increased macrocracks is unclear. Relevance to humans, however, has been questioned. Fracture healing in patients treated with chronic bisphosphonate therapy does not seem to be a problem, although there are few studies addressing this important issue.

LONG-TERM USE OF BISPHOSPHONATES

Randomized trials of duration up to about 4 years have shown fracture reductions, but the impact of longer-term therapy is not known. Two recent extension studies have shown that long-term use of alendronate continues to maintain BMD and continues to decrease bone remodeling for up to 10 years.[7,8] Similar data are available for as long as 7 years for risedronate. The two alendronate studies did not have long-term placebo, but fracture rates at the end of the studies were similar to those in the early periods, suggesting no increase in bone fragility with long-term use. The FIT Long-Term Extension study (FLEX),[8] a randomized, blinded trial, compared 5 years of continued alendronate followed by 5 years of placebo to 10 years of continuous use. This study found that BMD decreases slowly on cessation of alendronate and bone remodeling gradually increases. While clinical vertebral fractures were decreased among those who stopped alendronate compared with those who continued, other fracture rates were similar. These data suggest that clinicians might consider a "drug holiday" after 5 years of alendronate in some (probably lower risk) patients. There are no similar data for other bisphosphonates.

RELATIVE EFFICACY, SAFETY, AND TOLERABILITY

Bisphosphonate administration increases spine and hip BMD in the same range as estrogen, but more so than calcitonin or raloxifene. However, in head-to head trials, the bisphosphonates show less of an increase than PTH(1-34) (teriparatide) 20 μg/day and PTH(1-84) 100 μg/day.[45,46] There are no head-to-head trials comparing bisphosphonates with regard to fracture efficacy or comparing a bisphosphonate with any other drug with a fracture endpoint. Bisphosphonates are the only approved agents that have been shown to reduce the risk of hip fractures.[47] Both alendronate and risedronate were well tolerated in clinical trials, and recent data suggest no difference between the two once-weekly formulations in terms of upper gastrointestinal side effects (e.g., heartburn, pain on swallowing).[48] Ibandronate seems to have the same adverse event profile as alendronate and risedronate, although it is administered once monthly.

USE OF BISPHOSPHONATES IN COMBINATION WITH OTHER AGENTS

Because there are several classes of antiresorptive drugs, besides the bisphosphonates, the possibility of combining those with distinct mechanisms of action to enhance BMD or reduce fracture risk further has been considered. Several studies have shown that combining a bisphosphonate with estrogen or raloxifene produces a modestly greater change in BMD than a single agent alone,[49] and although this combination is probably safe, there are no fracture data to suggest any combination can reduce subsequent risk more than the bisphosphonates alone. Using two antiresorptive agents together increases the cost and probably increases the occurrence of side effects. For these reasons, combination therapy with antiresorptive drugs should probably be reserved for patients who have severe osteoporosis and perhaps for those who fail to respond to a single drug.[50]

Combining an anabolic agent (e.g., teriparatide) with bisphosphonate seems more appealing because these classes of drugs might complement each other. There is emerging literature from BMD studies examining this combination.[46,51–53] It seems that PTH added to on-going alendronate therapy somewhat blunts, but does not eliminate, the anabolic response in terms of BMD and bone remodeling.[52,54] However, simultaneous initiation of daily alendronate and PTH(1-84) in a randomized trial dramatically decreased the anabolic response to PTH.[46] Alendronate after the cessation of 1 year of PTH greatly increased BMD compared with cessation of PTH followed by placebo, where there were significant losses of bone mass.[51] These results suggest that a course of PTH therapy should be followed by a bisphosphonate or another antiresorptive drug. While there are no similar studies with other bisphosphonates, effects are presumably similar.

SUMMARY AND CONCLUSIONS

Bisphosphonates, as a class, are the most thoroughly studied agents for the prevention and treatment of osteoporosis. These drugs increase BMD at the lumbar spine and hip. In patients who have established osteoporosis, vertebral and nonvertebral fracture risk reduction is substantial. The bisphosphonates are currently the only approved treatments to reduce the risk of hip fractures in randomized prospective trials. Fracture risk reduction occurs relatively quickly. BMD increases are maintained over the course of 10 years of treatment, and there is no evidence for any long-term increase in bone fragility with long-term use. In general, the bisphosphonates are still considered first line agents for the treatment of most patients with osteoporosis.

Alendronate, ibandronate, and risedronate are approved by the FDA for prevention of bone loss in recently menopausal women. With respect to glucocorticoid-induced osteoporosis, alendronate and risedronate are approved for treatment and risedronate for prevention of bone loss. Alendronate is also approved for the treatment of osteoporosis in men. Other bisphosphonates (etidronate for oral use, pamidronate and zoledronate for intravenous infusion) are also available and can be used "off label" for patients who cannot tolerate approved agents. Although bisphosphonates combined with estrogen or raloxifene produce greater gains in bone mass compared with monotherapy, the use of two antiresorptive agents in combination cannot be recommended because the benefit on fracture risk has not been shown and because of increased cost and side effects. PTH added to ongoing bisphosphonate therapy blunts, but does not eliminate, the anabolic response, and it seems beneficial to follow a course of PTH therapy with a bisphosphonate.

REFERENCES

1. Papapoulos S 1996 Bisphosphonates: Pharmacology and use in the treatment of osteoporosis. In: Marcus R, Felman D, Kelsey J (eds.) Osteoporosis. Academic Press, San Diego, CA, USA, pp. 1209–1234.
2. Frith JC, Monkkonen J, Blackburn GM, Russell RG, Rogers MJ 1997 Clodronate and liposome-encapsulated clodronate are metabolized to a toxic ATP analog, adenosine 5'-(beta, gamma-dichloromethylene) triphosphate, by mammalian cells in vitro. J Bone Miner Res 12:1358–1367.
3. Rogers MJ, Frith JC, Luckman SP, Coxon FP, Benford HL, Monkkonen J, Auriola S, Chilton KM, Russell RG 1999 Molecular mechanisms of action of bisphosphonates. Bone 24(5 Suppl):73S–79S.
4. Green JR 2004 Bisphosphonates: Preclinical review. Oncologist 9(Suppl 4):3–13.
5. Cranney A, Tugwell P, Adachi J, Weaver B, Zytaruk N, Papaioannou A, Robinson V, Shea B, Wells G, Guyatt G 2002 Meta-analyses of therapies for postmenopausal osteoporosis. III. Meta-analysis of risedronate for the treatment of postmenopausal osteoporosis. Endocr Rev 23:517–523.
6. Liberman UA, Weiss SR, Broll J, Minne HW, Quan H, Bell NH, Rodriguez-Portales J, Downs RW, Jr, Dequeker J, Favus M 1995 Effect of oral alendronate on bone mineral density and the incidence of fractures in postmenopausal osteoporosis. The Alendronate Phase III Osteoporosis Treatment Study Group. N Engl J Med 333:1437–1443.
7. Bone HG, Hosking D, Devogelaer JP, Tucci JR, Emkey RD, Tonino RP, Rodriguez-Portales JA, Downs RW, Gupta J, Santora AC, Liberman UA 2004 Ten years' experience with alendronate for osteoporosis in postmenopausal women. N Engl J Med 350:1189–1199.
8. Black D, Schwartz A, Ensrud K, Ryback-Feiglin A, Gupta J, Lombardi A, Wallace R, Levis S, Quandt S, Satterfield S, Cauley J, Cummings S 2004 A 5 year randomized trial of the long-term efficacy and safety of alendronate: The FIT Longterm EXtension (FLEX). J Bone Miner Res 19:S45.
9. Schnitzer T, Bone HG, Crepaldi G, Adami S, McClung M, Kiel D, Felsenberg D, Recker RR, Tonino RP, Roux C, Pinchera A, Foldes AJ, Greenspan SL, Levine MA, Emkey R, Santora AC, 2nd, Kaur A, Thompson DE, Yates J, Orloff JJ 2000 Therapeutic equivalence of alendronate 70 mg once-weekly and alendronate 10 mg daily in the treatment of osteoporosis. Alendronate Once-Weekly Study Group. Aging (Milano) 12:1–12.
10. Black DM, Cummings SR, Karpf DB, Cauley JA, Thompson DE, Nevitt MC, Bauer DC, Genant HK, Haskell WL, Marcus R, Ott SM, Torner JC, Quandt SA, Reiss TF, Ensrud KE 1996 Randomized trial of effect of alendronate on risk of fracture in women with existing vertebral fractures. Fracture Intervention Trial Research Group. Lancet 348:1535–1541.
11. Cummings SR, Black DM, Thompson DE, Applegate WB, Barrett-Connor E, Musliner TA, Palermo L, Prineas R, Rubin SM, Scott JC, Vogt T, Wallace R, Yates AJ, LaCroix AZ 1998 Effect of alendronate on risk of fracture in women with low bone density but without vertebral fractures: Results from the Fracture Intervention Trial. JAMA 280:2077–2082.
12. Black DM, Thompson DE, Bauer DC, Ensrud K, Musliner T, Hochberg MC, Nevitt MC, Suryawanshi S, Cummings SR 2000 Fracture risk reduction with alendronate in women with osteoporosis: The Fracture Intervention Trial. FIT Research Group. J Clin Endocrinol Metab 85:4118–4124.
13. Pols HA, Felsenberg D, Hanley DA, Stepan J, Munoz-Torres M, Wilkin TJ, Qin-sheng G, Galich AM, Vandormael K, Yates AJ, Stych B 1999 Multinational, placebo-controlled, randomized trial of the effects of alendronate on bone density and fracture risk in postmenopausal women with low bone mass: Results of the FOSIT study. Foxamax International Trial Study Group. Osteoporos Int 9:461–468.
14. Nevitt MC, Thompson DE, Black DM, Rubin SR, Ensrud K, Yates AJ, Cummings SR 2000 Effect of alendronate on limited-activity days and bed-disability days caused by back pain in postmenopausal women with existing vertebral fractures. Fracture Intervention Trial Research Group. Arch Intern Med 160:77–85.

15. Ravn P, Weiss SR, Rodriguez-Portales JA, McClung MR, Wasnich RD, Gilchrist NL, Sambrook P, Fogelman I, Krupa D, Yates AJ, Daifotis A, Fuleihan GE 2000 Alendronate in early postmenopausal women: Effects on bone mass during long-term treatment and after withdrawal. Alendronate Osteoporosis Prevention Study Group. J Clin Endocrinol Metab 85:1492–1497.

16. Orwoll ES, Ettinger M, Weiss S, Miller P, Kendler D, Graham J, Adami S, Weber K, Lorenc R, Pietschmann P, Vandormael K, Lombardi A 2000 Alendronate for the treatment of osteoporosis in men. N Engl J Med 343:604–610.

17. Saag KG, Emkey R, Schnitzer TJ, Brown JP, Hawkins F, Goemaere S, Thamsborg G, Liberman UA, Delmas PD, Malice MP, Czachur M, Daifotis AG 1998 Alendronate for the prevention and treatment of glucocorticoid-induced osteoporosis. Glucocorticoid-Induced Osteoporosis Intervention Study Group. N Engl J Med 339:292–299.

18. Brown JP, Kendler DL, McClung MR, Emkey RD, Adachi JD, Bolognese MA, Li Z, Balske A, Lindsay R 2002 The efficacy and tolerability of risedronate once a week for the treatment of postmenopausal osteoporosis. Calcif Tissue Int 71:103-'11.

19. Harris ST, Watts NB, Genant HK, McKeever CD, Hangartner T, Keller M, Chesnut CH III, Brown J, Eriksen EF, Hoseyni MS, Axelrod DW, Miller PD 1999 Effects of risedronate treatment on vertebral and nonvertebral fractures in women with postmenopausal osteoporosis: A randomized controlled trial. Vertebral Efficacy With Risedronate Therapy (VERT) Study Group. JAMA 282:1344–1352.

20. Reginster J, Minne HW, Sorensen OH, Hooper M, Roux C, Brandi ML, Lund B, Ethgen D, Pack S, Ruumagnac I, Eastell R, for Vertebral Efficacy with Risedronate Therapy Study Group 2000 Randomized trial of the effects of risedronate on vertebral fractures in women with established postmenopausal osteoporosis. Vertebral Efficacy with Risedronate Therapy (VERT) Study Group. Osteoporos Int 11:83–91.

21. McClung MR, Geusens P, Miller PD, Zippel H, Bensen WG, Roux C, Adami S, Fogelman I, Diamond T, Eastell R, Meunier PJ, Reginster JY 2001 Effect of risedronate on the risk of hip fracture in elderly women. Hip Intervention Program Study Group. N Engl J Med 344:333–340.

22. Fogelman I, Ribot C, Smith R, Ethgen D, Sod E, Reginster JY 2000 Risedronate reverses bone loss in postmenopausal women with low bone mass: Results from a multinational, double-blind, placebo-controlled trial. BMD-MN Study Group. J Clin Endocrinol Metab 85:1895–1900.

23. Cohen S, Levy RM, Keller M, Boling E, Emkey RD, Greenwald M, Zizic TM, Wallach S, Sewell KL, Lukert BP, Axelrod DW, Chines AA 1999 Risedronate therapy prevents corticosteroid-induced bone loss: A twelve-month, multicenter, randomized, double-blind, placebo-controlled, parallel-group study. Arthritis Rheum 42:2309–2318.

24. Reid DM, Hughes RA, Laan RF, Sacco-Gibson NA, Wenderoth DH, Adami S, Eusebio RA, Devogelaer JP 2000 Efficacy and safety of daily risedronate in the treatment of corticosteroid-induced osteoporosis in men and women: A randomized trial. European Corticosteroid-Induced Osteoporosis Treatment Study. J Bone Miner Res 15:1006–1013.

25. Chesnut IC, Skag A, Christiansen C, Recker R, Stakkestad JA, Hoiseth A, Felsenberg D, Huss H, Gilbride J, Schimmer RC, Delmas PD 2004 Effects of oral ibandronate administered daily or intermittently on fracture risk in postmenopausal osteoporosis. J Bone Miner Res 19:1241–1249.

26. Delmas PD, Recker RR, Chesnut CH III, Skag A, Stakkestad JA, Emkey R, Gilbride J, Schimmer RC, Christiansen C 2004 Daily and intermittent oral ibandronate normalize bone turnover and provide significant reduction in vertebral fracture risk: Results from the BONE study. Osteoporos Int 15:792–798.

27. Miller PD, McClung MR, Macovei L, Stakkestad JA, Luckey M, Bonvoisin B, Reginster JY, Recker RR, Hughes C, Lewiecki EM, Felsenberg D, Delmas PD, Kendler DL, Bolognese MA, Mairon N, Cooper C 2005 Monthly oral ibandronate therapy in postmenopausal osteoporosis: 1-year results from the MOBILE study. J Bone Miner Res 20:1315–1322.

28. Storm T, Thamsborg G, Steiniche T, Genant HK, Sorenson OH 1990 Effect of intermittent cyclical etidronate therapy on bone mass and fracture rate in women with postmenopausal osteoporosis. N Engl J Med 322:1265–1271.

29. Watts NB, Harris ST, Genant HK, Wasnich RD, Miller PD, Jackson RD, Licata AA, Ross P, Woodson GC, Yanover MJ, Mysiw WJ, Kohse L, Rao MB, Steiger P, Richmond B, Chestnut CH 1990 Intermittent cyclical etidronate treatment of postmenopausal osteoporosis. N Engl J Med 323:73–79.

30. van Staa TP, Abenhaim L, Cooper C 1998 Use of cyclical etidronate and prevention of non-vertebral fractures. Br J Rheumatol 37:87–94.

31. Herd RJ, Balena R, Blake GM, Ryan PJ, Fogelman I 1997 The prevention of early postmenopausal bone loss by cyclical etidronate therapy: A 2-year, double-blind, placebo-controlled study. Am J Med 103:92–99.

32. Adachi JD, Bensen WG, Brown J, Hanley D, Hodsman A, Josse R, Kendler DL, Lentle B, Olszynski W, Ste-Marie LG, Tenenhouse A, Chines AA 1997 Intermittent etidronate therapy to prevent corticosteroid-induced osteoporosis. N Engl J Med 337:382–387.

33. Miller PD, Watts NB, Licata AA, Harris ST, Genant HK, Wasnich RD, Ross PD, Jackson RD, Hoseyni MS, Schoenfeld SL, Valent DJ, Chesnut CH III 1997 Cyclical etidronate in the treatment of postmenopausal osteoporosis: Efficacy and safety after seven years of treatment. Am J Med 103:468–476.

34. Peretz A, Body JJ, Dumon JC, Rozenberg S, Hotimski A, Praet JP, Moris M, Ham H, Bergmann P 1996 Cyclical pamidronate infusions in postmenopausal osteoporosis. Maturitas 25:69–75.

35. Boutsen Y, Jamart J, Esselinckx W, Devogelaer JP 2001 Primary prevention of glucocorticoid-induced osteoporosis with intravenous pamidronate and calcium: A prospective controlled 1-year study comparing a single infusion, an infusion given once every 3 months, and calcium alone. J Bone Miner Res 16:104–122.

36. Tyrrell CJ, Collinson M, Madsen EL, Ford JM, Coleman T 1994 Intravenous pamidronate: Infusion rate and safety. Ann Oncol 5(Suppl 7):S27–S29.

37. Bolognese M, Reid DM, Langdahl B, Hughes C, Ward P, Masanauskaite D, Olszynski WP 2005 Efficacy of intravenous ibandronate injections in postmenopausal osteoporosis: 1-year findings from DIVA. J Bone Miner Res 20:S96.

38. Reid IR, Brown JP, Burckhardt P, Horowitz Z, Richardson P, Trechsel U, Widmer A, Devogelaer JP, Kaufman JM, Jaeger P, Body JJ, Brandi ML, Broell J, Di Micco R, Genazzani AR, Felsenberg D, Happ J, Hooper MJ, Ittner J, Leb G, Mallmin H, Murray T, Ortolani S, Rubinacci A, Saaf M, Samsioe G, Verbruggen L, Meunier PJ 2002 Intravenous zoledronic acid in postmenopausal women with low bone mineral density. N Engl J Med 346:653–661.

39. Adami S, Bhalla AK, Dorizzi R, Montesanti F, Rosini S, Salvagno G, Lo Cascio V 1987 The acute-phase response after bisphosphonate administration. Calcif Tissue Int 41:326–331.

40. Zojer N, Keck AV, Pecherstorfer M 1999 Comparative tolerability of drug therapies for hypercalcaemia of malignancy. Drug Saf 21:389–406.

41. Drezner MK, Ste-Marie LG, Nuti R, Benhamou C, Leigh C, Ward P, Masanauskaite D, Lewiecki EM 2005 Safety and tolerability of intravenous ibandronate injections: DIVA 1-year analysis. J Bone Miner Res 20:S396.

42. Cadario B 2002 Alendronate: Suspected pancreatitis. Can Med Assoc J 166:86–91.

43. Rosen LS 2004 New generation of bisphosphonates: Broad clinical utility in breast and prostate cancer. Oncology (Williston Park) 18(5 Suppl 3):26–32.

44. Burr DB, Miller L, Grynpas M, Li J, Buyde A, Mashiba T, Hirano T, Johnston CC 2003 Tissue mineralization is increased following 1-year treatment with high doses of bisophosphonates in dogs. Bone 33:960–969.

45. Body JJ, Gaich GA, Scheele WH, Kulkarni PM, Miller PD, Peretz A, Dore RK, Correa-Rotter R, Papaioannou A, Cumming DC, Hodsman AB 2002 A randomized double-blind trial to compare the efficacy of teriparatide [recombinant human parathyroid hormone (1–34)] with alendronate in postmenopausal women with osteoporosis. J Clin Endocrinol Metab 87:4528–4535.

46. Black DM, Greenspan SL, Ensrud KE, Palermo L, McGowan JA, Lang TF, Garnero P, Bouxsein ML, Bilezikian JP, Rosen CJ 2003 The effects of parathyroid hormone and alendronate alone or in combination in postmenopausal osteoporosis. N Engl J Med 349:1207–1215.

47. Cranney A, Guyatt G, Griffith L, Wells G, Tugwell P, Rosen C 2002 Meta-analyses of therapies for postmenopausal osteoporosis. IX: Summary of meta-analyses of therapies for postmenopausal osteoporosis. Endocrinol Rev 23:570–578.

48. Rosen CJ, Hochberg MC, Bonnick SL, McClung M, Miller P, Broy S, Kagan R, Chen E, Petruschke RA, Thompson DE, de Papp AE 2005 Treatment with once-weekly alendronate 70 mg compared with once-weekly risedronate 35 mg in women with postmenopausal osteoporosis: A randomized double-blind study. J Bone Miner Res 20:141–151.

49. Greenspan SL, Emkey RD, Bone HG, Weiss SR, Bell NH, Downs RW, McKeever C, Miller SS, Davidson M, Bolognese MA, Mulloy AL, Heyden N, Wu M, Kaur A, Lombardi A 2002 Significant differential effects of alendronate, estrogen, or combination therapy on the rate of bone loss after discontinuation of treatment of postmenopausal osteoporosis. A randomized, double-blind, placebo-controlled trial. Ann Intern Med 137:875–883.

50. Compston JE, Watts NB 2002 Combination therapy for postmenopausal osteoporosis. Clin Endocrinol (Oxf) 56:565–569.

51. Black DM, Bilezikian JP, Ensrud KE, Greenspan SL, Palermo L, Hue T, Lang TF, McGowan JA, Rosen CJ 2005 One year of alendronate after one year of parathyroid hormone (1–84) for osteoporosis. N Engl J Med 353:555–565.

52. Cosman F, Nieves J, Zion M, Woelfert L, Luckey M, Lindsay R 2005 Daily and cyclic parathyroid hormone in women receiving alendronate. N Engl J Med 353:566–575.

53. Finkelstein JS, Hayes A, Hunzelman JL, Wyland JJ, Lee H, Neer RM 2003 The effects of parathyroid hormone, alendronate, or both in men with osteoporosis. N Engl J Med 349:1216–1226.

54. Ettinger B, Selby J, Citron JT, Vangessel A, Ettinger VM, Hendrickson MR 1994 Cyclic hormone replacement therapy using quarterly progestin. Obstet Gynecol 83:693–700.

Chapter 51.   Calcitonin

Stuart L. Silverman[1] and Charles H. Chesnut III[2]

[1]UCLA School of Medicine and Cedars-Sinai Medical Center, Beverly Hills, California; and [2]Osteoporosis Research Group, University of Washington Medical Center, Seattle, Washington

INTRODUCTION

Calcitonin, a 32 amino acid peptide secreted by the C cells in the thyroid and by the ultimobranchial gland in submammals, was originally identified as a hypocalcemic factor present in bovine serum.[1] It exerts its hypocalcemic effects by directly inhibiting osteoclast resorption. It is currently available as a parenteral or nasal spray (NS-CT) formulation, and for the future, an oral formulation.[2,3]

BASIC PHARMACOLOGY

Calcitonin inhibits bone resorption by osteoclasts.[4] Inhibition of osteoclastic bone resorption by calcitonin is mediated in part by binding to osteoclast receptors. After exposure to calcitonin in vitro, osteoclasts undergo flattening of their ruffled borders and withdraw from sites of active bone resorption. In the continued presence of calcitonin, escape from the inhibitory action of calcitonin may occur, possibly as a result of antibodies[5] or downregulation of receptors.[6]

The exact physiologic role of calcitonin in calcium homeostasis and skeletal metabolism in humans is not known. Interestingly, in genetically modified mouse models, a regulation of turnover including both bone resorption and formation has been suggested.[7]

Calcitonin knockout mice have been found to develop osteopenia. The exact mechanism is not known.[8]

EFFECTS OF CALCITONIN ON BMD

Postmenopausal Women

There are three small randomized clinical trials of injectable calcitonin on BMD in the treatment of osteoporosis[9] and two randomized clinical trials in the prevention of osteoporosis.[9] There are 12 published randomized clinical trials on the efficacy of nasal calcitonin on BMD for the prevention and treatment of postmenopausal osteoporosis.[6] In late postmenopausal women (>5 years after menopause), nasal calcitonin increased lumbar spine BMD by an average of 1–2%, significant over 2 years. There was no significant effect at cortical bone sites such as hip or forearm.

Men

There is an increase in lumbar BMD with nasal calcitonin in men.[10] There is no data with fracture as an endpoint.

Glucocorticoid-Induced Osteoporosis

A few small studies indicate that injectable calcitonin may reduce the rate of bone loss in lumbar spine and radius in patients both initiating and receiving corticosteroid therapy.[11]

Dr. Silverman has been on Speakers' Bureaus for Eli Lilly, Roche/GlaxoSmithKline, Kyphon, Merck, Novartis, and Proctor & Gamble, has received research funding from Eli Lilly, Merck, Novartis, Wyeth, Proctor & Gamble, and Roche, has been a consultant for Amgen, Roche/GlaxoSmithKline, Merck, Wyeth, Eli Lilly, and Novartis, and has been on the Advisory Boards for Amgen, Eli Lilly, Merck, Novartis, Proctor & Gamble, and Wyeth. Dr. Chestnut has been a consultant for Novartis Pharma.

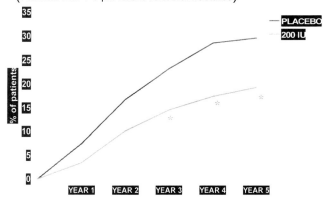

Cumulative Percent of Patients With New Vertebral Fractures By Year in PROOF
(Patients with 1-5 prevalent vertebral fractures)

* P < .05 vs placebo.

FIG. 1.   Cumulative percent of patients with new vertebral fractures by year in PROOF (patients with one to five prevalent vertebral fractures).

Data on bone loss prevention are conflicting with NS-CT. There is no data with fracture as an endpoint.

EFFECTS OF CALCITONIN ON FRACTURE

Data on the efficacy of injectable calcitonin on fracture are limited.[12,13] There have been no randomized controlled trials with injectable calcitonin using vertebral fracture as the primary endpoint.

There have been two randomized controlled trials of the efficacy of nasal calcitonin on fracture.[14,15] Both have shown vertebral fracture efficacy. None have shown hip fracture efficacy. A large multicenter trial involving 1255 postmenopausal women with lumbar spine T score < −2 studied the efficacy of NS-CT in the prevention of vertebral fractures.[15] The women, of whom 78% had prevalent vertebral fractures, were randomized to placebo nasal spray or 100 IU, 200 IU, or 400 IU NS-CT. All patients received 1000 mg calcium and 400 IU vitamin D.

In the women with prevalent vertebral fracture receiving 200 IU NS-CT, there was a 36% reduction in the risk of new vertebral fracture (RR = 0.64, 0.43–0.96) compared with placebo nasal spray (Fig. 1). In the entire cohort receiving 200 IU NS-CT, there was a 33% reduction in the risk of new vertebral fracture compared with placebo. There was no significant fracture reduction with the other two doses of NS-CT.

This multicenter study was not powered to examine the occurrence of hip fracture; however, when the data from the 100- and 200-IU doses were pooled, there was a 68% reduction in the risk of hip fracture compared with placebo.

BMD increased at the lumbar spine from baseline in all treatment groups over the 5 years of the trial (1.0–1.5%, $p = 0.01$) with no loss of bone at the hip. There was significant decrease in bone resorption as measured by serum C-telopeptide (CTX) in the 200- and 400-IU groups at 1 year (~25%, $p < 0.05$), with persistence of effect through 5 years.

Although no dose response for reduction of vertebral fracture risk was seen across doses in the intent to treat analysis, there was a significant fracture reduction with 400 IU in the valid completer analysis at 3 years.

A posthoc stratification analysis in older women showed a 53% reduction in the risk of vertebral fracture in women over age 70 and a 59% reduction in women over age 75.[16,17]

BONE QUALITY VERSUS QUANTITY WITH NASAL CALCITONIN

Nasal calcitonin (NS-CT) showed only a modest effect on BMD and bone turnover, yet NS-CT was associated with significant vertebral fracture reduction. This finding suggested that the therapeutic effect on fracture reduction might be mediated through effects on bone quality rather than on bone quantity. Chesnut et al.[18] examined the effects of NS-CT on trabecular microarchitecture as determined by high resolution MRI in a 2-year prospective placebo-controlled trial. A preservation at the distal radius of trabecular number and spacing and bone volume/total volume was noted in the NS-CT–treated group compared with significant losses in the placebo group; preservation of trabecular microarchitecture was also noted in the hip.

EFFECTS OF CALCITONIN IN PAGET'S DISEASE

Calcitonin injection is indicated for the treatment of symptomatic Paget's disease of bone.[19] The effectiveness of calcitonin salmon injection has been shown in individuals with moderate to severe disease characterized by involvement with elevated serum alkaline phosphatase and urinary hydroxyproline excretion. In these patients, >30% reduction in biochemical markers was observed, with similar decreases in pain.

EFFECTS OF CALCITONIN IN OSTEOARTHRITIS

In addition to its pronounced effect on bone resorption, oral salmon CT (sCT) may also reduce cartilage degradation as measured by urine CTX II and thereby provide therapeutic benefit in terms of chondroprotection. Women with high cartilage turnover are more likely to benefit from oral sCT treatment.[20]

ANALGESIC EFFECTS

Salmon calcitonin, both injectable and nasal, is unique among osteoporosis therapies in that it may have an analgesic effect on the bone pain of acute vertebral fracture.[21] This analgesic effect was most pronounced in the first weeks after vertebral fracture with a decrease in analgesic consumption by 3 days in one study. Calcitonin may also relieve bone pain in Paget's disease and bony metastasis.[19] Salmon calcitonin may have a role in the management of acute vertebral fracture by decreasing analgesic dependence and decreasing immobilization.[22]

CLINICAL USE

Indications

Salmon calcitonin is indicated for treatment of osteoporosis in postmenopausal women at least 5 years after menopause and may be of particular benefit in the elderly (>70 years). Salmon calcitonin may be considered for its analgesic efficacy.

Administration

Administration of SCT should be 200 IU of nasal calcitonin daily in alternating nostrils or 100 IU salmon calcitonin parenterally. Calcitonin should always be accompanied by optimal calcium and vitamin D.

Adverse Effects

Side effects with nasal calcitonin are minimal.[14] In a large multicenter study,[15] the only significant side effect was rhinitis. For parenteral calcitonin, facial flushing and/or nausea and vomiting can occur.

Monitoring

The increase in lumbar spine BMD with calcitonin is modest, as is the reduction in bone markers. BMD should be monitored at 2 years to assure no significant loss.

Clinical Use

Treatment with calcitonin should be considered for older women with osteoporosis on multiple medications or who fail to respond or cannot tolerate other treatments. Treatment with calcitonin should be considered as another treatment option in the management of acute vertebral fractures because of its analgesic effect and reduction of vertebral fracture risk..

REFERENCES

1. Azria M, Copp SH, Zanelli JM 1995 25 years of salmon calcitonin: From synthesis to therapeutic use. Calcif Tissue Int **57:**405–408.
2. Buclin T, Cosma Rochat M, Burckhardt P, Azria M, Attinger M 2002 Bioavailability and biological efficacy of a new oral formulation of salmon calcitonin in healthy volunteers J Bone Miner Res **17:**1478–1485.
3. Tanko LB, Bagger YZ, Alexanderson P, Devogelaer JP, Reginster JY, Chick R, Olson M, Benmammar H, Mindeholm L, Azria M, Christiansen C 2004 Safety and efficacy of a novel salmon calcitonin (sCT) technology based oral formulation in healthy postmenopausal women: Acute and 3 month effects on biomarkers of bone turnover. J Bone Miner Res **19:**1531–1538.
4. Chambers TJ, Moore A 1983 The sensitivity of isolated osteoclasts to morphological transformation by calcitonin. J Clin Endocrinol Metab **57:**819–824.
5. Singer FR, Aldred JP, Neer RM, Krane SM, Potts JT, Bloch KJ 1972 An evaluation of antibodies and clinical resistance to salmon calcitonin. J Clin Invest **51:**2331–2338.
6. Takahashi S, Goldring S, Katz M, Hilsenbeck S, Williams R, Roodman GD 1995 Downregulation of calcitonin receptor mRNA expression by calcitonin during human osteoclast-like cell differentiation. J Clin Invest **95:**167–171.
7. Voss A, Liese S, Priemel M, Catala-Lehnen P, Schilling AF, Mueldner C, Haberland M, Rueger JM, Emeson B, Gagel RF, Schinke T, Amling M 2005 Uncovering the physiologic function of calcitonin using genetically modified mouse models. J Bone Miner Res **20:**S1;S41.
8. Hoff AO, Thomas M, Cote GJ 1998 Generation of a calcitonin knockout mouse model. Bone **23:**1062.
9. Silverman SL 2002 Calcitonin. In: Cummings SR, Cosman F, Jamal SA (eds.) Osteoporosis: An Evidence Based Guide to Prevention and Management. American College of Physicians, Philadelphia, PA, USA, pp. 197–208.
10. Trovas GP, Lyritis GP, Galanos A, Raptou P, Constantelou E 2002 A randomized trial of nasal spray calcitonin in men with idiopathic osteoporosis: Effects on bone mineral density and bone markers. J Bone Miner Res **17:**521–527.
11. Reid IR 2002 Glucocorticoid-induced osteoporosis. In:Cummings SR, Cosman F, Jamal SA (eds.) Osteoporosis: An Evidence Based Guide to Prevention and Management. American College of Physicians, Philadelphia, PA, USA, pp. 223–240.
12. Rico H, Revilla M, Hernandez ER, Villa LF, Alvarez de Buergo M 1995 Total and regional bone mineral content and fracture rate in postmenopausal osteoporosis treated with salmon calcitonin. A prospective study. Calcif Tissue Int **47:**209–214.
13. Kanis JA, Johnell O, Gullberg B, Allander E, Dilsen G, Gennari C, Lopes

Vaz AA, Lyritis GP, Mazzuoli G, Miravet L 1992 Evidence for efficacy of drugs affecting bone metabolism in preventing hip fracture. BMJ **305:**1124–1128.

14. Chesnut CH, Silverman S, Andriano K, Genant H, Gimona A, Harris S, Kiel D, LeBoff M, Maricic M, Miller P, Moniz C, Peacock M, Richardson P, Watts N, Baylink D, for the PROOF Study Group 2000 A randomized trial of nasal spray calcitonin in postmenopausal women with established osteoporosis. The Prevent Recurrence of Osteoporotic Fractures Study. Am J Med **109:**267–276.

15. Overgaard K, Hansen MA, Jensen SB, Christiansen C 1992 Effect of calcitonin given intranasally on bone mass and fracture rates in established osteoporosis. A dose response study. BMJ **305:**556–561.

16. Silverman SL, Chesnut C, Baylink D, Gimona A, Adriano K, Mindeholm L 2001 Salmon calcitonin nasal spray (SCNS) is effective and safe in older osteoporotic women: Results from the PROOF Study. J Bone Miner Res **16:**S1;S530.

17. Olson M, Silverman SL, Mindeholm L, Azria M, Chesnut CH 2003 Discordance in vertebral fracture reduction in terms of age and fracture location in response to calcitonin nasal spray: Results from the PROOF study. J Bone Miner Res **18:**S1;S4351.

18. Chesnut CH, Majumdar S, Newitt DC, Shields A, Van Pelt , Laschansky E, Azria M, Kriegman A, Olson M, Erickson EF, Mindeholm L 2005 Effects of salmon calcitonin on trabecular microarchitecture as determined by magnetic resonance imaging:results from the QUEST study. J Bone Miner Res **20:**1548–1561.

19. Singer FR, Krane SM 1990 Pagets disease of bone. In: Avioli L, Krane SM (eds.) Metabolic Bone Disease and Clinically Related Disorders. WB Saunders, Philadelphia, PA, USA, pp. 588–595.

20. Bagger YZ, Tanko LB, Alexandersen P, Karsdal MA, Olson M, Mindeholm L, Azria M, Christiansen C 2005 Oral salmon calcitonin induced suppression of urinary collagen type II degradation in postmenopausal women: A new potential treatment of osteoarthritis. Bone **37:**425–430.

21. Silverman SL, Azria M 2002 The analgesic role of calcitonin following osteoporotic fracture. Osteoporos Int **13:**858–867.

22. Lyritis GP, Tsakalakos N, Magiasis B, Karachalios T, Yiatzides A, Tsekoura M 1991 Analgesic effect of salmon calcitonin in osteoporotic vertebral fractures: A double-blind placebo-controlled study. Calcif Tissue Int **49:**369–372.

Chapter 52.   PTH Treatment for Osteoporosis

Felicia Cosman

Clinical Research Center, Helen Hayes Hospital, West Haverstraw, New York; and Department of Clinical Medicine, Columbia College of Physicians and Surgeons, Columbia University, New York, New York

INTRODUCTION

As a result of its unique mechanism of action, PTH, the only approved anabolic therapy for bone, produces larger increments in bone mass (particularly in the spine) than those seen with antiresorptive therapies. PTH treatment first stimulates new bone formation and subsequently stimulates both bone resorption and formation, while the balance remains positive for bone formation, even in this latter phase of PTH activity.[1,2] The growth of new bone with PTH permits restoration of bone microarchitecture, including improved trabecular connectivity and enhanced cortical thickness.[3,4] Bone formation may also be induced on the outer periosteal surface,[5,6] possibly affecting bone size and geometry, with additional beneficial effects on bone strength.[5–10] For individuals with severe osteoporosis, PTH might produce bone benefits that afford a more substantial long-term reduction in risk of subsequent fractures, although at the present time, there are no long-term data to prove this concept.

This article reviews the clinical trial data using PTH as both monotherapy and in combination/sequence regimens with antiresorptive agents in women and in men and briefly overviews trials in a few special populations. PTH will be referred to as teriparatide when it is the recombinant human PTH(1-34) fragment produced by Lilly (Indianapolis, IN, USA); PTH(1-34) when it is the aminoterminal human fragment produced by biochemical synthetic methods (Bachem, CA, USA); and PTH(1-84) as the intact human recombinant molecule being produced and developed by NPS Pharmaceuticals (Salt Lake City, UT, USA). PTH without other designation denotes any of the three compounds.

CANDIDATES FOR ANABOLIC THERAPY

Good candidates for PTH are women and men who are at very high risk of future osteoporosis-related fractures. These include individuals who have had vertebral compression fractures (clinical or radiographic); other osteoporosis-related fractures, with BMD in the osteoporosis range; or very low BMD even in the absence of fractures (T score below −3). PTH should also be recommended for individuals who have been on prior antiresorptive agents, who have had a suboptimal response to treatment, defined as incident fractures or active bone loss during therapy, or who have persistent osteoporosis despite therapy. Individuals who might be at elevated risk for osteosarcoma, such as those with a history of Paget's disease, bone irradiation, unexplained elevations in alkaline phosphatase, and children with open epiphyses, should not receive PTH treatment. Furthermore, people with metastatic bone cancer, myeloma, hyperparathyroidism, and hypercalcemia should not receive PTH. The PTH treatment course is recommended to be no more than 2 years.

POSTMENOPAUSAL OSTEOPOROSIS

Teriparatide as Monotherapy

The largest study of teriparatide action was that of Neer et al.[11] in 1637 postmenopausal women with prevalent vertebral fractures, an average of 70 years of age, who were randomized to receive teriparatide, 20 or 40 μg, or placebo by daily subcutaneous injection. After a median treatment period of 19 months, teriparatide increased spine BMD by 9.7% (20-μg dose) and 13.7% (40-μg dose) and hip and total body bone densities to a lesser extent. A small decline in radius BMD was seen (significant only at the higher dose). Vertebral fracture risk reductions were similar for the two teriparatide groups, 65% and 69%, respectively, with an absolute vertebral fracture risk of 4% in women receiving the higher dose (19/434

Dr. Cosman has consulted for Merck, Lilly, Novartis, NPS, and Pfizer.

women) and 5% in women receiving the lower dose (22/444 women) versus 14% in women receiving placebo (64/448 women). There was also a reduction in the incidence of new or worsening back pain in both PTH groups. In patients with incident vertebral fractures, height loss was reduced in the teriparatide groups (mean 0.21 cm lost compared with 1.11 cm in those on placebo). Incident nonvertebral fractures were reduced by 40% (6% incidence in teriparatide groups versus 10% in placebo group) and by 50% for those defined as fragility fractures (with no differences between the two teriparatide groups). Despite the small decline in radius BMD, there was still an apparent reduction in wrist fracture occurrence in teriparatide-treated women (though too small a number to statistically evaluate this fracture alone). There were also numerically fewer hip fractures in teriparatide-treated patients, although again too few to evaluate statistically.

Although transient increases in serum calcium were common when measured within 6 h of the PTH injection, sustained increases (confirmed with at least one subsequent measurement) were seen in only 3% of patients assigned to the 20-μg group and 11% of those assigned to the 40-μg group. There were no significant differences between the teriparatide or placebo groups with respect to deaths, hospitalizations, cardiovascular disorders, renal stones, or gout, despite an average increase in 24-h urine calcium of 40 mg/day and an increase in serum uric acid of up to 25%. Animal studies have shown that administration of high-dose teriparatide to rodents is associated with an increase in osteogenic sarcoma, which is dependent on dose and duration of administration.[12,13] The relevance of this finding to humans is unclear. In patients with endogenous hyperparathyroidism or parathyroid cancer, there is no evidence of an increased risk of osteogenic sarcoma. Furthermore, there have been no cases of osteogenic sarcoma in any of the human studies with PTH or in the postmarketing experience, which currently exceeds >250,000 patients. Furthermore, in Neer et al.,[11] new cancer diagnoses occurred in fewer women assigned to the teriparatide groups (2% versus 4% in the placebo group), differences that seemed statistically significant ($p = 0.03$ for 20-μg and 0.07 for 40-μg group). The main side effects of teriparatide (20 μg) are dizziness, leg cramps, and redness and irritation at injection sites. Additional possible side effects include nausea, arthralgias, myalgias, lethargy, and weakness. Higher-dose teriparatide (40 μg) produced more side effects and withdrawals. Teriparatide-induced BMD changes in the trial of Neer et al. were not dependent on patient age, baseline BMD, or prior fracture history,[14] but were related to baseline biochemical bone turnover indices.[15] Furthermore, early PTH-induced changes in bone turnover markers (at 1 and 3 months) were predictive of ultimate change in spine BMD and bone structure.[15,16]

Two smaller studies have evaluated surrogate endpoints comparing teriparatide to alendronate.[1,10] In the first,[10] where 146 women were randomized to receive teriparatide (40 μg/day) versus alendronate (10 mg/day), spine BMD increased 15% in the teriparatide group versus 6% in the alendronate group after 1 year. Although there were fewer fractures in the teriparatide than the alendronate group at the end of 14 months (3/73 versus 10/73), several of the fractures were minor (toe fractures) and probably not attributable to osteoporosis. McClung et al.[1] studied 203 postmenopausal women with osteoporosis randomized to receive teriparatide (20 μg/day) or alendronate for 18 months. Biochemical markers of bone turnover increased substantially in the teriparatide group (formation earlier and to a greater degree than resorption) and declined substantially in the alendronate group (resorption earlier and to a greater degree than formation). In teriparatide-treated women, markers peaked within 6 months, despite ongoing administration of medication, suggesting developing resistance, as has been seen in many PTH trials. Spine BMD by DXA increased 10.3% in teriparatide-treated women versus 5.5% in the alendronate group. Volumetric spine BMD, performed in a subset of women by QCT, increased 19% in the teriparatide group versus 3.8% in alendronate-treated women. Femoral neck BMD by DXA increased similarly in both groups, although by QCT, cortical volumetric femoral neck BMD increased 7.7% in the alendronate group and declined 1.2% in the teriparatide group. The magnitude of spine BMD change was correlated with the aminoterminal propeptide of type 1 procollagen (P1NP) increment in the teriparatide group and with the P1NP decrement in the alendronate group ($r = 0.53$ and -0.51, respectively). Clinical fracture incidence was similar in the teriparatide (nine fractures) and alendronate (eight fractures) groups, but no radiographs were done to evaluate vertebral fractures. Moderate or severe back pain was reported significantly less often in women assigned to teriparatide versus alendronate (15% versus 33%, $p = 0.003$).

PTH(1-84) as Monotherapy

One study using the full intact PTH(1-84) molecule was performed in 217 women of mean age 64.5 years.[17] Patients were randomly assigned to receive placebo or one of three different PTH(1-84) doses (50, 75, or 100 μg). There was a dose-dependent increase in spine BMD; however, no increase in hip or total body BMD. Further studies involving PTH(1-84) have now been completed. The TOP (Treatment of Osteoporosis) trial was a 2-year study of 2532 postmenopausal women with osteoporosis randomized to 100 μg PTH(1-84) versus placebo.[18] To be enrolled, those 55 or older needed a BMD in the spine or hip of ≤ -2.5, or ≤ -2 with a prevalent vertebral fracture. Those in the 45- to 54-year age category required a T score of ≤ -3 or ≤ -2.5 with a fracture. Overall, mean age was 64, and 19% of subjects had a prevalent vertebral fracture. Average change in BMD was about 7% in PTH(1-84)-treated subjects compared with those on placebo. In the per protocol adherent population ($n = 1870$), new vertebral fracture incidence was 3.3% in the placebo group and 1.1% in the PTH group, yielding a relative risk reduction of 66%. The reduction in new vertebral fracture incidence was seen in both those with and without prevalent vertebral fracture at study enrollment. No data have yet been published to determine what effect PTH(1-84) had on nonvertebral fracture in the TOP trial. The incidence of hypercalcemia was significantly higher in PTH(1-84)–treated versus placebo-treated women (28.3% versus 4.7%).[19] An application for approval of PTH(1-84) therapy is currently being considered by the Food and Drug Administration (FDA). There have been no head to head trials comparing PTH(1-84) with teriparatide.

PTH and Antiresorptive Combination/Sequential Therapy

The rationale supporting the concept that PTH and antiresorptive agents could produce synergistic or at least additive benefits on BMD and on bone strength is as follows: PTH stimulates bone growth, restores microarchitecture, and seems to expand bone size, whereas antiresorptives decrease stress risers, decrease cortical porosity, and increase bone mineralization. Despite this strong rationale, recent studies on combination therapy in previously untreated women and men have produced results suggesting no clear benefit to starting PTH and alendronate together[20] or starting PTH after a brief course of alendronate.[21–22] Data also suggest that prior long-term alendronate treatment might blunt (but by no means eliminate) the magnitude of BMD accrual induced by PTH. These clini-

Combination Therapy in Treatment-Naïve Women: PTH and Alendronate

Black et al.[20] recently examined the potential additive or synergistic effect of co-administering PTH(1-84) with alendronate versus each agent alone in 238 previously treatment-naïve patients. BMD of the AP spine by DXA increased similarly in the PTH(1-84) alone and PTH(1-84) plus alendronate groups (6.3% and 6.1%, respectively). Total hip BMD (by DXA) increased in the combination group (1.9%) but not in the PTH(1-84) alone group (0.3%). Radial BMD declined more in the PTH(1-84) alone group (3.4%) versus the combination group (1.1%). QCT measured increase in the total spine and total hip were similar between the PTH(1-84) and combination groups, but trabecular spine BMD increased more with PTH(1-84) alone (25.5%) than with the combination (12.6%). In contrast, QCT-assessed cortical BMD declined in the hip (1.7% for total cortical hip BMD) with PTH(1-84) alone, but was unchanged in the combination group. Cortical volume of the femoral neck of the hip (but not the total hip) increased significantly in PTH(1-84)-treated women versus combination-treated women. These data provide no clear evidence of synergistic or additive effects when PTH(1-84) was combined with alendronate versus PTH(1-84) alone in previously untreated women, although which of the many outcomes assessed in this trial is the most highly predictive of bone strength is unknown. There were only a small number of fractures in this study, and no differences among groups were seen. Incident vertebral fractures were not reported.

Preliminary data from a study in women pretreated with alendronate for a 6-month period also suggested that spine BMD gain by DXA, and even more impressively by QCT, was lower in those given PTH(1-34) with continued alendronate compared with those given PTH(1-34) alone.[21] Based on this and the trial outlined above, at the current time, there is insufficient evidence to recommend using PTH with a bisphosphonate in patients being started anew for treatment of osteoporosis.

Combination Therapy in Women on Established Alendronate

Patients maintained and stabilized on long-term alendronate treatment are a distinct, but clinically very important, population, because many of these patients have fractures or do not achieve a BMD above the osteoporotic range, and thus might benefit from anabolic therapy. In patients who are on established alendronate, PTH can stimulate biochemical indices of bone formation without resorption over 6 weeks of treatment.[23] Two studies have presented longer-term data with BMD outcomes in women pretreated with long-term alendronate.[24,25] Our group randomized 126 women, average age 68 years, who had been on alendronate for at least 1 year (average, 3.2 years), to continue alendronate and to receive daily PTH(1-34), cyclic PTH(1-34) given in a 3-month-on/3-month-off regimen, or alendronate alone.[24] PTH(1-34) stimulated increments in bone formation rapidly and resorption markers more slowly, with percentage changes for bone formation substantially higher than for bone resorption. This difference was magnified in the cyclic group. Spine BMD rose 6.1% in the daily PTH(1-34) group and 5.4% in the cyclic PTH(1-34) group [$p < 0.001$ for each PTH(1-34) group, no group differ-

ence], whereas BMD was unchanged in the alendronate alone group. Although not powered for fracture outcome, a trend toward decreased vertebral fracture occurrence was seen in the PTH(1-34) groups (one patient in the daily group, two patients in the cyclic group, and four in the alendronate alone group had new or worsening vertebral deformities on radiograph, $p = 0.2$ group difference). Cyclic PTH administration might take advantage of the early phase of PTH action, characterized by more pure stimulation of bone formation, and avoid the latter phase of PTH action, characterized by stimulation of both formation and resorption. The clinical use of this approach deserves further study. Moreover, this study clearly shows that in patients on long-term alendronate, PTH can increase spine BMD substantially.

In an observational study where teriparatide was given to women after cessation of long-term alendronate or raloxifene,[25] bone turnover markers increased as did spine BMD, but these increases were somewhat delayed and blunted in patients pretreated with alendronate compared with those in patients pretreated with raloxifene. A transient reduction in hip BMD was seen at 6 months in the group previously on alendronate, but this reversed in the latter 12 months of administration. In contrast to the protocol above,[24] where alendronate was continued during treatment with PTH(1-34), in this study,[25] antiresorptive agents were discontinued when teriparatide was initiated. No studies have directly compared the relative benefits of continuing versus stopping alendronate when PTH is started in patients who were previously on long-term alendronate therapy.

These studies cannot directly address the issue of alendronate-induced blunting of subsequent PTH effect, because neither study had a PTH alone arm. Nevertheless, careful examination across studies of different design, age groups, severity of osteoporosis, and many other factors suggest that the BMD increment induced by PTH administration for up to 18 months, after established alendronate therapy, might not be as great as that of PTH followed by alendronate. There have been no published human trials of PTH in combination with other bisphosphonates, so it is unknown whether effects of alendronate on PTH action differ from those of risedronate, ibandronate, or zoledronic acid.

PTH and Hormone Therapy

In 52 women with osteoporosis, average age 60 years, treated with established long-term hormone therapy (HT),[26,27] daily PTH(1-34) produced rapid increases in markers of bone formation and delayed increases in markers of bone resorption.[26] This period of time, where augmentation of bone formation exceeds stimulation of bone resorption, has been referred to as the anabolic window and may represent the most efficient bone building opportunity with PTH. Furthermore, bone turnover levels remained elevated for only 18–24 months, after which, levels of both formation and resorption markers declined toward baseline.[27] The mechanism of this apparent resistance to PTH has still not been determined. BMD increased by about 14% over 3 years in women receiving PTH(1-34) + HT, with evidence of the most rapid rise in BMD within the first 6 months. Total body and total hip BMD increased by about 4% in patients on PTH(1-34) + HT. Although the study was not powered to assess fracture occurrence, after 3 years of treatment, vertebral deformity occurrence was significantly reduced in patients receiving PTH(1-34)+ HT compared with those on HT alone.[27]

Another study of similar design performed in women who had previously been treated with HT showed BMD increments by DXA in the PTH(1-34) group of 30% in the lumbar spine and 12% in the femoral neck versus placebo.[28] No fracture data were presented from this trial, and the data have never been published in a peer-reviewed journal. A third study was performed in 247 women, where one subgroup had been on prior HT (as in the previously discussed two trials and a second subgroup consisted of treatment-naïve women about to receive HT for the first time).[29] In the former group, there were BMD increments of 11% in the spine and 3% in the total hip in women randomized to teriparatide (40 μg/day). In the women receiving de novo HT, there were increases caused by HT itself (4% in the spine and 2% in the total hip), and larger increases in the group receiving HT with teriparatide (17% in the spine and 6% in the hip). The increases from teriparatide seemed additive to those of HT, although not synergistic. No fracture data were presented from this trial.

PTH and Raloxifene

Deal et al.[30] randomized 137 postmenopausal treatment-naive women to receive teriparatide or teriparatide plus raloxifene. The bone formation marker P1NP rose similarly in the two groups, whereas the bone resorption marker increment was lower in the women on teriparatide plus raloxifene versus teriparatide alone. Spine BMD increments were similar in the two groups, whereas hip BMD increased more in the group assigned to teriparatide plus raloxifene. Our group studied women ($n = 42$) on raloxifene for at least 1 year and randomized them to stay on raloxifene alone or to receive raloxifene plus PTH(1-34). The PTH(1-34) plus raloxifene group had an increment of about 12% in the lumbar spine and 3% in the total hip versus no BMD change in the raloxifene-only group.[31]

PTH TREATMENT OF MEN

In a small study, men with idiopathic osteoporosis were randomized to receive PTH (1-34) or placebo.[32] Biochemical markers of bone turnover increased rapidly with PTH(1-34) administration and spine BMD rose about 12%, with a plateau between 12 and 18 months. In the femoral neck and total hip, BMD increased 5% and 4%, respectively, and radius BMD did not change.

A subsequent multicenter trial of teriparatide[33] was performed in 437 men (mean age, 49 years) with primary idiopathic osteoporosis with no known secondary causes, except for low free testosterone levels in about 50% of the patients. Subjects were randomized to teriparatide 20 or 40 μg daily or placebo. After 1 year, spine BMD rose 5.4% and 8.5% in the 20- and 40-μg groups, respectively, with no change in the placebo group. There were also dose-dependent increases in BMD of the femoral neck, total hip, and total body bone mineral. Of the original enrollees, 355 men participated in an observational follow-up study. Lateral spine radiographs repeated after 18 months of follow-up (including use of antiresorptive therapy in a substantial proportion of the men) showed a 50% reduction in vertebral fracture risk in those men initially assigned to teriparatide compared with those who had received placebo ($p = 0.07$).[34]

In a third study, 83 men with osteoporosis were assigned to PTH(1-34) at 40 μg/day, alendronate alone, or PTH(1-34) after 6 months of alendronate pretreatment (with ongoing alendronate).[22] A substantial proportion of men in both PTH(1-34) groups had required dose adjustment (by 25–50%) caused by hypercalcemia or side effects. After a total of 24 months of PTH administration, spine BMD increased most in the PTH(1-34) alone group (18.1%) compared with that in the combination group (14.8%) or alendronate alone (7.9%). Similar trends were seen for the lateral spine and femoral neck, but for the total hip and total body, increases were similar in the three treatment groups. In contrast, in the radius, BMD declined in the PTH(1-34) alone group with slight increases in the other groups. Spine trabecular BMD on QCT increased 48% with PTH alone, 17% with the combination, and 3% with alendronate alone.

PTH IN SPECIAL POPULATIONS

Glucocorticoid-Treated Patients

Women with a variety of rheumatologic conditions on glucocorticoids and being treated with hormone therapy were randomized to PTH(1-34) + HT or continued HT alone.[35] PTH(1-34) resulted in a 12% increase in spine BMD by DXA and a smaller increase in femoral neck BMD. No fracture results were reported. PTH could conceivably be a preferred treatment for glucocorticoid osteoporosis, because some of the major pathophysiologic skeletal problems with glucocorticoid administration are reduced osteoblast function and lifespan, both of which might be counteracted by PTH. A large multicenter trial of teriparatide efficacy in glucocorticoid-treated individuals is ongoing.

Premenopausal Women

In premenopausal women with endometriosis being treated with a gonadotropin-releasing hormone (GnRH) analog to induce acute estrogen deficiency,[36] women randomized to PTH(1-34) maintained bone mass in the hip and increased bone mass in the lumbar spine, especially in the lateral spine, compared with bone loss at all sites in women receiving placebo over a 6- to 12-month treatment period.

PERSISTENCE OF EFFECT

A series of observational studies suggests that BMD is lost in individuals who do not take antiresorptive agents after cessation of teriparatide, synthetic PTH(1-34), or PTH(1-84), whereas antiresorptive therapy can maintain PTH-induced gains or even provide further increments in BMD after a course of PTH.[27,34,35,37–39] Black et al.[40] have provided clinical trial confirmation of this observation. Subjects originally randomized to 1 year of treatment with PTH(1-84) were subsequently randomized to receive alendronate or placebo. BMD increased further at all sites after 1 year of alendronate after 1 year of PTH(1-84) and declined significantly at all sites after 1 year of placebo after 1 year of PTH(1-84).

RECHALLENGE WITH PTH

Women originally randomized to daily or cyclic PTH(1-34) in addition to ongoing alendronate[24] were followed for a year after PTH(1-34) was discontinued.[41] BMD remained stable in these women during this year. A second 15-month course of PTH(1-34) was given to those volunteers who still had osteoporosis. The rechallenge with PTH produced similar biochemical and BMD changes to those seen during the first course of therapy.[41]

CONCLUSION

PTH is a unique approach to osteoporosis treatment. Because of the underlying effects it produces on the microarchitecture, macroarchitecture, and mass of bone, PTH may be able to ensure more long-term protection against fracture occurrence than antiresorptive agents alone; however, data proving this principle are lacking. Antiresorptive agents are clearly needed after PTH to maintain PTH-induced gains. There are still many unanswered questions concerning PTH therapy, including the optimal duration and regimen of therapy and the mechanism underlying resistance to PTH effect after 18 months. Different PTH peptides and alternative forms of delivery (oral, nasal, inhaled, transdermal) are currently under study.

REFERENCES

1. McClung MR, San Martin J, Miller PD, Civitelli R, Bandeira F, Omizo M, Donley DW, Dalsky GP, Eriksen EF 2005 Opposite bone remodeling effects of teriparatide and alendronate in increasing bone mass. Arch Intern Med 165:1762–1768.

2. Arlot M, Meunier PJ, Boivin G, Haddock L, Tamayo J, Correa-Rotter R, Jasqui S, Donley DW, Dalsky GP, Martin JS, Eriksen EF 2005 Differential effects of teriparatide and alendronate on bone remodeling in postmenopausal women assessed by histomorphometric parameters. J Bone Miner Res 20:1244–1253.

3. Jiang Y, Zhao JJ, Mitlak BH, Wang O, Genant HK, Eriksen EF 2003 Recombinant human parathyroid hormone (1–34) [teriparatide] improves both cortical and cancellous bone structure. J Bone Miner Res 18:1932–1941.

4. Dempster DW, Cosman F, Kurland ES, Zhou H, Nieves J, Woelfert L, Shane E, Plavetic K, Muller R, Bilezikian J, Lindsay R 2001 Effects of daily treatment with parathyroid hormone on bone microarchitecture and turnover in patients with osteoporosis: A paired biopsy study. J Bone Miner Res 16:1846–53.

5. Parfitt M 2002 PTH and periosteal bone expansion. J Bone Miner Res 17:1741–1743.

6. Burr D 2005 Does early PTH treatment compromise bone strength? The balance between remodeling, porosity, bone mineral, and bone size. Curr Osteoporos Rep 3:19–24.

7. Rehman Q, Lang TF, Arnaud CD, Modin GW, Lane NE 2003 Daily treatment with parathyroid hormone is associated with an increase in vertebral cross-sectional area in postmenopausal women with glucocorticoid-induced osteoporosis. Osteoporos Int 14:77–81.

8. Zanchetta JR, Bogado CE, Ferretti JL, Wang O, Wilson MG, Sato M, Gaich GA, Dalsky GP, Myers SL 2003 Effects of teriparatide [recombinant parathyroid hormone (1–34)] on cortical bone in postmenopausal women with osteoporosis. J Bone Miner Res 18:539–543.

9. Uusi-Rasi K, Semanick LM, Zanchetta JR, Bogado CE, Eriksen EF, Sato M, Beck TJ 2005 Effects of teriparatide [rhPTH(1–4)] treatment on structural geometry of the proximal femur in elderly osteoporotic women. Bone 36:948–958.

10. Body JJ, Gaich GA, Scheele WH, Kulkarni PM, Miller PD, Peretz A, Dore RK, Correa-Rotter R, Papaioannou A, Cumming DC, Hodsman AB 2002 A randomized double-blind trial to compare the efficacy of teriparatide [recombinant human parathyroid hormone (1–34)] with alendronate in postmenopausal women with osteoporosis. J Clin Endocrinol Metab 87:4528–4535.

11. Neer RM, Arnaud CD, Zanchetta JR, Prince R, Gaich GA, Reginster JY, Hodsman AB, Eriksen EF, Ish-Shalom S, Genant HK, Wang O, Mitlak BH 2001 Effect of parathyroid hormone (1–34) on fractures and bone mineral density in postmenopausal women with osteoporosis. N Engl J Med 344:1434–1441.

12. Vahle JL, Sato M, Long GG, Young JK, Francis PC, Engelhardt JA, Westmore MS, Linda Y, Nold JB 2002 Skeletal changes in rats given daily subcutaneous injections of rhPTH(1–34) for 2 years and relevance to human safety. Toxicol Pathol 30:312–321.

13. Vahle JL, Long GG, Sandusky G, Westmore M, Ma YL, Sato M 2004 Bone neoplasms in F344 rats given teriparatide [rhPTH (1–34)] are dependent on duration of treatment and dose. Toxicol Pathol 32:426–438.

14. Marcus R, Wang O, Satterwhite J, Mitlak B 2003 The skeletal response to teriparatide is largely independent of age, initial bone mineral density, and prevalent vertebral fractures in postmenopausal women with osteoporosis. J Bone Miner Res 18:18–23.

15. Chen P, Satterwhite JH, Licata AA, Lewiecki EM, Sipos AA, Misurski DM, Wagman RB 2005 Early changes in biochemical markers of bone formation predict BMD response to teriparatide in postmenopausal women with osteoporosis. J Bone Miner Res 20:962–970.

16. Dobnig H, Sipos A, Jiang Y, Fahrleitner-Pammer A, Ste-Marie LG, Gallagher JC, Pavo I, Wang J, Eriksen EF 2005 Early changes in biochemical markers of bone formation correlate with improvements in bone structure during teriparatide therapy. J Clin Endocrinol Metab 90:3970–3977.

17. Hodsman AB, Hanley DA, Ettinger MP, Bolognese MA, Fox J, Metcalfe AJ, Lindsay R 2003 Efficacy and safety of human parathyroid hormone-(1–84) in increasing bone mineral density in postmenopausal osteoporosis. J Clin Endocrinol Metab 88:5212–5220.

18. Ettinger MP, Greenspan SL, Marriott TB, Hanley DA, Zanchetta JR, Bone HG, Lindsay R 2004 PTH(1-84) prevents first vertebral fracture in postmenopausal women with osteoporosis: Results from the TOP study. Arthritis Rheum 50:3060.

19. Greenspan SL, Bone HG, Marriott TB, Zanchetta JR, Ettinger MP, Hanley DA, Drezner MK, Miller PD 2005 Preventing the first vertebral fracture in postmenopausal women with low bone mass using PTH(1-84): Results from the TOP study. J Bone Miner Res 20:S1;S56.

20. Black DM, Greenspan SL, Ensrud KE, Palermo L, McGowan JA, Lang TF, Garnero P, Bouxsein ML, Bilezikian JP, Rosen CJ, PaTH Study Investigators 2003 The effects of parathyroid hormone and alendronate alone or in combination in postmenopausal osteoporosis. N Engl J Med 349:1207–1215.

21. Neer R, Hayes A, Rao A, Finkelstein J 2002 Effects of parathyroid hormone, alendronate, or both on bone density in osteoporotic postmenopausal women. J Bone Miner Res 17:S1;1039.

22. Finkelstein JS, Hayes A, Hunzelman JL, Wyland JJ, Lee H, Neer RM 2003 The effects of parathyroid hormone, alendronate, or both in men with osteoporosis. N Engl J Med 349:1216–1226.

23. Cosman F, Nieves J, Woelfert L, Shen V, Lindsay R 1998 Alendronate does not block the anabolic effect of PTH in postmenopausal osteoporotic women. J Bone Miner Res 13:1051–1055.

24. Cosman F, Nieves J, Zion M, Woelfert L, Luckey M, Lindsay R 2005 Daily and cyclic parathyroid hormone in women receiving alendronate. N Engl J Med 353:566–575.

25. Ettinger B, San Martin J, Crans G, Pavo I 2004 Differential effects of teriparatide on BMD after treatment with raloxifene or alendronate. J Bone Miner Res 19:745–751.

26. Lindsay R, Nieves J, Formica C, Henneman E, Woelfert L, Shen V, Dempster D, Cosman F 1997 Randomised controlled study of effect of parathyroid hormone on vertebral-bone mass and fracture incidence among postmenopausal women on oestrogen with osteoporosis. Lancet 350:550–555.

27. Cosman F, Nieves J, Woelfert L, Formica C, Gordon S, Shen V, Lindsay R 2001 Parathyroid hormone added to established hormone therapy: Effects on vertebral fracture and maintenance of bone mass after parathyroid hormone withdrawal. J Bone Miner Res 16:925–931.

28. Roe EB, Sanchez SD, del Puerto GA, Pierini E, Bacchetti P, Cann CE, Arnaud CD 1999 Parathyroid hormone 1–34 (hPTH 1–34) and estrogen produce dramatic bone density increases in postmenopausal osteoporosis-results from a placebo-controlled randomized trial. J Bone Miner Res 12:S1;S137.

29. Ste-Marie LG, Schwartz SL, Hossain A, Dessiah D, Gaich GA 2006 Effect of teriparatide [rhPTH(1-34)] on BMD when given to postmenopausal women receiving hormone replacement therapy. J Bone Miner Res 21:283–291.

30. Deal C, Omizo M, Schwartz EN, Eriksen EF, Cantor P, Wang J, Glass EV, Myers SL, Krege JH 2005 Combination teriparatide and raloxifene therapy for postmenopausal osteoporosis: Results from a 6-month double-blind placebo-controlled trial. J Bone Miner Res 20:1905–1911.

31. Cosman F, Nieves J, Barbuto N, Zion M, Lindsay R 2004 Parathyroid hormone added to raloxifene and subsequent maintenance of BMD gain with raloxifene alone. J Bone Miner Res 19:S1;S98.

32. Kurland ES, Cosman F, McMahon DJ, Rosen CJ, Lindsay R, Bilezikian JP 2000 Parathyroid hormone as a therapy for idiopathic osteoporosis in men: Effects on bone mineral density and bone markers. J Clin Endocrinol Metab 85:3069–3076.

33. Orwoll ES, Scheele WH, Paul S, Adami S, Syversen U, Diez-Perez A, Kaufman JM, Clancy AD, Gaich GA 2003 The effects of teriparatide [human parathyroid hormone (1–34)] therapy on bone density in men with osteoporosis. J Bone Miner Res 18:9–17.

34. Kaufman JM, Orwoll E, Goemaere S, San Martin J, Hossain A, Dalsky GP, Lindsay R, Mitlak BH 2005 Teriparatide effects on vertebral fractures and bone mineral density in men with osteoporosis: Treatment and discontinuation of therapy. Osteo Int 16:510–516.

35. Lane NE, Sanchez S, Modin GW, Genant HK, Pierini E, Arnaud CD 2000 Bone mass continues to increase at the hip after parathyroid hormone treatment is discontinued in glucocorticoid-induced osteoporosis: Results of a randomized controlled clinical trial. J Bone Miner Res 15:944–951.

36. Finkelstein JS, Klibanski A, Arnold AL, Toth TL, Hornstein MD, Neer RM 1998 Prevention of estrogen deficiency-related bone loss with human parathyroid hormone-(1–34): A randomized, controlled trial. J Am Med Assoc 280:1067–1073.

37. Lindsay R, Scheele WH, Neer R, Pohl G, Adami S, Mautalen C, Reginster

JY, Stepan JJ, Myers SL, Mitlak BH 2004 Sustained vertebral fracture risk reduction after withdrawal of teriparatide in postmenopausal women with osteoporosis. Arch Intern Med **164**:2024–2030.

38. Kurland ES, Heller SL, Diamond B, McMahon DJ, Cosman F, Bilezikian JP 2004 The importance of bisphosphonate therapy in maintaining bone mass in men after therapy with teriparatide [human parathyroid hormone (1–34)]. Osteoporos Int **15**:992–997.

39. Rittmaster RS, Bolognese M, Ettinger MP, Hanley DA, Hodsman AB, Kendler DL, Rosen CJ 2000 Enhancement of bone mass in osteoporotic

women with parathyroid hormone followed by alendronate. J Clin Endocrinol Metab **85**:2129–2134.

40. Black DM, Bilezikian JP, Ensrud KE, Greenspan SL, Palermo L, Hue T, Lang TF, McGowan JA, Rosen CJ, PaTH Study Investigators 2005 One year of alendronate after one year of parathyroid hormone (1–84) for osteoporosis. N Engl J Med **353**:555–565.

41. Cosman F, Nieves JW, Zion M, Barbuto N, Lindsay R 2005 Effects of PTH(1–34) rechallenge 1 year after the first PTH course in patients on long-term alendronate. J Bone Miner Res **20**:S1;S21.

Chapter 53. Osteoporosis in Men

Eric S. Orwoll

Bone and Mineral Unit, Oregon Health and Science University, Portland, Oregon

INTRODUCTION

Osteoporosis in men was generally unrecognized 20 years ago, but it is now recognized as an important public health problem, the source of much discussion, and a very active research issue. There is now a much greater understanding of the disorder, and effective diagnostic, preventive, and treatment strategies have been developed. Moreover, the study of osteoporosis in men has revealed male–female differences that in turn have fostered a greater understanding of bone biology in general.

SKELETAL DEVELOPMENT

Bone mass accumulation in males occurs gradually during childhood and accelerates dramatically during adolescence. Peak bone mass is closely tied to pubertal development, and male–female differences in the skeleton appear during adolescence.[1] Peak bone mass is achieved somewhat later in boys than girls, and whereas trabecular bone accumulation is similar in boys and girls, boys generally develop thicker cortices and larger bones than do girls, even when adjusted for body size. These differences may provide important biomechanical advantages that could in part underlie the lower fracture risk observed in men later in life. The reasons for these sexual differences in skeletal development are unclear, but could be related to differences in sex steroid action (androgens may stimulate periosteal bone formation and bone expansion), growth factor concentrations, mechanical forces exerted on bone (for instance by greater muscle action or activity), etc.

EFFECTS OF AGING ON THE SKELETON IN MEN

As in women, aging is associated with large changes in bone mass and architecture in men.[2] Trabecular bone loss (for instance in the vertebrae and proximal femur) occurs during mid-life and accelerates in later life. The magnitude of these changes is similar, but probably slightly less, than those in women. Endocortical bone loss with resulting cortical thinning also takes place in long bones, but that process seems to be somewhat mitigated by a concomitant increase in periosteal bone expansion that tends to preserve the breaking strength of bone.[3] The increase in periosteal bone formation that occurs in

Dr. Orwoll has received an Honorarium from Merck and has been a consultant for Procter and Gamble, GlaxoSmithKline, Aventis, and TAP Pharmaceuticals.

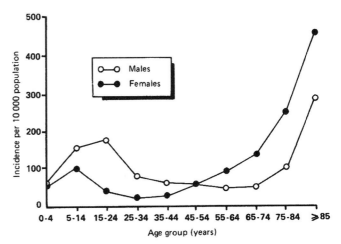

FIG. 1. Average annual fracture incidence rate per 10,000 population in Leicester, UK, by age, group, and sex.

men may be greater than that in women, and has been postulated to contribute to the lower fracture risk observed in older men.

FRACTURE EPIDEMIOLOGY

Fractures are common in men. The data concerning fractures in men are derived primarily from the study of white populations. In them, the incidence of fracture is bimodal, with a peak of fracture incidence in adolescence and young adulthood, a lower incidence in middle age, and a dramatic increase after the age of 70 years (Fig. 1).[4] The types of fractures sustained in younger and older men are different, with long bone fractures being common in younger men, whereas vertebral and hip fractures predominate in the elderly. These differences suggest that the etiologies of fractures at these two periods of life are distinct. In younger men, trauma may play a larger role, whereas in older men, skeletal fragility and fall propensity are likely to be major factors.

The exponential increase in fracture incidence in older men is as dramatic as the similar increase that occurs in women, but it begins 5–10 years later in life. This delay, combined with the longer life expectancy in women, underlies the greater burden of osteoporotic fractures in women. Nevertheless, the age-adjusted incidence of hip fracture in men is one third to one half that in women, and 20–25% of hip fractures occur in men [2] The consequences of fracture in men are at least as great as in women. In fact, elderly men seem to be more likely to die and to suffer disability than women after a hip fracture. Men suffer lower rates of long bone fractures than do women.[5] There is less information concerning vertebral fracture epidemiology in men, but the age-adjusted incidence seems to be high—~50% of that in women.[6] In younger men, the prevalence of vertebral fracture is actually greater in men than in women, at least in part the result of higher rates of spinal trauma experienced by men. Although there are inadequate data, the epidemiology of fracture in men seems to be dramatically influenced by both race and geography.[7,8] For instance, black men have a much lower likelihood of fractures than whites, and Asian men have a lower likelihood of suffering hip fracture than whites. Much more information is needed concerning these differences and their causation.

Fractures in men are related to a variety of risk factors. Certainly skeletal fragility (e.g., osteoporosis) makes fracture more likely. This trait is most commonly measured as reduced BMD, but almost certainly has other components (bone geometry, material properties, etc.). Aging and a previous history of fracture are independently associated with a higher probability of future fracture, and men of lower weight and those at risk for falling have a higher fracture risk.[2,9]

CAUSES OF OSTEOPOROSIS IN MEN

The causation of osteoporosis in men is commonly heterogeneous, and most osteoporotic men have several factors that contribute to the disease. One half to two thirds of men with osteoporosis have secondary osteoporosis—or that associated with other medical conditions, medications, or lifestyle factors that result in bone loss and fragility.[2,7] For instance, idiopathic hypercalciuria has been associated with low bone mass and abnormalities in bone remodeling.[10] The most important secondary causes include alcohol abuse, glucocorticoid excess, and hypogonadism. An important fraction of osteoporotic men, however, have idiopathic disease.

Idiopathic Osteoporosis

Osteoporosis of unknown etiology can present in men of any age,[-1] but is most dramatic in younger men who are otherwise unlikely to be affected. Several possible etiologies have been considered. Most prominent among them are genetic factors, because BMD and the risk of fracture are highly heritable. The specific genes that may be responsible are uncertain.

Hypogonadism

Sex steroids are clearly important for skeletal health in men, both for the attainment of peak bone mass as well as for the maintenance of bone strength in adults.[11] Hypogonadism is associated with low BMD. The development of hypogonadism results in increased bone remodeling and rapid bone loss, and hormone replacement increases BMD in hypogonadal men. One of the most important causes of severe hypogonadism is androgen deprivation therapy for prostate cancer. In that situation, bone loss is rapid. Gonadal function also declines with age in men, and it has been postulated that the decline may be related to age-related bone loss and fracture risk. This hypothesis has not been adequately tested.

The relative roles of estrogens and androgens in skeletal physiology in men are uncertain.[12–14] Estrogen is essential for normal bone development in young men, as evidenced by the immature development and low bone mass in men with aromatase deficiency and their reversal with estrogen therapy.

TABLE 1. CAUSES OF OSTEOPOROSIS IN MEN

Primary
  Aging
  Idiopathic
Secondary
  Hypogonadism
  Glucocorticoid excess
  Alcoholism, tobacco abuse
  Renal insufficiency
  Gastrointestinal, hepatic disorders, malabsorption
  Hyperparathyroidism
  Hypercalciuria
  Anticonvulsants
  Thyrotoxicosis
  Chronic respiratory disorders
  Anemias, hemoglobinopathies
  Immobilization
  Osteogenesis imperfecta
  Homocystinuria
  Systemic mastocytosis
  Neoplastic diseases
  Rheumatoid arthritis

Moreover, estrogen is correlated with bone remodeling, BMD, and rate of BMD loss in older men, apparently more strongly than is testosterone. However, testosterone is independently related to indices of bone resorption and formation and may stimulate periosteal bone formation.[15–17] The relative roles of estrogen and androgen must be better defined.

EVALUATION OF OSTEOPOROSIS IN MEN

Guidelines for the evaluation of osteoporosis in men are not well validated, but there are several recommendations that can be made confidently.

BMD Measurements

BMD measures are at least as effective in men as in women in predicting the risk of future fractures.[18] Unfortunately, in light of the prevalence of osteoporosis and the high incidence of fractures in men, BMD measures are performed too infrequently. Two groups of men clearly would benefit from BMD testing.

- Men over the age of 50 who have suffered a fracture, including those with vertebral deformity. Younger men who suffer low trauma fractures should also be assessed.
- Men who have known secondary causes of bone loss should have BMD determined. These include men treated with glucocorticoids or other medications associated with osteoporosis, with hypogonadism of any cause, or with alcoholism. Many other risk factors may also prompt BMD measures (Table 1).

Screening BMD measures in older men have been recommended (e.g., over age 70),[19] but the cost effectiveness of this approach hasn't been formally evaluated.

Currently, the presence of reduced BMD in men is commonly quantified with T scores and using a grading system parallel to that used in women (BMD T score −1.0 to −2.5 = low bone mass; BMD T score < −2.5 = osteoporosis). Whether BMD measurements in men should be interpreted using T scores based on a male-specific reference range or by using the same reference range used in women has been controversial. Until adequate data are available to confidently link

Table 2. Evaluation of Osteoporosis in Men—Laboratory Tests

Serum calcium, phosphorus, creatinine, alkaline phosphatase, liver
  function tests
Complete blood count (protein electrophoresis in those >50 years)
Serum 25(OH) vitamin D and PTH
Serum testosterone and luteinizing hormone
Twenty-four-hour urine calcium and creatinine
Targeted diagnostic testing in men with signs, symptoms, or other
  indications of secondary disorders

When an etiology is not apparent after the above, additional testing may be appropriate: thyroid function tests, 24-h urine cortisol, biochemical indices of remodeling.

fracture risk to BMD measures in men, the use of a male-specific reference range is suggested. The development of sufficient data to predict fracture risk from absolute levels of BMD in men would be very helpful.

Men who have been selected for androgen ablation therapy deserve special note because the risk of bone loss and fractures is clearly increased.[20] Men starting high-dose glucocorticoid therapy present the same challenges and should be similarly managed. When anti-androgen (or glucocorticoid) therapy is begun, a BMD assessment is appropriate. If it is normal, routine preventative measures are reasonable. A repeat BMD measurement should be done in 1–2 years. If BMD is reduced at the onset of therapy, more aggressive preventive measures should be considered (e.g., bisphosphonate therapy). In men with osteoporosis, prior to beginning anti-androgen (or glucocorticoid) therapy, pharmacologic approaches to prevent further bone loss or fractures are recommended.

The clinical evaluation of men found to have low BMD should include a careful history and physical examination designed to identify any factors that may contribute to deficits in bone mass. Attention should be paid to lifestyle factors, nutrition (especially calcium and vitamin D nutrition), activity level, and family history. A history of previous fracture should be identified, and fall risk should be assessed. This information should be used to formulate recommendations for prevention and treatment.

Laboratory Testing

In a man undergoing an evaluation for osteoporosis, laboratory testing is intended to identify correctable causes of bone loss. Appropriate tests are shown in Table 2.

OSTEOPOROSIS PREVENTION IN MEN

The essentials of fracture prevention in men are similar to those in women. In early life, excellent nutrition and exercise seem to have positive effects on bone mass. These principles and the avoidance of lifestyle factors known to be associated with bone loss (Table 1) remain important throughout life. Calcium and vitamin D probably provide beneficial effects on bone mass and fractures in men as in women. Recommendations for both sexes include 1000 mg of calcium for those 30–50 years of age and 1200 mg for those >50 years of age, with suggested vitamin D intakes of 1000 IU. In those at risk for falls (e.g., with reduced strength, poor balance, previous falls), attempts to increase strength and balance may be beneficial.

TREATMENT OF OSTEOPOROSIS IN MEN

Ensuring adequate calcium and vitamin D intake and appropriate physical activity are essential foundations for preserving and enhancing bone mass in men who have osteoporosis. Secondary causes of osteoporosis should be identified and treated. In addition, there are pharmacologic therapies that have been shown to enhance BMD, and in some cases reduce fracture risk in men. Although the available data are not as extensive as in women, these therapies seem to be as effective in affecting BMD and in reducing fracture risk in men. The treatment indications for these drugs are similar in men and women.

Idiopathic Osteoporosis

Alendronate, risedronate, and PTH are effective in improving BMD,[21,22] regardless of age or gonadal function. Although the trials are relatively small, each is also apparently effective in reducing vertebral fracture risk.

Glucocorticoid-Induced Osteoporosis

Bisphosphonate therapy (alendronate, risedronate) is effective in improving BMD, and although the data are not extensive, also probably reduces fracture risk.[23,24]

Hypogonadal Osteoporosis

Bisphosphonates and PTH therapy are effective in increasing BMD in hypogonadal men. Moreover, bisphosphonate treatment can prevent the bone loss that is common after androgen deprivation therapy for prostate cancer. Testosterone replacement therapy increases BMD in men with established hypogonadism,[2] but whether fracture risk is reduced is unknown. In older men with less severe, age-related reductions in gonadal function, the usefulness of testosterone is less certain. Relatively high doses (200 mg of intramuscular testosterone every 2 weeks) is associated with an increase in BMD and strength in older men with low testosterone levels,[25,26] but it's impact on fracture risk has not been examined. Lower doses seem to have lesser effects.[27] Moreover, the long-term risks of testosterone therapy in older men are unknown. Therefore, testosterone replacement therapy is appropriate for the management of the hypogonadal syndrome, but the treatment of osteoporosis in a man with low testosterone levels is most confidently undertaken with a bisphosphonate or with PTH.

REFERENCES

1. Seeman E 2001 Sexual dimorphism in skeletal size, density, and strength. J Clin Endocrinol Metab **86:**4576–4584.
2. Orwoll E, Klein R 2001 Osteoporosis in Men, 2nd ed. Academic Press, San Diego, CA, USA.
3. Seeman E 2002 Pathogenesis of bone fragility in women and men. Lancet **359:**1841–1850.
4. Donaldson LJ, Cook A, Thomson RG 1990 Incidence of fractures in a geographically defined population. J Epi Comm Health **44:**241–245.
5. Ismail AA, Pye SR, Cockerill WC, Lunt M, Silman AJ, Reeve J, Banzer D, Benevolenskaya LI, Bhalla A, Armas JB, Cannata JB, Cooper C, Delmas PD, Dequeker J, Dilsen G, Falch JA, Felsch B, Felsenberg D, Finn JD, Gennari C, Hoszowski K, Jajic I, Janott J, Johnell O, Kanis JA, Kragl G, Vaz AL, Lorenc R, Lyritis G, Marchand F, Masaryk P, Matthis C, Miazgowski T, Naves-Diaz M, Pols HAP, Poor G, Rapido A, Raspe HH, Reid DM, Reisinger W, Scheidt-Nave C, Stepan J, Todd C, Weber K, Woolf AD, O'Neill TW 2002 Incidence of limb fracture across Europe: Results from the European prospective osteoporosis study (EPOS). Osteoporos Int **13:**565–571.
6. Group EPOSE 2002 Incidence of vertebral fracture in Europe: Results from the European prospective osteoporosis study (EPOS). J Bone Miner Res **17:**716–724.
7. Amin S, Felson DT 2001 Osteoporosis in men. Osteoporos Int **27:**19–47.
8. Schwartz AV, Kelsey JL, Maggi S, Tuttleman M, Ho SC, Jonsson PV, Poor G, Sisson de Castro JA, Xu L, Matkin CC, Nelson LM, Heyse SP 1999 International variation in the incidence of hip fractures: Cross-

national project on osteoporosis for the world health organization proram for research aging. Osteoporos Int **9**:242–253.

9. Nguyen TV, Eisman JA, Kelly PJ, Sambrook PN 1996 Risk factors for osteoporotic fractures in elderly men. Am J Epidemiol **144**:258–261.

10. Pietschmann F, Breslau NA, Pak CYC 1992 Reduced vertebral bone density in hypercalciuric nephrolithiasis. J Bone Miner Res **7**:1383–1388.

11. Vanderschueren D, Boonen S, Bouillon R 2000 Osteoporosis and osteoportic fractures in men: A clinical perspective. Baillieres Best Pract Res Clin Endocrinol Metab **14**:299–315.

12. Khosla S, Melton III J 2002 Estrogen and the male skeleton. J Clin Endocrinol Metab **87**:1443–1450.

13. Vanderscheuren D, Boonen S, Bouillon R 1998 Action of androgens versus estrogens in male skeletal homeostasis. Bone **23**:391–394.

14. Orwoll ES 2003 Men, bone and estrogen: Unresolved issues. Osteoporos Int **14**:93–8.

15. Leder BZ, Le Blanc KM, Schoenfeld DA, Eastell R, Finkelstein J 2003 Differential effects of androgens and estrogens on bone turnover in normal men. J Clin Endocrinol Metab **88**:204–210.

16. Falahati-Nini A, Riggs, B.L., Atkinson, E.J., O'Fallon, W.M., Eastell, E., Khosla, S 2000 Relative contributions of testosterone and estrogen in regulating bone resorption and formation in normal elderly men. J Clin Invest **106**:1553–1560.

17. Orwoll ES 2001 Androgens: Basic biology and clinical implication. Calcif Tissue Int **69**:185–188.

18. Nguyen ND, Pongchaiyakul C, Center JR, Eisman JA, Nguyen TV 2005 Identification of high-risk individuals for hip fracture: A 14-year prospective study. J Bone Miner Res **20**:1921–1928.

19. Binkley NC, Schmeer P, Wasnich RD, Lenchik L 2002 What are the criteria by which a densitometric diagnosis of osteoporosis can be made in males and non-caucasians? J Clin Densitom **5**(Suppl):19–27.

20. Shahinian VB, Kuo YF, Freeman JL, Goodwin JS 2005 Risk of fracture after androgen deprivation for prostate cancer. N Engl J Med **352**:154–164.

21. Orwoll E, Ettinger M, Weiss S, Miller P, Kendler D, Graham J, Adami S, Weber K, Lorenc R, Pietschmann P, Vandormael K, Lombardi A 2000 Alendronate for the treatment of osteoporosis in men. N Engl J Med **343**:604–610.

22. Orwoll ES, Scheele WH, Paul S, Adami S, Syversen U, Diez-Perez A, Kaufman JM, Clancy AD, Gaich GA 2003 The effect of teriparatide [human parathyroid hormone (1–34)] therapy on bone density in men with osteoporosis. J Bone Miner Res **18**:9–17.

23. Adachi JD, Bensen WG, Brown J, Hanley D, Hodsman A, Josse R, Kendler DL, Lentle B, Olszynski W, Tenenhouse A, Chines AA 1997 Intermittent etidronate therapy to prevent corticosteroid-induced osteoporosis. N Engl J Med **337**:382–387.

24. Reid DM, Hughes RA, Laan RFJM, Sacco-Gibson NA, Wenderoth DH, S. A., Eusebio RA, Devogelaer JP 2000 Efficacy and safety of daily residronate in the treatment of corticosteroid-induced osteoporosis in men and women: A randomized trial. J Bone Miner Res **15**:1006–1013.

25. Page ST, Amory JK, Bowman FD, Anawalt BD, Matsumoto AM, Bremner WJ, Tenover JL 2005 Exogenous testosterone (T) alone or with finasteride increases physical performance, grip strength, and lean body mass in older men with low serum T. J Clin Endocrinol Metab **90**:1502–1510.

26. Amory JK, Watts NB, Easley KA, Sutton PR, Anawalt BD, Matsumoto AM, Bremner WJ, Tenover JL 2004 Exogenous testosterone or testosterone with finasteride increases bone mineral density in older men with low serum testosterone. J Clin Endocrinol Metab **89**:503–510.

27. Snyder PJ, Peachey H, Berlin JA, Hannoush P, Haddad G, Dlewati A, Santanna J, Loh L, Lenrow DA, Holmes JH, Kapoor SC, Atkinson LE, Strom BL 2000 Effects of testosterone replacement in hypogonadal men. J Clin Endocrinol Metab **85**:2670–2677.

Chapter 54. Juvenile Osteoporosis

Frank Rauch[1] and Nick Bishop[2]

[1]Genetics Unit, Shriners Hospital for Children, Montreal, Quebec, Canada; and [2]Sheffield Children's Hospital, University of Sheffield, Sheffield, United Kingdom

INTRODUCTION

Taken literally, "juvenile osteoporosis" means "osteoporosis in children and adolescents," and thus does not refer to any particular form of osteoporosis in this age group. However, in the scientific literature as well as in clinical practice, the term "juvenile osteoporosis" is usually used to refer to idiopathic juvenile osteoporosis (IJO). This chapter therefore discusses IJO rather than the entirety of osteoporotic conditions that may occur in young people.

Osteoporosis in childhood and adolescence is most commonly secondary to a spectrum of diverse conditions, such as osteogenesis imperfecta (OI), prolonged immobilization, and corticoid excess. Serious diseases such as leukemia also may temporarily present as osteoporosis. If no underlying cause can be detected, IJO is said to be present.

IJO was first described as a separate entity by Dent.[1] four decades ago. According to the classical description, IJO is a self-limiting disease that develops in a prepubertal, previously healthy child, leads to metaphyseal and vertebral compression fractures, and is characterized radiologically by radiolucent areas in the metaphyses of long bones, dubbed "neo-osseous osteoporosis."[2] However, it is clear that there are many children and adolescents who have low bone mass and who sustain fractures after minimal trauma but whose clinical findings do not correspond to the classical description of Dent. Medical science has not yet reserved a particular name for the condition of such patients, but logically, they should be diagnosed with IJO, if no other etiology for low bone mass and fractures is found. Thus, it may be useful to distinguish "classical IJO" (for patients whose presentation is similar to the description of Dent) from "IJO in the wider sense" (for patients who do not match the description of Dent, but nevertheless have unexplained fractures with low bone mass).

Most reviews on the topic state that IJO is an extremely rare disease, because <200 patients have been described in the literature under that label. This is probably because few patients present with the classical picture. However, most clinicians who see children and adolescents with fractures could probably list a few of their patients who have osteoporosis without recognizable etiology. In our clinical settings, IJO is ~10 times less common than OI.

PATHOPHYSIOLOGY

The etiology of IJO is unknown. One study found a normal rise in serum osteocalcin in six IJO patients after calcitriol was administered orally, which was postulated to indicate normal osteoblast function.[3] However, the fact that osteoblasts in this test released normal amounts of osteocalcin into the circulation

Dr. Bishop is a consultant for Procter & Gamble and Novartis. Dr. Rauch has reported no conflicts of interest.

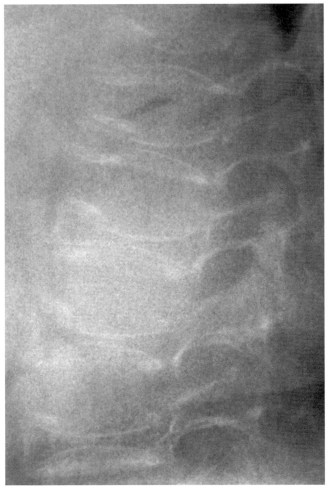

FIG. 1. Lateral lumbar spine radiograph of a 10-year-old girl with IJO. Compression fractures of all vertebral bodies and severe osteoporosis are evident. At the time of this radiograph, lumbar spine areal BMD Z score was −4.9 (at a height Z score of −2.5).

does not necessarily mean that they also deposited matrix on the bone surface in a normal fashion.

Early histomorphometric reports on IJO were limited to static methods to quantify bone metabolism, described single cases, or did not have adequate control groups.[4–8] No conclusive picture emerged from these reports. More recent studies using dynamic histomorphometry showed that IJO is characterized by a markedly reduced activation frequency and therefore low remodeling activity.[9] In addition, the amount of bone formed at each remodeling site was abnormally low. No evidence was found for increased bone resorption. Interestingly, the bone formation defect was limited to bone surfaces that were exposed to the bone marrow environment; no abnormalities were detected in intracortical and periosteal surfaces.[10] These results suggested that, in IJO, impaired osteoblast performance decreases the ability of cancellous bone to adapt to the increasing mechanical needs during growth. This results in load failure at sites where cancellous bone is essential for stability. The initial trigger of the decrease in osteoblast performance remains nevertheless elusive.

Two recent reports indicated that heterozygous mutations in the low density lipoprotein receptor–related protein 5 (LRP5) can result in low bone mass with fractures in some chil-

dren.[11,12] The frequency of such mutations in children with classical IJO as opposed to childhood osteoporosis generally remains to be determined.

CLINICAL FEATURES

Classical IJO typically develops in a prepubertal (mostly between 8 and 12 years of age), previously healthy child of either sex.[13] However, a series of 21 children who were presented as having IJO indicated a mean age at onset of 7 years, with a range of 1–13 years and no sex differences.[14]

Symptoms begin with an insidious onset of pain in the lower back, hips, and feet, and difficulty walking.[1] Knee and ankle pain and fractures of the lower extremities may be present, as well as diffuse muscle weakness. Vertebral compression fractures are frequent, resulting in a short back (Fig. 1). Long bone fractures, mostly at metaphyseal sites, may occur. Physical examination may be entirely normal or reveal thoracolumbar kyphosis or kyphoscoliosis, pigeon chest deformity, loss of height, deformities of the long bones, and limp.

RADIOLOGICAL FEATURES

Children with fully expressed classical IJO present with generalized osteopenia and collapsed or biconcave vertebrae. Disc spaces may be widened asymmetrically because of wedging of the vertebral bodies. Long bones usually have normal diameter and cortical width, unlike the thin, gracile bones of children with OI. The typical radiographic finding in IJO is neo-osseous osteoporosis, a radiolucent band at sites of newly formed metaphyseal bone. This localized metaphyseal weakness can give rise to fractures, often at the distal tibias and adjacent to the knee and hip joints.[7] Nevertheless, "neo-osseous osteoporosis" is not a prerequisite for diagnosing IJO.

TABLE 1. FORMS OF OSTEOPOROSIS IN CHILDREN ACCORDING TO CURRENT LITERATURE

I. Primary
  Osteogenesis imperfecta
  Idiopathic juvenile osteoporosis
II. Secondary
  Endocrine disorders
    Cushing syndrome
    Glucocorticoid therapy
    Thyrotoxicosis
    Gonadal dysgenesis
  Gastrointestinal disorders
    Biliary atresia
    Glycogen storage disease type 1
    Chronic hepatitis
    Malabsorption syndromes
  Inborn errors of metabolism
    Homocystinuria
  Other disorders
    Immobilization
    Anticonvulsant therapy
    Acute lymphoblastic leukemia
    Anorexia nervosa
    Thalassemia
    Severe congenital neutropenia
    Inflammatory bowel disease
    Cystic fibrosis

TABLE 2. DIFFERENTIAL DIAGNOSIS BETWEEN IJO AND OI TYPE I

	IJO	OI type I
Family history	Negative	Often positive
Onset	Late prepubertal	Birth or soon after
Duration	1–5 years	Lifelong
Clinical findings	Metaphyseal fractures	Long bone diaphyseal fractures
	No signs of connective tissue involvement	Blue sclerae, joint hyperlaxity, sometimes abnormal dentition
	Abnormal gait	
Growth rate	Normal	Normal or low
Radiologic findings	Vertebral compression fractures; long bones: predominantly metaphyseal involvement (neo-osseous osteoporosis)	Vertebral compression fractures; "narrow bones" (low diameter of diaphyses)
	No wormian bones	Wormian bones (skull)
Bone biopsy	Decreased bone turnover	Increased bone turnover
	Normal amount of osteocytes	Hyperosteocytosis
Genetic testing	LRP5 mutations in some patients	Mutations affecting collagen type I in most patients

BIOCHEMICAL FINDINGS

Biochemical studies of bone and mineral metabolism have not detected any consistent abnormality in children with IJO.[14–16]

BONE BIOPSY

Iliac bone biopsy specimens show low trabecular bone volume but largely preserved core width (i.e., a normal outer size of the biopsy specimen) and cortical width.[9,10] Tetracycline double-labeling reveals a low extent of mineralizing surface (a sign of decreased remodeling activity) and low mineral apposition rate (a sign of weakness of the individual osteoblast team at a remodeling site). There is no indication of a mineralization defect. Osteoclasts are normal in appearance and number.

DIFFERENTIAL DIAGNOSIS

The diagnosis of IJO is made by the exclusion of known etiologies for low bone mass and fractures. The list of conditions that may be associated with bone fragility in children and adolescents is rather long (Table 1). The exclusion of most of these disorders is usually not difficult. The most frequent diagnostic problem facing a clinician is probably to separate IJO from OI type I and adaptational problems during growth.

Table 2 presents the typical distinguishing features between IJO and OI type I. Apart from bone fragility and low bone mass, most patients with OI type I have associated extraskeletal connective tissue signs, such as bluish or grayish sclera, dentinogenesis imperfecta, joint hyperlaxity and Wormian bones (on skull X-rays). However, the extraskeletal involvement can be absent or too subtle to be clinically recognizable in some OI patients. In this situation, genetic analysis of the genes that code for the two collagen type Iα chains (COL1A1 and COL1A2) can be helpful. Mutations affecting a glycine residue in either gene or those leading to a quantitative defect in COL1A1 expression are diagnostic of OI (this issue was somewhat obfuscated by a case report of two brothers who had glycine mutations in the COL1A2 gene and therefore suffered from OI, but were presented as having IJO[17]). A negative collagen type I mutation analysis does not rule out OI, because false negative results can occur. LRP5 sequencing may be informative in some cases.

An iliac bone biopsy, preferably after tetracycline double-labeling, may also contribute to clarifying the diagnosis. Microscopically, a "lack of activity" is usually noted in IJO, whereas there is "hypercellularity" in OI. In histomorphometric terms, this translates into low activation frequency and bone surface based remodeling parameters in IJO and an increase in these values in OI. Also, hyperosteocytosis is a common feature in OI, whereas the amount of osteocytes seems to be normal in IJO.

Fractures and low bone mass may also occur in healthy prepubertal children. Indeed, during late prepuberty and early puberty, fracture rates are almost as high as in postmenopausal women.[18–20] Similar to IJO, such fractures frequently involve metaphyseal bone sites, especially the distal radius. This may reflect problems in the adaptation of the skeleton, in particular the metaphyseal cortex, to the increasing mechanical needs during growth.[21] Growing children and adolescents who had a few forearm fractures and who have borderline low areal BMD at the spine are frequently encountered in pediatric bone clinics. The medical literature is silent as to the distinction between IJO and patients who may have an "adaptational bone problem." We propose that IJO should only be diagnosed when vertebral compression fractures are present (with or without extremity fractures).

TREATMENT

There is no treatment with proven benefit to the patient. The effect of any kind of medical intervention is difficult to judge in IJO, because the disease is rare, has a variable course, and usually resolves without treatment. Nevertheless, given the current enthusiasm for pediatric bisphosphonate treatment, many IJO patients probably are receiving treatment with such drugs. A number of case reports have described increasing BMD and clinical improvement after treatment with bisphosphonates was started.[22–24] In any case, attempts at medical therapies should complement rather than replace orthopedic and rehabilitative measures, such as physiotherapy. Review at 6-month intervals is also warranted in children not receiving bisphosphonates. Changes in the shape of the spine should be monitored carefully, and early referral to a specialist pediatric spine surgeon should be made in any progressive cases.

PROGNOSIS

The disease process is only active in growing children, and spontaneous recovery is the rule after 3–5 years of evolution.[14] However, in some of the most severe cases reported to date, deformities and severe functional impairment persisted, which left them wheelchair bound and with cardiorespiratory abnormalities.[1,14]

REFERENCES

1. Dent CE, Friedman M 1965 Idiopathic juvenile osteoporosis. Q J Med 34:177–210.

2. Dent CE 1977 Osteoporosis in childhood. Postgrad Med J **53:**450–457.
3. Bertelloni S, Baroncelli GI, Di Nero G, Saggese G 1992 Idiopathic juvenile osteoporosis: Evidence of normal osteoblast function by 1,25-dihydroxyvitamin D3 stimulation test. Calcif Tissue Int **51:**20–23.
4. Cloutier MD, Hayles AB, Riggs BL, Jowsey J, Bickel WH 1967 Juvenile osteoporosis: Report of a case including a description of some metabolic and microradiographic studies. Pediatrics **40:**649–655.
5. Gooding CA, Ball JH 1969 Idiopathic juvenile osteoporosis. Radiology **93:**1349–1350.
6. Jowsey J, Johnson KA 1972 Juvenile osteoporosis: Bone findings in seven patients. J Pediatr **81:**511–517.
7. Smith R 1980 Idiopathic osteoporosis in the young. J Bone Joint Surg Br **62:**417–427.
8. Evans RA, Dunstan CR, Hills E 1983 Bone metabolism in idiopathic juvenile osteoporosis: A case report. Calcif Tissue Int **35:**5–8.
9. Rauch F, Travers R, Norman ME, Taylor A, Parfitt AM, Glorieux FH 2000 Deficient bone formation in idiopathic juvenile osteoporosis: A histomorphometric study of cancellous iliac bone. J Bone Miner Res **15:**957–963.
10. Rauch F, Travers R, Norman ME, Taylor A, Parfitt AM, Glorieux FH 2002 The bone formation defect in idiopathic juvenile osteoporosis is surface-specific. Bone **31:**85–89.
11. Toomes C, Bottomley HM, Jackson RM, Towns KV, Scott S, Mackey DA, Craig JE, Jiang L, Yang Z, Trembath R, Woodruff G, Gregory-Evans CY, Gregory-Evans K, Parker MJ, Black GC, Downey LM, Zhang K, Inglehearn CF 2004 Mutations in LRP5 or FZD4 underlie the common familial exudative vitreoretinopathy locus on chromosome 11q. Am J Hum Genet **74:**721–730.
12. Hartikka H, Makitie O, Mannikko M, Doria AS, Daneman A, Cole WG, Ala-Kokko L, Sochett EB 2005 Heterozygous mutations in the LDL receptor-related protein 5 (LRP5) gene are associated with primary osteoporosis in children. J Bone Miner Res **20:**783–789.
13. Teotia M, Teotia SP, Singh RK 1979 Idiopathic juvenile osteoporosis. Am J Dis Child **133:**894–900.
14. Smith R 1995 Idiopathic juvenile osteoporosis: Experience of twenty-one patients. Br J Rheumatol **34:**68–77.
15. Saggese G, Bertelloni S, Baroncelli GI, Perri G, Calderazzi A 1991 Mineral metabolism and calcitriol therapy in idiopathic juvenile osteoporosis. Am J Dis Child **145:**457–462.
16. Saggese G, Bertelloni S, Baroncelli GI, Di Nero G 1992 Serum levels of carboxyterminal propeptide of type I procollagen in healthy children from 1st year of life to adulthood and in metabolic bone diseases. Eur J Pediatr **151:**764–768.
17. Dawson PA, Kelly TE, Marini JC 1999 Extension of phenotype associated with structural mutations in type I collagen: Siblings with juvenile osteoporosis have an alpha2(I)Gly436 → Arg substitution. J Bone Miner Res **14:**449–455.
18. Landin LA 1997 Epidemiology of children's fractures. J Pediatr Orthop B **6:**79–83.
19. Cooper C, Dennison EM, Leufkens HG, Bishop N, van Staa TP 2004 Epidemiology of childhood fractures in Britain: A study using the general practice research database. J Bone Miner Res **19:**1976–1981.
20. Khosla S, Melton LJ III, Dekutoski MB, Achenbach SJ, Oberg AL, Riggs BL 2003 Incidence of childhood distal forearm fractures over 30 years: A population-based study. JAMA **290:**1479–1485.
21. Rauch F, Neu C, Manz F, Schoenau E 2001 The development of metaphyseal cortex—implications for distal radius fractures during growth. J Bone Miner Res **16:**1547–1555.
22. Hoekman K, Papapoulos SE, Peters AC, Bijvoet OL 1985 Characteristics and bisphosphonate treatment of a patient with juvenile osteoporosis. J Clin Endocrinol Metab **61:**952–956.
23. Brumsen C, Hamdy NA, Papapoulos SE 1997 Long-term effects of bisphosphonates on the growing skeleton. Studies of young patients with severe osteoporosis. Medicine (Baltimore) **76:**266–283.
24. Kauffman RP, Overton TH, Shiflett M, Jennings JC 2001 Osteoporosis in children and adolescent girls: Case report of idiopathic juvenile osteoporosis and review of the literature. Obstet Gynecol Surv **56:**492–504.

Chapter 55. Glucocorticoid-Induced Osteoporosis

Philip N. Sambrook

Institute of Bone and Joint Research, University of Sydney, Sydney, Australia

INTRODUCTION

Glucocorticoids (GCs) are widely used and effective agents for many inflammatory diseases, but bone loss and microarchitectural change causing increased fracture risk is a common problem associated with their long-term use. GC-induced osteoporosis (GIO) is the most common cause of secondary osteoporosis. GCs increase the risk of fracture generally throughout the skeleton, but especially in trabecular rich sites such as the spine and ribs. Glucocorticoid bone loss can now be effectively prevented or reversed by a number of proven therapies, especially the bisphosphonates.

CLINICAL FEATURES

Patients receiving pharmacologic doses of GCs commonly have a distinct clinical picture that includes centripetal obesity with peripheral subcutaneous fat atrophy, thinning of the skin with easy bruising, proximal muscle weakness, and hyperglycemia. It is unclear whether patients with these clinical manifestations are at higher risk of fracture. Moreover, there are quite marked interindividual differences in sensitivity to GCs, and some patients treated with GCs seem to lose little bone (as assessed by densitometry).

The author has reported no conflicts of interest.

PATHOPHYSIOLOGY

Most of the biological activities of GCs are mediated through binding with the GC receptor (GR). By this genomic mechanism, lipophilic GC passes across the cell membrane, attaches to the cytosolic GR, and after dimerization, the GR binds to conserved sequence motifs (called GC response elements [GREs]) to positively or negatively regulate specific gene transcription.[1] In addition, certain biological activities of GCs may be mediated through other transcription factors, such as activated protein 1 (AP-1) and NF-κB, independent of GR binding to DNA.[1] It seems likely that genetic variations in the GR may account for some of the differences in expression of GCs effects between individuals.[2]

Direct Effects on Bone Remodeling

Bone Formation. GCs affect bone through multiple pathways, influencing both bone formation and resorption (Fig. 1), but the most important effects seem to be a direct inhibitory effect on bone formation that has been well documented in histomorphometric studies.[3] For the most part, the decreased bone formation is caused by direct effects on cells of the osteoblastic lineage. GCs have complex effects on gene expression in bone cells, dependent on the stage of osteoblast growth and differentiation.[4] GCs decrease replication and repress type I collagen gene expression by osteoblasts by decreasing the rates of

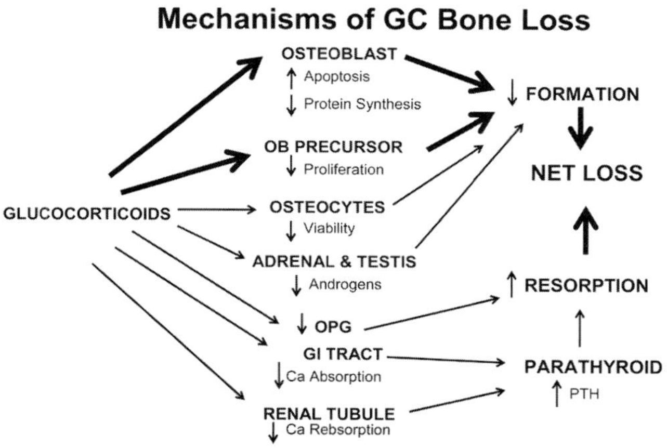

Mechanisms of GC Bone Loss

FIG. 1. Schematic diagram of effects of GCs on bone metabolism.

transcription and destabilizing type1 collagen mRNA. GCs also have complex effects on collagen degradation and regulate the synthesis of matrix metalloproteinases.

In addition, GCs affect the synthesis, release, receptor binding, or binding proteins of locally produced IGFs, leading to indirect effects on skeletal cells. Indeed IGF-I and IGF-II are among the most important local regulators of bone cell function because of their abundance and anabolic actions to increase type I collagen synthesis by the osteoblast and hence bone formation. GCs decrease IGF-I synthesis in osteoblasts by transcription mechanisms and inhibit IGF-II receptor expression in osteoblasts.[4,5] GCs have also been shown to decrease mRNA levels encoding for osteoblast products such as osteocalcin.

Enhanced osteoblast and osteocyte apoptosis has also been implicated as an important mechanism of GIO.[5] GCs have been shown to reduce the birth rate of osteoblasts and osteoclasts and cause earlier death of osteoblasts[5] and reduce osteocyte viability.[6]

Bone Resorption. Increased bone resorption is probably only a temporary phenomenon during the first 6 or 12 months of GC therapy and is in part caused by the effects of GCs on osteoprotegerin and its ligand, RANKL.[7] GCs increase the expression of RANKL and decrease osteoprotegerin expression in osteoblasts, leading to postponement of osteoclast apoptosis. In some patients, secondary hyperparathyroidism may also increase bone turnover and expand the remodeling space, but this does not usually persist. With long-term GC use, bone turnover is actually reduced.

PTH, Vitamin D, and Calcium Absorption. Another effect of GCs is to decrease intestinal absorption of calcium.[8,9] GCs increase urinary phosphate and calcium loss by direct effects on the kidney,[10–12] which, together with impaired calcium absorption, may lead to secondary hyperparathyroidism.[10] Numerous studies have looked for alterations in circulating vitamin D metabolites in patients receiving exogenous GCs or with Cushing's syndrome. Long-term excess GCs have been reported to produce varied effects on circulating vitamin D metabolites such as 25(OH)D or 1,25(OH)$_2$D, including reductions,[9,13,14] no change,[15–17] or small increases.[18,19] Recent reviews suggest a minor role for hyperparathyroidism in GIO[20] and little evidence that changes in vitamin D metabolism are involved in the pathophysiology of GIO.[21]

Gonadal Hormones. Serum concentrations of estradiol, estrone, dehydroepiandrosterone sulfate, and progesterone are decreased in women taking GCs,[22] and testosterone levels are decreased in

men taking GCs.[11] These changes in sex steroid production have indirect effects that also lead to decreased bone formation.

Effects on Microarchitecture

At any time during the lifespan of an osteoid seam, the number of osteoblasts depends both on the number initially assembled and the number that have escaped entrapment as osteocytes or death by apoptosis. With fewer cycles of remodeling and significant loss after each remodeling cycle, progressive degradation of microarchitecture occurs.

These effects are not only associated with trabecular thinning, but also perforation and major loss of trabecular connectivity in some patients,[23] indicating that changes in microarchitecture may be just as important as loss of bone mass or BMD in causing fractures in GC-treated patients.

Osteonecrosis

Osteonecrosis, also known as avascular necrosis, is a serious complication of GC treatment. Osteonecrosis most commonly occurs in the proximal femur, the head of the humerus, and the distal femur. Patients often complain of pain when they use the affected joint. The etiology of osteonecrosis is unclear but may be related to fat emboli,[24] oxidation injury,[25] and enhanced osteocyte apoptosis.[26] Because GCs also reduce the number of osteoblasts, the precursor to the osteocyte, the apoptotic osteocytes cannot be replaced, and changes in the bone structure may result in bone death or osteonecrosis.

Effects on Muscles

Loss of muscle mass and decreased muscle strength is a common side effect of GCs.[27] Muscle biopsy specimens performed in GC-treated patients show atrophy of type II muscle fibers and a decrease in the number of type I fibers in the presence of normal muscle enzymes.[28] Patients on GCs often complain of muscle pain and weakness and become less active. The combination of loss of muscle strength and reduced activity may contribute to glucocorticoid induced bone loss.[29]

EPIDEMIOLOGY

The risk of developing osteoporosis with GC therapy remains unclear but has been reported to occur in up to 50% of persons who require long-term therapy. Fractures can occur rapidly; however, prospective epidemiological fracture data in GC bone loss are generally limited. A large retrospective cohort study of 244,236 subjects receiving GCs identified in a primary care registry in the United Kingdom and matched with 244,235 control patients[30] reported a relative risk of clinical vertebral fracture during oral GC therapy to be 2.6, with the relative risk for hip fracture being 1.6 and for nonvertebral fracture being 1.3. Fracture risk was related to GCs dose,[30] and when GCs were discontinued, the fracture risk seemed to return to baseline.

The overall prevalence of vertebral fracture with GCs in cross-sectional studies is ~28%.[31,32] However, estimates of vertebral fracture incidence with GCs, derived from the calcium-treated control arms of randomized trials,[33–35] indicate they are highest in postmenopausal women and range from 13% to 22% in the first year of therapy. The incidence of vertebral fractures seems to be much lower in premenopausal women and men.

From a clinical point of view, fracture risk with GCs is determined by several factors[36] including the following:

- BMD, both the initial BMD before GC therapy and the amount of subsequent GC-induced loss; for example, bone loss of 10% from a baseline BMD of a premeno-

Timing of Intervention in Glucocorticoid Bone Loss

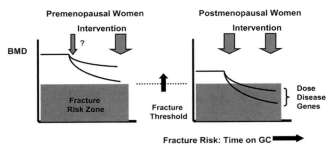

FIG. 2. Schematic diagram of how the degree of bone loss and risk of fracture from GCs varies according to age, dose, and underlying disease. The case for early intervention (primary prevention) is strongest in postmenopausal women and subjects with low BMD. Because fracture risk is a function of time on GCs, secondary prevention is appropriate to consider in men and pre- and postmenopausal women on long-term GCs with low BMD.

pausal woman creates a different fracture risk to bone loss of 10% from the BMD seen in a postmenopausal woman; Fig. 2). The greatest risk of vertebral fracture is in older postmenopausal women, and age is an independent risk factor for vertebral fracture.[31]

- glucocorticoid dose, because bone loss is dependent on cumulative and daily dosage.[30]
- duration of exposure (i.e., a short course of GCs will cause bone loss that is reversible on cessation, but long-term GCs therapy causes a sustained reduction in BMD increasing the likelihood that a fracture will occur eventually).
- the underlying disease for which GCs are used; these conditions may be independently associated with increased fracture risk.[37,38]

Although GIO is dose dependent, "low-dose" GCs have been reported to cause rapid initial bone loss in some patients. A longitudinal study observed loss averaging 9.5% over 20 weeks from spinal trabecular bone in patients receiving a mean dose of 7.5 mg prednisone/day.[39]

Inhaled steroids are less likely to have systemic effects than oral GCs, but in higher doses result in adrenal suppression and reduced BMD. In a large cross-sectional study in patients receiving long-term inhaled GCs for asthma, a significant inverse relationship between GC dose and duration of therapy and BMD at the spine and hip was observed.[40] An analysis of 170,818 inhaled GCs users in the primary care registry in the United Kingdom matched against an equal number of controls[41] reported that the relative risk of vertebral, hip, and nonvertebral fracture was 1.5, 1.2, and 1.2, respectively. No differences were found between inhaled and bronchodilator groups, and some of the increased risk related to the underlying disease rather than inhaled GCs.

INVESTIGATIONS

BMD

Effects of GCs on BMD can be measured precisely and accurately using DXA of the lumbar spine, hip, and distal forearm or QCT for the lumbar spine. The earliest changes of GC-induced bone loss are seen in the lumbar spine because of its high content of trabecular bone. Because the radiation exposure with QCT is higher than with DXA, it is recommended that physicians obtain a DXA measurement of the lumbar spine (antero-posterior scan) and femoral neck when

subjects first start GC treatment or soon thereafter. Lateral DXA measurement is not recommended because of positioning issues and its poorer precision and accuracy.

Some studies suggested that vertebral fractures caused by GCs occur at a higher BMD values than that observed in other types of osteoporosis.[32,42–44] In a study comparing 32 asthma patients with GC-related vertebral fractures and 55 postmenopausal patients with vertebral fractures, fracture thresholds were 1.17 and 0.98 g/cm^2, respectively.[42] Another study examined vertebral deformity prevalence in patients with rheumatoid arthritis treated with low-dose GCs. There was a 0.8 SD reduction in BMD values but a 6-fold increase in the prevalence of vertebral fractures compared with age-matched controls.[32] Other studies have similarly reported higher vertebral fracture risks in pre- and postmenopausal women taking GCs for given BMD levels.[43,44] In contrast, one study reported no increased risk of vertebral fracture in GC-treated patients compared with other causes of osteoporosis when cumulative fracture prevalence was compared with BMD.[45] If fracture risk is increased at higher BMD levels than in postmenopausal osteoporosis, and it can be anticipated that, in an individual starting GC therapy, BMD may drop by up to 10%, interventions may be appropriate at T score thresholds above the more conventional value of −2.5 usually applied in postmenopausal osteoporosis.

Bone loss with GCs is most rapid in the first 12–18 months after starting therapy, followed by a slower decline in patients on chronic GCs.[46–48] When high-dose GCs are used, rates of spinal bone loss in the spine range between 5% and 10% per year. Therefore, repeat DXA scans are recommended at 12-month intervals.

In patients on chronic low-dose therapy, continuing but much slower or even no bone loss may occur[49]; however, the overall reduction in BMD and change in microarchitecture with chronic GC therapy still increases the likelihood that a fracture will occur eventually. GC bone loss seems reversible, at least in part, in young patients, and recovery in BMD has been reported after successful treatment of Cushings syndrome.[50]

Biochemical Markers

The effects of GCs on bone metabolism are reflected in marked changes in biochemical markers of bone turnover.[10,51,52] Markers of bone formation such as serum osteocalcin fall within a few hours of treatment with GCs to as low as 30% of their pretreatment level,[52] with the degree of reduction significantly related to GC dose. Markers of bone resorption have been shown to rise after acute GC administration.[10] However, the role of such markers in diagnosis and management remains unclear.

Histomorphometry

Histomorphometry is mainly used as a research tool. Bone biopsy specimens from the iliac crest in GC-treated patients show a low mineral apposition rate, a reduction on mean trabecular wall thickness, and a decrease in the number of osteoid seams with a resultant decrease in bone volume.[53] Although an increase in eroded surface is observed with GCs compared with postmenopausal bone loss,[54] this is the result of the long delay between completion of resorption and onset of formation in each basic multicellular unit (BMU) rather than an actual increase bone resorption.[55] Moreover, the activation frequency, the best index of the overall degree of bone remodeling, is decreased with chronic GC therapy. In a serial histomorphometric study, treatment with prednisone (10–25 mg/day) resulted in a 27.1% decrease in iliac crest cancellous bone volume by 6 months; however, no further decline was observed at rebiopsy after 19 months.[48]

PREVENTION AND TREATMENT

Because the most rapid bone loss occurs in the first 6–12 months in patients commencing high-dose GCs, it is important to consider two different therapeutic situations: (1) primary prevention in patients starting GCs who have not yet lost bone and (2) treatment (or secondary prevention) in patients on chronic GCs who will generally have some significant degree of existing GC-related bone loss, with or without fractures.

Current therapeutic approaches to GC-induced bone loss include the following:

- use of the lowest dose possible
- minimize lifestyle risk factors (e.g., smoking and low dietary calcium intake)
- consider individualized exercise programs with the help of a physical therapist to prevent muscle loss and falls
- use of agents that have been studied for potential benefit, including antiresorptives (calcium, vitamin D and its metabolites, calcitonin, hormone replacement therapy, and bisphosphonates) and agents that stimulate bone formation such as PTH

Antiresorptive agents such as the bisphosphonates have generally shown the most consistent efficacy in clinical trials of GIO. Although the effects of GCs on bone formation seem more important than those on bone resorption, antiresorptives will reduce GC effects on bone remodeling and act to preserve microarchitecture. Bisphosphonates may also act to decrease GC-induced apoptosis.[56]

Hormone Replacement

Hormone replacement therapy is often recommended for GC-treated patients, but the evidence supporting its use is limited. There have been only two controlled trials in men. In a cross-over study of 15 men receiving chronic GCs for asthma, after 12 months, testosterone 250 mg/month increased lumbar BMD by 5% compared with the calcium group, which had no significant loss.[57] Similarly, testosterone was superior to both nandrolone and placebo in a trial of 51 men increasing lumbar BMD by 5.6% over 12 months.[58] In a randomized controlled trial in postmenopausal women with rheumatoid arthritis, which included a subgroup receiving chronic low-dose GCs, estrogen increased lumbar BMD by 3.8% over 2 years compared with 0.6% loss in the calcium-treated control group.[59] In a retrospective study, examining postmenopausal women treated with prednisone, spinal BMD was significantly higher in those women who were given estrogen and progesterone replacement compared with those not receiving hormone replacement.[60]

Calcium and Vitamin D

With respect to calcium, several studies suggest a benefit of calcium supplementation for secondary prevention in patients receiving chronic low-dose GCs. However, primary prevention trials in patients starting GCs, where calcium alone was used in the control arm, have observed rapid rates of loss.[61,62] It is therefore likely that calcium alone is not sufficient to prevent rapid bone loss in most patients starting high-dose GCs.

Calcium is often used in combination with vitamin D in GIO based on older studies that measured only forearm bone mass and studied patients on chronic GC treatment.[63] In a primary prevention study comparing 1000 mg calcium daily plus 50,000 U vitamin D weekly against placebo over 3 years in 62 patients starting GCs,[47] bone loss at the lumbar spine was not significantly different between calcium plus vitamin D group and placebo. However, a secondary prevention study in patients receiving chronic low-dose GCs for rheumatoid arthritis[64] observed an annual spinal loss of 2.0% in placebo-treated patients compared with 0.7% gain in calcium/vitamin D$_3$-treated patients (1000 mg plus 500 IU/day, respectively).

Vitamin D is sometimes used to refer to both the calciferols and active metabolites, but they have different therapeutic effects. The most commonly used active hormonal forms of vitamin D are calcitriol (1,25-dihydroxyvitamin D) and alfacalcidol (1α-hydroxyvitamin D). One study examined the effect of 12 months of calcium, calcitriol, or calcitonin in 103 patients starting GCs.[61] Patients treated with calcium lost bone rapidly at the lumbar spine (−4.3% in the first year), whereas patients treated with either calcitriol or calcitriol plus calcitonin lost at a much reduced rate (−1.3% and −0.2% per year, respectively). Both groups were significantly different from the calcium group. Another randomized double-blind controlled trial in 145 patients starting GCs compared alfacalcidol with calcium.[65] After 12 months, the change in spinal BMD with alfacalcidol was +0.4% compared with −5.7% with calcium. Hypercalcemia occurred in only 6.7% of alfacalcidol-treated patients[65] compared with 25% with calcitriol.[66] Whether active vitamin D metabolites have any advantage over simple vitamin D in the treatment of established GIO remains controversial with both positive and negative studies.[66–68]

Calcitonin

In patients receiving chronic GCs, salmon calcitonin has been reported to improve forearm bone mass in chronic obstructive lung disease, attenuate vertebral bone loss in sarcoidosis, and increase lumbar BMD in asthmatics.[69–71] Calcitonin has been studied in more recent trials in patients starting GCs.[61,72,73] In two primary prevention studies, there was a trend but no statistically significant additional benefit of adding calcitonin to calcitriol or cholecalciferol.[61,73]

Bisphosphonates

The first proper trial of bisphosphonates in GIO was with an oral formulation of pamidronate.[74] Since then, numerous trials have examined the efficacy of bisphosphonates on GC-induced bone loss with positive results. In a primary prevention study of 141 patients commencing GCs who received prophylaxis with either cyclical etidronate or 500 mg of calcium,[33] mean lumbar BMD change with etidronate was +0.6% compared with −3.2% in the calcium group at the end of 12 months. For postmenopausal women only, there was a significant difference in the incidence of new vertebral fractures favoring etidronate (21.9% versus 3.2%). In a secondary prevention study in 37 postmenopausal women who received GCs for at least 3 months, the mean change in lumbar BMD was +4.9% with etidronate versus −2.4% with placebo over 2 years, which was statistically significant.[75] There were no statistically significant differences for the femoral neck BMD or serum and urinary markers of turnover.

The combined results of two trials with alendronate in 477 GC-treated subjects who also received prophylaxis with calcium/vitamin D (800–1000 mg daily plus 250–500 IU daily, respectively) have been reported.[34] Patients were stratified according to their duration of prior GC treatment. Over 12 months of follow-up, the mean change in lumbar spine BMD in patients who received GCs for <4 months was +3.0% for alendronate 10 mg/day compared with −1% in the placebo group. In those who had received chronic GCs (>12 months), the increase with alendronate was +2.8% but also was +0.2% for calcium. These latter data suggest calcium/vitamin D is able to prevent further bone loss in patients on chronic low-dose GCs (secondary prevention). A posthoc analysis of incident

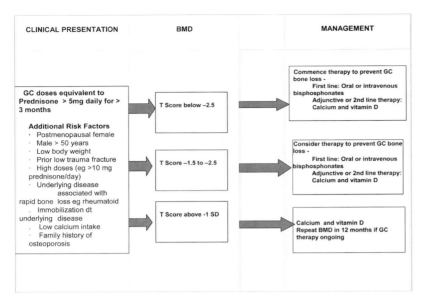

CLINICAL PRESENTATION	BMD	MANAGEMENT

GC doses equivalent to Prednisone > 5mg daily for > 3 months

Additional Risk Factors
· Postmenopausal female
· Male > 50 years
· Low body weight
· Prior low trauma fracture
· High doses (eg >10 mg prednisone/day)
· Underlying disease associated with rapid bone loss eg rheumatoid
. Immobilization dt underlying disease
. Low calcium intake
· Family history of osteoporosis

T Score below –2.5

Commence therapy to prevent GC bone loss -
First line: Oral or intravenous bisphosphonates
Adjunctive or 2nd line therapy: Calcium and vitamin D

T Score –1.5 to –2.5

Consider therapy to prevent GC bone loss -
First line: Oral or intravenous bisphosphonates
Adjunctive or 2nd line therapy: Calcium and vitamin D

T Score above -1 SD

Calcium and vitamin D
Repeat BMD in 12 months if GC therapy ongoing

FIG. 3. Algorithm for the diagnosis and management of GIO.

vertebral fractures favored alendronate in postmenopausal women (13% versus 4.4%). The effect of alendronate on bone histomorphometry has been assessed in 88 patients (52 women and 36 men; 22–75 years of age) from the above studies.[76] Iliac bone biopsy specimens were obtained after tetracycline double-labeling at the end of the first year of therapy. Osteoid thickness and volume were significantly lower in alendronate-treated patients, irrespective of the dose; however, mineral apposition rate was not altered. Significant decreases of mineralizing surfaces, activation frequency, and bone formation rate were also noted with alendronate treatment.

The results of a primary prevention trial with risedronate compared with calcium 500 mg daily in 224 GC-treated subjects have been reported.[62] Risedronate 5 mg daily prevented spinal bone loss (+0.6%) compared with calcium (−2.8%) over 12 months. Incident vertebral fracture rates were 17.3% with calcium and 5.7% for risedronate 5 mg ($p = 0.072$). Vertebral fractures were only seen in postmenopausal women and men but not in premenopausal women. The effects of risedronate in 290 patients receiving chronic GC treatment (prednisone $\geq$ 7.5 mg/day for $\geq$6 months) have also been reported.[35] Approximately one third of patients had vertebral fractures at baseline. The control group, who were treated with calcium 1000 mg and vitamin D 400 IU daily, maintained a stable BMD over 12 months. However, treatment with risedronate 5 mg/day significantly increased lumbar spine (+2.9%) and femoral neck (+1.8%) BMD. A pooling of the risedronate prevention and treatment studies showed a significant reduction in vertebral fractures after 1 year.[77]

Intermittent intravenous pamidronate and ibandronate have has also been reported as effective alternatives to oral bisphosphonates in GIO.[78,79]

PTH

PTH has the potential to increase osteoblast numbers by increasing both their replication rate and by decreasing apoptosis. A randomized controlled trial of PTH performed in postmenopausal women with GIO[80] reported that patients treated with PTH and estrogen had significant increases in bone mass (+35% for lumbar spine by QCT, +11% for lumbar spine by DXA, 1% hip) after 12 months, with no changes observed in the estrogen alone group. All study patients were followed for an additional year after the PTH was discontinued, and total hip and femoral neck bone mass

increased ~5% above baseline levels.[81] Treatment with PTH resulted in a dramatic increase in biochemical markers of bone turnover. Osteocalcin increased >150% above baseline levels within 1 month of starting the therapy and remained elevated for the remainder of the treatment period. Bone resorption increased to the same levels as osteocalcin after 6 months of therapy. The study was not powered to determine if PTH could reduce new vertebral fractures in GIO.

SUMMARY

Based on the summary evidence reviewed above, an algorithm for the diagnosis and management of GIO is shown in Fig. 3. Evidence from randomized controlled trials suggests that postmenopausal women receiving GC are at the greatest risk of rapid bone loss and consequent vertebral fracture and should be actively considered for prophylactic measures. In men and premenopausal women receiving GCs, the need to use osteoporosis prophylaxis is less straightforward and will depend on a number of factors including BMD, anticipated dose, duration of GCs, and other risk factors. Based on available evidence, the first choice for prevention would be a potent oral bisphosphonate such as alendronate or risedronate. In patients intolerant of oral bisphosphonates, intravenous bisphosphonates should be considered. Active vitamin D metabolites should be considered as second line therapy. Calcium alone seems unable to prevent rapid bone loss in patients starting GCs, but calcium plus vitamin D is appropriate adjunctive therapy. Testosterone should be considered in men if hypogonadism is present. Most trial data are limited to 1–2 years, but it is likely that prophylactic therapy needs to be continued while patients continue significant doses of GC therapy. In patients receiving chronic low-dose GCs, treatment with calcium and vitamin D may be sufficient to prevent further bone loss, but if BMD is substantially reduced, a bisphosphonate should be used or PTH considered, because fracture risk is a function of multiple factors including the degree of reduction in BMD and the duration of exposure to GCs.

REFERENCES

1. Buttergereit F, Straub RH, Wehling M, Burmester GR 2004 Glucocorticoids in the treatment of rheumatic diseases—an update on mechanism of action. Arthritis Rheum 50:3408–3417.

2. van Rossum EF, Lamberts SW 2004 Polymorphisms in the glucocorticoid receptor gene and their associations with metabolic parameters and body composition. Rec Prog Horm Res 59:333–357.

3. Dalle Carbonare L, Arlot ME, Chavassieux PM, Roux JP, Portero NR, Meunier PJ 2001 Comparison of trabecular bone microarchitecture and remodeling in glucocorticoid-induced and postmenopausal osteoporosis. J Bone Miner Res 16:97–103.

4. Canalis E, Bilezikian JP, Angeli A, Giustina A 2004 Perspectives on glucocorticoid-induced osteoporosis. Bone 34:593–598.

5. Weinstein RS, Jilka RL, Parfitt AF, Manalagas SC 1998 Inhibition of osteoblastogenesis and promotion of apoptosis of osteoblasts and osteocytes by glucocorticoids. J Clin Invest 102:272–282.

6. Sambrook PN, Hughes DR, Nelson AE, Robinson BG, Mason RS 2003 Osteocyte viability with glucocorticoid therapy: Relation to histomorphometry. Ann Rheum Dis 62:1215–1217.

7. Hofbauer L, Gori F, Riggs BL, Lacey DL, Dunstan CR, Spelsberg TC, Khosla S 1999 Stimulation of osteoprotegerin ligand and inhibition of osteoprotegerin production by glucocorticoids in human osteoblastic lineage cells: Potential paracrine mechanisms of glucocorticoid-induced osteoporosis. Endocrinology 140:4382–89.

8. Klein RG, Arnaud SB, Gallagher JC, DeLuca HF, Riggs BL 1977 Intestinal calcium absorption in exogenous hypercortisolism: Role of 25-hydroxyvitamin D and glucocorticoid dose. J Clin Invest 60:253–259.

9. Morris HA, Need AG, O'Loughlin PD, Horowitz M, Bridges A, Nordin BE 1990 Malabsorption of calcium in corticosteroid-induced osteoporosis. Calcif Tiss Int 46:305–308.

10. Cosman F, Nieves J, Herbert J, Shen V, Lindsay R 1994 High-dose glucocorticoids in multiple sclerosis patients exert direct effects on the kidney and skeleton. J Bone Miner Res 9:1097–1105.

11. Reid IR, France JT, Pybus J, Ibbertson HK 1985 Low plasma testosterone levels in glucocorticoid treated male patients. BMJ 291:574.

12. Reid IR, Ibbertson HK 1987 Evidence of decreased tubular resorption of calcium in glucocorticoid treated asthmatics. Horm Res 27:200–204.

13. Chesney RW, Mazess RB, Hamstra AJ, DeLuca HF, O'Reagan S 1978 Reduction of serum-1, 25-dihydroxyvitamin-D3 in children receiving glucocorticoids. Lancet 2:1123–1125.

14. Chesney RW, Hamstra A, Rose P, DeLuca HF 1984 Vitamin D and parathyroid hormone status in children with the nephrotic syndrome and chronic mild glomerulonephritis. Int J Pediat Neph 5:1–4.

15. Seeman E, Kumar R, Hunder GG, Scott M, Heath H, Riggs BL 1980 Production, degradation, and circulating levels of 1,25-dihydroxyvitamin D in health and in chronic glucocorticoid excess. J Clin Invest 66:664–669.

16. Slovik DM, Neer RM, Ohman JL, Lowell FC, Clark MB, Segre GV, Potts JT 1980 Parathyroid hormone and 25-hydroxyvitamin D levels in glucocorticoid-treated patients. Clin Endocrinol (Oxf) 12:243–248.

17. Prummel MF, Wiersinga WM, Lips P, Sanders GTB, Sauerwein HP 1991 The course of biochemical parameters of bone turnover during treatment with corticosteroids. J Clin Endocr Metab 72:382–387.

18. Findling JW, Adams ND, Lemann J, Gray RW, Thomas CJ, Tyrrell JB 1982 Vitamin D metabolites and parathyroid hormone in Cushing's syndrome: Relationship to calcium and phosphorus homeostasis. J Clin Endocr Metab 54:1039–1044.

19. Hahn TJ, Halstead LR, Baran DT 1981 Effects of short term glucocorticoid administration on intestinal calcium absorption and circulating vitamin D metabolite concentrations in man. J Clin Endocr Metab 52:111–115.

20. Rubin MR, Bilezikian JP 2002 The role of parathyroid hormone in the pathogenesis of glucocorticod induced osteoporosis—a re-examination of the evidence. J Clin Endocrinol Metab 87:4033–4041.

21. Sambrook PN 2004 Glucocorticoids and vitamin D. In: Feldman D, Glorieux F, Pike JW (eds.) Vitamin D, 2nd ed. Elsevier, Burlington, MA, USA, pp. 1239–1251.

22. Sambrook PN, Eisman JA, Champion GD, Pocock NA 1988 Sex hormone status and osteoporosis in postmenopausal women with rheumatoid arthritis. Arthritis Rheum 31:973–978.

23. Chappard D, Legrand E, Basle MF, Fromont P, Racineux JL, Rebel A, Audran M 1996 Altered trabecular architecture induced by glucocorticoids: A bone histomorphometric study. J Bone Miner Res 11:676–685.

24. Mankin HJ 1992 Nontraumatic osteonecrosis of bone. N Engl J Med 326:1473–1478.

25. Ichiseki T, Kaneuji A, Katsuda S, Ueda Y, Sugimori T, Matsumoto T 2005 DNA oxidation injury in bone early after steroid administration is involved in the pathogenesis of steroid-induced osteonecrosis. Rheumatology 44:456–460.

26. Weinstein RS, Nicholas RW, Manolagas SC 2000 Apoptosis of osteocytes in glucocorticoid-induced osteonecrosis of the hip. J Clin Endocr Metab 85:2907–2912.

27. Askari A, Vignos PJJ, Moskowitz RW 1976 Steroid myopathy in connective tissue diseases. Am J Med 61:485–492.

28. Danneskiold-Samsoe B, Grimby G 1986 The influence of prednisone on the muscle morphology and muscle enzymes in patients with rheumatoid arthritis. Clin Sci 71:693–701.

29. Afifi AK, Bergman RA, Harvey JC 1968 Steroid myopathy: Clinical, histologic, and cytological observations. John Hopkins Bed J 123:158–173.

30. Van Staa TP, Leufkens HGM, Abenhaim L, Zhang B, Cooper C 2000 Use of oral glucocorticoids and risk of fractures. J Bone Miner Res 15:993–1000.

31. Naganathan V, Jones G, Nash P, Nicholson GC, Eisman JA, Sambrook PN 2000 Vertebral Fracture risk with long term glucocorticoids: Prevalence, relationship to age, bone density and glucocorticoid use. Arch Int Med 160:2917–22.

32. Peel NFA, Moore DJ, Barrington NA 1995 Risk of vertebral fracture and relationship to bone mineral density in steroid treated rheumatoid arthritis. Ann Rheum Dis 54:801–806.

33. Adachi JD, Bensen WG, Brown J, Hanley D, Hodsman A, Josse R, Kendler DL, Lentle B, Olszynski W, Ste-Marie LG, Tenenhouse A, Chines AA 1997 Intermittent etidronate therapy to prevent glucocorticoid-induced osteoporosis. N Engl J Med 337:382–387.

34. Saag K, Emkey R, Schnitzler TJ, Brown JP, Hawkins F, Goemaere S, Thamsborg G, Liberman UA, Delmas PD, Malice MP, Czachur M, Daifotis AG 1998 Alendronate for the prevention and treatment of glucocorticoid induced osteoporosis. N Engl J Med 339:292–299.

35. Reid DM, Hughes RA, Laan RFJM, Sacco-Gibson NA, Wenderoth DH, Adami S, Eusebio R, Devogelaer JP 2000 Efficacy and safety of daily risedronate in the treatment of glucocorticoid induced osteoporosis in men and women: A randomised trial. J Bone Miner Res 15:1006–1013.

36. Sambrook PN 2000 Glucocorticoid osteoporosis: Practical implications of recent trials. J Bone Miner Res 15:1645–1649.

37. Pearce G, Ryan PF, Delmas PD, Tabensky DA, Seeman E 1998 The deleterious effects of low-dose corticosteroids on bone density in patients with polymyalgia rheumatica. Brit J Rheumatol 37:292–299.

38. Gough AK, Lilley J, Eyre S, Holder RL, Emery P 1994 Generalised bone loss in patients with early rheumatoid arthritis. Lancet 344:23–27.

39. Laan RFJM, Van Riel PLCM, Van de Putte LBA 1993 Low dose prednisone induces rapid reversible axial bone loss in patients with rheumatoid arthritis. Ann Intern Med 119:963–968.

40. Wong CA, Walsh LJ, Smith CJP, Wisniewski AF, Lewis SA, Hubbard R, Cawte S, Green DJ, Pringle M, Tattersfield AE 2000 Inhaled glucocorticoid use and bone mineral density in patients with asthma. Lancet 355:1399–1403.

41. Van Staa TP, Leufkins H, Cooper C 2001 Use of inhaled glucocorticoids and risk of fractures. J Bone Miner Res 16:581–588.

42. Luengo M, Picado C, Del Rio L, Guanabens N, Monstserrat JM, Setoain J 1991 Vertebral fractures in steroid dependent asthma and involutional osteoporosis: A comparative study. Thorax 46:8063–65.

43. Van Staa TP, Laan RF, Barton IP, Cohen S, Reid DM, Cooper C 2003 Bone density threshold and other predictors of vertebral fracture in patients receiving oral glucocorticoid therapy. Arthritis Rheum 48:3224–3229.

44. Kumagai S, Kawano S, Atsumi T, Inokuma S, Okada Y, Kanai Y, Kaburaki j, Kameda H, Suwa A, Hagiyama H, Hirohata S, Makino H, Hashimoto H 2005 Vertebral fracture and bone mineral density in women receiving high dose glucocorticoids for treatment of autoimmune diseases. J Rheumatol 32:863–868.

45. Selby PL, Halsey JP, Adams KRH, Klimiuk P, Knight SM, Pal B, Stewart IM, Swinson DR 2000 Glucocorticoids do not alter the threshold for vertebral fractures. J Bone Miner Res 15:952–956.

46. Sambrook PN, Kempler S, J B, Kelly PJ, Pocock NA, Yeates MG, Eisman JA 1990 Glucocorticoid effects on proximal femur bone loss. J Bone Miner Res 5:1211–1216.

47. Adachi JD, Bensen WG, Bianchi F, Cividino A, Pillersdorf S, Sebaldt RJ, Tugwell P, Gordon M, Steele M, Webber C, Goldsmith CH 1996 Vitamin D and calcium in the prevention of corticosteroid-induced osteoporosis: A three year follow up study. J Rheumatol 23:995–1000.

48. LoCascio V, Bonnucci E, Imbimbo B, Ballanti P, Adami S, Milani S, Tartarotti D, DellaRocca C 1992 Bone loss in response to long-term glucocorticoid therapy. Bone Miner 8:39–51.

49. Sambrook PN, Eisman JA, Champion GD, Cohen ML, Pocock N, Yeates MG 1989 Effect of low dose corticosteroids on bone mass in rheumatoid arthritis: A longitudinal study. Ann Rheum Dis 48:535–538.

50. Pocock NA, Eisman JA, Dunstan C, Evans R, Thomas DH, Huq NL 1987 Recovery from steroid-induced osteoporosis. Ann Intern Med 107:319–323.

51. Ebeling PR, Erbas B, Hopper JL, Wark JD, Rubinfeld A 1998 Bone mineral density and bone turnover in asthmatics treated with long term inhaled or oral glucocorticoids. J Bone Miner Res 13:1328–1389.

52. Kotowicz MA, Hall S, Hunder GG, Cedel SL, Mann KG, Riggs BL 1990 Relationship of glucocorticoid dosage to serum bone Gla-protein concentration in patients with rheumatologic disorders. Arthritis Rheum 33:1487–1492.

53. Dempster DW 1989 Bone histomorphometry in glucocorticoid osteoporosis. J Bone Miner Res 4:137–141.

54. Carbonare LD, Arlot ME, Chavassieux PM 2001 Comparison of trabecular bone microarchitecture and remodeling in glucocorticoid-induced and postmenopausal osteoporosis. J Bone Miner Res 16:97–103.

55. Parfitt AM 2001 Glucocorticoid osteoporosis—relations to BMU theory and to bone cell birth. IBMS BoneKey doi: 10.1138/2001026.

56. Plotkin LI, Weinstein RS, Parfitt AM 1999 Prevention of osteocyte and osteoblast apoptosis by bisphosphonates and calcitonin. J Clin Invest 104:1363–1367.

57. Reid IR, Wattie DJ, Evans MC, Stapleton JP 1996 Testosterone therapy in glucocorticoid-treated men. Arch Int Med **156:**1173–1177.
58. Crawford BAL, Liu PY, Bleasel JF, Handelsman DJ 2003 Randomised placebo-controlled trial of androgen effects on muscle and bone in men requiring long term systemic glucocorticoid treatment. J Clin Endocr Metab **88:**3167–3176.
59. Hall GM, Daniels M, Doyle DV, Spector TD 1994 The effect of hormone replacement therapy on bone mass in rheumatoid arthritis treated with and without steroids. Arthritis Rheum **37:**1499–1505.
60. Lukert BP, Johnson BE, Robinson RG 1992 Estrogen and progesterone replacement therapy reduces glucocorticoid-induced bone loss. J Bone Miner Res **9:**1063–1069.
61. Sambrook PN, Birmingham J, Kelly PJ, Kempler S, Pocock NA, Eisman JA 1993 Prevention of corticosteroid osteoporosis; a comparison of calcium, calcitriol and calcitonin. N Engl J Med **328:**1747–1752.
62. Cohen S, Levy RM, Keller M, Boling E, Emkey RD, Greenwald M, Zizic TM, Wallach S, Sewell KL, Lukert BP, Axelrod DW, Chines AA 1999 Residronate therapy prevents glucocorticoid-induced bone loss. Arthritis Rheum **42:**2309–2318.
63. Hahn TJ, Halstead LR, Teitelbaum SL, Hahn BH 1979 Altered mineral metabolism in glucocorticoid induced osteopenia: Effect of 25-hydroxyvitamin D administration. J Clin Invest **64:**655–665.
64. Buckley LM, Leib ES, Cartularo KS, Vacek PM, Cooper SM 1996 Calcium and vitamin D3 supplementation prevents bone loss in the spine secondary to low dose glucocorticoids in patients with rheumatoid arthritis. Ann Intern Med **125:**961–968.
65. Reginster JY, Kuntz D, Verdicht W, Wouters M, Guillevin L, Menkes CJ, Nielsen K 1999 Prophylactic use of alfacalcidol in glucocorticoid-induced osteoporosis. Osteoporos Int **9:**75–81.
66. Sambrook PN, Kotowicz M, Nash P, Styles CB, V N, Henderson-Briffa KN, Eisman JA, Nicholson GC 2003 Prevention and treatment of glucocorticoid induced osteoporosis: A comparison of calcitriol, vitamin D plus calcium and alendronate plus calcium. J Bone Miner Res **18:**919–924.
67. Ringe JD, Coster A, Meng T, Schacht E, Umbach R 1999 Treatment of glucocorticoid-induced osteoporosis with alfacalcidol/calcium versus vitamin D/calcium. Calcif Tiss Int **65:**337–340.
68. Ringe JD, Dorst A, Faber H, Schacht E, Rahlfs VW 2004 Superiority of alfacalcidol over plain vitamin D in the treatment of glucocorticoid-induced osteoporosis. Rheum Int **24:**63–70.
69. Luengo M, Picado C, Del Rio L, Guanabens N, Monserrat JM, Setoain J 1990 Treatment of steroid-induced osteopenia with calcitonin in corticosteroid-dependent asthma. Am Rev Respir Dis **142:**104–107.
70. Ringe JD, Welzel D 1987 Salmon calcitonin in the therapy of corticoid-induced osteoporosis. Eur J Clin Pharmacol **33:**35–39.
71. Rizzato G, Tosi G, Schiraldi G, Montemurro L, Zanni D, Sisti S 1988 Bone protection with salmon calcitonin (sCT) in the long term steroid therapy of chronic sarcoidosis. Sarcoidosis **5:**99–103.
72. Adachi JD, Bensen WG, Bell MJ, Bianchi FA, Cividino AA, Craig GL, Sturtridge WC, Sebalaldt RJ, Steele M, Gordon M, Themeles E, Tugwell R, Roberts R, Gent M 1997 Salmon calcitonin nasal spray in the prevention of corticosteroid-induced osteoporosis. Br J Rheumatol **36:**255–259.
73. Healey JH, Paget S, Williams-Russo P, Szatrowski TP, Schneider R, Spiera H, Mitnick H, Ales K, Schwartzberg P 1996 Randomised trial of salmon calcitonin to prevent bone loss in glucocorticoid treated temporal arteritis and polymyalgia rheumatica. Calcif Tiss Int **58:**73–80.
74. Reid IR, King AR, Alexander CJ, Ibbertson HK 1988 Prevention of steroid-induced osteoporosis with (3-amino-1-hydroxypropylidine)-1, 1-bisphosphonate (APD). Lancet **1:**143–146.
75. Geusens P, Dequeker J, Vanhoof J, Stalmans R, Boonen S, Joly J, Nijs J, Raus J 1997 Cyclical etidronate increases bone density in the spine and hip of postmenopausal women receiving long term corticosteroid treatment. A double blind, randomised placebo controlled study. Ann Rheum Dis **57:**724–727.
76. Chavassieux PM, Arlot ME, Roux JP, Portero N, Daifotis A, Yates AJ, Hamdy NA, Malice MP, Freedholm D, Meunier PJ 2000 Effects of alendronate on bone quality and remodelling in glucocorticoid-induced osteoporosis: A histomorphometric analysis of transiliac biopsies. J Bone Miner Res **15:**1754–1762.
77. Wallach S, Cohen S, Reid DM, Hughes RA, Hosking DJ, Laan RF, Doherty SM, Maricic M, Rosen C, Brown J, Barton I, Chines AA 2000 Effects of risedronate treatment on bone density and vertebral fracture in patients on corticosteroid therapy. Calcif Tiss Int **67:**277–285.
78. Ringe JD, Dorst A, Faber H, Ibach K, Sorenson F 2003 Intermittent intravenous ibandronate injections reduce vertebral fracture risk in corticosteroid-induced osteoporosis: Results from a long-term comparative study. Osteoporos Int **14:**801–807.
79. Boutsen Y, Jamart J, Esselinckx W, Stoffel M, Devogelaer JP 1997 Primary prevention of glucocorticoid-induced osteoporosis with intermittent intravenous pamidronate: A randomized trial. Calcif Tiss Int **61:**266–271.
80. Lane NE, Sanchez S, Modin GW, Genant HK, Pierini E, Arnaud CD 1998 Parathyroid hormone treatment can reverse glucocorticoid-induced osteoporosis. J Clin Invest **102:**1627–1633.
81. Lane NE, Pierini E, Modin G, Genant HK, Pierini E, Arnaud CD 2000 Bone mass continues to increase after parathyroid hormone treatment is stopped in glucocorticoid-induced osteoporosis. J Bone Miner Res **15:**944–951.

Chapter 56.   Transplantation Osteoporosis

Adi Cohen,[1] Peter Ebeling,[2] Stuart Sprague,[3] and Elizabeth Shane[1]

[1]*College of Physicians & Surgeons, Columbia University, New York, New York;* [2]*The Royal Melbourne Hospital, The University of Melbourne, Victoria, Australia; and* [3]*Evanston Northwestern Healthcare, Feinberg School of Medicine, Northwestern University, Evanston, Illinois*

INTRODUCTION

Transplantation is an established therapy for end-stage diseases of the kidney, heart, liver, and lung, and for certain hematologic conditions. Survival has improved dramatically and increased survival has been accompanied by greater awareness of complications such as osteoporosis. In this chapter, we discuss the various immunosuppressive medications that contribute to the pathophysiology of transplantation bone disease, the clinical features of transplantation osteoporosis, and the prevention and treatment of osteoporosis in transplant recipients.

This subject topic has been addressed in several recent chapters and reviews[1–4] that contain detailed references.

Dr. Sprague is a consultant for Abbott and Amgen and has received funding from Abbott, Amgen, and Novartis. All other authors have reported no conflicts of interest.

BONE DISEASE IN CANDIDATES FOR ORGAN TRANSPLANTATION

Candidates for kidney, heart, liver, lung, and bone marrow transplants are exposed to the unique skeletal effects of both their underlying disease and the agents used to treat them.[2,4–7] Pretransplant treatment with loop diuretics, anticoagulants, chemotherapy, radiation, or glucocorticoids (GCs) may have adverse effects on bone and mineral metabolism. Severely ill patients may experience bone loss because of hypothalamic hypogonadism, immobility, or vitamin D deficiency. Patients with cystic fibrosis, congestive heart or liver failure, or any severe chronic illness may be at increased risk for vitamin D deficiency and calcium malabsorption. In the setting of these illnesses and medications, abnormalities of bone metabolism may lead to bone loss caused by either high or low turnover bone disease. Thus, in each case, the bone pathology specific to organ transplantation is likely to occur on a background of previously existing bone disease.

TABLE 1. TRANSPLANTATION OSTEOPOROSIS

Type of transplant	Prevalence after transplantation		Bone loss: first post-transplant year	Fracture incidence
	Osteoporosis*	Fractures		
Kidney[†]	11–56%	Vertebral: 3–29%	Spine: 4–9%	Vertebral: 3–10%
		Peripheral: 11–22%	Hip: 8%	Peripheral: 10–50%
Heart	25–50%	Vertebral: 22–35%	Spine: 3–8%	10–36%
			Hip: 6–11%	
Liver	30–46%	Vertebral: 29–47%	Spine: 0–24%	Vertebral: 24–65%
			Hip: 2–4%	
Lung	57–73%	42%	Spine: 1–5%	18–37%
			Hip: 2–5%	
Bone marrow	4–15%	5%	Spine: 2–9%	1–16%
			Hip: 6–11%	

*Accepted definitions included BMD (by DXA) of the spine and/or hip with Z score ≤−2 or T score ≤−2.5.
[†]Definition of osteoporosis also included BMD of predominantly cortical sites such as the femoral shaft or proximal radius that are adversely affected by excessive PTH secretion.
From Cohen A, Shane E 2003 Osteoporosis after solid organ and bone marrow transplantation. Osteoporosis Int **14**:617–630. Copyright 2003, with kind permission from Springer Science and Business Media.

A more detailed discussion of pretransplant bone disease, specific to endstage kidney, liver, heart, and lung disease, can be found in a recent review.[2]

SKELETAL EFFECTS OF IMMUNOSUPPRESSIVE DRUGS USED AFTER TRANSPLANTATION

GCs

GCs in high doses (e.g., ≥50 mg/day of prednisone or prednisolone) are commonly prescribed immediately after transplantation, with subsequent dose reduction over several weeks and transient increases during rejection episodes. Exposure varies with the organ transplanted, the number and management of rejection episodes, and with the practice of transplantation programs. Recently, some programs have adopted steroid-free regimens. The introduction of cyclosporine A, tacrolimus, and more recently, rapamycin and daclizumab have reduced GC requirements. However, there is still sufficient exposure, particularly during the first few months after transplantation, to cause substantial bone loss.

The skeletal effects of GCs are discussed in detail elsewhere and will be reviewed only briefly here. GCs reduce BMD predominantly at trabecular sites, and even small doses are associated with markedly increased fracture risk. GCs cause direct and profound reductions in bone formation by decreasing osteoblast replication, differentiation, and lifespan and by inhibiting genes for type I collagen, osteocalcin, insulin-like growth factors, bone morphogenetic proteins and other bone matrix proteins, TGF-β, and RANKL. Direct effects of GCs on bone resorption are minor relative to formation. However, GCs may increase bone resorption indirectly, by inhibiting synthesis of gonadal steroids and inducing secondary hyperparathyroidism (HPT) from reduced intestinal and renal calcium absorption, although HPT is thought to be of minor importance in the pathogenesis of steroid-induced bone loss.

Calcineurin Inhibitors: Cyclosporine A and Tacrolimus

The introduction of cyclosporine (CsA), a calcineurin inhibitor (CI) with effects on T cell function, to transplantation regimens was associated with a marked reduction in rejection episodes and improved survival. Although in vitro studies showed that CsA inhibits bone resorption in cultured bone, in vivo rodent studies suggest that CsA has independent adverse effects on bone and mineral metabolism that could contribute to bone loss after organ transplantation.[8] In the rat, CsA administration caused severe bone loss, particularly in trabecular bone, that was associated with marked increases in resorption and formation and with increased levels of osteocalcin and 1,25(OH)$_2$D.[8] The CsA-mediated bone loss was associated with testosterone deficiency,[9] independent of renal function,[8] and attenuated by parathyroidectomy.[10] Antiresorptive agents such as estrogen, raloxifene, calcitonin, and alendronate prevented CsA-induced bone loss.[8] CsA may cause bone loss by direct effects on calcineurin genes expressed in osteoclasts or indirectly through alterations in T-cell function. These animal studies suggest that CsA could be responsible for the high-turnover aspects of post-transplantation bone disease.

The effects of CsA on the human skeleton are unclear. In a small group of kidney transplant recipients receiving long-term CsA monotherapy compared with those receiving prednisolone and azathioprine, there was no difference in extent of bone loss between the two groups.[11] In a prospective study, the cumulative CsA dose was associated with bone loss during the first 2 years after transplantation. This effect was independent of the steroid effect.[12] In contrast, there are several studies of kidney transplant patients receiving CsA in a steroid-free regimen[13–15] that did not lose bone.

Tacrolimus (FK506), another CI, also causes trabecular bone loss in the rat.[8] Fewer studies have evaluated the skeletal effects of FK506 in humans. Both cardiac[16] and liver[17] transplant recipients sustained rapid bone loss with FK506. However, FK506 may also cause less bone loss in humans than CsA.[18,19] Liver transplant recipients taking FK506 were exposed to less prednisone and had significantly higher femoral neck (FN) BMD 2 years after transplantation than those receiving CsA.[19] In a small group of kidney transplant recipients followed for 1 year, Goffin et al.[18] noted that those who received FK506 and low-dose steroids had a small net increase in bone density compared with a loss observed in those who received CsA and normal-dose steroids. Thus, FK506 based regimens may benefit the skeleton by allowing for the use of lower GC doses.

Other Immunosuppressive Agents

Limited information is available regarding the effects of other immunosuppressive drugs on BMD and bone metabolism. Azathioprine, sirolimus (rapamycin), and mycophenolate mofetil do not cause bone loss in the rat model. The skeletal effects of newer agents, such as daclizumab, have not been studied. However, by reducing GC requirements, they may be relatively beneficial to the skeleton.

CLINICAL FEATURES OF TRANSPLANTATION OSTEOPOROSIS

Information presented in the following sections is also summarized in Table 1.

Kidney Transplantation

In general, renal osteodystrophy improves after transplantation, with at least partial resolution of HPT during the first year. However, bone resorption remains elevated in a substantial proportion of kidney transplant recipients, and histomorphometric studies show osteoblast dysfunction and decreased mineral apposition rate, consistent with GC effect.[20,21] Persistent hyperphosphaturia with resultant hypophosphatemia may also predispose to bone loss. In some patients, this is the result of persistent or residual HPT. However, in many patients, it occurs in the absence of HPT and may persist for many years.

Cross-sectional studies of patients evaluated several years after kidney transplantation have reported osteoporosis (defined as a BMD Z score ≤ −2 or a T score ≤ −2.5) in 17–49% at the spine (LS), 11–56% at the FN, and 22–52% at the radius.[1,2,22,23] Several studies have shown a correlation between cumulative GC dose and BMD. However, it should be noted that low BMD measurements in such patients are not specific for osteoporosis and may reflect other metabolic bone diseases, such as osteomalacia, adynamic bone disease, and HPT.

The majority of bone loss occurs in the first 6–18 months after transplantation and ranges from 4% to 9% at the LS and 5% to 8% at the hip. Bone loss has not been consistently related to sex, patient age, cumulative GC dose, rejection episodes, activity level, or PTH levels.

Some longitudinal studies document ongoing, although less rapid, bone loss several years after kidney transplantation, whereas others do not.[24–29] In kidney transplant patients studied ~10 years after transplantation, GC withdrawal was associated with a significant increase in LS and FN BMD, an increase in markers of bone formation, and little change in markers of bone resorption.[30] Despite the improvements in BMD after the first post-transplant year noted in some reports, most studies show that BMD remains low up to 20 years after transplantation.

In kidney transplant patients, fractures affect appendicular sites (hips, long bones, ankles, feet) more commonly than axial sites (spine and ribs). Women and patients transplanted for diabetic nephropathy are at particularly increased risk of fractures. A recent cohort study of 101,039 patients with end-stage renal disease (ESRD) found that kidney transplantation was associated with a 34% greater risk of hip fracture compared with patients continuing on dialysis.[31] The majority of fractures occur within the first 3 years after transplantation.

Particularly severe osteoporosis has been documented in kidney–pancreas transplant recipients with type 1 diabetes. In patients evaluated a mean of 40 ± 23 months after kidney–pancreas transplantation, 23% had osteoporosis at the LS and 58% had osteoporosis at the FN.[32] Vertebral or nonvertebral fractures were documented in 45%.[32] Fracture prevalence varies from 26% to 49% several years after kidney–pancreas transplantation.[2,33]

Cardiac Transplantation

The prevalence of densitometric osteoporosis in long-term cardiac transplant recipients has been reported to be 28% at the LS and 20% at the FN. Observational studies have shown that the most rapid rate of bone loss occurs during the first year.[1,2,7] LS BMD declines by 6–10% during the first 6 months, followed by stabilization and partial recovery of LS BMD in later years. FN BMD falls by 6–11% in the first year and stabilizes thereafter in most cases. More recent studies suggest that there is less bone loss than documented in the late 1980s and early 1990s.[34]

Vertebral fracture prevalence rates range between 22% and 35% in long-term cardiac transplant recipients. Vertebral fracture incidence of 36% has been found during the first year after cardiac transplantation. The majority of fractures involved the spine and occurred within the first 6 months to 2 years.[35] A more recent study found the incidence of vertebral fractures to be 14% during the first post-transplant year.[34]

There are transient increases in markers of bone resorption and decreases in markers of bone formation (osteocalcin) soon after transplantation that return to the upper end of the normal range by 6–12 months after transplantation.

Liver Transplantation

Osteoporosis is also a common complication of liver transplantation, as has been discussed in several recent reviews.[5,36] The progression of osteoporosis after liver transplantation resembles that after cardiac transplantation.[35] Bone loss and fracture rates are highest in the first 6–12 months. Spine BMD declines by 2–24% during the first year in earlier studies. However, one recent study documented bone loss of only 2.3% at the FN, with preservation of spinal BMD during the first year after liver transplantation,[37] and another documented increases in BMD at 1 year.[38] Fracture rates range from 17% to 65% and, as with cardiac transplantation, ribs and vertebrae are the most common sites. Recovery of BMD at the LS and hip has been documented during the second and third years after transplantation in patients receiving no treatment for bone disease. In recent prospective studies, older age[39] and pretransplant BMD at the LS and FN[39,40] predicted post-transplant fractures and pretransplant vertebral fractures predicted post-transplant vertebral fractures.[35,41]

The high turnover state documented after liver transplantation contrasts with decreased bone formation and low turnover seen before transplantation. This change from low to high bone turnover may be caused by resolution of cholestasis or hypogonadism, increased PTH secretion, CsA, or FK506, or a combination of factors.

Lung Transplantation

The prevalence of osteoporosis is very high in lung transplant recipients, with rates as high as 73%. During the first year after lung transplantation, rates of bone loss at the LS and FN range from 2% to 5%.[1,2,22,23] Fracture rates are also high during the first year, ranging from 18% to 37%, even in patients who received antiresorptive therapy to prevent bone loss. Some, but not all, studies have found that bone loss correlates with GC dose. Bone turnover markers are consistent with increased resorption and formation.

Allogeneic Bone Marrow Transplantation

Osteoporosis after allogeneic bone marrow transplantation (BMT) has a complex pathogenesis that is related to effects of treatment and effects on the stromal cell compartment of the bone marrow.[6] Similar to solid organ transplantation, bone

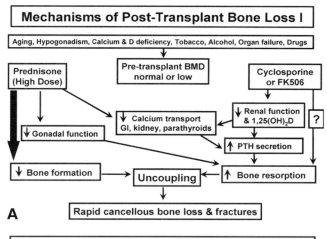

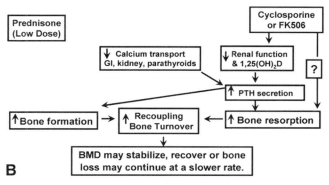

FIG. 1. (A) Mechanisms of bone loss in the early post-transplantation period. (B) Mechanisms of bone loss in the later post-transplantation period, after GC doses are tapered.

resorption increases, while bone formation decreases, resulting in early, rapid bone loss.

Small cross-sectional studies have shown decreased FN and LS BMD in adults and children after allogeneic (allo) BMT. Up to 29% and 52% of survivors have T scores < −1.0 at the LS and FN, respectively.[42] Osteoporosis is more common at proximal femur sites than at the spine. Patients who are <18 years of age at the time of BMT may fail to acquire adequate bone mass, and low BMD in this population may also be related to smaller bone size. Longitudinal studies have shown rapid bone loss in the first 6–12 months after BMT that is greater at the proximal femur than the spine and total body and is highly variable. Most studies suggest that little additional bone loss occurs after this time. Studies of long-term survivors of BMT have shown that the dramatic losses from the proximal femur are not regained. Spinal bone loss is less dramatic and partial recovery of bone mass occurs at this site from 6 to 12 months after BMT.

The pathogenesis of BMT-related bone loss is quite complex.[6] Contributing factors include cumulative GC exposure, whether given before BMT or for treatment of graft-versus-host disease (GVHD). Bone loss has been related to duration of CsA exposure and may also be a direct effect of GVHD itself on bone cells. Abnormal cellular or cytokine-mediated bone marrow function may affect bone turnover and BMD after BMT. Both myeloablative treatment and BMT stimulate the

early release of cytokines. BMT also has adverse effects on bone marrow osteoprogenitors. Osteocyte viability is decreased after BMT and osteocytes are replaced by differentiation of host stromal cells. Bone marrow stromal cells are damaged by high-dose chemotherapy, total body irradiation, GCs, and CsA, reducing osteoblastic differentiation from osteoprogenitor cells. Colony forming units-fibroblasts (CFU-f) are reduced for up to 12 years after BMT.

MECHANISMS OF POST-TRANSPLANTATION BONE LOSS

The body of research published over the past decade into the natural history and pathogenesis of transplantation osteoporosis has yielded fairly consistent data that now enable us to develop a unifying hypothesis regarding the mechanisms of post-transplantation bone loss and fracture. It seems very clear that the mechanisms differ according to the amount of time that has elapsed since transplantation. There seem to be two main phases of bone loss (Fig. 1) that can best be differentiated by the presence (Fig. 1A) or absence (Fig. 1B) of high-dose GCs in the immunosuppressive regimen.

During the first 6 months after transplantation, GC doses are generally high enough to profoundly suppress bone formation. Virtually every published study has found serum markers of bone formation, particularly osteocalcin, to be suppressed in the early post-transplant period. There are also consistent reports of increased urinary markers of bone resorption during the same time frame. This increase is probably due in part to effects of GCs to increase osteoblast synthesis of RANKL and decrease osteoblast synthesis of osteoprotegerin and to suppressive effects of GCs on the hypothalamic-pituitary-gonadal axis and on calcium transport across the intestinal, renal tubular, and parathyroid cell membranes. In addition, the well-known nephrotoxic effects of CsA and FK506 result in measurable declines in renal function and decreased synthesis of $1,25(OH)_2D$ that also inhibits calcium transport in the gut. Thus, both CIs and GCs have the potential to cause secondary increases in PTH secretion, which in turn increases osteoclast-mediated bone resorption. In addition, both CsA and FK506 may increase bone resorption directly. The concomitant administration of high dose GCs and CsA (or FK506) is therefore associated with uncoupling of resorption and formation. During this phase of the post-transplant period, there is rapid bone loss and high fracture rates.

As prednisone doses are tapered below 5 mg/day, osteoblast function recovers and the suppressive effects on bone formation are reversed (Fig. 1B). However, adverse effects of CsA and FK506 remain—both direct effects on the skeleton and indirect effects mediated by renal toxicity of these drugs that result in secondary HPT. Thus, resorption remains elevated. With tapering of GCs, bone formation increases also, resulting in "recoupling" of bone turnover. Rates of bone loss slow and there may even be some recovery, particularly at the spine. When steroid doses are increased for treatment of rejection or stress, the pathophysiologic picture resembles the first phase.

In addition to the effects of GCs and CIs, other factors may also play a role, such as decreasing kidney function with persistent and/or recurrent HPT, hypophosphatemia, and calcitriol deficiency

PREVENTION AND MANAGEMENT OF OSTEOPOROSIS

Before Transplantation

Because of the high prevalence of osteoporosis, osteopenia, and abnormal bone and mineral metabolism in patients awaiting transplantation and the morbidity caused by osteoporosis after transplantation, it is our position that all candidates for organ transplantation should have an evaluation of bone health. BMD of the hip and spine should be measured before transplantation, preferably at the time of acceptance to the waiting list. Spine radiographs should be performed to detect prevalent fractures. If BMD is low, an evaluation for secondary causes of osteoporosis should be undertaken and, if detected, should be treated specifically. All patients should receive the recommended daily allowance for calcium and vitamin D (1000–1500 mg of calcium and 400–800 IU of vitamin D). Patients with kidney failure should be evaluated and treated for renal osteodystrophy according to currently accepted standards.

Whether therapy for osteoporosis before transplantation reduces fracture risk after transplantation is presently unclear. Bisphosphonates, in particular, suppress bone resorption for up to 12 months after discontinuation of therapy. Transplantation with bisphosphonates already "on board" may prevent the increase in resorption that develops immediately after grafting and could theoretically mitigate post-transplant bone loss. Moreover, antiresorptive therapy clearly increases BMD and reduces fractures in other populations. Therefore, individuals awaiting lung, liver, and heart transplantation with osteoporosis or osteopenia should be evaluated and treated similarly to others with these conditions. The pretransplant waiting period is often long enough (1–2 years) to achieve significant improvements in BMD. The situation is clearly different and more complex in patients awaiting kidney transplantation. Because there are few published data on the use of antiresorptive drugs in patients with chronic kidney disease, it is not possible to make general recommendations for these individuals. Furthermore, the use of bisphosphonates in patients with kidney disease may increase the incidence of low bone turnover and adynamic bone disease.

After Organ Transplantation

Virtually all studies have shown that bone loss is most rapid immediately after transplantation. Fractures may occur very early and affect patients with both low and normal pretransplant BMD. Therefore, we believe that most patients (even those with normal BMD) should have preventive therapy instituted immediately after transplantation. In addition, there is an ever-enlarging population transplanted months or years before, yet never evaluated or treated for osteoporosis.

The majority of therapeutic trials have focused on the use of vitamin D metabolites and antiresorptive drugs, particularly bisphosphonates. In the discussions to follow, we will distinguish where possible between studies that focus on the early post-transplant period (prevention trials) and those that include mainly patients with established bone loss who are >6–12 months distant from transplantation and have thus passed the phase of most rapid demineralization (treatment trials).

Vitamin D and Analogs

Vitamin D metabolites are believed to mitigate post-transplantation bone loss by reversing glucocorticoid-induced impairment of intestinal calcium absorption and by curbing the resultant secondary HPT. It is also possible that these agents reduce glucocorticoid requirements because of their immunomodulatory effects.

Parent vitamin D, in doses of 400-1000 IU, does not prevent significant post-transplantation bone loss. Calcidiol [25(OH)D] has, however, been shown to prevent bone loss and increase LS BMD after cardiac transplantation.[3] Alfacalcidol prevents or attenuates LS and FN bone loss immediately after renal transplantation.[43,44]

$1,25(OH)_2D$ (calcitriol) has been studied in heart, lung, liver, and kidney transplant recipients. Although results of these trials have been contradictory, some studies have found beneficial effects with the use of 0.5 μg/day or more. Calcitriol, when initiated during the first year after kidney transplantation, was associated with an increase in BMD at the LS, FN, and distal radius (DR) after 1 year.[12] In another study of renal transplant recipients, intermittent calcitriol and calcium prevented total hip, but not LS, bone loss in comparison to calcium alone.[45] In a randomized placebo-controlled study of heart or lung transplant recipients who received placebo or calcitriol (0.5–0.75 μg/day) for either 12 or 24 months after transplantation,[46] LS bone loss did not differ between groups. FN bone loss at 24 months was significantly reduced only in those who had received calcitriol for the entire 24-month period. Although fracture rates were lower in the calcitriol-treated subjects, this study lacked sufficient statistical power to be certain. This study suggests that rapid bone loss resumes in heart and lung transplant recipients after cessation of calcitriol.[46] One study in long-term renal transplant patients found a benefit of calcitriol treatment compared with control,[47] whereas other studies of calcitriol in long-term kidney[26] and heart transplant recipients[48,49] found no benefit of calcitriol. Hypercalcemia and hypercalciuria, common side effects of vitamin D metabolites, may develop at any point during treatment. Frequent monitoring of urine and serum is required. In our opinion, active vitamin D metabolites should not be selected as first-line treatment because of their limited effectiveness and narrow therapeutic window.

Bisphosphonates

Several studies suggest that intravenous bisphosphonates prevent bone loss and fractures after transplantation. Repeated doses of intravenous pamidronate in heart,[50,51] kidney,[52,53] and lung[54,55] transplant recipients have been shown to prevent LS and FN bone loss. In a study that compared kidney transplant recipients treated with calcium and calcitriol to those treated with calcium, calcitriol, and intravenous pamidronate administered at transplantation and at months 1, 2, 3, and 6, there was no bone loss in the pamidronate-treated patients compared with a 4% to 6% loss in the other patients.[52] However, treatment with pamidronate resulted in a high incidence of adynamic bone disease as evidenced by bone biopsy specimens obtained after 6 months of therapy.[52] Some studies of intravenous bisphosphonates have reported fracture reduction, whereas others[54] have not. Recent randomized trials of the more potent intravenous bisphosphonates, ibandronate or zoledronic acid, in liver[56] and kidney[57,58] transplant recipients have also found a significant protective effect on BMD at 6–12 months.

Oral bisphosphonates have also been studied. Clodronate increases BMD in long-term cardiac transplant patients.[59] Alendronate has been compared with calcitriol in both immediate[34,60] and long-term[61–63] transplant recipients. In kidney transplant recipients, a regimen of alendronate (10 mg/day), calcium carbonate (2 g/day), and calcitriol (0.25 μg/day) was associated with a marked increase in LS BMD compared with a marked decrease with calcium and calcitriol alone.[60] In a 1-year trial, in which patients were randomized immediately after cardiac transplantation to receive either alendronate (10 mg/day) or calcitriol (0.25 μg, bid), bone loss at the LS and hip was prevented by both regimens compared with reference subjects who received only calcium and vitamin D (Fig. 2).[34] A 1-year trial comparing alendronate, calcitriol, and calcium to calcitriol and calcium treatment alone in kidney transplant recipients in whom therapy was begun an average of 5 years

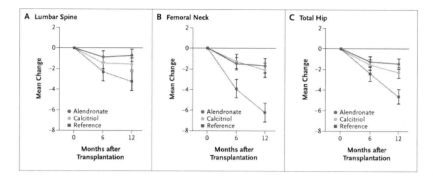

after transplantation reported significant improvements in LS and FN BMD in the alendronate-treated group[61]; BMD remained stable in the patients treated with calcitriol alone.

BMT deserves special consideration. Two large, randomized, prospective studies of intravenous pamidronate therapy have shown prevention of spinal bone loss and a reduction in proximal femoral bone loss after allogeneic BMT.[64,65] However, bone loss from the proximal femur was not entirely prevented, even using monthly doses of 90 mg in one study.[64] This may be caused by a failure of pamidronate to inhibit matrix metalloproteinase (MMP)-mediated bone resorption or to reverse the osteoblastic defect present after BMT.[66] Risedronate or intravenous zoledronate given 12 months after BMT prevent spinal and proximal femoral bone loss.[67,68] Zoledronate also increases ex vivo growth of the bone marrow CFU-f, suggesting that this potent bisphosphonate may be effective at improving osteoblast recovery and increasing osteoblast numbers after BMT.

In our opinion, bisphosphonates are the most promising approach for the management of transplantation osteoporosis. However, controversies remain regarding optimal administration of bisphosphonates. These include whether continuous or intermittent therapy should be used, duration of therapy, the level of renal impairment at which bisphosphonates should be avoided, whether they are safe in kidney transplant recipients with adynamic bone disease, and their use after pediatric transplantation.

Calcitonin

Calcitonin is relatively ineffective in preventing bone loss after transplantation.

Hormone Replacement Therapy

Hormone replacement therapy (HRT) protects the skeleton in women treated with GCs, as well as in women receiving liver, lung, and bone marrow transplantation. Because amenorrhea is a common sequela of BMT in women who are premenopausal, they should receive HRT whenever possible. The risks of HRT therapy, particularly with regard to breast cancer and cardiovascular disease, would likely outweigh the benefits in older women after other types of organ transplantation.

In cardiac transplant recipients, testosterone falls immediately after transplantation and normalizes 6–12 months later. In a recent study evaluating male cardiac transplant recipients treated with intravenous ibandronate, hypogonadal men who received testosterone supplementation showed an improved BMD response at 1 year compared with hypogonadal men who did not receive testosterone.[69] In general, testosterone replacement should be reserved for men with true hypogonadism, as defined by testosterone level and symptoms of hypogonadism.

Potential risks of testosterone therapy, such as prostatic hypertrophy, hyperlipidemia, and abnormal liver enzymes may have particular relevance for this population.

TABLE 2. MANAGEMENT SUMMARY

Principles of management
- Significant osteopenia and abnormal bone and mineral metabolism often antedate transplantation. Therefore, all patients should be evaluated for osteoporosis at time of acceptance to waiting list.
- Most rapid rates of bone loss and highest fracture incidence occur during the first 6–12 months. Therefore, efforts to prevent these complications should begin *before or immediately after* transplantation.
- Patients with normal pretransplant BMD fracture after transplantation. Therefore, prophylaxis of bone loss and fracture should be instituted in all organ transplant recipients, regardless of pretransplant BMD.

Before transplantation
- Begin recommended daily allowance of calcium and vitamin D.
- Encourage weight-bearing and strengthening exercises.
- Evaluate and treat prevalent osteoporosis or renal osteodystrophy according to current guidelines.

After transplantation
Prevention
- Rapid resumption of weight-bearing exercise; enrollment in organized rehabilitation program after transplantation
- Rapid reduction of glucocorticoid dose as permitted by clinical status
- Place all patients on elemental calcium (1000–1500 mg daily in divided doses) and at least 400–800 IU of vitamin D. Use the citrate salt as many transplant recipients are routinely prescribed antacids that may limit calcium absorption if given as the carbonate salt. Monitoring of urinary calcium may be appropriate in some glucocorticoid-treated patients.
- Begin oral or intravenous bisphosphonates as soon as practical after surgery.
- Calcitriol has also been shown to reduce bone loss, but monitoring of serum and urine calcium is necessary.

Treatment
- Bisphosphonates are effective first-line treatment for established bone loss in the later post-transplant period. These medications should be used with caution in patients with renal insufficiency.
- Calcitriol and calcitonin may also be used. Use of calcitriol requires monitoring of serum and urine calcium.
- Renal transplant recipients represent a special population. Bone biopsy may be required to exclude adynamic bone disease before initiating bisphosphonate therapy.

CONCLUSIONS

Pre-transplantation bone disease and post-transplantation immunosuppressive regimens, combining high doses of GCs (e.g., prednisone at >10 mg/day) and CIs (CsA or FK506), interact to produce a particularly severe form of osteoporosis characterized by rapid bone loss and increased fracture rates. Early rapid bone loss occurs in the setting of uncoupled bone turnover with many studies documenting increased bone resorption and decreased bone formation. Management of these patients should combine assessment and treatment of pre-transplantation bone disease with preventive therapy in the immediate post-transplantation period, because most bone loss occurs in the first months after grafting (Table 2). In addition, bone mass measurement and therapy for osteoporosis in the long-term organ transplant recipient should be addressed. There are no pre-transplantation variables that reliably predict post-transplantation bone loss and fracture in the individual patient. Therefore, all organ transplant recipients should be considered at risk for post-transplantation bone loss and fractures. Although newer studies suggest that rates of bone loss and fracture may be lower in more recently transplanted patients, morbidity from transplantation osteoporosis remains unacceptably high. Data from clinical trials suggests that bisphosphonates are the safest and most promising agents for the prevention and treatment of post-transplantation osteoporosis.

REFERENCES

1. Shane E 2003 Transplantation osteoporosis. In: Orwoll E, Bliziotes M (eds.) Osteoporosis: Pathophysiology and Clinical Management. Humana Press, Totowa, NJ, USA, pp. 537–567.
2. Cohen A, Shane E 2003 Osteoporosis after solid organ and bone marrow transplantation. Osteoporos Int 14:617–630.
3. Cohen A, Sambrook P, Shane E 2004 Management of bone loss after organ transplantation. J Bone Miner Res 19:1919–1932.
4. Maalouf NM, Shane E 2005 Osteoporosis after solid organ transplantation. J Clin Endocrinol Metab 90:2456–2465.
5. Hay JE 2003 Osteoporosis in liver diseases and after transplantation. J Hepatol 38:856–865.
6. Ebeling PR 2005 Bone disease after bone marrow transplantation. In: Compston J, Shane E. (eds.) Bone Disease of Organ Transplantation. Elsevier, Burlington, MA, USA, pp. 339–352.
7. Cohen A, Shane E 2005 Bone disease in patients before and after cardiac transplantation. In: Compston JE, Shane E (eds.) Bone Disease of Organ Transplantation. Elsevier, Burlington, MA, USA, pp. 287–301.
8. Epstein S 1996 Post-transplantation bone disease: The role of immunosuppressive agents on the skeleton. J Bone Miner Res 11:1–7.
9. Bowman AR, Sass DA, Dissanayake IR, Ma YF, Liang H, Yuan Z, Jee WS, Epstein S 1997 The role of testosterone in cyclosporine-induced osteopenia. J Bone Miner Res 12:607–615.
10. Epstein S, Dissanayake A, Goodman GR, Bowman A, Zhou H, Ma Y, Jee WS 2001 Effect of the interaction of parathyroid hormone and cyclosporine A on bone mineral metabolism in the rat. Calcif Tissue Int 68:240–247.
11. Cueto-Manzano AM, Konel S, Crowley V, France MW, Freemont AJ, Adams JE, Mawer B, Gokal R, Hutchison AJ 2003 Bone histopathology and densitometry comparison between cyclosporine a monotherapy and prednisolone plus azathioprine dual immunosuppression in renal transplant patients. Transplantation 75:2053–2058.
12. Josephson MA, Schumm LP, Chiu MY, Marshall C, Thistlethwaite JR, Sprague SM 2004 Calcium and calcitriol prophylaxis attenuates posttransplant bone loss. Transplantation 78:1233–1236.
13. Ponticelli C, Aroldi A 2001 Osteoporosis after organ transplantation. Lancet 357:1623.
14. Grotz W, Mundinger A, Gugel B, Exner V, Reichelt A, Schollmeyer P 1994 Missing impact of cyclosporine on osteoporosis in renal transplant recipients. Transplant Proc 26:2652–2653.
15. McIntyre HD, Menzies B, Rigby R, Perry-Keene DA, Hawley CM, Hardie IR 1995 Long-term bone loss after renal transplantation: Comparison of immunosuppressive regimens. Clin Transplant 9:20–24.
16. Stempfle HU, Werner C, Echtler S, Assum T, Meiser B, Angermann CE, Theisen K, Gartner R 1998 Rapid trabecular bone loss after cardiac

17. transplantation using FK506 (tacrolimus)-based immunosuppression. Transplant Proc 30:1132–1133.
17. Park KM, Hay JE, Lee SG, Lee YJ, Wiesner RH, Porayko MK, Krom RA 1996 Bone loss after orthotopic liver transplantation: FK 506 versus cyclosporine. Transplant Proc 28:1738–1740.
18. Goffin E, Devogelaer JP, Lalaoui A, Depresseux G, De Naeyer P, Squifflet JP, Pirson Y, van Ypersele de Strihou C 2002 Tacrolimus and low-dose steroid immunosuppression preserves bone mass after renal transplantation. Transplant Int 15:73–80.
19. Monegal A, Navasa M, Guanabens N, Peris P, Pons F, Martinez de Osaba MJ, Rimola A, Rodes J, Munoz-Gomez J 2001 Bone mass and mineral metabolism in liver transplant patients treated with FK506 or cyclosporine A. Calcif Tissue Int 68:83–86.
20. Julian BA, Laskow DA, Dubovsky J, Dubovsky EV, Curtis JJ, Quarrles LD 1991 Rapid loss of vertebral bone density after renal transplantation. N Engl J Med 325:544–550.
21. Monier-Faugere M, Mawad H, Qi Q, Friedler R, Malluche HH 2000 High prevalence of low bone turnover and occurrence of osteomalacia after kidney transplantation. J Am Soc Nephrol 11:1093–1099.
22. Epstein S, Shane E 2001 Transplantation osteoporosis. In: Marcus R, Feldman D, Kelsey J (eds.) Osteoporosis, vol. 2. Academic Press, San Diego, CA, USA, pp. 327–340.
23. Shane E, Epstein S 2001 Transplantation Osteoporosis. Transplant Rev 15:11–32.
24. Pichette V, Bonnardeaux A, Prudhomme L, Gagne M, Cardinal J, Ouimet D 1996 Long-term bone loss in kidney transplant recipients: A cross-sectional and longitudinal study. Am J Kidney Dis 28:105–114.
25. Nowacka-Cieciura E, Durlik M, Cieciura T, Lewandowska D, Baczkowska T, Kukula K, Lao M, Szmidt J, Rowinski W 2002 Steroid withdrawal after renal transplantation–risks and benefits. Transplant Proc 34:560–563.
26. Cueto-Manzano AM, Konel S, Freemont AJ, Adams JE, Mawer B, Gokal R, Hutchison AJ 2000 Effect of 1,25-dihydroxyvitamin D3 and calcium carbonate on bone loss associated with long-term renal transplantation. Am J Kidney Dis 35:227–236.
27. Grotz W, Rump AL, Niessen H, Schmidt-Gayt A, Reichelt G, Kirste G, Olchewski G, Schollmeyer P 1998 Treatment of osteopenia and osteoporosis after kidney transplantation. Transplantation 66:1004–1008.
28. Cruz DN, Wysolmerski JJ, Brickel HM, Gundberg CG, Simpson CA, Mitnick MA, Kliger AS, Lorber MI, Basadonna GP, Friedman AL, Insogna KL, Bia MJ 2001 Parameters of high bone-turnover predict bone loss in renal transplant patients: A longitudinal study. Transplantation 72:83–88.
29. Brandenburg VM, Ketteler M, Fassbender WJ, Heussen N, Freuding T, Floege J, Ittel TH 2002 Development of lumbar bone mineral density in the late course after kidney transplantation. Am J Kidney Dis 40:1066–1074.
30. Farmer CKT, Hampson G, Vaja S, Abbs IC, Hilton RM, Koffman G, Watkins J, Sacks SH, Fogelman I 2002 Late low dose steroid withdrawal in renal transplant recipients increases bone formation and bone mineral density without altering renal function: A randomized controlled trial. J Bone Miner Res 17:S1;S158.
31. Ball AM, Gillen DL, Sherrard D, Weiss NS, Emerson SS, Seliger SL, Kestenbaum BR, Stehman-Breen C 2002 Risk of hip fracture among dialysis and renal transplant recipients. JAMA 288:3014–3018.
32. Smets YF, van de Pijl JW, de Fijter JW, Ringers J, Lemkes HH, Hamdy NA 1998 Low bone mass and high incidence of fractures after successful simultaneous pancreas-kidney transplantation. Nephrol Dial Transplant 13:1250–1255.
33. Chiu MY, Sprague SM, Bruce DS, Woodle ES, Thistlethwaite JR, Jr., Josephson MA 1998 Analysis of fracture prevalence in kidney-pancreas allograft recipients. J Am Soc Nephrol 9:677–683.
34. Shane E, Addesso V, Namerow PB, McMahon DJ, Lo SH, Staron RB, Zucker M, Pardi S, Maybaum S, Mancini D 2004 Alendronate versus calcitriol for the prevention of bone loss after cardiac transplantation. N Engl J Med 350:767–776.
35. Leidig-Bruckner G, Hosch S, Dodidou P, Ritchel D, Conradt C, Klose C, Otto G, Lange R, Theilmann L, Zimmerman R, Pritsch M, Zeigler R 2001 Frequency and predictors of osteoporotic fractures after cardiac or liver transplantation: A follow-up study. Lancet 357:342–347.
36. Compston JE 2003 Osteoporosis after liver transplantation. Liver Transpl 9:321–330.
37. Ninkovic M, Love S, Tom BD, Bearcroft PW, Alexander GJ, Compston JE 2002 Lack of effect of intravenous pamidronate on fracture incidence and bone mineral density after orthotopic liver transplantation. J Hepatol 37:93–100.
38. Floreani A, Mega A, Tizian L, Burra P, Boccagni P, Baldo V, Fagiuoli S, Naccarato R, Luisetto G 2001 Bone metabolism and gonad function in

male patients undergoing liver transplantation: A two-year longitudinal study. Osteoporos Int **12**:749–754.

39. Monegal A, Navasa M, Guanabens N, Peris P, Pons F, Martinez de Osaba MJ, Ordi J, Rimola A, Rodes J, Munoz-Gomez J 2001 Bone disease after liver transplantation: A long-term prospective study of bone mass changes, hormonal status and histomorphometric characteristics. Osteoporos Int **12**:484–492.

40. Carey EJ, Balan V, Kremers WK, Hay JE 2003 Osteopenia and osteoporosis in patients with end-stage liver disease caused by hepatitis C and alcoholic liver disease: Not just a cholestatic problem. Liver Transpl **9**:1166–1173.

41. Ninkovic M, Skingle SJ, Bearcroft PW, Bishop N, Alexander GJ, Compston JE 2000 Incidence of vertebral fractures in the first three months after orthotopic liver transplantation. Eur J Gastroenterol Hepatol **12**:931–935.

42. Tauchmanova L, Serio B, Del Puente A, Risitano AM, Esposito A, De Rosa G, Lombardi G, Colao A, Rotoli B, Selleri C 2002 Long-lasting bone damage detected by dual-energy x-ray absorptiometry, phalangeal osteosonogrammetry, and in vitro growth of marrow stromal cells after allogeneic stem cell transplantation. J Clin Endocrinol Metab **87**:5058–5065.

43. El-Agroudy AE, El-Husseini AA, El-Sayed M, Ghoneim MA 2003 Preventing bone loss in renal transplant recipients with vitamin D. J Am Soc Nephrol **14**:2975–2979.

44. De Sevaux RG, Hoitsma AJ, Corstens FH, Wetzels JF 2002 Treatment with vitamin D and calcium reduces bone loss after renal transplantation: A randomized study. J Am Soc Nephrol **13**:1608–1614.

45. Torres A, Garcia S, Gomez A, Gonzalez A, Barrios Y, Concepcion MT, Hernandez D, Garcia JJ, Checa MD, Lorenzo V, Salido E 2004 Treatment with intermittent calcitriol and calcium reduces bone loss after renal transplantation. Kidney Int **65**:705–712.

46. Sambrook P, Henderson NK, Keogh A, MacDonald P, Glanville A, Spratt P, Bergin E, Ebeling P, Eisman J 2000 Effect of calcitriol on bone loss after cardiac or lung transplantation. J Bone Miner Res **15**:1818–1824.

47. Ugur A, Guvener N, Isiklar I, Karakayali H, Erdal R 2000 Efficiency of preventive treatment for osteoporosis after renal transplantation. Transplant Proc **32**:556–557.

48. Stempfle HU, Werner C, Echtler S, Wehr U, Rambeck WA, Siebert U, Uberfuhr P, Angermann CE, Theisen K, Gartner R 1999 Prevention of osteoporosis after cardiac transplantation: A prospective, longitudinal, randomized, double-blind trial with calcitriol. Transplantation **68**:523–530.

49. Stempfle HU, Werner C, Siebert U, Assum T, Wehr U, Rambeck WA, Meiser B, Theisen K, Gartner R 2002 The role of tacrolimus (FK506)-based immunosuppression on bone mineral density and bone turnover after cardiac transplantation: A prospective, longitudinal, randomized, double-blind trial with calcitriol. Transplantation **73**:547–552.

50. Bianda T, Linka A, Junga G, Brunner H, Steinert H, Kiowski W, Schmid C 2000 Prevention of osteoporosis in heart transplant recipients: A comparison of calcitriol with calcitonin and pamidronate. Calcif Tissue Int **67**:116–121.

51. Krieg M, Seydoux C, Sandini L, Goy JJ, Berguer DG, Thiebaud D, Bruckhardt P 2001 Intravenous pamidronate as a treatment for osteoporosis after heart transplantation: A prospective study. Osteoporos Int **12**:112–116.

52. Coco M, Glicklich D, Faugere MC, Burris L, Bognar I, Durkin P, Tellis V, Greenstein S, Schechner R, Figueroa K, McDonough P, Wang G, Malluche H 2003 Prevention of bone loss in renal transplant recipients: A prospective, randomized trial of intravenous pamidronate. J Am Soc Nephrol **14**:2669–2676.

53. Fan S, Almond MK, Ball E, Evans K, J.Cunningham 2000 Pamidronate therapy as prevention of bone loss following renal transplantation. Kidney Int **57**:684–690.

54. Aris RM, Lester GE, Renner JB, Winders A, Denene Blackwood A, Lark RK, Ontjes DA 2000 Efficacy of pamidronate for osteoporosis in patients with cystic fibrosis following lung transplantation. Am J Respir Crit Care Med **162**:941–946.

55. Trombetti A, Gerbase MW, Spiliopoulos A, Slosman DO, Nicod LP, Rizzoli R 2000 Bone mineral density in lung-transplant recipients before and after graft: Prevention of lumbar spine post-transplantation-accelerated bone loss by pamidronate. J Heart Lung Transplant **19**:736–743.

56. Hommann M, Abendroth K, Lehmann G, Patzer N, Kornberg A, Voigt R, Seifert S, Hein G, Scheele J 2002 Effect of transplantation on bone: Osteoporosis after liver and multivisceral transplantation. Transplant Proc **34**:2296–2298.

57. Grotz W, Nagel C, Poeschel D, Cybulla M, Petersen KG, Uhl M, Strey C, Kirste G, Olschewski M, Reichelt A, Rump LC 2001 Effect of ibandronate on bone loss and renal function after kidney transplantation. J Am Soc Nephrol **12**:1530–1537.

58. Haas M, Leko-Mohr Z, Roschger P, Kletzmayr J, Schwarz C, Mitterbauer C, Steininger R, Grampp S, Klaushofer K, Delling G, Oberbauer R 2003 Zoledronic acid to prevent bone loss in the first 6 months after renal transplantation. Kidney Int **63**:1130–1136.

59. Ippoliti G, Pellegrini C, Campana C, Rinaldi M, D'Armini A, Goggi C, Aiello M, Vigano M 2003 Clodronate treatment of established bone loss in cardiac recipients: A randomized study. Transplantation **75**:330–334.

60. Kovac D, Lindic J, Kandus A, Bren AF 2001 Prevention of bone loss in kidney graft recipients. Transplant Proc **33**:1144–1145.

61. Giannini S, Dangel A, Carraro G, Nobile M, Rigotti P, Bonfante L, Marchini F, Zaninotto M, Dalle Carbonare L, Sartori L, Crepaldi G 2001 Alendronate prevents further bone loss in renal transplant recipients. J Bone Miner Res **16**:2111–2117.

62. Jeffery JR, Leslie WD, Karpinski ME, Nickerson PW, Rush DN 2003 Prevalence and treatment of decreased bone density in renal transplant recipients: A randomized prospective trial of calcitriol versus alendronate. Transplantation **76**:1498–1502.

63. Koc M, Tuglular S, Arikan H, Ozener C, Akoglu E 2002 Alendronate increases bone mineral density in long-term renal transplant recipients. Transplant Proc **34**:2111–2113.

64. Grigg AC, Shuttleworth P, Reynolds J, Szer J, Schwarer AP, Roberts AW, Bradstock KF, Hui CH, Herrmann R, Ebeling PR 2004 Pamidronate therapy for one year after allogeneic bone marrow transplantation (AlloBMT) reduces bone loss from the lumbar spine, femoral neck and total hip. Blood **104**:A2253.

65. Kananen K, Volin L, Laitinen K, Alfthan H, Ruutu T, Valimaki MJ 2005 Prevention of bone loss after allogeneic stem cell transplantation by calcium, vitamin D, and sex hormone replacement with or without pamidronate. J Clin Endocrinol Metab **90**:3877–3885.

66. Ebeling PR 2005 Defective osteoblast function may be responsible for bone loss from the proximal femur despite pamidronate therapy. J Clin Endocrinol Metab **90**:4414–4416.

67. Tauchmanova L, Selleri C, Esposito M, Di Somma C, Orio F Jr, Bifulco G, Palomba S, Lombardi G, Rotoli B, Colao A 2003 Beneficial treatment with risedronate in long-term survivors after allogeneic stem cell transplantation for hematological malignancies. Osteoporos Int **14**:1013–1019.

68. Tauchmanova L, Ricci P, Serio B, Lombardi G, Colao A, Rotoli B, Selleri C 2005 Short-term zoledronic acid treatment increases bone mineral density and marrow clonogenic fibroblast progenitors after allogeneic stem cell transplantation. J Clin Endocrinol Metab **90**:627–634.

69. Fahrleitner A, Prenner G, Tscheliessnigg KH, Leb G, Piswanger-Solkner CJ, Obermayer-Pietsch B, Dimai HP, Dobnig H 2002 Testosterone supplementation has additional benefits on bone metabolism in cardiac transplant recipients receiving intravenous bisphosphonate treatment: A prospective study. J Bone Miner Res **17**:S1;S388.

Chapter 57.   Inflammation-Induced Bone Loss in the Rheumatic Diseases

Georg Schett, Kurt Redlich, and Josef Smolen

Division of Rheumatology, Department of Internal Medicine III, Medical University of Vienna, Vienna, Austria

Rheumatic diseases constitute a heterogeneous group of disorders, which describe inflammatory or degenerative changes of the connective tissue. Despite their heterogeneity, most rheumatic diseases share a common target structure—the diarthrodial joint. Articular structures are built by connective tissue, which bridges two or more neighboring skeletal margins. They usually contain hyaline cartilage covering the bony ends and a fibrous joint capsule, which spans the skeletal gap by inserting at the periosteum of both neighboring bones. Articular cartilage serves as elastic cushion, which largely consists of extracellular matrix molecules such as aggrecan and collagen type II. The fibrous capsule creates a unique inner compartment, containing a mesodermal derived synovial membrane, which produces the synovial fluid. This mucin-rich fluid lubricates the joint space and allows smooth motion of joints.

The etiology of rheumatic diseases is largely unknown, and current hypotheses suggest that an interplay of genetically determined increased susceptibility of the host to inflammatory stimuli and environmental factors, which trigger the onset of symptoms, is important. A disturbed balance of the immune function is a key observation in inflammatory rheumatic diseases and a clue to current strategies of therapeutic intervention. Based on this immune imbalance, rheumatic diseases such as rheumatoid arthritis (RA), ankylosing spondylitis (AS), and systemic lupus erythematosus (SLE) are not confined to joints but also lead to systemic effects including bone loss.

Skeletal damage is a hallmark of many rheumatic diseases and crucially influences our therapeutic strategies. Whereas in the case of short-lasting and self-limited disease, structural skeletal damage is highly unusual, its likelihood increases when inflammation turns to chronic. Thus, inflammation and bone loss are two related conditions, but they are not necessarily linked to each other. Viral infections, such as parvovirus-triggered arthritis, for instance, closely mimic rheumatoid arthritis, but they are self-limited and resolve without any structural damage. In contrast, chronic forms of arthritis, such as psoriatic arthritis or RA, often result in destruction of the architecture of the joint and end up in functional impairment.

Skeletal involvement is rheumatic diseases has been most extensively studied in RA. Apart from chronic inflammation of the synovial membrane, bone loss is a characteristic feature of RA. In fact, various forms of skeletal damage, which differ in their relative localization to the affected joint, are known: These are (1) local bone erosion, (2) periarticular bone loss, and (3) generalized osteopenia. Local bone erosion is the most typical example for inflammatory bone loss. These lesions affect the subchondral bone at the joint margins and emerge at the interphase between articular cartilage, the insertion of the synovial membrane at the periosteum, and the underlying bone. Bone erosions are characterized by a massive but localized loss of juxtaarticular bone as well as mineralized cartilage in direct proximity of the inflammatory synovium. Their typical appearance allowed their first scientific description as "caries of the joint ends" in the late 19th century, even before RA was recognized as a separate disease entity.[1]

Local bone erosions have similarities to bone metastases of tumors and lead to the destruction of the skeletal architecture of the affected joint (Fig. 1). In contrast to bone metastases, where transformed cells precipitate local bone loss, the driving force of inflammatory bone erosions is a dense cellular infiltrate, termed pannus, which consists of fibroblasts, macrophages, lymphocytes, and blood vessels. This accumulation of inflammatory cells creates a microenvironment, which creates a negative balance of bone resorption and formation. In fact, the histological analysis of the pannus–bone interphase has shown numerous multinucleated cells populating bone erosions, which fulfill all features of functional osteoclasts, such as expression of TRACP, cathepsin K, and the calcitonin receptor.[2,3] The functional role of osteoclasts within arthritic bone erosions has been established in experimental models of murine arthritis, showing that either a genetic deletion of osteoclasts or their pharmacologic blockade protects from bone erosion even if inflammatory arthritis is fully developed.[4–6] Moreover, TNF blocking agents exert a potent bone-sparing effect in patients with RA, which even exceeds their anti-inflammatory potential and attributes to the well-known co-stimulatory role of TNF in osteoclastogenesis.[7,8] Together with growing evidence for a bone protective role of bisphosphonates in arthritis, these observations suggest that osteoclast are the key mediators for the breakdown of periarticular skeletal structures in RA.[9]

Two important features of inflammatory arthritis facilitate differentiation of osteoclasts in inflammatory arthritis: one is the induced expression of cytokines, such as TNF, IL-1, and RANKL, which stimulate osteoclast formation.[8,10–13] The other is the accumulation of cells of the monocyte/macrophage lineage in synovial inflammatory tissue, which express receptors such as RANK, which allow responding to these signals and differentiating into mature osteoclasts. The observation that cells at various differentiation steps of the osteoclast lineage populate local bone erosions supports the notion that these cells differentiate in the inflamed synovium in situ.[3] Whether these cells emerge from monocytes or whether these cells already enter the synovial compartment as osteoclast precursors is a matter of uncertainty. Observations that cells capable to differentiate into mature osteoclasts are enriched in the peripheral blood of patients with psoriatic arthritis at least support certain influence of the latter mechanism.[14] Much less is known about bone formation in arthritic bone erosion. Functional osteoblasts and deposition of osteoid can indeed be detected in these lesions, but this attempt to form new bone can apparently not outweigh massive bone resorption.[3,15] It is likely that cytokines produced from synovial inflammatory tissue suppress adequate bone formation to some extent. In, fact, TNF, one of the key cytokines in RA, inhibits differentiation and metabolic activity of osteoblasts.[16] Similar effects are known in tumor cells, which express inhibitors of osteoblast differentiation such as dickkopf-1, but thus far, such mechanisms have not been studied in inflammatory bone lesions.[17]

The clinical importance of local bone erosion is shown by three important findings. First, the detection of bone erosion in X-ray analyses is part of the classification criteria.[18] Thus, destruction of the cortical lining is a clear sign for destructive arthritis. Second, local bone erosion is one of the key moni-

The authors have reported no conflicts of interest.

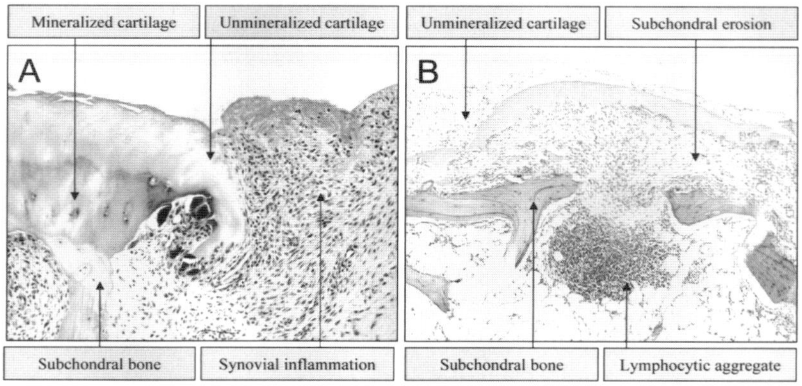

FIG. 1. (A) Decalcified paraffin-embedded tissue sections of a metacarpophalangeal joint of a patient with rheumatoid arthritis stained for TRACP. The image shows accumulation of osteoclasts (dark cells) at the site of local bone erosion. (B) Decalcified paraffin-embedded tissue sections of a metacarpophalangeal joint of a patient with rheumatoid arthritis stained by H&E. The image shows extensive resorption of mineralized cartilage and subchondral bone associated with full penetration of inflammatory synovial tissue through cortical bone into the marrow space. Within the marrow space, a lymphocytic aggregate is built up.

toring parameters for the efficacy of antirheumatic drugs to prevent, retard, or even arrest bone damage.[19] Third, bone erosion is associated with poor functional outcomes of RA patients.[20] Whereas functional impairment largely depends on swelling and pain in earlier disease stages, structural damage gains importance the longer disease lasts. High inflammatory disease activity is one of the most potent predictors of local bone erosions, pointing out the close relation of synovial inflammation and bone damage.[21] Importantly, the kinetics of emergence of bone lesions is fast in RA. Even with comparatively insensitive imaging techniques such as conventional radiographs, almost 50% of RA patients show bone erosions after 6 months of disease duration, which limits the time window to prevent skeletal damage to no more than a few months.[19] Subclinical bone erosions escaping detection by conventional radiographs might, in fact, form much earlier, even within days after onset of disease, as has been shown for osteoclast formation in experimental arthritis.[22]

Juxtaarticular osteopenia constitutes a second form of bone pathology in RA. It typically affects trabecular bone at the metaphyses near inflamed joints and is detected in hand radiographs of patients affected by RA. Juxtaarticular osteopenia is an early sign of disease. Thus, measurement of hand BMD has shown that RA patients lose bone mass early in disease, attributing to 5% loss of bone mass in the first year and another 5% in the following 2 years of disease.[23] The mechanism of juxtaarticular osteopenia is less clear, although its vicinity to arthritis suggests that synovial inflammation outside the cortical bone surface either directly or indirectly promotes a negative net effect on trabecular bone next to arthritic joints. Histological studies of specimen derived from joint replacement surgery of patients with RA have shown increased bone turnover at these trabecular sites.[24,25] There is also histomorphometric evidence for decreased bone volume and rarefaction of trabecular structures, which likely explains the osteopenic aspect of juxtaarticular bone in radiographs. Serial histological sections have also shown that local bone erosion can lead to a full penetration of the cortical barrier exposing the marrow space directly to synovial tissue.[25] Such interactions may be facilitated by Haversian channels, which tunnel cortical bone. When synovial inflammatory tissue reaches the bone marrow cavity, lymphocytic aggregates, predominantly consisting of B cells, form at the interphase between synovial inflammatory tissue and bone marrow adipocytes. These lesions are likely to be identical, with so-called "bone marrow edema" in MRI

scans of RA patients, which represent areas of reduced fat but increased water content in the marrow space, although a former proof for this is still lacking.[26] Interestingly, B cell–rich bone marrow aggregates not only express bone morphogenic proteins (BMPs), such as BMP-6, but are also associated with osteoblast accumulation and bone formation at the adjacent endosteum, which may be interpreted as a repair strategy to close the cortical bone damage.[27]

Generalized bone loss is another important feature of RA. Cross-sectional studies have shown a high prevalence of axial as well as appendicular osteoporosis in RA patients.[28] Roughly one third of RA patients are osteoporotic, and 10% face one or more vertebral fractures.[29] Longitudinal studies have shown that loss of systemic bone mass starts early in the course of disease. Thus, RA patients decrease in vertebral BMD by 2.5% and in hip BMD by 5% within the first year of disease and bone loss doubles after another year, if the disease is not adequately controlled.[30] Importantly, there is also clear evidence for an increased fracture risk of both vertebrae and at the hip.[31,32] Susceptibility to systemic bone loss and increased fracture risk among RA patients are partially identical with classical risk factors of bone loss, such as age, female gender, and postmenopausal state.[30]

Moreover, additional precipitators such as corticosteroid use and poor functional state add to the enhanced bone loss in RA. Thus, use of glucocorticoids increases the risk of peripheral fractures by the factor 2 and of vertebral fractures by the factor 5 compared with RA patients, which are not treated with glucocorticoids.[33] Whether this can also be applied to low-dose steroid therapy (<7.5 mg/day) is unclear and still a matter of controversy. Some authors suggest that the beneficial role of glucocorticoids in suppressing inflammation and restoring function may outweigh their deleterious effects.[30,34] Apart these secondary factors, there is still a direct link between RA and systemic bone loss. In fact, severity of disease as indicated by a high inflammatory disease activity is an independent risk factor for accelerated bone loss and increase fracture risk.[30,35–37] Disturbed bone turnover caused by the systemic presence of pro-inflammatory cytokines is the most likely explanation, but it remains thus far unclear whether increased bone resorption or decreased bone formation dominate this process. Whereas histomorphometric evaluation of bone of RA patients as well as the analysis of bone turnover in patients with juvenile arthritis suggests a decrease of bone formation as the primary event, other studies show evidence for systemically increased bone resorption.[38,39]

Although best studied in RA, bone loss is also a feature of other rheumatic diseases. AS is a systemic inflammatory disorder, which predominantly affects the axial skeleton. Although AS also manifests as an inflammation of synovial membrane, such as seen with affection of sacroiliac joints, inflammation of entheses and ligaments is pathognomonic. In the course of chronic inflammation, these tissues calcify and end up in fusion of neighboring skeletal structures, leading to stiffness as the classical clinical sign of disease. Despite clear signs for local bone formation and calcification, systemic bone mass in AS is low. Several studies have shown that the prevalence of vertebral osteoporosis is increased in AS and that there is an increased risk for vertebral but not peripheral fractures.[40] Typically clinical apparent vertebral fractures in disease lasting longer than two decades and a study by Cooper et al. have reported that fracture risk in AS can exceed those of normal individuals by the factor 7.[41] Major precipitators for vertebral fractures in AS are a low spinal mobility as well as a long disease duration, which both stress the lack of motion as a central trigger for vertebral bone loss.

SLE is another multisystem autoimmune disorder, which is characterized by chronic inflammation of skin, joints, and inner organs. Although arthritis is usually self-limited and nondestructive, mutilating forms of joint disease with destruction of the skeletal architecture (Jaccoud-Arthrpoathy) are known. More frequently, however, patients with SLE face systemic bone loss. The prevalence of osteopenia (up to 50%) and osteoporosis (up to 10%) is high, given that the average age of SLE patients is young.[42] Bone loss usually affects the trabecular bone of the hip and spine and leads to an increased risk of vertebral fractures, which occur in up to 20% of SLE patients.[42] As with chronic arthritis, the effects of chronic inflammation, drug therapy, low physical activity, and malnutrition add to osteoporosis in SLE.

In contrast to chronic inflammatory rheumatic diseases such as RA, AS, and SLE, the association of the most prevalent degenerative rheumatic disease, osteoarthritis (OA), with systemic bone loss is less clear. In the 1970s, Foss and Byers[43] reported on the absence of osteoarthritis changes in femoral heads of patients with osteoporotic hip fracture, which stimulated them to postulate an inverse relation of osteoarthritis and osteoporosis. Indeed, several cross-sectional studies and longitudinal studies of the Framing cohort confirmed an association between higher BMD and incident OA of the lower limbs.[44] However, this association seems to be more complex: Thus, (1) the inverse association between BMD and OA is only consistent in women and not in men, (2) is only valid for OA of the lower but not upper extremities, and (3) there is an apparent difference in the association with incidence or progression of OA. Thus, progression of OA is decreased rather than increased in patients with a high BMD; on the other hand, progression of bone loss is higher but not lower in patients with OA. Therefore, final conclusions on the interplay of OA and systemic bone mass need to be cautious unless further data are available.

Although, OA is currently considered as a primary disease of articular cartilage, changes in local bone turnover underneath the affected cartilage are well established. Several studies have shown an increased trabecular bone turnover and apparently bone formation is the predominant mechanism. Osteoarthritic bone shows radiological evidence for subchondral osteosclerosis.[45] Contrary to RA, the joint margins in OA show signs of bone formation. These lesions are termed osteophytes, which originate from chondroblastic and osteoblastic differentiation of periosteal cells. Experimental studies in animals have shown that these osteophytes depend on the presence of growth factors such as the BMP/TGF-β family, which enhance differentiation and metabolic activity of osteoblasts.[46]

REFERENCES

1. Weichselbaum A 1878 Die feineren Veränderungen des Gelenkknorpels bei fungöser Synovitis und Karies der Gelenkenden. Arch Pathol Anat Physiol Klin Med 73:461–475.
2. Bromley M, Woolley DE 1984 Chondroclasts and osteoclasts at subchondral sites of erosion in the rheumatoid joint. Arthritis Rheum 27:968–975.
3. Gravallese EM, Harada Y, Wang JT, Gorn AH, Thornhill TS, Goldring SR 1998 Identification of cell types responsible for bone resorption in rheumatoid arthritis and juvenile rheumatoid arthritis. Am J Pathol 152:943–951.
4. Redlich K, Hayer S, Ricci R, David JP, Tohidast-Akrad M, Kollias G, Steiner G, Smolen JS, Wagner EF, Schett G 2002 Osteoclasts are essential for TNF-alpha-mediated joint destruction. J Clin Invest 110:1419–1427.
5. Pettit AR, Ji H, von Stechow D, Müller R, Goldring SR, Choi Y, Benoist C, Gravallese EM 2001 TRANCE/RANKL knockout mice are protected from bone erosion in a serum transfer model of arthritis. Am J Pathol 159:1689–1699.
6. Kong YY, Feige U, Sarosi I, Bolon B, Tafuri A, Morony S, Capparelli C, Li J, Elliott R, McCabe S, Wong T, Campagnuolo G, Moran E, Bogoch ER, Van G, Nguyen LT, Ohashi PS, Lacey DL, Fish E, Boyle WJ, Penninger JM 1999 Activated T cells regulate bone loss and joint destruction in adjuvant arthritis through osteoprotegerin ligand. Nature 402:304–309.
7. Smolen JS, Han C, Bala M, Maini RN, Kalden JR, van der Heijde D, Breedveld FC, Furst DE, Lipsky PE, ATTRACT Study Group 2005 Evidence of radiographic benefit of treatment with infliximab plus methotrexate in rheumatoid arthritis patients who had no clinical improvement: A detailed subanalysis of data from the anti-tumor necrosis factor trial in rheumatoid arthritis with concomitant therapy study. Arthritis Rheum 52:1020–1030.
8. Lam J, Takeshita S, Barker JE, Kanagawa O, Ross FP, Teitelbaum SL 2000 TNF-alpha induces osteoclastogenesis by direct stimulation of macrophages exposed to permissive levels of RANK ligand. J Clin Invest 106:1481–1488.
9. Goldring SR, Gravallese EM 2004 Bisphosphonates: Environmental protection for the joint?. Arthritis Rheum 50:2044–2047.
10. Deleuren BW, Chu CG, Field M, Brennan FM, Katsikis P, Feldmann M, Maini RN 1992 Localization of interleukin-1 alpha, type 1 interleukin-1 receptor and interleukin-1 receptor antagonist in the synovial membrane and cartilage/pannus junction in rheumatoid arthritis. Br J Rheumatol 31:801–809.
11. Gravallese EM, Manning C, Tsay A, Naito A, Pan C, Amento E, Goldring SR 2000 Synovial tissue in rheumatoid arthritis is a source of osteoclast differentiation factor. Arthritis Rheum 43:250–258.
12. Shigeyama Y, Pap T, Kunzler P, Simmen BR, Gay RE, Gay S 2000 Expression of osteoclast differentiation factor in rheumatoid arthritis. Arthritis Rheum 43:2523–2530.
13. Wei S, Kitaura H, Zhou P, Ross FP, Teitelbaum SL 2005 IL-1 mediates TNF-induced osteoclastogenesis. J Clin Invest 115:282–290.
14. Ritchlin CT, Haas-Smith SA, Li P Hicks DG, Schwarz EM 2003 Mechanisms of TNF-alpha- and RANKL-mediated osteoclastogenesis and bone resorption in psoriatic arthritis. J Clin Invest 111:821–831.
15. Redlich, K, Görtz B, Hayer S, Zwerina J, Warmington K, Kostenuik P, Bergmeister H, Kollias G, Steiner G, Smolen JS, Schett G 2004 Repair of local bone erosions and reversal of systemic bone loss upon therapy with anti-TNF in combination with OPG or PTH in TNF-mediated arthritis. Am J Pathol 164:543–555.
16. Bertolini DR, Nedwin GE, Bringman TS, Smith DD, Mundy GR 1986 Stimulation of bone resorption and inhibition of bone formation in vitro by human tumour necrosis factors. Nature 319:516–518.
17. Tian E, Zhan F, Walker R, Rasmussen E, Ma Y, Barlogie B, Shaughnessy JD Jr 2003 The role of the Wnt-signaling antagonist DKK1 in the development of osteolytic lesions in multiple myeloma. N Engl J Med 349:2483–2494.
18. Arnett FC, Edworthy SM, Bloch DA, McShane DJ, Fries JF, Cooper NS, Healy LA, Kaplan SR, Liang MH, Luthra HS 1988 The American Rheumatism Association 1987 revised criteria for the classification of rheumatoid arthritis. Arthritis Rheum 31:315–324.
19. Van der Heijde DM 1995 Joint erosions and patients with early rheumatoid arthritis. Br J Rheumatol 34:74–78.
20. Scott DL, Pugner K, Kaarela K, Doyle DV, Woolf A, Holmes J, Hieke K

2000 The links between joint damage and disability in rheumatoid arthritis. Rheumatology (Oxf) **39**:122–132.

21. Van Leeuwen MA, van Rijswijk MH, van der Heide DM, Te Meerman GJ, van Riel PL, Houtman PM, van DE Putte LB, Limburg PC 1993 The acute phase response in relation to radiographic progression in early rheumatoid arthritis: A prospective study during the first three years of the disease. Br J Rheumatol **32**:9–13.

22. Schett G, Stolina M, Bolon B, Middleton S, Adlam M, Zack DJ, Brown H, Zhu L, Feige U 2005 Analysis of the kinetics of osteoclastogenesis in arthritic rats. Arthritis Rheum **52**:3192–3201.

23. Deodhar AA, Brabyn J, Pande I, Scott DL, Woolf AD 2003 Hand bone densitometry in rheumatoid arthritis, a five year longitudinal study: An outcome measure and a prognostic marker. Ann Rheum Dis **62**:767–770.

24. Shimizu S, Shiozawa S, Shiozawa K, Imura S, Fujita T 1985 Quantitative histologic studies on the pathogenesis of periarticular osteoporosis in rheumatoid arthritis. Arthritis Rheum **28**:25–31.

25. Jimenez-Boj E, Redlich K, Turk B, Hanslik-Schnabel B, Wanivenhaus A, Chott A, Smolen JS, Schett G 2005 Interaction between synovial inflammatory tissue and bone marrow in rheumatoid arthritis. J Immunol **175**:2579–2588.

26. Ostergaard, M, Peterfy C, Conaghan P, McQueen F, Bird P, Ejbjerg B, Shnier R, O'Connor P, Klarlund M, Emery P, Genant H, Lassere M, Edmonds J 2003 OMERACT rheumatoid arthritis magnetic resonance imaging studies. Core set of MRI acquisitions, joint pathology definitions, and the OMERACT RA-MRI scoring system. J Rheumatol **30**:1385–1386.

27. Görtz B, Hayer S, Redlich K, Zwerina J, Tohidast-Akrad M, Tuerk B, Hartmann C, Kollias G, Steiner G, Smolen JS, Schett G 2004 Arthritis induces lymphocytic bone marrow inflammation and endosteal bone formation. J Bone Miner Res **19**:990–998.

28. Woolf AD 1991 Osteoporosis in rheumatoid arthritis—the clinical viewpoint. Br J Rheumatol **30**:82–84.

29. Sinigaglia L, Nervetti A, Mela Q, Bianchi G, Del Puente A, Di Munno O, Frediani B, Cantatore F, Pellerito R, Bartolone S, La Montagna G, Adami S 2000 A multicenter cross sectional study on bone mineral density in rheumatoid arthritis. Italian Study Group on Bone Mass in Rheumatoid Arthritis. J Rheumatol **27**:2582–2589.

30. Gough AK, Lilley J, Eyre S, Holder RL, Emery P 1994 Generalized bone loss in patients with early rheumatoid arthritis. Lancet **344**:23–27.

31. Spector TD, Hall GM, McCloskey EV, Kanis JA 1993 Risk of vertebral fracture in women with rheumatoid arthritis. BMJ **306**:558.

32. Hooyman JR, Melton LJ III, Nelson AM, O'Fallon WM, Riggs BL 1984 Fractures after rheumatoid arthritis. A population-based study. Arthritis Rheum **27**:1353–1361.

33. Lems WF, Jahangier ZN, Raymakers JA, Jacobs JW, Bijlsma JW 1997

34. Kirwan Kirwan JR 1995 The effect of glucocorticoids on joint destruction in rheumatoid arthritis. The Arthritis and Rheumatism Council Low-Dose Glucocorticoid Study Group. N Engl J Med **333**:142–146.

35. Cooper C, Coupland C, Mitchell M 1995 Rheumatoid arthritis, corticosteroid therapy and hip fracture. Ann Rheum Dis **54**:49–52.

36. Peel NF, Spittlehouse AJ, Bax DE, Eastell R 1994 Bone mineral density of the hand in rheumatoid arthritis. Arthritis Rheum **37**:983–991.

37. Kvien TK, Haugeberg,G, Uhlig, T, Falch JA, Halse JI, Lems WF, Dijkmans BA, Woolf AD 2000 Data driven attempt to create a clinical algorithm for identification of women with rheumatoid arthritis at high risk of osteoporosis. Ann Rheum Dis **59**:805–811.

38. Compston JE, Vedi S, Croucher PI, Garrahan NJ, O'Sullivan MM 1994 Bone turnover in non-steroid treated rheumatoid arthritis. Ann Rheum Dis **53**:163–166.

39. Gough A, Sambrook P, Devlin J, Huissoon A, Njeh C, Robbins S, Nguyen T, Emery P 1998 Osteoclastic activation is the principal mechanism leading to secondary osteoporosis in rheumatoid arthritis. J Rheumatol **25**:1282–1289.

40. Ralston SH, Urquhart GD, Brzeski M, Sturrock RD 1990 Prevalence of vertebral compression fractures due to osteoporosis in ankylosing spondylitis. BMJ **300**:563–565.

41. Cooper C, Carbone L, Michet CJ, Atkinson EJ, O'Fallon WM, Melton LJ III 1994 Fracture risk in patients with ankylosing spondylitis: A population based study. J Rheumatol **21**:1877–1882.

42. Bultink IE, Lems WF, Kostense PJ, Dijkmans BA, Voskuyl AE 2005 Prevalence of and risk factors for low bone mineral density and vertebral fractures in patients with systemic lupus erythematosus. Arthritis Rheum **52**:2044–2050.

43. Foss MV, Byers PD 1972 Bone density, osteoarthrosis of the hip, and fracture of the upper end of the femur. Ann Rheum Dis **31**:259–264.

44. Zhang Y, Hannan MT, Chaisson CE Zhang Y, Niu J, Kelly-Hayes M, Chaisson CE, Aliabadi P, Felson DT 2002 Prevalence of symptomatic hand osteoarthritis and its impact on functional status among the elderly: The Framingham Study. Am J Epidemiol **156**:1021–1027.

45. Jordan GR, Loveridge N, Power J, Clarke MT, Parker M, Reeve J 2003 The ratio of osteocytic incorporation to bone matrix formation in femoral neck cancellous bone: An enhanced osteoblast work rate in the vicinity of hip osteoarthritis. Calcif Tissue Int **72**:190–196.

46. Scharstuhl A, Vitters EL, van der Kraan PM, van den Berg WB 2003 Reduction of osteophyte formation and synovial thickening by adenoviral overexpression of transforming growth factor beta/bone morphogenetic protein inhibitors during experimental osteoarthritis. Arthritis Rheum **48**:3442–3451.

Chapter 58.   Orthopedic Complications of Osteoporosis

Susan V. Bukata and Regis J. O'Keefe

Department of Orthopaedics, University of Rochester, Rochester, New York

INTRODUCTION

In the United States, >1.5 million fragility fractures occur annually and cost >17 billion dollars to treat, and the cost estimates do not include indirect costs associated with lost work days and the need for long-term care. Vertebral fractures are most common and account for 700,000 fractures. Other common osteoporotic fractures include the hip (300,000 fractures) and distal radius (250, 000 fractures), with a variety of others sites making up the additional 250,000 fractures related to osteoporosis annually.[1,2] Fractures in the setting of osteoporosis present a difficult challenge. The goal is to maintain as much function as possible during the healing process. Many patients are elderly with multiple medical problems that often interfere with healing and increase the rate of fracture and medical related complications, and slow rehabilitation. The decreased mechanical strength of bone makes surgical fixation of the skeleton more tenuous and frequently slows the rehabilitation process. Finally, multiple fragility fractures are often present simultaneously and occur at new sites during the process of rehabilitation, further complicating the recovery at any one particular site.[3,4]

LOWER EXTREMITY FRACTURES

The high morbidity and mortality associated with hip fractures make them the most serious osteoporotic fracture. One quarter of female patients and one third of the male patients die within a year of a hip fracture.[5] Furthermore, 50% of hip fracture patients suffer long-term disabilities, which include

Dr. Bukata has been on the Speakers Bureau for Eli Lilly. All other authors have reported no conflicts of interest.

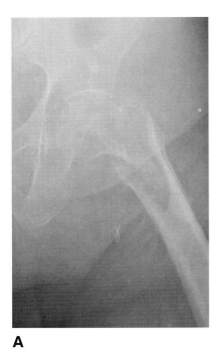

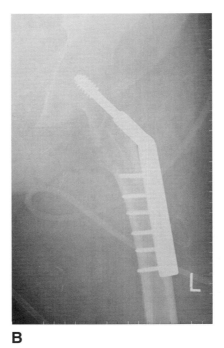

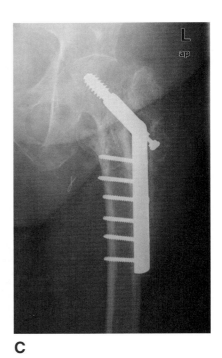

A　　　　　　　　　　**B**　　　　　　　　　　**C**

FIG. 1. Intertrochanteric hip fracture. (A) Preoperative. (B) Immediately postoperative. (C) Healed fracture. Note collapse of sliding hip screw to stable position.

chronic pain, diminished strength, the need for assistive devices for ambulation, and reduced functional status.[6] The capacity to perform activities of daily living such rising from a chair, getting into and out of bed, and climbing stairs are frequently impaired. Studies have shown that nearly 25% of hip fracture patients require long-term care, and an even larger percentage of patients will take a step down in their level of function, requiring increased assistance to complete activities of daily living and loss of independence.[7,8] Ideally, patients should be medically stabilized before surgery, but early fixation within 48 h of the fracture has been shown to minimize morbidity associated with both the surgery and the fracture. Longer delays are warranted if medical intervention can improve the condition of the patient and correct any acute issues that contributed to or resulted from the injury. The goal of any surgery is to allow early weight bearing and mobilization to decrease the complications associated with prolonged bedrest.[9–12]

Fragility fractures of the hip most commonly involve the femoral neck and the intertrochanteric region. These fractures require surgical management with the goal to provide pain relief, fracture stability, and the ability to mobilize the patient. Femoral neck fractures present as either displaced or nondisplaced and choice of fixation depends primarily on the degree of displacement of the fracture.[13] Nondisplaced or minimally displaced femoral neck fractures are most commonly treated with percutaneous screw fixation. Typically a cluster of three parallel screws are inserted from the proximal lateral cortex, just below the trochanter. The screws cross the fracture site and are inserted into the femoral head. With stable fixation, early weight bearing is possible and does not increase the risk of fixation failure or nonunion.[14]

Because femoral neck fractures with displacement have a high incidence of avascular necrosis of the femoral head, hemi-arthroplasty of the hip is typically the procedure of choice in patients with displaced hip fractures.[15–17] The femoral prosthesis is typically inserted using cement fixation, which permits the patient to resume full weight bearing as soon possible. Compared with percutaneous hip pinning, hemi-arthroplasty is a more lengthy procedure, has more blood loss, and a higher potential for perioperative complications.

Inter-trochanteric hip fractures also require surgical fixation and are anatomically defined by a fracture line that extends from the greater trochanter to the lesser trochanter. Inter-trochanteric fractures with this simple fracture pattern are further classified as two-part fractures. Additional fracture lines resulting in separation of the greater trochanter (three-part fractures) and both the greater trochanter and the lesser trochanter (four-part fractures) are frequently present and represent an inherently less stable fracture pattern.

The most common device used for fixation of inter-trochanteric hip fractures is the sliding hip screw and side plate.[18] Insertion of a large screw into the femoral neck and head provides fixation of the proximal fragment. The side plate has a barrel attached to it that permits the hip screw to "slide" relative to the plate (Fig. 1). The sliding action permits the proximal fragment to move relative to the distal fragment until a point is reach whereby bone contact provides resistance to further motion. In this manner, the sliding hip screw is a "load sharing" device; both the metal provides and host bone account for stabilization of the fracture. This device has a >95% rate of successful healing, and studies have shown that patients may return to full, unrestricted weight bearing as tolerated.[19,20] Intramedullary fixation provides another alternative to the sliding hip screw. Intramedullary also involve placement of a screw into the femoral neck and head for stabilization of the proximal segment, but the screw is subsequently fixed to an intramedullary implant. Because an intramedullary implant is closer to the center of rotation of the hip joint than a plate along the side of the bone, these devices receive less torque force and have more inherent stability. As such, they are sometimes used in fractures with less inherent stability, including in fractures that extend below the lesser trochanter into the femoral shaft (subtrochanteric region) and fractures with a "reverse obliquity" fracture line (extending from the femoral neck to the lateral cortex rather than from trochanter to trochanter).[21]

UPPER EXTREMITY FRACTURES

Fragility fractures occur at the proximal humerus, distal humerus, and elbow, but are most common at the wrist. Wrist fractures are often the first presenting fracture in osteoporosis. While these are often successfully treated with cast immobilization they frequently heal with residual deformity and typically result in decreased motion. When some healing has been obtained at the fracture site, patients can be shifted to a removable wrist splint and start working to regain motion.[22] Fractures that are unstable or have a displacement of the articular surface require operative fixation. Operative fixation can include plates and screws or placement of an external fixation device.[23] Screws in the distal metaphysis of the wrist may have relatively poor mechanical stability, and as with tibial plateau fractures, bone graft may be required to provide structural support for a damaged articular surface. External fixation uses soft tissues adjacent to the fracture including the ligaments, tendons, and muscles to pull the fractured fragments into position and maintain normal bone length by distraction (referred to as ligamentotaxis). This allows the fracture to be maintained in an acceptable position until healing can occur. Some external fixators for the wrist even allow for early motion while stabilizing the fracture in an effort to minimize joint stiffness.[24,25]

Most proximal humerus fractures are treated nonoperatively. The pattern of the fracture and displacement of the fragments determine whether open reduction and fixation is required to obtain adequate shoulder strength and range of motion to complete normal activities after healing. As with hip fractures, proximal humerus fractures are classified as two-part, three-part, or four-part fractures. Four-part fractures are the most severe and involve four major fragments: the head of the humerus, the humerus shaft, and the greater and lesser tuberosities of the humerus. Four-part fractures have a high risk of avascular necrosis of the humeral head and are treated with prosthetic replacement. Head splitting fractures that extend into the articular surface or damage all of the supporting bone below the articular surface are also treated with prosthetic replacement. Displaced two-part and three-part fractures can be surgically reduced and stabilized with plates and screws, but the fixation in osteoporotic bone may be tenuous. This has resulted in a relative reluctance to surgically treat these fractures, and poor fracture alignment is likely more often accepted in these patients with subsequent increased fracture morbidity.[26] More recently plates with locking screws have been used in the treatment of these fractures, but long-term clinical data on the results of these constructs are yet unknown. Tension bands can be used in the treatment of some fractures, taking advantage of the tissues of the rotator cuff to reapproximate the fracture fragments and compress these fragments to one another with motion of the shoulder. Tension bands pass through the bone of the proximal humerus and into the tissues of the rotator cuff, creating a "figure of 8" construct that helps to stabilize the fracture.[20,27] Fractures of the distal humerus and elbow also require open reduction and internal fixation if the position or integrity of the articular surface is affected. Loss of at least a portion of the normal range of motion of the elbow is commonly associated with these fractures.

PERIPROSTHETIC FRACTURES

Many elderly patients have undergone joint replacement surgery to treat arthritis and the presence of hardware has the potential to create areas of stress concentration in the setting of falls and other trauma. Fragility fractures adjacent to joint replacement implants present a special challenge. If the hip, knee, or proximal humerus implant has stable fixation to the bone, fracture treatment techniques involving the use of special plates and cables can be used to salvage the implants. If the fracture destabilizes the implant–bone interface, the implant frequently must be removed, the fracture is stabilized, and a longer implant extending further into the shaft of the bone or even replacing more of the original bone must be used to obtain a stable construct. Long stem hip replacements and special knee replacements that are used in revision joint surgery are frequently used to reconstruct the joint and the fractured bone. Bone graft or even larger allograft struts can provide a stable surface to hold hardware and encourage adequate bone healing in severely damaged areas.[28–30] Fractures of the supracondylar femur above a knee replacement can be treated with a retrograde femoral nail that is passed between the condyles of the knee replacement and up the femur. This construct depends heavily on the stability of the locking screws at proximal and distal ends of these femoral nails, but it provides an option for treating fractures around knee implants that maintains the prosthetic joint.[31]

PELVIC RING FRACTURES

Pelvic fragility (or insufficiency) fractures occur at high frequency in patients with low BMD. They occur after low-impact trauma and account for 55,000 hospitalizations per year in the United States. Fractures of the superior and inferior rami and the sacral ala can be quite debilitating and painful. As with hip fractures, women are more commonly affected than men and the mortality associated with pelvic fractures are similar to that observed in hip fractures: 10% at 1 year, 20% at 2 years, and 50% at 5 years.[32] Nondisplaced or minimally displaced pelvic fractures are typically treated conservatively with analgesics and activity limitation to minimize pain.

While patients are permitted to bear weight as tolerated on most of these fractures, pain often severely limits their ability to walk, stand, and change positions from lying down to seated to standing. Most fractures heal with time. However, elderly patients with pelvic fractures require substantial health care resources, have prolonged lengths of stay in hospitals and rehabilitation units, and have a increased need for health care services.[33–35] In these patients, mortality exceeds 12% per year.[36]

AUGMENTATION OF OSTEOPOROTIC BONE IN FRACTURE REPAIR

A substantial obstacle in the treatment of osteoporotic fractures is the innate weakness of the undamaged bone. In young bone with high mechanical strength, hardware can fail if a fracture does not heal. In osteoporotic bone, the weakest component of the repair construct is the bone itself. Instead of metal failure, the bone/implant interface fails, with pullout of the screws from the bone. Depending on the location of the fracture, between 10% and 50% of surgically treated patients can have a suboptimal result because of failure of the osteoporotic bone around the hardware.[37]

Several techniques can be used to improve the likelihood of success in treating fragility fractures. The use of larger diameter screws in cancellous bone and an emphasis on securing as much cortical purchase as possible helps to combat some of the difficulties presented by decreased BMD. Newer plates have locking threads for the heads of the screws preventing them from loosening within the plate and backing out of the bone.

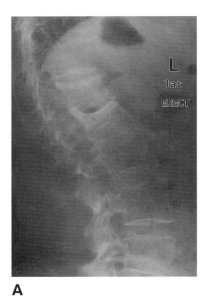

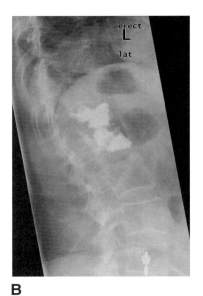

A   **B**

FIG. 2.   (A) L_1 and L_2 compression fractures. (B) L_1 and L_2 after kyphoplasty.

These locking plates are now being used more commonly in metaphyseal region fractures and severely comminuted fractures because they can function as fixed angle devices. They allow several smaller screws to grab multiple pieces of the fracture, often in a broader area than possible with the large cancellous screws used with standard plates where the heads of the screws are simply tightened against the surface of the plate. Polymethylmethacrylate cement (PMMA) can be used to augment screw fixation into osteoporotic bone. Bone allograft as crushed chips, small cubes, or cortical struts can be placed to help reinforce an area where there is not enough bone to securely support the hardware and the adjacent undamaged bone.[38–40]

VERTEBRAL FRACTURES

Although vertebral fractures are the most common osteoporotic fracture and occur much more frequently than hip fractures annually, they are often overlooked. Because the symptoms associated with these fractures resolve with rest, activity modification, and analgesic agents, many patients with back pain do not have X-ray identification of the fracture at the time that it occurs. In addition, nearly one half of the vertebral fractures are minimally symptomatic or do not present to health care professionals and thus go undiagnosed.[41]

Vertebral fractures can have a tremendous effect on quality of life, long after the pain from the fracture resolves. Chronic back pain, loss of height, and localized kyphosis affect patients with compression fractures. Compression fractures can also reduce the lung and abdominal volume, with a loss in ventilatory capacity and a protruding abdomen as contents move forward to make up for the lack of vertical space. Multiple lumbar vertebral fractures reduces the distance between the ribs and the pelvic iliac wings and ultimately can result in the rib cage resting on and rubbing against the ileum. This is a very painful condition, and long-term pain management is the only treatment for this problem.

Kyphosis, which is curvature of the spine in the sagittal plane, results in a change in the position of the head relative to the central axis of the body. To maintain balance, patients compensate by flexing their pelvis. This further decreases the volume of the abdominal cavity. Patients with kyphosis lean forward, and this posture increases the risk of falls and the development of additional osteoporotic fractures, lacerations, and head injuries. Changes in posture and loss of vertebral height result in reduced paraspinal muscle strength and chronic back pain as muscle demands are increased. Finally conformational changes in the spine frequently exacerbate other symptoms caused by spinal stenosis, arthritis, or nerve root compression.

Vertebral compression fractures typically present in one of three patterns. Most common is the anterior wedge fracture, where the anterior portion of the vertebral body collapses relative to the posterior elements. This results in loss of height as well as localized angulation of the spine and development of kyphosis. Crush fractures that result in the complete collapse of the entire vertebral body are less common, but can add the risk of pushing material from the posterior wall of the vertebrae into the spinal canal, reducing the space available for the spinal cord and nerve roots. Fortunately, significant compromise of the spinal canal is rare. The third type of fracture is a biconcave fracture in which the superior and inferior endplates of the vertebral body collapse into the central portion while the heights of the anterior and posterior portions of the vertebral body are relatively maintained. This has less effect on the structural integrity of the spinal column and is frequently an early sign of developing osteoporotic fractures in the spine. The biconcave fracture is often present in association with other fractures in the spinal column. Fractures occur most commonly in the thoracolumbar junction (T_{12} and L_1) and the midthoracic region (T_6–T_8), but can occur at any level in the spine.[42,43]

Clinically symptomatic fractures are managed in most patients with analgesics and activity modification. Hyperextension bracing can be used to help maintain posture during the early phases of healing, and when pain improves, physical therapy with an emphasis on extension exercises can be instituted.[44,45] Patients who do not respond to medical therapy and have persistent pain or continued fracture collapse are candidates for treatment with vertebroplasty or kyphoplasty. Both of these minimally invasive treatments use PMMA to provide mechanical stability for the fractured vertebrae and pain relief. In a vertebroplasty, a needle is introduced into the vertebral body through the pedicle or immediately adjacent to the pedicle (extrapedicular), and low-viscosity cement is injected directly into the fractured vertebral body under high pressure. In a kyphoplasty, an inflatable balloon is first passed into the vertebral body through a similar approach and inflated in an attempt to restore vertebral height and correct some of the angular deformity caused by the fracture. The balloon is then withdrawn, and the void created by it is filled with PMMA cement, using a lower pressure and more viscous cement (Fig. 2). Both vertebroplasty and kyphoplasty provide significant and almost immediate pain relief in 80% of patients. To date, no prospective, randomized, controlled trials comparing the two techniques has been performed to assess the relative efficacy of the two methods. Complication rates are very low with both techniques, with cement leakage, cerebrospinal fluid leak from a dural tear, and cement embolization reported.[46,47]

Long-term follow-up of kyphoplasty and vertebroplasty outcomes in patients with osteoporotic fractures show sustained pain relief at 2 and 3 years, respectively.[48–50] Fractures in adjacent vertebral bodies in patients with primary osteoporosis have been shown to increase in the first 2 months after the procedure. However, the ~2:1 ratio of adjacent to nonadjacent subsequent fractures is observed in both surgical and drug-treated patient populations. If cement augmentation was responsible for an increased risk of subsequent fractures, the ratio of adjacent fractures would be expected to be higher. Furthermore, after 6 months, other studies show a decrease in subsequent fractures compared with nonsurgically treated patients. Altogether, the literature suggests a beneficial effect of kyphoplasty and vertebroplasty in osteoporotic patients. However, patients with steroid-induced osteoporosis do seem to have an increased risk of subsequent vertebral fracture after cement augmentation. It is essential that patients undergoing cement augmentation also be placed on a medical regimen for their osteoporosis to obtain optimal results.[51,52]

MANAGEMENT OF METABOLIC BONE DISEASE

Despite growing public awareness of osteoporosis, there continues to be an abysmal record of management of metabolic bone disease in patients who have suffered osteoporotic fractures. In multiple studies of patients with hip fractures, therapy for osteoporosis was initiated in only 11–13% of patients after management of the hip fracture.[53,54] Thus, these patients remain unprotected and at extremely high risk for additional osteoporotic fractures. Patients are discharged without diagnosis or management of their underlying osteoporosis. Surgeons often assume that the patient's primary care physician will initiate diagnosis and management of osteoporosis, yet the issue commonly is never addressed by any of the patient's physicians. Intervention protocols have shown an improvement in treatment to 47–65%, but many barriers including denial of the disease by the patient, lack of work-up by the physicians, and lack of compliance with prescribed treatments contribute to the failures in treatment.[55,56] Thus, osteoporosis lags behind other common diseases such as hypertension in diagnosis and management, and this provides an extremely important window of opportunity to improve bone health in the next decade.

After a fragility fracture, patients should be started immediately on a regimen of daily calcium and vitamin D supplementation until a metabolic bone work-up is completed, provided that the fractures are not associated with malignancy and hypercalcemia. Controversy exists regarding the timing of bisphosphonate treatment after a fracture. Animal studies show an increase in fracture callus volume in bisphosphonate treated animals compared with controls, but the biomechanical strength of the callus is equal to that observed in the control animals. Minimal human data exists regarding fractures and bisphosphonates. Children with osteogenesis imperfecta

treated with bisphosphonates have normal healing after fractures, but have shown delayed healing after osteotomy to correct limb alignment. Thus, at doses used for osteoporosis treatment, humans do not have clear evidence of impaired fracture healing. Cancer patients and patients with Paget's disease receive much larger doses of bisphosphonates, but no information on fracture healing in these patients has been published.[57,58]

REFERENCES

1. Riggs BL, Melton LJ 1995 The worldwide problem of osteoporosis: Insights afforded by epidemiology. Bone **17:**S505–S511.
2. Chrischilles E, Shireman T, Wallace R 1994 Costs and health effects of osteoporotic fractures. Bone **15:**377–386.
3. Lucas TS, Einhorn TA 1993 Osteoporosis: The role of the orthopaedist. J Am Acad Orthop Surg **1:**48–56.
4. Cummings SR, Melton LJ 2002 Epidemiology and outcomes of osteoporotic fractures. Lancet **359:**1761–1767.
5. Center JR, Nguyen TV, Schneider D, Sambrook PN, Eisman JA 1999 Mortality after all major types of osteoporotic fracture in men and women: An observational study. Lancet **353:**878–882.
6. Zuckerman JD 1996 Hip fracture. N Engl J Med **334:**1519–1525.
7. Wehren LE, Magaziner J 2003 Hip fracture: Risk factors and outcomes. Curr Osteoporos Rep **1:**78–85.
8. Egol KA, Koval KJ, Zuckerman JD 1997 Functional recovery following hip fracture in the elderly. J Orthop Trauma **11:**594–599.
9. Kenzora JE, Mc Carthy RE, Lowell JD, Sledge CB 1984 Hip fracture mortality. Relation to age, treatment, preoperative illness, time of surgery, and complications. Clin Orthop **186:**45–56.
10. Zuckerman JD Skovron ML, Koval KJ, Aharonoff G, Frankel WH 1995 postoperative complications and mortality associated with operative delay in older patients who have a fracture of the hip. J Bone Joint Surg Am **77:**1551–1556.
11. Koval KJ, Zuckerman JD 1994 Functional recovery after fracture of the hip. J Bone Joint Surg Am **76:**955–962.
12. Borgquist L, Ceder L, Thorngren KG 1990 Function and social status 10 years after hip fracture. Prospective follow-up of 103 patients. Acta Orthop Scand **61:**404–410.
13. Chen WC, Yu SW, Tseng IC, Su JY, Tu YK, Chen WJ 2005 Treatment of undisplaced femoral neck fractures in the elderly. J Trauma **58:**1035–1039.
14. Koval KJ, Friend KD, Aharonoff GB, Zuckerman JD 1996 Weight bearing after hip fracture: A prospective series of 596 geriatric hip fracture patients. J Orthop Trauma **10:**526–530.
15. Tidermark J, Ponzer S, Svensson O, Soderqvist A, Tornkvist H 2003 Internal fixation compared with total hip replacement for displaced femoral neck fractures in the elderly. A randomized, controlled trial. J Bone Joint Surg Br **85:**380–388.
16. Rogmark C, Carlsson A, Johnell O, Sernbo I 2002 A prospective randomized trial of internal fixation versus arthroplasty for displaced fractures of the neck of the femur. Function outcome for 450 patients at two years. J Bone Joint Surg Br **84:**183–188.
17. Roden M, Schon M, Fredin H 2003 Treatment of displaced femoral neck fractures: A randomized minimum 5 year follow-up study of screws and bipolar hemiprostheses in 100 patients. Acta Orthop Scand **74:**42–44.
18. Kyle RF, Gustilo RB, Premer RF 1979 Analysis of six hundred and twenty-two intertrochanteric hip fractures. J Bone Joint Surg Am **61:**216–221.
19. Cornell C 2003 Internal fracture fixation in patients with osteoporosis. J Am Acad Orthop Surg **11:**109–119.
20. Lindskog DM, Baumgaertner MR 2004 Unstable intertrochanteric hip fractures in the elderly. J Am Acad Orthop Surg **12:**179–190.
21. Kummer FJ, Olsson O, Pearlman CA, Ceder L, Larsson S, Koval KJ 1998 Intramedullary versus extramedullary fixation of subtrochanteric fractures: A biomechanical study. Acta Orthop Scand **69:**580–584.
22. Fernandez DL 2005 Closed manipulation and casting of distal radius fractures. Hand Clin **21:**307–316.
23. Ring D, Jupiter JB 2005 Treatment of osteoporotic distal radius fractures. Osteoporos Int **16:** S80–S84.
24. Clyburn TA 1987 Dynamic external fixation for comminuted intra-articular fractures of the distal end of the radius. J Bone Joint Surg Am **69:**248–254.
25. Kaempffe FA, Walker KM 2000 External fixation for distal radius fractures: Effect of distraction on outcome. Clin Orthop **380:**220–225.
26. Szyszkowitz R, Seggl W, Schleifer P, Cundy PJ 1993 Proximal humeral

fractures: Management techniques and expected results. Clin Orthop **292:**13–25.

27. Cornell CN, Levine D, Pagnani MJ 1994 Internal fixation of proximal humerus fractures using the screw-tension band technique. J Orthop Trauma **8:**23–27.

28. Parvizi J, Rapuri VR, Purtill JJ, Sharkey PF, Rothman RH, Hozack WJ 2004 Treatment protocol for proximal femoral periprosthetic fractures. J Bone Joint Surg Am **86:**8–16.

29. Duwelius PJ, Schmidt AH, Kyle RF, Talbott V, Ellis TJ, Butler JB 2004 A prospective, modernized treatment protocol for periprosthetic femur fractures. Orthop Clin North Am **35:**485–492.

30. Ricci WM, Bolhofner BR, Loftus T, Cox C, Mitchell S, Borrelli J 2005 Indirect reduction and plate fixation, without grafting, for periprosthetic femoral shaft fractures about a stable intramedullary implant. J Bone Joint Surg Am **87:**2240–2245.

31. Tharani R, Nakasone C, Vince KG 2005 Periprosthetic fractures after total knee arthroplasty. J Arthroplasty **20:**27–32.

32. Hill RM, Robinson CM, Keating JF 2001 Fractures of the pelvic rami. Epidemiology and five year survival. J Bone Joint Surg Am **83:**1141–1144.

33. Ebraheim NA, Biyani A, Wong F 1998 Nonunion of pelvic fractures. J Trauma **44:**202–204.

34. Mears DC, Velyvis JH 2002 In situ fixation of pelvic nonunions following pathologic and insufficiency fractures. J Bone Joint Surg Am **84:**721–728.

35. Melton LJ, Sampson JM, Morrey BF, Ilstrup DM 1981 Epidemiologic features of pelvic fractures. Clin Orthoped Relat Res **155:**43–47.

36. Rossvol I, Finsen V 1989 Mortality after pelvic fractures in the elderly. J Orthop Trauma **3:**115–117.

37. Alho A 1993 Mineral and mechanics of bone fragility fractures: A review of fixation methods. Acta Orthop Scand **64:**227–232.

38. Stankewich CJ, Swiontkowski MF, Tencer AF, Yetkinler DN, Poser RD 1996 Augmentation of femoral neck fracture fixation with an injectable calcium-phosphate bone mineral cement. J Orthop Res **14:**786–793.

39. Schatzker J 1998 Fractures of the distal femur revisted. Clin Orthop **347:**43–56.

40. Haddad FS, Duncan CP 2003 Cortical onlay allograft struts in the treatment of periprosthetic femoral fractures. Instr Course Lect **52:**291–300.

41. Kado DM, Browner WS, Palermo L, Nevitt MC, Genant HK, Cummings SR 1999 Vertebral fractures and mortality in older women: A prospective study. Arch Intern Med **159:**1215–1220.

42. Cooper C, O'Neil T, Silman AJ 1993 The epidemiology of vertebral fractures. Bone **14:**S89–S97.

43. Haczyriski J, Jakimiuk AJ 2001 Vertebral fractures: A hidden problem of osteoporosis. Med Sci Monit **7:**1108–1117.

44. Lukert BP 1994 Vertebral compression fractures: How to manage pain, avoid disability. Geriatrics **49:**22–26.

45. Melton LJ 1997 Epidemiology of spinal osteoporosis. Spine **22:**2S–11S, 1997.

46. Tamayo-Orozco J, Arzac-Palumbo P, Peon-Vidales H, Mota-Bolfeta R, Fuentes F 1997 Vertebral fractures associated with osteoporosis: Patient management. Am J Med **103:**44S–50S.

47. Spivak JM, Johnson MG 2005 Percutaneous treatment of vertebral body pathology. J Am Acad Orthop Surg **13:**6–17.

48. Legroux-Gerot I, Lormeau C, Boutry N, Cotton A, Duquesnoy B, Cortet B 2004 Long-term follow-up of vertebral osteoporotic fractures treated by percutaneous vertebroplasty. Clin Rheumatol **23:**310–317.

49. Do HM, Kim BS, Marcellus ML, Curtis L, Marks MP 2005 Prospective analysis of clinical outcomes after percutaneous vertebroplasty for painful osteoporotic vertebral body fractures. Am J Neuroradiol **26:**1623–1628.

50. Ledlie JT, Renfro MB 2006 Kyphoplasty treatment of vertebral fractures: 2-year outcomes show sustained benefits. Spine **31:**57–64.

51. Fribourg D, Tang C, Sra P, Delamarter R, Bae H 2004 Incidence of subsequent vertebral fracture after kyphoplasty. Spine **29:**2270–2276.

52. Harrop JS, Prpa B, Reinhardt MK, Lieberman I 2004 Primary and secondary osteoporosis' incidence of subsequent vertebral compression fractures after kyphoplasty. Spine **29:**2120–2125.

53. Bouxsein ML, Kaufman J, Tosi L, Cummings S, Lane JM, Johnell O 2004 Recommendations for Optimal Care of the Fragility Fracture Patient to Reduce Risk of Future Fracture. J Am Acad Orthop Surg **12:**48–56.

54. Freedman KB, Kaplan FS, Bilker WB, Strom BL, Lowe RA 2000 Treatment of osteoporosis: Are physicians missing an opportunity? J Bone Joint Surg Am **82:**1063–1070.

55. Feldstein AC, Nichols GA, Elmer PJ, Smith DH, Aickin M, Herson M 2003 Older women with fractures: Patients falling through the cracks of guideline-recommended osteoporosis screening and treatment. J Bone Joint Surg Am **85:**2294–2302.

56. Gardner MJ. Brophy RH, Demetrakopoulos D, Koob J, Hong R, Rana A, Lin JT, Lane JM 2005 Interventions to improve osteoporosis treatment following hip fracture. A prospective, randomized trial. J Bone Joint Surg Am **87:**1–2.

57. Munns CF, Rauch F, Zeitlin L, Fassier F, Glorieux FH 2004 Delayed osteotomy but not fracture healing in pediatric osteogenesis imperfecta patients receiving pamidronate. J Bone Miner Res **19:**1779–1786.

58. Fleisch H 2001 Can bisphosphonates be given to patients with fractures? J Bone Miner Res **16:**437–440.

SECTION VII

Metabolic Bone Diseases
(Section Editors: Craig B. Langman and Michael P. Whyte)

Chapter 59.   Paget's Disease of Bone

Ethel S. Siris[1] and G. David Roodman[2]

[1]Department of Medicine, Columbia University College of Physicians and Surgeons, New York, New York; and [2]Department of Medicine, University of Pittsburgh, Pittsburgh, Pennsylvania

INTRODUCTION

Paget's disease of bone is a localized disorder of bone remodeling. The process is initiated by increases in osteoclast-mediated bone resorption, with subsequent compensatory increases in new bone formation, resulting in a disorganized mosaic of woven and lamellar bone at affected skeletal sites. This structural change produces bone that is expanded in size, less compact, more vascular, and more susceptible to deformity or fracture than is normal bone.[1] Clinical signs and symptoms will vary from one patient to the next depending on the number and location of affected skeletal sites, as well as on the degree and extent of the abnormal bone turnover. It is believed that most patients are asymptomatic, but a substantial minority may experience a variety of symptoms, including bone pain, secondary arthritic problems, bone deformity, excessive warmth over bone from hypervascularity, and a variety of neurological complications caused in most instances by compression of neural tissues adjacent to pagetic bone.

ETIOLOGY

Although Paget's disease is the second most common bone disease after osteoporosis, little is known about its pathogenesis—why it is highly localized, the potential role paramyxoviral infection might play, the basis for the unusual geographic distribution, and the contribution of a genetic component to the disease process.

It is abundantly clear that there is a strong genetic predisposition involved in the pathophysiology of Paget's disease. Paget's disease occurs commonly in families and can be transmitted vertically between generations in an affected family. In patients with Paget's disease described in several clinical series, 15–30% have positive family histories of the disorder.[2] An extensive study of relatives of 35 patients with Paget's disease in Madrid revealed that 40% of the patients had at least one first-degree relative affected with the disease.[3] Other studies have confirmed an autosomal dominant pattern of inheritance for Paget's disease.[4] Familial aggregation studies in a United States population[5] suggest that the risk of a first-degree relative of a pagetic subject developing the condition is seven times greater than is the risk for someone who does not have an affected relative.

Several genetic loci have been linked to familial Paget's disease. Cody et al.[6] described a predisposition locus on chromosome 18q in a large family with Paget's disease, and other groups[7,8] have identified different predisposition loci on chromosome 18, and on chromosome 6. No specific genes have been identified at these loci, and none are located on chromosome 13, which contains the *RANKL* gene. In a Japanese family with atypical Paget's disease, a mutation in the *RANK* gene has been reported,[9] but this mutation is not found in the overwhelming majority of patients with familial Paget's disease.[10]

Laurin et al.[11] in Quebec have mapped a mutation in a gene on 5q35-QTER, which encodes a ubiquitin binding protein, sequestasome-1 (SQSTM14/$p62^{ZIP}$), as a candidate gene for Paget's disease because of its association with the NF-κB signaling pathway. This mutation results in a proline to leucine substitution at amino acid 392 of the protein that was not found in 291 controls. The mutation was detected in 11 of 24 French-Canadian families with Paget's disease and 18 unrelated Paget's disease patients. Sequestasome-1 acts as an anchor protein and plays an important role in the NF-κB signaling pathway. It binds either TNF receptor–associated factor (TRAF)-6 in the interleukin (IL)-1 or receptor-interacting protein (RIP)-1 in the TNF signaling pathway to activate NF-κB. However, the $p62^{ZIP}$ mutation does not completely explain the pagetic phenotype. There is large phenotypic variability in patients with Paget's disease associated with the mutation in $p62^{ZIP}$. For example, one individual who is 77 years-old and carried this $p62^{ZIP}$ mutation had no signs of the disease.[12] Moreover, homozygotes and heterozygotes seem to be similarly affected, suggesting that other genetic and/or environmental factors such as a common viral infection may contribute to the variability and the severity of Paget's disease of bone.[12] Hocking et al.[8] studied a large group of patients with familial Paget's disease and found a mutation in the $p62^{ZIP}$ gene in 19% of the patients. A second mutation in $p62^{ZIP}$ in which a T insertion that introduces a stop code in position 396 was also found in 6% of the families, and a third mutation affecting a splice donor site in intron A was found in 2% of the families. Thus, 30% of patients with familial Paget's disease have mutations in the $p62^{ZIP}$ gene. These mutations are associated with a variable clinical phenotype, including no evidence of Paget's disease in at least one or two individuals, and they cannot explain the highly localized nature of the disease.

Ethnic and geographic clustering of Paget's disease also has been described, with the intriguing observation that the disorder is quite common in some parts of the world but relatively rare in others. Clinical observations indicate that the disease is most common in Europe, North America, Australia, and New Zealand. Studies surveying radiologists have computed prevalence rates in hospitalized patients >55 years in several European cities and found the highest percentages in England (4.6%) and France (2.4%), with other Western European countries reporting slightly lower prevalences (e.g., 0.7–1.7% in Ireland, 1.3% in Spain and West Germany, and 0.5% in Italy and Greece).[13] There is a remarkable focus of Paget's disease in Lancashire, England, where 6.3–8.3% of people >55 years in several Lancashire towns had radiographs revealing Paget's disease.[14]

Prevalence rates seem to decrease from north to south in Europe, except for the finding that Norway and Sweden have a particularly low rate (0.3%).[13] Few data are available from Eastern Europe, but Russian colleagues indicate that Paget's disease is not uncommon in that country. The disorder is seen in Australia and New Zealand at rates of 3–4%.[15] Paget's disease is distinctly rare in Asia, particularly in China, India, and Malaysia, although occasional cases of Indians living in the United States have been documented. Similar radiographic studies have described a prevalence of 0.01–0.02% in several areas of sub-Saharan Africa.[15] In Israel, the disease is seen predominantly in Jews[16] but was recently found to exist in Israeli Arabs as well.[17] In Argentina, the disease seems to be restricted to an area surrounding Buenos Aires and predominantly occurs in patients descended from European immi-

Dr. Siris is a consultant for Merck, Procter & Gamble, and Novartis, but not in the field of Paget's disease or its treatment. Dr. Roodman is a consultant for Scios, Merck, and Novartis.

grants.[18] It is estimated, based on very few studies, that 2–3% of people >55 years living in the United States have Paget's disease. It is believed that most Americans with Paget's disease are white and of Anglo-Saxon or European descent. The disorder is described in blacks, and most clinical series from hospitals in major American cities report having black patients.[2,19]

Some recent studies have remarked on an apparent decline in the frequency and severity of Paget's disease in both New Zealand and Great Britain.[20,21] The basis for this decline is unknown, but the changes are too rapid to be explained by a genetic cause and cannot be explained by migration patterns of persons with a predisposition to Paget's disease.

For >30 years, studies have suggested that Paget's disease may result from a chronic paramyxoviral infection. This is based on ultrastructural studies by Rebel et al.,[22] who showed that nuclear and, less commonly, cytoplasmic inclusions that were similar to nucleocapsids from paramyxoviruses were present in osteoclasts from Paget's disease patients. Mills et al.[23] also reported that the measles virus nucleocapsid antigen was present in osteoclasts from patients with Paget's disease, but not from patients with other bone diseases. In some specimens, both measles virus and respiratory syncytial virus nucleocapsid proteins were shown by immunocytochemistry on serial sections. Similarly, Basle et al.[24] have also shown the presence of measles virus nucleocapsid protein in patients with Paget's disease, but also found other paramyxoviral proteins as well.

Recently, Friedrichs et al.[25] have reported the full sequence of the measles virus nucleocapsid protein isolated from a patient with Paget's disease as well as 700 bp of measles virus nucleocapsid protein sequence from three other patients. In contrast, Gordon et al.,[26] using in situ hybridization studies, examined specimens from English patients with Paget's disease and found canine distemper virus nucleocapsid protein in 11 of 25 patients. Mee et al.,[27] using highly sensitive in situ PCR techniques, found that osteoclasts from 12 of 12 English patients with Paget's disease expressed canine distemper virus nucleocapsid transcripts.

Kurihara et al.[28] have provided in vitro evidence for a possible pathophysiologic role for measles virus in the abnormal osteoclast activity in Paget's disease. They transfected the measles virus nucleocapsid gene into normal human osteoclast precursors and showed that the osteoclasts that formed expressed many of the abnormal characteristics of pagetic osteoclasts. However, other workers have been unable to confirm the presence of measles virus or canine distemper virus in pagetic osteoclasts,[29] so that the role of a chronic paramyxoviral infection in Paget's disease remains controversial. Recently, Kurihara et al. targeted the measles virus nucleocapsid gene to cells in the osteoclast lineage in transgenic mice, and ~40% of these mice developed localized bone lesions that are similar to lesions seen in patients with Paget's disease. However, these results do not show a cause and effect relationship between measles virus and Paget's disease.[30]

Among the many questions that need to be explained to understand a putative viral etiology of Paget's disease are as follows. (1) Because paramyxoviral infections such as measles virus occur worldwide, why does Paget's disease have a very restricted geographic distribution? (2) How does the virus persist in osteoclasts in patients who are immunocompetent for such long periods of time, because measles virus infections generally occur in children rather than adults, and Paget's disease is usually diagnosed in elderly patients over the age of 55?

The presence of an acquired or inherited genetic component to explain Paget's disease has its limitations as well. It is very difficult to explain the variable phenotypic presentation of patients with familial Paget's disease, especially that some of these patients who carry the mutated gene do not have Paget's disease although they are >70 years of age. Furthermore, it is very difficult to explain how a mutation of a specific gene expressed in bone results in a highly focal disease such as Paget's disease. More likely, environmental factors and genetic factors are both required for patients to develop Paget's disease.

PATHOLOGY

Histopathologic Findings in Paget's Disease

The initiating lesion in Paget's disease is an increase in bone resorption. This occurs in association with an abnormality in the osteoclasts found at affected sites. Pagetic osteoclasts are more numerous than normal and contain substantially more nuclei than do normal osteoclasts, with up to 100 nuclei per cell noted by some investigators. In response to the increase in bone resorption, numerous osteoblasts are recruited to pagetic sites where active and rapid new bone formation occurs. It is generally believed that the osteoblasts are intrinsically normal,[31] but this has not been proven conclusively.

In the earliest phases of Paget's disease, increased osteoclastic bone resorption dominates, a picture appreciated radiographically by an advancing lytic wedge or "blade-of-grass" lesion in a long bone or by osteoporosis circumscripta, as seen in the skull. At the level of the bone biopsy, the structurally abnormal osteoclasts are abundant. After this, there is a combination of increased resorption and relatively tightly coupled new-bone formation, produced by the large numbers of osteoblasts present at these sites. During this phase, and presumably because of the accelerated nature of the process, the new bone that is made is abnormal. Newly deposited collagen fibers are laid down in a haphazard rather than a linear fashion, creating more primitive woven bone. The woven-bone pattern is not specific for Paget's disease, but it does reflect a high rate of bone turnover. The end product is the so-called mosaic pattern of woven bone plus irregular sections of lamellar bone linked in a disorganized way by numerous cement lines representing the extent of previous areas of bone resorption. The bone marrow becomes infiltrated by excessive fibrous connective tissue and by an increased number of blood vessels, explaining the hypervascular state of the bone. Bone matrix at pagetic sites is usually normally mineralized, and tetracycline labeling shows increased calcification rates. It is not unusual, however, to find areas of pagetic biopsy specimens in which widened osteoid seams are apparent, perhaps reflecting inadequate calcium/phosphorus products in localized areas where rapid bone turnover heightens mineral demands.

In time, the hypercellularity at a locus of affected bone may diminish, leaving the end product of a sclerotic, pagetic mosaic without evidence of active bone turnover. This is so-called burned out Paget's disease. Typically, all phases of the pagetic process can be seen at the same time at different sites in a particular subject. Scanning electron microscopy affords an excellent view of the chaotic architectural changes that occur in pagetic bone and provides the visual imagery that makes comprehensible the loss of structural integrity. Figure 1 compares the appearances of normal and of pagetic bone using this technique. Figure 2 show the mosaic pattern of disorganized bone in Paget's disease in most of the field, contrasted with a normal pattern of new bone deposition after restoration of normal turnover with bisphosphonate therapy.

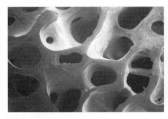

FIG. 1. Scanning electron micrographs with sections of normal bone (left) and pagetic bone (right). Both samples were taken from the iliac crest. The normal bone shows the trabecular plates and marrow spaces to be well preserved, whereas the pagetic bone has completely lost this architectural appearance. Extensive pitting of the pagetic bone is apparent, caused by dramatically increased osteoclastic bone resorption. [Photographs courtesy of Dr. David Dempster. The first photograph is reprinted from J Bone Miner Res 1986 **1**:15–21 with permission of the American Society for Bone and Mineral Research. The second photograph is reproduced from Siris ES, Canfield RE 1995 Paget's disease of bone. In: Becker KL (ed.) Principles and Practice of Endocrinology and Metabolism. 2nd ed. JB Lippincott, Philadelphia, PA, USA, pp. 585–594, with permission.]

Biochemical Parameters of Paget's Disease

Increases in the urinary excretion of biomarkers of bone resorption such as collagen cross-links and associated peptides (e.g., N-telopeptide of type 1 collagen [NTX], C-telopeptide of type 1 collagen [CTX], deoxypyridinoline [DPD])[32] reflect the primary lesion in Paget's disease, the increase in bone resorption. Increases in osteoblastic activity are associated with elevated levels of serum alkaline phosphatase. In untreated patients, the values of these two markers rise in proportion to each other, offering a reflection of the preserved coupling between resorption and formation. From the clinical perspective, the degree of elevation of these indices offers an approximation of the extent or severity of the abnormal bone turnover, with higher levels reflecting a more active, ongoing localized metabolic process. Interestingly, the patients with the highest alkaline phosphatase elevations (e.g., >10 times the upper limit of normal) typically have involvement of the skull as at least one site of the disorder. Active monostotic disease (other than skull) may have lower biochemical values than polyostotic disease. Lower values (e.g., less than three times the upper limit of normal) may reflect a lesser extent of involvement (i.e., fewer sites on bone scans or radiographs) or a lesser degree of increased bone turnover at affected skeletal sites. However, mild elevations in a patient with highly localized disease (e.g., the proximal tibia) may be associated with symptoms and clear progression of disease at the affected site over time. Indeed, a so-called "normal" alkaline phosphatase (e.g., a value a slightly less than the upper limit of normal for the assay) may not truly be normal for the pagetic patient. Today many would argue that to be confident that the value is normal (and the disease quiescent), a result in the middle of the normal range is required.

In addition to offering some estimate of the degree of increased bone turnover, measurement of a bone resorption marker and serum alkaline phosphatase is useful in observing the disorder over time and especially for monitoring the effects of treatment. Potent bisphosphonates are capable of normalizing the biochemical markers (i.e., producing a remission of the bone remodeling abnormality) in a majority of patients and bringing the markers to near normal in most others so that the monitoring role has heightened importance in assessing treatment effects. A urinary resorption marker such as the N- or C-telopeptide of collagen may become normal in days to a few weeks after bisphosphonate therapy is initiated. It is often most practical and least expensive, however, to monitor serum alkaline phosphatase as the sole biochemical endpoint, with a baseline measure and subsequent follow-up tests at intervals appropriate for the therapy used. If a patient has concomitant elevations of liver enzymes, a measurement of bone-specific alkaline phosphatase can be especially helpful. Serum osteocalcin, however, is not a useful measurement in Paget's disease.

Serum calcium levels are typically normal in Paget's disease, but they may become elevated in two special situations. First, if a patient with active, usually extensive Paget's disease is immobilized, the loss of the weight-bearing stimulus to new bone formation may transiently uncouple resorption and accretion, so that increasing hypercalciuria and hypercalcemia may occur. This is a relatively infrequent occurrence. Alternatively, when hypercalcemia is discovered in an otherwise healthy, ambulatory patient with Paget's disease, coexistent primary hyperparathyroidism may be the cause. Inasmuch as increased levels of PTH can drive the intrinsic pagetic remodeling abnormality to even higher levels of activity, correction of primary hyperparathyroidism in such cases is indicated.

Several investigators have commented on the 15–20% prevalence of secondary hyperparathyroidism (associated with normal levels of serum calcium) in Paget's disease, typically seen in patients with very high levels of serum alkaline phosphatase.[33,34] The increase in PTH is believed to reflect the need to increase calcium availability to bone during phases of very active pagetic bone formation, particularly in subjects in whom dietary intake of calcium is inadequate. Secondary hyperparathyroidism and transient decreases in serum calcium also can occur in some patients being treated with potent bisphosphonates such as pamidronate, alendronate, risedronate, or zoledronic acid. This results from the effective and rapid suppression of bone resorption in the setting of ongoing new-bone formation.[35] Later, as restoration of coupling occurs with time, PTH levels fall. The problem can be largely avoided by being certain that such patients are and remain replete in both calcium and vitamin D.

Elevations in serum uric acid and serum citrate have been described in Paget's disease and are of unclear clinical significance.[1] Gout has been noted in this disorder, but it is uncertain whether it is more common in pagetic patients than in nonpagetic subjects. Hypercalciuria may occur in some patients with Paget's disease, presumably because of the in-

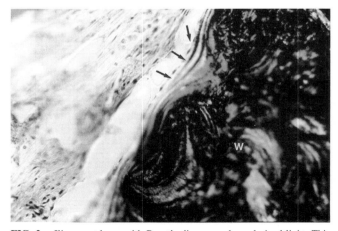

FIG. 2. Iliac crest bone with Paget's disease under polarized light. This patient had been treated with potent bisphosphonate therapy. Older bone is present in a pattern of woven bone (W), but new bone deposition after suppression of increased pagetic turnover shows a normal pattern of bone deposition (arrows).

creased bone resorption, and kidney stones are occasionally found as a consequence of this abnormality.[1]

Clinical Features of Paget's Disease

Paget's disease affects both men and women, with most series describing a slight male predominance. It is rarely observed to occur in individuals <25 years of age, it is thought to develop as a clinical entity after the age of 40 in most instances, and it is most commonly diagnosed in people over the age of 50. In a survey of >800 selected patients in the United States, 600 of whom had symptoms, the average age at diagnosis was 58 years.[36] It seems likely that many patients have the disorder for a period of time before any diagnosis is made, especially because it is often an incidental finding.

It is important to emphasize the localized nature of Paget's disease. It may be monostotic, affecting only a single bone or portion of a bone (Fig. 3), or may be polyostotic, involving two or more bones. Sites of disease are often asymmetric. A patient might have a pagetic right femur with a normal left, involvement of only one-half the pelvis, or involvement of several noncontiguous vertebral bodies. Clinical observation suggests that in most instances, sites affected with Paget's disease when the diagnosis is made are the only ones that will show pagetic change over time. Although progression of disease within a given bone may occur (Fig. 4), the sudden appearance of new sites of involvement years after the initial diagnosis is uncommon. This information can be very reassuring for patients who often worry about extension of the disorder to new areas of the skeleton as they age.

The most common sites of involvement include the pelvis, femur, spine, skull, and tibia. The bones of the upper extremity, as well as the clavicles, scapulae, ribs, and facial bones, are less commonly involved, and the hands and feet are only rarely affected. It is generally believed that most patients with Paget's disease are asymptomatic and that the disorder is most often diagnosed when an elevated serum alkaline phosphatase is noted on routine screening or when a radiograph taken for an unrelated problem reveals typical skeletal changes. The development of symptoms or complications of Paget's disease is influenced by the particular areas of involvement, the interrelationship between affected bone and adjacent structures, the extent of metabolic activity, and presence or absence of disease progression within an affected site.

Signs and Symptoms

Bone pain from a site of pagetic involvement, experienced either at rest or with motion, is probably the most common symptom. The direct cause of the pain may be difficult to characterize and requires careful evaluation. Pagetic bone associated with a high turnover state has an increased vascularity, leading to a sensation of warmth of the skin overlying bone (e.g., skull or tibia) that some patients perceive as an unpleasant sensation. Small transverse lucencies along the expanded cortices of involved weight-bearing bones or advancing, lytic, blade-of-grass lesions sometimes cause pain. It is postulated that microfractures frequently occur in pagetic bone and can cause discomfort for a period of days to weeks.

A bowing deformity of the femur or tibia can lead to pain for several possible reasons. A bowed limb is typically shortened, resulting in specific gait abnormalities that can lead to abnormal mechanical stresses. Clinically severe secondary arthritis can occur at joints adjacent to pagetic bone (e.g., the hip, knee, or ankle). The secondary gait problems also may lead to arthritic changes on the contralateral nonpagetic side, particularly at the hip.

Back pain in pagetic patients is another difficult symptom to

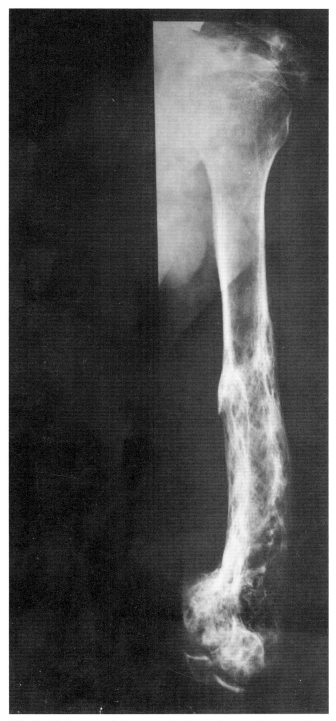

FIG. 3. Radiograph of a humerus showing typical pagetic change in the distal half, with cortical thickening, expansion, and mixed areas of lucency and sclerosis, contrasted with normal bone in the proximal half.

assess. Nonspecific aches and pains may emanate from enlarged pagetic vertebrae in some instances; vertebral compression fractures also may be seen at pagetic sites. In the lumbar area, spinal stenosis with neural impingement may arise, producing radicular pain and possibly motor impairment. Degenerative changes in the spine may accompany pagetic changes, and it is useful for the clinician to determine which symptoms arise as a consequence of the pagetic process and which result from degenerative disease of nonpagetic vertebrae. Kyphosis may occur, or there may be a forward tilt of the upper back, particularly when a compression fracture or spinal stenosis is present. Treatment options will differ, depending on the cause of the symptoms. When Paget's disease affects the thoracic spine, there may rarely be syndromes of direct spinal cord compression with motor and sensory changes. Several cases of apparent direct cord compression with loss of neural function have now been documented to have resulted from a vascular steal syndrome, whereby hypervascular pagetic bone "steals" blood from the neural tissue.[37]

Paget's disease of the skull, shown radiographically in Fig. 5, may be asymptomatic, but common complaints in up to one third of patients with skull involvement may include an increase in head size with or without frontal bossing or deformity, or headache, sometimes described as a band-like tightening around the head. Hearing loss may occur as a result of isolated or combined conductive or neurosensory abnormalities; recent data suggest cochlear damage from pagetic involvement of the temporal bone with loss of bone density in the cochlear capsule is an important component.[38] Cranial nerve palsies (such as in nerves II, VI, and VII) occur rarely. With extensive skull involvement, a softening of the base of the skull may produce platybasia, or flattening, with the development of basilar invagination, so that the odontoid process begins to extend upward as the skull sinks downward on it. This feature can be appreciated by various radiographic measures including skull radiographs and CT or MRI scans. Although many patients with severe skull changes may have radiographic evidence of basilar invagination, a relatively small number develop a very serious complication, such as direct brainstem compression or an obstructive hydrocephalus and increased intracranial pressure caused by blockage of cerebrospinal fluid flow. Pagetic involvement of the facial bones may cause facial deformity, dental problems, and, rarely, narrowing of the airway. Mechanical changes of these types may lead to a nasal intonation when the patient is speaking.

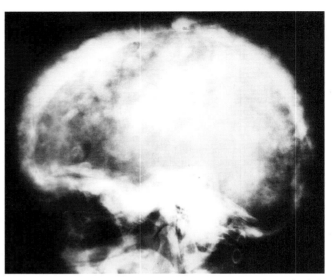

FIG. 5. Typical "cotton-wool" appearance of an enlarged pagetic skull with marked osteoblastic change. The patient had an increase in head size and deafness.

Fracture through pagetic bone is an occasional and serious complication. These fractures may be either traumatic or pathological, particularly involving long bones with active areas of advancing lytic disease; the most common involve the femoral shaft or subtrochanteric area.[39] The increased vascularity of actively remodeling pagetic bone (i.e., with a moderately increased serum alkaline phosphatase) may lead to substantial blood loss in the presence of fractures caused by trauma. Fractures also may occur in the presence of areas of malignant degeneration, a rare complication of Paget's disease. Far more common are the small fissure fractures along the convex surfaces of bowed lower extremities, which may be asymptomatic, stable, and persistent for years, but sometimes a more extensive transverse lucent area extends medially from the cortex and may lead to a clinical fracture with time. As described later, there are data indicating that blade-of-grass lytic areas as well as these larger transverse fractures may respond to antipagetic treatment and heal. These types of lesions warrant radiographic follow-up over time. Conversely, the smaller fissure fractures typically do not change with treatment and, in the absence of new pain, rarely require extensive radiographic monitoring. In most cases, fracture through pagetic bone heals normally, although some groups have reported as high as a 10% rate of nonunion.

Neoplastic degeneration of pagetic bone is a relatively rare event, occurring with an incidence of <1%. This abnormality has a grave prognosis, typically manifesting itself as new pain at a pagetic site. The most common site of sarcomatous change seems to be the pelvis, with the femur and humerus next in frequency.[40] Typically these lesions are destructive. The majority of the tumors are classified as osteogenic sarcomas, although both fibrosarcomas and chondrosarcomas are also seen. Current treatment regimens emphasize maximal resection of tumor mass and chemotherapy and sometimes radiotherapy. Unfortunately, in these typically elderly patients, death from massive local extension of disease or from pulmonary metastases occurs in the majority of cases in 1–3 years.

Benign giant-cell tumors also may occur in bone affected by Paget's disease. These lesions may present as localized masses at the affected site. Radiographic evaluation may disclose lytic changes. Biopsy reveals clusters of large osteoclast-like cells,

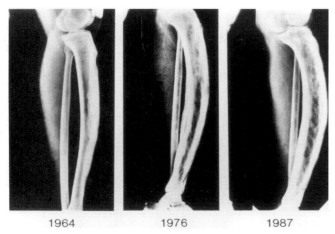

1964   1976   1987

FIG. 4. This series of radiographs of a pagetic tibia show progression of pagetic change and bowing deformity in an untreated patient. This individual's Paget's disease was limited to the tibia and was associated with a serum alkaline phosphatase level that was generally only mildly elevated to about twice the upper limit of normal. Note the distal progression of cortical thickening with time, as well as the worsening of the bowing deformity. (Reprinted from Siris ES, Feldman F 1997 Clinical vignette: Natural history of untreated Paget's disease of the tibia. J Bone Miner Res **12:**691–692, with permission of the American Society for Bone and Mineral Research.)

which some authors believe represent reparative granulomas.[41] These tumors may show a remarkable sensitivity to glucocorticoids, so in many instances, the mass will shrink or even disappear after treatment with prednisone or dexamethasone.[42]

DIAGNOSIS

When Paget's disease is suspected, the diagnostic evaluation should include a careful medical history and physical examination. The possibility of a positive family history and a symptom history should be ascertained. Gout, pseudogout, and arthritis are all possible complications of Paget's disease. Rarely patients with underlying intrinsic heart disease may develop congestive heart failure in the presence of severe Paget's disease. There are also reports suggesting that patients may have an increased incidence of calcific aortic disease.[43] Angioid streaks are seen on funduscopic examination of the eye in some patients with polyostotic Paget's disease. The physical examination also should note the presence or absence of warmth, tenderness, or bone deformity in the skull, spine, pelvis, and extremities, as well as evidence of loss of range of motion at major joints or leg length discrepancy.

Laboratory tests include measurement of serum alkaline phosphatase and in some cases a urinary marker of bone resorption, as described earlier. Radiographic studies (bone scans and conventional radiographs) complete the initial evaluation. Bone biopsy is not usually indicated, as the characteristic radiographic and laboratory findings are diagnostic in most instances.

Bone scans are the most sensitive means of identifying pagetic sites and are most useful for this purpose. Scans are nonspecific, however, and also can be positive in nonpagetic areas that have degenerative changes or, more ominously, may reflect metastatic disease. Plain radiographs of bones noted to be positive on the bone scan provide the most specific information, because the changes noted on the radiograph are usually characteristic to the point of being pathognomonic. Examples of these are shown in Figs. 3–5. Enlargement or expansion of bone, cortical thickening, coarsening of trabecular markings, and typical lytic and sclerotic changes may be found. Radiographs also provide data on the status of the joints adjacent to involved sites, identify fissure fractures, indicate the degree to which lytic or sclerotic lesions predominate, and show the presence or absence of deformity or fracture.

Repeated scans or radiographs are usually unnecessary in observing patients over time, unless new symptoms develop or current symptoms become significantly worse. The possibility of an impending fracture or, rarely, of sarcomatous change should be borne in mind in these situations. Although imaging studies such as CT or MRI scans are not usually required in routine cases, a CT scan may be helpful in the assessment of a fracture where radiographs are not sufficient, and MRI scans are quite useful in assessing the possibility of sarcoma, giant cell tumor, or metastatic disease at a site of Paget's disease, in which case discovery of an accompanying soft tissue mass aids in diagnosis.

The characteristic X-ray and clinical features of Paget's disease usually eliminate problems with differential diagnosis. However, an older patient may occasionally present with severe bone pain, elevations of the serum alkaline phosphatase and urinary N-telopeptide or deoxypyridinoline, a positive bone scan, and less-than-characteristic radiographic areas of lytic or blastic change. Here the possibility of metastatic disease to bone or some other form of metabolic bone disease (e.g., osteomalacia with secondary hyperparathyroidism) must be considered. Old radiographs and laboratory tests are very helpful in this setting, because normal studies a year earlier would make a diagnosis of Paget's disease less likely. A similar dilemma occurs when someone with known and established Paget's disease develops multiple painful new sites; here, too, the likelihood of metastatic disease must be carefully considered, and bone biopsy for a tissue diagnosis may be indicated.

TREATMENT

Antipagetic Therapy

Specific antipagetic therapy consists of those agents capable of suppressing the activity of pagetic osteoclasts. Currently approved agents available by prescription in the United States include six bisphosphonate compounds: orally administered etidronate, tiludronate, alendronate, and risedronate; intravenously administered pamidronate and zoledronic acid; and parenterally administered synthetic salmon calcitonin. Each of these is discussed later.

Between the mid-1970s, when treatments became available for the first time, and the mid-1990s, the mainstays of therapy were calcitonin and etidronate. However, these agents should generally be replaced as the first lines of therapy by the newer bisphosphonates, pamidronate, alendronate, risedronate and zoledronic acid, all progressively more potent than either etidronate or calcitonin, offering the potential for greater disease suppression and frank remission (i.e., normalization of pagetic indices) for prolonged periods. In addition to the newer bisphosphonates mentioned earlier, clodronate, more potent than etidronate and available in several other countries, has been shown to be effective in Paget's disease.[44] Olpadronate, neridronate, and ibandronate have significant activity in Paget's disease.[45-47] Gallium nitrate, approved in the United States for the treatment of cancer hypercalcemia, has been studied for efficacy in Paget's disease.[48] Other symptomatic treatments for Paget's disease, including analgesics, anti-inflammatory drugs, use of orthotics or canes, and selected orthopedic and neurosurgical interventions, have important roles in management in many patients.

Two logical indications for treatment of Paget's disease are to relieve symptoms and to prevent future complications. It has been clearly shown that suppression of the pagetic process by any of the available agents can effectively ameliorate certain symptoms in the majority of patients. Symptoms such as bone aches or pain (probably the most common complaints of Paget's disease), excessive warmth over bone, headache caused by skull involvement, low-back pain secondary to pagetic vertebral changes, and some syndromes of neural compression (e.g., radiculopathy and some examples of slowly progressive brainstem or spinal cord compression) are the most likely to be relieved. Pain caused by a secondary arthritis from pagetic bone involving the spine, hip, knee, ankle, or shoulder may or may not respond to antipagetic treatment. Filling in of osteolytic blade-of-grass lesions in weight-bearing bones has been reported in some treated cases with either calcitonin or bisphosphonates. On the other hand, a bowed extremity or other bone deformity will not change after treatment, and clinical experience indicates that deafness is unlikely to improve, although limited studies suggest that progression of hearing loss may be slowed[49] or even, in one case with pamidronate, reversed.[50]

A second indication for treatment is to prevent the development of late complications in those patients deemed to be at risk, based on their sites of involvement and evidence of active disease, as shown by elevated levels of bone turnover markers. Admittedly, it has not been proved that suppression of pagetic bone turnover will prevent future complications. However, as shown in Fig. 2, there is a restoration of normal patterns of new bone deposition in biopsy specimens after suppression of pagetic activity. It is also clear that active, untreated disease can continue to undergo a persistent degree of abnormal bone turnover for many years, with the possibility of severe bone deformity over time, as shown in Fig. 4. Indeed, substantial (e.g., 50%) but incomplete suppression of elevated indices of bone turnover with older therapies has been associated with disease progression[51]; with bisphosphonates such as pamidronate, alendronate, risedronate, and zoledronic acid, however, indices become normal after treatment for extended periods in the majority of patients and approach normal in most of the rest.

Thus, in the view of some investigators, the presence of asymptomatic but active disease (i.e., a serum alkaline phosphatase above normal) at sites where the potential for later problems or complications exists (e.g., weight-bearing bones, areas near major joints, vertebral bodies, extensively involved skull) is an indication for treatment.[52] The need for treatment in this setting may be particularly valid in patients who are younger, for whom many years of coexistence with the disorder is likely. However, even in the elderly, one can justify treatment if a degree of bone deformity is present that might create serious problems in the next few years. Others argue that the evidence does not yet support such use, because it has not been shown in clinical trials that disease suppression reduces progression of deformity.[53]

Although controlled studies are not available to prove effectiveness in this situation, the use of a potent bisphosphonate before elective surgery on pagetic bone also is recommended.[54] The goal here is to reduce the hypervascularity associated with moderately active disease (e.g., a 3-fold or more elevation in serum alkaline phosphatase) to reduce the amount of blood loss at operation.

Recently, recommendations for the management of Paget's disease have been published as guideline or management documents by consensus panels in the United States,[52] United Kingdom,[53] and Canada,[55] and the reader is referred to these thoughtful reviews.

Bisphosphonates

The discussion that follows will consider this class of drugs in their ascending order of potency and to some extent in terms of their historical development. It should be emphasized that while any of these medications might be chosen in a specific case, the agents that are considered to be first line at the time of this writing are pamidronate, alendronate, risedronate, and zoledronic acid.

Etidronate. Etidronate was the first bisphosphonate to have been used clinically in the United States for Paget's disease[56,57] and was one of the two mainstays of therapy (with salmon calcitonin) for nearly 20 years. It is the least potent of the currently available bisphosphonate drugs. Etidronate is commercially available as Didronel (Procter & Gamble, Mason, OH, USA) in a 200- or 400-mg tablet. Although only a small percentage of the administered dose is absorbed, 5 mg/kg/day will provide a 50% lowering of biochemical indices and a reduction in symptoms in the majority of patients.

All bisphosphonates have the capacity to impair mineralization of newly forming bone if high enough doses are used. The dose of etidronate is limited by the fact that the doses that most effectively reduce the increased bone resorption can also impair mineralization, compelling the use of lower doses given for no longer than 6 months at a time. Thus, the recommended regimen for the agent is 5 mg/kg/day (i.e., 400 mg in most

patients, taken with a small amount of water midway in a 4-h fast any time of day) for a 6-month period, followed by at least 6 months of no treatment. Etidronate is contraindicated in the presence of advancing lytic changes in a weight-bearing bone. Over several years of repeated 6-months-on, 6 months-off cycles, long-term benefit with maintenance of lower levels of pagetic biochemical activity has been observed in many patients, although others have become resistant to it after repeated courses. A failure to adhere to a cyclic low-dose regimen as described can induce bone pain and, occasionally, fracture caused by focal osteomalacia secondary to mineralization problems from excessive etidronate. However, careful cyclic management has been well tolerated by the majority of patients. Occasionally mild transient diarrhea may occur with etidronate, but this does not usually require more than a day or two of withholding the agent, after which it maybe taken again. More severe new pain in patients taking etidronate warrants stopping the drug and evaluating the patient before continuing therapy to be certain that lytic disease or impending fracture (particularly in a weight-bearing extremity) has not been exacerbated.

In summary, etidronate is generally well tolerated and relatively easy to administer, but it affords a less robust suppression of turnover than the newer bisphosphonates and has the associated risk of mineralization problems with over use.

Tiludronate. Tiludronate is about 10 times more potent than etidronate, and its use at effective doses is not associated with mineralization problems. Approved by the Food and Drug Administration (FDA) for Paget's disease in 1997, it is available as Skelid (Sanofi-Aventis, Bridgewater, NJ, USA) in a 200-mg tablet. The recommended dosage is 400 mg daily for 3 months with a 3-month post-treatment observation period, after which the serum alkaline phosphatase is likely to have reached its nadir. This approach led to a normal serum alkaline phosphatase at the 6-month point in 24–35% of moderately affected subjects in clinical trials.[58,59] It is generally well tolerated, with a minority of patients experiencing mild upper gastrointestinal upset. It seems to offer the benefits of etidronate without the risk of mineralization problems in patients for whom this might be a concern (e.g., those with lytic disease in lower extremities) and one half the total number of days of pills in a treatment course. As with etidronate, 400 mg of tiludronate should be taken with some water (in this case, 6–8 oz) at least 2 h away from food, and the patient should not lie down for the next 30 minutes. Patients also need to be calcium and vitamin D replete, but calcium supplements, like food, should not be taken within 2 h of the tiludronate dose.

Clinical experience with tiludronate is still relatively limited, with few data regarding duration of efficacy. It is a reasonable alternative to etidronate in patients with mild disease because it is well tolerated and requires only 3 months of active treatment. Patients who respond should have serum alkaline phosphatase measured at 3- to 4-month intervals and can be retreated when indices increase above normal or above a nadir level by 25% or more.

Pamidronate. Pamidronate is in the range of 100 times more potent than etidronate. With its availability in the mid-1990s, a new philosophy of and approach to management became available to the clinician. The greater potency of pamidronate (and also of the other newer agents, alendronate, risedronate, and zoledronic acid) allows a majority of patients to experience a normalization of pagetic indices rather than only partial suppression, as is seen with calcitonin, etidronate, and (in most cases) tiludronate. Second, the effects may be longer lasting, so a limited course of treatment may provide up to a year or more of disease suppression. Third, all of the potent newer bisphosphonates have a much more favorable ratio of inhibition of bone resorption to inhibition of mineralization, so the threat of focal osteomalacia should be markedly reduced if not eliminated.

With pamidronate there is an opportunity to individualize the dosing regimen to the needs of the specific patient, and there really is no single best dose. Indeed, the literature is replete with numerous approaches,[60–62] all of which seem to be effective. The package insert for pamidronate, available as Aredia (Novartis, East Hanover, NJ, USA), recommends three daily infusions of 30 mg each, over a period of 4 h each time, in 500 ml of normal saline or 5% dextrose in water. In clinical practice, experience has shown that this is probably not the best mode of administration. This dose is probably not high enough to achieve normalization of indices for many patients, and three daily infusions are highly impractical in most settings. Clinical experience indicates that patients with relatively mild disease may have a substantial reduction of alkaline phosphatase to normal or near normal with a single 60- to 90-mg infusion given over a 2-h period in 300–500 ml of 5% dextrose in water. Patients with more moderate to severe disease (e.g., serum alkaline phosphatase levels more than three to four times normal) may require multiple infusions of 60–90 mg infused as described and given on a once weekly or biweekly basis, primarily based on physician and patient convenience. Two to four 60-mg doses or three 90-mg doses may suffice in moderate disease (e.g., serum alkaline phosphatase in the range of four to five times normal). Total doses in the range of 300–500 mg may be required in some severe cases (serum alkaline phosphatase ~10–20 times normal), given over a number of weeks.

Suppression of urinary markers can often be noted within a few days after an infusion, but the serum alkaline phosphatase may take up to 2–3 months to reach its nadir. For moderate to severe cases, giving three to four 60-mg doses and then reassessing at 3 months with the possibility of more treatment is a reasonable approach. A successful course of therapy can result in 1 year or more of continued disease suppression with markers of turnover at normal or near-normal levels. Side effects may include a low-grade fever and flu-like symptoms in the first 24 h after the first ever infusion (decreasing in likelihood with repeated dosing) and the possibility of mild and transient hypocalcemia, hypophosphatemia, and lymphopenia. Venous irritation may arise, especially if an insufficient volume of fluid is used or if the fluid extravasates. It is desirable to provide oral calcium supplements at a dose of 500 mg, two or three times daily, and vitamin D_3, 800-1000 IU daily, to prevent or ameliorate a reduction in serum calcium and concomitant rise in PTH.

Overall, pamidronate offers the opportunity to titrate the dosage as required in the individual patient, with the possibility of normalization or near normalization of biochemical indices and the potential for substantial and prolonged reduction in disease progression in many patients. In our view, it is most useful in patients with mild disease, in whom a single infusion may afford long-term benefit in a very cost-effective manner, and in severe and refractory cases, in which delivery of drug by vein bypasses problems with oral absorption. It is also a drug of choice for individuals who experience esophageal symptoms from alendronate or risedronate. The need for outpatient intravenous administration of multiple doses may be expensive and inconvenient in some cases. However, the rapid onset of symptomatic improvement and overall potency of the agent make it an obvious choice for cases with neurologic compression syndromes, for severe and painful lytic disease with or without impending fracture, and as a pretreatment of active Paget's disease before elective surgery to shrink the hypervascularity

of the pagetic bone and decrease the amount of bleeding at operation. There has been one report of asymptomatic mineralization abnormalities with dosing in the usual clinical range,[63] but this is not the general experience. Recently, there has been a report of patients developing secondary resistance to pamidronate after repeated use.[64]

Alendronate. Approved by the FDA for the treatment of Paget's disease in the fall of 1995, alendronate, sold as Fosamax (Merck, West Point, PA, USA), is an orally administered aminobisphosphonate that is 700 times more potent than etidronate and is not associated with mineralization problems at therapeutically effective doses. In a study of 89 patients with moderate to severe disease who received 6 months of either alendronate, 40 mg daily, or etidronate, 400 mg/day, alendronate led to a normalized serum alkaline phosphatase in >63% of subjects compared with 17% for etidronate; overall, alendronate led to a mean fall in alkaline phosphatase of 79% compared with 44% with etidronate.[65] Alendronate seemed to be as well tolerated as etidronate in this study, although symptoms of upper gastrointestinal discomfort or nausea, or the less common but more serious complication of esophageal ulceration, should be watched for at the 40-mg dose. Biopsy specimens from patients treated with alendronate revealed normal patterns of deposition of new bone[65,66] and radiologic improvement.[66] The recommended dose is 40 mg daily for 6 months to be taken on arising in the morning after an overnight fast with 8 oz of tap water. The patient is instructed not to take anything else orally (except more water) and not to lie down for at least 30 minutes after the dose. It is important with alendronate, as with pamidronate and tiludronate, that patients be replete in vitamin D and have a daily calcium intake of 1 to 1.5 g to avoid hypocalcemia early in the treatment course. Biochemical remissions may persist for 12–18 months after a single course. Retreatment guidelines are incomplete as follow-up data are few, but many physicians have given repeat 6-month courses of alendronate once indices rise above normal with good success in re-establishing complete or partial biochemical remission.

Risedronate. More than 1000 times more potent than etidronate, risedronate was approved by the FDA for use in Paget's disease in 1998. Risedronate is available as Actonel (Procter & Gamble). Studies with risedronate have described the efficacy of a 30-mg dose given for 2[67] or 3[68] months to patients with moderately active disease. These short courses of therapy led to a nearly 80% reduction in serum alkaline phosphatase and normalization of indices of bone turnover in 50–70% of patients. Thus, 30 mg can be given daily for 2 months, with a follow-up measurement of serum alkaline phosphatase 1 month later; if the value is not yet normal or near normal, a third or fourth month could be offered with a good likelihood of normalcy or near normalcy of indices thereafter, with a prolonged period of disease suppression similar to that achieved with pamidronate or alendronate. Once again, adequacy of calcium and vitamin D intake is important to avoid hypocalcemia. The 30-mg risedronate dose is taken with 8 oz of water on arising in the morning after an overnight fast, with no other oral intake (except water) and no lying down for 30 minutes after the dose. In the clinical trials, the main side effects were mild upper gastrointestinal upset in 15% of patients; symptoms of esophageal irritation were not common in these clinical trials with the 30-mg dose but should be kept in mind by the physician until more data are available. A few cases of iritis were seen, something also reported rarely with pamidronate.

Zoledronic Acid. The newest of the available drugs for Paget's disease, this agent is expected to be approved for this indication by the FDA in 2006. More potent than the previously described bisphosphonates, it is given at a dose of 5 mg, administered as a single 15-minute intravenous infusion. Unlike pamidronate, which has been available for many years and has been administered in a variety of ways with respect to dose and dosing interval with success, the data on zoledronic acid for Paget's disease come primarily from a clinical trial comparing a single dose of 5 mg of zoledronic acid with 2 months of oral risedronate, 30 mg/day, in a group of 357 patients with a mean baseline serum alkaline phosphatase about four times greater than normal.[69] Six months after initiation of treatment, 89% of patients treated with zoledronic acid and 58% of those receiving risedronate had a normal serum alkaline phosphatase. The main side effects seen with zoledronic acid included a flu-like syndrome in 9.6% of patients with myalgia, fever, headache, rigors, and nausea each in about 7% of subjects and bone pain in 5% within the first 2–3 days after treatment, a finding similar to that seen with pamidronate. Eight patients who received zoledronic acid also had hypocalcemia that was mildly symptomatic in only two, neither of whom was taking the prescribed calcium or vitamin D. One hundred thirteen of the original 182 patients assigned to zoledronic acid were followed without further treatment after the end of the 6-month study; and at a mean of 190 days later (i.e., about 1 year after treatment), all but one still maintained a therapeutic response, defined as either a normal serum alkaline phosphatase or a reduction of at least 75% from baseline in the alkaline phosphatase excess (difference between the measured level and the mid-point of the reference range). Further studies will be needed to determine the typical durations of biochemical remission in clinical practice.

Osteonecrosis of the jaw has recently been described as a complication typically following dental extractions in patients receiving relatively high doses of potent bisphosphonates such as zoledronic acid and pamidronate given primarily for management of bone metastases. A few patients with Paget's disease have also been reported to have had this complication, but in some instances, these individuals received what seemed to be excessive amounts of bisphosphonate (e.g., 5 years of 40 mg/day of alendronate in one case, 18 months of monthly pamidronate 90 mg in another).[70]

Calcitonin

The polypeptide hormone, salmon calcitonin, is available therapeutically as a synthetic formulation for parenteral administration. It, like human and other calcitonins, was first shown to be efficacious in Paget's disease >30 years ago.[71,72] At present, the formulation approved for use in Paget's disease in the United States, sold as Miacalcin (Novartis), must be injected subcutaneously or intramuscularly. A nasal spray formulation of salmon calcitonin, approved by the FDA for use in postmenopausal osteoporosis, is available, although not specifically approved for treatment of Paget's disease.

The usual starting dose is 100 U (0.5 ml; the drug is available in a 2-ml vial), generally self-injected subcutaneously, initially on a daily basis. Symptomatic benefit may be apparent in a few weeks, and the biochemical benefit (typically about a 50% reduction from baseline in serum alkaline phosphatase) is usually seen after 3–6 months of treatment. After this period, many clinicians reduce the dose to 50–100 U every other day or three times weekly. Often, a dose of 50 U three times weekly after the first few months of therapy will maintain the achieved benefit. Patients with moderate to severe disease may require indefinite treatment to maintain a 50% reduction in the bio-

chemical indices and symptomatic relief, but milder or monostotic disease may allow discontinuation of treatment for prolonged periods.

Escape from the efficacy of salmon calcitonin may sometimes occur after a variable period of benefit. In some cases, this may be caused by a postulated downregulation of receptors, but in other instances, it may be a consequence of the development of neutralizing antibodies to the salmon polypeptide.[73] The main side effects of parenteral salmon calcitonin include, in a minority of patients, the development of nausea or queasiness, with or without flushing of the skin of the face and ears. These annoying side effects may last from a few minutes to several hours after each injection, although many patients can avoid them by experimenting with taking the agent at bedtime, with food, without food, and so on. Although these side effects are unpleasant, they do not seem to be serious or harmful, and most patients develop a tolerance to them. In summary, however, it is apparent that the newer bisphosphonates offer both greater effectiveness and ease of use, suggesting that this agent will be used in the future primarily by patients who do not tolerate oral or intravenous bisphosphonate therapy.

Intranasal calcitonin is available as Miacalcin Nasal Spray. It seems to have a lower incidence of the side effects described earlier. The optimal dose in Paget's disease with the present formulation is not known, but anecdotal evidence suggests that, in occasional patients with mild disease, the 200-U single spray dose given daily may lower biochemical indices and relieve mild symptoms, such as increased warmth in a pagetic tibia.

Other Therapies

Analgesics, nonsteroidal anti-inflammatory agents, and Cox-2 inhibitors may be tried empirically with or without antipagetic therapy to relieve pain. Pagetic arthritis (i.e., osteoarthritis caused by deformed pagetic bone at a joint space) may cause periods of pain that are often helped by these agents.

Surgery on pagetic bone[54] may be necessary in the setting of established or impending fracture. Elective joint replacement, more complex with Paget's disease than with typical osteoarthritis, is often very successful in relieving refractory pain. Rarely, osteotomy is performed to alter a bowing deformity in the tibia. Neurosurgical intervention is sometimes required in cases of spinal cord compression, spinal stenosis, or basilar invagination with neural compromise. Although medical management may be beneficial and adequate in some instances, all cases of serious neurological compromise require immediate neurological and neurosurgical consultation to allow the appropriate plan of management to be developed. As improved therapies emerge, long-term suppression of pagetic activity may have a preventive role in Paget's disease and, possibly, may obviate the need for surgical management in many cases.

REFERENCES

1. Kanis JA 1998 Pathophysiology and Treatment of Paget's Disease of Bone. 2nd ed. Martin Dunitz, London, UK.
2. Siris ES, Canfield RE, Jacobs TP 1980 Paget's disease of bone. Bull NY Acad Med **56:**285–304.
3. Morales-Piga AA, Rey-Rey JS, Corres-Gonzalez J, Garcia-Sagredo IM, Lopez-Abente G 1995 Frequency and characteristics of familial aggregation of Paget's disease of bone. J Bone Miner Res **10:**663–670.
4. McKusick VA 1972 Heritable disorders of connective tissue, 5th ed. CV Mosby, St. Louis, MO, USA, pp. 718–723.
5. Siris ES, Ottman R, Flaster E, Kelsey JL 1991 Familial aggregation of Paget's disease of bone. J Bone Miner Res **6:**495–500.
6. Cody JD, Singer FR, Roodman GD, Otterund B, Lewis TB, Leppert M

1997 Genetic linkage of Paget disease of bone to chromosome 18q. Am J Hum Genet **61:**1117–1122.

7. Good DA, Busfield F, Fletcher BH, Duffy DL, Kesting JB, Andersen J, Shaw JT 2002 Linkage of Paget disease of bone to a novel region on human chromosome 18q23. Am J Hum Genet **70:**517–525.

8. Hocking LJ, Herbert CA, Nicholls RK, Williams F, Bennett ST, Cundy T, Nicholson GC, Wuyts W, Van Hul W, Ralston SH 2001 Genomewide search in familial Paget disease of bone shows evidence of genetic heterogeneity with candidate loci on chromosomes 2q36, 10p13, and 5q35. Am J Hum Genet **69:**1055–1061.

9. Sparks AB, Peterson SN, Bell C, Loftus BJ, Hocking L, Cahill DP, Frassica FJ, Streeten EA, Levine MA, Fraser CM, Adams MD, Broder S, Venter JC, Kinzler KW, Vogelstein B, Ralston SH 2001 Mutation screening of the TNFRSF11A gene encoding receptor activator of NF kappa B (RANK) in familial and sporadic Paget's disease of bone and osteosarcoma. Calcif Tissue Int **68:**151–155.

10. Hocking L, Slee F, Haslam SI, Cundy T, Nicholson G, van Hul W, Ralston SH 2000 Familial Paget's disease of bone: Patterns of inheritance and frequency of linkage to chromosome 18q. Bone **26:**577–580.

11. Laurin N, Brown JP, Morissette J, Raymond V 2002 Recurrent mutation of the gene encoding sequestosome 1 (SQSTM1/p62) in Paget disease of bone. Am J Hum Genet 2002 **70:**1582–1588.

12. Laurin N, Morissette J, Raymond V, Brown JP 2002 Large phenotypic variability of Paget disease of bone caused by the P392L sequestasome 1/p62 mutation. J Bone Miner Res **17:**S1;S380.

13. Barker DJ 1984 The epidemiology of Paget's disease of bone. Br Med Bull **40:**396–400.

14. Barker DJP, Chamberlain AT, Guyer PH, Gardner MJ 1980 Paget's disease of bone: The Lancashire focus. BMJ **280:**1105–1107.

15. Barry HC 1969 Paget's Disease of Bone. E & S Livingstone, Edinburgh, Scotland.

16. Dolev E, Samuel R, Foldes J, Brickman M, Assia A, Liberman U 1994 Some epidemiological aspects of Paget's disease in Israel. Semin Arthritis Rheum **23:**228.

17. Lowenthal MN, Alkalay D, Abu Rabbia Y, Liel Y 1995 Paget's disease of bone in Negev Bedouin: Report of two cases. Isr J Med Sci **31:**628–629.

18. Mautalen C, Pumarino H, Blanco MC, Gonzalez D, Ghiringhelli G, Fromm G 1994 Paget's disease: The South American experience. Semin Arthritis Rheum **23:**226–227.

19. Guyer PH, Chamberlain AT 1980 Paget's disease of bone in two American cities. BMJ **280:**985.

20. Cundy T, McAnulty K, Wattie D, Gamble G, Rutland M, Ibbertson HK 1997 Evidence for secular changes in Paget's disease. Bone **20:**69–71.

21. Cooper C, Schafheutle K, Dennison E, Kellingray S, Guyer P, Barker D 1999 The epidemiology of Paget's disease in Britain: Is the prevalence decreasing?. J Bone Miner Res **14:**192–197.

22. Rebel A, Malkani K, Basle M, Bregeon C 1997 Is Paget's disease of bone a viral infection? Calcif Tissue Res **22**(Suppl)**:**283–286.

23. Mills BG, Singer FR, Weiner LP, Suffin SC, Stabile E, Holst P 1984 Evidence for both respiratory syncytial virus and measles virus antigens in the osteoclasts of patients with Paget's disease of bone. Clin Orthop **183:**303–311.

24. Basle M, Rebel A, Pouplard A, Kouyoumdjian S, Filmon R, Loepatezour A 1979 Demonstration by immunofluorescence and immunoperoxidase of an antigen of the measles type in the osteoclasts of Paget's disease of bone. Bull Assoc Anat **63:**263–272.

25. Friedrichs WE, Reddy SV, Bruder JM, Cundy T, Cornish J, Singer FR, Roodman GD 2002 Sequence analysis of measles virus nucleocapsid transcripts in patients with Paget's disease. J Bone Miner Res **17:**145–151.

26. Gordon MT, Mee AP, Sharpe PT 1994 Paramyxoviruses in Paget's disease. Semin Arthritis Rheum **23:**232–234.

27. Mee AP, Dixon JA, Hoyland JA, Davies M, Selby PL, Mawer EB 1998 Detection of canine distemper virus in 100% of Paget's disease samples by in situ-reverse transcriptase-polymerase chain reaction. Bone **23:**171–175.

28. Kurihara N, Reddy SV, Menaa C, Anderson D, Roodman GD 2000 Osteoclasts expressing the measles virus nucleocapsid gene display a pagetic phenotype. J Clin Invest 2000 **105:**607–614.

29. Ooi CG, Walsh CA, Gallagher JA, Fraser WD 2000 Absence of measles virus and canine distemper virus transcripts in long-term bone marrow cultures from patients with Paget's disease of bone. Bone **27:**417–421.

30. Kunihara N, Zhou H, Reddy SV, Garcia-Palacios V, Subler MA, Dempster DW, Windle JJ, Roodman GD 2006 Expression of measles virus nucleocapsid protein in osteoclasts indures Paget's disease–like bone lesions in mice. J Bone Miner Res **21:**446–455.

31. Rebel A, Basle M, Pouplard A, Malkani K. Filmon R, Lepatezour A 1980

32. Bone tissue in Paget's disease of bone: Ultrastructure and immunocytology. Arthritis Rheum **23:**1104–1114.

32. Calvo MS, Eyre DR, Gundberg CR 1996 Molecular basis and clinical application of biological markers of bone turnover. Endocr Rev **17:**333–368.

33. Meunier PJ, Coindre JM, Edouard CM, Arlot ME 1980 Bone histomorphometry in Paget's disease: Quantitative and dynamic analysis of pagetic and non-pagetic bone tissue. Arthritis Rheum **23:**1095–1103.

34. Siris ES, Clemens TP, McMahon D, Gordon AG, Jacobs TP, Canfield RE 1989 Parathyroid function in Paget's disease of bone. J Bone Miner Res **4:**75–79.

35. Siris ES, Canfield RE. 1994 The parathyroids and Paget's disease of bone. In: Bilezikian J, Levine M, Marcus R (eds.) The Parathyroids. Raven Press, New York, NY, USA, pp. 823–828.

36. Siris ES 1991 Indications for medical treatment of Paget's disease of bone. In: Singer FR, Wallach S (eds.) Paget's disease of bone: Clinical assessment: Present and future therapy. Elsevier, New York, NY, USA, pp. 44–56.

37. Herzberg L, Bayliss E 1980 Spinal cord syndrome due to non-compressive Paget's disease of bone: A spinal artery steal phenomenon reversible with calcitonin. Lancet **2:**13–15.

38. Monsell EM 2004 The mechanism of hearing loss in Paget's disease of bone. Laryngoscope **114:**598–606.

39. Barry HC 1980 Orthopedic aspects of Paget's disease of bone. Arthritis Rheum **23:**1128–1130.

40. Wick MR, Siegal GP, Unni KK, McLeod RA, Greditzer HB 1981 Sarcomas of bone complicating osteitis deformans (Paget's disease). Am J Surg PatholI **5:**47–59.

41. Upchurch KS, Simon LS, Schiller AL, Rosenthal DI, Campion EW, Krane SM 1983 Giant cell reparative granulomas of Paget's disease of bone: A unique clinical entity. Ann Intern Med **98:**35–40.

42. Jacobs TP, Michelsen J, Polay J, D' Adamo AC, Canfield RE 1979 Giant cell tumor in Paget's disease of bone: Familial and geographic clustering. Cancer **44:**742–747.

43. Strickenberger SA, Schulman SP, Hutchins GM 1987 Association of Paget's disease of bone with calcific aortic valve disease. Am J Med **82:**953–956.

44. Delmas PD,Chapuy MC, VignonE, Charon S, Briancon D, Alexandre C, Edouard C, Meunier PJ 1982 Long-term effects of dichloromethylene diphosphonate in Paget's disease of bone. J Clin Endocrinol Metab **54:** 837–844.

45. Gonzalez DC, Mautalen CA 1999 Short term therapy with oral olpadronate in active Paget's disease of bone. J Bone Miner Res **14:**2042–2047.

46. Adami S, Bevilacqua M, Broggini M, Filliponi P, Ortolani S, Palummeri E, Uliveri F, Nannipieri F, Braga V 2002 Short term intravenous therapy with neridronate in Paget's disease. Clin Exp Rheumatol **20:**55–58.

47. Woitge HW, Oberwittler H, Heichel S, Grauer A, Ziegler R, Seibel MJ 2000 Short- and long-term effects of ibandroante treatment on bone turnover in Paget disease of bone. Clin Chem **46:**684–690.

48. Bockman RS, Wilhelm F, Siris E, Singer F, Chausner A, Bitton R, Kotler J, Bosco BJ, Eyre DR, Levenson D 1995 A multi-center, prospective trial of gallium nitrate in patients with advanced Paget's disease of bone. J Clin Endocrinol Metab **80:**595–602.

49. EI-Sammaa M, Linthicum FH, House HP, House JW 1986 Calcitonin as treatment for hearing loss in Paget's disease. Am J Otol **7:**241–243.

50. Murdin L, Yeoh LH 2005 Hearing loss treated with pamidronate. J R Soc Med **98:**272–274.

51. Meunier PI, Vignot E 1995 Therapeutic strategy in Paget's disease of bone. Bone **17:**489S–49IS.

52. Lyles KW, Siris ES, Singer FR, Meunier PJ 2001 A clinical approach to the diagnosis and management of Paget's disease of bone. J Bone Miner Res **16:**1379–1387.

53. Selby PL, Davie MWJ, Ralston SH, Stone MD 2002 Guidelines on the management of Paget's disease of bone. Bone **31:**366–373.

54. Kaplan FS 1999 Surgical management of Paget's disease. J Bone Miner Res **14:**S2;34–38.

55. Drake WM, Kendler DL, Brown JP 2001 Consensus statement on the modern therapy of Paget's disease of bone from a Western Osteoporosis Alliance Symposium. Clin Ther **23:**620–626.

56. Altman RD, Johnston CC, Khairi MRA, Wellman H, Serafini AN, Sankey RR 1973 Influence of disodium etidronate on clinical and laboratory manifestations of Paget's disease of bone (osteitis deformans). N Engl J Med **289:**1379–1384.

57. Canfield R, Rosner W, Skinner J, McWhorter J, Resnick L, Feldman F, Kammerman S, Ryan K, Kunigonis M, Bohne W 1977 Diphosphonate therapy of Paget's disease of bone. J Clin Endocrinol Metab **44:**96–106.

58. Roux C, Gennari C, Farrerons J, Devogelaer JP, Mulder H, Kruse HP, Picot C, Titeux L, Reginster JY, Dougados M 1995 Comparative pro-

spective, double-blind, multi-center study of the efficacy of tiludronate and etidronate in the treatment of Paget's disease of bone. Arthritis Rheum 38:851–858.

59. McClung MR, Tou CPK, Goldstein NH, Picot C 1995 Tiludronate therapy for Paget's disease of bone. Bone 17:493S–496S.

60. Siris ES 1994 Perspectives: A practical guide to the use of pamidronate in the treatment of Paget's disease. J Bone Miner Res 9:303–304.

61. Harinck HI, Papapoulos SE, Blanksrna HJ, Moolenaar AJ, Vermeij P, Bijvoet OL 1987 Paget's disease of bone: Early and late responses to three different modes of treatment with aminohydroxypropylidene bisphosphonate (APD). BMJ 295:1301–1305.

62. Trombetti A, Arlot M, Thevenon J, Uebelhart B, Meunier PJ 1999 Effects of multiple intravenous pamidronate courses in Paget's disease of bone. Rev Rhum Engl Ed 66:467–476.

63. Adamson BB, Gallacher SJ, Byars J, Ralston SH, Boyle IT, Boyce BF 1993 Mineralisation defects with pamidronate therapy for Paget's disease. Lancet 342:1459–1460.

64. Gutteridge DH, Ward LC, Stewart GO, Retallack RW, Will RK, Prince RL, Criddle A, Bhagat CI, Stuckey BG, Price RI, Kent GN, Faulkner DL, Geelhoed E, Gan SK, Vasikaran S 1999 Paget's disease: Acquired resistance to one aminobisphosphonate with retained response to another. J Bone Miner Res 14:S2;79–84.

65. Siris E, Weinstein RS, Altman R, Conte JM, Favus M, Lombardi A, Lyles K, McIlwain H, Murphy WA Jr., Reda C, Rude R, Seton M, Tiegs R, Thompson D, Tucci JR, Yates AJ, Zimering M 1996 Comparative study of alendronate vs. etidronate for the treatment of Paget's disease of bone. J Clin Endocrinol Metab 81:961–967.

66. Reid IR, Nicholson GC, Weinstein RS, Hosking DJ, Cundy T, Kotowicz MA, Murphy WA Jr., Yeap S, Dufresne S, Lombardi A, Musliner TA, Thompson DE, Yates AJ 1996 Biochemical and radiologic improvement in Paget's disease of bone treated with alendronate: A randomized, placebo-controlled trial. Am J Med 171:341–348.

67. Miller PD, Adachi JD, Brown JP, Khairi RA, Lang R, Licata AA, McClung MR, Ryan WG, Singer FR, Siris ES, Tenenhouse A, Wallach S, Bekker PJ, Axelrod DW 1997 Risedronate vs. etidronate: Durable remission with only two months of 30 mg risedronate. J Bone Miner Res 12:S269.

68. Siris ES, Chines AA, Altman RD, Brown JP, Johnson CC Jr., Lang R, McClung MR, Mallette LE, Miller PD, Ryan WG, Singer FR, Tucci JR, Eusebio RA, Bekker PJ 1998 Risedronate in the treatment of Paget's disease: An open-label, multicenter study. J Bone Miner Res 13:1032–1038.

69. Reid IR, Miller P, Lyles K, Fraser W, Brown J, Saidi Y, Mesenbrink P, Su G, Pak J, Zelenakas K, Luchi M, Richardson P, Hosking D 2005 A single infusion of zoledronic acid improves remission rates in Paget's disease: A randomized controlled comparison with risedronate. N Engl J Med 353:898–908.

70. Carter G, Goss AN, Doecke C 2005 Bisphosphonates and avascular necrosis of the jaw: A possible association Med J Aust 182:413–415.

71. Woodhouse NJY, Bordier P, Fisher M, Joplin GF, Reiner M, Kalu DN, Foster GV, MacIntyre I 1971 Human calcitonin in the treatment of Paget's bone disease. Lancet 1:1139–1143.

72. DeRose J, Singer F, Avramides A, Flores A, Dziadiw R, Baker RK, Wallach S 1974 Response of Paget's disease to porcine and salmon calcitonins: Effects of long term treatment. Am J Med 56:858–866.

73. Singer FR, Ginger K 1991 Resistance to calcitonin. In: Singer FR, Wallach S (eds.) Paget's disease of bone: Clinical assessment, present and future therapy. Elsevier, New York, New York, USA, pp. 75–85.

Chapter 60. Nutritional and Drug-Induced Rickets and Osteomalacia

John M. Pettifor

MRC Mineral Metabolism Research Unit and the Department of Paediatrics, Chris Hani Baragwanath Hospital and the University of Witwatersrand, Johannesburg, South Africa

INTRODUCTION

Once a scourge for people living in cities of northern Europe, North America, and China, nutritional rickets and osteomalacia were considered by the latter half of the 20th century to have been all but eradicated from a number of countries except in a few at-risk groups such as preterm infants, the elderly, and the infirm. This was made possible through health education, the availability of vitamin D supplements, and the fortification of foods such as milk and margarine. However, over the past three decades, attention has been drawn to an apparent resurgence of the problem not only in the United States and the United Kingdom but also in a number of developing countries.

Rickets is a disorder associated with a failure of or delay in the mineralization of endochondral new bone formation at the growth plates, whereas osteomalacia is characterized by a failure of mineralization of newly formed osteoid at sites of bone turnover or periosteal and endosteal apposition. Thus, in children, whose growth plates (physes) are not closed, rickets and osteomalacia are found together, whereas in adults with fused growth plates, only osteomalacia will be noted. Although distinguishing between the two conditions might seem arbitrary, it is possible that the two conditions (endochondral calcification and osteoid mineralization) might respond differently to treatment as has been suggested in children with X-linked hypophosphatemic rickets.

The causes of rickets and osteomalacia are numerous, and many of the causes will be discussed in this and other chapters. In this chapter, nutritional and drug-induced causes will be described.

NUTRITIONAL CAUSES OF RICKETS/ OSTEOMALACIA

Nutritional rickets/osteomalacia may be caused by deficiencies of vitamin D, calcium, or phosphorus. While each of these causes will be considered separately, deficiencies of each may contribute to a greater or lesser degree to the disease in an individual patient.

Vitamin D Deficiency

Although considered to be a nutrient, vitamin D is found in only small quantities in the majority of natural foods, and these supplies are generally insufficient to meet the vitamin D requirements of humans. Vitamin D sufficiency is maintained in most populations through its formation in the skin from 7-dehydrocholesterol under the influence of UV-B irradiation from sunlight. In situations of impaired dermal synthesis, as may occur in countries of extreme latitude (e.g., in northern Europe, northern China, and northern North America), because of extensive clothing coverage of the skin (in the Middle

The author has reported no conflicts of interest.

Eastern region),[1] in darkly pigmented persons living in countries with limited UV-B irradiation (immigrants to Europe and blacks), in the elderly (because of decreased substrate being available for dermal synthesis of vitamin D), or because of the use of sunscreens, food fortification (infant milk formulas in most countries, cow's milk in the United States, and margarine) or vitamin D supplementation may be necessary to maintain an adequate vitamin D status.

Despite vitamin D fortification of foods in some countries and the recommendation of vitamin D supplementation in at-risk populations (particularly breastfed infants, the elderly, and the infirm), vitamin D deficiency rickets/osteomalacia continues to be public health problem in a number of countries: in the United States, increasing numbers of reports are highlighting rickets in infants of black parents, especially in those who have been breastfed for prolonged periods.[2] It is possible that in these toddlers low dietary calcium intakes during the weaning period may exacerbate the problem. In the United Kingdom and other northern European countries, Asian and immigrant populations (from Turkey and African countries) seem to be particularly at risk, where the disease affects not only breastfed infants but also occurs in adolescents and women. In the Middle East, a high prevalence of rickets and osteomalacia has been described in Muslim women and their infants.[3] In Tibet and Mongolia, clinical rickets has been described in >60% of young infants.[4] Other groups particularly at risk are those individuals living in areas of poor UV-B irradiation, who are vegan or vegetarian, or who have other extreme dietary restrictions such as macrobiotic diets. With the improvement in health care in many developed countries, life expectancy has increased dramatically, resulting in large numbers of elderly and infirm, often living in retirement villages or old-age homes, where there are limited opportunities of receiving adequate sunlight exposure. In such situations, vitamin D deficiency may develop insidiously, resulting in impaired muscle function, bone pain, and an increased risk of fractures.

Pathogenesis. Vitamin D, or more specifically the active metabolite $1,25(OH)_2D$, is essential for maintaining normocalcemia through ensuring adequate intestinal calcium absorption. Vitamin D deficiency also reduces intestinal phosphate absorption but not to the same extent as it affects calcium absorption. Inadequate intestinal calcium absorption, particularly in the growing child, leads to a fall in blood ionized calcium concentrations and secondary hyperparathyroidism. Low $1,25(OH)_2D$ levels may contribute to secondary hyperparathyroidism through the reduction of the suppressive effects of $1,25(OH)_2D$ on PTH gene transcription. Secondary hyperparathyroidism has a number of effects, which produces the typical biochemical changes seen in vitamin D deficiency. Through its actions on the kidney, urinary calcium excretion is decreased, and renal tubular phosphate loss is increased, reducing the tubular reabsorption of phosphate (TRP) and tubular maximum for phosphate (TmP/GFR). As a consequence of the increased phosphate loss, serum phosphate levels are typically reduced, despite an increase in phosphate release from bone. Increased bone resorption, which occurs through the indirect effect of PTH to increase both osteoclast numbers and activity, leads to osteopenia. Although $1,25(OH)_2D$ has effects on osteoblast differentiation and osteoclast precursors, it is thought that the major osseous features of vitamin D deficiency rickets and osteomalacia are as a result of the effects of hypocalcemia and hypophosphatemia on bone mineralization and of the effects of secondary hyperparathyroidism on bone turnover.

Clinical Features. The clinical features of rickets are more rapid in onset and generally of a more severe nature than those of osteomalacia, which may take several years to manifest. Although the features of rickets characteristically manifest as deformities of the skeletal system, other organ systems, such as the muscular and immune systems, are involved as well. In the young infant, symptoms and signs of hypocalcemia (tetany, apneic episodes, stridor, or convulsions) may be the only features.

The skeletal features in the infant and young child include skull abnormalities, such as a delay in closure of the anterior fontanelle, softening of the skull bones leading to craniotabes, and parietal and frontal bossing giving the hot-cross bun appearance. Chest deformities include enlargement of the costochondral junctions leading to the rachitic rosary, indrawing of the lower ribs at the sites of attachment of the diaphragm resulting in the Harrison's sulcus, and narrowing of the lateral diameter of the chest (violin case deformity). Softening of the ribs and enlargement of the costochondral junctions in association with muscular hypotonia and an inability to clear secretions may lead to severe respiratory distress and an increase in the severity and frequency of lower respiratory tract infections.[5] Weight bearing leads to deformities of the long bones and the characteristic enlargement of the growth plates, especially palpable at the wrist and knee. Deformities of the long bones depend on the stresses placed on the bones, such that in the young infant, bowing of the distal radius and ulna and anterior bowing of the tibia may occur. In the toddler, exaggeration of the normal bow legs (varus deformity) is frequent, whereas in the older child, knock-knees (valgus deformity) or mixed valgus and varus deformities of the legs (windswept deformity) may occur.[6] Long-standing rickets may result in deformities of the pelvis, with narrowing of the pelvic outlet and resultant increased risk of obstructed labor in females later in life. Minimal trauma fractures of the long bones may occur, particularly in the young infant and in the elderly with osteomalacia. Bone pain is often a feature in severe rickets/osteomalacia, which in the older patient may be confused with arthritis. Delay in the eruption of permanent dentition and enamel hypoplasia of both primary and secondary teeth may occur, depending on the age of the child when rickets occurred, because it must occur at the time of tooth and enamel formation.

Muscular hypotonia may be pronounced, resulting in a delay in gross motor milestones, whereas in older children and adults with osteomalacia, proximal muscle weakness may result in difficulties in getting out of chairs and climbing stairs. A waddling gait may also be present. Osteomalacia associated with muscle weakness and gait instability in the elderly may be responsible for an increase in the propensity to fall, thus increasing fracture risk over and above the risk associated with increased bone fragility.

Although in vitro studies clearly show a role for $1,25(OH)_2D$ in immune modulation,[7] there are few studies that have documented impaired immunity in subjects with vitamin D deficiency.[8]

Laboratory Investigations. The typical biochemical features of vitamin D deficiency rickets/osteomalacia are hypocalcemia, hypophosphatemia, and elevated PTH and alkaline phosphatase values. Although serum calcium and phosphorus values may occasionally be within the normal reference range for age before treatment, once treatment has commenced, values tend to rise. Serum 25-hydroxyvitamin D [25(OH)D] levels are typically lower than normal, with the majority of patients having values <5 ng/ml (12.5 nM). These low levels of 25(OH)D are a hallmark of vitamin D deficiency and help to differentiate the latter from other causes of rickets/osteomalacia. The measurement of serum $1,25(OH)_2D$ levels is

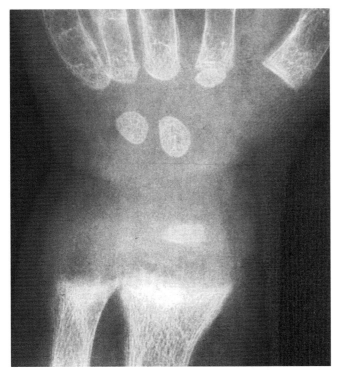

FIG. 1. X-ray of the wrist of an infant with vitamin D deficiency rickets. Note the widened growth plate, the fraying and splaying of the distal metaphyses of the radius and ulna, the poor developed ulna epiphysis, and the coarsening and sparseness of the metaphyseal trabeculae.

not particularly helpful in differentiating the various causes of nutritional rickets/osteomalacia because values may be low, normal, or elevated. Markers of bone turnover reflect the increased activity associated with secondary hyperparathyroidism. However, serum osteocalcin concentrations are typically within the normal range, despite elevated alkaline phosphatase values.[9] Urine calcium excretion is typically low, whereas the TRP and TmP/GFR are decreased. A generalized aminoaciduria and/or bicarbonaturia is also present.

Radiological Findings. The radiographic changes associated with rickets can develop very rapidly, which is different from those of osteomalacia, which may take years to become radiographically apparent. The classical features of rickets occur at the growth plates of long bones and are best seen at the distal end of the radius and ulna or at the tibial and femoral growth plates around the knee. The features at the growth plate include widening of the physis with fraying, cupping, and splaying of the metaphyses (Fig. 1) and underdevelopment of the epiphysis. The earliest sign at the wrist is considered to be a loss of the clear demarcation between the growth plate and the metaphysis, with loss of the provisional zone of calcification. The diaphyses of the long bones appear osteopenic and may show thinning of the cortices with periosteal new bone formation. Looser zones, which manifest as short radiolucent lines through the cortex perpendicular to the shaft, are typical of osteomalacia, although they may be seen rarely in other metabolic bone diseases. They are most frequently noted in the medial cortices of the femurs and in the pelvis and ribs. Because of secondary hyperparathyroidism, the trabecular pattern of the metaphyses becomes coarse and sparse, and subperiosteal erosions may be noted along the phalanges.

In adults with osteomalacia, the most common feature is that of osteopenia, which may be confused with osteoporosis. Only rarely may Looser zones be noted to suggest the diagnosis of osteomalacia. Thus, unlike the typical picture of rickets in children, osteomalacia in adults is difficult to diagnose radiographically and requires biochemical, and often, histological confirmation.[10]

Treatment. The mainstay of treatment is the provision of vitamin D (D_2 or D_3) to correct the vitamin deficiency. In infants and young children, vitamin D drops, 5000–15,000 IU/day (125–375 μg) for 1–2 months, effectively raise 25(OH)D levels to normal and correct serum calcium, phosphorus, and PTH values usually within 2–3 weeks, although the elevated alkaline phosphatase values and radiological abnormalities take longer to return to normal. An early radiographic sign of healing is the appearance of the provisional zone of calcification at the boundary between the physis and metaphysis, which appears as a well-defined sclerotic line. Older children and adults may be treated on a similar regimen, but compliance is probably better if a weekly dose of vitamin D 50,000 IU (1.25 mg) is taken orally for several months. In some countries, a single oral or intramuscular dose of vitamin D 600,000 IU (15 mg) is preferred. There is no indication for or advantage in using one of the vitamin D metabolites, 25(OH)D or 1,25-$(OH)_2$D, or the vitamin D analog, 1α-hydroxycholecalciferol, for the treatment of simple nutritional vitamin D deficiency. However, the metabolites may be more effective in the management of vitamin D deficiency resulting from intestinal malabsorption syndromes.[11] In this situation, UV irradiation of the skin may also be effective.

Calcium supplements (50 mg Ca/kg/day orally) may also be recommended in the initial stages of management, especially if dietary calcium intakes are poor, and advice on ensuring a dietary calcium intake near the adequate intake or recommended daily allowance (RDA) for age should be given. Initially symptomatic hypocalcemia may require parenteral calcium administration to correct the symptoms (1–2 mg Ca/kg, IV, as 10% calcium gluconate).

Prevention. Despite the availability of cheap and effective means of preventing vitamin D deficiency, it remains a public health problem in a number of countries in specific age or cultural groups. It is these groups that need to be targeted with educational messages, and possibly, vitamin D supplementation. Table 1 lists the recommended dietary intakes for vitamin D in the United Kingdom and North America. It should be noted that, in both countries, higher intakes are recommended in the elderly to compensate for possible decreased sun exposure, decreased dermal synthesis of vitamin D, and decreased responsiveness of the small intestine to vitamin D. In the

TABLE 1. RECOMMENDED VITAMIN D INTAKES IN THE UNITED KINGDOM AND NORTH AMERICA

Age	UK recommended nutrient intake (g/day)[54]	USA/Canadian adequate intake (g/day)[16]
0–6 months	8.5	5
7 months to 3 years	7	5
4–50 years	0*	5
50+ years	10 (61+ years)	10 (51–70 years)
		15 (71+ years)
Pregnancy and lactation	10	5

* The United Kingdom believes that healthy ambulatory persons should be able to obtain their vitamin D requirement from sunlight exposure.

United Kingdom, infants <6 months of age also have higher dietary recommendations because it is assumed that sunlight exposure is limited and that exclusively breastfed infants receive little vitamin D from breast milk.[12] The United Kingdom also recommends that all breastfed infants receive vitamin D supplements, whereas the American Academy of Pediatrics suggests that only at-risk infants should be considered for supplementation. In countries such as in the Middle East and Turkey or in communities such as Asians in the United Kingdom or blacks, where vitamin D deficiency is prevalent among mothers, it makes sense to supplement the mother during pregnancy to provide the breastfed newborn with stores of vitamin D and to reduce the incidence of neonatal hypocalcemia.[13] Although a daily supplement of 400 IU (10 μg) vitamin D is highly effective in preventing rickets in infants and young children, in situations where compliance may be a problem, intermittent high doses of vitamin D (100,000 IU [2.5 mg] every 3 months) have been shown to be successful.[14] Vitamin D supplementation should also be considered in the infirm and elderly because normal food sources and the limited sun exposure are generally insufficient to meet the vitamin D requirements of these groups. Over the last decade, considerable controversy has existed as to what might be considered optimal vitamin D status, particularly in the elderly. Evidence suggests that circulating 25(OH)D concentrations ≥75 nM (30 ng/ml) might be necessary to optimize BMD and muscle function and reduce falls and fractures.[15] To obtain such 25(OH)D concentrations, vitamin D intakes of 800-1600 IU/day might be needed; however, these are considerably higher than the adequate intake recommended by the Institute of Medicine.[16]

Dietary Calcium Deficiency

Over the past 20 or so years, growing interest has been shown in the role of low dietary calcium intakes in the pathogenesis of rickets in children. In the 1970s, a few isolated reports appeared of sick infants on highly modified low-calcium diets developing rickets, which responded to calcium supplements.[17] More recently, studies from South Africa,[18] Nigeria,[19] India,[20] and Bangladesh[21] have suggested that dietary calcium deficiency may be a major cause of rickets in children outside the infant age group living in developing countries. Characteristically, the children live in tropical or subtropical climates and are thus exposed to adequate amounts of sunshine. They consume a diet that is very low in calcium (estimated at ≈200 mg calcium daily or ~20% of the RDA) and is relatively monotonous, containing almost no dairy products but is high in phytates and oxalates.

Pathogenesis. It is suggested that the low dietary calcium intake, often exacerbated by a diet high in oxalate and phytate content that impairs intestinal calcium absorption, is unable to meet the demands of the growing skeleton. This results in a fall in serum ionized calcium concentration, which in turn stimulates secondary hyperparathyroidism and a cascade of biochemical changes similar to those described in vitamin D deficiency (Fig. 2). Dietary calcium deficiency may also affect vitamin D metabolism through stimulation of 1,25(OH)$_2$D production, which itself, in turn, leads to an increase in the catabolism of 25(OH)D. In situations of relative vitamin D insufficiency, this increased catabolism of 25(OH)D may precipitate vitamin D deficiency. Such increased catabolism of 25(OH)D has been proposed as the pathogenesis of the high prevalence of rickets in the Asian community in the United Kingdom.[22] There is some evidence that a similar mechanism may be important in the pathogenesis of rickets in black infants and toddlers.[23] It is important to point out that isolated dietary calcium deficiency and vitamin D deficiency are at the two

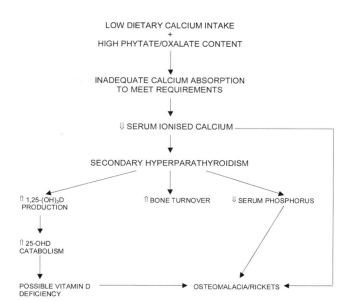

FIG. 2. The pathogenesis of rickets/osteomalacia caused by dietary calcium deficiency.

ends of the pole as far as the pathogenesis of nutritional rickets is concerned; in between these two poles are combinations of the two causes, such that vitamin D sufficiency may be converted to vitamin D deficiency by low dietary calcium intakes, and vitamin D insufficiency may precipitate dietary calcium deficiency by preventing optimal calcium absorption.[24] It is likely that many cases of nutritional rickets have a combination of these two deficiencies to varying degrees in their pathogenesis.

Clinical Presentation. Although calcium deficiency rickets has been described in young infants, these are the exception, because the majority of young infants are fed breast-milk or milk formulas, which are good calcium sources. Calcium deficiency rickets typically occurs after the weaning period, when calcium intakes fall as a result of the low calcium content of traditional diets of many communities in developing countries. In Nigeria, the mean age of presentation is around 4 years, although the onset of symptoms may have occurred several years earlier.[25] In South Africa, the mean age of presentation is older, around 8 years. The typical presentation is that of progressive lower limb deformities (bow legs, knock-knees, or windswept deformities; Fig. 3). The other features of rickets tend to be less pronounced than in vitamin D deficiency, although rachitic rosaries and enlarged wrists are useful clinical signs.[26] In the Nigerian study, delayed motor milestones were noted by the parents.[25] In the South African children, one of the striking differences between vitamin D deficiency and dietary calcium deficiency was noted to be the absence of muscle weakness in the calcium deficiency group.[27]

Laboratory Investigations and Radiological Features. The biochemical features of dietary calcium deficiency are very similar to those of vitamin D deficiency (i.e., hypocalcemia, variable hypophosphatemia, and elevated alkaline phosphatase and PTH values). However, the distinguishing features relate to differences in vitamin D status. In typical dietary calcium deficiency, serum 25(OH)D values are within the normal range (>10 ng/ml [>25 nM]) and 1,25(OH)$_2$D values are elevated, as would be expected in response to hypocalcemia.

The radiographic features of dietary calcium deficiency rick-

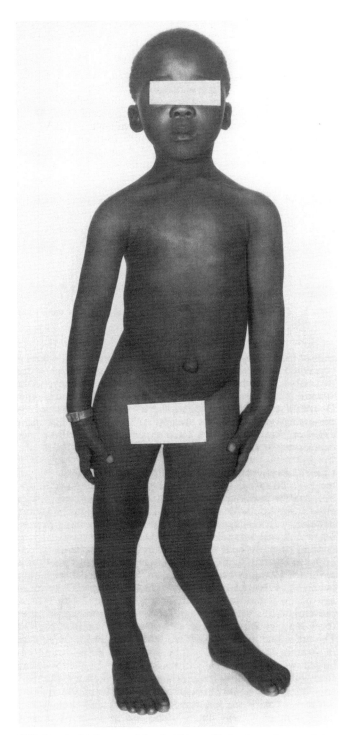

FIG. 3. A girl from rural South Africa suffering from dietary calcium deficiency rickets with windswept deformities of the legs.

ets are similar to those described for vitamin D deficiency with growth plate changes, osteomalacia, and features of secondary hyperparathyroidism (Fig. 4).

Treatment. A number of studies have documented the effectiveness of oral calcium supplements (1000 mg/day for 6 months) without supplemental need for vitamin D in the treat-

ment of dietary calcium deficiency rickets.[19] However, in communities in which it is unclear whether vitamin D insufficiency is playing a role or not, it is prudent to add vitamin D supplements to the regimen.

Prevention. In developing countries, where dietary calcium deficiency is prevalent, prevention of the disease by increase in the consumption of calcium-rich foods may be problematic, because dairy products are often scarce and too expensive for the affected communities. However, the use of locally available foods, such as ground dried fish with its bones, or the addition of limestone to the food, might be beneficial.

Phosphate Deficiency

Isolated nutritional phosphate deficiency is an uncommon cause of rickets/osteomalacia because phosphorus is ubiquitous in foods and the usual dietary intake of phosphate meets the recommended dietary allowances in most situations. However, such mineral deficiency may occur in the breastfed, very low birth weight (VLBW) infant,[28] during prolonged parenteral nutrition in sick patients,[29] and in patients on prolonged antacid therapy.[30] It should be noted that low serum phosphate levels may be a major contributing factor to the pathogenesis of rickets/osteomalacia caused by vitamin D deficiency. However, in that situation, phosphate depletion is dependent on secondary hyperparathyroidism that arises in response to impaired intestinal calcium absorption.

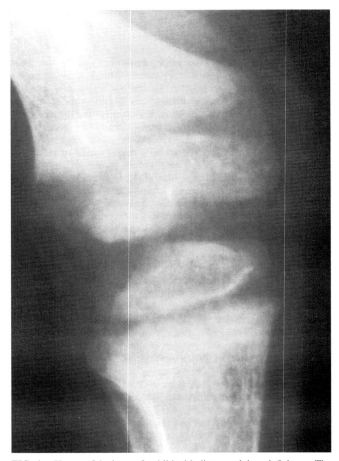

FIG. 4. X-rays of the knee of a child with dietary calcium deficiency. The changes are similar to those described in vitamin D deficiency, with widening of the growth plates and splaying and fraying of the metaphyses.

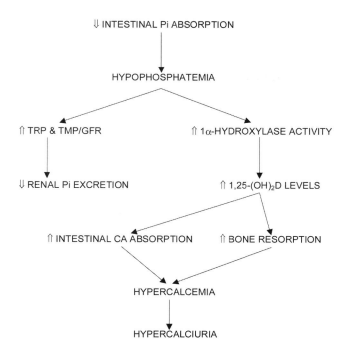

FIG. 5. The pathogenesis of the biochemical abnormalities in phosphate deficiency rickets/osteomalacia.

Pathogenesis. Phosphate deficiency induced by either dietary insufficiency or reduced intestinal absorption results in a fall in serum phosphate levels in association with increased renal reabsorption of phosphate (increased TRP or TmP/GFR). Hypophosphatemia stimulates renal 1α-hydroxylase with a consequent increase in serum $1,25(OH)_2D$ levels, which lead to increased bone resorption, intestinal calcium absorption, and hypercalciuria (Fig. 5). Unlike vitamin D deficiency, PTH levels and vitamin D status are normal in phosphate depletion syndromes. Hypophosphatemia results in impaired bone mineralization and the development of rickets and osteomalacia.

Clinical Presentation and Laboratory Investigations. Metabolic bone disease is a common problem in very low birth weight preterm infants. It typically manifests between 6 and 12 weeks postnatally, and has been estimated to occur radiologically in >50% of infants with birth weights <1000 g, and in >20% of those weighing <1500 g. The disease is most common in those infants who are breast-milk or soy-formula fed or in those who have had prolonged illnesses requiring periods of parenteral nutrition, corticosteroid, or diuretic administration. The clinical manifestations vary from a picture of mildly undermineralized bones to severe rickets with multiple fractures and deformities, which, if involving the ribs, may be severe enough to lead to respiratory distress. The biochemical changes associated with the development of the disease include a rise in alkaline phosphatase levels and the development of hypophosphatemia (<1.8 mM). It is difficult to give a cut-off value for alkaline phosphatase because different assays are used by various laboratories, but a value >7-fold that of the adult normal is highly suggestive of rickets in the preterm infant. Urine phosphate excretion is reduced while urine calcium excretion is increased.

The clinical picture and biochemical abnormalities in prolonged parenteral nutrition are very similar to those described above. The reasons for the development of metabolic bone disease relate to the difficulty in providing adequate amounts of calcium and phosphorus in total parenteral nutrition (TPN) solutions. These problems have been largely overcome in the newer parenteral nutrition solutions.

Treatment. Although the pathogenesis of metabolic bone disease in very low birth weight infants is multifactorial, the major factor seems to be an inadequate intake of phosphate. Soy-based formulas should be avoided, because their phosphorus content is generally less readily available, and if VLBW infants are fed breast milk, breast-milk fortifiers, which increase the Ca and Pi content of the intake (among other nutrients) should be provided until the infant is ready for discharge from hospital. An oral Pi intake of ≈120 mg/kg/day should be achieved. An adequate vitamin D intake of 200 IU/kg/day should also be ensured.[31]

Metabolic bone disease as a consequence of TPN should be treated by providing adequate amounts of Ca and Pi in the intravenous solutions. Furthermore, vitamin D sufficiency should also be maintained.

DRUG-INDUCED RICKETS/OSTEOMALACIA

The causes of drug-induced rickets/osteomalacia may be divided into three large groups: those that primarily result in hypocalcemia, those that primarily cause hypophosphatemia, and those that have a direct effect on the mineralization process. Drugs or medications may cause rickets/osteomalacia through each of the three mechanisms described above (Table 2).

Drugs Resulting in Hypocalcemia

Drugs that inhibit the production or intestinal absorption of vitamin D or interfere with its metabolism or action on its target organs may all produce hypocalcemia and consequent rickets/osteomalacia.

Sunscreens. With the increasing concern about the adverse effects of sunlight and particularly UV irradiation on the skin among health professionals and the general public, sunscreen use has become more prevalent. The extensive use of these products may impair vitamin D_3 formation in the skin, resulting in vitamin D deficiency rickets/osteomalacia, particularly in those subjects whose vitamin D status might normally be marginal. Recently rickets in children has been reported to be as a consequence of the use of sunscreens.[32]

TABLE 2. CAUSES OF DRUG-INDUCED RICKETS/OSTEOMALACIA

Drugs resulting in hypocalcemia
  Inhibitors of vitamin D formation or intestinal absorption
    Sunscreens
    Cholestyramine
  Increased catabolism of vitamin D or its metabolites
    Anticonvulsants
Drugs resulting in hypophosphatemia
  Inhibitors of intestinal phosphate absorption
    Aluminum containing antacids
  Impaired renal phosphate reabsorption
    Cadmium
    Ifosfamide
    Saccharated ferric oxide
Direct impairment of mineralization
  Parenteral aluminum
  Fluoride
  Etidronate

Cholestyramine. Similarly, impairment of vitamin D absorption from the gastrointestinal tract may also lead to osteomalacia as has been reported with the prolonged use of cholestyramine, an anion exchange resin used to bind bile salts in the gut in post-ileectomy diarrhea.[33]

Anticonvulsants. A number of drugs has been described to interfere with the normal metabolism of vitamin D to 25(OH)D and 1,25(OH)$_2$D, leading to alterations in calcium homeostasis and rickets/osteomalacia by increasing the catabolism of vitamin D and its metabolites through inducing hepatic cytochrome P450 enzymes. These include a number of anticonvulsants (phenobarbitone, phenytoin, and carbamazepine).[34] Phenytoin has been shown to have direct effects on decreasing calcium absorption and increasing bone resorption as well. The development of rickets/osteomalacia is more common in those subjects on anticonvulsant therapy who have limited exposure to sunlight such as those who are institutionalized[35] or handicapped, where the prevalence has been reported to be as high as 60%. Severe convulsions or spastic cerebral palsy may result in frequent long-bone fractures in such situations.

Typically, the biochemical abnormalities include hypocalcemia, low 25(OH)D levels, and elevated alkaline phosphatase and PTH values. It is unclear what the prevalence of anticonvulsant-associated bone disease is in ambulatory patients, because some studies have shown little effect of anticonvulsants on calcium homeostasis.[36] The disturbances in calcium homeostasis can be prevented or rapidly corrected by the use of vitamin D supplements (up to 4000 IU [100 μg] per day), although alkaline phosphatase levels may remain elevated, especially in phenobarbitone-treated subjects through induction of hepatic enzymes.

Drugs Resulting in Hypophosphatemia

Drugs may induce hypophosphatemia by either impairing phosphate absorption from the gastrointestinal tract or by increasing phosphate loss from the kidney.

Inhibitors of Intestinal Phosphate Absorption. As has been discussed earlier in this chapter, phosphate deficiency through an inadequate dietary intake is very unlikely to occur because phosphate is found ubiquitously in the diet. An important exception to this is found in the breast-fed VLBW infant, because breast milk contains inadequate phosphate, and possibly calcium, to meet the demands of the very rapidly growing infant during the first several months of life.

Inadequate intestinal phosphate absorption may occur through the inhibition of its absorption through the long-term use of aluminum containing antacids, which bind phosphate, thereby making it unavailable for absorption. The milk-alkali syndrome is characterized by clinical features of hypophosphatemia (muscle weakness and rickets/osteomalacia) and by hypercalcemia, elevated alkaline phosphatase levels, normal PTH values, and elevated 1,25(OH)$_2$D levels. Typically, such patients have a history of consuming large quantities of aluminum-containing antacids, often with the consumption of milk to manage chronic dyspeptic symptoms. Aluminum given parenterally over a prolonged period of time also causes osteomalacia, but the mechanism is thought to be different from that of oral aluminum administration. Phosphate depletion as a result of antacid ingestion can be effectively treated by removing the aluminum-containing antacids. Provision of oral Pi supplements may also be considered until the bone disease responds (clinical improvement in bone pain and muscle weakness, elevation of serum phosphorus values, and a fall in alkaline phosphatase concentrations).

Impaired Renal Phosphate Reabsorption. A number of heavy metals, such as cadmium,[37] and drugs, such as ifosfamide[38,39] and saccharated ferric oxide,[40] have been implicated in causing rickets/osteomalacia through damage to renal tubular function.

Cadmium. Cadmium exposure leads to Itai-Itai disease, which was first described in Japan.[41] The pathogenesis of the osteoporosis and osteomalacia in the disease is not completely elucidated, but cadmium exposure has been shown to lead to permanent damage to glomerular and tubular function, leading to low molecular proteinuria with the excretion of β_2-microglobulin, phosphaturia, and progressive renal failure. Hypophosphatemia and reduced levels of 1,25(OH)$_2$D are characteristic of the disease. Whether cadmium's direct effects on osteoclast and osteoblast function are important in the pathogenesis of the disease are unclear.

Ifosfamide. Ifosfamide, a chemotherapeutic agent used in the treatment of solid tumors, has been reported to produce a renal Fanconi syndrome and hypophosphatemic rickets/osteomalacia, particularly in children, although the complication has also been noted in adults.[31,32]

Saccharated Ferric Oxide. Prolonged intravenous use of saccharated ferric oxide (SFO) for the treatment of iron deficiency anemia causes reversible proximal renal tubular damage, hypophosphatemia, and depressed 1,25(OH)$_2$D levels, leading to osteomalacia.[33] SFO is also thought to inhibit mineralization directly. Cessation of therapy and the use of oral phosphate supplements correct the biochemical and histological abnormalities.

Impairment of Mineralization

A number of agents are known to produce rickets/osteomalacia through direct inhibition of mineralization at the mineralization front in bone and in the growth plate cartilage. These include aluminum,[42] fluoride,[43] and etidronate, a first generation bisphosphonate.[44]

Aluminum. The mechanism by which parenterally acquired aluminum causes rickets/osteomalacia is different from that associated with the oral use of aluminum containing antacids in subjects with normal renal function. The two major conditions, in which aluminum accumulation may occur, are TPN and hemodialysis. In both situations, the aluminum is acquired through contamination of the TPN or hemodialysis fluids. Aluminum may also accumulate through the use of aluminum phosphate binders in patients with impaired renal function. Aluminum inhibits PTH release and 1α-hydroxylase activity. Furthermore, it seems to have direct effects on bone, inhibiting osteoblastic activity and preventing mineralization of preformed osteoid. The net result of all these effects is the production of an adynamic bone disease or a low bone turnover osteomalacia/rickets.[45] The severity of the bone disease correlates with the extent of stainable aluminum at the bone surfaces. With the increased awareness of the importance of aluminum contamination as a cause of bone disease in patients receiving TPN or hemodialysis, regulations have been introduced to reduce the contamination.[42] This has been assisted by the removal of casein hydrolysates as the protein source in TPN solutions. Furthermore, aluminum-based phosphate binding agents have been replaced by the use of calcium-based oral medications, or other resins, in renal failure patients. Aluminum bone disease may respond to the use of deferoxamine, a chelating agent.

Fluoride. The attention of researchers in the developed world has been focused on the toxic effects of fluoride on bone since the introduction of oral fluoride as an experimental drug for the treatment of osteoporosis.[46] With the development of newer effective drugs for the treatment of osteoporosis, fluoride therapy has fallen into disrepute. However, in a number of developing countries, such as India, South Africa, and Kenya, which have areas of endemic fluorosis, the harmful effects of the excessive ingestion of fluoride have been known for many years.[47] Fluoride is incorporated in the newly formed hydroxyapatite crystal at the mineralization front, where it stabilizes the crystal and prevents its dissolution; furthermore, it stimulates osteoblastic activity but also inhibits mineralization. The mineralization defect is aggravated by low dietary calcium intakes. Although there is good evidence that fluoride therapy increases vertebral BMD, there is no good evidence that it reduces fracture rates in osteoporosis.[46]

Endemic fluorosis, after the long-term ingestion of water with fluoride contents of between 3 and 16 ppm, is associated with the insidious onset of generalized bone pain, stiffness, rigidity, and limitation of movement at the spine and the development of crippling deformities.[48] In children, endemic genu valgum and clinical features of rickets have been described.[49,50] Radiographically, osteosclerosis and irregular osteophyte formation are noted in the spine, with calcification of the intervertebral ligaments. The pelvis also shows osteosclerotic changes with calcification of the sacrotuberous and sacroiliac ligaments. Similarly, interosseous membrane calcification is noted in the forearms and lower limbs. In children, features of rickets at the growth plate[51] and osteomalacia with Looser zones may be noted. Histologically, widened osteoid seams, mineralization defects, poorly mineralized new bone formation, and features of increased bone turnover have been described together with areas of hypermineralization. Brown staining of the teeth is a characteristic feature in those subjects who were exposed to excessive fluoride intakes during the period of primary and secondary tooth formation.

Etidronate. The bisphosphonates have become established therapeutic agents in the management of osteoporosis, Paget's disease, and hypercalcemia of malignancy, among other generalized bone conditions. However, they are all analogs of pyrophosphate, an endogenous inhibitor of mineralization. Etidronate, the first bisphosphonate to be approved for clinical use, has been shown to induce impaired mineralization at high doses (20 mg/kg).[52] At lower doses, the incidence of osteomalacia was reduced markedly, but was still evident in biopsy specimens. The newer generations of bisphosphonates do not seem to have the same side effects and have been used extensively in the management of osteoporosis without evidence of impairing mineralization.

REFERENCES

1. Andiran N, Yordam N, Ozon A 2002 Risk factors for vitamin D deficiency in breast-fed newborns and their mothers. Nutrition 18:47–50.
2. Kreiter SR, Schwartz RP, Kirkman HN, Jr., Charlton PA, Calikoglu AS, Davenport ML 2000 Nutritional rickets in African American breast-fed infants. J Pediatr 137:153–157.
3. Sedrani SH 1986 Are Saudis at risk of developing vitamin D deficiency?. Saudi Med J 7:427–433.
4. Harris NS, Crawford PB, Yangzom Y, Pinzo L, Gyaltsen P, Hudes M 2001 Nutritional and health status of Tibetan children living at high altitudes. N Engl J Med 344:341–347.
5. Muhe L, Luiseged S, Mason KE, Simoes EAF 1997 Case-control study of the role of nutritional rickets in the risk of developing pneumonia in Ethiopian children. Lancet 349:1801–1804.
6. Oginni LM, Badru OS, Sharp CA, Davie MW, Worsfold M 2004 Knee Angles and Rickets in Nigerian Children. J Pediatr Orthop 24:403–407.
7. DeLuca HF, Cantorna MT 2001 Vitamin D: Its role and uses in immunology. FASEB J 15:2579–2585.
8. Lorente F, Fontan G, Jara P, Casas C, Garcia-Rodriguez MC, Ojeda JA 1976 Defective neutrophil motility in hypovitaminosis D rickets. Acta Paediatr Scand 65:695–699.
9. Daniels ED, Pettifor JM, Moodley GP 2000 Serum osteocalcin has limited usefulness as a diagnostic marker for rickets. Eur J Pediatr 159:730–733.
10. Parfitt AM 1997 Vitamin D and the pathogenesis of rickets and osteomalacia. In: Feldman D, Glorieux FH, Pike JW (eds.) Vitamin D. Academic Press, San Diego, CA, USA, pp. 645–662.
11. Basha B, Rao DS, Han ZH, Parfitt AM 2000 Osteomalacia due to vitamin D depletion: A neglected consequence of intestinal malabsorption. Am J Med 108:296–300.
12. Specker BL, Tsang RC, Hollis BW 1985 Effect of race and diet on human-milk vitamin D and 25-hydroxyvitiamin D. Am J Dis Child 139:1134–1137.
13. Andiran N, Yordam N, Ozon A 2002 Risk factors for vitamin D deficiency in breast-fed newborns and their mothers. Nutrition 18:47–50.
14. Zeghoud F, Ben-Mekhbi H, Djeghri N, Garabedian M 1994 Vitamin D prophylaxis during infancy: Comparison of the long-term effects of three intermittent doses (15, 5, or 2.5 mg) on 25-hydroxyvitamin D concentrations. Am J Clin Nutr 60:393–396.
15. Dawson-Hughes B 2005 The role of vitamin D in fracture prevention. Available online at http://www.bonekey-ibms.org/cgi/content/full/ibms. BoneKEy Osteovision 2:6–10.
16. Standing Committee on the Scientific Evaluation of Dietary Reference Intakes IoM 1997 Dietary Reference Intakes for Calcium, Phosphorus, Magnesium, Vitamin D, and Fluoride. National Academy Press, Washington, DC, USA.
17. Kooh SW, Fraser D, Reilly BJ, Hamilton JR, Gall D, Bell L 1977 Rickets due to calcium deficiency. N Engl J Med 297:1264–1266.
18. Marie PJ, Pettifor JM, Ross FP, Glorieux FH 1982 Histological osteomalacia due to dietary calcium deficiency in children. N Engl J Med 307:584–588.
19. Thacher TD, Fischer PR, Pettifor JM, Lawson JO, Isichei CO, Reading JC, Chan GM 1999 A comparison of calcium, vitamin D, or both for nutritional rickets in Nigerian children. N Engl J Med 341:563–568.
20. Balasubramanian K, Rajeswari J, Gulab, Govil YC, Agarwal AK, Kumar A, Bhatia V 2003 Varying role of vitamin D deficiency in the etiology of rickets in young children vs. adolescents in northern India. J Trop Pediatr 49:201–206.
21. Fischer PR, Rahman A, Cimma JP, Kyaw-Myint TO, Kabir AR, Talukder K, Hassan N, Manaster BJ, Staab DB, Duxbury JM, Welch RM, Meisner CA, Haque S, Combs GF Jr 1999 Nutritional rickets without vitamin D deficiency in Bangladesh. J Trop Pediatr 45:291–293.
22. Clements MR 1989 The problem of rickets in UK Asians. J Hum Nutr Diet 2:105–116.
23. DeLucia MC, Mitnick ME, Carpenter TO 2003 Nutritional rickets with normal circulating 25-hydroxyvitamin D: A call for reexamining the role of dietary calcium intake in North American infants. J Clin Endocrinol Metab 88:3539–3545.
24. Pettifor JM 1994 Privational rickets: A modern perspective. J Roy Soc Med 87:723–725.
25. Thacher TD, Fischer PR, Pettifor JM, Lawson JO, Isichei C, Chan GM 2000 Case-control study of factors associated with nutritional rickets in Nigerian children. J Pediatr 137:367–373.
26. Thacher TD, Fischer PR, Pettifor JM 2002 The usefulness of clinical features to identify active rickets. Ann Trop Paediatr 22:229–237.
27. Pettifor JM 1991 Dietary calcium deficiency. In: Glorieux FH (ed.) Rickets, vol. 21. Raven Press, New York, NY, USA, pp. 123–143.
28. Backstrom MC, Kuusela AL, Maki R 1996 Metabolic bone disease of prematurity. Ann Med 28:275–282.
29. Klein GL, Chesney RW 1986 Metabolic bone disease associated with total parenteral nutrition. In: Lebenthal E (ed.) Total Parenteral Nutrition: Indication, Utilization, Complications, and Pathophysiological Considerations, 1st ed. Raven Press, New York, NY, USA, pp. 431–443.
30. Pivnick EK, Kerr NC, Kaufman RA, Jones DP, Chesney RW 1995 Rickets secondary to phosphate depletion. A sequela of antacid use in infancy. Clin Pediatr (Phila) 34:73–78.
31. Backstrom MC, Maki R, Kuusela AL, Sievanen H, Koivisto AM, Ikonen RS, Kouri T, Maki M 1999 Randomised controlled trial of vitamin D supplementation on bone density and biochemical indices in preterm infants. Arch Dis Child Fetal Neonatal Educ 80:F161–F166.
32. Zlotkin S 1999 Vitamin D concentrations in Asian children living in

33. Compston JE, Horton LW 1978 Oral 25-hydroxyvitamin D₃ in the treatment of osteomalacia associated with ileal resection and cholestyramine therapy. Gastroenterology **74:**900–902.

34. Hahn TJ, Hendin BA, Scharp CR, Haddad JG 1972 Effect of chronic anticonvulsant therapy on serum 25-hydroxycalciferol levels in adults. N Engl J Med **287:**900–904.

35. Bischof F, Basu D, Pettifor JM 2002 Pathological long-bone fractures in residents with cerebral palsy in a long-term care facility in South Africa. Dev Med Child Neurol **44:**119–122.

36. Ala-Houhala M, Korpela R, Koivikko M, Koskinen T, Koskinen M, Koivula T 1986 Long-term anticonvulsant therapy and vitamin D metabolism in ambulatory pubertal children. Neuropediatrics **17:**212–216.

37. Berglund M, Akesson A, Bjellerup P, Vahter M 2000 Metal-bone interactions. Toxicol Lett **112–113:**219–225.

38. Kintzel PE 2001 Anticancer drug-induced kidney disorders. Drug Saf **24:**19–38.

39. Garcia AA 1995 Ifosfamide-induced Fanconi syndrome. Ann Pharmacother **29:**590–591.

40. Sato K, Shiraki M 1998 Saccharated ferric oxide-induced osteomalacia in Japan: Iron-induced osteopathy due to nephropathy. Endocr J **45:**431–439.

41. Jarup L 2002 Cadmium overload and toxicity. Nephrol Dial Transplant **17:**35–39.

42. Klein GL 1995 Aluminum in parenteral solutions revisited—again. Am J Clin Nutr **61:**449–456.

43. Kleerekoper M 1996 Fluoride and the skeleton. Crit Rev Clin Lab Sci **33:**139–161.

44. Silverman SL, Hurvitz EA, Nelson VS, Chiodo A 1994 Rachitic syndrome after disodium etidronate therapy in an adolescent. Arch Phys Med Rehabil **75:**118–120.

45. Tannirandorn P, Epstein S 2000 Drug-induced bone loss. Osteoporos Int **11:**637–659.

46. Haguenauer D, Welch V, Shea B, Tugwell P, Adachi JD, Wells G 2000 Fluoride for the treatment of postmenopausal osteoporotic fractures: A meta- analysis. Osteoporos Int **11:**727–738.

47. Mithal A, Trivedi N, Gupta SK, Kumar S, Gupta RK 1993 Radiological spectrum of endemic fluorosis: Relationship with calcium intake. Skeletal Radiol **22:**257–261.

48. Teotia SPS, Teotia M 1984 Endemic fluorosis in India: A challenging national health problem. J Assoc Physicians India **32:**347–352.

49. Krishnamachari KAVR, Sivakumar B 1976 Endemic genu valgum: A new dimension to the fluorosis in India. Fluoride **9:**185–200.

50. Pettifor JM, Schnitzler CM, Ross FP, Moodley GP 1989 Endemic skeletal fluorosis in children: Hypocalcemia and the presence of renal resistance to parathyroid hormone. Bone Miner **7:**275–288.

51. Khandare AL, Harikumar R, Sivakumar B 2005 Severe bone deformities in young children from vitamin D deficiency and fluorosis in Bihar-India. Calcif Tissue Int **76:**412–418.

52. Silverman SL, Hurvitz EA, Nelson VS, Chiodo A 1994 Rachitic syndrome after disodium etidronate therapy in an adolescent. Arch Phys Med Rehabil **75:**118–120.

53. Department of Health 1998 Nutrition and Bone Health, 49th ed. The Stationary Office, London, UK.

Chapter 61.   Rickets Caused by Impaired Vitamin D Activation and Hormone Resistance: Pseudovitamin D Deficiency Rickets and Hereditary Vitamin D–Resistant Rickets

Marie B. Demay

Endocrine Unit, Massachusetts General Hospital and Harvard Medical School, Boston, Massachusetts

INTRODUCTION

The clinical observation that rickets and osteomalacia could be cured with vitamin D repletion or sunlight led to the identification of a subset of affected individuals who were resistant to this therapeutic intervention. The skeletal abnormalities in patients who did not respond to this conventional therapy often resolved with pharmacologic doses of vitamin D or 25-hydroxyvitamin D. Subsequent clinical and basic studies showed that these patients could largely be subdivided into two categories: those in whom treatment with physiological doses of 1,25-dihydroxyvitamin D effected a cure and those in whom it did not. Characterization of biochemical and subsequently genetic abnormalities led to the identification of two rare autosomal recessive disorders: pseudovitamin D deficiency rickets (PDDR; OMIM 264700) and hereditary vitamin D–resistant rickets (HVDRR; OMIM 277440), previously known as VDDR types I and II.

PSEUDOVITAMIN D DEFICIENCY RICKETS

The identification of 1,25-dihydroxyvitamin D as the active metabolite of vitamin D led to studies that revealed a subset of patients with inherited rickets in whom treatment with this hormone effected a cure. Based on the biochemical parameters and the clinical response of these patients, it was postulated that this autosomal recessively inherited disorder was a consequence of impaired production of 1,25-dihydroxyvitamin D.[1,2] Studies in placental cells isolated from an affected individual confirmed an absence of 25-hydroxyvitamin D 1α-hydroxylase activity,[3] pointing directly to impaired enzyme activity as the cause of the disorder. The cloning of the *25-hydroxyvitamin D 1α-hydroxylase* gene[4–6] led to the identification of inactivating mutations in affected individuals,[7–9] thus confirming the hypothesis that had been proposed based on previous clinical and basic studies.

Individuals affected by this disorder usually present in the first year of life with rickets and osteomalacia and may also have hypocalcemic seizures. Although studies in rodent models have shown that intestinal calcium absorption is largely 1,25-dihydroxyvitamin D–independent the first 2 weeks of life, gradually being replaced by a 1,25-dihydroxvitamin D–dependent active transport mechanism,[10] it is not know whether an analogous transition occurs in humans that could account for the onset of the clinical disorder after the first 3 months of life. As a consequence of hypocalcemia, patients have secondary hyperparathyroidism that leads to the development of hypophosphatemia because of an increase in renal

---

The author has reported no conflicts of interest.

TABLE 1. CHARACTERISTICS OF PDDR AND HDVRR

Disorder	Gene mutated	Calcium	Phosphorus	PTH	25(OH)D	1,25(OH)$_2$D	Alopecia
PDDR	1α-hydroxylase	Low	Low	High	Normal	Low/undetectable	Absent
HVDRR	VDR	Low	Low	High	Normal	High	Variable

phosphate clearance. In addition to renal phosphate losses, amino aciduria may be observed, presumably because of secondary hyperparathyroidism. There is an increase in serum alkaline phosphatase levels, and radiological examination is notable for evidence of rickets. Unlike patients with nutritional rickets, affected individuals have normal circulating levels of 25-hydroxyvitamin D. However, levels of 1,25-dihydroxyvitamin D are undetectable or markedly reduced (Table 1). Bone biopsy specimens show the presence of osteomalacia and a decrease in mineral apposition in untreated individuals.[11] However, treatment with 1,25-dihydroxyvitamin D and calcium supplementation effectively cures the disorder by bypassing the enzymatic defect. Before the availability of 1α-hydroxylated vitamin D metabolites, patients were treated with pharmacologic amounts of vitamin D or 25-hydroxyvitamin D at doses that were ~100-fold those required to treat patients with nutritional vitamin D deficiency. The availability of 1,25-dihydroxyvitamin D led to the observation that restoration of normal serum levels of this hormone effected a cure.[11–13] In fact, treatment with 1α-hydroxylated vitamin D metabolites and calcium leads to an increase in serum calcium levels within 24 h and radiographic healing of rickets within 2–3 months.[12]

Although treatment of this disorder is uniformly effective, lifelong therapy is required, because discontinuation of therapy results in impaired intestinal calcium absorption, followed by clinical evidence of vitamin D deficiency within a few days. Therapeutic compliance and efficacy should be monitored by measurements of serum calcium, phosphorus, immunoreactive PTH (iPTH), and alkaline phosphatase. Although there may be an increase in alkaline phosphatase levels in the early stages of treatment, associated with healing of osteomalacic lesions, levels should return to normal within 6–12 weeks of therapy. Adequate calcium intake should be insured because studies in affected humans as well as in a mouse model of this disorder show that the skeletal abnormalities are a direct consequence of impaired intestinal calcium absorption.[14] Therapy should be adjusted to maintain serum calcium and iPTH levels within the normal range and to avoid hypercalciuria, because the latter may lead to nephrolithiasis. In growing children, monitoring should be performed every 6–8 weeks until a therapeutic response has been observed. Thereafter, monitoring should be performed at least every 6 months so that the therapeutic regimen can be adjusted to accommodate the mineral ion needs of a growing skeleton. Because the requirements of the adult skeleton are less variable, monitoring should be performed every 6–12 months once skeletal maturity has been achieved. More frequent monitoring, in both children and adults, is required during intercurrent illnesses, such as gastroenteritis, which can lead to a decrease in calcium intake or impaired intestinal calcium and 1,25-dihydroxyvitamin D absorption. Similarly, more frequent monitoring is required during pregnancy, and doses of 1,25-dihydroxyvitamin D often need to be increased by 50–100% to meet the needs of the fetus without further compromising the maternal skeleton.[13]

Treatment of PDDR is effective, and if instituted early, can prevent the skeletal and dental abnormalities that are a consequence of the disordered mineral ion homeostasis in these patients with 25-hydroxyvitamin D 1α-hydroxylase mutations.

Institution of treatment after the development of rickets leads to the cure of rickets and osteomalacia but is not uniformly associated with prevention of enamel hypoplasia in the dentition that develops postnatally.[15] Thus, although lifelong therapy is required, early clinical recognition permits institution of a safe and effective therapeutic regimen for this disorder.

HEREDITARY VITAMIN D–RESISTANT RICKETS

The observation that a group of patients with congenital rickets was not responsive to treatment with physiological doses of 1,25-dihydroxyvitamin D permitted the identification of a subset of rachitic patients with markedly elevated levels of this hormone, in whom resistance to the biological effects of this hormone were suspected.[16] Unlike fibroblasts isolated from normal individuals, which, when treated with 1,25-dihydroxyvitamin D, showed a decrease in proliferation and an increase in 24-hydroxylation of vitamin D metabolites, cells from affected individuals were not responsive to 1,25-dihydroxyvitamin D.[17–19] This impaired biological responsiveness to 1,25-dihydroxyvitamin D was associated with defective hormone binding or impaired nuclear uptake of radiolabeled 1,25-dihydroxyvitamin D.[20–22] Cloning of the vitamin D receptor (VDR) enabled studies directed at confirming that mutation of the vitamin D receptor was the molecular basis for this disorder.[23–26]

The VDR is a member of the nuclear receptor superfamily.[27] These nuclear receptors were originally thought to be ligand-dependent transcription factors, but studies directed at examining the in vitro and in vivo effects of these receptors have revealed a number of ligand-independent actions. Unlike the closely related thyroid and retinoid receptors, to date only one nuclear VDR isoform has been identified.[23] Analogous to other members of the nuclear receptor superfamily, the VDR has a DNA-binding domain comprised of two zinc fingers, a ligand binding domain, a domain required for heterodimerization with the retinoid-X receptor, and a transactivation domain that includes regions required for recruitment of nuclear receptor co-modulators.[27] Mutations in each of these functional domains have been found in affected patients.[28,29]

CLINICAL PRESENTATION

Like PDDR, HVDRR is an autosomal recessive disorder and is often associated with parental consanguinity.[28] The parents, who are obligate heterozygotes, are phenotypically normal. Affected individuals usually present in infancy with rickets and osteomalacia, accompanied by symptoms of hypocalcemia, including tetany and seizures. The clinical presentation is similar to that of patients with 25-hydroxyvitamin D 1α-hydroxylase mutations, with the exception that affected individuals in some kindreds with *VDR* mutations develop progressive alopecia beginning the first year of life, progressing to alopecia totalis. It was postulated that the development of alopecia was associated with a more severe clinical phenotype[30] and, in fact, all mutations in the DNA binding domain reported to date, are associated with alopecia.[28] However, some affected individuals with alopecia have been reported to have spontaneous remissions of their disordered mineral ion homeostasis,[31] suggesting either that they may have less severe hormone resistance or that other compensatory mechanisms are brought into play.

Radiological examination of affected individuals is analogous to that observed in patients with PDDR, including widened, radiolucent metaphyses characteristic of rickets and evidence of osteomalacia, including the presence of pseudofractures. Dental abnormalities, including enamel hypoplasia and oligodontia may also be seen.[32] Metabolic abnormalities include hypocalcemia, secondary hyperparathyroidism, and hypophosphatemia caused by a PTH-dependent increase in urinary phosphate clearance. The development of secondary hyperparathyroidism may be associated with aminoaciduria and osteitis fibrosa cystica. An increase in serum alkaline phosphatase levels is also observed. Recent studies in mice with targeted ablation of the VDR,[33] as well as in other hypophosphatemic mouse models,[34] point to hypophosphatemia as the etiological basis for the growth plate expansion. These studies show that hypophosphatemia is associated with impaired apoptosis of hypertrophic chondrocytes and that phosphate ions induce apoptosis of these cells in a differentiation-dependent fashion by activating the caspase 9–dependent mitochondrial apoptotic pathway.[33] Thus, normalizing serum phosphorus levels may be required to prevent rickets and to achieve normal growth.

The single parameter that distinguishes patients with HVDRR from PDDR is the presence of elevated levels of 1,25-dihydroxyvitamin D (Table 1). The dramatic increase in hormone levels is thought to reflect induction of the renal *25-hydroxyvitamin D 1α-hydroxylase* gene by the high PTH levels, as well as impaired inactivation of 1,25-dihydroxyvitamin D, because expression of the major enzyme involved in its inactivation, the vitamin D 24-hydroxylase, requires the receptor-dependent effects of 1,25-dihydroxyvitamin D for its activation.[35] Affected individuals have a dramatic impairment in intestinal calcium absorption,[36] despite markedly elevated serum levels of 1,25-dihydroxyvitamin D. Unlike patients affected by PDDR, in whom a uniformly successful treatment response is observed, treatment of patients with HVDRR often presents a challenge. In approximately one half of the patients impaired, receptor function is present rather than absent. In these individuals, pharmacologic doses of vitamin D or 1,25-dihydroxyvitamin D can overcome the resistance syndrome, ameliorating intestinal calcium absorption, and consequently, the clinical phenotype.[36] In other patients, this regimen is ineffective. In this subset of severely affected patients, skeletal manifestations can be treated by intravenous infusion with calcium, thus bypassing the defect in intestinal calcium absorption. The observation that these infusions can cure rickets and osteomalacia, as well as normalize the mineral apposition rate,[37] suggests that the receptor-dependent actions of 1,25-dihydroxyvitamin D are not essential for normal growth and skeletal homeostasis. In support of this hypothesis is the observation that prevention of abnormal mineral ion homeostasis in mice lacking functional VDRs results in a radiologically and histomorphometrically normal skeleton with normal biomechanical properties.[38]

Chronic therapy for this disorder is usually required. The mainstay of therapy is combined treatment with calcium and pharmacologic doses vitamin D metabolites. Although rare, sporadic remissions have been described in affected individuals during late adolescence, after the high mineral ion demands of the growing skeleton have abated. In children, the efficacy of the therapeutic regimen should be reassessed every 4–6 weeks by evaluation of serum calcium and phosphorus levels. Immunoreactive PTH levels and alkaline phosphatase levels should be measured every 2–3 months, because an increase in PTH

levels will antedate the decrease in serum calcium and allow therapeutic intervention in a more timely fashion. In patients in whom calcium infusions are required, these infusions should be continued until calcium, phosphorus, PTH, and alkaline phosphatase levels are normalized. Infusions should be resumed when these parameters become abnormal. In patients on chronic oral therapy, more frequent monitoring is required during intercurrent gastrointestinal illnesses or other situations where calcium intake or absorption may be compromised.

Patients with HVDRR are fertile; however, modification of the therapeutic regimen is usually required in the second and third trimesters because of the increased calcium requirements associated with pregnancy. The increased maternal calcium need continues through the period of lactation.

While appropriate treatment, whether oral or intravenous, ameliorates the skeletal consequences of *VDR* mutations, it does not affect the development of alopecia.[39] Studies in a mouse model of HVDRR showed that VDR expression in the keratinocyte component of the hair follicle is both necessary[40] and sufficient to prevent alopecia.[41] Interestingly, the actions of the VDR required to maintain normal hair are ligand-independent.[42] Clarifying the molecular actions of the VDR in this unique model system will undoubtedly elucidate novel molecular interactions of this nuclear receptor.

CONCLUSION

Investigations directed at elucidating the biochemical and molecular basis for these two autosomal recessive disorders provided considerable insight into the regulation of hormone synthesis and the molecular basis of hormone action. They also enabled the development of animal models to further elucidate novel actions of 1,25-dihydroxyvitamin D and its receptor. Analogous to other patients affected by hereditary disorders, genetic counseling should be offered to affected individuals and their parents. While the therapeutic regimen for patients affected by PDDR is effective, treatment of HVDRR still presents a challenge. Although parenteral calcium infusions have been successful in treating the skeletal sequelae of this disorder, a novel therapeutic regimen that would overcome the defect in intestinal calcium absorption would facilitate long-term compliance. In a similar fashion, characterization of the downstream effects of the VDR in the epidermal keratinocyte may enable the development of a therapeutic regimen directed at preventing alopecia in affected patients.

REFERENCES

1. Fraser D, Kooh SW, Kind HP, Holick MF, Tanaka Y, DeLuca HF 1973 Pathogenesis of hereditary vitamin-D-dependent rickets: An inborn error of vitamin D metabolism involving defective conversion of 25-hydroxyvitamin D to 1α,25-dihydroxyvitamin D. N Engl J Med 289:817–822.
2. Drezner MK, Feinglos MN 1977 Osteomalacia due to 1α,25-dihydroxycholecalciferol deficiency. J Clin Invest 60:1046–1053.
3. Glorieux FH, Arabian A, Delvin EE 1995 Pseudo-vitamin D deficiency: Absence of 25-hydroxyvitamin D 1α-hydroxylase activity in human placenta decidual cells. J Clin Endocrinol Metab 80:2255–2258.
4. St-Arnaud R, Messerliann S, Moir JM, Omdahl JL, Glorieux FH 1997 The 25-hydroxyvitamin D 1-alpha hydroxylase gene maps to the pseudovitamin D-deficiency rickets (PDDR) disease locus. J Bone Miner Res 12:1552–1559.
5. Fu GK, Lin D, Zhang MY, Bikle DD, Shackleton CH, Miller WL, Portale AA 1997 Cloning of human 25-hydroxyvitamin D-1 alpha-hydroxylase and mutations causing vitamin D-dependent rickets type 1. Mol Endocrinol 11:1961–1970.
6. Shinki T, Shimada H, Wakino S, Anazawa H, Hayashi M, Saruta T, DeLuca HF, Suda T 1997 Cloning and expression of rat 25-hydroxyvitamin D3 1-alpha-hydroxylase cDNA. Proc Natl Acad Sci USA 94:12920–12925.

7. Kitanaka S TK, Murayama A, Sato T, Okumura K, Nogami M, Hasegawa Y, Niimi H, Yanagisawa J, Tanaka T, Kato S 1998 Inactivating mutations in the 25-hydroxyvitamin D 1 alpha hydroxylase gene in patients with pseudovitamin D-deficiency rickets. N Engl J Med **338:**653–661.

8. Wang JT LC, Burridge SM, Fu GK, Labuda M, Portale AA, Miller WL 1998 Genetics of vitamin D 1alpha-hydroxylase deficiency in 17 families. Am J Hum Genet **63:**1694–1702.

9. Yoshida T MT, Tenenhouse HS, Goodyer P, Shinki T, Suda T, Wakino S, Hayashi M, Saruta T 1998 Two novel 1alpha-hydroxylase mutations in French-Canadians with vitamin D dependency rickets type I1. Kidney Int **54:**1437–1443.

10. Dostal LA, Toverud SU 1984 Effect of vitamin D_3 on duodenal calcium absorption in vivo during early development. Am J Physiol 246:G528–G534, 1984.

11. Delvin EE, Glorieux FH, Marie PJ, Pettifor JM 1981 Vitamin D dependency: Replacement therapy with calcitriol. Pediatrics **99:**26–34.

12. Reade TM, Scriver CR, Glorieux FH, Nogrady B, Delvin E, Poirier R, Holick MF, DeLuca HF 1975 Response to crystalline 1α-hydroxyvitamin D_3 in vitamin D dependency. Pediatr Res **9:**593–599.

13. Glorieux FH 1990 Calcitriol treatment in vitamin D-dependent and vitamin D-resistant rickets. Metabolism **39:**10–12.

14. Dardenne O, Prud'homme J, Glorieux FH, St-Arnaud R 2004 Rescue of the phenotype of CYP27B1 (1alpha-hydroxylase)-deficient mice. J Steroid Biochem Mol Biol **89–90:**327–330.

15. Arnaud C, Maijer R, Reade T, Scriver CR, Whelan DT 1970 Vitamin D dependency: An inherited postnatal syndrome with secondary hyperparathyroidism. Pediatrics **46:**871–880.

16. Brooks MH, Bell NH, Love L, Stern PH, Orfei E, Queener SF, Hamstra AJ, DeLuca HF 1978 Vitamin D-dependent rickets Type II: Resistance of target organs to 1,25-dihydroxyvitamin D. N Engl J Med **298:**996–999.

17. Clemens TL, Adams JS, Horiuchi N, Gilchrest BA, Cho H, Tsuchiya Y, Matsuo N, Suda T, Holick MF 1983 Interaction of 1,25-dihydroxyvitamin-D_3 with keratinocytes and fibroblasts from skin of normal subjects and a subject with vitamin-D-dependent rickets, type II: A mode of action of 1,25-dihydroxyvitamin D_3. J Clin Endocrinol Metab **56:**824–830.

18. Griffin JE, Zerwekh JE 1983 Impaired stimulation of 25-hydroxyvitamin D-24-hydroxylase in fibroblasts from a patient with vitamin D-dependent rickets, type II: A form of receptor-positive resistance to 1,25-dihydroxyvitamin D_3. J Clin Invest **72:**1190–1199.

19. Gamblin GT, Liberman UA, Eil C, Downs RW Jr, DeGrange DA, Marx SJ 1985 Vitamin D-dependent rickets type II: Defective induction of 25-hydroxyvitamin D_3-24-hydroxylase by 1,25-dihydroxyvitamin D in cultured skin fibroblasts. J Clin Invest **75:**954–960.

20. Feldman D, Chen T, Cone C, Hirst M, Shani S, Benderli A, Hochberg Z 1982 Vitamin D resistant rickets with alopecia: Cultured skin fibroblasts exhibit defective cytoplasmic receptors and unresponsiveness to 1,25(OH)$_2$$D_3$. J Clin Endocrinol Metab **55:**1020–1022.

21. Eil C, Liberman UA, Rosen JF, Marx SJ 1981 A cellular defect in hereditary vitamin-D-depenedent rickets type II: Defective nuclear uptake of 1,25-dihydroxyvitamin D in cultured skin fibroblasts. N Engl J Med **304:**1588–1591.

22. Eil C, Liberman UA, Marx SJ 1986 The molecular basis for resistance to 1,25-dihydroxyvitamin D: Studies in cells cultured from patients with hereditary hypocalcemic 1,25(OH)$_2$$D_3$-resistant rickets. Adv Exp Med Biol **196:**407–422.

23. Hughes MR, Malloy PJ, Kieback DG, Kesterson RA, Pike JW, Feldman D, O'Malley BW 1988 Point mutations in the human vitamin D receptor gene associated with hypocalcemic rickets. Science **242:**1702–1705.

24. Hughes MR, Malloy PJ, O'Malley BW, Pike JW, Feldmann D 1991 Genetic defects of the 1,25-dihydroxyvitamin D_3 receptor. J Recept Res **11:**699–716.

25. Malloy PJ, Hochberg Z, Pike JW, Feldman D 1989 Abnormal binding of vitamin D receptors to deoxyribonucleic acid in a kindred with vitamin D-dependent rickets, type II. J Clin Endocrinol Metab **68:**263–269.

26. Malloy PJ, Hochberg Z, Tiosano D, Pike JW, Hughes MR, Feldman D 1990 The molecular basis of hereditary 1,25-dihydroxyvitamin D_3 resistant rickets in seven related families. J Clin Invest **86:**2071–2079.

27. Haussler MR, Whitfield GK, Haussler CA, Hsieh JC, Thompson PD, Selznick SH, Dominguez CE, Jurutka PW 1998 The nuclear vitamin D receptor: Biological and molecular regulatory properties revealed. J Bone Miner Res **13:**325–349.

28. Malloy PJ, Pike JW, Feldman D 1999 The vitamin D receptor and the syndrome of hereditary 1,25- dihydroxyvitamin D-resistant rickets. Endocr Rev **20:**156–188.

29. Malloy PJ, Xu R, Peng L, Clark PA, Feldman D 2002 A novel mutation in helix 12 of the vitamin D receptor impairs coactivator interaction and causes hereditary 1,25-dihydroxyvitamin D-resistant rickets without alopecia. Mol Endocrinol **16:**2538–2546.

30. Marx SJ, Bliziotes MM, Nanes M 1986 Analysis of the relation between alopecia and resistance to 1,25-dihydroxyvitamin D. Clin Endocrinol (Oxf) **25:**373–381.

31. Takeda E, Yokota I, Kawakami I, Hashimoto T, Kuroda Y, Arase S 1989 Two siblings with vitamin-D-dependent rickets type II: No recurrence of rickets for 14 years after cessation of therapy. Eur J Pediatr **149:**54–57.

32. Bell NH 1980 Vitamin D-dependent rickets type II. Calcif Tissue Int **31:**89–91.

33. Sabbagh Y, Carpenter TO, Demay M 2005 Hypophosphatemia leads to rickets by impairing caspase-mediated apoptosis of hypertrophic chondrocytes. Proc Natl Acad Sci USA **102:**9637–9642.

34. Tu Q, Pi M, Karsenty G, Simpson L, Liu S, Quarles LD 2003 Rescue of the skeletal phenotype in CasR-deficient mice by transfer onto the Gcm2 null background. J Clin Invest **111:**1029–1037.

35. Kerry D, Dwivedi P, Hahn C, Morris H, Omdahl J, May B 1996 Transcriptional synergism between vitamin D-responsive elements in the rat 25-hydroxyvitamin D 24-hydroxylase (CYP24) promoter. J Biol Chem **22:**29715–29721.

36. Tsuchiya Y, Matsuo N, Cho H, Kumagai M, Yasaka A, Suda T, Orimo H, Shiraki M 1980 An unusual form of vitamin D-dependent rickets in a child: Alopecia and marked end-organ hyposensitivity to biologically active vitamin D. J Clin Endocrinol Metab **51:**685–690.

37. Balsan S, Garabedian M, Larchet M, Gorski A-M, Cournot G, Tau C, Bourdeau A, Silve C, Ricour C 1986 Long-term nocturnal calcium infusions can cure rickets and promote normal mineralization in hereditary resistance to 1,25-dihydroxyvitamin D. J Clin Invest **77:**1661–1667.

38. Amling M, Priemel M HT, Chapin K, Rueger JM, Baron R, Demay MB 1999 Rescue of the skeletal phenotype of vitamin D receptor ablated mice in the setting of normal mineral ion homeostasis: Formal histomorphometric and biomechanical analyses. Endocrinology **140:**4982–4987.

39. Al-Aqeel A, Ozand P, Sobki S, Sewairi W, Marx S 1993 The combined use of intravenous and oral calcium for the treatment of vitamin D dependent rickets type II (VDDRII). Clin Endocrinol (Oxf) **39:**229–237.

40. Sakai Y, Kishimoto J, Demay M 2001 Metabolic and cellular analysis of alopecia in vitamin D receptor knockout mice. J Clin Invest **107:**961–966.

41. Chen C, Sakai Y, Demay M 2001 Targeting expression of the human vitamin D receptor to the keratinocytes of vitamin D receptor null mice prevents alopecia. Endocrinology **142:**5386–5389.

42. Skorija K, Cox M, Sisk JM, Dowd DR, MacDonald PN, Thompson CC, Demay MB 2005 Ligand-independent actions of the vitamin D receptor maintain hair follicle homeostasis. Mol Endocrinol **19:**855–862.

Chapter 62.   Hypophosphatemic Vitamin D–Resistant Rickets

Uri S. Alon

Bone and Mineral Disorders Clinic, Section of Pediatric Nephrology, Children's Mercy Hospital, University of Missouri-Kansas City, School of Medicine, Kansas City, Missouri

INTRODUCTION

In the face of normal kidney function, all cases of rickets, other than a few with stage 1 vitamin D–deficient rickets, are characterized by hypophosphatemia.[1,2] Differentiation between primary hypophosphatemia and secondary, which is caused by hyperparathyroidism, can be easily achieved by measuring serum PTH concentration.[2] In cases of abnormalities in calcium homeostasis, and more frequently vitamin D metabolism, serum PTH is elevated, causing increased tubular loses of phosphate. Treatment of these cases is aimed at correcting the abnormalities in calcium and vitamin D metabolism and requires no phosphate supplementation. On the other hand, rickets caused by a primary abnormality in phosphate metabolism is characterized by the presence of normal serum PTH concentration. Its etiology, whether renal or extrarenal, can be determined by analyzing urine phosphate excretion in the face of normal dietary intake of the mineral. If elevated, the pathophysiology resides within the proximal renal tubule; if low, an extrarenal source should be investigated. If the renal tubule is to be implicated, either a primary genetic etiology or a secondary tubular damage (such as that after exposure to certain nephrotoxic agents) is the likely source of phosphate loss. The most common genetic form of hypophosphatemic rickets is the one transmitted as an X-linked dominant trait (XLH), described first by Albright and named by him "hypophosphatemic vitamin D–resistant rickets."[3]

Clinical and radiological features of all types of rickets are similar, but bone histology varies depending on the presence or absence of hyperparathyroidism.[4] In primary hypophosphatemic rickets and osteomalacia, histology shows accumulation of undermineralized osteoid with no evidence of increased osteoclast activity and excessive bone resorption. Consequently, bone mass is not always decreased. A DXA study in treated children and adolescents showed decreased BMD in the appendicular skeleton and increased BMD in the lumbar spine.[5]

GENETICS AND PATHOPHYSIOLOGY

Originally an abnormality at the sodium-dependent phosphate transporter (NaPi-2A) at the tubular brush border membrane was disclosed, but it became clear that this was not the primary source of the pathophysiology in XLH.[6] Further studies to define the genetic and molecular basis of the disease have led to the identification of *PHEX* (phosphate-regulating gene with homologies to endopeptidases on the X chromosome) located at Xp22.1–22.2. This gene encodes a membrane-bound endopeptidase primarily expressed in osteoblasts, osteocytes, odontoblasts, muscle, lung and ovary. Deletions affecting *phex*, the murine homolog of *PHEX*, were identified in the Hyp and Gy mice, the rodent analogs of human XLH.[7] Other mice strains with point mutations in *phex* also show tubular phosphate wasting, hypophosphatemia, and rickets.[7] More than 180 *PHEX* mutations have been identified (http://www.phexdb.mcgill.ca) in numerous XLH families and indi-

vidual cases, but some patients show no such abnormalities.[8] No phenotype–genotype correlation was established between the *PHEX* gene and disease pattern.[8,9] Furthermore, overexpression of the human *PHEX* gene did not fully correct abnormalities in the Hyp mouse.[7]

Both humans and the rodent mice model show insufficient production of 1,25-dihydroxyvitamin D in the face of low blood phosphate concentration (which normally stimulates increased production of the active vitamin D metabolite). Indeed, in the human autosomal recessive disease of hypophosphatemic rickets and hypercalciuria, patients exhibit high serum concentration of calcitriol, increased intestinal calcium absorption, and consequently, hypercalciuria and development of nephrocalcinosis and nephrolithiasis. Treatment of this disease, its genetic basis yet unknown, requires only oral phosphate supplementation.[10] In XLH, no cause and effect relationship has been established between the tubular phosphate leak and decreased calcitriol production.

The observation of development of hyperphosphaturia and hypophosphatemia in an XLH patient with end-stage kidney disease who received a kidney transplant from a healthy donor,[11] as well as studies on Hyp mice using parabiosis[12] and cross-renal transplantation,[13] provided evidence that the hyperphosphaturia in this disease is not caused by a primary defect in the kidney, but is caused by a circulating factor. Based on findings in patients with tumor-induced osteomalacia in whom a phosphaturic factor was extracted from the tumor, this factor was originally named "phosphatonin."[14–16] Multiple studies in recent years showed the presence of several phosphaturic agents, but at this point, abnormalities in fibroblast growth factor-23 (FGF-23) are at the center of attention.[17–20] Besides inhibiting tubular phosphate reabsorption, FGF-23 also inhibits 1,25-vitamin D production and stimulates 24,25-vitamin D production.[21] In Hyp mice, FGF-23 mRNA expression is increased in the bones, and circulating FGF-23 concentration is high.[19] Similarly, circulating levels of FGF-23 are elevated in many but not all XLH patients.[22] Although originally believed that it is the lack of PHEX-dependent endopeptidase that is causing the high FGF-23 level, some dispute this association.[21,23] Contrary to familial tumoral calcinosis where recessive mutations in FGF-23 were identified,[24,25] thus far, no functional FGF-23 mutations have been detected in XLH patients.[8]

CLINICAL MANIFESTATIONS

During the first year of life, before a child starts to walk, findings are minimal or nonexistent. In infants, diagnosis is established almost exclusively in those in whom XLH is suspected based on their family history. Once the child starts to walk, progressive deformities of the lower extremities and decrease in growth rate become evident and alert parents and health professionals. In later childhood, if still untreated, dental complications appear as well, because of poorly mineralized dentin, enlarged pulp chambers, and root canals, causing multiple periradicular abscesses in caries-free teeth that result in early teeth decay in the young adult.[26] In fact, in some adult carriers, history of dental abscesses might be the only clinical

---

The author has reported no conflicts of interest.

finding. In other female carriers, the only finding might be asymptomatic hypophosphatemia, making the latter the marker for this disease. Other manifestations in the adult patient may include involvement of the spine and ligaments and hearing impairment.[27,28] Although an earlier study suggested that hearing impairment may indicate the possibility of a variant of the disease equivalent to the situation in the Gy mouse,[29] more recent studies showed that hearing impairment is rarely seen in children with XLH but more commonly seen in adults and therefore may be part of the natural history of the disease.[28] It is possible that both the spinal nerve involvement and the neurosensory hearing loss are the result of bony changes. It is yet unknown whether these skeletal changes are the results of the disease itself of a complication of its treatment.[27] Besides the radiographic findings of rickets, diagnosis is based on the biochemical findings of hypophosphatemia, hyperphosphaturia, elevated serum alkaline phosphatase activity with normal serum creatinine, calcium, PTH, 25-hydroxyvitamin D, and inappropriately low 1,25-dihydroxyvitamin D concentrations.

TREATMENT

Because of our current inability to correct the tubular phosphate losses, the only way to correct hypophosphatemia is by providing the patients with large quantities of oral phosphate preparations. Each dose has a very short lifetime, so it is recommended to provide four to five doses a day. The recommended starting dose is 40 mg/kg/day, which can be adjusted up to a maximum of 100 mg/kg/day, not to exceed 3.0 g of elemental phosphate per day. Treatment with phosphate alone will result in mild hypocalcemia triggering increased secretion of PTH. This will further lower the tubular threshold for phosphate,[30] resulting in a vicious cycle that will require additional intake of phosphate and consequently further increase in PTH secretion. To offset this effect of phosphate administration, patients are concomitantly treated by supraphysiologic doses of 1,25-dihydroxyvitamin D. The recommended starting dose is 25 ng/kg/day, with a maximum of 70 ng/kg/day, divided to two doses. Because of tendency for nocturnal hyperparathyroidism, if calcitriol is divided unevenly, the higher dose should be given at night.[31] With the combined treatment, one can expect healing of the rickets, and in some patients, spontaneous improvement in leg deformities or good response to braces, minimizing the need for corrective orthopedic surgery. Biochemically, one should aim at keeping serum phosphate at the lower range of normal for age, with which alkaline phosphatase activity will decrease to normal or close to normal and bone radiographs will show healing of the rickets. Some patients will show improved growth rates, especially when treatment is started early.[32] In those not showing sufficient gain in height, growth hormone (GH) therapy might be considered. Although some researchers reported improved height with GH therapy,[33] others point to a possible increase in the discrepancy between body trunk and lower limbs growth.[34,35] Histologically, the phosphate and vitamin D combination was shown to improve and in some cases heal the mineralization defect on the trabecular surface.[4] Because of the fact that bone turnover is lower and epiphyseal plates are fused, the role of treatment of adults is still not fully clear. It seems, however, that symptomatic adults with osteomalacia do benefit from treatment[36]; it is as yet unknown, however, whether this treatment should be by 1,25-dihydroxyvitamin D alone or in combination with phosphate.[4]

A single study showed the beneficial effect of 24,25-dihydroxyvitamin D,[37] but as of now, this treatment has not become standard of care for XLH. Whereas treatment with dipyridamole was found to be effective in adult patients with

TABLE 1. PREPARATIONS FOR TREATMENT OF XLII

Calcitriol
  Oral solution
    Rocaltrol 1 μg/ml
  Capsules
    Rocaltrol: 0.25 μg, 0.5 μg
Phosphate
  Powder
    Neutra-Phos: phosphorus 250 mg (8 mmol), potassium 278 mg (7.125 mEq), sodium 164 mg (7.125 mEq)
    Neutra-Phos-K: phosphorus 250 mg (8 mmol), potassium 556 mg (14.25 mEq) (sodium free)
  Oral solution
    Fleet Phospho-Soda: phosphate 4 mmol, sodium 4.82 mEq/ml (equivalent to monobasic sodium phosphate monohydrate 2.4 g and dibasic sodium phosphate heptahydrate 0.9 g per 5 ml)
  Tablets
    K-Phos M/F: phosphorus 125.6 mg (4 mmol), potassium 44.5 mg (1.1 mEq), sodium 67 mg (2.9 mEq)
    K-Phos Neutral: phosphorus 250 mg (8 mmol), potassium 45 mg (1.1 mEq), sodium 298 mg (13 mEq)
    K-Phos No. 2: phosphorus 250 mg (8 mmol), potassium 88 mg (2.3 mEq), sodium 134 mg (5.8 mEq)
    K-Phos Original: phosphorus 114 mg (3.7 mmol), potassium 144 mg (3.7 mEq) (sodium free)
    Uro-KP-Neutral: phosphorus 258 mg (8 mmol), potassium 49.4 mg (1.27 mEq), sodium 262.4 mg (10.9 mEq)

tubular phosphate leak,[38] it was reported to be ineffective in XLH patients.[39] A recent study in the Hyp mouse showed the potential of indomethacin in reducing hyperphosphaturia and improving serum phosphate concentration without lowering glomerular filtration rate.[40] The application of this novel finding in humans awaits further research. Future treatment modalities might be aimed at lowering FGF-23 levels or blocking its activity.

COMPLICATIONS OF TREATMENT

Phosphate supplementation is usually well tolerated and can be provided in the form of liquid preparation to young children and as a tablet to older children and adults. At times, high doses of the phosphate can result in diarrhea. In such cases, it is recommended to stop treatment for a few days, start at a lower dose, and increase it gradually. It is also seems more reasonable to use K-phosphate preparations rather than Na-K-phosphate ones (Table 1). A high load of sodium may enhance calciuria with its potential bone and kidney complications, whereas potassium is known to have an anticalciuric effect and may augment urinary citrate.[41] Furthermore, sodium administration causes volume expansion that enhances phosphaturia, and finally, acidic K-phospate preparations (K-Phos Original; Beach Pharmaceuticals, Tampa, FL, USA) may lower urine pH, desirable in decreasing the risk of calcium phosphate precipitation in the kidneys.[42] Before the introduction of 1,25-dihydroxyvitamin D, patients were treated with large amounts of vitamin D, which often resulted in severe complications, including hypercalcemia, hypercalciuria, and kidney damage. On the other hand, insufficient dosing of vitamin D resulted in the development of secondary and at times tertiary hyperparathyroidism. The introduction of 1,25-dihydroxyvitamin D simplified treatment by allowing better dose adjustment.[27]

The two most common complications of therapy are nephrocalcinosis and hyperparathyroidism.[27] Nephrocalcinosis was reported in up to 60–100% of treated patients.[8,43,44] In the majority of patients, nephrocalcinosis is asymptomatic and does not tend to progress, but in some instances, it was reported to be associated with tubular dysfunction. Kidney biopsy specimens in XLH patients with nephrocalcinosis, as well as in Hyp mice treated with high doses of phosphate, showed the calcifications to be composed of calcium phosphate.[45] It is therefore reasonable to prefer the use of phosphate preparations that maintain the urine acidity, thus decreasing the risk of deposition of calcium phosphate precipitates in the kidney. Thiazide diuretics have been shown to arrest the progression of nephrocalcinosis.[46] Recently, nephrocalcinosis was reported to resolve in a few teenagers treated with thiazides/amiloride diuretics.[47] The combination thiazides/amiloride not only reduces calciuria and may reverse nephrocalcinosis, but it might also improve bone mineralization.[48] Hyperparathyroidism is detected in 20–25% of treated patients, and in some of them, may lead to hypertension and renal failure.[8,49] Although an abnormality in the *PHEX* chromosome in the parathyroid glands was reported in one patient,[50] and a few infant patients may present with mild hyperparathyroidism, in the vast majority of patients, hyperparathyroidism is believed to be caused by the repetitive hypocalcemic effect of phosphate administration. If detected early, secondary hyperparathyroidism can be reversed by medical means (decreased phosphate and increased vitamin D doses). Under some circumstances, all treatment has to be stopped for 4–6 weeks to normalize serum PTH concentration before treatment can be resumed. In some patients, secondary hyperparathyroidism may progress to autonomous, hypercalcemic, tertiary hyperparathyroidism, which requires parathyroidectomy.[51,52] In cases in which a subtotal parathyroidectomy was conducted, there might be a need to proceed to a total parathyroidectomy if the remaining gland develops hyperplasia by itself. The introduction of calcimimetic agents may assist in the prevention and treatment of hyperparathyroidism in this disorder.

CONCLUSION

As more and more evidence accumulates concerning the pathophysiology of hypophosphatemic vitamin–D resistant rickets, hope exists for new modes of treatment, in particular, preventing excess FGF-23 activity on bone and kidney. Until this futuristic treatment is available, current management continues with phosphate and vitamin D preparations. However, this treatment should be monitored carefully and routinely for possible side effects. In particular, routine measurements of kidney functions, serum PTH level, and urine calcium/creatinine ratio should be done every 3–4 months, combined with annual ultrasounds. Use of Ca-sparing diuretics seems to be beneficial in preventing renal complications, and calcimimetic agents may have a role in preventing and treating secondary hyperparathyroidism.

ACKNOWLEDGMENTS

This study was supported by the Sam and Helen Kaplan Research Fund in Pediatric Nephrology. I thank Regina Johnson for excellent administrative assistance.

REFERENCES

1. Srivastava T, Alon US 2002 Stage I vitamin D-deficiency rickets mimicking pseudohypoparathyroidism type II. Clin Pediatr 41:263–268.
2. Pattargarn A, Alon US 2001 Antacid-induced rickets in infancy. Clin Pediatr 40:389–393.
3. Albright F, Butlet AM, Bloomberg E 1937 Rickets resistant to vitamin D therapy. Am J Dis Child 54:529–535.
4. Glorieux FH 2003 Hypophospatemic vitamin D-resistant rickets. In Favus MJ (ed.) Primer on the Metabolic Bone Diseases and Disorders of Mineral Metabolism, 5th ed. American Society for Bone and Mineral Research, Washington, DC, USA, pp. 414–417.
5. Shore RM, Langman CB, Poznansk AK 2000 Lumbar and radial bone mineral density in children and adolescents with X-linked hypophosphatemia: Evaluation with dual X-ray. Skeletal Radiol 29:90–93.
6. Tenenhouse HS, Scriver CR, McInnes RR, Clorieux FH 1978 Renal handling of phosphate in vivo and in vitro by the X-linked hypophosphatemic male mouse (Hyp/Y): Evidence for a defect in the brush border membrane. Kidney Int 14:236–244.
7. Erben R, Dagmar M, Wever K, Jonsson K, Juppner H, Lanske B 2005 Overexpression of human PHEX under the β-actin promoter does not fully rescue the hype mouse phenotype. J Bone Miner Res 20:1149–1160.
8. Cho HY, Lee BH, Kang JH, Ha IS, Cheong HI, Choi, Y 2005 A clinical and molecular genetic study of hypophosphatemic rickets in children. Pediatr Res 58:329–333.
9. Holm IA, Nelson AE, Robinson BG, Mason RS, Marsh DJ, Cowell CT, Carpenter TO 2001 Mutational analysis and genotype-phenotype correlation of the PHEX gene in X-linked hypophosphatemic rickets. J Clin Endocrinol Metab 86:3889–3899.
10. Jones A, Tzenova J, Frappier D, Crumley M, Roslin N, Kos C, Tieder M, Langman C, Proesmans W, Carpenter T, Rice A, Anderson D, Morgan K, Fujiwara T, Tenenhouse H 2001 Hereditary hypophosphatemic rickets with hypercalciuria is not caused by mutations in the Na/Pi cotransporter NPT2 gene. J Am Soc Nephrol 12:507–514.
11. Morgan JM, Hawley WL, Chenoweth AI, Retan JW, Diethelm AG 1974 Renal transplantation in hypophosphatemia with vitamin D-resistant rickets. Arch Intern Med 134:549–552.
12. Meyer RA, Meyer MH, Gray RW 1989 Parabiosis suggests a humoral factor is involved in X-linked hypophosphatemia mice. J Bone Miner Res 4:493–500.
13. Nesbitt T, Coffman TM, Drezner MK 1992 Cross-transplantation of kidneys in normal and Hyp mice: Evidence that the Hyp phenotype is unrelated to an intrinsic renal defect. J Clin Invest 89:1453–1459.
14. Cai, Q, Hodgson ST, Kao PC, Lennon VA, Klee GG, Zinmiester AR, Kumar Rajiv 1994 Inhibition of renal phosphate transport by a tumor product in a patient with oncogenic osteomalacia. N Engl J Med 330:1645–1649.
15. Schiavi SC, Kumar R 2004 The phosphatonin pathway: New insights in phosphate homeostasis. Kidney Int 65:1–11.
16. Ward LM, Rauch F, White KE, Filler G, Matzinger MA, Letts M, Travers R, Econs MJ, Glorieux FH 2004 Resolution of severe, adolescent-onset hyphosphatemic rickets following resection of an FGF-23-producing tumour of the distal femur. Bone 34:905–911.
17. Rowe PS, Kumagai Y, Gutierrez G, Garrett IR, Blacher R, Rosen D, Cundy J, Navvab S, Chen D, Drezner MK, Quarles LD, Mundy GR 2004 MEPE has the properties of an osteoblastic phosphatonin and minhibin. Bone 34:303–319.
18. Shimada T, Urakawa I, Yamazaki Y, Hasegawa H, Hino R, Yoneya T, Takeuchi Y, Tasasaki T, Fukumoto S, Yamashita T 2004 FGF-23 transgenic mice demonstarate hypophosphatemic rickets with reduced expression of sodium phosphate cotransporter type IIa. Biochem Biophys Res Commun 314:409–414.
19. Shimada T, MIzutani S, Muto T, Yoneya T, Hino R, Takeda S. Takeuchi Y, Fujita T, Fukumoto S, Yamishita T 2001 Cloning and characterization of FGF23 as a causative factor of tumor-induced osteomalacia. Pro Natl Acad Sci USA 98:6500–6505.
20. Carpenter TO, Ellis BK, Insogna KL, Philbrick WM, Sterpka J, Shimkets R 2005 Fibroblast growth factor 7: An inhibitor of phosphate transport derived from oncogenic osteomalacia-causing tumors. J Clin Endocrinol Metab 90:1012–1020.
21. Shimada T, Hasegawa H, Yamazaki Y, Muto T, Hino R, Takeuchi Y, Fujita T, Nakahara K, Fukumoto S, Yamashita T 2004 FGF-23 is a potent regulator of vitamin D metabolism and phosphate homeostasis. J Bone Miner Res 19:429–435.
22. Jonsson KB, Zahradnik R, Larsson T, White KE, Sugimoto T, Imanishi Y, Yamamoto T, Hampson G, Koshiyama H, Ljuggren O, Oba K, Yang IM, Mijauchi A, Econs MJ, Lavigne J, Juppner H 2003 Fibroblast growth factor 23 in oncogenic osteomalacia and X-linked hypophosphatemia. N Engl J Med 348:1656–1663.
23. Benet-Pages A, Lorenz-Depiereux B, Zischka H, White KE, Econs MJ, Strom TM 2004 FGF23 is processed by proprotein convertases but not by PHEX. Bone 35:455–462.
24. Larsson T, Yu X, Davis SI. Draman MS, Mooney SD, Cullen MJ, White KE 2005 A novel recessive mutation in fibroblast growth factor causes familial tumoral calcinosis. J Clin Endocrinol Metab 90:2424–2427.
25. Benet-Pages A, Orlik P, Strom TM, Lorenz-Depiereux B 2005 An FGF23

missense mutation causes familial tumoral calcinosis with hyperphosphatemia. Hum Mol Genet **14**:385–390.

26. Pereira CM, de Andrade CR, Vargas PA, Coletta RD, de Almeida OP, Lopes MA 2004 Dental alterations associated with X-linked hypophosphatemic rickets. J Endod **30**:241–245.

27. Wilson DW, Alon U 1993 Renal hypophosphatemia. In: Alon U, Chan JCM (eds.) Phosphate in Pediatric Health and Disease. CRC Press, Boca Raton, FL, USA, pp. 159–192.

28. Fishman G, Miller-Hansen D, Jacobsen C, Singhal VK, Alon US 2004 Hearing impairment in familial X-linked hypophosphatemic rickets. Eur J Pediatr **163**:622–623.

29. Boneh A, Reade TM, Scriver CR, Rishikof E 1987 Audiometric evidence for two forms of X-linked hypophosphatemia in humans, apparent counterparts of Hyp and Gy mutations in mouse. Am J Med Genet **27**:997–1003.

30. Alon U, Chan JCM 1984 Effects of PTH and 1,25 dihydroxyvitamin D3 on tubular handling of phosphate in hypophosphatemic rickets. J Clin Endocrinol Metab **58**:671–675.

31. Carpenter TO, Mitnick MA, Ellison A, Smith C, Insogna KL 1994 Nocturnal hyperparathyroidism: A frequent feature of X-linked hypophosphatemia. J Clin Endocrinol Metab **78**:1378–1383.

32. Makitie O, Doria A, Kooh SW, Cole WG, Daneman A, Sochett E 2003 Early treatment improves growth and biochemical and radiographic outcome in X-linked hypophosphatemic rickets. J Clin Endrocrinol Metab **88**:3591–3597.

33. Baroncelli GI, Bertelloni S, Ceccarelli C, Saggese G 2001 Effect of growth hormone treatment on final height, phosphate metabolism, and bone mineral density in children with X-linked hypophosphatemic rickets. J Pediatr **138**:236–243.

34. Haffner D, Nissel R, Wuhl E, Mehls O 2004 Effects of growth hormone treatment on body proportions and final height among small children with X-linked hypophosphatemic rickets. Pediatr **11**:e593–e596.

35. Reusz GS, Miltényi G, Stubnya G, Szabó A, Horváth C, Byrd DJ, Péter F, Tulassay T 1997 X-linked hypophosphatemia: Effects of treatment with recombinant human growth hormone. Pediatr Nephrol **11**:573–577.

36. Sullivan W, Carpenter T, Glorieux FH, Travers R, Insogna K 1992 A prospective trial of phosphate and 1,25-dihydroxyvitamin D3 therapy in symptomatic adults with X-linked hypophasphatemic rickets. J Clin Endocrinol Metab **75**:879–885.

37. Carpenter TO, Keller M, Schwartz D, Mitnick M, Smith C, Ellison A, Carey D, Comite F, Horst R, Travers R, Glorieux FH, Gundberg CM, Poole AR, Insogna KL 1996 24,25-Dihydroxyvitamin D supplementation corrects hyperparathyroidism and improves skeletal abnormalities in X-linked hypophosphatemic rickets—a clinical research center study. J Clin Endocrinol Metab **81**:2381–2388.

38. Prié D, Blanchet FB, Essig M, Jourdain J, Friedlander G 1998 Dipyridamole decreases renal phosphate leak and augments serum phosphorus in patients with low renal phosphate threshold. J Am Soc Nephrol **9**:1264–1269.

39. Seikaly MG, Quigley R, Baum M 2000 Effect of dipyridamole on serum and urinary phosphate in x-linked hypophosphatemia. Pediatr Nephrol **15**:57–59.

40. Baum M, Loleh S, Seikaly M, Dwarakanath V, Quigley R 2003 Correction of proximal tubule phosphate transport defect in hyp mice in vivo and in vitro with indomethacin. Proc Natl Acad Sci USA **100**:11098–11103.

41. Osorio AV and Alon US 1997 The relationship between urinary calcium, sodium and potassium excretion and the role of potassium in treating idiopathic hypercalciuria. Pediatrics **100**:675–681.

42. Alon US, Moore W 2002 Effect of long-term treatment with acid phosphate on the development of nephrocalcinosis in familial hypophosphatemic rickets. Pediatric Academic Societies Annual Meeting, Baltimore, MD, USA, May 5–8, 2002.

43. Verge CF, Lam A, Simpson JM, Cowell CT, Howard NJ, Silink M 1991 Effects of therapy in X-lined hypophosphatemic rickets. N Engl J Med **325**:1843–1848.

44. Nehgme R, Fahey JT, Smith C, Carpenter TO 1997 Cardiovascular abnormalities in patients with X-linked hypophosphatemia. J Clin Endocrinol Metab **82**:2450–2454.

45. Alon U, Donaldson DL, Hellerstein S, Warady BA, Harris DJ 1992 Metabolic and histologic investigation of the nature of nephrocalcinosis in children with hypophosphatemic rickets and the Hyp mouse. J Pediatr **120**:899–905.

46. Seikaly MG, Baum M 2001 Thiazide diuretics arrest the progression of nephrocalcinosis in children with X-linked hypophosphatemia. Pediatrics **106**:e6–e12.

47. Auron A, Alon US 2005 Resolution of medullary nephrocalcinosis in children with metabolic bone disorders. Pediatr Nephrol **20**:1143–1145.

48. Alon U, Chan JCM 1985 The effects of hydrochlorothiazide and amiloride in renal hypophosphatemic rickets. Pediatrics **75**:754–763.

49. Alon US, Monzavi R, Lilien M, Rasoulpour M, Geffner ME, Yadin O 2003 Hypertension in hypophosphatemic rickets—role of secondary hyperparathyroidism. Pediatr Nephrol **18**:155–158.

50. Blydt-Hansen TD, Tenenhouse HS, Goodyer P 1999 PHEX expression in parathyroid gland and parathyroid hormone dysregulation in X-linked hypophasphatemia. Pediatr Nephrol **13**:617–611.

51. Chan JCM, Young RB, Alon U, Mamunes P 1983 Hypercalcemia in children with disorders of calcium and phosphate metabolism during long-term treatment with 1,25 dihydroxyvitamin D3. Pediatrics **72**:225–233.

52. Savio RM, Gosnell JE, Posen S, Reeve TS, Delbridge LW 2004 Parathyroidectomy for tertiary hyperparathyroidism associated with X-linked dominant hypophosphatemic rickets. Arch Surg **139**:218–222.

Chapter 63.   Tumor-Induced Osteomalacia

Suzanne M. Jan de Beur

Department of Medicine, The Johns Hopkins University School of Medicine, Baltimore, Maryland

INTRODUCTION

Tumor-induced osteomalacia (TIO), or oncogenic osteomalacia, is an acquired, paraneoplastic syndrome of renal phosphate wasting that resembles genetic forms of hypophosphatemic rickets. Since the initial observation by McCrance,[1] clinical and experimental studies implicate the humoral factor(s) that tumors produce in the profound biochemical and skeletal alterations that characterize TIO. TIO is a rare disorder; however, progress in understanding its pathogenesis is contributing to our understanding of hypophosphatemic disorders and of normal phosphate homeostatic mechanisms.

CLINICAL AND BIOCHEMICAL MANIFESTATIONS

Although the preponderance of patients with TIO is observed in adults (usually diagnosed in the sixth decade), this syndrome may present at any age. In the clinical setting, these patients report long-standing, progressive muscle and bone pain, weakness, and fatigue that often predate the fractures that complicate TIO. Children with TIO display rachitic features including gait disturbances, growth retardation, and skeletal deformities. The occult nature of TIO delays its recognition, and the average time from onset of symptoms to a correct diagnosis often exceeds 2.5 years.[2] Once the syndrome is recognized, an average of 5 years elapses from the time of diagnosis to the identification of the underlying tumor.[3] Until the underlying tumor is identified, other renal phosphate-wasting syndromes must be considered. There-

Dr. Jan de Beur has a consultant agreement with Genzyme.

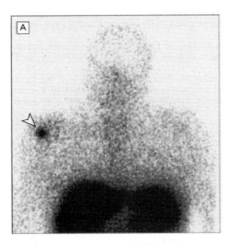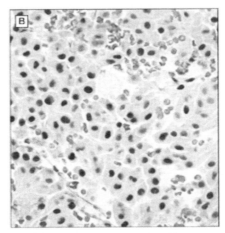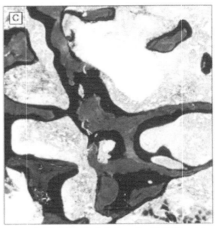

JAMA, 2005;294:1260-1267. © American Medical Association

FIG. 1. Radiographic and histological features of TIO. (A) Octreotide scan showing small mesenchymal tumor in the head of the humerus (arrowhead). (B) Hemangiopericytoma with numerous pericytes and vascular channels (H&E stain). Original magnification, ×100. (C) Bone biopsy with Goldner stain. Excessive osteoid or unmineralized bone matrix composed mainly of collagen stains pink (black). Mineralized bone stains blue (gray). Normal bone usually has a very thin, barely visible layer of osteoid. The presence of excessive osteoid is indicative of osteomalacia. This bone biopsy show severe osteomalacia. Original magnification, ×20.[46]

fore, it is important to note that, in patients with TIO, a family history of hypophosphatemia and bone disorders is absent. A rapid onset and severe clinical course may help differentiate TIO from X linked hypophosphatemic rickets (XLH). Identification of previously normal serum phosphorus level in an adult patient supports the diagnosis of TIO, although in rare instances patients with autosomal dominant hypophosphatemic rickets (ADHR) can present as adults. In situations when inherited hypophosphatemic rickets must be excluded, genetic testing for mutations in the *PHEX* gene and *FGF-23* gene is indicated. In the management of presumptive TIO, clinical diligence, serial physical examination, and appropriate imaging are required to successfully detect the underlying tumor.

One of the major obstacles to diagnosing TIO is that serum phosphorus measurements are no longer included in the standard comprehensive metabolic panel. Thus, hypophosphatemia is not identified unless it is ordered specifically by the clinician. The biochemical hallmarks of TIO are low serum concentrations of phosphorus, phosphaturia secondary to reduced proximal renal tubular phosphate reabsorption, and frankly low or inappropriate normal levels of serum calcitriol [$1,25(OH)_2D$] that are expected to be elevated in the face of hypophosphatemia. The degree of hypophosphatemia is usually profound and can range from 0.7 to 2.4 mg/dl.[2] However, serum calcium and 25-hydroxyvitamin D levels are invariably normal, and serum concentrations of intact PTH are only occasionally elevated. Alkaline phosphatase is typically elevated and derived primarily from bone. A more global proximal tubular defect that results in glucosuria, and amino aciduria may accompany the phosphaturia. Bone histomorphometry reveals severe osteomalacia with clear evidence of a mineralization defect with increased mineralization lag time and excessive osteoid (Fig. 1). The dual defect of renal phosphate wasting in concert with impaired calcitriol synthesis results in poor bone mineralization and fractures.[2,4] If untreated, severe osteomalacia leads to fractures of the long bones as well as vertebra and ribs with resultant chest wall deformity and respiratory compromise.

DIAGNOSTIC EVALUATION

Laboratory Studies

When evaluating a patient with suspected TIO, the work-up includes fasting serum phosphorus, a chemistry panel with

serum calcium, alkaline phosphatase, and creatinine, an intact PTH level, and serum $1,25(OH)_2D$. In addition, a fasting 2-h urine phosphorus, creatinine, calcium, amino acids, and glucose are measured. As an indication of renal tubular phosphate clearance, the maximum tubular reabsorption of phosphate factored for glomerular filtration rate (TmP/GFR) is calculated. In the setting of renal phosphate wasting, the TmP/GFR is lower than expected for the degree of hypophosphatemia. In some instances when confirmation of the diagnosis is warranted, a tetracycline double-labeled, iliac crest bone biopsy is obtained for bone histomorphometric studies.

Imaging

General. Plain radiographs exhibit characteristics of osteomalacia including generalized osteopenia, pseudofractures, and coarsened trabeculae. Radiographs of children with TIO show widened epiphyses and other features of rickets. Diffuse skeletal uptake, referred to as a "superscan," and focal uptake at sites of fractures are characteristic features on ^{99}Technecium bone scintigraphy. In general, plain films show features of osteomalacia; however, it is impossible to differentiate the underlying etiology of the osteomalacia with these modalities.

Tumor Localization. Detection and localization of the culprit tumor in TIO is imperative because complete surgical resection is curative. However, the mesenchymal tumors that cause this syndrome are often small, slow growing, and frequently situated in unusual anatomical sites; therefore, conventional imaging techniques often fail to localize them. Because in vitro studies show that many mesenchymal tumors express somatostatin receptors (SSTR),[5] ^{111}In-pentetreotide scintigraphy (octreotide scan), a scanning technique that uses a radiolabeled somatostatin analog, has been used to successfully detect and localize these tumors in some patients with TIO (Fig. 1).[3,6] The mesenchymal tumors that express SSTR are not limited to those associated with TIO; thus, careful biochemical confirmation of the syndrome is necessary before embarking on exhaustive imaging efforts.[7] Successful tumor localization has been reported in a few patients with other imaging techniques such as whole body MRI[8] and positron emission tomography.[9] In a single instance, venous sampling for fibroblast growth factor

(FGF)-23 was used to confirm an identified mass was the causative tumor in a patient with TIO.[10]

With conventional imaging such as magnetic resonance scanning or CT, special attention directed to craniofacial locations and the extremities is indicated because these are more common locations for tumors in TIO, although tumors have been found distributed through out the body.

DIFFERENTIAL DIAGNOSIS

Osteomalacia in adults and rickets in children can result from a variety of conditions including abnormal vitamin D metabolism (which in itself has a long differential diagnosis, abnormal bone matrix, enzyme defects, inhibitors of mineralization, calcium and phosphorus deficiency, and renal phosphate wasting. TIO is a syndrome of impaired renal phosphorus reabsorption; therefore, the discussion will focus on differentiating TIO from other renal phosphate-wasting disorders. In contrast to more common forms of osteomalacia that share clinical features with TIO, patients with TIO have normal serum calcium, normal serum 25-hydroxyvitamin D, normal intact PTH, low $1,25(OH)_2D$, and inappropriately elevated urine phosphorus. With the appropriate battery of tests, TIO is readily distinguishable from most common forms of osteomalacia. However, TIO is biochemically indistinguishable from several inherited forms of hypophosphatemic rickets: X linked hypophosphatemic rickets (XLH) and autosomal dominant hypophosphatemic rickets (ADHR).[11] Because patients with XLH and ADHR exhibit a variable age of onset, it is critical to take a careful family history in patients with hypophosphatemia. The clinical consequences of TIO are typically present for many years before the causal tumor is identified; this further obscures the clinical distinction between TIO and inherited forms of hypophosphatemic, vitamin D–resistant rickets. In contrast to XLH, patients with TIO exhibit symptoms of weakness, pain, and fractures that are more severe and disabling. Stress and insufficiency fractures are more typical of TIO, whereas lower extremity deformity and short stature are characteristic of XLH and ADHR. Serum FGF-23 levels are generally elevated in patients with TIO but are also elevated in patients with ADHR and some patients with XLH. Furthermore, normal serum FGF-23 levels do not eliminate the diagnosis of TIO.[11,12] The diagnosis of TIO is dependent on the identification of the culprit tumor and remission of the syndrome after complete tumor resection. Genetic testing of the *PHEX* and *FGF-23* genes, which are defective in XLH and ADHR, respectively, is commercially available and may be indicated when a definitive diagnosis is necessary.[13]

Another inherited renal phosphate-wasting syndrome, hereditary hypophosphatemic rickets with hypercalciuria (HHRH), is clinically similar to TIO, with bone pain, osteomalacia, and muscle weakness as prominent features; however, the distinction is easily made with biochemical testing.[14] Both syndromes are characterized by hypophosphatemia owing to decreased renal phosphorus reabsorption; however, patients with HHRH exhibit elevated levels of calcitriol and hypercalciuria that distinguish it from TIO, XLH, and ADHR. Recently, the molecular basis of this syndrome has been identified as biallelic mutations in *SLC34A3*, the gene that encodes the NaPiIIc sodium phosphate transporter.[15,16]

A new hypophosphatemic syndrome was described in two patients with hypophosphatemia secondary to renal phosphate wasting and osteopenia or nephrolithiasis. This was caused by heterozygous, dominant-negative, mutations in the renal type IIa sodium-phosphate co-transporter gene (*NPT-2*). The prominent symptoms of bone pain and muscle weakness seen in TIO are absent in those with *NPT-2* mutations. Furthermore, the presence of hypercalciuria and elevated calcitriol make these patients easily distinguishable from patients with TIO.[17]

TUMORS

The mesenchymal tumors that are associated with TIO are characteristically slow-growing, complex, polymorphous neoplasms that have been subdivided into four groups based on their histological features: (1) phosphaturic mesenchymal tumor, mixed connective tissue type (PMTMCT); (2) osteoblastoma-like tumors; (3) ossifying fibrous-like tumors; and (4) nonossifying fibrous-like tumors.[18] The PMTMCT subtype is the most common and comprises ~70–80% of the mesenchymal tumors associated with TIO.[18,19] Characterized by an admixture of spindle cells, osteoclast-like giant cells, prominent blood vessels, cartilage-like matrix, and metaplastic bone, these tumors occur equally in soft tissue and bone. Although typically benign, malignant variants of PMTMCT have been described.

FGF-23 message is abundantly expressed in these tumors,[20–22] and FGF-23 protein is detectable by immunoblot and immunohistochemistry.[23] In one series, 17 of 21 PMTMCT tumors had detectable FGF-23 protein expression.[19] The granular cytoplasm within the spindle cells exhibits the most consistent staining and seems to be the source of FGF-23.

These mesenchymal tumors are small, indolent and remotely located. Although found in a variety of anatomical locations, including the long bones, the nasopharynx, the sinuses, and the groin,[3] these tumors are most commonly located in the extremities and appendicular skeleton.[19] While tumor localization is frequently a prolonged and arduous task, once detected, the anatomical inaccessibility of the tumors make complete resection difficult. Successful tumor detection requires careful physical examination, diligent follow-up, and periodic imaging.

Although TIO is typically caused by benign mesenchymal tumors, the syndrome has also been associated with a variety carcinomas, neurofibromatosis, linear nevus syndrome, and fibrous dysplasia of bone. Because the multiplicity of lesions and resultant inability to completely resect the entire tumor burden, demonstration of biochemical and radiographic improvement with surgery has been lacking save for a few cases.

PATHOPHYSIOLOGY

Dual Defect: Renal Phosphate Wasting and Abnormal Vitamin D Metabolism

The basic pathophysiology of TIO is hypophosphatemia secondary to inhibition of renal phosphate reabsorption compounded by a vitamin D synthetic defect that blunts the compensatory rise in calcitriol in response to hypophosphatemia. Profound hypophosphatemia results in muscle pain and weakness, osteomalacia, and fractures. Experimental evidence suggests that the biochemical and skeletal defects in TIO are caused by a humoral factor (or factors), coined "phosphatonin," produced by mesenchymal tumors. Tumor extracts can inhibit phosphate transport in vitro,[23] produce phosphaturia and hypophosphatemia in vivo,[24] and inhibit renal 25-hydroxyvitamin D-1-α-hydroxylase activity in cultured kidney cells.[25] Furthermore, complete surgical resection of tumor tissue results in normalization of serum phosphate and calcitriol, reversal of renal phosphate loss, and eventually, remineralization of bone.[2,3]

Identifying "Phosphatonin": FGF-23

Although several groups have reported tumor cultures or tumor extracts inhibit phosphate transport, slow growth of cultured tumor cells and the frequent loss of phosphate-inhibitory activity in culture hampered the identification of the phosphaturic substance produced by these tumors. By examining highly expressed genes in TIO tumors,[21,26,27] several candidate genes for the phosphaturic substance(s) produced by these tumors have been identified. Included among these genes is *FGF-23*, a novel FGF, which was contemporaneously identified by positional cloning as the defective gene in ADHR.[28] In contrast to the low expression in normal tissues,[28] FGF-23 is highly expressed in TIO tumors.[21,28]

Conditioned media and purified FGF-23 can inhibit phosphate transport in opossum kidney cells (OK), a model of renal proximal tubular epithelium.[20,29] When injected into mice, FGF-23 reduces serum phosphate and increases fractional excretion of phosphorus.[27,30] Mice chronically exposed to FGF-23 become hypophosphatemic with increased renal phosphate clearance, show reduced bone mineralization, and have reduced expression of renal 25-hydroxyvitamin D-1-α-hydroxylase with decreased circulating levels of calcitriol.[27] The biochemical and skeletal abnormalities of transgenic mice that overexpress FGF-23 mimic human TIO.[31,32] Conversely, FGF-23–deficient mice exhibit growth retardation and early death, with biochemical abnormalities that include hyperphosphatemia, elevated calcitriol, and hypercalcemia.[33,34]

Circulating FGF-23 is detectable in human serum.[11,12] Individuals with TIO exhibit elevated serum levels of FGF-23 that plummet after complete tumor resection. However, some individuals with TIO have normal or only mildly elevated levels—underscoring the heterogeneous composition of "phosphatonin."

FGF-23 is also central in the pathogenesis of ADHR. Missense mutations in one of two arginine residues at positions 176 or 179 have been identified in affected members of four unrelated ADHR families.[28] This clustering of missense mutations suggests that they are activating mutations. Furthermore, the mutated arginine residues, located in the consensus proprotein convertase cleavage RXXR motif, prevent the degradation of FGF-23 and thus may result in prolonged or enhanced FGF-23 action.[20,31,35-37]

Amassing evidence suggests that FGF-23 may be key in the pathogenesis of XLH. XLH is caused by mutations in the *PHEX* gene,[38] which encodes an M13 metalloprotease. Speculation about the function of *PHEX* paired with data that implicate both an intrinsic osteoblast defect and a humoral factor in the pathogenesis of XLH led to the hypothesis that the substrate for PHEX is the humoral factor responsible for TIO. The endogenous substrate for PHEX remains unknown, and it remains unclear if PHEX modifies FGF-23 directly [20,39] or indirectly.[40]

It is clear that FGF-23 plays a central role in several disorders of renal phosphate wasting (Fig. 2). In TIO, tumors ectopically produce FGF-23 that inhibits renal tubular reabsorption of phosphate and downregulates the 25-hydroxyvitamin D-1-α-hydroxylase, resulting in hypophosphatemia and osteomalacia. In ADHR, FGF-23 bears mutations that enhance it biological activity and render it resistant to inactivation by proteolytic cleavage with resultant renal phosphate wasting, hypophosphatemia, bone deformity, and rickets. In XLH, mutated *PHEX* directly or indirectly leads to accumulation of FGF-23 that exerts its phosphaturic activity at the renal proximal tubule.

Other "Phosphatonin" Candidates

Secreted Frizzled Related Protein 4 (sFRP4).
Gene expression profiles of mesenchymal tumors associated with TIO[21] showed several genes that encoded secreted proteins that were highly and differentially expressed. This analysis revealed a second "phosphatonin" candidate, sFRP4. FRPs are a class of molecules that inhibit Wnt signaling by acting as a decoy receptor. Wnt signaling is important in development especially of the skeleton and kidney. Recently, two disorders of bone mass accrual have been linked to activation or inhibition of Wnt signaling through it co-receptor, LRP5. Thus, it is possible that modulation of Wnt signaling may be important in regulating determinants of bone mass including some aspects of mineral ion homeostasis. Several lines of evidence suggest sFRP4 has phosphaturic properties. sFRP4 inhibits phosphate transport in cultured renal epithelial cells, it reduces fractional excretion of phosphorus when infused into mice and rats, and with longer-term exposure, sFRP4 produces hypophosphatemia with blunting of the compensatory increase in 25-hydroxyvitamin D-1-α-hydroxylase expression.[41]

Matrix Extracellular Phosphoglycoprotein.
Matrix extracellular phosphoglycoprotein (MEPE)/osteoregulin is a recently identified secreted protein that displays structural features of an extracellular matrix protein and is highly expressed in bone marrow and differentiated osteoblasts.[26] Three independent investigators showed that MEPE is highly expressed in mesenchymal tumors associated with TIO.[20,26,27] MEPE-deficient mice exhibit increased BMD caused by enhanced bone mineralization,[42] whereas overexpression of MEPE in TIO is associated with impaired bone mineralization, suggesting that MEPE is an important negative regulator of bone mineralization. MEPE, when given intraperitoneally to mice, produced renal phosphate wasting and hypophosphatemia[43]; furthermore, MEPE inhibits phosphate transport in cultured human renal epithelial cells.[43] Intriguing data are emerging that MEPE may be a substrate for PHEX[20] or modify PHEX function by a nonproteolytic interaction.[44]

FGF-7.
Recently, Carpenter et al.[45] showed that FGF-7 is overexpressed in tumors associated with TIO and that it had phosphaturic activity in cultured cells.

TREATMENT

The definitive treatment for TIO is complete tumor resection. This results in rapid correction of the biochemical perturbations and remineralization of bone. However, even after the diagnosis of TIO is made, the tumor often remains obscure or incompletely resected. In the case of malignant tumors associated with TIO, such as prostate cancer, complete resection may not be possible. Therefore, many times, medical management of this disorder is necessary.

The current practice is to treat TIO with phosphorus supplementation in combination with calcitriol. The phosphorus supplementation serves to replace ongoing renal phosphorus loss and the calcitriol supplements replace insufficient renal production of 1,25-dihydroxyvitamin D and enhance renal and gastrointestinal phosphorus reabsorption. Generally, patients are treated with phosphorus (2 g/day), in divided doses, and calcitriol (1–3 μg/day).[2] In some cases, administration of calcitriol alone may improve the biochemical abnormalities seen in TIO and heal the osteomalacia. Therapy and dosing should be tailored to improve symptoms, maintain fasting phosphorus in the low normal range, normalize alkaline phosphatase, and control secondary hyperparathyroidism, without inducing hypercalcemia or hypercalciuria. With appropriate treatment, muscle and bone pain will improve, and healing of the osteomalacia will ensue.

Monitoring for therapeutic complications of high doses of calcitriol and phosphorus is important to prevent unintended

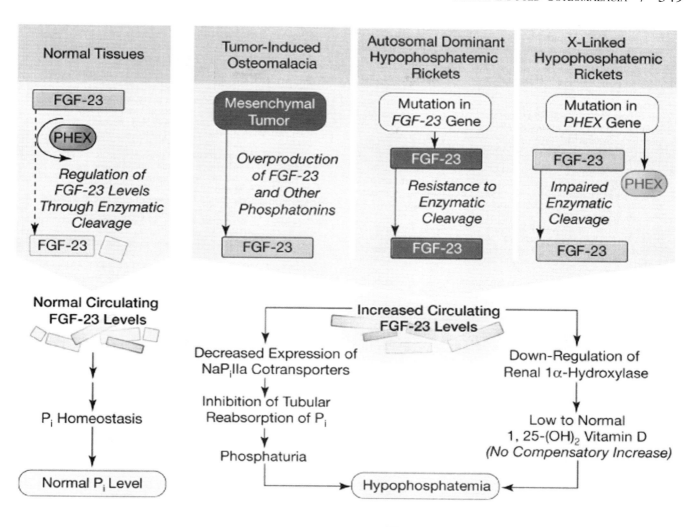

JAMA. 2005;294:1260-1267. © American Medical Association

FIG. 2. Mechanisms of FGF-23 excess in renal phosphate-wasting syndromes. In TIO, FGF-23 and other "phosphatonins" ectopically produced by a mesenchymal tumor lead to excess circulating FGF-23 levels. In ADHR, FGF-23 excess results from mutations in the *FGF-23* gene that render the protein resistant to cleavage and inactivation. In XLH, the mechanism of FGF-23 excess is more speculative; mutations in the *PHEX* endopeptidase (presumably located on osteoblasts or osteocytes) are thought to either directly or indirectly result in FGF-23 excess by interfering with processing and inactivation of FGF-23.[46]

hypercalcemia, nephrocalcinosis, and nephrolithiasis. Although parathyroid autonomy has been reported in only a few cases of TIO, the true incidence is likely higher with prolonged treatment with phosphorus (alone or in combination with vitamin D) because it stimulates parathyroid function that can eventually lead to autonomy. To assess safety and efficacy of therapy, monitoring of serum and urine calcium, renal function, and parathyroid status is recommended at least every 3 months.

Octreotide in vitro and in vivo has been shown to inhibit secretion of hormones by many neuroendocrine tumors. The expression of SSTRs that bind octreotide by some mesenchymal tumors provided the rationale for a therapeutic trial of octreotide in several patients with TIO and residual tumor. In one case, treatment with subcutaneous octreotide 50–100 μg three times a day resulted in correction of hypophosphatemia, improvement in phosphaturia, and reduction in alkaline phosphatase.[7] However, in two other patients, despite 8 weeks of treatment with subcutaneous octreotide up to 200 μg three times daily, serum levels of phosphorus and calcitriol failed to increase, and the tubular reabsorption of phosphate remained depressed.[4] Given the limited and mixed experience with octreotide treatment in TIO, this therapy should be reserved for the most severe cases that are refractory to current medical therapy.

As we understand the pathophysiology of this disorder more fully, specific therapies directed at attenuating the effect of excess FGF-23 and the other humoral factors elaborated in TIO no doubt will be developed.

REFERENCES

1. McCrance RA 1947 Osteomalacia with Looser's nodes (milkman's syndrome) due to a raised resistance to vitamin D acquired about the age of 15 years. Q J Med **16:**33–46.
2. Drezner MK 1999 Tumor-induced osteomalacia. In: Favus MJ (ed.) Primer on Metabolic Bone Diseases and Disorders of Mineral Metabolism, 4th ed. Lippincott-Raven, Philadelphia, PA, USA, pp. 331–337.
3. Jan de Beur SM, Streeten EA, Civelek AC, McCarthy EF, Uribe L, Watts N, Marx S, Sharon M, Levine MA 2002 Localization of mesenchymal tumors causing oncogenic osteomalacia with somatostatin receptor imaging. Lancet **359:**761–763.

4. Kumar R 2000 Tumor-induced osteomalacia and the regulation of phosphate homeostasis. Bone **27**:333–338.

5. Reubi JC, Waser B, Laissue JA, Gebbers JO 1996 Somatostatin and vasoactive intestinal peptide receptors in human mesenchymal tumors: *in vitro* identification. Cancer Res **56**:1922–1931.

6. Seufert J, Ebert K, Muller J, Eulert J, Hendrich C, Werner E, Schuuze N, Schulz G, Kenn W, Richtmann H, Palitzsch KD, Jakob F 2001 Octreotide therapy for tumor-induced osteomalacia. N Engl J Med **345**:1883–1888.

7. Jan de Beur SM, Levine MA 2002 Molecular pathogenesis of hypophosphatemic rickets. J Clin Endocrinol Metab **87**:2467–2473.

8. Avila NA, Skarulis M, Rubino DM, Doppman JL 1996 Oncogenic osteomalacia: Lesion detection by MR skeletal survey. Am J Roentgenol **167**:343–345.

9. Dupond JL, Mahammedi H, Prie D, Collin F, Gil H, Blagosklonov O, Ricbourg B, Meaux-Ruault N, Kantelip B 2005 Oncogenic osteomalacia: Diagnostic importance of fibroblast growth factor 23 and F-18 fluorodeoxyglucose PET/CT SCAN for the diagnosis and follow-up in one case. Bone **36**:375–378.

10. Takeuchi Y, Suzuki H, Ogura S, Imai R, Yamazaki Y, Yamashita T, Miyamoto Y, Okazaki H, Nakamura K, Nakahara K, Fukumoto S, Fujita T 2004 Venous sampling for fibroblast growth factor-23 confirms preoperative diagnosis of tumor-induced osteomalacia. J Clin Endocrinol Metab **89**:3979–3982.

11. Yamazaki Y, Okazaki R, Shibata M, Hasegawa Y, Satoh K, Tajima T, Takeuchi Y, Fujita T, Nakahara K, Yamashita T, Fukumoto S 2002 Increased circulatory level of biologically active full-length FGF23 in patients with hypophosphatemic rickets/osteomalacia. J Clin Endocrinol Metab **87**:4957–4960.

12. Jonsson KB, Zahradnik R, Larsson T, White KE, Sugimoto T, Imanishi Y, Yamamoto T, Hampson G, Koshiyama H, Ljunggren O, Oba K, Yang IM, Miyauchi A, Econs MJ, Lavigne J, Juppner H 2003 Fibroblast growth factor 23 in oncogenic osteomalacia and X-linked hypophosphatemia. N Engl J Med **348**:1656–1663.

13. Gene Dx Gene testing for XLH (PHEX) and ADHR (FGF23) are commercially available. Available online at www.genedx.com and www-.medichecks.com. Accessed March 28, 2006.

14. Teider M, Modai D, Samuel R 1985 Hereditary hypophosphatemic rickets with hypercalciuria. N Engl J Med **312**:611–617.

15. Lorenz-Depiereux B, Benet-Pages A, Eckstein G, Tenenbaum-Rakover Y, Wagenstaller J, Tiosano D, Gershoni-Baruch R, Albers N, Lichtner P, Schnabel D, Hochberg Z, Strom TM 2006 Hereditary hypophosphatemic rickets with hypercalciuria is caused by mutations in the sodium-phosphate cotransporter gene SLC34A3. Am J Hum Genet **78**:193–201.

16. Bergwitz C, Roslin NM, Tieder M, Loredo-Osti JC, Bastepe M, Abu-Zahra H, Frappier D, Burkett K, Carpenter TO, Anderson D, Garabedian M, Sermet I, Fujiwara TM, Morgan K, Tenenhouse HS, Juppner H 2006 LC34A3 mutations in patients with hereditary hypophosphatemic rickets with hypercalciuria predict a key role for the sodium-phosphate cotransporter NaPi-IIc in maintaining phosphate homeostasis. Am J Hum Genet **78**:179–192.

17. Prie D, Huart V, Bakouh N, Planelles G, Dellis O, Gerard B, Hulin P, Benque-Blanchet F, Silve C, Grandchamp B, Friedlander G 2002 Nephrolithiasis and osteoporosis associated with hypophosphatemia caused by mutations in the type 2a sodium-phosphate cotransporter. N Engl J Med **347**:983–991.

18. Weidner N, Santa CD 1987 Phosphaturic mesenchymal tumors. A polymorphous group causing osteomalacia or rickets. Cancer **59**:1442–1454.

19. Folpe AL, Fanburg-Smith JC, Weiss SW, the Phosphaturic Mesenchymal Tumor Study Group 2003 Most phosphaturic mesenchymal tumors are a single entity: An analysis of 31 cases. Mod Pathol **16**:12A.

20. Bowe A, Finnegan R, Jan de Beur SM, Vassiliadis J, Cho J, Levine MA, Kumar R, Schiavi SC 2001 FGF23 Inhibits phosphate transport *in vitro* and is a substrate for the PHEX endopeptidase. Biochem Biophys Res Commun **284**:977–981.

21. Jan de Beur SM, Finnegan RB, Vassiliadis J, Cook B, Barberio D, Estes S, Manavalon P, Petroziello J, Madden S, Cho JY, Kumar R, Levine MA, Schiavi SC 2002 Tumors associated with oncogenic osteomalacia express markers of bone and mineral metabolism. J Bone Miner Res **17**:1102–1110.

22. White KE, Jonsson KB, Carn G, Hampson G, Spector TD, Mannstadt M, Lorenz-Depiereux B, Miyauchi A, Yang IM, Ljunggren O, Meitinger T, Strom TM, Juppner H, Econs MJ 2001 The autosomal dominant hypophosphatemic rickets (ADHR) gene is a secreted polypeptide overexpressed by tumors that cause phosphate wasting. J Clin Endocrinol Metab **86**:497–500.

23. Cai Q, Hodgson SF, Kao PC, Lennon VA, Klee GG, Zinsmiester AR, Kumar R 1994 Brief report: Inhibition of renal phosphate transport by a tumor product in a patient with oncogenic osteomalacia. N Engl J Med **330**:1645–1649.

24. Popovtzer MM 1981 Tumor-induced hypophosphatemic osteomalacia (TIO): Evidence for a phosphaturic cyclic AMP-independent action of tumor extract. Clin Res **29**:418A.

25. Miyauchi A, Fukase M, Tsutsumi M, Fujita T 1998 Hemangiopericytoma-induced osteomalacia: Tumor transplantation in nude mice causes hypophosphatemia and tumor extracts inhibit renal 25-hydroxyvitamin D-1-hydroxylase activity. J Clin Endocrinol Metab **67**:46–53.

26. Rowe PS, de Zoysa PA, Dong R, Wang HR, White KE, Econs MJ, Oudet CL 2000 MEPE, a new gene expressed in bone marrow and tumors causing osteomalacia. Genomics **67**:54–68.

27. Shimada T, Mizutani S, Muto T, Yoneya T, Hino R, Takeda S, Takeuchi Y, Fujita T, Fukumoto S, Yamashita T 2001 Cloning and characterization of FGF23 as a causative factor of tumor-induced osteomalacia. Proc Natl Acad Sci USA **98**:6500–6505.

28. The ADHR Consortium 2000 Autosomal dominant hypophosphataemic rickets is associated with mutations in FGF 23. Nat Genet **26**:345–348.

29. Yamashita T, Konishi M, Miyake A, Inui Ki, Itoh N 2002 Fibroblast Growth Factor (FGF)-23 inhibits renal phosphate reabsorption by activation of the mitogen-activated protein kinase pathway. J Biol Chem **27**:28265–28270.

30. Shimada T, Muto T, Urakawa, Yoneya I, Yamazaki Y, Okawa K, Takeuchi Y, Fujita T, Fukumoto S, Yamashita T 2002 Mutant FGF23 responsible for autosomal dominant hypophosphatemic rickets is resistant to proteolytic cleavage and causes hypophophatemia in vivo. Endocrinology **143**:3179–3182.

31. Shimada T, Urakawa I, Yamazaki Y, Hasegawa H, Hino R, Yoneya T, Takeuchi Y, Fujita T, Fukumoto S, Yamashita T 2004 FGF-23 transgenic mice demonstrate hypophosphatemic rickets with reduced expression of sodium phosphate cotransporter type IIa. Biochem Biophys Res Commun **314**:409–414.

32. Larsson T, Marsell R, Schipani E, Ohlsson C, Ljunggren O, Tenenhouse HS, Juppner H, Jonsson KB 2004 Transgenic mice expressing fibroblast growth factor 23 under the control of the alpha1(I) collagen promoter exhibit growth retardation, osteomalacia, and disturbed phosphate homeostasis. Endocrinology **145**:3087–3094.

33. Sitara D, Razzaque M, Hesse M, Yoganathan S, Taguchi T, Erben R, Juppner H, Lanske B 2004 Homozygous ablation of fibroblast growth factor-23 results in hyperphosphatemia and impaired skeletogenesis, and reverses hypophosphatemia in *Phex*-deficient mice. Matrix Biol **23**:421–432.

34. Shimada T, Kakitani M, Yamazaki Y, Hasegawa H, Takeuchi Y, Fujita T, Fukumoto S, Tomizuka K, Yamashita T 2004 Targeted ablation of Fgf23 demonstrates an essential physiological role of FGF23 in phosphate and vitamin D metabolism. J Clin Invest **113**:561–568.

35. White KE, Carn G, Lorenz-Depiereux B, Benet-Pages A, Strom TM, Econs MJ 2001 Autosomal dominant hypophosphatemic rickets mutations stabilize FGF23. Kidney Int **60**:2079–2086.

36. Bai XY, Miao D, Goltzman D, Karaplis AC 2003 The autosomal dominant hypophosphatemic rickets R176Q mutation in fibroblast growth factor 23 resists proteolytic cleavage and enhances in vivo biological potency. J Biol Chem **278**:9843–9849.

37. Saito H, Kusano K, Kinosaki M, Ito H, Hirata M, Segawa H, Miyamoto K, Fukushima N 2003 Human fibroblast growth factor-23 mutants suppress Na+-dependent phosphate co-transport activity and 1alpha, 25-dihydroxyvitamin D3 production. J Biol Chem **278**:2206–2211.

38. The HYP Consortium 1995 A gene (PEX) with homologies to endopeptidases is mutated in patients with X-linked hypophosphatemic rickets. Nat Genet **11**:130–136.

39. Campos M, Couture C, Hirata IY, Juliano MA, Loisel TP, Crine P, Juliano L, Boileau G, Carmona AK 2003 Human recombinant PHEX has a strict S1' specificity for acidic residues and cleaves peptides derived from FGF23 and MEPE. Biochem J. **373**:271–279.

40. Guo R, Lui S, Spurney RF, Quarles LD 2001 Analysis of recombinant Phex: An endopeptidase in search of a substrate. Am J Physiol Endocrinol Metab **281**:E837–E847.

41. Berndt T, Craig TA, Bowe AE, Vassiliadis J, Reczek D, Finnegan R, Jan de Beur SM, Schiavi SC, Kumar R 2003 Frizzled Related Protein 4 is a potent phosphaturic agent: Properties of a novel phosphatonin-like substance. J Clin Invest **112**:785–794.

42. Gowen LC, Petersen DN, Mansolf AL, Qi H, Stock JL, Tkalcevic GT, Simmons HA, Crawford DT, Chidsey-Frink KL, Ke HZ, McNeish JD, Brown TA 2003 Targeted disruption of the osteoblast/osteocyte factor 45 gene (OF45) results in increased bone formation and bone mass. J Biol Chem **278**:1998–2007.

43. Rowe PS, Kumagai Y, Gutierrez G, Blacher R, Rosen D, Cundy J, Navvab S, Chen D, Drezner MK, Quarles LD, Mundy GR 2004 MEPE

has the properties of an osteoblastic phosphatonin and minihibin. Bone **34**:303–319.

44. Rowe PS, Garrett IR, Schwartz PM, Carnes DL, Lafer EM, Mundy GR, Gutierrez GE 2005 Surface Plasmon resonance confirms that MEPE binds to PHEX via the MEPE-ASARM motif: A model for impaired mineralization in X linked rickets (HYP). Bone **36**:33–46.

45. Carpenter TO, Ellis BK, Insogna KL, Philbrick WM, Sterpka J, Shimkets R 2004 Fibroblast growth factor 7: An inhibitor of phosphate transport derived from oncogenic osteomalacia-causing tumors. J Clin Endocrinol Metab **90**:1012–1020.

46. Jan de Beur SM 2005 Tumor-induced osteomalacia. JAMA **294**:1260–1267.

Chapter 64. Hypophosphatasia

Michael P. Whyte

Division of Bone and Mineral Diseases, Washington University School of Medicine at Barnes-Jewish Hospital and Center for Metabolic Bone Disease and Molecular Research, Shriners Hospitals for Children, St. Louis, Missouri

INTRODUCTION

Hypophosphatasia (OMIM 146300, 241500, 241510) is a rare, heritable type of rickets or osteomalacia that occurs in all races (although especially uncommon in blacks). The incidence for the severe forms is ~1 per 100,000 births; mild forms are more prevalent.[1,2] Approximately 300 cases have been reported. This inborn error of metabolism is characterized biochemically by subnormal activity of the tissue-nonspecific (bone/liver/kidney) isoenzyme of alkaline phosphatase (TNSALP). Activities of the tissue-specific intestinal, placental, and germ-cell ALP isoenzymes are not diminished.[3]

Although there is considerable overlap in severity among them, four principal clinical forms of hypophosphatasia are reported, depending on the age at which skeletal lesions are discovered: perinatal, infantile, childhood, and adult. When dental manifestations alone are present, the condition is called odontohypophosphatasia.[4]

Generally, the earlier the onset of skeletal problems, the more severe the clinical course.[1,2]

CLINICAL PRESENTATION

Although some TNSALP is normally present in all tissues, hypophosphatasia affects predominantly the skeleton and teeth. Severity of clinical expression is, however, remarkably variable (e.g., death may occur in utero or mild symptoms may go undiagnosed in adults).[1,2]

Perinatal hypophosphatasia manifests during gestation. Pregnancies may be complicated by polyhydramnios. Typically, extreme skeletal hypomineralization causes caput membranaceum and short, deformed limbs apparent at birth. Rarely, an unusual bony spur protrudes from a major long bone.[5] Most affected newborns survive only briefly while suffering increasing respiratory compromise and sometimes unexplained fever, anemia (perhaps from encroachment on the marrow space by excessive osteoid), failure to gain weight, irritability, periodic apnea with cyanosis and bradycardia, intracranial hemorrhage, and pyridoxine-dependent seizures. Survival is very rare.[1,2]

Infantile hypophosphatasia becomes clinically apparent before 6 months of age. Developmental milestones often seem normal until poor feeding, inadequate weight gain, hypotonia, and wide fontanels are noted.[6] Rachitic deformities then manifest. Hypercalcemia and hypercalciuria can cause recurrent vomiting, nephrocalcinosis and, occasionally, renal compro-

mise. Despite widely "open" fontanels (actually hypomineralized areas of calvarium), functional craniosynostosis can occur. Raised intracranial pressure may be associated with bulging of the anterior fontanel, proptosis, and papilledema. Mild hypertelorism and brachycephaly can appear. A flail chest predisposes to pneumonia. During the months after diagnosis, there may be spontaneous improvement or progressive skeletal deterioration. About 50% of patients die within 1 year.[6] Prognosis seems to improve if there is survival beyond infancy.[1,2]

Childhood hypophosphatasia varies greatly in severity. Premature loss of deciduous teeth (<5 years of age) from hypoplasia or aplasia of dental cementum is a major clinical hallmark. Odontohypophosphatasia is diagnosed when radiographs show no evidence of skeletal disease. The lower incisors are typically lost first, but in severe cases the entire dentition can be affected. Exfoliation occurs without root resorption; teeth slide out intact from sockets. Dental radiographs often show enlarged pulp chambers and root canals forming "shell teeth." The prognosis for the permanent dentition is more favorable. When rickets is present, delayed walking with a waddling gait, short stature, and a dolichocephalic skull with frontal bossing are often apparent. Static myopathy is a poorly understood complication. Childhood hypophosphatasia may improve spontaneously during puberty, but recurrence of skeletal symptoms is likely during adult life.[1,2]

Adult hypophosphatasia usually presents during middle age, often with painful and poorly healing, recurrent, metatarsal stress fractures.[7] Pain in the thighs or hips can reflect femoral pseudofractures. About 50% of patients give histories consistent with rickets and/or premature loss of deciduous teeth during childhood.[7] Chondrocalcinosis occurs frequently, and calcium pyrophosphate dihydrate crystal deposition disease and calcific periarthritis trouble some patients.[8] Femoral pseudofractures generally mend after intramedullary rodding.[9]

LABORATORY FINDINGS

Hypophosphatasia is diagnosed from a consistent clinical history and physical findings, radiographic or histopathological evidence of rickets or osteomalacia, and the presence of low serum ALP activity (hypophosphatasemia).[1] Diagnosticians must appreciate changes in the normal range for serum ALP activity with age and understand that rarely other conditions (including severe cases of osteogenesis imperfecta and cleidocranial dysplasia) and treatments can cause hypophosphatasemia.[1]

Rickets/osteomalacia in hypophosphatasia is distinctly unusual because serum levels of calcium and inorganic phosphate (Pi) are not reduced. In fact, hypercalcemia and hypercalciuria

---

The author has reported no conflicts of interest.

© 2006 American Society for Bone and Mineral Research

occur frequently in perinatal and infantile hypophosphatasia, apparently because of dyssynergy between gut absorption of calcium and defective skeletal growth and mineralization (severely affected patients may also show progressive skeletal demineralization).[6] Affected children and adults have serum Pi levels that are above mean levels for age-matched controls, and ~50% are hyperphosphatemic. Enhanced renal reclamation of Pi (increased transport maximum for phosphate [TmP]/ glomerular filtration rate [GFR]) accounts for this abnormality.[1] In serum, vitamin D metabolite concentrations are typically normal.[1] PTH levels may be suppressed.

At least three phosphocompounds accumulate endogenously in hypophosphatasia[1,3]: phosphoethanolamine (PEA), inorganic pyrophosphate (PPi), and pyridoxal 5′-phosphate (PLP). Demonstration of phosphoethanolaminuria supports the diagnosis but is not specific because PEA can be modestly increased in a variety of other disorders, and normal levels can occur in mild cases. Assay of PPi in plasma and urine is a research technique. If vitamin B_6 supplements are not taken, an elevated plasma level of PLP seems to be the most sensitive and specific test for hypophosphatasia among these markers. In general, the lower the serum level of ALP activity for age and the greater the plasma PLP level, the more severe the clinical manifestations.[1,3]

RADIOLOGIC FINDINGS

Perinatal hypophosphatasia manifests pathognomonic features.[10] In extreme cases, the skeleton may be so poorly calcified that only the base of the skull is visualized. In less remarkable patients, the calvarium may be ossified at central portions of individual membranous bones and give the illusion that the sutures are open and widely separated. Marked skeletal undermineralization occurs with severe rachitic changes. Segments of the spinal column may appear missing. Fractures are also common.

Infantile hypophosphatasia causes characteristic but less severe changes.[10] Abrupt transition from relatively normal appearing diaphyses to hypomineralized metaphyses can suggest a sudden metabolic deterioration. Worsening rickets with progressive skeletal demineralization and fracture heralds a lethal outcome. Skeletal scintigraphy may identify closed sutures that appear widened radiographically.

Childhood hypophosphatasia often features characteristic "tongues" of radiolucency that project from rachitic growth plates into metaphyses (Fig. 1). True, premature fusion of cranial sutures can cause a "beaten-copper" appearance of the skull.

Adult hypophosphatasia is associated with osteopenia, metatarsal stress fractures, chondrocalcinosis, and proximal femoral pseudofractures.

HISTOPATHOLOGIC FINDINGS

Nondecalcified sections of bone reveal histological features of rickets or osteomalacia (without secondary hyperparathyroidism) in all clinical forms of hypophosphatasia except odontohypophosphatasia.[1] However, biochemical or histochemical detection of low ALP activity in osseous tissue distinguishes hypophosphatasia from other disorders. Open cranial "sutures" are actually uncalcified osteoid. Dental histopathology shows aplasia or hypoplasia of cementum.[4] Enlarged pulp chambers indicate impaired dentinogenesis. Changes vary from tooth to tooth.

INHERITANCE

Perinatal and infantile hypophosphatasia are inherited as autosomal recessive traits. Parents of these severely affected

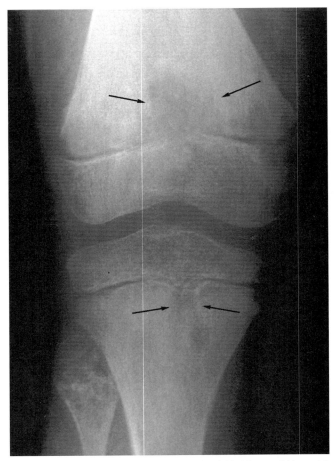

FIG. 1. The metaphysis of the proximal tibia of this 10-year-old boy with mild childhood hypophosphatasia shows a subtle but characteristic "tongue" of radiolucency (arrows). Note, however, that his rickets does not manifest with widening of the growth plate.

patients usually have low or low-normal serum ALP activity and sometimes mildly elevated plasma PLP levels and modest phosphoethanolaminuria. Challenge with vitamin B_6 (pyridoxine) orally is followed by a distinctly abnormal increment in plasma PLP levels in patients, and in some carriers.[1]

The mode of inheritance for the milder forms of hypophosphatasia (odontohypophosphatasia, childhood hypophosphatasia, and adult-onset disease) can be autosomal dominant or recessive.[1,11,12]

BIOCHEMICAL GENETIC DEFECT

In keeping with an inborn error of metabolism that selectively compromises the TNSALP isoenzyme, autopsy studies of perinatal and infantile hypophosphatasia show profound deficiency of ALP activity in bone, liver, and kidney, but not in the intestine or placenta. More than 170 different mutations have been identified worldwide in the TNSALP gene.[11–14]

PATHOGENESIS

Studies of vitamin B_6 metabolism in hypophosphatasia indicate that TNSALP regulates the extracellular concentration of a variety of phosphocompounds.[3] Accumulation of PPi, an inhibitor of hydroxyapatite crystal formation and growth, is increasingly incriminated in the impaired skeletal mineralization.[2,3,15,16] The TNSALP knockout mouse model, which recapitulates infantile hypophosphatasia,[17] is helping to clarify the physiological role of TNSALP.

TREATMENT

There is no established medical therapy for hypophosphatasia Marrow cell transplantation seemed to rescue and improve a patient with the infantile form.[6] Dietary Pi restriction to correct hyperphosphatemia and thereby reduce inhibition of TNSALP by Pi is being tested in milder cases.[18] A preliminary report suggests that teriparatide might stimulate TNSALP biosynthesis by osteoblasts and heal fractures.[19]

Unless there is documented deficiency, it seems important to avoid traditional treatments for rickets or osteomalacia (e.g., vitamin D sterols and mineral supplementation) because circulating levels of calcium, Pi, 25(OH)D, and 1,25(OH)$_2$D are usually not reduced.[1] Furthermore, traditional regimens may exacerbate any predisposition to hypercalcemia or hypercalciuria.

The hypercalcemia of perinatal or infantile hypophosphatasia may respond to restriction of dietary calcium and to salmon calcitonin and/or glucocorticoid therapy.[20] Fractures in children and adults usually mend; however, healing may be delayed, including after osteotomy. Placement of load-sharing intramedullary rods, rather than load-sparing plates, seems best for the acute or prophylactic treatment of fractures and pseudofractures in adults.[9] Expert dental care is important. Dentures may be necessary even for pediatric patients.

PRENATAL DIAGNOSIS

Perinatal hypophosphatasia can be detected in utero. Combined use of serial sonography (with attention to the limbs as well as to the skull) and radiologic study of the fetus have been successful in the second trimester.[21] First-trimester diagnosis is now based on DNA.[21] Importantly, however, some cases of childhood hypophosphatasia may manifest bowing in utero that does not reflect a lethal skeletal dysplasia and corrects postnatally.[5]

REFERENCES

1. Whyte MP 2001 Hypophosphatasia. In: Scriver CR, Beaudet AL, Sly WS, Valle D, Childs B, Vogelstein B (eds.) The Metabolic and Molecular Bases of Inherited Disease, 8th ed. McGraw-Hill, New York, NY, USA, pp. 5313–5329.
2. Caswell AM, Whyte MP, Russell RG 1992 Hypophosphatasia and the extracellular metabolism of inorganic pyrophosphate: Clinical and laboratory aspects. Crit Rev Clin Lab Sci 28:175–232.
3. Whyte MP 2002 Hypophosphatasia: Nature's window on alkaline phosphatase function in man. In: Bilezikian J, Raisz L, Rodan G (eds.) Principles of Bone Biology, 2nd ed. Academic Press, San Diego, CA, USA, pp. 1229–1248.
4. Van den Bos T, Handoko G, Niehof A, Ryan LM, Coburn SP, Whyte MP, Beertsen W 2005 Cementum and dentin in hypophosphatasia. J Dent Res 84:1021–1025.
5. Pauli RM, Modaff P, Sipes SL, Whyte MP 1999 Mild hypophosphatasia mimicking severe osteogenesis imperfecta in utero: Bent but not broken. Am J Med Genet 86:434–438.
6. Whyte MP, Kurtzberg J, McAlister WH, Mumm S, Podgornik MN, Coburn SP, Ryan LM, Miller CR, Gottesman GS, Smith AK, Douville J, Waters-Pick B, Armstrong RD, Martin PL 2003 Marrow cell transplantation for infantile hypophosphatasia. J Bone Miner Res 18:624–636.
7. Weinstein RS, Whyte MP 1981 Heterogeneity of adult hypophosphatasia: Report of severe and mild cases. Arch Intern Med 141:727–731.
8. Chuck AJ, Pattrick MG, Hamilton E, Wilson R, Doherty M 1989 Crystal deposition in hypophosphatasia: A reappraisal. Ann Rheum Dis 48:571–576.
9. Coe JD, Murphy WA, Whyte MP 1986 Management of femoral fractures and pseudofractures in adult hypophosphatasia. J Bone Joint Surg Am 68:981–990.
10. Shohat M, Rimoin DL, Gerber HE, Lachman RS 1991 Perinatal hypophosphatasia: Clinical, radiologic, and morphologic findings. Pediatr Radiol 21:421–427.
11. Henthorn PS, Raducha M, Fedde KN, Lafferty MA, Whyte MP 1992 Different missense mutations at the tissue-nonspecific alkaline phosphatase gene locus in autosomal recessively inherited forms of mild and severe hypophosphatasia. Proc Natl Acad Sci USA 89:9924–9928.
12. Mornet E 2000 Hypophosphatasia: The mutations in the tissue-nonspecific alkaline phosphatase gene. Hum Mutat 15:309–315.
13. Mornet E 2005 Tissue nonspecific alkaline phosphatase gene mutations database. Available online at http://www.sesep.uvsq.fr/Database.html. Accessed May 13, 2005.
14. Brun-Heath I, Taillandier A, Serre JL, Mornet E 2005 Characterization of 11 novel mutations in the tissue non-specific alkaline phosphatase gene responsible for hypophosphatasia and genotype-phenotype correlations. Mol Genet Metab 84:273–277.
15. Hessle L, Johnson KA, Anderson HC, Narisawa S, Sali A, Goding JW, Terkeltaub R, Millan JL 2002 Tissue-nonspecific alkaline phosphatase and plasma cell membrane glycoprotein-1 are central antagonistic regulators of bone mineralization. Proc Natl Acad Sci USA 99:9445–9449.
16. Harmey D, Hessle L, Narisawa S, Johnson KA, Terkeltaub R, Millan JL 2004 Concerted regulation of inorganic pyrophosphate and osteopontin by akp2, enpp1, and ank: An integrated model of the pathogenesis of mineralization disorders. Am J Pathol 164:1199–1209.
17. Fedde KN, Blair L, Silverstein J, Coburn SP, Ryan LM, Weinstein RS, Waymire K, Narisawa S, Millan JL, MacGregor GR, Whyte MP 1999 Alkaline phosphatase knock-out mice recapitulate the metabolic and skeletal defects of infantile hypophosphatasia. J Bone Miner Res 14:2015–2026.
18. Wenkert D, Podgornik MN, Coburn SP, Ryan LM, Mumm S, Whyte MP 2002 Dietary phosphate restriction therapy for hypophosphatasia: Preliminary observations. J Bone Miner Res 17:S384.
19. Deal C, Whyte MP 2005 Adult hypophosphatasia treated with teriparatide. J Bone Miner Res 20:S100.
20. Barcia JP, Strife CF, Langman CB 1997 Infantile hypophosphatasia: Treatment options to control hypercalcemia, hypercalciuria, and chronic bone demineralization. J Pediatr 130:825–828.
21. Henthorn PS, Whyte MP 1995 Infantile hypophosphatasia: Successful prenatal assessment by testing for tissue-nonspecific alkaline phosphatase gene mutations. Prenat Diagn 15:1001–1006.

Chapter 65. Fanconi Syndrome and Renal Tubular Acidosis

Peter J. Tebben,[1] Leslie F. Thomas,[2] and Rajiv Kumar[3]

[1]Department of Internal Medicine, Division of Endocrinology, Diabetes, Metabolism, and Nutrition, Mayo Clinic, Rochester, Minnesota; [2]Department of Internal Medicine, Mayo Clinic, Rochester, Minnesota; and [3]Mayo Proteomic Research Center, Department of Internal Medicine, Department of Biochemistry and Molecular Biology, Division of Nephrology, Division of Endocrinology, Diabetes, Metabolism, and Nutrition, Mayo Clinic, Rochester, Minnesota

DEFINITION AND PRESENTATION

Fanconi syndrome is a disorder of renal proximal tubules. The principle characteristics include decreased reabsorption of phosphorus, glucose, and amino acids. These findings are often accompanied by metabolic acidosis secondary to proximal tubular bicarbonate wasting (type II RTA). Although impaired handling of potassium, calcium, uric acid, sodium, water, and low-molecular-weight proteins have also been described,[1–5] these abnormalities are not necessary to establish the diagnosis. Laboratory findings include hypophosphatemia, hyperphosphaturia, and a low tubular maximum for inorganic phosphate; glycosuria with a normal plasma glucose concentration; generalized aminoaciduria; hypobicarbonatemia, excessive bicarbonate excretion in the urine and a low tubular maximum for bicarbonate; and elevated serum alkaline phosphatase, normal serum calcium, normal PTH, normal serum 25-hydroxyvitamin D [$25(OH)D_3$], and inappropriately low or normal serum $1\alpha,25$-dihydroxyvitamin D [$1\alpha,25(OH)_2D_3$] concentrations. Radiological studies reveal changes consistent with osteomalacia or rickets.

Children with Fanconi syndrome present clinically with growth failure and rickets. Lower extremity deformities including genu varus or valgum may be evident on exam. Radiographs show widened physeal plates and flared metaphyses. Fanconi syndrome has been associated with many diseases (Table 1), including the lysosomal storage disease, cystinosis, which is the most common inherited cause in the pediatric population. Adults present with osteomalacia, which manifests as bone pain, proximal muscle weakness, and spontaneous fractures. Pseudofractures can be seen on X-ray in various locations including the proximal femur. Multiple myeloma is the most common cause of Fanconi syndrome in adults. Showing the biochemical abnormalities noted above; hypophosphatemia and a reduced tubular maximum for phosphate, glycosuria with a normal plasma glucose concentration, generalized aminoaciduria, and hypobicarbonatemia can establish the diagnosis. Because some patients will have serum phosphorus values that fall within the low normal range, it is useful to calculate the fractional excretion of phosphorus that will be elevated in Fanconi syndrome.

PHYSIOLOGY OF SOLUTE TRANSPORT IN THE PROXIMAL TUBULE

The transport of filtered solute across the proximal tubular membrane requires multiple specialized transport proteins that are present in the luminal brush border. Reabsorption of inorganic phosphate (Pi) occurs primarily in the proximal tubule by a sodium–phosphate co-transporter system (NaPi-2).[6] The NaPi-2 co-transporter is located in the brush border of renal tubule epithelial cells and is influenced principally by dietary phosphate intake and PTH.[7] However, there are additional

TABLE 1. DISORDERS ASSOCIATED WITH FANCONI SYNDROME

Acquired
  Multiple myeloma
  Lymphoma
  Light chain nephropathy
  Amyloidosis
  Sjögrens syndrome
  Nephrotic syndrome
  Renal transplantation
  Balkan nephropathy
  Paroxysmal nocturnal hemoglobinuria
  Vitamin D deficiency
  Interstitial nephritis/uveitis syndrome
  Renal vein thrombosis
Drugs
  Outdated tetracycline
  Methyl-3-chromone
  6-Mercaptopurine
  Gentamicin
  Valproic acid
  Streptozocin
  Isophthalanilide
  Ifosphamide
  Cephalothin
Heavy metals
  Lead
  Cadmium
  Mercury
  Uranium
  Platinum
  Copper
  Bismuth
Other
  Parquat
  Lysol
  Toluene inhalation
Heritable
  Cystinosis
  Lowe syndrome
  Hereditary fructose intolerance
  Tyrosinemia
  Galactosemia
  Glycogen storage disease
  Wilson's disease
  Cytochrome oxidase deficiency
  Subacute necrotizing encephalomyelopathy
  Alport syndrome
  Leigh's syndrome
  Idiopathic (AD, AR, XLR)
  Fanconi-Bickel syndrome
  Dent's disease
  GRACILE syndrome
  Rod-cone dystrophy, sensorineural deafness, and renal dysfunction
  Pearson syndrome

The authors have reported no conflicts of interest.

factors that influence phosphate transport in the proximal renal tubule including vitamin D, fibroblast growth factor 23 (FGF23), and secreted frizzled related protein 4 (sFRP4).[8,9] Vitamin D enhances renal phosphate reabsorption, whereas PTH, FGF23, and sFRP4 decrease renal phosphate reclamation.[10] Amino acids are almost entirely reabsorbed in the proximal tubule by a variety of sodium-dependent transporters.[11] Transporters for acidic, basic, and neutral amino acids have been identified as well as carriers that are specific to single amino acids.[11] In Fanconi syndrome, all amino acids are lost in excess in the urine; however, urinary amino acid losses do not seem to be of clinical consequence. Glucose normally is reabsorbed with great efficiency by the proximal tubule. This is accomplished by sodium-dependent secondary active transport. Two separate transporters have been identified in the apical membrane: a high-capacity low-affinity transporter (SGLT2) in the S1 segment and a low-capacity high affinity transporter (SGLT1) in the S3 segment.[11,12] Glucose is transported out of the epithelial cell through the basolateral membrane by the sodium-glucose transporter GLUT2. Under normal conditions, very little glucose passes from the proximal tubule into the final urine. Glycosuria may contribute to the polyuria and polydipsia often seen in Fanconi syndrome but is otherwise clinically insignificant.

MECHANISMS OF ACIDIFICATION OF THE URINE

Acidification of the urine is accomplished by both the removal of base from, and the addition of acid to, the glomerular filtrate. Removal of base involves a process by which virtually all filtered HCO_3^- is reabsorbed. Addition of acid involves the combination of secreted H^+ with filtered weak acids that are not completely reabsorbed and with NH_3 that is produced in the kidney. The two main mechanisms used by the kidney to maintain acid–base balance include proximal tubule HCO_3^- reabsorption and distal tubule H^+ excretion.[13,14] Under physiologic conditions, 80–90% of filtered HCO_3^- is reabsorbed at the level of the proximal tubule through a carbonic anhydrase-dependent mechanism.[15] H^+ is secreted into the tubular lumen, principally through a Na^+-H^+ antiport, and combines with filtered HCO_3^-. H_2O and CO_2 are subsequently formed and passively diffuse across the luminal membrane into the cell. Intracellular H^+ and HCO_3^- are generated. The H^+ is recycled back into the lumen, and HCO_3^- is transported across the basolateral membrane through a Na^+-3(HCO_3^-) co-transporter. Concentration gradients that favor the action of apical Na^+ transporters, such as the Na^+H^+ antiport that secretes H^+ into the tubular lumen, and intracellular carbonic anhydrase that generates $HCO3^-$, are maintained by the basolateral Na^+K^+ ATPase and Na^+-3(HCO_3^-) co-transporter.[16,17] The majority of the remaining filtered HCO_3^- (10–20%) is reabsorbed distally through similar mechanisms. In the distal tubule, H^+ secretion takes place through a H^+-ATPase. HCO_3^- generated within the cells of the collecting tubule is directed into the systemic circulation through a basolateral membrane Cl^--HCO_3^- co-transporter. In addition, NH_3 generation by the kidney facilitates the secretion of H^+.[18] Renal tubular acidosis results from a failure to reabsorb bicarbonate in the proximal tubule or a failure to generate or secrete H^+ in the distal tubule.

Type II renal tubular acidosis (RTA), which is often associated with Fanconi syndrome, results from excessive loss of bicarbonate from the proximal tubule. The urine pH in type II RTA can be variable in contrast to type I RTA, in which it is consistently >5.5. This is because of the ability of the proximal tubule to reabsorb the filtered load of HCO_3^- once the serum

level falls below a given threshold. If untreated, the serum HCO_3^- will usually remain >12 mM, and the urine pH may fall below 5.5. Shortly after HCO_3^- is administered for treatment or for diagnostic purposes, the transport maximum for HCO_3^- will be exceeded, and the urine pH will rise significantly. The presence of type II RTA can be confirmed by measuring serum HCO_3^- and urine pH after an intravenous or oral load of bicarbonate. A urine pH >6.5 with a serum HCO_3^- of 22 mM or less will establish the diagnosis.[19]

In type I RTA, the distal tubule is unable to excrete hydrogen ion appropriately. As a result, the serum bicarbonate level can drop to <10 mM, and the urine pH is >5.5. Inappropriately maintaining a urine pH >5.5 after ammonium chloride administration (100 mg/kg orally) is consistent with the diagnosis of type I RTA. Hypokalemia and nephrolithiasis are common findings, and these characteristics can be used to help distinguish type I from type II RTA. Type I RTA can occur in Fanconi syndrome if there is damage to the distal tubule as well as the proximal tubule by the causal agent (e.g., drug or metal).

Hypoaldosteronism with associated hyperkalemia and a no-nanion gap metabolic acidosis is known as type IV RTA. In this condition, the action of aldosterone on the Na^+ reabsorbing cells of the collecting tubule is diminished. The normal reabsorption of Na^+, thought to contribute to luminal electronegativity and a favorable K^+ secretory gradient, does not occur and leads to persistent hyperkalemia.[20] The precise mechanism by which the mild nonanion gap metabolic acidosis occurs is not completely understood, although diminished NH_4^+ production plays a key role. Laboratory values consistent with type IV RTA include a plasma HCO_3^- concentration >17 mM and a urine pH usually <5.5. Type IV RTA is not commonly associated with Fanconi syndrome.

PATHOGENESIS OF HYPOPHOSPHATEMIA AND BONE DISEASE IN FANCONI SYNDROME

Renal proximal tubule epithelial cells have a high metabolic requirement. Because so many filtered solutes are affected in Fanconi syndrome, a generalized cellular toxicity seems more likely to account for the syndrome than multiple independent transport defects. Fanconi syndrome probably results from disrupted mitochondrial ATP production and/or Na^+/K^+-ATPase activity.[21–24] Either of these mechanisms could lead to a diminished sodium electrochemical gradient that drives the majority of solute transport across the luminal membrane. It is likely that multiple toxic proteins, drugs, insoluble metabolic products, or metals alter proximal tubule cell function in a global manner by diverse pathways. The end result is reduced solute reabsorption.

High fractional excretion of phosphate found in the setting of hypophosphatemia is a hallmark of Fanconi syndrome. Several mechanisms are likely responsible including those involving vitamin D, PTH, and the NaPi-2 co-transporter. Along with dietary intake, the extracellular pool of phosphorus is regulated by $1\alpha,25(OH)_2D_3$ and PTH.[9,25] $1\alpha,25(OH)_2D_3$ increases phosphate absorption in the intestine and phosphate reabsorption in the kidney.[26,27] $25(OH)D_3$ conversion to the more active metabolite, $1\alpha,25(OH)_2D_3$, can be stimulated by PTH alone or by a low serum Pi through a PTH-independent mechanism.[28] However, the expected elevation of $1\alpha,25(OH)_2D_3$ concentration in the face of hypophosphatemia is not seen in Fanconi syndrome. The result is a relative or absolute vitamin D deficiency. The $25(OH)_2D_3$ 1α-hydroxylase is a multicomponent mitochondrial enzyme located in the renal cortex, the activity of which is reduced in an experimental model of Fanconi syndrome.[29] Significant hepatic damage or reduced renal mass associated with many of the diseases listed in Table

TABLE 2. SERUM CALCIUM, PHOSPHORUS, PTH, 25(OH)D, AND 1,25(OH)$_2$D$_3$ CONCENTRATIONS AND URINE SOLUTE CONCENTRATIONS IN VARIOUS HYPOPHOSPHATEMIC CONDITIONS

Condition	sPi	sCa	sPTH	s25(OH)D	s1,25(OH)$_2$D	U$_{Pi}$	FE$_{Pi}$	U$_{Ca}$	FE$_{Ca}$	U$_{HCO3}$	FE$_{HCO3}$	U$_{Glu}$	FE$_{Glu}$	U$_{AA}$
Fanconi syndrome	D	N	N or I	N	D or N	I	I	N	N	I	I	I	I	I
Nutritional vitamin D deficiency, malabsorption	D	D	I	D	V	I	I	D	D	N or I	N or I	N	N	N or I
Impaired intestinal Pi absorption (use of binders)	D	N	N	N	I	D	D	I	I	N	N	N	N	N
X-linked hypophosphatemic rickets (XLH)	D	N	N	N	D or N	I	I	N	N	N	N	N	N	N
Autosomal dominant hypophosphatemic rickets (ADHR)	D	N	N	N	D or N	I	I	N	N	N	N	N	N	N
Tumor-induced osteomalacia	D	N	N	N	D or N	I	I	N	N	N	N	N	N	N
Vitamin D–dependent rickets (type 1)	D or low N	D	I	N	D	I	I	D	D	N or I	N or I	N	N	N or I
Vitamin D–dependent rickets (type 2)	D	D	I	N	I	I	I	D	D	N or I	N or I	N	N	N or I
Primary hyperparathyroidism	D or low N	I	I	N	N or I	I	I	I	D	N or I	N or I	N	N	N or I
Humoral hypercalcemia of malignancy	D or low N	I	D or N	N	D or N	I	I	I	D	N or I	N or I	N	N	N or I
Hereditary hypophosphatemic rickets with hypercalciuria	D	N	D or N	N	I	I	I	I	I	N	N	N	N	N

D, decreased; I, increased; N, normal; V, variable.

1 may also account for the vitamin D deficiency. However, vitamin D deficiency has been described in Fanconi syndrome patients without significant liver disease and with normal or minimally reduced glomerular filtration rates.[30,31] This would suggest that additional, poorly understood, mechanisms are contributing to the relatively low 1α,25(OH)$_2$D$_3$ concentration.

PTH, which is elevated in some patients with Fanconi syndrome, acts to reduce the number of NaPi-2 co-transporters in the luminal membrane, thereby reducing the tubular transport maximum for Pi, resulting in renal Pi loss. In addition, a maleic acid–induced model of Fanconi syndrome in rats causes downregulation of the NaPi-2 co-transporter,[32] offering another possible explanation for the phosphaturia and hypophosphatemia seen in human Fanconi syndrome.

Regardless of the mechanism of increased Pi losses in the urine, the diminished serum phosphorus will lead to poor bone mineralization. Inorganic phosphate plays a vital role in bone formation and is normally incorporated into the bone matrix produced by osteoblasts. This involves a complex process by which hydroxyapatite crystals [Ca$_5$(PO$_4$)$_3$OH] are formed within the matrix.[33] When Pi is not available in sufficient quantity, rickets/osteomalacia will result with thickened osteoid seams that are readily apparent on bone biopsy.[30]

The bone disease in Fanconi syndrome could be worsened by the presence of acidosis. Renal tubular acidosis is commonly seen in patients with Fanconi syndrome. It is generally a type II RTA, although defects in H$^+$ ion excretion may also be present.

The pathogenesis of bone disease in chronic metabolic acidosis is multifactorial. As previously discussed, Fanconi syndrome manifests as rickets in children and as osteomalacia in adults. It is assumed that phosphaturia and hypophosphatemia play a major role in the development of rickets/osteomalacia as seen in the other disorders such as X-linked hypophosphatemic rickets (XLH), oncogenic osteomalacia (OOM), and autosomal dominant hypophosphatemic rickets (ADHR). The bone disease in these phosphaturic disorders is well established but is not associated with metabolic acidosis. Acidosis can cause bone disease independent of phosphate wasting. Bone serves as a large reservoir of buffer for excess H$^+$.[34] Acute and chronic acidosis induce demineralization of bone and increased urinary losses of calcium.[34] Patients with RTA have lower BMD and increased osteoid volume compared with reference values.[35,36] Osteoblast-like cells cultured in an acidic environment show an increased response to PTH and increased mRNA for the PTH/ PTH-related peptide (PTHrP) receptor.[37] This would presumably increase bone turnover in favor of resorption. Cultured mouse calvaria exposed to an acidic environment show increased osteoclastic and decreased osteoblastic activity as determined by measurements of collagen synthesis, alkaline phosphatase activity, and β-glucuronidase activity compared with controls.[34,38] Impaired conversion of 25(OH)D$_3$ in the rat kidney exposed to a low pH show that vitamin D metabolism is impaired in an acidic environment.[39] Low 1α,25(OH)$_2$D$_3$ concentrations could also be caused by impaired delivery of substrate [25(OH)D$_3$] to the renal tubule epithelial cell if transport regulatory proteins are affected by acidosis or the underlying disorder causing Fanconi syndrome.[40,41] There are many pathways by which chronic acidosis seem to be inhibiting bone formation and enhancing demineralization.

DIFFERENTIAL DIAGNOSIS

Other disorders mimicking Fanconi syndrome are listed in Table 2. Hypophosphatemia is seen in several metabolic bone disorders that should be distinguished from Fanconi syndrome. This can usually be accomplished by determining serum phosphorus, calcium, PTH, and vitamin D (both metabolites) concentrations, as well as urine studies to measure excretion rates of several filtered solutes. Historical clues, such as inheritance patterns in familial disease, may also be useful in narrowing the differential diagnosis.

TREATMENT

Treatment of Fanconi syndrome–induced bone disease should be based on its underlying cause. If the associated disease can be treated or the offending agent removed (Table 1), Fanconi syndrome may resolve, and the metabolic bone disease remit. If the underlying cause of Fanconi syndrome cannot be identified or corrected, treatment with phosphorus, vitamin D, and/or bicarbonate may be necessary. The relative contribution of disordered phosphorus, vitamin D, and bicarbonate metabolism may vary in individual patients. Phosphate and calcium replacement have been reported to improve osteomalacia and rickets in Fanconi syndrome.[36,42–45] Large doses of phosphate may be required for healing of the rickets or osteomalacia and is available in several preparations (Table 3). Frequent doses throughout the day (four to five times) are preferred over larger, less frequent doses. This will minimize wide fluctuations in serum phosphorus that may lead to secondary hyperparathyroidism and undesirable gastrointestinal symptoms. Vitamin D replacement with vitamin D_2 or D_3 have been successfully used in the treatment of Fanconi syndrome.[30,36,42,46] Because many diseases associated with Fanconi syndrome are also characterized by renal failure, the relative potency and duration of toxicity of the specific form of vitamin D replacement should be taken into account. Ergocalciferol and calcitriol are readily available forms of vitamin D. Calcitriol is several-fold more potent than ergocalciferol; however, the duration of toxicity is considerably shorter. Alkali therapy alone can also improve RTA-associated osteomalacia.[47] Oral bicarbonate in doses of 10–20 mEq/kg/day are typically required to correct the acidosis caused by a proximal RTA with or without Fanconi syndrome. Bicarbonate replacement should be distributed during the day and not given as a single daily dose. Distal RTA bicarbonate requirements are considerably less (1–2 mEq/kg/day in divided doses). However, children with distal RTA may require significantly higher doses to achieve normal growth rates.[48] Many forms of alkali

TABLE 3. ORAL PHOSPHATE REPLACEMENT

	Content per dose		
	Phosphorus (mg)	Sodium (mEq)	Potassium (mEq)
K-Phos (tablet)			
Original	114	0	3.7
Neutral	250	13	1.1
MF	125	2.9	1.1
#2	250	5.8	2.3
Neutra-Phos (powder)	250	7.1	7.1
Neutra-Phos K (powder)	250	0	14.3
Uro-KP-Neutral (tablet)	250	10.9	1.3
Fleet phospho-soda (liquid)	128/ml	4.8/ml	0
Joulie's solution (liquid)	30.4/ml	0.76/ml	0

TABLE 4. ORAL BICARBONATE REPLACEMENT

Potassium citrate (Urocit-K)	
540 mg tablet	5 mEq per tablet
1080 mg tablet	10 mEq per tablet
Potassium citrate + citric acid	
Oral solution (Polycitra-K)	2 meq/1 ml
Crystals (Polycitra-K)	30 mEq per packet
Sodium citrate + citric acid (Bicitra or Shohl's solution)	1 meq/1 ml
Potassium citrate + sodium citrate + citric acid (Polycitra)	2 meq/1 ml
Sodium bicarbonate	
325 mg tablet	3.87 mEq per tablet
650 mg tablet	7.74 mEq per tablet
Baking soda	60 mEq/teaspoon

replacement are available (Table 4) and can be tailored to the individual patient needs. In type I RTA, it is often necessary to replace potassium before initiating alkali replacement, because correction of the acidosis will worsen hypokalemia. Treatment of type IV RTA includes a low potassium diet, alkali replacement, and occasionally a loop diuretic.

If long-term treatment with phosphorus and vitamin D are necessary, close monitoring of serum biochemistries and renal function is imperative. Secondary hyperparathyroidism is frequently seen in patients treated chronically with phosphorus and vitamin D therapy for various hypophosphatemic disorders.[49,50] Several reports of tertiary hyperparathyroidism requiring surgical intervention have also been published.[50–52] Periodic renal ultrasound may help identify patients at risk for significant renal impairment associated with treatment by identifying nephrocalcinosis[53,54] before obvious changes in serum creatinine or glomerular filtration rate are noted.

REFERENCES

1. Sebastian A, McSherry E, Morris RC Jr 1971 On the mechanism of renal potassium wasting in renal tubular acidosis associated with the Fanconi syndrome (type 2 RTA). J Clin Invest 50:231–243.
2. Rodriguez Soriano J, Houston IB, Boichis H, Edelmann CM Jr 1968 Calcium and phosphorus metabolism in the fanconi syndrome. J Clin Endocrinol Metab 28:1555–1563.
3. Rodriquez-Soriano J, Vallo A, Castillo G, Oliveros R 1980 Renal handling of water and sodium in children with proximal and distal renal tubular acidosis. Nephron 25:193–198.
4. Houston IB, Boichis H, Edelmann CM Jr 1968 Fanconi syndrome with renal sodium wasting and metabolic alkalosis. Am J Med 44:638–646.
5. Dillard MG, Pesce AJ, Pollak VE, Boreisha I 1971 Proteinuria and renal protein clearances in patients with renal tubular disorders. J Lab Clin Med 78:203–215.
6. Biber J, Custer M, Magagnin S, Hayes G, Werner A, Lotscher M, Kaissling B, Murer H 1996 Renal Na/Pi-cotransporters. Kidney Int 49:981–985.
7. Murer H, Lotscher M, Kaissling B, Levi M, Kempson SA, Biber J 1996 Renal brush border membrane Na/Pi-cotransport: Molecular aspects in PTH-dependent and dietary regulation. Kidney Int 49:1769–1773.
8. Berndt T, Craig TA, Bowe AE, Vassiliadis J, Reczek D, Finnegan R, Jan De Beur SM, Schiavi SC, Kumar R 2003 Secreted frizzled-related protein 4 is a potent tumor-derived phosphaturic agent. J Clin Invest 112:785–794.
9. Kumar R 2002 New insights into phosphate homeostasis: Fibroblast growth factor 23 and frizzled-related protein-4 are phosphaturic factors derived from tumors associated with osteomalacia. Curr Opin Nephrol Hypertens 11:547–553.
10. Schiavi SC, Kumar R 2004 The phosphatonin pathway: New insights in phosphate homeostasis. Kidney Int 65:1–14.
11. Moe OW, Berry CA, Rector FCJ 2000 Renal transport of glucose, amino acids, sodium, chloride, and water. In: Brenner BM, Rector FC (eds.) The Kidney, 6th ed., vol. 1. Saunders, Philadelphia, PA, USA, pp. 375–415.

12. Kanai Y, Lee WS, You G, Brown D, Hediger MA 1994 The human kidney low affinity Na+/glucose cotransporter SGLT2. Delineation of the major renal reabsorptive mechanism for D-glucose. J Clin Invest 93:397–404.

13. Kurtzman NA 2000 Renal tubular acidosis syndromes. South Med J 93:1042–1052.

14. Gluck SL, Iyori M, Holliday LS, Kostrominova T, Lee BS 1996 Distal urinary acidification from Homer Smith to the present. Kidney Int 49:1660–1664.

15. Rector FCJ, Carter NW, Seldin DW 1965 The mechanism of bicarbonate reabsorption in the proximal and distal tubules of the kidney. J Clin Invest 44:278–290.

16. Preisig PA, Ives HE, Cragoe EJ, Jr., Alpern RJ, Rector FC Jr 1987 Role of the Na+/H+ antiporter in rat proximal tubule bicarbonate absorption. J Clin Invest 80:970–978.

17. Soleimani M, Aronson PS 1989 Ionic mechanism of Na+-HCO3- co-transport in rabbit renal basolateral membrane vesicles. J Biol Chem 264:18302–18308.

18. Hamm LL, Simon EE 1987 Roles and mechanisms of urinary buffer excretion. Am J Physiol 253:F595–F605.

19. Gluck SL 1998 Acid-base. Lancet 352:474–479.

20. Rodriguez Soriano J 2002 Renal tubular acidosis: The clinical entity. J Am Soc Nephrol 13:2160–2170.

21. Guan S, el-Dahr S, Dipp S, Batuman V 1999 Inhibition of Na-K-ATPase activity and gene expression by a myeloma light chain in proximal tubule cells. J Invest Med 47:496–501.

22. Batuman V, Guan S, O'Donovan R, Puschett JB 1994 Effect of myeloma light chains on phosphate and glucose transport in renal proximal tubule cells. Ren Physiol Biochem 17:294–300.

23. Coor C, Salmon RF, Quigley R, Marver D, Baum M 1991 Role of adenosine triphosphate (ATP) and NaK ATPase in the inhibition of proximal tubule transport with intracellular cystine loading. J Clin Invest 87:955–961.

24. Castano E, Marzabal P, Casado FJ, Felipe A, Pastor-Anglada M 1997 Na+,K(+)-ATPase expression in maleic-acid-induced Fanconi syndrome in rats. Clin Sci (Lond) 92:247–253.

25. Berndt T, Knox FG 1992 Renal regulation of phosphate excretion. In: Seldin DW, Giebisch G (eds.) The Kidney: Physiology and Pathophysiology, 2 ed. Raven Press, New York, NY, USA, pp. 2511–2532.

26. Steele TH, Engle JE, Tanaka Y, Lorenc RS, Dudgeon KL, DeLuca HF 1975 Phosphatemic action of 1,25-dihydroxyvitamin D3. Am J Physiol 229:489–495.

27. Tanaka Y, Deluca HF 1974 Role of 1,25-dihydroxyvitamin D3 in maintaining serum phosphorus and curing rickets. Proc Natl Acad Sci USA 71:1040–1044.

28. Tanaka Y, Deluca HF 1973 The control of 25-hydroxyvitamin D metabolism by inorganic phosphorus. Arch Biochem Biophys 154:566–574.

29. Brewer ED, Tsai HC, Szeto KS, Morris RC Jr 1977 Maleic acid-induced impaired conversion of 25-(OH)D3 to 1,25(OH)2D3: Implications for Fanconi's syndrome. Kidney Int 12:244–252.

30. Clarke BL, Wynne AG, Wilson DM, Fitzpatrick LA 1995 Osteomalacia associated with adult Fanconi's syndrome: Clinical and diagnostic features. Clin Endocrinol (Oxf) 43:479–490.

31. Colussi G, De Ferrari ME, Surian M, Malberti F, Rombola G, Pontoriero G, Galvanini G, Minetti L 1985 Vitamin D metabolites and osteomalacia in the human Fanconi syndrome. Proc Eur Dial Transplant Assoc Eur Ren Assoc 21:756–760.

32. Haviv YS, Wald H, Levi M, Dranitzki-Elhalel M, Popovtzer MM 2001 Late-onset downregulation of NaPi-2 in experimental Fanconi syndrome. Pediatr Nephrol 16:412–416.

33. Neuman WF 1980 Bone material and calcification mechanisms. In: Urist MR (ed.) Fundamental and Clinical Bone Physiology. Lippincott, Philadelphia, PA, USA, pp. 83–107.

34. Bushinsky DA, Frick KK 2000 The effects of acid on bone. Curr Opin Nephrol Hypertens 9:369–379.

35. Domrongkitchaiporn S, Pongsakul C, Stitchantrakul W, Sirikulchayanonta V, Ongphiphadhanakul B, Radinahamed P, Karnsombut P, Kunkitti N, Ruang-raksa C, Rajatanavin R 2001 Bone mineral density and histology in distal renal tubular acidosis. Kidney Int 59:1086–1093.

36. Dalmak S, Erek E, Serdengecti K, Okar I, Ulku U, Basaran M 1996 A case study of adult-onset hypophosphatemic osteomalacia with idiopathic fanconi syndrome. Nephron 72:121–122.

37. Disthabanchong S, Martin KJ, McConkey CL, Gonzalez EA 2002 Metabolic acidosis up-regulates PTH/PTHrP receptors in UMR 106–01 osteoblast-like cells. Kidney Int 62:1171–1177.

38. Krieger NS, Sessler NE, Bushinsky DA 1992 Acidosis inhibits osteoblastic and stimulates osteoclastic activity in vitro. Am J Physiol 262:F442–F448.

39. Kawashima H, Kraut JA, Kurokawa K 1982 Metabolic acidosis suppresses 25-hydroxyvitamin in D3–1alpha-hydroxylase in the rat kidney. Distinct site and mechanism of action. J Clin Invest 70:135–140.

40. Nykjaer A, Fyfe JC, Kozyraki R, Leheste JR, Jacobsen C, Nielsen MS, Verroust PJ, Aminoff M, de la Chapelle A, Moestrup SK, Ray R, Gliemann J, Willnow TE, Christensen EI 2001 Cubilin dysfunction causes abnormal metabolism of the steroid hormone 25(OH) vitamin D(3). Proc Natl Acad Sci USA 98:13895–13900.

41. Nykjaer A, Dragun D, Walther D, Vorum H, Jacobsen C, Herz J, Melsen F, Christensen EI, Willnow TE 1999 An endocytic pathway essential for renal uptake and activation of the steroid 25-(OH) vitamin D3. Cell 96:507–515.

42. Zeier M, Ritz E 2000 The bedridden osteomalacic patient with Fanconi syndrome in pre-terminal renal failure. Nephrol Dialysis Transplant 15:1880–1882.

43. Long WS, Seashore MR, Siegel NJ, Bia MJ 1990 Idiopathic Fanconi syndrome with progressive renal failure: A case report and discussion. Yale J Biol Med 63:15–28.

44. Smith R, Lindenbaum RH, Walton RJ 1976 Hypophosphataemic osteomalacia and Fanconi syndrome of adult onset with dominant inheritance. Possible relationship with diabetes mellitus. Qtly J Med 45:387–400.

45. Harrison NA, Bateman JM, Ledingham JG, Smith R 1991 Renal failure in adult onset hypophosphatemic osteomalacia with Fanconi syndrome: A family study and review of the literature. Clin Nephrol 35:148–150.

46. Lambert J, Lips P 1989 Adult hypophosphataemic osteomalacia with Fanconi syndrome presenting in a patient with neurofibromatosis. Netherlands J Med 35:309–316.

47. Wrong OM, Richards P 1972 Treatment of osteomalacia of renal tubular acidosis by sodium bicarbonate alone. Lancet 2:998–999.

48. McSherry E, Morris RC Jr 1978 Attainment and maintenance of normal stature with alkali therapy in infants and children with classic renal tubular acidosis. J Clin Invest 61:509–527.

49. Makitie O, Kooh SW, Sochett E 2003 Prolonged high-dose phosphate treatment: A risk factor for tertiary hyperparathyroidism in X-linked hypophosphatemic rickets. Clin Endocrinol (Oxf) 58:163–168.

50. Alon U, Newsome H Jr, Chan JC 1984 Hyperparathyroidism in patients with X-linked dominant hypophosphatemic rickets–application of the calcium infusion test as an indicator for parathyroidectomy. Int J Pediatr Nephrol 5:39–43.

51. Rivkees SA, el-Hajj-Fuleihan G, Brown EM, Crawford JD 1992 Tertiary hyperparathyroidism during high phosphate therapy of familial hypophosphatemic rickets. J Clin Endocrinol Metab 75:1514–1518.

52. Savio RM, Gosnell JE, Posen S, Reeve TS, Delbridge LW 2004 Parathyroidectomy for tertiary hyperparathyroidism associated with X-linked dominant hypophosphatemic rickets. Arch Surg 139:218–222.

53. Goodyer PR, Kronick JB, Jequier S, Reade TM, Scriver CR 1987 Nephrocalcinosis and its relationship to treatment of hereditary rickets. J Pediatr 111:700–704.

54. Verge CF, Lam A, Simpson JM, Cowell CT, Howard NJ, Silink M 1991 Effects of therapy in X-linked hypophosphatemic rickets. N Engl J Med 325:1843–1848.

Chapter 66. Renal Osteodystrophy

Kevin J. Martin, Ziyad Al-Aly, and Esther A. Gonzalez

Division of Nephrology, Saint Louis University School of Medicine, St. Louis, Missouri

INTRODUCTION

Renal osteodystrophy is the skeletal component of a variety of abnormalities of bone and mineral metabolism that may occur as a complication of chronic kidney disease. These abnormalities may include abnormal values for serum calcium, phosphorus, PTH, and other bone markers, as well as extraskeletal calcification, and can be associated with bone pain, abnormal bone structure, and an increased incidence of fracture. The abnormalities in bone may vary widely from situations where bone turnover may be abnormally high as a manifestation of the effects of elevated levels of PTH on bone, and are manifested histologically by osteitis fibrosa, to the opposite end of the spectrum, where bone turnover may be abnormally low, which is often termed "adynamic bone." Either extreme may be accompanied by abnormal mineralization of bone, which can be manifested as osteomalacia. The patterns of skeleton abnormality commonly occur in combination and give rise to a term known as "mixed renal osteodystrophy," which is usually associated with some signs of the secondary hyperparathyroidism associated with mineralization defects. In the setting of chronic kidney disease, the skeleton may also be affected by other processes, such as the accumulation of β-2 microglobulin, and in addition, systemic therapy for kidney disease, such as corticosteroid therapy, or coincidental bone abnormalities from postmenopausal or other forms of osteoporosis, may also be present. Much has been learned about the pathogenesis of these abnormalities in recent years, and the understanding of these factors has lead to therapeutic strategies of minimize both the skeletal and extraskeletal pathology.

PATHOGENESIS OF RENAL OSTEODYSTROPHY

High Turnover Renal Osteodystrophy

High turnover renal osteodystrophy is the result of the effects of high levels of PTH on bone. Hyperplasia of the parathyroid glands and high levels of PTH are well known to occur early in the course of chronic kidney disease.[1–3] The development of hyperparathyroidism in this setting is the result of a variety of factors, which are shown in Fig. 1, and include retention of phosphorus as kidney function declines, reductions in the levels of calcitriol in serum, a number of intrinsic abnormalities in the parathyroid gland, disorders of parathyroid cell growth, abnormal control of serum calcium, and skeletal resistance to the calcemic actions of PTH.[4] These abnormalities are all closely interrelated and one or more may predominate in any given patient at different levels of renal insufficiency.

The importance of phosphate retention on the pathogenesis of secondary hyperparathyroidism has been shown by several studies over many years.[5,6] This has been accompanied by observations that dietary phosphate reduction in proportion to the decreased glomerular filtration rate (GFR) in experimental renal disease is associated with prevention of the development of hyperparathyroidism. While this observation is not in doubt and has been confirmed in many experimental systems, as well as in patients, the mechanism by which phosphorus affects the development of hyperparathyroidism continues to generate some controversy. The original hypothesis was that phosphorus retention with decreasing kidney function lead to decreases in ionized calcium, which would trigger a compensatory increase with PTH.[7] Subsequent studies, however, have shown that hypocalcemia is not necessary for hyperparathyroidism to occur,[8] and therefore, other mechanisms must be involved.

Because an additional consequence of phosphate retention is limitation of the production of calcitriol, it is possible that reductions in the levels of calcitriol allow hyperparathyroidism to occur and progress. Observations in experimental animals and humans have confirmed that there is a slow decline in the levels of calcitriol that begins early in the course of chronic kidney disease, and therefore, this is also a plausible hypothesis.[9]

Further studies have shown that phosphorus may directly affect the parathyroid gland by increasing PTH secretion and parathyroid growth, and conversely, prevention of phosphate retention is associated with prevention of these abnormalities in the parathyroid gland.[10–12]

The effect of phosphorus may well be directly on the parathyroid gland, but could also act through the calcitriol mechanism, because changes in the levels of serum phosphorus could alter the production of calcitriol by the kidney. The precise mechanism by which phosphorus could affect the parathyroid gland is not well understood at the present time. It has been shown, however, that phosphate retention or high phosphorus diets are associated with increased levels of PTH mRNA in parathyroid, and this effect seems to be caused by an effect on the stability of PTH mRNA.[13] The precise mechanism of this effect continues to be studied, and studies have shown that phosphate retention may be associated with alterations in proteins that are involved in regulating the degradation of PTH mRNA within the parathyroid.[14]

A potential signaling mechanism has been suggested by the demonstration that high extracellular phosphate concentrations may alter parathyroid function by reducing the production of arachadonic acid by parathyroid tissue.[15,16]

Phosphorus also seems to play an important role in the regulation of parathyroid growth. Thus, a high phosphorus diet has been shown to increase parathyroid hyperplasia. Conversely, a diet low in phosphorus is effective in preventing increased parathyroid growth in the setting of chronic kidney disease. A low phosphorus diet has been associated with upregulation of the cell cycle regulator, p21, which may play a role in the prevention of parathyroid hyperplasia.[17] A high phosphorus diet seems to be mediated by increases in the expression of TGF-α, which would work through the EGF receptor in stimulating parathyroid growth.[18] The mechanism by which phosphorus affects the parathyroid gland is not understood at the present time, and the search continues for a putative phosphate sensor that may trigger the cellular changes, but this has not been shown at the present time.

Because calcitriol is an important regulator of parathyroid function, it is also important to consider that phosphorus retention may affect parathyroid function by decreasing the production of calcitriol. In addition, recent data have suggested that phosphate retention may be associated with an increase in the levels of fibroblast growth factor (FGF)-23, which has also been shown to be a potent inhibitor of 1-α-hydroxylase activity, and accordingly, this mechanism could serve to limit the

Dr. Martin has had grant support from and served as a consultant for Abbott, Amgen, and Shire. All other authors have reported no conflicts of interest.

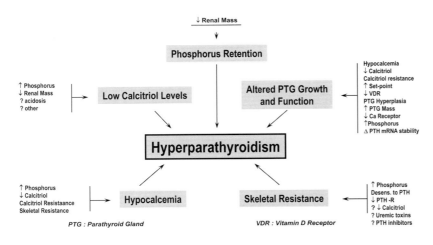

FIG. 1. Summary of factors that contribute to the secondary hyperparathyroidism of chronic renal failure. PTG, parathyroid glands; VDR, vitamin D receptor.

production of calcitriol by the kidney in the setting of chronic kidney disease.[19] Other factors associated with chronic kidney disease, such as acidosis, may also impact on the ability of the diseased kidney to increase calcitriol production.

In recent years, attention has been focused on an additional mechanism that could potentially limit the ability of the kidney to produce calcitriol. These data suggest that decreased delivery of the precursor, 25-hydroxyvitamin D, which circulates while bound to a vitamin D–binding protein, could impact on the ability of the kidney to produce calcitriol.[20] This 25-hydroxy-D-bound vitamin D–binding protein is filtered at the glomerulus and is taken up in the proximal tubule by a mechanism that involves megalin, which seems to be required for the internalization of the 25-hydroxyvitamin D–binding protein into the cell and is the rate-limiting step for the production of calcitriol by the 1-α-hydroxylase enzyme. This mechanism, obviously then, in the course of chronic kidney disease, may limit the ability of the kidney to produce increased calcitriol levels, even in circumstances where PTH levels are high.

In addition to deceases in the production of calcitriol, the setting of chronic kidney disease may also be associated with resistance to the peripheral actions of calcitriol, and it has been suggested that uremic serum contains factors that seem to decrease the ability of the vitamin D receptor to interact with the vitamin D responsive element on DNA.[21] Further studies have suggested that this may be caused by reductions in retinoid X receptor (RXR), the essential binding partner for the vitamin D receptor, and its interaction with the vitamin D response element (VDRE) on DNA.[22]

The principal regulator of PTH secretion is serum calcium, acting on the calcium-sensing receptor on the parathyroid. In the setting of chronic kidney disease, it has been shown that there seems to be reduced expression of the calcium-sensing receptor as the parathyroid glands enlarge and undergo hyperplasia.[23,24] The consequences of the reductions in the calcium-sensing receptor could lead to abnormal calcium-regulated PTH secretion.

An important issue as to whether parathyroid hyperplasia causes a reduction in expression of calcium-sensing receptor, or alternatively, whether the reduced calcium sensing receptor facilitated parathyroid growth, has been studied in experimental animals, with the results showing that the parathyroid proliferation seems to precede the reductions in the levels of the calcium-sensing receptor.[25] In some patients with severe hyperparathyroidism, an abnormal setpoint for calcium has been shown, which would consequently lead to abnormal calcium-regulated PTH secretion. The issue of parathyroid setpoint in uremia has been investigated by a number of studies, and it seems that the setpoint may be altered by multiple factors, including the baseline level of serum calcium, the rate of change of serum calcium, the magnitude of parathyroid hyperplasia, and polymorphisms of the calcium-sensing receptor gene.[26–30] Thus, with these multiple factors involved, heterogeneity of results is to be expected, and indeed, this has been found in clinical studies.

Calcitriol also has many effects on the parathyroid gland, which may contribute to many of the abnormalities. The effects of calcitriol on parathyroid function are summarized in Fig. 2. While these factors may play a role in the pathogenesis of the parathyroid abnormalities, these actions of calcitriol can also be exploited as a therapeutic agent, which is discussed below.

It has also been recognized that as a consequence of parathyroid growth, not only is there a decrease in the expression of the calcium sensing receptor, but there are also decreases in the expression of the vitamin D receptor as the parathyroid glands undergo proliferation.[31–33] Studies have shown that as parathyroid hyperplasia progresses, the glands take on a nodular appearance, and some of these nodules may represent monoclonal expansions of parathyroid cells.[34] Thus, similar to studies with the calcium-sensing receptor, the loss of vitamin D receptor expression may be a consequence of parathyroid growth. However, both pathways can be exploited therapeutically. Thus, evidence has been presented to show that administration of active vitamin D sterols can attenuate parathyroid cell growth in experimental models of uremia, and similarly, administration of calcimimetic agents has also been shown to suppress and prevent further parathyroid hyperplasia in experimental models of kidney disease.

An additional contributor to hyperparathyroidism in the setting of kidney disease may be related to the phenomenon of skeletal resistance to the calcemic actions of PTH, which were described many years ago. In essence, it was observed that the administration of PTH resulted in a lesser increase in serum calcium in patients or experimental animals with kidney disease.[35] Studies of the mechanisms involved have uncovered many potential contributors, such as phosphorus retention, decreased levels of calcitriol, downregulation of the PTH receptor, and potentially, PTH peptides, with truncations in their N terminus, a topic which is discussed in more detail below.

Pathogenesis of Low Turnover Renal Osteodystrophy

As mentioned above, low bone turnover can be seen in association with kidney disease and is characterized by extremely low rates of bone formation, and in some cases, with the severe mineralization defect of osteomalacia, which is manifested by an increased volume of unmineralized bone

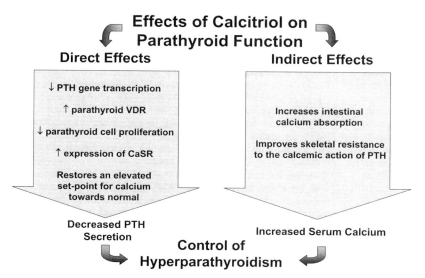

FIG. 2. Summary of direct and indirect effects of calcitriol administration to control PTH secretion in patients with chronic renal failure. Direct effects refer to changes in parathyroid cell synthesis and secretion of PTH, and indirect effects are actions of calcitriol on intestinal calcium absorption and skeletal response to PTH.

matrix. It now seems that the majority of cases of osteomalacia in the setting of chronic kidney disease have been caused by accumulation of aluminum at the mineralization front, and because the discontinuation of the use of aluminum-based phosphate binders, osteomalacia in the setting of chronic kidney disease is virtually nonexistent. However, a substantial number of patients have extremely low bone turnover not associated with osteomalacia, which is termed "adynamic bone." This is found with increasing frequency in patients on dialysis and seems to be especially prevalent among patients on peritoneal dialysis. The pathogenesis of adynamic bone is complex and includes a large number of factors, which are shown in Fig. 3. Many of these factors have in common that they serve to decrease the ambient levels of PTH, and thus induce a relative degree of hypoparathyroidism, which may be associated with decreasing bone formation rate.[36] The multiple factors involved show the complexity of the problem, but suggest that some therapeutic interventions for high bone turnover may facilitate the development of abnormally low bone turnover, such as the use of high levels of calcium-based phosphate binders, an elevated calcium intake, excess use of active vitamin D sterols, the presence of increasing age or diabetes, and a variety of other factors, which can all contribute. It is also possible that some of the disturbances in a variety of growth factors and cytokines could directly impact on bone formation rate.

Other Factors That May Play a Role in Renal Bone Disease

In addition to the broad histological types of skeletal abnormality outlined above, there are other associated metabolic abnormalities with chronic kidney disease that may adversely impact the skeleton. An important factor might be the presence of metabolic acidosis, which can affect the bone by liberation of bone mineral as the hydrogen ions are buffered by bone carbonate. Evidence is also being presented that acidosis can facilitate cell mediated bone resorption and therefore may alter the biological effects of PTH or vitamin D on bone.[37–39] The expression of the PTH receptor may also be affected by acidosis, as shown in osteoblast-like cells in vitro.[40] Acidosis can also affect the RANKL osteoprotogerin (OPG) system in a direction favoring bone resorption, and this, together with disturbances of other cytokines, such as interleukin-6 (IL-6) or IL-1, may contribute to the bony abnormalities associated with chronic kidney disease.[41]

It is important to remember that the skeleton may also be affected because of other systemic factors, such as reductions in sex hormones, which could contribute to an osteoporotic component of renal osteodystrophy in various patient groups. Similarly, the use of corticosteroids for treatment of the pre-existing kidney disease may also introduce a component of corticosteroid-induced osteoporosis that could complicate the manifestations of renal osteodystrophy.

Clinical Manifestations

Symptomatic bone disease in adult patients with advanced kidney disease is relatively unusual, and symptoms are only likely to appear late in the course. Children with renal osteodystrophy may manifest linear growth failure, deformities of the extremities, slipped epiphyses and fractures, and often at a relatively preserved GFR. In both adults and children, most

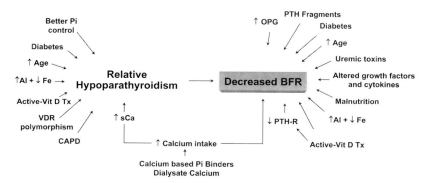

FIG. 3. Factors that contribute to relative hypoparathyroidism and decreased bone formation rate (BFR) in patients with chronic renal failure. Note that improvement in calcium intake and absorption or increased dialysate calcium may contribute to the relative hypoparathyroidism through an increase in serum calcium.

often, symptoms are nonspecific and insidious in nature, and by the time they appear, there are significant biochemical and histological changes. Pain or stiffness in long bones and round joints is common and is often associated with significant hyperparathyroidism. Periarthritis and arthritis may also occur and there may be calcium deposits around the affected joints, which can be revealed on X-ray. These manifestations can be confused with pseudo-gout or gout, but rather than treating with anti-inflammatory agents, consideration should be given to therapy directed at hyperparathyroidism. It should also be realized that erosive arthritis and joint effusions may also occur in association with β-2 microglobulin amyloidosis, for which intervention is problematic. Fractures may occur in vertebrae and long bones and ribs, often with minimal trauma, and should prompt detailed investigation and therapy when they occur.

Weakness of the proximal muscles is also relatively common. This can be a debilitating problem in patients with advanced kidney disease.[42] The principal differential diagnosis is secondary hyperparathyroidism, phosphate deficiency, or potentially, some manifestations of vitamin D deficiency. One must also consider the consequences on muscle of peripheral neuropathy, muscle weakness from electrolyte disturbances, or possibly carnitine deficiency in some circumstances.

Spontaneous rupture of tendons has also been noted in patients with long-standing kidney disease, often associated with severe hyperparathyroidism.[43] The development of spontaneous tendon rupture should alert the nephrologist that the control of secondary hyperparathyroidism may not be adequate and that further evaluation and therapy is indicated.

Itching is a common and troubling symptom in patients with kidney disease, particularly with those on hemodialysis. It may reflect the presence of an elevated calcium–phosphorus product, and in some cases, it has been noticed to disappear rapidly after parathyroidectomy. Some symptomatic relief can be seen after treatment with ultraviolet radiation, but in many cases, no specific diagnosis can be made, and treatment has been difficult.

Extraskeletal calcifications may be seen in association with the manifestation of renal osteodystrophy. These extraskeletal calcifications may include calcification of the vascular system, notably coronary arteries, aorta, femoral, and carotid arteries, as well as dystrophic calcification that may occur around joints. These extraskeletal calcifications may be associated with high bone turnover syndromes, and presumably represent the consequence of mobilizing excess quantities of calcium and phosphorus from bone. These extraskeletal calcifications may also be seen in association with low bone turnover renal osteodystrophy, and it has been hypothesized that with low bone turnover, there is inadequate amount of bone matrix being made to accommodate deposition of calcium and phosphorus in the bone mineralization process, and in these circumstances, precipitation may occur at extraskeletal sites. An extreme example of small vessel calcifications and extraskeletal calcification would be the syndrome of calcific uremic arteriolopathy, or calciphylaxis.[44] This is often manifested by the development of painful areas of the lower extremities and trunk or buttocks that become violaceous, indurated, and mottled, and may go on to frank ulceration. This syndrome is seen sporadically, but the general impression is that it has been seen with increasing frequency in recent years. It has been postulated that perhaps some of the current therapies for hyperparathyroidism, with the inclusion of large amounts of calcium-containing phosphate binders and active vitamin D sterols, may be contributing to the apparent increase and incidence. However, this is by no means clear at the present time. Some cases occur in association with severe hyperparathyroidism, but in many of these patients, hyperparathyroidism is not severe, and the patients tend to be obese with a high prevalence of diabetes. Because of the similarity with warfarin's skin necrosis, considerable attention has been given to the presence of pro-coagulant and anti-coagulant factors in serum, particularly in the protein C and protein S pathways in the final manifestations of this problem. Recent observations have suggested that decreased levels of the calcification inhibitor, fetuin A, may play an important role in this calciphylaxis syndrome.[45] Others have implicated a relative decrease in pyrophosphate levels in the vasculature as being an important contributor to vascular calcification.[46]

Calcification of the cardiovascular system, particularly the cardiac valves and coronary arteries, has been receiving increasing focus because of the high incidence of sudden death and coronary artery disease leading to death in this patient population. Most of the calcification seems to be of the medial type, and many risk factors for this have been uncovered, including uncontrolled hyperphosphatemia and elevation of the calcium–phosphorus product.[47,48]

Duration of dialysis is also a significant risk factor, and in addition, it is likely that excessive calcium load is contributory.[49] Studies have shown that withdrawal of the excess calcium load provided by calcium containing phosphate binders may be associated with a decreased rate of progression of coronary artery calcification in those that have calcification present at baseline.[50] Considerable interest surrounds this vascular calcification complication and studies have shown that phosphate may be a key regulator of these processes. Thus, it has been shown that phosphorus can lead to the transformation of cells within vasculature to an osteoblast-like phenotype with the expression of osteoblast-associated genes, such as CBFA-1 and matrix proteins. The process seems to involve the type III phosphate transporter, PIT-1, and in vitro, the process can be inhibited by inhibiting this phosphate transport system.[51–54] Active research continues in this area.

The deposition of β-2 microglobulin in articular and periarticular tissues may result in a disabling arthropathy that has been recognized for many years.[55] Usually, a considerable amount of time on dialysis is required before the manifestation of this type of amyloidosis becomes evident. The presentation usually involves either carpal tunnel syndrome or a swelling around joints of the hands. Onset is insidious, but tends to be progressive and usually presents with chronic pain in the joints and frequently involves the shoulders. Careful evaluation is necessary to distinguish this involvement of the cervical nerve roots. Evaluation is best performed with MRI, which shows thickening of the tendons or the subacromial bursa, and it can be associated with destructive arthropathies and with subchondral bone erosions in large joints. Large bone cysts may be seen, particularly in the vertebrae. The diagnosis can be made histologically, using Congo red, but can also be suspected on clinical grounds. Clinical management of this complication, in general, has been unsatisfactory, and sometimes surgical palliation can be useful. It seems that successful renal transplant may be associated with symptomatic relief in most patients, but there is no evidence to date that the soft tissue lesions actually regress.

Biochemical Abnormalities

Because of the nonspecific nature of the clinical signs and symptoms of renal osteodystrophy, diagnosis can often present a challenge. This is particularly so because a histological examination of undecalcified sections of bone remains the gold standard for the diagnosis of renal osteodystrophy, but this invasive technique is not in widespread use and may only be indicated in a limited set of clinical circumstances. Imaging studies may also be nonspecific, unless the manifestations are severe, and accordingly, much of the diagnosis revolves around probabilities from examination of abnormal biochemistries.

Gross abnormalities in serum calcium and phosphorus concentrations are important and must be frequently monitored. While, for the most part, serum calcium concentrations are preserved relatively normal, at least when corrected for albumin levels, hyperphosphatemia is frequently observed when GFRs fall below 20 ml/minute.

Control of hyperphosphatemia is of major importance in the management of kidney disease, not only because of its contribution to the development of secondary hyperparathyroidism, which is discussed above, but also because of its association with increased mortality and its role in facilitating vascular and extracellular calcifications. Hypocalcemia, if present, will require correction, because it is a powerful stimulus to PTH secretion and to parathyroid gland growth. Conversely, hypercalcemia may be seen in patients with low bone turnover syndrome, particularly when associated with vitamin D therapy.

The key to the assessment of bone and mineral metabolism in patients with chronic kidney disease is the accurate measurement of PTH in serum. The measurement of PTH has evolved considerably in recent years.[56] After the initial radioimmunoassays for PTH, usually directed toward the middle or C-terminal region of the PTH molecule, PTH assay evolved to two-site assays, which were believed to measure the 84 amino acid intact PTH molecule [PTH(1-84)]. Further refinement in PTH assays have now shown that these first-generation, two-site assays were not entirely specific for PTH(1-84) and that some peptides circulate in serum that are truncated at the N terminus, the prototype of which is PTH(7-84).[57] Therefore, further refinement in PTH assays have been able to exclude peptides such as PTH(7-84) for measurement, such that intact PTH(1-84) can now be measured reliably, and such assays are being used with increasing frequency in patients on hemodialysis.[58] This area of research has lead to additional considerations to understand the biology of these N-terminally truncated PTH peptides, following observations that the injection of PTH(7-84) in experimental animals seems to be associated with a fall in serum calcium and to blunt any rise in serum calcium induced by co-administration of PTH(1-84).[59,60] These observations have lead to efforts to try to understand the biology of PTH(7-84) and to begin to characterize receptors for this type of PTH peptides, which do not bind to the classical PTH receptor that mediates most of the classical biological activities of PTH. It is now known that peptides, such as PTH(7-84), arise both from the parathyroid gland themselves and also from the peripheral metabolism, and it is, therefore, important to try understand if such peptides have significant biological actions. Studies in vitro have shown that PTH(7-84) is a broad spectrum inhibitor of stimulated bone resorption by a variety of agents.[61,62] Studies in intact experimental animals have shown that PTH(7-84), when infused at high concentrations compared with PTH(1-84), a blunting of the expected effects of PTH(1-84) may occur.[63] Data obtained in vitro suggest that the receptor for these types of N-terminally truncated peptides may be located on osteocyte-like bone cells,[61] and this is an active field of study, to understand the clinical significance of this potentially biologically important and regulated system.

Markers of bone cell function may also be useful in the overall assessment of renal bone disease, and these markers may include total or bone-specific alkaline phosphatase, and measurements of osteocalcin, all of which seem to represent osteoblastic activity. Other marker peptides, such as pro-collagen, pro-peptides, or collagen breakdown products or TRACP, or C-terminal peptides from collagen, have also been studied, but at the present time, the routine clinical use of these markers is not well established.

Similarly, while cytokines and growth factors are clearly involved in the final manifestations of renal bone disease, one might envisage that measurements of some cytokines and growth factors might be helpful; however, at the present time, the clinical applications of such measurements have not been established.

If aluminum-related bone disease is felt to be a problem, the use of a desferrioxamine test may be used to try to uncover the presence of aluminum deposited in tissues, which may point the way for the need for the specific diagnosis of this type of problem.

Radiographic Features of Renal Osteodystrophy

The sensitivity of routine radiography for the evaluation of renal osteodystrophy is extremely limited in adults, and routine skeletal X-rays are not recommended, but are valuable and recommended for assessment of pediatric renal osteodystrophy. In its severe form, hyperparathyroid bone disease may be manifested by subperiosteal erosions, which may be seen in the tibia, the hands, the humerus, or the distal ends of the clavicles. A pepper pot skull is uncommonly seen nowadays. Severe hyperparathyroidism in the vertebrae may lead to "Rugger-Jersey" spine. Looser zones or pseudofractures may be seen in osteomalacic cases, particularly when caused by aluminum, and frank rickets may be seen in children. While the X-rays may not be revealing for the adult skeleton, routine X-rays may uncover the presence of vascular calcification, which may bring notice to this issue and perhaps modify treatment. Formal measurements of BMD are not routinely incorporated into the evaluation of renal osteodystrophy at this time. More sophisticated mechanisms, such as QCT, are also not routinely used.

PREVENTION AND MANAGEMENT OF RENAL OSTEODYSTROPHY

The objectives for the management of renal osteodystrophy in patients with kidney failure are to maintain the blood levels of calcium and phosphorus as close to normal as possible, prevent the development of parathyroid hyperplasia, or, if secondary hyperparathyroidism has already developed, to reduce the secretion of PTH to acceptable values. In addition, one needs to try to prevent extraskeletal depositions of calcium and to try and prevent or reverse accumulation of substances such as aluminum and iron that can adversely affect the skeleton. The specific treatment used and the intensity of treatment can vary with the stage of kidney disease and with the presence or absence of overt problems in the bone or cardiovascular systems. General guidelines are provided in Table 1, and clinical practice guidelines have been introduced to deal with the specifics of many of these issues in both adults and children.[64] It is now recommended that attention should be directed to the control of secondary hyperparathyroidism early in the course of chronic kidney disease when GFR is ~60 ml/minute. It is recommended that PTH levels should be measured at this stage of kidney dysfunction, and if elevated, one should proceed with a evaluation of vitamin D status and correct this if abnormal, before moving on to other measures. Consideration can be given to modest reductions in dietary phosphorus intake at this stage of kidney disease, and this has to be considered in the light of the necessity to maintain adequate protein intake.

TABLE 1. GENERAL GUIDELINE FOR MANAGEMENT OF RENAL OSTEODYSTROPHY

Begin management early in the course of renal disease
Monitor PTH, if elevated, evaluate vitamin D status
    Measure 25(OH)D levels
    Supplement if 25(OH)D is <30 ng/ml
    Ergocalciferol 50,000 units once a week ×4, then once per month
If PTH is elevated, and the levels of 25(OH)D are normal, begin dietary phosphate restriction within limits of adequate protein intake
Phosphate binders with meals (Maintain serum phosphorus 3.5–5.5 mg/dl)
    Calcium acetate
    Calcium carbonate
        Limit calcium intake to <2 g/day
    Magnesium carbonate
        If on dialysis, may need to decrease dialysate magnesium
    Sevelamer hydrochloride
    Lanthanum carbonate
    Aluminum based phosphate binders (short-term use only; monitor for toxicity)
Ensure adequate calcium intake
If on non–calcium-containing phosphate binder, and/or using dialysate calcium of 2.5 mEq/liter, give oral calcium supplement
Treat acidosis
Consider vitamin D sterols
    In predialysis chronic kidney disease, low-dose calcitriol, doxercalciferol paricalcitol or alphacalcidol
    Monitor closely for toxicity
On dialysis, oral or intravenous vitamin D sterols with close monitoring for toxicity
    Calcitriol
    Alfacalcidol or doxercalciferol
    Paricalcitol
Desired range for intact PTH 150–300 pg/ml. Preliminary estimates for the range for PTH(1–84) assays are 50–60% lower
Consider parathyroidectomy
    For severe hyperparathyroidism with
        Hypercalcemia
        Persistent hyperphosphatemia
        Failure to respond to therapy with vitamin D sterols and phosphate binders
        Persistently elevated calcium-phosphate product leading to Metastatic calcification
        Transplant candidate with living related donor
    Calciphylaxis

As kidney disease advances, further therapies may be necessary, and one might give additional consideration for the use of phosphate binders in the form of calcium carbonate or calcium acetate, when kidney disease is at stage III or IV. In patients on hemodialysis or peritoneal dialysis, aggressive use of phosphate binders is required, but the practice guidelines now limit the calcium intake from such agents to 1 g/day, and thus, often additional phosphate binders are required. Non–aluminum-, non–calcium-containing phosphate binders, such as sevelamer hydrochloride and lanthanum carbonate, are now available, and can be used to achieve effective control of serum phosphorus.[65,66] Consideration might also be given to the dialysis regimen, because longer-duration dialysis 6 days a week is usually sufficient to control hyperphosphatemia.

The practice guidelines provide specifics for how these issues should be managed, and provide biochemical targets to be achieved during the treatment. These targets are summarized in Table 2.

An important issue in the management of hyperparathyroidism during the course of chronic kidney disease is the use of vitamin D sterols. As indicated above, kidney disease is a risk factor for vitamin D deficiency, and this must be corrected before further measures are undertaken. As kidney disease advances, this may be insufficient to control hyperparathyroidism, and consideration should then be given to the use of active vitamin D sterols, or the use of vitamin D pro-hormones.[4]

Clinical studies in patients with CKD have shown that low dose calcitriol, α-calcidiol, doxercalciferol, or paricalcitol are useful for the control of hyperparathyroidism. Of these agents, it would seem that paricalcitol has the least effect on calcium and phosphorus metabolism, and thus, may be preferred.[67,68] One has to be cautious about inducing any toxicity with these active vitamin D sterols, because that would be detrimental to residual kidney function. The vitamin D pro-hormones, 1-α-hydroxyvitamin D₂ or 1-α-hydroxy-D₃, can also be used, but seem to have little advantage over their active counterparts.

In patients on hemodialysis in the United States, much of the use of vitamin D sterols is by parenteral administration, and paricalcitol is the most widely used of the vitamin D sterols. Its use is based on excellent safety profiles in experimental animals,[69] which, to some extent, have been corroborated in clinical studies.[67,70] This analog has lesser calcemic and phosphatemic potential than the native hormone, calcitriol, and yet seems to be effective at suppressing hyperparathyroidism.[71]

Recently, a new agent for the treatment of hyperparathyroidism, cinacalcet hydrochloride, an allosteric activator of the calcium-sensing receptor, has been introduced and seems to be extremely useful in decreasing the levels of PTH, and it has shown that, with the addition of this agent to the other strategies outlined above, there is significant improvement in our ability to reach the recommended practice guideline targets; thus, this agent provides an additional tool to provide effective control of hyperparathyroidism.[72]

Surgical removal of the parathyroid tissue may also be required if PTH levels remain excessively high. In addition, investigators in Japan have used percutaneous ablation of parathyroid tissue, which seems to have a role in the management of severe hyperparathyroidism.[73]

INTEGRATED MANAGEMENT OF RENAL OSTEODYSTROPHY

Based on the pathophysiology described above and the realization that hyperparathyroidism begins early in the course of renal insufficiency, one can develop an integrated and progressive scheme for management, which is shown in Fig. 4. In essence, this diagram summarizes the discussion above, to show that therapy should be started early and incremented as

TABLE 2. NKF/DOQI GUIDELINES FOR OPTIMAL SERUM LEVELS AND CALCIUM INTAKE FOR EACH OF THE STAGES OF RENAL INSUFFICIENCY

Stage	Ca (mg/dl)	P (mg/dl)	Ca × P (mg²/dl²)	iPTH (pg/ml)	Total elemental Ca intake
3	Within normal range of laboratory	2.7–4.6	<55	35–70	No more than 2 g (diet + binders)
4				70–110	
5	Preferred lower half of normal range	3.5–5.5	<55	150–300	

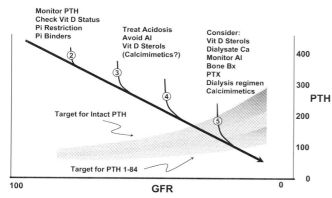

FIG. 4. Interventions and monitoring to prevent or reverse secondary hyperparathyroidism in patients with declining renal function at each stage of renal failure. Note that optimal PTH levels [shown as target for intact PTH and PTH(1–84)] change with stages of declining renal function.

kidney disease progresses to control this problem. It is hoped that with adequate attention to this problem and early intervention in the course of chronic kidney disease, this complication of kidney disease can be controlled and will ultimately lead to better patient outcomes.

REFERENCES

1. Reiss E, Canterbury JM, Kanter A 1969 Circulating parathyroid hormone concentration in chronic renal insufficiency. Arch Intern Med **124:**417–422.
2. Arnaud CD 1973 Hyperparathyroidism and renal failure. Kidney Int **4:**89–95.
3. Malluche H, Ritz E, Lange H 1976 Bone histology in incipient and advanced renal failure. Kidney Int **9:**355–362.
4. Martin KJ, Gonzalez EA, Slatopolsky E 2004 Renal osteodystrophy. In: Brenner BM (ed.) The Kidney, 7th ed., vol. 2. W.B. Saunders, Philadelphia, PA, USA. pp. 2255–2304.
5. Slatopolsky E, Caglar S, Pennell JP, Taggart DD, Canterbury JM, Reiss E, Bricker NS 1971 On the pathogenesis of hyperparathyroidism in chronic experimental renal insufficiency in the dog. J Clin Invest **50:**492–499.
6. Slatopolsky E, Finch J, Denda M, Ritter C, Zhong M, Dusso A, MacDonald PN, Brown AJ 1996 Phosphorus restriction prevents parathyroid gland growth. High phosphorus directly stimulates PTH secretion in vitro. J Clin Invest **97:**2534–2540.
7. Bricker NS 1972 On the pathogenesis of the uremic state. An exposition of the "trade-off hypothesis". N Engl J Med **286:**1093–1099.
8. Lopez-Hilker S, Galceran T, Chan YL, Rapp N, Martin KJ, Slatopolsky E 1986 Hypocalcemia may not be essential for the development of secondary hyperparathyroidism in chronic renal failure. J Clin Invest **78:**1097–1102.
9. Martinez I, Saracho R, Montenegro J, Llach F 1997 The importance of dietary calcium and phosphorous in the secondary hyperparathyroidism of patients with early renal failure. Am J Kidney Dis **29:**496–502.
10. Naveh-Many T, Rahamimov R, Livni N, Silver J 1995 Parathyroid cell proliferation in normal and chronic renal failure rats. The effects of calcium, phosphate, and vitamin D. J Clin Invest **96:**1786–1793.
11. Slatopolsky E, Brown A, Dusso A 2001 Role of phosphorus in the pathogenesis of secondary hyperparathyroidism. Am J Kidney Dis **37**(1 Suppl 2)**:**S54–S57.
12. Almaden Y, Canalejo A, Hernandez A, Ballesteros E, Garcia-Navarro S, Torres A, Rodriguez M 1996 Direct effect of phosphorus on PTH secretion from whole rat parathyroid glands in vitro. J Bone Miner Res **11:**970–976.
13. Moallem E, Kilav R, Silver J, Naveh-Many T 1998 RNA-Protein binding and post-transcriptional regulation of parathyroid hormone gene expression by calcium and phosphate. J Biol Chem **273:**5253–5259.
14. Yalcindag C, Silver J, Naveh-Many T 1999 Mechanism of increased parathyroid hormone mRNA in experimental uremia: Roles of protein RNA binding and RNA degradation. J Am Soc Nephrol **10:**2562–2568.
15. Almaden Y, Canalejo A, Ballesteros E, Anon G, Canadillas S, Rodriguez M 2002 Regulation of arachidonic acid production by intracellular cal-

16. Almaden Y, Canalejo A, Ballesteros E, Anon G, Rodriguez M 2000 Effect of high extracellular phosphate concentration on arachidonic acid production by parathyroid tissue in vitro. J Am Soc Nephrol **11:**1712–1718.
17. Dusso AS, Pavlopoulos T, Naumovich L, Lu Y, Finch J, Brown AJ, Morrissey J, Slatopolsky E 2001 p21(WAF1) and transforming growth factor-alpha mediate dietary phosphate regulation of parathyroid cell growth. Kidney Int **59:**855–865.
18. Dusso A, Lu Y, Pavlopoulos T, Slatopolsky E 1999 A role for enhanced expression of transforming growth factor alpha (TGF-α) in the mitogenic effects of high phosphorus on parathyroid cell growth. J Am Soc Nephrol **10:**617A.
19. Fukagawa M, Nii-Kono T, Kazama JJ 2005 Role of fibroblast growth factor 23 in health and in chronic kidney disease. Curr Opin Nephrol Hypertens **14:**325–329.
20. Nykjaer A, Dragun D, Walther D, Vorum H, Jacobsen C, Herz J, Melsen F, Christensen EI, Willnow TE 1999 An endocytic pathway essential for renal uptake and activation of the steroid 25-(OH) vitamin D3. Cell **96:**507–515.
21. Patel SR, Ke HQ, Vanholder R, Koenig RJ, Hsu CH 1995 Inhibition of calcitriol receptor binding to vitamin D response elements by uremic toxins. J Clin Invest **96:**50–59.
22. Sawaya BP, Koszewski NJ, Qi Q, Langub MC, Monier Faugere MC, Malluche HH 1997 Secondary hyperparathyroidism and vitamin D receptor binding to vitamin D response elements in rats with incipient renal failure. J Am Soc Nephrol **8:**271–278.
23. Gogusev J, Duchambon P, Hory B, Giovannini M, Goureau Y, Sarfati E, Drueke TB 1997 Depressed expression of calcium receptor in parathyroid gland tissue of patients with hyperparathyroidism. Kidney Int **51:**328–336.
24. Kifor O, Moore FD, Jr., Wang P, Goldstein M, Vassilev P, Kifor I, Hebert SC, Brown EM 1996 Reduced immunostaining for the extracellular Ca2+-sensing receptor in primary and uremic secondary hyperparathyroidism [see comments]. J Clin Endocrinol Metab **81:**1598–1606.
25. Ritter CS, Finch JL, Slatopolsky EA, Brown AJ 2001 Parathyroid hyperplasia in uremic rats precedes down-regulation of the calcium receptor. Kidney Int **60:**1737–1744.
26. De Cristofaro V, Colturi C, Masa A, Comelli M, Pedrini LA 2001 Rate dependence of acute PTH release and association between basal plasma calcium and set point of calcium-PTH curve in dialysis patients. Nephrol Dial Transplant **16:**1214–1221.
27. Borrego MJ, Felsenfeld AJ, Martin-Malo A, Almaden Y, Concepcion MT, Aljama P, Rodriguez M 1997 Evidence for adaptation of the entire PTH-calcium curve to sustained changes in the serum calcium in haemodialysis patients. Nephrol Dial Transplant **12:**505–513.
28. Indridason OS, Heath H III, Khosla S, Yohay DA, Quarles LD 1996 Non-suppressible parathyroid hormone secretion is related to gland size in uremic secondary hyperparathyroidism. Kidney Int **50:**1663–1671.
29. Yokoyama K, Shigematsu T, Tsukada T, Hara S, Yamada A, Kawaguchi Y, Hosoya T 2002 Calcium-sensing receptor gene polymorphism affects the parathyroid response to moderate hypercalcemic suppression in patients with end-stage renal disease. Clin Nephrol **57:**131–135.
30. Pahl M, Jara A, Bover J, Rodriguez M, Felsenfeld AJ 1996 The set point of calcium and the reduction of parathyroid hormone in hemodialysis patients. Kidney Int **49:**226–231.
31. Korkor AB 1987 Reduced binding of [3H]1,25-dihydroxyvitamin D3 in the parathyroid glands of patients with renal failure. N Engl J Med **316:**1573–1577.
32. Merke J, Hügel U, Zlotkowski A, Szabó A, Bommer J, Mall G, Ritz E 1987 Diminished parathyroid 1,25(OH)2D3 receptors in experimental uremia. Kidney Int **32:**350–353.
33. Brown AJ, Dusso A, Lopez-Hilker S, Lewis-Finch J, Grooms P, Slatopolsky E 1989 1,25-(OH)2D receptors are decreased in parathyroid glands from chronically uremic dogs. Kidney Int **35:**19–23.
34. Arnold A, Brown MF, Urena P, Gaz RD, Sarfati E, Drueke TB 1995 Monoclonality of parathyroid tumors in chronic renal failure and in primary parathyroid hyperplasia. J Clin Invest **95:**2047–2053.
35. Massry SG, Coburn JW, Lee DB, Jowsey J, Kleeman CR 1973 Skeletal resistance to parathyroid hormone in renal failure. Studies in 105 human subjects. Ann Intern Med **78:**357–364.
36. Couttenye MM, D'Haese PC, Verschoren WJ, Behets GJ, Schrooten I, De Broe ME 1999 Low bone turnover in patients with renal failure. Kidney Int **56**(Suppl 73)**:**S70–S76.
37. Martin KJ, Freitag JJ, Bellorin-Font E, Conrades MB, Klahr S, Slatopolsky E 1980 The effect of acute acidosis on the uptake of parathyroid hormone and the production of adenosine 3′,5′-monophosphate by isolated perfused bone. Endocrinology **106:**1607–1611.

38. Bushinsky DA 1995 The contribution of acidosis to renal osteodystrophy. Kidney Int **47:**1816–1832.

39. Cunningham J, Fraher LJ, Clemens TL, Revell PA, Papapoulos SE 1982 Chronic acidosis with metabolic bone disease. Effect of alkali on bone morphology and vitamin D metabolism. Am J Med **73:**199–204.

40. Disthabanchong S, Martin KJ, McConkey CL, Gonzalez EA 2002 Metabolic acidosis up-regulates PTH/PTHrP receptors in UMR 106–01 osteoblast-like cells. Kidney Int **62:**1171–1177.

41. Frick KK, Bushinsky DA 2002 Metabolic acidosis stimulates expression of rank ligand RNA. J Am Soc Nephrol **13:**576A.

42. Mallette LE, Patten BM, Engel WK 1975 Neuromuscular disease in secondary hyperparathyroidism. Ann Intern Med **82:**474–483.

43. De Franco P, Varghese J, Brown WW, Bastani B 1994 Secondary hyperparathyroidism, and not beta 2-microglobulin amyloid, as a cause of spontaneous tendon rupture in patients on chronic hemodialysis. Am J Kidney Dis **24:**951–955.

44. Angelis M, Wong LL, Myers SA, Wong LM 1997 Calciphylaxis in patients on hemodialysis: A prevalence study. Surgery **122:**1083–1090.

45. Ketteler M 2005 Fetuin-A and extraosseous calcification in uremia. Curr Opin Nephrol Hypertens **14:**337–342.

46. Lomashvili KA, Cobbs S, Hennigar RA, Hardcastle KI, O'Neill WC 2004 Phosphate-induced vascular calcification: Role of pyrophosphate and osteopontin. J Am Soc Nephrol **15:**1392–1401.

47. London G 2002 Cardiovascular disease in end-stage renal failure: Role of calcium-phosphate disturbances and hyperparathyroidism. J Nephrol **15:**209–210.

48. London GM, Marty C, Marchais SJ, Guerin AP, Metivier F, de Vernejoul MC 2004 Arterial calcifications and bone histomorphometry in end-stage renal disease. J Am Soc Nephrol **15:**1943–1951.

49. Goodman WG, Goldin J, Kuizon BD, Yoon C, Gales B, Sider D, Wang Y, Chung J, Emerick A, Greaser L, Elashoff RM, Salusky IB 2000 Coronary-artery calcification in young adults with end-stage renal disease who are undergoing dialysis. N Engl J Med **342:**1478–1483.

50. Chertow GM, Burke SK, Raggi P 2002 Sevelamer attenuates the progression of coronary and aortic calcification in hemodialysis patients. Kidney Int **62:**245–252.

51. Shanahan CM 2005 Mechanisms of vascular calcification in renal disease. Clin Nephrol **63:**146–157.

52. Farzaneh-Far A, Shanahan CM 2005 Biology of vascular calcification in renal disease. Nephron Exp Nephrol **101:**e134–e138.

53. Giachelli CM, Jono S, Shioi A, Nishizawa Y, Mori K, Morii H 2001 Vascular calcification and inorganic phosphate. Am J Kidney Dis **38**(4 Suppl 1):S34–S37.

54. Jono S, McKee MD, Murry CE, Shioi A, Nishizawa Y, Mori K, Morii H, Giachelli CM 2000 Phosphate regulation of vascular smooth muscle cell calcification. Circ Res **87:**E10–E17.

55. Bardin T 2001 Dialysis-associated amyloidosis. In: Drueke T, Salusky I (eds.) The Spectrum of Renal Osteodystrophy. Oxford University Press, New York, NY, USA, pp. 285–307.

56. Martin KJ, Gonzalez EA 2001 The evolution of assays for parathyroid hormone. Curr Opin Nephrol Hypertens **10:**569–574.

57. D'Amour P, Brossard JH, Rousseau L, Nguyen-Yamamoto L, Nassif E, Lazure C, Gauthier D, Lavigne JR, Zahradnik RJ 2005 Structure of non-(1–84) PTH fragments secreted by parathyroid glands in primary and secondary hyperparathyroidism. Kidney Int **68:**998–1007.

58. Brossard JH, Lepage R, Gao P, Cantor T, Rousseau L, D'amour P 1999 A new commercial whole-PTH assay free of interference by non-(1–84) parathyroid hormone fragments in uremic samples. J Bone Miner Res **14:**S444.

59. Slatopolsky E, Finch J, Clay P, Martin D, Sicard G, Singer G, Gao P, Cantor T, Dusso A 2000 A novel mechanism for skeletal resistance in uremia. Kidney Int **58:**753–761.

60. Nguyen-Yamamoto L, Rousseau L, Brossard JH, Lepage R, D'Amour P 2001 Synthetic carboxyl-terminal fragments of parathyroid hormone (pth) decrease ionized calcium concentration in rats by acting on a receptor different from the pth/pth-related peptide receptor. Endocrinology **142:**1386–1392.

61. Divieti P, Inomata N, Chapin K, Singh R, Juppner H, Bringhurst FR 2001 Receptors for the carboxyl-terminal region of pth(1–84) are highly expressed in osteocytic cells. Endocrinology **142:**916–925.

62. Divieti P, John MR, Juppner H, Bringhurst FR 2002 Human PTH-(7–84) inhibits bone resorption in vitro via actions independent of the type 1 PTH/PTHrP receptor. Endocrinology **143:**171–176.

63. Langub MC, Monier-Faugere MC, Wang G, Williams JP, Koszewski NJ, Malluche HH 2003 Administration of PTH-(7–84) antagonizes the effects of PTH(1–84) on bone in rats with moderate renal failure. Endocrinology **144:**1135–1138.

64. Eknoyan G, Levin A, Levin NW 2003 Bone metabolism and disease in chronic kidney disease. Am J Kidney Dis **42**(4 Suppl 3):1–201.

65. Chertow GM, Burke SK, Lazarus JM, Stenzel KH, Wombolt D, Goldberg D, Bonventre JV, Slatopolsky E 1997 Poly[allylamine hydrochloride] (RenaGel): A noncalcemic phosphate binder for the treatment of hyperphosphatemia in chronic renal failure. Am J Kidney Dis **29:**66–71.

66. Hutchison AJ 1999 Calcitriol, lanthanum carbonate, and other new phosphate binders in the management of renal osteodystrophy. Perit Dial Int **19**(Suppl 2):S408–S412.

67. Sprague SM, Llach F, Amdahl M, Taccetta C, Batlle D 2003 Paricalcitol versus calcitriol in the treatment of secondary hyperparathyroidism. Kidney Int **63:**1483–1490.

68. Teng M, Wolf M, Lowrie E, Ofsthun N, Lazarus JM, Thadhani R 2003 Survival of patients undergoing hemodialysis with paricalcitol or calcitriol therapy. N Engl J Med **349:**446–456.

69. Finch JL, Brown AJ, Slatopolsky E 1999 Differential effects of 1,25-dihydroxy-vitamin D3 and 19-nor-1,25-dihydroxy-vitamin D2 on calcium and phosphorus resorption in bone. J Am Soc Nephrol **10:**980–985.

70. Coyne DW, Grieff M, Ahya S, Giles K, Norwood K, Slatopolsky E 2000 Differential potencies of $1,25(OH)_2D_3$ and 19-Nor-$1,25(OH)_2D_2$ on bone resorption in hemodialysis patients. J Am Soc Nephrol **11:**574A.

71. Martin KJ, Gonzalez EA 2004 Vitamin D analogs: Actions and role in the treatment of secondary hyperparathyroidism. Semin Nephrol **24:**456–459.

72. Moe SM, Chertow GM, Coburn JW, Quarles LD, Goodman WG, Block GA, Drueke TB, Cunningham J, Sherrard DJ, McCary LC, Olson KA, Turner SA, Martin KJ 2005 Achieving NKF-K/DOQI bone metabolism and disease treatment goals with cinacalcet HCl. Kidney Int **67:**760–771.

73. Fukagawa M, Kitaoka M, Tominaga Y, Akizawa T, Kurokawa K 1999 Selective percutaneous ethanol injection therapy (PEIT) of the parathyroid in chronic dialysis patients—the Japanese strategy. Japanese Working Group on PEIT of Parathyroid, Tokyo, Japan. Nephrol Dial Transplant **14:**2574–2577.

Cancer and Bone
(Section Editors: Andrew F. Stewart and Theresa Guise)

Chapter 67. Skeletal Neoplasms

Michael P. Whyte

Division of Bone and Mineral Diseases, Washington University School of Medicine at Barnes-Jewish Hospital and Center for Metabolic Bone Disease and Molecular Research, Shriners Hospitals for Children, St. Louis, Missouri

GENERAL CONSIDERATIONS

Among the acquired disorders of cartilage and bone are a variety of neoplasms. Some are malignant and cause considerable morbidity and can metastasize and kill. Others are benign and may even heal spontaneously. Rarely, skeletal tumors behave as though "transitional," with both malignant and benign features. Diagnosis and treatment of bone tumors is a complex and specialized discipline. Only a brief overview is provided here. Additional resources include several comprehensive texts devoted to this topic.[1–7]

Classification of skeletal neoplasms begins with the apparent cell or tissue type of origin (Table 1). The source of the tumor is usually revealed by the kind of tissue that the neoplastic cells make, such as osteoid or cartilage. However, in a few instances (e.g., giant cell tumor of bone), the origin is less clear.[1,5] Chromosomal defects are detected more often in malignant than in benign skeletal neoplasms.[8]

Biological behavior of bone tumors importantly influences their classification. Within the two major categories, benign and malignant, there are different degrees of aggressiveness. Biological behavior reflects the capacity of the tumor to exceed its natural barriers. Such barriers may include a tumor capsule (the shell of fibrous tissue or bone around the neoplasm), a reactive zone (composed in part of fibrous tissue or bone that forms between the capsule and normal tissue), and any adjacent articular cartilage, cortical bone, or periosteum.[1,5,7]

Skeletal neoplasms will be properly managed only when there is a thorough understanding of their clinical presentation and natural history, as well as use of current staging procedures.[9] This often requires histopathological examination.[1,5,9] Proper choice of therapy may include medical and/or surgical approaches.[1–3,5,7,10–12] Optimum patient management can depend on multidisciplinary expertise.[1–7] Improved radiological imaging,[13,14] histopathological methods, cytogenetic and molecular testing, surgical techniques, and chemotherapeutic regimens have all contributed to better survival and function of patients with skeletal sarcomas. Chemotherapy has improved the treatment of early metastatic deposits.[12–18] Consequently, aggressive limb-salvaging procedures are now possible with survival rates that were previously achieved only by radical amputation.[16,19–22]

BENIGN BONE TUMORS

Benign skeletal tumors, with only rare exceptions, do not metastasize.[23,24] Nevertheless, as a group, their biological behavior can still be variable and may range from completely inactive to quite aggressive. Fortunately, their behavior can often be predicted by noting the clinical presentation and examining the radiological features of the specific neoplasm;[4,25,26] sometimes, histopathological inspection is also essential.[1,6] Benign tumors can be classified generally as "inactive," "active," or "aggressive."[1,6,23,24]

Inactive benign bone tumors are sometimes called "latent" or "static." They are encapsulated by mature fibrous tissue or by cortical bone-like material, and do not expand or deform surrounding skeletal tissue. Individual neoplasms will have only a minimal (if any) reactive zone, and their histopathological appearance is that of a benign tumor with a low cell-to-matrix ratio, a well-differentiated matrix, and no cellular hyperchromasia, anaplasia, or pleomorphism. Inactive benign tumors are usually asymptomatic.[1,6,23,24]

Active benign bone tumors can deform or destroy adjacent cortical bone or joint cartilage as they grow, but they do not metastasize. They are encapsulated within fibrous tissue, although a thin reactive zone can develop. These neoplasms generally cause mild symptoms, but may lead to pathological fractures.[1,6,23,24]

Aggressive benign bone tumors are not uncommon in children. They show invasive properties resembling low-grade malignancies. The reactive zone forms a capsule or pseudocapsule that prevents the neoplasm itself from extending directly into normal tissue, but the tumor can resorb and destroy adjacent bone and spread to nearby skeletal compartments. Despite their aggressive behavior, the cytological features are benign—including a well-differentiated matrix. These neoplasms cause symptoms and can engender pathological fractures.[1,6,23,24]

MALIGNANT BONE TUMORS

Malignant skeletal tumors may metastasize. Nevertheless, as a group, their biological behavior also varies considerably.[1–3,5,7] Some grow slowly with a low probability of spreading elsewhere, so that there is typically a long interval between the discovery of the primary neoplasm and the development and recognition of metastases. Others are very aggressive and not only cause rapid and extensive local tissue destruction, but also have a high incidence of metastases so that primary and metastatic lesions are frequently recognized simultaneously. The biological behavior of malignant skeletal tumors can usually be predicted by their clinical, radiological,[4,25,26] and histopathological features.[1,5,6] Assessment of the histopathological type and grade is currently the best predictor of biological activity and is of paramount importance for successful treatment and accurate prognostication.[1,5,6]

Low-grade sarcomas invade local tissues, but grow slowly and have a low risk of metastasizing. They are usually asymptomatic and manifest as gradually growing masses. Nevertheless, the histopathological features of malignancy are present, such as anaplasia, pleomorphism, and hyperchromasia, together with a

TABLE 1. COMMON SKELETAL NEOPLASMS*

Tissue origin	Benign	Malignant
Osseous		Classic osteosarcoma
		Parosteal osteosarcoma
		Periosteal osteosarcoma
Cartilaginous	Enchondroma	Primary chondrosarcoma
	Exostosis	Secondary chondrosarcoma
Fibrous	Nonossifying fibroma	Fibrosarcoma
		Malignant fibrous histiocytoma
Reticuloendothelial		Ewing's sarcoma
		Multiple myeloma
Unknown	Giant cell tumor in bone	

*See Refs. 1–7 for general reviews.

The author has reported no conflicts of interest.

few mitotic cells. The tumor capsule can be disrupted in many areas, and there may be an extensive reactive zone that forms a pseudocapsule and contains satellite tumor nodules that slowly erode the various natural barriers. Over time, and after repeatedly unsuccessful surgical excision with tumor recurrences, there is a risk of transformation to a high-grade sarcoma.[1,5,6]

High-grade sarcomas readily extend beyond their reactive zone. They seem to have minimal pseudoencapsulation. Their margins are poorly demarcated. Metastases may appear in seemingly uninvolved areas of the same bone and often in the medullary canal. Extension to nearby tissues destroys cortical bone, articular cartilage, and joint capsules. These tumors show all of the histopathological features that typify malignancy and produce a poorly differentiated (immature) matrix.[1,5,6]

DIAGNOSIS OF BONE TUMORS

A thorough medical history and complete physical examination are the foundation for successful delineation and management of skeletal neoplasms.[27] The patient's age, presence or absence of predisposing conditions (e.g., Paget's disease of bone), and anatomical site of the lesion provide important clues to the precise diagnosis.

Radiological studies should be selected both to help establish the tumor type and to provide staging information that will be critical for choosing treatment and for understanding the patient's prognosis.[4,28,29] The tumor "stage" reflects the neoplasm's location and extent, as well as its biological activity or grade, and is based in part on the presence or absence of metastases.[9] Radiographs establish the tumor location, often suggest the underlying histopathological type,[4,25,26] help assess its extent, and guide the selection of additional staging studies. Clinical and radiological examination is completed before biopsy or other surgical procedures.[1,3,7,9,27]

Bone scanning helps to determine if multiple areas of neoplasm are present and if the extent of skeletal involvement exceeds conventional radiographic findings. Avidity for radionuclide uptake generally reflects the tumor's biological activity.[25,26,28,29]

CT is especially useful for precisely defining the anatomical extent of the primary lesion, detecting destruction of spongy or cortical bone, assessing compartmental changes, and locating neurovascular structures that may be impinged on by tumor or located near planned surgery.[30] This technique also supplements conventional radiography for detecting pulmonary metastases.

MRI is particularly helpful for defining soft-tissue extension and for showing any disruption of the marrow space.[29,31,32] Positron emission tomography (PET) is also proving useful.[13,33]

Angiography can help plan limb-salvage operations, because this procedure may reveal involvement of major neurovascular bundles.[4]

Arthrography assists in showing joint involvement and is therefore useful for assessing whether a cartilaginous tumor is of intra-articular or extra-articular origin.[4]

Biopsy and histopathological study are essential for successful staging and treatment of many skeletal neoplasms.[1,2,34] Open (incisional) biopsy has been the technique of choice if a malignant lesion is suspected, because it secures sufficient tissue for examination.[1,2,34] However, this procedure carries a greater risk of tumor contamination of uninvolved tissues (e.g., by dissecting hematoma) compared with closed biopsy.[35] Accordingly, open biopsy can potentially compromise a limb-salvage procedure because of added risk of local recurrence. Hence, careful attention must be paid to where the incision for biopsy is made and to the surgical technique.[1–3] Increasingly, fine-needle aspiration biopsy is used.[36] Accessible benign tumors may be removed by incisional biopsy if they are intracapsular or with en bloc marginal incision.[1–3]

INDIVIDUAL TYPES OF SKELETAL NEOPLASIA

Benign and Transitional Bone Tumors

Benign skeletal neoplasms occasionally originate from marrow elements, but most often they arise from cartilage or bone.[37] Typically, these tumors develop before skeletal maturation is complete or during the early adult years, and they are most common in areas of rapid bone growth and cellular metabolism (i.e., epiphyses and metaphyses of major long bones).[38] In some patients or families with specific heritable disorders, benign skeletal tumors (e.g., enchondromas or exostoses) are multiple and have a significantly increased risk of malignant transformation.[39,40] Most benign skeletal tumors, however, are solitary lesions and have a good prognosis.[37] The following paragraphs describe the principal types.

Nonossifying fibroma is the most common bone tumor.[41,42] This lesion is often called a "fibrous cortical defect." It represents a focal, developmental abnormality in periosteal bone formation that results in an area of failed ossification. Nonossifying fibromas most commonly occur in the metaphyses of the distal femur or distal tibia and are located eccentrically in or near the bony cortex.[4,25,26] They are somewhat more prevalent in boys than in girls, develop in the older pediatric population, and are active lesions that enlarge throughout childhood yet typically do not cause symptoms. However, when most of the diameter of a long bone is involved, pathological fracture can occur.[41,42] Radiological study may show a well-demarcated radiolucent zone with apparent trabecularization that results in a multilocular or even in a septated appearance (Fig. 1). Some cortical bone erosion may be present. The radiographic pattern can be considered diagnostic, and further staging is typically unnecessary.[4,26,27] After puberty with skeletal maturation, nonossifying fibromas become inactive or latent and ultimately ossify. Surgical intervention is usually unnecessary unless pathological fracture is a significant risk.[43] Intracapsular curettage is effective, but bone grafting or other stabilizing techniques for fracture prevention or treatment may be required.[41,42] Rarely, nonossifying fibromas cause oncogenic rickets.

Enchondroma is a benign and typically asymptomatic tumor of cartilage caused by focal disruption of endochondral bone formation. It can be considered a dysplasia of the central growth plate.[23,44] Enchondromas seem to arise in metaphyses and may eventually become incorporated into the diaphysis. Solitary lesions are usually noted in adolescence or in early adulthood. They most commonly involve small tubular bones of the hands or feet or the proximal humerus. However, several distinct disorders feature multiple enchondromas (enchondromatosis, Ollier disease, and Maffucci syndrome). A mutant PTH/PTH-related peptide (PTHrP) type I receptor has been identified.[45] Fewer than 1% of the solitary asymptomatic tumors undergo malignant transformation, but with enchondromatosis the risk is estimated to be 10%.[37,42]

Radiographs show a medullary, radiolucent lesion with a well-defined (but only slightly thickened) bony margin (Fig. 2).[4,25,26] This defect may enlarge slowly during its active phase in adolescence but calcifies when the tumor becomes latent during the adult years. Then, it has a diffusely punctate or stippled appearance (Fig. 3). In time, enchondromas become surrounded by dense reactive osseous tissue. Skeletal scintigraphy typically reflects the tumor's biological activity and shows increased radioisotope uptake in the reactive zone (greatly increased uptake suggests malignant transformation). Accordingly, it is prudent to secure a "baseline" bone scan and radiographs for young adults with multiple enchondromas.

Biopsy is often not necessary because the lesion's identity is revealed by characteristic radiography.[4,25,26] Histopathologi-

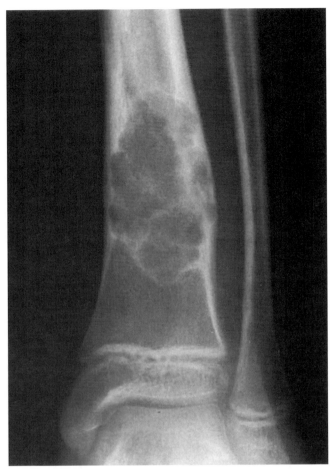

FIG. 1. Nonossifying fibroma. This 11-year-old boy has a typical, benign-appearing lesion of his distal left tibia. It is an ovoid, radiolucent, fibrous tumor located at the metadiaphyseal junction that is slightly expansile and has a multiloculated appearance with regions of cortical scalloping and thinning.

cal examination may be required, however, to distinguish benign from low-grade malignant enchondromas. Here, the patient's age is an especially important consideration.[44]

Solitary asymptomatic enchondromas are generally benign and require no treatment, although periodic follow-up is indicated. If they become symptomatic and begin to enlarge, careful surveillance is necessary.[44] Imaging techniques may be helpful to search for evidence of malignancy.[4,29,30] Surgical treatment would then be indicated.

Osteochondroma (osteocartilaginous exostosis) is a common dysplasia of cartilage involving the peripheral region of a growth plate.[23,38,44] Mutations within the *EXT1* or *EXT2* genes cause heritable forms of this disorder.[46–48] The lesion can arise in any bone that derives from cartilage, but it usually occurs in a long bone. Typically, either end of a femur, the proximal humerus or tibia, the pelvis, or the scapula is affected. Exostoses present as hard, painful masses that are fixed to bone. They enlarge during childhood but become latent in adulthood. These lesions can irritate overlying soft tissues and may form a fluid-filled bursa. A painful and enlarging exostosis during adult life, especially in the pelvis or shoulder girdle, should suggest malignant transformation to a chondrosarcoma.[38,40,44,49] Generally, exostoses are solitary, but multiple hereditary exostoses is a well-characterized, autosomal domi-

nant entity that can result in significant angular deformity of the lower limbs, clubbing of the radius, and short stature.[39]

Radiographs may show either a flat, sessile, or pedunculated metaphyseal bony lesion of variable density that is typically well defined and covered by a radiolucent cartilaginous cap (Fig. 4). Characteristically, there is continuity of tumor and metaphyseal bone.[4,26,27] The diagnosis is rarely difficult. However, after malignant transformation, there may be a soft tissue mass on CT or MRI, and a new bone scan will show suddenly or considerably increased tracer uptake.

The cartilaginous cap of an exostosis appears histopathologically like a poorly organized growth plate. The trabeculae are not remodeled and thus contain cartilage cores (primary spongiosa).

Excisional treatment of an active exostosis should include the cartilaginous cap and overlying perichondrium to minimize the chance of recurrence.[1,3,7,44] There is about a 5% recurrence rate after marginal excision of a solitary lesion. Malignant degeneration occurs in fewer than 1% of solitary lesions, but the likelihood is almost 10% for multiple hereditary exostoses.[39,40,44]

Giant cell tumor of bone (osteoclastoma) is a common benign bone neoplasm. The cellular origin, however, is unknown.[50–52] Men are more frequently affected than women,

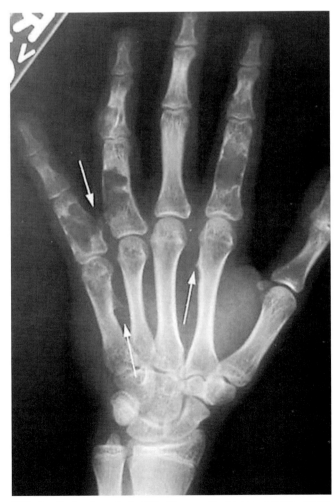

FIG. 2. Enchondromatosis. This 13-year-old girl has multiple, lucent, benign-appearing lesions of the phalanges. Each has produced expansion of the bone as well as cortical scalloping and thinning. Several periosteum-based chondromas are present that show reactive bone formation at their margins (arrows).

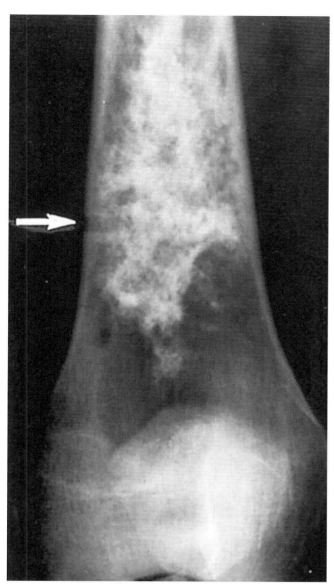

FIG. 3. Enchondroma. This 43-year-old woman has an extensively calcified lesion of the metadiaphyseal region of her distal femur. The calcification is amorphous and dense with little radiolucent component (arrow indicates a biopsy needle track). This lesion is differentiated from a bone infarction, which typically has a dense, linearly marginated periphery.

typically at 20–40 years of age. These tumors cause chronic and deep pain that mimics an arthropathy. Pathological fracture or effusion into the knee is a common presentation. Frequently, the epiphysis of a distal femur or a proximal tibia is affected. However, the distal radius, proximal humerus, distal tibia, and sacrum are also commonly involved. Often, giant cell tumors enlarge to occupy most of the epiphysis and portions of the adjacent metaphysis, and they can penetrate into subchondral bone and may even invade articular cartilage. In contrast to other benign skeletal neoplasms, they occasionally metastasize. Accordingly, giant cell tumors of bone are sometimes referred to as "transitional" neoplasms. Overexpression of the c-*myc* oncogene correlates with occurrence of metastasis.[52]

Radiographic studies show a relatively large lucent abnormality surrounded by an obvious reactive zone.[4,26,27] The cortex can appear eroded from the endosteal surface (Fig. 5). A

trabecular bone pattern may fill in the tumor cavity. Bone scanning can manifest decreased tracer uptake at the center of the lesion (the "doughnut" sign). Histopathological examination shows numerous, scattered, multinucleated giant cells in a proliferative stroma; mitoses are occasionally present.[1,6] The findings differ from the *extraskeletal osteoclastomas* that can affect exceptional patients with Paget's disease of bone.[53]

Curettage (with bone grafting or use of cement) deals with less advanced lesions. Recurrent or advanced tumors are removed with en bloc wide excision and reconstructive surgery.

Malignant Bone Tumors

Multiple myeloma, a neoplasm of marrow origin, is the most common cancer of the skeleton. However, a considerable variety of malignant tumors arise directly from bone, cartilage, fibrous tissue, histiocytes, and perhaps endothelial tissue in the skeleton itself.[1,2,5,6]

Malignant bone tumors typically cause skeletal pain that is noted particularly at night. Accordingly, this symptom, especially in adolescents or young adults, is reason for evaluation. Treatment of malignant bone tumors is complex and primarily based on the tumor grade and staging.[1,2,5,6] Only general comments are provided here and concern the principal entities.

Multiple myeloma typically develops during middle age and affects many skeletal sites. Constitutional symptoms can include bone pain, fever, malaise, fatigue, and weight loss. Often

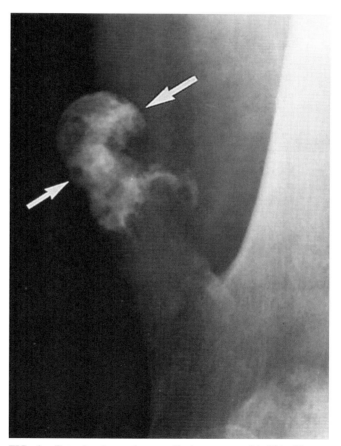

FIG. 4. Osteochondroma (osteocartilaginous exostosis). This 51-year-old woman has a typical pedunculated exostosis of her distal femur. The cortex and trabecular components of the exostosis are continuous with the host bone. Note how the exostosis slants away from the knee joint. The osteocartilaginous cap (arrows) is densely mineralized.

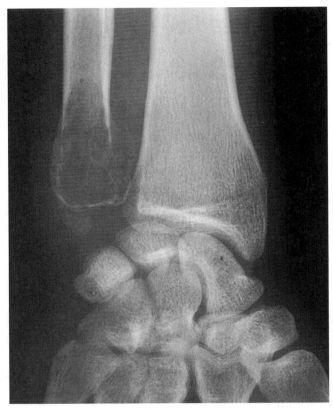

FIG. 5. Giant cell tumor. This 25-year-old man has an expansile, destructive, lucent lesion of the distal ulna. The lesion extends to the end of the bone.

there is anemia, thrombocytopenia, and renal failure.[54,55] Hypercalcemia, caused by elaboration of osteoclast-activating factors,[56] occurs in about 20–40% of patients.[57] The diagnosis is made by showing paraproteinemia using serum and urine immunoelectrophoresis and by examining bone marrow for plasmacytosis.[54] Infection with Kaposi's sarcoma-associated herpes virus[58] and overexpression of *DKK-1* leading to inactive bone formation[59] may be involved in the pathogenesis.

Radiographic findings classically include discrete, circular, osteolytic lesions, but generalized osteopenia is actually a more common presentation. Bone scintigraphy can seem unusual because of little tracer uptake in foci of osteolysis.[4,25,26,28]

Myeloma is radiation sensitive and treatable by chemotherapy. Reossification of tumor sites can occur within several months of therapy. Prevention of pathological fractures may require surgical stabilization.[54] The primary mechanism of bone destruction is increased osteoclastic action.[56] Bisphosphonate treatment has helped to decrease fractures and pain.[60,61]

Osteosarcoma (osteogenic sarcoma) is the most common primary malignancy of the skeleton.[1,7,62,63] There are about 1100–1500 new cases in the United States yearly. This cancer typically develops before age 30 and is somewhat more common in males than in females. Although most of the tumors are the "classic" variety, variants include parosteal, periosteal, and telangiectatic types that have different presentations and prognoses. Cytogenetic aberrations have been characterized.[63,64]

Classic osteosarcoma characteristically arises in the metaphysis of a long bone where there is the most rapid growth. Teenagers are usually affected. In about 50% of cases, these tumors develop near the knee in the distal femur or proximal tibia. Other commonly involved sites are the humerus, proximal femur, and pelvis, but they can begin de novo anywhere in the skeleton. Classic osteosarcomas also derive from malignant transformation of Paget's disease of bone.[65]

Typically, an osteosarcoma presents as a tender bony mass. Pain is severe and unremitting. Pathological fracture can occur. They are aggressive neoplasms that readily penetrate metaphyseal cortical bone, and the majority have already infiltrated surrounding soft tissues at the time of diagnosis. At presentation, about 50% of affected adolescents show penetration of their growth plates with epiphyseal involvement, about 20% have metastases elsewhere in the cancerous bone and, in approximately 10%, the tumor has spread to lymph nodes or to lung.[62]

Radiographic study shows a destructive lesion that is composed of amorphous osseous tissue with poorly defined margins.[4,25,26,66] Some osteosarcomas are predominantly osteoblastic and radiographically dense; others are predominantly osteolytic and radiolucent. Some have a mixed pattern.[25,26] Cortical bone destruction is often apparent (Fig. 6). A characteristic "sunburst" configuration results from spicules of amorphous neoplastic osseous tissue forming perpendicularly to the long axis of the affected bone. This is in contrast to the parallel

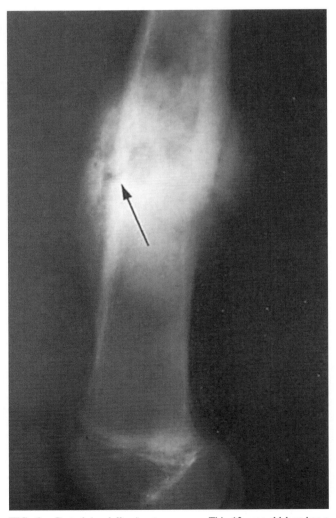

FIG. 6. Central (medullary) osteosarcoma. This 12-year-old boy has a sclerotic diaphyseal lesion that arose in the medullary cavity. It has penetrated the cortex and produced a densely mineralized mass surrounding the femur. Portions of the cortex seem to have been destroyed (arrow), whereas other regions are thickened.

or "onion skin" appearance of reactive periosteal new bone. Codman's triangle results from reaction and elevation of the periosteum that demarcates a triangular area of cortical bone (see Fig. 8). Bone scintigraphy shows intense uptake of tracer and may disclose more widespread disease than by conventional radiography.[65] CT, MRI, PET, and angiography are helpful, as discussed previously. Microscopic examination typically shows a very malignant stroma that produces an amorphous and immature osteoid in a trabecular pattern.[1–7]

Use of chemotherapy preoperatively[11,18,25,62] has significantly improved the prognosis for this malignancy, and has enabled many osteosarcoma patients to be managed by limb-salvage procedures instead of radical amputation.[7,10,21]

Parosteal osteosarcomas are juxtacortical (i.e., they develop between the bony cortex and the soft tissue as a surface neoplasm). Adolescents and young adults are most commonly affected by these slowly growing, low-grade tumors that typically occur as a fixed and painless mass posteriorly on the distal femur or medially on the proximal humerus. They are less aggressive than classic osteosarcomas and can remain separated for a considerable length of time from the parent bone by a narrow radiolucent region of soft tissue. Eventually, they may involve the underlying skeleton and degenerate into a high-grade osteosarcoma.[62]

Radiographic study typically reveals a densely ossified, broad-based, fusiform mass that seems to encircle the metaphyseal region of a long bone (Fig. 7).[4,25,26,66] Reactive tissue initially separates the neoplasm from the underlying bone that is destroyed once the tumor penetrates the normal cortex into the medullary canal. Parosteal osteosarcomas have mature trabeculae with cement lines resembling Paget's disease of bone,[10] however, a low-grade malignant stroma is present. This tumor is often misdiagnosed as benign. Limb-salvage with wide marginal excision is the usual treatment for less advanced disease. The prognosis is good. Chemotherapy is typically not used unless there has been dedifferentiation of the neoplasm.[10,18,62]

Periosteal osteosarcoma often presents as a painless growing mass that extends from the surface of a bone into soft tissue.[62] This uncommon variant of classic osteosarcoma typically affects young adults. Radiological study shows a poorly mineralized mass primarily on a bone surface in an area of cortical erosion. The crater-like lesion has irregular margins with periosteal reaction.[4,25,26] Penetration through cortical bone into the medullary canal occurs more rapidly than with parosteal osteosarcoma. If this complication has occurred, the likelihood of pulmonary metastasis is greater—contributing to its poorer prognosis. Bone scintigraphy shows avid tracer uptake.[66] CT reveals a mass that fills a shallow cortical bone defect but contains minimal calcification. Malignant mesenchymal stroma with neoplastic osteoid occurs in, and around, areas of mature cartilage.[4,6,25,26]

Periosteal osteosarcoma is often treated by excision with a wide margin.[56] Adjuvant chemotherapy is used when the tumor has regions of high-grade malignancy.[15,18]

Chondrosarcoma occurs most often between 40 and 60 years of age, when this neoplasm develops as a primary tumor.[44,67] About 25% of patients manifest malignant transformation in a pre-existing enchondroma or osteocartilaginous exostosis. Thus, chondrosarcomas usually involve the pelvis, proximal femur, or shoulder girdle. Patients initially experience a persistent dull ache that can mimic arthritis. Variants of the classic form of chondrosarcoma include a high-grade, dedifferentiated neoplasm, an intermediate-grade, clear cell type, and a low-grade, juxtacortical tumor. The particular designation depends on the histopathological pattern and anatomical location.[44,67]

Radiographs show a subtle radiolucent lesion that contains hazy or speckled calcification in a diffuse "salt and pepper" or

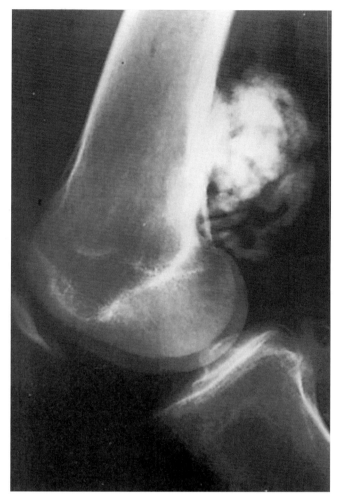

FIG. 7. Parosteal osteosarcoma. This 30-year-old woman has a very densely mineralized mass arising from the periosteal surface of the distal femoral metaphysis posteriorly. This tumor has lobular calcification and is attached to the femur by a broad pedicle.

"popcorn" pattern.[4,25,26] Primary chondrosarcomas can develop either within the medullary canal or on the surface of a bone where they may destroy the cortex and form a mass. On histopathological examination, it can be difficult to show that high-grade tumors are cartilaginous in origin, or that low-grade tumors are actually malignant.[44,50]

Treatment of chondrosarcomas depends on the tumor stage. Limb amputation may be necessary for higher grade tumors. Adjuvant chemotherapy or radiation therapy has been disappointing.[44]

Ewing sarcoma is a highly malignant neoplasm that arises from nonmesenchymal cells in the bone marrow.[68–71] This cancer usually harbors a pathognomonic t(11:12)(q24;q12) translocation[72] and represents a form of primitive neuroectodermal tumor.[66] It typically presents in 10- to 15-year-old children and more commonly affects boys than girls.[1,68–71] Initial manifestations include an enlarging and tender soft tissue swelling together with weight loss, malaise, fever, and lethargy. The erythrocyte sedimentation rate may be elevated, and there can be leukocytosis and anemia. The diaphysis of the femur is most commonly involved; alternatively, an ilium, tibia, fibula, or rib is affected. When this cancer occurs in the pelvis, it is usually found late and has an especially poor prognosis.[1,68–71]

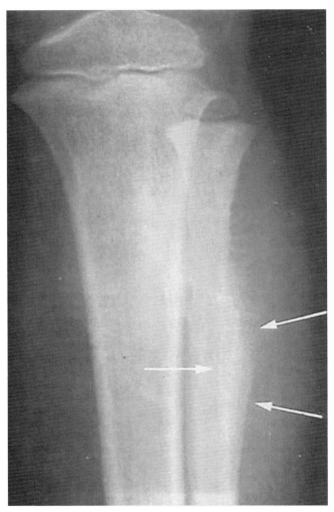

FIG. 8. Ewing sarcoma. This 5-year-old boy has a subtle permeative lesion of the proximal diaphysis of his fibula. The tumor is characterized by layered (onion skin) periosteal reaction forming a Codman's triangle (arrows) and by "sunburst" new bone formation more proximally, which is characteristically perpendicular to the bone's long axis. A large soft tissue mass is associated with the skeletal defects.

Radiological study typically reveals a diaphyseal lesion of patchy density that destroys cortical bone and frequently causes an "onion skin" appearance of reactive periosteum (Fig. 8).[4,25,26] Bone scanning may show intense tracer uptake that extends considerably beyond the radiographic abnormality.

Chemotherapy can be followed by wide excision or radiation therapy, depending on, among other factors, the anatomical site. Newer therapeutic approaches have reduced the incidence of pulmonary metastases and have markedly improved survival.[1,73] Zoledronic acid may be helpful.[74] Histological response to preoperative chemotherapy and tumor size are important predictors of event-free survival.[17]

Malignant fibrous histiocytoma occurs more frequently in soft tissues than in the skeleton and is less common than benign fibrous tumors.[1,3,42] This cancer affects adults and often originates in Paget's disease of bone or at the site of a skeletal infarct. Typically, this is an aggressive sarcoma that readily spreads within the lymphatics. Bone is infiltrated early on, and pathological fracture is a common presentation.

Radiological study reveals a poorly defined radiolucent le-

sion that causes cortical bone erosion.[4,23,25] The histopathological pattern is variable from area to area; extremely large and bizarre histiocytic cells are found in some sections, and undifferentiated cells that resemble histiocytic lymphoma are noted in others. Areas that contain fibrous tissue may suggest that the tumor is a fibrosarcoma. Special stains and electron microscopy can be required to establish the diagnosis.[5,6,75] Staging studies direct the therapy, which may require radical resection or amputation and perhaps chemotherapy.[1,44] The prognosis is guarded.[44,75]

Fibrosarcoma causes pain and typically arises in a major long bone of an adolescent or young adult.[1–5,42] Radiological study reveals a poorly defined and destructive lucent lesion in a metaphysis.[4,25,26] Low-grade and high-grade fibrosarcomas have similar radiological and histopathological appearances. Accordingly, electron microscopy may be necessary to reveal the collagenous composition of the matrix of a high-grade tumor.[6,42] Therapy depends on the staging results.[1,3,5]

Metastatic bone tumors are considerably more common than primary skeletal malignancies (with a ratio of about 25 to 1).[1,4,5] Prostate, breast, thyroid, lung, and kidney cancers are the principal neoplasms that metastasize to bone. There is predilection for malignant cells to deposit within blood-forming marrow spaces in the spine, ribs, skull, pelvis, and metaphyses of long bones (particularly the femur and humerus). In children, metastases within the skeleton usually reflect a neuroblastoma, leukemia, or Ewing sarcoma. In teenagers or young adults, lymphomas are the predominant source. After age 30, an adenocarcinoma is the likely primary. Osteoblastic metastases most commonly derive from carcinoma of the prostate or breast. Osteolytic metastases may come from the lung, thyroid, kidney, or gastrointestinal tract.[4,25,27] In a significant number of patients, the origin is not evident, and staging studies with biopsy[36] are performed to explore the possibility of an intrinsic skeletal sarcoma.[1–3,5,6]

REFERENCES

1. Dorfman HD, Czerniak B 1997 Bone Tumors. Mosby-Year Book, St. Louis, MO, USA.
2. Levesque J 1998 Clinical Guide to Primary Bone Tumors. Williams & Wilkins, Baltimore, MD, USA.
3. Simon M 1997 Surgery for Bone and Soft-Tissue Tumors. Lippincott-Raven Publishers, Philadelphia, PA, USA.
4. Wilner D 1997 Wilner's Radiology of Bone Tumors. W. B. Saunders, Philadelphia, PA, USA.
5. Unni K, Dahlin DC 1996 Dahlin's Bone Tumors: General Aspects and Data on 11,087 Cases, 5th ed. Lippincott-Raven, Philadelphia, PA, USA.
6. Greenspan A, Remagen W 1998 Differential Diagnosis of Tumors and Tumor-Like Lesions of Bones and Joints. Lippincott-Raven, Philadelphia, PA, USA.
7. Simon MA, Springfield DS 1998 Surgery for Bone and Soft-Tissue Tumors. Lippincott-Raven, Philadelphia, PA, USA.
8. Ozaki T, Wai D, Schaefer KL, Goshager G, Boecker W, Dockhorn-Dworniczak B, Poremba CH 2004 Genetic imbalances in benign bone tumors revealed by comparative genomic hybridization. Neoplasma. **51:** 456–459.
9. Heare TC, Enneking WF, Heare MM 1989 Staging techniques and biopsy of bone tumors. Orthop Clin North Am **20:**273–285.
10. Choong PF, Sim FH 1997 Limb-sparing surgery for bone tumors: New developments. Semin Oncol **13:**64–69.
11. Biermann JS, Baker LH 1997 The future of sarcoma treatment. Semin Oncol **24:**592–597.
12. Bielack SS, Machatschek JN, Flege S, Jurgens H 2004 Delaying surgery with chemotherapy for osteosarcoma of the extremities. Expert Opin Pharmacother **5:**1243–1256.
13. Dimitrakopoulou-Strauss A, Strauss LG, Heichel T, Wu H, Burger C, Bernd L, Ewerbeck V 2002 The role of quantitative (18)F-FDG PET studies for the differentiation of malignant and benign bone lesions. J Nucl Med **43:**510–518.
14. Littrell LA, Wenger DE, Wold LE, Bertoni F, Unni KK, White LM,

Kandel R, Sundaram M 2004 Radiographic, CT, and MR imaging features of dedifferentiated chondrosarcomas: A retrospective review of 174 de novo cases. Radiographics 24:1397–1409.

15. Jaffe N 1989 Chemotherapy for malignant bone tumors. Orthop Clin North Am 20:487–503.
16. Sweetnam R 1989 Malignant bone tumor management: 30 years of achievement. Clin Orthop 247:67–73.
17. Wunder JS, Paulian AG, Huvos AG, Heller G, Meyers PA, Healey JH 1998 The histological response to chemotherapy as a predictor of the oncological outcome of operative treatment of Ewing sarcoma. J Bone Joint Surg Am 80:1020–1033.
18. Bramwell VH 1997 The role of chemotherapy in the management of non-metastatic operable extremity osteosarcoma. Semin Oncol 24:561–571.
19. Nichter LS, Menendez LR 1993 Reconstructive considerations for limb salvage surgery. Orthop Clin North Am 24:511–521.
20. McDonald DJ 1994 Limb-salvage surgery for treatment of sarcomas of the extremities. Am J Roentgenol 163:509–513.
21. 1991 In: Langlais F, Tomeno B (eds.) Limb Salvage: Major Reconstruction in Oncologic and Nontumoral Conditions. Springer-Verlag, Berlin, Germany.
22. Weis LD 1999 The success of limb-salvage surgery in the adolescent patient with osteogenic sarcoma. Adolesc Med 10:451–458.
23. Scarborough MT, Moreau G 1996 Benign cartilage tumors. Orthop Clin North Am 27:583–589.
24. Yildiz C, Erler K, Atesalp AS, Basbozkurt M 2003 Benign bone tumors in children. Curr Opin Pediatr 15:58–67.
25. Edeiken J, Dalinka M, Karasick D 1990 Edeiken's Roentgen Diagnosis of Diseases of Bone, 4th ed. Williams and Wilkins, Baltimore, MD, USA.
26. Resnick D, Niwayama G 2002 Diagnosis of Bone and Joint Disorders, 4th ed. WB Saunders, Philadelphia, PA, USA.
27. Simon MA, Finn HA 1993 Diagnostic strategy for bone and soft-tissue tumors. J Bone Joint Surg Am 75:622–631.
28. Brown ML 1993 Bone scintigraphy in benign and malignant tumors. Radiol Clin North Am 31:731–738.
29. Murphy WA Jr 1991 Imaging bone tumors in the 1990s. Cancer 67:1169–1176.
30. Magid D 1993 Two-dimensional and three-dimensional computed tomographic imaging in musculoskeletal tumors. Radiol Clin North Am 31:425–447.
31. Berquist TM 1993 Magnetic resonance imaging of primary skeletal neoplasms. Radiol Clin North Am 31:411–424.
32. Redmond OM, Stack JP, Dervan PA, Hurson BJ, Carney DN, Ennis JT 1989 Osteosarcoma: Use of MR imaging and MR spectroscopy in clinical decision making. Radiology 172:811–815.
33. Cook GJ, Fogelman I 2001 The role of positron emission tomography in skeletal disease. Semin Nucl Med 31:50–61.
34. Simon MA, Biermann JS 1993 Biopsy of bone and soft-tissue lesions. J Bone Joint Surg Am 75:616–621.
35. Schwartz HS, Spengler DM 1997 Needle tract recurrences after closed biopsy for sarcoma: Three cases and review of the literature. Ann Surg Oncol 4:228–236.
36. Wedin R, Bauer HC, Skoog L, Soderlund V, Tani E 2000 Cytological diagnosis of skeletal lesions. Fine-needle aspiration biopsy in 110 tumours. J Bone Joint Surg Br 82:673–678.
37. Giudici MA, Moser RP Jr., Kransdorf MJ 1993 Cartilaginous bone tumors. Radiol Clin North Am 31:237–259.
38. Schubiner JM, Simon MA 1987 Primary bone tumors in children. Orthop Cl n North Am 18:577–595.
39. Wicklund CL, Pauli RM, Johnston D, Hecht JT 1995 Natural history study of hereditary multiple exostoses. Am J Med Genet 55:43–46.
40. Ozaki T, Hillmann A, Blasius S, Link T, Winkelmann W 1998 Multicentric malignant transformation of multiple exostoses. Skeletal Radiol 27:233–236.
41. Hudson TM, Stiles RG, Monson DK 1993 Fibrous lesions of bone. Radiol Clin North Am 31:279–297.
42. Marks KE, Bauer TW 1989 Fibrous tumors of bone. Orthop Clin North Am 20:377–393.
43. Jee WH, Choe BY, Kang HS, Suh KJ, Suh JS, Ryu KN, Lee YS, Ok IY, Kim JM, Choi KH, Shinn KS 1998 Nonossifying fibroma: Characteristics at MR imaging with pathological correlation. Radiology 209:197–202.
44. Greenspan A 1989 Tumors of cartilage origin. Orthop Clin North Am 20:347–366.
45. Hopyan S, Gokgoz N, Poor R, Gensure RC, Yu C, Cole WG, Bell RS, Juppner H, Andrulis IL, Wunder JS, Alman BA 2002 A mutant PTH/PTHrP type I receptor in enchondromatosis. Nat Genet 30:306–310.
46. McCormick C, Leduc Y, Martindale D, Mattison K, Esford LE, Dyer AP, Tufaro F 1998 The putative tumour suppressor EXT1 alters the expression of cell-surface heparan sulfate. Nat Genet 19:158–161.
47. Bridge JA, Nelson M, Orndal C, Bhatia P, Neff JR 1998 Clonal karyotypic abnormalities of the hereditary multiple exostoses chromosomal loci 8q24.1 (EXT1) and 11p11–12 (EXT2) in patients with sporadic and hereditary osteochondromas. Cancer 82:1657–1663.
48. McCormick C, Duncan G, Tufaro F 1999 New perspectives on the molecular basis of hereditary bone tumors. Mol Med Today 5:481–486.
49. Merchan EC, Sanchez-Herrera S, Gonzalez JM 1993 Secondary chondrosarcoma. Four cases and review of the literature. Acta Orthop Belg 59:76–80.
50. Manaster BJ, Doyle AJ 1993 Giant cell tumors of bone. Radiol Clin North Am 31:299–323.
51. Richardson MJ, Dickinson IC 1998 Giant cell tumor of bone. Bull Hosp Jt Dis 57:6–10.
52. Gamberi G, Benassi MS, Bohling T, Ragazzini P, Molendini L, Sollazzo MR, Merli M, Ferrari C, Magagnoli G, Bertoni F, Picci P 1998 Prognostic relevance of C-myc gene expression in giant-cell tumor of bone. J Orthop Res 16:1–7.
53. Ziambaras K, Totty WA, Teitelbaum SL, Dierkes M, Whyte MP 1997 Extraskeletal osteoclastomas responsive to dexamethasone treatment in Paget bone disease. J Clin Endocrinol Metab 82:3826–3834.
54. Osserman EF, Merlini G, Butler VP Jr 1987 Multiple myeloma and related plasma cell dyscrasias. JAMA 258:2930–2937.
55. Lacy MQ, Gertz MA, Hanson CA, Inwards DJ, Kyle RA 1997 Multiple myeloma associated with diffuse osteosclerotic bone lesions: A clinical entity distinct from osteosclerotic myeloma (POEMS syndrome). Am J Hematol 56:288–293.
56. Roodman GD 1997 Mechanisms of bone lesions in multiple myeloma and lymphoma. Cancer 80:1557–1563.
57. Mundy GR 1989 Calcium Homeostasis: Hypercalcemia and Hypocalcemia. Martin Dunitz, London, UK.
58. Berenson JR, Vescio RA, Said J 1998 Multiple myeloma: The cells of origin–a two-way street. Leukemia 12:121–127.
59. Tian E, Zhan F, Walker R, Rasmussen E, Ma Y, Barlogie B, Shaughnessy JD Jr 2003 The role of the Wnt-signaling antagonist DKK1 in the development of osteolytic lesions in multiple myeloma. N Engl J Med 349:2483–2494.
60. Bloomfield DJ 1998 Should bisphosphonates be part of the standard therapy of patients with multiple myeloma or bone metastases from other cancers? An evidence-based review. J Clin Oncol 16:1218–1225.
61. Ashcroft AJ, Davies FE, Morgan GJ 2003 Aetiology of bone disease and the role of bisphosphonates in multiple myeloma. Lancet Oncol 4:284–292.
62. Meyers PA 1987 Malignant bone tumors in children: Osteosarcoma. Hematol Oncol Clin North Am 1:655–665.
63. Meyers PA, Gorlick R 1997 Osteosarcoma. Pediatr Clin North Am 44:973–989.
64. Bridge JA, Nelson M, McComb E, McGuire MH, Rosenthal H, Vergara G, Maale GE, Spanier S, Neff JR 1997 Cytogenetic findings in 73 osteosarcoma specimens and a review of the literature. Cancer Genet Cytogenet 95:74–87.
65. Hadjipavlou A, Lander P, Srolovitz H, Enker IP 1992 Malignant transformation in Paget disease of bone. Cancer 70:2802–2808.
66. Fletcher BD 1997 Imaging pediatric bone sarcomas. Diagnosis and treatment-related issues. Radiol Clin North Am 35:1477–1494.
67. Welkerling H, Dreyer T, Delling G 1991 Morphological typing of chondrosarcoma: A study of 92 cases. Virchows Arch 418:419–425.
68. Horowitz ME, Tsokos MG, DeLaney TF 1992 Ewing's sarcoma. Cancer J 42:300–320.
69. Eggli KD, Quiogue T, Moser RP Jr 1993 Ewing's sarcoma. Radiol Clin North Am 31:325–337.
70. Lawlor ER, Lim JF, Tao W, Poremba C, Chow CJ, Kalousek IV, Kovar H, MacDonald TJ, Sorensen PH 1998 The Ewing tumor family of peripheral primitive neuroectodermal tumors expresses human gastrin-releasing peptide. Cancer Res 58:2469–2476.
71. Grier HE 1997 The Ewing family of tumors. Ewing's sarcoma and primitive neuroectodermal tumors. Pediatr Clin North Am 44:991–1004.
72. Maurici D, Perez-Atayde A, Grier HE, Baldini N, Serra M, Fletcher JA 1998 Frequency and implications of chromosome 8 and 12 gains in Ewing sarcoma. Cancer Genet Cytogenet 100:106–110.
73. Sandoval C, Meyer WH, Parham DM, Kun LE, Hustu HO, Luo X, Pratt CB 1996 Outcome in 43 children presenting with metastatic Ewing sarcoma; the St. Jude Children's Research Hospital experience, 1962 to 1992. Med Pediatr Oncol 26:180–185.
74. Zhou Z, Guan H, Duan X, Kleinerman ES 2005 Zoledronic acid inhibits primary bone tumor growth in Ewing sarcoma. Cancer 104:1713–1720.
75. Womer RB 1991 The cellular biology of bone tumors. Clin Orthop 262:12–21.

Chapter 68.   Mechanisms of Bone Destruction and Formation by Metastatic Tumors

Gregory A. Clines and Theresa A. Guise

Division of Endocrinology and Metabolism, Department of Medicine, The University of Virginia, Charlottesville, Virginia

INTRODUCTION

Cancer adversely affects bone and mineral metabolism through a broad spectrum of mechanisms. These include focal osteolysis at sites of metastases, hypercalcemia, and diffuse osteopenia. As early as 1889, Stephen Paget recognized the diversity of effects, stating that "in a cancer of the breast the bones suffer in a special way, which cannot be explained by any theory of embolism alone. . . the same thing is seen much more clearly in those cases of cancer of the thyroid body where secondary deposition occurs in bones with astonishing frequency." He further observed, "A general degradation of the bones sometimes occurs in carcinoma of the breast, yet without any distinct deposition of cancer in them." These were prescient observations, as it is now recognized that cancer affects bone through systemic humoral mechanisms and by direct metastatic invasion.[1,2] This review will focus on pathogenic bone remodeling as a consequence of cancer metastasis to bone.

The potential for tumor metastasis, especially to bone, is greater with certain types of cancers. Breast, prostate, lung, and renal cancers all frequently metastasize to bone, and bone metastases are present in nearly all patients with advanced breast or prostate cancer. Bone is the third most common site of metastasis of solid tumors after the liver and the lung. Metastatic bone disease is often classified as osteoblastic or osteolytic, but in reality, most bone lesions fall in between these two extremes. In fact, bone metastases may display extreme heterogeneity even in the same patient.[3]

Breast cancer is one of a limited number of primary neoplasms that display osteotropism, an extraordinary affinity to grow in bone. This property has provided a key paradigm for our understanding of the metastatic process. Paget, during his observations of breast cancer in 1889, proposed the "seed and soil" hypothesis to explain this phenomenon. "When a plant goes to seed, its seeds are carried in all directions; but they can only grow if they fall on congenial soil." In essence, the microenvironment of the organ to which the cancer cells metastasize may serve as a fertile soil on which the seeds (or cancer cells) may grow. This century-old concept remains a basic principle of our understanding of cancer metastasis, guiding current progress in the research of molecules produced by bones and tumor cells to enrich the vicious cycle of secondary tumor growth.

CHEMOTAXIS, INVASION, AND ADHESION

For metastasis to occur, a tumor cell must (1) detach from the primary site; (2) enter the systemic vasculature through the permeable neovasculature of the tumor; (3) survive host immune response and physical forces in the circulation; (4) arrest in a distant capillary bed; (5) escape the capillary bed; and (6) proliferate in the metastatic site.[1] A number of molecules have been identified that promote tumor cell escape, including E-cadherin, osteonectin, osteopontin, and urokinase. However, the chemokine system, integrins, and matrix metalloproteinases

have convincingly been shown to play a more direct role in bone metastasis. Platelets may also assist circulating cancer cells in the development of metastasis.

CXCR4

The chemokine receptor CXCR4 is abundantly expressed in breast cancer cells and involved in cellular migration. The CXCR4 ligand, stromal cell derived factor 1 (SDF-1) (CXCL12), is present in tissues that represent common sites of metastasis, including bone marrow. CXCR4 was one of a tool box of genes, upregulated in the highly bone metastatic MDA-MB-231 breast cancer,[4] that likely causes the breast cancer cells to home to bone. Neutralizing antibodies to CXCR4 impaired breast cancer metastasis to regional lymph nodes and lung in a mouse model,[5] as well as PC3 prostate cancer metastases to bone.[6] CXCR4-expressing prostate cancer cell lines adhered to bone marrow endothelial cells when treated with SDF-1 and migrated across an SDF-1 gradient.[7] Recent evidence indicates that bisphosphonates may affect this process because YM529 (minodoronate) decreased CXCR4 expression and invasiveness of prostate cancer cell lines in an animal model of bone metastasis.[8]

Integrins

Bone marrow stromal cells express the vascular cell adhesion molecule-1 (VCAM-1), a ligand for $\alpha_4\beta_1$ integrin.[9] CHO cells transfected with an $\alpha_4\beta_1$ integrin expression construct invaded bone and lung when inoculated intravenously into nude mice compared with lung invasion alone in mice inoculated with parental Chinese hamster ovary (CHO) cells.[10] Neutralizing antibodies to $\alpha_4\beta_1$ integrin or VCAM-1 inhibited development of these bone lesions. However, overexpression of $\alpha_3\beta_1$, $\alpha_6\beta_1$, or $\alpha_v\beta_1$ integrins did not produce similar results in this animal model. The $\alpha_v\beta_3$ integrin receptor binds the arginine-glycine-aspartic acid (RGD) peptide sequence present on a variety of extracellular matrix proteins, including osteopontin, vitronectin, and bone sialoprotein. This integrin is important in homing and, possibly, invasion of tumor cells into the bone endosteum.[11] In an animal model of bone metastasis, an $\alpha_v\beta_3$ antagonist suppressed the development of bone lesions after intracardiac inoculation of MDA-MB-435 breast cancer cells.[12]

Matrix Metalloproteinases

The matrix metalloproteinases (MMPs) are a family of at least 28 zinc-dependent proteinases that are either bound to the extracellular membrane or secreted within the local environment.[13] The expression of MMPs has been found to be increased in most cancer types including breast and prostate.[14,15] High levels of MMPs have been associated with poor prognosis.[16] MMPs participate in the progression of cancer metastasis not only by the degradation of matrix leading to invasion but also by the alteration of signaling molecules affecting tumor growth and migration. This process is manifested through the cleavage of tethered signaling molecules such as insulin-like growth factor binding protein 1, E-cadherin, fibroblast growth factor (FGF) receptor 1, and pro-TGF-β.[17–19] MMP-3 and MMP-7 cleave cell membrane-associated RANKL to a soluble form, resulting in osteoclast activation in an in

Dr. Guise is on the Board of Directors for IBMS and the Paget's Foundation and is a consultant for Novartis, Merck, and Abbott. Dr. Clines has reported no conflicts of interest.

vitro model, suggesting MMPs have a role in osteolytic bone metastasis.[20] Furthermore, MMP-1 was upregulated in the highly bone metastatic MDA-MB-231 breast cancer.[4] MMP-1 may contribute to osteolysis by promoting collagen degradation at the bone surface to make such a surface more attractive to osteoclastic bone resorption.

Platelets

Collective evidence from recent studies supports the role of platelets in promoting metastasis. While it has long been recognized that cancer patients are hypercoagulable, this association may be caused by direct and reciprocal interactions between the cancer cells and platelets. Platelets may "coat" circulating tumor cells thereby protecting them from attack from the immune system and enhancing their ability to adhere to disrupted vascular endothelium.[21] Cancer cell–mediated platelet aggregation may also result in the release of platelet vascular endothelial growth factor (VEGF), platelet-derived growth factor (PDGF), and thrombospondin-1 promoting cancer cell survival and angiogenesis. MDA-MB-231 breast cancer cells promote platelet aggregation and release of lysophosphatidic acid (LPA).[22] LPA receptors on cancer cells enhanced cellular proliferation, stimulated the production of osteolytic factors, such as interleukin (IL)-8, and increased the size of MDA-MB-231 subcutaneous tumors and osteolytic bone lesions in a mouse model of osteolytic bone metastasis. Moreover, integrilin, an $\alpha_{IIb}\beta_3$ antagonist and inhibitor of platelet aggregation, reduced osteolytic bone lesion area in this model.[22]

LOCAL TUMOR SYNDROMES IN BONE

Osteolytic Metastasis

Secondary tumor deposition in bone frequently causes osteolysis or bone destruction at the site of deposition. Breast cancer is the most common tumor type to do so, although prostate, lung, renal, and thyroid tumors are all associated with osteolytic lesions. The following discussion will focus on breast cancer as a model for cancer-mediated osteolysis.

Breast Cancer as the "Seed." Osteolysis is the ability to cause destruction of the hard, mineralized matrix. Breast cancer cells in vitro secrete proteolytic enzymes capable of destroying bone. In vivo, however, it seems that tumors cells are not active effectors of bone destruction, particularly during the establishment of metastasis. Histological analysis and scanning electron microscopy of osteolytic bone metastases indicate that osteoclasts adjacent to tumor cells actively resorb bone. This would suggest that breast cancer cells have the ability to stimulate osteoclastic bone resorption.

PTH-Related Peptide as a Mediator of Osteolysis. PTH-related peptide (PTHrP) plays a local paracrine role in the establishment and progression of breast cancer bone metastasis even in the absence of detectable increases in its plasma concentration with malignant hypercalcemia.[23] PTHrP is expressed by 50–60% of human primary breast cancers. In a mouse model of bone metastasis using the breast cancer cell line MDA-MB-231, a neutralizing antibody to PTHrP(1-34) reduced the number and size of osteolytic bone lesions. Histomorphometric analysis of long bones of mice treated with the PTHrP antibody revealed significantly fewer osteoclasts at the tumor–bone interface and less tumor than controls.[23] When mice with established osteolytic metastases caused by MDA-MB-231 were treated with the PTHrP antibody, an appreciable decrease in the rate of progression of disease compared with controls was observed.[24,25] Conversely, when MDA-MD-231

cells were engineered to overproduce PTHrP, an increase in the number of osteolytic lesions was seen.[26] The breast cancer cell line, MCF-7, does not express PTHrP and is not associated with osteolytic lesions. However, when engineered to overexpress PTHrP, MCF-7 cells induced marked bone destruction and increased osteoclast formation as compared with controls.[27]

Tumor-produced PTHrP drives the expression of RANKL and inhibits osteoprotegerin (OPG) secretion from osteoblasts and stromal cells. This stimulates osteoclastogenesis through the RANK located on osteoclast precursors.[2] While PTHrP expression by tumor cells within the bone microenvironment results in osteolysis, PTHrP expression by the primary tumor does not predict the development of bone metastasis. Overexpression of PTHrP in a murine primary mammary cancer in vivo resulted in the development of hypercalcemia but not bone metastasis.[28] Consistent with this, and in contrast to early, smaller clinical studies, are data from the largest prospective study of >300 breast cancer patients. Here, women with PTHrP-negative primary tumors were more likely to develop bone metastases than patients with PTHrP-positive primary tumors.[29]

Differences in PTHrP Expression Between Primary Tumor and Metastases. Interestingly, it is now known that PTHrP expression by tumor cells at the primary site differs significantly from PTHrP expression of tumor cells at sites of metastasis. PTHrP expression is higher in breast cancer cells that have metastasized to bone compared with nonbone sites.[1,2] Breast cancer tissue from primary tumors and bone metastases in three patients were analyzed. In these three cases, the bone metastases were PTHrP positive and the respective primary tumors were PTHrP negative. This is the only published study able to compare, in an individual patient, PTHrP expression in the primary tumor and at the metastatic site.[29] Two theories, which are not mutually exclusive, can be made from these observations. First, PTHrP stimulates osteolysis, thus promoting tumor growth in bone. Second, the bone microenvironment enhances expression of PTHrP in metastatic cancer cells. Studies with larger numbers of patients are needed to confirm these observations. Taken together, the data suggest that PTHrP is not important in the establishment of osteolytic bone metastases but is critical in the progression of osteolytic bone destruction.

Other Factors. Tumor cells also produce other important factors that lead to osteolysis. When IL-6, IL-11, and VEGF are secreted by osteolytic breast cancer cell lines after TGF-β stimulation, they potentiate the effects of PTHrP on osteoclastic bone resorption.[30,31] IL-8 production correlates with an increased metastatic potential in MDA-MB-231 cells but seems to be independent of PTHrP secretion.[32] IL-8, a potent osteolytic factor, is produced by tumor cells in response to activated platelet production of lysophosphatidic acid.[22] IL-11 was one of a cohort of genes upregulated in the highly bone metastatic MDA-MB-231 breast cancer cell line.[4] Its contribution to breast cancer osteolysis is obvious, by promoting osteoclastic bone resorption.

Interestingly, breast cancer cells express genes thought to be restricted to osteoblasts, bone sialoprotein and osteopontin; these genes are regulated by Runx2. The transcription factor Runx2 (Cbfa1) directs mesenchymal cells to the osteoblast lineage and is critical for osteoblast development. Stable expression of a dominant-negative Runx2 mutant or of a Runx2 mutant containing a point mutation in the nuclear matrix-targeting signal sequence in MDA-MB-231 cells blocked the cells' ability to form osteolytic bone lesions in animal models.[33,34] Thus, breast cancer cells may act as surrogate osteoblasts to support osteoclast formation.

Bone Microenvironment as the "Soil." Immobilized within the mineralized bone matrix is a rich trove of growth factors. These growth factors are released from the matrix by osteoclastic bone resorption during the normal course of physiological bone remodeling required to maintain structural integrity of bone. Thus, once tumor cells arrest in bone, the high concentrations of cytokines and growth factors in the microenvironment provide a fertile soil in which to grow. The environment is further enriched as the tumor cells stimulate osteoclastic bone resorption, leading to the release of more bone-derived growth factors that enhance survival and growth of the cancer, while simultaneously disrupting normal bone remodeling thus resulting in bone destruction.

TGF-β. TGF-β promotes invasion and metastasis in the transformed cancer cell and has a distinct role to promote bone metastasis through its effects to stimulate tumor production of osteolytic factors. TGF-β mobilized from the bone matrix increases metastasis of breast cancer by stimulating tumor production of PTHrP.[19] The signaling pathways by which TGF-β stimulates osteolytic factor production is cell and context specific. For example, the effects of TGF-β to stimulate PTHrP are mediated by both the Smad and p38 mitogen-activated protein kinase (MAPK) pathways in the MDA-MB-231 breast cancer cell line.[35] TGF-β stimulates production of the osteolytic factor, IL-11, and the pro-metastatic factor connective tissue growth factor (CTGF) through the Smad pathway in another variant of the MDA-MB-231 line.[4] Furthermore, knockdown of Smad4 through the siRNA approach reduced bone metastases by MDA-MB-231. Through immunohistochemical analysis of human breast cancer bone metastasis and functional imaging of the Smad pathway in this mouse xenograft model, Kang et al.[36] provided evidence for active Smad signaling in human and mouse bone metastatic lesions.

Other Osteolysis-Stimulating Factors. Osteoclastic resorption of bone releases high concentrations of ionized calcium and phosphate from the dissolution of the bone mineral. The calcium-sensing receptor (CaSR) is a G protein–coupled, seven-transmembrane domain receptor, which responds to small variations in the concentration of extracellular calcium.[37] CaSR is expressed by breast cancer cells and regulates tumor secretion of PTHrP,[38,39] an effect that is enhanced by TGF-β. Thus, the high concentrations of ionized calcium in bone may contribute to the vicious cycle by increasing PTHrP production and osteolysis. Small molecule agonists and antagonists of CaSR have been developed and are in clinical trials.[40] Such agents might be effective against breast cancer bone metastasis. The IGFs are also released into the local bone environment during osteolysis and likely also have a role in the proliferation of bone metastasis.[41,42] Hauschka et al.[43] found that IGF-II, then -I, was the most abundant factor in bone matrix, followed by TGF-β, after which were lower concentrations of bone morphogenetic proteins (BMPs), FGF-1 and -2, and PDGF.

Interactions Between Tumor and Bone—the "Vicious Cycle." The arrival of tumor cells in bone marks the beginning of complex interactions that occur with the bone-forming osteoblasts, bone-destroying osteoclasts, and the mineralized bone matrix (Fig. 1). Tumor cells secrete factors into the bone microenvironment that stimulate osteoclastic bone resorption directly (IL-8, TNF-α, and VEGF) or indirectly (PTHrP, IL-6,

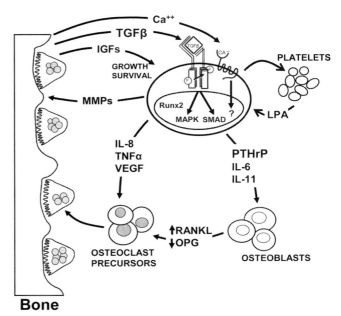

Bone

FIG. 1. Bone resorption in breast cancer osteolytic metastasis. Tumor cells secrete factors into the bone microenvironment that support osteoclastogenesis. Tumor-produced PTHrP, IL-6, and IL-11 increase osteoblast RANKL and decrease OPG activity, resulting in increased osteoclastogenesis. IL-8, TNF-α, and VEGF secreted by tumor cells also enhance osteoclast formation but are independent of the RANK/RANKL axis. MMPs produced from tumor cells may prime the bone surface for osteoclast attachment. The escalation in bone resorption leads to the release of factors immobilized in the mineralized bone matrix such as TGF-β. TGF-β stimulates tumor cells to produce even more osteolytic factors; thus, the "vicious cycle" of osteolytic bone metastases begins. The transcription factor Runx2 also plays a role in tumor cell activation. Other factors immobilized in bone that are released during osteoclast-mediated resorption include members of the IGF family. Increased calcium concentration as a consequence of enhanced bone resorption may also lead to tumor cell activation.

and IL-11) through the osteoblast through modulation of the RANK/RANKL axis. The dissolution of the bone matrix results in the release of a vast storehouse of matrix-immobilized growth factors, such as IGFs and TGF-β. These are synthesized by osteoblasts during the deposition of osteoid. Increasing concentrations of these factors in the bone metastasis microenvironment further stimulate nearby tumor cells to produce even more osteolytic factors. Therapies targeting this vicious cycle would be expected to reduce metastasis by decreasing growth factor concentrations in bone.

Multiple Myeloma

Although multiple myeloma bone disease is not a metastatic process per se, this malignancy shares similarities with breast cancer metastasis in that tumor-produced factors stimulate osteolysis resulting in the release of immobilized factors that further stimulate myeloma cells (Fig. 2). Almost all patients with multiple myeloma have extensive bone destruction that may occur either as discrete local lesions or as diffuse involvement throughout the axial skeleton. The increased bone resorption is responsible for a number of disabling features, including susceptibility to pathological fracture, intractable bone pain, and in some patients, hypercalcemia. Approximately 80% of patients with myeloma present with the chief complaint of bone pain. Hypercalcemia occurs in between 20% and 40% of patients at some time during the course of the disease.

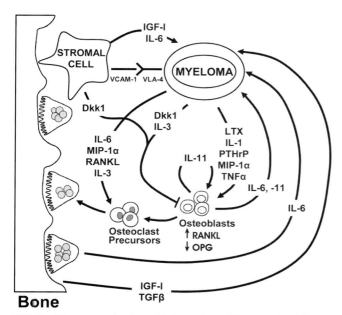

FIG. 2. Bone resorption in multiple myeloma. Numerous local factors have been identified in the bone microenvironment that contribute to increased bone resorption and osteolytic disease. IGF-I and IL-6 secreted by bone marrow stromal cells and the VLA-4/VCAM-1 interaction increase myeloma proliferation and survival. Myeloma cells produce IL-6, RANKL, and MIP-1α that ultimately lead to an increase in osteoclast activity and numbers. Myeloma cells also secrete Dkk1 and IL-3, resulting in suppression of osteoblast activity.

Stimulation of Myeloma Cells by the Bone Microenvironment. Identification of myeloma-stimulating factors within the bone microenvironment has been elusive. IL-6 produced by both osteoclasts and osteoblasts is mitogenic and reduces apoptosis in myeloma cells.[2] IGF-I produced by bone marrow stromal cells also contributes to myeloma survival and activates a signal transduction pathway that is independent of IL-6 signaling.[44] Osteoclast activity promotes myeloma survival; severe combined immunodeficient (SCID) mice inoculated with human myeloma cells show inhibition of myeloma growth in the presence of the bisphosphonates pamidronate and zoledronic acid.[45]

Stimulation of Osteoclastogenesis by Myeloma Cells. The bone destruction that occurs in myeloma is caused by an increase in the number and activity of osteoclasts. Myeloma cells in the marrow cavity produce cytokines that activate adjacent endosteal osteoclasts to resorb bone. IL-6 is secreted by myeloma cells and osteoblast precursors as a consequence of myeloma cell adherence. Myeloma cells also induce osteoblast production of IL-11. However, neither IL-11 nor IL-6 are potent bone-resorbing factors alone and likely cooperate with other factors. IL-3 is increased in multiple myeloma patients and promotes osteoclastogenesis.[46,47]

Myeloma-produced macrophage inflammatory protein-1α (MIP-1α) is a member of the RANTES family of chemokines. MIP-1α is a potent osteoclast stimulatory factor with an increased marrow plasma concentration in 70% of myeloma patients.[47] MIP-1α enhances osteoclast formation induced by IL-6, PTHrP, and RANKL.[48] MIP-1α neutralizing antibodies blocked osteoclast formation in bone marrow cultures treated with human myeloma bone marrow plasma[49] and reduced osteolysis in an in vivo mouse myeloma model.[50]

An important mediator of osteoclastogenesis in myeloma bone disease is RANKL. Association of this factor with RANK on osteoclast precursors is key to the development of mature osteoclasts. Marrow stromal cells from myeloma patients have increased expression of RANKL, presumably as a consequence of the myeloma cells.[51] Another source of RANKL is from myeloma cells themselves,[52] bypassing osteoblast and bone marrow stromal cell intermediaries. In a mouse model of multiple myeloma, a RANKL neutralizing antibody prevented myeloma bone destruction.[53]

Myeloma cells express the cell surface molecule VLA-4 (α4β1-integrin), a receptor that has affinity for fibronectin and vascular cell adhesion molecule-1 (VCAM-1). Bone marrow stromal cells express VCAM-1, thereby presumably promoting recruitment of myeloma to bone. Disruption of the VLA-4/VCAM-1 interaction in vitro resulted in decreased osteoclastic activity and was independent of other bone microenvironment cytokines, including IL-1, IL-6, TNF-α, and PTHrP.[9] The VLA-4/VCAM-1 system also has a role in the regulation of RANKL and OPG. Bone marrow stromal cells had increased RANKL and decreased OPG expression when co-cultured with myeloma cells, thereby promoting an environment for enhanced osteoclastogenesis. This imbalance of RANKL/OPG was inhibited in the presence of a VLA-4 neutralizing antibody.[54]

Suppression of Bone Formation in Myeloma Bone Disease. Dickkopf homolog 1 (Dkk1) is involved in the suppression of osteoblast activity in multiple myeloma.[55] Dkk1 mRNA concentrations were increased in plasma cells of patients with more advanced disease, and Dkk1 protein levels were higher in the bone marrow plasma and peripheral blood of patients with myeloma bone disease compared with controls. Dkk1 is a secreted inhibitor of the Wnt signaling pathway and binds to the LDL receptor–related proteins 5 and 6 (LRP5 and 6), preventing interaction of these co-receptors with the frizzled (Frz) receptor family.[56]

The Wnt pathway is important in the differentiation of mesenchymal stem cells to mature osteoblasts. Dkk1 seems to alter the bone microenvironment by suppressing osteoblast differentiation.[55] In vitro experiments support this statement. The addition of recombinant Dkk1 to osteoblast cultures decreased BMP-2–mediated increases in alkaline phosphatase, a marker of osteoblast differentiation.[55] Dkk1 also blocked the osteoblast proliferative effects of endothelin-1.[57] Low concentrations of this factor may have a role in promoting osteoblastic disease of prostate cancer and some breast cancers. Preclinical studies with a Dkk1 neutralizing antibody shows promise. In a mouse model of myeloma bone disease, an anti-Dkk1 antibody increased osteoblast activation and osteoclast inactivation and decreased bone loss and tumor burden.[58]

An additional role for Dkk1 in other osteolytic diseases is likely. Human prostate cancer PC-3 cells produce osteolytic lesions in a mouse model of bone metastasis. PC-3 cells abundantly expressed Dkk1 compared with the osteoblastic prostate cancer cell lines C4–2B and LuCaP-35. PC-3 cells were stably transfected with a Dkk1 siRNA construct and tested in an in vitro mineralization assay. These clones failed to stimulate mineralization. Furthermore, an opposite response was observed in C4–2B cells that overexpress Dkk1.[59]

Increased concentrations of IL-3 in the bone marrow plasma of myeloma patients stimulate osteoclast formation but may also inhibit osteoblast differentiation. In a recent report, IL-3 decreased osteoblast differentiation of murine stromal cell cultures and human bone marrow aspirates and blocked BMP-2–mediated osteoblast differentiation. Additionally, an IL-3 neutralizing antibody enhanced osteoblast differentiation from bone marrow plasma derived from myeloma patients.[60]

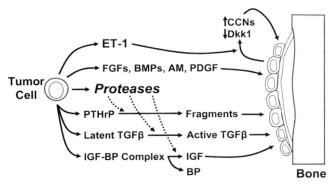

FIG. 3. Bone formation in prostate cancer osteoblastic metastasis. Prostate cancer cells stimulate osteoblast proliferation and new bone formation though secretion of factors into the bone microenvironment, including ET-1, FGFs, BMPs, adrenomedullin, and PDGF. Tumor-produced ET-1 stimulates osteoblast activity by decreasing secretion of the Wnt pathway inhibitor Dkk1. ET-1 may also lead to an increase in CCN proteins, which may further support osteoblastic bone metastasis. Tumor production of proteases, most notably prostate specific antigen, cleaves PTHrP, TGF-β, and IGF from its binding protein, resulting in the generation of fragments with osteoblast stimulating activity.

Osteoblastic Metastasis

Osteoblastic bone metastasis is commonly associated with prostate cancer and to a lesser degree with breast cancer. Just as with breast cancer–mediated osteolysis, the seed and soil hypothesis applies to prostate cancer in that the bone microenvironment readily supports the growth of prostate cancer cells. The key difference, however, is that prostate tumor cells secrete factors that stimulate bone formation rather than destruction (Fig. 3).

Endothelin-1. Endothelin-1 (ET-1) is a 21 amino acid peptide that was first identified as a potent vasoconstrictor but has since been found to have multiple physiologic functions and an important role in osteoblastic bone metastasis.[61] The biological actions of ET-1 are transmitted through activation of specific G protein–coupled receptors. Two receptors have been identified: the endothelin A receptor (ETAR) and the endothelin B receptor (ETBR).[61]

Tumor-produced ET-1 is implicated in the pathogenesis of osteoblastic metastasis.[62] The human breast cancer cell line ZR-75–1 produces osteoblastic bone lesions in nude mice and abundantly secretes ET-1. ET-1 stimulated osteoblast activity and new bone formation; these responses were blocked by an ETAR antagonist, ABT-627, but not by ETBR blockade. ABT-627 blocked development and progression of ZR-75–1 osteoblastic bone metastases in nude mice. The drug had no effect on mammary tumors or on bone metastases because of ET-1–negative MDA-MB-231 breast cancer cells. The former result suggests that ETAR blockade may have a bone-specific effect on metastasis, a fact that was borne out in clinical trials described below.

ET-1 also contributes to bone metastasis of human prostate cancer. (1) Prostate epithelial cells secrete large amounts of ET-1 into seminal fluid compared with plasma.[63,64] (2) ET-1 is secreted by the majority of prostate cancer cell lines.[65] (3) Plasma ET-1 concentrations are higher in men with advanced prostate cancer than in men with local disease or in age-matched controls.[65] (4) Prostate cancer expression of ETAR is higher in men with more aggressive disease.[66] (5) ETAR blockade benefits prostate cancer patients with bone metastases. In a phase II clinical study, the ETAR antagonist atrasentan (ABT-627) delayed progression and decreased prostate-specific antigen (PSA) compared with the control group in men with hormone refractory disease.[67] In addition, atrasentan reduced markers of bone formation (bone alkaline phosphatase) and bone resorption (N-telopeptide) in men with prostate cancer bone metastases.[68] In a large phase III placebo-controlled trial of atrasentan in men with advanced prostate cancer,[69] there was a significant decrease in the progression of bone metastasis but not in overall disease progression.[70] These clinical data again suggest that the effects of ETAR blockade are bone specific.

Results from animal and human clinical studies support a model in which tumor-produced ET-1 mediates pathological bone formation by acting on osteoblast ETAR. These findings also suggest that the effect of ET-1 to stimulate tumor growth is dependent on the osteoblast. The vicious cycle model predicts that osteoblasts, osteoclasts, and tumor cells cooperate to cause the pathology of bone metastases. The endothelin receptor antagonist blocks the activation of osteoblasts by tumor-produced ET-1. This reduction in osteoblast activity was associated with a reduction in bone resorption and suggests that the bone resorption associated with osteoblastic bone metastasis may be a secondary event because ETAR antagonists have no direct effects on osteoclastic bone resorption.[68]

Downstream mediators of the effects of ET-1 on the osteoblast were identified by microgene array analysis of ET-1–treated osteoblasts. ET-1 suppressed osteoblast production of Dkk1, and Dkk1 blocked osteoblast activation by ET-1. These results suggest that ET-1 mediates its effects on bone formation by activating the Wnt signaling pathway, findings that are consistent with dysregulation of this pathway in multiple myeloma. ET-1 also stimulated osteoblast production of IL-6 and CCN proteins, CTGF and Cyr61—factors that could contribute to the vicious cycle by affecting bone cell function, tumor growth, and angiogenesis.[57]

Other Osteoblastic Factors. Other factors that may contribute to osteoblastic metastasis include IGFs, PSA, and TGF-β. However, these factors remain to be critically tested. Such factors need to meet two initial criteria: (1) ability to stimulate osteoblastic new bone formation and (2) expression by cancer cells. Adrenomedullin (AM) is a 52 amino acid vasoactive peptide with potent bone stimulatory actions,[71] which is produced by many cancers.[72] In lung and prostate cancer cell lines, AM increases bone metastases in vivo.[73] It is also an autocrine growth factor for breast cancer cells,[74] but its role in breast cancer bone metastasis has not yet been investigated. Yi et al.[75] overexpressed platelet-derived growth factor B-chain (PDGF-BB) in MDA-MB-231 cells and observed osteosclerotic rather than osteolytic metastases.

A puzzling question has been the role of PTHrP in osteoblastic metastasis, especially those caused by prostate cancer, which nearly always express PTHrP. A partial explanation was provided by the observation that PSA is a serine proteinase, which cleaves PTHrP after residue 23.[1,2] The resulting fragment fails to activate the classical PTH/PTHrP receptor. It was later observed that the inactive fragment PTHrP1–16 increased cAMP in cardiomyocytes by activating ETAR. Binding was attributed to a four amino acid near-identity between the two peptides.[76] PTHrP-1–23 is a potent stimulator of new bone formation. The results suggest that PSA proteolysis, rather than inactivating PTHrP, converts it from an osteolytic factor to a potent osteoblastic one. This process may occur in breast and prostate cancer bone metastasis. Proteolytic cleavage of IGF from its binding protein and the processing of latent TGF-β to the active form may also contribute to osteoblast stimulation.[1,2]

Tumor cells may also secrete factors that oppose the development and progression of bone metastasis. IL-18, which decreases osteoclast formation, is one such factor made by cancer cells.[77,78] This unexplored territory may reveal exciting new approaches for future anti-metastatic therapies. Similarly, the role of the immune system in bone metastasis is understudied,[79] as is angiogenesis.[80]

REFERENCES

1. Mundy GR 2002 Metastasis to bone: Causes, consequences and therapeutic opportunities. Nature Rev Cancer **2:**584–593.
2. Roodman GD 2004 Mechanisms of bone metastasis. N Engl J Med **350:**1655–1664.
3. Roudier MP, Vesselle H, True LD, Higano CS, Ott SM, King SH, Vessella RL 2003 Bone histology at autopsy and matched bone scintigraphy findings in patients with hormone refractory prostate cancer: The effect of bisphosphonate therapy on bone scintigraphy results. Clin Exp Metast **20:**171–180.
4. Kang Y, Siegel PM, Shu W, Drobnjak M, Kakonen SM, Cordon-Cardo C, Guise TA, Massague AJ 2003 A multigenic program mediating breast cancer metastasis to bone. Cancer Cell **3:**537–549.
5. Muller A, Homey B, Soto H, Ge N, Catron D, Buchanan ME, McClanahan T, Murphy E, Yuan W, Wagner SN, Barrera JL, Mohar A, Verastegui E, Zlotnik A 2001 Involvement of chemokine receptors in breast cancer metastasis. Nature **410:**50–56.
6. Sun YX, Schneider A, Jung Y, Wang J, Dai J, Wang J, Cook K, Osman NI, Koh-Paige AJ, Shim H, Pienta KJ, Keller ET, McCauley LK, Taichman RS 2005 Skeletal localization and neutralization of the SDF-1(CXCL12)/CXCR4 axis blocks prostate cancer metastasis and growth in osseous sites in vivo. J Bone Miner Res **20:**318–329.
7. Taichman RS, Cooper C, Keller ET, Pienta KJ, Taichman NS, McCauley LK 2002 Use of the stromal cell-derived factor-1/CXCR4 pathway in prostate cancer metastasis to bone. Cancer Res **62:**1832–1837.
8. Miwa S, Mizokami A, Keller ET, Taichman R, Zhang J, Namiki M 2005 The bisphosphonate YM529 inhibits osteolytic and osteoblastic changes and CXCR-4-induced invasion of prostate cancer. Cancer Res **65:**8818–8825.
9. Michigami T, Shimizu N, Williams PJ, Niewolna M, Dallas SL, Mundy GR, Yoneda T 2000 Cell-cell contact between marrow stromal cells and myeloma cells via VCAM-1 and alpha(4)beta(1)-integrin enhances production of osteoclast-stimulating activity. Blood **96:**1953–1960.
10. Matsuura N, Puzon-McLaughlin W, Irie A, Morikawa Y, Kakudo K, Takada Y 1996 Induction of experimental bone metastasis in mice by transfection of integrin alpha 4 beta 1 into tumor cells. Am J Pathol **148:**55–61.
11. Felding-Habermann B, O'Toole TE, Smith JW, Fransvea E, Ruggeri ZM, Ginsberg MH, Hughes PE, Pampori N, Shattil SJ, Saven A, Mueller BM 2001 Integrin activation controls metastasis in human breast cancer. Proc Natl Acad Sci USA **98:**1853–1858.
12. Harms JF, Welch DR, Samant RS, Shevde LA, Miele ME, Babu GR, Goldberg SF, Gilman VR, Sosnowski DM, Campo DA, Gay CV, Budgeon LR, Mercer R, Jewell J, Mastro AM, Donahue HJ, Erin N, Debies MT, Meehan WJ, Jones AL, Mbalaviele G, Nickols A, Christensen ND, Melly R, Beck LN, Kent J, Rader RK, Kotyk JJ, Pagel MD, Westlin WF, Griggs DW 2004 A small molecule antagonist of the alpha(v)beta3 integrin suppresses MDA-MB-435 skeletal metastasis. Clin Exp Metast **21:**119–128.
13. Egeblad M, Werb Z 2002 New functions for the matrix metalloproteinases in cancer progression. Nature Rev Cancer **2:**161–174.
14. Bachmeier BE, Nerlich AG, Lichtinghagen R, Sommerhoff CP 2001 Matrix metalloproteinases (MMPs) in breast cancer cell lines of different tumorigenicity. Anticancer Res **21:**3821–3828.
15. Upadhyay J, Shekarriz B, Nemeth JA, Dong Z, Cummings GD, Fridman R, Sakr W, Grignon DJ, Cher ML 1999 Membrane type 1-matrix metalloproteinase (MT1-MMP) and MMP-2 immunolocalization in human prostate: Change in cellular localization associated with high-grade prostatic intraepithelial neoplasia. Clin Cancer Res **5:**4105–4110.
16. Nakopoulou L, Tsirmpa I, Alexandrou P, Louvrou A, Ampela C, Markaki S, Davaris PS 2003 MMP-2 protein in invasive breast cancer and the impact of MMP-2/TIMP-2 phenotype on overall survival. Breast Cancer Res Treat **77:**145–155.
17. Stamenkovic I 2003 Extracellular matrix remodelling: The role of matrix metalloproteinases. J Pathol **200:**448–464.
18. Dallas SL, Rosser JL, Mundy GR, Bonewald LF 2002 Proteolysis of latent transforming growth factor-beta (TGF-beta)-binding protein-1 by osteoclasts. A cellular mechanism for release of TGF-beta from bone matrix. J Biol Chem **277:**21352–21360.
19. Yin JJ, Selander K, Chirgwin JM, Dallas M, Grubbs BG, Wieser R, Massague J, Mundy GR, Guise TA 1999 TGF-beta signaling blockade inhibits PTHrP secretion by breast cancer cells and bone metastases development. J Clin Invest **103:**197–206.
20. Lynch CC, Matrisian LM 2003 Osteoprotegerin ligand is cleaved to a soluble functional form by MMP-3 and MMP-7. The IVth International Conference on Cancer-Induced Bone Diseases, San Antonio, TX, December 7–9, 2003.
21. Palumbo JS, Talmage KE, Massari JV, La Jeunesse CM, Flick MJ, Kombrinck KW, Jirouskova M, Degen JL 2005 Platelets and fibrin(ogen) increase metastatic potential by impeding natural killer cell-mediated elimination of tumor cells. Blood **105:**178–185.
22. Boucharaba A, Serre CM, Gres S, Saulnier-Blache JS, Bordet JC, Guglielmi J, Clezardin P, Peyruchaud O 2004 Platelet-derived lysophosphatidic acid supports the progression of osteolytic bone metastases in breast cancer. J Clin Invest **114:**1714–1725.
23. Guise TA, Yin JJ, Taylor SD, Kumagai Y, Dallas M, Boyce BF, Yoneda T, Mundy GR 1996 Evidence for a causal role of parathyroid hormone-related protein in the pathogenesis of human breast cancer-mediated osteolysis. J Clin Invest **98:**1544–1549.
24. Guise TA, Mundy GR 1996 Physiological and pathological roles of parathyroid hormone-related peptide. Curr Opin Nephrol Hypertens **5:**307–315.
25. Yin JJ, Taylor SD, Yoneda T, Dallas M, Boyce BF, Kumagai Y, Mundy GR, Guise TA 1995 Evidence that parathyroid hormone-related protein (PTHrP) cause osteolytic metastases without hypercalcemia. J Bone Miner Res **10:**S169.
26. Guise TA, Taylor SD, Yoneda T, Sasaki A, Wright KR, Boyce BF, Chirgwin JM, Mundy GR 1994 PTHrP expression by breast cancer cells enhance osteolytic bone metastases in vivo. J Bone Miner Res **9:**S128.
27. Thomas RJ, Guise TA, Yin JJ, Elliott J, Horwood NJ, Martin TJ, Gillespie MT 1999 Breast cancer cells interact with osteoblasts to support osteoclast formation. Endocrinology **140:**4451–4458.
28. Wysolmerski JJ, Dann PR, Zelazny E, Dunbar ME, Insogna KL, Guise TA, Perkins AS 2002 Overexpression of parathyroid hormone-related protein causes hypercalcemia but not bone metastases in a murine model of mammary tumorigenesis. J Bone Mine Res **17:**1164–1170.
29. Henderson M, Danks J, Moseley J, Slavin J, Harris T, McKinlay M, Hopper J, Martin T 2001 Parathyroid hormone-related protein production by breast cancers, improved survival, and reduced bone metastases. J Natl Cancer Inst **93:**234–237.
30. de la Mata J, Uy HL, Guise TA, Story B, Boyce BF, Mundy GR, Roodman GD 1995 Interleukin-6 enhances hypercalcemia and bone resorption mediated by parathyroid hormone-related protein in vivo. J Clin Invest **95:**2846–2852.
31. Kakonen SM, Kang Y, Carreon MR, Niewolna M, Kakonen RS, Chirgwin JM, Massague J, Guise TA 2002 Breast cancer cell lines selected from bone metastases have greater metastatic capacity and express increased vascular endothelial growth factor (VEGF), interleukin-11 (IL-11), and parathyroid hormone-related protein (PTHrP). J Bone Miner Metab **17:**M060.
32. Bendre MS, Gaddy-Kurten D, Mon-Foote T, Akel NS, Skinner RA, Nicholas RW, Suva LJ 2002 Expression of interleukin 8 and not parathyroid hormone-related protein by human breast cancer cells correlates with bone metastasis in vivo. Cancer Res **62:**5571–5579.
33. Barnes GL, Hebert KE, Kamal M, Javed A, Einhorn TA, Lian JB, Stein GS, Gerstenfeld LC 2004 Fidelity of Runx2 activity in breast cancer cells is required for the generation of metastases-associated osteolytic disease. Cancer Res **64:**4506–4513.
34. Javed A, Barnes GL, Pratap J, Antkowiak T, Gerstenfeld LC, van Wijnen AJ, Stein JL, Lian JB, Stein GS 2005 Impaired intranuclear trafficking of Runx2 (AML3/CBFA1) transcription factors in breast cancer cells inhibits osteolysis in vivo. Proc Natl Acad Sci USA **102:**1454–1459.
35. Kakonen SM, Selander KS, Chirgwin JM, Yin JJ, Burns S, Rankin WA, Grubbs BG, Dallas M, Cui YB, Guise TA 2002 Transforming growth factor-beta stimulates parathyroid hormone-related protein and osteolytic metastases via Smad and mitogen-activated protein kinase signaling pathways. J Biol Chem **277:**24571–24578.
36. Kang Y, He W, Tulley S, Gupta GP, Serganova I, Chen CR, Manova-Todorova K, Blasberg R, Gerald WL, Massague J 2005 Breast cancer bone metastasis mediated by the Smad tumor suppressor pathway. Proc Natl Acad Sci USA **102:**13909–13914.
37. Yamaguchi T, Chattopadhyay N, Brown EM 2000 G protein-coupled extracellular Ca2+ (Ca2+o)-sensing receptor (CaR): Roles in cell signaling and control of diverse cellular functions. Adv Pharmacol **47:**209–253.
38. Buchs N, Manen D, Bonjour JP, Rizzoli R 2000 Calcium stimulates parathyroid hormone-related protein production in Leydig tumor cells

through a putative cation-sensing mechanism. Eur J Endocrinol **142:**500–505.

39. Sanders JL, Chattopadhyay N, Kifor O, Yamaguchi T, Butters RR, Brown EM 2000 Extracellular calcium-sensing receptor expression and its potential role in regulating parathyroid hormone-related peptide secretion in human breast cancer cell lines. Endocrinology **141:**4357–4364.

40. Nemeth EF 2002 Pharmacological regulation of parathyroid hormone secretion. Curr Pharmaceut Design **8:**2077–2087.

41. Sachdev D, Yee D 2001 The IGF system and breast cancer. Endoc Relat Cancer **8:**197–209.

42. Yoneda T, Williams PJ, Hiraga T, Niewolna M, Nishimura R 2001 A bone-seeking clone exhibits different biological properties from the MDA-MB-231 parental human breast cancer cells and a brain-seeking clone in vivo and in vitro. J Bone Miner Res **16:**1486–1495.

43. Hauschka PV, Mavrakos AE, Iafrati MD, Doleman SE, Klagsbrun M 1986 Growth factors in bone matrix. Isolation of multiple types by affinity chromatography on heparin-Sepharose. J Biol Chem **261:**12665–12674.

44. Ferlin M, Noraz N, Hertogh C, Brochier J, Taylor N, Klein B 2000 Insulin-like growth factor induces the survival and proliferation of myeloma cells through an interleukin-6-independent transduction pathway. Br J Haematol **111:**626–634.

45. Yaccoby S, Pearse RN, Johnson CL, Barlogie B, Choi Y, Epstein J 2002 Myeloma interacts with the bone marrow microenvironment to induce osteoclastogenesis and is dependent on osteoclast activity. Br J Haematol **116:**278–290.

46. Lee JW, Chung HY, Ehrlich LA, Jelinek DF, Callander NS, Roodman GD, Choi SJ 2004 IL-3 expression by myeloma cells increases both osteoclast formation and growth of myeloma cells. Blood **103:**2308–2315.

47. Roodman GD 2005 Mechanisms of bone destruction in myeloma. Skeletal Complications of Malignancy IV, Bethesda, MD, USA, April 28–30, 2005.

48. Han JH, Choi SJ, Kurihara N, Koide M, Oba Y, Roodman GD 2001 Macrophage inflammatory protein-1alpha is an osteoclastogenic factor in myeloma that is independent of receptor activator of nuclear factor kappaB ligand. Blood **97:**3349–3353.

49. Choi SJ, Cruz JC, Craig F, Chung H, Devlin RD, Roodman GD, Alsina M 2000 Macrophage inflammatory protein 1-alpha is a potential osteoclast stimulatory factor in multiple myeloma. Blood **96:**671–675.

50. Oyajobi BO, Mundy GR 2003 Receptor activator of NF-kappaB ligand, macrophage inflammatory protein-1alpha, and the proteasome. Cancer **97:**813–817.

51. Roux S, Meignin V, Quillard J, Meduri G, Guiochon-Mantel A, Fermand JP, Milgrom E, Mariette X 2002 RANK (receptor activator of nuclear factor-kappaB) and RANKL expression in multiple myeloma. Br J Haematol **117:**86–92.

52. Sezer O, Heider U, Jakob C, Zavrski I, Eucker J, Possinger K, Sers C, Krenn V 2002 Immunocytochemistry reveals RANKL expression of myeloma cells. Blood **99:**4646–4647.

53. Pearse RN, Sordillo EM, Yaccoby S, Wong BR, Liau DF, Colman N, Michaeli J, Epstein J, Choi Y 2001 Multiple myeloma disrupts the TRANCE/ osteoprotegerin cytokine axis to trigger bone destruction and promote tumor progression. Proc Natl Acad Sci USA **98:**11581–11586.

54. Giuliani N, Bataille R, Mancini C, Lazzaretti M, Barille S 2001 Myeloma cells induce imbalance in the osteoprotegerin/osteoprotegerin ligand system in the human bone marrow environment. Blood **98:**3527–3533.

55. Tian E, Zhan F, Walker R, Rasmussen E, Ma Y, Barlogie B, Shaughnessy JDJ 2003 The role of the Wnt-signaling antagonist DKK1 in the development of osteolytic lesions in multiple myeloma. N Engl J Med **349:**2483–2494.

56. Mao B, Wu W, Li Y, Hoppe D, Stannek P, Glinka A, Niehrs C 2001 LDL-receptor-related protein 6 is a receptor for Dickkopf proteins. Nature **411:**321–325.

57. Clines GA, Mohaddad KS, Wessner LL, Chirgwin JM, Guise TA 2005 Endothelin-1 stimulates bone formation by regulating osteoblast secretion of the paracrine regulators IL-6, Cyr61, CTGF and Dkk1. J Bone Miner Res **20:**S249.

58. Yaccoby S, Zhan F, Barlogie B, Shaughnessy JD 2005 Blocking Dkk1 activity in primary myeloma-bearing SCID-rab mice is associated with increased osteoblast activity and bone formation, and inhibition of tumor growth. J Bone Miner Res **20:**S33.

59. Hall CL, Bafico A, Dai J, Aaronson SA, Keller ET 2005 Prostate cancer

cells promote osteoblastic bone metastases through Wnts. Cancer Res **65:**7554–7560.

60. Ehrlich LA, Chung HY, Ghobrial I, Choi SJ, Morandi F, Colla S, Rizzoli V, Roodman GD, Giuliani N 2005 IL-3 is a potential inhibitor of osteoblast differentiation in multiple myeloma. Blood **106:**1407–1414.

61. Masaki T 2000 The endothelin family: An overview. J Cardiovasc Pharmacol **35:**S3–S5.

62. Yin JJ, Mohammad KS, Kakonen SM, Harris S, Wu-Wong JR, Wessale JL, Padley RJ, Garrett IR, Chirgwin JM, Guise TA 2003 A causal role for endothelin-1 in the pathogenesis of osteoblastic bone metastases. Proc Natl Acad Sci USA **100:**10954–10959.

63. Casey ML, Byrd W, MacDonald PC 1992 Massive amounts of immunoreactive endothelin in human seminal fluid. J Clin Endocrinol Metab **74:**223–225.

64. Prayer-Galetti T, Rossi GP, Belloni AS, Albertin G, Battanello W, Piovan V, Gardiman M, Pagano F 1997 Gene expression and autoradiographic localization of endothelin-1 and its receptors A and B in the different zones of the normal human prostate. J Urol **157:**2334–2339.

65. Nelson JB, Hedican SP, George DJ, Reddi AH, Piantadosi S, Eisenberger MA, Simons JW 1995 Identification of endothelin-1 in the pathophysiology of metastatic adenocarcinoma of the prostate. Nat Med **1:**944–949.

66. Gohji K, Kitazawa S, Tamada H, Katsuoka Y, Nakajima M 2001 Expression of endothelin receptor a associated with prostate cancer progression. J Urol **165:**1033–1036.

67. Carducci MA, Padley RJ, Breul J, Vogelzang NJ, Zonnenberg BA, Daliani DD, Schulman CC, Nabulsi AA, Humerickhouse RA, Weinberg MA, Schmitt JL, Nelson JB 2003 Effect of endothelin-A receptor blockade with atrasentan on tumor progression in men with hormone-refractory prostate cancer: A randomized, phase II, placebo-controlled trial. J Clin Oncol **21:**679–689.

68. Nelson JB, Nabulsi AA, Vogelzang NJ, Breul J, Zonnenberg BA, Daliani DD, Schulman CC, Carducci MA 2003 Suppression of prostate cancer induced bone remodeling by the endothelin receptor A antagonist atrasentan. J Urol **169:**1143–1149.

69. Carducci MA, Nelson JB, Saad F, Schulman CC, Dearnaley DP, Sleep DJ, Hutling M, Isaacson JD, Allan AR, Nisen P 2004 Effects of atrasentan on disease progression and biological markers in men with metastatic hormone-refractory prostate cancer: Phase 3 study. J Clin Oncol **22:**384s.

70. Nelson JB 2005 Endothelin receptor antagonists. World J Urol **23:**19–27.

71. Cornish J, Naot D, Reid IR 2003 Adrenomedullin—a regulator of bone formation. Regul Pept **112:**79–86.

72. Zudaire E, Martinez A, Cuttitta F 2003 Adrenomedullin and cancer. Regul Pept **112:**175–183.

73. Mohammad KS, Wang Z, Martinez A, Corey E, Vessella RL, Guise TA, Chirgwin JM 2004 Adrenomedullin is made by prostate cancers and increases both osteolytic and osteoblastic bone metastases. J Bone Miner Res **19:**S25.

74. Miller MJ, Martinez A, Unsworth EJ, Thiele CJ, Moody TW, Elsasser T, Cuttitta F 1996 Adrenomedullin expression in human tumor cell lines. Its potential role as an autocrine growth factor. J Biol Chem **271:**23345–23351.

75. Yi B, Williams PJ, Niewolna M, Wang Y, Yoneda T 2002 Tumor-derived platelet-derived growth factor-BB plays a critical role in osteosclerotic bone metastasis in an animal model of human breast cancer. Cancer Res **62:**917–923.

76. Schluter KD, Katzer C, Piper HM 2001 A N-terminal PTHrP peptide fragment void of a PTH/PTHrP-receptor binding domain activates cardiac ET(A) receptors. Br J Pharmacol **132:**427–432.

77. Nakata A, Tsujimura T, Sugihara A, Okamura H, Iwasaki T, Shinkai K, Iwata N, Kakishita E, Akedo H, Terada N 1999 Inhibition by interleukin 18 of osteolytic bone metastasis by human breast cancer cells. Anticancer Res **19:**4131–4138.

78. Iwasaki T, Yamashita K, Tsujimura T, Kashiwamura S, Tsutsui H, Kaisho T, Sugihara A, Yamada N, Mukai M, Yoneda T, Okamura H, Akedo H, Terada N 2002 Interleukin-18 inhibits osteolytic bone metastasis by human lung cancer cells possibly through suppression of osteoclastic bone-resorption in nude mice. J Immunother **25:**S52–S60.

79. Roodman GD 2003 Role of stromal-derived cytokines and growth factors in bone metastasis. Cancer **97:**733–738.

80. van der Pluijm G, Lowik C, Papapoulos S 2000 Tumour progression and angiogenesis in bone metastasis from breast cancer: New approaches to an old problem. Cancer Treat Rev **26:**11–27.

Chapter 69. Treatment and Prevention of Bone Metastases and Myeloma Bone Disease

Jean-Jacques Body

Department of Internal Medicine, Institut J. Bordet, Université Libre de Bruxelles, Brussels, Belgium

CLINICAL ASPECTS

According to various large series, up to 90% of patients with advanced cancer will develop bone metastases. The skeleton is the most common site of metastatic disease. It is also the most frequent site of first distant relapse in breast and prostate cancers.

Breast Cancer

Metastatic bone disease causes considerable distress to breast cancer patients. Because of the long clinical course breast cancer may follow, morbidity caused by tumor bone disease also makes major demands on resources for health care provision. The term skeletal-related events (SREs) refers to the major complications of tumor bone disease, namely pathological fractures, need for radiotherapy, need for bone surgery, spinal cord compression, and hypercalcemia.[1,2] Such major complications will be observed in up to one third of the patients whose first relapse is in bone. Bone pain can be the source of great suffering, causing most patient concern and physician visits.[3] Hypercalcemia classically occurs in 10–15% of the cases, spinal cord compression in about 10%, and when long bones are invaded, fractures will occur in 10–20% of the cases.[4,5] Pathological fractures are a dramatic consequence of tumor bone disease and they occur with a median onset of 11 months from the initial diagnosis of bone involvement.[6] Across all tumor types, patients with breast cancer have the highest incidence of skeletal complications. Taken from data in placebo groups of randomized bisphosphonates trials, the mean skeletal morbidity rate (i.e., the mean number of SREs per year) varies between 2.2 and 4.0.[4–9] Patients who have metastases only in the skeleton have a higher rate of SREs than patients who have bone and visceral metastases (e.g., a 2- to 3-fold increase in pathological fractures).[9] The same authors also confirmed that survival from diagnosis of bone metastases was longest for patients with only bone metastases (median survival, 24 months) and was least for patients with concomitant bone and liver metastases (median survival, 5.5 months).[9]

Multiple Myeloma

Bone pain is a presenting feature in three fourths of patients with multiple myeloma. Back pain correlates with the presence of vertebral fractures that are present in more than one half of the patients at diagnosis. Extensive osteolytic lesions are frequent in this aggressive bone disease and, typically, they do not heal despite successful antineoplastic treatment.[10] Diffuse osteoporosis can also be a presenting and misleading feature. The increased fracture rate seems to be especially high around the time of diagnosis. In a large retrospective cohort study, fracture risk was increased 16-fold in the year before diagnosis and 9-fold thereafter. Fractures of the vertebrae and ribs were the most frequent, and oral corticosteroids were the most important predictor.[11]

Prostate Cancer

Surprisingly, there are only few studies to document the frequency and the nature of bone metastatic complications in hormone-refractory prostate cancer patients.[12–15] The incidence of SREs can probably be best estimated by analyzing the placebo group of the controlled trial that has shown the efficacy of the bisphosphonate zoledronic acid.[14,15] Inclusion criteria required that patients had at least one bone metastasis and an augmentation of prostate-specific antigen (PSA) levels while on hormonal therapy. During a follow-up period of 2 years, nearly one half of the patients developed one or more SREs, which were defined as the necessity of radiation therapy or surgery to bone, pathological fracture, spinal cord compression, or a change in antineoplastic therapy to treat bone pain. The two most frequent complications were the need for radiation therapy and the occurrence of pathological fractures. These fractures appeared more frequently at peripheral than at vertebral sites. The median time to the first SRE was 10.5 months, whereas the mean skeletal morbidity rate per year was nearly 1.5. The median survival was 9.5 months.[15]

The following sections relate to the use of bisphosphonates in tumor bone disease. The reader is referred to other sources for the other therapeutic modalities of bone metastases, namely analgesics,[16] radiotherapy,[17] radioisotopes,[18] surgery,[19] vertebroplasty,[20] or kyphoplasty.[21]

CURRENT USE OF BISPHOSPHONATES IN TUMOR BONE DISEASE

Bisphosphonates bind to active sites of bone remodeling, are released from the bone matrix during bone resorption, and are taken up by osteoclasts. They potently inhibit osteoclast-mediated bone resorption and eventually cause osteoclast apoptosis.[22]

Cancer Hypercalcemia

This complication of metastatic bone disease is reviewed elsewhere.

Metastatic Bone Pain

Bisphosphonates can relieve metastatic bone pain and improve patient functioning and quality of life even if the mechanism of this analgesic effect remains largely unknown. The relative inability of first-generation oral bisphosphonates to reduce metastatic bone pain has been confirmed in a placebo-controlled study of oral clodronate after a median time on study of almost 2 months in patients with progressing bone metastases.[23] In another short-term study, clodronate was inferior to intravenous pamidronate in relieving metastatic bone pain ($p < 0.01$) after 3 months.[24] The current opinion is that the intravenous route has to be selected to obtain optimal analgesic effects, but this statement is now challenged by the analgesic effects of oral ibandronate that have been shown in a placebo-controlled study.[25]

Short-term placebo-controlled trials have established that both clodronate and pamidronate given intravenously can exert significant and rapid analgesic effects.[26,27] A clinically meaningful relief of bone pain seems to occur in one

---

Dr. Body has a research grant from Roche and is a consultant for Amgen and Roche.

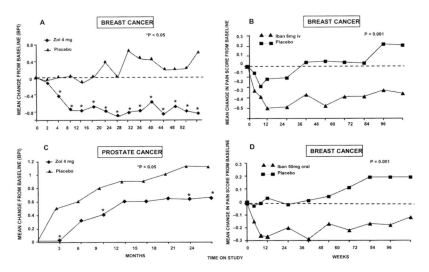

FIG. 1. Analgesic activity of long-term therapy with bisphosphonates in placebo-controlled trials. Effects of zoledronic acid (Zol) are shown in left panels (pain assessed by the Brief Pain Inventory score, quantitative 10-point scale): (A) breast cancer[33] and (C) prostate cancer[14,15]. Effects of ibandronate (Iban) in breast cancer are shown in the right panels (pain assessed on a qualitative five-point scale): (B) intravenous route[7] and (D) oral route.[34]

half to two thirds of the patients treated with pamidronate, and most of the effect is obtained after only one or two infusions.[1,27] More recently, open phase II studies have shown that intensive ibandronate dosing provides rapid and effective relief from severe metastatic bone pain.[28,29]

Over the long term, randomized placebo-controlled trials have shown that intravenous clodronate, pamidronate, ibandronate, and zoledronic acid exert useful pain relief. The American Society of Clinical Oncology (ASCO) panel considered it "reasonable" to start intravenous bisphosphonates in women with abnormal bone scans with localized pain and normal plain radiographs but not if the abnormal bone scan is asymptomatic.[30] In two randomized, placebo-controlled trials, mean pain scores and use of analgesics in patients treated with pamidronate 90 mg monthly for 2 years increased significantly less than in the placebo group.[31] In a phase III trial of patients with breast cancer, pain and analgesic scores were reduced to a similar extent with zoledronic acid 4 mg and pamidronate 90 mg at 13 months.[32] Performance status also improved in both groups. Bone pain levels were recently assessed in a randomized, placebo-controlled study of zoledronic acid in Japanese patients with breast cancer and bone metastases.[33] Patients receiving zoledronic acid 4 mg for 12 months experienced a significant decrease from baseline ($p < 0.001$) in their mean composite Brief Pain Inventory (BPI) score (Fig. 1A). In phase III trials of intravenous and oral ibandronate, bone pain was reduced and similarly maintained below baseline for 2 years (Figs. 1B and 1D).[34] There were also significant improvements in global quality of life and physical functioning with intravenous or oral ibandronate versus placebo.[35] Given the variations in the endpoints used between studies, direct comparative trials are warranted to further evaluate the efficacy of bisphosphonates against bone pain.

In prostate cancer, uncontrolled trials have often been positive, whereas placebo-controlled studies were usually negative, whether for clodronate or for pamidronate. Initial pamidronate uncontrolled trials reported impressive results,[36] but a more recent controlled trial suggests that pamidronate is no more effective than placebo in reducing bone pain or SREs over 6 months.[13] A posthoc analysis showed pain reduction in patients whose pain was "moderate" at baseline, although the effect was only transitory. In the large scale, placebo-controlled study of zoledronic acid, the effect on bone pain was not impressive (Fig. 1C)[14,15] compared with the analgesic effects observed in breast cancer. There was, however, a marked reduction in the frequency of SREs in the zoledronic acid group, which was not the case in the pamidronate trial.[13] However, the selection of bone pain (rather than SREs) as a primary endpoint in the latter study and the advanced disease state of the patients reduce the validity of cross-trial comparisons. In the placebo-controlled clinical trial in patients with bone metastases from other tumors, zoledronic acid had no significant effects on bone pain or quality of life.[37,38]

The analgesic effect of bisphosphonates is thus well established in patients with breast cancer or myeloma but seems to be less in patients with other tumor types. Last, the role of bisphosphonates as an alternative or an adjunct to radiotherapy remains unclear.

Prevention of Skeletal-Related Events

Breast Cancer. Bisphosphonates constitute a highly effective therapeutic option for the prevention of skeletal complications secondary to bone metastases in breast cancer. Several placebo-controlled trials and fewer comparative trials against another bisphosphonate have been performed. Assessment of treatment effects has often used the first-event analyses, such as the proportion of patients with at least one SRE or time to the first event. These are quite objective and conservative endpoints but they do not take into account all subsequent events that occur in any given patient. From a clinical perspective, an aggregate score of symptomatic SREs is more relevant. Skeletal morbidity rate (SMR) or skeletal morbidity period rate (SMPR, number of periods with at least one SRE) take into account the occurrence of multiple SREs. SMPR is better than SMR because events often occur in clusters and SMPR thus reduces the risk of multiple counting of the same event (e.g., fracture of a long bone, followed by surgery and radiotherapy). More recently, more sophisticated analyses have emerged. Multiple-event analyses are able to model all events and the time between events. Thus, Andersen-Gill multiple-event analysis calculates a hazard ratio that indicates the relative risk of skeletal events between two treatment groups.

Until quite recently, the bisphosphonates clodronate, in Europe, and pamidronate, in the United States and Europe, were most often used in practice. Clinical trials of these agents have established their effectiveness in breast cancer patients with bone metastases.[8,31,39–42] In these trials, clodronate has been shown to increase the time to the first event and to reduce the incidence of hypercalcemia and of vertebral fractures. However, clodronate is considered to be less effective than pamidronate for the prevention of SREs.[43] This has been shown in a limited comparative trial against pamidronate.[24] Two double-blind randomized placebo-controlled trials comparing 90 mg pamidronate infusions every 4 weeks to placebo infusions for up to 2 years in addition to chemo- or hormonal therapy in large series of breast cancer patients with at least one lytic bone metastasis showed that bisphosphonates can reduce SMR by more than one third, increase the median time to the occurrence of the first SRE by almost 50%, and reduce the proportion of patients having any SRE.[8,42] The results were more impressive in the chemotherapy trial[8] than in the hormone therapy trial,[42] probably because the skeletal disease was more aggressive at the beginning of the chemotherapy study.

In the past few years, more convenient and somewhat more effective aminobisphosphonates have emerged. Zoledronic acid is widely used for patients with bone metastases from various tumors,[14,32,37,38,44] and ibandronate has since been approved in many countries, but not in the United States, for the prevention of skeletal events in patients with breast cancer and bone metastases.

Three randomized double-blind multicenter trials assessed the efficacy of zoledronic acid in patients with breast cancer and multiple myeloma, in prostate cancer, and in lung or other solid tumors. The primary efficacy endpoint was the proportion of patients with at least one SRE, defined as pathological fracture, spinal cord compression, radiation therapy to bone, and surgery to bone. Secondary endpoints included time to first SRE, SMR, and Andersen-Gill multiple-event analysis. Patients with breast cancer or multiple myeloma ($n = 1648$) were randomized to a 15-minute infusion of zoledronic acid 4 or 8 mg or a 2-h infusion of pamidronate 90 mg every 3–4 weeks.[32,44] The proportion of patients with at least one SRE was similar in all treatment groups (46%, 44%, and 46% for zoledronic acid 8/4 mg, zoledronic acid 4 mg, and pamidronate, respectively). The pre-established criterion for non-inferiority of zoledronic acid to pamidronate was thus met. Zoledronic acid 8 mg was no more effective than the 4-mg dose but was associated with an increased frequency of renal adverse events, explaining why all patients in that treatment arm were switched to the lower dose of zoledronic acid during all zoledronic acid trials. Median time to first SRE was ~1 year in all three treatment groups, and SMRs were also not significantly different. A preplanned multiple-event analysis, according to the Andersen-Gill model, showed that zoledronic acid 4 mg reduced the risk of developing a skeletal complication by an additional 20% over that achieved by pamidronate 90 mg in the breast cancer subgroup ($p < 0.05$; Fig. 2, top).[44] The short infusion time (15-minutes compared with 1 or 2 h for pamidronate) offers a quite convenient therapy and is another advantage of zoledronic acid compared with pamidronate.[45]

The efficacy of intravenous and oral ibandronate has been assessed in randomized double-blind, placebo-controlled studies.[7,25] Breast cancer patients were randomized to ibandronate 6 mg or placebo infused over 1–2 h every 3–4 weeks in the intravenous trial. Oral ibandronate 50 mg was given once daily 1 h before breakfast in two trials of identical design that were pooled for analysis. The primary efficacy endpoint was the SMPR, loosely defined as the number of 12-week periods with skeletal complications (vertebral fractures, nonvertebral fractures, radiotherapy to bone, and surgery to bone) divided by the total observation time. Second-

ary endpoints also included a multiple-event analysis. Intravenous ibandronate 6 mg and oral ibandronate 50 mg significantly reduced SMPRs compared with placebo ($p < 0.005$ for both). Multiple-event Poisson regression analysis showed that intravenous ibandronate led to a statistically significant 40% reduction in the risk of SREs compared with placebo (Fig. 2, bottom; $p < 0.005$). The effect of oral ibandronate 50 mg on the risk of SREs was similar (Fig. 2, bottom; 38% reduction versus placebo; $p < 0.0001$). Posthoc Andersen-Gill analysis showed a 29% reduction in SREs for intravenous ibandronate ($p < 0.05$) and a 35–42% reduction for oral ibandronate ($p < 0.005$) compared with placebo.[46]

Myeloma. Bisphosphonates are of great benefit in myeloma patients. Chemotherapy may reduce tumor burden but has little effect on the underlying bone disease. A recent systematic review of the various therapeutic options for the management of multiple myeloma has considered the introduction of bisphosphonates as one of the two most important therapeutic advances for this disease, the other one being the use of high-dose chemotherapy.[47] Recently published ASCO guidelines recommend to start bisphosphonates in patients with lytic disease on plain X-rays and consider "reasonable" to start them in osteopenic patients without lytic disease. However, bisphosphonates are not suggested in other situations such as a solitary plasmacytoma or indolent myeloma.[48] The Cochrane Myeloma Review Group has reported a meta-analysis based on 11 trials and involving 2183 assessable patients. This review concluded that both pamidronate and clodronate reduce the incidence of hypercalcemia, the pain index, and the number of vertebral fractures in myeloma patients.[49]

The efficacy of repeated pamidronate infusions has been best shown in a placebo-controlled trial including 392 patients with at least one osteolytic lesion. Patients received either 90 mg pamidronate or placebo infusions monthly in addition to their antimyeloma regimen. The proportion of patients developing any SRE (defined as a pathological fracture, irradiation of bone, surgery on bone, hypercalcemia, or spinal cord compression) was significantly ($p < 0.001$) smaller in the pamidronate than in the placebo group (24% versus 41%). The effect was already evident after 3 months of therapy.[50] At the end of a second year extension of the trial, the mean number of skeletal events per year was 1.3 in the pamidronate group versus 2.2 in the placebo group.[51] Vertebral fractures were significantly reduced by pamidronate therapy, but nonvertebral fractures were not significantly affected, consistent with a better effect of bisphosphonates on trabecular than on cortical bone. Quality of life score, performance status, and pain score were all favorably affected by pamidronate therapy. The data also suggested a prolongation of survival in the pamidronate group in patients receiving second or subsequent lines of chemotherapy.[51]

The newer more potent bisphosphonate zoledronic acid has been shown to have a comparable efficacy to pamidronate in a randomized phase III trial including breast cancer and myeloma patients (Fig. 2, top).[44] Ibandronate has been tested in myeloma at a too low dose (2 mg monthly), but there was a significant reduction in SMR in ibandronate-treated patients who had a suppression of their bone resorption markers.[52] Although there is no direct comparative trial between clodronate and pamidronate or zoledronic acid, the ASCO Panel recommends only intravenous pamidronate or zoledronic acid in light of the use of the time to the first event as the primary endpoint and a more complete assessment of bony complications.[48]

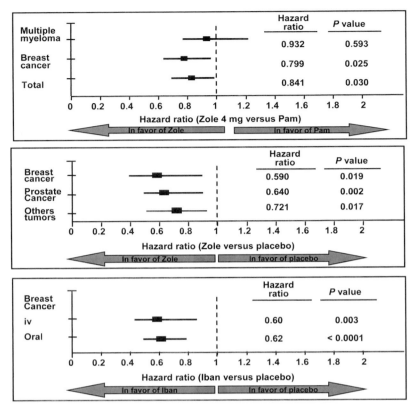

FIG. 2. Effects of long-term therapy with bisphosphonates on the risk of developing a skeletal complication in patients with bone metastases. Data are summarized by a multiple-event analysis (Andersen-Gill model for zoledronic acid and Poisson regression analysis for ibandronate). Hazard ratios (and 95% CI) are shown in the left part of each graph with corresponding p values indicated in the right parts. [Data from the top graph appear from Cancer **98**:1735–1744 (Ref. 44) with permission; data in the middle graph appear from Kohno N, Aogi K, Minami H, Nakamura S, Asaga T, Iino Y, Watanabe T, Goessl C, Ohashi Y, Takashima S 2005 Zoledronic acid significantly reduces skeletal complications compared with placebo in Japanese women with bone metastases from breast cancer: A randomized, placebo-controlled trial. J Clin Oncol **23**:3314–3321 (Ref. 33) with permission from the American Society of Clinical Oncology, Saad F, Gleason DM, Murray R, Tchekmedyian S, Venner P, Lacombe L, Chin JL, Vinholes JJ, Goas JA, Zheng M, Zoledronic Acid Prostate Cancer Study Group 2004 Long-term efficacy of zoledronic acid for the prevention of skeletal complications in patients with metastatic hormone-refractory prostate cancer. J Natl Cancer **96**:879–882 (Ref. 15) with permission from the Oxford University Press, and Rosen LS, Gordon D, Tchekmedyian S, Yanagihara R, Hirsch V, Krzakowski M, Pawlicki M, de Souza P, Zheng M, Urbanowitz G, Reitsma D, Seaman JJ 2003 Zoledronic acid versus placebo in the treatment of skeletal metastases in patients with lung cancer and other solid tumors: A phase II, double-blind, randomized trial—the Zoledronic Acid Lung Cancer and Other Solid Tumors Study Group. J Clin Oncol **21**:3150–3157 (Ref. 37) with permission from the American Society of Clinical Oncology; data in the bottom graph relate to ibandronate and appear from Body JJ 2006 Bisophosphonates for malignancy-related bone disease: Current status, future developments. Support Care Cancer (in press). (Ref. 46) with kind permission of Springer Science and Business Media.]

Prostate Cancer. Skeletal metastases from prostate cancer are typically osteoblastic. Therefore, it was traditionally not felt that this form of bone metastasis might respond to antiresorptive therapy. Meanwhile, histomorphometric analyses of bone biopsy specimens[53,54] and later studies on biochemical markers of bone turnover[54,55] showed that enhanced bone formation in osteoblastic lesions is accompanied by severe bone resorption. Levels of bone resorption markers could even be higher than for patients with breast cancer or other tumors with predominantly lytic bone metastases.[55]

In two studies where bone pain palliation was the primary endpoint and objective complications of bone metastases only secondary endpoints, neither oral clodronate nor intravenous pamidronate significantly reduced the need for radiotherapy[13,56] or the frequency of other SREs.[13] There is only one study whose primary objective was to show a reduction in the frequency of objective SREs after bisphosphonate therapy. Hormone-refractory prostate cancer patients with bone metas-

tases ($n = 643$) were randomized to intravenous zoledronic acid 8 mg or 4 mg or placebo every 3–4 weeks.[14,15] As mentioned above, the group receiving 8 mg was switched during the trial to 4 mg because of renal toxicity. At the end of the core trial, there was an absolute reduction of 11% corresponding to a relative reduction of 25% in the number of patients presenting an objective bone complication. Although the number of patients was much smaller, this difference was maintained at 24 months, as shown by a higher percentage of patients taking placebo who had SREs compared with those treated with zoledronic acid 4 mg (49% versus 38%; $p < 0.05$). In a multiple-event analysis, zoledronic acid 4 mg significantly decreased the risk of developing skeletal complications by 36% compared with placebo ($p < 0.005$; Fig. 2, middle). Other secondary endpoints, including the time to the first SRE or the percentage of patients who presented a fracture, were also significantly reduced in the 4 mg zoledronic acid group. One can speculate that part of the favorable effects of zoledronic acid, especially on the fracture rate, could be caused by effective therapy of castration-induced osteoporosis.

Other Solid Tumors. In a similar phase III study, patients with lung and other solid tumors ($n = 773$) received intravenous zoledronic acid 4 or 8 mg or placebo every 3–4 weeks.[37,38] The results were less impressive than in other cancers, but, because of the short survival of lung cancer patients, the median duration of treatment was only 4 months. At 9 months, the primary endpoint (percentage of patients with an SRE) was not significantly lower with zoledronic acid 4 mg than with placebo, but a multiple-event analysis indicated a favorable effect (Fig. 2, middle). Retrospective subset analysis of patients with kidney cancer suggested a marked efficacy in that particular tumor.[38]

Bisphosphonates as Adjuvant Therapy. Another potential major role for bisphosphonates is the prevention or at least a delay in the development of bone metastases. Bisphosphonates have the potential to reduce tumor burden in bone, whether indirectly by decreasing bone turnover or directly by one or several antitumor effects.[57] Published trials have only used clodronate thus far. The results of the two open studies are conflicting.[58,59] The only double-blind placebo-controlled trial involving >1000 unselected breast cancer patients after surgery treated for 2 years with 1600 mg clodronate or placebo indicates that clodronate can indeed reduce the incidence of bone metastases (by 31% at 5 years, $p = 0.043$) and may prolong survival ($p = 0.048$).[60]

An ongoing trial is comparing clodronate with placebo in the adjuvant setting (National Surgical Adjuvant Breast Project [NSABP] B-34 trial; $n = 3200$). The accrual is completed, and this study will prove to be the confirmatory trial for the effects of adjuvant clodronate. Newer aminobisphosphonates such as ibandronate and zoledronic acid are expected to inhibit bone metastases more effectively, and they are currently being tested in the adjuvant setting.

Practical Recommendations for Possible Individualized Use, Safety Aspects, and Perspectives

Breast Cancer. The indications of bisphosphonate therapy in breast cancer patients nowadays go from the correction of tumor-induced hypercalcemia to the prevention of cancer treatment–induced bone loss. Their main use is currently the prevention of SREs in patients with tumor bone disease. The fact that the efficacy of monthly 8-mg zoledronic acid infusions is not superior to the 4-mg dose[44,46] suggests that we have reached some form of a ceiling effect, at least with classical therapeutic schemes. The efficacy of new generation bisphosphonates looks quite similar (e.g., the comparable effects of zoledronic acid and ibandronate on markers of bone turnover in a 3-month study),[61] although comparative trials with clinical endpoints are needed to confirm this statement. Increasing the dose in patients who seem to respond poorly to standard doses of zoledronic acid cannot be recommended because of possible renal toxicity, and caution is probably mandatory with all bisphosphonates on a long-term basis.

There are few evidence-based medicine criteria for when bisphosphonate treatment should be started and stopped.[62] In an analysis of the subset of patients with breast cancer in the phase III comparative trial between zoledronic acid and pamidronate, patients who had experienced at least one SRE (68% of the total) had almost a 2-fold higher risk for the development of a subsequent SRE compared with patients who had no prior SREs (58% versus 32%, respectively). These high-risk patients seemed to benefit more from zoledronic acid than from pam-

idronate.[63] More importantly, this suggests that giving bisphosphonates early in patients with metastases from breast cancer might help to reduce skeletal complications. Current guidelines from ASCO recommend the routine use of intravenous pamidronate or zoledronic acid in patients with breast cancer and radiographic evidence of bone destruction, with additional consideration for patients who have an abnormal bone scan and localized bone pain.[30] However, the impact of an early treatment on quality of life has rarely been studied, and only ibandronate has shown a significant effect in phase III trials.[34,35] Oral bisphosphonates could be a preferred alternative for many patients on endocrine therapy to avoid the inconvenience of monthly infusions that may reduce quality of life, whereas the intravenous route will evidently be preferred for patients receiving chemotherapy.[62]

Based on the available data, it is thus reasonable to begin bisphosphonates immediately when there is lytic or mixed metastatic bone disease in weight-bearing bones or vertebrae, when painful site(s) correspond to areas of bone destruction as shown by imaging techniques, or when bone disease is multifocal on presentation. However, when starting therapy, clinicians might also need to consider the risk of an excessive anti-osteolytic therapy, in order not to induce "frozen bone" after prolonged bisphosphonate use in an asymptomatic patient with minimal bone disease and a good chance to respond to a first regimen of antineoplastic therapy. Animal data indicate that high-dose bisphosphonates for 1 year significantly increase microdamage accumulation and reduce bone toughness (i.e., its ability to absorb energy or sustain deformation without breaking). Both factors are significantly related to the suppression of bone turnover.[64] Although the clinical relevance of these data are unproven, cases of osteonecrosis of the jaw after prolonged bisphosphonate therapy[65] might, at least in part, be a symptom of excessive bone turnover inhibition and/or excessive suppression of angiogenesis.

ASCO guidelines recommend that, once initiated, intravenous bisphosphonates should be continued until there is a substantial decline in the patient's general performance status.[30] However, criteria are lacking to determine if and how long an individual patient benefits from their administration. Promoting lifelong therapy is somewhat in contradiction with the extreme paucity of data regarding the usefulness and the safety of treatment durations beyond 2 years. Biochemical markers of bone resorption might help identify patients who continue to benefit, particularly as a high rate of bone resorption is one of the factors indicating resistance to bisphosphonates.[66,67] Using bone markers to guide clinical decisions is not currently recommended by ASCO for the individual patient. However, with the growing number of studies indicating their value in predicting disease outcome and bisphosphonate efficacy, there may soon be enough evidence for clinicians to use bone markers to individualize and optimize therapeutic schemes.[67] For example, if bone turnover markers are suppressed in a patient whose bone disease is well controlled by antineoplastic therapy, it might be reasonable to consider a temporary arrest of bisphosphonates or a switch to intermittent infusions after prolonged administration. The benefits of such an approach are currently being tested. There is also a need for prospective cost-effectiveness assessments of bisphosphonates that take into account multiple endpoints such as SREs, bone pain, and quality of life.

Despite quite encouraging results with clodronate, the use of bisphosphonates in the adjuvant setting still has to be viewed as experimental and several randomized trials are ongoing. This should be one of the most promising avenues for the future, but it will be essential to select the patients at high risk of developing bone metastases before recommending a general primary preventive use of bisphosphonates.

Other Neoplasms. Myeloma patients should be treated with bisphosphonates when they present with lytic disease on plain X-rays, and it is reasonable to also treat osteopenic patients without lytic disease. The optimal duration of therapy is unknown, but patients should certainly be treated as long as the disease is active given the intimate relationship between bone cells and myeloma cells. However, it is unknown if bisphosphonates have to be continued when a complete remission has been obtained.

Although skeletal metastases from prostate cancer are typically osteoblastic, prolonged administration of zoledronic acid can significantly reduce the incidence of skeletal complications, particularly the need for radiation therapy and the occurrence of pathological fractures.[14,15] Bisphosphonates should probably be recommended for all patients with hormone-refractory prostate cancer and bone metastases, especially when they are symptomatic, even if part of the benefit is probably caused by effective prevention of cancer treatment–induced bone loss.

In other tumor types, it is reasonable to start bisphosphonates if the skeleton is one of (or the) predominant symptomatic metastatic site(s) and expected survival time is at least 4–6 months.

Safety Aspects. Although generally well tolerated, bisphosphonates are occasionally associated with adverse events. Hypocalcemia is a side effect that may occur with all bisphosphonates, regardless of administration method. It is advisable to administer calcium and vitamin D to all patients on prolonged bisphosphonate therapy to avoid hypocalcemia and the deleterious effects of chronic secondary hyperparathyroidism. Characteristic adverse events with oral bisphosphonates are gastrointestinal, such as epigastric pain and esophagitis, although oral clodronate and ibandronate have been shown to be well tolerated in controlled phase III trials.[25,39] Intravenous infusions can be associated with renal safety issues, injection site reactions, and flu-like syndromes.[68] Osteonecrosis of the jaw was more recently reported with some bisphosphonates.[65] Although sometimes devastating, it is a rare complication (probably around 1%), typically seen after dental extraction and/or concomitant corticosteroid therapy. The relationship with bisphosphonates is likely but needs further study.

The reported incidence of renal function deterioration in clinical trials of zoledronic acid was 10.7% in patients with multiple myeloma or breast cancer, not significantly different than the pamidronate figures in that trial.[44] Although most cases of renal deterioration were mild and reversible, the FDA subsequently reported 72 cases of renal failure with zoledronic acid observed in clinical practice.[69] Serum creatinine monitoring is thus recommended before each infusion of zoledronic acid, and recent updates to the product label advocate stepwise dose reductions when baseline creatinine clearance is 30–60 ml/minute. Zoledronic acid is not recommended in patients with severe renal deterioration or those taking nephrotoxic medications. Prolonged use of intravenous ibandronate in patients with breast cancer has shown a low incidence of renal adverse events that is comparable with placebo.[7] No cases of renal failure have been reported at the time of this writing, but the renal safety of ibandronate has also to be confirmed in routine clinical practice outside of clinical trials.

Other Short-Term Therapeutic Perspectives

Treatment of Severe Bone Pain. Patients with metastatic bone disease can present with very severe treatment-resistant bone pain, a cause of significant disability. First-line treatment tends to focus on opioids and/or radiotherapy to bone but many patients continue to experience bone pain despite these therapies.[70] Monitoring pain levels regularly in the clinic is likely to be an important step toward tailoring treatment to individual needs. Ibandronate renal safety could possibly allow the administration of higher doses in selected patients. While standard doses of bisphosphonates are typically associated with moderate bone pain-relief benefit, open trials suggest that loading doses of intravenous ibandronate could relieve severe or refractory metastatic bone pain in patients with various tumor types.[28,29] This suggests that we are yet to reach the limit of what can be achieved in terms of bone pain reduction with bisphosphonate use.

Inhibition of RANKL. Initial data indicate that blocking the RANK/RANKL system by osteoprotegerin (OPG) or an antiserum against RANKL could inhibit bone resorption for a longer period than pamidronate.[71,72] The antiserum against RANKL seems to be particularly promising because of its potency, the ease of its administration (subcutaneous route), and the apparent lack of toxicity.

REFERENCES

1. Body JJ, Bartl R, Burckhardt P, Delmas PD, Diel IJ, Fleisch H, Kanis JA, Kyle RA, Mundy GR, Paterson AHG, Rubens RD, for the International Bone and Cancer Study Group 1998 Current use of bisphosphonates in oncology. J Clin Oncol **16**:3890–3899.
2. Rubens RD 2000 Clinical aspects of bone metastases. In: Body JJ (ed.) Tumor Bone Diseases and Osteoporosis in Cancer Patients. Marcel Dekker, New York, NY, USA, pp. 85–96.
3. Cleeland CS, Janjan NA, Scott CB, Seiferheld WF, Curran WJ 2000 Cancer pain management by radiotherapists: A survey of radiation therapy oncology group physicians. Int J Radiat Oncol Biol Phys **47**:203–208.
4. Coleman R, Rubens R 1987 The clinical course of bone metastases from breast cancer. Br J Cancer **55**:61–66.
5. Body JJ 2000 Bisphosphonates in breast cancer and other solid tumors. In: Rubens RD, Mundy GR (eds.) Cancer and the Skeleton. Martin Dunitz, London, UK, pp. 231–243.
6. Lipton A 2000 Bisphosphonates and breast carcinoma: Present and future. Cancer **88**(12 Suppl):3033–3037.
7. Body JJ, Diel IJ, Lichinitser MR, Kreuser ED, Dornoff W, Gorbunova VA, Budde M, Bergstrom B, MF 4265 Study Group 2003 Intravenous ibandronate reduces the incidence of skeletal complications in patients with breast cancer and bone metastases. Ann Oncol **14**:1399–1405.
8. Hortobagyi GN, Theriault RL, Lipton A, Porter L, Blayney D, Sinoff C, Wheeler H, Simeone JF, Seaman JJ, Knight RD, Heffernan M, Mellars K, Reitsma DJ 1998 Long-term prevention of skeletal complications of metastatic breast cancer with pamidronate: Protocol 19 Aredia Breast Cancer Study Group. J Clin Oncol **16**:2038–2044.
9. Plunkett TA, Smith P, Rubens RD 2000 Risk of complications from bone metastases in breast cancer. implications for management. Eur J Cancer **36**:476–482.
10. Kanis JA, McCloskey EV 2000 Bisphosphonates in the treatment of multiple myeloma. In: Body JJ (ed.) Tumor Bone Diseases and Osteoporosis in Cancer Patients. Marcel Dekker, New York, NY, USA, pp. 457–481.
11. Melton LJ III, Kyle RA, Achenbach SJ, Oberg AL, Rajkumar SV 2005 Fracture risk with multiple myeloma: A population-based study. J Bone Miner Res **20**:487–493.
12. Berruti A, Dogliotti L, Bitossi R, Fasolis G, Gorzegno G, Bellina M, Torta M, Porpiglia F, Fontana D, Angeli A 2000 Incidence of skeletal complications in patients with bone metastatic prostate cancer and hormone refractory disease: Predictive role of bone resorption and formation markers evaluated at baseline. J Urol **164**:1248–1253.
13. Small EJ, Smith MR, Seaman JJ, Petrone S, Kowalski MO 2003 Combined analysis of two multicenter, randomized, placebo-controlled studies

of pamidronate disodium for palliation of bone pain in men with metastatic prostate cancer. J Clin Oncol 21:4277–4284.

14. Saad F, Gleason DM, Murray R, Tchekmedyian S, Venner P, Lacombe L, Chin JL, Vinholes JJ, Goas JA, Chen B, Zoledronic Acid Prostate Cancer Study Group, Zoledronic Acid Prostate Cancer Study Group 2002 A randomized, placebo-controlled trial of zoledronic acid in patients with hormone-refractory metastatic prostate carcinoma. J Natl Cancer Inst 94:1458–1468.

15. Saad F, Gleason DM, Murray R, Tchekmedyian S, Venner P, Lacombe L, Chin JL, Vinholes JJ, Goas JA, Zheng M, Zoledronic Acid Prostate Cancer Study Group 2004 Long-term efficacy of zoledronic acid for the prevention of skeletal complications in patients with metastatic hormone-refractory prostate cancer. J Natl Cancer Inst 96:879–882.

16. Ripamonti C, Fulfaro F 2000 Malignant bone pain: Pathophysiology and treatments. Curr Rev Pain 4:187–196.

17. McQuay HJ, Collins SL, Carroll D, Moore RA 2000 Radiotherapy for the palliation of painful bone metastases. Cochrane Database Syst Rev CD:001793.

18. Robinson RG, Preston DF, Schiefelbein M, Baxter KG 1995 Strontium 89 therapy for the palliation of pain due to osseous metastases. JAMA 274:420–424.

19. Harrington KD 1997 Orthopedic surgical management of skeletal complications of malignancy. Cancer 80(8 Suppl):1614–1627.

20. Peh WC, Gilula LA 2003 Percutaneous vertebroplasty: Indications, contraindications, and technique. Br J Radiol 76:69–75.

21. Dudeney S, Lieberman IH, Reinhardt MK, Hussein M 2002 Kyphoplasty in the treatment of osteolytic vertebral compression fractures as a result of multiple myeloma. J Clin Oncol 20:2382–2387.

22. Luckman SP, Hughes DE, Coxon FP, Graham R, Russell G, Rogers MJ 1998 Nitrogen-containing bisphosphonates inhibit the mevalonate pathway and prevent post-translational prenylation of GTP-binding proteins, including ras. J Bone Miner Res 13:581–589.

23. Robertson A, Reed N, Ralston S 1995 Effect of oral clodronate on metastatic bone pain: A double-blind, placebo-controlled study. J Clin Oncol 13:2427–2430.

24. Jagdev SP, Purohit P, Heatley S, Herling C, Coleman RE 2001 Comparison of the effect of intravenous pamidronate and oral clodronate on symptoms and bone resorption in patients with metastatic bone disease. Ann Oncol 12:1433–1438.

25. Body JJ, Diel IJ, Lichinitzer M, Lazarev A, Pecherstorfer M, Bell R, Tripathy D, Bergstrom B 2004 Oral ibandronate reduces the risk of skeletal complications in breast cancer patients with metastatic bone disease: Results from two randomised, placebo-controlled phase III studies. Br J Cancer 90:1133–1137.

26. Ernst DS, Brasher P, Hagen N 1997 A randomized, controlled trial of intravenous clodronate in patients with metastatic bone disease and pain. J Pain Symptom Manag 13:319–326.

27. Purohit OP, Anthony C, Radstone CR 1994 High-dose intravenous pamidronate for metastatic bone pain. Br J Cancer 70:554–558.

28. Mancini I, Dumon JC, Body JJ 2004 Efficacy and safety of ibandronate in the treatment of opioid-resistant bone pain associated with metastatic bone disease: A pilot study. J Clin Oncol 22:3587–3592.

29. Heidenreich A, Ohlmann C, Olbert P, Hegele A 2003 High-dose ibandronate is effective and well tolerated in the treatment of pain and hypercalcaemia due to metastatic urologic cancer. Eur J Cancer 1(Suppl 5):S270.

30. Hillner BE, Ingle JN, Chlebowski RT, Gralow J, Yee GC, Janjan NA, Cauley JA, Blumenstein BA, Albain KS, Lipton A, Brown S, American Society of Clinical Oncology 2003 American Society of Clinical Oncology 2003 update on the role of bisphosphonates and bone health issues in women with breast cancer. J Clin Oncol 21:4042–4057.

31. Lipton A, Theriault RL, Hortobagyi GN, Simeone J, Knight RD, Mellars K, Reitsma DJ, Heffernan M, Seaman JJ 2000 Pamidronate prevents skeletal complications and is effective palliative treatment in women with breast carcinoma and osteolytic bone metastases. Cancer 88:1082–1090.

32. Rosen LS, Gordon D, Kaminski M, Howell A, Belch A, Mackey J, Apffelstaedt J, Hussein M, Coleman RE, Reitsma DJ, Seaman JJ, Chen BL, Ambros Y 2001 Zoledronic acid versus pamidronate in the treatment of skeletal metastases in patients with breast cancer or osteolytic lesions of multiple myeloma: A phase III, double-blind, comparative trial. Cancer J 7:377–387.

33. Kohno N, Aogi K, Minami H, Nakamura S, Asaga T, Iino Y, Watanabe T, Goessl C, Ohashi Y, Takashima S 2005 Zoledronic acid significantly reduces skeletal complications compared with placebo in Japanese women with bone metastases from breast cancer: A randomized, placebo-controlled trial. J Clin Oncol 23:3314–3321.

34. Body JJ, Diel IJ, Bell R, Pecherstorfer M, Lichinitser MR, Lazarev AF, Tripathy D, Bergstrom B 2004 Oral ibandronate improves bone pain and preserves quality of life in patients with skeletal metastases due to breast cancer. Pain 111:306–312.

35. Diel IJ, Body JJ, Lichinitser MR, Kreuser ED, Dornoff W, Gorbunova VA, Budde M, Bergstrom B, MF 4265 Study Group 2004 Improved quality of life after long-term treatment with the bisphosphonate ibandronate in patients with metastatic bone disease due to breast cancer. Eur J Cancer 40:1704–1712.

36. Clarke NW, McClure J, George NJ 1992 Disodium pamidronate identifies differential osteoclastic bone resorption in metastatic prostate cancer. Br J Urol 69:64–70.

37. Rosen LS, Gordon D, Tchekmedyian S, Yanagihara R, Hirsh V, Krzakowski M, Pawlicki M, de Souza P, Zheng M, Urbanowitz G, Reitsma D, Seaman JJ 2003 Zoledronic acid versus placebo in the treatment of skeletal metastases in patients with lung cancer and other solid tumors: A phase III, double-blind, randomized trial–the Zoledronic Acid Lung Cancer and Other Solid Tumors Study Group. J Clin Oncol 21:3150–3157.

38. Lipton A, Zheng M, Seaman J 2003 Zoledronic acid delays the onset of skeletal-related events and progression of skeletal disease in patients with advanced renal cell carcinoma. Cancer 98:962–969.

39. Paterson AH, Powles TJ, Kanis JA, McCloskey E, Hanson J, Ashley S 1993 Double-blind controlled trial of oral clodronate in patients with bone metastases from breast cancer. J Clin Oncol 11:59–65.

40. Body JJ, Dumon JC, Piccart M, Ford J 1995 Intravenous pamidronate in patients with tumor-induced osteolysis: A biochemical dose-response study. J Bone Miner Res 10:1191–1196.

41. Kanis JA, Powles T, Paterson AH, McCloskey EV, Ashley S 1996 Clodronate decreases the frequency of skeletal metastases in women with breast cancer. Bone 19:663–667.

42. Theriault RL, Lipton A, Hortobagyi GN, Leff R, Gluck S, Stewart J F, Costello S, Kennedy I, Simeone J, Seaman JJ, Knight RD, Mellars K, Heffernan M, Reitsma DJ 1999 Pamidronate reduces skeletal morbidity in women with advanced breast cancer and lytic bone lesions: A randomized, placebo-controlled trial: Protocol 18 Aredia Breast Cancer Study Group. J Clin Oncol 17:846–854.

43. Lipton A 2003 Bisphosphonates and metastatic breast carcinoma. Cancer 97(Suppl):848–853.

44. Rosen LS, Gordon D, Kaminski M, Howell A, Belch A, Mackey J, Apffelstaedt J, Hussein MA, Coleman RE, Reitsma DJ, Chen BL, Seaman JJ 2003 Long-term efficacy and safety of zoledronic acid compared with pamidronate disodium in the treatment of skeletal complications in patients with advanced multiple myeloma or breast carcinoma: A randomized, double-blind, multicenter, comparative trial. Cancer 98:1735–1744.

45. Body JJ 2003 Zoledronic acid: An advance in tumour bone disease and a new hope for osteoporosis. Expert Opin Pharmacother 4:567–580.

46. Body JJ 2006 Bisphosphonates for malignancy-related bone disease: Current status, future developments. Support Care Cancer (in press).

47. Kumar A, Loughran T, Alsina M, Durie BG, Djulbegovic B 2003 Management of multiple myeloma: A systematic review and critical appraisal of published studies. Lancet Oncol 4:293–230.

48. Berenson JR, Hillner BE, Kyle RA, Anderson K, Lipton A, Yee GC, Biermann JS, American Society of Clinical Oncology Bisphosphonates Expert Panel 2002 American Society of Clinical Oncology clinical practice guidelines: The role of bisphosphonates in multiple myeloma. J Clin Oncol 20:3719–3736.

49. Djulbegovic B, Wheatley K, Ross J, Clark O, Bos G, Goldschmidt H, Cremer F, Alsina M, Glasmacher A 2002 Bisphosphonates in multiple myeloma. Cochrane Database Syst Rev 3:CD003188.

50. Berenson JR, Lichtenstein A, Porter L, Dimopoulos MA, Bordoni R, George S, Lipton A, Keller A, Ballester O, Kovacs MJ, Blacklock HA, Bell R, Simeone J, Reitsma DJ, Heffernan M, Seaman J, Knight RD 1996 Efficacy of pamidronate in reducing skeletal events in patients with advanced multiple myeloma. Myeloma Aredia Study Group. N Engl J Med 334:488–493.

51. Berenson JR, Lichtenstein A, Porter L, Dimopoulos MA, Bordoni R, George S, Lipton A, Keller A, Ballester O, Kovacs M, Blacklock H, Bell R, Simeone JF, Reitsma DJ, Heffernan M, Seaman J, Knight RD 1998 Long-term treatment of advanced multiple myeloma patients reduces skeletal events. J Clin Oncol 16:593–602.

52. Menssen HD, Sakalova A, Fontana A, Herrmann Z, Boewer C, Facon T, Lichinitser MR, Singer CR, Euller-Ziegler L, Wetterwald M, Fiere D, Hrubisko M, Thiel E, Delmas PD 2002 Effects of long-term intravenous ibandronate therapy on skeletal-related events, survival, and bone resorption markers in patients with advanced multiple myeloma. J Clin Oncol 20:2353–2359.

53. Charhon SA, Chapuy MC, Delvin EE, Valentin-Opran A, Edouard CM, Meunier PJ 1983 Histomorphometric analysis of sclerotic bone metastases from prostatic carcinoma special reference to osteomalacia. Cancer 51:918–924.

54. Percival RC, Urwin GH, Harris S, Yates AJ, Williams JL, Beneton M, Kanis JA 1987 Biochemical and histological evidence that carcinoma of the prostate is associated with increased bone resorption. Eur J Surg Oncol **13:**41–49.

55. Garnero P, Buchs N, Zekri J, Rizzoli R, Coleman RE, Delmas PD 2000 Markers of bone turnover for the management of patients with bone metastases from prostate cancer. Br J Cancer **82:**858–864.

56. Ernst DS, Tannock IF, Winquist EW, Venner PM, Reyno L, Moore MJ, Chi K, Ding K, Elliott C, Parulekar W 2003 Randomized, double-blind, controlled trial of mitoxantrone/prednisone and clodronate versus mitoxantrone/prednisone and placebo in patients with hormone-refractory prostate cancer and pain. J Clin Oncol **21:**3335–3342.

57. Fromigué O, Kheddoumi N, Body JJ 2003 Bisphosphonates antagonize bone growth factors effects on human breast cancer cells survival. British Journal of Cancer **89:**178–184.

58. Diel IJ, Solomayer EF, Costa SD, Gollan C, Goerner R, Wallwiener D, Kaufmann M, Bastert G 1998 Reduction in new metastases in breast cancer with adjuvant clodronate treatment. N Engl J Med **339:**357–363.

59. Saarto T, Blomqvist C, Virkkunen P, Elomaa I 2001 Adjuvant clodronate treatment does not reduce the frequency of skeletal metastases in node-positive breast cancer patients: 5-year results of a randomized controlled trial. J Clin Oncol **19:**10–17.

60. Powles T, Paterson S, Kanis JA, McCloskey E, Ashley S, Tidy A, Rosenqvist K, Smith I, Ottestad L, Legault S, Pajunen M, Nevantaus A, Mannisto E, Suovuori A, Atula S, Nevalainen J, Pylkkanen L 2002 Randomized, placebo-controlled trial of clodronate in patients with primary operable breast cancer. J Clin Oncol **20:**3219–3224.

61. Body JJ, Lichinitser M, Tjulandin SA, Budde M, Bergström B 2005 Effect of oral ibandronate versus intravenous (i.v.) zoledronic acid on markers of bone resorption in patients with breast cancer and bone metastases: Results from a comparative phase III trial. Proc ASCO **23:**12S.

62. Body JJ, Mancini I 2002 Bisphosphonates for cancer patients: Why, how, and when?. Support Care Cancer **10:**399–407.

63. Kaminski M, Rosen L, Gordon D, Zheng M, Hei YJ 2004 Zoledronic acid versus pamidronate in patients with breast cancer and multiple myeloma who are at high risk for skeletal complications. Proc Am Soc Clin Oncol **23:**90.

64. Mashiba T, Hirano T, Turner CH, Forwood MR, Johnston CC, Burr DB 2000 Suppressed bone turnover by bisphosphonates increases microdamage accumulation and reduces some biomechanical properties in dog rib. J Bone Miner Res **15:**613–620.

65. Ruggiero SL, Mehrotra B, Rosenberg TJ, Engroff SL 2004 Osteonecrosis of the jaws associated with the use of bisphosphonates: A review of 63 cases. J Oral Maxillofac Surg **62:**527–534.

66. Brown JE, Thomson CS, Ellis SP, Gutcher SA, Purohit OP, Coleman RE 2003 Bone resorption predicts for skeletal complications in metastatic bone disease. Br J Cancer **89:**2031–2037.

67. Coleman RE, Major P, Lipton A, Brown JE, Lee KA, Smith M, Saad F, Zheng M, Hei YJ, Seaman J, Cook R 2005 Predictive value of bone resorption and formation markers in cancer patients with bone metastases receiving the bisphosphonate zoledronic acid. J Clin Oncol **23:**4925–4935.

68. Body JJ 2001 Dosing regimens and main adverse events of bisphosphonates. Semin Oncol **28**(Suppl 11):49–53.

69. Chang JT, Green L, Beitz J 2003 Renal failure with the use of zoledronic acid. N Engl J Med **349:**1676–1679.

70. Yau V, Chow E, Davis L, Holden L, Schueller T, Danjoux C 2004 Pain management in cancer patients with bone metastases remains a challenge. J Pain Symptom Manag **27:**1–3.

71. Body JJ, Greipp P, Coleman RE, Facon T, Geurs F, Fermand JP, Harousseau JL, Lipton A, Marriette X, Williams CD, Nakanishi A, Holloway D, Dunstan CR, Bekker PJ 2003 A phase I study of AMGN-0007: A recombinant osteoprotegerin construct, in patients with multiple myeloma or breast carcinoma related bone metastases. Cancer **97**(3 Suppl):887–892.

72. Body JJ, Facon T, Coleman RE, Lipton A, Geurs F, Fan M, Holloway D, Peterson MC, Bekker PJ 2006 A study of the biologic receptor activator of nuclear factor-κB ligand inhibitor, Denosumab, in patients with multiple myeloma or bone metastases from breast cancer. Clin Cancer Res **12:**1221–1228.

Chapter 70.   Skeletal Complications of Breast and Prostate Cancer Therapies

Angela Hirbe, Elizabeth Morgan, Özge Uluçkan, and Katherine Weilbaecher

Departments of Medicine and Cellular Biology and Physiology, Division of Oncology, Washington University School of Medicine, St. Louis, Missouri

INTRODUCTION

Cancers of the breast and prostate are extremely common, with breast cancer accounting worldwide for 23% of cancer cases in women and prostate cancer accounting for 12% of cases in men. While advances in nonsurgical treatment options such as chemotherapy, hormonal therapy, and radiation are improving survival rates in patients with these diseases, these therapies also carry significant side effects. This chapter focuses on one such category of side effects—cancer treatment-induced skeletal complications such as bone loss, osteoporosis, and fractures, a growing cause of morbidity in this patient population.

SKELETAL COMPLICATIONS OF BREAST CANCER TREATMENT

Adjuvant Hormonal Therapy

In adults, the skeleton undergoes complete turnover every 10 years. Bone mass maintenance is a balance between the activity of osteoblasts, which form bone, and osteoclasts, which resorb it. Estrogen plays a key regulatory role in this cycle of bone remodeling by mediating effects through the estrogen receptor (ER), present on several cell types in the bone (Fig. 1). Estrogen stimulates osteoblasts to produce osteoprotegerin (OPG), a decoy receptor for RANK.[1] OPG blocks the binding of RANKL to RANK on osteoclasts, leading to impaired osteoclast activity and decreased bone resorption. Additionally, estrogen is believed to directly induce apoptosis of bone-resorbing osteoclasts.[2] Thus, in premenopausal women, estrogen both inhibits bone remodeling and suppresses bone resorption, contributing to bone strength. As estrogen levels decline in postmenopausal women, this regulation diminishes and bone resorption increases out of proportion to bone formation, leading to a net loss in bone and weakened bony microarchitecture. Despite the persistence of low levels of circulating estrogen in the postmenopausal state (produced by the conversion of peripheral tissue androgens to estrogen by the aromatase enzyme), bone mass can decrease by as much as 3% per year in the first 5 years after menopause.[3]

The ER is expressed by 70% of breast tumors,[4] and circulating estrogen promotes the growth of ER-positive tumors.

The authors have reported no conflicts of interest.

Control of Bone Remodeling: Androgens and Estrogens

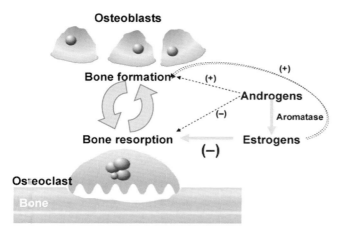

FIG 1. Contribution of estrogens and androgens to bone remodeling. Estrogen and androgens help to maintain a balance between bone formation and bone resorption. Estrogen inhibits osteoclast activity and contributes to osteoclast apoptosis; androgens are converted to estrogen by aromatization and may also directly affect osteoblast differentiation. As such, a decrease in estrogen and/or androgens leads to increased bone resorption and an imbalance in bone remodeling, which ultimately manifests as bone loss.[2,50] Printed with the permission of Postgraduate Institute for Medicine and Interlink Healthcare Communications, joint sponsors of the CME Lecture Series titled Skeletal Complications Across the Cancer Continuum Slide/Lecture Kit. Released June 2005.

Current breast cancer therapies exploit this relationship either by decreasing circulating estrogen levels or by blocking or downregulating the receptor itself. While some of the estrogen-mimicking agents seem to be bone-sparing, others that disrupt the estrogen–skeleton axis cause adverse effects on bone remodeling, leading to decreased BMD and an increased risk of osteoporosis and fracture (Fig. 2).

Selective Estrogen Receptor Modulators. Tamoxifen is a selective estrogen receptor modulator (SERM) that binds to the estrogen receptor and acts as an estrogen antagonist in breast tissue. Tamoxifen is routinely used as adjuvant therapy in patients with ER-positive breast cancers as well as a preventative in high-risk patients because of its anti-estrogen effects in the breast. In bone, tamoxifen has both positive and negative effects depending on the menopausal state; premenopausal women taking tamoxifen may experience bone loss, whereas the drug seems to have agonistic effects in postmenopausal women.[5,6]

Two placebo-controlled trials in postmenopausal women with breast cancer showed statistically significant increases in BMD in the groups receiving tamoxifen versus placebo.[3] The National Surgical Adjuvant Breast and Bowel Project P-1 study (NSABP-P1) showed 21% decrease in fracture risk in patients >50 years of age taking tamoxifen versus placebo for primary prevention of breast cancer, but this was not found to be statistically significant (hazard ratio = 0.79; 95% CI = 0.60–1.05).[7] The International Breast Cancer Intervention Study (IBIS-1), a randomized breast cancer prevention trial including both premenopausal and postmenopausal women, showed no difference in fracture incidence in the tamoxifen group versus placebo.[8]

Another SERM, the "fixed-ring" benzothiophene derivative raloxifene, is currently being studied as a potential breast

cancer preventative in The Study of Tamoxifen and Raloxifene (STAR) trial. This compound, approved for the prevention of osteoporosis in postmenopausal women in 1997, would likely also promote enhanced bone health in this patient population. In sum, SERMs do not seem to contribute to skeletal complications in postmenopausal women with breast cancer.

Aromatase Inhibitors. Postmenopausal women maintain a low level of circulating estrogen because of the aromatization of androgens to estrogen in tissues such as fat and muscle by the cytochrome P450 aromatase (P450arom) enzyme. Inhibitors of this enzyme are now commonly used for adjuvant endocrine therapy in postmenopausal women with breast cancer. There are two major classes of aromatase inhibitors: the nonsteroidal reversible inhibitors such as anastrozole and letrozole and the steroidal irreversible inhibitors such as exemestane.[9] Randomized clinical trials evaluating each of these aromatase inhibitors in the adjuvant therapy of breast cancer have shown decreased cancer recurrences and improved disease free survival in women who received aromatase inhibitors compared with tamoxifen, although no differences in overall survival have been reported to date.[3,10] Consequently, aromatase inhibitors are being commonly administered to postmenopausal women with ER$^+$ breast cancer.

Animal studies suggest that while the steroidal inhibitor exemestane may have bone-sparing effects in ovariectomized rats, the nonsteroidal inhibitor letrozole does not. In two separate studies, Goss et al.[11,12] showed that exemestane treatment prevented the bone loss that normally occurs in animals after ovariectomy, yet this effect was not observed after letrozole treatment. Exemestane may mediate its protective effect through androgenic effects. Both exemestane and its metabolite, 17-hydroxyexemestane, are proposed to have androgenic properties,[12] and androgens have been previously shown to be important for maintenance of BMD independent of their conversion to estrogen.[2]

In contrast, clinical trials have indicated that both classes of aromatase inhibitors result in bone loss to some extent (Fig. 2). However, there are no trials that compare the extent of bone loss in women on steroidal versus nonsteroidal aromatase inhibitors. As such, it is not possible to definitively conclude which would have the best skeletal side effect profile.

BMD Loss With Cancer Therapies

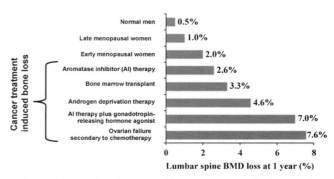

FIG. 2. Extent of bone loss caused by cancer therapy. Healthy men lose bone at a rate of 0.5% per year beginning at middle age, whereas menopausal women lose bone at a rate of 1–2% per year. Cancer treatments such as aromatase inhibitor therapy, androgen deprivation therapy, and chemotherapy accelerate this process, leading to significant bone loss and subsequent skeletal complications.[51–56] Printed with the permission of Postgraduate Institute for Medicine and Interlink Healthcare Communications, joint sponsors of the CME Lecture Series titled Skeletal Complications Across the Cancer Continuum Slide/Lecture Kit. Released June 2005.

A recent double-blind trial by Lonning et al.[13] compared the effects of exemestane versus placebo on BMD in 147 women after surgical resection of early breast cancer. They observed a slight increase in the annual rate of femoral neck BMD loss in the exemestane group (2.72% versus 1.48%, $p = 0.024$). However, there was not a significant increase in BMD loss in the lumbar spine for the exemestane group. This suggests that exemestane causes a modest loss of BMD.

Recent updates in the ATAC trial (Arimidex, Tamoxifen, Alone or in Combination) have indicated that while anastrazole (Arimidex) may have a milder overall side effect profile compared with tamoxifen, the effects on BMD may be more severe. Data have indicated that there is a statistically significant increase in fracture rate for women on anastrozole compared with tamoxifen (22.6 compared with 15.6 fratures per woman-year, $p < 0.0001$).[10]

A large ($N = 5187$), randomized, placebo-controlled phase III trial evaluated the aromatase inhibitor (AI) letrozole in postmenopausal women with primary breast cancer who had completed 5 years of adjuvant tamoxifen therapy.[14] Compared with placebo, patients receiving letrozole (2.5 mg) experienced more cases of patient-reported osteoporosis (8% versus 6% for placebo: $p = 0.003$).

In summary, clinical trials have indicated that aromatase inhibitors also lead to significant bone loss in women with breast cancer. As such, these women should be monitored carefully for changes in BMD and treated appropriately. Several multicenter randomized clinical trials are underway evaluating the role of bone targeted antiresorptive therapies to prevent bone loss associated with aromatase inhibitors.

Selective Estrogen Receptor Downregulators.

Recently a new class of endocrine agent, the selective estrogen receptor downregulators (SERDs), has been introduced. SERDs downregulate cellular levels of the ER and act as pure ER antagonists without any agonist effects. SERDs represent a potential treatment option for patients unable to tolerate the agonist effects of SERMs or who have tamoxifen or AI-resistant disease. Fulvestrant is currently the only SERD used in the clinics and is approved for second-line treatment of advanced breast cancer in postmenopausal women. The effect of fulvestrant on bone is controversial. In animal studies, fulvestrant was shown to increase bone turnover; however, the opposite results were obtained when the rats were ovariectomized.[2] Currently BMD is not an endpoint in clinical trials testing the efficacy of fulvestrant.

Chemotherapy

Chemotherapy is used as either neoadjuvant or adjuvant therapy in pre- and postmenopausal women diagnosed with breast cancer. Chemotherapy has both direct and indirect effects on the bone microenvironment, ultimately leading to decreased BMD.[15]

Direct Effects.

Animal studies[15] showed that male rats treated with methotrexate had decreased cancellous bone volume and decreased mineralizing surface compared with saline injected controls. Additionally, cortical cross-sectional area and periosteal mineralization rates were lower in the methotrexate group. Another study[15] examined the effects of chemotherapy on BMD in postmenopausal women with early stage breast cancer. The for-age bone density scores of postmenopausal women who received adjuvant chemotherapy were ~0.5 SD lower than women who had not received chemotherapy. These studies suggest that chemotherapy can have direct, nonhormonal effects on the skeleton.

Indirect Effects.

Breast cancer chemotherapy frequently induces primary ovarian failure in premenopausal women, which leads to a sudden decrease in estrogen production and early menopause (Fig. 2).[15–17] This drop in estrogen is believed to stimulate increased osteoclast survival and activity.[2] As a result, these women often develop osteopenia and are placed at an increased risk for developing osteoporosis.[15,18]

Several studies have shown a correlation between adjuvant chemotherapy and decreased BMD in women with breast cancer. One study[16] examined BMD of the lumbar spine in women with breast cancer who received adjuvant chemotherapy compared with women with breast cancer who did not receive chemotherapy. They showed that 71% of women who received chemotherapy experienced amenorrhea (loss of menses) at the time of BMD measurements compared with 16% of the women who did not receive chemotherapy. In addition, the BMD measurements of women in the chemotherapy group were significantly lower that those in the non-chemotherapy group (1.17 compared with 1.29 g/cm^2). Another study[16] also assessed BMD in women receiving adjuvant chemotherapy. They showed that women who became permanently amenorrheic as a result of chemotherapy had a BMD 14% lower than women who maintained menses after chemotherapy. These studies suggest that chemotherapy leads to an increased risk of entering early menopause and, subsequently, an increased risk of bone loss.

A more recent study[15] showed that chemotherapy-induced ovarian failure causes significant bone loss in the spine. This study examined 49 premenopausal women with stage I/II breast cancer receiving adjuvant chemotherapy. DXA scans and measurement of markers of skeletal turnover, namely osteocalcin and bone-specific alkaline phosphatase, were used to assess bone loss at baseline and 6, 12, and 24 months after initiation of chemotherapy. Thirty-five of these women were found to have ovarian failure, defined as a negative pregnancy test, >3 months of amenorrhea, and follicle-stimulating hormone (FSH) levels >30 MIU/ml at the 12-month evaluation. In turn, significant bone loss was observed by 6 months after initiation of chemotherapy. These women had an ~4% decrease in BMD in the spine ($p = 0.0001$) and increased serum levels of bone turnover markers. This bone loss continued at the 12-month interval.

Several groups have shown that bisphosphonates are able to reduce bone loss associated with breast cancer chemotherapy. One study[16] examined the effects of risedronate on BMD in 53 women who were postmenopausal because of chemotherapy or radiotherapy after breast cancer surgery. The annual rate of change in lumbar BMD in the risedronate group was $0.3 \pm 0.5\%$ compared with $-1.4 \pm 0.5\%$ in the placebo group ($p = 0.018$). Another group[16] conducted a large double-blind randomized two-center trial to examine BMD in 311 women with primary breast cancer who had received chemotherapy and/or tamoxifen and who were given an osteoclast-inhibiting bisphosphonate (clodronate) or placebo for 2 years. They showed that the change in BMD for the lumbar spine was only -0.16% at 2 years for the clodronate group compared with -1.88% for the placebo group ($p = 0.04$).

A more recent study[15] examined bone loss in 73 premenopausal women receiving the CMF regiment (cyclophosphomide, methotrexate, and 5-fluorouacil). The patients were randomized to oral clodronate daily for 3 years or to a control group. This study showed that women who lost menstrual function, indicative of ovarian failure, had increased bone loss compared with women who maintained menstrual function. Furthermore, the women in the clodronate group lost less lumbar BMD than the women in the control group (-3% compared with -7.4%, $p = 0.003$) at 3 years. Thus, adjuvant clodronate treatment significantly reduced bone loss.

In short, chemotherapy in the breast cancer setting has a negative impact on BMD in women undergoing treatment. This could be attributed to direct effects on the bone microenvironment as well as indirect effects caused by the decrease in estrogen that occurs after chemotherapy-induced primary ovarian failure.

SKELETAL COMPLICATIONS OF PROSTATE CANCER TREATMENT

Androgen Deprivation Therapy

Prostate cancer patients who are diagnosed with metastatic disease or whose other clinical features suggest a poor chance for cure often receive palliative therapy in the form of androgen deprivation therapy (ADT) as a first-line treatment. ADT includes surgical castration, pharmacologic castration with agents such as luteinizing hormone-releasing hormone agonists (LHRH-a), and antiandrogen therapy with agents such as flutamide, nilutamide, bicalutamide, or cyproterone.[19] One potential complication that can arise from surgical castration or gonadotropin-releasing hormone (GnRH) agonist therapy is a decrease in BMD[20,21] (Fig. 2). This is believed to be caused by a decrease in estrogen, because androgens can be converted to estrogen through aromatases, which is essential to maintain skeletal health.[22] A drop in estrogen is believed to lead to an increase in osteoclast survival and a subsequent increase in bone resorption as mentioned above.[23] In addition there may be a direct effect of androgens on osteoblast differentiation such that a decrease in androgens would lead to decreased bone formation.[24]

Several retrospective studies have shown this link between androgen deprivation therapy and increased bone loss.[20,21,25] One study[21] showed an increased risk of osteoporotic fractures in men treated with orchiectomy. Information was gathered on men with prostate cancer diagnosed between 1983 and 1990. Of the 235 men in the study, 10 had osteoporotic fractures—8 in the treated group and 2 in the untreated group (13.6% versus 1.1%, $p < 0.001$). Another retrospective study by Townsend et al. made use of chart reviews and phone interviews to assess the incidence of bone fractures in patients receiving LHRH-a for prostate cancer. They were able to show a 5% incidence of osteoporotic fractures in treated patients. Krupski et al.[20] used 1992–2001 claims data from a random sample of Medicare beneficiaries to investigate the link between ADT and bone complications in men with prostate cancer. They found that 45% of men who had received ADT for longer than the median duration (697 days) had sustained at least one fracture, whereas this was true for only 40% of men who received ADT for less than median treatment time of 697 days. This suggests that fracture risk may be related to the duration of ADT. Most recently, Shahinin et al.[25] performed a large retrospective study in which they examined records for 50,613 men diagnosed with prostate cancer between 1992 and 1997. They found that 19.4% of the men who received ADT suffered at least one fracture compared with 12.6% of men who did not receive ADT ($p < 0.001$). All of these data strongly suggests that ADT is a risk factor for osteoporosis and fracture in men with prostate cancer.

A number of recent studies have suggested that bisphosphonate therapy can reduce this increased risk for bone loss and subsequent fracture in men receiving ADT. Maorabito et al.[26] randomized 48 osteoporotic prostate cancer patients to receive either calcium supplements alone or calcium in combination with the bisphosphonate neridronate. While the patients receiving calcium alone had significant decreases in BMD as well as increased markers of bone turnover, the patients undergoing bisphosphonate treatment did not have any significant changes in BMD or markers of bone turnover. A double-blind randomized placebo controlled trial[27] was performed to assess the effect of the bisphosphonate zoledronic acid on BMD during ADT in 106 men with prostate cancer. While the men in the control group had a 2.2% decrease in BMD, the men in the zoledronic acid group had a 5.6% increase in BMD ($p < 0.001$). Both of these studies suggest a strong benefit of bisphosphonate therapy on skeletal health for men undergoing ADT.

The use of SERMs, which have agonistic effects on bone in postmenopausal women, may also combat bone loss in men receiving ADT. An open-label randomized controlled trial conducted by Smith et al.[28] compared BMD scores in 48 men with nonmetastatic prostate cancer who received 12 months of raloxifene (60 mg/day) or no raloxifene during concurrent treatment with a GnRH agonist. The mean duration of GnRH agonist therapy in the raloxifene group was 31 months compared with 37 months in the no raloxifene group. Men receiving raloxifene showed an increase in total hip BMD of $1.1 \pm 0.4\%$, whereas the no raloxifene group showed a decrease in total hip BMD of $2.6 \pm 0.7\%$ ($p < 0.001$). Further studies investigating SERM use at the initiation of ADT and the effect of SERMs on fracture rates will further contribute to our understanding of skeletal benefits of this therapy.

Antiandrogen compounds, which competitively inhibit activation of the androgen receptor by testosterone, can be used as prostate cancer treatment alone or in combination with other forms of ADT. In men with nonmetastatic prostate cancer, monotherapy with the nonsteroidal antiandrogen bicalutamide provides similar survival rates to castration.[29] The observation that bicalutamide monotherapy significantly increases serum concentrations of testosterone and estradiol compared with baseline[30] suggests that bicalutamide monotherapy may have a bone-protective effect in men with nonmetastatic prostate cancer. Several studies support this assertion. One group[31] found an increase in biochemical markers of bone turnover in men undergoing medical castration but not in men receiving bicalutamide monotherapy. Another group[32] reported lower BMD in men with nonmetastatic, locally advanced prostate cancer treated with castration compared with those receiving bicalutamide monotherapy. Sieber et al.[33] measured BMD in men with localized or locally advanced prostate cancer ($n = 103$) randomized to bicalutamide monotherapy or medical castration for 96 weeks; lumbar spine BMD was $+2.42\%$ and hip BMD was $+1.13\%$ in the bicalutamide group compared with lumbar spine BMD of -5.40% and hip BMD of -4.39% in the medical castration group (both $p < 0.0001$). Finally, Smith et al.[34] found that BMD increased significantly from baseline in men with nonmetastatic prostate cancer randomized to 12 months bicalutamide therapy; in comparison, BMD decreased significantly from baseline in the group randomized to treatment with leuprolide, a GnRH agonist. In sum, it seems that bicalutamide monotherapy may offer skeleto-protective benefits in men with nonmetastatic prostate cancer. An important next step will be to evaluate its effect on fracture rate compared with other forms of ADT.

RADIATION-INDUCED FRACTURES

Breast conservation surgery combined with radiotherapy has become the standard of care for patients with early-stage breast cancer.[35] One potential complication of this treatment is rib fracture after X-ray exposure, although few studies have investigated this phenomenon. A retrospective study by Pierce et al.[36] examined the incidence of various radiation-induced complications in 1624 patients with early stage breast cancer treated between 1968 and 1985. The median follow-up time for survivors was 79 months. They found that the incidence of rib fracture was between 0.4% and 2.2% depending on the type of linear accelerator used. Another retrospective study by Meric et al.[35] examined the incidence of radiation-induced complications in 294 women receiving surgery and radiotherapy treatment between 1990 and 1992. They found the risk of rib fractures to be 0.3%. These data suggest that radiotherapy for breast cancer may lead to a small risk of rib fracture.

Current recommendations for prostate cancer treatment suggest that brachytherapy (radiotherapy) is an option for non-metastatic patients with a long life expectancy (>5 years) or for patients for whom surgery is a contraindication.[37–39] While a possible side effect of brachytherapy could be pelvic fracture, there are no clinical studies examining this potential risk. There are, however, case reports documenting pelvic fracture in men who have received pelvic irradiation.[40]

OSTEONECROSIS OF THE JAW

Bisphosphonates are osteoclast inhibitors that are now widely used in cancer therapy to inhibit bone loss resulting from treatment or bone metastases. There are three classes of bisphosphonates: (1) first-generation compounds, such as clodronate, (2) second-generation compounds, which are stronger and contain a single nitrogen atom, such as pamidronate, and finally (3) third-generation compounds, such as zoledronic acid, which contain one or two nitrogen atoms in a ring form and are the most potent.[41] The first-generation bisphosphonates are metabolized into cytotoxic analogs of ATP inducing osteoclast cell death. The nitrogen-containing bisphosphonates, on the other hand, function by inhibiting the activity of farnesyl diphosphate (FPP) and geranylgeranyl diphosphate (GGPP). Because FPP and GGPP are required for post-translational lipid modification (prenylation) of small guanine triphosphatases (GTPases), bisphosphonates interfere with the function of GTPases such as Ras, Rac, and Rho. This leads to disruption of the actin cytoskeleton, altered tracking of intracellular components, and impaired integrin signaling within the osteoclast.[41] Second -and third-generation bisphosphonates do not have an effect on the osteoblast in vivo; thus, the bone formation is intact.[41] In addition, in vitro evidence suggests that bisphosphonates may have anti-angiogenic and antitumor properties, but these data have not been confirmed in vivo.[42,43]

In the last few years, zoledronic acid and pamidronate have been administered to >2.5 million cancer patients worldwide. In 2003, the first cases of osteonecrosis of the jaw (characterized by bone erosions and exposed bone) were reported in patients receiving chronic oral and intravenous bisphosphonate therapy for osteoporosis and bone metastases.[44,45] Osteonecrosis of the jaw is an extremely painful condition in which the mandible or the maxillary bones are exposed.[46,47] In addition to chronic bisphosphonate therapy, it is also associated with oral fungal infections, trauma, herpes zoster, and radiation therapy. In one study of 211 myeloma patients receiving zoledronic acid, 10% developed osteonecrosis of the jaw by 36 months, whereas 4% of 413 myeloma patients receiving pamidronate developed the disease by 36 months.[44]

Inhibition of the osteoclast by bisphosphonates is hypothesized to disrupt the critical balance between the osteoclast and the osteoblast. In a situation where healing of the bone is necessary, such as after chronic inflammation and infection associated with gum disease, the disruption of the dynamic and coupled processes of bone resorption and formation may contribute to the development of osteonecrosis of the jaw. The anti-angiogenic effects of the bisphosphonates are also hypothesized to contribute to the process of necrosis.[48] This complication is thought to become more likely if the patient is undergoing any manipulations in the oral cavity, such as tooth extractions and placement of oral implants.[49]

Meticulous oral hygiene, antibiotics, and the discontinuation of bisphosphonates is currently recommended for therapy of osteonecrosis of the jaw. The diagnosis of osteonecrosis of the jaw is a clinical diagnosis made by physical examination. Biopsy of the affected bone can be associated with worsening of the situation. More studies must be initiated to determine the exact mechanisms and cause of this complication and how it can be prevented and treated.[46–48]

CONCLUSION

Chemotherapy and hormonal therapies for breast and prostate cancer have the potential to lead to significant bone loss primarily through the disruption of estrogen's bone-enhancing properties. Current recommendations for avoiding the skeletal complications of cancer therapy include adequate intake of calcium and vitamin D, regular weight-bearing exercise, cessation of smoking, reduction in alcohol intake, and bisphosphonate therapy for osteoporotic patients.[16,31] Patients whose cancer is being treated with hormonal therapies are at increased risk for skeletal complications and should have regular BMD monitoring by DXA. The role of antiresorptive, osteoclast inhibitor therapy to prevent cancer therapy associated bone loss is under active study. It is recommended that patients who initiate bisphosphonate therapy receive a thorough oral examination and treatment for dental infections before initiating bisphosphonate therapy.[44,46–48] In addition to treating the cancer, careful monitoring of bone health is now an essential component of the treatment of both breast and prostate cancer.

REFERENCES

1. Hofbauer LC, Hicok KC, Chen D, Khosla S 2002 Regulation of osteoprotegerin production by androgens and anti-androgens in human osteoblastic lineage cells. Eur J Endocrinol 147:269–273.
2. Vanderschueren D, Vandenput L, Boonen S, Lindberg MK, Bouillon R, Ohlsson C 2004 Androgens and bone. Endocr Rev 25:389–425.
3. Lester J, Coleman R 2005 Bone loss and the aromatase inhibitors. Br J Cancer 93(Suppl 1):S16–S22.
4. Harvey JM, Clark GM, Osborne CK, Allred DC 1999 Estrogen receptor status by immunohistochemistry is superior to the ligand-binding assay for predicting response to adjuvant endocrine therapy in breast cancer. J Clin Oncol 17:1474–1481.
5. Delmas PD, Bjarnason NH, Mitlak BH, Ravoux AC, Shah AS, Huster WJ, Draper M, Christiansen C 1997 Effects of raloxifene on bone mineral density, serum cholesterol concentrations, and uterine endometrium in postmenopausal women. N Engl J Med 337:1641–1647.
6. Cosman F 2003 Selective estrogen-receptor modulators. Clin Geriatr Med 19:371–379.
7. Fisher B, Costantino JP, Wickerham DL, Redmond CK, Kavanah M, Cronin WM, Vogel V, Robidoux A, Dimitrov N, Atkins J, Daly M, Wieand S, Tan-Chiu E, Ford L, Wolmark N 1998 Tamoxifen for prevention of breast cancer: Report of the National Surgical Adjuvant Breast and Bowel Project P-1 Study. J Natl Cancer Inst 90:1371–1388.
8. Cuzick J, Forbes J, Edwards R, Baum M, Cawthorn S, Coates A, Hamed A, Howell A, Powles T 2002 First results from the International Breast Cancer Intervention Study (IBIS-I): A randomised prevention trial. Lancet 360:817–824.
9. Simpson ER, Dowsett M 2002 Aromatase and its inhibitors: Significance for breast cancer therapy. Recent Prog Horm Res 57:317–338.
10. Howell A, Cuzick J, Baum M, Buzdar A, Dowsett M, Forbes JF, Hoctin-Boes G, Houghton J, Locker GY, Tobias JS 2005 Results of the ATAC (Arimidex, Tamoxifen, Alone or in Combination) trial after completion of 5 years' adjuvant treatment for breast cancer. Lancet 365:60–62.
11. Goss PE, Qi S, Cheung AM, Hu H, Mendes M, Pritzker KP 2004 Effects of the steroidal aromatase inhibitor exemestane and the nonsteroidal

aromatase inhibitor letrozole on bone and lipid metabolism in ovariecto-mized rats. Clin Cancer Res 10:5717–5723.

12. Goss PE, Qi S, Josse RG, Pritzker KP, Mendes M, Hu H, Waldman SD, Grynpas MD 2004 The steroidal aromatase inhibitor exemestane prevents bone loss in ovariectomized rats. Bone 34:384–392.

13. Lonning PE, Geisler J, Krag LE, Erikstein B, Bremnes Y, Hagen AI, Schlichting E, Lien EA, Ofjord ES, Paolini J, Polli A, Massimini G 2005 Effects of exemestane administered for 2 years versus placebo on bone mineral density, bone biomarkers, and plasma lipids in patients with surgically resected early breast cancer. J Clin Oncol 23:5126–5137.

14. Goss PE, Ingle JN, Martino S, Robert NJ, Muss HB, Piccart MJ, Castiglione M, Tu D, Shepherd LE, Pritchard KI, Livingston RB, Davidson NE, Norton L, Perez EA, Abrams JS, Therasse P, Palmer MJ, Pater JL 2003 A randomized trial of letrozole in postmenopausal women after five years of tamoxifen therapy for early-stage breast cancer. N Engl J Med 349:1793–1802.

15. Lester J, Dodwell D, McCloskey E, Coleman R 2005 The causes and treatment of bone loss associated with carcinoma of the breast. Cancer Treat Rev 31:115–142.

16. Ramaswamy B, Shapiro CL 2003 Osteopenia and osteoporosis in women with breast cancer. Semin Oncol 30:763–775.

17. Shapiro CL, Phillips G, Van Poznak CH, Jackson R, Leboff MS, Woodard S, Lemeshow S 2005 Baseline bone mineral density of the total lumbar spine may predict for chemotherapy-induced ovarian failure. Breast Cancer Res Treat 90:41–46.

18. Howell SJ, Berger G, Adams JE, Shalet SM 1998 Bone mineral density in women with cytotoxic-induced ovarian failure. Clin Endocrinol (Oxf) 49:397–402.

19. Loblaw DA, Mendelson DS, Talcott JA, Virgo KS, Somerfield MR, Ben-Josef E, Middleton R, Porterfield H, Sharp SA, Smith TJ, Taplin ME, Vogelzang NJ, Wade JL, Jr., Bennett CL, Scher HI 2004 American Society of Clinical Oncology recommendations for the initial hormonal management of androgen-sensitive metastatic, recurrent, or progressive prostate cancer. J Clin Oncol 22:2927–2941.

20. Krupski TL, Smith MR, Lee WC, Pashos CL, Brandman J, Wang Q, Botteman M, Litwin MS 2004 Natural history of bone complications in men with prostate carcinoma initiating androgen deprivation therapy. Cancer 101:541–549.

21. Diamond TH, Higano CS, Smith MR, Guise TA, Singer FR 2004 Osteoporosis in men with prostate carcinoma receiving androgen-deprivation therapy: Recommendations for diagnosis and therapies. Cancer 100:892–899.

22. Hansen KA, Tho SP 1998 Androgens and bone health. Semin Reprod Endocrinol 16:129–134.

23. Hughes DE, Dai A, Tiffee JC, Li HH, Mundy GR, Boyce BF 1996 Estrogen promotes apoptosis of murine osteoclasts mediated by TGF-beta. Nat Med 2:1132–1136.

24. Vanderschueren D, Bouillon R 1995 Androgens and bone. Calcif Tissue Int 56:341–346.

25. Shahinian VB, Kuo YF, Freeman JL, Goodwin JS 2005 Risk of fracture after androgen deprivation for prostate cancer. N Engl J Med 352:154–164.

26. Morabito N, Gaudio A, Lasco A, Catalano A, Atteritano M, Trifiletti A, Anastasi G, Melloni D, Frisina N 2004 Neridronate prevents bone loss in patients receiving androgen deprivation therapy for prostate cancer. J Bone Miner Res 19:1766–1770.

27. Aapro MS 2004 Long-term implications of bone loss in breast cancer. Breast 13(Suppl 1):S29–S37.

28. Smith MR, Fallon MA, Lee H, Finkelstein JS 2004 Raloxifene to prevent gonadotropin-releasing hormone agonist-induced bone loss in men with prostate cancer: A randomized controlled trial. J Clin Endocrinol Metab 89:3841–846.

29. Pronzato P, Rondini M 2005 Hormonotherapy of advanced prostate cancer. Ann Oncol 16(Suppl 4):iv80–iv84.

30. Verhelst J, Denis L, Van Vliet P, Van Poppel H, Braeckman J, Van Cangh P, Mattelaer J, D'Hulster D, Mahler C 1994 Endocrine profiles during administration of the new non-steroidal anti-androgen Casodex in prostate cancer. Clin Endocrinol (Oxf) 41:525–530.

31. Saad F, Olsson C, Schulman CC 2004 Skeletal morbidity in men with prostate cancer: Quality-of-life considerations throughout the continuum of care. Eur Urol 46:731–739.

32. Tyrrell CJ, Blake GM, Iversen P, Kaisary AV, Melezinek I 2003 The non-steroidal antiandrogen, bicalutamide ('Casodex'), may preserve bone mineral density as compared with castration: Results of a preliminary study. World J Urol 21:37–42.

33. Sieber PR, Keiller DL, Kahnoski RJ, Gallo J, McFadden S 2004 Bicalutamide 150 mg maintains bone mineral density during monotherapy for localized or locally advanced prostate cancer. J Urol 171:2272–2276.

34. Smith MR, Goode M, Zietman AL, McGovern FJ, Lee H, Finkelstein JS 2004 Bicalutamide monotherapy versus leuprolide monotherapy for prostate cancer: Effects on bone mineral density and body composition. J Clin Oncol 22:2546–2553.

35. Meric F, Buchholz TA, Mirza NQ, Vlastos G, Ames FC, Ross MI, Pollock RE, Singletary SE, Feig BW, Kuerer HM, Newman LA, Perkins GH, Strom EA, McNeese MD, Hortobagyi GN, Hunt KK 2002 Long-term complications associated with breast-conservation surgery and radiotherapy. Ann Surg Oncol 9:543–549.

36. Pierce SM, Recht A, Lingos TI, Abner A, Vicini F, Silver B, Herzog A, Harris JR 1992 Long-term radiation complications following conservative surgery (CS) and radiation therapy (RT) in patients with early stage breast cancer. Int J Radiat Oncol Biol Phys 23:915–923.

37. Aus G, Abbou CC, Bolla M, Heidenreich A, Schmid HP, van Poppel H, Wolff J, Zattoni F 2005 EAU guidelines on prostate cancer. Eur Urol 48:546–551.

38. Pirtskhalaishvili G, Hrebinko RL, Nelson JB 2001 The treatment of prostate cancer: An overview of current options. Cancer Pract 9:295–306.

39. Nag S, Beyer D, Friedland J, Grimm P, Nath R 1999 American Brachytherapy Society (ABS) recommendations for transperineal permanent brachytherapy of prostate cancer. Int J Radiat Oncol Biol Phys 44:789–799.

40. Csuka M, Brewer BJ, Lynch KL, McCarty DJ 1987 Osteonecrosis, fractures, and protrusio acetabuli secondary to x-irradiation therapy for prostatic carcinoma. J Rheumatol 14:165–170.

41. Heymann D, Ory B, Gouin F, Green JR, Redini F 2004 Bisphosphonates: New therapeutic agents for the treatment of bone tumors. Trends Mol Med 10:337–343.

42. Wood J, Bonjean K, Ruetz S, Bellahcene A, Devy L, Foidart JM, Castronovo V, Green JR 2002 Novel antiangiogenic effects of the bisphosphonates compound zoledronic acid. J Pharmacol Exp Ther 302:1055–1061.

43. Croucher P, Jagdev S, Coleman R 2003 The anti-tumor potential of zoledronic acid. Breast 12(Suppl 2):S30–S36.

44. Durie BG, Katz M, Crowley J 2005 Osteonecrosis of the jaw and bisphosphonates. N Engl J Med 353:99–102.

45. Ruggiero SL, Mehrotra B, Rosenberg TJ, Engroff SL 2004 Osteonecrosis of the jaws associated with the use of bisphosphonates: A review of 63 cases. J Oral Maxillofac Surg 62:527–534.

46. Woo SB, Hande K, Richardson PG 2005 Osteonecrosis of the jaw and bisphosphonates. N Engl J Med 353:99–102.

47. Purcell PM, Boyd IW 2005 Bisphosphonates and osteonecrosis of the jaw. Med J Aust 182:417–418.

48. Jimenez-Soriano Y, Bagan JV 2005 Bisphosphonates, as a new cause of drug-induced jaw osteonecrosis: An update. Med Oral Patol Oral Cir Bucal 10(Suppl 2):E88–E91.

49. Lugassy G, Shaham R, Nemets A, Ben-Dor D, Nahlieli O 2004 Severe osteomyelitis of the jaw in long-term survivors of multiple myeloma: A new clinical entity. Am J Med 117:440–441.

50. Riggs BL, Khosla S, Melton LJ III 2002 Sex steroids and the construction and conservation of the adult skeleton. Endocr Rev 23:279–302.

51. Shapiro CL, Manola J, Leboff M 2001 Ovarian failure after adjuvant chemotherapy is associated with rapid bone loss in women with early-stage breast cancer. J Clin Oncol 19:3306–3311.

52. Maillefert JF, Sibilia J, Michel F, Saussine C, Javier RM, Tavernier C 1999 Bone mineral density in men treated with synthetic gonadotropin-releasing hormone agonists for prostatic carcinoma. J Urol 161:1219–1222.

53. Kanis J 1997 Pathogenesis of osteoporosis and fracture Osteoporosis. Blackwell Healthcare Communications, London, UK.

54. Eastell R, Hannon RA, Cuzick J, Clack G, Adams JE 2002 Effect of anastrozole on bone density and bone turnover: Results of the "Arimidex" (anastrozole), tamoxifen, aalone or in combination (ATAC) study. J Bone Miner Res 17:S1:S165.

55. Gnant M, Hausmaninger H, Samonigg H, Mlineritsch B, Taucher S, Luschin-Ebengreuth G, Jakesz R 2002 Changes in bone mineral density caused by anastrozole or tamoxifen in combination with goserelin (+/- zoledronate) as adjuvant treatment for hormone receptor-positive premenopausal breast cancer: Results of a randomized multicenter trial. 25th Annual San Antonio Breast Cancer Symposium, December 11, 2002, San Antonio, TX, USA.

56. Lee WY, Cho SW, Oh ES, Oh KW, Lee JM, Yoon KH, Kang MI, Cha BY, Lee KW, Son HY, Kang SK, Kim CC 2002 The effect of bone marrow transplantation on the osteoblastic differentiation of human bone marrow stromal cells. J Clin Endocrinol Metab 87:329–335.

Genetic, Developmental, and Dysplastic Skeletal Disorders
(Section Editor: Michael P. Whyte)

SECTION IX

Genetic, Developmental, and Dysplastic Skeletal Disorders

Michael P. Whyte

Division of Bone and Mineral Diseases, Washington University School of Medicine at Barnes-Jewish Hospital and Center for Metabolic Bone Disease and Molecular Research, Shriners Hospitals for Children, St. Louis, Missouri

INTRODUCTION

Physicians can encounter a great diversity of rare, genetic, developmental, or dysplastic skeletal disorders.[1-5] Some are mere radiographic curiosities; some are lethal. Some cause focal bony abnormalities; some feature generalized disturbances of skeletal growth, modeling, or remodeling leading to osteosclerosis, hyperostosis, or osteoporosis. A few are associated with overt derangements in mineral homeostasis. Most are important also because they harbor clues concerning factors and pathways that regulate mineral metabolism and skeletal homeostasis.[6] Cumulatively, the number of such patients is substantial.[1-5]

This section provides a concise overview of several of the more common or more revealing of the genetic, developmental, and dysplastic skeletal disorders beginning with those traditionally grouped as sclerosing bone dysplasias.[2-4] Subsequently, there are descriptions of a few additional important heritable or sporadic developmental and dysplastic conditions.

REFERENCES

1. Online Mendelian Inheritance in Man, OMIM 2000 McKusick-Nathans Institute for Genetic Medicine, Johns Hopkins University (Baltimore, MD) and National Center for Biotechnology Information, National Library of Medicine (Bethesda, MD). Available at http://www.ncbi.nlm.nih.gov/om.
2. Royce PM, Steinmann B (eds.) 2002 Connective Tissue and Its Heritable Disorders, 2nd ed. Wiley_Liss, New York, NY, USA.
3. Scriver CR, Beaudet AL, Sly WS, Valle D, Childs B, Vogelstein B (eds.) 2001 The Metabolic and Molecular Bases of Inherited Disease, 8th ed. McGraw-Hill, New York, NY, USA.
3. Whyte MP 1997 Skeletal disorders characterized by osteosclerosis or hyperostosis. In: Avioli LV, Krane SM (eds.) Metabolic Bone Disease, 2nd ed. Academic Press, San Diego, CA, USA, pp. 697–738.
5. Castriota-Scanderbeg A, Dallapiccola B 2005 Abnormal Skeletal Phenotypes: From Simple Signs To Complex Diagnoses. Springer, New York, NY, USA.
6. Van Hul W 2003 Recent progress in the molecular genetics of sclerosing bone dysplasias. Pediatr Pathol Mol Med 22:11–22.

Chapter 71.   Sclerosing Bone Disorders

Michael P. Whyte

Division of Bone and Mineral Diseases, Washington University School of Medicine at Barnes-Jewish Hospital and Center for Metabolic Bone Disease and Molecular Research, Shriners Hospitals for Children, St. Louis, Missouri

SCLEROSING BONE DISORDERS

Osteosclerosis and hyperostosis refer to trabecular and cortical bone thickening, respectively.[4] Increased skeletal mass is caused by many rare (often hereditary) dysplastic conditions,[1] as well as by a variety of dietary, metabolic, endocrine, hematologic, infectious, and neoplastic problems (Table 1).[4] The following sections describe the principal disorders among the bone dysplasias and other unusual conditions associated with localized or generalized osteosclerosis and hyperostosis.

OSTEOPETROSIS

Osteopetrosis (marble bone disease) was first described in 1904 by Albers-Schönberg.[7] More than 300 cases have been reported.[8] Traditionally, two major clinical forms are discussed: the autosomal dominant adult (benign) type that is associated with relatively few symptoms[9] and the autosomal recessive infantile (malignant) type that is typically fatal during infancy or early childhood if untreated.[10] A rarer "intermediate" form presents during childhood with some of the difficulties and signs of malignant osteopetrosis, but its impact on life expectancy is not known.[11] A fourth clinical type, also inherited as an autosomal recessive trait, was initially called the

syndrome of osteopetrosis with renal tubular acidosis and cerebral calcification, but is an inborn error of metabolism, carbonic anhydrase II deficiency.[8] Neuronal storage disease with malignant osteopetrosis has been reported in several patients and seems to represent a distinct entity.[12] There also seem to be especially rare forms of osteopetrosis called "lethal," "transient infantile," and "postinfectious."[8] A new syndrome of osteopetrosis, lymphedema, anhydrotic ectodermal dysplasia, and immunodeficiency (OL-EDA-ID) was characterized as an X-linked trait affecting boys.[13] The first report of drug-induced osteopetrosis was published in 2003 and concerned a boy who received a large amount of pamidronate.[14] Revelation of the genetic defects causing osteopetrosis promises an improved nosology.[15]

Although a diversity of clinical and hereditary types of osteopetrosis shows that defects in several different genes and a variety of biological disturbances cause this disorder in humans, the pathogenesis of all true forms involves failure of osteoclast-mediated resorption of the skeleton.[8,15] Consequently, primary spongiosa (calcified cartilage deposited during endochondral bone formation) persists as a histopathological marker.[16] Understandably, the term "osteopetrosis" has been used generically for some other conditions with radio-dense skeletons yet lacking this hallmark, but we should now be precise. In fact, it is crucial to recognize that therapeutic approaches for true forms of osteopetrosis, for which the patho-

---

The author has reported no conflicts of interest.

TABLE 1. DISORDERS THAT CAUSE HIGH BONE MASS

Dysplasias and dysostoses
  Autosomal dominant osteosclerosis
  Central osteosclerosis with ectodermal dysplasia
  Craniodiaphyseal dysplasia
  Craniometaphyseal dysplasia
  Dysosteosclerosis
  Endosteal hyperostosis (van Buchem disease and sclerosteosis)
  Frontometaphyseal dysplasia
  Infantile cortical hyperostosis (Caffey disease)
  Juvenile Paget's disease (osteoectasia with hyperphosphatasia or hyperostosis corticalis)
  Melorheostosis
  Metaphyseal dysplasia (Pyle disease)
  Mixed sclerosing bone dystrophy
  Oculodento-osseous dysplasia
  Osteodysplasia of Melnick and Needles
  Osteopathia striata
  Osteopetrosis
  Osteopoikilosis
  Progressive diaphyseal dysplasia (Engelmann disease)
  Pycnodysostosis
  Tubular stenosis (Kenny-Caffey syndrome)
Metabolic
  Carbonic anhydrase II deficiency
  Fluorosis
  Heavy metal poisoning
  Hepatitis C-associated osteosclerosis
  Hypervitaminosis A, D
  Hyper-, hypo-, and pseudohypoparathyroidism
  Hypophosphatemic osteomalacia
  LRP5 activation (high bone mass phenotype)
  Milk-alkali syndrome
  Renal osteodystrophy
  X linked hypophosphatemia
Other
  Axial osteomalacia
  Diffuse idiopathic skeletal hyperostosis (DISH)
  Erdheim-Chester disease
  Fibrogenesis imperfecta ossium
  Hypertrophic osteoarthropathy
  Ionizing radiation
  Leukemia
  Lymphomas
  Mastocytosis
  Multiple myeloma
  Myelofibrosis
  Osteomyelitis
  Osteonecrosis
  Paget disease
  Sarcoidosis
  Sickle cell disease
  Skeletal metastases
  Tuberous sclerosis

genesis is partly elucidated, may be hazardous for other sclerosing bone disorders.[8]

Clinical Presentation

Infantile osteopetrosis manifests during the first year of life.[30] Recurrence within sibships and an increased incidence of parental consanguinity implicate transmission as an autosomal recessive trait. Nasal stuffiness caused by malformation of the mastoid and paranasal sinuses is an early symptom. Also, cranial foramina do not widen fully, and this can gradually paralyze optic, oculomotor, and facial nerves. Hearing loss is common.[17] There is also failure to thrive. Eruption of the dentition is delayed. Bones may seem dense on radiographic study but are fragile. Some patients develop hydrocephalus or sleep apnea. Blindness can also be caused by retinal degeneration or raised intracranial pressure.[18] Recurrent infection and spontaneous bruising and bleeding are common problems from myelophthisis because of excessive bone, abundant osteoclasts, and fibrous tissue crowding the marrow spaces. Hypersplenism and hemolysis may exacerbate severe anemia. Physical examination shows short stature, a large head, frontal bossing, an "adenoid" appearance, nystagmus, hepatosplenomegaly, and genu valgum. Untreated children usually die during the first decade of life from hemorrhage, pneumonia, severe anemia, or sepsis.[10]

Intermediate osteopetrosis causes short stature. Some patients develop cranial nerve deficits, macrocephaly, ankylosed teeth that predispose to osteomyelitis of the jaw, recurrent fractures, and mild or occasionally moderately severe anemia.[11] A variant, CA II deficiency, is described in this section.

Adult osteopetrosis is a developmental disorder with radiographic abnormalities that appear during childhood. In some kindreds, generations are skipped, and carriers show no X-ray disturbances.[19] Although affected individuals can be asymptomatic,[9] the long bones are brittle and fractures do occur. Facial palsy, deafness, osteomyelitis of the mandible,[20] compromised vision or hearing, psychomotor delay, carpal tunnel syndrome, slipped capital femoral epiphysis, and osteoarthritis can be additional problems.[21] Two principal types of adult, autosomal dominant osteopetrosis have been proposed,[22] but so-called autosomal dominant osteopetrosis, type 1 (ADO 1) is essentially the high bone mass phenotype associated with LRP5 activation, whereas ADO 2 is Albers-Schönberg disease.[15,20]

Neuronal storage disease with osteopetrosis features severe skeletal manifestations and is characterized by the additional complications of epilepsy and neurodegenerative disease.[12] Lethal osteopetrosis manifests in utero and results in stillbirth.[8] Transient infantile osteopetrosis inexplicably resolves during the first few months of life.[8]

Radiological Features

Generalized, symmetrical increase in bone mass is the major radiographic finding in osteopetrosis.[23] Trabecular and cortical bone appear thickened. In the severe forms, all three principal components of skeletal development are disturbed; bone growth, modeling, and remodeling. Most of the skeleton is uniformly dense, but alternating sclerotic and lucent bands are commonly noted in the iliac wings and near the ends of the long bones. Metaphyses are typically broadened and may have a club shape or "Erlenmeyer flask" deformity (Fig. 1). Rarely, the distal phalanges in the hands are eroded (more common in pycnodysostosis). Pathological fracture of long bones is not rare. Rachitic-like changes in growth plates may occur,[24] perhaps reflecting secondary hyperparathyroidism. The skull is usually thickened and dense, especially at the base, and the paranasal and mastoid sinuses are underpneumatized (Fig. 2). Vertebrae may show, on lateral view, a "bone-in-bone" (endobone) configuration. Albers-Schönberg disease, the adult form of osteopetrosis, manifests with progressive osteosclerosis beginning in childhood, with selective thickening of the base of the skull together with typical vertebral end-plate accentuation that causes an endobone or "rugger jersey" appearance of the spine.[21,22] In the various forms of osteopetrosis, skeletal

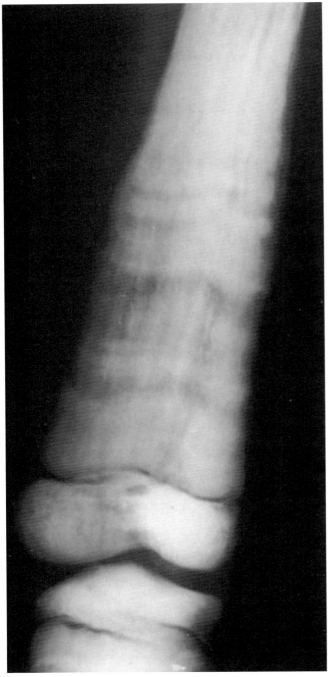

FIG. 1. Osteopetrosis. Anteroposterior radiograph of the distal femur of a 10-year-old boy shows a widened metadiaphyseal region with characteristic alternating dense and lucent bands. (Reprinted from Whyte MP, Murphy WA 1990 Osteopetrosis and other sclerosing bone disorders. In: Metabolic Bone Disease, with permission from Elsevier.)

scintigraphy can reveal fractures and osteomyelitis.[25] MRI may help to monitor patients with severe disease who undergo bone marrow transplantation, because successful engraftment will enlarge medullary spaces.[26] CT and MRI findings concerning the heads of affected infants and children have been detailed.[27]

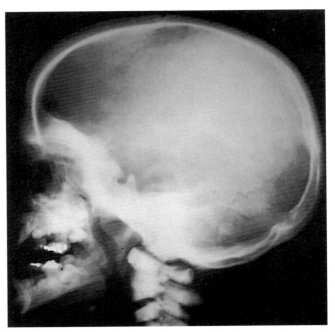

FIG. 2. Osteopetrosis. Lateral radiograph of the skull of a 13-year-old boy shows osteosclerosis especially apparent at the base. (Reprinted from Whyte MP, Murphy WA 1990 Osteopetrosis and other sclerosing bone disorders. In: Metabolic Bone Disease, with permission from Elsevier.)

Laboratory Findings

In infantile osteopetrosis, serum calcium levels generally reflect the dietary intake.[28] Hypocalcemia can occur and may be severe enough to engender rachitic changes in growth plates. Secondary hyperparathyroidism with elevated serum levels of calcitriol is commonly present.[29] Acid phosphatase (ACP) activity is often increased in serum. Presence of the brain isoenzyme of creatine kinase (BB-CK) in serum is a biochemical marker for genuine forms of osteopetrosis.[30] The ACP and apparently BB-CK originate from patient osteoclasts.[30,31] In adult osteopetrosis, standard biochemical indices of mineral homeostasis are usually unremarkable. However, PTH levels can be increased in serum.[22]

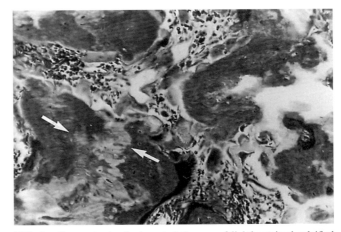

FIG. 3. Osteopetrosis. A characteristic area of lightly stained calcified primary spongiosa (arrows) is found within darkly stained mineralized bone.

Histopathological Findings

The radiographic features of the osteopetroses can be diagnostic.[23] Nevertheless, failure of osteoclasts to resorb skeletal tissue provides a histological finding that is pathognomonic[32]: that is, remnants of mineralized primary spongiosa persist as "islands" or "bars" of calcified cartilage within mature trabecular bone (Fig. 3).

Human osteopetroses may feature increased, normal, or decreased numbers of osteoclasts. In the infantile form, these cells are usually, but not always, abundant and are found at bone surfaces.[33] Their nuclei are especially numerous, yet the ruffled borders or clear zones that characterize healthy osteoclasts are absent.[34] Fibrous tissue often crowds the marrow spaces.[34] Adult osteopetrosis may show increased amounts of osteoid and osteoclasts can be few and lack ruffled borders, or they can be especially numerous and large.[35] A common histological finding is "woven" bone.[32] Hypernucleated osteoclasts off of bone surfaces occur with bisphosphonate-induced osteopetrosis.[14]

Etiology and Pathogenesis

The pathogenesis of all true forms of osteopetrosis involves diminished osteoclast-mediated skeletal resorption.[36,37] However, the potential causes of osteoclast failure are many and complex.[8,37] Abnormalities could occur in the osteoclast stem cell, its microenvironment, osteoclast precursor cells, or the mature heterokaryon, or the bone matrix.[8,16] In 1996, an osteoblast defect was reported in two severely affected patients.[38] Cases of osteopetrosis with neuronal storage disease (characterized by accumulation of ceroid lipofuscin) may involve a defect within lysosomes.[12,39] Virus-like inclusions have been found in the osteoclasts of a few sporadic cases of benign osteopetrosis, but their significance is uncertain.[40] Synthesis of an abnormal PTH,[41] or defective production of interleukin (IL)-2[42] or superoxide[43]—factors necessary for bone resorption—may also be pathogenetic defects. In fact, leukocyte function studies in the infantile form have revealed abnormalities in circulating monocytes and granulocytes.[43,44] Ultimately, impaired skeletal resorption causes fragility because fewer collagen fibrils properly connect osteons, and there is defective remodeling of woven bone to compact bone.[16]

Most forms of human osteopetrosis seem to be transmitted as autosomal traits. The molecular bases are increasingly understood.[8] Loss of the chloride channel 7 activity, as a result of deactivating mutations in the *CLCN7* gene on chromosome 16p13.3, has caused autosomal recessive malignant or intermediate osteopetrosis,[45] but more commonly explains autosomal dominant Albers-Schönberg disease.[8] Autosomal recessive infantile osteopetrosis has been found to most often represent mutations in *ATP6I* (*TCIRG1*) encoding the $\alpha 3$ subunit of the vacuolar proton pump.[46–49] In 2003, a defect in the *grey-lethal* (*GL*) gene was discovered to cause severe osteopetrosis.[50–52] Hence, deactivating mutations of three genes encoding CA II, the α_3 subunit of the vacuolar H^+ pump, and chloride channel 7 compromise acidification by osteoclasts.[8,15] The majority of patients with osteopetrosis reflect defects in osteoclast-mediated acidification. OL-EDA-ID is caused by a mutation in an essential modulator of NF-κB.[13]

Treatment

Because the etiology, pattern of inheritance, and prognosis for the various forms of osteopetrosis can differ, a correct diagnosis is crucial before therapy is attempted. Infants or young children with CA II deficiency may have radiographic features consistent with malignant osteopetrosis, yet subsequent X-ray studies can show spontaneous gradual resolution of their bony sclerosis.[8] Intermediate osteopetrosis is relatively benign compared with the infantile type. A precise diagnosis from among the various forms of osteopetrosis may require investigation of the family, careful evaluation of the patient's disease severity and progression, and gene studies.[8]

Bone Marrow Transplantation

Bone marrow transplantation (BMT) from human leukocyte antigen (HLA)-identical donors has remarkably improved some patients with infantile osteopetrosis.[53–57] Hypercalcemia can occur as osteoclast function begins.[58] Severe, acute, pulmonary hypertension is a frequent complication of stem cell transplantation.[59] In 1980, transplanted osteoclasts, but not osteoblasts, were shown to be of donor origin.[57] Such observations indicate that osteopetrosis is caused by defective osteoclast-mediated bone resorption and that osteoclast progenitor cells derive from marrow.[57] However, patients with severely crowded medullary spaces seem less likely to engraft after BMT. Hence, early intervention with BMT seems to be more successful.[55] Accordingly, histomorphometric studies of bone may help to assess the outcome of this procedure. Use of marrow from HLA-nonidentical donors warrants continued study. Purified progenitor cells in blood from HLA-haploidentical parents has been effective.[60] It is understandable that BMT may not benefit virtually all patients,[8] because defects not intrinsic to marrow could theoretically cause osteopetrosis.

Hormonal and Dietary Therapy

Some success in treating osteopetrosis has been reported with a calcium-deficient diet. Conversely, supplementation of dietary calcium may be necessary for symptomatic hypocalcemia in severely affected infants or children.[24] Large oral doses of calcitriol (1,25-dihydroxyvitamin D_3), together with limited dietary calcium intake (to prevent hypercalciuria/hypercalcemia), seems to occasionally improve infantile osteopetrosis.[61] Calcitriol may help by stimulating dormant osteoclasts. Nevertheless, some patients seem to become resistant to this treatment.[36,43] Long-term infusion of PTH helped one infant,[41] perhaps by enhancing calcitriol synthesis. The observation that leukocytes from severely affected individuals have diminished production of superoxide led to administration of recombinant human interferon γ-1b and clinical, laboratory, and histopathological evidence of benefit.[36,43] In 2000, IFN-γ-1b received Food and Drug Administration (FDA) approval in the United States for severe osteopetrosis.

High-dose glucocorticoid treatment stabilizes pediatric patients with pancytopenia and hepatomegaly. Prednisone and a low-calcium/high-phosphate diet may be an alternative to BMT.[62] One case report describes apparent cure of the malignant form using prednisone therapy.[63]

Supportive

Hyperbaric oxygenation can be an important adjunctive treatment for osteomyelitis of the jaw. Surgical decompression of the optic and facial nerves may benefit some patients.[39] Joint replacement can be helpful[64]; internal fixation may be necessary for femoral fractures.[65]

Early prenatal diagnosis of osteopetrosis by ultrasound has generally been unsuccessful. Conventional radiographic studies occasionally diagnose malignant osteopetrosis late in pregnancy.[66] Mutation detection is increasingly useful.[8]

CARBONIC ANHYDRASE II DEFICIENCY

In 1983, the autosomal recessive syndrome of osteopetrosis with renal tubular acidosis (RTA) and cerebral calcification was discovered to be an inborn error of metabolism caused by deficiency of the carbonic anhydrase II (CA II) isoenzyme.[67]

Clinical Presentation

Description of >50 cases of CA II deficiency has revealed considerable clinical variability among affected families.[68,69] The perinatal history is typically unremarkable, but in infancy or early childhood patients may sustain a fracture or manifest failure to thrive, developmental delay, or short stature. Mental subnormality is common, but not invariable. Compression of the optic nerves and dental malocclusion are additional complications. RTA may explain the hypotonia, apathy, and muscle weakness that trouble some patients. Periodic hypokalemic paralysis has been reported. Although fracture is unusual, recurrent breaks in long bones can cause significant morbidity.[68] Life expectancy does not seem to be shortened, but the oldest published cases have been young adults.[70–72]

Radiological Features

CA II deficiency resembles other forms of osteopetrosis on radiographic study, except that cerebral calcification develops during childhood and the osteosclerosis and defects in skeletal modeling diminish spontaneously (rather than increase) over years.[71] Skeletal radiographs are typically abnormal at diagnosis, although findings can be subtle at birth. CT has shown that the cerebral calcification appears between 2 and 5 years of age, increases during childhood, affects gray matter of the cortex and basal ganglia, and is similar if not identical to that of idiopathic hypoparathyroidism or pseudohypoparathyroidism.

Laboratory Findings

Bone marrow examination is unremarkable. If anemia is present, it is generally mild and of nutritional origin. Metabolic acidosis occurs as early as the neonatal period. Both proximal and distal RTA have been described[73]; distal (type I) RTA seems to be better documented. Additional understanding, however, is required.[73] Aminoaciduria and glycosuria are absent.[70]

Autopsy studies have not been reported.[70] Histopathological examination of bone from four individuals, who represented two affected families, revealed characteristic calcified primary spongiosa.[68]

Etiology and Pathogenesis

The CA isoenzymes accelerate the first step in the reaction $CO_2 + H_2O \leftrightarrow H_2CO_3 \rightarrow H^+ + HCO_3^-$. Accordingly, they function importantly in acid–base regulation. CA II is present in many tissues, such as brain, kidney, erythrocytes, cartilage, lung, and gastric mucosa.[74] The other CA isoenzymes have a more limited anatomic distribution.

All 21 patients from 12 unrelated kindreds of diverse ethnic and geographic origin were shown to have selective deficiency of CA II in erythrocytes.[70] In carriers, red cell CA II levels are approximately one-half normal.[67,69,70] Deactivating mutations in the gene encoding CA II in patients with osteopetrosis, RTA, and cerebral calcification indicate an important function for CA II in bone, kidney, and perhaps brain.[75] Further insight concerning CA II is provided by a knockout mouse model.[75]

Treatment

Transfusion of CA II–replete erythrocytes in one patient did not correct the systemic acidosis.[76] RTA in CA II deficiency has been treated with HCO_3^- supplementation, but the long-term impact is unknown. BMT corrected the osteopetrosis, slowed the cerebral calcification, but did not alter the RTA.[77]

PYCNODYSOSTOSIS

Pycnodysostosis may have afflicted the French impressionist painter Henri de Toulouse-Lautrec (1864–1901).[78,79] More than 100 cases from 50 families have been described since the disorder was delineated in 1962.[80] Pycnodysostosis is transmitted as an autosomal recessive trait; parental consanguinity has been reported for ~30% of patients. Most clinical descriptions have come from Europe or the United States, but the inborn error has been identified in Israelis, Indonesians, Asian Indians, and Africans. Pycnodysostosis seems to be especially common in the Japanese.[80–82] In 1996, the genetic defect, cathepsin K deficiency, was discovered.[83]

Clinical Presentation

Pycnodysostosis is generally diagnosed during infancy or early childhood because of disproportionate short stature associated with a relatively large cranium and dysmorphic features that include fronto-occipital prominence, obtuse mandibular angle, small facies and chin, high-arched palate, dental malocclusion with retained deciduous teeth, proptosis, bluish sclerae, and a beaked and pointed nose.[82,84] The anterior fontanel and other cranial sutures are usually open. Fingers are short and clubbed from acro-osteolysis or aplasia of terminal phalanges, fingernails are hypoplastic, and hands are small and square. The thorax is narrow and there may be pectus excavatum, kyphoscoliosis, and increased lumbar lordosis. Recurrent fractures typically involve the lower limbs and cause *genu valgum* deformity. Patients are, however, usually able to walk independently. Visceral manifestations and rickets have been described. Mental retardation affects ~10% of cases.[82,84] Adult height ranges from 4 ft 3 in to 4 ft 11 in. Recurrent respiratory infections and right heart failure, from chronic upper airway obstruction caused by micrognathia, trouble some patients.

Radiographic Features

Pycnodysostosis shares many radiographic features with osteopetrosis. For example, both conditions cause generalized osteosclerosis and are associated with recurrent fractures. Furthermore, the osteosclerosis is developmental, uniform, first becomes apparent in childhood, and increases with age. However, the marked modeling defects of the severe forms of osteopetrosis do not occur in pycnodysostosis, although long bones manifest hyperostosis and narrow medullary canals. Additional findings that help to differentiate pycnodysostosis include delayed closure of cranial sutures and fontanels (prominently the anterior; Fig. 4), obtuse mandibular angle, wormian bones, gracile clavicles that are hypoplastic at their lateral segments, hypoplasia or aplasia of the distal phalanges and ribs, and partial absence of the hyoid bone.[85] Endobones and radiodense striations are absent.[23] However, the calvarium and base of the skull are sclerotic, and the orbital ridges are radiodense. Hypoplasia of facial bones, sinuses, and terminal phalanges are characteristic. Vertebrae are dense, yet their transverse processes are uninvolved; anterior and posterior concavities occur. Lumbosacral spondylolisthesis is not uncommon, and lack of segmentation of the atlas and axis may be present. Madelung deformity can affect the forearms.

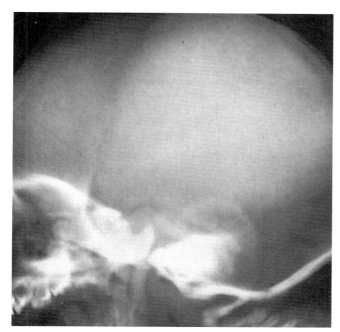

FIG. 4. Pycnodysostosis. Lateral radiograph of an infant skull shows markedly widened cranial sutures. The base is sclerotic. (Reprinted from Whyte MP, Murphy WA 1990 Osteopetrosis and other sclerosing bone disorders. In: Metabolic Bone Disease, with permission from Elsevier.)

Laboratory Findings

Serum calcium and inorganic phosphate levels and alkaline phosphatase activity are usually unremarkable. Anemia is not a problem. Histopathological study shows cortical bone structure that seems normal despite the appearance of diminished osteoclastic and osteoblastic activity.[86] Electron microscopy of bone from two patients suggested that degradation of collagen might be defective, perhaps from an abnormality in the bone matrix or in the osteoclast.[86] In chondrocytes, abnormal inclusions have been described.

Etiology and Pathogenesis

Early studies of pycnodysostosis indicated that absorption of dietary calcium may be increased. Both the rate of bone accretion and the size of the exchangeable calcium pool seemed reduced.[87] Accordingly, diminished rates of bone resorption potentially explained the osteosclerosis. Also, virus-like inclusions were found in the osteoclasts of two affected brothers.[88]

In 1993, the killing activity and IL-1 secretion of circulating monocytes were found to be low.[89] In 1996, defective growth hormone secretion and low serum insulin-like growth factor (IGF)-I levels were reported in five of six affected children.[90] In 1996, deactivating mutation of the gene encoding cathepsin K was discovered.[81] Cathepsin K, a lysosomal cysteine protease, is highly expressed in osteoclasts.[91] Impaired collagen degradation seems to be a fundamental pathogenetic defect.[83] Bone quality is compromised.[92]

Treatment

There is no known medical therapy for pycnodysostosis. Bone marrow transplantation has not been reported. Fractures of the long bones are typically transverse. They usually heal at a satisfactory rate, although delayed union and massive callus formation can occur. Internal fixation of long bones is formidable because of their hardness. Extraction of teeth is difficult; fracture of the jaw has occurred.[84] Osteomyelitis of the mandible may require treatment with a combined antibiotic and surgical approach. The orthopedic problems have been briefly reviewed.[93]

PROGRESSIVE DIAPHYSEAL DYSPLASIA (CAMURATI-ENGELMANN DISEASE)

Progressive diaphyseal dysplasia (PDD) was characterized by Cockayne in 1920.[94] Camurati discovered it is heritable. Engelmann described the severe typical form in 1929.[95] In 2001, mutations were identified in the $TGF-\beta1$ gene.[96]

PDD is transmitted as an autosomal dominant trait. All races are affected. Descriptions of >100 cases show that the clinical and radiographic expression is quite variable.[97,98] The characteristic feature is hyperostosis that occurs gradually on both the periosteal and endosteal surfaces of long bones. In severe cases, osteosclerosis is widespread, and the skull and axial skeleton are involved. Some carriers have no radiographic changes, but bone scintigraphy is abnormal.

Clinical Presentation

PDD typically presents during childhood with limping or a broad-based and waddling gait, leg pain, muscle wasting, and decreased subcutaneous fat in the extremities. Understandably, these features mimic muscular dystrophy.[99] Severely affected patients also have a characteristic body habitus that includes an enlarged head with prominent forehead, proptosis, and thin limbs with thickened bones and little muscle mass. Cranial nerve palsies may develop when the skull is affected. Puberty is sometimes delayed. Raised intracranial pressure can occur. Physical findings include palpable bony thickening and skeletal tenderness. Some patients have hepatosplenomegaly, Raynaud's phenomenon, and other findings suggestive of vasculitis.[100] Although radiological studies typically show progressive disease, the clinical course is variable, and remission of symptoms seems to occur in some patients during adult life.[101]

Radiological Features

The principal radiographic feature of PDD is hyperostosis of major long bone diaphyses caused by proliferation of new bone on both the periosteal and the endosteal surfaces.[23] The sclerosis is fairly symmetrical and gradually spreads to involve metaphyses. However, the epiphyses are characteristically spared (Fig. 5). The tibias and femora are most commonly involved; less frequently, the radii, ulnae, humeri and, occasionally, the short tubular bones are affected. The scapulae, clavicles, and pelvis may also become thickened. Typically, the shafts of long bones gradually widen and develop irregular surfaces. The age-of-onset, rate of progression, and degree of bony involvement are highly variable. With relatively mild disease, especially in adolescents or young adults, radiographic and scintigraphic abnormalities may be confined to the long bones of the lower limbs. Maturation of the new bone increases the degree of hyperostosis. However, in severely affected children, some areas of the skeleton can appear osteopenic.

Bone scanning typically reveals focally increased radionuclide accumulation in affected areas of the skeleton.[102] Clinical, radiographic, and scintigraphic findings are generally concordant. In some patients, however, bone scans are unremarkable despite considerable radiographic abnormality. This mismatch seems to reflect advanced but quiescent disease.[102] Markedly increased radioisotope accumulation with minimal radiographic findings can disclose active but early

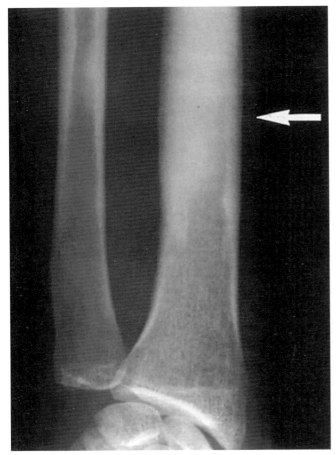

FIG. 5. Progressive diaphyseal dysplasia (Camurati-Engelmann disease). The distal radius of this 20-year-old woman has characteristic patchy thickening (arrow) of the periosteal and endosteal surfaces of the diaphysis.

skeletal disease.[13] MRI and CT findings delineating cranial involvement have been reported.[103]

Laboratory Findings

Routine biochemical parameters of bone and mineral metabolism are typically normal in PDD, although serum alkaline phosphatase activity and urinary hydroxyproline levels are elevated in some patients. Modest hypocalcemia and significant hypocalciuria occur in some affected individuals who have severe disease and seem to indicate markedly positive calcium balance.[101] Mild anemia and leukopenia and an elevated erythrocyte sedimentation rate may also be present.[100]

Histopathology shows new bone formation along diaphyses. Peripheral to the original bony cortex, there is disorganized, newly formed, woven bone undergoing centripetal maturation and then incorporation into the cortex.[97] Electron microscopy of muscle has shown myopathic changes and vascular abnormalities.[99]

Etiology and Pathogenesis

The clinical and laboratory features of severe PDD and its responsiveness to glucocorticoid treatment have led some investigators to suggest that this disorder is a systemic condition (i.e., an inflammatory connective tissue disease).[100] Some especially mild cases were believed to represent a separate, autosomal recessive, condition called Ribbing's disease.[104] However, sporadic cases of PDD do occur, and mild clinical

forms can be transmitted as an autosomal dominant trait with variable penetrance.[105]

Aberrant differentiation of monocytes/macrophages to fibroblasts, and hence to osteoblasts, has been discussed as a fundamental pathogenetic feature.[106]

Before its genetic basis became understood, PDD was thought to be more severe in ensuing generations (anticipation).[105] PDD is now known to involve mutations in the gene for TGF-β1. A "latency-associated peptide" encoded by this gene is altered and remains bound to TGF-β1 keeping it constitutively active in skeletal matrix.[96,107,108] Severity is variable among kindred members. Additionally, there seems to some locus heterogeneity.[109,110]

Treatment

PDD is a chronic and somewhat unpredictable condition.[111] Symptoms may remit during adolescence or adult life. Glucocorticoid therapy (typically prednisone given in small doses on alternate days) has become a well-documented, effective treatment that can relieve bone pain and apparently correct histological abnormalities in affected bone.[112] Complete relief of localized pain has followed surgical removal of diseased diaphyseal bone, forming a "cortical window."[113] Bisphosphonate therapy may increase bone pain.[114]

ENDOSTEAL HYPEROSTOSIS

In 1955, van Buchem et al.[115] first described the condition hyperostosis corticalis generalisata. Their report led to characterization of the disorders that are considered endosteal hyperostoses.

Van Buchem Disease

Van Buchem disease is an autosomal recessive, clinically severe condition[115] that is differentiated from an autosomal dominant, more benign form of endosteal hyperostosis (Worth type)[115,116] and an autosomal recessive, severe disorder called sclerosteosis. The entity is considerably less common than the cumulative number of case reports might suggest.[117]

Clinical Presentation. Van Buchem disease has been described in children and adults; sex distribution seems to be equal. Progressive asymmetrical enlargement of the jaw occurs during puberty. The adult mandible is markedly thickened with a wide angle, but there is no prognathism, and dental malocclusion is uncommon. Patients may be symptom free; however, recurrent facial nerve palsy, deafness, and optic atrophy from narrowing of cranial foramina are common and can begin as early as infancy. Long bones may become painful with applied pressure, but they are not fragile, and joint range-of-motion is generally normal. Sclerosteosis has been differentiated clinically from van Buchem disease because sclerosteosis patients are excessively tall and have syndactyly.[118]

Radiological Features. Endosteal cortical thickening that produces a dense and homogeneous diaphyseal cortex and narrows the medullary canal is the major radiographic feature of van Buchem disease. The hyperostosis is selectively endosteal; long bones are properly modeled. However, generalized osteosclerosis affects the base of the skull, facial bones, vertebrae, pelvis, and ribs. The mandible becomes enlarged (Fig. 6). Cranial CT features have been characterized.[119]

Laboratory Findings. Alkaline phosphatase activity in serum is primarily of skeletal origin and may be increased; calcium and inorganic phosphate levels are unremarkable. Van Buchem

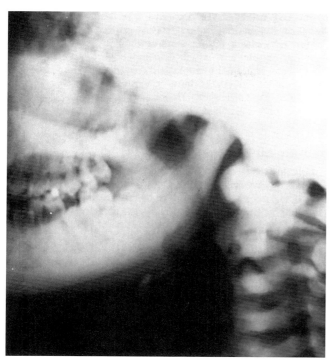

FIG 6. Endosteal hyperostosis. Lateral radiograph of the mandible and facial bones of a 9-year-old boy with van Buchem disease shows dense sclerosis of all osseous structures. (Reprinted from Whyte MP, Murphy WA 1990 Osteopetrosis and other sclerosing bone disorders. In: Metabolic Bone Disease, with permission from Elsevier.)

et al. suggested that the excessive bone was essentially of normal quality.

Etiology and Pathogenesis. Van Buchem disease and sclerosteosis were once predicated to be allelic disorders—their clinical/radiographic differences likely reflecting modifying genes.[118] Now, we know that deactivating mutations in the *SOST* gene cause sclerosteosis,[120] whereas van Buchem disease involves a 52-kb deletion that compromises a downstream enhancer of *SOST*.[121,122] Sclerostin promotes the apoptosis of osteoblasts[123] and binds to LRP5/6 and antagonizes canonical Wnt signaling.[124]

Treatment. There is no specific medical therapy. Surgical decompression of narrowed foramina may help cranial nerve palsies.[125] Surgery has also been used to recontour the mandible.[126]

Sclerosteosis

Sclerosteosis (cortical hyperostosis with syndactyly), like van Buchem disease, is an autosomal recessive form of endosteal hyperostosis. It occurs primarily in Afrikaners or others of Dutch ancestry.[118] Initially, sclerosteosis was distinguished from van Buchem disease by some radiographic differences and the presence of syndactyly. Subsequent clinical studies predicted both disorders were "allelic" and involved defects in the same gene.[118] We now know that the genetic defects are different.[120,121]

Clinical Presentation. At birth, only syndactyly may be noted.[127] During early childhood, overgrowth and sclerosis of the skeleton involves especially the skull and causes facial disfigurement. Patients are tall and heavy beginning in childhood. Understandably, the term "gigantism" has been used. However, deafness and facial palsy caused by nerve entrapment are also prominent problems. The mandible has a square configuration. Raised intracranial pressure and headache may be sequelae of a small cranial cavity. The brainstem can become compressed. Syndactyly from either cutaneous or bony fusion of the middle and index fingers is typical, but of variable severity. The fingernails are dysplastic. Patients are not prone to fracture, and their intelligence is normal. Life expectancy may be shortened.[128] The natural history has been reviewed.[129]

Radiological Features. Except when bony syndactyly is present, the skeleton is normal in early childhood. The principal radiographic feature is progressive bone thickening that causes widening of the skull and prognathism.[130] In the long bones, modeling defects occur and the cortices are thickened. The vertebral pedicles, ribs, pelvis, and tubular bones may also become somewhat dense. CT has shown fusion of the ossicles and narrowing of the internal auditory canals and cochlear aqueducts.[118]

Histopathological Findings. In an American kindred with sclerosteosis, dynamic histomorphometry of the skull of one patient showed thickened trabeculae and osteoidosis where the rate of bone formation was increased; osteoclastic bone resorption seemed to be quiescent.[131]

Etiology and Pathogenesis. Enhanced osteoblast activity with failure of osteoclasts to compensate for increased bone formation seems to explain the dense bone of sclerosteosis.[131] No abnormality of calcium homeostasis or of pituitary gland function has been documented.[132] The pathogenesis of the neurological defects has been described in detail.[131]

In 1998, van Buchem disease was mapped to chromosome 17q12-q21.[133] In 2000, deactivating mutations in a gene called *SOST* within this region were discovered in sclerosteosis patients of Afrikaner descent.[120]

Treatment. There is no specific medical treatment for sclerosteosis. Surgical correction of syndactyly is especially difficult if there is bony fusion. Prognathism cosmesis is complicated by dense mandibular bone. Management of associated neurological dysfunction has been reviewed.[131]

OSTEOPOIKILOSIS

Osteopoikilosis literally translated means spotted bones. This condition, usually a radiographic curiosity, is transmitted as an autosomal dominant trait with a high degree of penetrance.[134] Affected individuals may also have a form of connective tissue nevus called dermatofibrosis lenticularis disseminata; the disorder is then called the Buschke-Ollendorff syndrome.[135] The bony lesions are asymptomatic, but if not recognized, can precipitate studies for other important conditions, including metastatic disease to the skeleton.[136] Hence, family members at risk should be screened with a radiograph of the hand/wrist and knee after childhood.

Clinical Presentation

Osteopoikilosis is typically an incidental finding. Musculoskeletal pain, recorded in many cases, is sometimes coincidental. However, joint contractions and limb length inequality can occur, especially in individuals who also have radiographic changes of melorheostosis. The nevi usually involve the lower trunk or extremities and occur before puberty, sometimes congenitally. This dermatosis characteristically appears as small

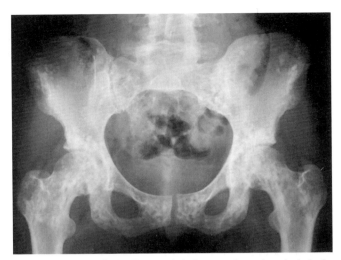

FIG. 7. Osteopoikilosis. Characteristic features shown here include the spotted appearance of the pelvis and metaepiphyseal regions of the femora. [Reproduced with permission from Whyte MP 1995 Rare disorders of skeletal formation and homeostasis. In: Becker KN (ed.) Principles and Practice of Endocrinology and Metabolism, 2nd ed. Lippincott-Raven Publishers, Philadelphia, PA, USA.]

asymptomatic papules; however, they are sometimes yellow or white discs or plaques, deep nodules, or streaks.[135]

Radiological Features

The characteristic radiographic finding is numerous small foci of osteosclerosis of variable shape (usually round or oval).[23] Commonly affected sites are the ends of the short tubular bones, the metaepiphyseal regions of the long bones, and the tarsal, carpal, and pelvic bones (Fig. 7). These foci do not change shape and size for decades, but they may mimic metastatic lesions. However, radionuclide accumulation is not increased on bone scanning.[136]

Histopathological Studies

Dermatofibrosis lenticularis disseminata is characterized by excessive amounts of unusually broad, markedly branched, interlacing elastin fibers in the dermis; the epidermis is normal.[135,137] The foci of osteosclerosis are thickened trabeculae that merge with surrounding normal bone or islands of cortical bone that include Haversian systems. Mature lesions seem to be remodeling slowly.[137] In 2004, deactivating mutations in the *LEMD3* gene were identified.[138]

OSTEOPATHIA STRIATA

Osteopathia striata is characterized by linear striations at the ends of long bones and in the ileum.[23] Like osteopoikilosis, it is a radiographic curiosity when the skeletal findings occur alone. However, osteopathia striata is also a feature of a variety of clinically important syndromes, including osteopathia striata with cranial sclerosis[139] and osteopathia striata with focal dermal hypoplasia.[140]

Clinical Presentation

Isolated osteopathia striata is transmitted as an autosomal dominant trait. The musculoskeletal symptoms that may have led to the radiographic studies are probably unrelated. However, when there is also sclerosis of the skull, cranial nerve palsies are common.[139] Until recently, this condition was considered an autosomal dominant trait, but now perhaps an X-linked dominant disorder.[141] Osteopathia striata with focal dermal hypoplasia (Goltz syndrome) is a serious X-linked recessive problem in which affected boys have widespread linear areas of dermal hypoplasia through which adipose tissue can herniate. They also have a variety of additional bony defects in their limbs.[140] Histopathological studies of bone have not been described.

Radiological Features

Gracile linear striations in the cancellous regions of the skeleton, particularly in the metaepiphyses of major long bones and in the periphery of the iliac bones, are the characteristic radiographic findings (Fig. 8).[23] The carpal, tarsal, and tubular bones of the hands and feet are less commonly and more subtly affected. The striations appear unchanged for years. Radionuclide accumulation is not increased during bone scanning.[136]

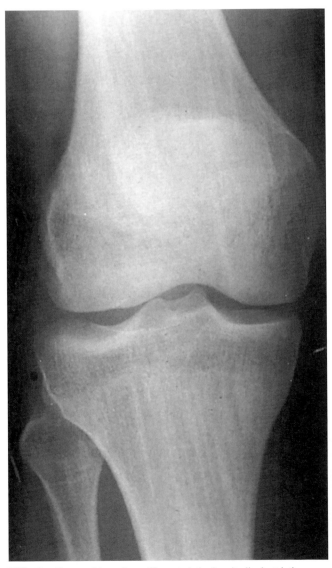

FIG. 8. Osteopathia striata. Characteristic longitudinal striations are present in the femur and tibia of this 17-year-old girl.

Treatment

The bone lesions are benign. Although unlikely to be misdiagnosed, radiographic screening after childhood of family members at risk would seem prudent. In one family with osteopathia striata and cranial sclerosis, the diagnosis was reportedly made prenatally by sonography.[142]

MELORHEOSTOSIS

Melorheostosis, from the Greek, refers to flowing hyperostosis of the limbs. The radiographic findings have been likened to hardened wax that had dripped down the side of a candle. First described in 1922,[143] ~200 cases have been reported.[144,145] True melorheostosis occurs sporadically. Melorheostosis-like changes can occur in some individuals with osteopoikilosis.

Clinical Presentation

Melorheostosis typically manifests during childhood. Usually there is monomelic involvement; bilateral disease, when it occurs, is generally asymmetrical. Cutaneous changes that overlie affected skeletal sites are not uncommon. Of 131 patients reported in one investigation, 17% had linear scleroderma-like patches and hypertrichosis. Fibromas, fibrolipomas, capillary hemangiomas, lymphangiectasia, and arterial aneurysms also occur.[146,147] Soft-tissue abnormalities are often noted before the hyperostosis is discovered. Pain and stiffness are the major symptoms. Affected joints can contract and deform. In affected children, leg length inequality occurs because of soft tissue contractures and premature fusion of epiphyses. The skeletal lesions seem to progress most rapidly during childhood. In the adult years, melorheostosis may or may not gradually extend.[148] Nevertheless, pain is a more frequent symptom in adults because of subperiosteal new bone formation.

Radiological Features

Dense, irregular, and eccentric hyperostosis of both the cortex and the adjacent medullary canal of a single bone, or several adjacent bones, is the characteristic radiographic finding in melorheostosis (Fig. 9).[23,145] Any anatomical region or bone may be affected, but the lower extremities are most commonly involved. Bone can also develop in soft tissues near affected skeletal areas, particularly near joints. Melorheostotic bone has increased blood flow and avidly accumulates radionuclide during bone scanning.[149]

Laboratory Findings

Routine laboratory studies (e.g., serum calcium and inorganic phosphate levels and alkaline phosphatase activity) are normal.

Histopathological Findings

The skeletal lesion in melorheostosis features endosteal thickening during infancy and childhood and then periosteal new bone formation during adult life.[145] Bony lesions are sclerotic with thickened irregular lamellae that may occlude Haversian systems. Marrow fibrosis may also be present.[145] Unlike in true scleroderma, the collagen of the scleroderma-like lesions of melorheostosis appear normal. Hence, this dermatosis has been called linear melorheostotic scleroderma.[146,150]

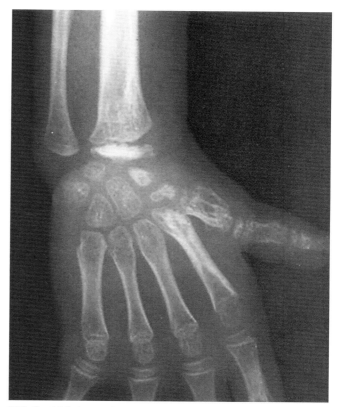

FIG. 9. Melorheostosis. Characteristic patchy osteosclerosis is most apparent in the radius and second metacarpal of this 8-year-old girl.

Etiology and Pathogenesis

The distribution of melorheostosis and its associated soft tissue lesions in sclerotomes, myotomes, and dermatomes suggests that a segmentary, embryogenetic defect explains this sporadic condition.[146,150] Linear scleroderma may reflect the primary abnormality that extends deep into the skeleton. Recent studies of affected skin suggest altered expression of several adhesion proteins.[151] Germline mutation of *LEMD3* is not the cause of classic sporadic melorheostosis.[152]

Treatment

Surgical correction of contractures can be difficult; recurrent deformity is common. Distraction techniques, however, have been promising.[153]

MIXED SCLEROSING BONE DYSTROPHY

Mixed sclerosing bone dystrophy is a rare skeletal dysplasia in which features of osteopoikilosis, osteopathia striata, melorheostosis, cranial sclerosis, or additional osseous defects occur together in various combinations in one individual.[154]

Clinical Presentation

Patients may experience the problems typically associated with the individual patterns of osteosclerosis; for example, cranial sclerosis may result in cranial nerve palsy, and melorheostosis can cause localized bone pain.[155]

Radiological Features

Two or more dense bone patterns are noted (osteopoikilosis, osteopathia striata, melorheostosis, cranial sclerosis, generalized cortical hyperostosis, focal osteosclerosis, or progressive diaphyseal dysplasia). However, just one region of the skeleton may be affected.

Bone scanning shows increased radionuclide uptake in the areas of greatest skeletal sclerosis.[154,155]

Histopathological Findings

Although the term "osteopetrosis" has been applied to the generalized osteosclerosis that occurs in some patients, histopathology has failed to show remnants of calcified primary spongiosa (see osteopetrosis).[154,155]

Etiology and Pathogenesis

Delineation of mixed sclerosing bone dystrophy suggests a common etiology and pathogenesis for its individual osteosclerotic patterns. However, osteopoikilosis from *LEMD3* mutation and most forms of osteopathia striata are heritable, whereas mixed sclerosing bone dystrophy, like melorheostosis, seems to be a sporadic disorder.[154,155]

Treatment

There is no medical treatment. Contractures or neurovascular compression by osteosclerotic lesions can require surgical intervention.

AXIAL OSTEOMALACIA

Axial osteomalacia is characterized radiographically by coarsening of the trabecular pattern of the axial but not the appendicular skeleton.[156] Fewer than 20 patients have been described. Most affected individuals have been sporadic cases, but dominant transmission has been reported.[153]

Clinical Presentation

Most patients with axial osteomalacia have been middle-aged or elderly men; a few middle-aged women have been described. However, radiographic manifestations are likely to be detectable earlier.[157] The majority of cases have presented with dull, vague, and chronic axial bone pain (often in the cervical region) that prompted radiographic study. Family histories are usually negative for skeletal disease.

Radiological Features

Abnormalities are confined essentially to the spine and pelvis, where trabeculae are coarsened and form a pattern resembling other types of osteomalacia.[158] However, Looser zones (a radiographic hallmark of osteomalacia) are not reported. The cervical spine and ribs seem to be the most severely affected; the lumbar spine is abnormal to a lesser degree. Several patients have also had features of ankylosing spondylitis.[159,160] Radiographic survey of the appendicular skeleton is unremarkable.

Laboratory Studies

In a few patients, serum inorganic phosphate levels tended to be low.[159,160]

For others, osteomalacia occurred despite normal serum levels of calcium, inorganic phosphate, 25-hydroxyvitamin D and 1,25-dihydroxyvitamin D. Serum alkaline phosphatase activity (bone isoenzyme) may be increased.

Histopathological Findings

Iliac crest specimens have distinct corticomedullary junctions, but the cortices can be especially wide and porous.

Trabeculae are of variable thickness; total bone volume may be increased. Collagen has a normal lamellar pattern on polarized-light microscopy. Increased width and extent of osteoid seams involves trabecular bone surfaces and cortical bone spaces. Tetracycline labeling confirms the defective skeletal mineralization and results in fluorescent "labels" that are single, irregular, and wide.[157] Osteoblasts are flat and inactive-appearing "lining" cells, with reduced Golgi zones and rough endoplasmic reticulum and increased amounts of cytoplasmic glycogen, but these cells do stain intensely for alkaline phosphatase. Changes of secondary hyperparathyroidism are absent.[157]

Etiology and Pathogenesis

Axial osteomalacia may be caused by an osteoblast defect.[161] Electron microscopy of iliac crest bone from one patient[157] revealed osteoblasts that had an inactive appearance but were able to form abundant osteoid with matrix vesicles.

Treatment

Effective medical therapy has not been reported. The natural history for axial osteomalacia, however, seems relatively benign. Methyltestosterone and stilbestrol have been tested without success.[161] Vitamin D_2 (as much as 20,000 U/day for 3 years) was similarly without beneficial effect.[161] Slight improvement in skeletal histology, but not in symptoms, was reported for calcium and vitamin D_2 therapy in a study of four cases.[159] Long-term follow-up of one patient showed that symptoms and radiographic findings did not change.[161]

FIBROGENESIS IMPERFECTA OSSIUM

Fibrogenesis imperfecta ossium was first described in 1950. Approximately 10 cases have been reported.[162,163] Although radiographic studies suggest generalized osteopenia, the coarse and dense appearance of trabecular bone explains why this condition fits among the osteosclerotic disorders. The clinical, biochemical, radiological, and histopathological features of fibrogenesis imperfecta ossium and axial osteomalacia have been carefully contrasted.[4]

Clinical Presentation

Fibrogenesis imperfecta ossium typically presents during middle age or later. Both sexes are affected. Gradual onset of intractable skeletal pain that rapidly progresses is the characteristic symptom. Subsequently, there is a debilitating course with progressive immobility. Spontaneous fractures are a prominent feature. Patients generally become bedridden. Physical examination shows marked bony tenderness.

Radiological Features

Radiographic changes are noted throughout the skeleton, except in the skull. Initially, there may be only osteopenia and a slightly abnormal appearance of trabecular bone.[163] Subsequently, the changes become more consistent with osteomalacia (i.e., further alterations of the trabecular bone pattern, heterogeneous bone density, and thinning of cortical bone). The corticomedullary junctions become indistinct as cortices are replaced by an abnormal pattern of trabecular bone. Areas of the skeleton may have a mixed lytic and sclerotic appearance.[162,163] The generalized osteopenia causes remaining trabeculae to appear coarse and dense in a "fish-net" pattern. Pseudofractures may develop. Deformities secondary to fractures can be present, although bony contours are typically normal. Some patients have a "rugger jersey" spine. Long bone shafts may show periosteal reaction. In fibrogenesis imperfecta ossium and axial osteomalacia, the distribution of the radiographic abnormalities (generalized versus axial, respectively) distinguishes the two conditions. Furthermore, the histopathological features are clearly different.[4]

Laboratory Findings

Serum calcium and inorganic phosphate concentrations are normal, but alkaline phosphatase is increased. Hydroxyproline levels in urine may be normal or elevated.[163] Typically, there is no aminoaciduria or other evidence of renal tubular dysfunction. Acute agranulocytosis and macroglobulinemia have been reported.

Histopathological Findings

The osseous lesion is a form of osteomalacia, although the amount of affected bone varies considerably from area to area.[163] Aberrant collagen is found in regions with abnormal mineralization patterns, but this protein is unremarkable in other tissues. Polarized-light microscopy shows that the abnormal collagen fibrils lack birefringence. Electron microscopy reveals that the collagen fibrils are thin and randomly organized in a "tangled" pattern. Cortical bone in the shaft of the femora and tibias may show the least abnormality. Osteoid seams are thick. Osteoblasts and osteoclasts can be abundant. In some regions, peculiar circular matrix structures of 300–500 nm diameter have been observed.[163] Unless bone specimens are viewed with polarized-light or electron microscopy, fibrogenesis imperfecta ossium can be mistaken for osteoporosis or other forms of osteomalacia.[163]

Etiology and Pathogenesis

The etiology is unknown. Genetic factors have not been implicated for this sporadic condition. It seems to be an acquired disorder of collagen synthesis in lamellar bone. Subperiosteal bone formation and collagen synthesis in nonosseous tissues appears to be normal.

Treatment

There is no recognized medical therapy. Temporary clinical improvement can occur.[163] Treatment with vitamin D (or an active metabolite) together with calcium supplementation has been tried without significant benefit. Indeed, ectopic calcification complicated high-dose vitamin D_2 therapy in one patient. Synthetic salmon calcitonin, sodium fluoride, and $24,25(OH)_2D$ have also been used without apparent benefit.[163] Treatment with melphalan and prednisolone seemed to help one patient.[164]

PACHYDERMOPERIOSTOSIS

Pachydermoperiostosis (hypertrophic osteoarthropathy: primary or idiopathic) causes clubbing of the digits, hyperhidrosis, and thickening of the skin, especially the face and forehead (cutis verticis gyrata), and periosteal new bone formation that occurs prominently in the distal limbs. Autosomal dominant inheritance with variable expression is established,[165] but autosomal recessive transmission also seems to occur.[166]

Clinical Presentation

Men seem to be more severely affected than women, and blacks more commonly than whites. The age at presentation is variable, but symptoms typically first manifest during adolescence.[165,166] All three principal features (clubbing, periostitis, and pachydermia) trouble some patients; others have just one or two of these findings. Clinical expression emerges over a

decade, but the disorder can then become quiescent.[167] Progressive gradual enlargement of the hands and feet may result in a "paw-like" appearance. Palms may be wet. Some affected individuals are described as "acromegalic." Arthralgias of the elbows, wrists, knees, and ankles are common. Occasionally, the small joints are also painful. Acro-osteolysis has been reported. Symptoms of pseudogout can occur. Chondrocalcinosis, with calcium pyrophosphate crystals in synovial fluid, troubled one patient. Stiffness and limited mobility of both the appendicular and the axial skeleton can develop. Compression of cranial or spinal nerves has been described. Cutaneous changes include coarsening, thickening, furrowing, pitting, and oiliness of especially the scalp and face. Fatigue is not uncommon. Myelophthisic anemia with extramedullary hematopoiesis may occur. Life expectancy is not compromised.[167]

Radiological Features

Severe periostitis that thickens the distal portions of the tubular bones—typically the radius, ulna, tibia, and fibula—is the principal radiographic abnormality (Fig. 10). The metacarpals, tarsals/metatarsals, clavicles, pelvis, base of the skull, and phalanges may also be affected. Clubbing is obvious, and acro-osteolysis can occur. The spine is rarely involved. Ankylosis of joints, especially in the hands and in the feet, may trouble older patients.[23]

The major diagnostic challenge is secondary hypertrophic osteoarthropathy (pulmonary or otherwise). The radiographic features of this condition are, however, somewhat different. In secondary hypertrophic osteoarthropathy, periosteal reaction typically has a smooth, undulating appearance.[168] In pachydermoperiostosis, periosteal proliferation is more exuberant, has an irregular appearance, and often involves epiphyses. Bone scanning in either condition reveals symmetrical, diffuse, regular uptake along the cortical margins of long bones, especially in the legs. This feature results in a "double stripe" sign.

Laboratory Findings

Periosteal new bone formation roughens the surface of cortical bone.[169] This newly synthesized osseous tissue undergoes cancellous compaction and can accordingly be difficult to distinguish on histopathological examination from the original cortex.[169] There may also be osteopenia of trabecular bone from quiescent formation.[23] Mild cellular hyperplasia and thickening of subsynovial blood vessels is found near synovial membranes.[170] Electron microscopy shows layered basement membranes. Typically, synovial fluid is unremarkable.

Etiology and Pathogenesis

Pachydermoperiostosis has not been mapped within the human genome. There are autosomal dominant and perhaps autosomal recessive forms. A controversial hypothesis suggests that initially some unknown circulating factor acts on vasculature to cause hyperemia and thus alters soft tissues; later, blood flow is reduced.[138] In one patient, skin fibroblasts reportedly synthesized decreased and increased amounts of collagen and decorin, respectively.[171]

Treatment

There is no established medical treatment. Painful synovial effusions may respond to nonsteroidal anti-inflammatory drugs.[172] Colchicine reportedly helped arthralgias, clubbing, folliculitis, and pachyderma in one patient.[173] Contractures or neurovascular compression by osteosclerotic lesions may require surgical intervention.

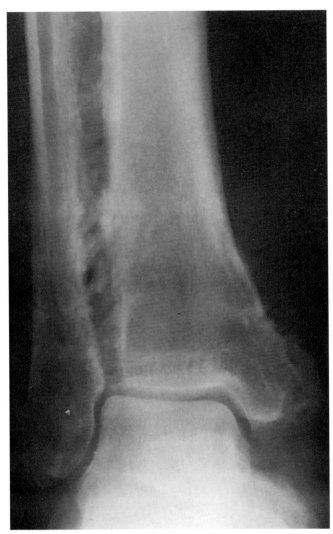

FIG. 10. Pachydermoperiostosis. Anteroposterior radiograph of the ankle shows ragged periosteal reaction along the interosseous membrane between the tibia and fibula (note also the proliferative bone formation along the medial malleolus). [Reproduced with permission from Whyte MP 1995 Rare disorders of skeletal formation and homeostasis. In: Becker KN (ed.) Principles and Practice of Endocrinology and Metabolism, 2nd ed. Lippincott-Raven Publishers, Philadelphia, PA, USA.]

HEPATITIS C–ASSOCIATED OSTEOSCLEROSIS

In 1992, a new syndrome was delineated that featured acquired, severe, generalized osteosclerosis and hyperostosis in former intravenous drug abusers infected with hepatitis C virus.[174] Approximately a dozen cases have been reported.

Periosteal, endosteal, and trabecular bone thickening occur throughout the skeleton, except, apparently, in the cranium (Fig. 11). During active disease, bones in the forearms and legs are painful. Osteodensitometry shows values 200–300% above age- and sex-matched control means. Bone remodeling seems, from biochemical markers, accelerated during active disease and may respond to pamidronate or to calcitonin therapy. Gradual, spontaneous remission of pain and normalization of bone turnover may occur. BMD may decrease. Exposure to blood contaminated with hepatitis C virus is the historical feature common to all patients.[175] Distinctive abnormalities in

the IGF system feature increased circulating levels of IGF binding protein 2[176] and "big" IGF II.[177]

HIGH BONE MASS PHENOTYPE

Certain mutations of the *LRP5* gene encoding low-density lipoprotein receptor–related protein 5 cause increased skeletal mass of good quality.[178,179] Some patients have torus palatinus.[180] This condition is not always benign—cranial nerve palsies and oropharyngeal exostoses may occur.[181] Uninhibited Wnt signaling stimulates osteoblasts.[180]

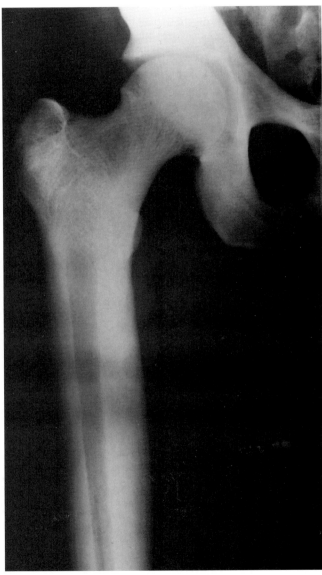

FIG. 11. Hepatitis C–associated osteosclerosis. Anteroposterior view of the proximal right femur of this middle-aged, former intravenous drug abuser shows diffuse bony sclerosis with marked cortical thickening. The medullary cavity is narrow and the periosteal margins of the cortex are mildly convex, suggesting endosteal and periosteal bone apposition, respectively. The cortices of the greater and lesser trochanters are relatively spared. The trabecular pattern in the femoral neck is especially prominent. (Reproduced from Whyte MP, Tertelbaum SL, Reinus WR 1996 Doubling skeletal mass during adult life: The syndrome of diffuse osteosclerosis after intravenous drug abuse. J Bone Miner Res **11:**554–558 with permission of the American Society for Bone and Mineral Research.)

OTHER SCLEROSING BONE DYSPLASIAS

Table 1 lists the relatively large number of conditions that cause focal or generalized increases in skeletal mass.[4,182] Of note, sarcoidosis characteristically causes cysts within coarsely reticulated bone; occasionally, however, sclerotic areas are found in the axial skeleton or in long tubular bones. These skeletal changes may develop well after the pulmonary disease is arrested. Although multiple myeloma typically presents with generalized osteopenia or with discrete osteolytic lesions, widespread osteosclerosis can occur in indolent forms. Lymphoma, myelofibrosis, and mastocytosis are additional hematologic causes of increased bone mass. Metastatic carcinoma, primarily prostatic, commonly causes dense bone. Diffuse osteosclerosis is also relatively frequent in secondary hyperparathyroidism (e.g., renal disease), but occurs rarely in primary hyperparathyroidism. Fluorosis, intoxication with vitamin A or vitamin D, heavy metal poisoning, milk-alkali syndrome, ionizing radiation, osteomyelitis, and osteonecrosis are additional explanations for increased bone mass.[4,182]

REFERENCES

1. McKusick-Nathans Institute for Genetic Medicine, Johns Hopkins University and National Center for Biotechnology Information, National Library of Medicine 2000 Online Mendelian Inheritance in Man, OMIM. Available online at http://www.ncbi.nlm.nih.gov/om. Accessed January 2, 2006.
2. Royce PM, Steinmann B (eds.) 2002 Connective Tissue and Its Heritable Disorders, 2nd ed. Wiley-Liss, New York, NY, USA.
3. Scriver CR, Beaudet AL, Sly WS, Valle D, Childs B, Vogelstein B (eds.) 2001 The Metabolic and Molecular Bases of Inherited Disease, 8th ed. McGraw-Hill, New York, NY, USA.
4. Whyte MP 1997 Skeletal disorders characterized by osteosclerosis or hyperostosis. In: Avioli LV, Krane SM (eds.) Metabolic Bone Disease, 2nd ed. Academic Press, San Diego, CA, USA, pp. 697–738.
5. Castriota-Scanderbeg A, Dallapiccola B 2005 Abnormal Skeletal Phenotypes: From Simple Signs To Complex Diagnoses. Springer, New York, NY, USA.
6. Van Hul W 2003 Recent progress in the molecular genetics of sclerosing bone dysplasias. Pediatr Pathol Mol Med 22:11–22.
7. Albers-Schönberg H 1904 Rontgenbilder einer seltenen, Knochenerkrankung. Meunch Med Wochenschr 51:365.
8. Whyte MP 2002 Osteopetrosis. In: Royce PM, Steinmann B (eds.) Connective Tissue and Its Heritable Disorders, 2nd ed. Wiley-Liss, New York, NY, USA, pp. 789–807.
9. Johnston CC Jr, Lavy N, Lord T, Vellios F, Merritt AD, Deiss WP Jr 1968 Osteopetrosis: A clinical, genetic, metabolic, and morphologic study of the dominantly inherited, benign form. Medicine (Baltimore) 47:149–167.
10. Loria-Cortes R, Quesada-Calvo E, Cordero-Chaverri E 1977 Osteopetrosis in children: A report of 26 cases. J Pediatr 91:43–47.
11. Kahler SG, Burns JA, Aylsworth AS 1984 A mild autosomal recessive form of osteopetrosis. Am J Med Genet 17:451–464.
12. Jagadha V, Halliday WC, Becker LE, Hinton D 1988 The association of infantile osteopetrosis and neuronal storage disease in two brothers. Acta Neuropathol (Berl) 75:233–240.
13. Dupuis-Girod S, Corradini N, Hadj-Rabia S, Fournet JC, Faivre L, Le Deist F, Durand P, Doffinger R, Smahi A, Israel A, Courtois G, Brousse N, Blanche S, Munnich A, Fischer A, Casanova JL, Bodemer C 2002 Osteopetrosis, lymphedema, anhidrotic ectodermal dysplasia, and immunodeficiency in a boy and incontinentia pigmenti in his mother. Pediatrics 109:1–6.
14. Whyte MP, Wenkert D, Clements KL, McAlister WH, Mumm S 2003 Bisphosphonate-induced osteopetrosis. N Engl J Med 394:455–461.
15. Tolar J, Teitelbaum SL, Orchard PJ 2004 Osteopetrosis. N Engl J Med 351:2839–2849.
16. Marks SC Jr 1987 Osteopetrosis. Multiple pathways for the interception of osteoclast function. Appl Pathol 5:172–183.
17. Dozier TS, Duncan IM, Klein AJ, Lambert PR, Key LL Jr 2005 Otologic manifestations of malignant osteopetrosis. Otol Neurotol 26:762–766.
18. Vanier V, Miller R, Carson BS 2000 Bilateral visual improvement after unilateral optic canal decompression and cranial vault expansion in a patient with osteopetrosis, narrowed optic canals, and increased intracranial pressure. J Neurol Neurosurg Psychiatry 69:405–406.
19. Campos-Xavier AB, Casanova JL, Doumaz Y, Feingold J, Munnich A, Cormier-Daire V 2005 Intrafamilial phenotypic variability of osteopetrosis due to chloride channel 7 (CLCN7) mutations. Am J Med Genet A 133:216–218.
20. Waguespack SG, Koller DL, White KE, Fishburn T, Carn G, Buckwalter KA, Johnson M, Kocisko M, Evans WE, Foroud T, Econs MJ 2003 Chloride channel 7 (ClCN7) gene mutations and autosomal dominant osteopetrosis, type II. J Bone Miner Res 18:1513–1518.
21. Benichou OD, Lareo JD, De Verenjoul MC 2000 Type II autosomal dominant osteopetrosis (Albers-Schönberg disease): Clinical and radiological manifestations in 42 patients. Bone 26:87–83.
22. Bollerslev J 1989 Autosomal dominant osteopetrosis: Bone metabolism and epidemiological, clinical and hormonal aspects. Endocr Rev 10:45–67.
23. Resnick D, Niwayama G 2002 Diagnosis of Bone and Joint Disorders, 4th ed. WB Saunders, Philadelphia, PA, USA.
24. Di Rocco M, Buoncompagni A, Loy A, Dellacqua A 2000 Osteopetrorickets: Case report. Eur J Paediatr Neurol 159:579–581.
25. Park H-M, Lambertus A 1977 Skeletal and reticuloendothelial imaging in osteopetrosis: Case report. J Nucl Med 18:1091–1095.
26. Rao VM, Dalinka MK, Mitchell DG, Spritzer CE, Kaplan F, August CS, Axel L, Kressel HY 1986 Osteopetrosis: MR characteristics at 1.5 T. Radiology 161:217–220.
27. Elster AD, Theros EG, Key LL, Chen MYM 1992 Cranial imaging in autosomal recessive osteopetrosis (parts I & II). Radiology 183:129–144.
28. Key LL, Carnes D, Cole S, Holtrop M, Bar-Shavit Z, Shapiro F, Arceci R, Steinberg J, Gundberg C, Kahn A, Teitelbaum S, Anast C 1984 Treatment of congenital osteopetrosis with high dose calcitriol. N Engl J Med 310:409–415.
29. Cournot G, Trubert-Thil CL, Petrovic M, Boyle A, Cormier C, Girault D, Fischer A, Garabedian M 1992 Mineral metabolism in infants with malignant osteopetrosis: Heterogeneity in plasma 1,25-dihydroxyvitamin D levels and bone histology. J Bone Miner Res 7:1–10.
30. Whyte MP, Chines A, Silva DP Jr., Landt Y, Ladenson JH 1996 Creatine kinase brain isoenzyme (BB-CK) presence in serum distinguishes osteopetrosis among the sclerosing bone disorders. J Bone Miner Res 11:1438–1443.
31. Alatalo SL, Ivaska KK, Waguespack SG, Econs MJ, Vaananen HK, Halleen JM 2004 Osteoclast-derived serum tartrate-resistant acid phosphatase 5b in Albers-Schönberg disease (type II autosomal dominant osteopetrosis). Clin Chem 50:883–890.
32. Revell PA 1986 Pathology of Bone. Springer-Verlag, Berlin, Germany.
33. Flanagan AM, Massey HM, Wilson C, Vellodi A, Horton MA, Steward CG 2002 Macrophage colony-stimulating factor and receptor activator NF-κB ligand fail to rescue osteoclast-poor human malignant infantile osteopetrosis in vitro. Bone 30:85–90.
34. Helfrich MH, Aronson DC, Everts V, Mieremet RHP, Gerritsen EJA, Eckhardt PG, Groot CG, Scherft JP 1991 Morphologic features of bone in human osteopetrosis. Bone 12:411–419.
35. Bollerslev J, Steiniche T, Melsen F, Mosekilde L 1986 Structural and histomorphometric studies of iliac crest trabecular and cortical bone in autosomal dominant osteopetrosis: A study of two radiological types. Bone 10:19–24.
36. Whyte MP 1995 Chipping away at marble bone disease. N Engl J Med 332:1639–1640.
37. Teitelbaum SL, Tondravi MM, Ross FP 1996 Osteoclast biology. In: Marcus R, Feldman D, Kelsey J (eds.) Osteoporosis. Academic Press, San Diego, CA, USA, pp. 61–94.
38. Lajeunesse D, Busque L, Ménard P, Brunette MG, Bonny Y 1996 Demonstration of an osteoblast defect in two cases of human malignant osteopetrosis. Correction of the phenotype after bone marrow transplant. Bone 98:1835–1842.
39. Steward CG 2003 Neurological aspects of osteopetrosis. Neuropathol Appl Neurobiol 29:87–97.
40. Mills BG, Yabe H, Singer FR 1988 Osteoclasts in human osteopetrosis contain viral-nucleocapsid-like nuclear inclusions. J Bone Miner Res 3:101–106.
41. Glorieux FH, Pettifor JM, Marie PJ, Delvin EE, Travers R, Shepard N 1981 Induction of bone resorption by parathyroid hormone in congenital malignant osteopetrosis. Metab Bone Dis Relat Res 3:143–150.
42. Key LL, Ries WL, Schiff R 1987 Osteopetrosis associated with interleukin-2 deficiency. J Bone Miner Res 2:S2;85.
43. Key LL, Rodriguiz RN, Willi SM, Wright NM, Hatcher HC, Eyre DR, Cure JK, Griffin PP, Ries WL 1995 Recombinant human interferon gamma therapy for osteopetrosis. N Engl J Med 332:1594–1599.
44. Beard CJ, Key L, Newburger PE, Ezekowitz RA, Arceci R, Miller B,

Proto P, Ryan T, Anast C, Simons ER 1986 Neutrophil defect associated with malignant infantile osteopetrosis. J Lab Clin Med **108**:498–505.

45. Campos-Xavier AB, Saraiva JM, Ribeiro LM, Munnich A, Cormier-Daire V 2003 Chloride channel 7 (CLCN7) gene mutations in intermediate autosomal recessive osteopetrosis. Hum Genet **112**:186–189.

46. Sobacchi C, Frattini A, Orchard P, Porras O, Tezcan I, Andolina M, Babul-Hirji R, Baric I, Canham N, Chitayat D, Dupuis-Girod S, Ellis I, Etzioni A, Fasth A, Fisher A, Gerritsen B, Gulino V, Horwitz E, Klamroth V, Lanino E, Mirolo M, Musio A, Matthijs G, Nonomaya S, Notarangelo LD, Ochs HD, Superti Furga A, Valiaho J, van Hove JL, Vihinen M, Vujic D, Vezzoni P, Villa A 2001 The mutational spectrum of human malignant autosomal recessive osteopetrosis. Hum Mol Genet **10**:1767–1773.

47. Scimeca JC, Quincey D, Parrinello H, Romatet D, Grosgeorge J, Gaudray P, Philip N, Fischer A, Carle GF 2003 Novel mutations in the TCIRG1 gene encoding the a3 subunit of the vacuolar proton pump in patients affected by infantile malignant osteopetrosis. Hum Mutat **21**:151–157.

48. Taranta A, Migliaccio S, Recchia I, Caniglia M, Luciani M, De Rossi G, Dionisi-Vici C, Pinto RM, Francalanci P, Boldrini R, Lanino E, Dini G, Morreale G, Ralston SH, Villa A, Vezzoni P, Del Principe D, Cassiani F, Palumbo G, Teti A 2003 Genotype-phenotype relationship in human ATP6i-dependent autosomal recessive osteopetrosis. Am J Pathol **162**:57–68.

49. Susani L, Pangrazio A, Sobacchi C, Taranta A, Mortier G, Savarirayan R, Villa A, Orchard P, Vezzoni P, Albertini A, Frattini A, Pagani F 2004 TCIRG1-dependent recessive osteopetrosis: Mutation analysis, functional identification of the splicing defects, and in vitro rescue by U1 snRNA. Hum Mutat **24**:225–235.

50. Chalhoub N, Benachenhou N, Rajapurohitam V, Pata M, Ferron M, Frattini A, Villa A, Vacher J 2003 Grey-lethal mutation induces severe malignant autosomal recessive osteopetrosis in mouse and human. Nat Med **9**:399–406.

51. Quarello P, Forni M, Barberis L, Defilippi C, Campagnoli MF, Silvestro L, Frattini A, Chalhoub N, Vacher J, Ramenghi U 2004 Severe malignant osteopetrosis caused by a GL gene mutation. J Bone Miner Res **19**:1194–1199.

52. Ramirez A, Faupel J, Goebel I, Stiller A, Beyer S, Stockle C, Hasan C, Bode U, Kornak U, Kubisch C 2004 Identification of a novel mutation in the coding region of the grey-lethal gene OSTM1 in human malignant infantile osteopetrosis. Hum Mutat **23**:471–476.

53. Kaplan FS, August CS, Fallon MD, Dalinka M, Axel L, Haddad JG 1988 Successful treatment of infantile malignant osteopetrosis by bone-marrow transplantation: A case report. J Bone Joint Surg Am **70**:617–623.

54. Schulz AS, Classen CF, Mihatsch WA, Sigl-Kraetzig M, Wiesneth M, Debatin KM, Friedrich W, Muller SM 2002 HLA-haploidentical blood progenitor cell transplantation in osteopetrosis. Blood **99**:3458–3460.

55. Driessen GJ, Gerritsen EJ, Fischer A, Fasth A, Hop WC, Veys P, Porta F, Cant A, Steward CG, Vossen JM, Uckan D, Friedrich W 2003 Long-term outcome of haematopoietic stem cell transplantation in autosomal recessive osteopetrosis: An EBMT report. Bone Marrow Transplant **32**:657–663.

56. Orchard PJ, Dickerman JD, Mathews CH, Frierdich S, Hong R, Trigg ME, Shahidi NT, Finlay JL, Sondel PM 1987 Haploidentical bone marrow transplantation for osteopetrosis. Am J Pediatr Hematol Oncol **9**:335–340.

57. Coccia PF, Krivit W, Cervenka J, Clawson C, Kersey JH, Kim TH, Nesbit ME, Ramsay NK, Warkentin PI, Teitelbaum SL, Kahn AJ, Brown DM 1980 Successful bone-marrow transplantation for infantile malignant osteopetrosis. N Engl J Med **302**:701–708.

58. Rawlinson PS, Green RH, Coggins AM, Boyle IT, Gibson BE 1991 Malignant osteopetrosis: Hypercalcaemia after bone marrow transplantation. Arch Dis Child **66**:638–639.

59. Steward CG, Pellier I, Mahajan A, Ashworth MT, Stuart AG, Fasth A, Lang D, Fischer A, Friedrich W, Schulz AS 2004 The Working Party on Inborn Errors of the European Blood and Marrow Transplantation Group. Severe pulmonary hypertension: A frequent complication of stem cell transplantation for malignant infantile osteopetrosis. Br J Haematol. **124**:63–71.

60. Tsuji Y, Ito S, Isoda T, Kajiwara M, Nagasawa M, Morio T, Mizutani S 2005 Successful nonmyeloablative cord blood transplantation for an infant with malignant infantile osteopetrosis. J Pediatr Hematol Oncol **27**:495–498.

61. Key LL Jr 1987 Osteopetrosis: A genetic window into osteoclast function. Cases Metab Bone Dis **2**:1–12.

62. Dorantes LM, Mejia AM, Dorantes S 1986 Juvenile osteopetrosis: Effects of blood and bone of prednisone and low calcium, high phosphate diet. Arch Dis Child **61**:666–670.

63. Iacobini M, Migliaccio S, Roggini M, Taranta A, Werner B, Panero A, Teti A 2001 Case Report: Apparent cure of a newborn with malignant osteopetrosis using prednisone therapy. J Bone Miner Res **16**:2356–2360.

64. Gwynne Jones DP, Hodgson BF, Hung NA 2004 Bilateral, uncemented total hip arthroplasty in osteopetrosis. J Bone Joint Surg Br **86**:276–278.

65. Chhabra A, Westerlund LE, Kline AJ, McLaughlin R 2005 Management of proximal femoral shaft fractures in osteopetrosis: A case series using internal fixation. Orthopedics **28**:587–592.

66. Ogur G, Ogur E, Celasun B, Baser I, Imirzalioglu N, Ozturk T, Alemdaroglut A 1995 Prenatal diagnosis of autosomal recessive osteopetrosis, infantile type, by x-ray evaluation. Prenat Diagn **15**:477–481.

67. Sly WS, Hewett-Emmett D, Whyte MP, Yu YS, Tashian RE 1983 Carbonic anhydrase II deficiency identified as the primary defect in the autosomal recessive syndrome of osteopetrosis with renal tubular acidosis and cerebral calcification. Proc Natl Acad Sci USA **80**:2752–2756.

68. Whyte MP 1993 Carbonic anhydrase II deficiency. Clin Orthop **294**:52–63.

69. Sly WS, Whyte MP, Sundaram V, Tashian RE, Hewett-Emmett D, Guibaud P, Vainsel M, Baluarte HJ, Graskin A, Al-Mosawi M 1985 Carbonic anhydrase II deficiency in 12 families with the autosomal recessive syndrome of osteopetrosis with renal tubular acidosis and cerebral calcification. N Engl J Med **313**:139–145.

70. Sly WS, Shah GN 2001 The carbonic anhydrase II deficiency syndrome: Osteopetrosis with renal tubular acidosis and cerebral calcification. In: Scriver CR, Beaudet AL, Sly WS, Valle D, Child B, Vogelstein B (eds.) The Metabolic and Molecular Bases of Inherited Disease, 8th ed. McGraw-Hill Book Company, New York, NY, USA, pp. 5331–5343.

71. Whyte MP, Murphy WA, Fallon MD, Sly WS, Teitelbaum SL, McAlister WH, Avioli LV 1980 Osteopetrosis, renal tubular acidosis and basal ganglia calcification in three sisters. Am J Med **69**:64–74.

72. Awad M, Al-Ashwal AA, Sakati N, Al-Abbad AA, Bin-Abbas BS 2002 Long-term follow up of carbonic anhydrase II deficiency syndrome. Saudi Med J **23**:25–29.

73. Sly WS, Whyte MP, Krupin T, Sundaram V 1985 Positive renal response to acetazolamide in carbonic anhydrase II-deficient patients. Pediatr Res **19**:1033–1036.

74. Roth DE, Venta PJ, Tashian RE, Sly WS 1992 Molecular basis of human carbonic anhydrase II deficiency. Proc Natl Acad Sci USA **89**:1804–1808.

75. Shah GN, Bonapace G, Hu PY, Strisciuglio P, Sly WS 2004 Carbonic anhydrase II deficiency syndrome (osteopetrosis with renal tubular acidosis and brain calcification): Novel mutations in CA2 identified by direct sequencing expand the opportunity for genotype-phenotype correlation. Hum Mutat **24**:272.

76. Whyte MP, Hamm LL III, Sly WS 1988 Transfusion of carbonic anhydrase-replete erythrocytes fails to correct the acidification defect in the syndrome of osteopetrosis, renal tubular acidosis, and cerebral calcification (carbonic anhydrase II deficiency). J Bone Miner Res **3**:385–388.

77. McMahon C, Will A, Hu P, Shah GN, Sly WS, Smith OP 2001 Bone marrow transplantation corrects osteopetrosis in the carbonic anhydrase II deficiency syndrome. Blood **97**:1947–1950.

78. Maroteaux P, Lamy M 1965 The malady of Toulouse-Lautrec. JAMA **191**:715–717.

79. Maroteaux P, Lamy M 1962 La pycnodysostose. Presse Med **70**:999–1002.

80. Sugiura Y, Yamada Y, Koh J 1974 Pycnodysostosis in Japan: Report of six cases and a review of Japanese literature. Birth Defects **10**:78–98.

81. Gelb BD, Brömme D, Desnick RJ 2001 Pycnodysostosis: Cathepsin K deficiency. In: Scriver CR, Beaudet AL, Sly WS, Valle D, Child B, Vogelstein B (eds.) The Metabolic and Molecular Bases of Inherited Disease, 8th ed. McGraw-Hill Book Company, New York, NY, USA, pp. 3453–3468.

82. Elmore SM 1967 Pycnodysostosis: A review. J Bone Joint Surg Am **49**:153–162.

83. Everts V, Hou WS, Rialland X, Tigchelaar W, Saftig P, Bromme D, Gelb BD, Beertsen W 2003 Cathepsin K deficiency in pycnodysostosis results in accumulation of non-digested phagocytosed collagen in fibroblasts. Calcif Tissue Int **73**:380–386.

84. Wolpowitz A, Matisson A 1974 A comparative study of pycnodysostosis, cleidocranial dysostosis, osteopetrosis and acro-osteolysis. S Afr Med J **48**:1011–1118.

85. Soto TJ, Mautalen CA, Hojman D, Codevilla A, Piqué J, Pangaro JA 1969 Pycnodysostosis, metabolic and histologic studies. Birth Defects **5**:109–115.

86. Everts V, Aronson DC, Beertsen W 1985 Phagocytosis of bone collagen by osteoclasts in two cases of pycnodysostosis. Calcif Tissue Int 37:25–31.

87. Cabrejas ML, Fromm GA, Roca JF, Mendez MA, Bur GE, Ferreyra ME, Demarchi C, Schurman L 1976 Pycnodysostosis: Some aspects concerning kinetics of calcium metabolism and bone pathology. Am J Med Sci 271:215–220.

88. Beneton MNC, Harris S, Kanis JA 1987 Paramyxovirus-like inclusions in two cases of pycnodysostosis. Bone 8:211–217.

89. Karkabi S, Reis ND, Linn S, Edelson G, Tzehoval E, Zakut V, Dolev E, Bar-Meir E, Ish-Shalom S 1993 Pyknodysostosis: Imaging and laboratory observations. Calcif Tissue Int 53:170–173.

90. Soliman AT, Rajab A, AlSalmi I, Darwish A, Asfour M 1996 Defective growth hormone secretion in children with pycnodysostosis and improved linear growth after growth hormone treatment. Arch Dis Child 75:242–244.

91. Motyckova G, Fisher DE 2002 Pycnodysostosis: Role and regulation of cathepsin K in osteoclast function and human disease. Curr Mol Med 2:407–21.

92. Fratzl-Zelman N, Valenta A, Roschger P, Nader A, Gelb BD, Fratzl P, Klaushofer K 2004 Decreased bone turnover and deterioration of bone structure in two cases of pycnodysostosis. J Clin Endocrinol Metab 89:1538–1547.

93. Edelson JG, Obad S, Geiger R, On A, Artul HJ 1992 Pycnodysostosis: Orthopedic aspects, with a description of 14 new cases. Clin Orthop 280:263–276.

94. Cockayne EA 1920 A case for diagnosis. Proc R Soc Med 13:132–136.

95. Engelmann G 1929 Ein fall von osteopathia hyperostotica (sclerotisans) multiplex infantilis. Fortschr Geb Roentgen 39:1101–1106.

96. Saito T, Kinoshita A, Yoshiura Ki, Makita Y, Wakui K, Honke K, Niikawa N, Taniguchi N 2001 Domain-specific mutations of a transforming growth factor (TGF)-β1 latency-associated peptide cause Camurati-Engelmann disease because of the formation of a constitutively active form of TGF-β1. J Biol Chem 276:11469–11472.

97. Hundley JD, Wilson FC 1973 Progressive diaphyseal dysplasia: Review of the literature and report of seven cases in one family. J Bone Joint Surg Am 55:461–474.

98. Wallace SE, Lachman RS, Mekikian PB, Bui KK, Wilcox WR 2004 Marked phenotypic variability in progressive diaphyseal dysplasia (Camurati-Engelmann disease): Report of a four-generation pedigree, identification of a mutation in TGFB1, and review. Am J Med Genet A 129:235–247.

99. Naveh Y, Ludatshcer R, Alon U, Sharf B 1985 Muscle involvement in progressive diaphyseal dysplasia. Pediatrics 76:944–949.

100. Crisp AJ, Brenton DP 1982 Engelmann's disease of bone: A systemic disorder?. Ann Rheum Dis 41:183–188.

101. Smith R, Walton RJ, Corner BD, Gordon IR 1977 Clinical and biochemical studies in Engelmann's disease (progressive diaphyseal dysplasia). Q J Med 46:273–294.

102. Kumar B, Murphy WA, Whyte MP 1981 Progressive diaphyseal dysplasia (Engelmann's disease): Scintigraphic-radiologic-clinical correlations. Radiology 140:87–92.

103. Applegate LJ, Applegate GR, Kemp SS 1991 MR of multiple cranial neuropathies in a patient with Camurati-Engelmann disease: Case report. Am Soc Neuroradiol 12:557–559.

104. Shier CK, Krasicky GA, Ellis BI, Kottamasu SR 1987 Ribbing's disease: Radiographic-scintigraphic correlation and comparative analysis with Engelmann's disease. J Nucl Med 28:244–248.

105. Saraiva JM 2000 Anticipation in progressive diaphyseal dysplasia. J Med Genet 37:394–395.

106. Labat ML, Bringuier AF, Seebold C, Moricard Y, Meyer-Mula C, Laporte P, Talmage RV, Grubb SA, Simmons DJ, Milhaud G 1991 Monocytic origin of fibroblasts: Spontaneous transformation of blood monocytes into neo-fibroblastic structures in osteomyelosclerosis and Engelmann's disease. Biomed Pharmacother 45:289–299.

107. Janssens K, Gershoni-Baruch R, Guanabens N, Migone N, Ralston S, Bonduelle M, Lissens W, Van Maldergem L, Vanhoenacker F, Verbruggen L, Van Hul W 2000 Mutations in the gene encoding the latency-associated peptide of TGF-β1 cause Camurati-Engelmann disease. Nat Genet 26:273–275.

108. Janssens K, ten Dijke P, Ralston SH, Bergmann C, Van Hul W 2003 Transforming growth factor-beta 1 mutations in Camurati-Engelmann disease lead to increased signaling by altering either activation or secretion of the mutant protein. J Biol Chem 278:7718–7724.

109. Hecht JT, Blanton SH, Broussard S, Scott A, Hall CR, Mlunsky JM 2001 Evidence for locus heterogeneity in the Camurati-Engelmann (DPD1) Syndrone. Clin Genet 59:198–200.

110. Makita Y, Nishimura G, Ikegawa S, Ishii T, Ito Y, Okuno A 2000 Intrafamilial phenotypic variability in Engelmann disease (ED): Are ED and Ribbing disease the same entity?. Am J Med Genet 91:153–156.

111. Kaftori JK, Kleinhaus U, Neveh Y 1987 Progressive diaphyseal dysplasia (Camurati-Engelmann): Radiographic follow-up and CT findings. Radiology 164:777–782.

112. Naveh Y, Alon U, Kaftori JK, Berant M 1985 Progressive diaphyseal dysplasia: Evaluation of corticosteroid therapy. Pediatrics 75:321–323.

113. Fallon MD, Whyte MP, Murphy WA 1980 Progressive diaphyseal dysplasia (Engelmann's disease): Report of a sporadic case of the mild form. J Bone Joint Surg Am 62:465–472.

114. Inaoka T, Shuke N, Sato J, Ishikawa Y, Takahashi K, Aburano T, Makita Y 2001 Scintigraphic evaluation of pamidronate and corticosteroid therapy in a patient with progressive diaphyseal dysplasia (Camurati-Engelmann disease). Clin Nucl Med 26:680–682.

115. Van Buchem FSP, Prick JJG, Jaspar HHJ 1976 Hyperostosis Corticalis Generalisata Familiaris (Van Buchem's Disease). Excerpta, Amsterdam, The Netherlands.

116. Perez-Vicente JA, Rodriguez de Castro E, Lafuente J, Mateo MM, Gimenez-Roldan S 1987 Autosomal dominant endosteal hyperostosis. Report of a Spanish family with neurological involvement. Clin Genet 31:161–169.

117. Eastman JR, Bixler D 1977 Generalized cortical hyperostosis (van Buchem disease): Nosologic considerations. Radiology 125:297–304.

118. Beighton P, Barnard A, Hamersma H, van der Wouden A 1984 The syndromic status of sclerostenosis and van Buchem disease. Clin Genet 25:175–181.

119. Hill SC, Stein SA, Dwyer A, Altman J, Dorwart R, Doppman J 1986 Cranial CT findings in sclerostenosis. Am J Neuroradiol 7:505–511.

120. Brunkow ME, Gardner JC, Van Ness J, Paeper BW, Kovacevich BR, Proll S, Skonier JE, Zhao L, Sabo PJ, Fu Y, Alisch RS, Gillett L, Colbert T, Tacconi P, Galas D, Hamersma H, Beighton P, Mulligan J 2001 Bone dysplasia sclerosteosis results from loss of the SOST gene product, a novel cystine knot-containing protein. Am J Hum Genet 68:577–589.

121. Balemans W, Patel N, Ebeling M, Van Hul E, Wuyts W, Lacza C, Dioszegi M, Dikkers FG, Hildering P, Willems PJ, Verheij JB, Lindpaintner K, Vickery B, Foernzler D, Van Hul W 2002 Identification of a 52 kb deletion downstream of the SOST gene in patients with van Buchem disease. J Med Gent 39:91–97.

122. Loots GG, Kneissel M, Keller H, Baptist M, Chang J, Collette NM, Ovcharenko D, Plajzer-Frick I, Rubin EM 2005 Genomic deletion of a long-range bone enhancer misregulates sclerostin in Van Buchem disease. Genome Res 15:928–935.

123. Sutherland MK, Geoghegan JC, Yu C, Turcott E, Skonier JE, Winkler DG, Latham JA 2004 Sclerostin promotes the apoptosis of human osteoblastic cells: A novel regulation of bone formation. Bone 35:828–835.

124. Li X, Zhang Y, Kang H, Liu W, Liu P, Zhang J, Harris SE, Wu D 2005 Sclerostin binds to LRP5/6 and antagonizes canonical Wnt signaling. J Biol Chem 280:19883–19887.

125. Ruckert EW, Caudill RJ, McCready PJ 1985 Surgical treatment of van Buchem disease. J Oral Maxillofac Surg 43:801–805.

126. Schendel SA 1988 van Buchem disease: Surgical treatment of the mandible. Ann Plast Surg 20:462–467.

127. Beighton P, Durr L, Hamersma H 1976 The clinical features of sclerostenosis: A review of the manifestations in twenty-five affected individuals. Ann Intern Med 84:393–397.

128. Barnard AH, Hamersma H, Kretzmar JH, Beighton P 1980 Sclerostenosis in old age. S Afr Med J 58:401–403.

129. Hamersma H, Gardner J, Beighton P 2003 The natural history of sclerostenosis. Clin Genet 63:192–197.

130. Beighton P, Cremin BJ, Hamersma H 1976 The radiology of sclerostenosis. Br J Radiol 49:934–939.

131. Stein SA, Witkop C, Hill S, Fallon MD, Viernstein L, Gucer G, McKeever P, Long D, Altman J, Miller NR, Teitelbaum SL, Schlesinger S 1983 Sclerostenosis, neurogenetic and pathophysiologic analysis of an American kinship. Neurology 33:267–277.

132. Epstein S, Hamersma H, Beighton P 1979 Endocrine function in sclerostenosis. S Afr Med J 55:1105–1110.

133. Van Hul W, Balemans W, Van Hul E, Dikkers FG, Obee H, Stokroos RJ, Hildering P, Vanhoenacker F, Van Camp G, Willems PJ 1998 Van Buchem disease (hyperostosis corticalis generalisata) maps to chromosome 17q12–q21. Am J Hum Genet 62:391–399.

134. Berlin R, Hedensio B, Lilja B, Linder L 1967 Osteopoikilosis: A clinical and genetic study. Acta Med Scand 18:305–314.

135. Uitto J, Santa Cruz DJ, Starcher BC, Whyte MP, Murphy WA 1981 Biochemical and ultrastructural demonstration of elastin accumulation in the skin of the Buschke-Ollendorff syndrome. J Invest Dermatol 76:284–287.

136. Whyte MP, Murphy WA, Seigel BA 1978 99m Tc-pyrophosphate bone imaging in osteopoikilosis, osteopathia striata, and melorheostosis. Radiology 127:439–443.

137. Lagier R, Mbakop A, Bigler A 1984 Osteopoikilosis: A radiological and pathological study. Skeletal Radiol 11:161–168.

138. Hellemans J, Preobrazhenska O, Willaert A, Debeer P, Verdonk PC, Costa T, Janssens K, Menten B, Van Roy N, Vermeulen SJ, Savarirayan R, Van Hul W, Vanhoenacker F, Huylebroeck D, De Paepe A, Naeyaert JM, Vandesompele J, Verschueren K, Coucke PJ, Mortier GR 2004 Loss-of-function mutations in LEMD3 result in osteopoikilosis, Buschke-Ollendorff syndrome and melorheostosis. Nat Genet 36:1213–1218.

139. Rabinow M, Unger F 1984 Syndrome of osteopathia striata, macrocephaly, and cranial sclerosis. Am J Dis Child 138:821–823.

140. Happle R, Lenz W 1977 Striation of bones in focal dermal hypoplasia: Manifestation of functional mosaicism?. Br J Dermatol 96:133–138.

141. Viot G, Lacombe D, David A, Mathieu M, de Broca A, Faivre L, Gigarel N, Munnich A, Lyonnet S, Le Merrer M, Cormier-Daire V 2002 Osteopathia striata cranial sclerosis: Non-random X-inactivation suggestive of X-linked dominant inheritance. Am J Med Genet 107:1–4.

142. Kornreich L, Grunebaum M, Ziv N, Shuper A, Mimouni M 1988 Osteopathia striata, cranial sclerosis with cleft palate and facial nerve palsy. Eur J Paediatr Neurol 147:101–103.

143. Leri A, Joanny J 1922 Une affection non decrite des os. Hyperostose "en coulee" sur toute la longueur d'un membre ou "melorheostose." Bull Mem Soc Med Hop Paris 46:1141–1145.

144. Murray RO, McCredie J 1979 Melorheostosis and sclerotomes: A radiological correlation. Skeletal Radiol 4:57–71.

145. Campbell CJ, Papademetriou T, Bonfiglio M 1968 Melorheostosis: A report of the clinical, roentgenographic, and pathological findings in fourteen cases. J Bone Joint Surg Am 50:1281–1304.

146. Miyachi Y, Horio T, Yamada A, Ueo T 1979 Linear melorheostotic scleroderma with hypertrichosis. Arch Dermatol 115:1233–1234.

147. Applebaum RE, Caniano DA, Sun CC, Azizkhan RA, Queral LA 1986 Synchronous left subclavian and axillary artery aneurysms associated with melorheostosis. Surgery 99:249–253.

148. Colavita N, Nicolais S, Orazi C, Falappa PG 1987 Melorheostosis: Presentation of a case followed up for 24 years. Arch Orthop Trauma Surg 106:123–125.

149. Davis DC, Syklawer R, Cole RL 1992 Melorheostosis on three-phase bone scintigraphy: Case report. Clin Nucl Med 17:561–564.

150. Wagers LT, Young AW Jr., Ryan SF 1972 Linear melorheostotic scleroderma. Br J Dermatol 86:297–230.

151. Kim JE, Kim EH, Han EH, Park RW, Park IH, Jun SH, Kim JC, Young MF, Kim IS 2000 A TGF-β-inducible cell adhesion moleculae, Big-h3, is downregulated in melorheostosis and involved in oseogeneis. J Cell Biochem 77:169–178.

152. Mumm S, Zhang X, McAlister WH, Wenkert D, Whyte MP 2005 Deactivating germline mutations in LEMD3 cause osteopoikilosis and Buschke-Ollendorff syndrome, but not melorheostosis. J Bone Miner Res 20:S1;S418.

153. Atar D, Lehman WB, Grant AD, Strongwater AM 1992 The Ilizarov apparatus for treatment of melorheostosis: Case report and review of the literature. Clin Orthop 281:163–167.

154. Whyte MP, Murphy WA, Fallon MD, Hahn TJ 1981 Mixed-sclerosing-bone-dystrophy: Report of a case and review of the literature. Skeletal Radiol 6:95–102.

155. Pacifici R, Murphy WA, Teitelbaum SL, Whyte MP 1986 Mixed-sclerosing-bone-dystrophy: 42-year follow-up of a case reported as osteopetrosis. Calcif Tissue Int 38:175–185.

156. Frame B, Frost HM, Ormond RS, Hunter RB 1961 Atypical axial osteomalacia involving the axial skeleton. Ann Intern Med 55:632–639.

157. Whyte MP, Fallon MD, Murphy WA, Teitelbaum SL 1981 Axial osteomalacia: Clinical, laboratory and genetic investigation of an affected mother and son. Am J Med 71:1041–1049.

158. Christmann D, Wenger JJ, Dosch JC, Schraub M, Wackenheim A 1981 L'osteomalacie axiale: Analyse compare avec la fibrogenese imparfaite. J Radiol 62:37–41.

159. Nelson AM, Riggs BL, Jowsey JO 1978 Atypical axial osteomalacia: Report of four cases with two having features of ankylosing spondylitis. Arthritis Rheum 21:715–722.

160. Cortet B, Berniere L, Solau-Gervais E, Hacene A, Cotton A, Delcambre B 2000 Axial osteomalacia with sacroiliitis and moderate phosphate diabetes: Report of a case. Clin Exp Rheumatol 18:625–628.

161. Condon JR, Nassim JR 1971 Axial osteomalacia. Postgrad Med 47:817–820.

162. Swan CH, Shah K, Brewer DB, Cooke WT 1976 Fibrogenesis imperfecta ossium. Q J Med 45:233–253.

163. Lang R, Vignery AM, Jenson PS 1986 Fibrogenesis imperfecta ossium with early onset: Observations after 20 years of illness. Bone 7:237–246.

164. Ralphs JR, Stamp TCB, Dopping-Hepenstal PJC, Ali SY 1989 Ultrastructural features of the osteoid of patients with fibrogenesis imperfecta ossium. Bone 10:243–249.

165. Rimoin DL 1965 Pachydermoperiostosis (idiopathic clubbing and periostosis). Genetic and physiologic considerations. N Engl J Med 272:923–931.

166. Matucci-Cerinic M, Lott T, Jajic IVO, Pignone A, Bussani C, Cagnoni M 1991 The clinical spectrum of pachydermoperiostosis (primary hypertrophic osteoarthropathy). Medicine 79:208–214.

167. Herman MA, Massaro D, Katz S 1965 Pachydermoperiostosis: Clinical spectrum. Arch Intern Med 116:919–923.

168. Ali A, Tetalman M, Fordham EW 1980 Distribution of hypertrophic pulmonary osteoarthropathy. Am J Roentgenol 134:771–780.

169. Vogl A, Goldfischer S 1962 Pachydermoperiostosis: Primary or idiopathic hypertrophic osteoarthropathy. Am J Med 33:166–187.

170. Lauter SA, Vasey FB, Huttner I, Osterland CK 1978 Pachydermoperiostosis: Studies on the synovium. J Rheumatol 5:85–95.

171. Wegrowski Y, Gillery P, Serpier H, Georges N, Combemale P, Kalis B, Maquart FX 1996 Alteration of matrix macromolecule synthesis by fibroblasts from a patient with pachydermoperiostosis. J Invest Dermatol 106:70–74.

172. Cooper RG, Freemont AJ, Riley M, Holt PJL, Anderson DC, Jayson MIV 1992 Bone abnormalities and severe arthritis in pachydermoperiostosis. Ann Rheum Dis 51:416–419.

173. Matucci-Cerinic M, Fattorini L, Gerini G, Lombardi A, Pignone A, Petrini N, Lotti T 1988 Cochicine treatment in a case of pachydermoperiostosis with acroosteolysis. Rheumatol Int 8:185–188.

174. Whyte MP, Teitelbaum SL, Reinus WR 1996 Doubling skeletal mass during adult life: The syndrome of diffuse osteosclerosis after intravenous drug abuse. J Bone Miner Res 11:554–558.

175. Shaker JL, Reinus WR, Whyte MP 1998 Hepatitis C-associated osteosclerosis: Late onset after blood transfusion in an elderly woman. J Clin Endocrinol Metab 84:93–98.

176. Khosla S, Hassoun AAK, Baker BK, Liu F, Zien NN, Whyte, MP, Reasner CA, Nippoldt TB, Tiegs RD, Hintz RL, Conover CA 1998 Insulin-like growth factor system abnormalities in hepatitis C-associated osteosclerosis: A means to increase bone mass in adults?. J Clin Invest 101:2165–2173.

177. Khosla S, Ballard FJ, Conover CA 2002 Use of site-specific antibodies to characterize the circulating form of big insulin-like growth factor II in patients with hepatitis C-associated osteosclerosis. J Clin Endocrinol Metab 87:3867–3870.

178. Little RD, Carulli JP, Del Mastro RG, Dupuis J, Osborne M, Folz C, Manning SP, Swain PM, Zhao SC, Eustace B, Lappe MM, Spitzer L, Zweier S, Braunschweiger K, Benchekroun Y, Hu X, Adair R, Chee L, FitzGerald MG, Tulig C, Caruso A, Tzellas N, Bawa A, Franklin B, McGuire S, Nogues X, Gong G, Allen KM, Anisowicz A, Morales AJ, Lomedico PT, Recker SM, Van Eerdewegh P, Recker RR, Johnson ML 2002 A mutation in the LDL receptor-related protein 5 gene results in the autosomal dominant high-bone-mass trait. Am J Hum Genet 70:11–19.

179. Van Wesenbeeck L, Cleiren E, Gram J, Beals RK, Benichou O, Scopelliti D, Key L, Renton T, Bartels C, Gong Y, Warman ML, De Vernejoul MC, Bollerslev J, Van Hul W 2003 Six novel missense mutations in the LDL receptor-related protein 5 (LRP5) gene in different conditions with an increased bone density. Am J Hum Genet 72:763–771.

180. Boyden LM, Mao J, Belsky J, Mitzner L, Farhi A, Mitnick MA, Wu D, Insogna K, Lifton RP 2002 High bone density due to a mutation in LDL-receptor-related protein 5. N Engl J Med 345:1513–1521.

181. Rickels MR, Zhang X, Mumm S, Whyte MP 2005 Oropharyngeal skeletal disease accompanying high bone mass and novel LRP5 mutation. J Bone Miner Res 20:878–885.

182. Frame B, Honasoge M, Kottamasu SR 1987 Osteosclerosis, Hyperostosis, and Related Disorders. Elsevier, New York, NY, USA.

Chapter 72. Fibrous Dysplasia

Michael T. Collins[1] and Paolo Bianco[2]

Craniofacial and Skeletal Diseases Branch, National Institute of Dental and Craniofacial Research, National Institutes of Health, Department of Health and Human Services, Bethesda, Maryland; and [2]Dipartimento di Medicina Sperimentale e Patologia, Universita' La Sapienza, Rome, Italy

INTRODUCTION

Fibrous dysplasia of bone (FD; OMIM#174800) is an uncommon skeletal disorder with a broad spectrum of clinical expressions, ranging from an incidentally discovered asymptomatic radiographic finding, involving a single skeletal site, to a severe disabling disease. The disease may involve one bone (monostotic), multiple bones (polyostotic FD), or even the entire skeleton (panostotic FD). In polyostotic disease, lesions of different limb bones are often (but not necessarily) ipsilateral.[1] FD may be associated with extraskeletal lesions or dysfunction, most commonly cutaneous pigmentation (Figs. 1A and 1B), and hyperfunctioning endocrinopathies, including precocious puberty, hyperthyroidism, growth hormone (GH) excess, and Cushing syndrome. FD in combination with one or more of the extraskeletal manifestations is known as McCune-Albright syndrome (MAS).[2] A renal tubulopathy, which includes renal phosphate wasting, is one of the most common extraskeletal dysfunctions associated with polyostotic disease.[3] More rarely, FD may be associated with myxomas of skeletal muscle (Mazabraud's syndrome)[4] or dysfunction of heart, liver, pancreas, or other organs within the context of the MAS.[5]

ETIOLOGY AND PATHOGENESIS

All forms of FD are caused by activating, missense mutations of the *GNAS* gene, encoding the α subunit of the stimulatory G protein, $G_s\alpha$.[6,7] Mutations occur postzygotically, are never inherited, and result in a somatic mosaic state. Time and location of mutation occurrence in development and size and viability of the mutated clone arising from the single, original mutated cell determine the variable distribution and frequency of the mutated cells in the postnatal organism and the extent and severity of disease.[1] Single base transitions lead to replacement of arginine at position 201 with histidine or cysteine (most commonly) or rarely with other amino acids.[8] As a consequence of the mutation, the catalysis of GTP to GDP by $G_s\alpha$ is significantly decreased. Constitutive activation of adenylyl cyclase by the mutated $G_s\alpha$ ensues, and the resulting excess cAMP mediates a number of pathological effects in mutated cells.[1] In bone, mutations impact on cells of the osteogenic lineage, with adverse effects both on osteoprogenitor cells and differentiated osteoblasts.[9,10] Expansion of the osteoprogenitor cell pool leads to their accumulation in marrow spaces, resulting in local loss of hematopoietic tissue and marrow fibrosis. Osteogenic cells derived from mutated skeletal progenitors are functionally and morphologically abnormal and deposit abnormal matrix. Bone trabeculae are abnormal in shape (so-called Chinese writing, alphabet soup patterns), collagen orientation, and biochemical composition,[9] and in many cases, are severely undermineralized and abnormally compliant[9,11] (Fig. 2E). Elevated serum levels of fibroblast growth factor (FGF)-23, a recently identified phosphate-regulating hormone produced by highly activated osteoblas-

tic cells in FD tissue, have been shown to be the etiology of the renal phosphate wasting commonly seen in association with FD.[12] The histological pattern may be significantly different at different skeletal sites, and peculiar patterns are seen in craniofacial bones.[13] The hormonal climate influences FD lesions,[14] and may significantly alter the local rate of bone remodeling.[11] FD tissue is highly vascularized and therefore prone to bleeding, leading to posthemorrhagic cysts.[15]

CLINICAL FEATURES

Pathological effects of $G_s\alpha$ mutations in osteogenic cells are most pronounced and evident during the phase of rapid bone growth and account for that fact that childhood or adolescence are the periods during which the disease most commonly presents, as well as the period of peak rate of fractures.[16,17] Presentation in infancy is rare, and usually heralds severe, widespread disease with multiorgan involvement. Pain, fracture, and deformity are the most common presenting features. In general, children are less likely to complain of pain, per se, and may instead report stiffness or tiredness. In adults, the complaint of pain is common, especially in the ribs, long bones, and craniofacial bones. It is often severe and may require narcotic analgesics. Lesions in the spine and pelvis are usually less painful. Pathological fractures or stress fracture of weight-bearing limb bones is a prime cause of morbidity. Deformity of limb bones is caused by expansion and abnormal compliance of lesional FD, fracture treatment failure, and local complications such as cyst formation.[1] Deformity of craniofacial bone is solely the result of the overgrowth of lesional bone.

Although any bone may be affected, the skull base and the proximal metaphysis of the femora are the two sites most commonly involved. Femoral disease usually presents in childhood with, limp, fracture, pain, and deformity, ranging from coxa vara to the classical shepherd's crook deformity (Fig. 2A). Radiographically, the lesion may be limited to the metaphysis or extend along the diaphysis for variable length.[15] The picture most commonly observed in children and adolescents consists of an expansile, deforming, medullary lesion, with cortical thinning and an overall "ground glass" density (Fig. 2A). The radiographic picture is significantly affected by the evolution of the lesion over time and by the appearance of superimposed changes, most commonly aneurysmal bone cysts. Hence, lesions observed in adults tend to appear more sclerotic and less homogeneous (Fig. 2B). Sclerosis in FD lesions of the femur and other limb bones, but not in craniofacial lesions, may signify less active disease.

In the skull, FD mostly involves the skull base and facial bones. The typical presentation is in childhood with facial asymmetry or a "bump" that persists, but symmetric expansion of the malar prominences and/or frontal bosses may also be seen. The disease can progress into adulthood and disfiguration may be marked. Abnormal growth and deformity of craniofacial bones may result in encroachment on cranial nerves. Severe adverse consequences are rare, but much more common in

The authors have reported no conflicts of interest.

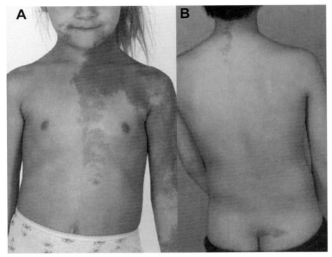

FIG. 1. Café-au-lait skin pigmentation. (A) A typical lesion on the face, chest, and arm of a 5-year-old girl with McCune-Albright syndrome that shows jagged "coast of Maine" borders and the tendency for the lesions to both respect the midline and follow the developmental lines of Blashko. (B) Typical lesions that are often found on the nape of the neck and crease of the buttocks are shown.

patients with associated growth hormone excess.[14,18] FD tissue in craniofacial bones is especially prone to bleeding, herniation through cranial foramina and vascular passages, as well as formation of posthemorrhagic cysts (Fig. 2D). These events may precipitate blindness when they occur in the vicinity of the optic nerves. Craniofacial FD may have a "ground glass" appearance, but a sclerotic "pagetoid" appearance is typical (Fig. 2C) and correlates with site-specific osteosclerotic histological changes.[13] Lesions in the spine, ribs, and pelvis are common, may be elusive on plain radiographs, but are easily detected by bone scintigraphy, the most sensitive imaging technique for the detection of FD lesions (Fig. 3). Disease in the spine is common and is frequently associated with scoliosis, may require surgery, and can be progressive into adulthood.[19]

Malignancy in FD is rare (<1%).[20] While there is an association with the development of cancer with prior treatment with high dose external beam radiation, it may occur independent of prior exposure to ionizing radiation. Rapid lesion expansion and cortical bone disruption should alert the clinician to the possibility of sarcomatous change. Osteogenic sarcoma is the most common, but not the only type of bone tumor that may complicate FD. The clinical course is usually aggressive, surgery is the primary treatment, and chemotherapeutic regimens do not seem to improve prognosis significantly.

MANAGEMENT AND TREATMENT

Diagnosis of FD must be established based on expert assessment of clinical, radiographic, and histopathological features. Markers of bone turnover are usually elevated.[3] The extent of the skeletal disease is best determined with total body bone scintigraphy, which can be used to assess the skeletal disease burden and predict functional outcome.[21] The metabolic derangements associated with FD, especially hypophosphatemia and growth hormone excess, are associated with a significantly worse clinical outcome, and therefore must be screened for and treated.[14,17,18,22]

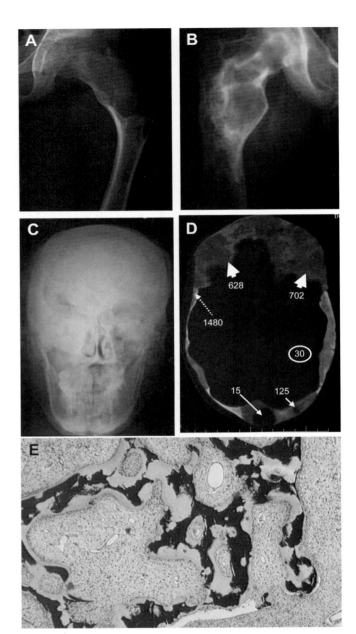

FIG. 2. Radiographic and histological appearance of FD. (A) A proximal femur with typical ground glass appearance and shepherd's crook deformity in a 10-year-old child is shown. (B) The appearance of FD in the femur of an untreated 40-year-old man shows the tendency for FD to appear more sclerotic with time. (C) The typical sclerotic appearance of FD in the craniofacial region is shown. (D) A CT image show thickened frontal bone with a mixed solid and cystic appearance (large arrowheads) and lesions in the occipital bone, one with "cystic" changes (small arrowhead) that represents an area of fibrous tissue, as well as a fluid-filled cyst (arrow). Normal bone is indicated by the dashed line. The Houndsfield unit (HU) measurements, which are quite useful in distinguishing soft tissue "cystic" lesions from true fluid-filled cysts, are indicated. The HU measurement of normal brain tissue is indicated in the oval. (E) Representative histological image of FD. The tissue was processed for undecalcified embedding, which enables demonstration of excess osteoid in the undermineralized fibrous dysplastic bone. The marrow spaces are filled with "fibrous" tissue, consisting of excess, abnormal marrow stromal cells.

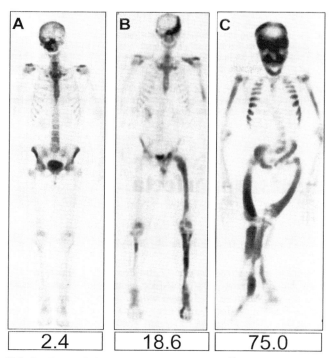

FIG. 3. Bone scintigraphy in FD. Representative ^{99}Tc-MDP bone scans that show tracer uptake at affected skeletal sites and the associated skeletal disease burden score[21] are shown. (A) A 50-year-old woman with monostotic FD confined to a single focus involving contiguous bones in the craniofacial region. (B) A 42-year-old man with polyostotic FD shows the tendency for FD to be predominantly (but not exclusively) unilateral and to involve the skull base and proximal femur. (C) A 16-year-old boy with McCune-Albright syndrome and involvement of virtually all skeletal sites (panostotic) is shown.

Mutation analysis may be helpful in distinguishing FD from unrelated fibro-osseous lesions of the skeleton, which may mimic FD both clinically and radiographically (osteofibrous dysplasia, ossifying fibromas of jawbones).[1] Multiple nonossifying fibromas, skeletal angiomatosis, and Ollier's disease may sometimes enter the differential diagnosis, which again relies on histology and mutation analysis.

Disease of the proximal femur, in which there is fracture or impending fracture, is often best treated by insertion of intramedullary nails in an effort to prevent serious deformity and limb length discrepancy.[15,23] Design of specific types of nails is felt to be necessary, and development of such devices is underway.[14] Surgery is not advocated for craniofacial disease unless hearing or vision loss are documented, and prophylactic optic nerve decompression seems to be contraindicated.[18] Treatment with bisphosphonates (pamidronate, etc.) has been advocated based on observational studies with claims of reduced pain, decreased serum and urine markers of bone metabolism, and improvement in the radiographic appearance of the disease.[24,25] However, a recently completed open label, prospective study with appropriate histological, radiographic, and clinical endpoint(s), showed pain relief but no benefit radiographically or histologically.[26] Ongoing placebo controlled studies in the United States and Europe may help to better define the role of bisphosphonates in treating FD.

REFERENCES

1. Bianco P, Gehron Robey P, Wientroub S 2003 Fibrous dysplasia. In: Glorieux F, Pettifor J, Juppner H (eds.) Pediatric Bone: Biology and disease. Academic Press/Elsevier, New York, NY, USA, pp. 509–539.
2. Danon M, Crawford JD 1987 The McCune-Albright syndrome. Ergeb Inn Med Kinderheilkd **55:**81–115.
3. Collins MT, Chebli C, Jones J, Kushner H, Consugar M, Rinaldo P, Wientroub S, Bianco P, Robey PG 2001 Renal phosphate wasting in fibrous dysplasia of bone is part of a generalized renal tubular dysfunction similar to that seen in tumor- induced osteomalacia. J Bone Miner Res **16:**806–813.
4. Cabral CE, Guedes P, Fonseca T, Rezende JF, Cruz Junior LC, Smith J 1998 Polyostotic fibrous dysplasia associated with intramuscular myxomas: Mazabraud's syndrome. Skeletal Radiol **27:**278–282.
5. Shenker A, Weinstein LS, Moran A, Pescovitz OH, Charest NJ, Boney CM, Van Wyk JJ, Merino MJ, Feuillan PP, Spiegel AM 1993 Severe endocrine and nonendocrine manifestations of the McCune-Albright syndrome associated with activating mutations of stimulatory G protein GS. J Pediatr **123:**509–518.
6. Weinstein LS, Shenker A, Gejman PV, Merino MJ, Friedman E, Spiegel AM 1991 Activating mutations of the stimulatory G protein in the McCune-Albright syndrome. N Engl J Med **325:**1688–1695.
7. Bianco P, Riminucci M, Majolagbe A, Kuznetsov SA, Collins MT, Mankani MH, Corsi A, Bone HG, Wientroub S, Spiegel AM, Fisher LW, Robey PG 2000 Mutations of the GNAS1 gene, stromal cell dysfunction, and osteomalacic changes in non-McCune-Albright fibrous dysplasia of bone. J Bone Miner Res **15:**120–128.
8. Riminucci M, Fisher LW, Majolagbe A, Corsi A, Lala R, De Sanctis C, Robey PG, Bianco P 1999 A novel GNAS1 mutation, R201G, in McCune-Albright syndrome. J Bone Miner Res **14:**1987–1989.
9. Riminucci M, Fisher LW, Shenker A, Spiegel AM, Bianco P, Gehron Robey P 1997 Fibrous dysplasia of bone in the McCune-Albright syndrome: Abnormalities in bone formation. Am J Pathol **151:**1587–1600.
10. Bianco P, Kuznetsov S, Riminucci M, Fisher LW, Spiegel AM, Gehron Robey P 1998 Reproduction of human fibrous dysplasia of bone in immunocompromised mice by transplanted mosaics of normal and Gs-alpha mutated skeletal progenitor cells. J Clin Invest **101:**1737–1744.
11. Corsi A, Collins MT, Riminucci M, Howell PGT, Boyde A, Robey PG, Bianco P 2005 Osteomalacic and hyperparathyroid changes in fibrous dysplasia of bone: Core biopsy studies and clinical correlations. J Bone Miner Res **18:**1235–1246.
12. Riminucci M, Collins MT, Fedarko NS, Cherman N, Corsi A, White KE, Waguespack S, Gupta A, Hannon T, Econs MJ, Bianco P, Gehron Robey P 2003 FGF-23 in fibrous dysplasia of bone and its relationship to renal phosphate wasting. J Clin Invest **112:**683–692.
13. Riminucci M, Liu B, Corsi A, Shenker A, Spiegel AM, Gehron Robey P, Bianco P 1999 The histopathology of fibrous dysplasia of bone in patients with activating mutations of the Gs al[ha gene: Site-specific patterns and recurrent histological hallmarks. J Pathol **187:**249–258.
14. Akintoye SO, Chebli C, Booher S, Feuillan P, Kushner H, Leroith D, Cherman N, Bianco P, Wientroub S, Robey PG, Collins MT 2002 Characterization of gsp-mediated growth hormone excess in the context of McCune-Albright syndrome. J Clin Endocrinol Metab **87:**5104–5112.
15. Ippolito E, Bray EW, Corsi A, De Maio F, Exner UG, Robey PG, Grill F, Lala R, Massobrio M, Pinggera O, Riminucci M, Snela S, Zambakidis C, Bianco P 2003 Natural history and treatment of fibrous dysplasia of bone: A multicenter clinicopathologic study promoted by the European Pediatric Orthopaedic Society. J Pediatr Orthop B **12:**155–177.
16. Harris WH, Dudley HR, Barry RJ 1962 The natural history of fibrous dysplasia. An orthopedic, pathological, and roentgenographic study. J Bone Joint Surg Am **44:**207–233.
17. Leet AI, Chebli C, Kushner H, Chen CC, Kelly MH, Brillante BA, Robey PG, Bianco P, Wientroub S, Collins MT 2004 Fracture incidence in polyostotic fibrous dysplasia and the McCune-Albright syndrome. J Bone Miner Res **19:**571–577.
18. Lee JS, FitzGibbon E, Butman JA, Dufresne CR, Kushner H, Wientroub S, Robey PG, Collins MT 2002 Normal vision despite narrowing of the optic canal in fibrous dysplasia. N Engl J Med **347:**1670–1676.
19. Leet AI, Magur E, Lee JS, Wientroub S, Robey PG, Collins MT 2004 Fibrous dysplasia in the spine: Prevalence of lesions and association with scoliosis. J Bone Joint Surg Am **86:**531–537.
20. Ruggieri P, Sim FH, Bond JR, Unni KK 1994 Malignancies in fibrous dysplasia. Cancer **73:**1411–1424.

21. Collins MT, Kushner H, Reynolds JC, Chebli C, Kelly MH, Gupta A, Brillante B, Leet AI, Riminucci M, Robey PG, Bianco P, Wientroub S, Chen CC 2005 An instrument to measure skeletal burden and predict functional outcome in fibrous dysplasia of bone. J Bone Miner Res **20:**219–226.

22. Corsi A, Collins MT, Riminucci M, Howell PG, Boyde A, Robey PG, Bianco P 2003 Osteomalacic and hyperparathyroid changes in fibrous dysplasia of bone: Core biopsy studies and clinical correlations. J Bone Miner Res **18:**1235–1246.

23. Keijser LC, Van Tienen TG, Schreuder HW, Lemmens JA, Pruszczynski M, Veth RP 2001 Fibrous dysplasia of bone: Management and outcome of 20 cases. J Surg Oncol **76:**157–168.

24. Liens D, Delmas PD, Meunier PJ 1994 Long-term effects of intravenous pamidronate in fibrous dysplasia of bone. Lancet **343:**953–954.

25. Chapurlat RD, Delmas PD, Liens D, Meunier PJ 1997 Long-term effects of intravenous pamidronate in fibrous dysplasia of bone. J Bone Miner Res **12:**1746–1752.

26. Plotkin H, Rauch F, Zeitlin L, Munns C, Travers R, Glorieux FH 2003 Effect of pamidronate treatment in children with polyostotic fibrous dysplasia of bone. J Clin Endocrinol Metab **88:**4569–4575.

Chapter 73.   Osteogenesis Imperfecta

Joan C. Marini

NICHD, Bone and Extracellular Matrix Branch, National Institutes of Health, Bethesda, Maryland

INTRODUCTION

Osteogenesis imperfecta (OI), also known as brittle bone disease, is a genetic disorder of connective tissue characterized by fragile bones and a susceptibility to fracture from mild trauma or even acts of daily living.[1,2] The clinical range of this condition is extremely broad, ranging from a form that is lethal in the perinatal period to a form that may be difficult to detect and can present as early osteoporosis. Defects in type I collagen, the major structural component of the extracellular matrix of bone, skin, and tendon, are responsible for the full clinical range of OI.[3] Reflecting the broad tissue distribution of type I collagen, individuals with OI may have varying combinations of growth deficiency, defective tooth formation (dentinogenesis imperfecta), hearing loss, macrocephaly, blue coloration of sclerae, scoliosis, barrel chest, and ligamentous laxity. OI is generally described using the Sillence classification,[4] a nomenclature based on clinical and radiographic features, which was first proposed in 1979. Subsequent biochemical and molecular studies have shown that the mild Sillence type of OI is caused by quantitative defects in type I collagen,[5] whereas the moderate and severe types are caused by structural defects in either of the two chains that form the type I collagen heterotrimer. OI is an autosomal dominant condition. Most recurrences of OI in the children of unaffected parents are caused by parental mosaicism,[6] although extremely rare recessive forms of OI have been described.

CLINICAL PRESENTATION

Because the four types of OI vary widely in symptoms and in the timing of their onset, the diagnosis and its differential varies with the age of the individual in question. A positive family history is usually not present, because most mutations occur de novo. Prenatally, severe type II or III OI may be difficult to distinguish from thanatophoric dysplasia, camptomelic dysplasia, and achondrogenesis type I. Neonatally, type III OI and infantile hypophosphatasia may have an overlapping presentation, but infantile hypophosphatasia has the radiographic distinction of spurs extending from sides of knee and elbow joints and the biochemical distinction of a low alkaline phosphatase level. In childhood diagnoses of the milder forms of OI, the major distinctions are with juvenile and idiopathic osteoporosis and child abuse. The key diagnostic element for OI is the generalized nature of the connective tissue defect, with facial features (flat mid-face, triangular shape, bluish sclerae, yellowish or opalescent teeth), relative macrocephaly, thoracic configuration (barrel chest or pectus excavatum), joint laxity, vertebral compressions, and growth deficiency present in variable combinations in each case. When a diagnosis is still in doubt, DNA sequencing of type I collagen provides helpful information on the presence of a mutation.

CLINICAL TYPES

The classification proposed by Sillence (Table 1) is based on clinical and radiographic criteria and distinguished four types. Although both clinical and laboratory practice have subsequently evolved, the classification has continued to be useful and is still in general use in a modified form. The major modifications involve inheritance and scleral hue. The recessive form described by Sillence is almost always caused by parental mosaicism for a dominantly inherited mutation. Scleral hue has a broad range in each OI type. While scleral hue is helpful in the general diagnosis, it is not useful as a major distinguishing criterion.

Type I OI is the mildest form of the disorder. There is postnatal onset of fractures, usually after ambulation is attained and even beginning in early middle age when type I OI can present as early onset osteoporosis. Fractures decrease markedly after puberty. Individuals with type I OI often have blue sclerae and easy bruising. They may have hearing loss (onset as early as late childhood, usually in their 20s) or joint hyperextensibility. Growth deficiency, long bone deformity, and dentinogenesis imperfecta are not usual.

Type II OI is the most severe form of OI .[7] This form is generally lethal in the perinatal period, although survival for months is not uncommon, and survival to a year or more has been noted. These individuals are often born prematurely and are small for gestational age. Legs are usually held in the frog leg position with hips abducted and knees flexed. Radiographically, long bones are extremely osteoporotic, with in utero fractures and abnormal modeling (often a crumpled cylindrical shape). The skull is severely undermineralized with wide-open anterior and posterior fontanels. Scleral hue is blue-gray. The bones of these infants are composed predominantly of woven bone without haversian canals or organized lamellae. Demise is generally of pulmonary origin, especially respiratory insufficiency and pneumonias.

Type III OI[8] contains the most severe survivors and is known as the progressive deforming type. The presentation at

---

The author has reported no conflicts of interest.

TABLE 1. CLASSIFICATION OF OSTEOGENESIS IMPERFECTA BY TYPE*

OI type	Clinical features	Inheritance
I	Normal stature, little or no deformity, blue sclerae, hearing loss in 50% of families. Dentinogenesis imperfecta is rare and may distinguish a subset.	ADI
II	Lethal in the perinatal period; minimal calvarial mineralization, beaded ribs, compressed femurs, marked long bone deformity, platyspondyly	AD (new mutations) Parental mosaicism
III	Progressively deforming bones, usually with moderate deformity at birth. Scleral hue varies, often lightening with age. Dentinogenesis imperfecta common, hearing loss common. Stature very short.	AD AR (rare) Parental mosaicism
IV	Mild to moderate bone deformity and variable short stature; dentinogenesis imperfecta is common and hearing loss occurs in some families. White or blue sclerae.	AD Parental mosaicism
Non-collagenous types of OI		
V	Phenotypically indistinguishable from type IV OI. Distinctive histology of irregular arrangement or meshlike appearance of lamellae. Also have triad of hypertrophic callus formation, dense metaphyseal bands, and ossification of the interosseus membranes of the forearm. Normal type I collagen; no mutations detected.	Unknown
VI	Phenotypically indistinguishable from type IV OI. Diagnosed on basis of unique histological features. Elevated alkaline phosphatase activity. "Fish-scale" appearance of bone under the microscope.	Unknown
VII	Moderate to severe bone disease. Bluish sclerae and rhizomelia. Found only in a First Nations community in northern Quebec.	AR

* Modified from Sillence DO, Senn A, Danks DM 1979 Genetic heterogeneity in osteogenesis imperfecta. J Med Genet **16**:101–116 with permission from the BMJ Publishing Group.

AD, autosomal dominant; AR, autosomal recessive.

birth may be similar to the milder end of the type II OI spectrum. They have extremely fragile bones and will have dozens to hundreds of fractures over a lifetime. The long bones are also soft and will deform from normal muscle tension as well as subsequent to fractures. These individuals have extreme growth deficiency; final stature is in the range of a prepubertal child. Almost all type III cases develop scoliosis. Radiographically, metaphyseal flaring, and "popcorn" formation at growth plates are seen in addition to osteoporosis. They require intensive physical rehabilitation and orthopedic care to attain assisted ambulation; many will require wheelchairs for mobility.[9] This form is compatible with a full life span, although many individuals have respiratory insufficiency and cor pulmonale in middle age, and some die in infancy and childhood from respiratory causes.

Type IV OI is the moderately severe form. The diagnosis may be made at birth or delayed until the toddler or school ages. Scleral hue is variable. These children often have several fractures a year and bowing of their long bones. Fractures decrease after puberty. Essentially all type IV individuals have short final stature, often in the range of pubertal children; many of these children are responsive to growth hormone for significant additional height. Radiographically, they have osteoporosis and mild modeling abnormalities. They may have platybasia. Many develop vertebral compressions and scoliosis. With consistent rehabilitation intervention and orthopedic management, these individuals should be able to attain independent mobility.[9] This form is compatible with a full lifespan.

OI/EDS is a discrete subgroup of patients who have an overlap of the skeletal symptoms of OI (types IV, usually, or III) and the joint laxity of Ehlers-Danlos syndrome.[10] Hip dysplasia occurs in some patients and early progressive scoliosis in others. Tissue is friable, requiring extra intervention for spinal fixation. They have mutations in the amino terminal region of the type I collagen chains.

Recently, types V–VII OI have been proposed. Although these types have continued the Sillence numeration, they are based on bone histology distinctions and generally have a phenotype that would be included in Sillence type IV. These individuals do not have defects in type I collagen.

Type V OI[11] is associated with a triad of findings. First, there is a radiographically dense band adjacent to the growth plate of long bones. Second, they develop hypertrophic calluses at the sites of fractures or surgical procedures. Finally, there is calcification of the membrane between the radius and ulna, leading to restricted rotation. They have normal teeth and white sclerae. On microscopy, the bony lamellae are meshlike.

Type VI OI[12] can be distinguished only on bone biopsy. The lamellae have a "fish-scale" like appearance under the microscope. These individuals have moderate to severe skeletal disease, with normal teeth and sclerae. Alkaline phosphatase is slightly elevated.

Type VII OI[13] is an autosomal recessive form in an isolated First Nations community in northern Quebec. Bone disease is moderate to severe. Affected individuals have bluish sclerae and rhizomelia.

RADIOGRAPHIC FEATURES

The skeletal survey in OI reveals generalized osteopenia. Long bones have thin cortices and a gracile appearance. In moderately to severely affected patients, long bones have bowing and modeling deformities, including cylindrical configuration from an apparent lack of modeling, metaphyseal flaring, and "popcorn" appearance[14] at the metaphyses. Long bones of the upper extremity often seem milder than those of the lower extremity, even without weight bearing. Vertebrae often have central compressions even in mild type I OI; these often appear first at the T_{12}–L_2 level, consistent with weight-bearing stress. In moderate to severe OI, vertebrae will have central and anterior compressions and may appear compressed throughout. The compressions are generally consistent with the patient's L_1–L_4 DXA Z score, but do not correlate in a straightforward manner with scoliosis. In the lateral plane film of the spine, it is not easy to assess the asymmetry of vertebral collapse, which, along with paraspinal ligamentous laxity, is generally the root of OI scoliosis. The skull of OI patients with a wide range of severity has wormian bones, although this is not unique to OI. Patients with type III and IV OI may also have platybasia, which should be followed with periodic CT studies for basilar impression and invagination.[15]

Bone densitometry by DXA (L_1–L_4) is useful over a wide age and severity range of OI. It aids diagnosis in milder cases and facilitates longitudinal patient follow-up in moderate to severe forms. There is a general correlation of Z score and severity of OI. Type I individuals are generally in the −1 to −2 range, type IV Z scores cluster in the −2 to −4 range, whereas type III spans −3 to −6. It is important to remember that the Z score compares the mineral quantity of the bone being studied to bone with a normal matrix structure and crystal alignment. In OI, many mutations result in irregular crystal alignment on the abnormal matrix, in addition to reduced mineral quantity. DXA does not measure bone quality, which includes bone geometry, histomorphometry, and mechanical properties.

LABORATORY FINDINGS

Serum chemistry related to bone and mineral metabolism are generally normal. Alkaline phosphatase may be elevated after a fracture. Hormones of the growth axis have normal levels.[16]

Bone histomorphometry[17] reveals defects in bone modeling and in production and thickening of trabeculae. Cortical width and cancellous bone volume are decreased in all types; trabecular number and width are decreased. Bone remodeling is increased, as are osteoblast and osteoclast surfaces. When viewed under polarized light, the lamellae of OI bone are thinner and less smooth than in controls. Mineral apposition rate is normal; crystal disorganization may contribute to bone weakness.

ETIOLOGY AND PATHOGENESIS

More than 90% of patients who have clinical OI have abnormalities of type I collagen, the major structural protein of the bone extracellular matrix. Patients with types V, VI, and VII OI and a small group of unclassified patients with clinical OI do not have mutations in type I collagen.

Cultured dermal fibroblasts are convenient cells in which to examine the collagen biochemistry of probands using gel electrophoresis. Probands with type I OI, who synthesize a reduced amount of structurally normal type I collagen from a null COL1A1 allele, display a relative increase in the COL3/COL1 ratio.[5] Probands with the clinically significant types II, III, and IV OI synthesize a mixture of normal collagen and collagen with a structural defect. With rare exceptions, the structural defects are either substitutions for one of the glycine residues that occur at every third position along the chain and are essential for proper helix folding (80%) or alternative splicing of an exon (20%), resulting in an in-frame deletion of a section of the chain. Structural abnormalities delay helix folding, expose the constituent chains to modifying enzymes for a longer time, and result in overmodification detectable as slower electrophoretic migration. The biochemical test does not accurately detect abnormalities in the amino one third of the $\alpha 1(I)$ chain or amino one half of the $\alpha 2(I)$ chain.[18]

Mutation detection by direct sequencing is more sensitive than the biochemical test, although it does not provide functional information. Collagen sequencing is available either as exon-by-exon sequencing of DNA or transcript sequencing as cDNA.

Genotype–phenotype modeling of the >800 mutations currently available has yielded different patterns for the two chains,[19] supporting distinct roles in maintaining matrix integrity.

About one third of the substitutions in $\alpha 1(I)$ are lethal, especially those to residues with a branched or charged side chain. Two exclusively lethal regions coincide with the proposed major ligand-binding regions for the collagen monomer with integrins, matrix metalloproteinases (MMPs), fibronectin, and cartilage oligomeric matrix protein (COMP). For the $\alpha 2(I)$ chain, only one fifth of substitutions are lethal; these substitutions are clustered in eight regularly spaced regions along the chain, coinciding with the proteoglycan binding regions on the collagen fibril.

TREATMENT

Early and consistent rehabilitation intervention is the basis for maximizing the physical potential of individuals with OI.[20] Physical therapy should begin in infancy for the severest types, promoting muscle strengthening, aerobic conditioning and, if possible, protected ambulation. Programs to assure that children have muscle strength to lift a limb against gravity should continue between orthopedic interventions using isotonic and aerobic conditioning. Swimming should be encouraged.

Orthopedic care should be in the hands of a surgeon with experience in OI. Fractures should not be allowed to heal without reduction to prevent loss of function. The goals of orthopedic surgery are to correct deformity for ambulation and to interrupt a cycle of fracture and refracture. The classic osteotomy procedure requires fixation with an intramedullary rod. The hardware currently in use includes telescoping rods (Bailey-Dubow or Fassier-Duval rods[21,22]) and non-elongating rods (Rush rods). Important considerations include selection of a rod with the smallest diameter suited to the situation to avoid cortical atrophy. Children who are anticipated to have significant growth may require fewer rod revisions with either of the extensible rods.

The secondary features of OI, including abnormal pulmonary function, hearing,[23] and basilar invagination, are best managed in a specialized coordinated care program. The severe growth deficiency of OI is responsive to exogenous growth hormone administration in about one half of cases of type IV OI[24] and most type I OI[25]; some treated children can attain heights within the normal growth curves. Responders to rGH also experience increased L_1–L_4 DXA, bone volume per total volume (BV/TV), and bone formation rate (BFR). Growth hormone remains under study for its effects on OI skeletal integrity.

Four controlled trials have revealed the benefits and limitations of bisphosphonate treatment for OI.[26–29] The trabecular bone of vertebral bodies has the most positive response. Bone density is increased, although the functional meaning of this measurement is difficult to assess because it also includes retained mineralized cartilage; the increase in Z score tapers after 1- to 2-year treatment.[27] More importantly, the vertebral ability to resist compressive forces is shown as increased vertebral area and decreased central vertebral compressions. The effect of bisphosphonate treatment on predominantly cortical long bone is more equivocal. There is a combination of increased stiffness and load bearing that is balanced by weakened bone quality.[30] There is, at best, a trend toward reduced fracture incidence or a reduced relative risk rather than a clear statistical benefit. The functional changes in ambulation, muscle strength, and bone pain reported in the uncontrolled trials have been shown to be placebo effects.[26,27] Our current management of bisphosphonates for OI is to treat for 2–3 years and then discontinue the drug but continue to follow the patient.

REFERENCES

1. Marini JC 2004 Osteogenesis imperfecta. In: Behrman RE, Kliegman EM, Jenson HB (eds.) Nelson Textbook of Pediatrics, 17th ed. Saunders, Philadelphia, PA, USA, pp. 2336–2338.
2. Byers PH, Cole WG 2002 Osteogenesis imperfecta. In: Royce PM, Steinman B (eds.) Connective Tissue and Its Heritable Disorders. Wiley-Liss, New York, NY, USA, pp. 385–430.
3. Kuivaniemi H, Tromp G, Prockop DJ 1997 Mutations in fibrillar collagens (Types I, II, III, and XI), fibril-associated collagen (Type IX), and network forming collagen (Type X) cause a spectrum of diseases of bone, cartilage, and blood vessels. Human Mutat 9:300–315.
4. Sillence DO, Senn A, Danks DM 1979 Genetic heterogeneity in osteogenesis imperfecta. J Med Genet 16:101–116.
5. Willing MC, Pruchno CJ, Byers PH 1993 Molecular heterogeneity in osteogenesis imperfecta type I. Am J Med Genet 45:223–227.
6. Cohn DH, Starman BJ, Blumberg B, Byers PH 1990 Recurrence of lethal osteogenesis imperfecta due to parental mosaicism for a dominant mutation in a human type I collagen gene (COLIA). Am J Hum Genet 45:591–601.
7. Sillence DO 1981 Osteogenesis imperfecta: An expanding panorama of variants. Clin Ortho and Rel Res 159:11–25.
8. Sillence DO, Barlow KK, Cole WG, Dietrich S, Garber AP, Rimoin, DL 1986 Osteogenesis imperfecta type III. Delineation of the phenotype with reference to genetic heterogeneity. Am J Med Genet 23:821–832.
9. Gerber LH, Binder H, Weintrob J, Grange DK, Shapiro J, Fromherz W, Berry R, Conway A, Nason S, Marini JC 1990 Rehabilitation of children and infants with osteogenesis imperfecta. A program for ambulation. Clin Orthop 251:254–262.
10. Cabral WA, Makareeva E, Colige A, Letocha AD, Ty JM, Yeowell HN, Pals G, Leikin S, Marini JC 2005 Mutations near amino end α(I) collagen cause combined osteogenesis imperfecta/Ehlers-Danlos syndrome by interference with N-propeptide processing. J Biol Chem 15:19259–1269.
11. Glorieux FH, Rauch F, Plotkin H, Ward L, Travers R 2000 Type V osteogenesis imperfecta: A new form of brittle bone disease. J Bone Miner Res 15:1650–1658.
12. Glorieux FH, Ward LM, Bauch F, Lalic L, Roughley PJ, Travers R 2000 Osteogenesis imperfecta type VI: A form of brittle bone disease with a mineralization defect. J Bone Miner Res 17:12–18.
13. Ward LM, Rauch F, Travers R, Chabot G, Azouz FM, Lalic I, Roughley PJ, Glorieux FH 2002 Osteogenesis imperfecta type VII: An autosomal recessive form of brittle bone disease. Bone 31:12–18.
14. Goldman AB, Davison D, Pawlor H, Bullough PG 1980 "Popcorn" cacifications: A prognostic sign in osteogenesis imperfecta. Radiology 136:351–358.
15. Charnas LR, Marini JC 1993 Communicating hydrocephalus, basilar invagination and other neurologic features in osteogenesis imperfecta. Neurology 43:2603–2608.
16. Marini JC, Bordenick S, Heavner G, Rose S, Hintz R, Rosenfeld R, Chrousos GF 1993 The growth hormone and somatomedin axis in short children with osteogenesis imperfecta. J Clin Endocrin Metab 76:251–256.
17. Rauch F, Travers R, Parfitt AM, Glorieux FH 2000 Static and dynamic bone histomorphometry in children with osteogenesis imperfecta. Bone 26:581–589.
18. Cabral WA, Milgrom S, Moriarty E, Marini JC 2005 Detection of glycine substitutions in the amino end of type I collagen by biochemical screening of fibroblast collagen requires supplementation by direct sequencing for osteogenesis imperfecta probands. Am J Hum Genet 77:A1173.
19. Marini JC, Forlino A, Cabral W, Barnes A, San Antonio J, Milgrom S, Hyland J, Korkko J, Prockop D, DePaepe A, Coucke P, Glorieux F, Roughley P, Lund A, Kuurila K, Cohn D, Krakow D, Mottes M, Dalgleish R, Byers P 2005 Consortium for osteogenesis imperfecta mutations: Lethal regions in the helical portion of type I collagen chains align with collagen binding sites for integrin and proteoglycans. Am J Hum Genet 78:A1174.
20. Binder H, Conway A, Hason S, Gerber LH, Marini JC, Weintrob J 1993 Comprehensive rehabilitation of the child with osteogenesis imperfecta. Am J Med Genet 45:265–269.
21. Zionts LE, Ebramzadeh E, Stott NS 1998 Complications in the use of the Bailey-Dubow extensible nail. Clin Orthop Rel Res 348:186–195.
22. Fassier F 2005 Experience with the Fassier-Duval rod: Effectiveness and complications. 9th International Conference on Osteogenesis Imperfecta, Annapolis, MD, USA, June 13–16, 2005.
23. Kuurila K, Grenman R, Johansson R, Kaitila I 2000 Hearing loss in children with osteogenesis imperfecta. Eur J Pediatr 159:515–519.
24. Marini JC, Hopkins E, Glorieux FH, Chrousos GP, Reynolds JC, Gundberg CM, Reing CM 2003 Positive linear growth and bone responses to growth hormone treatment in children with types III and IV osteogenesis imperfecta: High predictive value of the carboxyterminal propeptide of type I procollagen. J Bone Miner Res 18:237–243.
25. Antoniazzi F, Bertoldo F, Mottes M, Valli M, Sirpresi S, Zamboni G, Valentini R, Tato L 1996 Growth hormone treatment in osteogenesis imperfecta with quantitative defect of type I collagen synthesis. J Pediatr 129:432–439.
26. Sakkers R, Kok D, Engelbert R, van Dongen A, Jansen M, Pruijs H, Verbout A, Schweitzer D, Uiterwaal C 2004 Skeletal effects and functional outcome with olpadronate in children with osteogenesis imperfecta: A 2 year randomized placebo-controlled study. Lancet 363:1427–1431.
27. Letocha AD, Cintas HL, Troendle JF, Reynolds JC, Cann CE, Chernoff EJ, Hill SC, Gerber LH, Marini JC 2005 Controlled trial of pamidronate in children with types III and IV osteogenesis imperfecta confirms vertebral gains but not short-term functional improvement. J Bone Miner Res 20:977–986.
28. Glorieux FH, Rauch F, Ward LM, Smith P, Verbruggen N, Heyden N, Lombardi A 2004 Alendronate in the treatment of pediatric osteogenesis imperfecta. J Bone Miner Res 19:S1;1043.
29. Gatti D, Antoniazzi F, Prizzi R, Braga V, Rossini M, Tato L, Viapiana O, Adami S 2005 Intravenous neridronate in children with osteogenesis imperfecta: A randomized controlled study. J Bone Miner Res 5:758–763.
30. Uveges TE, Kozloff KM, Ty JM, Gronowicz G, Ledgard F, Goldstein SA, Marini JC 2004 Alendronate treatment of the Brtl mouse model for osteogenesis imperfecta improved bone geometry and loading before fracture but decreased bone material quality and alters osteoblast morphology. Eur J Hum Genet 12:P1208.

Chapter 74.   Chondrodystrophies and Mucopolysaccharidoses

Michael P. Whyte

Division of Bone and Mineral Diseases, Washington University School of Medicine at Barnes-Jewish Hospital and Center for Metabolic Bone Disease and Molecular Research, Shriners Hospitals for Children, St. Louis, Missouri

INTRODUCTION

Beginning in the 1960s, efforts to classify the skeletal dysplasias led to reports of >80 such entities.[1] Most seemed to be heritable, yet the nosology at that time was essentially descriptive because the biochemical bases were unknown for nearly all of these disorders, and the genetic defects were unapproachable. The early nomenclature was based largely on inheritance patterns and the parts of the skeleton that appeared most disturbed on radiographic study.[1–4]

Now, various genetic approaches have revealed the molec-

The author has reported no conflicts of interest.

Table 1. Gene Defects in Osteochondrodysplasias

Disorder	Gene	Protein
1. Achondroplasia group		
Thanatophoric dysplasia, Type I	FGFR3	Fibroblast growth factor receptor 3
Thanatophoric dysplasia, Type II	"	"
Achondroplasia	"	"
Hypochondroplasia	"	"
2. Diastrophic dysplasia group		
Diastrophic dysplasia	DTDST	Sulfate transporter
Achondrogenesis I B	"	"
Atelosteogenesis, Type II	"	"
3. Type II collagenopathies		
Achondrogenesis II (Langer-Saldino)	COL2AI	Type II collagen
Hypochondrogenesis	"	"
Kniest dysplasia	"	"
Spondyloepiphyseal dysplasia (SED) congenita	"	"
Spondyloepimetaphyseal dysplasia (SEMD) Strudwick type	"	"
SED with brachydactyly	"	"
Mild SED with premature onset arthrosis	"	"
Stickler dysplasia (heterogeneous, some not linked to COL2A1)	"	"
4. Type XI collagenopathies		
Stickler dysplasia (heterogeneous)	COL11A1	Type XI collagen
Otospondylomegaepiphyseal dysplasia (OSMED)	COL11A2	"
5. Multiple epiphyseal dysplasias and pseudoachondroplasia		
Pseudoachondroplasia	COMP	Cartilage oligomeric-matrix protein
Multiple epiphyseal dysplasia (MED) (Fairbanks and Ribbing types)	"	"
Other MEDs	COL9A2	Type IX collagen
6. Chondrodysplasia punctata (stippled epiphyses group)		
Rhizomelic type	PEX7	Peroxin-7
Zellweger syndrome	PEX	Peroxin 1, 2, 5, 6
Conradi-Hünermann type	CPXD	
X-linked recessive type	CPXR	
Brachytelephalangic type	ARSE	Arylsulfatase E
7. Metaphyseal dysplasias		
Jansen type	PTHR	PTHR/PTHRP
Schmid type	COL10A1	COL10 α chain
8. Acromelic and acromesomelic dysplasias		
Trichorhinophalangeal dysplasia, type I	TRPS1	
" , type II (Langer-Giedion)	TRPS1 + EXT1	
Grebe dysplasia	CDMP1	Cartilage-derived morphogenic protein 1
Hunter-Thompson dysplasia	"	"
Brachydactyly type C	"	"
Pseudohypoparathyroidism (Albright Hereditary Osteodystrophy)	GNAS1	Guanine nucleotide binding protein of adenylate cyclase α-subunit
9. Dysplasias with prominent membranous bone involvement		
Cleidocranial dysplasia	CBFA1	Core binding factor α1-subunit
10. Bent-bone dysplasia group		
Campomelic dysplasia	SOX9	SRY-box 9
11. Multiple dislocations with dysplasias		
Larsen syndrome	LAR1	
12. Dysostosis multiplex group		
Mucopolysaccharidosis IH	IDA	α-1-Iduronidase
" IS	"	"
" II	IDS	Iduronidate-2-sulfatase
" IIIA	HSS	Heparan sulfate sulfatase
" IIID	GNS	N-Ac-glucosamine-6-sulfatase
" IVA	GSLNS	Galactose-6-sulfatase
" IVB	GLB1	β-Galactosidase
" VI	ARSB	Arylsulfatase B
" VII	GUSB	β-Glucuronidase
Fucosidosis	FUCA	α-Fucosidase
A-Mannosidosis	MAN	α-Mannosidase
B-Mannosidosis	MANB	β-Mannosidase
Aspartyglucosaminuria	AgA	Aspartyglucosaminidase

Table 1. Gene Defects in Osteochondrodysplasias (Continued)

Disorder	Gene	Protein
GMI Gangliosidosis, several forms	GLB1	β-Galactosidase
Sialidosis, several forms	NEU	α-Neuraminidase
Sialic acid storage disease	SIASD	
Galactosialidosis, several forms	PPGB	β-Galactosidase protective protein
Multiple sulfatase deficiency		Multiple sulfatases
Mucolipidosis II, III	GNPTA	N-Ac-Glucosamine-phosphotransferase
13. Dysplasias with decreased bone density		
Osteogenesis imperfecta	COL1A1 & A2	Type I procollagen
Juvenile Paget's disease	TNFRSF11B	Osteoprotegerin
14. Dysplasias with defective mineralization		
Hypophosphatasia	TNSALP (ALPL)	Alkaline phosphatase
Hypophosphatemic rickets	PHEX	X-linked hypophosphatemia protein
Neonatal hyperparathyroidism	CASR	Calcium sensor
Transient neonatal hyperparathyroidism with hypocalciuric hypercalcemia	"	"
15. Increased bone density without modification of bone shape		
Osteopetrosis with renal tubular acidosis	CA2	Carbonic anhydrase II
Pycnodysostosis	CTSK	Cathepsin K
16. Disorganized development of cartilaginous and fibrous components of the skeleton		
Multiple cartilaginous exostoses	EXT1	Exostosin-1
Fibrous dysplasia (McCune-Albright and others)	GNAS1	Guanine nucleotide protein, α-subunit
17. Patella dysplasias		
Nail patella dysplasia	NPS1	
18. Paget's disease of bone (PDB)	SQSTM1	Sequestosome 1
Familial expansile osteolysis, expansile skeletal hyperphosphatasia, and early onset PDB in Japan	TNFRSF11A	RANK

Modified from Lachman RS 1998 International nomenclature and classification of the osteochondrodysplasias. Pediatr Radiol **28**:737–744, copyright 1998, with kind permission of Springer Science and Business Media.

ular bases of many of these conditions and significantly improved our understanding and their classification by showing that a considerable number are "allelic" problems involving surprisingly few genes.[5] Notably, these advances are increasing the spectrum of disorders that can be considered "metabolic bone diseases" and are shifting classification to a molecular foundation (Table 1).[5,6] Nevertheless, radiographic investigation, often using a skeletal survey, remains sufficient for diagnosis for many of these conditions, but usually requires expert interpretation that increasingly can be supplemented by biochemical and mutation analysis.[7]

OSTEOCHONDRODYSPLASIAS

The term osteochondrodysplasia encompasses a large group of seemingly distinctive entities among the skeletal dysplasias.[8–10] Each is characterized by abnormal growth or development of bone and/or cartilage.[1,8–10] In turn, osteochondrodysplasias are subdivided into several groups, some of which feature defects in the growth of tubular bones and/or the spine. These disorders are frequently referred to as chondrodysplasias.[1] The anatomic region of the long bones that is disturbed most (epiphyses, metaphyses, or diaphyses) is the basis for their further subclassification into epiphyseal, metaphyseal, or diaphyseal dysplasias.[1–3] When the vertebrae too are deformed, these conditions are grouped as spondyloepiphyseal dysplasia, and so on (Fig. 1).

Chondrodysplasias that feature primarily metaphyseal defects (metaphyseal dysplasia and spondylometaphyseal dysplasia) may be confused, from their clinical and radiographic appearances, with forms of rickets (Fig. 2). However, biochemical parameters of bone and mineral metabolism are typically undisturbed, and the skeleton is generally well mineralized (Jansen syndrome, caused by activating mutations in the PTH/

PTH-related peptide [PTHrP] receptor and leading to hypercalcemia, is an interesting exception[5]). Indeed, the configuration of the metaphyseal defects has led to the useful subclassification scheme devised by experienced radiologists. When

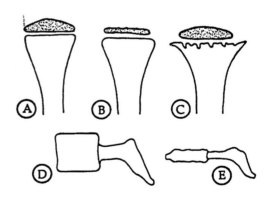

Involvement	Disease Category
A+D	Normal
B+D	Epiphyseal dysplasia
C+D	Metaphyseal dysplasia
B+E	Spondyloepiphyseal dysplasia
C+E	Spondylometaphyseal dysplasia
B+C+E	Spondyloepimetaphyseal dysplasia

FIG. 1. Chondrodysplasias. Classification based on radiographic involvement of long bones and vertebrae.[1] (Reprinted from Rimoin DL, Lachman RS 1996 Emery and Rimoin's Principles and Practice of Medical Genetics, p. 2796 with permission from Elsevier.)

abnormalities of the spine are present (Fig. 3), diagnosis of dysplasia and not rickets should be especially evident.

DNA-based technology has mapped and characterized many of the genes and the mutations that cause skeletal dysplasias (Table 1). Our understanding of the molecular/biochemical bases of these disorders is growing rapidly.[1,5,6,9] Defects in a variety of genes reveal that many proteins are essential for human skeletal development.[6] Abnormalities in type I, II, IX, and X collagen genes cause osteogenesis imperfecta, spondyloepiphyseal dysplasia, multiple epiphyseal dysplasia, and metaphyseal dysplasia (Schmid type), respectively.[1,9,10] Cartilage-oligomeric-matrix–protein gene mutations can engender multiple epiphyseal dysplasia and pseudoachondroplasia. Fibroblast growth factor (FGF) receptor-3 gene defects cause achondroplasia.[1,5,9,10] The elastin and fibrillin genes are involved in Williams and Marfan syndromes, respectively.[5] Remarkably, however, the majority of skeletal dysplasias are "allelic" disorders involving relatively few genes, but especially those encoding type II collagen and the FGF receptor-3.[10] Nevertheless, the number of "metabolic bone diseases" will continue to grow.

MUCOPOLYSACCHARIDOSES

Mucopolysaccharidoses are inborn errors of metabolism caused by diminished activity of the lysosomal enzymes that degrade glycosaminoglycans (acid mucopolysaccharides; Ta-

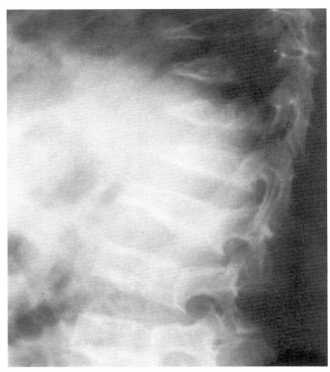

FIG. 3. Spondylometaphyseal dysplasia. Characteristic dysplastic changes at 11 years of age are present in the vertebrae of the patient shown in Fig. 2 and establish a spondylometaphyseal rather than a metaphyseal dysplasia.

ble 1).[11,12] Accumulation of these complex carbohydrates within marrow cells leads to skeletal alterations that are generally referred to by radiologists as dysostosis multiplex.[13] However, the severity and precise bony manifestations vary according to the specific enzymopathy and the underlying mutations.[1–5,13] Each mucopolysaccharidosis manifests with a broad continuum of severity.[14]

Patients with dysostosis multiplex share the following radiographic features: osteoporosis with coarsened trabeculae, macrocephaly, dyscephaly, a J-shaped sella turcica, oar-shaped ribs, widened clavicles, oval or hook-shaped vertebral bodies, dysplasia of the capital femoral epiphyses, coxa valga, epiphyseal and metaphyseal dysplasia, proximal tapering of the second and fifth metacarpals, and dysplasia of long tubular bones.[3,4,13] Enzyme assays or genetic testing are available and necessary for diagnosis of this group of disorders.[14]

Mucopolysaccharidoses are increasingly treated by stem cell transplantation and enzyme replacement therapy.[15]

REFERENCES

1. Rimoin DL, Lachman RS, Unger S 2002 Chondrodysplasias. In: Rimoin DL, Connor JM, Pyeritz RE (eds.) Emery and Rimoin's Principles and Practice of Medical Genetics, 4th ed. Churchill Livingstone, London, UK, pp. 4071–4115.
2. Wynne-Davies R, Hall CM, Apley AG 1985 Atlas of Skeletal Dysplasias. Churchill Livingstone, Edinburgh, UK.
3. Resnick D, Niwayama G 2002 Diagnosis of Bone and Joint Disorders, 4th ed. WB Saunders, Philadelphia, PA, USA.
4. Taybi H, Lachman RS 1996 Radiology of Syndromes, Metabolic Disorders, and Skeletal Dysplasias, 4th ed. Mosby, St. Louis, MO, USA.
5. McKusick-Nathans Institute for Genetic Medicine, Johns Hopkins University, and National Center for Biotechnology Information, National Library of Medicine 2000 Online Mendelian Inheritance in Man, OMIM.

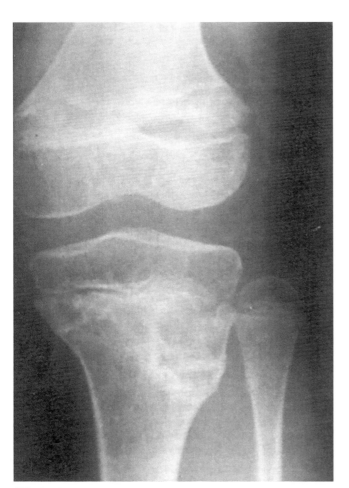

FIG. 2. Spondylometaphyseal dysplasia. The irregularity of the metaphyses in the knees of this 9-year-old girl are sometimes mistaken for rickets.

Available online at http://www.ncbi.nlm.nih.gov/omim. Accessed January 2, 2006.

6. Spranger, J 2001 Changes in clinical practice with the unravelling of diseases: Connective-tissue disorders. J Inherit Metab Dis 24:117–126.

7. University of Washington 2006 GeneTests. Available online at http://www.genetests.com/. Accessed January 2, 2006.

8. Lachman RS 1998 International nomenclature and classification of the osteochondrodysplasias. Pediatr Radiol 28:737–744.

9. Rimoin DL, Lachman RS 1993 Genetic disorders of the osseous skeleton. In: Beighton P (ed.) McKusick's Heritable Disorders of Connective Tissue, 5th ed. CV Mosby, St. Louis, MO, USA, pp. 557–689.

10. Horton WA, Hecht JT 2001 Chondrodysplasias: Disorders of cartilage matrix proteins. In: Royce PM, Steinmann B (eds.) Connective Tissue and Its Heritable Disorders, 2nd ed. Wiley-Liss, New York, NY, USA, pp. 909–937.

11. Leroy JG, Wiesmann U 2001 Disorders of lysosomal enzymes. In: Royce PM, Steinmann B (eds.) Connective Tissue and Its Heritable Disorders. Wiley-Liss, New York, NY, USA, pp. 8494–8499.

12. Neufeld EF, Muenzer J 2001 The mucopolysaccharidoses. In: Scriver CR, Beaudet AL, Sly WS, Valle D, Childs B, Vogelstein B (eds.) The Metabolic and Molecular Bases of Inherited Disease, 8th ed. McGraw-Hill, New York, NY, USA, pp. 3421–3452.

13. Markowitz, RI 2001 A pragmatic approach to the radiologic diagnosis of pediatric syndromes and skeletal dysplasias. Radiol Clin North Am 39:197–802.

14. Muenzer J 2004 The mucopolysaccharidoses: A heterogeneous group of disorders with variable pediatric presentations. J Pediatr 144:S27–S34.

15. Schiffmann R, Brady RO 2002 New prospects for the treatment of lysosomal storage diseases. Drugs 62:733–742.

SECTION X

Acquired Disorders of Cartilage and Bone
(Section Editor: Michael P. Whyte)

Acquired Disorders of Cartilage and Bone

Michael P. Whyte

*Division of Bone and Mineral Diseases, Washington University School of Medicine at Barnes-Jewish Hospital and Center for
Metabolic Bone Disease and Molecular Research, Shriners Hospitals for Children, St. Louis, Missouri*

INTRODUCTION

Physicians who care for patients with metabolic bone diseases encounter a considerable number and variety of acquired skeletal disorders. Among these conditions are problems that result from disruption of the vascular supply to the skeleton and diseases that are characterized by proliferation or infiltration of the marrow space by specific types of cells. Certain metabolic disturbances can cause skeletal ischemia (e.g., Cushing's syndrome, storage diseases), and infiltrative marrow disorders may be associated with aberrant mineral homeostasis (e.g., sarcoidosis). This section provides an overview of some of the principal acquired disorders of cartilage and bone.

Chapter 75.   Ischemic Bone Disease

Michael P. Whyte

*Division of Bone and Mineral Diseases, Washington University School of Medicine at Barnes-Jewish Hospital and Center for
Metabolic Bone Disease and Molecular Research, Shriners Hospitals for Children, St. Louis, Missouri*

INTRODUCTION

Regional interruption of blood flow to the skeleton can cause ischemic (aseptic or avascular) necrosis—an important acquired disorder affecting bone and cartilage.[1–7] Ischemia, if sufficiently severe and prolonged, will kill osteoblasts and chondrocytes. Clinical problems arise if subsequent resorption of necrotic tissue during skeletal repair compromises bone strength enough to cause fracture.[1–7]

A focal change in skeletal density is the principal radiographic feature of ischemic bone disease.[2,3] However, alterations may take several months to appear. Characteristic signs include crescent-shaped subchondral radiolucencies, patchy areas of sclerosis and lucency, bone collapse, and diaphyseal periostitis. Joint space is initially preserved despite the epiphyseal disease.

A variety of conditions cause ischemic bone disease (Table 1), and a great number of clinical presentations occur based primarily on the affected skeletal site.[1,7] Legg-Calvé-Perthes disease is discussed in some detail here, because it represents an archetypal form. A few additional important clinical presentations are mentioned subsequently, including the recently recognized entity of osteonecrosis of the jaw after primarily intravenous bisphosphonate therapy.[8]

LEGG-CALVÉ-PERTHES DISEASE

Legg-Calvé-Perthes disease (LCPD) can be defined as idiopathic ischemic necrosis (osteonecrosis) of the capital femoral epiphysis in children.[9–11] It is a common, complex, and controversial problem that affects boys more frequently than girls (~5:1). Typically, LCPD presents between 2 and 12 years of age; the mean age at diagnosis is 7 years. When it manifests later in life, the term "adolescent ischemic necrosis" is used to indicate the poorer prognosis compared with adults who suffer ischemic bone disease. Usually, one hip is involved. However, bilateral LCPD troubles ~20% of patients where our experience suggests that an epiphyseal dysplasia should be considered as an alternative explanation for the radiographic findings. Familial incidence varies from 1% to 20%.[9–11]

Although the etiology of LCPD is unknown, the pathogenesis is fairly well understood. Interruption of blood flow to the capital femoral epiphysis is the fundamental skeletal insult. However, ischemia at this site in children can have many causes including raised intracapsular pressure resulting from congenital or developmental abnormalities, episodes of synovitis, venous thrombosis, or perhaps increased blood viscosity.[9–11] Most, if not all, of the capital femoral epiphysis is rendered ischemic. Consequently, osteoblasts, osteocytes,

TABLE 1. CAUSES OF ISCHEMIC NECROSIS OF CARTILAGE AND BONE

Endocrine/metabolic
  Alcohol abuse
  Bisphosphonate therapy
  Glucocorticoid therapy
  Cushing's syndrome
  Gout
  Osteomalacia
Storage diseases (e.g., Gaucher's disease)
Hemoglobinopathies (e.g., sickle cell disease)
Trauma (e.g., dislocation, fracture)
Dysbaric conditions
Collagen vascular disorders
HIV infection
Irradiation
Pancreatitis
Renal transplantation
Idiopathic, familial

The author has reported no conflicts of interest.

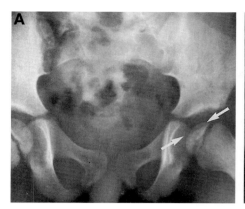
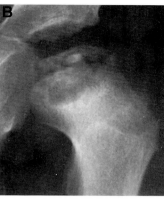

FIG. 1. Legg-Calvé-Perthes disease. (A) The affected left capital femoral epiphysis of this 4-year-old boy is denser and smaller than the contralateral normal side. It shows a radiolucent area that forms the "crescent sign" (arrows) indicative of subchondral bone collapse. (B) Seven months later, there is flattening of the capital femoral epiphysis with widening and irregularity of the femoral neck.

and marrow cells may die. Endochondral ossification ceases temporarily because blood flow to chondrocytes in the growth plate is impaired. Articular cartilage, however, remains intact initially because synovial fluid provides nourishment. Revascularization of necrosed areas follows and proceeds from the periphery to the center of the epiphysis. New bone is deposited on the surface of subchondral cortical or central trabecular osseous debris. Subsequently, removal of necrotic bone begins, during which time the rate of bone resorption exceeds the rate of reparative new bone formation. Consequently, subchondral bone is weakened.

If there is no fracture in the area of reparative bone resorption, the child may remain asymptomatic and eventually heal. If, however, fracture occurs, there will be symptoms. Furthermore, trabecular bone collapse can cause a second episode of ischemia.[9–11] Longitudinal growth of the proximal femur can be stunted, because the disrupted blood flow disturbs the physis and metaphysis. Premature closure of the growth plate may ensue.

Children with LCPD typically limp, complain of pain in a knee or anterior thigh, and have limited mobility of the hip (especially with abduction or internal rotation). The Trendelenburg sign may be positive. If treatment is not successful, adduction and flexion contractures of the hip can develop, and thigh muscles may atrophy.

Radiographic examination, which should include anteroposterior and "frog" lateral views for diagnosis and follow-up, often reveals a bone age that is 1–3 years delayed.[2,3] Sequential studies typically show cessation of growth of the capital femoral epiphysis, resorption of necrotic bone, subchondral fracture, reossification and, finally, healing (Fig. 1). MRI is helpful because signal intensity patterns change with circulatory compromise, soft tissues as well as bone are visualized, and containment of the femoral head can be assessed.[12]

The short-term prognosis for LCPD depends on the severity of femoral head deformity at the completion of the healing phase. The long-term outcome is conditioned by how much secondary degenerative osteoarthritis develops. As reossification of the epiphysis proceeds, the femoral head will remold its shape according to impacting mechanical forces.[2,3,9–11] Generally, the more extensive the involvement of the capital femoral epiphysis, the worse the prognosis. Girls seem to have poorer outcomes than boys, because they tend to have greater disruption of the capital femoral epiphysis and they mature earlier (sexual maturation means less time for femoral head modeling before closure of the growth plates). Onset at 2–6 years of age leads to the least femoral head deformity; onset after 10 years of age has a poor outcome.[9–13]

Treatment for LCPD is directed principally by the orthopedic surgeon.[14] Prevention of femoral head deformity is a major goal. Significant distortion, not mild, predisposes to

osteoarthritis. Degenerative joint disease seems most for children who lose containment of the femoral head by the acetabulum. Improved coverage of the femoral head by the acetabulum is sought, allowing the acetabulum to act as a mold during reparative reossification.[9–11] Appropriate management may be observation alone, intermittent treatment of symptoms with periodic bed rest, stretching exercises to maintain hip range-of-motion, and early or late surgical prevention or correction of deformity.[14,15] Bed rest does not seem to decrease compressive forces that may stimulate healing and bone modeling if properly distributed.[9–11,14,15] Periodic radiographic follow-up is essential, and arthrography, bone scintigraphy, and especially MRI can be useful.[10–12] The long-term results of these treatments remain controversial. Whether containment is useful, and how best to achieve it, are being studied.[9–11,14,15]

OSTEONECROSIS OF THE JAW

Recently, >800 cases of "osteoradionecrosis of the jaw" have been described in adults who have received bisphosphonate treatment, especially intravenous zoledronate and pamidronate.[8] With tooth extraction, a "dry socket" ensues, but the problem can occur without dental surgery. Accordingly, it seems prudent that patients about to receive bisphosphonates should be counseled to have dental work, including extractions, performed first.

OTHER CLINICAL PRESENTATIONS

A considerable variety of perturbations can cause ischemic necrosis (Table 1). This now includes HIV infection in adults and children[16] and primarily intravenous bisphosphonate therapy in adults.[17] Numerous clinical presentations are possible (Table 2),[1–3] now perhaps including regional migratory osteoporosis.[18] Symptoms result primarily from skeletal disintegration. The specific diagnosis, however, depends on the patient's age, the anatomic site, and the size of the area of bone where blood flow has been interrupted. LCPD illustrates particularly well how disruption of the microvasculature of the skeleton predisposes especially subchondral bone to infarction. However, several mechanisms for vascular insufficiency may lead to ischemic bone disease, such as traumatic rupture, internal obstruction, or external pressure compromising blood flow. Arteries, veins, or sinusoids may be involved causing "ischemic," "avascular," "aseptic," or "idiopathic" necrosis.[1–3,6]

The pathogenesis of disrupted blood flow in ischemic bone disease is, however, incompletely understood.[1–3,6] For many types of nontraumatic ischemic necrosis, the predisposed sites seem to reflect the physiological conversion of red marrow to

TABLE 2. COMMON SITES OF OSTEOCHONDROSIS AND ISCHEMIC NECROSIS
OF BONE

Adult skeleton
  Osteochondritis dissecans (König)
  Osteochondrosis of lunate (Kienböck)
  Fractured head of femur (Axhausen, Phemister)
  Proximal fragment of fractured carpal scaphoid
  Fractured head of humerus
  Fractured talus
  Osteonecrosis of the knee (spontaneous or idiopathic ischemic
    necrosis)
  Idiopathic ischemic necrosis of the femoral head
Developing skeleton
  Osteochondrosis of femoral head (Legg-Calvé-Perthes)
  Slipped femoral epiphysis
  Vertebral epiphysitis affecting secondary ossification centers
    (Scheuermann)
  Vertebral osteochondrosis of primary ossification centers (Calvé)
  Osteochondrosis of tibial tuberosity (Osgood-Schlatter)
  Osteochondrosis of tarsal scaphoid (Köhler)
  Osteochondrosis of medial tibial condyle (Blount)
  Osteochondrosis of primary ossification center of patella (Köhler) and
    of secondary ossification center (Sinding Larsen)
  Osteochondrosis of os calcis (Sever)
  Osteochondrosis of head of second metatarsal (Freiberg) and of other
    metatarsals and metacarpals
  Osteochondrosis of the humeral capitellum (Panner)

Reproduced with permission from Edeiken J, Dalinka M, Karasic D (eds).
1990 Edeiken's Roentgen Diagnosis of Diseases of Bone, 4th ed. Williams &
Wilkins, Baltimore, MD, USA, p. 937.

fatty marrow with aging.[2] This process occurs from distally to proximally in the appendicular skeleton. As the transition occurs, marrow blood flow decreases. Accordingly, disorders that increase the size and/or number of adipocytes within critical areas of medullary space (e.g., alcohol abuse, Cushing's syndrome) may ultimately compress sinusoids and infarct bone. However, fat embolization, hemorrhage, and abnormalities in the quality of susceptible bone tissue may also be pathogenetic factors in some types of traumatic or nontraumatic ischemic necrosis.[2]

Radiographic features of ischemic bone disease depend on the amount of skeletal revascularization, reossification, and resorption of infarcted bone.[2,3] Revascularization occurs within 6–8 weeks of the ischemic event and may cause trabecular bone resorption (radiolucent bands near necrotic areas). New bone formation then occurs on dead bone surfaces. Over months or years, dead bone may, or may not, be slowly resorbed. Osteosclerosis will occur if new bone encases dead bone and/or if there is bony collapse.

Histopathological study is consistent with the pathogenesis that is suggested radiographically. It shows that these various processes of skeletal death and repair are focal and may be occurring simultaneously (Fig. 2).[4]

After infarction, necrotic bone does not change density for at least 10 days.[2] Currently, MRI is the most sensitive way to detect ischemic necrosis of the skeleton. It is therefore particularly useful early on, although occasionally false negatives do occur.[8,19–21] Bone scintigraphy with [99m]technetium diphosphonate, although not specific, can also detect osteonecrosis before radiographic changes are apparent.[22–24] Before the process of revascularization, the infarcted area shows decreased radioisotope uptake. Later, increased tracer accumulation will occur. CT is especially helpful for detecting ischemic necrosis of the femoral head, because the bony structure centrally has an "asterisk" shape that is distorted by new bone formation.[25]

The various clinical presentations of ischemic bone disease (Table 2) are sometimes divided into two major anatomic categories: diaphysometaphyseal and epiphysometaphyseal.[2,7]

Diaphysometaphyseal ischemia can be caused by dysbaric disorders, hemoglobinopathies, collagen vascular diseases, thromboembolic problems, gout, storage disorders (e.g., Gaucher's disease), acute or chronic pancreatitis, pheochromocytoma, and other conditions. Typically, large bones (especially the distal femur or proximal tibia) are involved where radiographic changes extend into the metaphysis. Lesions are often symmetrical; however, the size can vary considerably. Small bones may be affected, for example, in the hands and feet of infants with sickle cell anemia. New bone deposition delineates infarcted bone especially well on radiographic study.

Epiphysometaphyseal infarcts can result from dysbaric conditions, sickle cell disease, Cushing's syndrome, gout, trauma, storage problems, and other disorders. When the lesions are

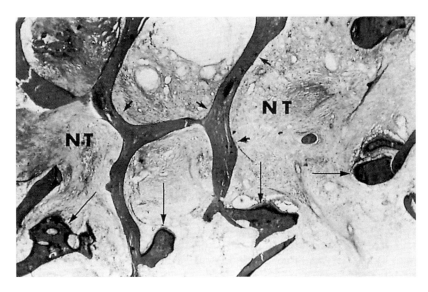

FIG. 2. Ischemic necrosis. This undecalcified section from an affected femoral head shows a typical area of dead bone (arrows) with a smooth acellular surface. A band of necrotic tissue (NT) is visible. Reparative bone formation is occurring in adjacent areas where darkly stained, newly synthesized osteoid is covered by osteoblasts (arrowheads; Goldner stain, ×160).

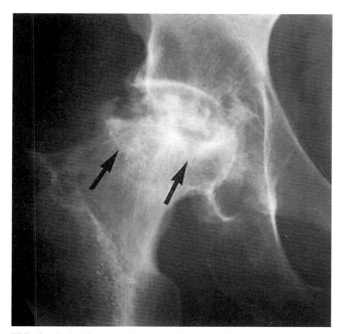

FIG. 3. Ischemic (avascular) necrosis. This 50-year-old man has advanced avascular necrosis of the femoral head. Note that much of the femoral head has been resorbed, causing collapse of the articular surface. The necrotic area is fragmented. A sclerotic zone of reparative tissue (arrows) indicates the interface between viable and necrotic tissues. The acetabular cartilage is focally thin. This finding indicates that he is developing secondary osteoarthritis.

small, they typically affect children or young adults and occur without a history of injury, although occult trauma may actually be important in their pathogenesis. Thrombosis, disease of arterial walls, or abnormalities within adjacent bone, such as those occurring in Gaucher's disease or histiocytosis-X, may cause this category of ischemic necrosis.

Osteochondrosis refers to atraumatic ischemic necrosis that typically affects an ossification ("growth") center.[2,7] Osteochondritis dissecans describes a small epiphysometaphyseal infarct that can cause fracture immediately adjacent to a joint space. This lesion appears as a small, dense, button-like area of osseous tissue separated from the intact bone by a radiolucent band. This skeletal fragment can become loose and enter the joint, but it may also heal in place. Larger infarcts are often also idiopathic, occur frequently in adults, and typically involve the hip and the femoral condyles. Large areas of ischemic bone can collapse, thus flattening joint surfaces and destroying articular cartilage. Ultimately, this complication will lead to osteoarthritis (Fig. 3). Very extensive epiphysometaphyseal infarction results from trauma or systemic disease and frequently involves the femoral head (e.g., LCPD).[2,7]

Eponyms for specific presentations of osteochondrosis or ischemic necrosis of the skeleton are numerous and popular (e.g., Blount's disease, Scheuermann's disease). However, classification according to the involved anatomic site is more informative. Table 2 matches the eponym with the affected skeletal region and helps to show that the patient's age is an important factor for where the skeleton is at risk.[2,7]

Treatment of ischemic bone disease varies according to the site and size of the lesion and the patient's age, and various aspects remain controversial. Conservative or surgical approaches may be appropriate.[1,26,27]

REFERENCES

1. Pavelka K 2000 Osteonecrosis. Clin Rheumatol **14:**399–414.
2. Edeiken J, Dalinka M, Karasick D 1990 Edeiken's Roentgen Diagnosis of Diseases of Bone, 4th ed. Williams and Wilkins, Baltimore, MD, USA.
3. Resnick D, Niwayama G 2002 Diagnosis of Bone and Joint Disorders, 4th ed. WB Saunders, Philadelphia, PA, USA.
4. Plenk H Jr, Hofmann S, Eschberger J, Gstettner M, Kramer J, Schneider W, Engel A 1997 Histomorphology and bone morphometry of the bone marrow edema syndrome of the hip. Clin Orthop **334:**73–84.
5. Assouline-Dayan Y, Chang C, Greenspan A, Shoenfeld Y, Gershwin ME 2002 Pathogenesis and natural history of osteonecrosis. Semin Arthritis Rheum **32:**94–124.
6. Jones LC, Hungerford DS 2004 Osteonecrosis: Etiology, diagnosis, and treatment. Curr Opin Rheumatol **16:**443–449.
7. Steinberg ME, Steinberg DR 2004 Classification systems for osteonecrosis: An overview. Orthop Clin North Am **35:**273–283.
8. Merigo E, Manfredi M, Meleti M, Corradi D, Vescovi P 2005 Jaw bone necrosis without previous dental extractions associated with the use of bisphosphonates (pamidronate and zoledronate): A four-case report. J Oral Pathol Med **34:**613–617.
9. Katz JE 1984 Legg-Calvé-Perthes Disease. Praeger, New York, NY, USA.
10. Conway JJ 1993 A scintigraphic classification of Legg-Calvé-Perthes disease. Semin Nucl Med **23:**274–295.
11. Thompson GH, Price CT, Roy D, Meehan PL, Richards BS 2002 Legg-Calve-Perthes disease: Current concepts. Instr Course Lect **51:**367–384.
12. Lang P, Genant HK, Jergesen HE, Murray WR 1992 Imaging of the hip joint. Computed tomography versus magnetic resonance imaging. Clin Orthop **274:**135–153.
13. Mukherjee A, Fabry G 1990 Evaluation of the prognostic indices in Legg-Calvé-Perthes disease: Statistical analysis of 116 hips. J Pediatr Orthop **10:**153–158.
14. Herring JA 1994 The treatment of Legg-Calvé-Perthes disease. A critical review of the literature. J Bone Joint Surg Am **76:**448–458.
15. Paterson DC, Leitch JM, Foster BK 1991 Results of innominate osteotomy in the treatment of Legg-Calvé-Perthes disease. Clin Orthop **266:**96–103.
16. Gaughan DM, Mofenson LM, Hughes MD, Seage GR III, Ciupak GL, Oleske JM, Pediatric AIDS Clinical Trials Group Protocol 219 Team 2002 Osteonecrosis of the hip (Legg-Calvé-Perthes disease) in human immunodeficiency virus-infected children. Pediatrics **109:**1–8.
17. Qaqish RB, Sims KA 2004 Bone disorders associated with the human immunodeficiency virus: Pathogenesis and management. Pharmacotherapy **24:**1331–1346.
18. Trevisan C, Ortolani S, Monteleone M, Mrinoni EC 2002 Case Report: Regional migratory osteoporosis. A pathogenetic hypothesis based on three cases and a review of the literature. Clin Rheumatol **21:**418–425.
19. Watson RM, Roach NA, Dalinka MK 2004 Avascular necrosis and bone marrow edema syndrome. Radiol Clin North Am **42:**207–219.
20. Saini A, Saifuddin A 2004 MRI of osteonecrosis. Clin Radiol **59:**1079–1093.
21. Mitchell DG, Rao VM, Dalinka MK, Spritzer CE, Alavi A, Steinberg ME, Fallon M, Kressel HY 1987 Femoral head avascular necrosis: Correlation of MR imaging, and clinical findings. Radiology **162:**709–715.
22. Mitchell MD, Kundel HL, Steinberg ME, Kressel HY, Alavi A, Axel L 1986 Avascular necrosis of the hip: Comparison of MR, CT, and scintigraphy. Am J Roentgenol **147:**67–71.
23. Bonnarens F, Hernandez A, D'Ambrosia RD 1985 Bone scintigraphic changes in osteonecrosis of the femoral head. Orthop Clin North Am **16:**697–703.
24. Spencer JD, Maisey M 1985 A prospective scintigraphic study of avascular necrosis of bone in renal transplant patients. Clin Orthop **194:**125–135.
25. Dihlmann W 1982 CT analysis of the upper end of the femur: The asterisk sign and ischemic bone necrosis of the femoral head. Skeletal Radiol **8:**251–258.
26. Canale ST 1998 Campbell's Operative Orthopaedics, 9th ed. CV Mosby, St. Louis, MO, USA.
27. Smith SW, Fehring TK, Griffin WL, Beaver WB 1995 Core decompression of the osteonecrotic femoral head. J Bone Joint Surg Am **77:**674–680.

Chapter 76. Infiltrative Disorders of Bone

Michael P. Whyte

Division of Bone and Mineral Diseases, Washington University School of Medicine at Barnes-Jewish Hospital and Center for Metabolic Bone Disease and Molecular Research, Shriners Hospitals for Children, St. Louis, Missouri

INTRODUCTION

Several important skeletal disorders feature excessive proliferation or infiltration of specific cell types within marrow spaces. Reviewed briefly here are systemic mastocytosis and histiocytosis-X.

SYSTEMIC MASTOCYTOSIS

Systemic mastocytosis, one of several disorders characterized by increased numbers of mast cells,[1] involves the viscera—principally the liver, spleen, gastrointestinal tract, and lymph nodes.[1–5] Additionally, the skin can contain numerous hyperpigmented macules that reflect dermal mast cell accumulation, a condition called urticaria pigmentosa (Fig. 1). Bone marrow is also typically involved and increasingly recognized to cause skeletal pathology. Patients often succumb to a granulocytic neoplasm.[1–3,6]

Symptoms of systemic mastocytosis result primarily from release of mediator substances by the mast cells and include generalized pruritus, urticaria, flushing, episodic hypotension, diarrhea, weight loss, peptic ulcer, and syncope.[1–5] With cutaneous involvement, histamine release occurs from stroking the skin causing urtication (Darier's sign). Skeletal complications develop relatively infrequently but include bone pain or tenderness from deformity resulting from fracture.[1–5,7–10] Serum tryptase elevation is a good, but not disease-specific, marker for systemic mastocytosis.[1] Urinary *N*-methylhistamine increase is an indicator of bone marrow involvement.[11]

Radiographic abnormalities of the skeleton are common in systemic mastocytosis (~70% of patients). The disturbances have been thoroughly characterized.[12,13] Radiographs classically show diffuse, poorly demarcated, sclerotic, and lucent areas where red marrow is present (i.e., axial skeleton) (Fig. 2). However, circumscribed lesions can occur especially in the skull and in the extremities. These focal findings may be mistaken for metastatic disease. Lytic areas are often small and have a surrounding rim of osteosclerosis; rarely, they are large and can lead to fracture. Progression of the radiographic changes can occur as regional involvement becomes generalized.[12,13] Focal bony changes may be absent despite extensive accumulation of mast cells in the skeleton. Generalized osteopenia (without discrete bony abnormalities) is also a common presentation,[7,8,10] but has a relatively benign prognosis.[14] Bone scintigraphy helps detect involved skeletal areas[15] and can provide information regarding disease activity and prognosis.[16] Reportedly, hip bone density correlates positively with urinary excretion of the histamine metabolite, methylimidazoleacetic acid.[17]

Histopathological correlates of systemic mastocytosis within the skeleton are also well characterized.[2,7,18,19] In fact, it is increasingly apparent that examination of undecalcified sections of bone can be an especially effective way to establish the diagnosis. Transiliac crest biopsy may be superior for this purpose to bone marrow aspiration or biopsy.[7,18,19] Undecalcified sections of iliac crest show multiple nodules 150–450 μm in diameter that resemble granulomas (mast cell granulo-

mas). Within the granulomas are characteristic oval or spindle-shaped mast cells, eosinophils, lymphocytes, and plasma cells. The spindle-shaped cells resemble histiocytes or fibroblasts, but they contain granules that stain metachromatically and are actually a type of mast cell (Fig. 3). In addition, the marrow contains increased numbers of these mast cells, individually or in small aggregates.[7,18,19] Tetracycline-based histomorphometry shows rapid skeletal remodeling.[18,19]

The etiology of systemic mastocytosis is emerging.[1–5] Persistence of mast cell disease after bone marrow transplantation (for an additional condition) suggests that a defective myeloid precursor cell is not the cause.[20,21] The disorder seems to be a multitopic, monoclonal proliferation of cytologically and/or functionally abnormal tissue mast cells.[3] Many patients have a mutation in the *C-KIT* proto-oncogene in abnormal mast cells.[22]

Treatment of systemic mastocytosis is discussed in a number of reviews[1–5,22–26] and must be "tailored" in individual patients.[25,26] Severe bone pain from advanced bone disease has been reported to respond to radiotherapy.[27] Bisphosphonates have controlled pain and improved bone density in early trials.[28]

HISTIOCYTOSIS-X

Histiocytosis-X is the term coined in 1953 to unify what had been regarded as three distinct entities: Letterer-Siwe disease, Hand-Schüller-Christian disease, and eosinophilic granuloma.[29,30] An immature, clonal Langerhans cell is considered the pathognomonic and linking feature, and the condition is now called Langerhans cell histiocytosis.[29,30] Histiocytosis-X seems to result from some poorly understood dysfunction of the immune system.[29] There is an increased amount of TNF-α and other cytokines in the lesions.[30] It is an extremely heterogeneous condition that includes an association with major congenital malformations. Nevertheless, the tripartite distinction for histiocytosis-X continues to be used because of the generally different clinical courses and prognoses.[29,30]

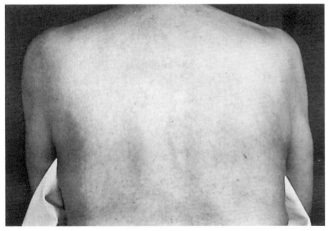

FIG. 1.   Systemic mastocytosis. Numerous characteristic hyperpigmented macules (urticaria pigmentosa) are present on the back of this 61-year-old woman.

The author has reported no conflicts of interest.

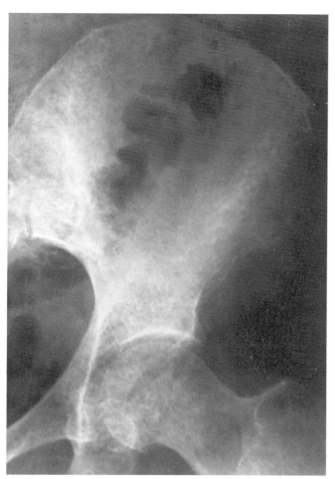

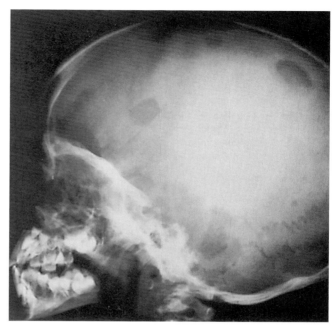

FIG. 4. Hand-Schüller-Christian disease. This 2-year-old boy has multiple, well-defined, beveled-edge, lucent lesions of the skull. Note the extensive destruction of the paranasal sinuses and at the base of the skull.

FIG. 2. Systemic mastocytosis. This 81-year-old woman has characteristic diffuse punctuate radiolucencies of her pelvis and hip that indicate a permeative process in the bone marrow.

About 1200 cases of histiocytosis-X are diagnosed yearly in the United States. Sex incidence is equal. Northern Europeans are affected more commonly than Hispanics, and the condition is rare in blacks. Many tissues and organs can be involved, including brain, lung, oropharynx, gastrointestinal tract, skin, and bone marrow. Diabetes insipidus is common because of

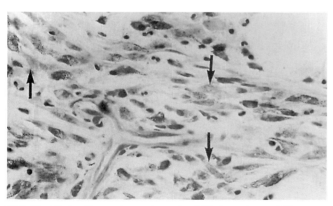

FIG. 3. Mast cell granuloma. A nondecalcified specimen of iliac crest shows a characteristic mast cell granuloma that contains numerous spindle-shaped mast cells (arrows; Toluidine blue stain, ×20).

pituitary infiltration. Prognosis is age-related; infants and the elderly have poorer outcomes. The signs and symptoms of the three principal clinical forms also differ.

Letterer-Siwe disease presents between several weeks and 2 years of age with hepatosplenomegaly, lymphadenopathy, anemia, hemorrhagic tendency, fever, failure to grow, and skeletal lesions. It has ended fatally after just several weeks.[29,30]

Hand-Schüller-Christian disease is a chronic condition that begins in early childhood, although symptoms may not manifest until the third decade.[29,30] The classic triad of findings consists of exophthalmos, diabetes insipidus, and bony lesions. However, this presentation occurs in only 10% of cases. The most common skeletal manifestation is osteolytic lesions in the skull, with overlying soft tissue nodules (Fig. 4).[30,31] Proptosis is associated with destruction of orbital bones. There may be spontaneous remissions and exacerbations. Soft tissue nodules may remit without treatment.

Eosinophilic granuloma occurs most frequently in children between 3 and 10 years of age, and it is rare after the age of 15 years.[29] A solitary and painful lesion in a flat bone is the most common finding.[30,31] There may be a soft tissue mass. The calvarium is usually affected, although any bone can be involved. The prognosis is excellent, with monostotic lesions healing spontaneously or responding well to X-ray therapy.

The radiographic findings in the skeleton are similar in the three disorders.[11,12,30,31] Single bony foci are most prevalent. Nevertheless, multiple areas can be affected and show progressive enlargement. Individual lesions are well defined (i.e., "punched-out," osteolytic, and destructive with scalloped edges). They vary from a few millimeters to several centimeters in diameter. Fewer than one half of these radiolucencies show marginal reactive osteosclerosis. Membranous bones as well as long bones can be affected. In the long bones, defects occur in the medullary canal where there is erosion of the endosteal cortex (commonly in the metaphyseal or epiphyseal regions). Periosteal reaction is frequent and produces a solid layer of new bone. In the skull, the bony tables can be eroded.

Destruction of orbital bones may or may not be associated with exophthalmos. Vertebra plana (i.e., flattened vertebra) can result from spinal involvement in young children. Radionuclide accumulation is poor during bone scanning.[11,12] Biochemical parameters of mineral homeostasis are usually normal.

Histiocytosis-X tends to be benign and self-limiting when there is no systemic involvement. Treatment for severe disease includes chemotherapy, radiation therapy, and immunotherapy.[32,33] Methylprednisolone injected into lesions is an effective procedure.[31] Central nervous system involvement is often treated by radiation therapy. Allogeneic bone marrow transplantation was reportedly successful in a severe case with poor prognosis.[34]

REFERENCES

1. Akin C and Metcalfe DD 2004 Systemic mastocytosis. Annu Rev Med 55:419–432.
2. Pardanani A 2005 Systemic mastocytosis: Bone marrow pathology, classification, and current therapies. Acta Haematol 114:41–51.
3. Akin C 2005 Clonality and molecular pathogenesis of mastocytosis. Acta Haematol 114:61–69.
4. Valent, P, Akin C, Sperr WR, Horny HP, Arock M, Lechner K, Bennett JM, Metcalfe DD 2003 Diagnosis and treatment of systemic mastocytosis: State of the art. Br J Haematol 122:695–717.
5. Valent P, Akin C, Sperr WR, Mayerhofer M, Fodinger M, Fritsche-Polanz R, Sotlar K, Escribano L, Arock M, Horny HP, Metcalfe DD 2005 Mastocytosis: Pathology, genetics, and current options for therapy. Leuk Lymphoma 46:35–48.
6. Lawrence JB, Friedman BS, Travis WD, Chinchilli VM, Metcalfe DD, Gralnick HR 1991 Hematologic manifestations of systemic mast cell disease: A prospective study of laboratory and morphologic features and their relation to prognosis. Am J Med 91:612–624.
7. Fallon MD, Whyte MP, Teitelbaum SL 1981 Systemic mastocytosis associated with generalized osteopenia: Histopathological characterization of the skeletal lesion using undecalcified bone from two patients. Hum Pathol 12:813–820.
8. Harvey JA, Anderson HC, Borek D, Morris D, Lukert BP 1989 Osteoporosis associated with mastocytosis confined to bone: Report of two cases. Bone 10:237–241.
9. Cook JV, Chandy J 1989 Systemic mastocytosis affecting the skeletal system. J Bone Joint Surg Br 71:536.
10. Lidor C, Frisch B, Gazit D, Gepstein R, Hallel T, Mekori YA 1990 Osteoporosis as the sole presentation of bone marrow mastocytosis. J Bone Miner Res 5:871–876.
11. Oranje AP, Riezebos P, van Toorenenbergen AW, Mulder PGH, Heide R, Tank B 2002 Urinary N-methylhistamine as an indicator of bone marrow involvement in mastocytosis. Clin Exp Dermatol 27:502–506.
12. Edeiken J, Dalinka M, Karasick D 1990 Edeiken's Roentgen Diagnosis of Diseases of Bone, 4th ed. Williams and Wilkins, Baltimore, MD, USA.
13. Resnick D, Niwayama G 2002 Diagnosis of Bone and Joint Disorders, 4th ed. WB Saunders, Philadelphia, PA, USA.
14. Andrew SM, Freemont AJ 1993 Skeletal mastocytosis. J Clin Pathol 46:1033–1035.
15. Arrington ER, Eisenberg B, Hartshorne MF, Vela S, Dorin RI 1989 Nuclear medicine imaging of systemic mastocytosis. J Nucl Med 30:2046–2048.
16. Chen CC, Andrich MP, Mican JM, Metcalfe DD 1994 A retrospective analysis of bone scan abnormalities in mastocytosis: Correlation with disease category and prognosis. J Nucl Med 35:1471–1475.
17. Johansson C, Roupe G, Lindstedt G, Mellstrom D 1996 Bone density, bone markers and bone radiological features in mastocytosis. Age Ageing 25:1–7.
18. de Gennes C, Kuntz D, de Vernejoul MC 1991 Bone mastocytosis. A report of nine cases with a bone histomorphometric study. Clin Orthop 279:281–291.
19. Chines A, Pacifici R, Avioli LV, Teitelbaum SL, Korenblat PE 1991 Systemic mastocytosis presenting as osteoporosis: A clinical and histomorphometric study. J Clin Endocrinol Metab 72:140–144.
20. Ronnov-Jessen D, Nielsen PL, Horn T 1991 Persistence of systemic mastocytosis after allogeneic bone marrow transplantation in spite of complete remission of the associated myelodysplastic syndrome. Bone Marrow Transplant 8:413–415.
21. Van Hoof A, Criel A, Louwagie A, Vanvuchelen J 1991 Cutaneous mastocytosis after autologous bone marrow transplantation. Bone Marrow Transplant 8:151–153.
22. Fritsche-Polanz R, Jordan JH, Feix Al, Sperr WR, Sunder-Plassmann G, Valent P, Födinger M 2001 Mutation analysis of C-KIT in patients with myelodysplastic syndromes without mastocytosis and cases of systemic mastocytosis. Br J Haematol 113:357–364.
23. Gasior-Chrzan B, Falk ES 1992 Systemic mastocytosis treated with histamine H1 and H2 receptor antagonists. Dermatology 184:149–152.
24. Metcalfe DD 1991 The treatment of mastocytosis: An overview. J Invest Dermatol 96:55S–59S.
25. Valent, P, Ghannadan M, Akin C, Krauth MT, Selzer E, Mayerhofer M, Sperr WR, Arock M, Samorapoompichit P, Horny HP, Metcalfe DD 2004 On the way to targeted therapy of mast cell neoplasms: Identification of molecular targets in neoplastic mast cells and evaluation of arising treatment concepts. Eur J Clin Invest 34(Suppl 2):41–52.
26. Krokowski M, Sotlar K, Krauth MT, Fodinger M, Valent P, Horny HP 2005 Delineation of patterns of bone marrow mast cell infiltration in systemic mastocytosis: Value of CD25, correlation with subvariants of the disease, and separation from mast cell hyperplasia. Am J Clin Pathol 124:560–568.
27. Johnstone PA, Mican JM, Metcalfe DD, DeLaney TF 1994 Radiotherapy of refractory bone pain due to systemic mast cell disease. Am J Clin Oncol 17:328–330.
28. Brumsen C, Hamady NAT, Papapoulos SE 2002 Osteoporosis and bone marrow mastocytosis: Dissociation of skeletal responses and mast cell activity during long-term bisphosphonate therapy. J Bone Miner Res 17:567–569.
29. Lam KY 1997 Langerhans cell histiocytosis (histiocytosis X). Postgrad Med J 73:391–394.
30. Coppes-Zantinga A, Egeler RM 2002 The Langerhans cell histiocytosis X files revealed. Br J Haematol 116:3–9.
31. Alexander JE, Seibert JJ, Berry DH, Glasier CM, Williamson SL, Murphy J 1988 Prognostic factors for healing of bone lesions in histiocytosis X. Pediatr Radiol 18:326–332.
32. Bollini G, Jouve JL, Gentet JC, Jacquemier M, Bouyala JM 1991 Bone lesions in histiocytosis X. J Pediatr Orthop 11:469–477.
33. Greenberger JS, Crocker AC, Vawter G, Jaffe N, Cassady JR 1981 Results of treatment of 127 patients with systemic histiocytosis (Letterer-Siwe syndrome, Schüller-Christian syndrome and multifocal eosinophilic granuloma). Medicine (Baltimore) 60:311–388.
34. Ringdén O, Aohström L, Lönnqvist B, Boaryd I, Svedmyr E, Gahrton G 1987 Allogeneic bone marrow transplantation in a patient with chemotherapy-resistant progressive histiocytosis X. N Engl J Med 316:733–735.

Extraskeletal (Ectopic) Calcification and Ossification
(Section Editors: Michael P. Whyte and Frederick S. Kaplan)

Extraskeletal (Ectopic) Calcification and Ossification

Michael P. Whyte

Division of Bone and Mineral Diseases, Washington University School of Medicine at Barnes-Jewish Hospital and Center for Metabolic Bone Disease and Molecular Research, Shriners Hospitals for Children, St. Louis, Missouri

INTRODUCTION

A significant number and variety of disorders cause extraskeletal deposition of calcium and phosphate (Table 1). In some, mineral is precipitated as amorphous calcium phosphate or as crystals of hydroxyapatite; in others, osseous tissue is formed. The pathogenesis of ectopic mineralization is generally attributed to one of three mechanisms (Table 1). First, a supranormal "calcium-phosphate solubility product" in extracellular fluid can cause metastatic calcification. Second, mineral may be deposited as dystrophic calcification into metabolically impaired or dead tissue despite normal serum levels of calcium and phosphate. Third, ectopic ossification (or true bone formation) occurs in a few disorders for which the pathogenesis is becoming increasingly understood.

Discussed briefly in this introduction are these three mechanisms for extraskeletal calcification or ossification. Subsequently, there follows a description of disorders that illustrate each pathogenesis.

MECHANISMS FOR EXTRASKELETAL CALCIFICATION AND OSSIFICATION

Calcium and inorganic phosphate are normally present in serum or extracellular fluid at concentrations that form a "metastable" solution. That is, their levels are too low for spontaneous precipitation but sufficiently great to cause hydroxyapatite $[Ca_{10}(PO_4)_6(OH)_2]$ formation once crystal nucleation has begun.[1] In health, the presence of a variety of inhibitors of mineralization, such as inorganic pyrophosphate, helps to prevent ectopic calcification.[2]

The pathogenesis of metastatic and dystrophic calcification at the cell level is partially understood. Both processes typically involve mineral accumulation within matrix vesicles and sometimes within mitochondria.[2] Conversely, the mechanisms which initiate ectopic ossification are less clear, but studies of progressive osseous heteroplasia (POH) identified deactivating mutations in *GNAS* (which also causes pseudohypoparathyroidism type IA).[3] Calcification and ossification within the vasculature is now being investigated intensely.[4]

Metastatic calcification can occur from significant hypercalcemia or hyperphosphatemia (especially both) of any etiology (Table 1). In fact, therapy with phosphate supplements during mild hypercalcemia or treatment with vitamin D or calcium during mild hyperphosphatemia may trigger this problem. Mineral deposition can also occur ectopically from hyperphosphatemia despite concomitant hypocalcemia.[5]

Direct precipitation of mineral occurs when the calcium–phosphate solubility product in extracellular fluid is exceeded. A value of 75 (mg/dl × mg/dl) is commonly taken as the limit that, if surpassed, causes mineral precipitation. However, the critical value for renal calcification is not precisely defined and may vary with age.[5] In adults, some consider 70 to be the maximal safe level for the kidney. Possibly, children tolerate a somewhat higher value because they have greater serum phosphate concentrations compared with adults. However, this is not well established.[5]

The material that comprises metastatic calcification may be amorphous calcium phosphate initially, but hydroxyapatite is deposited soon after.[2] The anatomic pattern of deposition varies somewhat between hypercalcemia and hyperphosphatemia, but occurs irrespective of the specific underlying condition or mechanism for the disturbed mineral homeostasis. Additionally, there is a predilection for certain tissues.

Hypercalcemia is typically associated with mineral deposits in the kidneys, lungs, and fundus of the stomach. In these "acid-secreting" organs, a local alkaline milieu may account for the calcium deposition. In addition, the media of large arteries, elastic tissue of the endocardium (especially the left atrium), conjunctiva, and periarticular soft tissues are often affected. However, why these sites are predisposed is not well understood. In the kidney, hypercalciuria may cause calcium phosphate casts to form within the tubule lumen, or calculi to develop in the calyces or pelvis. Furthermore, calcium phosphate may precipitate in peritubular tissues. In the lung, calcification affects the alveolar walls and the pulmonary venous system. Well-established causes of metastatic calcification mediated by hypercalcemia include the milk-alkali syndrome, hypervitaminosis D, sarcoidosis, and hyperparathyroidism (Table 1).

TABLE 1. DISORDERS ASSOCIATED WITH EXTRASKELETAL CALCIFICATION OR OSSIFICATION

A. Metastatic calcification
  I. Hypercalcemia
    a. Milk-alkali syndrome
    b. Sarcoidosis
    d. Hyperparathyroidism
    e. Renal failure
  II. Hyperphosphatemia
    a. Tumoral calcinosis
    b. Hypoparathyroidism
    c. Pseudohypoparathyroidism
    d. Cell lysis after chemotherapy for leukemia
    e. Renal failure
B. Dystrophic calcification
  I. Calcinosis (universalis or circumscripta)
    a. Childhood dermatomyositis
    b. Scleroderma
    c. Systemic lupus erythematosis
  II. Post-traumatic
C. Ectopic ossification
  I. Myositis ossificans (post-traumatic)
    a. Burns
    b. Surgery (joint replacement)
    c. Neurologic injury
  II. Fibrodysplasia (myositis) ossificans progressiva (FOP)
  III. Progressive osseous heteroplasia (POH)
  IV. Osteoma cutis

The author has reported no conflicts of interest.

Hyperphosphatemia of sufficient severity to cause metastatic calcification occurs in idiopathic hypoparathyroidism or pseudohypoparathyroidism and with the massive cell lysis (release of cellular phosphate) that can follow chemotherapy for leukemia (Table 1). Renal insufficiency is commonly associated with metastatic calcification—the mechanism may involve hyperphosphatemia, hypercalcemia, or both.[6] Of interest (but unexplained), ectopic calcification is more common in pseudohypoparathyroidism (type I) than in idiopathic hypoparathyroidism despite comparable elevations in serum phosphate levels. Furthermore, the location of ectopic calcification in pseudohypoparathyroidism and hypoparathyroidism (e.g., cerebral basal ganglion) is different from observations in hypercalcemia. With hyperphosphatemia, calcification of periarticular subcutaneous tissues is characteristic and may be related to tissue trauma from the movement of joints.[6]

Dystrophic calcification occurs despite a normal serum calcium–phosphate solubility product.[7] Injured tissue of any kind is predisposed to this type of extraskeletal calcification. Apparently, tissues can release material that has nucleating properties. One classic example is the caseous lesion of tuberculosis. However, what local factor predisposes to the precipitation of calcium salts is unknown. Indeed, several mechanisms seem likely. It is clear that mineral precipitation into injured tissue is even more striking and more severe when either the calcium or phosphate level in extracellular fluid is also increased. The deposited mineral, as for metastatic calcification, may be either amorphous calcium phosphate or crystalline hydroxyapatite.

The term "calcinosis" refers to an important type of dystrophic calcification that commonly occurs in (or under) the skin from connective tissue disorders—particularly dermatomyositis, scleroderma, or systemic lupus erythematosus.[7] As the symptoms and the inflammatory process in the subcutaneous tissues from the acute connective tissue disease subside, painful masses of calcium phosphate appear under the skin. Calcinosis may involve a relatively localized area with small deposits in the skin and subcutaneous tissues, especially over the extensor aspects of the joints and the fingertips (calcinosis circumscripta); or, it may be widespread and not only in the skin and subcutaneous tissues, but deeper in periarticular regions as well as areas of trauma (calcinosis universalis). The lesions of calcinosis are small or medium-sized hard nodules that can cause muscle atrophy and contractures. Other etiologies for calcinosis include metastases or trauma that produce necrotic tissue.

Ectopic ossification is associated with two principal etiologies. It occurs sporadically with the fasciitis that follows neurological injury, surgery, burns or trauma, when it is called myositis ossificans. It also occurs as the major feature of a separate, heritable entity—fibrodysplasia (myositis) ossificans progressiva—where the pathogenesis is becoming understood. Some ascribe the ectopic bone formation in this latter, genetic disorder to be a muscle abnormality (myositis ossificans progressiva), whereas others favor a connective tissue defect (fibrodysplasia ossificans progressiva). In all of these conditions, osseous tissue is formed. The bone is lamellar, is actively remodeled by osteoblasts and osteoclasts, has haversian systems, and sometimes contains marrow. Apparently, the injured or diseased tissue has the necessary inductive signals and precursor cells to form cartilage and bone.

Described in the following chapters are tumoral calcinosis, dermatomyositis, fibrodysplasia ossificans progressiva (FOP), and vascular diseases, which represent the principal examples of each type of ectopic mineralization.

REFERENCES

1. Fawthrop FW, Russell RGG 1993 Ectopic calcification and ossification. In: Nordin BEC, Need AG, Morris HA (eds.) Metabolic Bone and Stone Disease, 3rd ed. Churchill Livingstone, Edinburgh, UK, pp. 325–338.
2. Anderson HC 1983 Calcific diseases: A concept. Arch Pathol Lab Med **107:**341–348.
3. Eddy MC, Jan de Beur SM, Yandow SM, McAlister WH, Shore EM, Kaplan FS, Whyte MP, Levine MA 2000 Deficiency of the α-subunit of the stimulatory G protein and severe extraskeletal ossification. J Bone Miner Res **15:**2074–2083.
4. Collett GD, Canfield AE 2005 Angiogenesis and pericytes in the initiation of ectopic calcification. Circ Res **96:**930–938.
5. Harrison HE, Harrison HC 1979 Disorders of Calcium and Phosphate Metabolism in Childhood and Adolescence. WB Saunders, Philadelphia, PA, USA.
6. Hamada J, Tamai K, Ono W, Saotome K 2006 Uremic tumoral calcinosis in hemodialysis patients: Clinicopathological findings and identification of calcific deposits. J Rheumatol **33:**119–126.
7. Boulman N, Slobodin G, Rozenbaum M, Rosner I 2005 Calcinosis in rheumatic diseases. Semin Arthritis Rheum **34:**805–812.

Chapter 77.   Tumoral Calcinosis

Michael P. Whyte

Division of Bone and Mineral Diseases, Washington University School of Medicine at Barnes-Jewish Hospital and Center for Metabolic Bone Disease and Molecular Research, Shriners Hospitals for Children, St. Louis, Missouri

INTRODUCTION

Tumoral calcinosis, first described in 1899, is a heritable disorder that features periarticular metastatic calcification.[1] Hyperphosphatemia is a pathogenetic factor in many patients.[2-4] Mineral deposition manifests as soft tissue masses around the major joints. Typically, the hips and shoulders are affected, although additional joints can be involved.[5] Visceral calcification does not occur, but segments of vasculature may contain deposits.[5] The differential diagnosis includes periarticular metastatic calcification from hypercalcemia associated with renal failure, milk-alkali syndrome, sarcoidosis, and vitamin D intoxication.

CLINICAL PRESENTATION

Most patients in North America with this disorder have black ancestry. About one third of cases are familial. Autosomal recessive inheritance is usually described, although autosomal dominant transmission has also been reported.[1-6] There is no gender preference.

The author has reported no conflicts of interest.

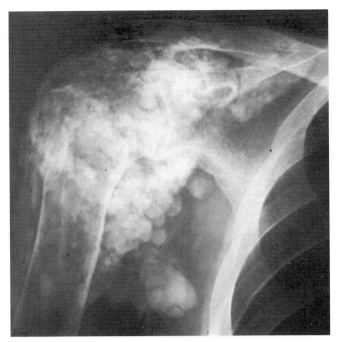

FIG. 1. Tumoral calcinosis. Lobular, periarticular calcifications are present at the right shoulder of this middle-aged man.

Tumoral calcinosis often presents in childhood, but characteristic masses have been discovered in infancy and in old age. Hyperphosphatemic patients are usually black, have a positive family history, manifest the disease before 20 years of age, and have multiple lesions.[3]

The soft tissue calcifications are typically painless and grow at variable rates.[7] After 1 or 2 years, the masses may be the size of an orange or grapefruit and weigh 1 kg or more. Often they are hard, lobulated, and firmly attached to deep fascia. Occasionally, the swellings infiltrate into muscles and tendons.[3] The major clinical complications are related to the tumors that occur around joints and the sequelae in skin, marrow, teeth, and blood vessels. Because the deposits are extracapsular, joint range of motion is not impaired unless the tumors are particularly large. There can, however, be compression of adjacent neural structures. The lesions can also ulcerate the skin and form a sinus tract that drains a chalky fluid; this complication may lead to infection. Other potential secondary problems include anemia, low-grade fever, regional lymphadenopathy, splenomegaly, and amyloidosis. Some patients have characteristics of *pseudoxanthoma elasticum* (i.e., skin and vascular calcifications and angioid streaks in the retina). A dental abnormality, featuring short bulbous tooth roots and calcific deposits that often obliterate pulp chambers, is a hallmark.[6,8] Recurrent episodes of bone inflammation have been characterized.[9] This is a lifelong disorder.

RADIOGRAPHIC EXAMINATION

The tumors typically appear as large aggregations of irregular, densely calcified lobules that are confined to soft tissues (Fig. 1). Radiolucent fibrous septae account for the lobular appearance.[10] Occasionally, fluid layers are seen within the masses. The joints per se are unaffected. Bone texture and density are also unremarkable.

A "diaphysitis" has been recognized using radiographs, CT, or MRI in some cases of tumoral calcinosis. New bone forma-tion occurs along the endosteal surface of the diaphysis, perhaps from calcific myelitis.[7] This finding may be confused with osteomyelitis or a neoplasm.[11] When only calcific myelitis is present, CT and MRI are excellent tools for diagnosis.[11] Bone scanning, however, is the best method to detect and localize the calcified masses.[12]

Periarticular masses that are radiologically indistinguishable from those of tumoral calcinosis occur in chronic renal failure when mineral homeostasis is poorly controlled.

LABORATORY FINDINGS

Serum calcium levels and alkaline phosphatase activity are usually normal. Hyperphosphatemia and increased serum calcitriol levels occur in some patients.[3,13] The TmP/GFR (phosphate transport maximum/glomerular filtration rate) may be supranormal, but renal function is otherwise unremarkable. Patients are in positive calcium/phosphate balance. Urinary studies reflect both the ongoing calcium and phosphate retention, and some patients are frankly hypocalciuric.

The chalky fluid in lesions is predominantly hydroxyapatite.[14,15]

HISTOPATHOLOGY

The masses of tumoral calcinosis are essentially foreign body granuloma reactions that form multilocular, cystic structures.[16] The early lesion may involve hemorrhage and histiocyte accumulation.[16,17] There are ill-defined, perivascular, reactive-like, solid cell nests admixed with mononuclear and iron-loaded macrophages, or well-organized, variably-sized, fibrohistiocytic nodules embedded in a dense collagenous stroma.[16] The cysts have tough connective tissue capsules, and their fibrous walls contain numerous foreign body giant cells. Mature lesions are filled with calcareous material in a viscous milky fluid. Occasionally, spicules of spongy bone and cartilage are found as well.

ETIOLOGY AND PATHOGENESIS

The genetic basis for tumoral calcinosis has recently been revealed with deactivating mutations identified in the *FGF23* and *GALNT3* genes.[18,19] The pathogenesis involves a deficiency of phosphaturia mediated by the kidney tubule cell. Increased renal reclamation of filtered phosphate becomes an important pathogenetic factor.[2,4] In hyperphosphatemic patients, enhanced kidney tubular reabsorption of phosphate occurs independently of suppressed serum PTH levels.[3,13] Deranged regulation of the renal 25-hydroxyvitamin D, 1-hydroxylase causes increased calcitriol synthesis. Consequently, dietary calcium absorption is enhanced, and serum PTH levels are suppressed.[3,13]

The masses may begin as calcific bursitis but then grow into adjacent fascial planes. Tissue damage with fat necrosis can be a pathogenetic factor.[15]

TREATMENT

Surgical removal of subcutaneous calcified masses may be helpful if they are painful, interfere with function, or are cosmetically unacceptable. When tumor excision is complete, recurrence seems unlikely.[20]

Radiation therapy and cortisone treatment have not been effective. Although it might seem that large masses of apatite crystals would be refractory to dissolution, success with aluminum hydroxide therapy (together with dietary phosphate and calcium deprivation) has been reported.[2,21,22] Furthermore, reduction of phosphate levels in extracellular fluid could help to prevent reformation of mineral deposits.[2] Preliminary studies indicate that calcitonin therapy may also be efficacious by enhancing phosphaturia.[23] Acetazolamide, together with aluminum hydroxide, seemed to be helpful for one patient.[24]

REFERENCES

1. McKusick-Nathans Institute for Genetic Medicine 2000 Online Mendelian Inheritance in Man McKusick-Nathans Institute for Genetic Medicine, Johns Hopkins University, Baltimore, MD, USA and National Center for Biotechnology Information, National Library of Medicine, Bethesda, MD, USA.
2. Yu X, White KE 2005 FGF23 and disorders of phosphate homeostasis. Cytokine Growth Factor Rev 16:221–232.
3. Prince MJ, Schaefer PC, Goldsmith RS, Chausmer AB 1982 Hyperphosphatemic tumoral calcinosis. Association with elevation of serum 1,25-dihydroxy-cholecalciferol concentrations. Ann Intern Med 96:586–591.
4. Smack D, Norton SA, Fitzpatrick JE 1996 Proposal for a pathogenesis-based classification of tumoral calcinosis. Int J Dermatol 35:265–271.
5. Martinez S 2002 Tumoral calcinosis: 12 years later. Semin Musculoskelet Radiol 6:331–339.
6. Lyles KW, Burkes EJ, Ellis GJ, Lucas KJ, Dolan EA, Drezner MK 1985 Genetic transmission of tumoral calcinosis: Autosomal dominant with variable clinical expressivity. J Clin Endocrinol Metab 60:1093–1096.
7. Narchi H 1997 Hyperostosis with hyperphosphatemia: Evidence of familial occurrence and association with tumoral calcinosis. Pediatrics 99:745–748.
8. Burkes EJ Jr, Lyles KW, Dolan EA, Giammara B, Hanker J 1991 Dental lesions in tumoral calcinosis. J Oral Pathol Med 20:222–227.
9. Blay P, Fernandez-Martinez JM, Diaz-Lopez B 2001 Vertebral involvement in hyperphosphatemic tumoral calcinosis. Bone 28:316–318.
10. Steinbach LS, Johnston JO, Tepper EF, Honda GD, Martel W 1995 Tumoral calcinosis: Radiologic-pathologic correlation. Skeletal Radiol 24:573–578.
11. Martinez S, Vogler JB, Harrelson JM, Lyles KW 1990 Imaging of tumoral calcinosis: New observations. Radiology 174:215–222.
12. Le Stanc E, Vilain D, Tainturier C 2004 Tumoral calcinosis appearances on skeletal scintigraphy. Clin Nucl Med 29:821–822.
13. Lyles KW, Halsey DL, Friedman NE, Lobaugh B 1988 Correlations of serum concentrations of 1,25-dihydroxyvitamin D, phosphorus, and parathyroid hormone in tumoral calcinosis. J Clin Endocrinol Metab 67:88–92.
14. Boskey AL, Vigorita VJ, Sencer O, Stuchin SA, Lane JM 1983 Chemical, microscopic and ultrastructural characterization of mineral deposits in tumoral calcinosis. Clin Orthop 178:258–270.
15. Kindbolm L-G, Gunterberg B 1988 Tumoral calcinosis: An ultrastructural analysis and consideration of pathogenesis. Acta Pathol Microbiol Immunol Scand 96:368–376.
16. Pakasa NM, Kalengayi RM 1997 Tumoral calcinosis: A clinicopathological study of 111 cases with emphasis on the earliest changes. Histopathology 31:18–24.
17. Slavin RE, Wen J, Kumar WJ, Evans EB 1993 Familial tumoral calcinosis. A clinical, histopathologic, and ultrastructural study with an analysis of its calcifying process and pathogenesis. Am J Surg Pathol 17:788–802.
18. Chefetz I, Heller R, Galli-Tsinopoulou A, Richard G, Wollnik B, Indelman M, Koerber F, Topaz O, Bergman R, Sprecher E, Schoenau E 2005 A novel homozygous missense mutation in FGF23 causes familial tumoral calcinosis associated with disseminated visceral calcification. Hum Genet 118:261–266.
19. Ichikawa S, Lyles KW, Econs M 2005 A novel GALNT3 mutation in a pseudoautosomal dominant form of tumoral calcinosis: Evidence that the disorder is autosomal recessive. J Clin Endocrinol Metab 90:2420–2423.
20. Noyez JF, Murphree SM, Chen K 1993 Tumoral calcinosis, a clinical report of eleven cases. Acta Orthop Belg 59:249–254.
21. Davies M, Clements MR, Mawer EB, Freemont AJ 1987 Tumoral calcinosis: Clinical and metabolic response to phosphorus deprivation. Q J Med 242:493–503.
22. Gregosiewicz A, Warda E 1989 Tumoral calcinosis: Successful medical treatment. J Bone Joint Surg Am 71:1244–1249.
23. Salvi A, Cerudelli B, Cimino A, Zuccato F, Giustina G 1983 Phosphaturic action of calcitonin in pseudotumoral calcinosis. Horm Metab Res 15:260.
24. Yamaguchi T, Sugimoto T, Imai Y, Fukase M, Fujita T, Chihara K 1995 Successful treatment of hyperphosphatemic tumoral calcinosis with long-term acetazolamide. Bone 16:247S–250S.

Chapter 78. Dermatomyositis in Children

Michael P. Whyte

Division of Bone and Mineral Diseases, Washington University School of Medicine at Barnes-Jewish Hospital and Center for Metabolic Bone Disease and Molecular Research, Shriners Hospitals for Children, St. Louis, Missouri

INTRODUCTION

Dermatomyositis is a multisystem connective tissue disorder caused by small vessel vasculitis.[1,2] Acute and chronic, nonsuppurative inflammation involves especially the skin and striated muscles. Dystrophic calcification can follow episodes of inflammation and can be severely debilitating.[3–6]

CLINICAL PRESENTATION

There are more female than male patients and two peak ages of incidence: childhood (5–15 years) and adulthood (50–60 years). When the disorder manifests before age 16 years, it is called juvenile or childhood dermatomyositis.[1,2] The adult form is associated with malignancy.[3]

In juvenile dermatomyositis, the patient's sex and the age-of-onset of symptoms seem unrelated to the severity of any calcinosis, although increased time to diagnosis and treatment worsen this complication.[4] Calcification is generally noted 1–3 years after the disease onset and occurred in 25–50% of patients before intensive therapeutic regimens became available for dermatomyositis.

Calcinosis may predate the myopathy.[6] Mineral deposits develop over 1–3 years. In calcinosis universalis (see below), calcification occurs throughout the subcutaneous tissues, but primarily in periarticular regions or in areas that are subject to trauma (Fig. 1). In calcinosis circumscripta, the deposits are more localized and typically occur around joints. The ectopic mineralization can cause pain, ulcerate the skin, limit mobility, result in contractures, and predispose to abscess formation. Although the dystrophic calcification then typically remains stable, rarely some spontaneous resolution is reported.[1,2] Dystrophic calcification is rare in adults with dermatomyositis.[3]

LABORATORY FINDINGS

Although hypercalcemia with hypercalciuria and hyperphosphaturia may occur in juvenile dermatomyositis, parameters of mineral homeostasis are usually normal.[7] Elevated levels of γ-carboxyglutamic acid have been found in the urine of af-

The author has reported no conflicts of interest.

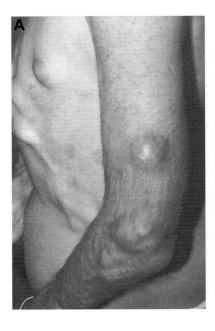
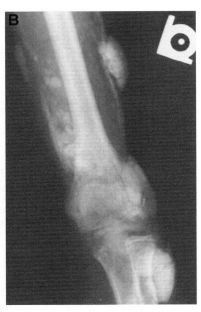

FIG. 1. Calcinosis universalis in childhood dermatomyositis. (A) Characteristic subcutaneous nodules are apparent in the left arm and anterior chest wall of this 15-year-old boy. (B) The nodules in this boy's arm are composed of dense lobular calcifications. In addition, the muscles of the upper arm are encased in a characteristic calcified sheath.

fected children—especially if there is calcinosis.[8] Hydroxyapatite comprises the nucleus of the calcinosis deposits, but other factors (including cytokines and macrophages) are also present.[9]

RADIOGRAPHIC FINDINGS

In juvenile dermatomyositis, four types of dystrophic calcification occur.[10]

1. Superficial masses (small circumscribed nodules or plaques) within the skin
2. Deep, discrete, subcutaneous, nodular masses (Fig. 1) near joints that can impair movement (calcinosis circumscripta)
3. Deep, linear, sheet-like deposits within intramuscular fascial planes (calcinosis universalis)
4. Lacy reticular subcutaneous deposits that encase the torso to form a generalized "exoskeleton"

Children with severe disease refractory to medical therapy seem especially prone to developing exoskeleton-like calcifications. In turn, the exoskeleton is associated with severe calcinosis and poor physical function. Skeletal scintigraphy can be useful.[11] MRI is also helpful for diagnosis by showing muscle edema.[12]

ETIOLOGY AND PATHOGENESIS

Juvenile dermatomyositis seems to be a form of complement-mediated microangiopathy.[13] HLA-DQA1*051 may be a predisposing factor.[14] The precise cause of the dystrophic calcification is unknown. However, immune deficiencies may predispose the patient to this complication.[15] Calcinosis seems to occur in the majority of long-term survivors and may reflect a scarring process. This hypothesis is supported by the observation that mineral deposition appears primarily in the muscles that were most severely affected during the disease's acute phase. Electron microscopy shows that the calcification consists of hydroxyapatite crystals,[16] but other important factors and cells seem to be significant constituents.[9] μCT and X-ray diffraction reveal hydroxyapatite with varied microstructures.[17]

A variety of mechanisms considered for the dystrophic calcification include release of alkaline phosphatase or free fatty acids from diseased muscle that, in turn, directly precipitate calcium or first bind acid mucopolysaccharides. Increased urinary levels of γ-carboxylated peptides suggest that calcium-binding proteins may be responsible for the mineral deposition.

TREATMENT

High-dose prednisone therapy soon after the onset of symptoms seems to be important for minimizing the risk of calcinosis and for ensuring good, functional recovery.[1,2,18,19] If the response is incomplete, consideration is given to additional immunosuppressive agents, including methotrexate and cyclosporine.[20] In a small clinical trial, warfarin treatment to decrease γ-carboxylation was not associated with changes in calcium or phosphorus excretion or in a reduction of calcinosis.[21] Phosphate-binding antacid therapy may reverse the mineral deposition.[22] Remarkable resolution of calcinosis can occur with probenecid therapy to improve renal handling of phosphate.[23] Positive responses to alendronate[24] and increasingly positive responses to diltiazem treatment are reported.[25] Troublesome calcium deposits can be removed surgically.

PROGNOSIS

The clinical course of dermatomyositis in children is variable. Some have long-term relapsing or persistent disease, whereas others recover. When recovery is incomplete, there may be severe residual weakness, joint contractures, and calcinosis. The calcinosis may be the principal cause of long-term disability.[1–6,23]

REFERENCES

1. Cassidy JT, Lindsley CB 2005 Juvenile dermatomyositis. In: Cassidy JT, Petty RE (eds.). Textbook of Pediatric Rheumatology, 5th ed. WB Saunders, Philadelphia, PA, USA, pp. 407–441.
2. Pachman LM 1995 Juvenile dermatomyositis. Pathophysiology and disease expression. Pediatr Clin North Am **42:**1071–1098.

3. Jayalakshmi SS, Borgohain R, Mohandas S 2000 Dystrophic calcification in adult dermatomyositis: Neuroimage. Neurol India **48:**407.
4. Pachman LM, Hayford JR, Chung A, Daugherty CA, Pallansch MA, Fink CW, Gewanter HL, Jerath R, Lang BA, Sinacore J, Szer IS, Dyer AR, Hochberg MC 1998 Juvenile dermatomyositis at diagnosis: Clinical characteristics of 79 children. J Rheumatol **25:**1198–1204.
5. Fisler RE, Liang MG, Fuhlbrigge RC, Yalcindag A, Sundel RP 2002 Aggressive management of juvenile dermatomyositis results in improved outcome and decreased incidence of calcinosis. J Am Acad Dermatol **47:**505–511.
6. Wananukul S, Pongprasit P, Wattanakrai P 1997 Calcinosis cutis presenting years before other clinical manifestations of juvenile dermatomyositis: Report of two cases. Australas J Derm **38:**202–205.
7. Perez MD, Abrams SA, Koenning G, Stuff JE, O'Brien KO, Ellis KJ 1994 Mineral metabolism in children with dermatomyositis. J Rheumatol **21:**2364–2369.
8. Lian JB, Pachman LM, Gundberg CM, Partridge REH, Maryjowski MC 1982 Gamma-carboxyglutamate excretion and calcinosis in juvenile dermatomyositis. Arthritis Rheum **25:**1094–1100.
9. Mukamel M, Horev G, Mimouni M 2001 New insight into calcinosis of juvenile dermatomyositis: A study of composition and treatment. J Pediatr **138:**763–766.
10. Blane CE, White SJ, Braunstein EM, Bowyer SL, Sullivan DB 1984 Patterns of calcification in childhood dermatomyositis. Am J Roentgenol **142:**397–400.
11. Bar-Sever Z, Mukamel M, Harel L, Hardoff R 2000 Scintigraphic evaluation of calcinosis in juvenile dermatomyositis with Tc-99m MDP. Clin Nucl Med **25:**1013–1016.
12. Samson C, Soulen RL, Gursel E 2000 Milk of calcium fluid collections in juvenile dermatomyositis: MR characteristics. Pediatr Radiol **30:**28–29.
13. Kissel JT, Mendell JR, Rammohan KW 1986 Microvascular deposition of complement membrane attack complex in dermatomyositis. N Engl J Med **314:**329–334.
14. Reed AM, Pachman LM, Hayford J, Ober C 1998 Immunogenetic studies in families of children with juvenile dermatomyositis. J Rheumatol **25:**1000–1002.
15. Moore EC, Cohen F, Douglas SD, Gutta V 1992 Staphylococcal infec-
tions in childhood dermatomyositis association with the development of calcinosis, raised IgE concentrations and granulocyte chemotactic defect. Ann Rheum Dis **51:**378–383.
16. Landis WJ 1995 The strength of a calcified tissue depends in part on the molecular structure and organization of its constituent mineral crystals in their organic matrix. Bone **116:**533–544.
17. Stock S, Ignatiev K, Lee P, Abbott K, Pachman L 2004 Pathological calcification in juvenile dermatomyositis (JDM): MicroCT and synchrotron x-ray diffraction reveal hydroxyapatite with varied microstructures. Connect Tissue Res **45:**248–256.
18. Bowyer SL, Blane CE, Sullivan DB, Cassidy JT 1983 Childhood dermatomyositis: Factors predicting functional outcome and development of dystrophic calcification. J Pediatr **103:**882–888.
19. DeSilva TN, Kress DW 1998 Management of collagen vascular diseases in childhood. Dermatol Clin **6:**579–592.
20. Reiff A, Rawlings DJ, Shaham B, Franke E, Richardson L, Szer IS, Bernstein BH 1997 Preliminary evidence for cyclosporin A as an alternative in the treatment of recalcitrant juvenile rheumatoid arthritis and juvenile dermatomyositis. J Rheumatol **24:**2436–2443.
21. Moore SE, Jump AA, Smiley JD 1986 Effect of warfarin sodium therapy on excretion of 4-carboxy-l-glutamic acid in scleroderma, dermatomyositis, and myositis ossificans progressiva. Arthritis Rheum **29:**344–351.
22. Wang W-J, Lo W-L, Wong CK 1988 Calcinosis cutis-juvenile dermatomyositis: Remarkable response to aluminum hydroxide therapy. Arch Dermatol **124:**1721–1722.
23. Harel L, Harel G, Korenreich L, Straussberg R, Amir J 2001 Treatment of calcinosis in juvenile dermatomyositis with probenecid: The role of phosphorus metabolism in the development of calcifications. J Rheumatol **28:**1129–1132.
24. Ambler GR, Chaitow J, Rogers M, McDonald DW, Ouvrier RA 2005 Rapid improvement of calcinosis in juvenile dermatomyositis with alendronate therapy. J Rheumatol **32:**1837–1839.
25. Ichiki Y, Akiyama T, Shimozawa N, Suzuki Y, Kondo N, Kitajima Y 2001 An extremely severe case of cutaneous calcinosis with juvenile dermatomyositis, and successful treatment with diltiazem. Br J Dermatol **144:**894–897.

Chapter 79.   Vascular Calcification

Dwight A. Towler[1] and Linda L. Demer[2]

[1]*Department of Medicine, Division of Bone and Mineral Diseases, Washington University School of Medicine, St. Louis, Missouri; and* [2]*Department of Medicine, Division of Cardiology, David Geffen School of Medicine, University of California at Los Angeles, Los Angeles, California*

INTRODUCTION

The details of tissue calcium homeostasis in the skeleton are beginning to emerge. Interactions between a functional triumvirate of endothelial, mesenchymal, and hematopoietic cell lineages control bone formation and bone resorption—entrained to morphogenetic, metabolic, inflammatory, and mechanical demands placed on the skeleton. However, with advancing age, vascular inflammation, hypertension, and certain dysmetabolic states (diabetes, dyslipidemia, uremia, hyperphosphatemia), calcium accumulates to a substantial extent in another venue—the arterial macrovasculature.[1,2] Mechanistic studies of vascular calcification and vascular calcium metabolism significantly lag behind those of skeletal mineral physiology. Recent data show that "osteogenic" and "chondrogenic" mechanisms resembling those of craniofacial or endochondral bone formation control vascular mineral deposition.[1,2] As in bone, cells of endothelial, mesenchymal, and hematopoietic

cell lineages control vascular mineral metabolism, entrained to morphogenetic, metabolic, inflammatory, and mechanical demands experienced by any particular vascular segment. This chapter provides a very brief overview of vascular calcification, organized into histoanatomic categories that highlight known or probable differences in pathobiology, and thus may potentially guide future development of effective pharmacotherapeutic approaches.

ATHEROSCLEROTIC CALCIFICATION

The most common form of vascular calcification is atherosclerotic calcification (Table 1), in which hydroxyapatite mineral forms inside intimal plaque in association with lipid deposits and monocyte–macrophage infiltration. Until recently, atherosclerotic vascular calcification was considered an uncommon, passive, degenerative, inevitable process of aging. Textbook examples seldom included calcification, and pathologists classified calcified plaque as a category Vb lesion, giving the impression that it is limited to end-stage disease processes.[3] Selection bias may have occurred as a result of investigator avoidance of significantly calcified plaques, be-

Dr. Towler is a consultant for Eli Lilly. Dr. Demer has reported no conflicts of interest.

TABLE 1. Histoanatomic Types of Vascular Calcification

Atherosclerotic intimal calcification (type Vb atherosclerotic plaque)
Medial artery calcification of diabetes and chronic kidney disease
Elastocalcinotic medial artery calcification (Marfan's syndrome,
    pseudoxanthoma elasticum)
Cardiac valve calcification (native and bioprosthetic)
Calcific uremic arteriolopathy ("cutaneous calciphylaxis")
Cardiac annulus calcification
Post-infarct myocardial calcification
Pericardial calcification
Soft tissue calciphylaxis including vessels (acute hyperphosphatemia and
    renal failure)
Calcifying primary cardiac tumors
Portal vein calcification
Pelvic vein pleboliths

cause these plaques can damage both scalpels and microtomes and require prolonged decalcification or plastic embedding. However, with growing use of cardiac gated electron beam CT scanning (EBCT), calcium deposits have been found in ~20% of young adults, 60% of middle-aged adults, and 90% of the elderly.[4]

Pathobiology of Atherosclerotic Calcification

Inflammatory Milieu of Atherosclerotic Lesion. Atherosclerosis is an inflammatory vascular disease, which might more accurately be termed "atheroscleritis." The process is initiated by a breach in the endothelial barrier or by high serum lipids, resulting in accumulation of lipoprotein particles in the subendothelial space between the endothelial monolayer and the underlying internal elastic lamina (Fig. 1).[1,2] When the retained lipoproteins undergo non-enzymatic oxidation, they generate bioactive phospholipids and oxysterols, which induce chemotactic influx of smooth muscle cells from the vessel wall as well as monocytes and T lymphocytes from the circulation.[1,2] These inflammatory lipids can also induce osteogenic differentiation and mineralization of vascular smooth muscle cells.[5] Earliest sites of atherosclerotic calcification are lipid nucleated and located along the internal elastic laminae between the endothelial and medial layers. Proteases are generated in atherosclerosis and degrade elastin, apparently opening sites of lipid and calcium binding. Normally the extracellular matrix of arteries includes collagen type III and collagen type I, but greater collagen I is produced in atherosclerosis. Loss of elastin with upregulation of type I collagen may promote osteogenic phenotypic differentiation by oxylipids.

Ectopic Bone in Atherosclerosis. Although it is well known that calcium deposits in the artery wall are generally composed of hydroxyapatite mineral, it is little known that ~15% of calcified plaques contain fully formed lamellar bone.[6] As Virchow noted in 1863, some cases of vascular calcification are not mere calcification, but "ossification with real plates of bone."[7] A prerequisite for bone formation within arteries is angiogenic invasion, driven by vascular endothelial growth factor, as in endochondral vascularization, which provides a scaffold for bone tissue development. Sites of atherosclerotic ossification frequently include marrow spaces with fat tissue and hematopoietic cells, as well as multinucleated cells that are positive for osteoclast markers.[8] Usually, the bone tissue is associated with and appears to arise from calcified matrix. The mature bone tissue does not usually appear until vascular invasion of the deposit. It is remarkable to note that, in its mature stage, atherosclerotic calcification actually contains vessels within bone structures that are, themselves, within a vessel. Thus, angiogenesis and biology of the vasa vasorum play important roles in the formation of advanced atherosclerotic calcification.

Molecular Mechanisms, Vascular Stem Cells, and Relationships to Bone Formation. As with skeletal bone formation and remodeling, vascular mineralization is subject to both positive and negative regulation. Pathological calcification in arteries and valves shares many features with normal skeletal mineralization. Matrix vesicles are found in human and animal atherosclerotic calcification,[9] along with bone regulatory proteins, such as osteopontin, osteocalcin, osteonectin, matrix Gla protein (MGP), and bone sialoprotein.[2] Human and animal

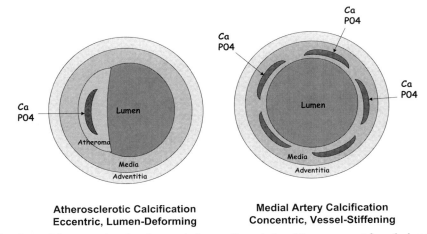

Atherosclerotic Calcification
Eccentric, Lumen-Deforming

Medial Artery Calcification
Concentric, Vessel-Stiffening

FIG. 1. Arterial calcification. In arterial cross-section, three layers—intima, media, and adventitia—are present from the lumen outward. In atherosclerosis, eccentric, subintimal atheroma formation, cholesterol deposition with inflammation, fibrosis, compromise of the internal elastic lamina, apoptic body formation, and calcium deposition herald formation of the type Vb calcified atherosclerotic plaque.[3] Atherosclerosis deforms the lumen and potentially provides a focus for thrombosis and acute occlusion. In medial artery calcification, calcium deposition is concentric, compromising vascular compliance without lumen deformation. Low-grade adventitial inflammation, elastinolysis, and vascular smooth muscle cell matrix vesicle formation drive concentric disease processes. Of note, vascular calcification is only one component of the pathobiology that contributes to reduced vascular compliance.[68] Myofibroblast proliferation, vascular monocyte–macrophage infiltration, and microvessel formation (angiogenesis) are key components of osteogenic vascular calcification responses in macrovascular settings.[1,2,6] CaPO4, apatitic calcium phosphate deposition.

calcific arterial lesions also contain osteogenic regulatory and transcription factors such as BMP2, Msx2, Runx2, Osterix, and Wnts.[1,2,10] Current evidence indicates that, in vascular cells, BMP2 signaling initiates ectopic osteoblastic differentiation.[2]

In addition to bone, atherosclerotic lesions may contain cartilage tissue, amorphous calcification, marrow-like tissue, and adipose tissue. The origin of all these tissues is not clear, but the possibilities are intriguing. One consideration is that there are resident mesenchymal stem cells in the artery wall.[11] The smooth muscle cells of the tunica media contain heterogeneous subpopulations. Some, including aortic myofibroblasts, bovine aortic calcifying vascular cells (CVCs), and microvascular pericytes, are now known to have multilineage potential in vitro, generating osteogenic, chondrogenic, leiomyogenic, marrow stromal, and adipogenic lineages under regulation of BMP2 and Wnt signaling. It is also possible that the multipotential cells in the artery wall arise from the adventitial layer.[10,12] Adventitial cells, in turn, may originate in the bone as marrow stromal cells and immigrate to the atherosclerotic plaque through the circulation entering through the adventitial vasa vasorum. Recent evidence that atherosclerotic plaques derive in part from progenitor cells in the adventitia and circulation. However, the relative contributions of regional vascular mesenchymal progenitors versus circulating marrow-derived mesenchymal progenitors has yet to be determined.

In Vitro Models of Vascular Calcification. A variety of cells harvested from the artery wall, with the exception of endothelial cells, produce hydroxyapatite mineral in vitro.[13,14] Unselected medial smooth muscle cells, in the same manner as osteoblastic cells, mineralize the film of extracellular matrix overlying cellular monolayers in the presence of exogenous phosphate donors. Occasionally, these cultures will produce a 3D cellular aggregate containing mineral. Such mineralized aggregates are produced in cultures of bovine microvascular pericytes, human aortic smooth muscle cells, and bovine aortic smooth muscle cells. The spatial frequency of nodules is increased several-fold in about one third of single-cell derived subcultures of bovine aortic smooth muscle cells (SMCs) termed CVCs.[14] The nodules range widely in size—from about 100 to 1500 mm in diameter—and contain irregularly shaped hydroxyapatite mineral deposits within their core. The regular spacing of the nodules seems to be mediated by a reaction–diffusion process involving the morphogens BMP2 and one of its inhibitors, matrix GLA protein (MGP).[15] Bovine pericytes, retinal microvascular smooth muscle cells, require several weeks to produce calcified nodules; bovine cloned CVCs and human SMCs require about 10–14 days. The rate is affected by exogenous ascorbic acid, presumably caused by the changes in extracellular type I collagen production.

In Vivo Models of Atherosclerotic Calcification. Mice deficient in apolipoprotein E develop spontaneous vascular calcification, primarily in the form of cartilaginous metaplasia.[16] Interestingly, these mice also have increased BMD, presumably related to deficiencies in vitamin K delivery. Most severely affected are the great vessels of the heart, especially the brachiocephalic (innominate) artery.[16] Mice deficient in the low-density lipoprotein receptor (LDLR) develop hyperlipidemia and vascular calcification when exposed to a high-fat diabetogenic diets.[17] Mice expressing the human *LPA* gene develop calcified aortic lesions.[18] Certain strains of mice are more predisposed to develop spontaneous vascular calcification through endochondral calcific metaplasia.[19] Atherosclerotic calcification can be induced by vitamin D and calcium supplements in hyperlipidemic rabbits.[20] Vitamin D also enhances

TABLE 2. EVIDENCE LINKING HYPERLIPIDEMIA WITH CORONARY AND VALVULAR CALCIFICATION

Coronary calcification correlates with LDL—independently of age	Pohle et al. 2001
Cardiac valve calcification progression correlates with LDL	Mohler et al. 2001 Pohle et al. 2001
High-fat diet induces matrix vesicles	Hsu et al. 2001
Coronary calcification correlates inversely with HDL and positively with LDL	Kuller et al. 1999
Lipid-lowering treatment inhibits coronary calcification in monkeys and in humans	Williams et al. 1998 Callister et al. 1998
Hyperlipidemia induces and lipid-lowering inhibits, aortic valve calcification	Rajamannan et al. 2003, 2005

warfarin-induced vascular calcification in rats,[21] but without atherosclerosis (see medial artery calcification below).

Role of Hyperlipidemia and Inflammatory Lipids in Atherosclerotic Vascular Calcification. Atherosclerosis and atherosclerotic vascular calcification associate epidemiologically with hyperlipidemia (Table 2). In young adults with homozygous familial hypercholesterolemia, atherosclerotic coronary calcification is essentially universal, and its severity correlates with the severity and duration of the hypercholesterolemia as measured in cholesterol-years.[22] In coronary artery disease patients, progression of coronary calcification correlates with the severity of hyperlipidemia.[23] Conversely, when patients successfully lower their cholesterol levels with lipid-lowering agents, the rate of progression of coronary calcification is reduced.[24] This epidemiological evidence together with the close physical relationship between vascular calcification and atherosclerotic lesions strongly suggest that the two are mechanistically related. Lipid may directly contribute to hydroxyapatite mineral proliferation. At the ultrastructural level, hydroxyapatite mineral crystals from atherosclerotic lesions are physically associated with microcrystals of cholesterol.[25] Boskey and Posner[26] showed that phospholipids form complexes with calcium and phosphate in mineral initiation, and the phospholipids in matrix vesicles may be crucial in nidus formation. One of the earliest sites of calcification in atherosclerosis is in the elastin layer, where dietary lipids incorporate into the molecular structure.[27] While it is generally assumed that the calcium deposits follow from inflammatory effects of the cholesterol deposits, some data suggest that calcium hydroxyapatite crystals trigger the inflammatory reaction in atherosclerosis rather than vice versa[28]; such responses have the tremendous potential to fuel rapid vascular disease progression through procalcific "feedforward" mechanisms. In vitro, interleukin-6 (IL-6), TNF-α, 25-hydroxycholesterol, TGF-β, fibronectin and collagen I, and inflammatory lipoproteins/phospholipids induce osteoblastic differentiation in vascular smooth muscle cells.[5,29] In vivo, mice with hyperlipidemia develop both atherosclerosis and vascular calcification.[16] Apoptosis occurs in atherosclerotic plaques, producing apoptotic bodies that nucleate mineral deposition through mechanisms similar to those used by the geometrically smaller matrix vesicle.[30]

Clinical Issues in Atherosclerotic Calcification

Clinical Significance. The correlation between the degree of calcification and atherosclerosis is strong enough that the "calcium score" is a reliable clinical marker for coronary artery disease, predicting cardiovascular events independently and more accurately than some conventional risk factors.[31] As might be expected, the degree of calcification correlates quantitatively with the volume of atherosclerotic plaque burden. Clinical consequences of vascular calcification primarily stem from perturbed endothelial antithrombotic function and mechanical rigidity of the aortic arch and cardiac valves. Normally highly resilient and rich in elastin, these structures develop high flow impedance once calcified, resulting in hypertension, left ventricular hypertrophy, heart failure, aortic stenosis, coronary ischemia, complications of cardiovascular surgery and procedures, as well as possible acute coronary syndrome and myocardial infarction. Aortic recoil is required for maintaining diastolic aortic pressure, which, in turn, is required for coronary perfusion. Calcified aortas lack recoil, resulting in attenuated diastolic perfusion, high pulse pressure, and coronary insufficiency. It remains controversial whether calcified plaques convey mechanical stability or instability to atherosclerotic lesions. Although most plaques that rupture are calcified, and numerous calcium deposits increase the risk of rupture,[32] ~80% of significantly narrowed plaques are calcified.[33] Real-time imaging during human angioplasty and engineering considerations suggest that solid mechanical failure stresses are concentrated at the edges of calcium deposits.[2]

Inhibition of Atherosclerotic Calcification. If lipids promote vascular calcification, an obvious approach to inhibition would be lipid-lowering agents. Patients who successfully lower their cholesterol levels significantly reduce progression of their coronary calcification.[24] Atherogenic effects of oxidized lipids are also blocked by high-density lipoprotein (HDL) and in vitro vascular calcification. In an entirely different mechanism, osteopontin seems to inhibit mineralization both at the physico-chemical level of stearic inhibition of crystal growth, as well as at the level of cellular genetic regulation.[34] An in vivo model for regression of ectopic calcification has been developed using an allograft of glutaraldehyde-fixed cardiac valvular tissue implanted subcutaneously in mice. Using this model, Steitz et al.[35] showed that osteopontin blocks ectopic calcification; in addition, osteopontin promotes calcium egress by inducing invading monocyte/macrophage carbonic anhydrase II, thus acidifying the extracellular matrix and enhancing calcium mobilization. Given that atherosclerotic lesions are already rich in osteoclast progenitors in the form of diapedetic monocytes, it is conceivable that existing atherosclerotic calcification could be reversed by local induction of osteoclastic resorption—essentially by eliciting osteoporosis in the artery wall. Indeed, osteoclast-like cells have been identified histopathologically in calcified atherosclerotic lesions.[8] These multinucleated cells stain positively for tartrate resistant acid phosphatase and cathepsin K, but it remains to be established whether they are bona fide osteoclasts. The net effects of augmenting "vascular osteoclast" activity on vascular health and integrity is as yet unknown.

CARDIAC VALVE CALCIFICATION

Cardiac valve leaflets are remarkably thin and pliable, yet strong and inelastic, consisting of two layers of interstitial cell myofibroblasts surrounded on either side by endothelial monolayers.[36] Valvular sclerosis (fibrosis) is a common occurrence during hypertension, inflammation, diabetes, dyslipidemia, and advanced age, and can occur in the absence of narrowing of the valvular opening. Once the scarring becomes sufficiently advanced to narrow the orifice (i.e., stenotic), it is usually calcified. Hence, a common disorder is calcific cardiac valve stenosis. Stenosis is most clinically apparent in calcific aortic sclerosis because the aortic valve is in a high pressure system,

supplies coronary and systemic circulation, and hence can rapidly threaten hemodynamic stability when severe. Calcification is primarily on the aortic face of the valve, the layer known as the fibrosa. The two other layers, the spongiosa and ventricularis, which face the ventricle, are generally spared.[36] The primary cell type, known as the valvular interstitial cell, is intermediate between fibroblasts and vascular smooth muscle cells. Valve interstitial cell myofibroblasts resemble the aortic adventitial myofibroblasts that contribute to medial artery calcification.[1,2]

Pathobiology of Cardiac Valve Calcification

Native Cardiac Valve Calcification. For years, cardiac valvular stenosis had been attributed solely to mechanical "wear and tear." Indeed, the endothelium on the two faces are heterogeneous, both in development and in adult valves, which have reduced expression of calcification inhibitors on the high-pressure, aortic face of the leaflets.[37] However, recent evidence converges to support the concept that most aortic calcific valvular stenosis is atherosclerotic. Many of the same molecular and cellular processes driving atherosclerotic calcification have now been shown to enhance valvular calcification. Atherosclerotic and coronary risk factors also convey risk for calcific aortic stenosis. As with atherosclerotic calcification, most of these factors can be categorized as inflammatory or oxidative stressors. In early lesions, increases in subendothelial thicknesses on the aortic face, with myofibroblast intracellular lipid accumulation, expansion of the valve interstitial valve fibrosus, diffuse stippled calcium deposition, and monocyte–macrophage infiltration histologically evident.[36] Of note, whether valvular calcification arises in response to atherosclerotic stimuli or the hemodynamic stresses such as those experienced with bicuspid aortic valves, inflammatory T-cell infiltrates are observed during the later stages of disease progression. As in atherosclerotic calcification, mature lamellar or endochondral bone tissue is found in ~15% of stenotic cardiac valves.[6] Calcified aortic valves express many of the same osteogenic processes as atherosclerotic calcification, including osteopontin at the mRNA and protein level, BMP2, RANKL, tenascin C, osteocalcin, and alkaline phosphatase activity.[2]

Bioprosthetic Cardiac Valve Calcification. Cardiac valves can be replaced by mechanical or biological tissue protheses. The biological prostheses are usually fashioned from devitalized, glutaraldehyde treated, allograft or xenograft (porcine, bovine) valve or pericardium. Glutaraldehyde treatment is believed to reduce immunogenicity. Bioprosthetic valves have the advantage of not requiring long-term anticoagulation; however, the greatest concern in these valves is ultimate mechanical failure because of mineralization. The observations that cell-free bioprosthetic valves and vascular matrix can mineralize in vitro with inorganic phosphate supplementation[38] has generated some confusion about whether vascular calcification is "cell-regulated." A clarifying point is that even normal, physiological calcification occurs outside of cells, as in cartilage calcification that occurs after apoptotic death of hypertrophic chondrocytes. Interestingly, the valve fixation procedure does not usually remove lipids; however, when lipids are removed experimentally, ex vivo mineralization is reduced.[39] Thus, the cellular regulation occurs at the level of removing PPi-like mineralization inhibitors and generating matrix:lipid complexes that nucleate mineral deposition. As such, valve calcification occurs through cell-regulated mechanisms similar to those directing skeletal mineralization. Of note, vascular and valvular cells require no more, and possibly less, exogenous organic phosphate than skeletal-derived osteoblastic primary cells or cell lines; some vascular cells require no supplemental organic phosphate to mineralize in vitro.[2]

Models of Valve Calcification. Myofibroblastic valve interstitial cells can be harvested from human, canine, lapine, or ovine aortic valves obtained at surgery.[2] Rajamannan et al.[40] developed a rabbit model for studying calcific valvuloplasty elicited by diet-induced hyperlipidemia. As with mural vascular cells, these valvular cells incorporate calcium and deposit hydroxyapatite mineral in their matrix. Osteogenic calcification is enhanced by oxysterols, RANKL, and canonical Wnt signaling.[41] However, it is as yet unclear whether these models fully recapitulate the pathobiology and pharmacology of established human cardiac valve calcification.

Clinical Issues in Cardiac Valve Calcification

Clinical Significance of Calcific Valvular Stenosis and Bioprosthetic Valve Calcification. Calcific aortic stenosis is the most frequent cardiac valve disorder in developed countries and the primary valve disorder in the elderly. It confers high morbidity and mortality.[42] Valvular calcification can be diagnosed by ultrasonic imaging (echocardiography), but the narrowing of the orifice is ideally assessed by Doppler techniques. Recent evidence suggests that valve calcification can be reliably quantified by EBCT. While bioprosthetic valves do not require long-term anticoagulation, the life span of these implants is generally limited to about 10 years because of calcification that results in stenosis and insufficiency.

Inhibition of Cardiac Valve Calcification. Several strategies have been evaluated in preclinical and clinical models to inhibit cardiac valve calcification. Osteopontin, known to be inhibitory in vascular calcification, is also inhibitory in the in vivo model of valvular calcification developed by Steitz et al.[35] and colocalizes with mineralization in valves. Another inhibitor validated in vivo is pulsatile teriparatide, a PTH/PTH-related peptide (PTHrP) receptor agonist and bone anabolic agent that concomitantly inhibited cardiac valve calcification in LDL receptor null mice.[43] Etidronate, used to inhibit heterotopic bone formation after hip surgery, seems to inhibit progression of aortic calcification in patients with end-stage renal disease (ESRD).[44] Some evidence suggests that lipid lowering may reduce valvular calcification. In the hyperlipidemic rabbit model, treatment to lower serum lipids levels reduced the severity of calcification[40] through effects on the LDL receptor related protein, LRP5, and canonical Wnt signaling.[41] Aortic valve calcification progresses more rapidly in subjects with high LDL levels.[23] However, strategies aggressively focused on LDL-cholesterol reduction with statin therapy seem insufficient to prevent vascular calcification progression once the disease has been initiated.[45]

MEDIAL ARTERY CALCIFICATION (MONCKEBERG'S MEDIAL CALCIFIC SCLEROSIS)

Medial artery calcification is a highly characteristic feature of diabetes and ESRD.[1] Although diabetes is the leading cause of ESRD, diabetes is also an independent risk factor for vascular calcification[46]; indeed, even in the presence of chronic renal insufficiency, the extent of medial artery calcification increases with worsening glycemic control.[47] Uremic and diabetic medial artery calcification proceed through matrix vesicle–dependent mineralization processes.[30] Medial artery calcification also occurs in the setting of Marfan's syndrome and pseudoxanthoma elasticum, characterized by primary deficiencies in elastin-based extracellular matrix metabolism and elastocalcinosis (i.e., not through matrix vesicle formation [vide infra]). While both types of medial artery calcification are sometimes denoted as Monckeberg's medial calcific sclerosis, the emerging differences in pathobiology are highlighted by individual consideration below.

Pathobiology of Medial Artery Calcification

Medial Artery Calcification of Diabetes and Uremia. Medial artery calcification is characterized by the deposition of apatitic calcium phosphate in the tunica media of large vessels—with the notable absence of neointima formation. Medial artery calcium deposition is nucleated by lipidaceous matrix vesicles that arise from a minimum of two sources: (1) the apoptotic bodies of dying vascular smooth muscle cells (VSMCs) reminiscent of hypertrophic chondrocyte mineralization and (2) the regulated extrusion of mineralizing matrix vesicles from viable VSMCs.[30] The latter process closely resembles the mineralization of membranous bone formation during craniofacial skeletogenesis. Importantly, Reynolds et al.[48] have convincingly shown that matrix vesicles can promote or inhibit calcium deposition, dependent on whether serum-derived inhibitors such as fetuin are recruited into MGP-containing complexes. Serum fetuin is taken up by VSMCs and packaged into matrix vesicles that serve to inhibit calcium deposition. Besides inhibiting matrix vesicle nucleation, fetuin promotes VSMC "phagocytosis" of pro-osteogenic matrix vesicles; this highlights the complexity of VSMC-regulated vesicle metabolism that controls the initiation and propagation of vascular calcification. Importantly, production of pro-osteogenic matrix vesicles entails the upregulation of bone alkaline phosphatase (ALP), a key osteoblast ectoenzyme that promotes deposition of calcified extracellular matrix. ALP (a.k.a. tissue nonspecific alkaline phosphatase) is of particular importance. Inorganic pyrophosphate (PPi) is a cell-generated organic anion that inhibits mineralization-and is a physiologically relevant substrate for ALP hydrolysis. Johnson and Terkeltaub[49] have elegantly shown that loss of extracellular PPi derived from (1) the extracellular enzyme NPP1 (ectonucleotide pyrophosphatase/phosphodiesterase I) or (2) the cellular PPi exporter ANK predisposes to massive arterial calcification in murine models. Intriguingly, extracellular pyrophosphate is required to stabilize the myogenic phenotype of VSMCs; VSMCs incapable of generating a PPi-replete extracellular milieu undergo phenotypic drift and begin to express molecular markers of the chondrogenic lineage. Importantly, chondrogenic "trans-differentiation" and tissue mineralization are inhibited by treatment with nanomolar concentrations of PPi.[49] Of note, in the setting of ESRD, circulating PPi levels are reduced.[50] Thus, along with the prevalent glucose intolerance, hyperphosphatemia, and fetuin deficiency, reduction in PPi synergistically promotes the profound calcific vasculopathy that assails patients with ESRD.[1] Strategies that seek to restore serum PPi "tone" using non-hydrolyzable bisphosphonate PPi analogs may in fact inhibit progression of vascular calcification.[44]

Molecular Mechanisms, Vascular Stem Cells, and Relationships to Bone Formation. The molecular mechanisms that regulate vascular calcification in diabetes are beginning to be understood. High-fat diets that induce obesity, insulin-resistant diabetes, and dyslipidemia promote vascular calcification in male LDLR-deficient mice.[17] In this physiologically relevant model of type II diabetes, the high fat Western diet—a stimulus for obesity and vascular matrix vesicle formation[51]—activates an aortic adventital BMP2-Msx2 signaling cascade. Cell culture studies have shown that Msx2 enhances osteogenic differentiation (ALP induction, calcification) of aortic myofibroblasts through Osterix-dependent signals. Analysis of conditioned media from Msx2-expressing 10T1/2 mesenchymal cells revealed the elaboration of a pro-osteogenic signal characteristic of a canonical Wnt ligand.[10] Canonical Wnts signal through the heteromeric LDLR-related protein receptors LRP5 and LRP6 to activate osteogenic gene expression through nuclear β-catenin–dependent transcription. Similarly, Msx2-expressing cells express a factor that enhances nuclear accumulation of β-catenin and upregulates activity of β-catenin–dependent transcription driven by a T-cell transcription factor/lymphoid enhancer binding factor (TCF/LEF) optimal promoter (TOP)-reporter construct.[10] Pro-osteogenic activities of Msx2 were reversed by treatment with Dkk1, an inhibitory ligand for LRP5 and LRP6 signaling. Similar results were observed in vivo in studies of cytomegalovirus immediate early promoter (CMV)-Msx2 transgenic mice,[10] a model previously validated in studies of Msx2-dependent ectopic calvarial bone formation. Aortic Wnt3a and Wnt7a were upregulated by the Msx2 transgene, with concomitant suppression of aortic Dkk1. Immunohistochemistry showed Msx2 accumulation in the aortic adventitia but induction of ALP in the tunica media. Calcium deposition coincides with ALP expression. Thus, a working model has emerged in which a paracrine BMP2-Msx2-Wnt signaling cascade, initiated by the adventitial oxidative stressors of type 2 diabetes, controls the osteogenic differentiation and mineralization of vascular progenitors through non-endochondral processes.[10] The vector of mural microvascular flow is concentric, with the vasa vasorum coursing from the tunica adventitia to the tunica media. The concentric medial calcification of diabetes arises in part from the anatomic relationship between (1) the Msx2 expressing cells of the periaortic adventitia that elaborate a Wnt-laden osteogenic milieu[10] and (2) CVCs of Demer in the tunica media that undergo osteogenic differentiation in response to signals or cells conveyed through the vasa vasorum.[11] The precise origins of the Msx2-expressing cells and CVCs are not known; however, a Sca1+ stem cell population has recently been shown to reside within the aortic adventitia.[12] Whether these cells arise from circulating progenitors[52] or aortic mesoangioblast-like cells is also unclear.

In uremia, a "perfect storm" of calcific vasculopathy occurs. Approximately 5% of Americans have impaired renal function, and three million patients have clinically relevant chronic kidney disease (CKD). In this common clinical setting, phosphate retention, secondary hyperparathyroidism, and the accumulation of PTH fragments that perturb normal calcium phosphate homeostasis drive tremendous vascular calcium loads.[53] The phosphate retention of CKD presents opportunity for intervention[54]-but confounds simple interpretation of disease pathophysiology and progression. Hyperphosphatemia stimulates vascular matrix accumulation of procalcific VSMC matrix vesicles.[30] Consistent with this, Giachelli et al.[55] have provided evidence that inhibition of the cellular phosphate transporter, Pit-1, inhibits VSMC calcification and subsequent osteo-/chondrogenic differentiation. Moreover, Vyavahare et al.[39] showed that paracrine vascular PTHrP limits VSMC calcification, consistent with results obtained with pulsatile PTH(1-34) administration in vivo[43]; thus, the widespread use of calcitriol to limit secondary and tertiary hyperparathyroidism may exert unintended deleterious consequences on vascular calcium load[56] through suppression of vascular PTHrP.[57] A proteolytic fragment of PTH, PTH(7-84), that accumulates in ESRD and functions to induce resistance to PTH binds the PTH1R and does not elicit signaling cascades; instead it downregulates cell surface expression by enhancing dynamin-dependent internalization.[58] Thus, if PTH1R signaling plays important roles in promoting skeletal mineral accumulation while simultaneously limiting vascular calcium accumulation, the accumulation of such antagonistic PTH fragments may contribute to the calcific vasculopathy of CKD.

Elastocalcinotic Vascular Calcification: A Distinct Form of Medial Artery Calcification. Recently, it has become apparent that vascular calcification associated with primary alterations in elastin metabolism may in fact represent a unique entry point in a feedforward cycle of medial artery calcification.[59] Large muscular arteries contain elastin as a major extracellular matrix constituent. Aberrant elastin organization and metabolism is characterized by aortic root dilatation, aneurysm formation, and medial calcification and degeneration. This is perhaps most evident in Marfan's syndrome, where deficiencies in fibrillin 1 (1) cause homeostatic failure in the microfibrillar array of the tunica adventitia to withstand physiological hemodynamic stress; and (2) result in disruption of the tunica media elastin network, smooth muscle cell phenotypic modulation, metalloproteinase induction, and calcification as secondary events.[59] Elastolytic calcification—unlike medial artery calcification of diabetes—is not initially associated with matrix vesicle formation; instead, calcium phosphate deposition occurs in association with degenerating elastin fibrils of the tunica media. As such, it is a form of medial artery calcification. While molecular mechanisms are not understood, it is apparent that elastinolytic matrix remodeling processes degrading vascular tropoelastin and elastin enhance vascular matrix calcium deposition. During the progression of any form of medial calcification, perturbations in elastin metabolism likely contribute to vascular calcium load. Interestingly, elastin glycoxidation products such as pentosidine accumulate in ESRD, increase vessel stiffness, and enhance matrix calcium binding.[60] However, matrix vesicles are clearly evident in medial calcification of ESRD, and as such progresses through mechanisms overlapping those of diabetic medial artery calcification.[30,48]

Elastin-nucleated calcification also occurs in the setting of pseudoxanthoma elasticum (PXE), arising from mutations in the *ABCC6* gene that causes fragmentation of elastic lamina.[61] Mechanisms are again unknown. Electron microscopy confirms deposition of calcium along thickened elastin fibers in the absence of matrix vesicle formation. A murine model of *ABCC6* deficiency has been recently reported.[61] Detailed study of this model should provide further insights into the pathobiology of elastocalcinotic medial artery calcification.

In Vivo Models of Medial Artery Calcification. Several models of medial artery calcification have been developed. The best appreciated models are those associated with vitamin D excess with warfarin + menadione or hypervitaminosis D plus nicotine administration.[62,63] These treatments result in an elastocalcinotic medial artery calcification but may also suppress vascular PTHrP, a paracrine inhibitor of vascular osteogenic differentiation.[57] Other models include genetic osteoprotegerin (OPG) deficiency and high-fat diet administration to nephrectomized LDLR$^{-/-}$ mice[64] or C57Bl/6 mice possessing the CMV-Msx2 transgene.[10] With OPG deficiency, intimal and medial artery calcification arises,[65] potentially related to unopposed actions of RANKL on vascular myofibroblasts.[66] Pro-osteogenic Wnt signaling cascades are activated by aortic *Msx2* gene expression, with calcification triggered by high-fat diabetogenic diet (vide supra).[10] Induction of chronic renal insufficiency, with attendant phosphate retention, profoundly accelerates calcification in LDLR$^{-/-}$ mice.[64] Side-by-side comparisons have yet to be performed with these models to clarify mechanistic similarities and differences.

Clinical Issues in Medial Artery Calcification

Clinical Significance of Medial Artery Calcification. Epidemiological studies have clearly shown that medial artery calcification increases the risk of cardiovascular morbidity and mortality in patients with diabetes[67] and uremia.[53] The excess risk for lower extremity amputation and cardiovascular mortality may arise from a type of vascular "diastolic" dysfunction that arises with reduced vascular compliance of elastic arteries. During systole, potential energy is stored within large elastic arteries such as the aorta. Kinetic energy is subsequently released during the relaxation phase of the cardiac cycle, providing diastolic perfusion of the myocardium and sustained perfusion of distal vascular beds.[68] With vessel stiffening, elevated pulse pressure and highly pulsatile flow kinetics interact with elevated systolic blood pressure and increased myocardial oxygen consumption to increase workload and decrease distal tissue perfusion.[68] Compromised elastic artery compliance is likely a major contributor to the increased risk for lower extremity amputation of patients with type 2 diabetes.[67]

Inhibition or Regression of Medial Artery Calcification. Very few studies have explored whether medial artery calcification is preventable or reversible. Price et al.[63] have shown that vitamin D plus warfarin-induced vascular calcification in the rat is inhibited by treatment with OPG. Giachelli et al.[55] have provided evidence that inhibition of the phosphate transporter, Pit-1, inhibits smooth muscle cell calcification and osteo-/chondrogenic differentiation. The phosphate binding resin sevelamer inhibits the endochondral vascular calcification of apoE null mice.[69] Moreover, aggressive lipid-lowering therapy with statins suppresses cardiovascular calcification and associated canonical Wnt signaling in dyslipidemic rabbits.[41] However, in human studies, only sevelamer has been unambiguously shown to decrease progression of vascular calcification.[54] A very recent study showed that administration of the endothelin receptor antagonist darusentan induced regression of elastocalcinotic medial calcification in rodents by upregulation of carbonic anhydrase[62]; whether this exciting new strategy is effective in other preclinical models of vascular calcification has yet to be determined.

CALCIFIC UREMIC ARTERIOLOPATHY (CUTANEOUS CALCIPHYLAXIS)

A particularly severe and mercifully uncommon form of vascular calcification is calcemic uremic arteriolopathy (CUA), observed in the setting of ESRD. Unlike the highly common macrovascular medial artery and atherosclerotic calcification of ESRD, CUA afflicts much smaller arteries, most notably the arterioles of the dermis.[70] Clinically, it presents as a vasculitis, with *livido reticularis* followed by cord-like dermal thickening and subsequent "dry" cutaneous necrosis. The histopathology is medial arteriolar (100–600 micron diameter) calcification with concomitant (1) endovascular, fibroproliferative neointimal constriction; (2) frequent small vessel thrombosis; and (3) fat necrosis with panniculitis and acute inflammatory changes. Similar histopathology can occur in intestinal mesenteric arterioles, and contributes to poor clinical outcome.[70] The pathobiology of CUA is poorly understood. Antecedent hyperphosphatemia and elevated calcium-phosphate product is prevalent but insufficient to explain the disease process. However, treatment with warfarin before onset of CUA is observed in one half of the afflicted patients.[70] MGP is a highly important modulator of BMP signaling and inhibitor of osteo/chondrogenic vascular calcification. BMPs are powerful bone morphogens that promote osteogenic differentiation and ALP induction.

Zebboudj et al.[71] first showed that MGP forms an inhibitory complex with BMPs that precludes ALP induction; this bioactivity is dependent on modification of MGP by Gla residues. Moreover, as shown by Shanahan et al.,[48] MGP–fetuin complexes assembled by vascular smooth muscle cells form vesicles that can actually inhibit vascular calcium deposition. Of note, recent data suggest that undercarboxylated MGP is associated with the risk of calcific vascular disease in patients with normal renal function.[72] Thus, given the above data, we speculate that MGP–fetuin deficiencies associated with weight loss and warfarin treatment in patients with CUA contributes to pathogenesis. However, until a robust animal model of CUA is developed, these notions are again speculative; as previously noted,[70] the original calciphylaxis model of Selye that causes skin necrosis in experimental animals does not recapitulate the histopathology of CUA. Thus, the use of the term "cutaneous calciphylaxis" to connote CUA should probably be discontinued. Future studies will no doubt address whether patients with CUA are particularly deficient in the formation of these novel inhibitory MGP:fetuin vesicles.[48] Infusion of sodium thiosulfate has been used to treat severe calcific uremic arteriolopathy,[73] but no randomized control trial of thiosulfate therapy in any form of vascular calcification has been reported.

MYOCARDIAL, PERICARDIAL, AND ANNULAR CALCIFICATION

Calcium deposits also develop in human myocardial and pericardial tissue in a variety of conditions; these include myocardial infarction—especially with aneurysm formation, pericarditis, and myocarditis. Myocardial dystrophic calcification is visible by chest X-ray in ~5–10% of patients who have survived 5+ years after a left ventricular infarct.[74] In mice, spontaneous calcification of the myocardial tissue, known as dystrophic cardiac calcinosis, can be induced by a high-fat diet in certain strains. Using intercrosses of resistant C57Bl/6J and susceptible C3H/HeJ inbred mice, Ivandic et al.[75] identified a major predisposing quantitative trait locus, Dyscalc1, on proximal chromosome 7. Granulomatous diseases (tuberculosis, histoplasmosis, sarcoidosis) were historically the common causes of pericardial calcification; with the incidence of tuberculosis in decline, granulomatous pericardial calcification has also declined.[76] Uremia, systemic lupus, and postviral, postirradiation, or post-hemopericardium pericardial inflammation are the more common settings in which pericardial calcification is seen today.[76] The stiffening of this tissue produces clinically significant hemodynamic abnormalities leading to restrictive heart failure. The valve annulus, a fibrous ring embedded in the myocardium surrounding each valve, often undergoes calcification through endochondral metaplasia. Cardiac annulus calcification is commonly observed after middle age in women (mitral) or in the setting of uremia and aortic valve calcification. Rarely, primary cardiac tumors such as rhabdomyomas, endotheliomas, and myxomas can also calcify.

VENOUS VASCULAR CALCIFICATION

Calcification does occur in the venous vasculature; indeed, calcified pelvic venous thromboliths are commonly observed on plain film, but have little known clinical consequence. However, venous vasculature exposed to elevated transmural pressures may become subject to "arterialization" and thus clinically relevant macrovascular calcification in certain disease settings. Calcification of saphenous vein grafts used for coronary bypass certainly represents a visible and relevant example. However, orthotopic venous calcification has been uniformly reported in another common clinical setting—portal hypertension. Verma et al.[77] have recently identified that ~11% of patients with cirrhosis have portal and mesenteric venous calcification. The pathobiology and clinical consequences have yet to be evaluated, but a detailed understanding of how venous Wnt/LRP signaling and splanchnic venous matrix remodeling responds to elevated transmural pressure promises to be fruitful.

SUMMARY

The above pathogenetic mechanisms—reduced tissue pyrophosphate, elevated serum phosphate levels, enhanced vascular inflammation and oxylipid formation with reduced serum fetuin, activated vascular BMP2-Msx2-Wnt signaling, and diminished vascular PTH/PTHrP receptor signaling–offer multiple potential therapeutic strategies. However, in humans, only sevelamer has been unambiguously shown to decrease progression of vascular calcification[54]; clinical studies of bisphosphonates and statins have been either too small[44] or disappointing.[45] There are a number of biological and epidemiologic links between the diseases of osteoporosis and atherosclerosis, suggesting common pathophysiological mechanisms and, thus, potential therapeutic linkage.[78] Given that bone has vascular channels, lipids deposits in subendothelial spaces of bone tissue and resultant oxidative stress may contribute to both disorders.[79] Of note, maintaining bone anabolism is important to diminish the risk of vascular calcification in ESRD; excessive reductions in serum PTH in hemodialysis patients results in low-turnover osteoporosis and profound vascular calcification.[80,81] Indeed, in murine models bone anabolic agents inhibit vascular calcium deposition.[43,64] The pulsatile PTH responses elicited by calcium receptor antagonists in chronic renal insufficiency may thus help normalize both vascular and skeletal calcium homeostasis.[56] However, the biological heterogeneity of vascular calcification demonstrates that carefully crafted, controlled and monitored translational research studies are desperately needed to address the tremendous unmet clinical need in this bone and mineral disease.

ACKNOWLEDGMENTS

The authors are supported by grants from the National Institutes of Health (D.A.T., L.L.D), the American Diabetes Association (D.A.T.), and the American Heart Association (L.L.D.).

REFERENCES

1. Vattikuti R, Towler DA 2004 Osteogenic regulation of vascular calcification: An early perspective. Am J Physiol Endocrinol Metab **286**:E686–E696.
2. Abedin M, Tintut Y, Demer LL 2004 Vascular calcification: Mechanisms and clinical ramifications. Arterioscler Thromb Vasc Biol **24**:1161–1170.
3. Stary HC, Chandler AB, Dinsmore RE, Fuster V, Glagov S, Insull W Jr, Rosenfeld ME, Schwartz CJ, Wagner WD, Wissler RW 1995 A definition of advanced types of atherosclerotic lesions and a histological classification of atherosclerosis. A report from the Committee on Vascular Lesions of the Council on Arteriosclerosis, American Heart Association. Arterioscler Thromb Vasc Biol **15**:1512–1531.
4. Newman AB, Naydeck BL, Sutton-Tyrrell K, Feldman A, Edmundowicz D, Kuller LH 2001 Coronary artery calcification in older adults to age 99: Prevalence and risk factors. Circulation **104**:2679–2684.
5. Parhami F, Morrow AD, Balucan J, Leitinger N, Watson AD, Tintut Y, Berliner JA, Demer LL 1997 Lipid oxidation products have opposite effects on calcifying vascular cell and bone cell differentiation. A possible explanation for the paradox of arterial calcification in osteoporotic patients. Arterioscler Thromb Vasc Biol **17**:680–687.
6. Mohler ER III, Gannon F, Reynolds C, Zimmerman R, Keane MG, Kaplan FS 2001 Bone formation and inflammation in cardiac valves. Circulation **103**:1522–1528.
7. Virchow R 1863 Cellular Pathology as Based Upon Physiological and Pathological Histology. Dover Publications, New York, NY, USA.
8. Hunt JL, Fairman R, Mitchell ME, Carpenter JP, Golden M, Khalapyan T, Wolfe M, Neschis D, Milner R, Scoll B, Cusack A, Mohler ER III 2002 Bone formation in carotid plaques: A clinicopathological study. Stroke **33**:1214–1219.
9. Tanimura A, McGregor DH, Anderson HC 1983 Matrix vesicles in atherosclerotic calcification. Proc Soc Exp Biol Med **172**:173–177.
10. Shao JS, Cheng SL, Pingsterhaus JM, Charlton-Kachigian N, Loewy AP, Towler DA 2005 Msx2 promotes cardiovascular calcification by activating paracrine Wnt signals. J Clin Invest **115**:1210–1220.
11. Tintut Y, Alfonso Z, Saini T, Radcliff K, Watson K, Bostrom K, Demer LL 2003 Multilineage potential of cells from the artery wall. Circulation **108**:2505–2510.
12. Hu Y, Zhang Z, Torsney E, Afzal AR, Davison F, Metzler B, Xu Q 2004 Abundant progenitor cells in the adventitia contribute to atherosclerosis of vein grafts in ApoE-deficient mice. J Clin Invest **113**:1258–1265.
13. Schor AM, Allen TD, Canfield AE, Sloan P, Schor SL 1990 Pericytes derived from the retinal microvasculature undergo calcification in vitro. J Cell Sci **97**:449–461.
14. Bostrom K, Watson KE, Horn S, Wortham C, Herman IM, Demer LL 1993 Bone morphogenetic protein expression in human atherosclerotic lesions. J Clin Invest **91**:1800–1809.
15. Garfinkel A, Tintut Y, Petrasek D, Bostrom K, Demer LL 2004 Pattern formation by vascular mesenchymal cells. Proc Natl Acad Sci USA **101**:9247–9250.
16. Rattazzi M, Bennett BJ, Bea F, Kirk EA, Ricks JL, Speer M, Schwartz SM, Giachelli CM, Rosenfeld ME 2005 Calcification of advanced atherosclerotic lesions in the innominate arteries of ApoE-deficient mice: Potential role of chondrocyte-like cells. Arterioscler Thromb Vasc Biol **25**:1420–1425.
17. Towler DA, Bidder M, Latifi T, Coleman T, Semenkovich CF 1998 Diet-induced diabetes activates an osteogenic gene regulatory program in the aortas of low density lipoprotein receptor-deficient mice. J Biol Chem **273**:30427–30434.
18. Teivainen PA, Eliassen KA, Berg K, Torsdalen K, Svindland A 2004 Atherogenesis and vascular calcification in mice expressing the human LPA gene. Pathophysiology **11**:113–120.
19. Qiao JH, Fishbein MC, Demer LL, Lusis AJ 1995 Genetic determination of cartilaginous metaplasia in mouse aorta. Arterioscler Thromb Vasc Biol **15**:2265–2272.
20. Demer LL 1991 Effect of calcification on in vivo mechanical response of rabbit arteries to balloon dilation. Circulation **83**:2083–2093.
21. Price PA, Faus SA, Williamson MK 2000 Warfarin-induced artery calcification is accelerated by growth and vitamin D. Arterioscler Thromb Vasc Biol **20**:317–327.
22. Hoeg JM, Feuerstein IM, Tucker EE 1994 Detection and quantitation of calcific atherosclerosis by ultrafast computed tomography in children and young adults with homozygous familial hypercholesterolemia. Arterioscler Thromb **14**:1066–1074.
23. Pohle K, Maffert R, Ropers D, Moshage W, Stilianakis N, Daniel WG, Achenbach S 2001 Progression of aortic valve calcification: Association with coronary atherosclerosis and cardiovascular risk factors. Circulation **104**:1927–1932.
24. Callister TQ, Raggi P, Cooil B, Lippolis NJ, Russo DJ 1998 Effect of HMG-CoA reductase inhibitors on coronary artery disease as assessed by electron-beam computed tomography. N Engl J Med **339**:1972–1978.
25. Hirsch D, Azoury R, Sarig S, Kruth HS 1993 Colocalization of cholesterol and hydroxyapatite in human atherosclerotic lesions. Calcif Tissue Int **52**:94–98.
26. Boskey AL, Posner AS 1977 The role of synthetic and bone extracted Ca-phospholipid-PO4 complexes in hydroxyapatite formation. Calcif Tissue Res **23**:251–258.
27. Noma A, Takahashi T, Wada T 1981 Elastin-lipid interaction in the arterial wall. Part 2. In vitro binding of lipoprotein-lipids to arterial elastin and the inhibitory effect of high density lipoproteins on the process. Atherosclerosis **38**:373–382.
28. Nadra I, Mason JC, Philippidis P, Florey O, Smythe CD, McCarthy GM, Landis RC, Haskard DO 2005 Proinflammatory activation of macrophages by basic calcium phosphate crystals via protein kinase C and MAP kinase pathways: A vicious cycle of inflammation and arterial calcification?. Circ Res **96**:1248–1256.
29. Tintut Y, Patel J, Parhami F, Demer LL 2000 Tumor necrosis factor-alpha promotes in vitro calcification of vascular cells via the cAMP pathway. Circulation **102**:2636–2642.
30. Reynolds JL, Joannides AJ, Skepper JN, McNair R, Schurgers LJ, Proud-

foot D, Jahnen-Dechent W, Weissberg PL, Shanahan CM 2004 Human vascular smooth muscle cells undergo vesicle-mediated calcification in response to changes in extracellular calcium and phosphate concentrations: A potential mechanism for accelerated vascular calcification in ESRD. J Am Soc Nephrol 15:2857–2867.

31. Raggi P, Callister TQ, Cooil B, He ZX, Lippolis NJ, Russo DJ, Zelinger A, Mahmarian JJ 2000 Identification of patients at increased risk of first unheralded acute myocardial infarction by electron-beam computed tomography. Circulation 101:850–855.

32. Ehara S, Kobayashi Y, Yoshiyama M, Shimada K, Shimada Y, Fukuda D, Nakamura Y, Yamashita H, Yamagishi H, Takeuchi K, Naruko T, Haze K, Becker AE, Yoshikawa J, Ueda M 2004 Spotty calcification typifies the culprit plaque in patients with acute myocardial infarction: An intravascular ultrasound study. Circulation 110:3424–3429.

33. Honye J, Mahon DJ, Jain A, White CJ, Ramee SR, Wallis JB, al-Zarka A, Tobis JM 1992 Morphological effects of coronary balloon angioplasty in vivo assessed by intravascular ultrasound imaging. Circulation 85:1012–1025.

34. Wada T, McKee MD, Steitz S, Giachelli CM 1999 Calcification of vascular smooth muscle cell cultures: Inhibition by osteopontin. Circ Res 84:166–178.

35. Steitz SA, Speer MY, McKee MD, Liaw L, Almeida M, Yang H, Giachelli CM 2002 Osteopontin inhibits mineral deposition and promotes regression of ectopic calcification. Am J Pathol 161:2035–2046.

36. Otto CM, Kuusisto J, Reichenbach DD, Gown AM, O'Brien KD 1994 Characterization of the early lesion of 'degenerative' valvular aortic stenosis. Histological and immunohistochemical studies. Circulation 90:844–853.

37. Simmons CA, Grant GR, Manduchi E, Davies PF 2005 Spatial heterogeneity of endothelial phenotypes correlates with side-specific vulnerability to calcification in normal porcine aortic valves. Circ Res 96:792–799.

38. Hamlin NJ, Price PA 2004 Mineralization of decalcified bone occurs under cell culture conditions and requires bovine serum but not cells. Calcif Tissue Int 75:231–242.

39. Vyavahare NR, Jones PL, Hirsch D, Schoen FJ, Levy RJ 2000 Prevention of glutaraldehyde-fixed bioprosthetic heart valve calcification by alcohol pretreatment: Further mechanistic studies. J Heart Valve Dis 9:561–566.

40. Rajamannan NM, Subramaniam M, Springett M, Sebo TC, Niekrasz M, McConnell JP, Singh RJ, Stone NJ, Bonow RO, Spelsberg TC 2002 Atorvastatin inhibits hypercholesterolemia-induced cellular proliferation and bone matrix production in the rabbit aortic valve. Circulation 105:2660–2665.

41. Rajamannan NM, Subramaniam M, Caira F, Stock SR, Spelsberg TC 2005 Atorvastatin inhibits hypercholesterolemia-induced calcification in the aortic valves via the Lrp5 receptor pathway. Circulation 112:I229–I234.

42. Rosenhek R, Binder T, Porenta G, Lang I, Christ G, Schemper M, Maurer G, Baumgartner H 2000 Predictors of outcome in severe, asymptomatic aortic stenosis. N Engl J Med 343:611–617.

43. Shao JS, Cheng SL, Charlton-Kachigian N, Loewy AP, Towler DA 2003 Teriparatide (human parathyroid hormone (1–34)) inhibits osteogenic vascular calcification in diabetic low density lipoprotein receptor-deficient mice. J Biol Chem 278:50195–50202.

44. Nitta K, Akiba T, Suzuki K, Uchida K, Watanabe R, Majima K, Aoki T, Nihei H 2004 Effects of cyclic intermittent etidronate therapy on coronary artery calcification in patients receiving long-term hemodialysis. Am J Kidney Dis 44:680–688.

45. Cowell SJ, Newby DE, Prescott RJ, Bloomfield P, Reid J, Northridge DB, Boon NA 2005 A randomized trial of intensive lipid-lowering therapy in calcific aortic stenosis. N Engl J Med 352:2389–2397.

46. Reaven PD, Sacks J 2005 Coronary artery and abdominal aortic calcification are associated with cardiovascular disease in type 2 diabetes. Diabetologia 48:379–385.

47. Ishimura E, Okuno S, Kitatani K, Kim M, Shoji T, Nakatani T, Inaba M, Nishizawa Y 2002 Different risk factors for peripheral vascular calcification between diabetic and non-diabetic haemodialysis patients—importance of glycaemic control. Diabetologia 45:1446–1448.

48. Reynolds JL, Skepper JN, McNair R, Kasama T, Gupta K, Weissberg PL, Jahnen-Dechent W, Shanahan CM 2005 Multifunctional roles for serum protein fetuin-a in inhibition of human vascular smooth muscle cell calcification. J Am Soc Nephrol 16:2920–2930.

49. Johnson K, Terkeltaub R 2005 Inorganic pyrophosphate (PPI) in pathologic calcification of articular cartilage. Front Biosci 10:988–997.

50. Lomashvili KA, Khawandi W, O'Neill WC 2005 Reduced plasma pyrophosphate levels in hemodialysis patients. J Am Soc Nephrol 16:2495–2500.

51. Hsu HH, Camacho NP, Sun F, Tawfik O, Aono H 2000 Isolation of calcifiable vesicles from aortas of rabbits fed with high cholesterol diets. Atherosclerosis 153:337–348.

52. Eghbali-Fatourechi GZ, Lamsam J, Fraser D, Nagel D, Riggs BL, Khosla S 2005 Circulating osteoblast-lineage cells in humans. N Engl J Med 352:1959–1966.

53. London GM, Marchais SJ, Guerin AP, Metivier F 2005 Arteriosclerosis, vascular calcifications and cardiovascular disease in uremia. Curr Opin Nephrol Hypertens 14:525–531.

54. Chertow GM, Burke SK, Raggi P 2002 Sevelamer attenuates the progression of coronary and aortic calcification in hemodialysis patients. Kidney Int 62:245–252.

55. Giachelli CM 2003 Vascular calcification: In vitro evidence for the role of inorganic phosphate. J Am Soc Nephrol 14:S300–S304.

56. Henley C, Colloton M, Cattley RC, Shatzen E, Towler DA, Lacey D, Martin D 2005 1,25-Dihydroxyvitamin D3 but not cinacalcet HCl (Sensipar/Mimpara) treatment mediates aortic calcification in a rat model of secondary hyperparathyroidism. Nephrol Dial Transplant 20:1370–1377.

57. Jono S, Nishizawa Y, Shioi A, Morii H 1998 1,25-Dihydroxyvitamin D3 increases in vitro vascular calcification by modulating secretion of endogenous parathyroid hormone-related peptide. Circulation 98:1302–1306.

58. Sneddon WB, Magyar CE, Willick GE, Syme CA, Galbiati F, Bisello A, Friedman PA 2004 Ligand-selective dissociation of activation and internalization of the parathyroid hormone (PTH) receptor: Conditional efficacy of PTH peptide fragments. Endocrinology 145:2815–2823.

59. Bunton TE, Biery NJ, Myers L, Gayraud B, Ramirez F, Dietz HC 2001 Phenotypic alteration of vascular smooth muscle cells precedes elastolysis in a mouse model of Marfan syndrome. Circ Res 88:37–43.

60. Sakata N, Noma A, Yamamoto Y, Okamoto K, Meng J, Takebayashi S, Nagai R, Horiuchi S 2003 Modification of elastin by pentosidine is associated with the calcification of aortic media in patients with end-stage renal disease. Nephrol Dial Transplant 18:1601–1609.

61. Klement JF, Matsuzaki Y, Jiang QJ, Terlizzi J, Choi HY, Fujimoto N, Li K, Pulkkinen L, Birk DE, Sundberg JP, Uitto J 2005 Targeted ablation of the abcc6 gene results in ectopic mineralization of connective tissues. Mol Cell Biol 25:8299–8310.

62. Essalihi R, Dao HH, Gilbert LA, Bouvet C, Semerjian Y, McKee MD, Moreau P 2005 Regression of medial elastocalcinosis in rat aorta: A new vascular function for carbonic anhydrase. Circulation 112:1628–1635.

63. Price PA, June HH, Buckley JR, Williamson MK 2001 Osteoprotegerin inhibits artery calcification induced by warfarin and by vitamin D. Arterioscler Thromb Vasc Biol 21:1610–1616.

64. Davies MR, Lund RJ, Hruska KA 2003 BMP-7 is an efficacious treatment of vascular calcification in a murine model of atherosclerosis and chronic renal failure. J Am Soc Nephrol 14:1559–1567.

65. Bucay N, Sarosi I, Dunstan CR, Morony S, Tarpley J, Capparelli C, Scully S, Tan HL, Xu W, Lacey DL, Boyle WJ, Simonet WS 1998 Osteoprotegerin-deficient mice develop early onset osteoporosis and arterial calcification. Genes Dev 12:1260–1268.

66. Kaden JJ, Bickelhaupt S, Grobholz R, Haase KK, Sarikoc A, Kilic R, Brueckmann M, Lang S, Zahn I, Vahl C, Hagl S, Dempfle CE, Borggrefe M 2004 Receptor activator of nuclear factor kappaB ligand and osteoprotegerin regulate aortic valve calcification. J Mol Cell Cardiol 36:57–66.

67. Lehto S, Niskanen L, Suhonen M, Ronnemaa T, Laakso M 1996 Medial artery calcification. A neglected harbinger of cardiovascular complications in non-insulin-dependent diabetes mellitus. Arterioscler Thromb Vasc Biol 16:978–983.

68. Zieman SJ, Melenovsky V, Kass DA 2005 Mechanisms, pathophysiology, and therapy of arterial stiffness. Arterioscler Thromb Vasc Biol 25:932–943.

69. Phan O, Ivanovski O, Nguyen-Khoa T, Mothu N, Angulo J, Westenfeld R, Ketteler M, Meert N, Maizel J, Nikolov IG, Vanholder R, Lacour B, Drueke TB, Massy ZA 2005 Sevelamer prevents uremia-enhanced atherosclerosis progression in apolipoprotein E-deficient mice. Circulation 112:2875–2882.

70. Coates T, Kirkland GS, Dymock RB, Murphy BF, Brealey JK, Mathew TH, Disney AP 1998 Cutaneous necrosis from calcific uremic arteriolopathy. Am J Kidney Dis 32:384–391.

71. Zebboudj AF, Imura M, Bostrom K 2002 Matrix GLA protein, a regulatory protein for bone morphogenetic protein-2. J Biol Chem 277:4388–4394.

72. Schurgers LJ, Teunissen KJ, Knapen MH, Kwaijtaal M, van Diest R, Appels A, Reutelingsperger CP, Cleutjens JP, Vermeer C 2005 Novel conformation-specific antibodies against matrix gamma-carboxyglutamic acid (Gla) protein: Undercarboxylated matrix Gla protein as marker for vascular calcification. Arterioscler Thromb Vasc Biol 25:1629–1633.

73. Cicone JS, Petronis JB, Embert CD, Spector DA 2004 Successful treatment of calciphylaxis with intravenous sodium thiosulfate. Am J Kidney Dis 43:1104–1108.

74. Kelley MJ, Newell JD 1983 Chest radiography and cardiac fluoroscopy in coronary artery disease. Cardiol Clin **1:**575–595.
75. Ivandic BT, Qiao JH, Machleder D, Liao F, Drake TA, Lusis AJ 1996 A locus on chromosome 7 determines myocardial cell necrosis and calcification (dystrophic cardiac calcinosis) in mice. Proc Natl Acad Sci USA **93:**5483–5488.
76. Ling LH, Oh JK, Breen JF, Schaff HV, Danielson GK, Mahoney DW, Seward JB, Tajik AJ 2000 Calcific constrictive pericarditis: Is it still with us?. Ann Intern Med **132:**444–450.
77. Verma V, Cronin DC II, Dachman AH 2001 Portal and mesenteric venous calcification in patients with advanced cirrhosis. AJR Am J Roentgenol **176:**489–492.
78. Tanko LB, Christiansen C, Cox DA, Geiger MJ, McNabb MA, Cummings SR 2005 Relationship between osteoporosis and cardiovascular disease in postmenopausal women. J Bone Miner Res **20:**1912–1920.
79. Tintut Y, Morony S, Demer LL 2004 Hyperlipidemia promotes osteoclastic potential of bone marrow cells ex vivo. Arterioscler Thromb Vasc Biol **24:**e6–e10.
80. London GM, Marty C, Marchais SJ, Guerin AP, Metivier F, de Vernejoul MC 2004 Arterial calcifications and bone histomorphometry in end-stage renal disease. J Am Soc Nephrol **15:**1943–1951.
81. Chertow GM, Raggi P, Chasan-Taber S, Bommer J, Holzer H, Burke SK 2004 Determinants of progressive vascular calcification in haemodialysis patients. Nephrol Dial Transplant **19:**1489–1496.

Chapter 80. Fibrodysplasia (Myositis) Ossificans Progressiva

Frederick S. Kaplan, David L. Glaser, and Eileen M. Shore

Division of Molecular Orthopaedics, Department of Orthopaedic Surgery, The University of Pennsylvania School of Medicine, Philadelphia, Pennsylvania

INTRODUCTION

Fibrodysplasia ossificans progressiva (FOP) is a rare heritable disorder of connective tissue disease characterized by (1) congenital malformations of the great toes and (2) recurrent episodes of painful soft-tissue swelling that lead to heterotopic ossification.[1,2]

Post-traumatic myositis ossificans, a different disorder, also features heterotopic bone and cartilage formation within soft tissues. Heterotopic ossification may also follow hip replacement, spinal cord injury, and brain injury.

FOP was first described in 1692; >600 cases have been reported.[1,2] This disorder is among the rarest of human afflictions, with an estimated incidence of one per two million live births.[1,2] All races are affected.[2] Autosomal dominant transmission with variable expressivity is established.[3] However, reproductive fitness is low, and most cases are sporadic. Gonadal mosaicism has been described.[4]

CLINICAL PRESENTATION

If the typical congenital skeletal malformations are recognized, FOP can be suspected at birth before soft tissue lesions occur.[1,2] The characteristic feature is short great toes, caused by malformation (hallux valgus) of the cartilaginous anlage of the first metatarsal and proximal phalanx (Fig. 1). In some cases, the thumbs also are strikingly short. Synostosis and hypoplasia of the phalanges is typical.[1,2] FOP is usually diagnosed when soft tissue swellings and radiographic evidence of heterotopic ossification are first noted, although misdiagnosis is common.[1,2]

The severity of FOP differs significantly among patients,[3,5] although most become immobilized and confined to a wheelchair by the third decade of life.[1,2,6] Typically, episodes of soft tissue swelling begin during the first decade of life (Fig. 1),[7] although occasionally, the onset occurs as late as early adulthood.

Painful, tender, and rubbery soft tissue lesions appear spontaneously or may seem to be precipitated by minor trauma

including intramuscular injections and influenza-like illnesses.[2,8,9] Swellings develop rapidly during the course of several days. Typically, lesions affect the paraspinal muscles in the back or in the limb girdles and may persist for several months.[10] Aponeuroses, fascia, tendons, ligaments, and connective tissue of voluntary muscles may be affected. Although some swellings may regress spontaneously, most mature through an endochondral pathway, engendering true heterotopic bone.[10] The episodes of induration recur with unpredictable frequency. Some patients seem to have periods of quiescent disease. However, once ossification develops, it is permanent.

Gradually, bony masses immobilize joints and cause contractures and deformity, particularly in the neck and shoulders. Ossification around the hips, typically present by the third decade of life, often prevents ambulation.[6] Involvement of the muscles of mastication (frequently the outcome of injection of local anesthetic or overstretching of the jaw during dental procedures) can severely limit movement of the mandible and ultimately impair nutrition.[11,12] Ankylosis of the spine and rib cage further restricts mobility and may imperil cardiopulmonary function (Fig. 1).[1,2,6,13] Scoliosis is common and associated with heterotopic bone that asymmetrically connects the rib cage to the pelvis.[14] Hypokyphosis results from ossification of the paravertebral musculature. Restrictive lung disease and predisposition to pneumonia may follow. However, the vocal muscles, diaphragm, extraocular muscles, heart, and smooth muscles are characteristically spared.[1] Although secondary amenorrhea may develop, reproduction has occurred.[1–3] Hearing impairment (beginning in late childhood or adolescence) manifests with increased frequency.[15]

RADIOLOGIC FEATURES

Skeletal anomalies and soft tissue ossification are the characteristic radiologic features of FOP.[16] The principal malformations involve the great toe, although other anomalies of digits in the feet and hands may occur. Exostoses are frequent.[10] A remarkable feature of FOP is progressive fusion of cervical vertebrae that may be confused with Klippel-Feil syndrome.[1,17] The femoral necks may be broad yet short.

The authors have reported no conflicts of interest.

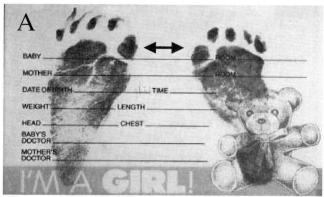

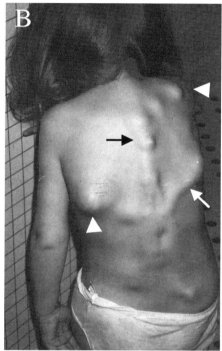

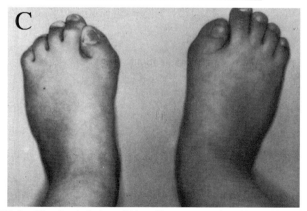

FIG. 1. Fibrodysplasia (myositis) ossificans progressiva. Characteristic features of FOP are seen in early childhood. The presence of short malformed great toes at birth (A, arrows) heralds the later spontaneous appearance of the preosseous soft tissue lesions on the neck and back (B, arrowheads) and should provoke suspicion of FOP even before the transformation to heterotopic bone (arrows). An inspection of the toes (C) will confirm the diagnosis and may alleviate the need for a lesional biopsy (trauma) that could exacerbate the condition [from Kaplan FS and Smith RM 1997 Clinical vignette: Fibrodysplasia ossificans progressiva (FOP). J Bone Miner Res **12:**855 with permission of the American Society for Bone and Mineral Research].

However, the remainder of the skeleton is generally unremarkable.[16]

Ectopic ossification in FOP progresses in several regular patterns or gradients (involvement is generally proximal before distal, axial before appendicular, cranial before caudal, and dorsal before ventral).[7] Paraspinal muscles are involved early in life, with subsequent spread to the shoulders and hips. The ankles, wrists, and jaw may be affected at later stages.[7]

Radiographic and bone scan findings suggest normal modeling and remodeling of heterotopic bone.[18] Fractures are not increased and respond similarly in either the heterotopic or normotopic skeleton.[19]

Bone scans are abnormal before ossification can be shown by conventional radiographs.[18] CT and MRI of early lesions have been described.[20]

LABORATORY FINDINGS

Routine biochemical studies of mineral metabolism are usually normal, although alkaline phosphatase activity in serum may be increased, especially during disease "flare-ups," (i.e., periods of active heterotopic bone formation).[1,2,21] Urinary basic fibroblast growth factor (FGF) levels may be elevated during disease flare-ups and coincide with the preosseous angiogenic fibroproliferative lesions.[22]

HISTOPATHOLOGY

The earliest stage of FOP lesion formation consists of an intense aggregation of B and T lymphocytes in the perivascular spaces of otherwise normal-appearing skeletal muscle.[23] Subsequently, a nearly pure T cell occurs between edematous muscle fibers at the leading edge of an angiogenic fibroproliferative lesion, which is indistinguishable from aggressive juvenile fibromatosis.[23,24] Immunostaining with a monoclonal antibody against bone morphogenetic protein (BMP)-2/4 is intense in FOP lesions, but not in aggressive fibromatosis.[24] Mast cell infiltration is seen at all stages of FOP flare-ups.[25] Endochondral ossification is the major pathway for heterotopic bone formation.[10] Mature osseous lesions have haversian systems and can contain hematopoietic tissue.

ETIOLOGY AND PATHOGENESIS

Similarities between FOP and the effects of *Drosophila* decapentaplegic gene (*BMP4* homolog) mutations have suggested involvement of the BMP signaling pathway in the pathogenesis of FOP [26]. In fact, the BMP signaling pathway is highly dysregulated in FOP cells.[27–31] FOP cells overexpress BMP4, and are unable to appropriately upregulate the expression of multiple BMP antagonists, including Noggin and Gremlin, in response to a BMP challenge.[27,29,30] Additionally, FOP cells exhibit a defect in BMP receptor internalization and increased activation of downstream signaling, suggesting that altered BMP receptor trafficking underlies ectopic bone formation in this disease.[31] Recently, BMP4 transgenic mice that develop an FOP-like phenotype have been described.[32]

An initial genome-wide linkage analysis mapped FOP to 4q27-31; however, subsequent DNA sequence analysis of candidate genes in this and other regions did not identify any mutations.[33,34] With the discovery of additional pedigrees, a more conservative genome-wide linkage analysis excluded the 4q27-31 region and identified linkage of FOP to 2q23-24, a locus that includes the activin A type I receptor gene, ACVR1, a receptor for bone morphogenetic protein.[35] An identical heterozygous missense mutation (c.617G>A; R206H) in the glycine-serine (GS) activation domain of ACVR1 was identified in all affected individuals with classic features of either sporadic or inherited FOP.[35] Protein modeling predicts destabilization of the GS domain, consistent with constitutive activation of ACVR1 as the underlying cause of the ectopic chondrogenesis, osteogenesis, and joint fusions seen in FOP.[35]

TREATMENT

There is no established medical treatment for FOP.[1,2] The disorder's rarity, variable severity, and fluctuating clinical course pose substantial uncertainties when evaluating experimental therapies. Binders of dietary calcium, radiotherapy, and warfarin are ineffective.[1,2,36] Limited benefits have been reported using corticosteroids and disodium etidronate together during flare-ups or using isotretinoin to prevent disease activation.[37,38] However, these impressions reflect uncontrolled studies. Accordingly, medical intervention is currently supportive. Nevertheless, physical therapy to maintain joint mobility may be harmful by provoking or exacerbating lesions.[1,2] Surgical release of joint contractures is unsuccessful and risks new, trauma-induced heterotopic ossification.[1,2] Removal of FOP lesions is often followed by significant recurrence. Osteotomy of ectopic bone to mobilize a joint is uniformly counterproductive because additional heterotopic ossification develops at the operative site. Spinal bracing is ineffective, and surgical intervention is associated with numerous complications.[14] Dental therapy should preclude injection of local anesthetics and stretching of the jaw.[1,2,11,12] In fact, newer dental techniques for focused administration of anesthetic are available. Guidelines for general anesthesia have been reported.[11] Intramuscular injections should be avoided.[8] Prevention of falls is crucial.[39] Measures against recurrent pulmonary infections and onset of cardiopulmonary complications of restrictive lung disease are important. More focused efforts based on inhibition of BMP signaling may offer hope for the future.[40]

PROGNOSIS

Despite widespread heterotopic ossification and severe disability, some patients live productive lives into the seventh decade. Most, however, die earlier from pulmonary complications including pneumonia, secondary to restricted ventilation from chest wall involvement.[1,2,13]

PROGRESSIVE OSSEOUS HETEROPLASIA

Research on FOP led to the discovery of progressive osseous heteroplasia (POH), a distinct developmental disorder of heterotopic ossification.[41–43] Like FOP, POH is an autosomal dominant genetic disorder of heterotopic ossification within soft connective tissues. However, unlike in FOP, heterotopic ossification in POH commonly occurs within the dermis and forms by an intramembraneous, rather than an endochondral pathway.[43] Identification of two patients with POH-like features who also had Albright hereditary osteodystrophy suggested the possibility of a genetic link between the two conditions,[43,44] which was confirmed in a third patient with pure POH.[45] These discoveries led to the rapid identification of paternally inherited inactivating mutations of the *GNAS* gene as the genetic cause of POH.[46] Reduced expression of $G_s\alpha$, one of several proteins encoded by *GNAS*, can induce an osteoblast-like phenotype in human mesenchymal stem cells.[47]

REFERENCES

1. Connor JM, Evans DAP 1982 Fibrodysplasia ossificans progressiva: The clinical features and natural history of 34 patients. J Bone Joint Surg Br **64**:76–83.

2. Kaplan FS, Shore EM, Connor JM 2002 Fibrodysplasia ossificans progressiva. In: Royce PM, Steinmann B (eds.) Connective Tissue and Its Heritable Disorders: Molecular, Genetic, and Medical Aspects, 2nd ed. John Wiley & Sons, New York, NY, USA, pp. 827–840.

3. Delatycki M, Rogers JG 1998 The genetics of fibrodysplasia ossificans progressiva. Clin Orthop **346**:15–18.

4. Janoff HB, Muenke M, Johnson LO, Rosenberg A, Shore EM, Okereke E, Zasloff M, Kaplan FS 1996 Fibrodysplasia ossificans progressiva in two half-sisters. Evidence for maternal mosaicism. Am J Med Genet **61**:320–324.

5. Janoff HB, Tabas JA, Shore EM, Muenke M, Dalinka MK, Schlesinger S, Zasloff MA, Kaplan FS 1995 Mild expression of fibrodysplasia ossificans progressiva: A report of 3 cases. J Rheumatology **22**:976–978.

6. Rocke DM, Zasloff M, Peeper J, Cohen RB, Kaplan FS 1994 Age and joint-specific risk of initial heterotopic ossification in patients who have fibrodysplasia ossificans progressiva. Clin Orthop **301**:243–248.

7. Cohen RB, Hahn GV, Tabas JA, Peeper J, Levitz CL, Sando A, Sando N, Zasloff M, Kaplan FS 1993 The natural history of heterotopic ossification in patients who have fibrodysplasia ossificans progressiva. A study of 44 patients. J Bone Joint Surg Am **75**:215–219.

8. Lanchoney TF, Cohen RB, Rocke DM, Zasloff MA, Kaplan FS 1995 Permanent heterotopic ossification at the injection site after diphtheria-tetanus-pertussis immunizations in children who have fibrodysplasia ossificans progressiva. J Pediatr **126**:762–764.

9. Scarlett RF, Rocke DM, Kantanie S, Patel JB, Shore EM, Kaplan FS 2004 Influenza-like viral illnesses and flare-ups of fibrodysplasia ossificans progressiva (FOP). Clin Orthop Rel Res **423**:275–279.

10. Kaplan FS, Tabas JA, Gannon FH, Finkel G, Hahn GV, Zasloff MA 1993 The histopathology of fibrodysplasia ossificans progressiva: An endochondral process. J Bone Joint Surg Am **75**:220–230.

11. Luchetti W, Cohen RB, Hahn GV, Rocke DM, Helpin M, Zasloff M, Kaplan FS 1996 Severe restriction in jaw movement after routine injection of local anesthetic in patients who have progressiva. Oral Surg Oral Med Oral Pathol Oral Radiol Endod **81**:21–25.

12. Janoff HB, Zasloff M, Kaplan FS 1996 Submandibular swelling in patients with fibrodysplasia ossificans progressiva. Otolaryngol Head Neck Surg **114**:599–604.

13. Kussmaul WG, Esmail AN, Sagar Y, Ross J, Gregory S, Kaplan FS 1998 Pulmonary and cardiac function in advanced fibrodysplasia ossificans progressiva. Clin Orthop **346**:104–109.

14. Shah PB, Zasloff MA, Drummond D, Kaplan FS 1994 Spinal deformity in patients who have fibrodysplasia ossificans progressiva. J Bone Joint Surg Am **76**:1442–1450.

15. Levy CE, Lash AT, Janoff HB, Kaplan FS 1999 Conductive hearing loss in individuals with fibrodysplasia ossificans progressiva. Am J Audiol **8**:29–33.

16. Mahboubi S, Glaser DL, Shore EM, Kaplan FS 2001 Fibrodysplasia ossificans progressiva (FOP). Pediatr Radiol **31**:307–314.

17. Schaffer AA, Kaplan FS, Tracy MR, O'Brien ML, Dormans JP, Shore EM, Harland RM, Kusumi K 2005 Developmental anomalies of the cervical spin in patients with fibrodysplasia ossificans progressiva are distinctly different from those in patients with Klippel-Feil syndrome. Spine **30**:1379–1385.

18. Kaplan FS, Strear CM, Zasloff MA 1994 Radiographic and scintigraphic features of modeling and remodeling in the heterotopic skeleton of patients who have fibrodysplasia ossificans progressiva. Clin Orthop **304**:238–247.

19. Einhorn TA, Kaplan FS 1994 Traumatic fractures of heterotopic bone in patients who have fibrodysplasia ossificans progressiva. Clin Orthop **308**:173–177.

20. Shirkhoda A, Armin A-R, Bis KG, Makris J, Irwin RB, Shetty AN 1995 MR imaging of myositis ossificans: Variable patterns at different stages. J Magn Reson Imaging **65**:287–292.

21. Lutwak L 1964 Myositis ossificans progressiva: Mineral, metabolic, and radioactive calcium studies of the effects of hormones. Am J Med **37**:269–293.

22. Kaplan F, Sawyer J, Connors S, Keough K, Shore E, Gannon F, Glaser D, Rocke D, Zasloff M, Folkman J 1998 Urinary basic fibroblast growth factor: A biochemical marker for preosseous fibroproliferative lesions in patients with FOP. Clin Orthop **346**:59–65.

23. Gannon FH, Valentine BA, Shore EM, Zasloff MA, Kaplan FS 1998 Acute lymphocytic infiltration in an extremely early lesion of fibrodysplasia ossificans progressiva. Clin Orthop **346**:19–25.

24. Gannon F, Kaplan FS, Olmsted E, Finkel G, Zasloff M, Shore EM 1997 Differential immunostaining with bone morphogenetic protein (BMP) 2/4 in early fibromatous lesions of fibrodysplasia ossificans progressiva and aggressive juvenile fibromatosis. Hum Pathol **28**:339–343.

25. Gannon FH, Glaser D, Caron R, Thompson LD, Shore EM, Kaplan FS

2001 Mast cell involvement in fibrodysplasia ossificans progressiva. Hum Pathol 32:842–848.

26. Kaplan F, Tabas JA, Zasloff MA 1990 Fibrodysplasia ossificans progressiva: A clue from the fly? Calcif Tissue Int 47:117–125.

27. Shafritz AB, Shore EM, Gannon FH, Zasloff MA, Taub R, Muenke M, Kaplan FS 1996 Dysregulation of bone morphogenetic protein 4 (BMP4) gene expression in fibrodysplasia ossificans progressiva. N Engl J Med 335:555–561.

28. Lanchoney TF, Olmsted EA, Shore EM, Gannon FA, Rosen V, Zasloff MA, Kaplan FS 1998 Characterization of bone morphogenetic protein 4 receptors in fibrodysplasia ossificans progressiva. Clin Orthop 346:38–45.

29. Olmsted EA, Kaplan FS, Shore EM 2003 Bone morphogenetic protein-4 regulation in fibrodysplasia ossificans progressiva. Clin Orthop 408:331–343.

30. Ahn J, Serrano de La Peña L, Shore EM, Kaplan FS 2003 Paresis of a bone morphogenetic protein antagonist response in a genetic disorder of heterotopic skeletogenesis. J Bone Joint Surg Am 85:667–674.

31. Serrano de la Peña L, Billings PC, Fiori JL, Ahn J, Kaplan FS, Shore EM 2005 Fibrodysplasia ossificans progressiva (FOP), a disorder of ectopic osteogenesis, misregulates cell surface expression and trafficking of BMPRIA. J Bone Miner Res 20:1168–1176.

32. Kan L, Hu M, Gomes WA, Kessler JA 2004 Transgenic mice overexpressing BMP4 develop a fibrodysplasia ossificans progressiva (FOP)-like phenotype. Am J Pathol 165:1107–1115.

33. Feldman G, Li M, Martin S, Urbanek M, Urtizberea JA, Fardeau M, LeMerrer M, Connor JM, Triffitt J, Muenke M, Kaplan FS, Shore EM 2000 Fibrodysplasia ossificans progressiva (FOP), a heritable disorder of severe heterotopic ossification, maps to human chromosome 4q27-31. Am J Human Genet 66:128–135.

34. Xu MQ, Feldman G, Le Merrer M, Shugart YY, Glaser DL, Urtizberea JA, Fardeau M, Connor JM, Triffitt J, Smith R, Shore EM, Kaplan FS 2005 Linkage exclusion and mutational analysis of the noggin gene in patients with fibrodysplasia ossificans progressiva. Clin Genet 58:291–298.

35. Shore EM, Xu M, Feldman GJ, Fenstermacher DA, The FOP International Research Consortium, Brown MA, Kaplan FS 2006 A recurrent mutation in the BMP type I receptor ACVR1 causes inherited and sporadic fibrodysplasia ossificans progressiva. Nat Genet 38:525–527.

36. Moore SE, Jump AA, Smiley JD 1986 Effect of warfarin sodium therapy on excretion of 4-carboxy-L-glutamic acid in scleroderma, dermatomyositis, and myositis ossificans progressiva. Arthritis Rheum 29:344–351.

37. Brantus J-F, Meunier PJ 1998 Effects of intravenous etidronate and oral corticosteroids in fibrodysplasia ossificans progressiva. Clin Orthop 346:117–120.

38. Zasloff MA, Rocke DM, Crofford LJ, Hahn GV, Kaplan FS 1998 Treatment of patients who have fibrodysplasia ossificans progressiva with isotretinoin. Clin Orthop 346:121–129.

39. Glaser DM, Rocke DM, Kaplan FS 1998 Catastrophic falls in patients who have fibrodysplasia ossificans progressiva. Clin Orthop 346:110–116.

40. Glaser DL Economides AN, Wang L, Liu X, Kimble RD, Fandl JP, Wilson JM, Stahl, N, Kaplan FS, Shore EM 2003 In vivo somatic cell gene transfer or an engineered noggin mutein prevents BMP4-induced heterotopic ossification. J Bone Joint Surg Am 85:2332–2342.

41. Kaplan FS, Craver R, MacEwen GD, Gannon FH, Finkel G, Hahn G, Tabas J, Gardner RJ, Zasloff MA 1994 Progressive osseous heteroplasia: A distinct developmental disorder of heterotopic ossification. J Bone Joint Surg Am 76:425–436.

42. Rosenfeld SR, Kaplan FS 1995 Progressive osseous heteroplasia in male patients. Clin Orthop 317:243–245.

43. Kaplan FS, Shore EM 2000 Progressive osseous heteroplasia. J Bone Miner Res 15:2084–2094.

44. Eddy MC, Jan De Beur SM, Yandow SM, McAlister WH, Shore EM, Kaplan FS, Whyte MP, Levine MA 2000 Deficiency of the alpha-subunit of the stimulatory G protein and severe extraskeletal ossification. J Bone Miner Res 15:2074–2083.

45. Yeh GL, Mathur S, Wivel A, Li M, Gannon FH, Ulied A, Audi L, Olmstead EA, Kaplan FS, Shore EM 2000 GNAS1 mutation and Cbfa1 misexpression in a child with severe congenital platelike osteoma cutis. J Bone Miner Res 15:2063–2073.

46. Shore EM, Ahn J, Jan de Beur S, Li M, Xu M, Gardner RJ, Zasloff MA, Whyte MP, Levine MA, Kaplan FS 2002 Paternally-inherited inactivating mutations of the GNAS1 gene in progressive osseous heteroplasia. N Engl J Med 346:99–106.

47. Leitman SA, Ding C, Cooke DW, Levine MA 2005 Reduction in Gs-alpha induces osteogenic differentiation in human mesenchymal stem cells. Clin Orthop Rel Res 434:231–238.

SECTION XII

Hypercalciuria and Kidney Stones
(Section Editor: Murray J. Favus)

Chapter 81.   Calcium Nephrolithiasis

David A. Bushinsky

*Department of Medicine and of Pharmacology and Physiology, University of Rochester School of Medicine, Division of Nephrology,
Strong Memorial Hospital, Rochester, New York*

INTRODUCTION

Nephrolithiasis refers to the formation of a solid phase within the kidney, which generally leads to considerable morbidity but rare mortality.[1-3] Stones tend to form in the renal papilla and collecting system but are also commonly found within the ureters and bladder. Stones are composed of calcium oxalate (~26%), calcium phosphate (~7%), mixed calcium oxalate and calcium phosphate (~37%), uric acid (~5%), magnesium ammonium phosphate (struvite, ~22%), and/or cystine (~2%).[4-6] Patients with nephrolithiasis often present with renal colic but may also commonly present with hematuria or urinary tract infection.[7] The severity of the clinical presentation is dependent on the location, size, and type of stone. The severe pain of renal colic can lead to frequent hospitalizations, shock-wave lithotripsy, and/or invasive surgical procedures.

Males are affected more than females, and the peak age of onset is in the third to fourth decade.[8] The incidence of nephrolithiasis seems to be increasing over the last few decades and is ~3 per 1000 per year in men and between 1 and 2 per 1000 per year in women. The prevalence is between 4% and 9% in men and 2% and 4% in women. The lifetime risk of kidney stones in men seems to be between 10% and 12% in men and somewhat lower in women.

PATHOGENESIS

A kidney stone can only form in urine that is supersaturated with respect to the specific components of the stone.[1,2,4-6] For example, a calcium oxalate stone will only form in urine that is supersaturated with respect to the calcium oxalate solid phase. Supersaturation is dependent on the product of the free ion activities of the stone components. While increases in concentration will tend to increase free ion activity, factors such as the presence of inhibitors of crystallization or alterations in pH will decrease it.

Stones will not form in urine that is undersaturated with respect to the components of the stone.[1,2,4-6] As the ion activity product is increased, for example, by adding calcium or oxalate, a concentration is reached where a previously formed stone will neither shrink nor grow. This is termed the equilibrium solubility product; however, a new stone will not yet form. The ion activity product must increase further in this now supersaturated, metastable solution to the so-called formation product (or the upper limit of metastability), which will permit a new stone to form. The ions will come together, nucleate, to form a more stable, solid phase. The spontaneous formation of a new solid phase in supersaturated urine is unusual. Generally a new crystal will form by heterogeneous nucleation when a solid phase forms on a pre-existing surface such as cellular debris or another crystal. For example uric acid crystals are excellent heterogeneous nuclei for calcium oxalate crystals. For crystals to become a clinically significant stone they must grow to sufficient size to irritate the urothelium or obstruct a lumen. Crystals generally increase in size by aggregating with other similar crystals.

The glomerular ultrafiltrate passes through the renal tubule so rapidly that it would be impossible for a clinically significant kidney stone to spontaneously form in the tubule.[9] Recent evidence suggests that in patients with calcium oxalate nephrolithiasis, the initial crystal phase forms in the interstitium around the thin limbs of the loop of Henle.[10] This solid phase, which contains only calcium phosphate, and not calcium oxalate, increases in size and finally erodes into the urinary space forming a so-called Randalls' plaque. Calcium oxalate crystals may adhere to the Randalls' plaque increasing in size and finally breaking off, leading to clinically significant stone disease.

CLINICAL PRESENTATION

Patients with nephrolithiasis often describe severe flank pain of increasing intensity that is abrupt in onset and is caused by the passage of a stone from the renal pelvis into the ureter.[7] The pain may migrate from the anterior abdomen to the testicle or labia majora as the stone moves through the ureter. The patient may complain of nausea and may vomit. The mere presence of a stone on a radiograph does not exclude that the patient has another acute abdominal or pelvic emergency. The pain may be associated with hematuria; however, hematuria has many causes and again must not be attributed to a kidney stone until other causes are studied and excluded. The pain and hematuria often do not resolve until the stone is passed into the bladder. Stones <5 cm in diameter generally will pass spontaneously, especially when the patient is vigorously hydrated. Although the acute presentation is common, some kidney stones are asymptomatic and only found serendipitously.

Radiographic studies are integral in determining if a patient has a kidney stone.[5] A traditional KUB (kidneys ureter and bladder) may detect calcium-containing stones but will often miss those composed of uric acid and those obscured by bone and cannot indicate whether the stone is causing obstruction. A renal ultrasound avoids radiation and is useful for finding stones in the renal parenchyma and for detecting obstruction. An IVP (IV pyelogram) can detect obstructing stones regardless of the composition but requires contrast and will miss smaller stones. Whether the contrast-induced osmotic diuresis is superior to forced hydration in moving the stone through the ureter is not yet clear. A helical (spiral) CT is highly sensitive and specific for detecting small stones, including those composed of uric acid, and those in the ureters and does not require contrast. Many consider a helical CT the radiographic procedure of choice in evaluating a patient with nephrolithiasis, although it does expose the patient to more radiation that either a KUB or IVP.

EVALUATION AFTER A SINGLE STONE

The intensity of the evaluation after a single stone is dependent on the likelihood of recurrence. Were the rate of recurrence low, the benefit of an extensive evaluation would not be warranted. Conversely, were the rate of recurrence high, most would argue for a complete evaluation, especially if it could be shown that the resulting data would lead to effective treatment. Recurrence rates of untreated patients vary with different studies, but it is generally felt that 40-50% of patients will have a recurrent stone in 5 years. Once a patient has a recurrent stone, the next recurrence will occur in a shorter interval than the first. Many, including an National Institutes of Health consensus

The author has reported no conflicts of interest.

conference on the Prevention and Treatment of Kidney Stones, suggest a basic evaluation after an adult forms a single stone.[11] Children, patients with growing stones, and non-calcium stone formers merit a more extensive evaluation as detailed below. Often easily corrected factors are found in the basic evaluation, which can lead to a marked reduction in stone formation.

The basic evaluation consists of a basic medical history, family history, stone history, and an extensive review of medications, diet, fluid intake, and occupation.[1,3,5,12]

Basic Medical History

A number of systemic diseases clearly increase the predisposition to forming kidney stones. For example granulomatous diseases such as sarcoid can lead to a $1,25(OH)_2D_3$-mediated increase in intestinal calcium absorption and urine calcium excretion. Intestinal malabsorption caused by inflammatory bowel disease or a short bowel can increase oxalate absorption and excretion.

Family History

Idiopathic hypercalciuria seems to be an inherited polygenic disorder. Certain autosomal recessive disorders such as primary hyperoxaluria and cystinuria lead to nephrolithiasis at a young age.

Stone History

A chronology of stone events including age at the first stone, stone type and size, and the frequency of subsequent stones will guide the subsequent evaluation and therapy. Early first stone formation suggests a genetic disorder and formation of repeated unilateral stones suggests an anatomic disorder.

Medications

A large number of medications, by increasing excretion of the ions that make up the solid phase, forming a solid phase themselves, or altering the urinary environment, can promote stone formation. For example, calcium-containing medications increase the total amount of calcium absorbed and subsequently excreted and loop diuretics increase calcium excretion. Indinavir, acyclovir, and triamterene themselves can precipitate and form stones. The carbonic anhydrase inhibitors, such as acetazolamide, increase urine pH, and promote calcium phosphate and calcium oxalate precipitation.

Occupation

In many occupations, the need to urinate may be disruptive. Surgeons and airline pilots, for example, may consume scant amounts of fluid in an effort to decrease urination. In others outdoor activity in a hot, dry climate may increase insensible fluid losses that are not compensated for by increased oral hydration. A concentrated urine, more prone to crystal formation, results.

Diet

The diet of many individuals leads directly to stone formation. A dietary history is often the most revealing aspect of the initial evaluation. Sodium-induced hypercalciuria can often be traced to consumption of processed foods that are high in salt. Hyperoxaluria can often be traced to excessive chocolate or nut consumption and occasionally to rhubarb pies. A paucity of fluid intake may reflect habit more than a conscious desire not to be inconvenienced by urination. A surfeit of protein resulting in metabolism to metabolic acids and hypercalciuria and hypocitraturia is a fixture of many American diets.

LABORATORY EXAMINATION

In general, all patients should have a creatinine to determine the level of renal function, a bicarbonate and potassium to exclude renal tubular acidosis, a calcium and phosphorus to exclude hyperparathyroidism and a uric acid to exclude hyperuricemia. A urine analysis will give an indication of hematuria and increased urine concentration, often associated with stones, and pH, which may be high in the presence of urea splitting organisms and struvite and low in the presence of excessive protein intake.

All available stones should be analyzed for ion content and crystal phases optimally by X-ray diffraction crystallography or infrared spectroscopy. This inexpensive, risk-free analysis is often the single most important guide to therapy.

A 24-h collection for ion excretion and supersaturation is generally only performed when a patient has formed more than one stone, if stones are found to be enlarging or increasing in number, or in children. The collection should, at a minimum, be analyzed for volume, calcium, oxalate, sodium, uric acid, phosphorus, citrate, and creatinine. There are several laboratories in the United States who will perform further analyses and calculate the supersaturation with respect to the mineral phases calcium oxalate, calcium phosphate, and uric acid. The supersaturation can be used to guide therapy. The goal of all therapy directed at preventing kidney stones is to lower the prevailing urinary supersaturation with respect to the solid phase formed. Except in specific research settings, there is general consensus that there is no use in attempting to separate those patients who absorb excessive amounts of calcium from those whose kidneys cannot adequately reabsorb filtered calcium.

GENERAL ADVICE TO AVOID STONES

If a patient has only formed a single stone most physicians opt not to collect a 24-h urine for ion excretion and supersaturation.

Patients are told to increase fluid intake, reduce dietary sodium, protein, and eat an age- and sex-appropriate amount of calcium.[13–15] The fluid intake should be increased so that the patient excretes at least 2–2.5 liters of urine a day, which will lead to a reduction in urinary supersaturation. Urine calcium excretion is directly correlated with dietary and thus urinary sodium excretion. Patients are instructed to limit sodium intake to less than 3 g/day. Finally animal protein causes an increase in metabolic acid production that leads to increased urine calcium excretion and decreased urine citrate excretion, both of which promote calcium stone formation. A low calcium diet promotes stone formation. This general advice can reduce recurrence of the next stone by ~60% at 5 years.

MECHANISMS AND DIRECTED THERAPY FOR CALCIUM NEPHROLITHIASIS

Approximately 70% of all kidney stones contain calcium usually with oxalate or with phosphate or urate. The principle mechanisms by which calcium containing kidney stones form are hypercalciuria, hyperoxaluria, hyperuricosuria, hypocitraturia, and renal tubular acidosis (Table 1).[1,5,12,16]

Hypercalciuria

Hypercalciuria (>250 mg/24 h in females and >300 mg/24 h in males) is the most consistent metabolic abnormality found in patients with calcium nephrolithiasis. Idiopathic hypercalci-

TABLE 1. CAUSES OF CALCIUM STONE FORMATION

Hypercalciuria
  Idiopathic hypercalciuria
  Hypercalcemic disorders
    Primary hyperparathyroidism
    Malignancy
    Granulomatous diseases
      Sarcoid
    Immobilization
    Thyrotoxicosis
    Milk-alkali syndrome
  Medications that promote calcium stone formation
    Loop diuretics
    Calcium supplements
    Vitamin D
    Glucocorticoids
    Theophylline
    ? Vitamin C
    Acetazolamide
    Amphotericin B
  Medications that may precipitate into stones or crystals
    Indinavir
    Acyclovir (when infused rapidly intravenously)
    Triamterene
Hyperoxaluria
  Dietary hyperoxaluria (oxalate 40–60 mg/day)
  Enteric oxaluria (oxalate 60–100 mg/day)
    Malabsorptive disorders
      Crohn's disease
      Sprue (celiac disease)
      Jejuno-ilial bypass
      Chronic pancreatitis
      Biliary obstruction
  Primary hyperoxaluria types 1 and 2 (oxalate 80–300 mg/day)
Hyperuricosuria
Hypocitraturia
  Dietary protein excess
  Metabolic acidosis
  Hypokalemia
  Exercise
  Infection
  Starvation
  Hypomagnesemia
  Androgens
Renal tubular acidosis (distal, type 1)
Anatomic abnormalities of the genitourinary tract
  Medullary sponge kidney
  Tubular ectasia
  Congenital megacalyx

Modified from Refs. 1, 5, 12, and 16.

uria, which is defined as excess calcium excretion with no identifiable metabolic cause, is found in up to 40% of stone-formers but has an incidence of <10% in the overall population.[17] Excess urinary calcium leads to increased supersaturation with respect to a solid phase, generally calcium oxalate or calcium phosphate, which increases the probability for stone formation.

Idiopathic hypercalciuria is an inherited metabolic abnormality;[18–20] up to 75% of children with kidney stones have a family history of nephrolithiasis. Of patients with hypercalciuria, the prevalence of nephrolithiasis in the family history was 69%.[17] Supporting a genetic basis for hypercalciuria is our ability to breed a strain of rats with this disorder. After almost 70 generations of inbreeding, all of the rats are

hypercalciuric: they excrete ~8–10 times as much calcium as control animals and almost uniformly form kidney stones.[21–23]

Mechanisms of Hypercalciuria

Idiopathic hypercalciuria is thought to be caused by dysregulation of mineral ion transport at sites where large ion fluxes must be precisely controlled, which are the intestine, kidney, and bone.[3,17] Excessive absorption of calcium by the gastrointestinal tract would lead to an increase in serum calcium that would suppress PTH secretion [and $1,25(OH)_2D_3$], which, along with the increased filtered load of calcium to the kidneys, would result in hypercalciuria. A primary defect in renal calcium reabsorption would lead directly to hypercalciuria and result in a fall in serum calcium that would stimulate production of PTH and $1,25(OH)_2D_3$ resulting in enhanced intestinal calcium absorption. Hypercalciuria could also develop as a result of a renal defect in phosphorus reabsorption as the resultant hypophosphatemia would lead to increased $1,25(OH)_2D_3$ and stimulation of intestinal calcium and phosphorus absorption. The increased filtered load of calcium in the setting of suppressed PTH, because of the increased calcium, would also lead to hypercalciuria. Enhanced bone demineralization would increase the serum calcium concentration, which in turn, would suppress PTH production. The increase in the filtered load of calcium would result in hypercalciuria.

Analysis of human data indicates that while some patients have a single, specific genetic defect resulting in hypercalciuria,[24–26] most do not have a specific site of mineral ion transport dysregulation, rather they have a systemic disorder of mineral ion homeostasis resulting in hypercalciuria.[1,5] Attempts to categorize patients into a specific site of dysregulation leads not only to inconsistent results in the best research laboratories, but the danger of placing a patient wrongly presumed to have increased intestinal calcium transport on a low calcium diet, leading to bone demineralization.[6]

An animal model of idiopathic hypercalciuria has been developed to aid in the understanding of this disorder. Through almost 70 generations of inbreeding of the most hypercalciuric progeny of hypercalciuric rats, we have established a strain of rats each of which excrete 8–10 times as much urine calcium as the wildtype rats.[5,21,22] The principal mechanism for the hypercalciuria in these rats is increased intestinal calcium absorption. However, when these hypercalciuric rats are deprived of dietary calcium, their urine calcium excretion remains elevated, indicating a defect in renal calcium reabsorption and/or an increase in bone resorption. Bone from these rats releases more calcium, compared with bone of control rats, when exposed to increasing amounts of $1,25(OH)_2D_3$. There is also a primary defect in renal calcium reabsorption. The intestine, bone, and kidney of these hypercalciuric rats have been shown to have an increased number of vitamin D receptors. Thus, these hypercalciuric rats have a systemic abnormality in calcium homeostasis; they absorb more intestinal calcium, they resorb more bone and they fail to adequately reabsorb filtered calcium, similar to observations in humans. As each of these hypercalciuric rats forms renal stones, we have termed the rats genetic hypercalciuric stone-forming (GHS) rats. Our studies suggest that an increased number of vitamin D receptors may be the underlying mechanism for hypercalciuria in these rats.[27] Initial studies have shown an increased number of vitamin D receptors in the monocytes of humans with idiopathic hypercalciuria.[28]

Patients with persistent hypercalciuria despite a diet low in sodium often benefit from the hypocalciuric action of a thiazide diuretic. Chlorthalidone is generally used as it requires only daily dosing at an initial dose is 25 mg. Thiazides increase serum lipid levels. In patients for whom this is a concern, indapamide at an initial dose of 1.25 mg can be used. Thiazides also lower serum potassium. If an increase in potassium-rich foods does not lead to an increase in serum potassium, patients are often started on potassium citrate, which is available as a wax matrix tablet. The potassium citrate provides base, which will increase excretion of the stone inhibitor citrate. If hypokalemia persists, a potassium-sparing diuretic may be used. Amiloride, at a starting dose of 5 mg, is usually used as triamterene itself can precipitate into stones.

Hyperoxaluria

Oxalate is produced through endogenous metabolism of glyoxylate and, to a lesser extent, ascorbic acid or derived from dietary sources, such as rhubarb, cocoa, nuts, tea, and certain leafy green vegetables.[1,5,6] Oxalate is excreted in the urine and raises urinary supersaturation with respect to calcium oxalate. Hyperoxaluria (>45 mg/24 h) accounts for the formation of ~5% of all calcium stones. Hyperoxaluria results from excessive oxalate ingestion (dietary oxaluria), malabsorptive gastrointestinal disorders (enteric oxaluria), or excessive endogenous metabolism of oxalate caused by a hepatic enzyme deficiency (primary hyperoxaluria). The antifreeze ethylene glycol is metabolized to oxalate and ingestion of this toxic compound frequently leads to nephrolithiasis.

Dietary oxaluria results in moderate increases in levels of urinary oxalate (40–60 mg/day). Treatment consists of avoiding foods that contain large amounts of oxalate. Intestinal calcium binds oxalate and calcium supplementation at the time of meals is often used to decrease oxalate absorption.

Enteric oxaluria often causes higher urinary oxalate levels (60–100 mg/day). Gastrointestinal malabsorptive disorders associated with normal colonic function often lead to enteric oxaluria. Here the malabsorbed fatty acids bind intestinal calcium, freeing oxalate for colonic absorption. The malabsorbed bile acids increase colonic permeability. When possible, treatment consists of correcting the underlying disorder, or if that is not possible, treating the steatorrhea with measures such as a low fat diet, cholestyramine, and medium-chain triglycerides. As for dietary oxaluria, an oxalate restriction coupled to calcium supplementation should be suggested. These patients are also at risk for low urinary volumes and hypocitraturia, increasing the risk of nephrolithiasis. The acidic, concentrated urine increases the risk of uric acid stones.

Primary hyperoxaluria (PH) is caused by hepatic enzyme deficiencies that lead to massive endogenous oxalate production, tissue deposition, and severe hyperoxaluria (80–300 mg/day).[29] PH type 1 is caused by a deficiency of the hepatic enzyme alanine:glyoxylate aminotransferase (AGT).[30] PH type 2 is caused by a lack of d-glycerate reductase (DGDH) and glyoxylate reductase (GR). PH 1 patients benefit from pyridoxine (vitamin B_6) therapy, as it reduces oxalate production. PH patients should consume large amount of fluids and be treated with potassium citrate, magnesium, and orthophosphate. The latter inhibits calcium-oxalate crystallization but should be avoided with chronic kidney disease. In PH 1 patients, liver transplantation will be curative. The development of renal failure, from oxalate deposition, often necessitates renal transplantation as dialysis is not as effective as a functioning kidney in oxalate removal. Combined liver–kidney transplantation is sometimes necessary.

Hyperuricosuria

Uric acid crystals may form the nidus of calcium oxalate stones. These patients often have elevated urinary uric acid levels (>750 mg/24 h) with relatively normal urinary calcium

and oxalate levels. As opposed to the typical patient with uric acid stones who has a very acid urinary pH, these patients tend to have a higher urinary pH (>5.5).[31,32] They are generally treated with dietary purine restriction, increased fluid intake and, if necessary, allopurinol, 100–300 mg/day.

Hypocitraturia

Citrate binds calcium and forms a soluble complex reducing supersaturation with respect to both calcium oxalate and calcium phosphate. Consumption of large amounts of dietary protein, metabolic acidosis, exercise, infection, starvation, androgens, and acetazolamide are leading causes of hypocitraturia (<400 mg/24 h).[15] Treatment consists of addressing the underlying cause, which in the United States is often moderating dietary protein intake. If this is not successful, potassium citrate (30–75 mEq/day) is prescribed as a wax matrix formulation to increase palatability. Potassium and bicarbonate levels should be closely monitored, especially in patients with chronic kidney disease.

Renal Tubular Acidosis

In distal renal tubular acidosis (type 1 RTA), distal tubular hydrogen ion excretion is impaired, which results in a nonanion gap metabolic acidosis and a persistently alkaline urine. The acidemia increases calcium and phosphate efflux from bone and enhanced proximal tubular reabsorption of citrate. Excretion of calcium and phosphate increases; there is severe hypocitraturia, and an alkaline urine pH, all of which promote calcium–phosphate precipitation. Patients often present with nephrocalcinosis (renal parenchymal calcification). Therapy consists of potassium citrate or potassium bicarbonate supplementation, often 1–2 mEq/kg/day, to treat both the metabolic acidosis and hypocitraturia.

ACKNOWLEDGMENTS

This work was supported in part by National Institutes of Health Grants DK 56788 and AR 46289.

REFERENCES

1. Monk RD, Bushinsky DA 2003 Comprehensive Clinical Nephrology. Mosby, London, UK.
2. Asplin JR, Favus MJ, Coe FL 2000 The Kidney. W.B. Saunders, Philadelphia, PA, USA.
3. Bushinsky DA 1998 Nephrolithiasis. J Am Soc Nephrol 9:917–924.
4. Bushinsky DA 2000 Kelly's Textbook of Medicine. Lippincott Williams & Wilkens, New York, NY, USA.
5. Monk RD, Bushinsky DA 2003 Williams Textbook of Endocrinology. W. B.Saunders, Philadelphia, PA. USA.
6. Coe FL, Evan A, Worcester E 2005 Kidney stone disease. J Clin Invest 115:2598–2608.
7. Teichman JMH 2004 Acute renal colic from ureteral calculus. N Engl J Med 350:684–693.
8. Stamatelou KK, Francis ME, Jones CA, Nyberg LM, Curhan GC 2003 Time trends in reported prevalence of kidney stones in the United States: 1976–1994. Kidney Int 63:1817–1823.
9. Bushinsky DA 2003 Nephrolithiasis: Site of the initial solid phase. J Clin Invest 111:602–605.
10. Evan AP, Lingeman JE, Coe FL, Parks JH, Bledsoe SB, Shao Y, Sommer AJ, Paterson RF, Kuo RL, Grynpas M 2003 Randall plaque of patients with nephrolithiasis begins in basement membranes of thin loops of Henle. J Clin Invest 111:607–616.
11. Consensus Conference 1988 Prevention and treatment of kidney stones. JAMA 260:977–981.
12. Monk RD 1996 Clinical approach to adults. Semin Nephrol 16:375–388.
13. Borghi L, Schianchi T, Meschi T, Guerra A, Allegri F, Maggiore U, Novarini A 2002 Comparison of two diets for the prevention of recurrent stones in idiopathic hypercalciuria. N Engl J Med 346:77–84.

14. Bushinsky DA 2002 Recurrent hypercalciuric nephrolithiasis—does diet help? N Engl J Med **346:**124–125.
15. Meschi T, Schianchi T, Ridolo E, Adorni G, Allegri F, Guerra A, Novarini A, Borghi L 2004 Body weight, diet and water intake in preventing stone disease. Urol Int **72:**29–33.
16. Bushinsky DA, Monk RD 1998 Calcium. Lancet **352:**306–311.
17. Frick KK, Bushinsky DA 2003 Molecular mechanisms of primary hypercalciuria. J Am Soc Neph **14:**1082–1095.
18. Harangi F, Mehes K 1993 Family investigatons in idiopathic hypercalciuria. Eur J Pediatr **152:**64–68.
19. Bushinsky DA 1996 Genetic hypercalciuric stone forming rats. Semin Nephrol **16:**448–457.
20. Bushinsky DA 2006 Genetic hypercalciuric stone-forming rats. Curr Opin Nephrol Hypertens (in press).
21. Bushinsky DA, Asplin JR, Grynpas MD, Evan AP, Parker WR, Alexander KM, Cole FL 2002 Calcium oxalate stone formation in genetic hypercalciuric stone-forming rats. Kidney Int **61:**975–987.
22. Bushinsky DA, Asplin JR 2005 Thiazides reduce brushite, but not calcium oxalate, supersaturation and stone formation in genetic hypercalciuric stone-forming rats. J Am Soc Nephrol **16:**417–424.
23. Hoopes RR Jr, Reid R, Sen S, Szpirer C, Dixon P, Pannett AA, Thakker RV, Bushinsky DA, Scheinman SJ 2003 Quantitative trait loci for hypercalciuria in a rat model of kidney stone disease. J Am Soc Nephrol **14:**1844–1850.
24. Moe OW, Bonny O 2005 Genetic hypercalciuria. J Am Soc Nephrol **16:**729–745.
25. Sayer JA, Carr G, Simmons NL 2004 Nephrocalcinosis: Molecular insights into calcium precipitation within the kidney. Clin Sci **106:**549–561.
26. Gambaro G, Vezzoli G, Casari G, Rampoldi L, D'Angelo A, Borghi L 2004 Genetics of hypercalciuria and calcium nephrolithiasis: From the rare monogenic to the common polygenic forms. Am J Kid Dis **44:**963–986.
27. Karnauskas AJ, van Leeuwen JP, van den Bemd GJ, Kathpalia PP, DeLuca HF, Bushinsky DA, Favus MJ 2005 Mechanism and function of high vitamin D receptor levels in genetic hypercalciuric stone-forming rats. J Bone Miner Res **20:**447–454.
28. Favus MJ, Karnauskas AJ, Parks JH, Coe FL 2004 Peripheral blood monocyte vitamin D receptor levels are elevated in patients with idiopathic hypercalciuria. J Clin Endocrinol Metab **89:**4937–4943.
29. Milliner DS 2005 The primary hyperoxalurias: An algorithm for diagnosis. Am J Nephrol **25:**154–160.
30. Danpure CJ 2005 Molecular etiology of primary hyperoxaluria type 1: New direction for treatment. Am J Nephrol **25:**303–310.
31. Marangella M 2005 Uric acid elimination in the urine. Pathophysiological implications. Contrib Nephrol **147:**132–148.
32. Maalouf NM, Cameron MA, Moe OW, Sakhaee K 2004 Novel insights into the pathogenesis of uric acid nephrolithiasis. Curr Opin Nephrol Hypertens **13:**181–189.

Chapter 82. Urologic Aspects of Nephrolithiasis Management

Nicole L. Miller, Brian R. Matlaga, Ramsay L. Kuo, Samuel C. Kim, and James E. Lingeman

Methodist Hospital Institute for Kidney Stone Disease and Indiana University School of Medicine, Indianapolis, Indiana

INTRODUCTION

Urologic management of nephrolithiasis has steadily evolved with the introduction of shock wave lithotripsy (SWL) and advances in endoscopic technology. Presently, SWL and other endourological procedures, such as ureteroscopy (URS) and percutaneous nephrolithotomy (PNL), have supplanted the use of open stone procedures. These minimally invasive techniques currently allow the safe removal of urinary calculi regardless of composition, location, or stone burden.

Although there are many surgical options for the treatment of urolithiasis, the fundamental principle that ultimately guides decision-making is the goal of maximizing stone clearance while minimizing patient morbidity. Most of the recommendations delineated by the National Institutes of Health Consensus Conference in 1988 and the American Urological Association (AUA) Ureteral Stones Clinical Guidelines Panel in 1997 still apply today.[1,2] Furthermore, the 2005 AUA Nephrolithiasis Committee has published recommendations for the management of patients with staghorn calculi based on a meta-analysis of outcome data. Recent advances in endoscopic equipment and the development of adjunctive technologies, such as the holmium laser, have expanded the role of flexible URS in the treatment paradigm for patients with urinary calculi, especially patients with comorbidities precluding alternate surgical therapy.

When treating nephrolithiasis, surgical decisions can be simplified by stratifying stones into clinical categories that direct treatment selection (Table 1). The initial distinction is identifying the general location of the stone burden—renal or ureteral.

RENAL CALCULI

Stone-related characteristics (size, number, location, and composition), renal anatomy, and patient clinical factors should all be considered, in conjunction with equipment availability and procedural morbidity, when selecting a surgical approach for renal calculi (Table 2). Diagnostic evaluation and metabolic classification, as outlined elsewhere, is important when choosing therapy as previous stones containing significant amounts of calcium oxalate monohydrate, brushite, cystine, or soft matrix will be resistant to fragmentation with SWL. With the availability of multiple minimally invasive techniques for the treatment of kidney stones such as SWL, URS, PNL, and laparoscopic stone surgery, the current challenge for the urologist is not whether the calculus can be removed endoscopically but rather selecting the appropriate approach.

SIMPLE RENAL CALCULI

SWL has streamlined the treatment protocol for nephrolithiasis, because the majority of simple renal calculi (80–85%) can be successfully treated with SWL.[3] However, there are several factors that have been associated with resistance to SWL and poor stone clearance rates: large renal calculi (mean,

Dr. Lingeman has been a consultant/advisor and meeting participant/lecturer for Lumenis, an investor, meeting participant/lecturer, and was involved in a scientific study/trial for Boston Scientific, a consultant/advisor for Olympus, and a meeting participant/lecturer for Karl Storz. Dr. Kuo has been a meeting participant/lecturer for Lumenis, Boston Scientific, and Karl Storz. All other authors have reported no conflicts of interest.

TABLE 1. Classification System for Patients With Nephrolithiasis

Renal calculi
  Simple
    Stone burden < 2 cm
    Normal renal anatomy
  Complex
    Stone burden > 2 cm
    Staghorn stone
    Lower pole calculus
    Abnormal renal anatomy
      Dilated calyx
      Ureteropelvic junction obstruction
      Horseshoe kidney
      Pelvic kidney
      Calyceal diverticulum
    Infection and obstruction
    Stones difficult to fragment
      Cystine
      Brushite
      Calcium oxalate monohydrate
Ureteral calculi
  Proximal/mid
    Less than 1 cm
    Greater than 1 cm
  Distal
    Less than 1 cm
    Greater than 1 cm

22.2 mm), stones within dependent or obstructed portions of the collecting system, stone composition (mostly calcium oxalate monohydrate, brushite and cystine), obesity or a body habitus that inhibits imaging, and unsatisfactory targeting of the stone.[4] Clearly, larger stone burdens increase the number of treatment sessions and ancillary procedures while decreasing stone-free rates.[5,6]

PNL, a more invasive approach, results in a significantly higher stone-free rate and lower retreatment rate than that of SWL.[6] However, because of increased patient morbidity, PNL should be limited to kidneys with a larger stone burden (>2.0 cm) or those stones known to be resistant to SWL, including cystine, brushite, and, to a lesser extent, calcium oxalate monohydrate.[5,7,8] As a result, the 1988 National Institutes of Health Consensus Conference recommendations that simple renal calculi (see Table 1) can be effectively treated with SWL and that complex renal calculi are better managed with PNL still hold true.[1]

Advances in endoscopic technology and equipment have been introduced since publication of the above guideline panels. Currently, retrograde endoscopic procedures with the new generation of flexible ureteroscopes are increasingly used. URS, in conjunction with laser lithotripsy, has been success-

fully used in settings of SWL failure, complex renal calculi, and lower pole renal calculi.[4,9] URS is especially attractive when patient factors, such as coagulopathy or morbid obesity, preclude alternate approaches.

COMPLEX RENAL CALCULI

Complex renal calculi (Table 1) present a greater challenge than simple calculi. This category includes not only stones of large size, such as staghorn stones, but also encompasses kidneys with abnormal anatomy and stones that are difficult to fragment. Ureteroscopic techniques can be used in upper urinary tract stones >2 cm; however, stone clearance is significantly less than with PNL, and stone recurrence is rapid (16% over 6 months).[9] For this reason, PNL still remains the treatment of choice for most complex renal stones.[1,5,10] The combination of PNL and SWL for complex stones was commonplace in the 1990s. PNL techniques have improved, and the need for SWL during percutaneous procedures has declined.[11] Even the largest of staghorn calculi can be cleared percutaneously with the aid of secondary PNL and/or multiple accesses as needed (Table 3).

SPECIAL CONSIDERATIONS

An area of controversy continues to be the management of lower pole calyceal calculi. SWL results in significantly lower clearance of lower pole calyceal stones when compared with PNL.[12] A prospective randomized multicenter trial clearly showed the superiority of PNL over SWL in clearance of lower pole calculi >10 mm (stone free rates of 91% versus 21% for PNL and SWL, respectively).[12] Retreatment rates (16% versus 9%) and ancillary treatment rates (14% versus 2%) were also higher for the SWL group. However, for lower pole calculi <1 cm, a recent prospective randomized trial failed to show a statistically significant difference in stone-free rates between SWL and URS.[13] The impact of various lower pole anatomic features on stone clearance after SWL (infundibulopelvic angle, infundibular length, and infundibular width) is unclear at present.[12]

Aberrant renal anatomy merits special consideration when addressing urinary calculi. Horseshoe and pelvic kidneys, ureteropelvic junction obstructions (UPJOs) and calyceal diverticuli are often associated with nephrolithiasis and can present a treatment challenge. Although SWL may be used as initial treatment for renal calculi in horseshoe kidneys, stone-free rates vary greatly.[14–18] Because stone burden and urinary drainage play important roles in stone clearance, SWL is appropriate only for horseshoe kidneys with smaller renal calculi with normal urinary drainage; PNL produces better results for larger stones or when impaired drainage is present.[19]

Pelvic kidneys can create positioning difficulties for SWL. The retroperitoneal position of the kidney and blockage by the

TABLE 2. Factors Affecting the Management of Renal Stones[19]

Stone	Renal anatomy	Clinical
Size	Obstruction/stasis	Infection
Number	Hydronephrosis	Body habitus
Composition	Ureteropelvic junction obstruction	Renal failure
Location (lower pole)	Calyceal diverticulum	Coagulopathy
	Horseshoe kidney/ectopic/fusion abnormality	Age (pediatric/elderly)
		Hypertension

Adapted from Lingeman JE, Matlaga BR, Evan AP. Surgical management of urinary lithiasis. In: Walsh PC, Retik AB, Vaughan ED, Wein AJ (eds.) Campbell's Urology (in press) with permission from Elsevier.[19]

bony pelvis may require SWL to be performed prone.[15] If SWL fails or the stone burden is large, laparoscopic-assisted percutaneous procedures or flexible URS are options.[20]

UPJO can cause urinary stasis in the renal collecting system and can thus contribute to stone formation. Metabolic issues must also be addressed because patients with concomitant UPJO and calcium nephrolithiasis commonly have metabolic abnormalities.[21,22] When UPJO and renal calculi are present, PNL with endopyelotomy is a successful approach to remove the stone burden and endoscopically treat the UPJO.[23–25] Laparoscopic pyeloplasty with pyelolithotomy may be appropriate for some patients.[26,27]

Calyceal diverticula are non–urine-producing congenital urothelial-lined outpouchings that are commonly complicated by urinary calculi. Often, the neck of the diverticulum is quite small and does not allow passage of fragments after SWL.[28] For this reason, stone-free rates after SWL are poor.[28,29] On the other hand, PNL accomplishes both stone removal and ablation of the diverticular cavity—an option unavailable with SWL.[30]

Although SWL is quite versatile, certain clinical scenarios are either not amenable to SWL or increase the potential for complications. The presence of obstruction and/or infection requires prompt attention and precludes primary SWL. Immediate intervention is compulsory if obstruction occurs in a solitary kidney or concomitant obstruction and infection secondary to a calculus occur in any kidney. Once the obstruction and/or infection has been appropriately treated with a combination of decompression and antimicrobial therapy, the offending calculus can be definitively treated per the above guidelines.

One of the more significant complications of SWL is perinephric hematoma. Risk factors identified as increasing the risk of this complication include age, obesity, pre-existing hypertension, diabetes mellitus, coronary artery disease, thrombocytopenia, and coagulopathy. SWL may be safely used to treat patients with coagulation disorders if the bleeding diathesis can be corrected.[31] However, if the patient's coagulopathy is the result of a pharmacologic therapy that cannot be safely discontinued, URS with holmium laser lithotripsy is the preferable approach.[32]

URETERAL CALCULI

For ureteral calculi, stone-related factors, clinical parameters, and other technical issues differ considerably from those for renal calculi because ureteral stones tend to be more resistant to SWL and can be easily treated with flexible URS (Table 4).[2,33] Most ureteral calculi are <5 mm in diameter and have a high likelihood of spontaneous passage if symptoms are

TABLE 4. FACTORS AFFECTING THE MANAGEMENT OF URETERAL STONES

Stone	Renal anatomy	Clinical
Size	Solitary kidney	Symptom severity
Location	Abnormal ureteral anatomy (i.e., strictures)	Infection
Composition	Obstruction	Equipment availability

Adapted from Lingeman JE, Matlaga BR, Evan AP. Surgical management of urinary lithiasis. In: Walsh PC, Retik AB, Vaughan ED, Wein AJ (eds.) Campbell's Urology (in press) with permission from Elsevier.[19]

tolerable.[2] When ureteral stones are larger in size, become increasingly symptomatic, or are unable to pass spontaneously, appropriate surgical intervention can be undertaken (Table 5).

PROXIMAL URETERAL CALCULI

Multiple endourologic options are available for the treatment of proximal ureteral stones: SWL with or without stone manipulation, URS, and PNL. The AUA Ureteral Stones Guidelines Panel in 1997 recommended SWL (in situ or push back) as the treatment of choice for stones 1 cm or smaller in the proximal ureter.[2] As SWL is noninvasive and can achieve up to 85% stone-free rates for ureteral calculi, SWL remains a reasonable treatment option for proximal and distal ureteral stones <1 cm in size.[2]

Flexible URS has become increasingly popular as primary therapy for proximal ureteral stones <1 cm because of its higher stone-free rates than with SWL. Furthermore, URS is effective for patients with stones difficult to fragment, distal ureteral obstruction, impacted stones, and medical conditions precluding other approaches (such as obesity and coagulopathy).[34] Current endoscopic equipment, in conjunction with holmium laser lithotripsy and stone baskets, allows the urologist to treat proximal ureteral stones of all sizes.[9,34]

As in renal stone disease, stone burden affects SWL results

TABLE 5. ADAPTED FROM THE AUA GUIDELINES PANEL SUMMARY REPORT FOR URETERAL STONES

Goals
  Stone free with single procedure preferred
  Avoid unplanned secondary procedures
  Minimize morbidity
Recommendations for all ureteral stones
  Stones 5 mm or less in diameter have a good chance of spontaneous passage
  Routine stent placement for SWL not necessary
Proximal/midureteral stone 1 cm or less
  SWL and Flexible URS both acceptable therapy
  URS if SWL inappropriate or as salvage for failed SWL
Proximal/midureteral stone greater than 1 cm
  PNL/SWL/URS all acceptable
  URS not affected by stone size compared with SWL
Distal ureteral stone 1 cm or less
  Blind basketing without fluoroscopy/guidewire not preferred
  SWL/URS both effective; URS more widely available
Distal ureteral stone greater than 1 cm
  Blind basketing without fluoroscopy/guidewire not preferred
  SWL/URS both options
  URS preferred if multiple SWL sessions necessary for fragmentation

Adapted from Segura JW, Preminger GM, Assimos DG, et al. 1997 Ureteral stones clinical guidelines panel summary report on the management of ureteral calculi. The American Urological Association. J Urol 158:1915–1921 with permission from the American Urological Association.[21]

TABLE 3. ADAPTED FROM THE AUA GUIDELINES PANEL SUMMARY FOR STAGHORN STONES

Recommendations
  Newly diagnosed struvite staghorn calculi require active treatment intervention
  Percutaneous stone removal is preferred (includes secondary percutaneous procedure and/or multiple accesses)
  SWL monotherapy and open surgery should not be used as initial therapy
  Nephrectomy may be appropriate for a nonfunctioning kidney

Adapted from Preminger GM, Assimos DG, Lingeman JE, et al. AUA guideline on management of staghorn calculi: Diagnosis and treatment recommendations. J Urol 173:1991–2000 with permission from the American Urological Association.[10]

TABLE 6. CLINICAL FACTORS FAVORING URS OVER SWL

Radiolucent calculi
Anatomic abnormalities
Calyceal diverticula
Renal ectopia
Impaired drainage
UPJ obstruction
Lower pole
Anticoagulation/bleeding diathesis
Morbid obesity
Stone composition (cystine, brushite, COM)
Pregnancy

when treating ureteral stones. Proximal ureteral stones >1 cm undergoing SWL have lower stone-free rates than those <1 cm.[2,35] The development of flexible ureteroscopes and adjunctive laser lithotripsy has allowed proximal ureteral stones, even those >1 cm, to be successfully treated with minimal morbidity; PNL is reserved for large or impacted proximal ureteral stones.[4,9]

DISTAL URETERAL CALCULI

Although the likelihood of spontaneous passage of stones is highest in the distal ureter, intervention with URS or SWL often is necessary. For symptomatic ureteral calculi <1 cm, both SWL and URS are excellent options. Previous randomized control trials comparing SWL and URS have reached conflicting conclusions.[36,37] URS is not influenced by stone size and can effectively treat distal ureteral calculi >1 cm, a size that would be ineffectively treated by SWL.[38] Many institutions have limited access to a lithotriptor, and therefore patient treatment may be delayed; URS is widely available, and treatment can be promptly instituted.

The indications for URS (Table 6) are ever increasing, and the number of URSs performed annually is steadily on the rise.[3] URS is effective in treating impacted ureteral stones and as salvage therapy for failed SWL of ureteral or renal stones. The low success rate of repeat SWL for ureteral stones after failed initial SWL makes URS a particularly attractive option.[35]

CONCLUSIONS

Although most urinary calculi are best treated initially with SWL, endourologic techniques play an important adjunctive role. Percutaneous procedures are instrumental in eliminating complex renal calculi, and URS is increasingly used for the treatment of ureteral and renal stones. As endoscopic technology and equipment continue to improve, the role of URS in treating ureteral and renal calculi is likely to further expand. Although multiple minimally invasive procedures can safely treat urinary calculi, prevention of future stone events through appropriate metabolic testing and medical treatment remains paramount.

REFERENCES

1. Conference NC 1988 Prevention and treatment of kidney stones. JAMA **260:**977.
2. Segura JW, Preminger GM, Assimos DG, Dretler SP, Kahn RI, Lingeman JE, Macaluso JN Jr 1997 Ureteral stones clinical guidelines panel summary report on the management of ureteral calculi. The American Urological Association. J Urol **158:**1915–1921.
3. Kerbl K, Rehman J, Landman J, Lee D, Sundaram C, Clayman RV 2002 Current management of urolithiasis: Progress or regress? J Endourol **16:**281–288.
4. Grasso M, Loisides P, Beaghler M, Bagley D 1995 The case for primary endoscopic management of upper urinary tract calculi: I. A critical review of 121 extracorporeal shock-wave lithotripsy failures. Urology **45:**363–371.
5. Lam HS, Lingeman JE, Barron M, Newman DM, Mosbaugh PG, Steele RE, Knapp PM, Scott JW, Nyhuis A, Woods JR 1992 Staghorn calculi: Analysis of treatment results between initial percutaneous nephrolithotomy and extracorporeal shock wave lithotripsy monotherapy with reference to surface area. J Urol **147:**1219–1225.
6. Lingeman JE, Coury TA, Newman DM, Kahnoski RJ, Mertz JH, Mosbaugh PG, Steele RE, Woods JR 1987 Comparison of results and morbidity of percutaneous nephrostolithotomy and extracorporeal shock wave lithotripsy. J Urol **138:**485–490.
7. Parks JH, Worcester EM, Coe FL, Evan AP, Lingeman JE 2004 Clinical implications of abundant calcium phosphate in routinely analyzed kidney stones. Kidney Int **66:**777–785.
8. Klee LW, Brito CG, Lingeman JE 1991 The clinical implications of brushite calculi. J Urol **145:**715–718.
9. Grasso M, Conlin M, Bagley D 1998 Retrograde ureteropyeloscopic treatment of 2 cm. or greater upper urinary tract and minor Staghorn calculi. J Urol **160:**346–351.
10. Preminger GM, Assimos DG, Lingeman JE, Nakada SY, Pearle MS, Wolf JS Jr 2005 Chapter 1: AUA guideline on management of staghorn calculi: Diagnosis and treatment recommendations. J Urol **173:**1991–2000.
11. Lam HS, Lingeman JE, Mosbaugh PG, Steele RE, Knapp PM, Scott JW, Newman DM 1992 Evolution of the technique of combination therapy for staghorn calculi: A decreasing role for extracorporeal shock wave lithotripsy. J Urol **148:**1058–1062.
12. Albala DM, Assimos DG, Clayman RV, Denstedt JD, Grasso M, Gutierrez-Aceves J, Kahn RI, Leveillee RJ, Lingeman JE, Macaluso JN, Jr., Munch LC, Nakada SY, Newman RC, Pearle MS, Preminger GM, Teichman J, Woods JR 2001 Lower pole I: A prospective randomized trial of extracorporeal shock wave lithotripsy and percutaneous nephrostolithotomy for lower pole nephrolithiasis-initial results. J Urol **166:**2072–2080.
13. Pearle MS, Lingeman JE, Leveillee R, Kuo R, Preminger GM, Nadler RB, Macaluso J, Monga M, Kumar U, Dushinski J, Albala DM, Wolf JS Jr, Assimos D, Fabrizio M, Munch LC, Nakada SY, Auge B, Honey J, Ogan K, Pattaras J, McDougall EM, Averch TD, Turk T, Pietrow P, Watkins S 2005 Prospective, randomized trial comparing shock wave lithotripsy and ureteroscopy for lower pole caliceal calculi 1 cm or less. J Urol **173:**2005–2009.
14. Esuvaranathan K, Tan EC, Tung KH, Foo KT 1991 Stones in horseshoe kidneys: Results of treatment by extracorporeal shock wave lithotripsy and endourology. J Urol **146:**1213–1215.
15. Kupeli B, Isen K, Biri H, Sinik Z, Alkibay T, Karaoglan U, Bozkirli I 1999 Extracorporeal shockwave lithotripsy in anomalous kidneys. J Endourol **13:**349–352.
16. Lampel A, Hohenfellner M, Schultz-Lampel D, Lazica M, Bohnen K, Thurof JW 1996 Urolithiasis in horseshoe kidneys: Therapeutic management. Urology **47:**182–186.
17. Kirkali Z, Esen AA, Mungan MU 1996 Effectiveness of extracorporeal shockwave lithotripsy in the management of stone-bearing horseshoe kidneys. J Endourol **10:**13–15.
18. Theiss M, Wirth MP, Frohmuller HG 1993 Extracorporeal shock wave lithotripsy in patients with renal malformations. Br J Urol **72:**534–538.
19. Lingeman JE, Matlaga BR, Evan AP 2006 Surgical management of urinary lithiasis. In: Walsh PC, Petik AB, Vaughan ED, Wein AJ (eds.) Campbell's Urology. Saunders, Philadelphia, PA, USA (in press).
20. Matlaga BR, Kim SC, Watkins S, Kuo RL, Munch LC, Lingeman JE 2005 Percutaneous nephrolithotomy for ectopic kidneys: Over, around or through. Urology (in press).
21. Husmann DA, Milliner DS, Segura JW 1995 Ureteropelvic junction obstruction with a simultaneous renal calculus: Long-term followup. J Urol **153:**1399–1402.
22. Matin SF, Streem SB 2000 Metabolic risk factors in patients with ureteropelvic junction obstruction and renal calculi. J Urol **163:**1676–1678.
23. Oshinsky GS, Jarrett TW, Smith AD 1996 New technique in managing ureteropelvic junction obstruction: Percutaneous endoscopic pyeloplasty. J Endourol **10:**147–151.
24. Kletscher BA, Segura JW, LeRoy AJ, Patterson DE 1995 Percutaneous antegrade endopyelotomy: Review of 50 consecutive cases. J Urol **153:**701–703.
25. Motola JA, Badlani GH, Smith AD 1993 Results of 212 consecutive endopyelotomies: An 8-year followup. J Urol **149:**453–456.
26. Ramakumar S, Lancini V, Chan DY, Parsons JK, Kavoussi LR, Jarrett

TW 2002 Laparoscopic pyeloplasty with concomitant pyelolithotomy. J Urol **167:**1378–1380.

27. Siqueira TM Jr, Nadu A, Kuo RL, Paterson RF, Lingeman JE, Shalhav AL 2002 Laparoscopic treatment for ureteropelvic junction obstruction. Urology **60:**973–978.

28. Jones JA, Lingeman JE, Steidle CP 1991 The roles of extracorporeal shock wave lithotripsy and percutaneous nephrostolithotomy in the management of pyelocaliceal diverticula. J Urol **146:**724–727.

29. Streem SB, Yost A 1992 Treatment of caliceal diverticular calculi with extracorporeal shock wave lithotripsy: Patient selection and extended followup. J Urol **148:**1043–1046.

30. Kim SC, Kuo RL, Tinmouth WW, Watkins S, Lingeman JE 2005 Percutaneous nephrolithotomy for caliceal diverticular calculi: A novel single stage approach. J Urol **173:**1194–1198.

31. Streem SB, Yost A 1990 Extracorporeal shock wave lithotripsy in patients with bleeding diatheses. J Urol **144:**1347–1348.

32. Watterson JD, Girvan AR, Cook AJ, Beiko DT, Nott L, Auge BK, Preminger GM, Denstedt JD 2002 Safety and efficacy of holmium: YAG laser lithotripsy in patients with bleeding diatheses. J Urol **168:**442–445.

33. Turk TM, Jenkins AD 1999 A comparison of ureteroscopy to in situ extracorporeal shock wave lithotripsy for the treatment of distal ureteral calculi. J Urol **161:**45–47.

34. Tawfiek ER, Bagley DH 1999 Management of upper urinary tract calculi with ureteroscopic techniques. Urology **53:**25–31.

35. Pace KT, Weir MJ, Tariq N, Honey RJ 2000 Low success rate of repeat shock wave lithotripsy for ureteral stones after failed initial treatment. J Urol **164:**1905–1907.

36. Pearle MS, Nadler R, Bercowsky E, Chen C, Dunn M, Figenshau RS, Hoenig DM, McDougall EM, Mutz J, Nakada SY, Shalhav AL, Sundaram C, Wolf JS Jr, Clayman RV 2001 Prospective randomized trial comparing shock wave lithotripsy and ureteroscopy for management of distal ureteral calculi. J Urol **166:**1255–1260.

37. Peschel R, Janetschek G, Bartsch G 1999 Extracorporeal shock wave lithotripsy versus ureteroscopy for distal ureteral calculi: A prospective randomized study. J Urol **162:**1909–1912.

38. Pardalidis NP, Kosmaoglou EV, Kapotis CG 1999 Endoscopy vs. extracorporeal shockwave lithotripsy in the treatment of distal ureteral stones: Ten years' experience. J Endourol **13:**161–164.

SECTION XIII

Dental Biology
(Section Editor: Pamela Gehron Robey)

Chapter 83.   Craniofacial Development

Andrew Ravanelli and John Klingensmith

Department of Cell Biology, Duke University Medical Center, Durham, North Carolina

OVERVIEW

In this chapter, we provide a brief overview of human craniofacial development. The head is one of the first structures to arise in the embryo, with morphologically distinct primordia apparent by the end of the third week of pregnancy. Here we describe key events in the development of the head and its major compartments, focusing on skeletal structures. We also consider the major congenital malformations arising from defects in head formation.

EARLY EMBRYOGENESIS

The embryo develops from conception into a trilayered disc of cells. These germ layers are called the ectoderm, mesoderm, and endoderm. Organ systems begin to form as these layers fold to create two tubes. The neural ectoderm folds dorsally to become the neural tube. The anterior end of the neural tube expands to form the brain rudiments: the prosencephalon, mesencephalon, and rhombencephalon (Fig. 1A). The endoderm folds ventrally to create the gut tube. The anterior end is the foregut, which gives rise to the majority of the oral cavity and pharynx. The brain and foregut of the early embryo are the centers around which the head is formed, and each is a source of signals that direct development of craniofacial tissues.

Many tissues of the head are formed from neural crest cells (NCCs), a pluripotential migratory cell type in the midgestation embryo. During neurulation, NCCs arise from the converging crests of the neural folds as they fuse dorsally to form the neural tube. The NCCs undergo an epithelial-to-mesenchymal transition, delaminate, and migrate through the mesoderm to populate various structures of the embryo (Fig. 1A). Cranial NCCs migrate to the head to eventually form the bulk of the facial tissues, many bones of the skull, the dental papillae of the teeth, and much of the muscular, nervous, and vascular tissue of the head and neck.

The mesoderm also contributes substantially to the early head. Paraxial mesoderm segments and condenses into somitomeres, just lateral to the neural folds. As the trunk somitomeres condense further, they form a series of segmented units (somites). The first seven cranial somitomeres never fully condense to form definitive somites. In all cases, these units each consist of three compartments: dermatome, myotome, and sclerotome. The dermatome contributes to the dermis of the skin. Myotomes give rise to the skeletal muscles of the body, limbs, and head. Sclerotome derivatives form the bones of the axial skeleton, including the base of the skull.[1]

PHARYNGEAL ARCHES

A large portion of the head and neck derives from the pharyngeal arches (Fig. 1B). These are five, bilaterally paired swellings formed along the pharyngeal foregut in the fourth week, as the rostral neuropore is closing. The arches are numbered 1, 2, 3, 4, and 6 by homology to the primitive gill arches of lower vertebrates. An early rostrocaudal subdivision of the first arch yields the maxillary and mandibular prominences. Each arch is composed of a mesodermal core lined with endoderm and ectoderm. Endodermal pouches and ectodermal

clefts separate the arches. NCCs migrate into the arches, filling them with mesenchyme.

Each pharyngeal arch gives rise to a variety of specific structures of the head and neck (Table 1). In general, the mesodermal cores yield skeletal structures of the neck and lower head. The clefts and pouches form the epithelial linings of the many of the organs, ducts, and mucosa of the mouth and neck. The cranial neural crest differentiates into bones, cartilages, nerves, tooth rudiments, and many other craniofacial tissues.[1]

Within each arch, a cranial nerve (CN), an aortic arch artery, and an arch cartilage develops. Their derivatives are listed in Table 1. The cranial nerves innervate the structures derived from the arches in which they form. The left and right arteries of the arches undergo differential development and regression in a very complex morphogenetic progression, ultimately forming components of the aortic system. The arch cartilages form a variety of small bones and cartilages, primarily in the middle ear and neck.

NEUROCRANIUM

The bones and muscles of the skull that encase the brain comprise the neurocranium (Fig. 1C), consisting largely of the membranous bones that form the cranial vault and the cartilaginous neurocranium forming the floor of the skull. The thin, broad bones of the membranous neurocranium derive from cranial NCCs that migrate from brain regions to form the mesenchyme covering the sides and top of the brain. This mesenchyme condenses and differentiates directly into osteoblasts that secrete osteoid and form bone (intramembranous ossification). The resulting calvarial bones are separated by dense, connective tissue seams (sutures), leaving open spaces (the fontanelles). These flexible junctures accommodate deformation during birth and brain enlargement during infancy.

The cartilaginous neurocranium, or neural chondrocranium, is formed by the fusion of cartilages, composed primarily of cells from the sclerotome of cranial somitomeres and occipital somites. The cartilage models then undergo endochondral ossification. Some undergo regression as membranous bone.[2] The resulting bones comprise some of the facial bones, including the sphenoid, ethmoid, temporal, and the caudal portion of the occipital bone. These bones have complex origins: The ethmoid and sphenoid cartilages are formed from somitomeric mesoderm and NCC derivatives, whereas the caudal portion of the occipital bone is formed from the somatic sclerotomes of the first three occipital somites and the cranial half of the first cervical somite. The sensory capsules, also part of the cartilaginous neurocranium, encase the nasal passages, the eyes, and the inner ear.[1]

VISCEROCRANIUM

The viscerocranium is the skeleton of the face. These cartilages and bones form the skeletal structures of the mouth and the supporting structures of the orphopharynx and trachea. The bones of the viscerocranium are also formed by either intramembranous or endochondral ossification (Fig. 1C). The membranous viscerocranium consists of the maxilla, the palatine bones, the zygoma, the squamous temporal bones, and the mandible. The latter is formed by ossification of NCC-derived mesenchyme that condenses around the mesodermal core of the

---

The authors have reported no conflicts of interest.

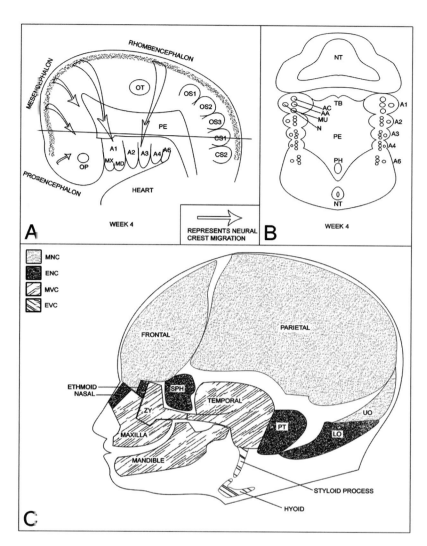

FIG. 1. Head precursors and skull derivatives. (A) The human embryo depicting formed pharyngeal arches (A1–A6), regions of the brain, optic vesicle (OP), otic vesicle (OT), occipital somites (OS1-OS3), the first two cervical somites (CS1-CS2), pharyngeal endoderm tube (PE), heart, and a schematic generalization of neural crest migration. MX and MD represent the maxillary and mandibular divisions of arch 1. Bisecting line represents plane of section for B. (B) Cross-section of embryo showing the pharyngeal endoderm (PE) and arch core components. NT, neural tube; TB, tongue bud; AC, arch cartilage; AA, arch artery; MU, arch muscle; N, arch nerve; PH, pharynx. (C) Bones of the skull. Shadings represent membranous neurocranium (MNC), neural chondrocranium (ENC), membranous viscerocranium (MVC), and endochondral viscerocranium (EVC). ZY, zygoma; SPH, sphenoid; PT, petrous temporal; UO and LO, upper and lower occipital.

mandibular prominence (Meckel's cartilage). The endochondral (cartilaginous) viscerocranium arises from the first two arches and consists of the middle ear bones, the styloid process of the temporalis, and the hyoid bone. The laryngeal cartilages are derived mainly from arches 4 and 6.

FACIAL MORPHOGENESIS

Mesenchymal masses of NCC derivatives yield the features and structures of the face from five primary swellings: two maxillary and two mandibular prominences derived from the first arch and a single frontonasal mass derived from head mesenchyme (Fig. 2A). These are organized around the stomodeum, the future opening to the mouth. Rapid facial growth occurs from the fourth to eighth weeks. The frontonasal mass forms the bulk of tissues rostral to the stomodeum, forming structures such as the forehead. The maxillary prominences form lateral tissues, ultimately producing much of the upper face. The mandibular prominences primarily form the tissues just caudal to the stomodeum, including the chin.

The buccopharyngeal membrane, separating the stomodeum from the anterior foregut tube, ruptures at day 24 to create a broad, slit-like, embryonic mouth (the orphopharynx). This early mouth is reduced laterally by the fusion of the mandibular and maxillary prominences to form the cheeks. Nasal placodes thicken on the frontonasal mass and develop nasal pits that divide each side of the process into the medial and lateral nasal processes (Fig. 2B). The medial nasal processes grow down into the stomodeum and fuse with the maxillary processes (Fig. 2C). These medial nasal processes then expand and fuse to form the intermaxillary process, thus forming the primitive upper lip and philtrum (Fig. 2D). Proliferating mesenchyme fills in the mandibular fusion to form the lower lip.[1,3]

ORONASAL CAVITY AND PALATOGENESIS

The oronasal cavity is created as the frontonasal mass enlarges and the first arches grow together to form the stomodeum. As the nasal pits invaginate, they create the nasal passage, which grows inward toward the pharyngeal endoderm. The oronasal membrane, a layer of tissue separating the oral and nasal compartments, breaks down to form openings between the oral and nasal cavities (the primitive choana).

The oral and nasal cavities become separated by the palate, which has several components. The primary palate is a small anterior domain contributed by the medial nasal processes, whereas the secondary palate comprises most of the soft and hard tissues of the roof of the mouth (Fig. 3C). The hard (bony) portion of the palate arises as palatine shelves grow together

TABLE 1. STRUCTURES DERIVED FROM PHARYNGEAL ARCH TISSUES

Pharyngeal tissue	Major structures	Cranial nerve	Cartilages and bone	Skeletal muscles	Arch artery
Arch 1	Mandibular arch, maxillary prominence	Trigeminal (V)	Palatopterygoid, maxilla, palatine, zygoma, squamous, temporal, incus	All muscles of mastication: masseter, temporalis, pterygoids	Terminal branch of maxillary artery
	Mandibular prominence		Meckel's, mandible, malleus	Mylohyoid, anterior digastric, tensor veli palatini, tensor tympani	
Pouch 1/Cleft 1	Linings of auditory tube and external auditory meatus and tympanic membrane				
Arch 2	Hyoid arch	Facial (VII)	Reichert, styloid, hyoid, stapes, stylohyoid ligament	All muscles of facial expression, Posterior digastric, stylohyoid, stapedius	Stapedial artery, corticotympanic artery
Pouch 2	Lining of palatine tonsils				
Arch 3		Glossopharyngeal (IX)	Hyoid	Stylopharyngeus	Common carotid artery, root of internal carotid
Pouch and Cleft 3— dorsal tissues —ventral tissues	Cells of inferior parathyroid gland Components of thymus gland				
Arch 4		Vagus: superior, laryngeal branch (X) Pharyngeal Branch (X)	All laryngeal cartilages: thyroid, cricoid, arytenoids, corniculate, cuneiform, epiglottis (4 and 6)	Pharyngeal constrictors All soft palate muscles except tensor veli, palatini All intrinsic laryngeal muscles (4 and 6)	Arch of aorta, right subclavian artery, base of pulmonary arteries
Pouch 4—dorsal tissues —ventral tissues	Cells of superior parathyroid gland Parafollicular cells of thymus				
Arch 6		Recurrent laryngeal branch (X)			Ductus arteriosus, roots of definitive pulmonary arteries

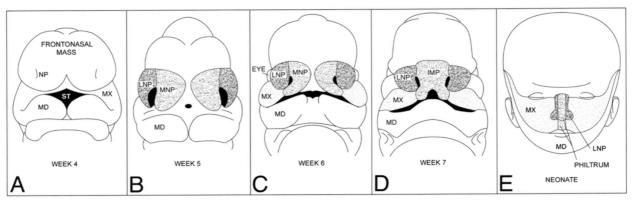

FIG. 2. Facial morphogenesis. This figure shows the progression of the facial primordial. NP, nasal pit; MD, mandible; MX, maxilla; ST, stomodeum; LNP and MNP, lateral and medial nasal processes; IMP, intermaxillary process.

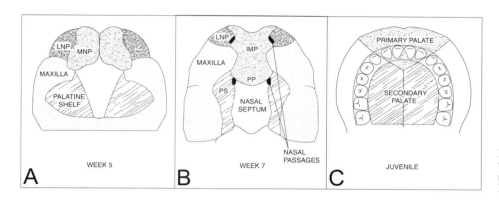

FIG. 3. Palatogenesis. This figure shows the movement of the primary palate (PP) and secondary palatine shelves (PS). LNP and MNP, lateral and medial nasal processes.

from the maxillary processes (Fig. 3A). As the secondary palatine shelves grow together, they become positioned above the tongue to allow for fusion in the midline. They also fuse anteriorly to the primary palate (Fig. 3B). Fusion of the palatine shelves with each other and with the nasal septum separates the nasal cavities from the oral cavity. The posterior parts of the palatine shelves do not ossify, but fuse to form the soft palate. This is the fleshy portion of the mouth's roof, extending posteriorly from the hard palate.

The tongue arises as a swelling from the floor of the pharynx in the fourth week. A medial and two lateral lingual buds swell and fuse to form the tongue primordium. The lateral buds outgrow the medial bud to form the oral portion of the tongue. The base of the tongue is formed with contributions from the second, third, and fourth arches.

The teeth are formed from ectodermal (oral epithelium) and mesenchymal (neural crest derived) tissues of the mandibular and maxillary prominences. Each tooth bud is composed of an ectodermal dental lamina and a basal, mesenchymal dental papilla.[4,5] Their development into mature teeth is described elsewhere.

CRANIOFACIAL BIRTH DEFECTS

The head is most sensitive to developmental perturbations from 3 to 8 weeks of gestation, the period when most of the cranial tissues and precursors of head structures are forming. The complexity of cell types contributing to the head and their dynamic reorganizations create many opportunities for error. Depending on when and how severe the insult is, a wide range of defects can occur—ranging from minor cosmetic concerns to serious medical disasters. Significant birth defects occur in ~1 per 50 live births, a third involving craniofacial malformations. Collectively, birth defects are the leading cause of infant mortality in the Western world.[6] In the United States, congenital malformations, deformations, and chromosomal abnormalities accounted for one-fifth of all infant deaths in 2002, as reported in the National Vital Statistics Report by the CDC.[6] Head malformations account for many of these deaths and often lead to significant disability in those who survive infancy.

Structural anomalies of craniofacial development have a varied etiology. They can result from genetic mutation(s) or from environmental disruption of developmental pathways. Such an environmental disruption could be chemical exposure to the mother, physical stress to the pregnancy, or anything else exogenous to the embryo. Increasingly, it seems likely that many malformations might result from an unfortunate interaction between a compromising allele of some key gene and an environmental trigger, neither of which would necessarily cause a birth defect on its own. A birth defect can occur as an isolated malformation or as part of a syndrome, in which

multiple defects occur in a group of organs and structures. The latter case, a syndromic association of birth defects, is likely to reflect a disruption in a key developmental process or population of precursor cells. For example, a mutation causing a defect in the migration of NCCs could cause major malformations of the face, skull, heart, and many other structures. In contrast, a mutation in a gene required for palatal fusion might result in cleft palate but no other defects. Here we describe several representative classes of craniofacial birth defects and their origins (Table 2).

HOLOPROSENCEPHALY

This major class of birth defects occurs because of insufficient tissue along the midline of the ventral prosencephalon and/or facial precursors. This deficiency of midline structures can show varying levels of severity. Defects can range from a single central upper incisor (Fig. 4A), to close-set eyes (hypotelorism), to either no nose (arhinia) or a single nostril (cebocephaly; Fig. 4B), or even to cyclopia, with a nose-like proboscis above the eye field (Fig. 4C). Alcohol consumption by pregnant females can result in midline facial deficiencies and mental retardation in the developing progeny. Unfortunately, pregnant women are normally unaware of their pregnancy during the critical period for forebrain formation, during weeks 3 and 4 of gestation. Holoprosencephalies occur in as many as 1 in 250 conceptuses and 1 in 5000–16,000 live births.[3,7]

PHARYNGEAL ARCH DEFECTS

Arch defects often involve the tissues of the viscerocranium and are frequently caused by improper development of NCC derivatives. These defects include micrognathia (Fig. 4E), agnathia, and palatal or mandibular clefting. Mandibulofacial dysostoses are included in a large number of syndromes, including Treacher-Collins, Hallerman-Streiff, and Franceschetti's syndromes.[3,4]

TISSUE FUSION DEFECTS

Facial fusion defects occur when the epithelia of the facial primordia fail to fuse properly, causing facial clefting. The facial cleft sequence can involve a combination of complete or incomplete, bilateral or unilateral clefting of the lip, palate, or nostril (Fig. 4D). It can also include failure of fusion of the mandibular processes or the mandible to the maxilla, causing improper lateral restriction of the mouth. These defects often cause problems in eating and breathing and require corrective plastic surgery.[3]

TABLE 2. REPRESENTATIVE CONGENITAL MALFORMATIONS OF THE HEAD

Structure	Birth defect	Major origin	References Embryological	Molecular	Clinical
Skull vault	Craniosynostosis Apert Syndrome Pfeiffer Syndrome Crouzon Syndrome	Premature fusion of the cranial sutures	3	8	9
	Microcephaly	Severe underdevelopment of the skull and cerebrum			
Jaw	Micrognathia Agnathia DiGeorge Syndrome	Dysgenesis of the mandible	13, 14	4, 14	9, 10
Palate/mouth	Cleft lip/palate	Failure of fusion of a combination of the nasal and maxillary processes	12, 14	4, 11, 14	9
	Pierre Robin Sequence	U-shaped cleft palate, micrognathia, retracted tongue			
	DiGeorge Syndrome				
Face	Microsomia	Velocardiofacial defects Underdevelopment of various facial features	13, 14	7, 14	9
	Apert Syndrome Pfeiffer Syndrome Crouzon Syndrome	Abnormal fusion of facial bones			
	DiGeorge Syndrome	Velocardiofacial defects			
	Holoprosencephaly	Midline deletions			
Teeth	Ectodermal dysplasia	Two or more ectodermal anomalies	3	4, 5	9

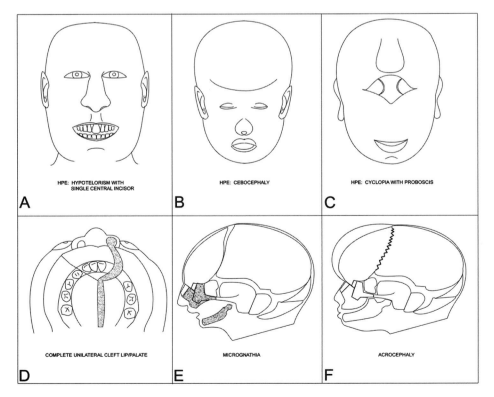

FIG. 4. Examples of craniofacial birth defects. This figure shows schematic diagrams of some craniofacial defects, including (A–C) examples of holoprosencephaly (HPE) midline defects, (D) facial clefting, (E) pharyngeal arch defect, and (F) cranial synostosis. Affected tissues are shaded.

VASCULAR DEFECTS

A defect in vascular development or blood flow can cause a variety of craniofacial defects involving hypoplasia of head tissues. For example, hemifacial microsomia (underdevelopment of one side of the face) is caused by a unilateral insufficiency of blood supply during facial development. This can result in clefting defects caused by underdevelopment of tissues that grow together and fuse. Vascular defects are also a cause of Goldenhar syndrome.[3]

SKELETAL DYSPLASIAS

This class of defects is caused by improper bone growth. Dysplasias that affect the head may involve cranial synostoses or premature fusion of the cranial sutures. This inhibits bone growth and puts pressure on the brain, which is forced to grow improperly and protrude where it can. Such defects include tower skull, or acrocephaly (Fig. 4F), and meningohydroencephaloceles. Skeletal dysplasias often involve other areas of the body including limbs, digits, and vertebrae. Some of the more common are Crouzon, Pfeiffer, Saethre-Chotzen, and Apert's syndromes.[3,8]

CONCLUSIONS

Experimental manipulations and genetic studies in mice are identifying many of the genes and pathways that control both normal craniofacial development and its anomalies. Most of the genes to date have been intercellular signaling factors, their transducers, or their targets, highlighting the prime importance of cell interactions to normal head formation. Genetic association and expression studies in humans can test whether these candidate genes are mutated or misexpressed in human congenital malformations. Rapidly advancing genomic, embryological, and medical technologies promise to bring soon a better understanding of the basis of craniofacial development and approaches toward minimizing its defects.

REFERENCES

1. Larsen WJ 1997 Human Embryology, 2nd ed. Churchill Livingstone, New York, NY, USA.
2. Holmbeck K, Bianco P, Chrysovergis K, Yamada S, Birkedal-Hansen H 2003 MT1-MMP-dependent, apoptotic remodeling of unmineralized cartilage: A critical process in skeletal growth. J Cell Biol 163:661–671.
3. Thorogood P 1997 The head and face. In: Thorogood P (ed.) Embryos, Genes and Birth Defects. John Wiley & Sons, Chichester, West Sussex, UK, pp. 197–229.
4. Cobourne MT, Sharpe PT 2003 Tooth and jaw: Molecular mechanisms of patterning in the first branchial arch. Arch Oral Biol 48:1–14.
5. Laurikkala J, Mikkola M, Mustonen T, Aberg T, Koppinen P, Pispa J, Nieminen P, Galceran J, Grosschedl R, Thesleff I 2001 TNF signaling via the ligand-receptor pair ectodysplasin and edar controls the function of epithelial signaling centers and is regulated by Wnt and activin during tooth organogenesis. Dev Biol 229:443–455.
6. Anderson RN, Smith BL 2005 Deaths: Leading causes for 2002. Natl Vital Stat Rep 53:17.
7. Wallis D, Muenke M 2000 Mutations in holoprosencephaly. Hum Mutat 16:99–108.
8. Yu HM, Jerchow B, Sheu TJ, Liu B, Costantini F, Puzas JE, Birchmeier W, Hsu W 2005 The role of Axin2 in calvarial morphogenesis and craniosynostosis. Development 132:1995–2005.
9. Jones KL 1988 Smith's Recognizable Patterns of Human Malformation, 4th ed. W.B. Saunders, Philadelphia, PA, USA.
10. Singh DJ, Bartlett SP 2005 Congenital mandibular hypoplasia: Analysis and classification. J Craniofac Surg 16:291–300.
11. Houdayer C, Portnoi M, Vialard F, Soupre V, Crumiere C, Taillemite J, Couderc R, Vasquez M, Bahuau M 2001 Pierre robin sequence and interstitial deletion 2q32.3-q33.2. Am J Med Genet 102:219–226.
12. Schubert J, Jahn H, Berginski M 2005 Experimental aspects of the pathogenesis of robin sequence. Cleft Palate Craniofac J 42:372–376.
13. Hunt JA, Hobar PC 2003 Common craniofacial abnormalities: The facial dysostoses. Plast Reconstr Surg 112:606–615.
14. Goodman FR 2003 Congenital abnormalities of body patterning: Embryology revisited. Lancet 362:651–662.

Chapter 84. Development and Structure of Teeth and Periodontal Tissues

Alan Boyde and Sheila J. Jones

Centre for Oral Growth and Development, Queen Mary, University of London, London, United Kingdom

NORMAL DENTAL DEVELOPMENT

Three of the five distinct types of mineralized tissues found in the human body, enamel, dentine, and cementum, only occur in teeth. Because turnover in these tissues is nonexistent or minimal, they form a valuable, permanent record of conditions prevailing at their time of formation; this extends throughout fetal life and up to adulthood. Moreover, the enamel and dentine of the crowns of the deciduous teeth are available for analysis without surgical intervention when the teeth are shed naturally. Enamel is a surface tissue of epithelial origin, whereas dentine and cementum are avascular connective tissues of mesenchymal origin. Teeth form at special locations within the jaws mapped out by the overlapping of molecular signals common to many developmental processes.[1] Tooth development is rigorously controlled by regulatory genes determining tooth type (incisor, canine, premolar, or molar) and shape.[2] Sequential local interactions at the interface between epithelium over the facial processes and mesenchyme derived from the cranial neural crest play a crucial role in tooth morphogenesis,[3] the main signaling molecules being members of the Hedgehog, bone morphogenetic protein, fibroblast growth factor, Wnt (wingless), and TNF families.[4-7]

The embryonic tooth germ passes through three morphological stages, described as bud, cap, and bell, and has three main components, the enamel organ, the dental papilla, and the dental follicle. The epithelial enamel organ differentiates into a four-layered structure, within which the enamel knot is the signaling center that regulates tooth shape and size.[6] A complex sequence of epithelial–mesenchymal interactions results in waves of differentiation that start at the eventual enamel–dentine junction underlying the cusp tips—determined by the spatio-temporal induction of secondary enamel knots—and

The authors have reported no conflicts of interest.

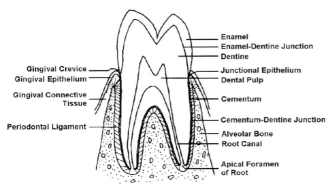

FIG. 1. Organization of dental and periodontal tissues in the erupted tooth.

incisal central mammelons (rounded prominences on biting edges when incisors first erupt) and spread away, eventually delineating the whole junction between the tissues as the tooth germ grows. The expression of secretory signaling molecules varies continuously in the different cell types during tooth initiation and construction.[8] Odontoblasts, which make dentine, are postmitotic cells that differentiate from mesenchymal cells of the dental papilla at the interface with the inner enamel epithelial cells of the enamel organ, which themselves differentiate into pre-ameloblasts. Dentine formation triggers the pre-ameloblasts to differentiate into ameloblasts, the cells that produce enamel.[9] A bilayer of epithelial cells, the epithelial root sheath, extends from the enamel organ at the base of the developing crown to map out the dentine–cementum junction and initiate the differentiation of the odontoblasts of the root. The third tissue type, cementum, is the product of both fibroblasts and cementoblasts, which differentiate from mesenchymal cells of the dental follicle adjacent to the dentine once epithelial cells of the root sheath have moved away from the interface.[8] In human teeth, a small amount of afibrillar cementum may form on the enamel surface close to the junction between the crown and the root if there are interruptions in the covering layer of epithelial cells once enamel formation has been completed. Within the developing tooth, a core of loose connective tissue remains and eventually forms the dental pulp.

The dental follicle, also derived from cells of the cranial neural crest, gives rise to three components of the periodontium: cementum, alveolar bone, and the intervening periodontal ligament. The tooth germs are partially enclosed by the developing alveolar bone—this is initially typical woven bone, formed by osteoblasts, with enclosed osteocytes, and is remodeled to accommodate the growing teeth by osteoclasts of hematopoietic origin. The follicle, a sac of loose connective tissue that separates the developing tooth from its bony crypt, is essential for eruption and will become the periodontal ligament on tooth eruption.[11] This tissue contributes extrinsic collagen fibers to the cementum and alveolar bone, and its main cell type is the fibroblast (see Fig. 1 for a diagram of a mature tooth and its components).

NORMAL DENTAL STRUCTURE

Enamel

Enamel matrix is delicate when first secreted, at which time it is protected by the soft enamel organ. The mature, erupted enamel—the hardest of the hard tissues—is acellular and may contain 98% by weight or 93% by volume of an apatitic calcium phosphate of variable composition.[12,13] The final

strength of enamel partly derives from the dentine mold on which it grows. The junction between these tissues is ill-defined and irregular on a microscopic scale, with tongues of dentine projecting into the enamel, crystals of indeterminate provenance at the common boundary, and many fine, short enamel tubules marking where ameloblast processes once contacted odontoblasts. Spindles, expanded continuations of dentine tubules within enamel, most likely result from the envelopment of individual ameloblasts that died as amelogenesis commenced. The extracellular proteinaceous matrix of developing enamel is secreted by ameloblasts, which are highly polarized, tall cells. Its main component is amelogenin, a tissue-specific protein rich in proline, leucine, histidine, and glutamyl residues. Other, nonacidic proteins include enamelin, tuftelin, and ameloblastin (amelin, sheathlin): this 3D protein array is thought to control crystal growth.[14] To achieve enamel's high degree of mineralization, much of its organic matrix is degraded by neutral metalloproteinases and serine proteases and removed, even while ameloblasts are still secretory.[15] Enamel crystals are, even initially, very long and slender, with centers richer in carbonate; however, the net carbonate content falls as they thicken. In humans, relatively large amounts of mineral accumulate at early stages of development, and the enamel has a long postsecretory maturation period during which it becomes hard and the ameloblasts remain active. The maturation phase may last 5 years or more in human third permanent molars. In species with rapid enamel development, cyclical changes in morphology of the maturation ameloblasts are seen to coincide with episodic matrix removal. Enamel's final composition and mechanical properties are not uniform.

The most notable feature of enamel is the organization of the crystals into enamel "prisms" about 6 μm across and up to the enamel thickness in length, demarcated by a sharp change in crystal orientation (Figs. 2 and 3). Enamel crystals grow mainly with their long c-axes nearly parallel to each other and the larger sides of their flattened hexagonal cross-sections parallel within groups. Where the rate of formation is low, as in the superficial enamel, the secretory interface is nearly flat, and there is little variation in the underlying crystal orientation. However, during most of enamel formation, the secretory (Tomes') process of each ameloblast is lodged in a pit at the interface. Enamel matrix is released below a continuous belt of

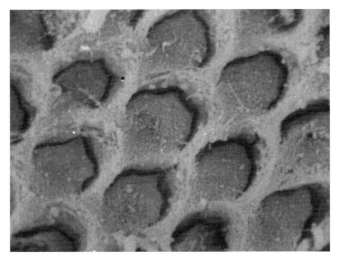

FIG. 2. External surface of cervical region of developing human permanent molar tooth, showing the morphology of the interface between ameloblasts and their calcified secretory product, the enamel. Scanning electron micrograph (SEM), field width 25 μm.

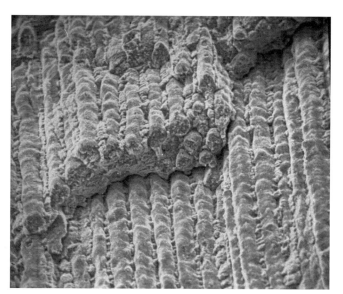

FIG. 3. Human enamel fractured to show the form of the prisms that are ~6 μm across. SEM, field width 82 μm.

intercellular attachments so as to maintain the relatively constant shape of the interface between cells and matrix (Fig. 2).[16,17] The interpit phase is continuous and the crystals have their long axes perpendicular to the general plane of the developing enamel surface. In human enamel, the dividing lines of the prism junctions are generally incomplete, and the interlocking prisms are described as keyhole-shaped. The concentration of the cleavage products of the enamel proteins at the discontinuities in crystal orientation increases relatively during enamel maturation. Tufts and lamellae are other regions that finally contain less mineral and higher concentrations of proteins.[17]

As ameloblasts move away from the dentine, they travel in groups across the surface that they make. This results in decussation (crossing in an X fashion) of the enamel prisms, with zones of prisms with contrasting 3D courses forming the Hunter-Schreger bands. The sides of the prisms show varicosities (Fig. 3) with the same period as cross-striations in the prisms, which are thought to be caused by circadian changes in the composition of the mineral component.[17] A prominence of the cross-striations occurs at 7- to 10-day intervals (the regular striae of Retzius), and major life events, such as birth (the neonatal line) or severe illness during enamel formation, may be recorded as conspicuous incremental lines. At the finished enamel surface, perikymata or imbrication lines are outcrops of the internal growth layers. They grade from horizontal bands displaying pits alternating with smoother regions at more incisal or occlusal levels, to near the neck of the tooth, small steps at the sharp boundary between the imbricating layers.

The unerupted crown is protected from resorption by a layer of cells termed the reduced enamel epithelium, comprising remnants of mature ameloblasts. These are lost once the tooth erupts. As the tooth wears during function, the surface features of the enamel become abraded, microcracks develop particularly along developmental faults, and the chemistry of the mineral exposed to the oral environment changes.

Dentine

Dentine forms the bulk of the tooth and extends within both crown and root. It is a pale creamy yellow color, in contrast to the much whiter, harder enamel. Dentine is tough and elastic,

and its prime feature is its penetration by odontoblast tubules that radiate out from the dental pulp to the periphery (Fig. 4). These, with their many side branches that remain in the tubules within the dentine, are analogous to the canaliculi that house osteocyte processes in bone. The peripheral, first formed dentine is termed mantle dentine, and the inner layer is termed circumferential dentine. After differentiating from cells of the dental papilla, the odontoblasts retreat centripetally as a cone-shaped monolayer sheet, depositing a collagenous predentine matrix and leaving lengthening cell processes.[18] The curved paths that the cell bodies take are therefore recorded in the extracellular matrix. This is similar to that of bone, comprising mainly type I collagen, acidic proteins, and proteoglycans. The predominant noncollagenous protein in dentine is the highly phosphorylated dentine phosphoprotein (phosphophoryn). This and dentine sialoprotein[19] are cleavage products of dentine sialophosphoprotein and are formed during the maturation of predentine into dentine. Dentine matrix protein 1 and other sialic acid–rich phosphoproteins common to dentine and bone are also present. Decorin, biglycan, lumican, and fibromodulin are the main proteoglycans in predentine.[20] The predentine matrix matures progressively, and the collagen fibrils thicken and compact and mineralize after a lag time of ~4 days.[21]

Dentine contains ~70% mineral (wet weight). Carbonate-rich calcium phosphate (hydroxyapatite) crystals initially form in relation to submicroscopic vesicles shed by the odontoblasts in the mantle layer or at sites on collagen fibrils rich in noncollagenous proteins. Mineralization extends radially from initial nucleation sites in the matrix, possibly by a process of secondary nucleation, forming regions of dentine known as calcospherites. These may fail to fuse, leaving unmineralized interglobular dentine between them. In a second, concurrent pattern of mineralization, crystals extend along the fine type I collagen fibrils that lie in a feltwork parallel to the incremental surface. Peritubular dentine is deposited within the tubules, partially or sometimes completely occluding them. It contains a negligible amount of collagen and mineralizes to a higher degree than the surrounding bulk intertubular dentine.

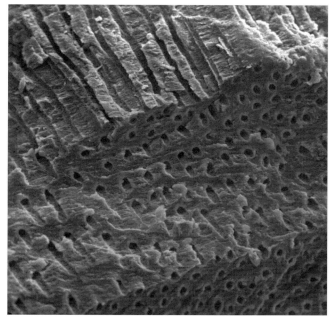

FIG. 4. Human dentine fractured to display the tubules that are ~2 μm across. SEM, field width 88 μm.

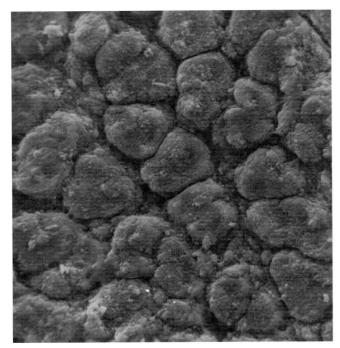

FIG. 5. Human cementum surface, made anorganic, showing mineralized ends of extrinsic fibers, ~6 μm diameter, separated by intrinsic fibers. SEM, field width 30 μm.

Because it is harder and more wear-resistant than intertubular dentine, it stands proud on teeth worn through to dentine.

Like enamel, dentine is deposited rhythmically, leaving lines marking daily and approximately weekly increments.[22] Major life events, such as birth (the neonatal line) and illness, or dietary deficiencies are recorded as disturbances in the structure of the tissue forming at the time. Once eruption has occurred and root formation is complete, further dentine formation occurs as slowly deposited, regular secondary dentine or, irregularly, as a response of the pulp–dentine complex to attrition or disease. Nerves pass from the dental pulp between odontoblasts and extend into the dentine tubules for variable distances. Dentine is acquisitively painful if touched or subjected to large temperature or osmotic changes.

Like any other loose connective tissue, the dental pulp shows signs of aging, which may include diffuse or local calcifications and the formation of dental stones. In the roots of human teeth, occlusion of the tubules with peritubular dentine extends coronally from the root apex; the resulting transparent dentine can be used as a guide to the age of the tooth.

Cementum

Cementum is a calcified connective tissue that is deposited initially on the newly mineralized dentine matrix of the root by cells derived from the dental follicle.[10] Secretory proteins from the cells of the epithelial root sheath may be included in the first-formed matrix. Cementum is laid down centrifugally from the cement–dentine junction and is marked by incremental lines that are close together, continuous, and evenly spaced where apposition was slow and patchy and irregular otherwise. The tissue is similar to bundle (Sharpey fiber) bone in that it incorporates extrinsic collagen fibers formed by fibroblasts.[23] These fibers may be very closely packed, comprising the whole tissue in slowly forming acellular cementum (Fig. 5), or be separated from each other by intervening intrinsic collagen fibers, of cementoblast

origin, which lie in the plane of the developing root surface (Fig. 3). Where cementum is deposited very rapidly, it is cellular, containing cementocytes that resemble the osteocytes of bundle bone (Fig. 6). In heavily remodeled root apices, there may be patches of cellular cementum without extrinsic fibers. Only in cementum-containing intrinsic fibers may a well-defined region of unmineralized precementum, equivalent to osteoid, be present at the surface of the tissue. The collagen of both the extrinsic and intrinsic fibers is type I. The main non-collagenous proteins of cementum identified so far (bone sialoprotein, osteopontin, osteocalcin, and α-2-HS-glycoprotein) vary in amount and distribution in the types of cementum and do not distinguish it from other calcified connective tissues[24,25] (Table 1).

Cementum mineralization reflects the rate of formation and the composition of the matrix. In afibrillar coronal cementum, the layer of noncollagenous proteins adsorbed on to the enamel surface mineralizes fully. At the cementum–dentine junction, collagen fibrils and non-collagenous constituents of the two tissues mingle without a regular, distinct border or osteopontin-rich hypermineralized cement line. The extrinsic fibers of slowly forming cementum mineralize completely, the advancing mineralized front across the fibers being relatively flat and defining a border between cementum and the dental sac or periodontal ligament. This type of cementum is more highly mineralized, more translucent, and paler than dentine. Where only a small proportion of intrinsic fibers exists in acellular cementum, the extrinsic fibers lead the mineralization front. As the rate of deposition of cementum increases and proportionately more intrinsic fibers are deposited, the likelihood that the extrinsic fibers will retain unmineralized cores increases. During periods of fast cellular cementogenesis, even the intrinsic fibers may retain unmineralized centers, and the mineralization front becomes irregular, with the extrinsic component lagging behind the intrinsic. This cementum type is the softest and least well mineralized of the calcified dental tissues. The mineralization front can be read to estimate the current rate of formation and the degree of mineralization of the fibers within the tissue

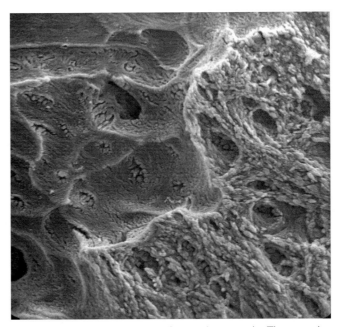

FIG. 6. Human alveolar bone surface made anorganic. The resorption lacunae reveal that the extrinsic (Sharpey's) fibers were only partly mineralized. The remainder of the surface was forming, as evidenced by incomplete mineralization of intrinsic and extrinsic fibers. SEM, field width 110 μm.

TABLE 1. Main Constituents of Dental Tissues

	Enamel	Dentine	Cementum
Proteins	Amelogenin: major protein in immature enamel, secreted by ameloblasts, then degraded and removed. Non-amelogenin proteins (enamelins): includes Enamelin and Tuftelin; secreted by ameloblasts. Ameloblastin: also known as amelin or sheathlin, secreted by ameloblasts and odontoblasts	Collagen type 1 Dentine sialophosphoprotein (DSPP): in predentine, then degraded Dentine sialoprotein (DSP): in dentine, processed from DSPP Dentine phosphoprotein (DPP): in dentine, processed from DSPP Dentine matrix protein 1 (DMP1)	Collagen type 1 Bone sialoprotein Osteopontin Osteocalcin α2HS-glycoprotein
Proteoglycans		Decorin: chondroitin-sulphate-rich Biglycan: chondroitin-sulphate-rich Lumican: keratan-sulphate-rich Fibromodulin: keratan-sulphate-rich	Decorin: in cellular cementum only Biglycan: in cellular cementum only, in incremental lines Lumican: in cellular cementum only Versican: in cementocyte lacunae only
Proteinases	Enamelysin (MMP-20): metalloprotease in immature enamel, processes enamel proteins in secretory phase of amelogenesis Kallikrein 4 (KLK4): also known as Enamel matrix serine protease-1 (EMSP1); in immature enamel, also secreted by odontoblasts, clears enamel proteins during enamel maturation phase	Matrix metalloproteinases (MMP2): in predentine, degrade and process dentine proteins secreted by odontoblasts	

indicates past rates.[23] The carbonate-rich apatite phase is similar to bone salt.

INTERRELATIONSHIPS OF TEETH, PERIODONTAL TISSUES, AND ALVEOLAR BONE

Teeth are a highly specialized part of an integrated functional unit (see Fig. 1), the primary (but not sole) purpose of which is the mastication of food. Unique among the human calcified tissues, enamel is destined to be exposed to an external environment. As the tooth erupts, the alveolar bone is resorbed to allow its passage, its root develops, and the crown pierces the oral mucosa that finally contributes to a tight ring seal of epithelial cells on the enamel close to the junction of crown and root. The complex molecular signaling cascades in the dental follicle controlling eruption and root growth are unclear.[11] At emergence, the root of the tooth is not yet fully formed, and the pulpal aspect of the root end (apex) resembles a large closing cone in bone. Root completion takes ~18 months more in the deciduous teeth and up to 3 years in the permanent teeth. During root development, the follicle becomes organized into the periodontal ligament that supports the tooth, provides nutrition and mechanosensation, and allows physiological tooth movement. Through the groups of fibers of the periodontal ligament, comprising types I and III collagen, functioning teeth are linked to each other, the gingiva, and the alveolar bone. On either side of the ligament, its principal fibers are incorporated within cementum and bundle bone; within the ligament, there is constant adaptive remodeling of the soft tissue.

Cementum in permanent teeth sees little remodeling, but the surface of alveolar bone (Fig. 6) is continually resorbing and forming to allow the tooth to move in response to eruption, growth drift, or changing functional forces. Resorption of deciduous tooth roots begins shortly after their completion, appearing first and most extensively on the aspect adjacent to the successional tooth. Interspersed between resorptive bursts are occasional short periods of repair by cemento(osteo)blasts.

Odontoclasts—typical osteoclasts—resorb both cementum and dentine and, in deciduous molars, a small mount of enamel.

REFERENCES

1. Thesleff I 2000 Genetic basis of tooth development and dental defects. Acta Odontol Scand **58:**191–194.
2. Jernvall J, Thesleff I 2000 Reiterative signaling and patterning during mammalian tooth morphogenesis. Mech Dev **92:**19–29.
3. Miletich I, Sharpe PT 2004 Neural crest contribution to mammalian tooth formation. Birth Defects Res C Embryo Today **72:**200–212.
4. James CT, Ohazama A, Tucker AS, Sharpe PT 2002 Tooth development is independent of a Hox patterning programme. Dev Dyn **225:**332–335.
5. Thesleff I, Mikkola M 2002 The role of growth factors in tooth development. Int Rev Cytol **217:**93–135.
6. Mustonen T, Tummers M, Mikami T, Itoh N, Zhang N, Grindley T, Thesleff I 2002 Lunatic fringe, FGF, and BMP regulate the Notch pathway during epithelial morphogenesis of teeth. Dev Biol **248:**281–293.
7. Ohazama A, Sharpe PT 2004 TNF signalling in tooth development. Curr Opin Genet Dev **14:**513–519.
8. Smith AJ, Lesot H 2001 Induction and regulation of crown dentinogenesis: Embryonic events as a template for dental tissue repair?. Crit Rev Oral Biol Med **12:**425–437.
9. Thesleff I, Åberg T 1997 Tooth morphogenesis and the differentiation of ameloblasts. In: Chadwick D, Cardew G (eds.) Dental Enamel. Wiley, Chichester, UK, pp. 1–17.
10. Diekwisch TG 2001 The developmental biology of cementum. Int J Dev Biol **45:**695–706.
11. Wise GE, Frazier-Bowers S, D'Souza RN 2002 Cellular, molecular, and genetic determinants of tooth eruption. Crit Rev Oral Biol Med **13:**323–334.
12. Elliott JC 1997 Structure, crystal chemistry and density of enamel apatites. In: Chadwick D, Cardew G (eds.) Dental Enamel. Wiley, Chichester, UK, pp. 54–67.
13. Elliott JC, Wong FS, Anderson P, Davis GR, Dowker SE 1998 Determination of mineral concentration in dental enamel from X-ray attenuation measurements. Connect Tiss Res **38:**61–79.
14. Diekwisch TGH, Berman BJ, Anderton X, Gurinsky B, Ortega AJ, Satchell PG, Williams M, Arumugham C, Luan X, McIntosh JE, Yamane A, Carlson DS, Sire J-Y, Shuler CF 2002 Membranes, minerals, and proteins of developing vertebrate enamel. Microsc Res Tech **59:**373–395.
15. Simmer JP, Hu JC 2002 Expression, structure, and function of enamel proteinases. Connect Tiss Res **43:**441–449.

16. Boyde A 1997 Microstructure of enamel. In: Chadwick D, Cardew G (eds.) Dental Enamel. Wiley, Chichester, UK, pp. 18–31.
17. Boyde A 1989 Enamel. In: Oksche A, Vollrath L (eds.) Handbook of Microscopic Anatomy. Springer Verlag, Berlin, Germany, pp. 309–473.
18. Sasaki T, Garant PR 1996 Structure and organization of odontoblasts. Anat Rec 245:235–249.
19. Butler WT, Brunn JC, Qin C, McKee MD 2002 Extracellular matrix proteins and the dynamics of dentin formation. Connect Tiss Res 43:301–307.
20. Embery G, Hall R, Waddington R, Septier D, Goldberg M 2001 Proteoglycans in dentinogenesis. Crit Rev Oral Biol Med 12:331–349.
21. Linde A, Goldberg M 1993 Dentinogenesis. Crit Rev Oral Biol Med 4:679–728.
22. Dean MC, Scandrett AE 1996 The relation between long-period incremental markings in dentine and daily cross-striations in enamel in human teeth. Arch Oral Biol 41:233–241.
23. Jones SJ 1989 Cement. In: Osborn JW (ed.) Dental Anatomy and Embryology. Blackwell Scientific, Boston, MA, USA, pp. 193–205 and 286–294.
24. McKee MD, Zalzal S, Nanci A 1996 Extracellular matrix in tooth cementum and mantle dentin: Localization of osteopontin and other noncollagenous proteins, plasma proteins and glycoconjugates by electron microscopy. Anat Rec 245:293–312.
25. Sasano Y, MaruyaY, Sato H, Zhu JX, Takahashi I, Mizoguchi I, Kagayama M 2001 Distinctive expression of extracellular matrix molecules at mRNA and protein levels during formation of cellular and acellular cementum in the rat. Histochem J 33:91–99.

Chapter 85. Dental Manifestations of Disorders of Bone and Mineral Metabolism

Paul H. Krebsbach and James P. Simmer

Department of Biologic and Materials Sciences, School of Dentistry, University of Michigan, Ann Arbor, Michigan

ORAL MANIFESTATIONS OF GENETIC SKELETAL DISORDERS

The skeleton contains two of the five mineralized tissues in the body: bone and calcified cartilage. The other three mineralized tissues, dentin, enamel, and cementum, are found in teeth. The mineral in each of these hard tissues is a biological apatite resembling calcium hydroxyapatite $Ca_{10}^{2+}(PO_4^{3-})_6(OH^-)_2$ in structure, with the most common substitutions being carbonate (CO_3^{2-}) for phosphate (PO_4^{3-}), and fluoride (F^-) for hydroxyl (OH^-). Therefore, disorders involving the regulation of calcium and phosphate metabolism potentially affect multiple hard tissues. In every mineralizing tissue, biomineralization occurs in a defined extracellular space. Establishing these extracellular mineralizing environments involves the synthesis and secretion of extracellular matrix proteins, the transport of ions, and matrix turnover. While each mineralizing tissue is in many ways unique, there are common elements that, when defective, lead to pathologies in multiple hard tissues. Changes in the dentition and its supporting oral structures may occur in response to disorders of mineral metabolism. The clinical presentations in these disorders may vary from mild asymptomatic changes to alterations that severely alter the form and function of craniofacial structures. In some cases, the oral phenotype may be the earliest or most obvious sign of a broader syndrome involving bone and mineral metabolism and lead to the original diagnosis. This chapter provides a concise overview of the dental manifestations of selected disorders of bone and mineral metabolism.

Osteogenesis Imperfecta, Dentinogenesis Imperfecta, and Dentin Dysplasia

Defects in either the $\alpha1$ chains or $\alpha2$ chain of type I collagen can cause osteogenesis imperfecta (OI). OI is associated with assorted dentin defects that are collectively designated as dentinogenesis imperfecta (DGI).[1] In rare cases, the dentin defects are the only prominent phenotype.[2] It has been reported that 10–50% of patients afflicted with OI also have DGI. This assessment, however, may underestimate the true prevalence because mild forms of DGI may require microscopic analysis for diagnosis.[3] Dental abnormalities have been described in several subtypes of OI, but are most prevalent in OI types IB, IC, and IVB.[4] The range of dental defects observed in osteogenesis imperfecta are similar to those observed in kindreds with DGI and dentin dysplasia (DD).

The most abundant noncollagenous proteins in dentin are proteolytic cleavage products of a large chimeric protein known as dentin sialophosphoprotein (DSPP). The intact DSPP protein has never been identified in dentin, but three cleavage products spanning the entire length of DSPP have been isolated and partially characterized. Dentin sialoprotein (DSP) is a proteoglycan with both N- and O-linked glycosylations and two glycosaminoglycan attachments comprised of long chondroitin 6-sulfate chains.[5] Dentin glycoprotein DGP is a small, phosphorylated glycoprotein.[6] Dentin phosphoprotein (DPP) is highly phosphorylated protein, with the lowest (most acidic) isoelectric point (∼1) of any known protein. DPP is thought to participate in the nucleation of hydroxyapatite crystallites on collagen.[7] In the past few years, nine different *DSPP* (4q21.3) mutations have been linked to inherited dentin defects in kindreds with DD-type II, DGI-type II, and DGI-type III phenotypes.[8–14] No mutations in candidate genes encoding other extracellular matrix proteins, such as osteopontin, bone sialoprotein, and dentin matrix protein-1, have been identified. Like type I collagen, the *DSPP* gene is expressed in bone, as well as dentin. Despite this, no bony defects have been reported in any of the kindreds with dentin defects linked to *DSPP* mutations.

The clinical classification system most often used to categorize inherited defects of dentin was established >30 years ago, before recent discoveries concerning their genetic etiologies, and divided the phenotypes into two disease groups with five subtypes: dentinogenesis imperfecta (DGI, types I–III) and dentin dysplasia (DD, types I and II), with all forms showing an autosomal dominant pattern of inheritance.[15] Type I DGI is a collective designation for OI with DGI and has largely been abandoned in deference to the current OI classification system. An alternative designation for isolated inherited dentin defects is hereditary opalescent dentin.[16] Type II DGI is the most prevalent inherited dentin phenotype. Clinically, the teeth of individuals with DGI are characterized by an amber-like appearance (Fig. 1). The teeth are narrower at the cervical margins and thus exhibit a bulbous or bell-shaped crown. Micro-

The authors have reported no conflicts of interest.

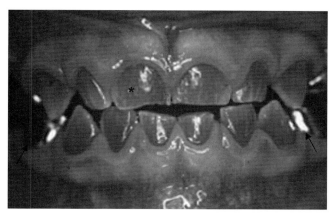

FIG. 1. Dental manifestations of teeth from a patient with dentinogenesis imperfecta. The permanent teeth of this patient exhibit the characteristic blue-gray or opalescent appearance associated with dentinogenesis imperfecta (asterisks). The enamel of the posterior teeth has fractured and the underlying dentin has undergone severe attrition. Crowns have been made to control further destruction (arrows).

scopic anomalies of affected dentin include fewer and irregular dentin tubules containing vesicles and abnormally thick collagen fibers.[17] The mineral content of DGI teeth is reduced, being about 30% less than normal dentin and intrafibrillar collagen mineralization is absent. The structurally abnormal dentin may not provide adequate support for the overlying enamel. Although enamel is chemically and structurally normal in individuals with DGI, the lack of support from dentin leads to fracturing and severe attrition of the teeth, the distinguishing clinical feature of type II DGI. Type III DGI is a rare form that is also known as the "Brandywine isolate," after the prototype kindred identified in Brandywine, Maryland. This form features multiple pulp exposures in the deciduous teeth, which show considerable variation radiographically, ranging from shell teeth, to normal pulp chambers, to pulpal obliteration. The permanent teeth are the same as in type II DGI. In type I dentin dysplasia both the permanent and deciduous teeth seem to have a normal shape and color clinically. Dental radiographs, however, show the teeth have short roots with periapical radiolucencies in noncarious teeth (Fig. 2). The primary teeth show total obliteration of the pulp. Type II dentin dysplasia seems to be a mild form of type II DGI, featuring amber tooth coloration with total pulpal obliteration in the primary teeth and a thistletube pulp configuration with ubiquitous pulp stones and normal to near normal coloration in the permanent teeth.[15,18,19]

Osteopetrosis

The lack of appropriate bone resorption observed in osteopetrosis has several implications in the craniofacial region. The jawbones are abnormally dense at the expense of cancellous bone and these changes may affect normal tooth development. Because normal tooth eruption is dependent on resorption of alveolar bone surrounding the developing tooth germ, inadequate resorptive function in osteopetrosis may limit the eruptive mechanisms and place altered forces on the erupting teeth. Dental findings associated with osteopetrosis include congenitally absent teeth, unerupted and malformed teeth, delayed eruption, and enamel hypoplasia.[20] There is a reduced calcium-phosphorous ratio in both enamel and dentin that may alter hydroxyapatite crystal formation and contribute to an increased caries index, as has been reported in several cases. Additionally, there are deviations in amino acid content, indicative of altered matrix composition.[20] Perhaps the most serious dental complication of osteopetrosis is the propensity

to develop osteomyelitis.[21] Because the vascular supply to the jaws is compromised, avascular necrosis and infection after dental extractions may lead to osteomyelitis that is difficult to treat. Thus, extraction of teeth must be performed as atraumatically as possible.

Mucopolysaccharidoses

Lysosomal storage disorders comprise >40 inherited diseases that are caused primarily by defects in genes encoding lysosomal enzymes.[22,23] Among the lysosomal storage disorders are the mucopolysaccharidoses (MPS), which are characterized by the accumulation of partially degraded glycosaminoglycans (previously called mucopolysaccharides) within lysosomes, as well as in the urine. There are 10 enzymes involved in the stepwise degradation of glycosaminoglycans, and deficiencies in these activities give rise to the MPS.[24] There are seven MPS types: I, II, III, IV, VI, VII, and IX (types V and VIII have been retired and type IX is extremely rare). The mucopolysaccharidoses are distinguished from each other based on genetic, biochemical, and clinical analyses.[4] Although heterogeneous, several craniofacial characteristics are similar between the different types. The oral manifestations may include a short and broad mandible with abnormal condylar development and limited temporomandibular joint function. The teeth are often peg-shaped and exhibit increased interdental spacing perhaps because of the frequently observed gingival hyperplasia and macroglossia. Some forms of MPS have abnormally thin enamel covering the clinical crowns or radiographic evidence of cystic lesions surrounding the molar teeth that contain excessive dermatan sulfate and collagen.[25–28]

Mucopolysaccharidosis type IVA (Morquio A syndrome, MPS IVA) is an autosomal recessive disorder caused by deficiency of the lysosomal hydrolase, *N*-acetylgalactosamine 6-sulfatase (GALNS), encoded by a gene on human chromosome 16q24.3.[29,30] Mucopolysaccharidosis type IVA is the only MPS associated with dental enamel malformation,[31] although mucopolysaccharides accumulate in the developing teeth in other MPS syndromes, such as Hurler (MPS I),[32,33] Hunter (MPS II), and Maroteaux-Lamy (MPS VI) syndromes. In MPS IVA, enamel malformations are a consistent feature. The enamel is dull gray in color, thin, pitted, and tends to flake off from the underlying dentin. The thin enamel layer is of normal hardness and radiodensity. MPS IVA patients often show severe bone dysplasia and dwarfism.

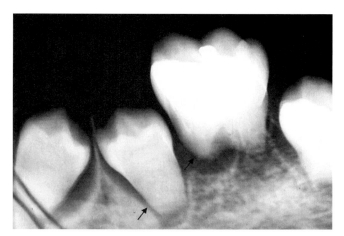

FIG. 2. Radiograph of teeth from a patient with dentin dysplasia. The roots are abnormally short or absent (arrows) and the pulp chamber is obliterated (Courtesy of Dr. Sharon Brooks).

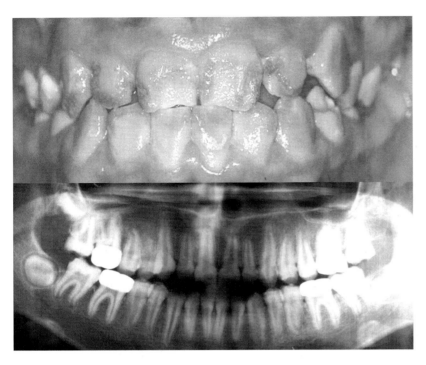

FIG. 3. Dental manifestations of vitamin D–dependent rickets type I. The oral photograph shows the dental presentation of a Hispanic patient having short stature for her age.[10] Both the enamel and the dentin are affected throughout the dentition. The oral radiograph (Panorex) shows that the teeth generally had short roots with large pulp chambers. The radiodensity of the enamel crown is similar to that of the underlying dentin. Chronic periodontal disease is often associated with this condition (Contributed by Dr. Jan C-C. Hu).

Cherubism

Cherubism is a rare autosomal dominant disorder that manifests as bilateral jaw enlargement primarily involving the mandible of children. The condition affects boys twice as often as girls, and the clinical symptoms generally are not present until the affected children reach 2–7 years of age. The clinical features of cherubism include painless, bilateral expansion of the posterior mandible, and upward turning of the eyes that impart the cherubic facies from which this rare developmental jaw condition gets its name. Radiographically, the lesions appear as multilocular, expansile radiolucencies that can interfere with normal tooth eruption. The histopathologic features may not help in the definitive diagnosis of cherubism because the fibrous lesion containing multinucleated giant cells may resemble giant cell granuloma and fibrous dysplasia.[34] However, cherubism may now be more clearly distinguished from these other conditions because a mutation associated with cherubism has been identified in the c-Abl-binding protein SH3BP2.[35] Cherubism is also a component of the Noonan-like/multiple giant cell lesion syndrome, which has additional craniofacial and skeletal abnormalities.[36] A common problem in understanding the genetic underpinnings of craniofacial disorders such as cherubism is the genetic mutation, or genotype, does not always correlate with the phenotype. That is, a mutation in one gene may result in one of several different craniosyostoses. Therefore, with our current understanding of genetic and epigenetic events, it may be more appropriate to state that a certain gene mutation is associated with the syndromic phenotype rather than state that the gene mutation causes the specific condition.

ORAL MANIFESTATIONS OF METABOLIC BONE DISEASES

Metabolic diseases of bone are disorders of bone remodeling that characteristically involve the entire skeleton and are often manifest in the oral cavity, which can lead to the diagnosis of the underlying systemic disease. Numerous studies suggest that subclinical derangements in calcium homeostasis and bone metabolism may also contribute to a variety of dental abnormalities including alveolar ridge resorption and periodontal bone loss in predisposed individuals. The significance of this spectrum of diseases and their overall impact on oral health and dental management are likely to increase as the elderly segment of the population increases in the coming decades.[37]

Vitamin D Deficiency

In vitamin D–resistant rickets, the primary oral abnormality is similar to dentin dysplasia. Enamel is usually reported to be normal, but in some instances may be hypoplastic. Patients also suffer from delayed tooth eruption, and radiographically, teeth often display enlarged pulp chambers. Other salient radiographic findings include decreased alveolar bone density, thinning of bone trabeculae, loss of lamina dura, and retarded tooth calcification.[34] In familial hypophosphatemia, dental findings are often the first clinically noticeable signs of the disease and resemble those seen in rickets and osteomalacia. Patients may present with abscessed primary or permanent teeth that have no signs of dental caries.[38] Although the enamel is reported to be normal, microbial infection of the pulp is thought to occur though invasion of dentinal tubules exposed by attrition of enamel or through enamel microfractures.[39]

Vitamin D–dependent rickets type I is an autosomal recessive defect in vitamin D metabolism caused by mutations in the *CYP27B1* gene (12q13.3-q14) encoding 25-hydroxyvitamin D-1α-hydroxylase. Decreased 1,25(OH)$_2$ vitamin D results in teeth with yellow-brown color, pitted enamel, short roots, and a tendency to develop chronic periodontal disease (Fig. 3).[40]

Hypophosphatasia

Hypophosphatasia is an inherited disorder caused by a defect in the *alkaline phosphatase (ALPL)* gene. Osteoblasts show the highest level of ALPL expression, and profound skeletal hypomineralization occurs in the severest forms of hypophosphatasia. The hard tissue that seems to be most sensitive to an ALPL defect is cementum. The classic oral presentation of hypophosphatasia is the premature loss of fully rooted primary

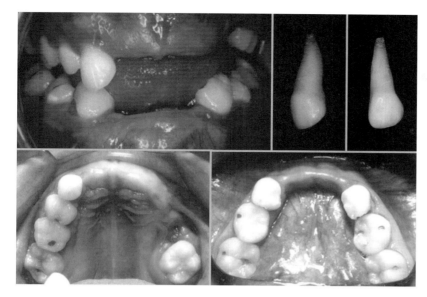

FIG. 4. Exfoliation of fully rooted primary teeth in hypophosphatasia. Oral photographs show the dental condition of a patient with childhood hypophosphatasia at the age of 6. The maxillary cuspid and incisor (top right) were brought by the parents to the visit and had fallen out naturally about 2 years previously. This patient is also showed periodontal attachment problems in her primary posterior teeth, which were mobile. Some childhood hypophosphatasia patients present with enamel hypoplasia. These dental findings are diagnostic of childhood hypophosphatasia and is often the first symptom leading to the diagnosis (Contributed by Dr. Jan C-C. Hu).

teeth (Fig. 4). Histological examination indicates that these teeth lack cementum on their root surface, so that the attachment apparatus fails to develop properly. The periodontal ligament fibers do not connect the alveolar bone to the root, and the teeth exfoliate prematurely. In the permanent teeth, large pulp spaces, late eruption, and delayed apical closure are often observed. Bone loss is primarily horizontal, and in the adult form of the disease, there may be widespread dental caries.

Paget's Disease

Paget's disease, also known as osteitis deformans, a disorder of bone remodeling,[41,42] is characterized by the presence of irregular islands of bone with prominent internal cement lines that create a mosaic pattern. In the craniofacial bones, radiographic lesions usually progress from irregular lytic lesions to areas of sclerosis that present with a distinctive cotton-wool appearance. Involvement of the maxilla is more common than the mandible where patients often present with alveolar ridge enlargement and hypercementosis. In extreme cases, the expanding alveolar ridges can lead to the separation of teeth and poor denture adaptation in the edentulous patient. As the disease progresses, there may be extensive bone deformity with nerve compression and altered blood flow, conditions that can make tooth extraction problematic.

ORAL MANIFESTATIONS OF ACQUIRED DISORDERS

Benign Non-Odontogenic Neoplasms of the Jaws

Benign fibro-osseous lesions of the jaw are a heterogeneous group of disorders characterized by the replacement of normal trabecular bone and marrow with cellular fibrous connective tissue and a disorganized array of randomly oriented mineralized tissue. The most common group of lesions is known collectively as the cemento-osseous dysplasias,[43] so named because they contain spherical calcifications believed to be of cemental origin and randomly oriented mineralized structures, sometimes resembling bone. In some cases, these lesions are also associated with long bone fragility (gnatho-diaphyseal dysplasia).[44] Two other conditions included in this category are fibrous dysplasia of bone and cherubism, which are of greater clinical significance because they tend to attain a larger

size and have the potential for producing greater facial disfigurement and severe malocclusion.

Among the cemento-osseous dysplasias, the most common is a condition known as periapical cemental dysplasia. This asymptomatic lesion presents radiographically as a mixed radiolucent/radiopaque lesion that involves a single mandibular quadrant in middle-aged women. It is frequently encountered below the apices of the mandibular incisors. The involved teeth are vital, and no treatment is required. Florid cemento-osseous dysplasia is a more extensive form of periapical cemental dysplasia that invariably involves multiple jaw quadrants. Fibrous dysplasia is a disorder that can affect single (monostotic) or multiple (polyostotic) bones and can occur as part of the McCune-Albright syndrome, where it is associated with skin pigmentation and endocrinopathies. When it occurs in the absence of endocrine abnormalities it is referred to as Jaffe syndrome. The underlying cause of fibrous dysplasia and the McCune-Albright syndrome are activating mutations in the $Gs\alpha$ gene, resulting in abnormal accumulation and maturation of precursor osteogenic cells to osteoblast cells and formation of sclerotic lesions in craniofacial bones.[45] Caries prevalence in these patients is higher than in the normal population, and prevalent dental anomalies included malocclusion, tooth rotation, oligodontia, and taurodontism.[46] Other benign expansile lesions of the jaw include the fibro-osseous tumors associated with hyperparathyroidism-jaw tumor syndrome, an autosomal dominant, multineoplasia disorder associated with primary parathyroid tumors and caused by mutation of the parafibromin gene, $HRPT2$,[47] and the exostoses seen in torus mandibularis that may be related to loss of function mutations in the gene for low-density lipoprotein receptor-related protein 5.[48]

Malignant Non-Odontogenic Neoplasms of the Jaws

Osteosarcoma is the most common malignant neoplasm derived from bone cells, occurring in 1 of every 100,000 people.[34] The peak incidence when it occurs in the jaws is ~10 years later than the peak incidence in the long bones. The radiographic appearance of osteosarcoma varies considerably depending on the histological type. Osteosarcomas that produce large amount of mineralized bone-like tissue will present as large areas of radiopacity within a diffuse radiolucent background. A characteristic finding in jaw lesions is widening of the periodontal ligament in adjacent teeth. Although this finding is not unique to osteosarcoma, it is sufficiently consistent to be of diagnostic value. Occlusal radiographs may also reveal a sunburst pattern of radiopacity radiating from the periosteum and may be of assistance diagnostically.

Bisphosphonate-Induced Osteonecrosis of the Jaw

Although intravenous bisphosphonate therapy is the standard of care for the management of hypercalcemia of malignancy and metastatic osteolytic lesions associated with multiple myeloma and other solid tumors such as in breast, prostate, and lung cancer,[49,50] recent findings point to potential complications in the jaw bones of patients undergoing this form of cancer therapy. Several groups have identified a cohort of patients that presented with exposed bone in the maxilla and mandible that resembled refractory osteomyelitis or osteoradionecrosis that is occasionally observed in patients who have received high dose radiation therapy to the jaws. In each case, patients were nonresponsive to noninvasive treatments and were receiving intravenous bisphosphonate therapy.[51–54] Conservative treatment for such avascular, necrotic lesions of the jaw involves the use of antibiotic and anti-inflammatory therapy. In more severe cases, surgical intervention has been advocated, but the results have not been consistent. At this time, because of the lack of any prospective controlled data on the success rate of different treatment modalities, conservative management is strongly recommended.

REFERENCES

1. O'Connell AC, Marini JC 1999 Evaluation of oral problems in an osteogenesis imperfecta population. Oral Surg Oral Med Oral Pathol Oral Radiol Endod 87:189–196.
2. Pallos D, Hart PS, Cortelli JR, Vian S, Wright JT, Korkko J, Brunoni D, Hart TC 2001 Novel COL1A1 mutation (G559C) [correction of G599C] associated with mild osteogenesis imperfecta and dentinogenesis imperfecta. Arch Oral Biol 46:459–470.
3. Waltimo J, Ojanotko-Harri A, Lukinmaa PL 1996 Mild forms of dentinogenesis imperfecta in association with osteogenesis imperfecta as characterized by light and transmission electron microscopy. J Oral Pathol Med 25:256–264.
4. Gorlin RJ, Cohen MMJ, Levin LS 1990 Syndromes of the head and neck. In: Motulsky AG, Harper PS, Bobrow M, Scriver C (eds.) Oxford Monographs on Medical Genetics, 3rd ed. Oxford University Press, New York, NY, USA, pp 155–166.
5. Yamakoshi Y, Hu JC, Fukae M, Iwata T, Kim JW, Zhang H, Simmer JP 2005 Porcine dentin sialoprotein is a proteoglycan with glycosaminoglycan chains containing chondroitin 6-sulfate. J Biol Chem 280:1552–1560.
6. Yamakoshi Y, Hu JC, Fukae M, Zhang H, Simmer JP 2005 Dentin glycoprotein: The protein in the middle of the dentin sialophosphoprotein chimera. J Biol Chem 280:17472–17479.
7. George A, Bannon L, Sabsay B, Dillon JW, Malone J, Veis A, Jenkins NA, Gilbert DJ, Copeland NG 1996 The carboxyl-terminal domain of phosphophorin contains unique extended triplet amino acid repeat sequences forming ordered carboxyl-phosphate interaction ridges that may be essential in the biomineralization process. J Biol Chem 271:32869–32873.
8. Dong J, Gu T, Jeffords L, MacDougall M 2005 Dentin phosphoprotein compound mutation in dentin sialophosphoprotein causes dentinogenesis imperfecta type III. Am J Med Genet A 132:305–309.
9. Kim JW, Hu JC, Lee JI, Moon SK, Kim YJ, Jang KT, Lee SH, Kim CC, Hahn SH, Simmer JP 2005 Mutational hot spot in the DSPP gene causing dentinogenesis imperfecta type II. Hum Genet 116:186–191.
10. Kim JW, Nam SH, Jang KT, Lee SH, Kim CC, Hahn SH, Hu JC, Simmer JP 2004 A novel splice acceptor mutation in the DSPP gene causing dentinogenesis imperfecta type II. Hum Genet 115:248–254.
11. Malmgren B, Lindskog S, Elgadi A, Norgren S 2004 Clinical, histopathologic, and genetic investigation in two large families with dentinogenesis imperfecta type II. Hum Genet 114:491–498.
12. Rajpar MH, Koch MJ, Davies RM, Mellody KT, Kielty CM, Dixon MJ 2002 Mutation of the signal peptide region of the bicistronic gene DSPP affects translocation to the endoplasmic reticulum and results in defective dentine biomineralization. Hum Mol Genet 11:2559–2565.
13. Xiao S, Yu C, Chou X, Yuan W, Wang Y, Bu L, Fu G, Qian M, Yang J, Shi Y, Hu L, Han B, Wang Z, Huang W, Liu J, Chen Z, Zhao G, Kong X 2001

14. Zhang X, Zhao J, Li C, Gao S, Qiu C, Liu P, Wu G, Qiang B, Lo WH, Shen Y 2001 DSPP mutation in dentinogenesis imperfecta Shields type II. Nat Genet 27: 151–152.
15. Shields ED, Bixler D, el-Kafrawy AM 1973 A proposed classification for heritable human dentine defects with a description of a new entity. Arch Oral Biol 18:543–553.
16. Witkop CJ Jr 1971 Manifestations of genetic diseases in the human pulp. Oral Surg Oral Med Oral Pathol 32:278–316.
17. Waltimo J 1994 Hyperfibers and vesicles in dentin matrix in dentinogenesis imperfecta (DI) associated with osteogenesis imperfecta (OI). J Oral Pathol Med 23:389–393.
18. Giansanti JS, Allen JD 1974 Dentin dysplasia, type II, or dentin dysplasia, coronal type. Oral Surg Oral Med Oral Pathol 38:911–917.
19. Lukinmaa PL, Ranta H, Ranta K, Kaitila I, Hietanen J 1987 Dental findings in osteogenesis imperfecta: II. Dysplastic and other developmental defects. J Craniofac Genet Dev Biol 7:127–135.
20. Dick HM, Simpson WJ 1972 Dental changes in osteopetrosis. Oral Surg Oral Med Oral Pathol 34:408–416.
21. Dyson DP 1970 Osteomyelitis of the jaws in Albers-Schonberg disease. Br J Oral Surg 7:178–187.
22. Meikle PJ, Hopwood JJ, Clague AE, Carey WF 1999 Prevalence of lysosomal storage disorders. JAMA 281:249–254.
23. Winchester B, Vellodi A, Young E 2000 The molecular basis of lysosomal storage diseases and their treatment. Biochem Soc Trans 28:150–154.
24. Neufeld E, Muenzer J 1995 The Mucopolysaccharidoses. In: Scriver C, Beaudet A, Sly W, Valle D (eds.) The Metabolic and Molecular Bases of Inherited Disease. McGraw-Hill, New York, NY, USA, pp. 2465–2494.
25. Downs AT, Crisp T, Ferretti G 1995 Hunter's syndrome and oral manifestations: A review. Pediatr Dent 17:98–100.
26. Keith O, Scully C, Weidmann GM 1990 Orofacial features of Scheie (Hurler-Scheie) syndrome (alpha-L- iduronidase deficiency). Oral Surg Oral Med Oral Pathol 70:70–74.
27. Kinirons MJ, Nelson J 1990 Dental findings in mucopolysaccharidosis type IV A (Morquio's disease type A). Oral Surg Oral Med Oral Pathol 70:176–179.
28. Smith KS, Hallett KB, Hall RK, Wardrop RW, Firth N 1995 Mucopolysaccharidosis: MPS VI and associated delayed tooth eruption. Int J Oral Maxillofac Surg 24:176–180.
29. Baker E, Guo XH, Orsborn AM, Sutherland GR, Callen DF, Hopwood JJ, Morris CP 1993 The morquio A syndrome (mucopolysaccharidosis IVA) gene maps to 16q24.3. Am J Hum Genet 52:96–98.
30. Masuno M, Tomatsu S, Nakashima Y, Hori T, Fukuda S, Masue M, Sukegawa K, Orii T 1993 Mucopolysaccharidosis IV A: Assignment of the human N-acetylgalactosamine-6-sulfate sulfatase (GALNS) gene to chromosome 16q24. Genomics 16:777–778.
31. Pedrini V, Lennzi L, Zambotti V 1962 Isolation and identification of keratosulphate in urine of patients affected by Morquio-Ullrich disease. Proc Soc Exp Biol Med 110:847–849.
32. Witkop C, Sauk JJ 1976 Heretable defects in enamel. In: Steward RE, Presscott GH (eds.) Oral Facial Genetics. C.V. Mosby Co., St. Louis, MO, USA, pp. 151–226.
33. Gardner DG 1971 The oral manifestations of Hurler's syndrome. Oral Surg Oral Med Oral Pathol 32:46–57.
34. Neville BW, Damm DD, Allen CM 1995 Oral and Maxillofacial Pathology. 1st ed. W.B.Saunders, Philadelphia, PA, USA.
35. Ueki Y, Tiziani V, Santanna C, Fukai N, Maulik C, Garfinkle J, Ninomiya C, doAmaral C, Peters H, Habal M, Rhee-Morris L, Doss JB, Kreiborg S, Olsen BR, Reichenberger E 2001 Mutations in the gene encoding c-Abl-binding protein SH3BP2 cause cherubism. Nat Genet 28:125–126.
36. Cohen MM Jr, Gorlin RJ 1991 Noonan-like/multiple giant cell lesion syndrome. Am J Med Genet 40:159–166.
37. Solt DB 1991 The pathogenesis, oral manifestations, and implications for dentistry of metabolic bone disease. Curr Opin Dent 1:783–791.
38. Goodman JR, Gelbier MJ, Bennett JH, Winter GB 1998 Dental problems associated with hypophosphataemic vitamin D resistant rickets. Int J Paediatr Dent 8:19–28.
39. Hillmann G, Geurtsen W 1996 Pathohistology of undecalcified primary teeth in vitamin D-resistant rickets: Review and report of two cases. Oral Surg Oral Med Oral Pathol Oral Radiol Endod 82:218–224.
40. Zambrano M, Nikitakis NG, Sanchez-Quevedo MC, Sauk JJ, Sedano H, Rivera H 2003 Oral and dental manifestations of vitamin D-dependent rickets type I: Report of a pediatric case. Oral Surg Oral Med Oral Pathol Oral Radiol Endod 95:705–709.
41. Carter LC 1991 Paget's disease: Important features for the general practitioner. Comp Contin Educ Dent 11:662–669.
42. Merkow RL, Lane JM 1990 Paget's disease of bone. Orthop Clin North Am 21:171–189.

43. Waldron CA 1993 Fibro-osseous lesions of the jaws. J Oral Maxillofac Surg 51:828–835.
44. Riminucci M, Collins MT, Corsi A, Boyde A, Murphey MD, Wientroub S, Kuznetsov SA, Cherman N, Robey PG, Bianco P 2001 Gnathodiaphyseal dysplasia: A syndrome of fibro-osseous lesions of jawbones, bone fragility, and long bone bowing. J Bone Miner Res 16:1710–1718.
45. Riminucci M, Liu B, Corsi A, Shenker A, Spiegel AM, Robey PG, Bianco P 1999 The histopathology of fibrous dysplasia of bone in patients with activating mutations of the Gs alpha gene: Site-specific patterns and recurrent histological hallmarks. J Pathol 187:249–258.
46. Akintoye SO, Lee JS, Feimster T, Booher S, Brahim J, Kingman A, Riminucci M, Robey PG, Collins MT 2003 Dental characteristics of fibrous dysplasia and McCune-Albright syndrome. Oral Surg Oral Med Oral Pathol Oral Radiol Endod 96:275–282.
47. Carpten JD, Robbins CM, Villablanca A, Forsberg L, Presciuttini S, Bailey-Wilson J, Simonds WF, Gillanders EM, Kennedy AM, Chen JD, Agarwal SK, Sood R, Jones MP, Moses TY, Haven C, Petillo D, Leotlela PD, Harding B, Cameron D, Pannett AA, Hoog A, Heath H, James-Newton LA, Robinson B, Zarbo RJ, Cavaco BM, Wassif W, Perrier ND, Rosen IB, Kristoffersson U, Turnpenny PD, Farnebo LO, Besser GM, Jackson CE, Morreau H, Trent JM, Thakker RV, Marx SJ, Teh BT, Larsson C, Hobbs MR 2002 HRPT2, encoding parafibromin, is mutated in hyperparathyroidism-jaw tumor syndrome. Nat Genet 32:676–680.
48. Boyden LM, Mao J, Belsky J, Mitzner L, Farhi A, Mitnick MA, Wu D, Insogna K, Lifton RP 2002 High bone density due to a mutation in LDL-receptor-related protein 5. N Engl J Med 346:1513–1521.
49. Berenson JR, Hillner BE, Kyle RA, Anderson K, Lipton A, Yee GC, Biermann JS, American Society of Clinical Oncology Bisphosphonates Expert Panel 2002 American Society of Clinical Oncology clinical practice guidelines: The role of bisphosphonates in multiple myeloma. J Clin Oncol 20:3719–3736.
50. Hillner BE, Ingle JN, Chlebowski RT, Gralow J, Yee GC, Janjan NA, Cauley JA, Blumenstein BA, Albain KS, Lipton A, Brown SJ, American Society of Clinical Oncology 2003 2003 update on the role of bisphosphonates and bone health issues in women with breast cancer. Clin Oncol 1:4042–4057.
51. Bagan JV, Murillo J, Jimenez Y, Poveda R, Milian MA, Sanchis JM, Silvestre FJ, Scully C 2005 Avascular jaw osteonecrosis in association with cancer chemotherapy: Series of 10 cases. J Oral Pathol Med 34:120–123.
52. Ficarra G, Beninati F, Rubino I, Vannucchi A, Longo G, Tonelli P, Pini Prato G 2005 Osteonecrosis of the jaws in periodontal patients with a history of bisphosphonates treatment. J Clin Periodontol 32:1123–1128.
53. Migliorati CA, Schubert MM, Peterson DE, Seneda LM 2005 Bisphosphonate-associated osteonecrosis of mandibular and maxillary bone: An emerging oral complication of supportive cancer therapy. Cancer 104:83–93.
54. Ruggiero SL, Mehrotra B, Rosenberg TJ, Engroff SL 2004 Osteonecrosis of the jaws associated with the use of bisphosphonates: A review of 63 cases. J Oral Maxillofac Surg 62:527–534.

Chapter 86. Periodontal Diseases and Bone

Marjorie K. Jeffcoat and Sundaye O. Akintoye

School of Dental Medicine, University of Pennsylvania, Philadelphia, Pennsylvania

INTRODUCTION

Periodontal diseases fall into two broad categories: gingivitis and periodontitis. Gingivitis is characterized by gingival inflammation. Its major etiologic factor is bacterial plaque accumulation on the teeth. The response to the plaque may be modified by systemic or genetic diseases and a myriad of drugs. One of the major features distinguishing gingivitis from periodontitis is the absence of alveolar bone loss in the former. Periodontitis is characterized by loss of soft tissue attachment to the tooth along with alveolar bone loss, resulting in decreased support of the tooth (Fig. 1).

DIAGNOSIS

Table 1 shows the terminology used to distinguish the various forms of periodontitis,[1] according to the American Academy of Periodontology. This chapter focuses on periodontitis, because one of the hallmarks of periodontitis is alveolar bone loss. Periodontal diseases are classified by clinical syndromes, because to date there are no definitive tests for periodontitis. The current system in the United States uses rate of progression of attachment and bone loss as the key classifying factors. In Europe, the European Academy of Periodontology uses age as the primary classifying factor.

ETIOLOGY

Periodontitis is a multifactorial disease. While the bacteria in the plaque biofilm are considered the major causative agent, susceptibility of the host plays an important role. This interaction is shown in Fig. 2. There are ~500 microbiological species that have been isolated from the oral cavity. At the gingival crevice, there is a shift from a gram-positive aerobic flora in a state of health to gram-negative anaerobic or gram-negative facultative species, which have been implicated in the pathogenesis of periodontal diseases. The bacteria in biofilm were categorized into clusters. The "red cluster," consisting of *Porphyromones gingivalis, Baceroides forsythus,* and *Treptonema denticola,* are most often associated with inflammation and attachment loss.[2]

The pathogenicity of the microbiological biofilm associated with disease is enabled by the virulence factors of the gram-negative and facultative species once they invade the tissue. The predominant virulence factors that play a role in host interaction are endotoxin, exotoxin, and bacterial enzymes.

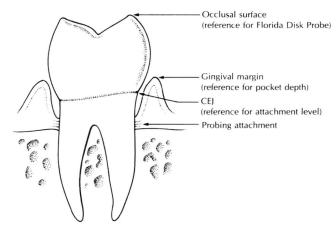

FIG. 1. Anatomy of the tooth. The soft tissue attachment is assessed clinically by measuring the distance from the cemento-enamel junction (CEJ) and pocket base. In health, the alveolar bone crest is no more than 2–3 mm apical of the CEJ.

The authors have reported no conflicts of interest.

TABLE 1. CLASSIFICATION OF PERIODONTAL DISEASES

Disease	Age	Progression	Replaces old terminology
Chronic periodontitis	Any	Slow	Adult periodontitis
Aggressive periodontitis	Any	Rapid	Juvenile, prepubertal, rapidly progressive periodontitis
Necrotizing ulcerative periodontitis	Any	Rapid	Necrotizing ulcerative periodontitis
Periodontitis as a manifestation of systemic disease	Any	Any rate	Not in older classifications

Gram-negative (lipopolysaccharide [LPS]) endotoxin produces cytotoxic effects on host tissue, resulting in tissue necrosis and bone resorption through osteoclast stimulation.[3] The exotoxins excreted by the bacteria are metabolic end products such as organic acids, amines, indole, ammonia, and sulfur compounds that produce local cytotoxic and host defense inhibitory effects. The bacterial enzymes such as collagenase, hyaluronidase, and proteinase lead to increased intracellular spaces and permeability and further enable tissue invasion.[4]

Periodontal diseases are initiated by bacteria, and the bacteria may directly interact with the host tissues in mediating the destruction. In general, there is a well-regulated host response mediated through inflammatory cells that control the spread of bacterial infection. However, the host response itself may establish a chronic inflammatory state and may play a role in the local destruction of the supporting structures of the teeth. Mediators produced as part of the inflammatory host response that contribute to tissue destruction include proteinases, cytokines, and prostaglandins. Matrix metalloproteinases are considered the primary proteinases involved in periodontal tissue destruction by degradation of extracellular molecules.[5] At least two pro-inflammatory cytokines, interleukin (IL)-1 and TNF, seem to have a central role in periodontal destruction. The properties of these cytokines that relate to tissue destruction involve the stimulation of bone resorption by IL-1 and induction of tissue-degrading proteinases by TNF.[6] Prostaglandins, especially PGE_2, seem to be partially responsible for the bone loss associated with periodontal diseases. Prostaglandins are arachidonic acid metabolites generated by cyclo-oxygenses. Cyclo-oxygenase production of PGE_2 that is associated with inflammation is upregulated by IL-1, TNF, and bacterial LPS. Clinical trials have indicated that bone loss associated with periodontitis was partially prevented by administration of inhibitors of prostaglandin synthesis.[7,8]

DIAGNOSTIC TOOLS

The diagnostic tools used today for the diagnosis of periodontal disease are primarily based on the anatomy of the lesions. Visual inspection reveals superficial signs of gingival inflammation such as edema and redness of the tissues. Periodontal probing uses a 0.5-mm probe that is placed between the tooth root and the gingiva in the pocket or sulcus. Probing depth, the distance between the base of the pocket and the gingival margin, provides some indication of prior disease progression and alerts the practitioner to the depth of the anaerobic chamber the pocket provides for growth of gram-negative anaerobic bacteria. This measure is of importance in

planning treatment because deep pockets are more difficult to clean. Probing attachment levels (or clinical attachment leads), which measure the distance from the base of the pocket to a fixed landmark such as the cemento-enamel junction, give an estimate of prior soft tissue attachment.

Radiographs are used to determine the extent of alveolar bone loss in teeth at risk. Both radiographs and probing examinations do not provide an indication of current disease activity. Rather, they represent the sum total of disease and healing that has occurred over the lifespan of the tooth. Prior studies have shown, however, that the absence of inflammation, lack of radiographic indication of bone loss, and shallow pockets are associated with a low risk of future progression.

Microbial tests aim to detect the presence of putative periodontal pathogens in a given pocket. In many cases, cultural methods have been replaced by newer ELISA and DNA testing.[2] Only cultural methods can be used to determine which antibiotics may be used to successfully treat a given bacterial infection. At present, these tests are not routinely used in the diagnosis of periodontitis but may be useful for treatment planning in aggressive or refractory disease.

Gingival crevicular fluid is a transudate of plasma. The quantity of gingival crevicular fluid is associated with inflammation. Biochemical profiles of inflammatory markers and mediators have also been studied extensively.[8] Markers such as aspartate aminotransferase, β-glucuronidase, elastase, and many cytokines are elevated in periodontitis and in progressive periodontitis.

Genetic testing has become a reality for periodontal disease. Certain IL-1β polymorphisms are associated with a higher risk of periodontitis.[9] Other cytokine polymorphisms are under study.

TREATMENT

Treatment of periodontitis is usually divided into two types: surgical and nonsurgical. While this is a helpful categorization for patients, insurance companies, and clinicians, it does not address the mechanism of each treatment modality. Therefore, treatment will be discussed in reference to Fig. 2 (treatment may be directed at the bacteria or the host).

Treatment Directed Against the Bacteria

This mode of treatment includes self-care, such as brushing and flossing, and professionally administered care (Table 2).

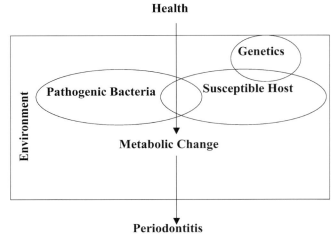

FIG. 2. Etiology of periodontal disease. Periodontal disease occurs when a pathogenic bacterial biofilm is present in a susceptible host. Genetic and environmental factors modify the ultimate response to the bacteria.

TABLE 2. NONSURGICAL THERAPY—PERIODONTITIS

Category of treatment	Treatment	Strengths	Availability
Targeted at bacteria by nonsurgical mechanical means			
Professional mechanical therapy—used in the treatment of gingivitis and periodontitis	Scaling and root planing—with manual instrument and ultrasonics	Decreases gingival inflammation by 40–60% Decreases probing depth Facilitates gain in clinical attachment level	Widespread
Targeted at bacteria by non-surgical chemotherapy			
Chemical plaque control with mouthrinses and tooth pastes	Chlorhexidine Triclosan co-polymer or triclosan zinc-citrate Essential oils Stabilized CPC	Significant reductions in gingival inflammation No evidence that there is a substantial long-term benefit for periodontitis except to control co-existing inflammation	Widespread
Sustained release antimicrobials	Intrapocket resorbable or nonresorbable delivery systems containing a tetracycline antibiotic, or chlorhexidine	When used as an adjunct to scaling and root planing, gains in clinical attachment level, and decreases in probing depth and bleeding	Widespread
Systemic antibiotics	Tetracyclines, metranidazole, spiromycin, clindamycin, azithromycin, ciproflocaxin and combinations such as metranidazole and amoxicillin	Not indicated for most adult periodontitis patients May be useful to treat aggressive destructive periodontitis	Widespread

TABLE 3. SURGICAL PERIODONTAL THERAPY—SELECTED PROCEDURE

Category and goal	Procedures	Strengths	Availability
Pocket therapy—provides access to root surfaces and bony defects, reduces probing depths, facilitates plaque control and enhances restorative and cosmetic dentistry	Gingival flap to provide access to roots and bony defects for debridement	Improvement in clinical attachment level	Widespread
Regeneration—procedures to facilitate growth of new periodontal ligament, cementum and bone over previously diseased root surfaces	Extraoral autogeneous bone grafts	High potential for bone growth	Limited
	Intraoral autogenous grafts (i.e., maxillary tuberosity, healing extraction sites, osseous coagulum)	Case reports indicate bone gain of >50% Controlled studies comparing to nongrafted bone show improved clinical attachment levels and bone, but not as great as in case reports	Widespread
	Allografts—tissue transferred from one individual to another Freeze dried bone allograft	Bone fill has been reported in a high proportion of defects, but is variable Osteogenic potential may vary from vial to vial, patient differences, and clinician variability	Widespread
	Alloplasts—synthetic grafts Absorbable: plaster, calcium carbonates, ceramics such as tricalcium phosphate and absorbable HA Nonabsorbable: dense HA, porous HA, bioglass	Improved probing depth and attachment level	Widespread
Barrier membranes	Resorbable and nonresorbable membranes	Improve attachement levels relative to flap surgery alone	Widespread

TABLE 4. GROWTH FACTORS AND BIOLOGICS

Category and goal	Procedures	Strengths	Availability
Formation of new bone and cementum	Bone morphogenetic proteins	In experimental systems forms new cementum and bone	Not commercially available
Growth factors	Platelet derived growth factor, isulin like growth factor, transforming growth factor, fibroblast growth factor	Improve healing although some studies show mixed results May be influenced by delivery system	Available from spun plasma Insulin-like factor recently approved
Improve bone fill and attachment	Enamel matrix proteins Anorganic bovine derived hydroxyapatite matrix cell-binding peptide	Fill in infrabony osseous defects	Approved
Putative collagen binding protein	Anorganic bovine-derived matrix and syntheic clone of 15 amino acid sequence of type I collagen	Limited trials have shown hard tissue fill	Cleared for marketing

TABLE 5. NONSURGICAL THERAPY—PERIODONTITIS

Category of treatment	Treatment	Strengths	Availability
MMP inhibitors low dose tetracyclines	Used in adult or chronic periodontitis	Slow the progression of attachment loss	Approved
Nonsteroidal inflammatory drugs	Used in adult or chronic periodontitis in research	Slow the progression of attachment loss	Research
Bisphosphonates	Used in adult or chronic periodontitis research	Increase bone mineral density and Slow the progression of attachment loss	Research

Targeted the host response.

Professional mechanical therapy, such as scaling and root planing, removes plaque biofilm from the tooth surface, as well as removing calculus (tartar), and it decreases endotoxin on the root surface cementum. Scaling and root planing, when performed with hand or ultrasonic instrumentation, decreases gingival inflammation, decreases probing depth, and facilitates gain in clinical attachment levels.[10] This therapy must be distinguished from a dental prophylaxis. The goal of scaling and root planing is to remove plaque, calculus, and endotoxin as far into the periodontal pocket as possible, where a prophylaxis (conventional tooth cleaning) is more superficial. In cases of mild to moderate periodontitis, scaling and root planing may be the definitive therapy for the average patient, as well as for patients with complex medical problems or with end-stage periodontitis.

The bacteria in plaque biofilm may be controlled using chemical agents in mouth rinses, toothpastes, and intrapocket delivery systems. Both antiseptics and antibiotics are available. Antiseptics are the agent of choice for gingivitis because of the unfavorable risk to benefit ratio of antibiotics for the treatment of inflammation. At present, the gold standard antiseptic is chlorhexidine gluconate. In the United States, chlorhexidine gluconate is available in mouth rinse form. When used in a 30-s rinse, chlorhexidine gluconate reduces gingival inflammation up to 60%. Other antiseptics include triclosan copolymer or triclosan zinc-citrate, essential oils, and stabilized cetylpridinium chloride (CPC).

Sustained release antimicrobial agents are in the forms of gels chips or microspheres. They are placed in the periodontal pocket and deliver antimicrobials (chlorhexidine or one of the tetracyclines) from a sustained release matrix.[10–14] When used as an adjunct to scaling and root planing, improvements in clinical attachment levels, decreases in probing depth, and gingival inflammation have been shown. Systemic antibiotics do not automatically kill sensitive plaque bacteria, because the bacteria are in the form of a biofilm necessitating high doses of antimicrobial for efficacy. Tetracyclines, metronidazole, clindamycin, spiramycin, and combinations such as metronidazole and amoxicillin have been tested with mixed results.[13] Systemic antibiotics are not indicated for gingivitis in most cases of chronic periodontitis but may be used to treat aggressive destructive periodontitis.

Surgical Techniques

Periodontal surgical therapy aims to facilitate patient plaque control through pocket reduction and improved clinical attachment (Table 3). Simple mucoperiosteal flap elevation provides access to bony defects for more thorough debridement than closed scaling and root planing may provide. The flap may be apically positioned with or without recontouring of the underlying bone. Bone grafting techniques may involve materials that are osteoconductive or osteoinductive.[15,16] Alloplasts or synthetic grafts are generally osteoconductive. Autogenous bone grafts have the highest potential for bone growth. Osteoinductive materials include freeze-dried bone allografts from a tissue bank. Allografts should be tested to avoid transmission of pathogenic viruses from donor to recipient. Barrier membranes,[17] either nonresorbable or resorbable, may be used alone or in conjunction with graft materials. The goal of the barrier membrane is to exclude epithelium from the healing surgical wound, thereby promoting periodontal regeneration.

Biological agents to promote the growth of new periodontal ligament, cementum, and bone are increasingly available. These are detailed in Table 4.

Bone morphogenetic proteins[18] have been tested in experimental systems and in limited clinical trials. Formation of bone and cementum has been shown. Other growth factors such as platelet-derived growth factor and insulin-like growth factors have also been tested. Autogenous platelet- derived growth factors may be delivered using the patient's own plasma. Most recently, the Food and Drug Administration approved a biologic including insulin-like growth factor and platelet-derived growth factor for regeneration in periodontal defects.[19]

Enamel matrix protein has been shown to increase bone fill in intraosseous defects.[20] As well, an anorganic bovine-derived hydroxyapatite matrix cell-binding peptide (P-15) has been shown to increase bone fill in intraosseous defects.[21] The patient's own growth factors are used when a membrane is used to cover the osseous defect and blood clot, thereby promoting osseous fill.

Therapy Directed at the Host Response

A newer concept is therapy directed at the host response (Table 5). Low-dose tetracycline therapy has been shown to improve attachment levels in patients with periodontitis.[22] This therapy is relatively long-term, and its mechanism of action is believed to be inhibition of matrix metalloproteinases. Other therapies directed at the host response are used in research. These include nonsteroidal anti-inflammatory drugs that slow the progression of alveolar bone loss.[14] Bisphosphonates have also been shown to increase alveolar bone density while slowing the rate of bone loss.[23]

FUTURE DIRECTIONS

Current research is focused on eliminating pathogens and improving host response to bacteria with the aim of moderating bone and attachment loss. As well, bone grafts with allographs, alloplasts, and biologics are coming into the armamentaria for periodontal therapy with the aim of improving the predictability of fill of osseous defects.

REFERENCES

1. Armitage GC 1999 Development of a classification system for periodontal diseases and conditions. Ann Periodontol 4:1–6.
2. Socransky SS, Haffajee AD, Cugini MA, Smith C, Kent RL Jr 1998 Microbial complexes in subgingival plaque. J Clin Periodontol 25:134–144.
3. Offenbacher S, Salvi GE 1999 Induction of prostaglandin release from macrophages by bacterial endotoxin. Clin Infect Dis 28:505–513.
4. Curtis MA, Kuramitsu HK, Lantz M, Macrina FL, Nakayama K, Potempa J, Reynolds EC, Aduse-Opoku J 1999 Molecular genetics and nomenclature of proteases of Porphyromonas gingivalis.. J Periodontal Res 34:464–472.
5. Romanelli R, Mancini S, Laschinger C, Overall CM, Sodek J, McCulloch CA 1999 Activation of neutrophil collagenase in periodontitis. Infect Immun 67:2319–2326.
6. Graves DT 1999 The potential role of chemokines and inflammatory cytokines in periodontal disease progression. Clin Infect Dis 28:482–490.
7. Jeffcoat MK, Reddy MS, Haigh S, Buchanan W, Doyle MJ, Meredith MP, Nelson SL, Goodale MB, Wehmeyer KR 1995 A comparison of topical ketorolac, systemic flurbiprofen, and placebo for the inhibition of bone loss in adult periodontitis. J Periodontol 66:329–338.
8. Armitage GC 1996 Periodontal diseases: Diagnosis. Ann Periodontol 1:37–215.
9. Kornman KS, di Giovine FS 1998 Genetic variations in cytokine expression: A risk factor for severity of adult periodontitis. Ann Periodontol 3:327–338.
10. Cobb CM 1996 Non-surgical pocket therapy: Mechanical. Ann Periodontol 1:443–490.
11. Jeffcoat MK, Bray KS, Ciancio SG, Dentino AR, Fine DH, Gordon JM, Gunsolley JC, Killoy WJ, Lowenguth RA, Magnusson NI, Offenbacher S, Palcanis KG, Proskin HM, Finkelman RD, Flashner M 1998 Adjunctive use of a subgingival controlled-release chlorhexidine chip reduces probing depth and improves attachment level compared with scaling and root planing alone. J Periodontol 69:989–997.
12. Garrett S, Johnson L, Drisko CH, Adams DF, Bandt C, Beiswanger B, Bogle G, Donly K, Hallmon WW, Hancock EB, Hanes P, Hawley CE, Kiger R, Killoy W, Mellonig JT, Polson A, Raab FJ, Ryder M, Stoller NH, Wang HL, Wolinsky LE, Evans GH, Harrold CQ, Arnold RM, Southard GL 1999 Two multi-center studies evaluating locally delivered doxycycline hyclate, placebo control, oral hygiene, and scaling and root planing in the treatment of periodontitis. J Periodontol 70:490–503.
13. Williams RC, Paquette DW, Offenbacher S, Armitage GC, Bray K, Caton J, Cochran DL, Drisko CH, Fiorellini JP, Giannobile WV, Grossi S, Guerrero DM, Johnson GK, Lamster IB, Magnusson I, Oringer RJ, Persson GR, Van Dyke TE, Wolff LF, Santucci EA, Rodda BE, Lessem J 2001 Treatment of periodontitis by local administration of minocycline microspheres: A controlled trial. J Periodontol 72:1535–1544.
14. Elter JR, Lawrence HP, Offenbacher S, Beck JD 1997 Meta-analysis of the effect of systemic metronidazole as an adjunct to scaling and root planing for adult periodontitis. J Periodontal Res 32:487–496.
15. Academy Report 2005 Periodontal regeneration. J Periodontol 76:1601–1622.
16. Nasr HF, Aichelmann-Reidy ME, Yukna RA 2000 Bone and bone substitutes. Periodontology 19:74–86.
17. Murphy K, Gunsolley J 2003 Guided tissue regeneration for the treatment of periodontal intrabony and furcation defects. A systematic review. Ann Periodontol 8:266–302.
18. Sorensen RG, Polimeni G, Kinoshita A, Wozney JM, Wikesjo UM 2004 Effect of recombinant human bone morphogenetic protein-12 (rhBMP-12) on regeneration of peridontal attachment following tooth replantation in dogs. J Clin Periodont 31:654–661.
19. Howell TH, Fiorellini JP, Paquette DW, Offenbacher S, Giannobile WV, Lynch SE 1997 A Phase I/II clinical trial to evaluate a combination of recombinant human platelet derived growth factor-BB and recombinant human insulin-like growth factor-I in patients with periodontal disease. J Periodontol 68:1186–1193.
20. Giannobile W, Somerman M 2003 Growth and amelogeninlike factors in periodontal wound healing. A systematic review. Ann Periodontol 8:193–204.
21. Yukna RA, Callan DP, Krauser JT, Evan GH, Aichelmann-Reidy ME, Moore K, Cruz R, Scott JB 1998 Multi-center clinical evaluation of combination anorganic bovine derived hydroxyapatite matrix (ABM)/cell-binding peptide (P-15) as a bone replacement graft material in human periodontal osseous defects: 6 month results. J Periodontol 69:655–663.
22. Caton JG, Ciancio SG, Blieden TM, Bradshaw M, Crout RJ, Hefti AF, Massaro JM, Polson AM, Thomas J, Walker C 2000 Treatment with subantimicrobial dose doxycycline improves the efficacy of scaling and root planing in patients with adult periodontitis. J Periodontol 71:521–532.
23. MK Jeffcoat, Cizza G, Shi J, Genco R, Lombardi A 2005 Efficacy of bisphosphonates for the control of alveolar bone loss in periodontitis. J Int Acad Periodontol (in press).

Chapter 87.   Oral Bone Loss and Osteoporosis

Jean Wactawski-Wende

Social and Preventive Medicine, University at Buffalo, Buffalo, New York

INTRODUCTION

Osteoporosis is a skeletal disorder characterized by compromised bone strength predisposing to increased risk of fracture, with bone strength determined by both bone density and bone quality.[1] Periodontitis is an infection-mediated process characterized by resorption of the alveolar bone as well as loss of the soft tissue attachment to the tooth and is a major cause of tooth loss and edentulousness in adults.[2] The primary etiology of periodontal disease as a bacterial infection has been established. Several subgingival bacteria including *Porphyromonas gingivalis, Prevotella intermedia, Bacteroides forsythus, Actinobacillus actinomycetemcomitans*, and others are leading candidates as etiologic agents in periodontal disease.[3] The loss of soft tissue attachment and resorption of alveolar bone as a result of bacterial infection lead to tooth loss and edentulousness, which, in turn, result in the resorption of the remaining residual ridge and continued loss of oral bone. Oral bone loss has been shown to be associated with osteoporosis and low skeletal BMD. The interaction of host infection and host susceptibility (i.e., osteoporosis) in the incidence and progression of oral bone loss and periodontal disease continues to be an area of intensive investigation, with most published studies supporting a positive association. However, many of these studies are cross-sectional in nature, include relatively small sample sizes and have inadequate control of potential confounding factors, limiting our understanding of the nature of the relationship between these common conditions.

METHODS TO ASSESS SYSTEMIC OR POSTCRANIAL BONE

Interpretation of published findings is complicated by various methods to assess both postcranial and oral bone loss. Techniques used to assess systemic BMD include single and dual photon absorptiometry (SPA and DPA), single- and dual-energy absorptiometry (SXA and DXA), QCT, radiographic absorptiometry (RA), and ultrasound (US). Systemic density can be measured at various skeletal sites, each including differing proportions of cortical and trabecular bone that may more (i.e., wrist) or less (i.e., spine) approximate that found in the oral cavity. Not all studies of oral bone loss and osteoporosis rely on some measure of BMD. Some use clinical observations, such as history of bone fracture.

METHODS TO ASSESS ORAL BONE

There are several techniques used to assess oral bone and bone loss, and all typically involve use of radiographic measures of the oral bones. The commonly used assessments of oral bone include measures of loss of alveolar crestal height (ACH), measures of resorption of the residual ridge after tooth loss (RRR), and assessment of oral BMD.

ACH is assessed using oral radiographs. In this technique, oral radiographs (bitewings) are taken in regions of the oral cavity that include intact teeth. These radiographs are typically digitized, and distance measurements are made from fixed points on the teeth (the cemento-enamel junction [CEJ]) to the top of the alveolar bone (crest) adjacent to the tooth (Fig. 1).

The author has reported no conflicts of interest.

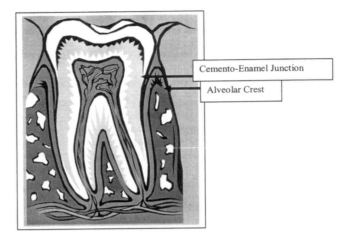

FIG. 1.   Alveolar crestal height.

ACH is usually measured at two sites per tooth (mesial and distal) and is often reported as the average loss of bone height in all teeth measured in the mouth (mean ACH). The larger the mean ACH reported, the worse the bone loss surrounding the teeth. However, ACH may be reported in other ways (e.g., the number or the percent of teeth measured with ACH loss beyond a certain millimeter threshold; Fig. 1).[4]

Cross-sectional assessments of bone height can be troublesome because ACH values can be affected by tooth loss. Teeth that have been lost because of periodontal disease no longer contribute to ACH assessments. As such, the teeth with the worst periodontal destruction (and presumably the worst oral bone) are lost, no longer contributing to average ACH measures, resulting in assessments that seem to be better than they actually are. Prospective studies are less prone to the affects of tooth loss on measures of ACH. Methods to account for periodontal related tooth loss in measures of ACH have been proposed; however, no overall consensus on methodologies to deal with this issue have been reached, and most published studies to date have not accounted for the impact of tooth loss on these ACH loss estimates.

After a tooth is lost, there is resorption or recession of the oral bone in that region. This phenomenon is called RRR. Most often the extent of RRR is described in edentulous subjects, but RRR can be described in dentate subjects that have lost one or more teeth in the region of tooth loss. RRR can be described in cross-sectional studies, but more meaningful information can be obtained in prospective studies where the rate of RRR after tooth loss or extraction is described.

Measurement of oral bone density has been assessed using a variety of techniques that include measurement of absolute bone density (DXA, DPA, QCT, RA) of oral bones and studies that approximate change in oral density over time, such as computer-assisted densitometric image analysis (CADIA). All techniques used to assess oral bone density are limited to some extent by either cost or precision. QCT provides perhaps the best assessment of oral density because it allows for assessment of density in various regions of the oral bones without obstruction by teeth; however, this technique is relatively expensive and includes relatively high exposure to radiation. Both DPA and DXA have been used to assess oral bone density; however, positioning and reproducibility of oral density is difficult. RA has been used in several studies using bitewing radiographs taken with a calibrated step-wedge of known density in the field of X-ray. Reproducibility of this method is good when positioning aids are used.

Region of the oral bone measured varies by technique to assess oral density. Density assessments in human cadavers have shown variation across regions of the mandible by edentulation and by age and gender.[5] QCT can measure virtually any region. RA is restricted to regions that can accessed by bitewing radiographs. DXA and DPA can measure the mandible; however, obstruction by teeth in dentate subjects makes measurement of the basal bone easier to access and reproduce than regions surrounding the teeth. Most measurements are made in the in the mandible because of easier access. Within the mandible, subregions that may be measured include molar, premolar, or incisor regions. Each region has the potential to be of different cortical thickness, which may affect density, especially techniques that are two-dimensional and sensitive to thickness differences. Most (DXA, RA) but not all (QCT) measures of oral density are two dimensional. Ability to measure oral bone density is restricted at least in part by whether or not teeth are present, with edentulous subjects being easier to measure without potential for tooth obstruction. However, edentulous subjects may have marked resorption of the residual ridge, which in turn affects the area of comparison and ultimately density. Attempts to use radiomorphometrical indices in panoramic radiographs to predict skeletal density have been largely disappointing.

Although tooth loss is the ultimate endpoint of periodontal destruction, it can also be used as a proxy measure of oral bone loss. Teeth are held in place by oral bone and surrounding soft tissue. Loss of oral bone will impact tooth stability and eventual loss. Reason for tooth loss is complex, and in addition to periodontal destruction, can include caries and trauma and is often determined by extraction practices of the dentist. There are other measures used to assess extent of periodontal disease that are not directly measures of oral bone. These include probing measures to assess loss of soft tissue attachment surrounding the teeth such as the clinical attachment level (CAL) and pocket depth (PD). Although assessment of loss of soft tissue attachment is a primary means to assess periodontal disease by dental professionals, discussion within this chapter will be limited to measures of oral bone loss. Further discussion on the relation of CAL and PD to osteoporosis can be found elsewhere.[6] Finally, any review of evidence on the relation of oral bone loss and osteoporosis should consider both demographic makeup of the population under study (age, gender, race) and control of potential confounding variables that can vary markedly across studies and impact both the findings and interpretation.

STUDIES OF OSTEOPOROSIS, ACH, AND RRR

Most but not all studies of the relationship between osteoporosis or low skeletal BMD and ACH have shown an association. However, the studies published to date are limited in number and are largely cross-sectional in nature. Loss of ACH and RRR is more predominant in females than males and most predominant in older subjects. Presumably, the stronger consistent association found in older female subjects is associated with by lower BMD in these groups.

Humphries et al.[7] showed that age was an important factor in loss of height in the residual ridge in edentulous adult mandibles in females but not in males. Ortman et al.[8] assessed a random sample of 459 radiographs from edentulous patients and found a significantly higher percentage of women with severe RRR than men. Older female subjects (>55 years) were more likely to be edentulous than older males and both male and female younger subjects. Hirai et al.[9] found skeletal osteoporosis strongly affects RRR in edentulous patients ($r = -0.42$, $p < 0.01$), as did female gender and increasing age.

Loss of ACH was assessed in 70 postmenopausal women to determine its relation to systemic BMD.[10] Complete dental and BMD assessments (DXA) were performed, and a comprehensive medical and dental history was taken. Lower BMD of the femur was significantly correlated with worse mean ACH and was persistent after control for confounding.

In a more recent cross-sectional cohort of postmenopausal women from this same group, the relationship between osteoporosis and severity of alveolar crestal bone loss was studied. This well-controlled study of >1300 postmenopausal women showed a strong association between T score category and ACH, with those in the osteoporotic category having the worst ACH. This association was most evident in women 70 years of age or older who were over three times more likely to have moderate or severe ACH levels if they were osteoporotic.[11]

Studies that have included younger subjects have not found a consistent association between skeletal BMD and ACH. Elders et al.[12] assessed the association between alveolar bone height, spinal BMD, and metacarpal cortical thickness (MCT) in 286 women 46–55 years of age, 21% of which were edentulous. The MCT and spinal BMD of dentate and edentulous subjects was not found to be different. In the dentate subjects, mean ACH was not correlated with spinal BMD, MCT, age, and years since menopause. The lack of an association may be limited by selection of relatively young subjects (46–55 years) when prevalence of osteoporosis may be low. Similarly, Ward and Manson[13] were unable to show a significant relationship between ACH and metacarpal BMD in a younger group (mean age, 41 years). However, "rapidity" (alveolar bone loss divided by age) was associated with the metacarpal bone index in females but not males.

Prospective studies of the association of ACH and skeletal BMD are limited. However, one small but well-designed 2-year longitudinal study in 59 postmenopausal women determined that smokers ($n = 21$) had a higher frequency of ACH loss and worse oral density in the crestal and subcrestal regions than nonsmokers ($n = 38$). A significant interaction between spinal BMD and smoking on change in alveolar BMD was found, with the nonsmoking subjects with normal spine BMD gaining oral density over time, and subjects with low BMD who smoked losing oral BMD over time.[14]

OSTEOPOROSIS AND ORAL BONE DENSITY

Studies have found that oral bone density is correlated with systemic bone density and osteoporosis. Mandibular BMD has assessed using DPA and was found in a series of studies to be associated with total skeletal mass in osteoporotic women.[15–17] Mandibular density assessed by DPA was shown to be highly accurate and precise.[18] Using this technique, von Wowern et al.[17] found that women had significantly lower BMC of the forearm and mandible compared with men and that, in older subjects, mandibular density varied by sex and age. Rates of BMC loss were greater over time in older women than men.

Osteoporotic women were found to have significantly lower mandibular and forearm BMC values than controls in a case-control study of 12 women with a history of osteoporotic fractures and 14 normal controls.[15] Mandibular BMC values in osteoporotic women were 2 SD below those for young "normal" women in 92% of the osteoporotic group and in 64% of the controls, suggesting a large portion of the controls also had mandibular osteopenia.

A series of studies has been conducted to determine the relationship between osteoporosis and oral bone density and other indicators of oral health in postmenopausal women using a reproducible microdensitometry technique to determine mandibular density.[19] In one study, 30 postmenopausal women 55–71 years of age with history of vertebral fracture taking part in a larger randomized clinical trial had significant associations between RRR and bone height and radius density. Height of the mandible was correlated with tooth loss but not with density of the forearm regions or the mandible ($r = 0.21$). Mandibular density was correlated with total body calcium ($r = 0.89$) and forearm density ($r = 0.60$) in edentulous women ($n = 7$); however, only the correlation with total body calcium was statistically significant. A significant correlation was found to exist between forearm density and oral bone density.[20] In another study, mandibular bone mass and cortical thickness at the gonion was found to be significantly correlated with BMD of the spine ($r = 0.39$) and radius ($r = 0.33$) in 50 women, 20–90 years of age, without vertebral fractures noted at enrollment. Associations were most apparent in the older (>50 years) women. However, when spinal trabecular density was measured using QCT, only the association with cortical thickness at the gonion persisted.[21] In 112 women 50–85 years of age with or without prevalent vertebral fracture, women with vertebral fracture had significantly lower mandibular bone mass and density. Cortical thickness at the gonion was significantly higher in the normal subjects.[22] Kribbs et al.[23] and others further showed that mandibular mass was correlated with all skeletal measures in osteoporotic women. The height of the edentulous ridge correlated with total body calcium and mandibular BMD.

Postmortem studies in edentulous female ($n = 24$) and male subjects ($n = 26$) found the specific gravity of the mandible and radius decreased with increasing age. Females had lower densities than males, and mandibular and radius measures were highly correlated ($r = 0.634$, $p < 0.01$).[24] BMC in 25 edentulous mandibles taken from cadavers by DPA was found to increase in male subjects with advancing age, whereas mandibular BMC of female subjects tended to decrease with advancing age.[25] Mandibular density measured by QCT differed between partially and totally edentulous postmenopausal women who had been edentulous >12 years, suggesting years edentulous may be important when assessing the relationship between skeletal and mandibular density.[26]

Hormone therapy and endogenous hormone levels have been assessed in their role in BMD of oral and skeletal regions. Hormone therapy's effect on future BMD was assessed in a prospective study of 69 women. The relationship between spinal density (DPA) and mandibular density (RA) was significantly yet moderately correlated at baseline and at an average 5-year follow-up in 28 of the subjects. Change in density in the jaw and spine were also significantly correlated.[27] In a small study ($N = 24$) measuring estrogen levels (17-β-estradiol [E2]) among postmenopausal women, alveolar BMD was assessed using CADIA to measure the relative change in density in crestal and subcrestal regions of posterior interproximal alveolar bone. A net gain in alveolar density was found in E2-sufficient women compared with those who were E2-deficient ($p < 0.001$); however, the number of sites gaining/losing density were similar. CADIA does not allow calculation of absolute density changes.[28] In a 2-year study of the oral bone density and bone height changes in 38 nonsmoking postmenopausal women with periodontal disease, women with low BMD had higher rates of density loss and ACH loss than those with higher BMD. Estrogen deficiency was also found to be associated with greater loss of both oral BMD and ACH in women overall and for crestal region density in osteopenic women.[29]

These findings were supported by results of a 3-year double-blind randomized clinic trial of hormone therapy that revealed that both oral and postcranial BMD were increased in postmenopausal women taking oral estrogen therapy compared with placebo. In addition to the positive change in BMD, a significant increase in ACH was observed.[30]

A 28-month prospective study of the mandibular BMD (DXA), hip BMD (DXA) and ultrasound assessment of the calcaneus and hand in 18 postmenopausal edentulous women found the largest change in density occurring in the mandible with other significant loss seen in the femoral neck and Ward's triangle. Insignificant changes were seen in the trochanteric region and in all regions assessed by US. The change in mandibular density in this study was 7.54% per year. Although small, this study provided evidence of differential loss of BMD by region.[31]

Several important questions remain regarding the correlation between systemic and oral bone density including determination of normal ranges of mandibular density by age and sex, further comparison of mandibular density in normal and osteoporotic women, assessment of longitudinal progression of mandibular bone loss, comparison of the rate of bone loss in the mandible compared with other skeletal regions, and the effects of different therapies on mandibular density compared with other skeletal sites. Further study of measurement error in various techniques to assess oral density is also needed.

OSTEOPOROSIS AND TOOTH LOSS

Numerous studies have looked at the relationship between osteoporosis and tooth loss, and most have found a positive association. A cross-sectional study of mandibular BMD in osteoporotic women found tooth loss and edentulism were significantly more common in the osteoporotic group.[21] On average, the osteoporotic women had lost 6.9 mandibular teeth compared with 4.5 teeth in women with normal BMD ($p < 0.05$). In a second study, osteoporotic subjects were reported to be edentulous more often than normal subjects (20% versus 7%), although the differences were statistically insignificant.[22] In a previously reported study of osteoporotic women, 20% of all women studied were edentulous.[23]

Taguchi et al.[32] has studied the relation between tooth loss and oral bone density. The first study included 269 subjects, 99 men and 170 women, 3–88 years of age. In males, no relationship was seen between mandibular cortical width and tooth loss; however, in female subjects, a decrease in mandibular cortical bone width was positively correlated with tooth loss. In women past their seventh decade of life, the association was most apparent. In a cross-sectional study of 64 women 50–70 years of age, tooth loss was found to be highly correlated with prevalence of spinal fracture.[33] A positive relationship between loss of the posterior teeth and alveolar and spinal bone density has been reported; however, no association was found between anterior teeth and density of the spine or oral cavity.[34]

A large cross-sectional study of the association of tooth loss to BMD of the spine and hip in 608 men and 874 women found skeletal BMD in male subjects correlated with self-reported tooth loss, after controlling for age, body mass index (BMI), and smoking. However, the association of tooth loss with BMD was insignificant in the females studied after controlling for the affects of age, BMI, and smoking. Overall, 24% of the men and 27% of the women were edentulous, less than expected from previous estimates from this region. No information was available on the use of hormone therapy in females.[35]

Krall et al.[36] found a significant positive relationship between number of teeth and BMD of the spine ($p < 0.05$) and radius ($p < 0.01$) in a cross-sectional study of 329 postmenopausal women. The association persisted after control for pack-years of smoking, years since menopause, education, and body mass. A subsequent analysis of participants of one of three prospective clinical trials of calcium and vitamin D assessed the relationship between bone loss in the hip, spine, and total body and tooth loss in healthy, white, dentate, postmenopausal women.[37] In 189 women followed, 45 had lost at least one tooth during the next 7 years. Those who had lost teeth were significantly more likely than those who retained their teeth to lose BMD in the whole body, femur, and spine (relative risk = 4.83, 1.50, and 1.45, respectively), after controlling for years since menopause, BMI, number of teeth at baseline, smoking, and intervention assignment. Interestingly, all women enrolled had relatively normal spinal BMD values at baseline (i.e., no osteoporosis); therefore, the relation of systemic bone loss to tooth loss would be predicted to be low over the 7-year study period. Of note was that one-half the women recruited reported ≤400 mg daily calcium dietary intake at baseline.

A related study of estrogen use after menopause and tooth retention in 488 women found estrogen users had more teeth than nonusers (12.5 versus 10.7, $p = 0.046$), and duration of estrogen use independently predicted number of remaining teeth ($p = 0.05$). Long-term users of estrogen had more teeth than never users (14.3 versus 10.7, $p < 0.02$). Estrogen use was shown to be protective for tooth loss, regardless of type of tooth or location in the mouth. Users of estrogen (1–4 years) had 1.1 more teeth than nonusers.[38]

A 3-year prospective Swedish study of 14,375 older men and women found that women with the fewest teeth at baseline (lowest tertile) had a risk of hip fracture that was twice that of the women in the highest two tertiles. The association between tooth loss and hip fracture was stronger in the men studied, with the risk of fracture 3-fold higher in men with the fewest teeth at baseline, although the absolute number of hip fractures was greatest in women.[39] A recent 10-year prospective study found alveolar bone loss (ACH) at baseline was the strongest independent predictor of incident tooth loss in postmenopausal women.[40] For every millimeter of ACH loss, there was a 3-fold increase in incidence of tooth loss in these older women.

Not all studies have found an association between BMD and tooth loss. Klemetti[41] did not find an association with tooth loss and BMD in a group of 355 Finnish women; however, dental practices in Finland may have led to extractions for preventative purposes rather than as a result of underlying disease. One-half of all women studied had all their maxillary teeth, and 25% of women had all their mandibular teeth extracted before the age of 30, suggesting reason for tooth loss was likely not periodontal in nature.

Several studies of younger women have not shown an association between BMD and periodontal disease. Hildebolt et al.[42] found no association between spine or femur BMD and number of remaining teeth among 135 subjects enrolled in a hormone therapy study trial. Subjects were relatively young postmenopausal women who had 10 or more teeth present and no periodontal pockets deeper than 5 mm at enrollment, limiting the ability to detect an association between BMD and tooth loss. Earnshaw et al.[43] found no relationship between BMD and tooth number in 1365 white women 45–59 years of age, who were within 12 years of menopause. Analysis included adjustment for age, years since menopause, hormone therapy use, and center. This was a fairly large well-controlled study; however, the underlying risk of tooth loss in this relatively young population may have been too small to observe in this study. A recent prospective study of a subgroup of participants from the Study of Osteoporotic Fractures found absolute BMD and percentage change in BMD were similar in women dentate and edentulous at baseline examination.[44] Additional studies are needed to further define this relationship in larger cohorts of women, especially prospective cohorts, where temporality can be established.

POTENTIAL MECHANISMS AND THE BIOLOGICAL BASIS

Based on our knowledge of osteopenia and periodontal disease and the risk factors that affect both, it is reasonable to propose the following hypothesis: periodontitis results from bacteria that produce factors that cause loss of collagenous support of the tooth, as well as loss of alveolar bone. Systemic factors can lead to loss of BMD throughout the body, including loss in the maxilla and mandible. The resulting local reduction of BMD in the jawbones could set the stage for more rapid ACH loss because a comparable challenge of bacterial bone-resorbing factors could be expected to result in greater alveolar crestal loss than in an individual with good bone mass. There are, in addition, systemic risk factors such as smoking, diabetes, diet, and hormone levels that affect systemic bone level and may also affect periodontitis. Although periodontal disease has historically been thought to be the result of a local infectious process, others have suggested that periodontal disease may be an early manifestation of generalized osteopenia.[45]

Mechanisms by which osteoporosis or systemic bone loss may be associated with periodontal attachment loss, loss of alveolar bone height or density, and tooth loss continue to be explored. Several potential mechanisms have been proposed.[10] First, low BMD in the oral bones may be a associated with low systemic bone. This low BMD or loss of BMD may lead to more rapid resorption of alveolar bone after insult by periodontal bacteria. With less dense oral bone to start, loss of bone surrounding the teeth may occur more rapidly. Second, systemic factors affecting bone remodeling may also modify local tissue response to periodontal infection. Persons with systemic bone loss are known to have increased systemic production of cytokines (i.e., interleukin-1, interleukin-6) that may have effects on bone throughout the body, including the bones of the oral cavity. Periodontal infection has been shown to increase local cytokine production that, in turn, increases local osteoclast activity resulting in increased bone resorption. Third, genetic factors that predispose a person to systemic bone loss also influence or predispose an individual to periodontal destruction. Last, certain lifestyle factors such as cigarette smoking and suboptimal calcium intake, among others, may put individuals at risk for development of both systemic osteopenia and oral bone loss.

Prospective study of the association between osteoporosis and oral bone loss is needed in large cohorts where temporal sequence can be established and where adequate assessment and control of confounding variables can be done. Both osteoporosis and periodontal disease are major health concerns in the United States, especially in older populations. As the population ages, the impact of both osteoporosis and periodontal disease will be more profound. Studies that improve our understanding of the mechanisms by which osteoporosis and oral bone loss are associated are needed and will be increasingly important in the prevention of morbidity and mortality related to these two very prevalent disorders in older Americans.

REFERENCES

1. National Institutes of Health 2000 Osteoporosis prevention, diagnosis, and therapy. NIH Consensus Statement. **17:**1–36.
2. American Academy of Periodontology. 1992 Glossary of Periodontal

Terms, 3rd ed. American Academy of Periodontology, Chicago, IL, USA, 1992.

3. Socransky SS, Haffajee AD 1997 The nature of periodontal diseases Ann Periodontol **2:**3–10.

4. Armitage GC 2002 Classifying periodontal diseases—a long-standing dilemma. Periodontology **30:**9–23.

5. D'Amelio P, Panattoni GL, DiStefano M, Nassisi R, Violino D, Isaia GC 2002 Densitometric study of dry human mandible. J Clin Densitometry **5:**363–367.

6. Wactawski-Wende J 2001 Periodontal disease and osteoporosis: Association and mechanisms. Ann Periodontal **6:**197–208.

7. Humphries S, Devlin H, Worthington H 1989 A radiographic investigation into bone resorption of mandibular alveolar bone in elderly edentulous adults. J Dent **17:**94–96.

8. Ortman LF, Hausmann E, Dunford RG 1989 Skeletal osteopenia and residual ridge resorption. J Prosthet Dent **61:**321–325.

9. Hirai T, Ishijima T, Hashikawa Y, Yajima T 1993 Osteoporosis and reduction of residual ridge in edentulous patients. J Prosthet Dent **69:**49–56.

10. Tezal M, Wactawski-Wende J, Grossi SG, Ho AW, Dunford R, Genco RJ 2000 The relationship between bone mineral density and periodontitis in postmenopausal women. J Periodontol **71:**1492–1498.

11. Wactawski-Wende J, Hausmann E, Hovey K, Trevisan M, Grossi S, Genco R 2005 The relationship between bone mineral density and alveolar crest height loss in postmenopausal women. J Periodontol **76:**2116–2124.

12. Elders PJM, Habets LLMH, Netelenbos JC, van der Linden LWJ, van der Stelt PF 1992 The relation between periodontitis and systemic bone mass in women between 46 and 55 years of age. J Clin Periodontol **19:**492–496.

13. Ward VJ, Manson JD 1973 Alveolar bone loss in periodontal disease and the metacarpal index. J Periodontol **44:**763–769.

14. Payne JB, Reinhardt RA, Nummikoski PV, Dunning DG, Patil KD 2000 The association of cigarette smoking with alveolar bone loss in postmenopausal females. J Clin Periodontol **27:**658–664.

15. von Wowern N, Klausen B, Kollerup G 1994 Osteoporosis: A risk factor in periodontal disease. J Periodontol **65:**1134–1138.

16. von Wowern N, Klausen B, Hylander E 1996 Bone loss and oral state in patients on home parenteral nutrition. J Parenter Enter Nutr **20:**105–109.

17. von Wowern N 1988 Bone mineral content of mandibles: Normal reference values—rate of age related bone loss. Calcif Tissue Int **43:**193–198.

18. von Wowern N 1985 Dual-photon absorptiometry of mandibles: In vitro test of a new method. Scand J Dent Res **93:**169–177.

19. Kribbs PJ, Smith DE, Chesnut CH 1983 Oral findings in osteoporosis. Part I: Measurement of mandibular bone density. J Prosthet Dent **50:**576–579.

20. Kribbs PJ, Smith DE, Chesnut CH 1983 Oral findings in osteoporosis. Part II: Relationship between residual ridge and alveolar bone resorption in generalized skeletal osteopenia. J Prosthet Dent **50:**719–724.

21. Kribbs PJ, Chesnut CH, Ott SM, Kilcoyne RF 1990 Relationships between mandibular and skeletal bone in a population of normal women. J Prosthet Dent **63:**86–89.

22. Kribbs PJ 1990 Comparison of mandibular bone in normal and osteoporotic women. J Prosthet Dent **63:**218–222.

23. Kribbs PJ, Chesnut CH, Ott SM, Kilcoyne RF 1989 Relationships between mandibular and skeletal bone in an osteoporotic population. J Prosthet Dent **62:**703–707.

24. Henrikson P-A, Wallenius K 1974 The mandible and osteoporosis (1). A qualitative comparison between the mandible and the radius. J Oral Rehab **1:**67–74.

25. Solar P, Ulm CW, Thornton B, Matejka M 1994 Sex-related differences in the bone density of atrophic mandibles. J Prosthet Dent **71:**345–349.

26. Klemetti E, Vainio P, Lassila V 1994 Mineral density in the mandibles of partially and totally edentate postmenopausal women. Scand J Dent Res **102:**64–67.

27. Jacobs R, Ghyselen J, Koninckx P, van Steenberghe D 1996 Long-term bone mass evaluation of mandible and lumbar spine in a group of women receiving hormone replacement therapy. Eur J Oral Sci **104:**10–16.

28. Payne JB, Zachs NR, Reinhardt RA Nummikoski PV, Patil K 1997 The association between estrogen status and alveolar bone density changes in postmenopausal women with a history of periodontitis. J Periodontol **68:**24–31.

29. Payne JB, Reinhardt RA, Nummikoski PV, Patil KD 1999 Longitudinal alveolar bone loss in postmenopausal osteoporotic/osteopenic women. Osteoporos Int **10:**34–40.

30. Civitelli R, Pilgram TK, Dotson M, Muckerman J, Lewandowski N, Armamento-Villareal R, Yokoyama-Crothers N, Kardaris EE, Hauser J, Cohen S and Hildebolt CF 2002 Alveolar and postcranial bone density in postmenopausal women receiving hormone/estrogen replacement therapy: A randomized, double-blind, placebo-controlled trial. Arch Int Med **162:**1409–1415.

31. Drozdzowska B, Pluskiewicz W 2002 Longitudinal changes in mandibular bone mineral density compared with hip bone mineral density and quantitative ultrasound at calcaneus and hand phalanges. Brit J Radiol **75:**743–747.

32. Taguchi A, Tanimoto K, Suei Y, Wada T 1995 Tooth loss and mandibular osteopenia. Oral Surg Oral Med Oral Pathol Oral Radiol Endod **79:**127–132.

33. Taguchi A, Tanimoto K, Suei Y, Otani K, Wada T 1995 Oral signs as indicators of possible osteoporosis in older women. Oral Surg Oral Med Oral Pathol Oral Radiol Endod **80:**612–616.

34. Taguchi A, Suei Y, Ohtsuka M, Tanimoto K, Hollender LG 1999 Relationship between bone mineral density and tooth loss in elderly Japanese women. Dentomaxillofacial Radiol **28:**219–223.

35. May H, Reader R, Murphy S, Khaw K-T 1995 Self-reported tooth loss and bone mineral density in older men and women. Age Ageing **24:**217–221.

36. Krall EA, Dawson-Hughes B, Papas A, Garcia RI 1994 Tooth loss and skeletal bone density in healthy postmenopausal women. Osteoporos Int **4:**104–109.

37. Krall EA, Garcia RI, Dawson-Hughes B 1996 Increased risk of tooth loss is related to bone loss at the whole body, hip, and spine. Calcif Tissue Int **59:**433–437.

38. Krall EA, Dawson-Hughes B, Hannan MT, Wilson PWF, Kiel DP 1997 Postmenopausal estrogen replacement and tooth retention. Am J Med **102:**536–542.

39. Aström J, Bäckström C, Thidevall G 1990 Tooth loss and hip fractures in the elderly. J Bone Joint Surg Br **72:**324–325.

40. Tezal M, Wactawski-Wende J, Grossi S, Dmochowski J, Genco R 2005 Periodontal disease and the incidence of tooth loss in postmenopausal women. J Periodontol **76:**1123–1128.

41. Klemetti E, Vainio P 1993 Effect of bone mineral density in skeleton and mandible on extraction of teeth and clinical alveolar height. J Prosthet Dent **70:**21–25.

42. Hildebolt CF, Pilgram TK, Dotson M, Yokoyama-Crothers N, Muckerman J, Hauser J, Cohen S, Kardaris E, Vannier MW, Hanes P, Shrout MK, Civitelli R 1997 Attachment loss with postmenopausal age and smoking. J Periodontal Res **32:**619–625.

43. Earnshaw SA, Keating N, Hosking DJ, Chilvers CE, Ravn P, McClung M, Wasnich RD for the EPIC Study Group 1998 Tooth counts do not predict bone mineral density in early postmenopausal Caucasian women. Int J Epidemiol **27:**479–483.

44. Famili P, Cauley J, Suzuki JB, Weyant R 2005 Longitudinal study of periodontal disease and edentulism with rates of bone loss in older women. J Periodontol **76:**11–15.

45. Whalen JP, Krook L 1996 Periodontal disease as the early manifestation of osteoporosis. Nutrition **12:**53–54.

SECTION XIV

Appendix
(Section Editors: Michael Kleerekoper and Daniel D. Bikle)

Laboratory Values related to Calcium Metabolism/Metabolic Bone Disease [a]

Test	Source of specimen	Reference population	Reference Range	Reference Range (SI units)
Calcium, ionized	Serum or plasma	Cord	5.5±0.3 ng/dL	1.37±0.07 mmol/L
		Newborn 3-24 h	4.3-5.1 mg/dL	1.07-1.27 mmol/L
		Newborn 24-48 h	4.0-4.7 mg/dL	1.00-1.17 mmol/L
		Adult	4.48-4.92 mg/dL	1.12-1.23 mmol/L
		Adult >60 yr		1.13-1.30 mmol/L
Calcium, total	Serum[b]	Child	8.8-10.8 mg/dL	2.2-2.7 mmol/L
		Adult	8.4-10.2 mg/dL	2.1-2.55 mmol/L
	Urine	Ca in diet		
		Free Ca	5-40 mg/dL	0.13-1.0 mmol/d
		Low to average	50-150 mg/dL	1.25-3.8 mmol/d
		Average (20 mmol/d)	100-300 mg/dL	2.1-7.5 mmol/d
Magnesium	Feces	Average 0.64 g/d		16 mmol/d
	Serum	1.3-2.1 mEq/d (higher during menses)		0.65-1.05 mmol/d
	Urine, 24h	6.0-100 mEq/d		3.0-5.0 mmol/d
Phosphatase, acid				
Prostatic (RIA)	Serum		<3.0 ng/ml	<3.0 µg/L
Roy, Brower & Hayden 37C			0.11-0.60 U/L	0.11-0.60 U/L
Phosphatase, acid tartrate resistant (TRAP 5.6) Suomen	Serum		2.5-45 U/L	
Phosphatase, alkaline				
p-Nitrophenyl phosphate, carbonate buffer, 30 C	Serum	Infant		50-165 U/L
		Child		20-150 U/L
		Adult		20-70 U/L
		>60 yr		30-75 U/L
Bowers & McComb IFCC, 30C	Serum	Male		30-90 U/L
		Female		20-80 U/L
Bone-specific alkaline phosphatase				
Hybritech/Beckman IRMA, ELISA	Serum	Male	6.9-20.1 ng/mL	
		Female – premenopausal	4.6-14.3 ng/mL	
		Female -- postmenopausal	7.3-22.4 ng/mL	
Metra Biosystems, ELISA	Serum	Male	15.0-41.3 U/L	
		Female – premenopausal	11.6-29.6 U/L	
Phosphorus, inorganic	Serum	Cord	3.7-8.1 mg/dL	1.2-2.6 nmol/L
		Child	4.5-5.5 mg/dL	1.45-1.78 nmol/L
		Adult	2.7-4.5 mg/dL	0.87-1.45 nmol/L
		>60 year Male	2.3-3.7 mg/dL	0.74-1.2 nmol/L
		>60 year Female	2.8-4.1 mg/dL	0.9-1.3 nmol/L
	Urine	Adult on diet containing .9-1.5 g P and 10 mg Ca/kg: <1.0 g/d		<32 mmol/d
		Unrestricted diet 0.4-1.3 g/d		13-42 mmol/d
Tubular reabsorption of phosphate	Urine, 4-h (0600 – 1200 h), and serum		82-95%	Fraction reabsorbed: 0.82-0.95
Vitamin A				
(Quest Diagnostics/Nichols)	Serum	Child 1-6 yr	20-43 µg/dL	
		Child 7-12 yr	26-49 µg/dL	
		Child 13-19 yr	26-72 µg/dL	
		Adult >19 yr	38-98 µg/dL	
Retinol (Mayo Medical)	Serum		360-1200 µg/dL	
Retinyl esters (Mayo Medical)			≤10 µg/dL	
Vitamin D, 25 hydroxy (Mayo Medical Labs)	Serum	Summer (total):	15-80 ng/mL	37-200 nmol/L
		Winter (total):	14-42 ng/mL	
Vitamin D, 25 hydroxy (RIA, DiaSorin)	Serum/Plasma	Adults	9.0-37.6 ng/mL (mean 23.0 ng/mL)	35-105 nmol/L
Vitamin D, 1,25 dihydroxy (Mayo)	Serum	Adults	25-45 pg/mL	12-46 µmol/L
Vitamin D,1,25 dihydroxy (RIA DiaSorin)	Serum/Plasma	Adults	15.9-55.6 pg/mL (mean 35.7pg/mL)	
Calcitonin				
Quest Diagn/Nichols two-site ICMA	Serum	Basal Male	≤8 pg/mL	
		Basal Female	≤4 pg/mL	
		Pentagastrin/Ca Male	10-491 pg/mL	
		Pentagastrin/Ca Female	≤70 pg/mL	
CIS Biointernational two-site IRMA	Serum	Basal Male	<10 pg/mL	
		Basal Female	<10 pg/mL	
		Pentagastrin Male	<30 pg/mL	
		Pentagastrin Female	<30 pg/mL	
Mayo Medical Labs	Plasma	Basal Male	<19 pg/mL	
		Basal Female	<14 pg/mL	
		Pentagastrin Male	<110 pg/mL	
		Pentagastrin Female	<30 pg/mL	
RIA, DiaSorin	Serum	Adult	0-95 pg/mL (mean 47 pg/mL)	

Test	Source of specimen	Reference population	Reference Range	Reference Range (SI units)
Parathyroid hormone (Intact) [c]				
Mayo Medical Labs	Serum	Basal		1.0-5.2 pmol/L
Quest Diagnostics/Nichols	Serum	Basal	10-65 pg/mL	
IRMA, DiaSorin	Serum/Plasma		13-54 pg/mL (mean 26 pg/mL)	
Scantibodies	Serum	Basal		0.9-6.3 pmol/L
Osteocalcin [c]				
Quest/Nichols, CIS Bio	Serum	Male	8.0-52.0 ng/mL	
		Female premenopausal	5.8-41.0 ng/mL	
		Female postmenopausal	8.0-56.0 ng/mL	
Mayo Medical Labs, CIA	Serum	Male 20-50 yr	2-15 ng/mL	
		Male 51-70 yr	2-10 ng/mL	
		Female 20-50 yr	2-15 ng/mL	
		Female 51-80 yr	6-22 ng/mL	
RMA, DiaSorin	Serum	Male	3.2-12.2 ng/mL (mean 6.25ng/mL)	
		Female	2.7-11.5 ng/mL (mean 5.58ng/mL)	
ELISA, Metra Biosystems	Serum	Male	3.4-8.6 ng/mL	
		Female	3.8-10.0 ng/mL	
ELISA, N-Mid, Osteometer BioTech A/S	Serum/Plasma	Male	23.2±7.2 ng/mL	
		Female premenopausal	17.7±6.4 ng/mL	
		Female postmenopausal	28.9±9.7 ng/mL	
RMA, N-Mid, Osteometer BioTech A/S	Serum/Plasma	Male	23.0±9.7 ng/mL	
		Female premenopausal	18.4±8.9 ng/mL	
		Female postmenopausal	29.9±11.5 ng/mL	
PTHrP [c]				
Quest Diagnostic/Nichols Institute	Serum	Basal		<1.3 pmol/L
RMA, DiaSorin	Plasma	Adults		<1.5 pmol/L
Collagen cross-links				
Free deoxypyridinoline (DPD)				
Metra Biosystems, ELISA	Urine	Male		2.3-5.4 nmol/mmol creatinine
		Female premenopausal		3.0-7.4 nmol/mmol creatinine
Free pyridinoline (Pyd)				
Metra Biosystems, ELISA	Urine	Male		12.8-25.6 nmol/mmol creatinine
		Female		16.0-37.0 nmol/mmol creatinine
	Serum	Male		1.59±0.38 nmol/L
		Female		1.55±0.26 nmol/L
Total deoxypyridinoline (DPD)				
Metra Biosystems, HPLC	Urine	Male		4-19 nmol/mmol creatinine
		Female		4-21 nmol/mmol creatinine
Total pyridinoline (Pyd)				
Metra Biosystems, HPLC	Urine	Male		20-61 nmol/mmol creatinine
		Female		22-89 nmol/mmol creatinine
C-telopeptide (CTx)				
Osteometer Biotech A/S, ELISA	Urine	Male		207±128 µg/mmol creatinine
		Female premenopausal		220±128 µgmmol creatinine
		Female postmenopausal		363±160 µg/mmol creatinine
Osteometer Biotech A/S, RIA	Urine	Male		290±120 µg/mmol creatinine
		Female premenopausal		227±90 µg/mmol creatinine
		Female postmenopausal		429±225 µg/mmol creatinine
N-telopeptide (NTx)				
Ostex International, ELISA	Urine	Male		3-63 nM BCE/mM creatinine
		Female premenopausal		5-65 nM BCE/mM creatinine
		Female postmenopausal		17-188 nM BCE/mM creatinine
	Serum	Male		5.4-24.2 nM BCE
		Female premenopausal		6.2-19.0 nM BCE
		Female postmenopausal		8.1-38.7 nM BCE

ELISA, enzyme-linked immunosorbent assay; RIA, radioimmunoassay; IRMA, immunoradiometric assay; ICMA, immunochemiluminescent assay; IFCC, International Federation of Clinical Chemistry; BCE, bone collagen equivalents

[a] Selected laboratory values in this table were kindly compiled by Barry C. Kress, Ph.D., Hybritech Incorporated, a subsidiary of Beckman Coulter, Inc., San Diego, CA. Every effort was made to include values for all known companies for the various categories.

[b] Divide by 2 to get mEq/L. The total serum calcium can be corrected for alterations in the serum protein concentration by the following formula: Corrected total serum calcium (mg/dL) – observed total serum calcium + [(the normal mean albumin concentration – the observed albumin concentration) x 0.8]. In most situations, the normal mean albumin concentration equals 4 g/dL.

[c] The normal values listed include commercial assays. These are listed not to provide an endorsement for these assays, but because they are representative of values available for daily clinical use. It is likely that normal values in other research or commercial assays will vary to some extent; where ± values are given, the mean plus or minus one standard deviation is given.

Formulary of Drugs Commonly Used In Treatment of Mineral Disorders [a]

Drug	Application in treatment of bone and mineral disorders	Dosage (adult) [b]	Rx Cat[c]	Notes
Hormones and Analogs				
1. Calcitonin				
Human (Cibacalcin) im or SQ (0.5-mg vials)	Paget's disease	0.25-0.5 mg im or SQ; q24h	Rx	
Salmon (Calcimar, Miacalcin) im or SQ (100, 200 IU/mL) (SQ preferred)	Paget's disease, osteoporosis, hypercalcemia	50-100 IU, im or SQ; qod or qd for Paget's or osteoporosis; 4-6 IU/kg im or SQ; qid for hypercalcemia	Rx	Modestly effective and short-lived in treatment of hypercalcemia
Nasal spray (200 IU/spray)	Osteoporosis		Rx	
2. Estrogens				
Estinyl estradiol po (0.02, 0.05, 0.5 mg)	Postmenopausal osteoporosis (prevention and treatment)	0.02 – 0.05 mg; qd 3/4 wk	Rx	To reduce risk of endometrial cancer, estrogens can be cycled with progesterone during last 7-10 days or given concurrent with a progestin throughout the cycle (less breakthrough bleeding). In women who have not had a hysterectomy, a progesterone should be used with the estrogen and does not appear to alter the skeletal effectiveness of estrogen. Recent data from the Women's Health Initiative discourage the use of estrogen for purposes other than menopausal symptoms short term.
17β estradiol (Estrace) po (0.5, 1.2 mg)		0.5 mg qd	Rx	
Transderm patch (Estraderm)		0.05-0.1 mg 2x/wk	Rx	
Esterified estrogens (Estratab) po (0.3, 0.625, 2.5)		0.3-1.25 mg qd	Rx	
Estropipate (Ortho-Est .625) po (0.75, 1.5 mg)		0.75 mg qd	Rx	
Conjugated equine estrogens (Premarin) po (0.3, 0.625, 0.9, 1.25, 2.5 mg)		0.625-1.25 mg qd 3/4 wk	Rx	0.3 mg conjugated equine estrogens (CEE) with calcium also may be effective
Conjugated equine estrogen with medroxyprogesterone acetate (MPA)				
(Premphase)		0.625 mg estrogen qd on days 1-14 and 0.625 mg estrogen with 5 mg MPA qd on days 15-26	Rx	
(Prempro)		0.625 mg estrogen with 2.5 or 5 mg MPA qd	Rx	
3. Selective estrogen-receptor modulators (SERMs)				
Raloxifene (Evista)	Postmenopausal osteoporosis (prevention)	60 mg qd	Rx	Aggravates hot flashes. Decreased risk of endometrial and breast cancer.
4. Glucocorticoids				
Prednisone (Deltasone), po (2.5, 5, 10, 20, 50 mg)	Hypercalcemia due to sarcoidosis, vitamin D intoxication, and certain malignancies such as multiple myeloma and related lymphoproliferative disorders	10-60 mg qd	Rx	Long-term use results in osteoporosis and adrenal suppression. Other glucocorticoids with minimal mineralocorticoid activity can be used.
5. Parathyroid Hormone				
Teriparatide (Forteo)	Osteoporosis	20 µg SQ daily	Rx	

Drug	Application in treatment of bone and mineral disorders	Dosage (adult) [b]	Rx Cat[c]	Notes
6. Testosterone				
Testosterone cypionate	Male hypogonadism	200-300 mg im q2-3 wk	Rx	
Testosterone enanthate		200-300 mg im q2-3wk	Rx	
Transdermal patch				
Testoderm TTS		5 mg body patch q 24h	Rx	
Androderm		5 mg body patch q 24h	Rx	
Androgel 1%		5 mg topical q day	Rx	
7. Vitamin D preparations				
Cholecalciferol or D₃, p.o (125, 250, 400 U, often in combination with calcium)	Nutritional vitamin D deficiency, osteoporosis, malabsorption, hypoparathyroidism, refractory rickets	400-1000 U; as dietary supplement	OTC	D_2 (or D_3) has been shown to reduce fractures and increase BMD in elderly women in 400-1000 U doses
Ergocalciferol or D2 (Calciferol), po (8000 U/mL drops; 25,000, 50,000 U tabs)		25,000-100,000 U; 3x/wk to qd	Rx	$25(OH)D_3$ may be useful in treatment of steroid-induced osteoporosis
Calcitriol or 1,25(OH)2D3 (Rocaltrol), po (0.25, 0.5 µg); (Calcijex), iv (1 or 2 µg/mL)	Renal osteodystrophy, hypoparathyroidism, refractory rickets	0.25-1.0 µg; qd to bid	Rx	Role of calcitriol in treatment of osteoporosis, psoriasis and certain malignancies is being evaluated, primarily with new analogs
Dihydrotachysterol (DHT), po (0.125, 0.2, 0.4 mg)	Renal osteodystrophy, hypoparathyroidism, refractory rickets	0.2-1.0 mg; qd	Rx	
Doxercalciferol (Hectrol) 0.5 µg, 2.5 µg capsules po , 2 µg/ml iv	Secondary hyperparathyroidism	10-20 µg 3x/week	Rx	
Paricalcitol (Zemplar) 5 µg/mL iv, 1, 2, 4 µg capsules po	Secondary hyperparathyroidism	0.04-0.1 µg/kg iv qod-initial. May increase to 0.24 µg/kg 2-4 µg po 3x/week	Rx	
Bisphosphonates				
1. Etidronate (Didronel), po (200, 400 mg); iv (300 mg/6 mL vial)	Paget's disease, heterotopic ossification, hypercalcemia of malignancy	po, 5 mg/kg qd for 6/12 mo for Paget's disease; 20 mg/kg, qd 1 mo before to 3 mo after total hip replacement; 10/20 mg/kg qd for 3 mo after spinal cord injury for heterotopic ossification iv, 7.5 mg/kg, qd for 3 d, given in 250-500 mL normal saline for hypercalcemia of malignancy; 5 mg qd for osteoporosis prevention	Rx Rx	Etidronate is a first-generation bisphosphonate. High doses may cause a mineralization disorder not seen with newer bisphosphonates. This is seldom used anymore.
2. Alendronate (Fosamax) po (5, 10, 35, 40, 70 mg)	Osteoporosis treatment, Paget's disease	10 mg qd or 70 mg q wk for osteoporosis treatment; 40 mg qd for Paget's disease	Rx	Ingest 30 min before breakfast with 1 glass water; remain upright. Esophagitis is a risk. Not recommended for creatinine decrease <35 ml/min. Jaw osteonecrosis is a potential problem
3. Pamidronate (Aredia), iv (30-90 mg/10 mL)	Hypercalcemia of malignancy, Paget's disease	60-90 mg given as a single ivinfusion over 2-4 h for hypercalcemia of malignancy; 30 mg doses over 2 h on 3 consecutive days for a total of 90 mg for Paget's disease	Rx	complications as per alendronate

Drug	Application in treatment of bone and mineral disorders	Dosage (adult) [b]	Rx Cat [c]	Notes
Bisphosphonates (cont.)				
4. Risedronate (Actonel) (5, 30, 35 mg)	Osteoporosis, Paget's disease	5 mg po qd or 35 mg q wk for osteoporosis; 30 mg qd for 2 mo for Paget's	Rx	complications as per alendronate
5. Tiludronate (Skelid)	Paget's disease	400 mg qd for 3 mo	Rx	
6. Zoledronate (Zometa)	Hypercalcemia of malignancy; osteolytic metastases	4 mg iv over 15 min; may repeat in 7 d for hypercalcemia; 4 mg iv over 15 min q 3-4 week for bony metastases	Rx	complications as per alendronate
7. Ibandronate (Boniva) 2.5, 150 mg po	Osteoporosis	2.5 mg po qd 150 mg po qmo	Rx	
Minerals				
1. Bicarbonate, sodium, po (325, 527, 650 mg)	Chronic metabolic acidosis leading to bone disease	Must be titrated for each patient	Rx, OTC	
2. Calcium preparations				
Calcium carbonate (40% Ca), po (500, 650 mg)	Hypocalcemia (if symptomatic should be treated iv), osteoporosis, rickets, osteomalacia, chronic renal failure, hypoparathyroidism, malabsorption, enteric oxaluria	po 400-2000 mg elemental Ca in divided doses; qd	OTC	Calcium carbonate is the preferred form because it has the highest percentage of calcium and is the least expensive, although calcium citrate may be somewhat better absorbed. In normal subjects, the solubility of the calcium salt has not been shown to affect its absorption from the intestine, in achlorhydric subjects, $CaCO_3$ should be given with meals.
Calcium citrate (21% Ca) po (950-1500 mg)			OTC	
Calcium chloride (36% Ca), iv (100% solution)			Rx	
Calcium bionate (6.5% Ca), po (1.8 g in 5 mL)			Rx	
Calcium gluconate (9% Ca), po (500, 600, 1000 mg), iv (10% solution, 0.465 mEq/mL)		iv, 2-20 mL 10% calcium gluconate over several hours	Rx	Calcium gluconate is the preferred iv form because, unlike calcium chloride, it does not burn.
Calcium lactate (13% Ca), po (325, 650 mg)			OTC	
Calcium phosphate, dibasic (23% Ca), po (486 mg)			OTC	
Tricalcium phosphate (39% Ca) po (300, 600 mg)			OTC	
3. Magnesium preparations				
Magnesium oxide (Mag-Ox, Uro-Mag), po (84.5, 241.3 mg Mg)	Hypomagnesemia	240-480 mg elemental Mg	OTC	Low magnesium often coexists with low calcium in alcoholics and malabsorbers. Also found in many antacids and vitamin formulations.
4. Phosphate preparations				
Neutra-Phos, po (250 mg P, 278 mg K, 164 mg Na)	Hypophosphatemia, vitamin D resistant rickets, hypercalcemia, hypercalciuria	po, 1-3 g in divided doses; qd	Rx, OTC	
Neutra-Phos K, po (250 mg P, 556 mg K)			Rx	
Fleet Phospha-Soda, po (815 mg P, 760 mg Na in 5 mL)			Rx, OTC	
In-Phos, iv (1 g P in 40 mL)		iv, 1.5 g over 6-8 h	Rx	iv phosphorus is seldom necessary and can be toxic if infusion is too rapid
Hyper-Phos-K, iv (1 g P in 15 mL)			Rx	

Drug	Application in treatment of bone and mineral disorders	Dosage (adult) [b]	Rx Cat[c]	Notes
Diuretics				
1. Thiazides				
Hydrochlorothiazide, po (25, 50, 100 mg)	Hypercalciuria, nephrolithiasis	25-50 mg; qd or bid	Rx	Other thiazides may also be effective but are less commonly used for this purpose. These uses are not FDA approved.
Chlorhalidone, po (25, 50 mg)				
2. Loop Diuretics				
Furosemide, po (20, 40, 80 mg), iv (10 mg/mL)	Hypercalcemia; if symptomatic, use iv	po 20-80 mg, q6h as necessary	Rx	Ethacrynic acid may also be effective but is less commonly used for this purpose. These uses are not FDA approved.
Miscellaneous				
1. Mithramycin or plicamycin (Mithracin), iv (2.5 mg/vial)	Hypercalcemia of malignancy	25 µg in 1 L D5W or normal saline over 4-8 hr	Rx	Has been used in treatment of severe Paget's disease, but toxicity makes it treatment of last resort for this purpose

BMD, bone mineral density; FDA, Food and Drug Administration; PTH, parathyroid hormone

[a] This table is not intended to be an official guideline. See PDR or package insert for more complete information. Selected information kindly provided by Daniel D. Bikle, M.D., Ph.D., Professor, Departments of Medicine and Dermatology, University of California, San Francisco, and Co-Director Special Diagnostic and Treatment Unit, Department of Medicine, Veterans Affairs Medical Center, San Francisco, California.

[b] qd, every day; qo, every other day; bid, twice a day; tid, 3 times a day; qid, 4 times a day; SQ, subcutaneously; im, intramuscularly; po, orally; iv, intravenously; IU, International Units.

[c] Rx Cat, prescription category; Rx, prescriptions required; OTC, over-the-counter preparations available

Summary of Gene Disorders of Serum Mineral Metabolism or Skeleton Formation

Genetic Disorder	OMIM Syndrome #	Gene	Protein	OMIM Gene #
Associated Hypocalcemia				
Albright osteodystrophy	103580	GNAS	G-Protein, α subunit	139320
Autoimmune polendocrinopathy syndrome, type 1	240300	AIRE	Autoimmune regulator	607358
DiGeorge syndrome	188400	DGCR	22q11.2, DiGeorge syndrome region	168450
Hypocalcemia, autosomal dominant	146200	PTH	Parathyroid hormone	601199
		CaSR	Calcium sensing receptor	168450
Hypoparathyroidism, autosomal dominant	601198	PTH	Parathyroid hormone	601199
		CaSR	Calcium sensing receptor	601199
Hypomagnesemia with 2° hypocalcemia	602014	TRPM6	Receptor cation channel	607009
Hypoparathyroidism-retardation-dysmorphism syndrome	241410	TBCE	Tubulin-specific chaperone E	604934
Hypoparathyroidism, sensorineural deafness renal dysplasia	146255	GATA3	GATA-binding protein	131320
Kenny-Caffey syndrome, type 1	244460	TBCE	Tubulin-specific chaperone E	604934
Osteopetrosis, autosomal recessive	259700	TCIRG1	T-cell immune regulator	604592
Primary hypomagnesemia	248250	PCLN1	Paracellin-1	603959
Pseudohypoparathyroidism, type 1B	603233	GNAS	G-Protein, α subunit	139320
Pseudovitamin D-deficient rickets, type 1	264700	CYP27B1	25(OH)D-1-α-hydroxylase	264700
Renal tubular acidosis, autosomal dominant distal	179800	SLC4A1	Solute carrier 4, anion exchanger	109270
Vitamin D-resistant rickets, type IIA	277440	VDR	Vitamin D receptor	601769
Associated Hypercalcemia				
Familial hypocalciuric hypercalcemia	145980	CaSR	Calcium sensing receptor	601199
Familial isolated hyperparathyroidism, type 1	145000	HPRT2	Parafibromin	607393
		MEN1	Menin	131100
Familial isolated hyperparathyroidism, type 2 (jaw tumor)	145001	HPRT2	Parafibromin	607393
Metaphyseal chondrodysplasia, Jansen type	156400	PTHR1	Parathyroid hormone receptor	168468
Multiple endocrine neoplasia, type 1	131100	MEN1	Menin	131100
Multiple endocrine neoplasia, type 2	171400	RET	RET proto-oncogene	164761
Neonatal hyperparathyroidism	239200	CaSR	Calcium sensing receptor	601199
Williams-Beuren syndrome	194050	ELN	Elastin	130160
		LIMK1	LIM kinase-1	601329
Associated Hypophosphatemia				
Albright osteodystrophy	103580	GNAS	G-Protein, α subunit	139320
Dent disease, Nephrolithiasis, X-linked, type 2	300009	CLCN5	Choride channel 5	300008
Fanconi-Bickel syndrome	227810	SCL2A2	Solute carrier family 2	138160
Hypophosphatasia, Adult type	146300	ALPL	Alkaline phosphatase	171760
Hypophosphatasia, Infantile type	241500	ALPL	Alkaline phosphatase	171760
Hypophosphatemic rickets, autosomal dominant	193100	FGF23	Fibroblast growth factor-23	605380
Hypophosphatemic rickets, X-linked, type 2	307800	PHEX	X-linked endopeptidase	307800
Hypophosphatemic rickets, X-linked, type 3	300008	CLCN5	Choride channel 5	300008
Hypophosphatemic urolithiasis	182309	SLC34A1	Solute carrier family 34, Member 1	182309
Hypophosphatemic osteoporosis	182309	SLC34A1	Solute carrier family 34, Member 1	182309
Metaphyseal chondrodysplasia, Jansen type	156400	PTHR1	Parathyroid hormone receptor	168468
Neonatal hyperparathyroidism	239200	CaSR	Calcium sensing receptor	601199
Nephrolithiasis, X-linked, type 1	310468	CLCN5	Choride channel 5	300008
Nephropathic cystinosis	219800	CTNS	Cystinosin	606272
Pseudovitamin D-deficient rickets, type 1	264700	CYP27B1	25(OH)D-1-α-hydroxylase	264700
Associated Hyperphosphatemia				
Albright osteodystrophy	103580	GNAS	G-Protein, α subunit	139320
Hypoparathyroidism, autosomal dominant	601198	PTH	Parathyroid hormone gene	168450
		CaSR	Calcium sensing receptor	601199
Hypoparathyroidism-retardation-dysmorphism syndrome	241410	TBCE	Tubulin-specific chaperone E	604934
Kenny-Caffey syndrome, type 1	244460	TBCE	Tubulin-specific chaperone E	604934
Paget disease, juvenile	239000	TNFRSF11B	Osteoprotegerin	602643
Pseudohypoparathyroidism, type 1B	603233	GNAS	G-Protein, α subunit	139320

Summary of Gene Disorders of Serum Mineral Metabolism or Skeleton Formation

Genetic Disorder	OMIM Syndrome #	Gene	Protein	OMIM Gene #
Associated Hypomagnesia				
Bartter syndrome, type 1	601678	SLC12A1	Sodium-potassium-chloride cotransporter-2	600839
Bartter syndrome, Gitelman variant	263800	SLC12A3	Thiazide-sensitive Na-Cl cotransporter	600968
Hypomagnesemia with 2° hypocalcemia	602014	TRPM6	Receptor cation channel	607009
Primary hypomagnesemia	248250	PCLN1	Paracellin-1	603959
Renal hypomagnesemia, type 2	154020	FXYD2	Na+,K+-ATPase gamma subunit	601814
Osteochondrodysplasias				
1. Achondroplasias				
Achondroplasia	100800	FGFR3	Fibroblast growth factor receptor-3	134934
Hypochondroplasia	146000	FGFR3	Fibroblast growth factor receptor-3	134934
SADDAN dysplasia	134934	FGFR3	Fibroblast growth factor receptor-3	134934
Thanatophoric dysplasia, type 1	187600	FGFR3	Fibroblast growth factor receptor-3	134934
Thanatophoric dysplasia, type 2	187600	FGFR3	Fibroblast growth factor receptor-3	134934
4. Short-rib dysplasias				
Ellis-van Creveld syndrome	225500	EVC / EVC2	EVC gene product / EVC2 gene product	604831 / 607261
5. Atelosteogenesis-omodysplasias				
Neonatal osseous dysplasia	256050	SLC26A2	Diastrophic dysplasia sulfate transporter	606718
6. Diastrophic dysplasias				
Achondrogenesis, type 1B	600972	SLC26A2	Diastrophic dysplasia sulfate transporter	606718
Diastrophic dysplasia	222600	SLC26A2	Diastrophic dysplasia sulfate transporter	606718
Multiple epiphyseal dysplasia, type 4	226900	SLC26A2	Diastrophic dysplasia sulfate transporter	606718
7. Dyssegmental dysplasias				
Dyssegmental dysplasia, Silverman-Handmaker type	224410	HSPG2	Perlecan	142461
Dyssegmental dwarfism	224400	HSPG2	Perlecan	142461
8. Type II collagenopathies				
Achondrogenesis, type II	200610	COL2A1	Collagen-2-A1	120140
Hypochondrogenesis	120140	COL2A1	Collagen-2-A1	120140
Kniest dysplasia	156550	COL2A1	Collagen-2-A1	120140
Spondyloepiphyeal dysplasia, congenital	183900	COL2A1	Collagen-2-A1	120140
Spondyloepimetaphyeal dysplasia, Strudwick type	184250	COL2A1	Collagen-2-A1	120140
Spondylometaphyseal dysplasia	184252	COL2A1	Collagen-2-A1	120140
Spondyloperipheral dysplasia	271700	COL2A1	Collagen-2-A1	120140
Stickler syndrome, type 1	108300	COL2A1	Collagen-2-A1	120140
9. Type XI collagenopathies				
Marshall syndrome	154780	COL11A1	Collagen-11-A1	120280
Otospondylomegaepiphyseal dysplasia	215150	COL11A1	Collagen-11-A2	120290
Stickler syndrome, type 2	604841	COL11A1	Collagen-11-A1	120280
Stickler syndrome, type 3	184840	COL11A1	Collagen-11-A2	120290
10. Other spondyloepi-(meta)-physeal dysplasias				
Dyggve-Melchior-Clausen dysplasia	223800	FLJ90130	Unknown	607461
Progressive pseudorheumatoid dysplasia	208230	WISP3	Wnt1 signalling protein	603400
Immunoosseous dysplasia, Schimke type	242900	SMARCAL1	SMARCA-like protein 1	606622
Schwartz-Jampel syndrome	255800	HSPG2	Perlecan	142461
Smith-McCort dysplasia	607326	FLJ90130	Unknown	607461
Spondyloepimetaphyseal dysplasia, Pakistani	603005	PAPSS2	PAPS synthase	603005
Spondyloepiphyseal dysplasia tarda	313400	SEDL	Sedlin	300202
Wolcott-Rallison syndrome	226980	EIF2AK3	EIF 2A kinase	604032

Summary of Gene Disorders of Serum Mineral Metabolism or Skeleton Formation

Genetic Disorder	OMIM Syndrome #	Gene	Protein	OMIM Gene #
11. Multiple epiphyseal dysplasias & pseudoachondroplasia				
Pseudoachondroplasia	177170	COMP	Cartilage oligomeric matric protein-1	600310
Multiple epiphyseal dysplasia, COL9A1-related	120140	COL9A1	Collagen-9-A1	120140
Multiple epiphyseal dysplasia, type 1	132400	COMP	Cartilage oligomeric matric protein-1	600310
Multiple epiphyseal dysplasia, type 2	600204	COL9A2	Collagen-9-A2	120260
Multiple epiphyseal dysplasia, type 3	600969	COL9A3	Collagen-9-A3	120270
Multiple epiphyseal dysplasia, type 5	607078	MATN3	Matrilin 3	602109
12. Chondrodysplasia punctata (CDP)				
CHILD syndrome	308050	NSDHL	NAD(P)H steroid dehydrogenase-like protein	300275
Chondrodysplasia punctata with coagulation deficiency	277450	GGCX	γ-Glutamyl carboxylase	137167
Chondrodysplasia punctata, X-linked dominant	302960	EBP	Emopamil-binding protein	300205
Chondrodysplasia punctata, X-linked recessive	302950	ARSE	Arylsulfatase E	300180
Desmosterolosis	602398	DHCR24	24-Dehydrocholesterol reductase gene	606418
Moth-eaten skeletal dysplasia	215140	LBR	Lamin B receptor	600024
Rhizomelic chondrodysplasia punctata, type 1	215100	PEX7	Peroxin-7	601757
Rhizomelic chondrodysplasia punctata, type 2	222765	GNPAT	Glyceronephosphate acyltransferase	602744
Rhizomelic chondrodysplasia punctata, type 3	600121	AGPS	Alkyl-DHAP synthase gene	603051
Smith Lemli Opitz syndrome, type 1	270400	DHCR7	Sterol delta-7-reductase gene	602858
Smith Lemli Opitz syndrome, type 2	268670	DHCR7	Sterol delta-7-reductase gene	602858
Zellweger syndrome	214100	PEX1	Peroxin-1	602136
		PEX2	Peroxin-2	170993
		PEX3	Peroxin-3	603164
		PEX5	Peroxin-5	600414
		PEX6	Peroxin-6	601498
		PEX12	Peroxin-12	601758
13. Metaphyseal dysplasias				
Adenosine deaminase deficiency	102700	ADA	Adenosine deaminase	102700
Jansen type	156400	PTHR1	Parathyroid hormone receptor	168468
Schmid type	156500	COL10A1	Collagen-10-A1	120110
Shwachman-Diamond syndrome	260400	SBDS	Unknown	607444
McKusick type (Cartilage-Hair-Hypoplasia)	250250	RMRP	Mitochondrial RNA-processing endoribonuclease	157660
16. Mesomelic dysplasias				
Langer mesomelic dysplasia	249700	SHOX	Short stature homeo box	312865
Leri-Weill dyschondrosteosis	127300	SHOX	Short stature homeo box	312865
Robinow syndrome, recessive	268310	ROR2	NTRKR2/RTK-like orphan receptor 2	602337
Short Stature, idiopathic	604271	SHOX	Short stature homeo box	312865
		SHOXY	Short stature homeo box	400020
17. Acromelic dysplasias				
Albright osteodystrophy	103580	GNAS	G-Protein, α subunit	139320
Brachydactyly, type A1	112500	IHH	Indian hedgehog	600726
Brachydactyly, type B1	113000	ROR2	NTRKR2/RTK-like orphan receptor 2	602337
Brachydactyly, type C	113100	GDF5	Cartilage-derived morphogenetic protein	601146
Brachydactyly, type D	113200	HOXD13	Homeo box 4I	142989
Brachydactyly, type E	113300	HOXD13	Homeo box 4I	142989
Noonan syndrome	163950	PTPN11	Protein tyrosine phosphatase	176876
Trichorhinophalangeal syndrome, type 1	190350	TRPS1	Putative transcription factor	605386
Trichorhinophalangeal syndrome, type 2	150230	TRPS1/EXT1	Putative transcription factor/Exostosin-1	605386/133700
Trichorhinophalangeal syndrome, type 3	190351	TRPS1	Putative transcription factor	605386
18. Acromesomelic dysplasias				
Grebe chondrodysplasia	200700	GDF5	Cartilage-derived morphogenetic protein	601146
Hunter-Thompson type chondrodysplasia	201250	GDF5	Cartilage-derived morphogenetic protein	601146
Du Pan syndrome	228900	GDF5	Cartilage-derived morphogenetic protein	601146

Summary of Gene Disorders of Serum Mineral Metabolism or Skeleton Formation

Genetic Disorder	OMIM Syndrome #	Gene	Protein	OMIM Gene #
19. Dysplasias with predominant membranous bone involvement				
Cleidocranial dysplasia syndrome	119600	RUNX2	Core-binding factor, α subunit 1	600211
Parietal foramina, type 1	168500	MSX2	Muscle segment homeo box	123101
Parietal foramina, type 2	168500	ALX4	Aristaless-like 4	605420
20. Bent-bone dysplasia				
Campomelic dysplasia	114290	SOX9	SRY box-related-9	211970
22. Dysostosis multiplex				
Aspartylglucosaminuria	208400	AGA	Aspartylglucosaminidase	208400
Fucosidosis	230000	FUCA1	α-L-fucosidase	230000
Galactosialidosis	256540	PPGB	β-galactosidase protective protein	256540
α-Mannosidosis	248500	MAN2B1	α-D-Mannosidase	248500
β-Mannosidosis	248510	MANBA	β-D-Mannosidase	248510
Mucopolysaccharidosis, type I	252800	IDUA	α-L-iduronidase	252800
Mucopolysaccharidosis, type II	309900	IDS	Iduronate sulfatase	309900
Mucopolysaccharidosis, type IIIA	252900	SGSH	Heparan sulfate sulfatase	605270
Mucopolysaccharidosis, type IIID	252940	GNS	N-acetylglucosamine-6-sulfatase	607664
Mucopolysaccharidosis, type IVA	253000	GALNS	Galactosamine-6-sulfatase	253000
Mucopolysaccharidosis, type IVB/Gangliosidosis	253010	GLB1	β-galactosidase	230500
Mucopolysaccharidosis, type VI	253200	ARSB	Arylsulfatase B	253200
Mucopolysaccharidosis, type VII	253220	GUSB	β-glucuronidase	253220
Sialidosis	256550	NEU1	α-neuraminidase	256550
Sialuria, infantile	269920	SLC17A5	Sialin	604322
Sialuria, Finnish type	604369	SLC17A5	Sialin	604322
Sialuria, French type	269921	GNE	UDP-GlcNAc 2-epimerase	603824
24. Dysplasias with decreased bone density				
Gaucher disease	230800	GBA	Acid-beta glucosidase	606463
Homocystinuria	236200	CBS	Cystathionine beta-synthase	236200
Osteogenesis imperfecta, type I	166200	COL1A1	Collagen-1-A1	120150
		COL1A1	Collagen-1-A2	120160
Osteogenesis imperfecta, type II	166210	COL1A1	Collagen-1-A1	120150
		COL1A1	Collagen-1-A2	120160
Osteogenesis imperfecta, type III	259420	COL1A1	Collagen-1-A1	120150
		COL1A1	Collagen-1-A2	120160
Osteogenesis imperfecta, type IV	166220	COL1A1	Collagen-1-A1	120150
		COL1A1	Collagen-1-A2	120160
Osteoporosis-pseudoglioma syndrome	259770	LRP5	Lipoprotein receptor-related protein 5	603506
25. Dysplasias with defective mineralization				
Familial hypocalciuric hypercalcemia	145980	CaSR	Calcium sensing receptor	601199
Hypophosphatasia, Adult type	146300	ALPL	Alkaline phosphatase	171760
Hypophosphatasia, Infantile type	241500	ALPL	Alkaline phosphatase	171760
Hypophosphatemic rickets, autosomal dominant	193100	FGF23	Fibroblast growth factor-23	605380
Hypophosphatemic rickets, X-linked, type 2	307800	PHEX	X-linked endopeptidase	307800
Hypophosphatemic rickets, X-linked, type 3	300008	CLCN5	Choride channel 5	300008
Neonatal hyperparathyroidism	239200	CaSR	Calcium sensing receptor	601199
26. Increase bone density without modification of bone shape				
High bone mass trait, autosomal dominant	601884	LRP5	Lipoprotein receptor-related protein 5	603506
Netherton syndrome	256500	SPINK5	LEKTI	605010
OLEDAID syndrome	300301	IKBKG	NEMO	300248
Osteopetrosis, autosomal recessive	259700	CLCN7	Chloride channel 7	602727
		GL	Grey-lethal	607649
		TCIRG1	T-cell immune regulator	604592
Osteopetrosis with renal tubular acidosis	259730	CA2	Carbonic anhydrase II	259730
Osteopetrosis, type I	607634	LRP5	Lipoprotein receptor-related protein 5	603506

Summary of Gene Disorders of Serum Mineral Metabolism or Skeleton Formation

Genetic Disorder	OMIM Syndrome #	Gene	Protein	OMIM Gene #
Osteopetrosis, type II	166600	CLCN7	Chloride channel 7	602727
Pycnodysostosis	265800	CTSK	Cathepsin-K	601105
27. Increased bone density with diaphyseal involvement				
Diaphyseal dysplasia (Camurati-Engelmann disease)	131300	TGFB1	Transforming growth factor-β-1	190180
Kenny-Caffey syndrome, type 1	244460	TBCE	Tubulin-specific chaperone E	604934
Oculodentodigital dysplasia	164200	GJA1	Gap junction protein 1	121014
Osteosclerosis, autosomal dominant	144750	LRP5	Lipoprotein receptor-related protein 5	603506
Paget disease, juvenile	239000	TNFRSF11B	Osteoprotegerin	602643
Paget disease, type 2	602080	TNFRSF11A	RANK	603499
Paget disease, type 3	602080	SQSTM1	Sequestosome 1	601530
Sclerosteosis	269500	SOST	Sclerostin	605740
Trichodentoosseous dysplasia	190320	DLX3	Distal-less homeo box 3	600525
Van Buchem, type 2	607363	LRP5	Lipoprotein receptor-related protein 5	603506
28. Increased bone density with metaphyseal involvement				
Craniometaphyseal dysplasia, autosomal dominant	123000	ANKH	Ankylosis gene	605145
29. Craniotubular digital dysplasias				
Frontometaphyseal dysplasia	305620	FLNA	Filamin A	300017
Osteodysplasty, Melnick-Needles	309350	FLNA	Filamin A	300017
Otopalatodigital syndrome, type I	311300	FLNA	Filamin A	300017
Otopalatodigital syndrome, type II	304120	FLNA	Filamin A	300017
30. Neonatal severe osteosclerotic dysplasias				
Chondrodysplasia, Blomstrand type	215045	PTHR1	Parathyroid hormone receptor	168468
31. Disorganized development of cartilaginous and fibrous components of the skeleton				
Cherubism	118400	SH3BP2	SH3 domain-binding protein	602104
Fibromatosis, gingival	135300	SOS1	SOS homolog 1	182530
Fibrodysplasia ossificans progressiva	135100	ACVR1	Activin A Receptor, Type 1	102576
McCune-Albright syndrome	174800	GNAS	G-Protein, α subunit	139320
Multiple endochondromatosis	166000	PTHR1	Parathyroid hormone receptor	168468
Multiple exostoses, type 1	133700	EXT1	Exostosin-1	133700
Multiple exostoses, type 2	133701	EXT2	Exostosin-2	133701
Osseous heteroplasia	166350	GNAS	G-Protein, α subunit	139320
32. Osteolyses				
Familial expansile osteolysis	174810	TNFRSF11A	RANK	603499
Mandibuloacral dysplasia	248370	LMNA	Lamin A/C	150330
Osteolysis, idiopathic, Saudi type	605156	MMP2	Matrix metalloproteinase-2	120360
33. Patella dysplasias				
Nail-patella	161200	LMX1B	Lim homeodomain	602575
Localized Skeletal Malformations (Dysotoses)				
A. Localized disorders with predominant cranial and facial involvement				
Antley-Bixler syndrome	207410	FGFR2	Fibroblast growth factor receptor-2	176943
Apert syndrome	101200	FGFR2	Fibroblast growth factor receptor-2	176943
Beare-Stevenson cutis gyrata syndrome	123790	FGFR2	Fibroblast growth factor receptor-2	176943
Craniofacial-deafness-hand syndrome	122880	PAX3	Paired homeo box 3	606597
Craniosynostosis, Boston type	604757	MSX2	MSX2 homeo box gene	123101
Craniosynostosis, Muenke type	602849	FGFR3	Fibroblast growth factor receptor-3	134934
Crouzon syndrome	123500	FGFR2	Fibroblast growth factor receptor-2	176943
Greig cephalopolysyndactyly syndrome	175700	GLI3	GLI-Kruppel member 3	165240
Jackson-Weiss syndrome	123150	FGFR2	Fibroblast growth factor receptor-2	176943
Orofaciodigital syndrome I	311200	CXORF5	X open reading frame	300170
Pfeiffer syndrome	101600	FGFR1	Fibroblast growth factor receptor-1	136350
		FGFR2	Fibroblast growth factor receptor-2	176943

Summary of Gene Disorders of Serum Mineral Metabolism or Skeleton Formation

Genetic Disorder	OMIM Syndrome #	Gene	Protein	OMIM Gene #
Robinow-Sorauf syndrome	180750	TWIST	Twist	601622
Saethre-Chotzen syndrome	101400	TWIST	Twist	601622
Shprintzen-Goldberg syndrome	182212	FBN1	Fibrillin-1	134797
Treacher Collins syndrome	154500	TCOF1	Treacle	606847
Waardenburg syndrome, type 1	193500	PAX3	Paired homeo box 3	606597
Waardenburg syndrome, type 2A	193510	MITF	Microphtalmia-associated transcription factor	156845
Waardenburg syndrome, type 3	148820	PAX3	Paired homeo box 3	606597
B. Localized disorders with predominant axial involvement				
Robinow syndrome, recessive also in 16	268310	ROR2	NTRKR2/RTK-like orphan receptor 2	602337
Spondylocostal dysostosis	277300	DLL3	Delta-like 3	602768
Weyers acrodental dysostosis	193530	EVC	EVC gene product	604831
C. Localized disorders with predominant involvement of the extremities				
Bardet-Biedl syndrome, type 1	209900	BBS1	Unknown	209901
Bardet-Biedl syndrome, type 2	209900	BBS2	Unknown	606151
Bardet-Biedl syndrome, type 4	209900	BBS4	Unknown	600374
Bardet-Biedl syndrome, type 6	209900	MKKS	Unknown	604896
Contractural arachnodactyly	121050	FBN2	Fibrillin-2	121050
Fanconi Anemia	227650	FANCA	FA complement	607139
		FANCB	FA complement	227660
		FANCC	FA complement	227645
		FANCD1	FA complement	605724
		FANCD2	FA complement	227646
		FANCE	FA complement	600901
		FANCF	FA complement	603467
		FANCG	FA complement	602956
Guttmacher syndrome	176305	HOXA13	Homeo box A13	142959
Hand foot uterus syndrome	140000	HOXA13	Homeo box A13	142959
Heart-hand syndrome	142900	TBX5	T-Box 5	601620
McKusick-Kaufman syndrome	236700	MKKS	Unknown	604896
Multiple synostosis syndrome 1	186500	NOG	Noggin	602991
Pallister-Hall syndrome	146510	GLI3	GLI-Kruppel member 3	165240
Postaxial polydactyly, type A	174200	GLI3	GLI-Kruppel member 3	165240
Preaxial polydactyly type IV	174700	GLI3	GLI-Kruppel member 3	165240
Rubinstein syndrome	180849	CREBBP	CREB-binding protein	600140
Split-hand malformation 4	605289	TP73L	p63	603273
Syndactyly, type 2	186000	HOXD13	Homeo box 4I	142989
Tarsal-carpal coalition syndrome	186570	NOG	Noggin	602991
Ulnar-mammary syndrome	181450	TBX3	T-Box 3	601621

Information identifying the disorders and their respective affected genes was obtained by a key-word search of the Online Mendelian Inheritance in Man, OMIM(TM), Center for Medical Genetics, Johns Hopkins University (Baltimore, MD) and National Center for Biotechnology Information, National Library of Medicine (Bethesda, MD), 1997. World Wide Web URL: http://www.ncbi.nlm.nih.gov/omim. The classification into groups based on associated serum mineral defects is based on the OMIM clinical synopsis provided for each disorder. The remaining classifications are in part based on the International Nosology and Classification of Constitutive Disorders of Bone (2001)(Hall, C.M. Amer. J. Med. Genet. 113:65-77, 2002). Disorders are separated into two major classifications, osteochondrodysplasias, which comprise 33 numbered groups, and dysostoses, which comprise 3 groups identified alphabetically. The absence of Groups 2, 3, 14, 15, 21 and 23 is due to the lack of defined genetic mutations for disorders in these groups. More detailed information on individual disorders or genes can be obtained by using the OMIM numbers provided to perform a key-word search (http://www.ncbi.nlm.nih.gov/Omim/searchomim.html).

Subject Index

NOTES

NOTES